Financial Institutions and Markets

Financial Institutions and Markets

9TH EDITION

JEFF MADURA
Florida Atlantic University

SOUTH-WESTERN
CENGAGE Learning

Australia • Brazil • Japan • Korea • Mexico • Singapore • Spain • United Kingdom • United States

SOUTH-WESTERN
CENGAGE Learning

**Financial Institutions and Markets,
9th Edition
Jeff Madura**

VP of Editorial, Business: Jack W. Calhoun

Publisher: Joe Sabatino

Executive Editor: Michael R. Reynolds

Developmental Editor: Kendra Brown

Sr. Marketing Comm. Manager: Jim Overly

Marketing Coordinator: Suellen Ruttkay

Marketing Manager: Nate Anderson

Content Project Manager: Scott Dillon

Manager of Technology, Editorial:
Matt McKinney

Manager of Media, Editorial: John Barans

Media Editor: Scott Fidler

Sr. Frontlist Buyer, Manufacturing: Kevin Kluck

Production Service/Compositor: Integra

Copyeditor: Pat Lewis

Proofreader: Ann Whetstone

Sr. Editorial Assistant: Adele Scholtz

Sr. Art Director: Michelle Kunkler

Cover Image: © Shutterstock

For product information and technology assistance, contact us at
Cengage Learning Customer & Sales Support, 1-800-354-9706
For permission to use material from this text or product,
submit all requests online at **www.cengage.com/permissions**
Further permissions questions can be emailed to
permissionrequest@cengage.com

International Student Edition PKG: ISBN 13: 978-1-4390-3887-1
International Student Edition PKG: ISBN 10: 1-4390-3887-2

Cengage Learning International Offices

Asia
cengageasia.com
tel: (65) 6410 1200

Australia/New Zealand
cengage.com.au
tel: (61) 3 9685 4111

Brazil
cengage.com.br
tel: (011) 3665 9900

India
cengage.co.in
tel: (91) 11 30484837/38

Latin America
cengage.com.mx
tel: +52 (55) 1500 6000

UK/Europe/Middle East/Africa
cengage.co.uk
tel: (44) 207 067 2500

Represented in Canada by Nelson Education, Ltd.
nelson.com
tel: (416) 752 9100 / (800) 668 0671

For product information: **www.cengage.com/international**
Visit your local office: **www.cengage.com/global**
Visit our corporate website: **www.cengage.com**

Printed in China by China Translation & Printing Services Limited
2 3 4 5 6 7 13 12 11 10

This text is dedicated to Best Friends Animal Sanctuary in Kanab, Utah, for its commitment to, compassion for, and care of more than 1,500 animals, many of which were previously homeless. Most of the royalties the author receives from this text will be invested in an estate that will ultimately be donated to Best Friends.

Brief Contents

PART 1: Overview of the Financial Environment   1

1   Role of Financial Markets and Institutions, 3
2   Determination of Interest Rates, 29
3   Structure of Interest Rates, 49

PART 2: The Fed and Monetary Policy   79

4   Functions of the Fed, 81
5   Monetary Policy, 99

PART 3: Debt Security Markets   123

6   Money Markets, 125
7   Bond Markets, 149
8   Bond Valuation and Risk, 173
9   Mortgage Markets, 205

PART 4: Equity Markets   227

10   Stock Offerings and Investor Monitoring, 229
11   Stock Valuation and Risk, 263
12   Market Microstructure and Strategies, 303

PART 5: Derivative Security Markets   323

13   Financial Futures Markets, 325
14   Options Markets, 353
15   Swap Markets, 391
16   Foreign Exchange Derivative Markets, 417

PART 6: Commercial Banking   459

17   Commercial Bank Operations, 461
18   Bank Regulation, 481
19   Bank Management, 499
20   Bank Performance, 527

PART 7: Nonbank Operations   543

21   Thrift Operations, 545
22   Finance Operations, 567
23   Mutual Fund Operations, 579
24   Securities Operations, 615
25   Insurance and Pension Fund Operations, 641

Appendix A: Comprehensive Project, 677
Appendix B: Using Excel to Conduct Analyses, 687
Glossary, 691
Index, 705

Contents

Preface, xxxi
About the Author, xxxvii

PART 1: Overview of the Financial Environment 1

1: ROLE OF FINANCIAL MARKETS AND INSTITUTIONS 3

Role of Financial Markets, 3
  Types of Financial Markets, 4
  How Financial Markets Facilitate Corporate Finance, 5
Securities Traded in Financial Markets, 6
  Money Market Securities, 6
  Capital Market Securities, 6
  Using the Wall Street Journal: Assessing Stock Performance, 8
  Derivative Securities, 8
  Valuation of Securities in Financial Markets, 9
  Market Efficiency, 10
  Financial Market Regulation, 11
Global Financial Markets, 12
  International Corporate Governance, 12
  Global Integration, 13
  Role of the Foreign Exchange Market, 13
Role of Financial Institutions, 13
  Role of Depository Institutions, 14
  Role of Nondepository Financial Institutions, 15
  Comparison of Roles among Financial Institutions, 16
  Relative Importance of Financial Institutions, 18
  Consolidation of Financial Institutions, 19
  Impact of the Internet on Financial Institutions, 21
  Global Expansion by Financial Institutions, 21
Impact of the Credit Crisis on Financial Institutions, 21
Summary, 22
Point Counter-Point: Will Computer Technology Cause Financial Intermediaries to Become Extinct? 23
Questions and Applications, 23
  Advanced Questions, 24
  Interpreting Financial News, 24
  Managing in Financial Markets, 24
Flow of Funds Exercise: Roles of Financial Markets and Institutions, 25
Internet/Excel Exercises, 25
WSJ Exercise: Differentiating between Primary and Secondary Markets, 26
Term Paper on the Credit Crisis, 27

2: DETERMINATION OF INTEREST RATES   29

Loanable Funds Theory, 29

Household Demand for Loanable Funds, 29

Business Demand for Loanable Funds, 30

Government Demand for Loanable Funds, 31

Foreign Demand for Loanable Funds, 32

Aggregate Demand for Loanable Funds, 32

Supply of Loanable Funds, 34

Equilibrium Interest Rate, 35

Factors That Affect Interest Rates, 36

Impact of Economic Growth on Interest Rates, 37

Impact of Inflation on Interest Rates, 38

Impact of Monetary Policy on Interest Rates, 39

Impact of the Budget Deficit on Interest Rates, 39

Impact of Foreign Flows of Funds on Interest Rates, 40

Summary of Forces That Affect Interest Rates, 41

Forecasting Interest Rates, 43

Summary, 45

Point Counter-Point: Does a Large Fiscal Budget Deficit Result in Higher Interest Rates? 45

Questions and Applications, 45

Advanced Questions, 46

Interpreting Financial News, 46

Managing in Financial Markets, 46

Problems, 47

Flow of Funds Exercise: How the Flow of Funds Affects Interest Rates, 47

Internet/Excel Exercises, 47

WSJ Exercise: Forecasting Interest Rates, 48

3: STRUCTURE OF INTEREST RATES   49

Why Debt Security Yields Vary, 49

Credit (Default) Risk, 49

Liquidity, 51

Tax Status, 51

Term to Maturity, 52

Explaining Actual Yield Differentials, 53

Yield Differentials of Money Market Securities, 53

Yield Differentials of Capital Market Securities, 53

Estimating the Appropriate Yield, 54

Using the Wall Street Journal: Assessing the Yield Curve, 56

A Closer Look at the Term Structure, 56

Pure Expectations Theory, 56

Liquidity Premium Theory, 61

Segmented Markets Theory, 63

Research on Term Structure Theories, 64

Integrating the Theories of the Term Structure, 65

Uses of the Term Structure, 66

Why the Slope of the Yield Curve Changes, 67

How the Yield Curve Has Changed over Time, 68

International Structure of Interest Rates, 68

Summary, 70

Point Counter-Point: Should a Yield Curve Influence a Borrower's Preferred Maturity of a Loan? 70

Questions and Applications, 71

   Advanced Questions, 71

   Interpreting Financial News, 72

   Managing in Financial Markets, 72

Problems, 72

Flow of Funds Exercise: Influence of the Structure of Interest Rates, 73

Internet/Excel Exercises, 74

WSJ Exercise: Interpreting the Structure of Interest Rates, 74

Part 1 Integrative Problem: Interest Rate Forecasts and Investment Decisions, 76

Questions, 77

PART 2: The Fed and Monetary Policy 79

4: FUNCTIONS OF THE FED 81

Organizational Structure of the Fed, 81

   Federal Reserve District Banks, 81

   Member Banks, 83

   Board of Governors, 83

   Federal Open Market Committee (FOMC), 83

   Advisory Committees, 83

   Integration of Federal Reserve Components, 84

How the Fed Controls the Money Supply, 84

   Open Market Operations, 84

   Role of the Fed's Trading Desk, 86

   How Fed Operations Affect All Interest Rates, 88

   Using the Wall Street Journal: The Federal Funds Rate, 89

   Adjusting the Reserve Requirement Ratio, 90

   Adjusting the Fed's Loan Rate, 91

The Fed's Lending Role during the Credit Crisis, 92

   Facilities Created by the Fed, 92

Global Monetary Policy, 93

   A Single Eurozone Monetary Policy, 93

   Global Central Bank Coordination, 95

Summary, 95

Point Counter-Point: Should There Be a Global Central Bank? 96

Questions and Applications, 96

   Interpreting Financial News, 97

   Managing in Financial Markets, 97

Flow of Funds Exercise: Monitoring the Fed, 97

Internet/Excel Exercise, 98

WSJ Exercise: Reviewing Fed Policies, 98

5: MONETARY POLICY 99

Mechanics of Monetary Policy, 99

   Indicators of Economic Growth, 99

   Using the Wall Street Journal: The Consumer Price Index, 101

   Indicators of Inflation, 101

   How Monetary Policy Corrects the Economy, 102

   Limitations of Monetary Policy, 103

Tradeoff in Monetary Policy, 107
Impact of Other Forces on the Tradeoff, 107
Shifts in Monetary Policy 2001–2008, 109
How Monetary Policy Responds to Fiscal Policy, 110
Proposals to Focus on Inflation, 110
Impact of Monetary Policy, 111
Impact on Financial Markets, 112
Impact on Financial Institutions, 115
Global Monetary Policy, 115
Impact of the Dollar, 115
Impact of Global Economic Conditions, 116
Transmission of Interest Rates, 116
Summary, 117
Point Counter-Point: Can the Fed Prevent U.S. Recessions? 117
Questions and Applications, 117
Advanced Questions, 118
Interpreting Financial News, 119
Flow of Funds Exercise: Anticipating Fed Actions, 119
Internet/Excel Exercises, 119
WSJ Exercise: Market Assessment of Fed Policy, 120
Part 2 Integrative Problem: Fed Watching, 121
Questions, 122

PART 3: Debt Security Markets   123

6: MONEY MARKETS   125

Money Market Securities, 125
Treasury Bills, 126
Commercial Paper, 129
Negotiable Certificates of Deposit (NCDs), 131
Repurchase Agreements, 132
Federal Funds, 133
Banker's Acceptances, 133

Using the Wall Street Journal: Rates on Banker's Acceptances, 134
Institutional Use of Money Markets, 135
Valuation of Money Market Securities, 137
Impact of Changes in Credit Risk, 139
Interest Rate Risk, 139
Globalization of Money Markets, 141
Eurodollar Securities, 141
International Interbank Market, 143
Performance of Foreign Money Market Securities, 143
Summary, 145
Point Counter-Point: Should Firms Invest in Money Market Securities? 145
Questions and Applications, 145
Advanced Questions, 146
Interpreting Financial News, 146
Managing in Financial Markets, 146
Problems, 147

Flow of Funds Exercise: Financing in the Money Markets, 148
Internet/Excel Exercises, 148
WSJ Exercise: Assessing Yield Differentials of Money Market Securities, 148

7: BOND MARKETS   149

Background on Bonds, 149
  Institutional Use of Bond Markets, 149
  Bond Yields, 150
Treasury and Federal Agency Bonds, 151
  Treasury Bond Auction, 152
  Trading Treasury Bonds, 152
  Treasury Bond Quotations, 153
  Stripped Treasury Bonds, 153
  Inflation-Indexed Treasury Bonds, 154
  Savings Bonds, 154
  Federal Agency Bonds, 155
Municipal Bonds, 155
  Credit Risk, 155
  Characteristics of Municipal Bonds, 156
  Trading and Quotations, 156
  Yields Offered on Municipal Bonds, 156
Corporate Bonds, 158
  Corporate Bond Offerings, 158
  Characteristics of Corporate Bonds, 159
  Corporate Bond Yields and Risk, 161
  Using the Wall Street Journal: Bond Yields, 162
  Secondary Market for Corporate Bonds, 163
  Junk Bonds, 164
  How Corporate Bonds Finance Restructuring, 165
Globalization of Bond Markets, 166
  Eurobond Market, 167
Other Types of Long-Term Debt Securities, 167
  Structured Notes, 167
  Exchange-Traded Notes, 168
  Auction-Rate Securities, 168
Summary, 169
Point Counter-Point: Should Financial Institutions Invest in Junk Bonds? 169
Questions and Applications, 169
  Advanced Questions, 170
  Interpreting Financial News, 170
  Managing in Financial Markets, 170
Problems, 171
Flow of Funds Exercise: Financing in the Bond Markets, 171
Internet/Excel Exercise, 172
WSJ Exercise: Impact of Treasury Financing on Bond Prices, 172

8: BOND VALUATION AND RISK   173

Bond Valuation Process, 173
  Impact of the Discount Rate on Bond Valuation, 174
  Impact of the Timing of Payments on Bond Valuation, 175
  Valuation of Bonds with Semiannual Payments, 175
  Relationships between Coupon Rate, Required Return, and Bond Price, 176

Explaining Bond Price Movements, 178
Factors That Affect the Risk-Free Rate, 178
Factors That Affect the Credit (Default) Risk Premium, 180
Summary of Factors Affecting Bond Prices, 181
Implications for Financial Institutions, 182

Using the Wall Street Journal: Bond Values, 183
Sensitivity of Bond Prices to Interest Rate Movements, 184
Bond Price Elasticity, 184
Duration, 185
Bond Investment Strategies, 189
Matching Strategy, 189
Laddered Strategy, 189
Barbell Strategy, 189
Interest Rate Strategy, 189
Valuation and Risk of International Bonds, 190
Influence of Foreign Interest Rate Movements, 190
Influence of Credit Risk, 190
Influence of Exchange Rate Fluctuations, 191
International Bond Diversification, 191
Summary, 192
Point Counter-Point: Does Governance of Firms Affect the Prices of Their Bonds? 193
Questions and Applications, 193
Advanced Questions, 194
Interpreting Financial News, 195
Managing in Financial Markets, 195
Problems, 195
Flow of Funds Exercise: Interest Rate Expectations, Economic Growth, and Bond Financing, 197
Internet/Excel Exercises, 198

Appendix 8: Forecasting Bond Prices and Yields   199

9: MORTGAGE MARKETS   **205**
Background on Mortgages, 205
How Mortgage Markets Facilitate the Flow of Funds, 205
Criteria Used to Measure Creditworthiness, 207
Classification of Mortgages, 207
Types of Residential Mortgages, 208
Fixed-Rate Mortgages, 208
Adjustable-Rate Mortgages (ARMs), 209

Using the Wall Street Journal: Mortgage Rates, 210
Graduated-Payment Mortgages (GPMs), 210
Growing-Equity Mortgages, 211
Second Mortgages, 211
Shared-Appreciation Mortgages, 211
Balloon Payment Mortgages, 21l
Valuation and Risk of Mortgages, 211
Risk from Investing in Mortgages, 212
Mortgage-Backed Securities, 213
The Securitization Process, 213
Mortgage-Backed Securities within CDOs, 214
Types of Mortgage-Backed Securities, 214
Risk of Mortgage-Backed Securities, 216

Mortgage Credit Crisis, 217
  Who Is to Blame? 217
  Contagion Effects of the Credit Crisis, 219
  Government Programs Implemented in Response to the Crisis, 219
  Impact of the Credit Crisis on Fannie Mae and Freddie Mac, 219
  Government Bailout of Financial Institutions, 221
Summary, 221
Point Counter-Point: Is the Trading of Mortgages Similar to the Trading of Corporate Bonds? 222
Questions and Applications, 222
  Advanced Questions, 222
  Interpreting Financial News, 223
  Managing in Financial Markets, 223
Problem, 224
Flow of Funds Exercise: Mortgage Financing, 224
Internet/Excel Exercise, 224
WSJ Exercise: Explaining Mortgage Rate Premiums, 224
Part 3 Integrative Problem: Asset Allocation, 225
Questions, 225

PART 4: Equity Markets   227

10: STOCK OFFERINGS AND INVESTOR MONITORING   229
Private Equity, 229
  Financing by Venture Capital Funds, 229
  Financing by Private Equity Funds, 230
Public Equity, 230
  Ownership and Voting Rights, 232
  Preferred Stock, 232
  Participation in Stock Markets, 232
Initial Public Offerings, 234
  Process of Going Public, 234
  Underwriter Efforts to Ensure Price Stability, 236
  Timing of IPOs, 237
  Initial Returns of IPOs, 237
  Using the Wall Street Journal: Recent IPO Performance, 238
  Google's IPO, 238
  Abuses in the IPO Market, 240
  Long-Term Performance Following IPOs, 240
  Impact of the Sarbanes-Oxley Act on IPOs, 241
Secondary Stock Offerings, 241
  Shelf-Registration, 242
Stock Repurchases, 242
Stock Exchanges, 242
  Organized Exchanges, 242
  Over-the-Counter Market, 244
  Electronic Stock Exchanges, 245
  Extended Trading Sessions, 245
  Stock Quotations Provided by Exchanges, 245
  Using the Wall Street Journal: Late Trading, 246
  Stock Index Quotations, 248
  Using the Wall Street Journal: Stock Market Review, 249

Monitoring Publicly Traded Companies, 249
Role of Analysts, 250
Accounting Irregularities, 250
Sarbanes-Oxley Act, 250
Shareholder Activism, 252
Limited Power of Governance, 254
Market for Corporate Control, 254
Use of LBOs to Achieve Corporate Control, 255
Barriers to the Market for Corporate Control, 255
Globalization of Stock Markets, 256
Foreign Stock Offerings in the United States, 256
International Placement Process, 256
Global Stock Exchanges, 257
Emerging Stock Markets, 258
Methods Used to Invest in Foreign Stocks, 258
Summary, 260
**Point Counter-Point: Should a Stock Exchange Enforce Some Governance
Standards on the Firms Listed on the Exchange? 260**
Questions and Applications, 260
Advanced Questions, 261
Interpreting Financial News, 261
Managing in Financial Markets, 261
Problem, 262
**Flow of Funds Exercise: Contemplating an Initial Public
Offering (IPO), 262**
Internet/Excel Exercises, 262
WSJ Exercise: Assessing Stock Market Movements, 262

11: STOCK VALUATION AND RISK   263
Stock Valuation Methods, 263
Price-Earnings (PE) Method, 263
Dividend Discount Model, 264
Adjusting the Dividend Discount Model, 265
Free Cash Flow Model, 266
Required Rate of Return on Stocks, 267
Capital Asset Pricing Model, 267
Arbitrage Pricing Model, 269
Factors That Affect Stock Prices, 269
Economic Factors, 269
Market-Related Factors, 271
Firm-Specific Factors, 272

Using the Wall Street Journal: Stock Market Indexes, 273
Integration of Factors Affecting Stock Prices, 274
Stock Risk, 274
Volatility of a Stock, 275
Beta of a Stock, 276
Value at Risk, 279
Forecasting Stock Volatility and Beta, 281
Methods of Forecasting Stock Price Volatility, 281
Forecasting a Stock Portfolio's Volatility, 282
Forecasting a Stock Portfolio's Beta, 282

Risk-Adjusted Stock Performance, 283
  Sharpe Index, 283
  Treynor Index, 283
Stock Market Efficiency, 284
  Forms of Efficiency, 284
  Tests of the Efficient Market Hypothesis, 285
Foreign Stock Valuation and Performance, 286
  Valuation of Foreign Stocks, 286
  International Market Efficiency, 286
  Measuring Performance from Investing in Foreign Stocks, 287
  Performance from Global Diversification, 287
Summary, 288
Point Counter-Point: Is the Stock Market Efficient? 289
Questions and Applications, 289
  Advanced Questions, 290
  Interpreting Financial News, 290
  Managing in Financial Markets, 290
Problems, 291
Flow of Funds Exercise: Valuing Stocks, 292
Internet/Excel Exercises, 292
WSJ Exercise: Reviewing Abrupt Shifts in Stock Valuation, 293
  Appendix 11: The Link between Accounting and Stock Valuation, 294

12: MARKET MICROSTRUCTURE AND STRATEGIES   **303**
Stock Market Transactions, 303
  Placing an Order, 303
  Margin Trading, 305
  Short Selling, 306
How Stock Transactions Are Executed, 309
  Floor Brokers, 309
  Specialists, 309
  The Spread on Stock Transactions, 311
  Electronic Communication Networks (ECNs), 312
  Program Trading, 314
Regulation of Stock Trading, 315
  Circuit Breakers, 316
  Trading Halts, 316
  Securities and Exchange Commission (SEC), 316
Trading International Stocks, 318
  Reduction in Transaction Costs, 318
  Reduction in Information Costs, 318
  Reduction in Exchange Rate Risk, 318
Summary, 319
Point Counter-Point: Is a Specialist or a Market-Maker Needed? 319
Questions and Applications, 320
  Advanced Questions, 320
  Interpreting Financial News, 320
  Managing in Financial Markets, 320
Problems, 320
Flow of Funds Exercise: Shorting Stocks, 321

Internet/Excel Exercises, 321

Part 4 Integrative Problem: Stock Market Analysis, 322

Questions, 322

PART 5: Derivative Security Markets   323

13: FINANCIAL FUTURES MARKETS   325

Background on Financial Futures, 325

  Purpose of Trading Financial Futures, 325

  Structure of the Futures Market, 326

  Trading Futures, 327

Interpreting Financial Futures Tables, 327

Valuation of Financial Futures, 328

  Using the Wall Street Journal: Interest Rate Futures, 329

  Impact of the Opportunity Cost, 329

Explaining Price Movements of Bond Futures Contracts, 330

Speculating with Interest Rate Futures, 331

  Impact of Leverage, 332

Closing Out the Futures Position, 332

Hedging with Interest Rate Futures, 333

  Using Interest Rate Futures to Create a Short Hedge, 333

  Using Interest Rate Futures to Create a Long Hedge, 336

  Hedging Net Exposure, 336

Bond Index Futures, 336

Stock Index Futures, 337

  Valuing Stock Index Futures Contracts, 338

  Speculating with Stock Index Futures, 339

  Hedging with Stock Index Futures, 339

  Using the Wall Street Journal: Stock Index Futures Contracts, 340

  Dynamic Asset Allocation with Stock Index Futures, 341

  Prices of Stock Index Futures versus Stocks, 342

  Arbitrage with Stock Index Futures, 342

  Circuit Breakers on Stock Index Futures, 343

Single Stock Futures, 343

Risk of Trading Futures Contracts, 344

  Market Risk, 344

  Basis Risk, 344

  Liquidity Risk, 345

  Credit Risk, 345

  Prepayment Risk, 345

  Operational Risk, 345

Regulation in the Futures Markets, 346

Institutional Use of Futures Markets, 346

Globalization of Futures Markets, 347

  Non-U.S. Participation in U.S. Futures Contracts, 347

  Foreign Stock Index Futures, 347

  Currency Futures Contracts, 348

Summary, 349

Point Counter-Point: Has the Futures Market Created More
  Uncertainty for Stocks? 349

Questions and Applications, 349
Advanced Questions, 350
Interpreting Financial News, 350
Managing in Financial Markets, 351
Problems, 351
Flow of Funds Exercise: Hedging with Futures Contracts, 351
Internet/Excel Exercises, 352

1 4: OPTIONS MARKETS   353
Background on Options, 353
Markets Used to Trade Options, 354
How Option Trades Are Executed, 355
Types of Orders, 355
Stock Option Quotations, 355
Speculating with Stock Options, 356
Speculating with Call Options, 356
Speculating with Put Options, 357
Excessive Risk from Speculation, 360
Determinants of Stock Option Premiums, 361
Determinants of Call Option Premiums, 361
Determinants of Put Option Premiums, 362
Explaining Changes in Option Premiums, 364
Indicators Monitored by Participants in the Options Market, 365
Hedging with Stock Options, 365
Hedging with Call Options, 365
Hedging with Put Options, 367
Using Options to Measure a Stock's Risk, 367
Options on ETFs and Stock Indexes, 368
Hedging with Stock Index Options, 368
Dynamic Asset Allocation with Stock Index Options, 369
Using Index Options to Measure the Market's Risk, 370
Options on Futures Contracts, 370
Speculating with Options on Futures, 371
Hedging with Options on Futures, 372
Hedging with Options on Interest Rate Futures, 372
Hedging with Options on Stock Index Futures, 373
Institutional Use of Options Markets, 375
Options as Compensation, 375
Globalization of Options Markets, 376
Currency Options Contracts, 377
Summary, 377
Point Counter-Point: If You Were a Major Shareholder of a Publicly Traded Firm, Would You Prefer That Stock Options Be Traded on That Stock? 378
Questions and Applications, 378
Advanced Questions, 378
Interpreting Financial News, 379
Managing in Financial Markets, 379
Problems, 380
Flow of Funds Exercise: Hedging with Options Contracts, 381
Internet/Excel Exercises, 382
WSJ Exercise: Assessing Stock Option Information, 382
Appendix 14: Option Valuation, 383

15: SWAP MARKETS   **391**

Background, 391

Use of Swaps for Hedging, 392

Use of Swaps for Speculating, 393

Participation by Financial Institutions, 393

Types of Interest Rate Swaps, 394

Plain Vanilla Swaps, 394

Forward Swaps, 396

Callable Swaps, 397

Putable Swaps, 397

Extendable Swaps, 398

Zero-Coupon-for-Floating Swaps, 398

Rate-Capped Swaps, 400

Equity Swaps, 400

Other Types of Swaps, 401

Risks of Interest Rate Swaps, 402

Basis Risk, 402

Credit Risk, 402

Sovereign Risk, 403

Pricing Interest Rate Swaps, 403

Prevailing Market Interest Rates, 403

Availability of Counterparties, 403

Credit and Sovereign Risk, 404

Factors Affecting the Performance of Interest Rate Swaps, 404

Interest Rate Caps, Floors, and Collars, 404

Interest Rate Caps, 405

Interest Rate Floors, 406

Interest Rate Collars, 407

Credit Default Swaps, 408

Development of the CDS Market, 409

Payments on a Credit Default Swap, 409

How CDSs Affect Debtor-Creditor Negotiations, 409

Impact of the Credit Crisis on the CDS Market, 409

Globalization of Swap Markets, 410

Currency Swaps, 411

Summary, 413

Point Counter-Point: Should Financial Institutions Engage in Interest Rate Swaps for Speculative Purposes? 414

Questions and Applications, 414

Advanced Questions, 415

Interpreting Financial News, 415

Managing in Financial Markets, 415

Problems, 415

Flow of Funds Exercise: Hedging with Interest Rate Derivatives, 416

Internet/Excel Exercises, 416

WSJ Exercise: Impact of Interest Rates on a Swap Arrangement, 416

16: FOREIGN EXCHANGE DERIVATIVE MARKETS   **417**

Foreign Exchange Markets, 417

Institutional Use of Foreign Exchange Markets, 417

Exchange Rate Quotations, 418

Types of Exchange Rate Systems, 419

Factors Affecting Exchange Rates, 420
Differential Inflation Rates, 420
Differential Interest Rates, 421
Central Bank Intervention, 421
Foreign Exchange Controls, 423
Forecasting Exchange Rates, 423
Technical Forecasting, 423
Fundamental Forecasting, 424
Market-Based Forecasting, 424
Mixed Forecasting, 424
Foreign Exchange Derivatives, 425
Forward Contracts, 425
Currency Futures Contracts, 426
Currency Swaps, 426
Currency Options Contracts, 426

Using the Wall Street Journal: Currency Futures Contracts, 427
Use of Foreign Exchange Derivatives for Speculating, 429
International Arbitrage, 431
Locational Arbitrage, 431
Triangular Arbitrage, 431
Covered Interest Arbitrage, 432
Summary, 433
**Point Counter-Point: Do Financial Institutions Need to Consider Foreign
 Exchange Market Conditions When Making Domestic Security Market Decisions? 434**
Questions and Applications, 434
Advanced Questions, 435
Interpreting Financial News, 435
Managing in Financial Markets, 435
Problems, 435
Flow of Funds Exercise: Hedging with Foreign Exchange Derivatives, 436
Internet/Excel Exercises, 436
WSJ Exercise: Assessing Exchange Rate Movements, 436

Appendix 16A: Impact of the Asian Crisis on Foreign Exchange Markets
 and Other Financial Markets, 437

Appendix 16B: Currency Option Pricing, 447

Part 5 Integrative Problem: Choosing among Derivative Securities, 451
Questions, 451
Midterm Self-Exam, 453
Midterm Review, 453
Midterm Self-Exam, 454
Answers to Midterm Self-Exam, 456

PART 6: Commercial Banking 459

17: COMMERCIAL BANK OPERATIONS 461

Background on Commercial Banks, 461
Bank Market Structure, 461
Bank Sources of Funds, 462
Transaction Deposits, 463
Savings Deposits, 463

Time Deposits, 463

Money Market Deposit Accounts, 464

Federal Funds Purchased, 464

Borrowing from the Federal Reserve Banks, 465

Repurchase Agreements, 465

Eurodollar Borrowings, 466

Bonds Issued by the Bank, 466

Bank Capital, 466

Distribution of Bank Sources of Funds, 467

Uses of Funds by Banks, 467

Cash, 468

Bank Loans, 468

Using the Wall Street Journal: Prime Rates, 470

Investment in Securities, 472

Federal Funds Sold, 473

Repurchase Agreements, 473

Eurodollar Loans, 473

Fixed Assets, 473

Summary of Bank Uses of Funds, 473

Off-Balance Sheet Activities, 475

Loan Commitments, 476

Standby Letters of Credit, 476

Forward Contracts on Currencies, 476

Interest Rate Swap Contracts, 477

Credit Default Swap Contracts, 477

International Banking, 477

Global Competition in Foreign Countries, 477

Impact of the Euro on Global Competition, 478

Summary, 478

Point Counter-Point: Should Banks Engage in Other Financial Services Besides Banking? 479

Questions and Applications, 479

Interpreting Financial News, 479

Managing in Financial Markets, 479

Flow of Funds Exercise: Services Provided by Financial Conglomerates, 480

Internet/Excel Exercise, 480

18: BANK REGULATION   **481**

Background, 481

Background Structure, 481

Regulators, 482

Regulation of Bank Ownership, 482

Regulation of Bank Operations, 482

Regulation of Deposit Insurance, 482

Regulation of Deposits, 484

Regulation of Bank Loans, 484

Regulation of Bank Investment in Securities, 485

Regulation of Securities Services, 485

Regulation of Insurance Services, 486

Regulation of Off-Balance Sheet Transactions, 486

Regulation of the Accounting Process, 487

Regulation of Capital, 488
Basel I Accord, 488
Basel II Accord, 488
Use of the VAR Method to Determine Capital Requirements, 490
How Regulators Monitor Banks, 491
CAMELS Ratings, 491
Corrective Action by Regulators, 494
Funding the Closure of Failing Banks, 494
Global Bank Regulations, 496
Summary, 496
Point Counter-Point: Should Regulators Intervene to Take Over Weak Banks? 497
Questions and Applications, 497
Interpreting Financial News, 498
Managing in Financial Markets, 498
Flow of Funds Exercise: Impact of Regulation and Deregulation on Financial Services, 498
Internet/Excel Exercise, 498
WSJ Exercise: Impact of Bank Regulations, 498

19: BANK MANAGEMENT   **499**

Bank Management Goals and Structures, 499
Board of Directors, 499
Overview of Bank Management, 500
Management of Operations, 500
Managing Liquidity, 500
Use of Securitization to Boost Liquidity, 501
Liquidity Problems, 501
Managing Interest Rate Risk, 501
Methods Used to Assess Interest Rate Risk, 502
Whether to Hedge Interest Rate Risk, 507
Methods Used to Reduce Interest Rate Risk, 507
International Interest Rate Risk, 511
Managing Credit Risk, 512
Measuring Credit Risk, 512
Tradeoff between Credit Risk and Return, 513
Reducing Credit Risk, 513
Managing Market Risk, 514
Measuring Market Risk, 515
Methods Used to Reduce Market Risk, 515
Integrated Bank Management, 516
Application, 516
Managing Risk of International Operations, 519
Exchange Rate Risk, 519
Settlement Risk, 520
Participation in Financial Markets, 520
Summary, 521
Point Counter-Point: Can Bank Failures Be Avoided? 521
Questions and Applications, 521
Advanced Questions, 522
Interpreting Financial News, 522
Managing in Financial Markets, 522

Problems, 523
Flow of Funds Exercise: Managing Credit Risk, 525
Internet/Excel Exercises, 526
WSJ Exercise: Bank Management Strategies, 526

20: BANK PERFORMANCE   527

Valuation of a Commercial Bank, 527
  Factors That Affect Cash Flows, 527
  Factors That Affect the Required Rate of Return by Investors, 529
Performance of Banks, 530
  Interest Income and Expenses, 530
  Noninterest Income and Expenses, 531
  Net Income, 533
How to Evaluate a Bank's Performance, 533
  Examination of Return on Assets (ROA), 534
  Application, 535
Summary, 537
Point Counter-Point: Does a Bank's Income Statement Clearly Indicate the Bank's
  Performance? 537
Questions and Applications, 537
  Interpreting Financial News, 538
  Managing in Financial Markets, 538
Problem, 538
Flow of Funds Exercise: How the Flow of Funds Affects Bank Performance, 539
Internet/Excel Exercises, 539
WSJ Exercise: Assessing Bank Performance, 539
Part 6 Integrative Problem: Forecasting Bank Performance, 540
Questions, 541

PART 7: Nonbank Operations   543

21: THRIFT OPERATIONS   545

Background on Savings Institutions, 545
  Ownership of Savings Institutions, 545
Regulation of Savings Institutions, 546
  Regulatory Assessment of Savings Institutions, 546
  Deregulation of Services, 546
Sources and Uses of Funds, 546
  Sources of Funds, 547
  Uses of Funds, 548
  Balance Sheet of Savings Institutions, 549
Exposure to Risk, 550
  Liquidity Risk, 550
  Credit Risk, 551
  Interest Rate Risk, 552
Management of Interest Rate Risk, 553
  Adjustable-Rate Mortgages (ARMs), 553
  Interest Rate Futures Contracts, 554
  Interest Rate Swaps, 554
  Conclusions about Interest Rate Risk, 554

Interaction with Other Financial Institutions, 555
Participation in Financial Markets, 555
Valuation of a Savings Institution, 556
Factors That Affect Cash Flows, 556
Factors That Affect the Required Rate of Return, 557
Exposure of Savings Institutions to Crises, 557
Savings Institution Crisis in the Late 1980s, 557
The Credit Crisis, 559
Credit Unions, 560
Ownership of Credit Unions, 560
Advantages and Disadvantages of Credit Unions, 561
Credit Union Sources of Funds, 561
Credit Union Uses of Funds, 562
Regulation of Credit Unions, 562
Exposure of Credit Unions to Risk, 563
Summary, 563
Point Counter-Point: Can All Savings Institutions Avoid Failure? 564
Questions and Applications, 564
Interpreting Financial News, 565
Managing in Financial Markets, 565
Flow of Funds Exercise: Market Participation by Savings Institutions, 566
Internet/Excel Exercises, 566
WSJ Exercise: Assessing Performance of Savings Institutions, 566

2 2: FINANCE OPERATIONS   **567**
Types of Finance Companies, 567
Consumer Finance Companies, 567
Business Finance Companies, 567
Captive Finance Subsidiaries, 568
Sources and Uses of Funds, 568
Sources of Funds, 568
Uses of Finance Company Funds, 569
Risks Faced by Finance Companies, 571
Liquidity Risk, 571
Interest Rate Risk, 571
Credit Risk, 572
Valuation of a Finance Company, 572
Factors That Affect Cash Flows, 572
Factors That Affect the Required Rate of Return, 573
Interaction with Other Financial Institutions, 573
Participation in Financial Markets, 574
Multinational Finance Companies, 575
Summary, 575
Point Counter-Point: Will Finance Companies Be Replaced by Banks? 576
Questions and Applications, 576
Interpreting Financial News, 576
Managing in Financial Markets, 576
Flow of Funds Exercise: How Finance Companies Facilitate the Flow of Funds, 577
Internet/Excel Exercises, 577
WSJ Exercise: Finance Company Performance, 577

2 3: MUTUAL FUND OPERATIONS 579

Background on Mutual Funds, 579
Types of Funds, 579
Comparison to Depository Institutions, 581
Regulation, 581
Estimating the Net Asset Value, 582
Distributions to Shareholders, 582
Mutual Fund Classifications, 583
Management of Mutual Funds, 583
Expenses Incurred by Shareholders, 584
Sales Load, 585
12b-1 Fees, 586
Governance of Mutual Funds, 586
Late Trading Scandal, 587
Corporate Control by Mutual Funds, 587

Mutual Fund Categories, 587
Stock Mutual Fund Categories, 588
Bond Mutual Fund Categories, 589
Asset Allocation Funds, 591
Growth and Size of Mutual Funds, 591

Performance of Mutual Funds, 593
Performance of Stock Mutual Funds, 593

Using the Wall Street Journal: Performance of Mutual Fund Indexes, 594

Performance from Diversifying among Mutual, 595
Performance of Closed-End Stock Funds, 595
Performance of Bond Mutual Funds, 595
Research on Mutual Fund Performance, 596

Money Market Funds, 596
Asset Composition of Money Market Funds, 598
Maturity of Money Market Funds, 598
Risk of Money Market Funds, 599
Management of Money Market Funds, 600
Regulation and Taxation of Money Market Funds, 600

Other Types of Funds, 600
Exchange-Traded Funds, 601
Venture Capital Funds, 602
Private Equity Funds, 602
Hedge Funds, 604
Real Estate Investment Trusts, 607

Interaction with Other Financial Institutions, 607
Use of Financial Markets, 608

Globalization through Mutual Funds, 609
Summary, 610
Point Counter-Point: Should Mutual Funds Be Subject to More Regulation? 610
Questions and Applications, 610
Advanced Questions, 611
Interpreting Financial News, 611
Managing in Financial Markets, 611

Flow of Funds Exercise: How Mutual Funds Facilitate the Flow of Funds, 612
Internet/Excel Exercises, 612
WSJ Exercise: Finance Company Performance, 613

2 4: SECURITIES OPERATIONS   **615**

Services Provided by Securities Firms, 615

Facilitating New Stock Offerings, 615

Facilitating New Bond Offerings, 617

Facilitating Leveraged Buyouts, 618

Facilitating Arbitrage, 619

Facilitating Corporate Restructuring, 620

Providing Brokerage Services, 621

Investing Their Own Funds, 623

Summary of Services Provided, 624

Interaction with Other Financial Institutions, 625

Participation in Financial Markets, 625

Regulation of Securities Firms, 625

Financial Services Modernization Act, 627

Regulation FD, 628

Analyst Compensation and Ratings, 628

Rules Preventing Abuses in the IPO Market, 629

Repeal of the Trade-Through Rule, 629

Risks of Securities Firms, 629

Market Risk, 629

Interest Rate Risk, 629

Credit Risk, 630

Exchange Rate Risk, 630

Valuation of a Securities Firm, 630

Factors That Affect Cash Flows, 630

Factors That Affect the Required Rate of Return, 631

Impact of the Credit Crisis on Securities Firms, 631

Government Assistance to Bear Stearns, 631

Failure of Lehman Brothers, 634

Impact of the Crisis on Regulatory Reform, 635

Globalization of Securities Firms, 636

Growth in International Joint Ventures, 636

Growth in International Securities Transactions, 636

Summary, 637

Point Counter-Point: Should Analysts Be Separated from Securities Firms to Prevent Conflicts of Interest? 638

Questions and Applications, 638

Interpreting Financial News, 638

Managing in Financial Markets, 639

Flow of Funds Exercise: How Securities Firms Facilitate the Flow of Funds, 639

Internet/Excel Exercises, 639

WSJ Exercise: Performance of Securities Firms, 640

2 5: INSURANCE AND PENSION FUND OPERATIONS   **641**

Background, 641

Determinants of Insurance Premiums, 641

Investments by Insurance Companies, 643

Regulation of Insurance Companies, 643

Life Insurance Operations, 644

Ownership, 645

Types of Life Insurance, 645

Sources of Funds, 645

Uses of Funds, 646

Asset Management of Life Insurance Companies, 648

Other Types of Insurance Operations, 649

Property and Casualty Insurance, 650

Health Care Insurance, 651

Business Insurance, 652

Bond Insurance, 652

Mortgage Insurance, 653

Interaction with Other Financial Institutions, 653

Participation in Financial Markets, 654

Exposure to Risk, 655

Interest Rate Risk, 655

Credit Risk, 655

Market Risk, 655

Liquidity Risk, 655

Valuation of an Insurance Company, 655

Factors That Affect Cash Flows, 656

Factors That Affect the Required Rate of Return by Investors, 656

Impact of the Credit Crisis, 657

Indicators of Value and Performance, 658

Multinational Insurance Companies, 659

Background on Pension Funds, 660

Public Pension Funds, 660

Private Pension Plans, 660

Pension Fund Participation in Financial Markets, 661

Pension Regulations, 662

Pension Fund Management, 664

Management of Insured versus Trust Portfolios, 664

Management of Portfolio Risk, 665

Corporate Control by Pension Funds, 665

Performance of Pension Funds, 665

Pension Fund's Stock Portfolio Performance, 666

Pension Fund's Bond Portfolio Performance, 666

Performance Evaluation, 667

Performance of Pension Portfolio Managers, 667

Performance during the Credit Crisis, 667

Summary, 668

Point Counter-Point: Should Pension Fund Managers Be More Involved with Corporate Governance? 668

Questions and Applications, 668

Interpreting Financial News, 669

Managing in Financial Markets, 669

Flow of Funds Exercise: How Insurance Companies Facilitate the Flow of Funds, 670

Internet/Excel Exercises, 670

WSJ Exercise: Insurance Company Performance, 670

Part 7 Integrative Problem: Assessing the Influence of Economic Conditions across a Financial Conglomerate's Units, 671

Questions, 671

Final Self-Exam, 672

Final Review, 672
Final Self-Exam, 673
Answers to Final Self-Exam, 674

Appendix A: Comprehensive Project   677
Appendix B: Using Excel to Conduct Analyses   687
Glossary   691
Index   705

Preface

Financial markets finance much of the expenditures by corporations, governments, and individuals. Financial institutions are the key intermediaries in financial markets because they transfer funds from savers to those who need funds. *Financial Institutions and Markets,* Ninth Edition, describes financial markets and the financial institutions that serve those markets. It provides a conceptual framework that can be used to understand why markets exist. Each type of financial market is described, with a focus on the securities that are traded in that market and the participation by financial institutions.

Today, many financial institutions offer all types of financial services, such as banking, securities services, mutual fund services, and insurance services. Each type of financial service is unique, however. Therefore, the discussion of financial services in this book is organized by type of financial service that can be offered by financial institutions.

The credit crisis has had an adverse effect across financial markets and institutions. Accordingly, this text gives special attention to the impact of the credit crisis on each type of financial market and financial institution.

INTENDED MARKET

This text is suitable for both undergraduate and master's level courses in financial markets, financial institutions, or both. To maximize students' comprehension, some of the more difficult questions and problems should be assigned, along with the special applications at the end of each chapter and the Comprehensive Project. A term paper on the credit crisis may also be a valuable exercise, and several possible topics for this paper are provided.

ORGANIZATION OF THE TEXT

Part 1 (Chapters 1 through 3) introduces the key financial markets and financial institutions, explains interest rate movements in the financial markets, and explains why yields vary among securities. Part 2 (Chapters 4 and 5) describes the functions of the Federal Reserve System (the Fed) and explains how its monetary policy influences interest rates and other economic conditions. Part 3 (Chapters 6 through 9) covers the major debt security markets, Part 4 (Chapters 10 through 12) describes equity securities markets, and Part 5 (Chapters 13 through 16) covers the derivative security markets. Each chapter in Parts 3 through 5 focuses on a particular market. The integration of each market with other markets is stressed throughout these chapters. Part 6 (Chapters 17 through 20) concentrates on commercial banking, and Part 7 (Chapters 21 through 25) covers all other types of financial services.

Courses that emphasize financial markets should focus on the first five parts (Chapters 1 through 16); however, some chapters in the section on commercial banking are also relevant. Courses that emphasize financial institutions and financial services should focus on Parts 1, 2, 6, and 7, although some background on securities markets (Parts 3, 4, and 5) may be helpful.

Professors who emphasize financial markets and institutions in their courses may wish to focus on certain chapters of this book and skip others, depending on the other courses available to their students. For example, if a course on derivative securities is commonly offered, Part 5 of this text may be ignored. Alternatively, if an investments course provides a thorough background on types of securities, Parts 3 and 4 can be given less attention.

Chapters can be rearranged without a loss in continuity. Regardless of the order in which chapters are studied, it is highly recommended that the special exercises and selected questions in each chapter be assigned. These exercises may serve as a focal point for class discussion.

The credit crisis receives considerable emphasis in the mortgage markets chapter (Chapter 9) because it was primarily caused by activities in the mortgage market. The crisis has had an impact on every type of financial market and institution, however, so it is covered in each chapter as it applies to the contents of that chapter.

COVERAGE OF MAJOR CONCEPTS AND EVENTS

Numerous concepts relating to recent events and current trends in financial markets are discussed throughout the chapters, including the following:

- Causes of the credit crisis

- Effects of the credit crisis

- Government rescues of financial institutions during the credit crisis

- Credit default swaps

- Behavioral finance

- Private equity funding

- Venture capitalists

- Backdating of options

- Governance in financial markets

- The Fed's impact on financial markets

- Role of analysts

- Value-at-risk measurements

- Asymmetric information

- Valuation of financial institutions

- Regulatory reform in financial services

- Modified duration

- Collateralized mortgage obligations (CMOs)

- Portfolio insurance strategies

Each chapter is self-contained, so professors can use classroom time to focus on the more complex concepts and rely on the text to cover the other concepts.

MAJOR CONTENT CHANGES

Discussions of the causes and effects of the credit crisis are integrated throughout the text. Much attention is also given to innovations in financial markets and government intervention in financial markets.

FEATURES OF THE TEXT

The features of the text are as follows:

- *Part-Opening Diagram.* A diagram is provided at the beginning of each part to illustrate generally how the key concepts in that part are related. This offers information about the organization of chapters in that part.

- *Objectives.* A bulleted list at the beginning of each chapter identifies the key concepts in that chapter.

- *Examples* Examples are provided to reinforce key concepts.

- *Credit Crisis.* A Credit Crisis icon in the margin indicates a discussion of the credit crisis as it applies to the topics covered in the chapter.

- *Global Aspects.* A Global Aspects icon in the margin indicates international coverage of the topic being discussed.

- *Summary.* A bulleted list at the end of each chapter summarizes the key concepts. This list corresponds to the list of objectives at the beginning of the chapter.

- *Point Counter-Point.* A controversial issue is introduced, along with opposing arguments, and students are asked to determine which argument is correct and explain why.

- *Questions and Applications.* The Questions and Applications section at the end of each chapter tests students' understanding of the key concepts and may serve as homework assignments or study aids in preparation for exams.

- *Flow of Funds Exercise.* A running exercise is provided at the end of each chapter to illustrate how a manufacturing company relies on all types of financial markets and financial services provided by financial institutions.

- *Interpreting Financial News.* At the end of each chapter, students are challenged to interpret comments made in the media about the chapter's key concepts. This gives students practice in interpreting announcements by the financial media.

- *Internet/Excel Exercises.* At the end of each chapter, there are exercises that introduce students to applicable information available on various websites, enable the application of Excel to related topics, or a combination of these. For example, the exercises allow students to assess yield curves, risk premiums, and stock volatility.

- *Managing in Financial Markets.* At the end of each chapter, students are placed in the position of financial managers and must make decisions about specific situations related to the key concepts in that chapter.

- *Problems.* Selected chapters include problems to test students' computational skills.

- *WSJ Exercise.* This exercise, which appears at the end of selected chapters, gives students an opportunity to apply information provided in *The Wall Street Journal* to specific concepts explained in that chapter.

- *Integrative Problems.* An integrative problem at the end of each part integrates the key concepts of chapters within that part.

- *Term Paper on the Credit Crisis.* Several topics for term papers on the credit crisis are suggested at the end of Chapter 1.

- *Comprehensive Project.* This project, found in Appendix A, requires students to apply real data to several key concepts described throughout the book.

- *Midterm and Final Self-Examinations.* At the end of Chapter 16, a midterm self-exam is offered to test students' knowledge of financial markets. At the end of Chapter 25, a final self-exam is offered to test students' knowledge of financial institutions. An answer key is provided so that students can evaluate their answers after they take the exam.

The concepts in each chapter can be reinforced by using one or more of the above features. Professors' use of the features will vary depending on the level of their students and the focus of the course. A course that focuses mostly on financial markets may emphasize tools such as the WSJ Exercises and Part 1 of the Comprehensive Project (on taking positions in securities and derivative instruments). Conversely, a course that focuses on financial institutions may assign an exercise in which students have to review recent annual reports (see Part 2 of the Comprehensive Project) to determine how a particular financial institution's performance is affected by its policies, industry regulations, and economic conditions. In addition, the Internet/Excel Exercises on financial institutions give students practice in assessing the operations and performance of financial institutions.

SUPPLEMENTS TO THE TEXT

The following supplements are available:

- The **website** for *Financial Institutions and Markets,* Ninth Edition, can be found at **www.cengage.com/international**. This robust site contains Internet exercises, updated URLs, downloadable PowerPoint slides, and links to finance sites.

- Revised by Joe Greco of California State University–Fullerton for this edition, **PowerPoint** lecture slides are available on the text website and the Instructor's Resource CD (IRCD) as a lecture aid for instructors and a study aid for students. In addition, key figures from the text are also provided in a separate PowerPoint package, also included on the website and IRCD.

- The **Instructor's Manual** contains the chapter outline for each chapter and a summary of key concepts for discussion as well as answers to the end-of-chapter Questions, Problems, Managing in Financial Markets, and Interpreting Financial News. The Instructor's Manual is also available to instructors on the text website and the Instructor's Resource CD.

- The **Test Bank** is available on the text website and Instructor's Resource CD.

- The **ExamView**™ computerized testing program contains all of the questions in the Test Bank. It is easy-to-use test creation software that is compatible with Microsoft® Windows. Instructors can add or edit questions, instructions, and answers and select questions by previewing them on the screen. Instructors can also create and administer quizzes online, whether over the Internet, a local area network (LAN), or a wide area network (WAN). ExamView™ is available on the Instructor's Resource CD.

- The **WSJ Subscription** is a special, 15-week subscription offer to *The Wall Street Journal* that is available to students of instructors adopting this text. *The Wall Street Journal* is the unprecedented resource for financial information in the marketplace, which the text integrates throughout. Contact your Cengage Learning sales representative for subscription package pricing and ordering information.

ACKNOWLEDGMENTS

The motivation to write this textbook came primarily from the encouragement of E. Joe Nosari (Florida State University). Several professors helped develop the text outline and offered suggestions on which of the concepts from earlier editions of this book should be covered in this edition. They are acknowledged in alphabetical order:

Ibrihim Affaneh, Indiana University of Pennsylvania

Henry C. F. Arnold, Seton Hall University

James C. Baker, Kent State University

Gerald Bierwag, Florida International University

Carol Billingham, Central Michigan University

Randy Billingsley, Virginia Tech University

Rita M. Biswas, State University of New York–Albany

Howard W. Bohnen, St. Cloud State University

Paul J. Bolster, Northeastern University

M. E. Bond, University of Memphis

Carol Marie Boyer, Long Island University, C.W. Post Campus

Alka Bramhandkar, Ithaca College

Emile J. Brinkman, University of Houston–University Park

Christopher L. Brown, Western Kentucky University

Sarah Bryant, George Washington University

Bill Brunsen, Eastern New Mexico University

James B. Burnham, Duquesne University

Deanne Butchey, Florida International University

William Carner, University of Missouri–Columbia

Joseph Cheng, Ithaca College

William T. Chittenden, Northern Illinois University

C. Steven Cole, University of North Texas

M. Cary Collins, University of Tennessee

Mark Correll, University of Colorado

Wayne C. Curtis, Troy State University

Steven Dobson, California Polytechnic State University

Robert M. Donchez, University of Colorado–Boulder

Richard J. Dowen, Northern Illinois University

Imad Elhaj, University of Louisville

James Felton, Central Michigan University

Stuart Fletcher, Appalachian State University

Clifford L. Fry, University of Houston

Edward K. Gill, California State University–Chico

Claire G. Gilmore, St. Joseph's University

Owen Gregory, University of Illinois–Chicago

Paul Grier, State University of New York–Binghamton

Ann Hackert, Idaho State University

John Halloran, University of Notre Dame

Gerald A. Hanweck, George Mason University

Hildegard R. Hendrickson, Seattle University

Bradley K. Hobbs, Ph.D., Florida Gulf Coast University

Jerry M. Hood, Loyola University–New Orleans

Ronald M. Horowitz, Oakland University

Paul Hsueh, University of Central Florida

Carl D. Hudson, Auburn University

John S. Jahera, Jr., Auburn University

Robert James, Babson College

Mel Jameson, University of Nevada

Shane Johnson, Bowling Green State University

Richard H. Keehn, University of Wisconsin–Parkside

James B. Kehr, Miami University of Ohio

David F. Kern, Arkansas State University

Elinda F. Kiss, University of Maryland Robert H Smith School of Business

James W. Kolari, Texas A&M University

Vladimir Kotomin, University of Wisconsin–Eau Claire

Robert A. Kunkel, University of Wisconsin–Oshkosh

George Kutner, Marquette University

Robert Lamy, Wake Forest University

David J. Leahigh, King's College

David N. Leggett, Bentley College

William Lepley, University of Wisconsin–Green Bay

Morgan Lynge, Jr., University of Illinois

Judy E. Maese, New Mexico State University

Timothy A. Manuel, University of Montana

L. R. Martindale, Texas A&M University

Joseph S. Mascia, Adelphi University

Robert W. McLeod, University of Alabama

Kathleen S. McNichol, LaSalle University

James McNulty, Florida Atlantic University

Charles Meiburg, University of Virginia

Jose Mercado-Mendez, Central Missouri State University

Kenneth Moran, Harding University

J. K. Mullen, Clarkson University

Neil Murphy, Virginia Commonwealth University

Hossein Noorain, Boston University & Wentworth Institute of Technology

Dale Osborne, University of Texas–Dallas

Coleen Pantalone, Northeastern University

Thomas H. Payne, University of Tennessee–Chattanooga

Sarah Peck, University of Iowa

Chien-Chih Peng, Morehead State University

D. Anthony Plath, University of North Carolina–Charlotte

Barbara Poole, Roger Williams University

Rose Prasad, Central Michigan University

Mitchell Ratner, Rider University

David Rayome, Northern Michigan University

Alan Reichert, Cleveland State University

Kenneth L. Rhoda, LaSalle University

Antonio J. Rodriguez, Texas A&M International University

Lawrence C. Rose, Massey University

Jack Rubens, Bryant College

Atul K. Saxena, Georgia Gwinnett College

Robert Schweitzer, University of Delaware

Mehmet Sencicek, University of New Haven

Kilman Shin, Ferris State University

Ahmad Sorhabian, California State Polytechnic University–Pomona

Andrew Spieler, Hofstra University

K. P. Sridharan, Delta State University

S. R. Stansell, East Carolina University

Richard W. Stolz, University of South Carolina Upstate

Richard S. Swasey, Northeastern University

John Thornton, Kent State University

Olaf J. Thorp, Babson College

James D. Tripp, University of Tennessee–Martin

K. C. Tseng, California State University–Fresno

Harry J. Turtle, University of Manitoba

Cevdet Uruk, University of Memphis

Geraldo M. Vasconcellos, Lehigh University

Michael C. Walker, University of Cincinnati

Fang Wang, West Virginia University

Bruce Watson, Wellesley College

David A. Whidbee, Washington State University

Colin Young, Bentley College

Stephen Zera, California State University–San Marcos

Mei "Miranda" Zhang, Mercer University

Other colleagues who offered suggestions for clarification include Jarrod Johnston (Appalachian State University), Victor Kalafa (Cross Country Staffing), Marek Marciniak (Florida Atlantic University), Thanh Ngo (University of Texas–Pan American), Oliver Schnusenberg (University of North Florida), John Taylor (Florida Atlantic University), and John Walker (Kutztown University).

This text also benefited from the research departments of several Federal Reserve district banks, the Federal National Mortgage Association, the National Credit Union Administration, the American Council of Life Insurance, the Investment Company Institute, and the Chicago Mercantile Exchange.

I acknowledge the help and support from the people at South-Western, including Mike Reynolds (Executive Editor), Nathan Anderson (Marketing Manager), Kendra Brown (Developmental Editor), Adele Scholtz (Senior Editorial Assistant), and Suellen Ruttkay (Marketing Coordinator). A special thanks is due to Scott Dillon (Content Project Manager) and Pat Lewis (Copyeditor) for their efforts to ensure a quality final product.

About the Author

Jeff Madura is the SunTrust Bank Professor of Finance at Florida Atlantic University. He has written several highly regarded textbooks, including *International Financial Management*. His research on international finance has been published in numerous journals, including the *Journal of Financial and Quantitative Analysis; Journal of Money, Credit and Banking; Financial Management; Journal of Financial Research;* and *Financial Review.* He has received multiple awards for excellence in teaching and research and has served as a consultant for international banks, securities firms, and other multinational corporations. He has also served as director for the Southern Finance Association and Eastern Finance Association and as president of the Southern Finance Association.

PART 1

Overview of the Financial Environment

Part 1 focuses on the flow of funds across financial markets, interest rates, and security prices. Chapter 1 introduces the key financial markets and the financial institutions that participate in those markets. Chapter 2 explains how various factors influence interest rates and how interest rate movements in turn affect the values of securities purchased by financial institutions. Chapter 3 identifies factors other than interest rates that influence security prices. Participants in financial markets use this information to value securities and make investment decisions within financial markets.

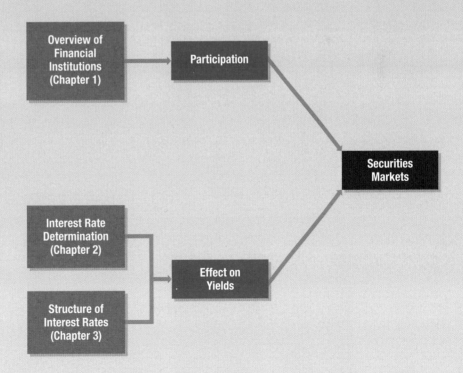

1

Role of Financial Markets and Institutions

CHAPTER OBJECTIVES

The specific objectives of this chapter are to:

- describe the types of financial markets that facilitate the flow of funds,

- describe the types of securities traded within financial markets,

- describe the role of financial institutions within financial markets, and

- identify the types of financial institutions that facilitate transactions in financial markets.

A **financial market** is a market in which financial assets (securities) such as stocks and bonds can be purchased or sold. Funds are transferred in financial markets when one party purchases financial assets previously held by another party. Financial markets facilitate the flow of funds and thereby allow financing and investing by households, firms, and government agencies. This chapter provides a background on financial markets and the financial institutions that participate in them.

ROLE OF FINANCIAL MARKETS

Financial markets transfer funds from those who have excess funds to those who need funds. They enable college students to obtain student loans, families to obtain mortgages, businesses to finance their growth, and governments to finance many of their expenditures. Without financial markets, many students could not go to college, many families could not purchase a home, corporations could not grow, and the government would not have been able to provide funding to corporations. Households and businesses that supply funds to financial markets earn a return on their investment; the return is necessary to ensure that funds are supplied to the financial markets. If funds were not supplied, the financial markets would not be able to transfer funds to those who need them.

Those participants who receive more money than they spend are referred to as **surplus units** (or investors). They provide their net savings to the financial markets. Those participants who spend more money than they receive are referred to as **deficit units** (or borrowers). They access funds from financial markets so that they can spend more money than they receive. Many individuals provide funds to financial markets in some periods and access funds in other periods.

EXAMPLE

College students are typically deficit units, as they often borrow from financial markets to support their education. After they obtain their degree, they earn more income than they spend and thus become surplus units. A few years later, they may become deficit units again by purchasing a home. At this stage, they may provide funds to and access funds from financial markets simultaneously. That is, they may periodically deposit savings in a financial institution, but also borrow money from a financial institution to buy a home. ●

Many deficit units such as firms and government agencies access funds from financial markets by issuing securities. **Securities** represent a claim on the issuer. **Debt securities** represent debt (also called credit, or borrowed funds) incurred by the issuer. Deficit units issue the securities to surplus units and pay interest to the surplus units on a periodic basis (such as every six months). Debt securities have a maturity date, when the surplus units can redeem them, receiving the principal (face value) from the issuer. **Equity securities** (also called stocks) represent equity or ownership in the issuer. Some businesses issue equity securities as an alternative way of raising funds.

Issuing securities enables corporations and government agencies to obtain money from surplus units and thus to spend more money than they receive from normal operations.

EXAMPLE

If the U.S. government wants to spend $70 billion more than it receives in taxes this month, it can issue U.S. Treasury securities to net savers. The U.S. government is a major deficit unit and therefore frequently relies on financial markets. The Treasury securities that it issues are a form of debt owed by the Treasury to the net savers who purchased the securities. Other government agencies also commonly issue debt securities to obtain funds.

Similarly, if Google wants to spend $40 million more than it receives in revenue this month, it can issue corporate debt securities to net savers. Alternatively, it can issue equity securities to raise funds. Each method of raising funds has distinct advantages and disadvantages, as will be discussed in later chapters. ●

Types of Financial Markets

Each financial market is created to satisfy particular preferences of market participants. For example, some participants may want to invest funds for a short-term period, whereas others want to invest for a long-term period. Some participants are willing to tolerate a high level of risk when investing, whereas others need to avoid risk. Some participants that need funds prefer to borrow, whereas others prefer to issue stock. There are many different types of financial markets, and each market can be distinguished by the maturity structure and trading structure of its securities.

Money versus Capital Markets

The financial markets that facilitate the transfer of debt securities are commonly classified by the maturity of the securities. Those financial markets that facilitate the flow of short-term funds (with maturities of one year or less) are known as **money markets,** while those that facilitate the flow of long-term funds are known as **capital markets.**

Primary versus Secondary Markets

Money market securities are debt securities that have a maturity of one year or less. They have a relatively high degree of liquidity, due to their short maturities, and because they typically have an active secondary market. Whether referring to money market securities or capital market securities, it is necessary to distinguish between transactions in the primary market and transactions in the secondary market. **Primary markets** facilitate the issuance of new securities. **Secondary markets** facilitate the trading of existing securities, which allows for a change in the ownership of the securities. Primary market transactions provide funds to the initial issuer of securities; secondary market transactions do not. The issuance of new corporate stock or new Treasury securities is a primary market transaction, while the sale of existing corporate stock or Treasury security holdings by one investor to another is a secondary market transaction.

An important characteristic of securities that are traded in secondary markets is **liquidity,** which is the degree to which securities can easily be liquidated (sold) without a loss of value. Some securities have an active secondary market, meaning that there are many willing buyers and sellers of the security at a given point in time. Investors prefer liquid securities so that they can easily sell the securities whenever they want (without a loss in value). If a security is illiquid, investors may not be able to find a willing buyer for it in the secondary market and may have to sell the security at a large discount just to attract a buyer. During the credit crisis in 2008 and 2009, investors were less willing to invest in many debt securities because they were concerned that these securities might default, meaning that the investors would not receive the interest and principal payments they expected. As the investors reduced their investments, the secondary markets for some debt securities became illiquid. Thus, investors who were holding these securities could not easily sell them.

How Financial Markets Facilitate Corporate Finance

Finance is commonly partitioned into three segments as shown in Exhibit 1.1: (1) corporate finance, (2) investment management, and (3) financial markets and institutions. Corporate finance involves decisions such as how much funding to obtain and how to invest the proceeds to expand operations.

The financial markets attract funds from investors and channel the funds to corporations. Thus, they serve as the means by which corporations finance their existing operations and their growth. The money markets enable corporations to borrow funds on a short-term basis so that they can support their existing operations. The capital markets enable corporations to obtain long-term funds to support corporate expansion. The decisions by the managers of publicly traded firms affect a firm's performance and stock price, which affects the returns to the investors who provided funding in the capital markets by purchasing the stock.

How Financial Markets Facilitate Investing   Investment management involves decisions by investors regarding how to invest their funds. The financial markets offer investors a wide variety of investment opportunities, including securities issued by the U.S. Treasury and government agencies as well as corporate securities. A major part of investment management is deciding which securities to purchase. When investing in stock, investors assess the financial management of various firms. They look for firms that are currently undervalued and have the potential to improve. They monitor and may even attempt to influence the financial management of the firms in which they invest to ensure that the financial managers make decisions that maximize the stock price. The market price of the stock serves as a measure of how well each publicly traded firm is being managed by its managers.

Financial institutions (discussed later in this chapter) are shown in Exhibit 1.1. They serve as intermediaries that execute the transactions within the financial markets so that funds from investors are channeled to corporations. They also commonly serve as investors and channel their own funds to corporations.

Exhibit 1.1 How Financial Markets Facilitate Corporate Finance and Investment Management

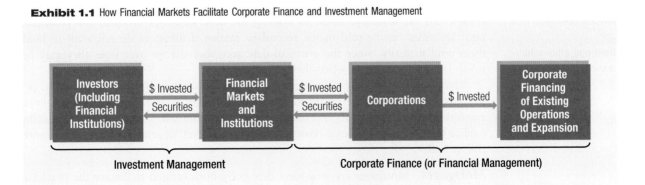

SECURITIES TRADED IN FINANCIAL MARKETS

Each type of security tends to have specific return and risk characteristics, as described in detail in the chapters covering financial markets. The term *risk* is used here to represent the uncertainty surrounding the expected return. The more uncertain the expected return, the greater the risk is. When investors have funds available for one year, for example, they can purchase one-year Treasury securities and know exactly what return they will receive on their investment. Alternatively, they can attempt to earn higher returns by investing in debt securities issued by firms, but there is a risk that they will never receive payments if those firms go bankrupt. Equity securities are also risky because their values depend on the future performance of the firms that issued them.

Investors differ with respect to the risk they are willing to incur, the amount of liquidity they desire, and their tax status, making some types of securities more desirable to some investors than to others. Normally, investors attempt to balance the objective of high return with their particular preference for low risk and adequate liquidity. Some investors are much more willing than others to invest in risky securities, as long as the potential return is sufficiently high.

Securities can be classified as money market securities, capital market securities, or derivative securities.

Money Market Securities

Money market securities are debt securities that have a maturity of one year or less. They generally have a relatively high degree of liquidity. Money market securities tend to have a low expected return but also a low degree of risk. Common types of money market securities include Treasury bills (issued by the Treasury), commercial paper (issued by corporations), and negotiable certificates of deposit (issued by depository institutions).

Capital Market Securities

Securities with a maturity of more than one year are called **capital market securities.** Capital market securities are commonly issued to finance the purchase of capital assets, such as buildings, equipment, or machinery. Three common types of capital market securities are bonds, mortgages, and stocks.

Bonds   Bonds are long-term debt securities issued by corporations and government agencies to support their operations. They provide a return to investors in the form of interest income (coupon payments) every six months. Since bonds represent debt, they specify the amount and timing of interest and principal payments to investors who purchase them. At maturity, investors holding the debt securities are paid the principal. Debt securities can be sold in the secondary market if investors do not want to hold them until maturity. Since the prices of debt securities change over time, they may be worth less when sold than when they were purchased.

Some debt securities are risky because the issuer could default on its obligation to repay the debt. Under these circumstances, the debt security will not provide the entire amount of coupon payments and principal that was promised. Long-term debt securities tend to have a higher expected return than money market securities, but they have more risk as well.

Mortgages   Mortgages are long-term debt obligations created to finance the purchase of real estate. Some mortgages are riskier than others. Lenders try to assess the likelihood of loan repayment using various criteria such as the borrower's income level relative to the value of the home. They offer prime mortgages to borrowers who qualify based on these criteria. Subprime mortgages are offered to some borrowers who do not have sufficient income to qualify for prime mortgages or are unable to make a down payment. The subprime mortgages exhibit a higher risk of default, and therefore the lenders providing the mortgages charge a higher interest rate and additional up-front fees to compensate for the higher level of risk. Subprime mortgages have recently received much attention because of their high default rates, which led to the major credit crisis that began in 2008.

Mortgage-Backed Securities   Mortgage-backed securities are debt obligations representing claims on a package of mortgages. There are many forms of mortgage-backed securities, but in the simplest form, the investors who purchase these securities receive monthly payments that are made by the homeowners on the mortgages backing the securities.

EXAMPLE

Mountain Savings Bank originates 100 residential mortgages for home buyers and will service the mortgages by processing the monthly payments. However, the bank does not want to use its own funds to finance the mortgages. It issues mortgage-backed securities that represent this package of 100 mortgages to eight financial institutions that are willing to purchase all of these securities. Each month, when Mountain Savings Bank receives interest and principal payments on the mortgages, it passes those payments on to the eight financial institutions that purchased the mortgage-backed securities and thereby provided the financing to the homeowners. If some of the homeowners default on their payments, the payments will be reduced and therefore so will the return on investment earned by the financial institutions that purchased the mortgage-backed securities. The securities they purchased are backed (collateralized) by the mortgages.

In many cases, the financial institution that originates the mortgage is not accustomed to the process of issuing mortgage-backed securities. If Mountain Savings Bank is unfamiliar with the process, another financial institution may participate by bundling Mountain's 100 mortgages with mortgages originated by other institutions. Then the financial institution issues mortgage-backed securities that represent all the mortgages in the bundle. Thus, any investor that purchases these mortgage-backed securities is partially financing the 100 mortgages at Mountain Savings Bank and all the other mortgages in the bundle that are backing these securities. Because of the high default rate on mortgages, mortgage-backed securities performed poorly during the credit crisis in 2008 and 2009. Some financial institutions that held a large amount of mortgage-backed securities suffered major losses at this time. ●

Stocks   Stocks (also referred to as equity securities) represent partial ownership in the corporations that issued them. They are classified as capital market securities because they have no maturity and therefore serve as a long-term source of funds. Some corporations provide income to their stockholders by distributing a portion of their quarterly earnings in the form of dividends. Other corporations retain and reinvest all of their earnings, which allows them more potential for growth.

Equity securities differ from debt securities in that they represent partial ownership. As corporations grow and increase in value, the value of the stock increases, and investors can earn a capital gain from selling the stock for a higher price than they paid for it. Thus, investors can earn a return from stocks in the form of periodic dividends (if there are any) and a capital gain when they sell the stock. Investors can experience a negative return, however, if the corporation performs poorly and its stock price declines over time as a result. Equity securities have a higher expected return than most long-term debt securities, but they also exhibit a higher degree of risk.

USING THE WALL STREET JOURNAL

Assessing Stock Performance

The Wall Street Journal provides information on how stocks performed recently. It shows charts for various stock indexes, such as the one shown here for the Dow Jones Industrial Average (an index representing stocks of 30 large well-known companies).

Notice that the range (from low to high) of index prices are also shown, so that you can assess the volatility of the index prices over time. In addition, the daily trading volume of all stocks on the New York Stock Exchange is disclosed, in billions of shares.

Source: Republished with permission of Dow Jones & Company, Inc., from The Wall Street Journal, January 1, 2009, p. C4; permission conveyed through the Copyright Clearance Center, Inc.

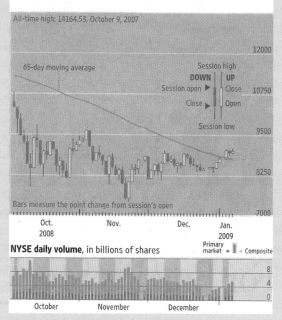

Dow Jones Industrial Average

9015.10 ▲ 62.21, or 0.69%
High, low, open and close for each trading day of the past three months.

	Last	Year ago
Trailing P/E ratio	18.83	44.39
P/E estimate *	10.62	15.36
Dividend yield	3.48	2.39
Current divisor	0.125552709	

All-time high: 14164.53, October 9, 2007

Derivative Securities

In addition to money market and capital market securities, derivative securities are also traded in financial markets. **Derivative securities** are financial contracts whose values are derived from the values of underlying assets (such as debt securities or equity securities). Many derivative securities enable investors to engage in speculation and risk management.

Speculation   Derivative securities allow an investor to speculate on movements in the value of the underlying assets without having to purchase those assets. Some derivative securities allow investors to benefit from an increase in the value of the underlying assets, whereas others allow investors to benefit from a decrease in the assets' value. Investors who speculate in derivative contracts can achieve higher returns than if they had speculated in the underlying assets, but they are also exposed to higher risk.

Risk Management   Derivative securities can be used in a manner that will generate gains if the value of the underlying assets declines. Consequently, financial institutions and other firms can use derivative securities to adjust the risk of their existing investments in securities. If a firm maintains investments in bonds, for example, it can take specific positions in derivative securities that will generate gains if bond values decline. In this way, derivative securities can be used to reduce a firm's risk. The loss on the bonds is offset by the gains on these derivative securities.

Valuation of Securities in Financial Markets

Each type of security generates a unique stream of expected cash flows to investors. In addition, each security has a unique level of uncertainty surrounding the expected cash flows that it will provide to investors and therefore surrounding its return. The valuation of a security is measured as the present value of its expected cash flows, discounted at a rate that reflects the uncertainty. Since the cash flows and the uncertainty surrounding the cash flows for each security are unique, the value of each security is unique.

EXAMPLE

Nike stock provides cash flows to investors in the form of quarterly dividends and its stock price at the time investors sell the stock. Both the future dividends and the future stock price are uncertain. Thus, the cash flows that Nike stock will provide to investors in the future are also uncertain. Investors can attempt to estimate the future cash flows that they will receive by obtaining information that may indicate Nike's future performance, such as reports about the athletic shoe industry, announcements by Nike about its recent sales, and published opinions about Nike's management ability. The valuation process is illustrated in Exhibit 1.2. ●

Impact of Information on Valuations   Although all investors rely on valuation to make investment decisions, different investors may interpret and use information in different ways. Thus, they may derive different valuations of a security based on the available information. Some investors rely mostly on economic or industry information to value a security, while others rely more on published opinions about the firm's management.

When investors receive new information about a security that clearly indicates the likelihood of higher cash flows or less uncertainty, they revise their valuations of that

Exhibit 1.2 Use of Information to Make Investment Decisions

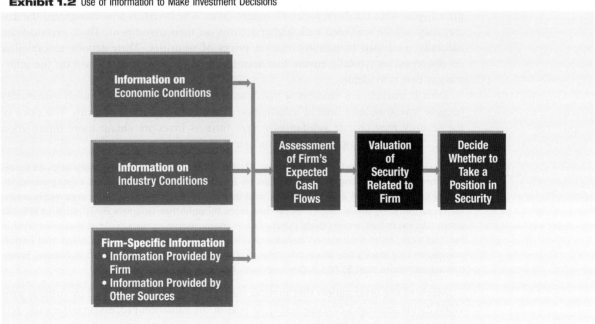

security upward. Consequently, the prevailing price is no longer in equilibrium, as most investors now view the security as undervalued at that price. The demand for the security increases at that price, and the supply of that security for sale decreases. As a result, the market price rises to a new equilibrium level.

Conversely, when investors receive unfavorable information, they reduce the expected cash flows or increase the discount rate used in valuation. All of the valuations of the security are revised downward, which results in shifts in the demand and supply conditions and a decline in the equilibrium price.

Announcements that do not contain any valuable new information will not elicit a market response. Sometimes, market participants take a position in anticipation of a particular announcement. If an announcement is fully anticipated, there will be no market response when the announcement occurs.

WEB

http://finance.yahoo
.com
Market quotations and
overview of financial
market activity.

Impact of the Internet on the Valuation Process   The Internet has improved the valuation of securities in several ways. Prices of securities are quoted online and can be obtained at any given moment by investors. For some securities, investors can track the actual sequence of transactions. Because much more information about the firms that issue securities is available online, securities can be priced more accurately. Furthermore, orders to buy or sell many types of securities can be submitted online, which expedites the adjustment in security prices to new information.

Market Efficiency

Because securities have market-determined prices, their favorable or unfavorable characteristics as perceived by the market are reflected in their prices. When security prices fully reflect all available information, the markets for these securities are referred to as efficient.

In an efficient market, securities are rationally priced. If a security is clearly undervalued based on public information, some investors will capitalize on the discrepancy by purchasing that security. This strong demand for the security will push the security's price higher until the discrepancy no longer exists. The investors who recognized the discrepancy will be rewarded with higher returns on their investment. Thus, investors are naturally motivated to monitor market prices of securities. Their actions to capitalize on discrepancies typically ensure that securities are properly priced, based on the information that is available.

Even if markets are efficient, a firm's security's price is subject to much uncertainty because investors have limited information available to value the security. The price of the security may change substantially over time as investors obtain more information about the firm's management, or its industry, or the economy.

EXAMPLE   When Google first issued stock on August 18, 2004, there was much uncertainty as to its value. Investors knew that Google's stock would be affected by factors such as its management, industry conditions (such as competition), and economic conditions, but there was much uncertainty surrounding these factors. Some investors thought that Google's initial price of $85 per share was excessive, while others purchased as many shares as they could at that price. Within the first year, more information became available about Google's business plans and performance, and its stock price more than tripled. Thus, for every $1,000 invested in Google, investors earned more than $3,000 within one year. ●

Much of the information that investors use to value securities issued by firms is provided by the managers of those firms. As part of the valuation process, investors also rely on accounting reports of a firm's revenue and expenses as a base for estimating its future cash flows. Although firms with publicly traded stock are required to disclose financial information and accounting statements, a firm's managers still possess information about its financial condition that is not necessarily available to investors. This situation is referred to as asymmetric information. Even when information is disclosed, an asymmetric information problem may still exist if some of the information provided by the firm's managers is misleading.

In some cases, a security is mispriced because of the psychology involved in the decision making. **Behavioral finance** is the application of psychology to make financial decisions. It explains why markets are not always efficient.

A positive report about Nadal Company's earnings caused the demand for Nadal stock to increase. The stock's price rose by 2 percent, an adjustment in the stock's price that was justified by the new information. As other media reported the same positive news, however, investors'-demand for Nadal stock increased again, causing the stock price to rise an additional 4 percent. The next day there was more media buzz about how well Nadal's stock was performing, and this caused a further increase in demand, and the share price increased another 3 percent. Thus, the stock's price increased much more than was justified because some investors based their investment decisions on the degree of media exposure that the stock received rather than on the actual information. The stock's price declined once the media hype subsided, but the point is that the stock was temporarily priced improperly as a result of the psychology used by investors to make their decisions. ●

Various conditions can affect the psychology used by investors or corporate managers to make decisions. Consequently, behavioral finance can sometimes explain the movements of a security's price or even the entire stock market.

Financial Market Regulation

In general, securities markets are regulated to ensure that the participants are treated fairly. Many regulations were enacted in response to fraudulent practices before the Great Depression.

Disclosure   Since the use of incorrect information can result in poor investment decisions, many regulations attempt to ensure that businesses disclose accurate information. Similarly, when information is disclosed to only a small set of investors, those investors have a major advantage over other investors. Thus, another regulatory goal is to provide all investors with equal access to disclosures by firms. The Securities Act of 1933 was intended to ensure complete disclosure of relevant financial information on publicly offered securities and to prevent fraudulent practices in selling these securities. The Securities Exchange Act of 1934 extended the disclosure requirements to secondary market issues. It also declared illegal a variety of deceptive practices, such as misleading financial statements and trading strategies designed to manipulate the market price. In addition, it established the Securities and Exchange Commission (SEC) to oversee the securities markets, and the SEC has implemented additional regulations over time. Securities laws do not prevent investors from making poor investment decisions but only attempt to ensure full disclosure of information and thus protect against fraud.

Regulatory Response to Financial Scandals   The financial scandals that occurred in the 2001–2002 period proved that the existing regulations were not sufficient to prevent fraud. Several well-known companies such as Enron and WorldCom misled investors by exaggerating their earnings. They also failed to disclose relevant information that would have adversely affected the prices of their stock and debt securities. Firms that have issued stock and debt securities must hire independent auditors to verify that their financial information is accurate. However, in some cases, the auditors who were hired to ensure accuracy were not meeting their responsibility.

In response to the financial scandals, the Sarbanes-Oxley Act (discussed throughout this text) was passed to require firms to provide more complete and accurate financial information. It also imposed restrictions to ensure proper auditing by auditors and proper oversight by the firm's board of directors. These rules were intended to regain the trust of investors who supply the funds to the financial markets. Through these measures, regulators tried to eliminate or reduce the asymmetric information problem.

Given the potential wealth that may be earned in financial markets when regulations are circumvented, it is safe to say that unethical behavior of some sort will occur in the future. New financial scandals will result in new regulations, which will be followed by new types of scandals that circumvent the latest regulations. Often the most naive (least informed) investors are those most adversely affected by financial scandals. In 2008, financial problems at financial institutions such as Bear Stearns, Lehman Brothers, and American International Group (AIG) caught many investors by surprise and renewed concerns that the information provided by firms to investors is very limited. The limited financial disclosure by firms is a major reason why there is much uncertainty surrounding their valuations.

GLOBAL FINANCIAL MARKETS

Financial markets are continuously being developed throughout the world to improve the transfer of funds from surplus units to deficit units. The financial markets are much more developed in some countries than in others, however, and vary in terms of the volumes of funds that are transferred from surplus units to deficit units and the types of funding that are available. Some countries have had financial markets for a long time, but other countries have converted to market-oriented economies and established financial markets relatively recently.

EXAMPLE

Since the early 1990s, many private businesses have been established in developing countries. The governments of these countries have allowed **privatization,** or the sale of government-owned firms to individuals. In addition, some businesses have issued stock, which allows many other investors who do not work in the business to participate in the ownership. Financial markets have been established in these countries to ensure that these businesses can obtain funding from surplus units. With these changes, private businesses are now able to obtain funds by borrowing or by issuing stock to investors. In addition, individuals in these countries have the opportunity to provide credit (loans) to some businesses or become stockholders of other businesses. ●

International Corporate Governance

Since financial markets channel funds from surplus units to deficit units, they can function only if surplus units are willing to provide funds to the markets. If there is a lack of information about the securities traded in the market, or a lack of safeguards to ensure that investors are treated fairly, surplus units will not participate. Consequently, the financial markets will not be liquid.

Financial markets have developed slowly in some developing countries for several reasons. First, the issuers of debt securities do not provide much financial information to indicate how they intend to repay the investors who would buy the securities. Second, regulatory agencies provide very little enforcement to ensure that the financial information provided by the issuers is correct. Third, businesses that do not repay the investors are rarely prosecuted. Fourth, courts in these countries do not provide an efficient system that investors can use to obtain the funds they believe they are owed.

Global Integration

Many financial markets are globally integrated, allowing participants to move funds out of one country's markets and into another's. Foreign investors serve as key surplus units in the United States by purchasing U.S. Treasury securities and other types of securities issued by businesses. Conversely, some investors based in the United States serve as key surplus units for foreign countries by purchasing securities issued by foreign corporations and government agencies. In addition, investors assess the potential return and the risk of securities in financial markets across countries and invest in the market that satisfies their return and risk preferences.

With these more integrated financial markets, U.S. market movements may have a greater impact on foreign market movements, and vice versa. Because interest rates are influenced by the supply of and demand for available funds, they are now more susceptible to foreign lending or borrowing activities.

EXAMPLE

The most pronounced progress in global financial market integration has occurred in Europe. Numerous regulations have been eliminated so that surplus and deficit units in one European country can now use financial markets throughout Europe. Some stock exchanges in different European countries have merged, making it easier for investors to conduct all of their stock transactions on one exchange. Since 1999, the adoption of the euro as the currency by 16 European countries (the so-called eurozone) has contributed significantly to financial market integration within Europe because transactions between these countries are now denominated in euros. In addition, securities issued within these countries are now denominated in euros. Thus, consumers and investors in any of these countries do not have to convert their currency when purchasing products or securities within the eurozone. ●

Role of the Foreign Exchange Market

International financial transactions (except for those within the eurozone) normally require the exchange of currencies. The **foreign exchange market** facilitates the exchange of currencies. Many commercial banks and other financial institutions serve as intermediaries in the foreign exchange market by matching up participants who want to exchange one currency for another. Some of these financial institutions also serve as dealers by taking positions in currencies to accommodate foreign exchange requests.

Like securities, most currencies have a market-determined price (exchange rate) that changes in response to supply and demand conditions. If there is a sudden shift in the aggregate demand by corporations, government agencies, and individuals for a given currency, or a shift in the aggregate supply of that currency for sale (to be exchanged), the price will change.

ROLE OF FINANCIAL INSTITUTIONS

If financial markets were **perfect,** all information about any securities for sale in primary and secondary markets (including the creditworthiness of the security issuer) would be continuously and freely available to investors. In addition, all information identifying investors interested in purchasing securities as well as investors planning to sell securities would be freely available. Furthermore, all securities for sale could be broken down (or unbundled) into any size desired by investors, and security transaction costs would be nonexistent. Under these conditions, financial intermediaries would not be necessary.

Because markets are **imperfect,** securities buyers and sellers do not have full access to information. Individual who have funds available normally do not have a means of identifying creditworthy borrowers to whom they could lend their funds. In addition, they do not have the expertise to assess the creditworthiness of potential borrowers. Financial institutions are needed to resolve the problems caused by market imperfections. They accept funds from surplus units and channel the funds to deficit units. Without financial institutions, the information and transaction costs of financial market transactions would be excessive. Financial institutions can be classified as depository and nondepository institutions.

Role of Depository Institutions

Depository institutions accept deposits from surplus units and provide credit to deficit units through loans and purchases of securities. They are popular financial institutions for the following reasons:

- They offer deposit accounts that can accommodate the amount and liquidity characteristics desired by most surplus units.
- They repackage funds received from deposits to provide loans of the size and maturity desired by deficit units.
- They accept the risk on loans provided.
- They have more expertise than individual surplus units in evaluating the creditworthiness of deficit units.
- They diversify their loans among numerous deficit units and therefore can absorb defaulted loans better than individual surplus units could.

To appreciate these advantages, consider the flow of funds from surplus units to deficit units if depository institutions did not exist. Each surplus unit would have to identify a deficit unit desiring to borrow the precise amount of funds available for the precise time period in which funds would be available. Furthermore, each surplus unit would have to perform the credit evaluation and incur the risk of default. Under these conditions, many surplus units would likely hold their funds rather than channel them to deficit units. Thus, the flow of funds from surplus units to deficit units would be disrupted.

When a depository institution offers a loan, it is acting as a creditor, just as if it had purchased a debt security. The more personalized loan agreement is less marketable in the secondary market than a debt security, however, because the loan agreement contains detailed provisions that can differ significantly among loans. Any potential investors would need to review all provisions before purchasing loans in the secondary market.

A more specific description of each depository institution's role in the financial markets follows.

Commercial Banks In aggregate, commercial banks are the most dominant depository institution. They serve surplus units by offering a wide variety of deposit accounts, and they transfer deposited funds to deficit units by providing direct loans or purchasing debt securities. Commercial banks serve both the private and public sectors, as their deposit and lending services are utilized by households, businesses, and government agencies. Some commercial banks, such as Bank of America, J.P. Morgan Chase, Citigroup, and SunTrust Banks, have more than $100 billion in assets.

Some commercial banks receive more funds from deposits than they need to make loans or invest in securities. Other commercial banks need more funds to accommodate customer requests than the amount of funds that they receive from deposits. The **federal funds market** facilitates the flow of funds between banks. A bank that has excess funds can lend to a bank with deficient funds for a short-term period, such as one to five days. Thus, the federal funds market facilitates the flow of funds from banks that have excess funds to banks that are in need of funds.

Savings Institutions   Savings institutions, which are sometimes referred to as thrift institutions, are another type of depository institution. Savings institutions include savings and loan associations (S&Ls) and savings banks. Like commercial banks, S&Ls offer deposit accounts to surplus units and then channel these deposits to deficit units. Whereas commercial banks have concentrated on commercial loans, however, S&Ls have concentrated on residential mortgage loans. This difference in the allocation of funds has caused the performance of commercial banks and S&Ls to differ significantly over time. In recent decades, however, deregulation has permitted S&Ls more flexibility in allocating their funds, so their functions have become more similar to those of commercial banks. Although S&Ls can be owned by shareholders, most are mutual (depositor owned).

Savings banks are similar to S&Ls, except that they have more diversified uses of funds. Over time, however, this difference has narrowed. Like S&Ls, most savings banks are mutual. Like commercial banks, savings institutions rely on the federal funds market to lend their excess funds or to borrow funds on a short-term basis.

Credit Unions   Credit unions differ from commercial banks and savings institutions in that they (1) are nonprofit and (2) restrict their business to the credit union members, who share a common bond (such as a common employer or union). Because of the common bond characteristic, credit unions tend to be much smaller than other depository institutions. They use most of their funds to provide loans to their members. Some of the largest credit unions, such as the Navy Federal Credit Union, the State Employees Credit Union of North Carolina, and the Pentagon Federal Credit Union, have assets of more than $5 billion.

Role of Nondepository Financial Institutions

Nondepository institutions generate funds from sources other than deposits but also play a major role in financial intermediation. These institutions are briefly described here and are covered in more detail in Part 7.

Finance Companies   Most finance companies obtain funds by issuing securities, then lend the funds to individuals and small businesses. The functions of finance companies and depository institutions overlap, although each type of institution concentrates on a particular segment of the financial markets (explained in the chapters devoted to these institutions). Many large finance companies are owned by large multinational corporations, including American Express and General Electric.

Mutual Funds   Mutual funds sell shares to surplus units and use the funds received to purchase a portfolio of securities. They are the dominant nondepository financial institution when measured in total assets. Some mutual funds concentrate their investment in capital market securities, such as stocks or bonds. Others, known as **money market mutual funds,** concentrate in money market securities. Typically, mutual funds purchase securities in minimum denominations that are larger than the savings of an individual surplus unit. By purchasing shares of mutual funds and money market mutual funds, small savers are able to invest in a diversified portfolio of securities with a relatively small amount of funds.

Securities Firms   Securities firms provide a wide variety of functions in financial markets. Some securities firms use their information resources to act as a **broker,** executing securities transactions between two parties. Many financial transactions are standardized to a degree. For example, stock transactions are normally in multiples of 100 shares. To expedite the securities trading process, the delivery procedure for each security transaction is also somewhat standard.

Brokers charge a fee for executing transactions. The fee is reflected in the difference (or **spread**) between their **bid** and **ask** quotes. The markup as a percentage of the transaction amount will likely be higher for less common transactions, as more time is needed to match up buyers and sellers. It will also likely be higher for transactions involving relatively small amounts to provide the broker with adequate compensation for the time required to execute the transaction.

In addition to brokerage services, securities firms also provide investment banking services. Some securities firms place newly issued securities for corporations and government agencies; this task differs from traditional brokerage activities because it involves the primary market. When securities firms **underwrite** newly issued securities, they may sell the securities for a client at a guaranteed price, or they may simply sell the securities at the best price they can get for their client.

Furthermore, securities firms often act as **dealers,** making a market in specific securities by adjusting their inventory of securities. Although a broker's income is mostly based on the markup, the dealer's income is influenced by the performance of the security portfolio maintained. Some dealers also provide brokerage services and therefore earn income from both types of activities.

Another investment banking activity offered by securities firms is advisory services on mergers and other forms of corporate restructuring. Securities firms may not only help a firm plan its restructuring but also execute the change in the firm's capital structure by placing the securities issued by the firm. Some securities firms, such as Morgan Stanley and Goldman Sachs, play a major role in brokerage, underwriting, and advisory services.

Insurance Companies   Insurance companies provide individuals and firms with insurance policies that reduce the financial burden associated with death, illness, and damage to property. They charge premiums in exchange for the insurance that they provide. They invest the funds that they receive in the form of premiums until the funds are needed to cover insurance claims. Insurance companies commonly invest the funds in stocks or bonds issued by corporations or in bonds issued by the government. In this way, they finance the needs of deficit units and thus serve as important financial intermediaries. Their overall performance is linked to the performance of the stocks and bonds in which they invest. Large insurance companies include State Farm Group, Allstate Insurance, Travelers Group, CNA Insurance, and Liberty Mutual.

Pension Funds   Many corporations and government agencies offer pension plans to their employees. The employees, their employers, or both periodically contribute funds to the plan. Pension funds provide an efficient way for individuals to save for their retirement. The pension funds manage the money until the individuals withdraw the funds from their retirement accounts. The money that is contributed to individual retirement accounts is commonly invested by the pension funds in stocks or bonds issued by corporations or in bonds issued by the government. In this way, pension funds finance the needs of deficit units and thus serve as important financial intermediaries.

Comparison of Roles among Financial Institutions

The role of financial institutions in facilitating the flow of funds from individual surplus units (investors) to deficit units is illustrated in Exhibit 1.3. Surplus units are shown on the left side of the exhibit, and deficit units are shown on the right side. Three different flows of funds from surplus units to deficit units are shown in the exhibit. One set of flows represents deposits from surplus units that are transformed by depository institutions into loans for deficit units. A second set of flows represents purchases of securities (commercial paper) issued by finance companies that are transformed into finance com-

Exhibit 1.3 Comparison of Roles among Financial Institutions

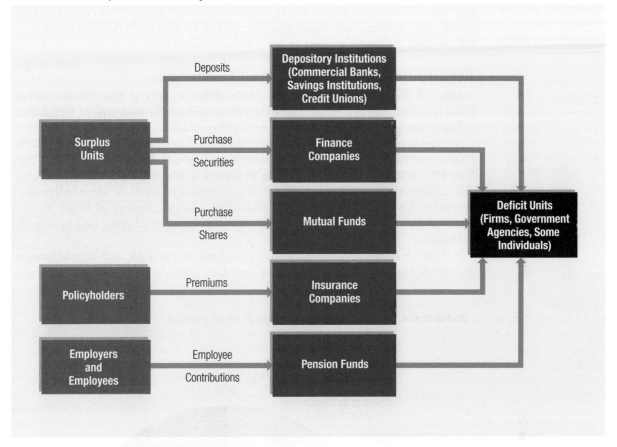

pany loans for deficit units. A third set of flows reflects the purchases of shares issued by mutual funds, which are used by the mutual funds to purchase debt and equity securities of deficit units.

The deficit units also receive funding from insurance companies and pension funds. Because insurance companies and pension funds purchase massive amounts of stocks and bonds, they finance much of the expenditures made by large deficit units, such as corporations and government agencies. Since financial institutions commonly serve the role of investing funds that they have received from surplus units, they are referred to as institutional investors.

Securities firms are not shown in Exhibit 1.3, but they play a very important role in facilitating the flow of funds. Many of the transactions between the financial institutions and deficit units are executed by securities firms. Furthermore, some funds flow directly from surplus units to deficit units as a result of security transactions, with securities firms serving as brokers.

Role as a Monitor of Publicly Traded Firms
In addition to the roles just described, financial institutions also serve as monitors of publicly traded firms. Because insurance companies, pension funds, and some mutual funds are major investors in stocks, they can have some influence over the management of publicly traded firms. In recent years, many large institutional investors have publicly criticized the management of specific firms, which has resulted in corporate restructuring or even the firing of executives

in some cases. Thus, institutional investors not only provide financial support to companies but exercise some degree of corporate control over them. By serving as activist shareholders, they can help ensure that managers of publicly held corporations are making decisions that are in the best interests of the shareholders.

Relative Importance of Financial Institutions

Exhibit 1.4 illustrates the relative sizes of the different types of financial institutions, based on assets. The percentage next to the dollar amount for each type of financial institution indicates its proportion of the total dollars in assets held by all financial institutions. Together, all of these financial institutions hold assets equal to about $46 trillion. Commercial banks hold the largest amount of assets of any depository institution. They have $11.2 trillion in assets, representing 24 percent of the total assets held by all financial institutions. Mutual funds hold the largest amount of assets of any nondepository institution. They have about the same amount of assets as commercial banks. Pension funds have about $10 trillion in assets, or about 22 percent of all assets held by financial institutions.

Exhibit 1.5 summarizes the main sources and uses of funds for each type of financial institution. Households with savings are served by depository institutions. Households

Exhibit 1.4 Asset Sizes of Financial Institutions (in Billions of Dollars)

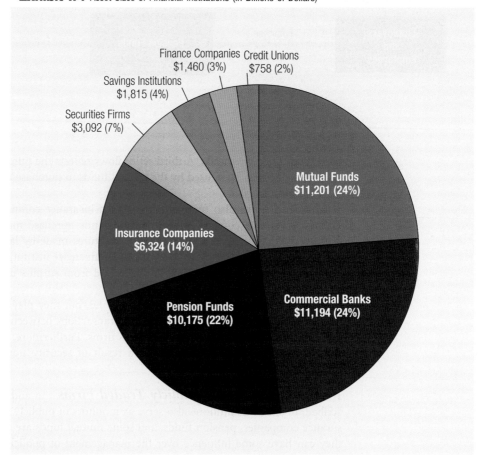

Source: *Board of Governors, Federal Reserve System, 2009.*

Exhibit 1.5 Summary of Institutional Sources and Uses of Funds

FINANCIAL INSTITUTIONS	MAIN SOURCES OF FUNDS	MAIN USES OF FUNDS
Commercial banks	Deposits from households, businesses, and government agencies	Purchases of government and corporate securities; loans to businesses and households
Savings institutions	Deposits from households, businesses, and government agencies	Purchases of government and corporate securities; mortgages and other loans to households; some loans to businesses
Credit unions	Deposits from credit union members	Loans to credit union members
Finance companies	Securities sold to households and businesses	Loans to households and businesses
Mutual funds	Shares sold to households, businesses, and government agencies	Purchases of long-term government and corporate securities
Money market funds	Shares sold to households, businesses, and government agencies	Purchases of short-term government and corporate securities
Insurance companies	Insurance premiums and earnings from investments	Purchases of long-term government and corporate securities
Pension funds	Employer/employee contributions	Purchases of long-term government and corporate securities

with deficient funds are served by depository institutions and finance companies. Large corporations and governments that issue securities obtain financing from all types of financial institutions. Several different regulatory agencies regulate the various types of financial institutions, and these differential regulations can cause some financial institutions to have a comparative advantage over others.

Consolidation of Financial Institutions

In recent years, commercial banks have acquired other commercial banks so that they can generate a higher volume of business supported by a given infrastructure. By increasing the volume of services produced, the average cost of providing the services (such as loans) can be reduced. Savings institutions have consolidated to achieve economies of scale for their mortgage lending business. Insurance companies have consolidated so that they can reduce the average cost of providing insurance services.

From the early 1980s through the early 2000s, the regulations imposed on financial institutions were relaxed, allowing different types of financial institutions to expand the types of services they offer and capitalize on economies of scope. As a result of this reduction in regulation, commercial banks have merged with savings institutions, securities firms, finance companies, mutual funds, and insurance companies. Although the operations of each type of financial institution are commonly managed separately, a financial conglomerate offers advantages to customers who prefer to obtain all of their financial services from a single financial institution. Since a financial conglomerate is more diversified, it may be less exposed to a possible decline in customer demand for any single financial service.

EXAMPLE   Wells Fargo is a classic example of the evolution in financial services. It originally focused on commercial banking, but has expanded its nonbank services to include mortgages, small business loans, consumer loans, real estate, brokerage, investment banking, online financial services, and insurance. In a recent annual report, Wells Fargo stated:

Our diversity in businesses makes us much more than a bank. We're a diversified financial services company. We're competing in a highly fragmented and fast growing industry: Financial Services. This helps us weather downturns that inevitably affect any one segment of our industry. ●

Typical Structure of a Financial Conglomerate A typical organizational structure of a financial conglomerate is shown in Exhibit 1.6. Historically, each of the financial services (such as banking, mortgages, brokerage, and insurance) had significant barriers to entry, so only a limited number of firms competed in that industry. The barriers prevented most firms from offering a wide variety of these services. In recent years, the barriers to entry have been reduced, allowing firms that had specialized in one service to more easily expand into other financial services. Many firms expanded by acquiring other financial services firms. Thus, many financial conglomerates are composed of various financial institutions that were originally independent, but are now units (or subsidiaries) of the conglomerate.

Impact of Consolidation on Competition As financial institutions spread into other financial services, the competition for customers desiring the various types of financial services increased. Prices of financial services declined in response to the competition. In addition, consolidation has provided more convenience. Individual customers can rely on the financial conglomerate for convenient access to life and health insurance, brokerage, mutual funds, investment advice and financial planning, bank deposits, and personal loans. A corporate customer can turn to the financial conglomerate for property and casualty insurance, health insurance plans for employees, business loans, advice on restructuring its businesses, issuing new debt or equity securities, and management of its pension plan.

Exhibit 1.6 Organizational Structure of a Financial Conglomerate

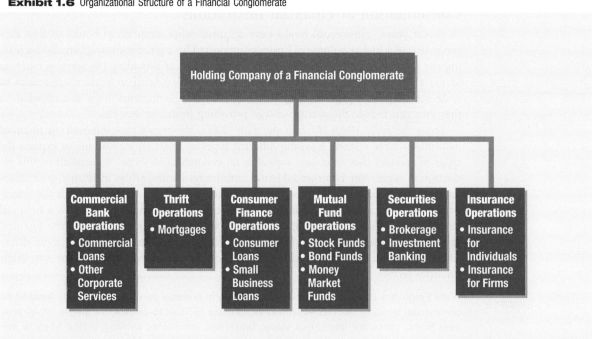

Impact of the Internet on Financial Institutions

The Internet has also led to more intense competition among financial institutions. Some commercial banks have been created solely as online entities. Because they have lower costs, they can offer higher interest rates on deposits and lower rates on loans. Other banks also offer online services, which can reduce costs, increase efficiency, and intensify banking competition. Some insurance companies conduct much of their business online, which reduces their operating costs and forces other insurance companies to price their services competitively. Some brokerage firms conduct much of their business online, which reduces their operating costs; because these firms can lower the fees they charge, they force other brokerage firms to price their services competitively. The Internet has also made it possible for corporations and municipal governments to circumvent securities firms by conducting security offerings online and selling directly to investors. This capability forces securities firms to be more competitive in the services they offer to issuers of securities.

Global Expansion by Financial Institutions

In addition to consolidating, many financial institutions have expanded internationally to capitalize on their expertise. Commercial banks, insurance companies, and securities firms have expanded through international mergers. An international merger between financial institutions enables the merged company to offer the services of both entities to its entire customer base. For example, a U.S. commercial bank may have specialized in lending while a European securities firm specialized in services such as underwriting securities. A merger between the two entities allows the U.S. bank to provide its services to the European customer base (clients of the European securities firm), while the European securities firm can offer its services to the U.S. customer base. By combining specialized skills and customer bases, the merged financial institutions can offer more services to clients and have an international customer base.

The adoption of the euro by 16 European countries has increased business between European countries and created a more competitive environment in Europe. European financial institutions, which had primarily competed with other financial institutions based in their own country, recognized that they would now face more competition from financial institutions in other countries.

Many financial institutions have attempted to benefit from opportunities in emerging markets. For example, some large securities firms have expanded into many countries to offer underwriting services for firms and government agencies. The need for this service has increased most dramatically in countries where businesses have been privatized. In addition, commercial banks have expanded into emerging markets to provide loans.

IMPACT OF THE CREDIT CRISIS ON FINANCIAL INSTITUTIONS

Following the abrupt increase in home prices in the 2004–2006 period, many financial institutions increased their holdings of mortgages and mortgage-backed securities whose performance was based on the mortgage payments made by homeowners. Some financial institutions (especially commercial banks and savings institutions) applied liberal standards when originating new mortgages and did not carefully assess the risk of default by the homeowners. In addition, some financial institutions including commercial banks, savings institutions, insurance companies, securities firms, and pension funds purchased large bundles of mortgages and mortgage-backed securities in the secondary market without carefully assessing the risk of these securities. In the 2007–2008 period, mortgage defaults increased, and home values declined substantially. As a result, the value of the property collateral backing many mortgages was less than the outstanding mortgage amount. By January 2009, at least 10 percent of all American homeowners were either behind on their mortgage payments or had defaulted on their mortgages.

The mortgage defaults led to the credit crisis, which affected financial institutions in several ways. First, the mortgages and mortgage-backed securities held by financial institutions experienced a major decline in value. Second, some financial institutions lost much of their business because their customers were afraid that the institutions might fail. The flow of funds through financial institutions relies on funding from surplus units who trust that that the institutions are safe. During the credit crisis, the flow of funds in financial markets was disrupted because some investors were no longer willing to invest in financial institutions. Because only very limited information about the potential risk of financial institutions was available, investors became extremely cautious and avoided even institutions that were in good financial condition.

On October 3, 2008, Congress enacted the Emergency Economic Stabilization Act of 2008 (also referred to as the bailout act), which was intended to resolve the liquidity problems of financial institutions and to restore the confidence of the investors who invest in them. The act directed the Treasury to inject $700 billion into the financial system, primarily by investing money into the banking system by purchasing preferred stock of financial institutions. In this way, the Treasury provided large commercial banks with capital to cushion their losses, thereby reducing the likelihood that the banks would fail. The credit crisis and the subsequent government intervention to resolve the crisis had a major impact on financial markets and institutions, as explained throughout this text.

Several of the financial institutions that either failed or were rescued by the government during the credit crisis suffered financial problems because they had taken on excessive risk through their holdings of mortgage-related products. The credit crisis illustrated the need for improved regulations that could ensure the safety of the financial institutions.

SUMMARY

- Financial markets facilitate the transfer of funds from surplus units to deficit units. Because funding needs vary among deficit units, various financial markets have been established. The primary market allows for the issuance of new securities, while the secondary market allows for the sale of existing securities.

- Securities can be classified as money market (short-term) securities or capital market (long-term) securities. Common capital market securities include bonds, mortgages, mortgage-backed securities, and stocks. The valuation of a security represents the present value of future cash flows that it is expected to generate. New information that indicates a change in expected cash flows or degree of uncertainty affects prices of securities in financial markets.

- Depository and nondepository institutions help to finance the needs of deficit units. Depository institutions can serve as effective intermediaries within financial markets because they have greater information on possible sources and uses of funds, they are capable of assessing the creditworthiness of borrowers, and they can repackage deposited funds in sizes and maturities desired by borrowers. Nondepository institutions are major purchasers of securities and therefore provide funding to deficit units.

- The main depository institutions are commercial banks, savings institutions, and credit unions. The main nondepository institutions are finance companies, mutual funds, pension funds, and insurance companies. Many financial institutions have been consolidated (due to mergers) into financial conglomerates, where they serve as subsidiaries of the conglomerate while conducting their specialized services. Thus, some financial conglomerates are able to provide all types of financial services. Consolidation allows for economies of scale and scope, which can enhance cash flows and increase the financial institution's value. In addition, consolidation

can diversify the institution's services and increase its value through the reduction in risk.
- The credit crisis in 2008 and 2009 had a profound effect on financial institutions. Those institutions that were heavily involved in originating or invest-

ing in mortgages suffered major losses. Many investors were concerned that the institutions might fail and therefore avoided them, which disrupted the ability of financial institutions to facilitate the flow of funds.

POINT COUNTER-POINT

Will Computer Technology Cause Financial Intermediaries to Become Extinct?

Point Yes. Financial intermediaries benefit from access to information. As information becomes more accessible, individuals will have the information they need before investing or borrowing funds. They will not need financial intermediaries to make their decisions.

Counter-Point No. Individuals rely not only on information, but also on expertise. Some financial intermediaries specialize in credit analysis so that they can make loans. Surplus units will continue to provide

funds to financial intermediaries rather than make direct loans, because they are not capable of credit analysis, even if more information about prospective borrowers is available. Some financial intermediaries no longer have physical buildings for customer service, but they still require people who have the expertise to assess the creditworthiness of prospective borrowers.

Who Is Correct? Use the Internet to learn more about this issue. Offer your own opinion on this issue.

QUESTIONS AND APPLICATIONS

1. Securities Firms What are the functions of securities firms? Many securities firms employ brokers and dealers. Distinguish between the functions of a broker and those of a dealer, and explain how each is compensated.

2. Impact of Privatization on Financial Markets Explain how the privatization of companies in Europe can lead to the development of new securities markets.

3. International Flow of Funds In what way could the international flow of funds cause a decline in interest rates?

4. Mutual Funds What is the function of a mutual fund? Why are mutual funds popular among investors? How does a money market mutual fund differ from a stock or bond mutual fund?

5. International Barriers If barriers to international securities markets are reduced, will a country's interest rate be more or less susceptible to foreign lending or borrowing activities? Explain.

6. Nondepository Institutions Compare the main sources and uses of funds for finance companies, insurance companies, and pension funds.

7. Securities Laws What was the purpose of the Securities Act of 1933? What was the purpose of the Securities Exchange Act of 1934? Do these laws prevent investors from making poor investment decisions? Explain.

8. Credit Unions With regard to the profit motive, how are credit unions different from other financial institutions?

9. Efficient Markets Explain the meaning of efficient markets. Why might we expect markets to be efficient most of the time? In recent years, several securities firms have been guilty of using inside information when purchasing securities, thereby achieving returns well above the norm (even when accounting for risk). Does this suggest that the security markets are not efficient? Explain.

10. Depository Institutions How have the asset compositions of savings and loan associations differed from those of commercial banks? Explain why and how this distinction may change over time.

11. Imperfect Markets Distinguish between perfect and imperfect security markets. Explain why the existence of imperfect markets creates a need for financial intermediaries.

12. **Marketability** Commercial banks use some funds to purchase securities and other funds to make loans. Why are the securities more marketable than loans in the secondary market?

13. **Types of Markets** Distinguish between primary and secondary markets. Distinguish between money and capital markets.

14. **Standardized Securities** Why is it necessary for securities to be somewhat standardized? Explain why some financial flows of funds cannot occur through the sale of standardized securities. If securities were not standardized, how would this affect the volume of financial transactions conducted by brokers?

15. **Surplus and Deficit Units** Explain the meaning of surplus units and deficit units. Provide an example of each. Which types of financial institutions do you deal with? Explain whether you are acting as a surplus unit or a deficit unit in your relationship with each financial institution.

Advanced Questions

16. **Regulation of Financial Institutions** Financial institutions are subject to regulationto ensure that they do not take excessive risk and can safely facilitate the flow of funds through financial markets. Nevertheless, during the credit crisis, individuals were concerned about using financial institutions to facilitate their financial transactions. Why do you think the existing regulations were ineffective at ensuring a safe financial system?

17. **Role of Accounting in Financial Markets** Integrate the roles of accounting, regulation, and financial market participation. That is, explain how financial market participants rely on accounting and why regulatory oversight of the accounting process is necessary.

18. **Impact of Credit Crisis on Institutions** Explain why mortgage defaults during the credit crisis adversely affected financial institutions that did not originate the mortgages. What role did these institutions play in financing the mortgages?

19. **Financial Intermediation** Look in a business periodical for news about a recent financial transaction involving two financial institutions. For this transaction, determine the following:

a. How will each institution's balance sheet be affected?

b. Will either institution receive immediate income from the transaction?Who is the ultimate user of funds?

c. Who is the ultimate user of funds?

d. Who is the ultimate source of funds?

20. **Impact of Credit Crisis on Liquidity** Explain why the credit crisis caused a lack of liquidity in the secondary markets for many types of debt securities. Explain how such a lack of liquidity would affect the prices of the debt securities in the secondary markets.

21. **Comparing Financial Institutions** Classify the types of financial institutions mentioned in this chapter as either depository or nondepository. Explain the general difference between depository and nondepository institution sources of funds. It is often said that all types of financial institutions have begun to offer services that were previously offered only by certain types. Consequently, the operations of many financial institutions are becoming more similar. Nevertheless, performance levels still differ significantly among types of financial institutions. Why?

Interpreting Financial News

"Interpreting Financial News" tests your ability to comprehend common statements made by Wall Street analysts and portfolio managers who participate in the financial markets. Interpret the following statements made by Wall Street analysts and portfolio managers:

a. "The price of IBM stock will not be affected by the announcement that its earnings have increased as expected."

b. "The lending operations at Bank of America should benefit from strong economic growth."

c. "The brokerage and underwriting performance at Goldman Sachs should benefit from strong economic growth."

Managing in Financial Markets

Utilizing Financial Markets As a financial manager of a large firm, you plan to borrow $70 million over the next year.

a. What are the more likely ways in which you can borrow $70 million?

b. Assuming that you decide to issue debt securities, describe the types of financial institutions that may purchase these securities.

c. How do individuals indirectly provide the financing for your firm when they maintain deposits at depository institutions, invest in mutual funds, purchase insurance policies, or invest in pensions?

FLOW OF FUNDS EXERCISE

Roles of Financial Markets and Institutions

This continuing exercise focuses on the interactions of a single manufacturing firm (Carson Company) in the financial markets. It illustrates how financial markets and institutions are integrated and facilitate the flow of funds in the business and financial environment. At the end of every chapter, this exercise provides a list of questions about Carson Company that require the application of concepts presented in the chapter, as they relate to the flow of funds.

Carson Company is a large manufacturing firm in California that was created 20 years ago by the Carson family. It was initially financed with an equity investment by the Carson family and 10 other individuals. Over time, Carson Company has obtained substantial loans from finance companies and commercial banks. The interest rate on the loans is tied to market interest rates and is adjusted every six months. Thus, Carson's cost of obtaining funds is sensitive to interest rate movements. It has a credit line with a bank in case it suddenly needs additional funds for a temporary period. It has purchased Treasury securities that it could sell if it experiences any liquidity problems.

Carson Company has assets valued at about $50 million and generates sales of about $100 million per year. Some of its growth is attributed to its acquisitions of other firms. Because of its expectations of a strong U.S. economy, Carson plans to grow in the future by expanding its business and by making more acquisitions. It expects that it will need sub-stantial long-term financing and plans to borrow additional funds either through loans or by issuing bonds. It is also considering issuing stock to raise funds in the next year. Carson closely monitors conditions in financial markets that could affect its cash inflows and cash outflows and therefore affect its value.

a. In what way is Carson a surplus unit?

b. In what way is Carson a deficit unit?

c. How might finance companies facilitate Carson's expansion?

d. How might commercial banks facilitate Carson's expansion?

e. Why might Carson have limited access to additional debt financing during its growth phase?

f. How might investment banks facilitate Carson's expansion?

g. How might Carson use the primary market to facilitate its expansion?

h. How might it use the secondary market?

i. If financial markets were perfect, how might this have allowed Carson to avoid financial institutions?

j. The loans that Carson has obtained from commercial banks stipulate that Carson must receive the bank's approval before pursuing any large projects. What is the purpose of this condition? Does this condition benefit the owners of the company?

INTERNET/EXCEL EXERCISES

1. Review the information for the common stock of IBM, using the website http://finance.yahoo.com. Insert the ticker symbol "IBM" in the box and click on "Get Quotes." The main goal at this point is to become familiar with the information that you can obtain at this website. Review the data that are shown for IBM stock. Compare the price of IBM based on its last trade with the price range for the year. Is the price near its high or low price? What is the total value of IBM stock (market capitalization)? What is the average daily trading volume (Avg Vol) of IBM stock? Click on "5y" just below the stock price chart to see IBM's stock price movements over the last five years. Describe the trend in IBM's stock over this period. At what points was the stock price the highest and lowest?

2. Repeat the questions in exercise 1 for the Children's Place Retail Stores (symbol is PLCE). Explain how the market capitalization and trading volume for PLCE differ from IBM.

WSJ EXERCISE

Differentiating between Primary and Secondary Markets

Review the different tables relating to stock markets and bond markets that appear in Section C of *The Wall Street Journal*. Explain whether each of these tables is focused on the primary or secondary markets.

Term Paper on the Credit Crisis

Write a term paper on one of the following topics or on a topic assigned by your professor. Details such as the due date and the length of the paper will be provided by your professor.

Each of the topics listed below can be easily researched because considerable media attention has been devoted to the subject. While this text offers a brief summary of each topic, much more information is available at online sources that you can find by using a search engine and inserting a few key terms or phrases.

1. **Impact of Lehman Brothers' Bankruptcy on Individual Wealth**. Explain how the bankruptcy of Lehman Brothers (the largest bankruptcy ever) affected the wealth and income of many different types of individuals whose money was invested by institutional investors (such as pension funds) in Lehman Brothers' debt.

2. **Impact of the Credit Crisis on Financial Market Liquidity**. Explain the link between the credit crisis and the lack of liquidity in the debt markets. Offer some insight as to why the debt markets became inactive. How were interest rates affected? What happened to inititial public offering (IPO) activity during the credit crisis? Why?

3. **Transparency of Financial Institutions during the Credit Crisis**. Select a financial institution that had serious financial problems as a result of the credit crisis. Review the media stories about this institution during the six months before its financial problems were publicized. Were there any clues that the financial institution was having problems? At what point do you think that the institution recognized that it was having financial difficulties? Did its previous annual report indicate serious problems? Did it announce its problems, or did another media source reveal the problems?

4. **Cause of Problems for Financial Institutions during the Credit Crisis**. Select a financial institution that had serious financial problems as a result of the credit crisis. Determine the main underlying causes of the problems experienced by that financial institution. Explain how these problems might have been avoided.

5. **Mortgage-Backed Securities and Risk Taking by Financial Institutions**. Do you think that institutional investors that purchased mortgage-backed securities containing subprime mortgages were following reasonable investment guidelines? Address this issue for various types of financial institutions such as pension funds, commercial banks, insurance companies, and mutual funds. Your answer might differ with the type of institutional investor. If financial institutions are taking on too much risk, how should regulations be changed to limit such excessive risk taking?

6. **Pension Fund Investments in Lehman Brothers' Debt**. At the time that Lehman Brothers filed for bankruptcy, financial institutions serving municipalities in California were holding more than $300 billion in debt issued by Lehman. Do you think that municipal pension funds that purchased commercial paper and other debt securities issued by Lehman Brothers were following reasonable investment guidelines? If a pension fund is taking on too much risk, how should regulations be changed to limit such excessive risk taking?

7. **Future Valuation of Mortgage-Backed Securities**. Commercial banks are required to periodically mark their assets to market in order to determine the capital that they need. Identify some advantages and disadvantages of this method, and propose a solution that would be fair to both commercial banks and regulators.

8. **Future Structure of Fannie Mae**. Fannie Mae plays an important role in the mortgage market, but it suffered major problems during the credit crisis. Discuss the underlying causes of the problems at Fannie Mae, beyond what is discussed in this text. Should Fannie Mae be owned completely by the government? Or should it be privatized? Offer your opinion on a structure for Fannie Mae that would avoid its previous problems and enable it to serve the mortgage market.

9. **Future Structure of Ratings Agencies**. Rating agencies rated the tranches of mortgage-backed securities that were sold to institutional investors. Explain why the performance of these agencies was criticized. Then defend against this criticism on behalf of the agencies. Was the criticism of the agencies justified? How could rating agencies be structured or regulated in a different manner in order to prevent the problems that occurred during the credit crisis?

10. **Future Structure of Credit Default Swaps**. Explain how credit default swaps may be partially responsible for the credit crisis. Offer a proposal as to how they could be structured in the future to ensure that they are used to enhance the safety of the financial system.

11. **Sale of Bear Stearns**. Review the arguments that have been made for the government-orchestrated sale of Bear Stearns. If Bear Stearns had been allowed to fail, what types of financial institutions would have been adversely affected? That is, who benefited from the government's action to prevent the failure of Bear Stearns? Do you think Bear Stearns should have been allowed to fail? Explain your opinion.

12. **Bailout of AIG**. Review the arguments that have been made for the bailout of American International Group (AIG). If AIG had been allowed to fail, what types of financial institutions would have been adversely affected? That is, who benefited from the bailout of AIG? Do you think AIG should have been allowed to fail? Explain your opinion.

13. **Executive Compensation at Financial Institutions**. Discuss the compensation received by executives at some financial institutions that experienced financial problems such as AIG, Bear Stearns, Lehman Brothers, Merrill Lynch, and Washington Mutual. Should these executives be allowed to retain the bonuses that they received in the 2007–2008 period? Should executive compensation at financial institutions be capped?

14. **Impact of the Credit Crisis on Commercial Banks versus Securities Firms**. Both commercial banks and securities firms were adversely affected by the credit crisis, but for different reasons. Discuss the reasons for the adverse effects on commercial banks and securities firms and explain why the reasons were different.

15. **Role of the Treasury and the Fed in the Credit Crisis**. Summarize the various ways in which the U.S. Treasury and the Fed intervened to resolve the credit crisis. Discuss the pros and cons of their interventions. Offer your own opinion about whether they should have intervened.

2
Determination of Interest Rates

CHAPTER OBJECTIVES

The specific objectives of this chapter are to:

- apply the loanable funds theory to explain why interest rates change,

- identify the most relevant factors that affect interest rate movements, and

- explain how to forecast interest rates.

WEB

www.bloomberg.com
Information on interest rates in recent months.

Interest rate movements have a direct influence on the market values of debt securities, such as money market securities, bonds, and mortgages, and have an indirect influence on equity security values. Thus, participants in financial markets attempt to anticipate interest rate movements when restructuring their positions. Interest rate movements also affect the value of most financial institutions. The cost of funds to depository institutions and the interest received on some loans by financial institutions are affected by interest rate movements. In addition, the market values of securities (such as bonds) held by depository institutions or nondepository institutions are affected as well. Thus, managers of financial institutions attempt to anticipate interest rate movements so that they can capitalize on favorable movements or reduce their institution's exposure to unfavorable movements.

LOANABLE FUNDS THEORY

The **loanable funds theory,** commonly used to explain interest rate movements, suggests that the market interest rate is determined by the factors that control the supply of and demand for loanable funds. The theory is especially useful for explaining movements in the general level of interest rates for a particular country. Furthermore, it can be used along with other concepts to explain why interest rates among some debt securities of a given country vary, which is the focus of the next chapter. The phrase "demand for loanable funds" is widely used in financial markets to refer to the borrowing activities of households, businesses, and governments. This chapter looks first at the sectors that commonly affect the demand for loanable funds and then describes the sectors that supply loanable funds to the markets. Finally, the demand and supply concepts are integrated to explain interest rate movements.

Household Demand for Loanable Funds

Households commonly demand loanable funds to finance housing expenditures. In addition, they finance the purchases of automobiles and household items, which results in installment debt. As the aggregate level of household income rises over time, so does installment debt. The level of installment debt as a percentage of disposable income has been increasing since 1983. It is generally lower in recessionary periods.

Exhibit 2.1 Relationship between Interest Rates and Household Demand (D_h) for Loanable Funds at a Given Point in Time

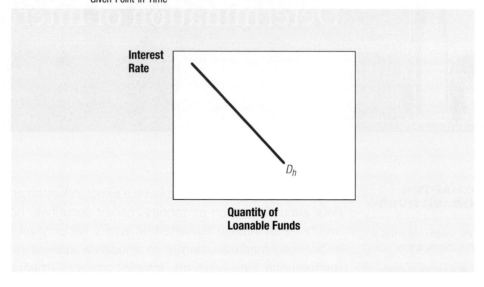

If households could be surveyed at any given point in time to indicate the quantity of loanable funds they would demand at various interest rate levels, there would be an inverse relationship between the interest rate and the quantity of loanable funds demanded. This simply means that at any point in time, households would demand a greater quantity of loanable funds at lower rates of interest.

EXAMPLE

Consider the household demand-for-loanable-funds schedule shown in Exhibit 2.1. This schedule depicts the amount of funds that would be demanded at various possible interest rates at a given point in time. Various events can cause household borrowing preferences to change and thereby shift the demand schedule. For example, if tax rates on household income are expected to decrease significantly in the future, households might believe that they can more easily afford future loan repayments and thus be willing to borrow more funds. For any interest rate, the quantity of loanable funds demanded by households would be greater as a result of the tax rate change. This represents an outward shift (to the right) in the demand schedule. ●

Business Demand for Loanable Funds

Businesses demand loanable funds to invest in long-term (fixed) and short-term assets. The quantity of funds demanded by businesses depends on the number of business projects to be implemented. Businesses evaluate a project by comparing the present value of its cash flows to its initial investment, as follows:

$$NPV = -INV + \sum_{t=1}^{n} \frac{CF_t}{(1+k)^t}$$

where
$$NPV = \text{net present value of project}$$
$$INV = \text{initial investment}$$
$$CF_t = \text{flow in period } t$$
$$k = \text{required rate of return on project}$$

Projects with a positive net present value (NPV) are accepted because the present value of their benefits outweighs the costs. The required return to implement a given project will be lower if interest rates are lower because the cost of borrowing funds to support the project will be lower. Consequently, more projects will have positive NPVs, and businesses will

Exhibit 2.2 Relationship between Interest Rates and Business Demand (D_b) for Loanable Funds at a Given Point in Time

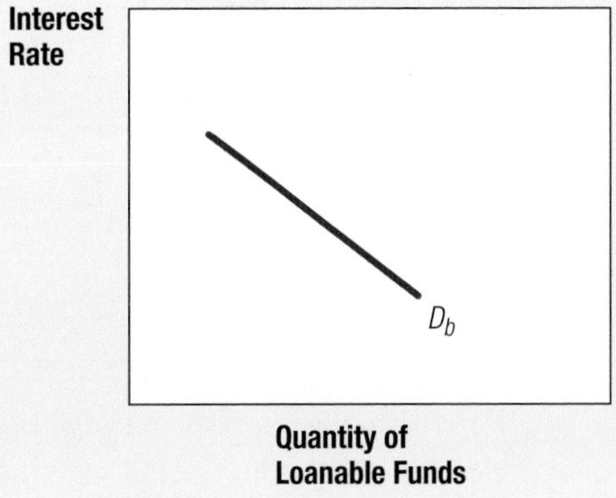

need a greater amount of financing. This implies that businesses will demand a greater quantity of loanable funds when interest rates are lower, as illustrated in Exhibit 2.2.

In addition to long-term assets, businesses also invest in short-term assets (such as accounts receivable and inventory) in order to support ongoing operations. Any demand for funds resulting from this type of investment is positively related to the number of projects implemented and thus is inversely related to the interest rate. The opportunity cost of investing in short-term assets is higher when interest rates are higher. Therefore, firms generally attempt to support ongoing operations with fewer funds during periods of high interest rates. This is another reason that a firm's total demand for loanable funds is inversely related to interest rates at any point in time. Although the demand for loanable funds by some businesses may be more sensitive to interest rates than others, all businesses are likely to demand more funds if interest rates are lower at a given point in time.

Shifts in the Demand for Loanable Funds The business demand-for-loanable-funds schedule can shift in reaction to any events that affect business borrowing preferences. If economic conditions become more favorable, the expected cash flows on various proposed projects will increase. More proposed projects will have expected returns that exceed a particular required rate of return (sometimes called the hurdle rate). Additional projects will be acceptable as a result of more favorable economic forecasts, causing an increased demand for loanable funds. The increase in demand will result in an outward shift in the demand curve (to the right).

Government Demand for Loanable Funds

WEB

www.treasurydirect.gov
Information on the U.S. government's debt.

Whenever a government's planned expenditures cannot be completely covered by its incoming revenues from taxes and other sources, it demands loanable funds. Municipal (state and local) governments issue municipal bonds to obtain funds, while the federal government and its agencies issue Treasury securities and federal agency securities. These securities represent government debt.

The federal government's expenditure and tax policies are generally thought to be independent of interest rates. Thus, the federal government's demand for funds is said to

Exhibit 2.3 Impact of Increased Government Deficit on the Government Demand for Loanable Funds

Interest
Rate

D_{g1} D_{g2}

Quantity of
Loanable Funds

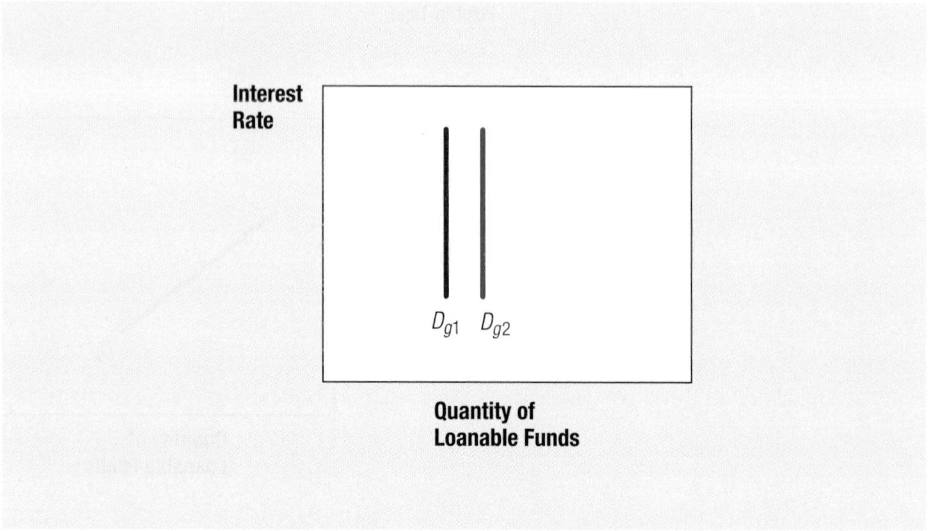

be **interest-inelastic,** or insensitive to interest rates. In contrast, municipal governments sometimes postpone proposed expenditures if the cost of financing is too high, implying that their demand for loanable funds is somewhat sensitive to interest rates.

Like household and business demand, government demand for loanable funds can shift in response to various events.

EXAMPLE

The federal government's demand-for-loanable-funds schedule is D_{gl} in Exhibit 2.3. If new bills are passed that cause a net increase of $200 billion in the deficit, the federal government's demand for loanable funds will increase by that amount. The new demand schedule is D_{g2} in the exhibit. ●

Foreign Demand for Loanable Funds

The demand for loanable funds in a given market also includes foreign demand by foreign governments or corporations. For example, the British government may obtain financing by issuing British Treasury securities to U.S. investors, representing a British demand for U.S. funds. Because foreign financial transactions are becoming so common, they can have a significant impact on the demand for loanable funds in any given country. A foreign country's demand for U.S. funds is influenced by the differential between its interest rates and U.S. rates (along with other factors). Other things being equal, a larger quantity of U.S. funds will be demanded by foreign governments and corporations if their domestic interest rates are high relative to U.S. rates. Therefore, for a given set of foreign interest rates, the quantity of U.S. loanable funds demanded by foreign governments or firms will be inversely related to U.S. interest rates.

The foreign demand schedule can shift in response to economic conditions. For example, assume the original foreign demand schedule is D_{f1} in Exhibit 2.4. If foreign interest rates rise, foreign firms and governments will likely increase their demand for U.S. funds, as represented by the shift from D_{f1} to D_{f2}.

WEB

www.bloomberg.com/
markets
Interest rate
information.

Aggregate Demand for Loanable Funds

The aggregate demand for loanable funds is the sum of the quantities demanded by the separate sectors at any given interest rate, as shown in Exhibit 2.5. Because most of these sectors are likely to demand a larger quantity of funds at lower interest rates (other

Exhibit 2.4 Impact of Increased Foreign Interest Rates on the Foreign Demand for U.S. Loanable Funds

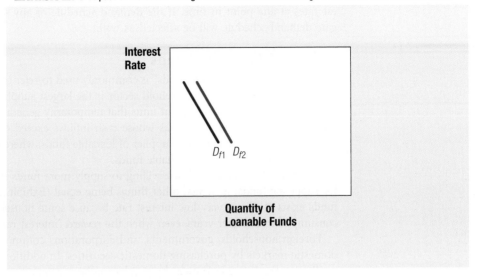

Exhibit 2.5 Determination of the Aggregate Demand Schedule for Loanable Funds

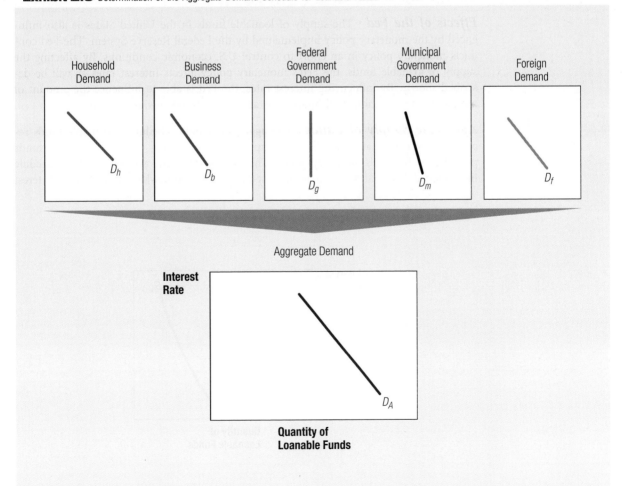

things being equal), the aggregate demand for loanable funds is inversely related to interest rates at any point in time. If the demand schedule of any sector changes, the aggregate demand schedule will be affected as well.

Supply of Loanable Funds

The term "supply of loanable funds" is commonly used to refer to funds provided to financial markets by savers. The household sector is the largest supplier, but loanable funds are also supplied by some government units that temporarily generate more tax revenues than they spend or by some businesses whose cash inflows exceed outflows. Households as a group, however, represent a net supplier of loanable funds, whereas governments and businesses are net demanders of loanable funds.

Suppliers of loanable funds are willing to supply more funds if the interest rate (reward for supplying funds) is higher, other things being equal (Exhibit 2.6). A supply of loanable funds exists at even a very low interest rate because some households choose to postpone consumption until later years, even when the reward (interest rate) for saving is low.

Foreign households, governments, and corporations commonly supply funds to their domestic markets by purchasing domestic securities. In addition, they have been a major creditor to the U.S. government by purchasing large amounts of Treasury securities. The large foreign supply of funds to the U.S. market is partially attributed to the high saving rates of foreign households.

Effects of the Fed   The supply of loanable funds in the United States is also influenced by the monetary policy implemented by the Federal Reserve System. The Fed conducts monetary policy in an effort to control U.S. economic conditions. By affecting the supply of loanable funds, the Fed's monetary policy affects interest rates as will be described shortly. By influencing interest rates, the Fed is able to influence the amount of money that corporations and households are willing to borrow and spend.

Aggregate Supply of Funds   The aggregate supply schedule of loanable funds represents the combination of all sector supply schedules along with the supply of funds provided by the Fed's monetary policy. The steep slope of the aggregate supply schedule in Exhibit 2.6 indicates that it is interest-inelastic, or somewhat insensitive to interest

Exhibit 2.6 Aggregate Supply Schedule for Loanable Funds

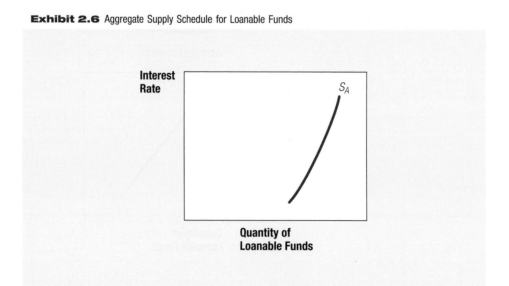

rates. The quantity of loanable funds demanded is normally expected to be more elastic, meaning more sensitive to interest rates, than the quantity of loanable funds supplied.

The supply curve can shift in or out in response to various conditions. For example, if the tax rate on interest income is reduced, the supply curve will shift outward, as households save more funds at each possible interest rate level. Conversely, if the tax rate on interest income is increased, the supply curve will shift inward, as households save fewer funds at each possible interest rate level.

Note that minimal attention has been given to financial institutions in this section. Although financial institutions play a critical intermediary role in channeling funds, they are not the ultimate suppliers of funds. Any change in a financial institution's supply of funds results only from a change in habits by the households, businesses, or governments that supply the funds.

Equilibrium Interest Rate

An understanding of equilibrium interest rates is necessary to assess how various events can affect interest rates. In reality, there are several different interest rates because some borrowers pay a higher rate than others. At this point, however, the focus is on the forces that cause the general level of interest rates to change, as interest rates across borrowers tend to change in the same direction. The determination of an equilibrium interest rate is presented first from an algebraic perspective and then from a graphic perspective. Following this presentation, several examples are offered to reinforce the concept.

Algebraic Presentation   The equilibrium interest rate is the rate that equates the aggregate demand for funds with the aggregate supply of loanable funds. The aggregate demand for funds (D_A) can be written as

$$D_A = D_h + D_b + D_g + D_m + D_f$$

where
D_h = household demand for loanable funds
D_b = business demand for loanable funds
D_g = federal government demand for loanable funds
D_m = municipal government demand for loanable funds
D_f = foreign demand for loanable funds

The aggregate supply of funds (S_A) can be written as

$$S_A = S_h + S_b + S_g + S_m + S_f$$

where
S_h = household supply of loanable funds
S_b = business supply of loanable funds
S_g = federal government supply of loanable funds
S_m = municipal government supply of loanable funds
S_f = foreign supply of loanable funds

In equilibrium, $D_A = S_A$. If the aggregate demand for loanable funds increases without a corresponding increase in aggregate supply, there will be a shortage of loanable funds. Interest rates will rise until an additional supply of loanable funds is available to accommodate the excess demand. If the aggregate supply of loanable funds increases without a corresponding increase in aggregate demand, there will be a surplus of loanable funds. Interest rates will fall until the quantity of funds supplied no longer exceeds the quantity of funds demanded.

 As an example, when the credit crisis began in 2008, many individual and institutional investors liquidated their investments in mortgage-related securities and invested their funds in more liquid Treasury securities or in short-term bank deposits. This resulted in a large supply of short-term funds in financial markets and placed downward pressure on short-term interest rates.

Exhibit 2.7 Interest Rate Equilibrium

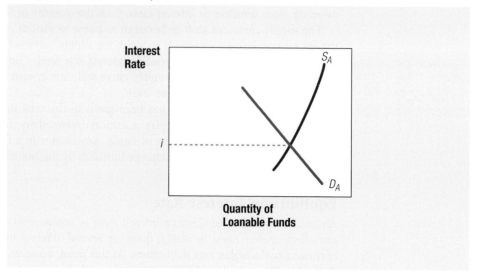

In many cases, both supply and demand for loanable funds are changing. Given an initial equilibrium situation, the equilibrium interest rate should rise when $D_A > S_A$ and fall when $D_A < S_A$.

Graphic Presentation   By combining the aggregate demand and aggregate supply schedules of loanable funds (refer to Exhibits 2.5 and 2.6), it is possible to compare the total amount of funds that would be demanded to the total amount of funds that would be supplied at any particular interest rate. Exhibit 2.7 illustrates the combined demand and supply schedules. At the equilibrium interest rate of i, the supply of loanable funds is equal to the demand for loanable funds.

At any interest rate above i, there is a surplus of loanable funds. Some potential suppliers of funds will be unable to successfully supply their funds at the prevailing interest rate. Once the market interest rate decreases to i, the quantity of funds supplied is sufficiently reduced and the quantity of funds demanded is sufficiently increased such that there is no longer a surplus of funds. When a disequilibrium situation exists, market forces should cause an adjustment in interest rates until equilibrium is achieved.

If the prevailing interest rate is below i, there will be a shortage of loanable funds. Borrowers will not be able to obtain all the funds that they desire at that rate. Because of the shortage of funds, the interest rate will increase, causing two reactions. First, more savers will enter the market to supply loanable funds now that the reward (interest rate) is higher. Second, some potential borrowers will decide not to demand loanable funds at the higher interest rate. Once the interest rate rises to i, the quantity of loanable funds supplied has increased and the quantity of loanable funds demanded has decreased to the extent that a shortage no longer exists. An equilibrium position is achieved once again.

FACTORS THAT AFFECT INTEREST RATES

Although it is useful to identify those who supply or demand loanable funds, it is also necessary to recognize the underlying economic forces that cause a change in the supply of or the demand for loanable funds. The following economic factors influence the demand for or supply of loanable funds and therefore influence interest rates.

Impact of Economic Growth on Interest Rates

Changes in economic conditions cause a shift in the demand schedule for loanable funds, which affects the equilibrium interest rate.

EXAMPLE

When businesses anticipate that economic conditions will improve, they revise upward the cash flows expected for various projects under consideration. Consequently, businesses identify more projects that are worth pursuing, and they are willing to borrow more funds. Their willingness to borrow more funds at any given interest rate reflects an outward shift in the demand schedule (to the right).

The supply-of-loanable-funds schedule may also shift in response to economic growth, but it is more difficult to know how it will shift. It is possible that the increased expansion by businesses will lead to more income for construction crews and others who service the expansion. In this case, the quantity of savings, and therefore of loanable funds supplied at any possible interest rate, could increase, causing an outward shift in the supply schedule. There is no assurance that the volume of savings will actually increase, however. Even if a shift occurs, it will likely be of smaller magnitude than the shift in the demand schedule.

Overall, the expected impact of the increased expansion by businesses is an outward shift in the demand schedule and no obvious change in the supply schedule (Exhibit 2.8). The shift in the aggregate demand schedule to D_{A2} in the exhibit causes an increase in the equilibrium interest rate to i_2. ●

Just as economic growth puts upward pressure on interest rates, an economic slowdown puts downward pressure on the equilibrium interest rate.

EXAMPLE

A slowdown in the economy will cause the demand schedule to shift inward (to the left), reflecting less demand for loanable funds at any possible interest rate. The supply schedule may possibly shift a little, but the direction of its shift is uncertain. One could argue that a slowdown should cause increased saving at any possible interest rate as households prepare for possible layoffs. At the same time, the gradual reduction in labor income that occurs during an economic slowdown could reduce households' ability to save. Historical data support this latter expectation. Any shift that does occur will likely be minor relative to the shift in the demand schedule. Therefore, the equilibrium interest rate is expected to decrease, as illustrated in Exhibit 2.9.

During the credit crisis that began in 2008, many corporations noticed a decline in consumer spending and therefore reduced their plans for expansion. Consequently, they reduced their demand for loanable funds, which placed downward pressure on short-term interest rates. Interest rates declined substantially in the fall of 2008. ●

Exhibit 2.8 Impact of Increased Expansion by Firms

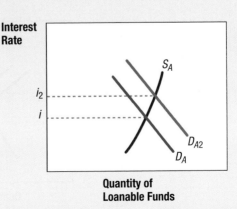

Exhibit 2.9 Impact of an Economic Slowdown

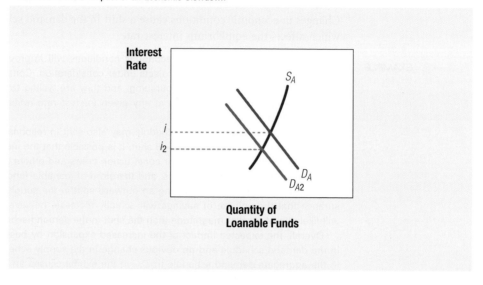

Impact of Inflation on Interest Rates

Changes in inflationary expectations can affect interest rates by affecting the amount of spending by households or businesses. Decisions to spend affect the amount saved (supply of funds) and the amount borrowed (demand for funds).

EXAMPLE

Assume the U.S. inflation rate is expected to increase. Households that supply funds may reduce their savings at any interest rate level so that they can make more purchases now before prices rise. This shift in behavior is reflected by an inward shift (to the left) in the supply curve of loanable funds. In addition, households and businesses may be willing to borrow more funds at any interest rate level so that they can purchase products now before prices increase. This is reflected by an outward shift (to the right) in the demand curve for loanable funds. These shifts are illustrated in Exhibit 2.10. The new equilibrium interest rate is higher because of the shifts in saving and borrowing behavior. ●

Exhibit 2.10 Impact of an Increase in Inflationary Expectations on Interest Rates

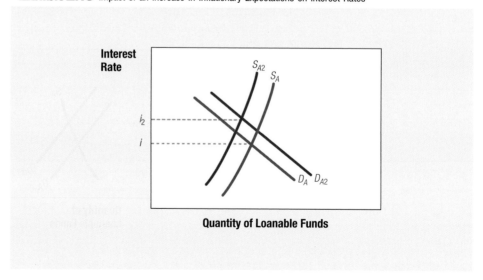

Fisher Effect   More than 70 years ago, Irving Fisher proposed a theory of interest rate determination that is still widely used today. It does not contradict the loanable funds theory but simply offers an additional explanation for interest rate movements. Fisher proposed that nominal interest payments compensate savers in two ways. First, they compensate for a saver's reduced purchasing power. Second, they provide an additional premium to savers for forgoing present consumption. Savers are willing to forgo consumption only if they receive a premium on their savings above the anticipated rate of inflation, as shown in the following equation:

$$i = E(\text{INF}) + i_R$$

where
$$i = \textbf{nominal or quoted rate of interest}$$
$$E(\text{INF}) = \textbf{expected inflation rate}$$
$$i_R = \textbf{real interest rate}$$

This relationship between interest rates and expected inflation is often referred to as the **Fisher effect.** The difference between the nominal interest rate and the expected inflation rate is the real return to a saver after adjusting for the reduced purchasing power over the time period of concern. It is referred to as the **real interest rate** because, unlike the nominal rate of interest, it adjusts for the expected rate of inflation. The preceding equation can be rearranged to express the real interest rate as

$$i_R = i - E(\text{INF})$$

When the inflation rate is higher than anticipated, the real interest rate is relatively low. Borrowers benefit because they were able to borrow at a lower nominal interest rate than would have been offered if inflation had been accurately forecasted. When the inflation rate is lower than anticipated, the real interest rate is relatively high and borrowers are adversely affected.

Throughout the text, the term *interest rate* will be used to represent the nominal, or quoted, rate of interest. Keep in mind, however, that because of inflation, purchasing power is not necessarily increasing during periods of rising interest rates.

WEB

www.federalreserve
.gov/monetarypolicy/
fomc.htm
Information on how the
Fed controls the money
supply.

Impact of Monetary Policy on Interest Rates

The Federal Reserve can affect the supply of loanable funds by increasing or reducing the total amount of deposits held at commercial banks or other depository institutions. The process by which the Fed adjusts the money supply is described in Chapter 4. When the Fed increases the money supply, it increases the supply of loanable funds, which places downward pressure on interest rates.

EXAMPLE

When the credit crisis intensified during the fall of 2008, the Fed increased the money supply. Consequently, financial institutions had more funds available that they could lend. The increase in the supply of loanable funds placed downward pressure on interest rates. Since the demand for loanable funds decreased during this period (as explained earlier), the downward pressure on interest rates was even more pronounced. Interest rates declined substantially in the fall of 2008 due to both forces. ●

If the Fed reduces the money supply, it reduces the supply of loanable funds. Assuming no change in demand, this action places upward pressure on interest rates.

Impact of the Budget Deficit on Interest Rates

When the federal government enacts fiscal policies that result in more expenditures than tax revenue, the budget deficit is increased. The U.S. government is a major participant in the demand for loanable funds due to large budget deficits in recent years. A higher

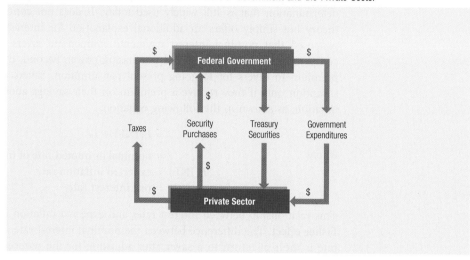

Exhibit 2.11 Flow of Funds between the Federal Government and the Private Sector

federal government deficit increases the quantity of loanable funds demanded at any prevailing interest rate, causing an outward shift in the demand schedule. Assuming that all other factors are held constant, interest rates will rise. Given a certain amount of loanable funds supplied to the market (through savings), excessive government demand for these funds tends to "crowd out" the private demand (by consumers and corporations) for funds. The federal government may be willing to pay whatever is necessary to borrow these funds, but the private sector may not. This impact is known as the **crowding-out effect.** Exhibit 2.11 illustrates the flow of funds between the federal government and the private sector.

There is a counterargument that the supply schedule might shift outward if the government creates more jobs by spending more funds than it collects from the public (this is what causes the deficit in the first place). If this were to occur, the deficit might not necessarily place upward pressure on interest rates. Much research has investigated this issue and, in general, has shown that when holding other factors constant, higher budget deficits place upward pressure on interest rates.

Impact of Foreign Flows of Funds on Interest Rates

The interest rate for a specific currency is determined by the demand for funds denominated in that currency and the supply of funds available in that currency.

EXAMPLE

The supply and demand schedules for the U.S. dollar and for Brazil's currency (the real) are compared for a given point in time in Exhibit 2.12. Although the demand schedule for loanable funds should be downward sloping for every currency and the supply schedule should be upward sloping, the actual positions of these schedules vary among currencies. First, notice that the demand and supply curves are farther to the right for the dollar than for the Brazilian real. The amount of dollar-denominated loanable funds supplied and demanded is much greater than the amount of Brazilian real–denominated loanable funds because the U.S. economy is much larger than Brazil's economy.

Also notice that the positions of the demand and supply schedules for loanable funds are much higher for the Brazilian real than for the dollar. The supply schedule for loanable funds denominated in the Brazilian real shows that hardly any amount of savings would be supplied at low interest rate levels because the relatively high inflation in Brazil encourages households to spend more of their disposable income before prices increase. It discourages households

Exhibit 2.12 Demand and Supply Schedules for Loanable Funds Denominated in U.S. Dollars and Brazilian Real

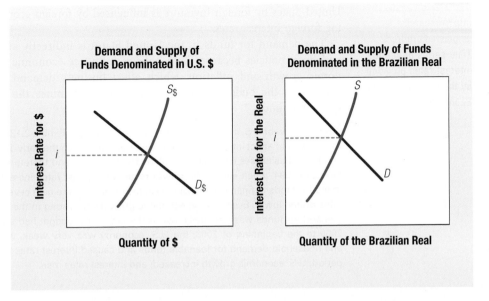

from saving unless the interest rate is sufficiently high. In addition, the demand for loanable funds in the Brazilian real shows that borrowers are willing to borrow even at relatively high rates of interest because they want to make purchases now before prices increase. Firms are willing to pay 15 percent interest on a loan to purchase machines whose prices may have increased by 20 percent by next year.

Because of the different positions of the demand and supply schedules for the two currencies shown in Exhibit 2.12, the equilibrium interest rate is much higher for the Brazilian real than for the dollar. As the demand and supply schedules change over time for a specific currency, so will the equilibrium interest rate. For example, if Brazil's government could substantially reduce the local inflation, the supply schedule of loanable funds denominated in real would shift out (to the right) while the demand schedule of loanable funds would shift in (to the left), which would result in a lower equilibrium interest rate. ●

In recent years, massive flows of funds have shifted between countries, causing abrupt adjustments in the supply of funds available in each country and therefore affecting interest rates. In general, the shifts are driven by large institutional investors seeking a high return on their investments. These investors commonly attempt to invest funds in debt securities in countries where interest rates are high. However, many countries that typically have relatively high interest rates also tend to have high inflation, which can weaken their local currencies. Since the depreciation (decline in value) of a currency can more than offset a high interest rate in some cases, investors tend to avoid investing in countries with high interest rates if the threat of inflation is very high.

Summary of Forces That Affect Interest Rates

In general, economic conditions are the primary forces behind a change in the supply of savings provided by households or a change in the demand for funds by households, businesses, or the government. The saving behavior of the households that supply funds in the United States is partially influenced by U.S. fiscal policy, which determines the taxes paid by U.S. households and thus determines the level of disposable income. The

Federal Reserve's monetary policy also affects the supply of funds in the United States because it determines the U.S. money supply. The supply of funds provided to the United States by foreign investors is influenced by foreign economic conditions, including foreign interest rates.

The demand for funds in the United States is indirectly affected by U.S. monetary and fiscal policies because these policies influence economic conditions such as economic growth and inflation, which affect business demand for funds. Fiscal policy determines the budget deficit and therefore determines the federal government demand for funds.

EXAMPLE

A brief review of U.S. interest rates over recent decades in Exhibit 2.13 illustrates how these forces can interact to affect interest rates. Interest rates declined in the early 1990s as the economy weakened, and businesses cut back their plans for expansion and therefore reduced their demand for funds. In 1994, when economic growth resumed, interest rates increased, and the business demand for funds to finance expansion also increased. For the next several years, however, interest rates drifted lower. Even though economic growth was strong in the late 1990s, the government demand for funds was unusually low as the U.S. fiscal budget had a surplus at that time. From 2000 to the beginning of 2003, the U.S. economy was very weak, which reduced the business and household demand for loanable funds and caused interest rates to decline. In the 2005–2007 period, U.S. economic growth increased, and interest rates rose.

Exhibit 2.13 Interest Rate Movements Over Time

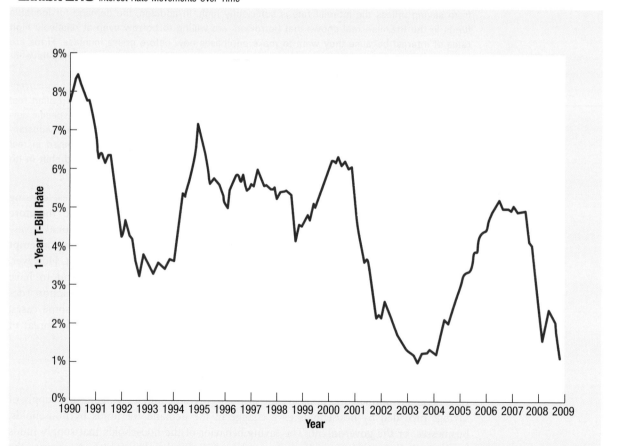

The credit crisis that began in 2008, however, caused the economy to weaken substantially, and interest rates declined to very low levels. During the crisis, the federal government experienced a very large budget deficit as it was bailing out some firms and increasing its spending in various ways to stimulate the economy. While the large government demand for funds placed upward pressure on interest rates, this pressure was offset by a weak demand for funds by firms (as businesses canceled their plans to expand). In addition, the Federal Reserve increased the money supply at this time in order to push interest rates lower in an attempt to encourage businesses and households to borrow and spend money. ●

This summary does not cover every possible interaction among the forces that can affect interest rate movements, but it does illustrate how some key factors have an influence on interest rates over time. Since the prices of some securities are influenced by interest rate movements, they are affected by the factors discussed here, as explained in other chapters.

FORECASTING INTEREST RATES

WEB

http://research
.stlouisfed.org/fred2
Quotations of current
interest rates and
trends of historical in-
terest rates for various
debt securities.

Exhibit 2.14 summarizes the key factors that are evaluated when forecasting interest rates. With an understanding of how each factor affects interest rates, it is possible to forecast how interest rates may change in the future. When forecasting household demand for loanable funds, it may be necessary to assess consumer credit data to determine the borrowing capacity of households. The potential supply of loanable funds provided by households may be determined in a similar manner by assessing factors that affect the earning power of households.

Business demand for loanable funds can be forecast by assessing future plans for corporate expansion and the future state of the economy. Federal government demand for loanable funds could be influenced by the future state of the economy because it affects tax revenues to be received and the amount of unemployment compensation to be paid out, factors that affect the size of the government deficit. The Federal Reserve System's money supply targets may be assessed by reviewing public statements about the Fed's future objectives, although those statements are somewhat vague.

To forecast future interest rates, the net demand for funds *(ND)* should be forecast:

$$ND = D_A - S_A$$
$$= (D_h + D_b + D_g + D_m + D_f) - (S_h + S_b + S_g + S_m + S_f)$$

If the forecasted level of *ND* is positive or negative, a disequilibrium will exist temporarily. If *ND* is positive, the disequilibrium will be corrected by an upward adjustment in interest rates. If *ND* is negative, the disequilibrium will be corrected by a downward adjustment. The larger the forecasted magnitude of *ND*, the larger the adjustment in interest rates.

Some analysts focus more on changes in D_A and S_A than on estimating the aggregate level of D_A and S_A. For example, assume that today the equilibrium interest rate is 7 percent. This interest rate will change only if D_A and S_A change to create a temporary disequilibrium. If the government demand for funds (D_g) is expected to increase substantially, and no other components are expected to change, D_A will exceed S_A, placing upward pressure on interest rates. Thus, the forecast of future interest rates can be derived without estimating every component comprising D_A and S_A.

Exhibit 2.14 Framework for Forecasting Interest Rates

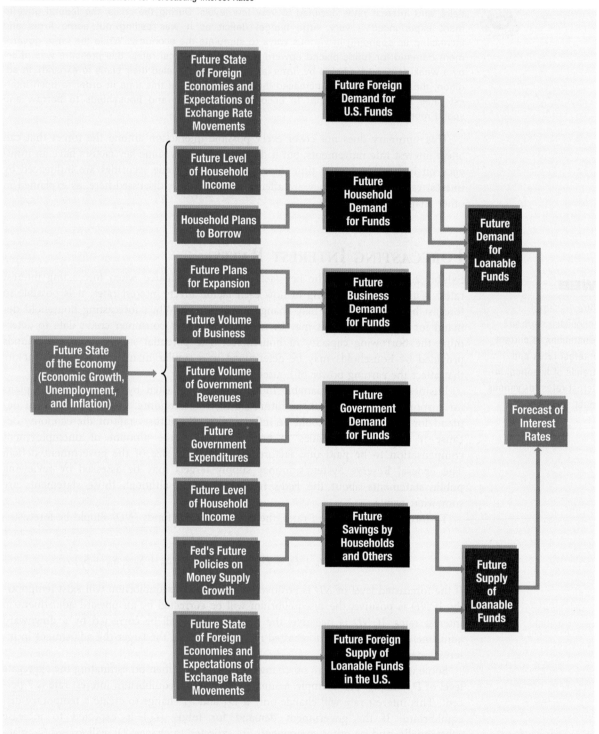

SUMMARY

- The loanable funds framework shows how the equilibrium interest rate is dependent on the aggregate supply of available funds and the aggregate demand for funds. As conditions cause the aggregate supply or demand schedules to change, interest rates gravitate toward a new equilibrium.
- The relevant factors that affect interest rate movements include changes in economic growth, inflation, the budget deficit, foreign interest rates, and the money supply. These factors can have a strong impact on the aggregate supply of funds or on the aggregate demand for funds and therefore can affect

the equilibrium interest rate. In particular, economic growth has a strong influence on the demand for loanable funds, and changes in the money supply have a strong impact on the supply of loanable funds.

- Given that the equilibrium interest rate is determined by supply and demand conditions, changes in the interest rate can be forecasted by forecasting changes in the supply of or the demand for loanable funds. Thus, the factors that influence the supply of and the demand for funds must be forecasted in order to forecast interest rates.

POINT COUNTER-POINT

Does a Large Fiscal Budget Deficit Result in Higher Interest Rates?

Point No. In some years (such as 2008), the fiscal budget deficit was large, but interest rates were very low.

Counter-Point Yes. When the federal government borrows large amounts of funds, it can crowd out

other potential borrowers, and the interest rates are bid up by the deficit units.

Who Is Correct? Use the Internet to learn more about this issue. Offer your own opinion on this issue.

QUESTIONS AND APPLICATIONS

1.   Impact of the Economy Explain how the expected interest rate in one year is dependent on your expectation of economic growth and inflation.

2.   Forecasting Interest Rates Why do forecasts of interest rates differ among experts?

3.   Impact of a Recession Explain why interest rates tend to decrease during recessionary periods. Review historical interest rates to determine how they reacted to recessionary periods. Explain this reaction.

4.   Real Interest Rate Estimate the real interest rate over the last year. If financial market participants overestimate inflation in a particular period, will real interest rates be relatively high or low? Explain.

5.   Impact of Government Spending If the federal government planned to expand the space program, how might this affect interest rates?

6.   Nominal versus Real Interest Rate What is the difference between the nominal interest rate and the real interest rate? What is the logic behind the Fisher effect's implied positive relationship between expected inflation and nominal interest rates?

7.   Interest Elasticity Explain what is meant by interest elasticity. Would you expect the federal government's demand for loanable funds to be more or less interest-elastic than household demand for loanable funds? Why?

8.   Impact of Exchange Rates on Interest Rates Assume that if the U.S. dollar strengthens, it can place downward pressure on U.S. inflation. Based on this information, how might expectations of a strong dollar affect the demand for loanable funds in the United States and U.S. interest rates? Is there any reason to think that expectations of a strong dollar could also affect the supply of loanable funds? Explain.

9.   Interest Rate Movements Explain why interest rates changed as they did over the past year.

10.   Impact of the Money Supply Should increasing money supply growth place upward or downward pressure on interest rates?

Advanced Questions

11.   Impact of War A war tends to cause significant reactions in financial markets. Why would a war in Iraq place upward pressure on U.S. interest rates? Why might some investors expect a war like this to place downward pressure on U.S. interest rates?

12.   Forecasting Interest Rates Based on Prevailing Conditions Consider the prevailing conditions for inflation (including oil prices), the economy, the budget deficit, and the Fed's monetary policy that could affect interest rates. Based on prevailing conditions, do you think interest rates will likely increase or decrease during this semester? Offer some logic to support your answer. Which factor do you think will have the biggest impact on interest rates?

13.   Global Interaction of Interest Rates Why might you expect interest rate movements of various industrialized countries to be more highly correlated in recent years than in earlier years?

14.   Impact of Government Spending Jayhawk Forecasting Services analyzed several factors that could affect interest rates in the future. Most factors were expected to place downward pressure on interest rates. Jayhawk also felt that although the annual budget deficit was to be cut by 40 percent from the previous year, it would still be very large. Thus, Jayhawk believed that the deficit's impact would more than offset the other effects and therefore forecast interest rates to increase by 2 percentage points. Comment on Jayhawk's logic.

15.   Impact of Expected Inflation How might expectations of higher oil prices affect the demand for loanable funds, the supply of loanable funds, and interest rates in the United States? Will the interest rates of other countries be affected in the same way? Explain.

16.   Decomposing Interest Rate Movements The interest rate on a one-year loan can be decomposed into a one-year risk-free (free from default risk) compo-

nent and a risk premium that reflects the potential for default on the loan in that year. A change in economic conditions can affect the risk-free rate and the risk premium. The risk-free rate is normally affected by changing economic conditions to a greater degree than the risk premium. Explain how a weaker economy will likely affect the risk-free component, the risk premium, and the overall cost of a one-year loan obtained by (a) the Treasury and (b) a corporation. Will the change in the cost of borrowing be more pronounced for the Treasury or for the corporation? Why?

17.   Impact of Stock Market Crises During periods when investors suddenly become fearful that stocks are overvalued, they dump their stocks, and the stock market experiences a major decline. During these periods, interest rates tend to decline. Use the loanable funds framework discussed in this chapter to explain how the massive selling of stocks leads to lower interest rates.

18.   Impact of September 11 Offer an argument for why the terrorist attack on the United States on September 11, 2001, could have placed downward pressure on U.S. interest rates. Offer an argument for why the terrorist attack could have placed upward pressure on U.S. interest rates.

Interpreting Financial News

Interpret the following comments made by Wall Street analysts and portfolio managers.

a. "The flight of funds from bank deposits to U.S. stocks will pressure interest rates."

b. "Since Japanese interest rates have recently declined to very low levels, expect a reduction in U.S. interest rates."

c. "The cost of borrowing by U.S. firms is dictated by the degree to which the federal government spends more than it taxes."

Managing in Financial Markets

Forecasting Interest Rates As the treasurer of a manufacturing company, your task is to forecast the direction of interest rates. You plan to borrow funds and may use the forecast of interest rates to determine whether you should obtain a loan with a fixed interest rate or a floating interest rate. The following information can be considered when assessing the future direction of interest rates:

- Economic growth has been high over the last two years, but you expect that it will be stagnant over the next year.

- Inflation has been 3 percent over each of the last few years, and you expect that it will be about the same over the next year.

- The federal government has announced major cuts in its spending, which should have a major impact on the budget deficit.

- The Federal Reserve is not expected to affect the existing supply of loanable funds over the next year.

- The overall level of savings by households is not expected to change.

a. Given the preceding information, determine how the demand for and the supply of loanable funds would be affected (if at all), and determine the future direction of interest rates.

b. You can obtain a one-year loan at a fixed rate of 8 percent or a floating-rate loan that is currently at 8 percent but would be revised every month in accordance with general interest rate movements. Which type of loan is more appropriate based on the information provided?

c. Assume that Canadian interest rates have abruptly risen just as you have completed your forecast of future U.S. interest rates. Consequently, Canadian interest rates are now 2 percentage points above U.S. interest rates. How might this specific situation place pressure on U.S. interest rates? Considering this situation along with the other information provided, would you change your forecast of the future direction of U.S. interest rates?

PROBLEMS

1. Nominal Rate of Interest Suppose the real interest rate is 6 percent and the expected inflation rate is 2 percent. What would you expect the nominal rate of interest to be?

2. Real Interest Rate Suppose that Treasury bills are currently paying 9 percent and the expected inflation rate is 3 percent. What is the real interest rate?

FLOW OF FUNDS EXERCISE

How the Flow of Funds Affects Interest Rates

Recall that Carson Company has obtained substantial loans from finance companies and commercial banks. The interest rate on the loans is tied to market interest rates and is adjusted every six months. Thus, Carson's cost of obtaining funds is sensitive to interest rate movements. Because of its expectations that the U.S. economy will strengthen, Carson plans to grow in the future by expanding and by making acquisitions. Carson expects that it will need substantial long-term financing to finance its growth and plans to borrow additional funds either through existing loans or by issuing bonds. It is also considering issuing stock to raise funds in the next year.

a. Explain why Carson should be very interested in future interest rate movements.

b. Given Carson's expectations, do you think that the company expects interest rates to increase or decrease in the future? Explain.

c. If Carson's expectations of future interest rates are correct, how would this affect its cost of borrowing on its existing loans and on its future loans?

d. Explain why Carson's expectations about future interest rates may affect its decision about when to borrow funds and whether to obtain floating-rate or fixed-rate loans.

INTERNET/EXCEL EXERCISES

1. Go to http://research.stlouisfed.org/fred2. Under "Categories," select "Interest rates" and then select the three-month Treasury bill series (secondary market). Describe how this rate has changed in recent months.

Using the information in this chapter, explain why the interest rate changed as it did.

2. Using the same website, retrieve data at the beginning of the last 20 quarters for interest rates (based on the three-month Treasury bill rate) and the producer price index for all commodities and place the data in two columns of an Excel spreadsheet. Derive the change in interest rates on a quarterly basis. Then derive the percentage change in the producer price index on a quarterly basis, which serves as a measure of inflation. Apply regression analysis in which the change in interest rates is the dependent variable and inflation is the independent variable (see Appendix B for information about applying regression analysis). Explain the relationship that you find. Does it appear that inflation and interest rate movements are positively related?

WSJ EXERCISE

Forecasting Interest Rates

Review information about the credit markets in a recent issue of *The Wall Street Journal*. Identify the factors that are given attention because they may affect future interest rate movements. Then create your own forecasts as to whether interest rates will increase or decrease from now until the end of the school term, based on your assessment of any factors that affect interest rates. Explain your forecast.

3

Structure of Interest Rates

CHAPTER OBJECTIVES

The specific objectives of this chapter are to:

- describe how characteristics of debt securities cause their yields to vary,

- demonstrate how to estimate the appropriate yield for any particular debt security, and

- explain the theories behind the term structure of interest rates (relationship between the term to maturity and the yield of securities).

The annual interest rate offered by debt securities at a given point in time varies among debt securities. Individual and institutional investors must understand why quoted yields vary so that they can determine whether the extra yield on a given security outweighs any unfavorable characteristics. Financial managers of corporations or government agencies in need of funds must understand why quoted yields of debt securities vary so that they can estimate the yield they would have to offer in order to sell new debt securities.

WHY DEBT SECURITY YIELDS VARY

Debt securities offer different yields because they exhibit different characteristics that influence the yield to be offered. In general, securities with unfavorable characteristics will offer higher yields to entice investors. Some debt securities, however, have favorable features as well. The yields on debt securities are affected by the following characteristics:

- Credit (default) risk

- Liquidity

- Tax status

- Term to maturity

The yields on bonds may also be affected by special provisions, as described in Chapter 7.

Credit (Default) Risk

Because most securities are subject to the risk of default, investors must consider the creditworthiness of the security issuer. Although investors always have the option of purchasing risk-free Treasury securities, they may prefer some other securities if the yield compensates them for the risk. Thus, if all other characteristics besides credit (default) risk are equal, securities with a higher degree of risk will have to offer higher yields to be purchased. Credit risk is especially relevant for longer-term securities that expose creditors to the possibility of default for a longer time.

Credit risk premiums of 1 percent, 2 percent, or more may not seem significant. But for a corporation borrowing $30 million through the issuance of bonds, an extra percentage point as a premium reflects $300,000 in additional interest expenses per year.

Investors may personally assess the creditworthiness of corporations that issue bonds, or they may use bond ratings provided by rating agencies. These ratings are based on a financial assessment of the issuing corporation. The higher the rating, the lower the perceived credit risk. As time passes, economic conditions can change, and the perceived credit risk of a corporation can change as well. Thus, bonds previously issued by a firm may be rated at one level, while a subsequent issue from the same firm is rated at a different level. The ratings can also differ if the collateral provisions differ among the bonds.

Rating Agencies   Rating agencies charge the issuers of debt securities a fee for assessing the default risk of their securities. The ratings are then provided through various financial media outlets at no cost to investors who wish to use the ratings. The most popular rating agencies are Moody's Investors Service and Standard & Poor's Corporation. A summary of their rating classification schedules is provided in Exhibit 3.1. Moody's ratings range from Aaa for highest quality to C for lowest quality, and Standard & Poor's range from AAA to D. Because these rating agencies use different methods to assess the creditworthiness of firms and state governments, a particular bond could be assigned a different rating by each agency; nevertheless, differences are usually small.

Some financial institutions such as commercial banks are required by law to invest only in **investment-grade bonds**, that is, bonds that are rated as Baa or better by Moody's and BBB or better by Standard & Poor's. This requirement is intended to limit the portfolio risk of the financial institutions.

Accuracy of Credit Ratings   The ratings issued by the agencies are opinions, not guarantees. In general, credit ratings have served as reasonable indicators of the likelihood of default. Bonds assigned a low credit rating experience default more frequently than bonds assigned a high credit rating. Nevertheless, credit rating agencies do not always detect firms' financial problems. For example, they did not recognize Enron's financial problems until shortly before Enron filed for bankruptcy in 2001. Their inability to detect Enron's problems may be partially attributed to Enron's fraudulent financial statements that the credit agencies presumed were accurate. When the credit crisis began in 2008, ratings agencies were slow to downgrade debt securities issued by some financial institutions that experienced financial problems.

Exhibit 3.1 Rating Classification by Rating Agencies

DESCRIPTION OF SECURITY	RATINGS ASSIGNED BY:	
	MOODY'S	STANDARD & POOR'S
Highest quality	Aaa	AAA
High quality	Aa	AA
High-medium quality	A	A
Medium quality	Baa	BBB
Medium-low quality	Ba	BB
Low quality (speculative)	B	B
Poor quality	Caa	CCC
Very poor quality	Ca	CC
Lowest quality (in default)	C	DDD, D

Liquidity

Investors prefer securities that are *liquid,* meaning that they could be easily converted to cash without a loss in value. Thus, if all other characteristics are equal, securities with less liquidity will have to offer a higher yield to be preferred. Securities with a short-term maturity or an active secondary market have greater liquidity. For investors who will not need their funds until the securities mature, less liquidity is tolerable. Other investors, however, are willing to accept a lower return in exchange for a high degree of liquidity.

Tax Status

Investors are more concerned with after-tax income than before-tax income earned on securities. If all other characteristics are similar, taxable securities will have to offer a higher before-tax yield to investors than tax-exempt securities to be preferred. The extra compensation required on such taxable securities depends on the tax rates of individual and institutional investors. Investors in high tax brackets benefit most from tax-exempt securities.

When assessing the expected yields of various securities with similar risk and maturity, it is common to convert them into an after-tax form, as follows:

$$Y_{at} = Y_{bt}(1-T)$$

where
$$Y_{at} = \text{after-tax yield}$$
$$Y_{bt} = \text{before-tax yield}$$
$$T = \text{investor's marginal tax rate}$$

Investors retain only a percentage $(1-T)$ of the before-tax yield once taxes are paid.

EXAMPLE

Consider a taxable security that offers a before-tax yield of 14 percent. When converted into after-tax terms, the yield will be reduced by the tax percentage. The precise after-tax yield is dependent on the tax rate (T). If the tax rate of the investor is 20 percent, the after-tax yield will be

$$Y_{at} = Y_{bt}(1-T)$$
$$Y_{at} = 14\%(1-.2)$$
$$= 11.2\%$$

Exhibit 3.2 presents after-tax yields based on a variety of tax rates and before-tax yields. For example, a taxable security with a before-tax yield of 6 percent will generate an after-tax yield of 5.4 percent to an investor in the 10 percent tax bracket, 5.10 percent to an investor in the 15 percent tax bracket, and so on. This exhibit shows why investors in high tax brackets are attracted to tax-exempt securities. ●

Computing the Equivalent Before-Tax Yield In some cases, investors wish to determine the before-tax yield necessary to match the after-tax yield of a tax-exempt

Exhibit 3.2 After-Tax Yields Based on Various Tax Rates and Before-Tax Yields

	BEFORE–TAX YIELD				
TAX RATE	6%	8%	10%	12%	14%
10%	5.40%	7.20%	9.00%	10.80%	12.60%
15	5.10	6.80	8.50	10.20	11.90
25	4.50	6.00	7.50	9.00	10.50
28	4.32	5.76	7.20	8.64	10.08
35	3.90	5.20	6.50	7.80	9.10

security that has a similar risk and maturity. This can be done by rearranging the terms of the previous equation:

$$Y_{bt} = \frac{Y_{at}}{(1-T)}$$

Suppose that a firm in the 20 percent tax bracket is aware of a tax-exempt security that is paying a yield of 8 percent. To match this after-tax yield, taxable securities must offer a before-tax yield of

$$Y_{bt} = \frac{Y_{at}}{(1-T)} = \frac{8\%}{(1-.2)} = 10\%$$

State taxes should be considered along with federal taxes in determining the after-tax yield. Treasury securities are exempt from state income tax, and municipal securities are sometimes exempt as well. Because states impose different income tax rates, a particular security's after-tax yield may vary with the location of the investor.

Term to Maturity

Maturity differs among debt securities and is another reason that debt security yields differ. The **term structure of interest rates** defines the relationship between the term to maturity and the annualized yield of debt securities at a specific point in time, holding other factors such as risk constant.

EXAMPLE

Assume that as of today, the annualized yields for federal government securities (free from default risk) of varied maturities are as shown in Exhibit 3.3. The curve created by connecting the

Exhibit 3.3 Example of Relationship between Maturity and Yield of Treasury Securities (as of January 4, 2009)

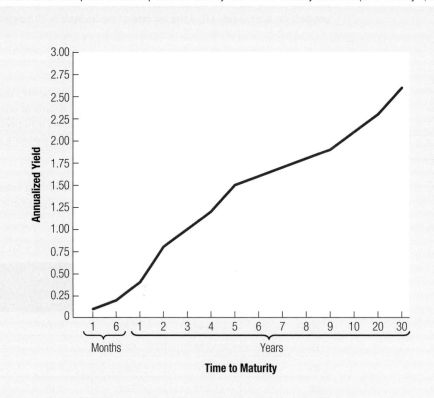

points plotted in the exhibit is commonly referred to as a yield curve. Notice that the yield curve exhibits an upward slope.

The term structure of interest rates in Exhibit 3.3 shows that securities that are similar in all ways except their term to maturity may offer different yields. Because the demand and supply conditions for securities may vary among maturities, so may the price (and therefore the yield) of securities. A comprehensive explanation of the term structure of interest rates is provided later in this chapter. ●

Since the yield curve in Exhibit 3.3 is based on Treasury securities, the curve is not influenced by default risk. A yield curve for AA-rated corporate bonds would typically have a slope similar to that of the Treasury yield curve, but the yield at any term to maturity would be higher to reflect the risk premium.

WEB
www.bloomberg.com
Assess the most recent yield curve.

EXPLAINING ACTUAL YIELD DIFFERENTIALS

Even small differentials in yield can be relevant to financial institutions that are borrowing or investing millions of dollars. Yield differentials are sometimes measured in basis points; a basis point equals .01 percent, and 100 basis points equals 1 percent. If a security offers a yield of 4.3 percent while the a risk-free security offers a yield of 4.0 percent, the yield differential is .30 percent or 30 basis points. Yield differentials are described for money market securities next, followed by capital market securities.

Yield Differentials of Money Market Securities

The yields offered on commercial paper (short-term securities offered by creditworthy firms) are typically just slightly higher than T-bill (Treasury bill) rates, as investors require a slightly higher return (such as 10 to 40 basis points on an annualized basis) to compensate for default risk and less liquidity. Negotiable certificates of deposit rates are slightly higher than yields on Treasury bills with the same maturity at a given point in time because of their lower degree of liquidity and higher degree of default risk.

Market forces cause the yields of all securities to move in the same direction. To illustrate, assume the budget deficit increases substantially and the Treasury issues a large number of T-bills to finance the increased deficit. This action creates a large supply of T-bills in the market, placing downward pressure on the price and upward pressure on the T-bill yield. As the yield begins to rise, it approaches the yield of other short-term securities. Businesses and individual investors are now encouraged to purchase T-bills rather than these risky securities because they can achieve about the same yield while avoiding default risk. The switch to T-bills lowers the demand for risky securities, thereby placing downward pressure on their price and upward pressure on their yields. Thus, the risk premium on risky securities would not disappear completely.

Yield Differentials of Capital Market Securities

With regard to capital market securities, municipal bonds have the lowest before-tax yield, yet their after-tax yield is typically above that of Treasury bonds from the perspective of investors in high tax brackets. Treasury bonds are expected to offer the lowest yield because they are free from default risk and can easily be liquidated in the secondary market. Investors prefer municipal or corporate bonds over Treasury bonds only if the after-tax yield is sufficiently higher to compensate for default risk and a lower degree of liquidity.

Exhibit 3.4 Yield Differentials of Corporate Bonds

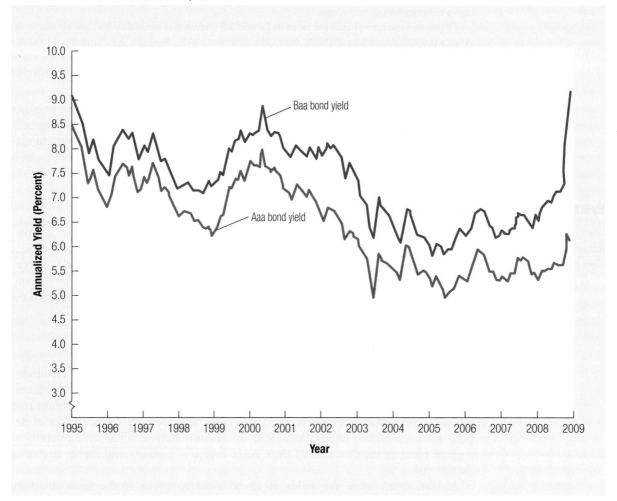

To illustrate how capital market security yields can vary because of default risk, Exhibit 3.4 shows yields of corporate bonds in two different risk classes. The yield differentials among capital market securities can change over time as perceptions of risk change. Notice that the yield differential between Baa bonds and Aaa bonds was relatively large in the 2000–2003 period when economic conditions were weak. In this period, corporations had to pay a relatively high premium if their bonds were rated Baa. The yield differential narrowed in the 2004–2007 period when economic conditions improved. During the credit crisis in the 2008–2009 period, however, the yield differential increased substantially. Many corporations whose bonds are rated Baa or below were unwilling to issue bonds because of the very high credit risk premium they would have to pay to bondholders.

ESTIMATING THE APPROPRIATE YIELD

The discussion up to this point suggests that the appropriate yield to be offered on a debt security is based on the risk-free rate for the corresponding maturity, with adjustments to capture various characteristics. This model is specified below:

$$\Upsilon_n = R_{f,n} + DP + LP + TA$$

where

$\Upsilon_n =$ **yield of an *n*-day debt security**
$R_{f,n} =$ **yield of an *n*-day Treasury (risk-free) security**
$DP =$ **default premium to compensate for credit risk**
$LP =$ **liquidity premium to compensate for less liquidity**
$TA =$ **adjustment due to the difference in tax status**

These are the characteristics identified earlier that explain yield differentials among securities (special provisions applicable to bonds may also be included, as described in Chapter 7). Although maturity is another characteristic that can affect the yield, it is not included here because it is controlled for by matching the maturity of the risk-free security to that of the security of concern.

EXAMPLE

Suppose that the three-month T-bill's annualized rate is 8 percent and Elizabeth Company plans to issue 90-day commercial paper. Elizabeth will need to determine the default premium *(DP)* and liquidity premium *(LP)* to offer on its commercial paper to make it as attractive to investors as a three-month (13-week) T-bill. The federal tax status of commercial paper is the same as for T-bills. Income earned from investing in commercial paper is subject to state taxes, however, whereas income earned from investing in T-bills is not. Investors may require a premium for this reason alone if they reside in a location where state and local income taxes apply.

Assume that Elizabeth Company believes that a 0.7 percent default risk premium, a 0.2 percent liquidity premium, and a 0.3 percent tax adjustment are necessary to sell its commercial paper to investors. The appropriate yield to be offered on the commercial paper (called Υ_{cp}) is

$$\begin{aligned} \Upsilon_{cp,n} &= R_{f,n} + DP + LP + TA \\ &= 8\% + .7\% + .2\% + .3\% \\ &= 9.2\% \end{aligned}$$ ●

As time passes, the appropriate commercial paper rate will change, perhaps because of changes in the risk-free rate, default premium, liquidity premium, and tax adjustment.

Some corporations may postpone plans to issue commercial paper until the economy improves and the required premium for credit risk is reduced. Yet even then, the market rate of commercial paper may increase if interest rates increase.

EXAMPLE

If the default risk premium decreases from 0.7 percent to 0.5 percent but $R_{f,n}$ increases from 8 percent to 8.7 percent, the appropriate yield to be offered on commercial paper (assuming no change in the previously assumed liquidity and tax adjustment premiums) would be

$$\begin{aligned} \Upsilon_{cp} &= R_{f,n} + DP + LP + TA \\ &= 8.7\% + .5\% + .2\% + .3\% \\ &= 9.7\% \end{aligned}$$

The strategy to postpone issuing commercial paper would backfire in this example. Even though the default premium decreased by 0.2 percent, the general level of interest rates rose by 0.7 percent, so the net change in the commercial paper rate is + 0.5 percent. ●

As this example shows, the increase in a security's yield over time does not necessarily mean that the default premium has increased.

The assessment of yields as described here could also be applied to long-term securities. If, for example, a firm desires to issue a 20-year corporate bond, it will use the yield of a new 20-year Treasury bond as the 20-year risk-free rate and add on the premiums for credit risk, liquidity risk, and so on, to determine the yield at which it can sell corporate bonds.

USING THE WALL STREET JOURNAL

Assessing the Yield Curve

The Wall Street Journal provides a graph of the prevailing yield curve, as shown here. Notice that the curve is upward sloping. A yield curve as of one year ago is also plotted so that financial market participants can review how the yields to maturity have changed over time. Firms that plan to borrow assess the yield curve in order to determine the difference in the cost of financing among different maturities. Investors assess the yield curve in order to determine the difference in rates of return among maturities if they purchase Treasury securities and hold them until maturity. The Treasury may use the yield curve when deciding what maturity to select when issuing new securities to raise additional funds.

_____

Source: Republished with permission of Dow Jones & Company, Inc., from *The Wall Street Journal*, January 7 , 2009, p. C4; permission conveyed through the Copyright Clearance Center, Inc.

Bonds, Rates, & Yields

Benchmark Yields and Rates

Treasury yield curve

Yield to maturity of current bills, notes and bonds

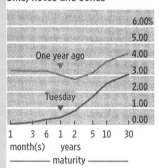

*Semiannual swaps maturing in 2 yrs–30 yrs   Sources: Ryan ALM; ICAP plc.

A simpler and more general relationship is that the yield offered on a debt security is positively related to the prevailing risk-free rate and the security's risk premium (*RP*). This risk premium captures any risk characteristics of the security, including credit risk and liquidity risk. A more detailed model for the yield of a debt security could be applied by including additional characteristics that can vary among bonds, such as whether the bond is convertible into stock, and whether it contains a call premium. The conversion option is favorable for investors, so that could reduce the yield that needs to be offered on a bond. The call premium is unfavorable for investors, so that could increase the yield that needs to be offered on a bond.

A Closer Look at the Term Structure

Of all the factors that affect the yields offered on debt securities, the factor that is most difficult to understand is the term to maturity. For this reason, a more comprehensive explanation of the relationship between term to maturity and annualized yield (referred to as the term structure of interest rates) is necessary.

Various theories have been used to explain the relationship between maturity and annualized yield of securities, including the pure expectations theory, liquidity premium theory, and segmented markets theory. Each of these theories is explained here.

Pure Expectations Theory

According to the **pure expectations theory,** the term structure of interest rates (as reflected in the shape of the yield curve) is determined solely by expectations of future interest rates.

Impact of an Expected Increase in Interest Rates To under stand how interest rate expectations may influence the yield curve, assume that the annualized yields of short-term and long-term risk-free securities are similar; that is, the yield curve is flat. Then assume that investors begin to believe that interest rates will rise. They will respond by investing their funds mostly in the short term so that they can soon reinvest their funds at higher yields after interest rates increase. When investors flood the short-term market and avoid the long-term market, they may cause the yield curve to adjust as shown in Panel A of Exhibit 3.5. The large supply of funds in the short-term markets will force annualized yields down. Meanwhile, the reduced supply of long-term funds forces long-term yields up.

Even though the annualized short-term yields become lower than annualized long-term yields, investors in short-term funds are satisfied because they expect interest rates to rise. They will make up for the lower short-term yield when the short-term securities mature, and they reinvest at a higher rate (if interest rates rise) at maturity.

Assuming that the borrowers who plan to issue securities also expect interest rates to increase, they will prefer to lock in the present interest rate over a long period of time. Thus, borrowers will generally prefer to issue long-term securities rather than short-term securities. This results in a relatively small demand for short-term funds. Consequently, there is downward pressure on the yield of short-term funds. There is also an increase in the demand for long-term funds by borrowers, which places upward pressure on long-term funds. Overall, the expectation of higher interest rates changes the demand for funds and the supply of funds in different maturity markets, which forces the original flat yield curve (labeled YC_1) to pivot upward (counterclockwise) and become upward sloping (YC_2).

Impact of an Expected Decline in Interest Rates If investors expect interest rates to decrease in the future, they will prefer to invest in long-term funds rather than short-term funds, because they could lock in today's interest rate before interest rates fall. Borrowers will prefer to borrow short-term funds so that they can reborrow at a lower interest rate once interest rates decline.

Based on the expectation of lower interest rates in the future, the supply of funds provided by investors will be low for short-term funds and high for long-term funds. This will place upward pressure on short-term yields and downward pressure on long-term yields as shown in Panel B of Exhibit 3.5. Overall, the expectation of lower interest rates causes the shape of the yield curve to pivot downward (clockwise).

Algebraic Presentation Investors monitor the yield curve to determine the rates that exist for securities with various maturities. They can purchase either a security with a maturity that matches their investment horizon or a security with a shorter term and reinvest the proceeds at maturity. If a particular investment strategy is expected to generate a higher return over the investment horizon, investors may use that strategy. This could affect the prices and yields of securities with different maturities, realigning the rates so that the expected return over the entire investment horizon would be similar, regardless of the strategy used. If investors were indifferent to security maturities, they would want the return of any security to equal the compounded yield of consecutive investments in shorter-term securities. That is, a two-year security should offer a return that is similar to the anticipated return from investing in two consecutive one-year securities. A four-year security should offer a return that is competitive with the expected return from investing in two consecutive two-year securities or four consecutive one-year securities, and so on.

Exhibit 3.5 How Interest Rate Expectations Affect the Yield Curve

Panel A: Impact of a Sudden Expectation of Higher Interest Rates

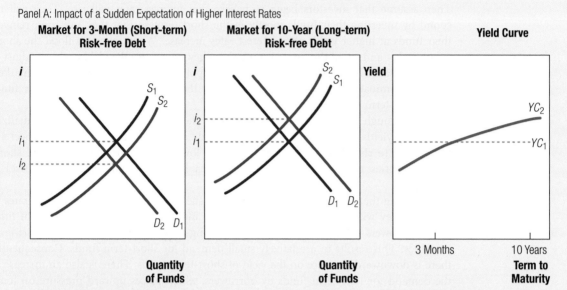

E($\uparrow i$) → Supply of funds provided by investors ↑ in short-term (such as 3-month) markets, and ↓ in long-term (such as 10-year) markets. Demand for funds by borrowers ↑ in long-term markets and ↓ in short-term markets. Therefore, the yield curve becomes upward sloping as shown here.

Panel B: Impact of a Sudden Expectation of Lower Interest Rates

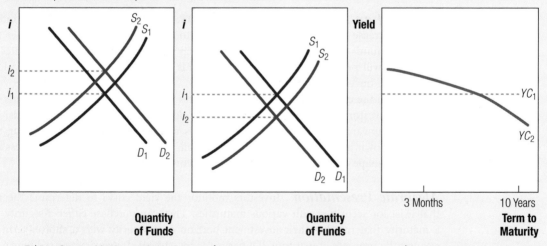

E($\downarrow i$) → Supply of funds provided by investors ↑ in long-term (such as 10-year) markets, and ↓ in short-term (such as 3-month) markets. Demand for funds by borrowers ↑ in short-term markets and ↓ in long-term markets. Therefore, the yield curve becomes downward sloping as shown here.

To illustrate these equalities, consider the relationship between interest rates on a two-year security and a one-year security as follows:

$$(1 + {}_t i_2)^2 = (1 + {}_t i_1)(1 + {}_{t+1} r_1)$$

where ${}_t i_2 =$ **known annualized interest rate of a two-year security as of time** *t*
         ${}_t i_1 =$ **known annualized interest rate of a one-year security as of time** *t*
    ${}_{t+1} r_1 =$ **one-year interest rate that is anticipated as of time** *t* $+ 1$
           (**one year ahead**)

The term *i* represents a quoted rate, which is therefore known, whereas *r* represents a rate to be quoted at some point in the future, which is therefore uncertain. The left side of the equation represents the compounded yield to investors who purchase a two-year security, while the right side of the equation represents the anticipated compounded yield from purchasing a one-year security and reinvesting the proceeds in a new one-year security at the end of one year. If time *t* is today, ${}_{t+1} r_1$ can be estimated by rearranging terms:

$$1 + {}_{t+1} r_1 = \frac{(1 + {}_t i_2)^2}{(1 + {}_t i_1)}$$

$$_{t+1} r_1 = \frac{(1 + {}_t i_2)^2}{(1 + {}_t i_1)} - 1$$

The term ${}_{t+1} r_1$ referred to as the **forward rate,** is commonly estimated in order to represent the market's forecast of the future interest rate. As a numerical example, assume that as of today (time *t)* the annualized two-year interest rate is 10 percent, while the one-year interest rate is 8 percent. The forward rate is estimated as follows:

$$_{t+1} r_1 = \frac{(1 + .10)^2}{(1 + .08)} - 1$$

$$= .1203704$$

Conceptually, this rate implies that one year from now, a one-year interest rate must equal about 12.037 percent in order for consecutive investments in two one-year securities to generate a return similar to that of a two-year investment. If the actual one-year rate beginning one year from now (at period *t* + 1) is above (below) 12.037 percent, the return from two consecutive one-year investments will exceed (be less than) the return on a two-year investment. ●

    The forward rate is sometimes used as an approximation of the market's consensus interest rate forecast, because if the market had a different perception, demand and supply of today's existing two-year and one-year securities would adjust to capitalize on this information. Of course, there is no guarantee that the forward rate will forecast the future interest rate with perfect accuracy.

    The greater the difference between the implied one-year forward rate and today's one-year interest rate, the greater the expected change in the one-year interest rate. If the term structure of interest rates is solely influenced by expectations of future interest rates, the following relationships hold:

SCENARIO	STRUCTURE OF YIELD CURVE	EXPECTATIONS ABOUT THE FUTURE INTEREST RATE
1. ${}_{t+1} r_1 > {}_t i_1$	Upward slope	Higher than today's rate
2. ${}_{t+1} r_1 = {}_t i_1$	Flat	Same as today's rate
3. ${}_{t+1} r_1 < {}_t i_1$	Downward slope	Lower than today's rate

Forward rates can be determined for various maturities. The relationships described here can be applied when assessing the change in the interest rate of a security with any particular maturity.

The previous example can be expanded to solve for other forward rates. The equality specified by the pure expectations theory for a three-year horizon is

$$(1 + {}_ti_3)^3 = (1 + {}_ti_1)(1 + {}_{t+1}r_1)(1 + {}_{t+2}r_1)$$

where ${}_ti_3$ = **annualized rate on a three-year security as of time** t

   ${}_{t+2}r_1$ = **one-year interest rate that is anticipated as of time** $t + 2$ **(two years)**

All other terms were already defined. By rearranging terms, we can isolate the forward rate of a one-year security beginning two years from now:

$$1 + {}_{t+2}r_1 = \frac{(1 + {}_ti_3)^3}{(1 + {}_ti_1)(1 + {}_{t+1}r_1)}$$

$$_{t+2}r_1 = \frac{(1 + {}_ti_3)^3}{(1 + {}_ti_1)(1 + {}_{t+1}r_1)} - 1$$

If the one-year forward rate beginning one year from now $({}_{t+1}r_1)$ has already been estimated, this estimate along with actual one-year and three-year interest rates can be used to estimate the one-year forward rate two years from now. Recall that our previous example assumed ${}_ti_1$ = 8 percent and estimated ${}_{t+1}r_1$ to be about 12.037 percent.

EXAMPLE

Assume that a three-year security has an annualized interest rate of 11 percent $({}_ti_3$ = 11 percent). Given this information, the one-year forward rate two years from now is

$$_{t+2}r_1 = \frac{(1 + {}_ti_3)^3}{(1 + {}_ti_1)(1 + {}_{t+1}r_1)} - 1$$

$$= \frac{(1 + .11)^3}{(1 + .08)(1 + .12037)} - 1$$

$$= \frac{1.367631}{1.21} - 1$$

$$= 13.02736\%$$

Thus, the market anticipates a one-year interest rate of 13.02736 percent as of two years from now. ●

The yield curve can also be used to forecast annualized interest rates for periods other than one year. For example, the information provided in the last example could be used to determine the two-year forward rate beginning one year from now.

According to the pure expectations theory, a one-year investment followed by a two-year investment should offer the same annualized yield over the three-year horizon as a three-year security that could be purchased today. This equality is shown as follows:

$$(1 + {}_{t+1}i_3)^3 = (1 + {}_ti_1)(1 + {}_{t+1}r_2)^2$$

where

   ${}_{t+1}r_2$ = **annual interest rate of a two-year security anticipated as of time** $t + 1$

By rearranging terms, ${}_{t+1}r_2$ can be isolated:

$$(1 + {}_{t+1}r_2)^2 = \frac{(1 + {}_ti_3)^3}{(1 + {}_ti_1)}$$

EXAMPLE

Recall that today's annualized yields for one-year and three-year securities are 8 percent and 11 percent, respectively. With this information, $_{t+1}r_2$ is estimated as follows:

$$(1 + {}_{t+1}r_2)^2 = \frac{(1 + {}_ti_3)^3}{(1 + {}_ti_1)}$$

$$= \frac{(1 + .11)^3}{(1 + .08)}$$

$$= 1.266325$$

$$(1 + {}_{t+1}r_2) = \sqrt{1.266325}$$

$$= 1.1253$$

$$_{t+1}r_2 = .1253$$

Thus, the market anticipates an annualized interest rate of about 12.53 percent for two-year securities beginning one year from now. ●

Pure expectations theory is based on the premise that the forward rates are unbiased estimators of future interest rates. If forward rates are biased, investors could attempt to capitalize on the bias.

EXAMPLE

In the previous numerical example, the one-year forward rate beginning one year ahead was estimated to be about 12.037 percent. If the forward rate was thought to contain an upward bias, the expected one-year interest rate beginning one year ahead would be less than 12.037 percent. Therefore, investors with funds available for two years would earn a higher yield by purchasing two-year securities rather than purchasing one-year securities for two consecutive years. Their actions would cause an increase in the price of two-year securities and a decrease in that of one-year securities. The yields of the securities would move inversely with the price movements. The attempt by investors to capitalize on the forward rate bias would essentially eliminate the bias. ●

If forward rates are unbiased estimators of future interest rates, financial market efficiency is supported, and the information implied by market rates about the forward rate cannot be used to generate abnormal returns. As new information develops, investor preferences would change, yields would adjust, and the implied forward rate would adjust as well.

If a long-term rate is expected to equal a geometric average of consecutive short-term rates covering the same time horizon (as is suggested by pure expectations theory), long-term rates would likely be more stable than short-term rates. As expectations about consecutive short-term rates change over time, the average of these rates is less volatile than the individual short-term rates. Thus, long-term rates are much more stable than short-term rates.

Liquidity Premium Theory

Some investors may prefer to own short-term rather than long-term securities because a shorter maturity represents greater liquidity. In this case, they may be willing to hold long-term securities only if compensated with a premium for the lower degree of liquidity. Although long-term securities can be liquidated prior to maturity, their prices are more sensitive to interest rate movements. Short-term securities are normally considered to be more liquid because they are more likely to be converted to cash without a loss in value.

The preference for the more liquid short-term securities places upward pressure on the slope of a yield curve. Liquidity may be a more critical factor to investors at particular points in time, and the liquidity premium will change over time accordingly. As it does, so will the yield curve. This is the **liquidity premium theory** (also sometimes referred to as the liquidity preference theory).

Exhibit 3.6 combines the simultaneous existence of expectations theory and a liquidity premium. Each graph shows different interest rate expectations by the market. Regardless

Exhibit 3.6 Impact of Liquidity Premium on the Yield Curve under Three Different Scenarios

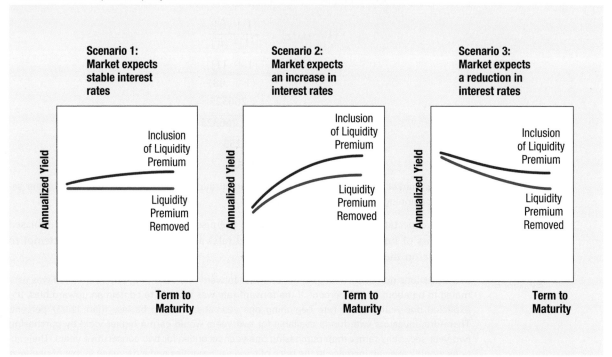

of the interest rate forecast, the yield curve is affected in a somewhat similar manner by the liquidity premium.

Estimation of the Forward Rate Based on a Liquidity Premium   When expectations theory is combined with the liquidity theory, the yield on a security will not necessarily be equal to the yield from consecutive investments in shorter-term securities over the same investment horizon. For example, the yield on a two-year security can be determined as

$$(1 + {}_ti_2)^2 = (1 + {}_ti_1)(1 + {}_{t+1}r_1) + LP_2$$

where LP_2 represents the liquidity premium on a two-year security. The yield generated from the two-year security should exceed the yield from consecutive investments in one-year securities by a premium that compensates the investor for less liquidity. The relationship between the liquidity premium and term to maturity can be expressed as follows:

$$0 < LP_1 < LP_2 < LP_3 < \cdots < LP_{20}$$

where the subscripts represent years to maturity. This implies that the liquidity premium would be more influential on the difference between annualized interest rates on one-year and 20-year securities than on the difference between one-year and two-year securities.

If liquidity influences the yield curve, the forward rate overestimates the market's expectation of the future interest rate. A more appropriate formula for the forward rate would account for the liquidity premium. By rearranging the terms of the previous equation, the one-year forward rate can be derived as follows:

$${}_{t+1}r_1 = \frac{(1 + {}_ti_2)^2}{(1 + {}_ti_1)} - 1 - [LP_2/(1 + {}_ti_1)]$$

Reconsider the example where i_1 = 8 percent and i_2 = 10 percent. Assume that the liquidity premium on a two-year security is 0.5 percent. The one-year forward rate can be derived from this information:

$$_{t+1}r_1 = \frac{(1 + {}_ti_2)^2}{(1 + {}_ti_1)} - 1 - [LP_2/(1 + {}_ti_1)]$$

$$_{t+1}r_1 = \frac{(1.10)^2}{1.08} - 1 - [.005/(1 + .08)]$$

$$= .11574$$

This estimate of the one-year forward rate is below the estimate derived in the previous related example in which the liquidity premium was not considered. The previous estimate (12.037 percent) of the forward rate should overstate the market's expected interest rate, because it did not account for a liquidity premium. Forecasts of future interest rates implied by a yield curve are reduced slightly when accounting for the liquidity premium. ●

Even with the existence of a liquidity premium, yield curves could still be used to interpret interest rate expectations. A flat yield curve would be interpreted to mean that the market is expecting a slight decrease in interest rates (without the effect of the liquidity premium, the yield curve would have had a slight downward slope). A slight upward slope would be interpreted as no expected change in interest rates because if the liquidity premium were removed, this yield curve would be flat.

Segmented Markets Theory

According to the **segmented markets theory,** investors and borrowers choose securities with maturities that satisfy their forecasted cash needs. Pension funds and life insurance companies may generally prefer long-term investments that coincide with their long-term liabilities. Commercial banks may prefer more short-term investments to coincide with their short-term liabilities. If investors and borrowers participate only in the maturity market that satisfies their particular needs, markets are segmented. That is, investors (or borrowers) will shift from the long-term market to the short-term market or vice versa only if the timing of their cash needs changes. According to the segmented markets theory, the choice of long-term versus short-term maturities is predetermined according to need rather than expectations of future interest rates.

Assume that most investors have funds available to invest for only a short period of time and therefore desire to invest primarily in short-term securities. Also assume that most borrowers need funds for a long period of time and therefore desire to issue mostly long-term securities. The result will be downward pressure on the yield of short-term securities and upward pressure on the yield of long-term securities. Overall, the scenario described would create an upward-sloping yield curve.

Now consider the opposite scenario in which most investors wish to invest their funds for a long period of time, while most borrowers need funds for only a short period of time. According to the segmented markets theory, there will be upward pressure on the yield of short-term securities and downward pressure on the yield of long-term securities. If the supply of funds provided by investors and the demand for funds by borrowers were better balanced between the short-term and long-term markets, the yields of short- and long-term securities would be more similar. ●

The example separated the maturity markets into just short term and long term. In reality, several maturity markets may exist. Within the short-term market, some investors may prefer maturities of one month or less, while others prefer maturities of one to three months. Regardless of how many maturity markets exist, the yields of securities with various maturities should be somewhat influenced by the desires of investors and borrowers to participate in the maturity market that best satisfies their needs. A corporation that needs additional funds for 30 days would not consider issuing long-term bonds for such a purpose. Savers with short-term funds would avoid some long-term investments, such as 10-year certificates of deposit, that cannot be easily liquidated.

Limitation of the Theory   A limitation of the segmented markets theory is that some borrowers and savers have the flexibility to choose among various maturity markets. Corporations that need long-term funds may initially obtain short-term financing if they expect interest rates to decline. Investors with long-term funds may make short-term investments if they expect interest rates to rise. Some investors with short-term funds available may be willing to purchase long-term securities that have an active secondary market.

Some financial institutions focus on a particular maturity market, but others are more flexible. Commercial banks obtain most of their funds in short-term markets but spread their investments into short-, medium-, and long-term markets. Savings institutions have historically focused on attracting short-term funds and lending funds for long-term periods. If maturity markets were completely segmented, an adjustment in the interest rate in one market would have no impact on other markets. However, there is clear evidence that interest rates among maturity markets move closely in tandem over time, proving that there is some interaction among markets, which implies that funds are being transferred across markets. Note that this theory of segmented markets conflicts with the general presumption of the pure expectations theory that maturity markets are perfect substitutes for one another.

Implications   Although markets are not completely segmented, the preference for particular maturities can affect the prices and yields of securities with different maturities and therefore affect the yield curve's shape. Therefore, the segmented markets theory appears to be a partial explanation for the yield curve's shape, but not the sole explanation.

A more flexible perspective of the segmented markets theory, called the **preferred habitat theory,** offers a compromise explanation for the term structure of interest rates. This theory suggests that although investors and borrowers may normally concentrate on a particular natural maturity market, certain events may cause them to wander from it. For example, commercial banks that obtain mostly short-term funds may select investments with short-term maturities as a natural habitat. However, if they wish to benefit from an anticipated decline in interest rates, they may select medium- and long-term maturities instead. Preferred habitat theory acknowledges that natural maturity markets may influence the yield curve but recognizes that interest rate expectations could entice market participants to stray from preferred maturities.

Research on Term Structure Theories

An abundance of research has been conducted on the term structure of interest rates, offering insight into the various theories. Researchers have found that interest rate expectations have a strong influence on the term structure of interest rates. However, the forward rate derived from a yield curve does not accurately predict future interest rates. This may suggest that other factors are relevant. The liquidity premium, for example, could cause consistent positive forecasting errors, meaning that forward rates tend to overestimate future interest rates. Studies have documented variation in the yield-maturity relationship that cannot be explained by interest rate expectations or liquidity. Thus, the variation could be attributed to different supply and demand conditions for particular maturity segments.

General Research Implications   Although the results of research differ, there is some evidence that expectations theory, liquidity premium theory, and segmented markets theory all have some validity. Thus, if the term structure is used to assess the market's expectations of future interest rates, investors should first net out the liquidity premium and any unique market conditions for various maturity segments.

Integrating the Theories of the Term Structure

To illustrate how all three theories can simultaneously affect the yield curve, assume the following conditions:

1. Investors and borrowers who select security maturities based on anticipated interest rate movements currently expect interest rates to rise.

2. Most borrowers are in need of long-term funds, while most investors have only short-term funds to invest.

3. Investors prefer more liquidity to less.

The first condition, related to expectations theory, suggests the existence of an upward-sloping yield curve, other things being equal. This is shown in Exhibit 3.7 as Curve E. The segmented markets information (condition 2) also favors the upward-sloping yield curve. When conditions 1 and 2 are considered simultaneously, the appropriate yield curve may look like Curve E + S. The third condition relating to liquidity would then place a higher premium on the longer-term securities because of their lower degree of liquidity. When this condition is included with the first two, the yield curve may look like Curve E + S + L.

In this example, all conditions placed upward pressure on long-term yields relative to short-term yields. In reality, there will sometimes be offsetting conditions, as one condition places downward pressure on the slope of the yield curve while the others place upward pressure on the slope. If condition 1 were revised to suggest the expectation of lower interest rates in the future, this condition by itself would result in a downward-sloping yield curve. When combined with the other conditions that favor an upward-sloping curve, it would create a partial offsetting effect. This yield curve would exhibit a downward slope if the effect of the interest rate expectations dominated the combined liquidity premium and segmented markets effects. Conversely, an upward slope would exist if the liquidity premium and segmented markets effects dominated the effects of interest rate expectations.

Exhibit 3.7 Effect of Conditions in Example of Yield Curve

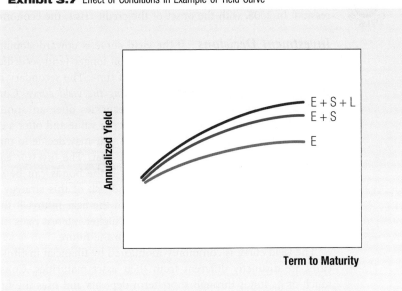

Uses of the Term Structure

The term structure of interest rates is used to forecast interest rates, forecast recessions, and make investment and financing decisions, as explained next.

Forecast Interest Rates   At any point in time, the shape of the yield curve can be used to assess the general expectations of investors and borrowers about future interest rates. Recall from expectations theory that an upward-sloping yield curve generally results from the expectation of higher interest rates, while a downward-sloping yield curve generally results from the expectation of lower interest rates. Expectations about future interest rates must be interpreted cautiously, however, because liquidity and specific maturity preferences could influence the yield curve's shape. It is generally believed, though, that interest rate expectations are a major contributing factor to the yield curve's shape, and the curve's shape should provide a reasonable indication (especially if the liquidity premium effect is accounted for) of the market's expectations about future interest rates.

Although investors can use the yield curve to interpret the market's consensus expectation of future interest rates, they may have their own interest rate projections. By comparing their projections to those implied by the yield curve, they can attempt to capitalize on the difference. For example, if an upward-sloping yield curve exists, suggesting a market expectation of increasing rates, investors expecting stable interest rates could benefit from investing in long-term securities. From their perspective, long-term securities are undervalued because they reflect the market's expectation of higher interest rates. Strategies such as this are effective only if the investor can consistently forecast better than the market.

Forecast Recessions   Some analysts believe that flat or inverted yield curves indicate a recession in the near future. The rationale is that given a positive liquidity premium, such yield curves reflect the expectation of lower interest rates. This is commonly associated with expectations of a reduced demand for loanable funds, which could be attributed to expectations of a weak economy.

The yield curve became flat or slightly inverted in 2000. At that time, the shape of the curve indicated expectations of a slower economy, which would result in lower interest rates. In 2001, the economy weakened considerably. In March 2007, the yield curve exhibited a slight negative slope, which caused some market participants to forecast a recession. In 2008, with the onset of the credit crisis, the economy weakened substantially.

Investment Decisions   If the yield curve is upward sloping, some investors may attempt to benefit from the higher yields on longer-term securities, even though they have funds to invest for only a short period of time. The secondary market allows investors to attempt this strategy, referred to as *riding the yield curve.* Consider an upward-sloping yield curve such that some one-year securities offer an annualized yield of 7 percent while 10-year bonds can be purchased at par value and offer a coupon rate of 10 percent. An investor with funds available for one year may decide to purchase the bonds and sell them in the secondary market after one year. The investor earns 3 percent more than was possible on the one-year securities, if the bonds can be sold after one year at the price at which they were purchased. The risk of this strategy is the uncertainty of the price at which the security can be sold in the near future. If the upward-sloping yield is interpreted as the market's consensus of higher interest rates in the future, the price of a security would be expected to decrease in the future.

The yield curve is commonly monitored by financial institutions whose liability maturities are distinctly different from their asset maturities. Consider a bank that obtains much of its funds through short-term deposits and uses the funds to provide long-term loans or purchase long-term securities. An upward-sloping yield curve is favorable to the bank because annualized short-term deposit rates are significantly lower than annualized long-term investment rates. The bank's spread is higher than it would be if the yield curve were flat. However, if the bank believes that the upward slope of the yield curve indicates higher interest rates in the future (as reflected in the expectations theory), it will expect its cost of liabilities to increase over time, as future deposits would be obtained at higher interest rates.

Financing Decisions   The yield curve is also useful for firms that plan to issue bonds. By assessing the prevailing rates on securities for various maturities, firms can estimate the rates to be paid on bonds with different maturities. This may enable them to decide the maturity for the bonds they issue.

Why the Slope of the Yield Curve Changes

If interest rates at all maturities are affected in the same manner by existing conditions, the slope of the yield curve would remain the same. However, conditions may cause short-term yields to change in a manner that differs from the change in long-term yields.

Exhibit 3.8 Potential Impact of Treasury Shift from Long-Term to Short-Term Financing

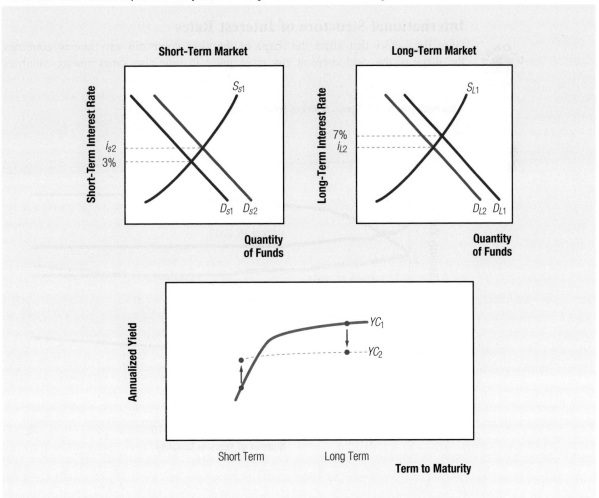

EXAMPLE

Assume that last July the yield curve had a large upward slope as shown by yield curve YC_1 in Exhibit 3.8. Since then, the Treasury decided to restructure its debt by retiring $300 billion of long-term Treasury securities and increasing its offering of short-term Treasury securities. This caused a large increase in the demand for short-term funds and a large decrease in the demand for long-term funds. The increase in the demand for short-term funds caused an increase in short-term interest rates and therefore increased yields offered on newly issued short-term securities. Conversely, the decline in the demand for long-term funds caused a decrease in long-term interest rates and therefore reduced yields offered on newly issued long-term securities. Today, the yield curve is YC_2 and is much flatter than it was last July. ●

How the Yield Curve Has Changed over Time

The yield curves at various points in time are illustrated in Exhibit 3.9. The slope of the yield curve is usually upward sloping, but a slight downward slope has existed at some points in time, such as March 21, 2007 (shown in the exhibit). Notice that the yield curve for January 3, 2009, is below the other yield curves shown in the exhibit, which means that the yield to maturity was relatively low regardless of the maturity considered. This curve existed during the credit crisis, when economic conditions were very weak.

International Structure of Interest Rates

Since the factors that affect the shape of the yield curve can vary among countries, the shape of the yield curve at any given point in time also varies among countries.

Exhibit 3.9 Yield Curves at Various Points in Time

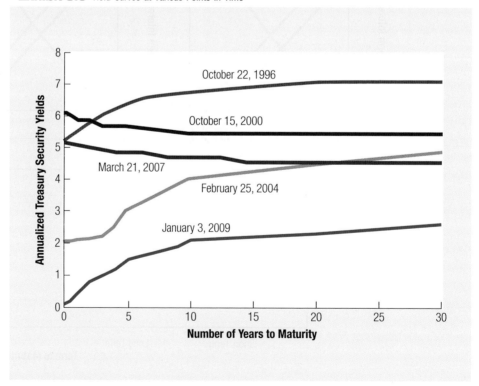

Source: *FRBNY Quarterly Review,* various issues.

Exhibit 3.10 Yield Curves among Foreign Countries (as of January 2009)

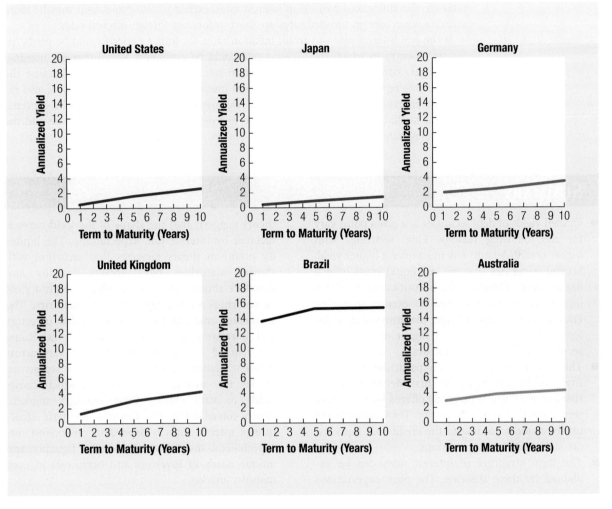

Exhibit 3.10 shows the yield curve for six different countries at a given point in time. Each country with a different currency has its own interest rate levels for various maturities. Each country's interest rates are based on supply and demand conditions.

Interest rate movements across countries tend to be positively correlated as a result of internationally integrated financial markets. Nevertheless, the actual interest rates may vary significantly across countries at a given point in time. This implies that the differential in interest rates is primarily attributed to general supply and demand conditions across countries rather than differences in default premiums, liquidity premiums, or other factors unique to the individual securities.

Because forward rates (as defined in this chapter) reflect the market's expectations of future interest rates, the term structure of interest rates for various countries should be monitored for the following reasons. First, with the integration of financial markets, movements in one country's interest rate can affect interest rates in other countries. Thus, some investors may estimate the forward rate in a foreign country to predict the foreign interest rate, which in turn may affect domestic interest rates. Second, foreign securities and some domestic securities are influenced by foreign economies, which are dependent on foreign interest rates. If the foreign forward rates can be used to forecast foreign interest rates, they can enhance forecasts of foreign economies. Because exchange rates are also influenced by foreign interest rates, exchange rate projections may be more accurate when foreign forward rates are used to forecast foreign interest rates.

If the real interest rate was fixed, inflation rates for future periods could be predicted for any country in which the forward rate could be estimated. Recall that the nominal interest rate consists of an expected inflation rate plus a real interest rate. Because the forward rate represents an expected nominal interest rate for a future period, it also represents an expected inflation rate plus a real interest rate in that period. The expected inflation in that period is estimated as the difference between the forward rate and the real interest rate.

SUMMARY

- Quoted yields of debt securities at a given point vary for the following reasons. First, securities with higher credit (default) risk must offer a higher yield. Second, securities that are less liquid must offer a higher yield. Third, taxable securities must offer a higher before-tax yield than tax-exempt securities. Fourth, securities with longer maturities offer a different yield (not consistently higher or lower) than securities with shorter maturities.

- The appropriate yield for any particular debt security can be estimated by first determining the risk-free yield that is currently offered by a Treasury security with a similar maturity. Then, adjustments can be made according to the credit risk, liquidity, tax status, and other provisions.

- The term structure of interest rates can be explained by three theories. The pure expectations theory suggests that the shape of the yield curve is dictated by interest rate expectations. The liquidity premium theory suggests that securities with shorter maturities have greater liquidity and therefore should not have to offer as high a yield as securities with longer terms to maturity. The segmented markets theory suggests that investors and borrowers have different needs, which cause the demand and supply conditions to vary across different maturities; that is, there is a segmented market for each term to maturity, which causes yields to vary among these maturity markets. When consolidating the theories, the term structure of interest rates is dependent on interest rate expectations, investor preferences for liquidity, and unique needs of investors and borrowers in each maturity market.

POINT COUNTER-POINT

Should a Yield Curve Influence a Borrower's Preferred Maturity of a Loan?

Point Yes. If there is an upward-sloping yield curve, a borrower should pursue a short-term loan to capitalize on the lower annualized rate charged for a short-term period. The borrower can obtain a series of short-term loans rather than one loan to match the desired maturity.

Counter-Point No. The borrower will face uncertainty regarding the interest rate charged on subse-

quent loans that are needed. An upward-sloping yield curve suggests that interest rates may rise in the future, which will cause the cost of borrowing to increase. Overall, the cost of borrowing may be higher when using a series of loans than when matching the debt maturity to the time period in which funds are needed.

Who Is Correct? Use the Internet to learn more about this issue. Offer your own opinion on this issue.

QUESTIONS AND APPLICATIONS

1. Yield Curve What factors influence the shape of the yield curve? Describe how financial market participants use the yield curve.

2. Forward Rate What is the meaning of the forward rate in the context of the term structure of interest rates? Why might forward rates consistently overestimate future interest rates? How could such a bias be avoided?

3. Preferred Habitat Theory Explain the preferred habitat theory.

4. Pure Expectations Theory Explain how a yield curve would shift in response to a sudden expectation of rising interest rates, according to the pure expectations theory.

5. Segmented Markets Theory If the segmented markets theory causes an upward-sloping yield curve, what does this imply? If markets are not completely segmented, should we dismiss the segmented markets theory as even a partial explanation for the term structure of interest rates? Explain.

6. Tax Effects on Yields Do investors in high tax brackets or those in low tax brackets benefit more from tax-exempt securities? Why? Do municipal bonds or corporate bonds offer a higher before-tax yield at a given point in time? Why? Which has the higher after-tax yield? If taxes did not exist, would Treasury bonds offer a higher or lower yield than municipal bonds with the same maturity? Why?

7. Impact of Liquidity Premium on Forward Rate Explain how consideration of a liquidity premium affects the estimate of a forward interest rate.

8. Impact of Liquidity on Yield Discuss the relationship between the yield and liquidity of securities.

9. Segmented Markets Theory If a downward-sloping yield curve is mainly attributed to segmented markets theory, what does that suggest about the demand for and supply of funds in the short-term and long-term maturity markets?

10. Impact of Credit Risk on Yield What effect does a high credit risk have on securities?

11. Liquidity Premium Theory Explain the liquidity premium theory.

12. Characteristics That Affect Security Yields Identify the relevant characteristics of any security that can affect the security's yield.

13. Pure Expectations Theory Assume there is a sudden expectation of lower interest rates in the future. What would be the effect on the shape of the yield curve? Explain.

Advanced Questions

14. Applying the Yield Curve to Risky Debt Securities Assume that the yield curve for Treasury bonds has a slight upward slope, starting at 6 percent for a 10-year maturity and slowly rising to 8 percent for a 30-year maturity. Create a yield curve that you believe would exist for A-rated bonds. Create a yield curve that you believe would exist for B-rated bonds.

15. Multiple Effects on the Yield Curve Assume that (1) investors and borrowers expect that the economy will weaken and that inflation will decline, (2) investors require a small liquidity premium, and (3) markets are partially segmented and the Treasury currently has a preference for borrowing in short-term markets. Explain how each of these forces would affect the term structure, holding other factors constant. Then explain the effect on the term structure overall.

16. Assessing Interest Rate Differentials among Countries In some countries where there is high inflation, the annual interest rate is more than 50 percent, while in other countries, such as the United States and many European countries, the annual interest rates are typically less than 10 percent. Do you think such a large interest rate differential is primarily attributed to the difference in the risk-free rates or to the difference in the credit risk premiums between countries? Explain.

17. Global Interaction among Yield Curves Assume that the yield curves in the United States, France, and Japan are flat. If the U.S. yield curve then suddenly becomes positively sloped, do you think the yield curves in France and Japan would be affected? If so, how?

18. How the Yield Curve May Respond to Prevailing Conditions Consider how economic conditions affect the default risk premium. Do you think the default risk premium will likely increase or decrease during this semester? How do you think the yield curve will change during this semester? Offer some logic to support your answers.

19.   Yield Curve If liquidity and interest rate expectations are both important for explaining the shape of a yield curve, what does a flat yield curve indicate about the market's perception of future interest rates?

20.   Effect of Crises on the Yield Curve
During some crises, investors shift their funds out of the stock market and into money market securities for safety, even if they do not fear rising interest rates. Explain how and why these actions by investors affect the yield curve. Is the shift due to the expectations theory, liquidity premium theory, or segmented markets theory?

21.   Segmented Markets Theory Suppose that the Treasury decides to finance its deficit with mostly long-term funds. How could this decision affect the term structure of interest rates? If short-term and long-term markets are segmented, would the Treasury's decision have a more or less pronounced impact on the term structure? Explain.

Interpreting Financial News

Interpret the following comments made by Wall Street analysts and portfolio managers:

a. "An upward-sloping yield curve persists because many investors stand ready to jump into the stock market."

b. "Low-rated bond yields rose as recession fears caused a flight to quality."

c. "The shift from an upward-sloping yield curve to a downward-sloping yield curve is sending a warning about a possible recession."

Managing in Financial Markets

Monitoring Yield Curve Adjustments As an analyst of a bond rating agency, you have been asked to interpret the implications of the recent shift in the yield curve. Six months ago, the yield curve exhibited a slight downward slope. Over the last six months, long-term yields declined, while short-term yields remained the same. Analysts said that the shift was due to revised expectations of interest rates.

a. Given the shift in the yield curve, does it appear that firms increased or decreased their demand for long-term funds over the last six months?

b. Interpret what the shift in the yield curve suggests about the market's changing expectations of future interest rates.

c. Recently, an analyst argued that the underlying reason for the yield curve shift is that many large U.S. firms anticipate a recession. Explain why an anticipated recession could force the yield curve to shift as it has.

d. What could the specific shift in the yield curve signal about the ratings of existing corporate bonds? What types of corporations would be most likely to experience a change in their bond ratings as a result of the specific shift in the yield curve?

PROBLEMS

1.   Debt Security Yield

a. Determine how the appropriate yield to be offered on a security is affected by a higher risk-free rate. Explain the logic of this relationship.

b. Determine how the appropriate yield to be offered on a security is affected by a higher default risk premium. Explain the logic of this relationship.

2.   After-Tax Yield You need to choose between investing in a one-year municipal bond with a 7 percent yield and a one-year corporate bond with an 11 percent yield. If your marginal federal income tax rate is 30 percent and no other differences exist

between these two securities, which one would you invest in?

3.   After-Tax Yield Determine how the after-tax yield from investing in a corporate bond is affected by higher tax rates, holding the before-tax yield constant. Explain the logic of this relationship.

4.   Forward Rate If $_ti_1 > _ti_2$, what is the market consensus forecast about the one-year forward rate one year from now? Is this rate above or below today's one-year interest rate? Explain.

5.   Forward Rate

a. Determine the forward rate for various one-year interest rate scenarios if the two-year interest rate is

8 percent, assuming no liquidity premium. Explain the relationship between the one-year interest rate and the one-year forward rate, holding the two-year interest rate constant.

b. Determine the one-year forward rate for the same one-year interest rate scenarios as in question (a), assuming a liquidity premium of 0.4 percent. Does the relationship between the one-year interest rate and the forward rate change when considering a liquidity premium?

c. Determine how the one-year forward rate would be affected if the quoted two-year interest rate rises, holding the quoted one-year interest rate constant. Also hold the liquidity premium constant. Explain the logic of this relationship.

d. Determine how the one-year forward rate would be affected if the liquidity premium rises, holding the quoted one-year interest rate constant. Also, hold the two-year interest rate constant. Explain the logic of this relationship.

6.   Forward Rate Assume that as of today, the annualized interest rate on a three-year security is 10 percent, while the annualized interest rate on a two-year security is 7 percent. Use only this information to estimate the one-year forward rate two years from now.

7.   Commercial Paper Yield

a. A corporation is planning to sell its 90-day commercial paper to investors offering an 8.4 percent yield. If the three-month T-bill's annualized rate is 7 percent, the default risk premium is estimated to be 0.6 percent, and there is a 0.4 percent tax adjustment, what is the appropriate liquidity premium?

b. If due to unexpected changes in the economy the default risk premium increases to 0.8 percent, what is the appropriate yield to be offered on the commercial paper (assuming no other changes occur)?

8.   Forward Rate

a. Assume that as of today, the annualized two-year interest rate is 13 percent, while the one-year interest rate is 12 percent. Use only this information to estimate the one-year forward rate.

b. Assume that the liquidity premium on a two-year security is 0.3 percent. Use this information to reestimate the one-year forward rate.

9.   Deriving Current Interest Rates Assume that interest rates for one-year securities are expected to be 2 percent today, 4 percent one year from now, and 6 percent two years from now. Using only the pure expectations theory, what are the current interest rates on two-year and three-year securities?

FLOW OF FUNDS EXERCISE

Influence of the Structure of Interest Rates

Recall that Carson Company has obtained substantial loans from finance companies and commercial banks. The interest rate on the loans is tied to the six-month Treasury bill rate (and includes a risk premium) and is adjusted every six months. Thus, Carson's cost of obtaining funds is sensitive to interest rate movements. Because of its expectations that the U.S. economy will strengthen, Carson plans to grow in the future by expanding its business and by making acquisitions. Carson expects that it will need substantial long-term financing to finance its growth and plans to borrow additional funds either through loans or by issuing bonds. It is also considering issuing stock to raise funds in the next year.

a. Assume that the market's expectations for the economy are similar to Carson's expectations.

Also assume that the yield curve is primarily influenced by interest rate expectations. Would the yield curve be upward sloping or downward sloping? Why?

b. If Carson could obtain more debt financing for 10-year projects, would it prefer to obtain credit at a long-term fixed interest rate or at a floating rate? Why?

c. If Carson attempts to obtain funds by issuing 10-year bonds, explain what information would help to estimate the yield it would have to pay on 10-year bonds. That is, what are the key factors that would influence the rate it would pay on the 10-year bonds?

d. If Carson attempts to obtain funds by issuing loans with floating interest rates every six months, explain what information would help to estimate the yield it would have to pay over the next 10 years. That is, what are the key factors that would influence the rate it would pay over the 10-year period?

e. An upward-sloping yield curve suggests that the initial rate that financial institutions could charge on a long-term loan to Carson would be higher than the initial rate that they could charge on a loan that floats in accordance with short-term interest rates. Does this imply that creditors should prefer to provide a fixed-rate loan rather than a floating-rate loan to Carson? Explain why Carson's expectations of future interest rates are not necessarily the same as those of some financial institutions.

INTERNET/EXCEL EXERCISES

1. Assess the shape of the yield curve, using the website www.bloomberg.com. Click on "Market data" and then on "Rates & bonds." Is the Treasury yield curve upward or downward sloping? What is the yield of a 90-day Treasury bill? What is the yield of a 30-year Treasury bond?

2. Based on the various theories attempting to explain the shape of the yield curve, what could explain the difference between the yields of the 90-day Treasury bill and the 30-year Treasury bond? Which theory, in your opinion, is the most reasonable? Why?

WSJ EXERCISE

Interpreting the Structure of Interest Rates

a. Explaining Yield Differentials Using the most recent issue of *The Wall Street Journal,* review the yields for the following securities:

TYPE	MATURITY	YIELD
Treasury	10-year	_____
Corporate: high-quality	10-year	_____
Corporate: medium-quality	10-year	_____
Municipal: (tax-exempt)	10-year	_____

If credit (default) risk is the only reason for the yield differentials, what is the default risk premium on the corporate high-quality bonds? On the medium-quality bonds?

During a recent recession, high-quality corporate bonds offered a yield of 0.8 percent above Treasury bonds, and medium-quality bonds offered a yield of about 3.1 percent above Treasury bonds. How do these yield differentials compare to the differentials today? Explain the reason for the change in yield differentials.

Using the information in the previous table, complete the table below. In Column 2, indicate the before-tax yield necessary to achieve the existing after-tax yield of tax-exempt bonds. In Column 3, answer this question: If the tax-exempt bonds have the same risk and other fea-

tures as high-quality corporate bonds, which type of bond is preferable for investors in each tax bracket?

MARGINAL TAX BRACKET OF INVESTORS	COLUMN 2	COLUMN 3
10%	_____	_____
15%	_____	_____
20%	_____	_____
28%	_____	_____
34%	_____	_____

b. Examining Recent Adjustments in Credit Risk Using the most recent issue of *The Wall Street Journal,* review the corporate debt section showing the high-yield issue with the biggest price decrease.

- Why do you think there was such a large decrease in price?

- How does this decrease in price affect the expected yield for any investors who buy bonds now?

c. Determining and Interpreting Today's Term Structure Using the most recent issue of *The Wall Street Journal,* review the yield curve to determine the approximate yields for the following maturities:

TERM TO MATURITY	ANNUALIZED YIELD
1 year	_____
2 years	_____
3 years	_____

Assuming that the differences in these yields are solely because of interest rate expectations, determine the one-year forward rate as of one year from now and the one-year forward rate as of two years from now.

d. *The Wall Street Journal* provides a "Treasury Yield Curve." Use this curve to describe the market's expectations about future interest rates. If a liquidity premium exists, how would this affect your perception of the market's expectations?

Interest Rate Forecasts and Investment Decisions

This problem requires an understanding of how economic conditions affect interest rates and bond yields (Chapters 1, 2, and 3).

Your task is to use information about existing economic conditions to forecast U.S. and Canadian interest rates. The following information is available to you:

1. Over the past six months, U.S. interest rates have declined, and Canadian interest rates have increased.

2. The U.S. economy has weakened over the past year, and the Canadian economy has improved.

3. The U.S. savings rate (proportion of income saved) is expected to decrease slightly over the next year, while the Canadian savings rate will remain stable.

4. The U.S. and Canadian central banks are not expected to implement any policy changes that would have a significant impact on interest rates.

5. You expect the U.S. economy to strengthen considerably over the next year but still be weaker than it was two years ago. You expect the Canadian economy to remain stable.

6. You expect the U.S. annual budget deficit to increase slightly from last year but be significantly less than the average annual budget deficit over the past five years. You expect the Canadian budget deficit to be about the same as last year.

7. You expect the U.S. inflation rate to rise slightly, but still remain below the relatively high levels of two years ago. You expect the Canadian inflation rate to decline.

8. Based on some events last week, most economists and investors around the world (including yourself) expect the dollar to weaken against the Canadian dollar and other foreign currencies over the next year. This expectation was already accounted for in your forecasts of inflation and economic growth.

9. The yield curve in the United States currently exhibits a consistent downward slope. The yield curve in Canada currently exhibits an upward slope. You believe that the liquidity premium on securities is quite small.

Questions

1. Using the information available to you, forecast the direction of U.S. interest rates.

2. Using the information available to you, forecast the direction of Canadian interest rates.

3. Assume that the perceived risk of corporations in the United States is expected to increase. Explain how the yield of newly issued U.S. corporate bonds will change to a different degree than the yield of newly issued U.S. Treasury bonds.

PART 2
The Fed and Monetary Policy

The chapters in Part 2 explain how the Federal Reserve System (the Fed) affects economic conditions. Because the policies implemented by the Fed can influence securities prices, they are closely monitored by financial market participants. By assessing the Fed's policies, market participants can more accurately value securities and make more effective investment and financing decisions.

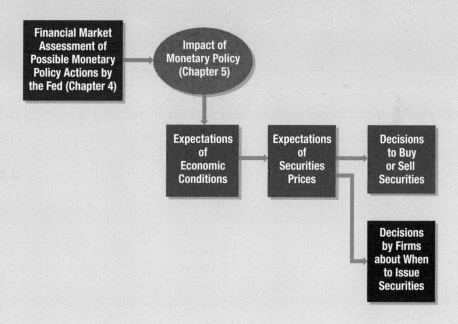

4

Functions of the Fed

CHAPTER OBJECTIVES

The specific objectives of this chapter are to:

- describe the organizational structure of the Fed,

- describe how the Fed influences monetary policy,

- explain how the Fed revised its lending role in response to the credit crisis, and

- explain how monetary policy is used in other countries.

WEB

www.clevelandfed.org
Features economic and banking topics.

The **Federal Reserve System** (the Fed), as the central bank of the United States, has the responsibility for conducting national monetary policy. This policy influences interest rates and other economic variables that determine the prices of securities. Hence, participants in the financial markets closely monitor the Fed's monetary policy. It is important for them to understand how the Fed's actions may influence security prices so that they can manage their security portfolios in response to the Fed's policies.

ORGANIZATIONAL STRUCTURE OF THE FED

During the late 1800s and early 1900s, the United States experienced several banking panics, culminating with a major crisis in 1907. This motivated Congress to establish a central bank. Accordingly, in 1913 the Federal Reserve Act was passed, establishing reserve requirements for those commercial banks that chose to become members. It also specified 12 districts across the United States as well as a city in each district where a Federal Reserve district bank was to be established. Initially, each district bank had the ability to affect the money supply (as will be explained later in this chapter). Each district bank focused on its particular district, without much concern for other districts. Over time, the system became more centralized, and money supply decisions were assigned to a particular group of individuals rather than across 12 district banks.

The Fed earns most of its income in the form of interest on its holdings of U.S. government securities (to be discussed shortly). It also earns some income from providing services to financial institutions. Most of its income is transferred to the Treasury.

The Fed is involved (along with other agencies) in regulating commercial banks. It also conducts monetary policy, adjusting the money supply in an attempt to achieve full employment and price stability (low or zero inflation) in the United States.

The Fed as it exists today has five major components:

- Federal Reserve district banks

- Member banks

- Board of Governors

- Federal Open Market Committee (FOMC)

- Advisory committees

Federal Reserve District Banks

The 12 Federal Reserve districts are identified in Exhibit 4.1, along with the city where each district bank is located. The New York district bank is considered the most

Exhibit 4.1 Locations of Federal Reserve District Banks

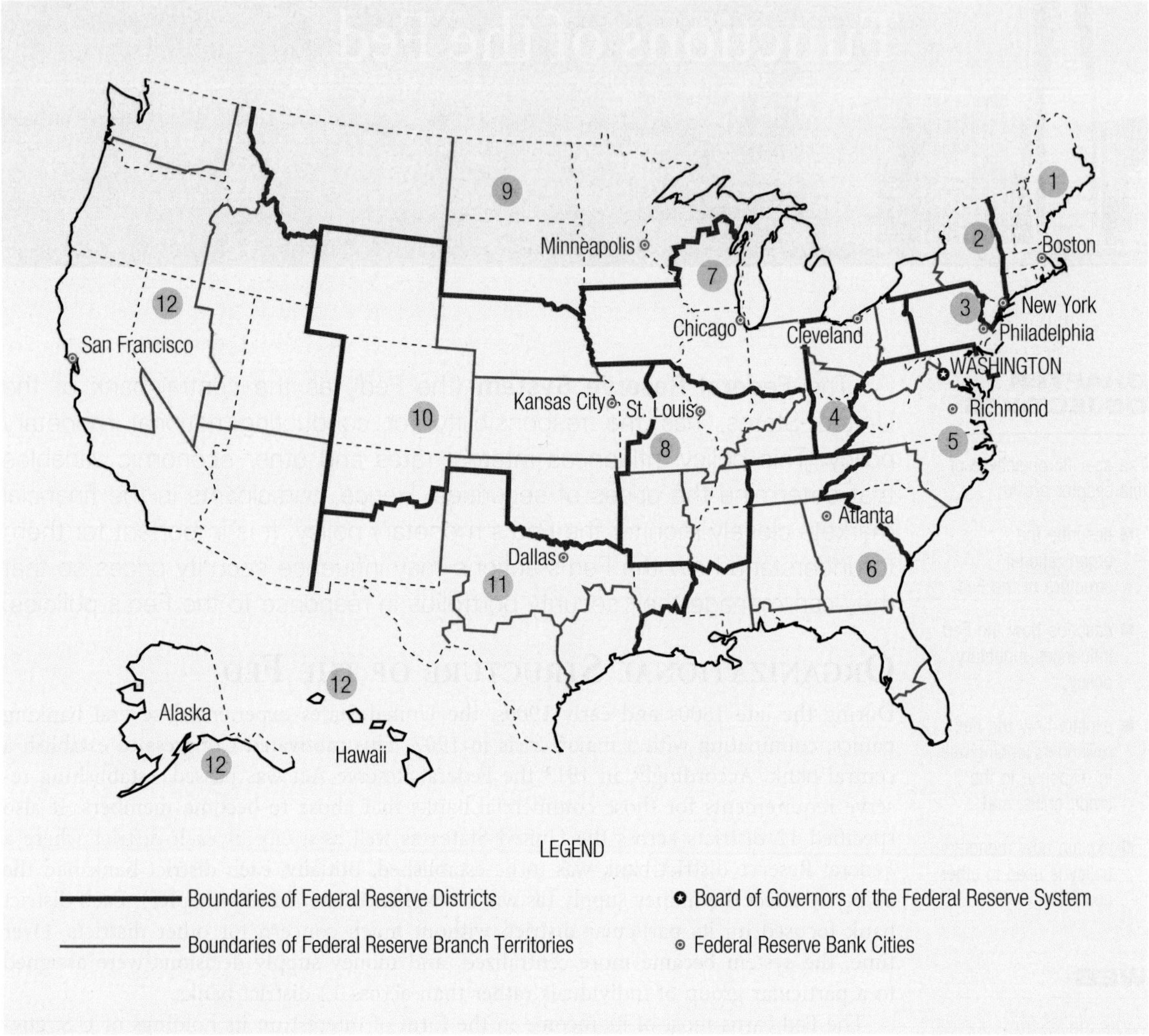

LEGEND

———— Boundaries of Federal Reserve Districts   ⊙ Board of Governors of the Federal Reserve System

———— Boundaries of Federal Reserve Branch Territories   ⊚ Federal Reserve Bank Cities

Source: *Federal Reserve Bulletin.*

important because many large banks are located in this district. Commercial banks that become members of the Fed are required to purchase stock in their **Federal Reserve district bank.** This stock, which is not traded in a secondary market, pays a maximum dividend of 6 percent annually.

Each Fed district bank has nine directors. Six are elected by member banks in that district. Of these six directors, three are professional bankers and three are engaged in business. The other three directors are appointed by the Board of Governors (to be discussed shortly). The nine directors appoint the president of their Fed district bank.

Fed district banks facilitate operations within the banking system by clearing checks, replacing old currency, and providing loans (through the discount window) to depository institutions in need of funds. They also collect economic data and conduct research projects on commercial banking and economic trends.

Member Banks

Commercial banks can elect to become member banks if they meet specific requirements of the Board of Governors. All national banks (chartered by the Comptroller of the Currency) are required to be members of the Fed, but other banks (chartered by their respective states) are not. Currently, about 35 percent of all banks are members; these banks account for about 70 percent of all bank deposits.

Board of Governors

The **Board of Governors** (sometimes called the Federal Reserve Board) is made up of seven individual members with offices in Washington, D.C. Each member is appointed by the President of the United States and serves a nonrenewable 14-year term. This long term is thought to reduce political pressure on the governors and thus encourage the development of policies that will benefit the U.S. economy over the long run. The terms are staggered so that one term expires in every even-numbered year.

One of the seven board members is selected by the President to be the Federal Reserve chairman for a four-year term, which may be renewed. The chairman has no more voting power than any other member, but may have more influence. Paul Volcker (chairman from 1979 to 1987), Alan Greenspan (chairman from 1987 to 2006), and Ben Bernanke (whose term began in 2006) were regarded as very persuasive.

The board has two main roles: (1) regulating commercial banks and (2) controlling monetary policy. It supervises and regulates commercial banks that are members of the Fed and bank holding companies. It oversees the operation of the 12 Federal Reserve district banks as they provide services to depository institutions and supervise specific commercial banks. It also establishes regulations on consumer finance. In addition, the board participates in setting credit controls, such as margin requirements (percentage of a purchase of securities that must be paid with nonborrowed funds).

With regard to monetary policy, the board has the power to revise reserve requirements imposed on depository institutions. The board can also control the money supply by participating in the decisions of the Federal Open Market Committee, discussed next.

Federal Open Market Committee (FOMC)

The **Federal Open Market Committee (FOMC)** is made up of the seven members of the Board of Governors plus the presidents of five Fed district banks (the New York district bank plus 4 of the other 11 Fed district banks as determined on a rotating basis). Presidents of the seven remaining Fed district banks typically participate in the FOMC meetings but are not allowed to vote on policy decisions. The chairman of the Board of Governors serves as chairman of the FOMC.

The main goals of the FOMC are to achieve stable economic growth and price stability (low inflation). Achievement of these goals would stabilize financial markets and interest rates. The FOMC attempts to achieve its goals through control of the money supply, as described shortly.

Advisory Committees

The Federal Advisory Council consists of one member from each Federal Reserve district. Each district's member is elected each year by the board of directors of the respective district bank. The council meets with the Board of Governors in Washington, D.C., at least four times a year and makes recommendations about economic and banking issues.

The Consumer Advisory Council is made up of 30 members, representing the financial institutions industry and its consumers. This committee normally meets with the Board of Governors four times a year to discuss consumer issues.

Exhibit 4.2 Integration of Federal Reserve Components

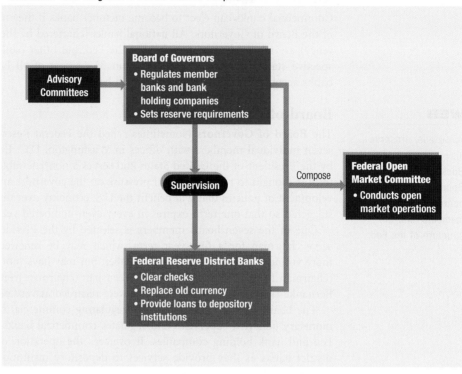

The Thrift Institutions Advisory Council is made up of 12 members, representing savings banks, savings and loan associations, and credit unions. Its purpose is to offer views on issues specifically related to these institutions. It meets with the Board of Governors three times a year.

Integration of Federal Reserve Components

Exhibit 4.2 shows the relationships among the various components of the Federal Reserve System. The advisory committees advise the board, while the board oversees operations of the district banks. The board and representatives of the district banks make up the FOMC.

How the Fed Controls Money Supply

The Fed controls the money supply in order to affect interest rates and thereby affect economic conditions. Financial market participants closely monitor the Fed's actions so that they can anticipate how the money supply will be affected. They then use this information to forecast economic conditions and securities prices. The relationship between the money supply and economic conditions is discussed in detail in the following chapter. First, it is important to understand *how* the Fed controls the money supply.

Open Market Operations

The FOMC meets eight times a year. At each meeting, the target money supply growth level and interest rate level are determined, and actions are taken to implement the

WEB
___

www.federal
reserve.gov/monetary
policy/fomccalendars
.htm
Provides minutes of
FOMC meetings.
Notice from the
minutes how much
attention is given to
any economic
indicators that can be
used to anticipate
future economic
growth or inflation.

monetary policy dictated by the FOMC. If the Fed wants to consider changing its targets for money growth or interest rates before its next scheduled meeting because of unusual circumstances, it may hold a conference call meeting.

Pre-Meeting Economic Report   About two weeks before the FOMC meeting, FOMC members are sent the **Beige Book,** which is a consolidated report of regional economic conditions in each of the 12 districts. Each Federal Reserve district bank is responsible for reporting its regional conditions, and all of these reports are consolidated to compose the Beige Book.

Economic Presentations   The FOMC meeting is conducted in the boardroom of the Federal Reserve Building in Washington, D.C. The seven members of the Board of Governors, the 12 presidents of the Fed district banks, and staff members (typically economists) of the Board of Governors are in attendance. The meeting begins with presentations by the staff members about current economic conditions and recent economic trends. They provide data and trends for wages, consumer prices, unemployment, gross domestic product, business inventories, foreign exchange rates, interest rates, and financial market conditions.

The staff members also assess production levels, business investment, residential construction, international trade, and international economic growth. This assessment is conducted to predict economic growth and inflation in the United States, assuming that the Fed does not adjust its monetary policy. For example, a decline in business inventories may lead to an expectation of stronger economic growth, as firms will need to boost production in order to replenish inventories. Conversely, an increase in inventories may indicate that firms will reduce their production and possibly their workforces as well. An increase in business investment indicates that businesses are expanding their production capacity and are likely to increase production in the future. An increase in economic growth in foreign countries is important because a portion of the rising incomes in those countries will be spent on U.S. products or services. The Fed uses this information to determine whether U.S. economic growth is adequate.

Much attention is also given to any factors that can affect inflation. For example, oil prices are closely monitored because they affect the cost of producing and transporting many products. A decline in business inventories when production is near full capacity may indicate an excessive demand for products that will pull prices up. This condition indicates the potential for higher inflation because firms may raise the prices of their products when they are producing near full capacity and experience shortages. If firms attempt to expand capacity under these conditions, they will have to raise wages to obtain additional qualified employees. They will incur higher costs from raising wages and therefore raise the prices of their products. The Fed becomes concerned when several indicators suggest that higher inflation is likely.

The staff members typically base their forecasts for economic conditions on the assumption that the prevailing monetary growth level will continue in the future. When it is highly likely that the monetary growth level will be changed, they provide forecasts for economic conditions under different monetary growth scenarios. Their goal is to provide facts and economic forecasts, not to make judgments about the appropriate monetary policy. The members normally receive some economic information a few days before the meeting so that they are prepared when the staff members make their presentations.

FOMC Decisions   Once the presentations are completed, each FOMC member has a chance to offer recommendations as to whether the prevailing monetary growth and interest rate targets should be changed and, if so, how they should be changed. Even the nonvoting members may offer their views. The chairman of the Fed may also offer a recommendation and usually has some influence over the other members. After all members have provided their recommendations, the voting members of the FOMC vote on whether the prevailing money supply and interest rate target levels should be revised. Most FOMC decisions on monetary policy are unanimous, although it is not unusual for some decisions to have one or two dissenting votes.

Role of the Fed's Trading Desk

If the FOMC determines that a change in its monetary policy is appropriate, its decision is forwarded to the **Trading Desk** (or the **Open Market Desk**) at the New York Federal Reserve District Bank through a statement called the **policy directive**. The FOMC specifies a desired target for the federal funds rate, the rate charged by banks on short-term loans to each other. Even though this rate is determined by the banks that participate in the federal funds market, it is subject to the supply and demand for funds in the banking system. Thus, the Fed influences the federal funds rate by revising the amount of funds in the banking system.

Since all short-term interest rates are affected by the supply of and demand for funds, they tend to move together. Thus, the Fed's actions affect all short-term interest rates that are market determined and may even affect long-term interest rates as well.

WEB

www.treasurydirect
.gov
Treasury note and
bond auction results.

After receiving the policy directive from the FOMC, the manager of the Trading Desk instructs traders who work at that desk on the amount of Treasury securities to buy or sell in the secondary market based on the directive. The buying and selling of government securities (through the Trading Desk) is referred to as **open market operations.** Even though the Trading Desk at the Federal Reserve Bank of New York receives a policy directive from the FOMC only eight times a year, it continuously conducts open market operations to control the money supply in response to ongoing changes in bank deposit levels. The FOMC is not limited to issuing new policy directives only on its scheduled meeting dates. It can hold additional meetings any time it wants to consider changing the federal funds rate.

Fed Purchase of Securities   When traders at the Trading Desk at the New York Fed are instructed to lower the federal funds rate, they purchase Treasury securities in the secondary market. First, they call government securities dealers to obtain their list of securities for sale, including the denomination and maturity of each security, and the dealer's ask quote (the price at which the dealer is willing to sell the security). From this list, the traders attempt to purchase those Treasury securities that are most attractive (lowest prices for whatever maturities are desired) until they have purchased the amount requested by the manager of the Trading Desk. The accounting department of the New York Fed then notifies the government bond department to receive and pay for those securities.

When the Fed purchases securities through the government securities dealers, the bank account balances of the dealers increase, and therefore the total deposits in the banking system increase. The increase in the supply of funds places downward pressure on the federal funds rate. The Fed increases the total amount of funds at the dealers' banks until the federal funds rate declines to the new targeted level. This activity initiated by the FOMC's policy directive represents a loosening of money supply growth.

The Fed's purchase of government securities has a different impact than a purchase by another investor would have because the Fed's purchase results in additional bank funds and increases the ability of banks to make loans and create new deposits. An increase in funds can allow for a net increase in deposit balances and therefore an increase in the money supply. Conversely, the purchase of government securities by someone other than the Fed (such as an investor) results in offsetting account balance positions at commercial banks. For example, as investors purchase Treasury securities in the secondary market, their bank balances decline while the bank balances of the sellers of the Treasury securities increase.

Fed Sale of Securities   If the Trading Desk at the New York Fed is instructed to increase the federal funds rate, its traders sell government securities (obtained from previous purchases) to government securities dealers. The securities are sold to the dealers that submit the highest bids. As the dealers pay for the securities, their bank account balances are reduced. Thus, the total amount of funds in the banking system is reduced by the market value of the securities sold by the Fed. The reduction in the supply of funds in the banking system places upward pressure on the federal funds rate. This activity initiated by the FOMC's policy directive is referred to as a tightening of money supply growth.

Fed Trading of Repurchase Agreements   In some cases, the Fed may wish to increase the aggregate level of bank funds for only a few days to ensure adequate liquidity in the banking system on those days. Under these conditions, the Trading Desk may trade **repurchase agreements** rather than government securities. It purchases Treasury securities from government securities dealers with an agreement to sell back the securities at a specified date in the near future. Initially, the level of funds rises as the securities are sold; it is then reduced when the dealers repurchase the securities. The Trading Desk uses repurchase agreements during holidays and other such periods to correct temporary imbalances in the level of bank funds. To correct a temporary excess of funds, the Trading Desk sells some of its Treasury securities holdings to securities dealers and agrees to repurchase them at a specified future date.

Control of M1 versus M2   When the Fed conducts open market operations to adjust the money supply, it must also consider the measure of money on which it will focus. For the Fed's purposes, the optimal form of money should (1) be controllable by the Fed and (2) have a predictable impact on economic variables when adjusted by the Fed. The most narrow form of money, known as **M1,** includes currency held by the public and checking deposits (such as demand deposits, NOW accounts, and automatic transfer balances) at depository institutions. M1 does not include all funds that can be used for transactions purposes. For example, checks can be written against a **money market deposit account (MMDA)** offered by depository institutions or against a money market mutual fund. In addition, funds can easily be withdrawn from savings accounts to make transactions. For this reason, a broader measure of money, called **M2,** also deserves consideration. It includes everything in M1 as well as savings accounts and small time deposits, MMDAs, and some other items. Another measure of money, called **M3,** includes everything in M2 as well as large time deposits and other items. Although there are even a few broader measures of money, M1, M2, and M3 receive the most attention. A comparison of M1, M2, and M3 is provided in Exhibit 4.3.

Exhibit 4.3 Comparison of Money Supply Measures

MONEY SUPPLY MEASURES
M1 = currency + checking deposits
M2 = M1 + savings deposits, MMDAs, overnight repurchase agreements, Eurodollars, noninstitutional money market mutual funds, and small time deposits
M3 = M2 + institutional money market mutual funds, large time deposits, and repurchase agreements and Eurodollars lasting more than one day

The M1 money measure is more volatile than M2 or M3. Since M1 can change simply because of changes in the types of deposits maintained by households, M2 and M3 are more reliable measures for monitoring and controlling the money supply.

Consideration of Technical Factors   The money supply can shift abruptly as a result of so-called technical factors, such as currency in circulation and Federal Reserve float. When the amount of currency in circulation increases (such as during the holiday season), the corresponding increase in net deposit withdrawals reduces funds. When it decreases, the net addition to deposits increases funds. Federal Reserve float is the amount of checks credited to bank funds that have not yet been collected. A rise in float causes an increase in bank funds, and a decrease in float causes a reduction in bank funds.

The manager of the Trading Desk incorporates the expected impact of technical factors on funds into the instructions to traders. If the policy directive calls for growth in funds but technical factors are expected to increase funds, the instructions will call for a smaller injection of funds than if the technical factors did not exist. Conversely, if technical factors are expected to reduce funds, the instructions will call for a larger injection of funds to offset the impact of the technical factors.

Dynamic versus Defensive Open Market Operations   Depending on the intent, open market operations can be classified as either **dynamic** or **defensive.** Dynamic operations are implemented to increase or decrease the level of funds; defensive operations offset the impact of other conditions that affect the level of funds. For example, if the Fed expects a large inflow of cash into commercial banks, it could offset this inflow by selling some of its Treasury security holdings.

How Fed Operations Affect All Interest Rates

Even though most interest rates are market determined, the Fed can have a strong influence on these rates by controlling the supply of loanable funds. The use of open market operations to increase bank funds can affect various market-determined interest rates. First, the federal funds rate may decline because some banks have a larger supply of excess funds to lend out in the federal funds market. Second, banks with excess funds may offer new loans at a lower interest rate in order to make use of these funds. Third, these banks may also lower interest rates offered on deposits because they have more than adequate funds to conduct existing operations.

The Federal Funds Rate

The Wall Street Journal provides quotes on the federal funds rate, as shown here. The Federal Reserve conducts monetary policy in order to control the federal funds rate. In the table shown here, the first column shows the latest quote while the second column shows the rate one week ago. The third column discloses the highest rate over the last year, while the fourth column provides the lowest rate over the last year.

Federal funds

Effective rate	**0.13**	0.16	4.28	0.12
High	**0.5000**	0.5000	10.0000	0.5000
Low	**0.0313**	0.0300	4.1875	0.0000
Bid	**0.0313**	0.0313	4.2500	0.0000
Offer	**0.0625**	0.0625	7.0000	0.0500

Source: Republished with permission of Dow Jones & Company, Inc., from *The Wall Street Journal*, January 7, 2009; p. C9; permission conveyed through the Copyright Clearance Center, Inc.

Since open market operations commonly involve the buying or selling of Treasury bills, the yields on Treasury securities are influenced along with the yields (interest rates) offered on bank deposits. For example, when the Fed buys Treasury bills as a means of increasing the money supply, it places upward pressure on their prices. Since these securities offer a fixed value to investors at maturity, a higher price translates into a lower yield for investors who buy them and hold them until maturity. While Treasury yields are affected directly by open market operations, bank rates are also affected because of the change in the money supply that open market operations bring about.

As the yields on Treasury bills and bank deposits decline, investors search for alternative investments such as other debt securities. As more funds are invested in these securities, the yields will decline. Thus, open market operations used to increase bank funds influence not only bank deposit and loan rates but also the yields on other debt securities. The reduction in yields on debt securities lowers the cost of borrowing for the issuers of new debt securities. This can encourage potential borrowers (including corporations and individuals) to borrow and make expenditures that they might not have made if interest rates were higher.

If open market operations are used to reduce bank funds, the opposite effects occur. There is upward pressure on the federal funds rate, on the loan rates charged to individuals and firms, and on the rates offered to bank depositors. As bank deposit rates rise, some investors may be encouraged to create bank deposits rather than invest in other debt securities. This activity reduces the amount of funds available for these debt instruments, thereby increasing the yield offered on the instruments.

Open Market Operations in Response to the Economy During the 2001–2003 period, when economic conditions were weak, the Fed frequently used open market operations to reduce interest rates. In the 2004–2007 period, the economy improved, and the Fed's concern shifted from a weak economy to high inflation. Therefore, it used a policy of raising interest rates in an attempt to keep the economy from overheatingand to reduce inflationary pressure. When the credit crisis began in 2008, economic conditions weakened, and the Fed used open market operations to reduce interest rates in an attempt to stimulate the economy. The impact of monetary policy on economic conditions is given much more attention in the following chapter.

Adjusting the Reserve Requirement Ratio

Depository institutions are subject to a **reserve requirement ratio,** which is the proportion of their deposit accounts that must be held as required reserves (funds held in reserve). This ratio is set by the Board of Governors. Depository institutions have historically been forced to maintain between 8 and 12 percent of their transactions accounts (such as checking accounts) and a smaller proportion of their other savings accounts as required reserves. The **Depository Institutions Deregulation and Monetary Control Act (DIDMCA)** of 1980 established that all depository institutions are subject to the Fed's reserve requirements. Required reserves were held in a non-interest-bearing form until 2008, when the rule was changed. Now the Fed pays interest on required reserves maintained by depository institutions.

Because the reserve requirement ratio affects the degree to which the money supply can change, it is considered a monetary policy tool. By changing it, the Board of Governors can adjust the money supply. When the board reduces the reserve requirement ratio, it increases the proportion of a bank's deposits that can be lent out by depository institutions. As the funds loaned out are spent, a portion of them will return to the depository institutions in the form of new deposits. The lower the reserve requirement ratio, the greater the lending capacity of depository institutions, so any initial change in bank required reserves can cause a larger change in the money supply. In 1992, the Fed reduced the reserve requirement ratio on transactions accounts from 12 percent to 10 percent, where it has remained.

Impact of Reserve Requirements on Money Growth   An adjustment in the reserve requirement ratio changes the proportion of financial institution funds that can be lent out, which, in turn, affects the degree to which the money supply can grow.

EXAMPLE

Assume the following conditions in the banking system:

Assumption 1. Banks obtain all their funds from demand deposits and use all funds except required reserves to make loans.

Assumption 2. The public does not store any cash; any funds withdrawn from banks are spent; and any funds received are deposited in banks.

Assumption 3. The reserve requirement ratio on demand deposits is 10 percent.

Based on these assumptions, 10 percent of all bank deposits are maintained as required reserves, and the other 90 percent are loaned out (zero excess reserves). Now assume that the Fed initially uses open market operations by purchasing $100 million worth of Treasury securities.

As the Treasury securities dealers sell securities to the Fed, their deposit balances at commercial banks increase by $100 million. Banks maintain 10 percent of the $100 million, or $10 million, as required reserves and lend out the rest. As the $90 million lent out is spent, it returns to banks as new demand deposit accounts (by whoever received the funds that were spent). Banks maintain 10 percent, or $9 million, of these new deposits as required reserves and lend out the remainder ($81 million). The initial increase in demand deposits (money) multiplies into a much larger amount. This process, illustrated in Exhibit 4.4, will not continue forever. Every time the funds lent out return to a bank, a portion (10 percent) is retained as required reserves. Thus, the amount of new deposits created is less for each round. Under

Exhibit 4.4 Illustration of Multiplier Effect

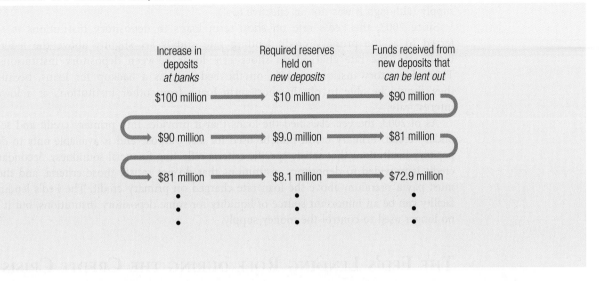

the previous assumptions, the initial money supply injection of $100 million would multiply by l/(reserve requirement ratio), or 1/.10, to equal 10, so the total change in the money supply once the cycle is complete is $100 million × 10 = $1 billion. ●

As this simplified example demonstrates, an initial injection of funds will multiply into a larger amount. The reserve requirement controls the amount of loanable funds that can be created from new deposits. A higher reserve requirement ratio causes an initial injection of funds to multiply by a smaller amount. Conversely, a lower reserve requirement ratio causes it to multiply by a greater amount. In this way, the Fed can adjust money supply growth by changing the reserve requirement ratio.

In reality, households sometimes hold cash, and banks sometimes hold excess reserves, contradicting the assumptions of banks holding only demand deposits and zero excess reserves. Consequently, major leakages occur, and money does not multiply to the extent shown in the example. The money multiplier can change over time because of changes in the excess reserve level and in household preferences for demand deposits versus time deposits (which are not included in the most narrow definition of money). This complicates the task of forecasting how an initial adjustment in bank required reserves will ultimately affect the money supply level. Another disadvantage of using the reserve requirement as a monetary policy tool is that an adjustment in the reserve requirement ratio can cause erratic shifts in the money supply. Thus, the probability of missing the target money supply level is higher when using the reserve requirement ratio. Because of these limitations, the Fed normally relies on open market operations rather than adjustments in the reserve requirement ratio when controlling the money supply.

Adjusting the Fed's Loan Rate

The Fed has traditionally provided short-term loans to depository institutions through its so-called discount window. Before 2003, the Fed set its loan rate (then called the "discount rate") at low levels when it wanted to encourage banks to borrow, as this activity increased the amount of funds injected into the financial system. The discount rate was viewed as a monetary policy tool, because it could have been used to affect the money supply (although it was not an effective tool).

Since 2003, the Fed's rate on short-term loans to depository institutions is referred to as the primary credit lending rate and is set slightly above the federal funds rate (the rate charged on short-term loans between depository institutions). Thus, depository institutions rely on the Fed only as a backup for loans, because they should be able to obtain short-term loans from other institutions at a lower interest rate.

As of 2003, the Fed classified the loans that it provides into primary credit and secondary credit. Primary credit may be used for any purpose and is available only to depository institutions that satisfy specific criteria reflecting financial soundness. Secondary credit is provided to depository institutions that do not satisfy those criteria, and they must pay a premium above the loan rate charged on primary credit. The Fed's lending facility can be an important source of liquidity for some depository institutions, but it is no longer used to control the money supply.

THE FED'S LENDING ROLE DURING THE CREDIT CRISIS

Normally, depository institutions use the federal funds market rather than the Fed's discount window to borrow short-term funds. During the credit crisis in 2008, however, some depository institutions that were unable to obtain credit in the federal funds market were allowed to obtain funding from the Fed's discount window. In March 2008, the Fed's discount window provided funding to enable Bear Stearns, a large securities firm, to avoid having to file for bankruptcy. Bear Stearns was not a depository institution and therefore ordinarily would not have been allowed to borrow funds from the Fed. However, it was a major provider of clearing operations for many types of financial transactions conducted by firms and individuals. If it had gone bankrupt, these financial transactions might have been delayed, potentially creating liquidity problems for many individuals and firms that were to receive cash as a result of the transactions. On March 16, 2008, the Fed's discount window provided a loan to J.P. Morgan Chase that was passed through to Bear Stearns. This ensured that the clearing operations would continue and avoided liquidity problems.

Facilities Created by the Fed

In response to the credit crisis, the Fed also created various facilities for providing funds to financial institutions and other corporations. These facilities were created because of concerns about a lack of liquidity in financial markets and were intended to ensure that healthy firms could easily access funds.

Primary Dealer Credit Facility The Fed established the Primary Dealer Credit Facility (PDCF) so that primary dealers that serve as financial intermediaries for bonds and other securities could obtain overnight loans from the Fed. The dealers were required to provide collateral such as investment-grade corporate securities, municipal securities, and highly rated mortgage-backed securities. The PDCF was expected to be available as long as the Fed believed it could improve the functioning of financial markets.

Term Auction Facility The Term Auction Facility allows depository institutions to borrow funds from the Federal Reserve for a 35-day period. The Fed makes a specified amount of funds available, and depository institutions that wish to borrow can participate in an auction in which they bid the rate they are willing to pay. Thus, the funds are essentially allocated based on prevailing market interest rates. The borrowers must be in good financial condition and must post collateral.

Term Securities Lending Facility   In the Term Securities Lending Facility (TSLF), banks package high-risk mortgage-backed securities and other high-risk loans and swap them with the Fed for Treasury securities for periods up to 28 days. At the end of the swap period, the swap of securities is reversed. Thus, during the period in which the securities are swapped, the banks have more liquid securities and therefore have more liquidity. The counterparty is accountable if the assets lose value. However, the Fed is exposed to the risk that the counterparty could fail.

Commercial Paper Facility   In November 2008, the Federal Reserve created a facility to participate in the commercial paper (short-term debt) market. When Lehman Brothers had filed for bankruptcy two months earlier, it defaulted on its commercial paper. Consequently, many institutional investors stopped purchasing commercial paper because of fear of additional defaults by firms that issue commercial paper. The Fed's commercial paper facility allowed it to invest in commercial paper issued by highly rated firms. Its intervention was intended to encourage other institutional investors to participate in the commercial paper market again in order to restore activity and ensure that firms could obtain funds in that market.

GLOBAL MONETARY POLICY

Each country has its own central bank that conducts monetary policy. The central banks of industrialized countries tend to have somewhat similar goals, which essentially reflect price stability (low inflation) and economic growth (low unemployment). Resouces and conditions vary among countries, however, so a given central bank may focus more on a particular economic goal.

Like the Fed, central banks of other industrialized countries use open market operations and reserve requirement adjustments as monetary tools. They also make adjustments in the interest rate they charge on loans to banks as a monetary policy tool. The monetary policy tools are generally used as a means of affecting local market interest rates in order to influence economic conditions.

Because country economies are integrated, the Fed must consider economic conditions in other major countries when assessing the U.S. economy. The Fed may be most effective when it coordinates its activities with those of central banks of other countries. Central banks commonly work together when they intervene in the foreign exchange market, but coordinating monetary policies can be difficult because of conflicts of interest.

A Single Eurozone Monetary Policy

One of the goals of the European Union (EU) has been to establish a single currency for its members. In 2002, the following European countries replaced their national currencies with the euro: Austria, Belgium, Finland, France, Germany, Greece, Ireland, Italy, Luxembourg, the Netherlands, Portugal, and Spain. Since that time four more countries have also adopted the euro—Slovenia in 2007, Cyprus and Malta in 2008, and Slovakia in 2009. When the euro was introduced, three of the EU's members at that time (Denmark, Sweden, United Kingdom) decided not to participate in the euro, but they may join later. Since the euro was introduced, 12 emerging countries in Europe have joined

WEB

www.federalreserve
.gov

Provides links on the
European Central Bank
and other foreign cen-
tral banks.

the EU (10 countries, including the Czech Republic and Hungary, joined in 2004, and Bulgaria and Romania joined in 2007). While four of these new members have already adopted the euro, others may eventually participate if they satisfy the limitations imposed on government deficits.

The European Central Bank (ECB), based in Frankfurt, is responsible for setting monetary policy for all European countries that participate in the euro. Its objective is to control inflation in the participating countries and to stabilize (within reasonable boundaries) the value of the euro with respect to other major currencies. Thus, the ECB's monetary goals of price stability and currency stability are somewhat similar to those of individual countries around the world, but differ in that they are focused on a group of countries rather than a single country. Because participating countries are subject to the monetary policy imposed by the ECB, a given country no longer has full control over the monetary policy implemented within its borders at any given time. The implementation of a common monetary policy may lead to more political unification among participating countries and encourage them to develop similar national defense and foreign policies.

Impact of the Euro on Monetary Policy   As just described, the use of a common currency forces countries to abide by a common monetary policy. Any changes in the money supply affect all European countries using the euro as their form of money. Having a single currency also means that the interest rate offered on government securities must be similar across the participating European countries. Any discrepancy in rates would encourage investors within these countries to invest in the country with the highest rate, which would realign the interest rates among the countries.

Although having a single monetary policy may allow for more consistent economic conditions across the eurozone countries, it prevents any participating country from solving local economic problems with its own unique monetary policy. Eurozone governments may disagree on the ideal monetary policy for their local economies, but they must nevertheless agree on a single monetary policy. Yet any given policy used in a particular period may enhance economic conditions in some countries and adversely affect others. Each participating country is still able to apply its own fiscal policy (tax and government expenditure decisions), however.

One concern about the euro is that each of the participating countries has its own agenda, which may prevent unified decisions about the future direction of the eurozone economies. Each country was supposed to show restraint on fiscal policy spending so that it could improve its budget deficit situation. Nevertheless, some countries have ignored restraint in favor of resolving domestic unemployment problems. The euro's initial instability was partially attributed to political maneuvering as individual countries tried to serve their own interests at the expense of the other participating countries. This lack of solidarity is exactly the reason why there was some concern about using a single currency (and therefore monetary policy) among several European countries. Disagreements over policy intensified as the European economies weakened during 2008 and 2009.

Variations in the Value of the Euro   Since the euro was introduced in 1999, it has experienced volatile movements. Its value initially declined substantially against the British pound, the dollar, and many other currencies. By October 2001, its value was $.90, or about 25 percent less than its value when it was introduced. The weakness was partially attributed to capital outflows from Europe. More money was flowing out of Europe and into U.S. and other financial markets than was flowing from these countries to Europe. The net outflows from Europe were partially caused by lack of confidence in the euro. Investors preferred to hold assets denominated in dollars than in euros.

Then, from October 2001 to August 2008, the euro reversed course, appreciating by more than 70 percent. One reason for its strength in this period was that the interest rate on euro-denominated debt securities was typically higher than the rate on dollar-denominated securities. Thus, capital flowed to the eurozone to take advantage of the higher interest rate. However, as the credit crisis intensified in September 2008, there were signals that Europe's economy would weaken in the near future. Speculators moved their money out of euros, and the euro depreciated by 20 percent within two months.

Global Central Bank Coordination

In some cases, the central banks of various countries coordinate their efforts for a common cause. Shortly after the terrorist attack on the United States on September 11, 2001, central banks of several countries injected money denominated in their respective currencies into the banking system to provide more liquidity. This strategy was intended to ensure that sufficient money would be available in case customers began to withdraw funds from banks or cash machines. On September 17, 2001, the Fed's move to reduce interest rates before the U.S. stock market reopened was immediately followed by similar decisions by the Bank of Canada (Canada's central bank) and the European Central Bank.

Sometimes, however, central banks have conflicting objectives. For example, it is not unusual for two countries to simultaneously experience weak economies. In this situation, each central bank may consider intervening to weaken its home currency, which could increase foreign demand for exports denominated in that currency. If both central banks attempt this type of intervention simultaneously, however, the exchange rate between the two currencies will be subject to conflicting forces.

EXAMPLE

Today, the Fed plans to intervene directly in the foreign exchange market by selling dollars for yen in an attempt to weaken the dollar. Meanwhile, the Bank of Japan plans to sell yen for dollars in the foreign exchange market in an attempt to weaken the yen. The effects are offsetting. One central bank can attempt to have a more powerful impact by selling more of its home currency in the foreign exchange market, but the other central bank may respond to offset that force. ●

Global Monetary Policy during the Credit Crisis   During 2008, the effects of the credit crisis began to spread internationally. In the August–October period, stock market prices in the United States, Canada, China, France, Germany, Italy, Japan, Mexico, Russia, Spain, and many other countries declined by more than 25 percent. On October 8, 2008, central banks of several countries reduced interest rates in a unified effort to stimulate the world economies. The central bank actions were not effective in the short run, however, because there were many indicators that a global recession was coming, which created negative investor sentiment in stock markets around the world.

SUMMARY

■ The key components of the Federal Reserve System are the Board of Governors and the Federal Open Market Committee. The Board of Governors determines the reserve requirements on account balances at depository institutions. It is also an important subset of the Federal Open Market Committee (FOMC), which determines U.S. monetary policy. The FOMC's monetary policy has a major influence on interest rates and other economic conditions.

- The Fed uses open market operations (the buying and selling of securities) as a means of adjusting the money supply. The Fed purchases securities as a means of increasing the money supply, whereas it sells them as a means of reducing the money supply.
- In response to the credit crisis, the Fed provided indirect funding to Bear Stearns (a large securities firm) so that it did not have to file for bankruptcy. It also created various facilities for providing funds to financial institutions and other corporations. One facility allowed primary dealers that serve as finan-cial intermediaries for bonds and other securities to obtain overnight loans. Another facility purchased commercial paper issued by corporations. A third facility allowed depository institutions to obtain loans for a 35-day period.
- Each country has its own central bank, which is responsible for conducting monetary policy to achieve economic goals such as low inflation and low unemployment. Sixteen countries in Eur-ope have adopted a single currency, which causes all of these countries to be subject to the same monetary policy.

POINT COUNTER-POINT

Should There Be a Global Central Bank?

Point Yes. A global central bank could serve all coun-tries in the manner that the European Central Bank now serves several European countries. With a single central bank, there could be a single monetary policy across all countries.

Counter-Point No. A global central bank could create a global monetary policy only if a single currency was used throughout the world. Moreover, all countries would not agree on the monetary policy that would be appropriate.

Who Is Correct? Use the Internet to learn more about this issue. Offer your own opinion on this issue.

QUESTIONS AND APPLICATIONS

1. The Fed versus Congress. Should the Fed or Congress decide the fate of large financial institu-tions that are near bankruptcy?

2. Reserve Requirements How is money sup-ply growth affected by an increase in the reserve re-quirement ratio?

3. Discount Window Lending during Credit Crisis Explain how and why the Fed extended its discount window lending to nonbank financial insti-tutions during the credit crisis.

4. Beige Book What is the Beige Book, and why is it important to the FOMC?

5. Effect on Money Supply Why do the Fed's open market operations have a different effect on the money supply than transactions between two deposi-tory institutions?

6. Policy Directive What is the policy directive, and who carries it out?

7. Open Market Operations Explain how the Fed can use open market operations to reduce the money supply.

8. Open Market Operations Explain how the Fed increases the money supply through open market operations.

9. FOMC Economic Presentations What is the purpose of economic presentations during an FOMC meeting?

10. FOMC What are the main goals of the Federal Open Market Committee (FOMC)? How does it at-tempt to achieve these goals?

11. Control of Money Supply Describe the characteristics that a measure of money should have if it is to be manipulated by the Fed.

12. The Fed Briefly describe the origin of the Federal Reserve System. Describe the functions of the Fed district banks.

13. Bailouts by the Fed Do you think that the Fed should have bailed out large financial institutions during the credit crisis?

Interpreting Financial News

Interpret the following statements made by Wall Street analysts and portfolio managers:

a. "The Fed's future monetary policy will be dependent on the economic indicators to be reported this week."

b. "The Fed's role is to take the punch bowl away just as the party is coming alive."

c. "Inflation will likely increase because real short-term interest rates currently are negative."

Managing in Financial Markets

Anticipating the Fed's Actions As a manager of a large U.S. firm, one of your assignments is to monitor U.S. economic conditions so that you can forecast the demand for products sold by your firm. You recognize that the Federal Reserve attempts to implement monetary policy to affect economic growth and inflation. In addition, you recognize that the federal government implements spending and tax policies (fiscal policy) to affect economic growth and inflation. It is difficult to achieve high economic growth without igniting inflation, however. Although the Federal Reserve is often said to be independent of the administration in Washington, D.C., there is much interaction between monetary and fiscal policies.

Assume that the economy is currently stagnant, and some economists are concerned about the possibility of a recession. Some industries, however, are experiencing high growth, and inflation is higher this year than in the previous five years.Assume that the Federal Reserve chairman's term will expire in four months and that the President of the United States will have to appoint a new chairman (or reappoint the existing chairman). It is widely known that the existing chairman would like to be reappointed. Also assume that next year is an election year for the administration.

a. Given the circumstances, do you expect that the administration will be more concerned about increasing economic growth or reducing inflation?

b. Given the circumstances, do you expect that the Fed will be more concerned about increasing economic growth or reducing inflation?

c. Your firm is relying on you for some insight on how the government will influence economic conditions and therefore the demand for your firm's products. Given the circumstances, what is your forecast of how the government will affect economic conditions?

FLOW OF FUNDS EXERCISE

Monitoring the Fed

Recall that Carson Company has obtained substantial loans from finance companies and commercial banks. The interest rate on the loans is tied to market interest rates and is adjusted every six months. Because of its expectations of a strong U.S. economy, Carson plans to grow in the future by expanding its business and by making acquisitions. It expects that it will need substantial long-term financing and plans to borrow additional funds either through loans or by issuing bonds. It is also considering issuing stock to raise funds in the next year.

Given its large exposure to interest rates charged on its debt, Carson closely monitors Fed actions. It subscribes to a special service that attempts to monitor the Fed's actions in the Treasury security markets. It recently received an alert from the service that suggested the Fed has been selling large holdings of its Treasury securities in the secondary Treasury securities market.

a. How should Carson interpret the actions by the Fed? That is, will these actions place upward or downward pressure on Treasury securities prices? Explain.

b. Will these actions place upward or downward pressure on Treasury yields? Explain.

c. Will these actions place upward or downward pressure on interest rates? Explain.

INTERNET/EXCEL EXERCISE

Assess the current structure of the Federal Reserve System, using the website www.federalreserve.gov/monetarypolicy/fomc.htm.

Go to the minutes of the most recent meeting. Who is the current chairman? Who is the current vice chairman? How many people attended the meeting? Describe the main issues discussed at the meeting.

WSJ EXERCISE

Reviewing Fed Policies

Review recent issues of *The Wall Street Journal* and search for any comments that relate to the Fed. Does it appear that the Fed may attempt to revise the federal funds rate? If so, how and why?

5

Monetary Policy

CHAPTER
OBJECTIVES

The specific objectives of this chapter are to:

■ describe the mechanics of monetary policy,

■ explain the tradeoffs involved in monetary policy,

■ describe how financial market participants respond to the Fed's policies, and

■ explain how monetary policy is affected by the global environment.

The previous chapter discussed the Federal Reserve System and how it controls the money supply, information essential to financial market participants. It is just as important for participants to know how changes in the money supply affect the economy, which is the subject of this chapter.

MECHANICS OF MONETARY POLICY

The monetary policy goals of most central banks are focused on stabilizing the economy. Recall that the Fed's goals are to achieve a low level of inflation and a low level of unemployment. Given the Fed's goals of controlling economic growth and inflation, it assesses indicators of these economic variables before it determines its monetary policy.

Indicators of Economic Growth

The Fed monitors indicators of economic growth because high economic growth creates a more prosperous economy and can result in lower unemployment. Gross domestic product (GDP), which measures the total value of goods and services produced during a specific period, is measured each month. It serves as the most direct indicator of economic growth in the United States. The level of production adjusts in response to changes in consumers' demand for goods and services. A high production level indicates strong economic growth and can result in an increased demand for labor (lower unemployment).

The Fed also monitors national income, which is the total income earned by firms and individual employees during a specific period. A strong demand for U.S. goods and services results in a large amount of income to firms and employees.

The unemployment rate is monitored as well, because one of the Fed's primary goals is to maintain a low rate of unemployment in the United States. The unemployment rate does not necessarily indicate the degree of economic growth, however, because it measures only the number and not the types of jobs that are being filled. It is possible to have a substantial reduction in unemployment during a period of weak economic growth if new low-paying jobs are created during that period.

Several other indexes serve as indicators of growth in specific sectors of the U.S. economy, including an industrial production index, a retail sales index, and a home sales index. A composite index combines various indexes to indicate economic growth across sectors. In addition to the many indicators reflecting recent conditions, the Fed may also use forward-looking indicators, such as consumer confidence surveys, to forecast future economic growth.

Index of Leading Economic Indicators   Among the economic indicators widely followed by market participants are the indexes of leading, coincident, and lagging economic indicators, which are published by the Conference Board. **Leading economic indicators** are used to predict future economic activity. Usually, three consecutive monthly changes in the same direction in these indicators suggest a turning point in the economy. **Coincident economic indicators** tend to reach their peaks and troughs at the same time as business cycles. **Lagging economic indicators** tend to rise or fall a few months after business-cycle expansions and contractions.

The Conference Board is an independent, not-for-profit membership organization whose stated goal is to create and disseminate knowledge about management and the marketplace to help businesses strengthen their performance and better serve society. The Conference Board conducts research, convenes conferences, makes forecasts, assesses trends, and publishes information and analyses. A summary of the Conference Board's leading, coincident, and lagging indexes is provided in Exhibit 5.1.

Exhibit 5.1 The Conference Board's Indexes of Leading, Coincident, and Lagging Indicators

Leading Index
1. Average weekly hours, manufacturing
2. Average weekly initial claims for unemployment insurance
3. Manufacturers' new orders, consumer goods and materials
4. Vendor performance, slower deliveries diffusion index
5. Manufacturers' new orders, nondefense capital goods
6. Building permits, new private housing units
7. Stock prices, 500 common stocks
8. Money supply, M2
9. Interest rate spread, 10-year Treasury bonds less federal funds
10. Index of consumer expectations
Coincident Index
1. Employees on nonagricultural payrolls
2. Personal income less transfer payments
3. Industrial production
4. Manufacturing and trade sales
Lagging Index
1. Average duration of unemployment
2. Inventories to sales ratio, manufacturing and trade
3. Labor cost per unit of output, manufacturing
4. Average prime rate
5. Commercial and industrial loans
6. Consumer installment credit to personal income ratio
7. Consumer price index for services

USING THE WALL STREET JOURNAL

The Consumer Price Index

As shown here, *The Wall Street Journal* provides information on the consumer price index, which is used to measure inflation. The Fed attempts to monitor inflation because its monetary policy is influenced by the prevailing inflation. In general, the Fed uses a more restrictive monetary policy when it decides that inflation must be reduced.

Source: Republished with permission of Dow Jones & Company, Inc., from *The Wall Street Journal,* January 7, 2009; p.C9; permission conveyed through the Copyright Clearance Center, Inc.

Inflation

	Nov. index level	CHG FROM (%) Oct. '08	Nov. '07
U.S. consumer price index			
All items	**212.425**	−1.9	1.1
Core	**216.690**	−0.2	2.0

Indicators of Inflation

The Fed closely monitors price indexes and other indicators to assess the U.S. inflation rate.

Producer and Consumer Price Indexes The producer price index represents prices at the wholesale level, and the consumer price index represents prices paid by consumers (retail level). There is a lag time of about one month after the period being measured due to the time required to compile price information for the indexes. Nevertheless, financial markets closely monitor the price indexes because they may be used to forecast inflation, which affects nominal interest rates and the prices of some securities. Agricultural price indexes reflect recent price movements in grains, fruits, and vegetables. Housing price indexes reflect recent price movements in homes and rental properties.

Other Inflation Indicators In addition to price indexes, there are several other indicators of inflation. Wage rates are periodically reported in various regions of the United States. Because wages and prices are highly correlated over the long run, wages can indicate price movements. Oil prices can signal future inflation because they affect the costs of some forms of production, as well as transportation costs and the prices paid by consumers for gasoline.

The price of gold is closely monitored because gold prices tend to move in tandem with inflation. Some investors buy gold as a hedge against future inflation. Therefore, a rise in gold prices may signal the market's expectation that inflation will increase.

In some cases, indicators of economic growth are also used to indicate inflation. For example, the release of several favorable employment reports may arouse concern that the economy will overheat, leading to **demand-pull inflation,** which occurs when excessive spending pulls up prices. Although these reports offer favorable information about economic growth, their information about inflation is unfavorable. The financial markets can be adversely affected by such reports, as investors anticipate that the Fed will have to increase interest rates to reduce the inflationary momentum.

How Monetary Policy Corrects the Economy

Once the Fed assesses economic conditions, it can decide on a monetary policy. It changes the money supply in order to influence interest rates, which affect the level of aggregate borrowing and spending by households and firms. The level of aggregate spending affects demand for products and services, and therefore affects price levels (inflation) and the unemployment level. This can be illustrated using the loanable funds framework described in Chapter 2. Recall that the interaction of the supply of loanable funds available and the demand for loanable funds determines the interest rate charged on loanable funds. Much of the demand for loanable funds is by households, corporations, and government agencies that need to borrow money. Recall that the demand schedule indicates the quantity of funds that would be demanded (at that time) at various possible interest rates. This schedule is downward sloping because many potential borrowers would borrow a larger quantity of funds at lower interest rates.

The supply schedule of loanable funds indicates the quantity of funds that would be supplied (at that time) at various possible interest rates. This schedule is upward sloping because suppliers of funds tend to supply a larger amount of funds when the interest rate is higher. Assume that as of today, the demand and supply schedules for loanable funds are represented by D_1 and S_1 in the left graph of Exhibit 5.2. Based on these schedules, the equilibrium interest rate is i_1. The right graph of Exhibit 5.2 represents the typical relationship between the interest rate on loanable funds and the level of business investment as of today. The relation is inverse because corporations are more willing to expand when interest rates are relatively low. Given today's equilibrium interest rate of i_1, the level of business investment is B_1. The Fed can influence the level of business investment and therefore aggregate spending in the economy by adjusting the supply of loanable funds.

Exhibit 5.2 Effects of an Increased Money Supply

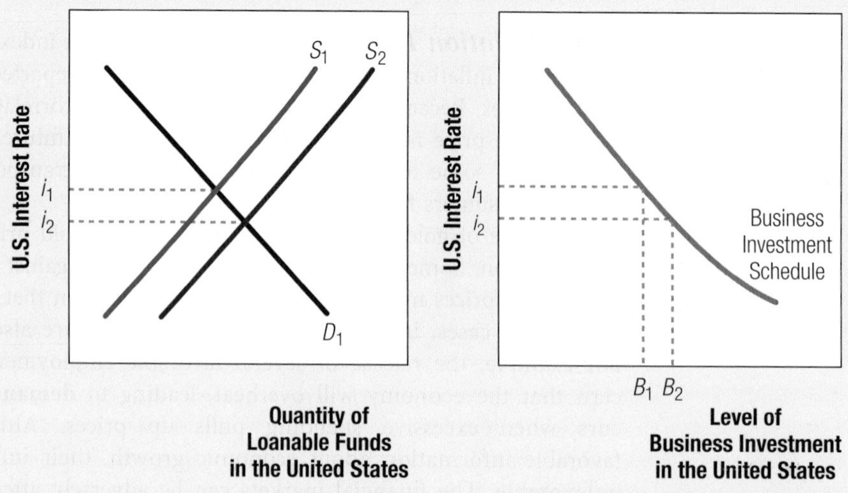

Correcting a Weak Economy   If the economy is weak, the Fed can increase the level of spending as a means of stimulating the economy. It uses open market operations to increase the money supply, a move that is intended to reduce interest rates and encourage more borrowing and spending.

The Fed can attempt to stimulate the economy by using a loose-money policy. It purchase Treasury securities in the secondary market. As the investors who sell their Treasury securities receive payment from the Fed, their account balances at financial institutions increase, without any offsetting decrease in the account balances of any other financial institutions. Thus, there is a net increase in the supply of loanable funds. If the Fed's action results in an increase of $5 billion in loanable funds, the quantity of loanable funds supplied will now be $5 billion higher at any possible interest rate level. This means that the supply schedule for loanable funds shifts outward to S_2 in Exhibit 5.2. The difference between S_2 and S_1 is that S_2 incorporates the $5 billion of loanable funds added as a result of the Fed's actions.

Given the shift in the supply schedule for loanable funds, the quantity of loanable funds supplied exceeds the quantity of loanable funds demanded at the interest rate level i_1. Thus, the interest rate will decline to i_2, the level at which the quantities of loanable funds supplied and demanded are equal.

The lower interest rate level causes an increase in the level of business investment from B_1 to B_2. The increase in business investment represents new business spending that was triggered by lower interest rates, which reduced the corporate cost of financing new projects. ●

Correcting High Inflation   If excessive inflation is the main concern, the Fed can institute a tight-money policy by using open market operations to reduce money supply growth. A portion of the inflation may be due to demand-pull inflation. The Fed can reduce this type of inflation by slowing economic growth and thereby reducing the excessive spending that can lead to demand-pull inflation.

To slow economic growth and reduce inflationary pressures, the Fed can sell some of its holdings of Treasury securities in the secondary market. As investors make payments to purchase these Treasury securities, their account balances decrease, without any offsetting increase in the account balances of any other financial institutions. Thus, there is a net decrease in deposit accounts (money), which results in a net decrease in the quantity of loanable funds. Assume that the Fed's action causes a decrease of $5 billion in loanable funds. The quantity of loanable funds supplied will now be $5 billion lower at any possible interest rate level. This reflects an inward shift in the supply schedule from S_1 to S_2, as shown in Exhibit 5.3.

Given the inward shift in the supply schedule for loanable funds, the quantity of loanable funds demanded exceeds the quantity of loanable funds supplied at the original interest rate level (i_1). Thus, the interest rate will increase to i_2, the level at which the quantities of loanable funds supplied and demanded are equal. The higher interest rate level increases the corporate cost of financing new projects and therefore causes a decrease in the level of business investment from B_1 to B_2. As economic growth is slowed by the reduction in business investment, inflationary pressure may be reduced. ●

Exhibit 5.4 summarizes how the Fed (as the central bank of the United States) can affect economic conditions through its influence on the supply of loanable funds. The top part of the exhibit illustrates a stimulative (loose-money) monetary policy intended to boost economic growth, and the bottom part illustrates a restrictive (tight-money) monetary policy intended to reduce inflation.

Limitations of Monetary Policy

Monetary policy has limitations, which may prevent the Fed from achieving its goals. Some of the more important limitations are mentioned here.

Exhibit 5.3 Effects of a Reduced Money Supply

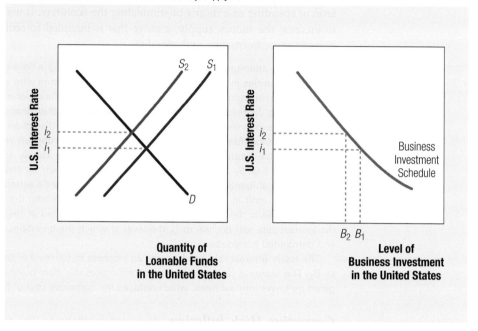

Exhibit 5.4 How Monetary Policy Can Affect Economic Conditions

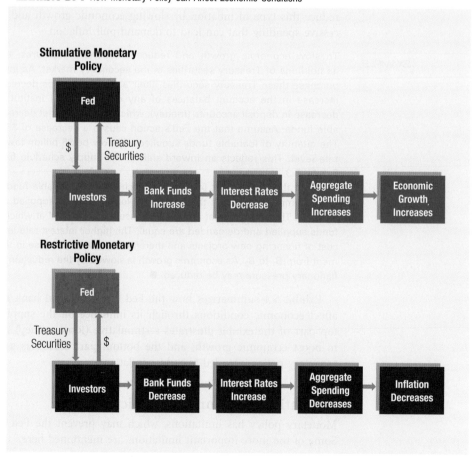

Impact of a Credit Crunch   The effects of monetary policy on the economy are dependent on the willingness of depository institutions to lend funds. Even if the Fed increases the level of bank funds during a weak economy, banks may be unwilling to extend credit to some potential borrowers, and the result is a *credit crunch*. If banks do not lend out the newly created funds, the economy will not be stimulated. The banks are reluctant to lend out sufficient funds because they are concerned that the weak economy will make it less likely that loans will be repaid. Banks provide loans only after confirming that the borrower's future cash flows will be adequate to make loan repayments. In a weak economy, the future cash flows of many potential borrowers are more uncertain, causing a reduction in loan applications (demand for loans) and in the number of qualified loan applicants.

Banks and other lending institutions have a responsibility to their depositors, shareholders, and regulators to avoid loans that are likely to default. Because default risk rises during a weak economy, some potential borrowers will be unable to obtain loans. Others may qualify only if they pay high-risk premiums to cover their default risk. Thus, the effects of the Fed's monetary policy may be limited if potential borrowers do not qualify or are unwilling to incur the high-risk premiums.

EXAMPLE

During the credit crisis that began in 2008, the Fed attempted to stimulate the economy by using monetary policy to reduce interest rates. Initially, however, the effect of the monetary policy was negligible. Firms were unwilling to borrow even at low interest rates because they did not want to expand while economic conditions were so weak. In addition, commercial banks raised the standards necessary to qualify for loans so that they would not repeat the mistakes (liberal lending standards) that caused the credit crisis. ●

Lagged Effects of Monetary Policy   Another reason that monetary policy may not achieve the desired results is that there are lags between the time that an economic problem occurs and the time that the monetary policy is implemented and has an effect. Three specific lags are involved. First, there is a **recognition lag,** or the lag between the time a problem arises and the time it is recognized. Most economic problems are initially revealed by statistics, not actual observation. Because economic statistics are reported only periodically, they will not immediately signal a problem. For example, the unemployment rate is reported monthly. A sudden increase in unemployment may not be detected until the end of the month when statistics reveal the problem. If unemployment increases slightly each month for two straight months, the Fed may not necessarily act on this information, because the information may not appear to be significant. Only after a few more months of steadily increasing unemployment might the Fed recognize that a serious problem exists. In such a case, the recognition lag may be four months or longer.

The lag from the time a serious problem is recognized until the time the Fed implements a policy to resolve it is known as the **implementation lag.** Then, even after the Fed implements a policy, there will be an **impact lag** until the policy has its full impact on the economy. For example, an adjustment in money supply growth may have an immediate impact on the economy to some degree, but its full impact may not occur until a year or so after the adjustment.

These lags hinder the Fed's control of the economy. Suppose the Fed uses a loose-money policy to stimulate the economy and reduce unemployment. By the time the implemented monetary policy begins to take effect, the unemployment rate may have already reversed itself and may now be trending downward as a result of some other outside factors (such as a weakened dollar that increased foreign demand for U.S. goods and created U.S. jobs). Without monetary policy lags, implemented policies would have a higher rate of success.

Impact of a Stimulative Policy on Expected Inflation   When a stimulative monetary policy is used, the effect of an increase in money supply growth may be disrupted due to an increase in inflationary expectations.

Assume that the U.S. economy is very weak, and the Fed responds by using open market operations (purchasing Treasury securities) to increase the supply of loanable funds. This action is supposed to reduce interest rates and increase the level of borrowing and spending. However, there is some evidence that high money growth may also lead to higher inflation over time. To the extent that businesses and households recognize that an increase in money growth will cause higher inflation, they will revise their inflationary expectations upward as a result. This effect is often referred to as the **theory of rational expectations**. Higher inflationary expectations encourage businesses and households to increase their demand for loanable funds (as explained in Chapter 2), in order to borrow and make planned expenditures before price levels increase. This increase in demand reflects a rush to make planned purchases now.

These effects of the Fed's monetary policy are shown in Exhibit 5.5 The result is an increase in both the supply of loanable funds and the demand for loanable funds. The effects are offsetting, so the Fed may not be able to reduce interest rates for a sustained period of time. If the Fed cannot force interest rates lower with an active monetary policy, it is unable to stimulate an increase in the level of business investment. Business investment will increase only if the cost of financing is reduced, making some proposed business projects feasible. If the increase in business investment does not occur, economic conditions will not improve. ●

Given the limitations of an active monetary policy illustrated here, an alternative approach is a passive monetary policy that allows the economy to correct itself rather than rely on the Fed's intervention. Even if the Fed is passive, interest rates should ultimately decline in a weak economy because the demand for loanable funds should decline as economic growth weakens. In this case, interest rates would have declined without a corresponding increase in inflationary expectations, so the rates may stay lower for a sustained period of time. Consequently, the level of business in-

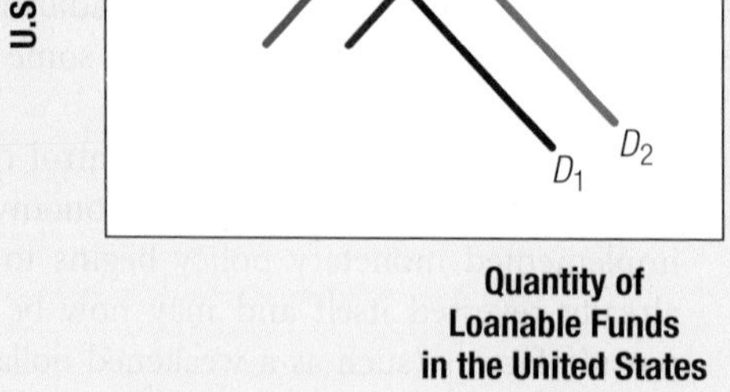

Exhibit 5.5 Effects of an Increased Money Supply According to the Rational Expectations Theory

vestment should ultimately increase, which should lead to a stronger economy and more jobs. The major criticism of a passive monetary policy is that the weak economy could take years to correct itself. Many people would prefer that the Fed take an active role in improving economic conditions rather than hope that the economy will correct itself.

How the Fed Deals with the Limitations   The economists who work at the Fed tend to believe that monetary policy can be an effective tool for controlling economic growth, inflation, and the unemployment level. Therefore, they periodically revise money supply growth in order to fine-tune the economy. Nevertheless, they are aware of the potential limitations. In particular, they recognize that a stimulative monetary policy will not always cure a high unemployment rate and could even ignite inflation. They also recognize that a restrictive monetary policy will not always reduce inflation. The effects of monetary policy are dependent on other existing conditions that also affect the economy. These conditions are discussed in more detail in the following section.

TRADEOFF IN MONETARY POLICY

Ideally, the Fed would like to achieve both a very low level of unemployment and a very low level of inflation in the United States. The U.S. unemployment rate should be low in a period when U.S. economic conditions are strong. Inflation will likely be relatively high at this time, however, because wages and price levels tend to increase when economic conditions are strong. Conversely, inflation may be lower when economic conditions are weak, but unemployment will be relatively high. There is an inverse relationship between the inflation rate and the unemployment rate, as shown in Exhibit 5.6. Therefore, it is difficult, if not impossible, for the Fed to cure both problems simultaneously.

When inflation is higher than the Fed deems acceptable, the Fed may consider implementing a tight-money policy to reduce economic growth. As economic growth slows, producers cannot as easily raise their prices and still maintain sales volume. Similarly, workers are not in demand and do not have much bargaining power on wages. Thus, the use of a tight-money policy to slow economic growth can reduce the inflation rate. A possible cost of the lower inflation rate is higher unemployment. If the economy becomes stagnant because of the tight-money policy, sales decrease, inventories accumulate, and firms may reduce their workforces to reduce production.

Given that a loose-money policy can reduce unemployment whereas a tight-money policy can reduce inflation, the Fed must determine whether unemployment or inflation is the more serious problem. It may not be able to solve both problems simultaneously. In fact, it may not be able to fully eliminate either problem. Although a loose-money policy can stimulate the economy, it does not guarantee that unskilled workers will be hired. Although a tight-money policy can reduce inflation caused by excessive spending, it cannot reduce inflation caused by such factors as an agreement by the members of the oil cartel to keep oil prices high.

Impact of Other Forces on the Tradeoff

Other forces may also affect the tradeoff faced by the Fed. Consider a situation where because of specific cost factors (such as higher energy and insurance costs), inflation will be at least 3 percent. This amount of inflation will exist no matter what type of monetary policy the Fed implements. Also assume that because of the number of unskilled workers and people between jobs, the unemployment rate will be at least 4 percent. A loose-money policy will stimulate the economy sufficiently to maintain unemployment at that minimum level of 4 percent. However, such a stimulative policy may also cause additional inflation beyond the 3 percent level. A tight-money policy could maintain inflation at the 3 percent minimum, but unemployment would likely rise above the 4 percent minimum.

This tradeoff is illustrated in Exhibit 5.6. Here the Fed can use a very stimulative (loose-money) policy that is expected to result in Point A (9 percent inflation and 4 percent unemployment). Alternatively, it can use a very restrictive (tight-money) policy that is expected to result in Point B (3 percent inflation and 8 percent unemployment). Or it can implement a compromise policy that will result in some point along the curve between A and B.

Historical data on annual inflation and unemployment rates show that when one of these problems worsens, the other does not automatically improve. Both variables can rise or fall simultaneously over time. Nevertheless, this does not refute the tradeoff faced by the Fed. It simply means that some outside factors have affected inflation or unemployment or both.

EXAMPLE

Recall that the Fed could have achieved Point A, Point B, or somewhere along the curve connecting these points during a particular time period. Now assume that oil prices have increased substantially and several major product liability lawsuits have occurred. These events will affect consumer prices such that the minimum inflation rate will be, say, 6 percent. In addition, assume that various training centers for unskilled workers have been closed, leaving a higher number of unskilled workers. This forces the minimum unemployment rate to 6 percent. Now the Fed's tradeoff position has changed. The Fed's new set of possibilities is shown as Curve CD in Exhibit 5.7. Note that the points reflected on Curve CD are not as desirable as the points along Curve AB that were previously attainable. No matter what type of monetary policy the Fed uses, both the inflation rate and the unemployment rate will be higher than in the previous time period. This is not the Fed's fault. In fact, the Fed is still faced with a tradeoff between Point C (11 percent inflation, 6 percent unemployment), Point D (6 percent inflation, 10 percent unemployment), or somewhere within those points along Curve CD. ●

Exhibit 5.6 Tradeoff between Reducing Inflation and Unemployment

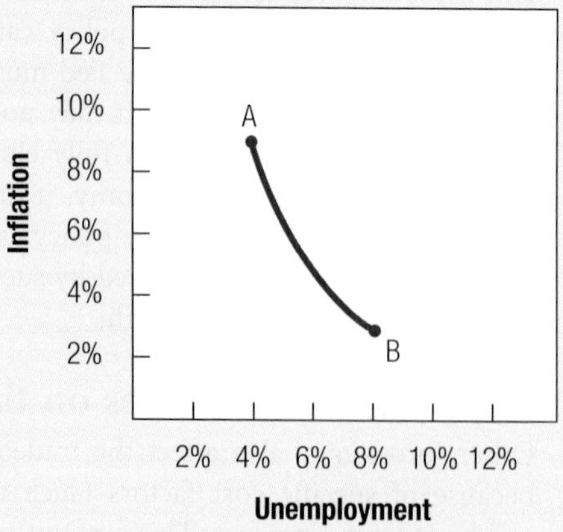

Exhibit 5.7 Adjustment in the Tradeoff between Unemployment and Inflation over Time

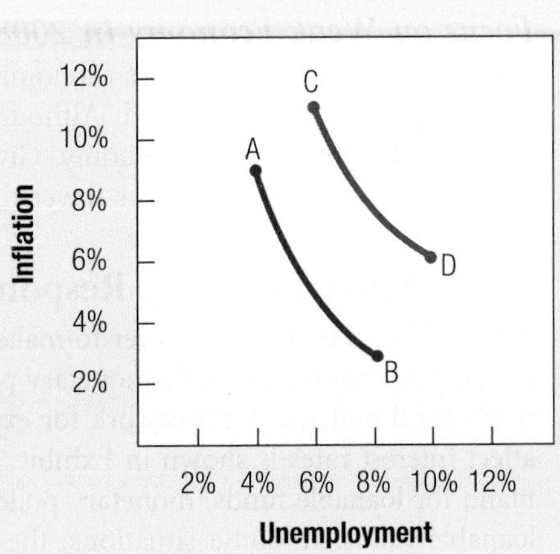

When FOMC members are primarily concerned with either inflation or unemployment, they tend to agree on the type of monetary policy that should be implemented. When both inflation and unemployment are relatively high, however, there is more disagreement among the members about the proper monetary policy to implement. Some members would likely argue for a tight-money policy to prevent inflation from rising, while other members would suggest that a loose-money policy should be implemented to reduce unemployment even if it results in higher inflation.

Shifts in Monetary Policy 2001–2008

The tradeoffs involved in monetary policy can be understood by considering the Fed's decisions during the 2001–2008 period.

Focus on Weak Economy in 2001–2003 In 2001 when economic conditions were weak, the Fed reduced the targeted federal funds rate 10 times, resulting in a cumulative decline of 4.25 percent in the targeted federal funds rate. As the federal funds rate was reduced, other market interest rates declined as well. Despite these interest rate reductions, the economy did not respond. The Fed's effects on the economy might have been stronger had it been able to reduce long-term interest rates. After the economy failed to respond as hoped in 2001, the Fed reduced the federal funds target rate twice more in 2002 and 2003. Finally, in 2004 the economy began to show some signs of improvement.

WEB

www.newyorkfed.org
Shows recent changes in the federal funds target rate.

Focus on Inflation in 2004–2007 The Fed's focus then began to shift from concern about the economy to concern about the potential for higher inflation. It raised the federal funds target rate 17 times over the period from mid-2004 to the summer of 2006. The typical adjustment in the target rate was 0.25 percent. By adjusting in small increments, as it did during this period, the Fed is unlikely to overadjust. After making each small adjustment, it monitors the economic effects and decides whether additional adjustments are needed at the next meeting. During the 2004–2007 period, there were periodic indications of rising prices, mostly due to high oil prices. While the Fed's monetary policy could not control oil prices, it wanted to prevent any inflation that could be triggered if the economy became very strong and there was excessive demand for products or labor shortages. Thus, the Fed tried to maintain economic growth, without letting the growth become so strong that it could cause higher inflation.

 Focus on Weak Economy in 2008–2009   Near the end of 2008, the credit crisis developed, resulting in a severe economic slowdown. The Fed implemented a stimulative monetary policy in this period. Although it reduced market interest rates, this did not immediately stimulate the economy. Given the weak economy, many corporations were unwilling to expand even at the lower financing rates.

How Monetary Policy Responds to Fiscal Policy

Although the Fed has the power to make decisions without the approval of the presidential administration, the Fed's monetary policy is commonly influenced by the administration's fiscal policies. A framework for explaining how monetary policy and fiscal policies affect interest rates is shown in Exhibit 5.8. Although fiscal policy typically shifts the demand for loanable funds, monetary policy normally has a larger impact on the supply of loanable funds. In some situations, the administration has enacted a fiscal policy that causes the Fed to reassess its tradeoff between focusing on inflation versus unemployment, as explained below.

Proposals to Focus on Inflation

Recently, some have proposed that the Fed should focus more on controlling the inflation rate than on unemployment. Ben Bernanke, the current chairman of the Fed, has made some arguments in favor of inflation targeting. If this proposal was adopted in its strictest form, the Fed would no longer face a tradeoff between controlling inflation and controlling unemployment. It would not have to consider responding to any fiscal policy actions such as those shown in Exhibit 5.8. It might be better able to control inflation if it could concentrate on that problem without having to worry about the unemployment rate. In addition, the Fed's role would be more transparent, and there would be less uncertainty in the financial markets about how the Fed would respond to specific economic conditions.

Nevertheless, inflation targeting also has some disadvantages. First, if the U.S. inflation rate deviated substantially from the Fed's target inflation rate, the Fed could lose credibility. Factors such as oil prices could cause high inflation regardless of the Fed's targeted inflation rate. Second, focusing only on inflation could result in a much higher unemployment level. Bernanke has argued, however, that inflation targeting could be flexible enough that the employment level would still be given consideration. He believes that inflation targeting may not only satisfy the inflation goal, but could also achieve the employment stabilization goal in the long run. For example, if unemployment was slightly higher than normal, while inflation was at the peak of the target range, an inflation targeting approach might be to leave monetary policy unchanged. In this situation, stimulating the economy with lower interest rates might reduce the unemployment rate temporarily, but could ultimately lead to excessive inflation. This would require the Fed to use a tight-money policy (higher interest rates) to correct the inflation, which could ultimately lead to a slower economy and an increase in unemployment. In general, the inflation targeting approach would discourage such "quick fix" strategies to stimulate the economy.

Although some Fed members have publicly said that they do not believe in inflation targeting, their opinions are not necessarily much different from those of Bernanke. Flexible inflation targeting would allow changes in monetary policy to increase employment. The differences in opinion among Fed members are about how bad unemployment

Exhibit 5.8 Framework for Explaining How Monetary Policy and Fiscal Policy Affect Interest Rates over Time

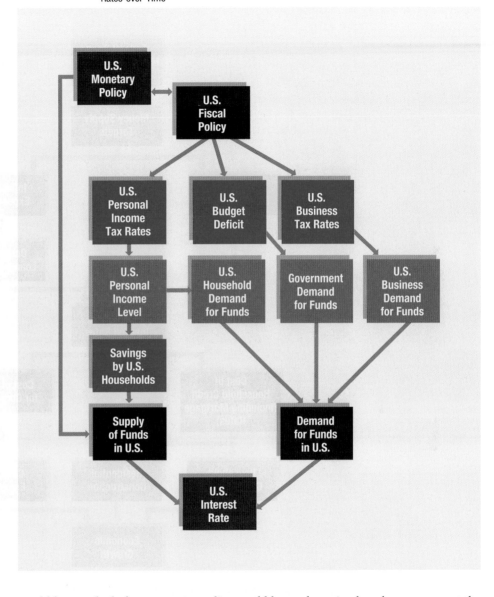

would have to be before monetary policy would be used to stimulate the economy, at the risk of raising inflation. In fact, discussion of inflation targeting declined during the credit crisis when the economy weakened and unemployment increased in the United States. This suggests that while some Fed members might argue for an inflation targeting policy in the long run, they tend to change their focus toward reducing unemployment when the United States is experiencing very weak economic conditions.

IMPACT OF MONETARY POLICY

The Fed's monetary policy affects many parts of the economy as shown in Exhibit 5.9. The effects of monetary policy can vary with the perspective. Households monitor the Fed because their loan rates on cars and mortgages will be affected. Corporations

Exhibit 5.9 How Monetary Policy Affects Financial Conditions

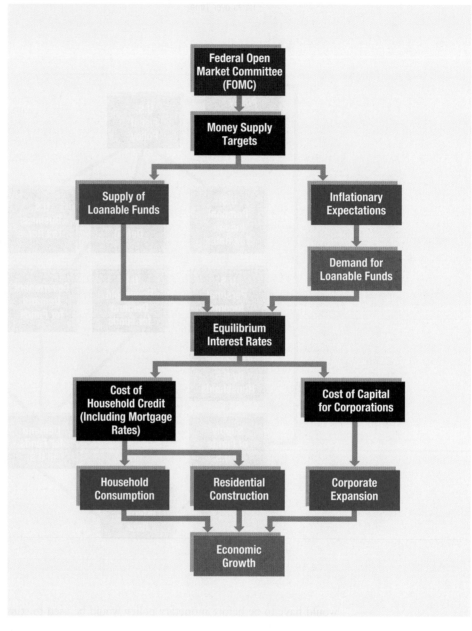

monitor the Fed because their cost of borrowing from loans and from issuing new bonds will be affected. Some corporations are affected to a greater degree if their businesses are more sensitive to interest rate movements. The Treasury monitors the Fed because its cost of financing the budget deficit will be affected.

Impact on Financial Markets

Because monetary policy can have a strong influence on interest rates and economic growth, it affects the valuation of most securities traded in financial markets. The values of existing bonds are inversely related to interest rate movements. Thus, investors who own Treasury, corporate, or municipal bonds are adversely affected when the Fed raises interest rates, and they are favorably affected when the Fed reduces interest rates (as explained in Chapter 8).

The values of stocks (discussed in Chapter 11) also are commonly affected by interest rate movements, but the effects are not as consistent as they are for bonds.

EXAMPLE

If the Fed lowers interest rates because the economy is weak, and investors anticipate that this action will enhance economic growth, they may expect that corporations will generate higher sales and earnings in the future. Thus, the values of stocks would increase due to this favorable information. However, the Fed's decision to reduce interest rates could make investors realize that economic conditions are worse than they thought. In this case, the Fed's actions could signal that corporate sales and earnings may weaken, and the values of stocks will decline due to this negative information. ●

WEB

www.federalreserve
.gov/monetary policy/
fomccalendars.htm
Schedule of FOMC
meetings and minutes
of previous FOMC
meetings.

To appreciate the potential impact of the Fed's actions on financial markets, go to any financial news website during the week in which the FOMC holds its meeting, and you will see predictions of whether the Fed will change the target federal funds rate, by how much, and how that change will affect the financial markets. Sometimes the markets fully anticipate the Fed's actions. In this case, prices of securities should adjust to the anticipated news before the meeting, and they will not adjust further when the Fed's decision is announced.

Fed's Communication to the Markets

When the Fed holds a meeting, it announces its monetary policy through a press release. The press releases issued after previous meetings are available at www.federalreserve.gov (click on "News & Events" and then on "Press Releases"). The following is an example of a typical press release.

The Federal Open Market Committee decided to raise its target for the federal funds rate by .25% to 5.00%.

Economic growth has been strong so far this year. The Committee expects that growth will continue at a more sustainable pace, partly reflecting a cooling of the housing market.

Energy prices have had a modest impact on inflation. Unit labor costs have been stable. Energy prices have the potential to add to inflation.

The Committee judges that some further policy firming may be needed to address inflation risks, but emphasizes that the extent and timing of any firming will depend on the evolution of the economic outlook as implied by future information. The Committee will respond to changes in economic prospects as needed to support the attainment of its objectives.

Voting for the FOMC monetary policy action were [list of voting members provided here].

Financial market participants closely review the press release to interpret the Fed's future plans. Some institutions hire economists to focus on assessing monetary policy so that they can determine how their various securities portfolios will be affected.

EXAMPLE

When a press release uses the phrase "further policy firming may be needed," this implies that the Fed stands ready to tighten monetary policy further in the future if it senses more upward pressure on inflation. The Fed is saying that it wants to achieve stable economic growth and price stability (low inflation), but based on existing conditions, it is more worried about price

Exhibit 5.10 Impact of Monetary Policy across Financial Markets

TYPE OF FINANCIAL MARKET	RELEVANT FACTORS INFLUENCED BY MONETARY POLICY	KEY INSTITUTIONAL PARTICIPANTS
Money market	• Secondary market values of existing money market securities • Yields on newly issued money market securities	Commercial banks, savings institutions, credit unions, money market funds, insurance companies, finance companies, pension funds
Bond market	• Secondary market values of existing bonds • Yields offered on newly issued bonds	Commercial banks, savings institutions, bond mutual funds, insurance companies, finance companies, pension funds
Mortgage market	• Demand for housing and therefore the demand for mortgages • Secondary market values of existing mortgages • Interest rates on new mortgages • Risk premium on mortgages	Commercial banks, savings institutions, credit unions, insurance companies, pension funds
Stock market	• Required return on stocks and therefore the market values of stocks • Projections for corporate earnings and therefore stock values	Stock mutual funds, insurance companies, pension funds
Foreign exchange	• Demand for currencies and therefore the values of currencies, which in turn affect currency option prices	Institutions that are exposed to exchange rate risk

stability. Therefore, it is biased toward a tight money policy (raising interest rates) in the future. If financial market participants had not anticipated the Fed's bias, the news would probably arouse concerns that interest rates would increase in the future.

Alternatively, consider the following press release by the Fed: "The reduced growth in aggregate demand should help to limit the inflation pressure over time. However, if the economy shows further signs of weakening, the Committee anticipates that some stimulus may be needed." In this case, the Fed is suggesting that inflation is not such a threat and that it is more concerned about a weak economy. Thus, the Fed has a bias toward loosening the money supply. If financial market participants had not anticipated this information, the press release would probably cause expectations of lower interest rates in the future. ●

The type of influence that monetary policy can have on each financial market is summarized in Exhibit 5.10.

Impact of the Fed's Response to Oil Shocks   A month rarely goes by without the financial press reporting a potential inflation crisis, such as a hurricane that could affect oil production and refining in Louisiana or Texas, or friction in the Middle East or Russia that could disrupt oil production there. Whenever an event occurs that could affect the world's production of oil, people presume that there will be an oil shortage. If their expectations are correct, inflation will be higher, because oil prices affect the prices of gasoline and airline fuel, which affect the costs of transporting many products and supplies. Oil is also used in the production of some products. Firms that experience higher costs due to higher oil expenses may raise their prices. An increase in inflation puts pressure on the Fed to tighten monetary policy. The Fed does not have control over oil prices, but it reasons that it can at least dampen any inflationary pressure on prices if it slows economic growth. In other words, if the economy is weak, firms are less likely to increase the prices of their products because they know that their sales may drop if they raise prices.

The concerns that an oil price shock will occur and that the Fed will raise interest rates to offset the high oil prices tend to have the following effects. First, bond markets react strongly because bond prices are inversely related to interest rates. The fear of rising interest rates is enough to cause a major sell-off of bonds, which reduces bond prices. Stock prices are affected by expectations of corporate earnings. If corporations will incur higher costs of production and transportation due to higher oil prices, their earnings could decrease. In addition, if the Fed increases interest rates in order to slow economic growth (to reduce inflationary pressure), corporations will experience an increase in the cost of financing. This also would reduce their earnings. Consequently, investors who expect a reduction in earnings may sell their holdings of stock, and stock prices will decline.

In some cases, the fears of higher oil prices turn out to be correct, and the Fed decides that it has no choice but to slow economic growth. The prices of bonds and stocks tend to suffer as a result. In many other cases, the fears of an oil price shock subside, the Fed does not need to adjust its monetary policy, and the prices of bonds and stocks rise back toward their previous levels. Nevertheless, some investors will have incurred losses because they sold their bonds and stocks after prices declined in financial markets due to the possible effects of an oil price shock. By the time the fears have subsided and they invest in bonds and stocks again, bond and stock prices may have increased.

Impact on Financial Institutions

Many depository institutions obtain most of their funds in the form of short-term loans and then use some of their funds to provide long-term fixed-rate mortgage loans. When interest rates rise, their cost of funds rises faster than the return they receive on their loans. Thus, they are adversely affected when the Fed increases interest rates.

Financial institutions such as commercial banks, bond mutual funds, insurance companies, and pension funds maintain large portfolios of bonds, so their portfolios are adversely affected when the Fed raises interest rates. Financial institutions such as stock mutual funds, insurance companies, and pension funds maintain large portfolios of stocks, and their stock portfolios are also susceptible to changes in the Fed's monetary policy.

GLOBAL MONETARY POLICY

Financial market participants must recognize that the type of monetary policy implemented by the Fed is somewhat dependent on various international factors, as explained next.

Impact of the Dollar

A weak dollar can stimulate U.S. exports because it reduces the amount of foreign currency needed by foreign companies to obtain dollars in order to purchase U.S. exports. A weak dollar also discourages U.S. imports because it increases the dollars needed to obtain foreign currency in order to purchase imports. Thus, a weak dollar can stimulate the U.S. economy. In addition, it tends to exert inflationary pressure in the United States because it reduces the foreign competition. If economic conditions are weak, the Fed may not need to be as aggressive with a stimulative monetary policy if the dollar is weak, because a weak dollar can provide some stimulus to the U.S. economy. Conversely, a strong dollar tends to reduce inflationary pressure but also dampens the U.S. economy. Therefore, if U.S. economic conditions are weak, a strong dollar will not provide the stimulus needed to improve condtions, and the Fed may need to implement a stimulative monetary policy.

Impact of Global Economic Conditions

The Fed recognizes that economic conditions are integrated across countries, so it considers prevailing global economic conditions when conducting monetary policy. When global economic conditions are strong, foreign countries purchase more U.S. products and can stimulate the U.S. economy. When global economic conditions are weak, the foreign demand for U.S. products weakens.

During the credit crisis that began in 2008, the United States and many other countries experienced very weak economic conditions The Fed's decision to lower U.S. interest rates and stimulate the U.S. economy was partially driven by these weak global economic conditions. The Fed recognized that the United States would not receive any stimulus from other countries (such as a strong demand for U.S. products) where income and aggregate spending levels were also relatively low.

Transmission of Interest Rates

Each country has its own currency (with the exception of countries in the eurozone) and its own interest rate, which is based on the supply of and demand for loanable funds in that currency. Investors residing in one country may attempt to capitalize on high interest rates in another country. If there is upward pressure on U.S. interest rates that can be offset by foreign inflows of funds, the Fed may not feel compelled to use a loose-money policy. However, if foreign investors reduce their investment in U.S. securities, the Fed may be forced to intervene to prevent interest rates from rising.

Given the international integration in money and capital markets, a government's budget deficit can affect interest rates of various countries. This concept, referred to as **global crowding out,** is illustrated in Exhibit 5.11. An increase in the U.S. budget deficit causes an outward shift in the federal government's demand for U.S. funds and therefore in the aggregate demand for U.S. funds (from D_1 to D_2). This crowding-out effect forces the U.S. interest rate to increase from i_1 to i_2 if the supply curve (S) is unchanged. As U.S. rates rise, they attract funds from investors in other countries, such as Germany and Japan. As foreign investors use more of their funds to invest in U.S. securities, the supply of available funds in their respective countries declines. Consequently, there is upward pressure on non-U.S. interest rates as well. The impact will be most pronounced in those countries whose investors are most likely to be attracted to the higher U.S. interest rates. The possibility of global crowding out has caused national governments to criticize one another for large budget deficits.

Exhibit 5.11 Illustration of Global Crowding Out

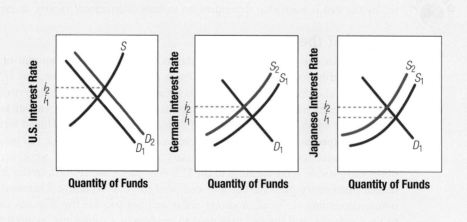

SUMMARY

- By using monetary policy, the Fed can affect the interaction between the demand for money and the supply of money, which affects interest rates, aggregate spending, and economic growth. As the Fed increases the money supply, interest rates should decline, which results in more aggregate spending (because of cheaper financing rates) and higher economic growth. As the Fed decreases the money supply, interest rates should increase, which results in less aggregate spending (because of higher financing rates), lower economic growth, and lower inflation.

- A stimulative monetary policy can increase economic growth, but it could ignite demand-pull inflation. A restrictive monetary policy is likely to reduce inflation, but may also reduce economic growth. Thus, the Fed faces a tradeoff when implementing monetary policy. Given a possible tradeoff, the Fed tends to pinpoint its biggest concern (unemployment versus inflation) and assesses whether the potential benefits of any proposed monetary policy outweigh the potential adverse effects.

- The Fed's monetary policy is commonly influenced by the prevailing fiscal policy. Whereas fiscal policy typically shifts the demand for loanable funds, monetary policy normally has a larger impact on the supply of loanable funds. It has been proposed that the Fed should focus more on controlling the inflation rate than on unemployment. If the Fed adopted such an inflation targeting policy, it would not have to consider responding to fiscal policy actions.

- Financial market participants attempt to forecast the Fed's future monetary policies and the effects of these policies on economic conditions. When the Fed implements monetary policy, financial market participants attempt to assess how their security holdings will be affected and adjust their security portfolios accordingly.

- The Fed's monetary policy must take into account the global economic environment. A weak dollar may increase U.S. exports and thereby stimulate the U.S. economy. In addition, if economies of other countries are strong, this can also enhance U.S. exports and the U.S. economy. Thus, the Fed may not have to implement a stimulative monetary policy if international conditions may provide some stimulus to the U.S. economy. Conversely, the Fed may consider a more aggressive monetary policy to fix a weak U.S. economy if international conditions are weak, and the Fed cannot rely on other economies to boost the U.S. economy.

POINT COUNTER-POINT

Can the Fed Prevent U.S. Recessions?

Point Yes. The Fed has the power to reduce market interest rates and can therefore encourage more borrowing and spending. In this way, it stimulates the economy.

Counter-Point No. When the economy is weak, individuals and firms are unwilling to borrow regardless of the interest rate. Thus, the borrowing (by those who are qualified) and spending will not be influenced by the Fed's actions. The Fed should not intervene, but should let the economy work itself out of a recession.

Who Is Correct? Use the Internet to learn more about this issue. Offer your own opinion on this issue.

QUESTIONS AND APPLICATIONS

1. Lagged Effects of Monetary Policy Compare the recognition lag and the implementation lag.

2. Fed Response to Fiscal Policy. Explain why the Fed's monetary policy could be dependent on the fiscal policy that is implemented.

3. Passive Monetary Policy Describe a passive monetary policy.

4. Confounding Effects What factors might be considered by financial market participants who are assessing whether an increase in money supply growth will affect inflation?

5.   Fed Control Why may the Fed have difficulty controlling the economy in the manner desired? Be specific.

6.   Impact of Money Supply Growth Explain why an increase in the money supply can affect interest rates in different ways. Include the potential impact of the money supply on the supply of and the demand for loanable funds when answering this question.

7.   Active Monetary Policy Describe an active monetary policy.

8.   Monetary Policy during the Credit Crisis. Describe the Fed's monetary policy response to the credit crisis.

9.   Choice of Monetary Policy When does the Fed use a loose-money policy, and when does it use a tight-money policy? What is a criticism of a loose-money policy? What is the risk of using a monetary policy that is too tight?

10.   Monitoring Money Supply Why do financial market participants closely monitor money supply movements?

11.   Tradeoffs of Monetary Policy Describe the economic tradeoff faced by the Fed in achieving its economic goals.

12.   Fed's Control of Inflation Assume that the Fed's primary goal is to cure inflation. How can it use open market operations to achieve its goal? What is a possible adverse effect of this action by the Fed (even if it achieves its goal)?

13.   Impact of Monetary Policy How does the Fed's monetary policy affect economic conditions?

Advanced Questions

14.   Economic Indicators Stock market conditions serve as a leading economic indicator. Assuming the U.S. economy is currently in a recession, discuss the implications of this indicator. Why might this indicator possibly be inaccurate?

15.   The Fed's Impact on the Housing Market In some periods when home prices declined substantially, some homeowners blamed the Fed. In other periods when home prices increased, homeowners gave credit to the Fed. How can the Fed have such a large impact on home prices? Why would news that the general inflation level has increased substantially possibly affect the Fed's monetary policy and therefore affect home prices?

16.   Monetary Policy during the War in Iraq Consider the likely discussion that was occurring in the FOMC meetings when the war in Iraq began in 2003. The U.S. economy was weak at that time. Do you think the FOMC should have proposed a loose-money policy or a tight-money policy once the war began? This war could have resulted in major damage to oil wells. Explain why this possible effect would have received much attention at the FOMC meetings. If this possibility was perceived to be highly likely at the time of the meetings, explain how it may have complicated the decision about monetary policy at that time. Given the conditions stated in this question, would you have suggested that the Fed use a tight-money policy, a loose-money policy, or a stable-money policy? Support your decision with logic and acknowledge any adverse effects of your decision.

17.   Predicting the Fed's Actions Assume these existing conditions. The last time the FOMC met, it decided to raise interest rates. At that time economic growth was very strong, and as a result of the strong economy, inflation was relatively high. Since the last meeting, economic growth has weakened, and the unemployment rate will likely rise by 0.5 percentage point over the quarter. The FOMC's next meeting is tomorrow. Do you think the FOMC will revise its targeted federal funds rate, and if so, how?

18.   Impact of Foreign Policies Why might a foreign government's policies be closely monitored by investors in other countries, even if the investors plan no investments in that country? Explain how monetary policy in one country can affect interest rates in other countries.

19.   Impact of Inflation Targeting by the Fed Assume the Fed adopts an inflation targeting strategy. Describe how the Fed's monetary policy would be affected by an abrupt 15 percent rise in oil prices in response to an oil shortage. Do you think an inflation targeting strategy would be more or less effective in this situation than a strategy of balancing inflation concerns with unemployment concerns? Explain.

20.   Monetary Policy Today Assess the economic situation today. Is the administration more concerned with reducing unemployment or inflation? Does the Fed have a similar opinion? If not, is the administration publicly criticizing the Fed? Is the Fed publicly criticizing the administration? Explain.

21.   How the Fed Should Respond to Prevailing Conditions Consider the current economic conditions, including inflation and economic growth. Do you think the Fed should increase interest rates, reduce interest rates, or leave interest rates at their present levels? Offer some logic to support your answer.

22. Interpreting the Fed's Monetary Policy

When the Fed increases the money supply to lower the federal funds rate, will the cost of capital to U.S. companies be reduced? Explain how the segmented markets theory regarding the term structure of interest rates could influence the degree to which the Fed's monetary policy affects long-term interest rates.

Interpreting Financial News

Interpret the following statements made by Wall Street analysts and portfolio managers:

a. "Lately, the Fed's policies are driven by gold prices and other indicators of the future rather than by recent economic data."

b. "The Fed cannot boost money growth at this time because of the weak dollar."

c. "The Fed's fine-tuning may distort the economic picture."

Managing in Financial Markets

Forecasting Monetary Policy As a manager of a firm, you are concerned about a potential increase in interest rates, which would reduce the demand for your firm's products. The Fed is scheduled to meet in one week to assess economic conditions and set monetary policy. Economic growth has been high, but inflation has also increased from 3 percent to 5 percent (annualized) over the last four months. The level of unemployment is very low and cannot possibly go much lower.

a. Given the situation, is the Fed likely to adjust monetary policy? If so, how?

b. Recently, the Fed has allowed the money supply to expand beyond its long-term target range. Does this affect your expectation of what the Fed will decide at its upcoming meeting?

c. Assume that the Fed has just learned that the Treasury will need to borrow a larger amount of funds than originally expected. Explain how this information may affect the degree to which the Fed changes the monetary policy.

FLOW OF FUNDS EXERCISE

Anticipating Fed Actions

Recall that Carson Company has obtained substantial loans from finance companies and commercial banks. The interest rate on the loans is tied to market interest rates and is adjusted every six months. Because of its expectations of a strong U.S. economy, Carson plans to grow in the future by expanding the business and by making acquisitions. It expects that it will need substantial long-term financing and plans to borrow additional funds either through loans or by issuing bonds. It also considers issuing stock to raise funds in the next year.

An economic report just noted the strong growth in the economy, which has caused the economy to be close to full employment. In addition, the report estimated that the annualized inflation rate increased to 5 percent, up from 2 percent last month. The factors that caused the higher inflation (shortages of products and shortages of labor) are expected to continue.

a. How will the Fed's monetary policy change based on the report?

b. How will the likely change in the Fed's monetary policy affect Carson's future performance? Could it affect Carson's plans for future expansion?

c. Explain how a tight monetary policy could affect the amount of funds borrowed at financial institutions by deficit units such as Carson Company. How might it affect the credit risk of deficit units such as Carson Company? How might it affect the performance of financial institutions that provide credit to deficit units such as Carson Company?

INTERNET/EXCEL EXERCISES

1. Go to the website www.federalreserve.gov/monetarypolicy/fomc.htm to review the activities of the FOMC. Succinctly summarize the minutes of the last FOMC meeting. What did the FOMC discuss at the last meeting? Did the FOMC make any changes in the current monetary policy? What is the FOMC's current monetary policy?

2. Is the Fed's present policy focused more on stimulating the economy or on reducing inflation? Or is the present policy evenly balanced? Explain.

3. Using the website www.research.stlouisfed.org/fred2/, retrieve interest rate data at the beginning of the last 20 quarters for the federal funds rate and the three-month Treasury bill (T-bill) rate, and place the data in two columns of an Excel spreadsheet. Derive the change in interest rates on a quarterly basis. Apply regression analysis in which the quarterly change in the T-bill rate is the dependent variable (see Appendix B for more information about using regression analysis). If the Fed's effect on the federal funds rate influences other interest rates (such as the T-bill rate), there should be a positive and significant relationship between the interest rates. Is there a positive relationship? Explain.

WSJ EXERCISE

Market Assessment of Fed Policy

Review a recent issue of *The Wall Street Journal*. Summarize the market's expectations about future interest rates. Are these expectations based primarily on the Fed's monetary policy or on other factors?

Fed Watching

This problem requires an understanding of the Fed (Chapter 4) and monetary policy (Chapter 5). It also requires an understanding of how economic conditions affect interest rates and securities' prices (Chapters 2 and 3).

Like many other investors, you are a "Fed watcher," who constantly monitors any actions taken by the Fed to revise monetary policy. You believe that three key factors affect interest rates. Assume that the most important factor is the Fed's monetary policy. The second most important factor is the state of the economy, which influences the demand for loanable funds. The third factor is the level of inflation, which also influences the demand for loanable funds. Because monetary policy can affect interest rates, it affects economic growth as well. By controlling monetary policy, the Fed influences the prices of all types of securities.

The following information is available:

- Economic growth has been consistently strong over the past few years but is beginning to slow down.

- Unemployment is as low as it has been in the past decade but has risen slightly over the past two quarters.

- Inflation has been about 5 percent per year for the past few years.

- The dollar has been strong.

- Oil prices have been very low.

Yesterday, an event occurred that you believe will cause much higher oil prices in the United States and a weaker U.S. economy in the near future. You plan to determine whether the Fed will respond to the economic problems that are likely to develop.

You have reviewed previous economic slowdowns caused by a decline in the aggregate demand for goods and services and found that each slowdown precipitated a loose-money policy by the Fed. Inflation was 3 percent or less in each of the previous economic slowdowns. Interest rates generally declined in response to these policies and the U.S. economy improved.

Assume that the Fed's philosophy regarding monetary policy is to maintain economic growth and low inflation. There does not appear to be any major fiscal policy forthcoming that will have a major effect on the economy. Thus, the future economy is up to the Fed. The Fed's present policy is to maintain a 2 percent annual growth rate in the money supply. You believe that the economy is headed toward a recession unless the Fed uses a very stimulative monetary policy, such as a 10 percent annual growth rate in the money supply.

The general consensus of economists is that the Fed will revise its monetary policy to stimulate the economy for three reasons: (1) it recognizes the potential costs of higher unemployment if a recession occurs, (2) it has consistently used a stimulative policy in the past to prevent recessions, and (3) the administration has been pressuring the Fed to use a stimulative monetary policy. Although you will consider the economists' opinions, you plan to make your own assessment of the Fed's future policy. Two quarters ago, GDP declined by 1 percent. Last quarter, GDP declined again by 1 percent. Thus, there is clear evidence that the economy has recently slowed down.

Questions

1. Do you think that the Fed will use a stimulative monetary policy at this point? Explain.

2. You maintain a large portfolio of U.S. bonds. You believe that if the Fed does not revise its monetary policy, the U.S. economy will continue to decline. If the Fed stimulates the economy at this point, you believe that you would be better off with stocks than with bonds. Based on this information, do you think you should switch to stocks? Explain.

PART 3

Debt Security Markets

Part 3 focuses on how debt security markets facilitate the flow of funds from surplus units to deficit units. Chapter 6 focuses on money markets for investors and borrowers trading short-term securities. Chapters 7 and 8 focus on the bond markets, and Chapter 9 focuses on the mortgage markets. Because some financial market participants trade securities in all of these markets, there is much interaction among these markets, as emphasized throughout the chapters.

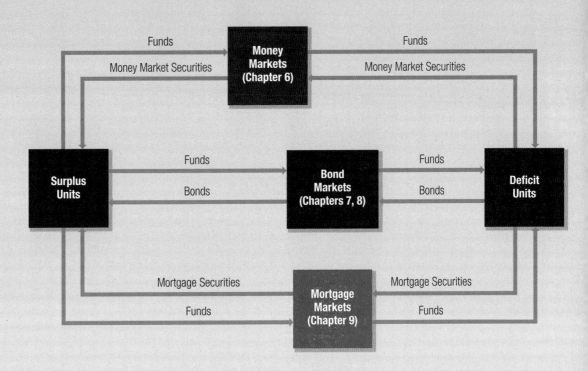

6

Money Markets

The specific objectives of this chapter are to:

- describe the features of the most popular money market securities,

- explain how money markets are used by institutional investors,

- explain the valuation and risk of money market securities, and

- explain how money markets have become globally integrated.

Money markets are used to facilitate the transfer of short-term funds from individuals, corporations, or governments with excess funds to those with deficient funds. Even investors who focus on long-term securities tend to hold some money market securities. Money markets enable financial market participants to maintain liquidity.

MONEY MARKET SECURITIES

Money market securities are debt securities with a maturity of one year or less. They are issued in the primary market through a telecommunications network by the Treasury, corporations, and financial intermediaries that wish to obtain short-term financing. The means by which money markets facilitate the flow of funds are illustrated in Exhibit 6.1. The U.S. Treasury issues money market securities (Treasury bills) and uses the proceeds to finance the budget deficit. Corporations issue money market securities and use the proceeds to support their existing operations or to expand their operations. Financial institutions issue money market securities and bundle the proceeds to make loans to households or corporations. Thus, the funds are channeled to support household purchases, such as cars and homes, and to support corporate investment in buildings and machinery. The Treasury and some corporations commonly pay off their debt from maturing money market securities with the proceeds from issuing new money market securities. In this way, they are able to finance expenditures for long periods of time even though money market securities have short-term maturities. Overall, money markets allow households, corporations, and the U.S. government to increase their expenditures; thus, the markets finance economic growth.

Money market securities are commonly purchased by households, corporations (including financial institutions), and government agencies that have funds available for a short-term period. Because money market securities have a short-term maturity and can typically be sold in the secondary market, they provide liquidity to investors. Most firms and financial institutions maintain some holdings of money market securities for this reason.

The more popular money market securities are

- Treasury bills
- Commercial paper
- Negotiable certificates of deposit
- Repurchase agreements
- Federal funds
- Banker's acceptances

Each of these instruments is described in turn.

Exhibit 6.1 How Money Markets Facilitate the Flow of Funds

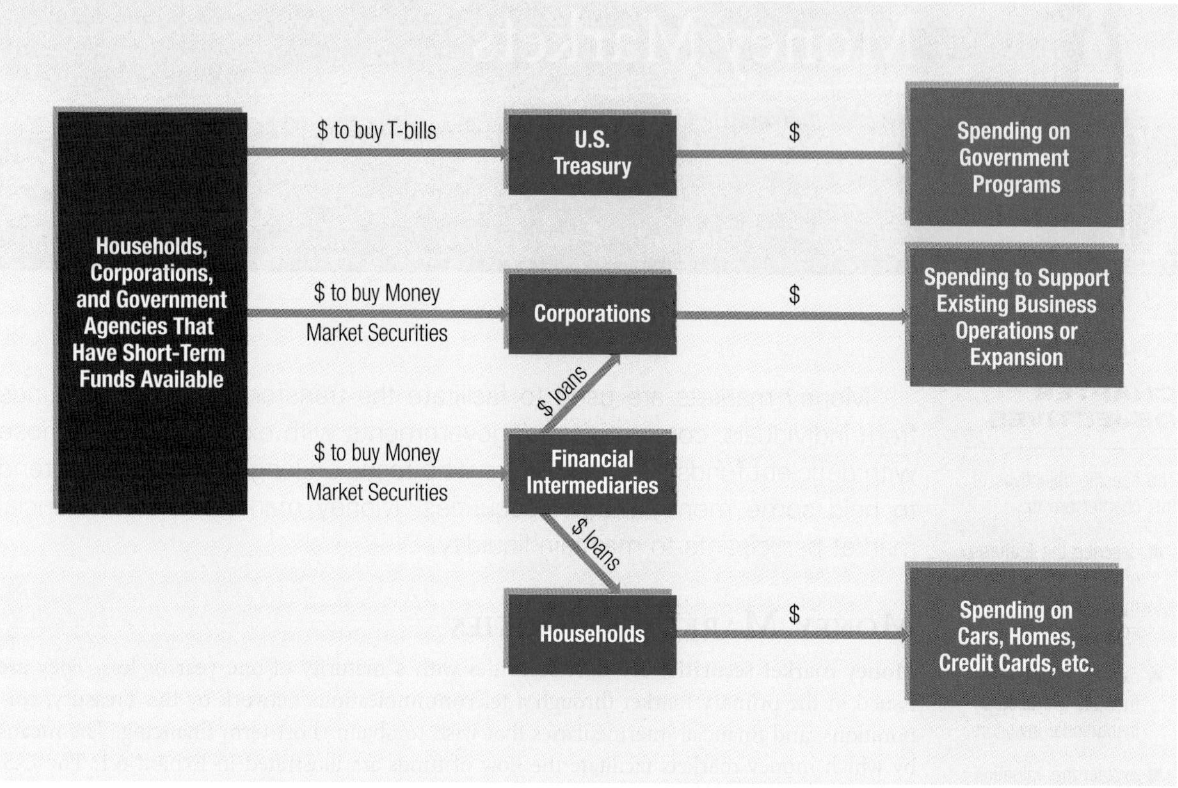

Treasury Bills

When the U.S. government needs to borrow funds, the U.S. Treasury frequently issues short-term securities known as Treasury bills (or T-bills). The Treasury issues T-bills with 4-week, 13-week, and 26-week maturities on a weekly basis. It periodically issues T-bills called cash management bills that have shorter-term maturities. It also issues T-bills with a one-year maturity on a monthly basis. T-bills used to be issued in paper form but are now maintained electronically. The par value (amount received by investors at maturity) of T-bills was historically a minimum of $10,000, but is now $1,000 and in multiples of $1,000 thereafter. Since T-bills do not pay interest, they are sold at a discount from par value, and the gain to an investor holding a T-bill until maturity is the difference between par value and the price paid.

T-bills are attractive to investors because they are backed by the federal government and therefore are virtually free of credit (default) risk. Another attractive feature of T-bills is their liquidity, which is due to their short maturity and strong secondary market. Existing T-bills can be sold in the secondary market through government securities dealers, who profit by purchasing the bills at a slightly lower price than the price at which they sell them.

Investors in Treasury Bills   Depository institutions commonly invest in T-bills so that they can retain a portion of their funds in assets that can easily be liquidated if they suddenly need to accommodate deposit withdrawals. Other financial institutions also invest in T-bills in the event that they need cash because cash outflows exceed cash inflows. Individuals with substantial savings invest in T-bills for liquidity purposes. Many individuals invest in T-bills indirectly by investing in money market funds, which in turn purchase large amounts of T-bills. Corporations invest in T-bills so that they have easy access to funding if they suddenly incur unanticipated expenses.

Pricing Treasury Bills   As mentioned, T-bills do not pay interest, but are priced at a discount from their par value. The price that an investor will pay for a T-bill with a particular maturity is dependent on the investor's required rate of return on that T-bill. That price is determined as the present value of the future cash flows to be received. Since the T-bill does not generate interest payments, the value of a T-bill is the present value of the par value. Thus, investors are willing to pay a price for a one-year T-bill that ensures that the amount they receive a year later will generate their desired return.

EXAMPLE

If investors require a 7 percent annualized return on a one-year T-bill with a $10,000 par value, the price that they are willing to pay is

$$P = \$10,000/1.07$$
$$= \$9,345.79$$

If the investors require a higher return, they will discount the $10,000 at that higher rate of return, which will result in a lower price that they are willing to pay today. You can verify this by estimating the price based on a required return of 8 percent and then on a required return of 9 percent. ●

To price a T-bill with a maturity shorter than one year, the annualized return can be reduced by the fraction of the year in which funds will be invested.

EXAMPLE

If investors require a 6 percent annualized return on a six-month T- bill, this reflects a 3 percent unannualized return over six months. The price that they will be willing to pay for a T-bill with a par value of $10,000 is

$$P = \$10,000/1.03$$
$$= \$9,708.74$$ ●

Treasury Bill Auction   The primary T-bill market is an auction. Individual investors can submit bids online for newly issued T-bills at www.treasurydirect.gov.

Financial institutions can submit their bids for T-bills (and other Treasury securities) online using the Treasury Automated Auction Processing System (TAAPSLink*).* Individuals and financial institutions can set up an account with the Treasury. Then they can select the specific maturity and face value that they desire and submit their bids electronically. Payments to the Treasury are withdrawn electronically from the account, and payments received from the Treasury when the securities mature are deposited electronically into the account.

At the auctions, investors have the option of bidding competitively or noncompetitively. The Treasury has a specified amount of funds that it plans to borrow, which dictates the amount of T-bill bids that it will accept for that maturity. Investors who wish to ensure that their bids will be accepted can use noncompetitive bids. Noncompetitive bidders are limited to purchasing T-bills with a maximum par value of $5 million per auction, however. Consequently, large corporations typically make competitive bids so that they can purchase larger amounts.

After accounting for noncompetitive bids, the Treasury accepts the highest competitive bids first and works it way down until it has generated the amount of funds from competitive bids that it needs. Any bids below that cutoff point are not accepted. The Treasury applies the lowest accepted bid price to all competitive bids that are accepted and to all noncompetitive bids. Thus, the price paid by competitive and noncompetitive bidders reflects the lowest price of the competitive bids. Competitive bids are still submitted because, as noted above, many bidders want to purchase more T-bills than the maximum that can be purchased on a noncompetitive basis.

WEB

www.treasurydirect .gov
Results of recent Treasury bill auctions.

The results of the weekly auction of 13-week and 26-week T-bills are summarized in the financial media each Tuesday and are also provided online at the Treasury's TreasuryDirect website. Some of the more commonly reported statistics are the dollar amount of applications and Treasury securities sold, the average price of the accepted competitive bids, and the coupon equivalent (annualized yield) for investors who paid the average price.

Exhibit 6.2 Example of Treasury Bill Auction Results

	13-WEEK TREASURY BILL AUCTION	26-WEEK TREASURY BILL AUCTION
Applications	\$44,685,977,000	\$45,991,246,000
Accepted bids	\$19,022,977,000	\$18,005,496,000
Average price of accepted bids (per \$100 par value)	\$98.792	\$97.508
Coupon equivalent (yield)	4.918%	5.139%

Source: *The Wall Street Journal.* See *The Wall Street Journal* on any Tuesday for the information pertaining to Monday's Treasury bill auction.

WEB

www.federalreserve.gov/econresdata
Click on "Statistical Releases and Historical Data" to find a database of Treasury bill rates over time.

WEB

http://research.stlouisfed.org
Obtain yields offered on T-bills and various other money market securities.

An example of results from a recent T-bill auction are shown in Exhibit 6.2. At each auction, the prices paid for six-month T-bills are significantly lower than the prices paid for three-month T-bills because the investment term is longer. The lower price results in a higher unannualized yield that compensates investors for their longer-term investment.

Estimating the Yield As explained earlier, T-bills do not offer coupon payments but are sold at a discount from par value. Their yield is influenced by the difference between the selling price and the purchase price. If an investor purchases a newly issued T-bill and holds it until maturity, the return is based on the difference between the par value and the purchase price. If the T-bill is sold prior to maturity, the return is based on the difference between the price for which the bill was sold in the secondary market and the purchase price.

The annualized yield from investing in a T-bill (Y_T) can be determined as

$$Y_T = \frac{SP - PP}{PP} \times \frac{365}{n}$$

where SP = **selling price**
PP = **purchase price**
n = **number of days of the investment (holding period)**

EXAMPLE

An investor purchases a T-bill with a six-month (182-day) maturity and \$10,000 par value for \$9,600. If this T-bill is held to maturity, its yield is

$$Y_T = \frac{\$10{,}000 - \$9{,}600}{\$9{,}600} \times \frac{365}{182} = 8.36\%$$

If the T-bill is sold prior to maturity, the selling price and therefore the yield are dependent on market conditions at the time of the sale.

Suppose the investor plans to sell the T-bill after 120 days and forecasts a selling price of \$9,820 at that time. The expected annualized yield based on this forecast is

$$Y_T = \frac{\$9{,}820 - \$9{,}600}{\$9{,}600} \times \frac{365}{120} = 6.97\%$$

The higher the forecasted selling price, the higher the expected annualized yield. ●

Estimating the Treasury Bill Discount Some business periodicals quote the T-bill discount along with the T-bill yield. The T-bill discount represents the percent discount of the purchase price from par value (Par) for newly issued T-bills and is computed as

$$\text{T-bill discount} = \frac{\text{Par} - PP}{\text{Par}} \times \frac{360}{n}$$

A 360-day year is used to compute the T-bill discount.

EXAMPLE

Using the information from the previous example, the T-bill discount is

$$\text{T-bill discount} = \frac{\$10{,}000 - \$9{,}600}{\$10{,}000} \times \frac{360}{182} = 7.91\%$$

For a newly issued T-bill that is held to maturity, the T-bill yield will always be higher than the discount. The difference occurs because the purchase price is the denominator of the yield equation, while the par value is the denominator of the T-bill discount equation, and the par value will always exceed the purchase price of a newly issued T-bill. In addition, the yield formula uses a 365-day year versus a 360-day year for the discount computation.

Commercial Paper

WEB

www.federalreserve
.gov/releases/cp/
about.htm

Provides valuable information about commercial paper.

Commercial paper is a short-term debt instrument issued only by well-known, creditworthy firms and is typically unsecured. It is normally issued to provide liquidity or finance a firm's investment in inventory and accounts receivable. The issuance of commercial paper is an alternative to short-term bank loans. Financial institutions such as finance companies and bank holding companies are major issuers of commercial paper.

The minimum denomination of commercial paper is usually $100,000. The typical denominations are in multiples of $1 million. Maturities are normally between 20 and 45 days but can be as short as one day or as long as 270 days. The 270-day maximum is due to a Securities and Exchange Commission (SEC) ruling that paper with a maturity exceeding 270 days must be registered.

Because of the high minimum denomination, individual investors rarely purchase commercial paper directly although they may invest in it indirectly by investing in money market funds that have pooled the funds of many individuals. Money market funds are major investors in commercial paper. An active secondary market for commercial paper does not exist. However, it is sometimes possible to sell the paper back to the dealer who initially helped to place it. In most cases, investors hold commercial paper until maturity. The secondary market for commercial paper is very limited.

Ratings   Since commercial paper is issued by corporations that are susceptible to business failure, the commercial paper could possibly default. The risk of default is influenced by the issuer's financial condition and cash flow. Investors can attempt to assess the probability that commercial paper will default by monitoring the issuer's financial condition. The focus is on the issuer's ability to repay its debt over the short term because the payments will be completed within a short-term period. The rating serves as an indicator of the potential risk of default. Money market funds can invest only in commercial paper that has a top-tier or second-tier rating, and second-tier paper cannot represent more than 5 percent of their assets. Thus, corporations can more easily place commercial paper that is assigned a top-tier rating. The ratings are assigned by rating agencies such as Moody's Investors Service, Standard & Poor's Corporation, and Fitch Investor Service. Some commercial paper (called **junk commercial paper**) is rated low or not rated at all.

Credit Risk during the Credit Crisis   Although issuers of commercial paper are subject to possible default, historically the percentage of issues that have defaulted is very low, as most issuers of commercial paper are very strong financially. In addition, the short time period of the credit reduces the chance that an issuer will suffer financial problems before repaying the funds borrowed. However, during the credit crisis in 2008, Lehman Brothers (a large securities firm) failed, which made investors more cautious before purchasing securities, as discussed later in this chapter.

Placement Some firms place commercial paper directly with investors. Other firms rely on commercial paper dealers to sell their commercial paper, at a transaction cost of about one-eighth of 1 percent of the face value. This transaction cost is generally less than it would cost to establish a department within the firm to place commercial paper directly. Companies that frequently issue commercial paper may reduce expenses by creating an in-house department, however. Most nonfinancial companies use commercial paper dealers rather than in-house resources to place their commercial paper. Their liquidity needs, and therefore their commercial paper issues, are cyclical, so they would use an in-house direct-placement department only a few times during the year. Finance companies typically maintain an in-house department because they frequently borrow in this manner.

Backing Commercial Paper Issuers of commercial paper typically maintain backup lines of credit in case they cannot roll over (reissue) commercial paper at a reasonable rate because, for example, their assigned rating was lowered. A backup line of credit provided by a commercial bank gives the company the right (but not the obligation) to borrow a specified maximum amount of funds over a specified period of time. The fee for the line can either be a direct percentage of the total accessible credit (such as 0.5 percent) or be in the form of required compensating balances (such as 10 percent of the line).

Estimating the Yield Like T-bills, commercial paper does not pay interest, but is priced at a discount from par value. At a given point in time, the yield on commercial paper is slightly higher than the yield on a T-bill with the same maturity because commercial paper carries some credit risk and is less liquid. The nominal return to investors who retain the paper until maturity is the difference between the price paid for the paper and the par value. Thus, the yield received by a commercial paper investor can be determined in a manner similar to the T-bill yield, although a 360-day year is usually used.

EXAMPLE

If an investor purchases 30-day commercial paper with a par value of $1,000,000 for a price of $990,000, the yield ($Y_{cp}$) is

$$Y_{cp} = \frac{\$1,000,000 - \$990,000}{\$990,000} \times \frac{360}{30}$$

$$= 12.12\%$$

When a firm plans to issue commercial paper, the price (and therefore yield) to investors is uncertain. Thus, the cost of borrowing funds is uncertain until the paper is issued. Consider the case of a firm that plans to issue 90-day commercial paper with a par value of $5,000,000. It expects to sell the commercial paper for $4,850,000. The yield it expects to pay investors (its cost of borrowing) is estimated to be

$$Y_{cp} = \frac{Par - PP}{PP} \times \frac{360}{n}$$

$$= \frac{\$5,000,000 - \$4,850,000}{\$4,850,000} \times \frac{360}{90}$$

$$= 12.37\%$$

WEB

www.federalreserve
.gov/releases/cp
Provides information on current commercial paper rates as well as a database of commercial paper rates over time.

When firms sell their commercial paper at a lower (higher) price than projected, their cost of raising funds will be higher (lower) than they initially anticipated. For example, if the firm had initially sold the commercial paper for $4,865,000, the cost of borrowing would have been about 11.1 percent. (Check the math as an exercise.)

Ignoring transaction costs, the cost of borrowing with commercial paper is equal to the yield earned by investors holding the paper until maturity. The cost of borrowing can be adjusted for transaction costs (charged by the commercial paper dealers) by subtracting the nominal transaction fees from the price received.

Some corporations prefer to issue commercial paper rather than borrow from a bank because it is usually a cheaper source of funds. Nevertheless, even the large creditworthy corporations that are able to issue commercial paper normally obtain some short-term loans from commercial banks in order to maintain a business relationship with them.

Commercial Paper Yield Curve   The commercial paper yield curve represents the yield offered on commercial paper at various maturities. The curve is typically established for a maturity range from 0 to 90 days because most commercial paper has a maturity within that range. This yield curve is important because it may influence the maturity that is used by firms that issue commercial paper and by the institutional investors that purchase commercial paper. The shape of this yield curve could be roughly drawn from the short-term range of the traditional Treasury yield curve. However, that curve is graphed over a long time period, so it is difficult to derive the precise shape of a yield curve over a three-month range from that graph.

The same factors that affect the Treasury yield curve affect the commercial paper yield curve, but are applied to very short-term horizons. In particular, expectations of interest over the next few months can influence the commercial paper yield curve.

Negotiable Certificates of Deposit (NCDs)

Negotiable certificates of deposit (NCDs) are certificates that are issued by large commercial banks and other depository institutions as a short-term source of funds. The minimum denomination is $100,000, although a $1 million denomination is more common. Nonfinancial corporations often purchase NCDs. Although NCD denominations are typically too large for individual investors, they are sometimes purchased by money market funds that have pooled individual investors' funds. Thus, money market funds allow individuals to be indirect investors in NCDs, creating a more active NCD market.

Maturities on NCDs normally range from two weeks to one year. A secondary market for NCDs exists, providing investors with some liquidity. However, institutions prefer not to have their newly issued NCDs compete with their previously issued NCDs that are being resold in the secondary market. An oversupply of NCDs for sale can force them to sell their newly issued NCDs at a lower price.

Placement   Some issuers place their NCDs directly; others use a correspondent institution that specializes in placing NCDs. Another alternative is to sell NCDs to securities dealers, who in turn resell them. A portion of unusually large issues is commonly sold to NCD dealers. Normally, however, NCDs can be sold to investors directly at a higher price.

Premium   NCDs must offer a premium above the T-bill yield to compensate for less liquidity and safety. The premiums are generally higher during recessionary periods. The premiums also reflect the market's perception about the safety of the financial system.

Yield   NCDs provide a return in the form of interest along with the difference between the price at which the NCD is redeemed (or sold in the secondary market) and the purchase price. Given that an institution issues an NCD at par value, the annualized yield that it will pay is the annualized interest rate on the NCD. If investors purchase this NCD and hold it until maturity, their annualized yield is the interest rate. However, the annualized yield can differ from the annualized interest rate for investors who either purchase or sell the NCD in the secondary market instead of holding it from inception until maturity.

An investor purchased an NCD a year ago in the secondary market for $970,000. He redeems it today upon maturity and receives $1,000,000. He also receives interest of $40,000. His annualized yield (Y_{NCD}) on this investment is

$$Y_{NCD} = \frac{SP - PP + \text{interest}}{PP}$$
$$= \frac{\$1,000,000 - \$970,000 + \$40,000}{\$970,000}$$
$$= 7.22\%$$

Repurchase Agreements

With a repurchase agreement (or repo), one party sells securities to another with an agreement to repurchase the securities at a specified date and price. In essence, the repo transaction represents a loan backed by the securities. If the borrower defaults on the loan, the lender has claim to the securities. Most repo transactions use government securities, although some involve other securities such as commercial paper or NCDs. A **reverse repo** refers to the purchase of securities by one party from another with an agreement to sell them. Thus, a repo and a reverse repo can refer to the same transaction but from different perspectives. These two terms are sometimes used interchangeably, so a transaction described as a repo may actually be a reverse repo.

Financial institutions such as banks, savings and loan associations, and money market funds often participate in repurchase agreements. Many nonfinancial institutions are active participants as well. The size of the repo market is about $4.5 trillion. Transaction amounts are usually for $10 million or more. The most common maturities are from one day to 15 days and for one, three, and six months. A secondary market for repos does not exist. Some firms in need of funds will set the maturity on a repo to be the minimum time period for which they need temporary financing. If they still need funds when the repo is about to mature, they will borrow additional funds through new repos and use these funds to fulfill their obligation on maturing repos.

Placement   Repo transactions are negotiated through a telecommunications network. Dealers and repo brokers act as financial intermediaries to create repos for firms with deficient and excess funds, receiving a commission for their services.

When the borrowing firm can find a counterparty to the repo transaction, it avoids the transaction fee involved in having a government securities dealer find the counterparty. Some companies that commonly engage in repo transactions have an in-house department for finding counterparties and executing the transactions. These same companies that borrow through repos may, from time to time, serve as the lender. That is, they purchase the government securities and agree to sell them back in the near future. Because the cash flow of any large company changes on a daily basis, it is not unusual for a firm to act as an investor one day (when it has excess funds) and a borrower the next (when it has a cash shortage).

Impact of the Credit Crisis   During the credit crisis in 2008, the values of mortgage securities declined, and financial institutions participating in the housing market were exposed to more risk. Consequently, many financial institutions that relied on the repo market for funding were not able to obtain funds. Investors became more concerned about the securities that were posted as collateral. Bear Stearns, a large securities firm, relied heavily on repos for funding and used mortgage securities as collateral. But the valuation of these types of securities was subject to much uncertainty because of the credit crisis. Consequently, investors were unwilling to provide funding, and Bear Stearns could not obtain sufficient financing. It avoided bankruptcy only with the aid of the federal government. The lesson of this example is that repo market funding requires collateral that is trusted by investors, and when economic conditions are weak, some securities may not serve as adequate collateral to obtain funding.

Estimating the Yield   The repo rate is determined by the difference between the initial selling price of the securities and the agreed-on repurchase price, annualized with a 360-day year.

EXAMPLE   An investor initially purchased securities at a price *(PP)* of $9,852,217, with an agreement to sell them back at a price *(SP)* of $10,000,000 at the end of a 60-day period. The yield (or repo rate) on this repurchase agreement is

$$\begin{aligned} \text{Repo rate} &= \frac{SP - PP}{PP} \times \frac{360}{n} \\ &= \frac{\$10{,}000{,}000 - \$9{,}852{,}217}{\$9{,}852{,}217} \times \frac{360}{60} \\ &= 9\% \end{aligned}$$

Federal Funds

WEB

www.federalreserve
.gov/fomc/fundsrate
.htm

Provides an excellent
summary of the Fed's
adjustment in the fed-
eral funds rate over
time.

The federal funds market allows depository institutions to effectively lend or borrow short-term funds from each other at the so-called **federal funds rate.** The federal funds rate is the rate charged on federal funds transactions. It is influenced by the supply of and demand for funds in the federal funds market. The Federal Reserve adjusts the amount of funds in depository institutions in order to influence the federal funds rate (as explained in Chapter 4) and several other short-term interest rates. All types of firms closely monitor the federal funds rate because the Federal Reserve manipulates it to affect general economic conditions. Many market participants view changes in the federal funds rate as an indicator of potential changes in other money market rates.

The federal funds rate is normally slightly higher than the T-bill rate at any point in time. A lender in the federal funds market is subject to credit risk, since it is possible that the financial institution borrowing the funds could default on the loan. Once a loan transaction is agreed upon, the lending institution can instruct its Federal Reserve district bank to debit its reserve account and to credit the borrowing institution's reserve account by the amount of the loan. If the loan is for just one day, it will likely be based on an oral agreement between the parties, especially if the institutions commonly do business with each other.

Commercial banks are the most active participants in the federal funds market. Federal funds brokers serve as financial intermediaries in the market, matching up institutions that wish to sell (lend) funds with those that wish to purchase (borrow) them. The brokers receive a commission for their service. The transactions are negotiated through a telecommunications network that links federal funds brokers with the participating institutions. Most loan transactions are for $5 million or more and usually have a one- to seven-day maturity (although the loans may often be extended by the lender if the borrower desires more time).

The volume of interbank loans on commercial bank balance sheets over time is an indication of the importance of lending between depository institutions. The interbank loan volume outstanding now exceeds $200 billion.

Banker's Acceptances

A **banker's acceptance** indicates that a bank accepts responsibility for a future payment. Banker's acceptances are commonly used for international trade transactions. An exporter that is sending goods to an importer whose credit rating is not known will often prefer that a bank act as a guarantor. The bank therefore facilitates the transaction by stamping ACCEPTED on a draft, which obligates payment at a specified point in time. In turn, the importer will pay the bank what is owed to the exporter along with a fee to the bank for guaranteeing the payment.

Exporters can hold a banker's acceptance until the date at which payment is to be made, but they frequently sell the acceptance before then at a discount to obtain cash immediately. The investor who purchases the acceptance then receives the payment guaranteed by the bank in the future. The investor's return on a banker's acceptance, like that on commercial paper, is derived from the difference between the discounted price paid for the acceptance and the amount to be received in the future. Maturities

USING THE WALL STREET JOURNAL

Rates on Banker's Acceptances

The Wall Street Journal provides rates on banker's acceptances (as shown here), the federal funds rate, Treasury bill rates, and rates of other money market securities for various maturities. For the banker's acceptance shown here, the first column shows the latest quote while the second column shows the rate one week ago. The third column discloses the highest rate over the last year, and the fourth column discloses the lowest rate over the last year. Some institutional investors assess rates of banker's acceptances, Treasury bills, and other money market securities when considering whether to make investments in these types of securities.

Bankers acceptances				
30 days	**0.50**	0.75	5.13	0.50
60 days	**1.25**	1.00	5.13	0.88
90 days	**1.25**	1.33	5.00	1.13
120 days	**1.50**	1.50	5.00	1.50
150 days	**1.50**	1.50	5.00	1.50
180 days	**1.75**	1.75	5.00	1.75

on banker's acceptances often range from 30 to 270 days. Because there is a possibility that a bank will default on payment, investors are exposed to a slight degree of credit risk. Thus, they deserve a return above the T-bill yield as compensation.

Because acceptances are often discounted and sold by the exporting firm prior to maturity, an active secondary market exists. Dealers match up companies that wish to sell acceptances with other companies that wish to purchase them. A dealer's bid price is less than its ask price, which creates the spread, or the dealer's reward for doing business. The spread is normally between one-eighth and seven-eighths of 1 percent.

Steps Involved in Banker's Acceptances   The sequence of steps involved in a banker's acceptance is illustrated in Exhibit 6.3. To understand these steps, consider the example of a U.S. importer of Japanese goods. First, the importer places a purchase order for the goods (Step 1). If the Japanese exporter is unfamiliar with the U.S. importer, it may demand payment before delivery of goods, which the U.S. importer may be unwilling to make. A compromise may be reached through the creation of a banker's acceptance. The importer asks its bank to issue a **letter of credit (L/C)** on its behalf (Step 2). The L/C represents a commitment by that bank to back the payment owed to the Japanese exporter. Then the L/C is presented to the exporter's bank (Step 3), which informs the exporter that the L/C has been received (Step 4). The exporter then sends the goods to the importer (Step 5) and sends the shipping documents to its bank (Step 6), which passes them along to the importer's bank (Step 7). At this point, the banker's acceptance is created, which obligates the importer's bank to make payment to the holder of the banker's acceptance at a specified future date. The banker's acceptance may be sold to a money market investor at a discount. Potential purchasers of acceptances are short-term investors. When the acceptance matures, the importer pays its bank, which in turn pays the money market investor who presents the acceptance.

The creation of a banker's acceptance allows the importer to receive goods from an exporter without sending immediate payment. The selling of the acceptance creates financing for the exporter. Even though banker's acceptances are often created to facilitate international transactions, they are not limited to money market investors with international experience. Investors who purchase acceptances are more concerned with the

Exhibit 6.3 Sequence of Steps in the Creation of a Banker's Acceptance

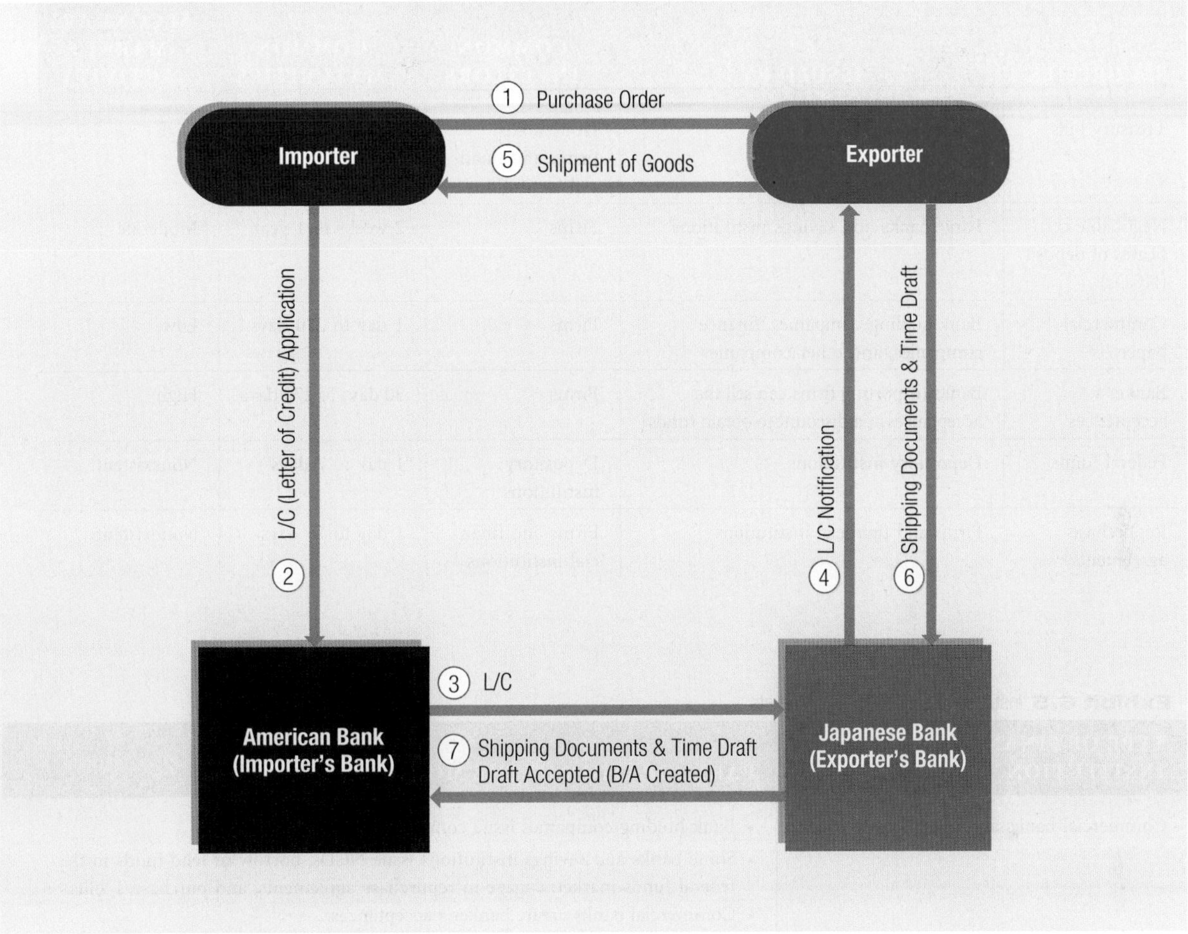

credit of the bank that guarantees payment than with the credit of the exporter or importer. For this reason, the credit risk on a banker's acceptance is somewhat similar to that of NCDs issued by commercial banks. Because acceptances have the backing of the bank as well as the importing firm, however, they may be perceived as having slightly less credit risk than NCDs.

The money market securities are summarized in Exhibit 6.4. When money market securities are issued to obtain funds, the type of securities issued depends on whether the issuer is the Treasury, a depository institution, or a corporation. When investors decide which type of money market securities to invest in, their choice is dependent on the desired return and liquidity characteristics.

INSTITUTIONAL USE OF MONEY MARKETS

The institutional use of money market securities is summarized in Exhibit 6.5. Financial institutions purchase money market securities in order to simultaneously earn a return and maintain adequate liquidity. They issue money market securities when experiencing a temporary shortage of cash. Because money markets serve businesses, the average transaction is very large and is typically executed through a telecommunications network.

Exhibit 6.4 Survey of Commonly Issued Money Market Securities

SECURITIES	ISSUED BY	COMMON INVESTORS	COMMON MATURITIES	SECONDARY MARKET ACTIVITY
Treasury bills	Federal government	Households, firms, and financial institutions	13 weeks, 26 weeks, 1 year	High
Negotiable certificates of deposit (NCDs)	Large banks and savings institutions	Firms	2 weeks to 1 year	Moderate
Commercial paper	Bank holding companies, finance companies, and other companies	Firms	1 day to 270 days	Low
Banker's acceptances	Banks (exporting firms can sell the acceptances at a discount to obtain funds)	Firms	30 days to 270 days	High
Federal funds	Depository institutions	Depository institutions	1 day to 7 days	Nonexistent
Repurchase agreements	Firms and financial institutions	Firms and financial institutions	1 day to 15 days	Nonexistent

Exhibit 6.5 Institutional Use of Money Markets

TYPE OF FINANCIAL INSTITUTION	PARTICIPATION IN THE MONEY MARKETS
Commercial banks and savings institutions	• Bank holding companies issue commercial paper. • Some banks and savings institutions issue NCDs, borrow or lend funds in the federal funds market, engage in repurchase agreements, and purchase T-bills. • Commercial banks create banker's acceptances. • Commercial bank provide backup lines of credit to corporations that issue commercial paper.
Finance companies	• Issue large amounts of commercial paper.
Money market mutual funds	• Use proceeds from shares sold to invest in T-bills, commmercial paper, NCDs, repurchase agreements, and banker's acceptances.
Insurance companies	• May maintain a portion of their investment portfolio as money market securities for liquidity.
Pension funds	• May maintain a portion of their investment portfolio as money market securities that may be liquidated when portfolio managers desire to increase their investment in bonds or stocks.

Money market securities can be used to enhance liquidity in two ways. First, newly issued securities generate cash. The institutions that issue new securities have created a short-term liability in order to boost their cash balance. Second, institutions that previously purchased money market securities will generate cash upon liquidation of the securities. In this case, one type of asset (the security) is replaced by another (cash).

Most financial institutions maintain sufficient liquidity by holding either securities that have very active secondary markets or securities with short-term maturities. T-bills are the most popular money market instrument because of their marketability, safety, and short-term maturity. Although T-bills are purchased through an auction, other money market instruments are commonly purchased through dealers or specialized brokers. For example, commercial paper is purchased through commercial paper dealers or directly from the issuer, NCDs are usually purchased through brokers specializing in NCDs, federal funds are purchased (borrowed) through federal funds brokers, and repurchase agreements are purchased through repo dealers.

Financial institutions whose future cash inflows and outflows are more uncertain will generally maintain additional money market instruments for liquidity. For this reason, depository institutions such as commercial banks allocate a greater portion of their asset portfolio to money market instruments than pension funds usually do.

Financial institutions that purchase money market securities are acting as a creditor to the initial issuer of the securities. For example, when they hold T-bills, they are creditors to the Treasury. The T-bill transactions in the secondary market commonly reflect a flow of funds between two nongovernment institutions. T-bills represent a source of funds for those financial institutions that liquidate some of their T-bill holdings. In fact, this is the main reason that financial institutions hold T-bills. Liquidity is also the reason financial institutions purchase other money market instruments, including federal funds (purchased by depository institutions), repurchase agreements (purchased by depository institutions and money market funds), banker's acceptances, and NCDs (purchased by money market funds).

Some financial institutions issue their own money market instruments to obtain cash. For example, depository institutions issue NCDs, and bank holding companies and finance companies issue commercial paper. Depository institutions also obtain funds through the use of repurchase agreements or in the federal funds market.

Many money market transactions involve two financial institutions. For example, a federal funds transaction involves two depository institutions. Money market funds commonly purchase NCDs from banks and savings institutions. Repurchase agreements are frequently negotiated between two commercial banks.

VALUATION OF MONEY MARKET SECURITIES

The market price of money market securities (P_m) should equal the present value of their future cash flows. Since money market securities normally do not make periodic interest payments, their cash flows are in the form of one lump-sum payment of principal. Therefore, the market price of a money market security can be determined as

$$P_m = Par/(1+k)^n$$

where Par = par value or principal amount to be provided at maturity
             k = required rate of return by investors
             n = time to maturity

Since money market securities have maturities of one year or less, n is measured as a fraction of one year.

A change in P_m can be modeled as

$$\Delta P_m = f(\Delta k) \text{ and } \Delta k = f(\Delta R_f, \Delta RP)$$

where R_f = risk-free interest rate
                                    RP = risk premium
Therefore,

$$\Delta P_m = f(\Delta R_f, \Delta RP)$$

Exhibit 6.6 Framework for Pricing Money Market Securities

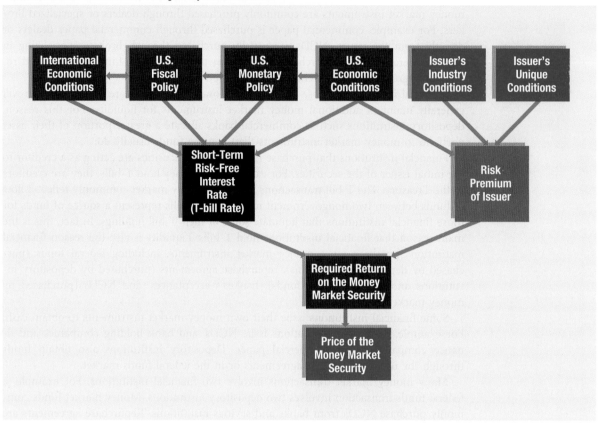

This illustrates how the prices of money market securities would change in response a change in the required rate of return, which is influenced by the risk-free interest rate and the perceived credit risk over time. Exhibit 6.6 identifies the underlying forces that can affect the short-term risk-free interest rate (the T-bill rate) and the risk premium, and can therefore affect the required return and prices of money market securities over time.

In general, the money markets are widely perceived to be efficient, in that the prices reflect all available public information. Investors closely monitor economic indicators that may signal future changes in the strength of the economy, which can affect short-term interest rates and therefore the required return from investing in money market securities. Some of the more closely monitored indicators of economic growth include employment, gross domestic product, retail sales, industrial production, and consumer confidence. A favorable movement in these indicators tends to create expectations of increased economic growth, which could place upward pressure on market interest rates (including the risk-free rate for short-term maturities) and downward pressure on prices of money market securities.

Investors also closely monitor indicators of inflation, such as the consumer price index and the producer price index. An increase in these indexes may create expectations of higher interest rates and places downward pressure on money market prices.

In addition to the indicators, investors also assess the financial condition of the firms that are issuing commercial paper. Their intent is to ensure that the issuing firm is financially healthy and therefore capable of paying off the debt at maturity.

Impact of Changes in Credit Risk

If investors want to avoid credit risk, they can purchase T-bills. When investing in other money market securities, they must weigh the higher potential return against the exposure to credit risk. Investors commonly invest in money market securities such as commercial paper amd NCDs that offer a slightly higher yield than T-bills and are very unlikely to default. The perception of credit risk can change over time, which affects the required return and therefore the price of money market securities.

Credit Risk Following Lehman's Default The credit crisis of 2008 had a major impact on the perceived risk of money market securities. As Lehman Brothers filed for bankruptcy in September 2008, it defaulted on hundreds of millions of dollars of commercial paper that it had issued. This shocked the commercial paper market since defaults on commercial paper are very rare. Suddenly, institutional investors were less willing to invest in commercial paper because of concerns that other firms might default. As a result, many firms were no longer able to rely on the commercial paper market for short-term funding. In the two months following the bankruptcy of Lehman Brothers, the volume of commercial paper declined by about $370 billion. Those firms that were still able to sell commercial paper had to pay higher risk premiums to compensate for the higher credit risk perceived by investors.

On October 3, 2008, the Emergency Economic Stabilization Act of 2008 (also referred to as the bailout act) was enacted, which helped to stabilize the money markets. The act directed the Treasury to inject $700 billion into the financial system. This allowed the Treasury to invest in the large commercial banks as a means of providing the banks with capital to cushion their losses and therefore reduce their risk. Since financial institutions are major participants in the money markets, the liquidity of the money markets increased after the Treasury took action.

In November 2008, the Federal Reserve began to purchase commercial paper issued by highly rated firms. The Fed normally does not participate as an investor in the commercial paper market, but this new form of participation was intended to restore activity and therefore increase liquidity in the commercial paper market.

Risk Premiums among Money Market Securities Exhibit 6.7 shows the yields of money market securities over time. Notice that T-bills consistently offer slightly lower yields than the other securities because they are very liquid and free from credit risk. As the exhibit illustrates, the other money market securities must offer a higher yield to compensate for credit risk.

During periods of heightened uncertainty about the economy, investors tend to shift from risky money market securities to Treasury securities. This so-called flight to quality creates a greater differential between yields, as risky money market securities must provide a larger risk premium to attract investors. During the credit crisis in 2008, the failure of Lehman Brothers increased the risk premium that some financial institutions had to pay when issuing commercial paper or NCDs. In the period shortly after Lehman's collapse, institutional investors were willing to purchase these money market securities only if the yield was sufficiently high to compensate for possible default risk.

Interest Rate Risk

If short-term interest rates increase, the required rate of return on money market securities will increase, and the prices of money market securities will decrease. Although money market security values are sensitive to interest rate movements in the same direction as bonds, they are not as sensitive as bond values to interest rate movements. The lower degree of sensitivity is primarily attributed to the shorter term to maturity. With money market securities, the principal payment will occur in the next year, whereas the

Exhibit 6.7 Money Market Yields (3-Month Maturity)

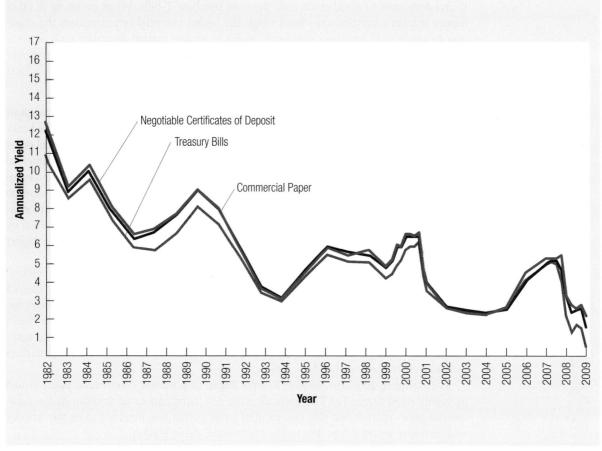

Source: *Federal Reserve Bulletin.*

principal payment on bonds may be 10 or 20 years away. In other words, an increase in interest rates is not as harmful to a money market security because it will mature soon anyway, and the investor can reinvest the proceeds at the prevailing rate at that time.

Measuring Interest Rate Risk   Participants in the money markets can use sensitivity analysis to determine how the value of money market securities may change in response to a change in interest rates.

Assume that Long Island Bank has money market securities with a par value of $100 million that will mature in nine months. Since the bank will need a substantial amount of funds in three months, it wants to know how much cash it will receive from selling these securities three months from now. Assume that it expects the unannualized required rate of return on those securities for the remaining six months to be 3 percent, or 3.5 percent, or 3.8 percent with a 33.3 percent chance for each of these three scenarios.

Exhibit 6.8 shows the probability distribution of the proceeds that Long Island Bank will receive from selling the money market securities in three months, based on the possible scenarios for the required rate of return at that time. As this exhibit shows, the bank expects that it will receive at least $96,339,113, but it could receive more if interest rates (and therefore the required rate of return) are relatively low in three months. By deriving a probability distribution of outcomes, the bank can anticipate whether the proceeds to be received will be sufficient to cover the amount of funds that it needs in three months. ●

Exhibit 6.8 Probability Distribution of Proceeds from Selling Money Market Securities

SCENARIO FOR REQUIRED RATE OF RETURN	PROBABILITY	VALUE OF SECURITIES IF SCENARIO OCCURS
3%	33.3%	$97,087,379
3.5%	33.3%	$96,618,357
3.8%	33.3%	$96,339,113

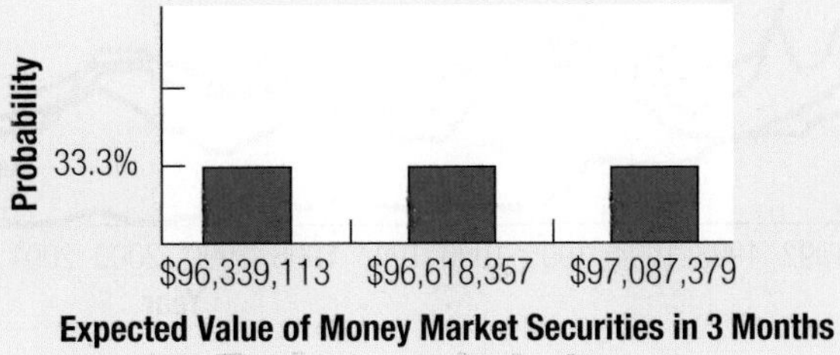

Probability

33.3%

$96,339,113 $96,618,357 $97,087,379

Expected Value of Money Market Securities in 3 Months

GLOBALIZATION OF MONEY MARKETS

As international trade and financing have grown, money markets have developed in Europe, Asia, and South America. Corporations commonly accept foreign currencies as revenue if they will need those currencies to pay for imports in the future. Since a corporation may not need to use funds at the time it receives them, it deposits the funds to earn interest until they are needed. Meanwhile, other corporations may need funds denominated in foreign currencies and therefore may wish to borrow those funds from a bank. International banks facilitate the international money markets by accepting deposits and providing loans in a wide variety of currencies.

The flow of funds between countries has increased as a result of tax differences among countries, speculation on exchange rate movements, and a reduction in government barriers that were previously imposed on foreign investment in securities. Consequently, international markets are integrated. Market interest rates vary among countries, as shown in Exhibit 6.9. Notice in the exhibit how money market rates are correlated among countries. Money market rates among several countries increased during the 2005–2006 period when many economies were growing. However, money market rates declined in most countries during the latter half of 2008 when the credit crisis intensified. The interest rates of several European countries are the same as a result of the conversion of their currencies to the euro.

Eurodollar Securities

As corporations outside the United States (especially in Europe) increasingly engaged in international trade transactions in U.S. dollars, U.S. dollar deposits in non-U.S. banks grew. Furthermore, because interest rate ceilings were historically imposed on dollar deposits in U.S. banks, corporations with large dollar balances often deposited their funds

Exhibit 6.9 International Money Market Rates over Time

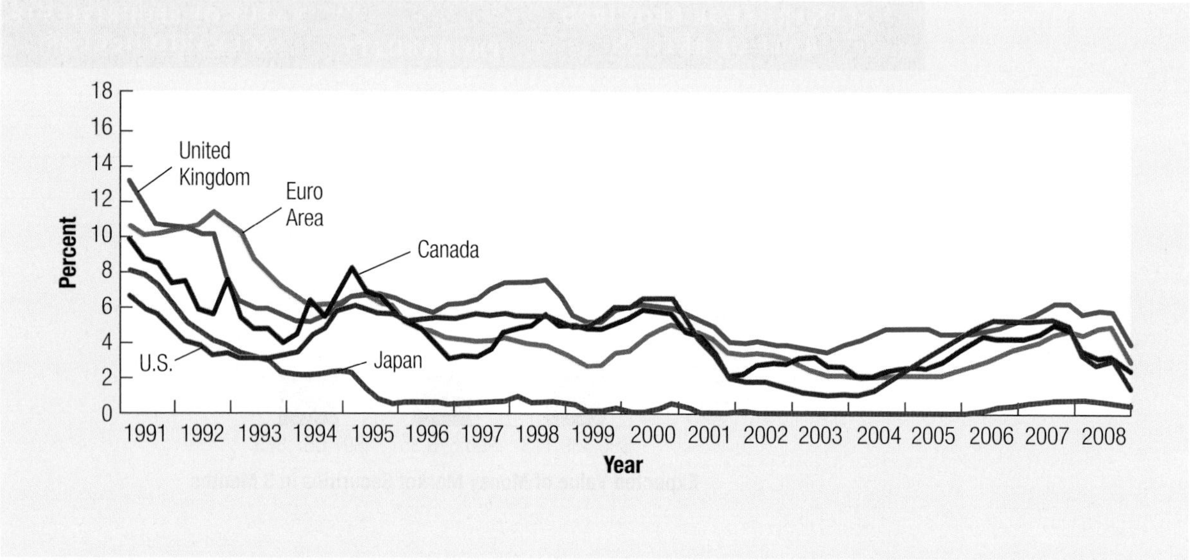

Source: *Federal Reserve.*

in Europe to receive a higher yield. These dollar deposits in Europe were referred to as **Eurodollars.** Several types of money market securities utilize Eurodollars.

Eurodollar CDs   **Eurodollar certificates of deposit** are large dollar-denominated deposits (such as $1 million) accepted by banks in Europe. Eurodollar CD volume has grown substantially over time, as the U.S. dollar is used as a medium of exchange in a significant portion of international trade and investment transactions. Some firms overseas receive U.S. dollars as payment for exports and invest in Eurodollar CDs. Because these firms may need dollars to pay for future imports, they retain dollar-denominated deposits rather than convert dollars to their home currency.

In the so-called **Eurodollar market**, banks channel the deposited funds to other firms that need to borrow them in the form of Eurodollar loans. The deposit and loan transactions in Eurodollars are typically $1 million or more per transaction, so only governments and large corporations participate in this market. Because transaction amounts are large, investors in the market avoid some costs associated with the continuous small transactions that occur in retail-oriented markets. In addition, Eurodollar CDs are not subject to reserve requirements, which means that banks can lend out 100 percent of the deposits that arrive. For these reasons, the spread between the rate banks pay on large Eurodollar deposits and what they charge on Eurodollar loans is relatively small. Consequently, interest rates in the Eurodollar market are attractive for both depositors and borrowers. The rates offered on Eurodollar deposits are slightly higher than the rates offered on NCDs.

A secondary market for Eurodollar CDs exists, allowing the initial investors to liquidate their investment if necessary. The growth in Eurodollar volume has made the secondary market more active.

Investors in fixed-rate Eurodollar CDs are adversely affected by rising market interest rates, while issuers of these CDs are adversely affected by declining rates. To deal with this interest rate risk, **Eurodollar floating-rate CDs** (called **FRCDs**) have been used in recent years. The rate adjusts periodically to the London Interbank Offer Rate (LIBOR), which is the interest rate charged on international interbank loans. As with other floating-rate instruments, the rate on FRCDs ensures that the borrower's cost and the investor's return reflect prevailing market interest rates.

Euronotes   Short-term **Euronotes** are short-term securities issued in bearer form, with common maturities of one, three, and six months. Typical investors in Euronotes often include the Eurobanks (banks that accept large deposits and make large loans in foreign currencies) that are hired to place the paper. These Euronotes are sometimes underwritten in a manner that guarantees the issuer a specific price.

Euro-Commercial Paper   **Euro-commercial paper (Euro-CP)** is issued without the backing of a banking syndicate. Maturities can be tailored to satisfy investors. Dealers that place commercial paper have created a secondary market by being willing to purchase existing Euro-CP before maturity.

The Euro-CP rate is typically between 50 and 100 basis points above LIBOR. Euro-CP is sold by dealers, at a transaction cost ranging between 5 and 10 basis points of the face value. This market is tiny compared to the U.S. commercial paper market. Nevertheless, some European companies that want short-term funding in dollars can more easily place their paper here, where they have a household name.

International Interbank Market

Some international banks periodically have an excess of funds beyond the amount that other corporations want to borrow. Other international banks may be short of funds because their client corporations want to borrow more funds than the banks have available. An international interbank market facilitates the transfer of funds from banks with excess funds to those with deficient funds. This market is similar to the federal funds market in the United States, but it is worldwide and conducts transactions in a wide variety of currencies. Some of the transactions are direct from one bank to another, while others are channeled through large banks that serve as intermediaries between the lending bank and the borrowing bank. Historically, international banks in London carried out many of these transactions.

The rate charged for a loan from one bank to another in the international interbank market is the LIBOR, which is similar to the federal funds rate in the United States. The LIBOR varies among currencies and is usually in line with the prevailing money market rates in the currency. It varies over time in response to changes in money market rates in a particular currency, which are driven by changes in the demand and supply conditions for short-term money in that currency. The term LIBOR is still frequently used, even though many international interbank transactions do not pass through London.

Performance of Foreign Money Market Securities

The performance of an investment in a foreign money market security is measured by the **effective yield** (yield adjusted for the exchange rate), which is dependent on the (1) yield earned on the money market security in the foreign currency and (2) the exchange rate effect. The yield earned on the money market security (Y_f) is

$$Y_f = \frac{SP_f - PP_f}{PP_f}$$

where SP_f = selling price of the foreign money market security in the foreign currency

PP_f = purchase price of the foreign money market security in the foreign currency

The exchange rate effect (denoted as %ΔS) measures the percentage change in the spot exchange rate (in dollars) from the time the foreign currency was obtained to invest in the foreign money market security until the time the security was sold and the foreign currency was converted into the investor's home currency. Thus, the effective yield is

$$Y_e = (1 + Y_f) \times (1 + \%\Delta S) - 1$$

EXAMPLE

A U.S. investor obtains Mexican pesos when the peso is worth \$.12 and invests in a one-year money market security that provides a yield (in pesos) of 22 percent. At the end of one year, the investor converts the proceeds from the investment back to dollars at the prevailing spot rate of \$.13 per peso. In this example, the peso increased in value by 8.33 percent, or .0833. The effective yield earned by the investor is

$$\begin{aligned} Y_e &= (1 + Y_f) \times (1 + \%\Delta S) - 1 \\ &= (1.22) \times (1.0833) - 1 \\ &= 32.16\% \end{aligned}$$

●

The effective yield exceeds the yield quoted on the foreign currency whenever the currency denominating the foreign investment increases in value over the investment horizon.

To illustrate the potential effects of exchange rate movements, the effective yield for a U.S. investor that invests in British money market securities is shown in Exhibit 6.10. The effective yield was higher than the alternative domestic yields for U.S. investors during certain periods when the pound strengthened, such as in the 2006–2007 period. Conversely, the effective yield on British money market securities was low or even negative in periods when the pound depreciated substantially, such as in the third quarter of 2008. The results displayed in Exhibit 6.10 show both the high potential yields and the risk from investing in foreign money market securities. The risk could be reduced somewhat by spreading the investment across securities denominated in several currencies.

Exhibit 6.10 Comparison of Effective Yields between U.S. and British Money Market Yields for a U.S. Investor

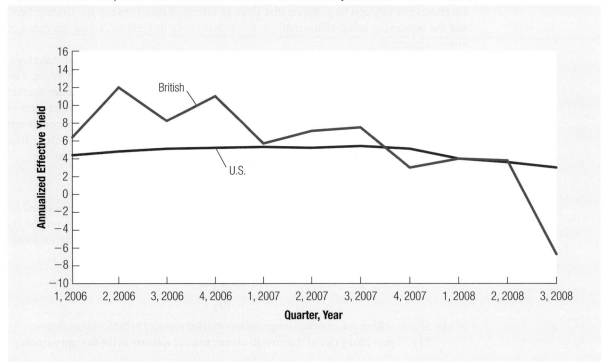

SUMMARY

- The main money market securities are Treasury bills, commercial paper, NCDs, repurchase agreements, federal funds, and banker's acceptances. These securities vary according to the issuer. Consequently, their perceived degree of credit risk can vary. They also have different degrees of liquidity. Therefore, the quoted yields at any given point in time vary among money market securities.

- Financial institutions manage their liquidity by participating in money markets. They may issue money market securities when they experience cash shortages and need to boost liquidity. They can also sell holdings of money market securities to obtain cash.

- The value of a money market security represents the present value of future cash flows generated by that security. Since money market securities represent debt, their expected cash flows are typically known. However, the pricing of money market securities changes in response to a shift in the required rate of return by investors. The required rate of return changes in response to interest rate movements or to a shift in the security's credit risk.

- Interest rates vary among countries. Some investors are attracted to high interest rates in foreign countries, which cause funds to flow to those countries. Consequently, money markets have become globally integrated. Investments in foreign money market securities are subject to exchange rate risk because the foreign currency denominating the securities could depreciate over time.

POINT COUNTER-POINT

Should Firms Invest in Money Market Securities?

Point No. Firms are supposed to use money in a manner that generates an adequate return to shareholders. Money market securities provide a return that is less than that required by shareholders. Thus, firms should not be using shareholder funds to invest in money market securities. If firms need liquidity, they can rely on the money markets for short-term borrowing.

Counter-Point Yes. Firms need money markets for liquidity. If they do not hold any money market securities, they will frequently be forced to borrow to cover unanticipated cash needs. The lenders may charge higher risk premiums when lending so frequently to these firms.

Who Is Correct? Use the Internet to learn more about this issue. Offer your own opinion on this issue.

QUESTIONS AND APPLICATIONS

1.   Negotiable CDs How can small investors participate in investments in negotiable certificates of deposits (NCDs)?

2.   Commercial Paper Yield Curve How do you think the shape of the yield curve for commercial paper and other money market instruments compares to the yield curve for Treasury securities? Explain your logic.

3.   Commercial Paper Ratings Why do ratings agencies assign ratings to commercial paper?

4.   Risk and Return of Commercial Paper You have the choice of investing in top-rated commercial paper or commercial paper that has a lower risk rating. How do you think the risk and return performances of the two investments differ?

5.   Commercial Paper Rates Explain how investors' preferences for commercial paper change during a recession. How should this reaction affect the difference between commercial paper rates and T-bill rates during recessionary periods?

6.   Motive to Issue Commercial Paper The maximum maturity of commercial paper is 270 days. Why would a firm issue commercial paper instead of longer-term securities, even if it needs funds for a long period of time?

7.   Commercial Paper Who issues commercial paper? What types of financial institutions issue commercial paper? Why do some firms create a department that can directly place commercial paper? What criteria affect the decision to create such a department?

8.   Foreign Money Market Yield Explain how the yield on a foreign money market security would be affected if the foreign currency denominating that security declines to a greater degree.

9.   Secondary Market for T-bills Describe the activity in the secondary T-bill market. How can this degree of activity benefit investors in T-bills? Why might a financial institution sometimes consider T-bills as a potential source of funds?

10.   Banker's Acceptances Explain how each of the following would use banker's acceptances: (a) exporting firms, (b) importing firms, (c) commercial banks, and (d) investors.

11.   T-bill Auction How can investors using the primary T-bill market be assured that their bid will be accepted? Why do large corporations typically make competitive bids rather than noncompetitive bids for T-bills?

12.   Repurchase Agreements Based on what you know about repurchase agreements, would you expect them to have a lower or higher annualized yield than commercial paper? Why?

13.   Primary Market Explain how the Treasury uses the primary market to obtain adequate funding.

Advanced Questions

14.   Impact of Credit Crisis on Risk Premiums Explain how the credit crisis affected the credit risk premium in the commercial paper market.

15.   How Money Market Rates May Respond to Prevailing Conditions How have money market rates changed since the beginning of the semester? Consider the current economic conditions. Do you think money market rates will increase or decrease during the semester? Offer some logic to support your answer.

16.   Bear Stearns and the Repo Market Explain the lesson to be learned about the repo market based on the experience of Bear Stearns.

17.   Applying Term Structure Theories to Commercial Paper Apply the term structure of interest rate theories that were discussed in Chapter 3 to explain the shape of the existing commercial paper yield curve.

18.   Impact of Credit Crisis on Liquidity Explain why the credit crisis affected the ability of financial institutions to access short-term financing in the money markets.

19.   Influence of Money Market Activity on Working Capital Assume that interest rates for most maturities are unusually high. Also, assume that the net working capital (defined as current assets minus current liabilities) levels of many corporations are relatively low in this period. Explain how the money markets play a role in the relationship between the interest rates and the level of net working capital.

20.   Impact of Lehman Brothers Failure Explain how the bankruptcy of Lehman Brothers (a large securities firm) reduced the liquidity of the commercial paper market.

Interpreting Financial News

Interpret the following statements made by Wall Street analysts and portfolio managers:

a. "Money markets are not used to get rich, but to avoid being poor."

b. "Until conditions are more favorable, investors are staying on the sidelines."

c. "My portfolio is overinvested in stocks because of the low money market rates."

Managing in Financial Markets

Money Market Portfolio Dilemma As the treasurer of a corporation, one of your jobs is to maintain investments in liquid securities such as Treasury securities and commercial paper. Your goal is to earn as high a return as possible but without taking much of a risk.

a. The yield curve is currently upward sloping, such that 10-year Treasury bonds have an annualized yield 3 percentage points above the annualized yield of three-month T-bills. Should you consider using some of your funds to invest in 10-year Treasury securities?

b. Assume that you have substantially more cash than you would possibly need for any liquidity problems.

Your boss suggests that you consider investing the excess funds in some money market securities that have a higher return than short-term Treasury securities, such as negotiable certificates of deposit (NCDs). Even though NCDs are less liquid, this would not cause a problem if you have more funds than you need. Given the situation, what use of the excess funds would benefit the firm the most?

c. Assume that commercial paper is currently offering an annualized yield of 7.5 percent, while Treasury securities are offering an annualized yield of 7 percent. Economic conditions have been stable, and you expect conditions to be very favorable over the next six months. Given this situation, would you prefer to hold a diversified portfolio of commercial paper issued by various corporations or T-bills?

d. Assume that commercial paper typically offers a premium of 0.5 percent above the T-bill rate. Given that your firm typically maintains about $10 million in liquid funds, how much extra will you generate per year by investing in commercial paper versus T-bills? Is this extra return worth the risk that the commercial paper could default?

PROBLEMS

1.   T-bill Yield The Treasury is selling 91-day T-bills with a face value of $10,000 for $8,800. If the investor holds them until maturity, calculate the yield.

2.   Return on T-bills Current T-bill yields are approximately 2 percent. Assume an investor considering the purchase of a newly issued three-month T-bill expects interest rates to increase within the next three months and has a required rate of return of 2.5 percent. Based on this information, how much is this investor willing to pay for a three-month T-bill?

3.   T-bill Yield You paid $98,000 for a $100,000 T-bill maturing in 120 days. If you hold it until maturity, what is the T-bill yield? What is the T-bill discount?

4.   Return on NCDs Phil purchased an NCD a year ago in the secondary market for $980,000. The NCD matures today at a price of $1 milllion, and Phil received $45,000 in interest. What is Phil's return on the NCD?

5.   Repurchase Agreement Stanford Corporation arranged a repurchase agreement in which it purchased securities for $4.9 million and will sell the securities back for $5 million in 40 days. What is the yield (or repo rate) to Stanford Corporation?

6.   Effective Yield A U.S. investor obtains British pounds when the pound is worth $1.50 and invests in a one-year money market security that provides a yield of 5 percent (in pounds). At the end of one year, the investor converts the proceeds from the investment back to dollars at the prevailing spot rate of $1.52 per pound. Calculate the effective yield.

7.   Commercial Paper Yield Assume an investor purchased six-month commercial paper with a face value of $1 million for $940,000. What is the yield?

8.   T-bill yield

a. Determine how the annualized yield of a T-bill would be affected if the purchase price is lower. Explain the logic of this relationship.

b. Determine how the annualized yield of a T-bill would be affected if the selling price is lower. Explain the logic of this relationship.

c. Determine how the annualized yield of a T-bill would be affected if the number of days is shorter, holding the purchase price and selling price constant. Explain the logic of this relationship.

9.   T-bill Discount Newly issued three-month T-bills with a par value of $10,000 sold for $9,700. Compute the T-bill discount.

10.   Required Rate of Return A money market security that has a par value of $10,000 sells for $8,816.60. Given that the security has a maturity of two years, what is the investor's required rate of return?

11.   T-bill Yield Assume an investor purchased a six-month T-bill with a $10,000 par value for $9,000 and sold it 90 days later for $9,100. What is the yield?

Flow of Funds Exercise

Financing in the Money Markets

Recall that Carson Company has obtained substantial loans from finance companies and commercial banks. The interest rate on the loans is tied to market interest rates and is adjusted every six months. Carson has a credit line with a bank in case it suddenly needs to obtain funds for a temporary period. It previously purchased Treasury securities that it could sell if it experiences any liquidity problems. If the economy continues to be strong, Carson may need to increase its production capacity by about 50 percent over the next few years to satisfy demand. It is concerned about a possible slowing of the economy because of potential Fed actions to reduce inflation. It needs funding to cover payments for supplies. It is also considering issuing stock or bonds to raise funds in the next year.

a. The prevailing commercial paper rate on paper issued by large publicly traded firms is lower than the rate Carson would pay when using a line of credit. Do you think that Carson could issue commercial paper at this prevailing market rate?

b. Should Carson obtain funds to cover payments for supplies by selling its holdings of Treasury securities or by using its credit line? Which alternative has a lower cost? Explain.

Internet/Excel Exercises

1. Go to http://research.stlouisfed.org/fred2. Under "Categories," select "Interest rates." Compare the yield offered on a T-bill with the yield offered by another money market security with a similar maturity. What is the difference in yields? Why do you think the yields differ?

2. How has the risk premium on a specific risky money market security (versus the T-bill) changed since one year ago? Is the change due to a change in economic conditions? Explain.

3. Using the same website, retrieve interest rate data at the beginning of the last 20 quarters for the three-month T-bill and another money market security and place the data in two columns of an Excel spreadsheet. Derive the change in interest rates for both money market securities on a quarterly basis. Apply regression analysis in which the quarterly change in the interest rate of the risky money market security is the dependent variable and the quarterly change in the T-bill rate is the independent variable (see Appendix B for more information about using regression analysis). Is there a positive and significant relationship between the interest rate movements? Explain.

WSJ Exercise

Assessing Yield Differentials of Money Market Securities

Use the "Money Rates" section of *The Wall Street Journal* to determine the 30-day yield (annualized) of commercial paper, certificates of deposit, banker's acceptances, and T-bills. Which of these securities has the highest yield? Why? Which of these securities has the lowest yield? Why?

7

Bond Markets

CHAPTER OBJECTIVES

The specific objectives of this chapter are to:

- provide a background on bonds,

- describe the different types of bonds and their characteristics,

- explain how bond markets have become globally integrated, and

- describe other types of long-term debt securities.

From this chapter through Chapter 12, the focus is on capital market securities. These chapters are distinctly different from the previous chapter on money market securities in that they focus on a long-term rather than a short-term perspective. This chapter and the following chapter focus on bond markets, which facilitate the flow of long-term debt from surplus units to deficit units.

BACKGROUND ON BONDS

Bonds are long-term debt securities that are issued by government agencies or corporations. The issuer of a bond is obligated to pay interest (or coupon) payments periodically (such as annually or semiannually) and the par value (principal) at maturity. An issuer must be able to show that its future cash flows will be sufficient to enable it to make its coupon and principal payments to bondholders. Investors will consider buying bonds for which the repayment is questionable only if the expected return from investing in the bonds is sufficient to compensate for the risk.

Bonds are often classified according to the type of issuer. Treasury bonds are issued by the U. S. Treasury, federal agency bonds are issued by federal agencies, municipal bonds are issued by state and local governments, and corporate bonds are issued by corporations.

Most bonds have maturities of between 10 and 30 years. Bonds are classified by the ownership structure as either bearer bonds or registered bonds. **Bearer bonds** require the owner to clip coupons attached to the bonds and send them to the issuer to receive coupon payments. **Registered bonds** require the issuer to maintain records of who owns the bond and automatically send coupon payments to the owners.

Bonds are issued in the primary market through a telecommunications network. Exhibit 7.1 shows how bond markets facilitate the flow of funds. The U.S. Treasury issues bonds and uses the proceeds to support deficit spending on government programs. Federal agencies issue bonds and use the proceeds to buy mortgages that are originated by financial institutions. Thus, they indirectly finance purchases of homes. Corporations issue bonds and use the proceeds to expand their operations. Overall, by allowing households, corporations, and the U.S. government to increase their expenditures, bond markets finance economic growth.

Institutional Use of Bond Markets

All types of financial institutions participate in the bond markets, as summarized in Exhibit 7.2. Commercial banks, savings institutions, and finance companies commonly issue bonds in order to raise capital to support their operations. Commercial banks,

Exhibit 7.1 How Bond Markets Facilitate the Flow of Funds

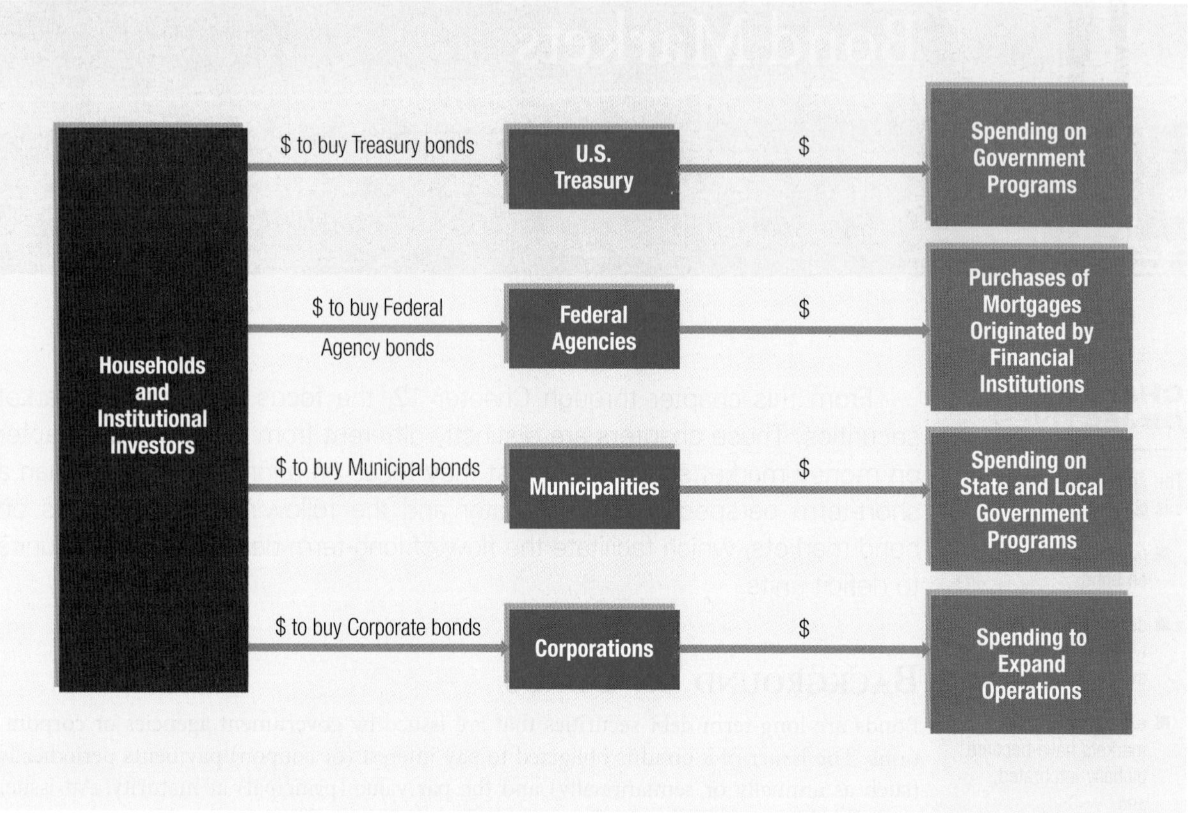

savings institutions, bond mutual funds, insurance companies, and pension funds are investors in the bond market. Financial institutions dominate the bond market in that they purchase a very large proportion of bonds issued.

Bond Yields

The yield on a bond may depend on whether it is viewed from the perspective of the issuer of the bond who is obligated to make payments on the bond until maturity or from the perspective of the investors who purchase the bond.

Yield from the Issuer's Perspective   The issuer's cost of financing with bonds is commonly measured by the **yield to maturity**, which reflects the annualized yield that is paid by the issuer over the life of the bond. The yield to maturity is the annualized discount rate that equates the future coupon and principal payments to the initial proceeds received from the bond offering. It is based on the assumption that coupon payments received can be reinvested at the same yield.

EXAMPLE

Consider an investor who can purchase bonds with 10 years until maturity, a par value of $1,000, and an 8 percent annualized coupon rate for $936. The yield to maturity on this bond can be determined by using a financial calculator as follows:

INPUT	10	936	80	1000		
Function Key	N	PV	PMT	FV	CPT	I
Answer						9%

Exhibit 7.2 Participation of Financial Institutions in Bond Markets

FINANCIAL INSTITUTION	PARTICIPATION IN BOND MARKETS
Commercial banks and savings and loan associations (S&Ls)	• Purchase bonds for their asset portfolio. • Sometimes place municipal bonds for municipalities. • Sometimes issue bonds as a source of secondary capital.
Finance companies	• Commonly issue bonds as a source of long-term funds.
Mutual funds	• Use funds received from the sale of shares to purchase bonds. Some bond mutual funds specialize in particular types of bonds, while others invest in all types.
Brokerage firms	• Facilitate bond trading by matching up buyers and sellers of bonds in the secondary market.
Investment banking firms	• Place newly issued bonds for governments and corporations. They may place the bonds and assume the risk of market price uncertainty or place the bonds on a best-efforts basis in which they do not guarantee a price for the issuer.
Insurance companies	• Purchase bonds for their asset portfolio.
Pension funds	• Purchase bonds for their asset portfolio.

Notice that the yield paid to investors is composed of two components: (1) a set of coupon payments and (2) the difference between the par value that the issuer must pay to investors at maturity versus the price it received when selling the bonds. In this example and in most cases, the biggest component of the yield to maturity is the set of coupon payments. The yield to maturity does not include the transaction costs associated with issuing the bonds. When those transaction costs are considered, the issuer's actual cost of borrowing is higher than the yield to maturity. ●

Yield from the Investor's Perspective   An investor who invests in a bond when it is issued and holds it until maturity will earn the yield to maturity. Many investors, however, do not hold a bond to maturity and therefore focus on their holding period return, or the return from their investment over a particular holding period. If they hold the bond for a very short time period (such as less than one year), they may estimate their holding period return as the sum of the coupon payments plus the difference between the selling price and the purchase price of the bond, as a percentage of the purchase price. For relatively long holding periods, a better approximation of the holding period yield is the annualized discount rate that equates the payments received to the initial investment. Since the selling price to be received by investors is uncertain if they do not hold the bond to maturity, their holding period yield is uncertain at the time they purchase the bond. Consequently, an investment in bonds is subject to the risk that the holding period return will be less than expected. The valuation and return of bonds from the investor's perspective are discussed more thoroughly in the following chapter.

WEB

http://money.cnn.com/ markets/bondcenter
Yields and information on all types of bonds for various maturities.

TREASURY AND FEDERAL AGENCY BONDS

The U.S. Treasury commonly issues Treasury notes or Treasury bonds to finance federal government expenditures. The minimum denomination for Treasury notes or bonds is $1,000. The key difference between a note and a bond is that note maturities are less than 10 years, whereas bond maturities are 10 years or more. An active over-the-counter secondary market allows investors to sell Treasury notes or bonds prior to maturity.

The yield from holding a Treasury bond, as with other bonds, depends on the coupon rate and on the difference between the purchase price and the selling price. Investors in Treasury notes and bonds receive semiannual interest payments from the Treasury.

WEB

www.treasurydirect .gov
Details about Treasury bonds.

Although the interest is taxed by the federal government as ordinary income, it is exempt from state and local taxes, if any exist. Domestic and foreign firms and individuals are common investors in Treasury notes and bonds.

Since 2006, the Treasury has issued 30-year Treasury bonds and 10-year Treasury bonds to finance the U.S. budget deficit. From October 2001 until 2006, however, the Treasury relied only on 10-year Treasury bonds instead of issuing both 10-year and 30-year bonds as it had done previouly.

Treasury Bond Auctions

The Treasury obtains long-term funding through Treasury bond offerings, which are conducted through periodic auctions. Treasury bond auctions are normally held in the middle of each quarter. The Treasury announces its plans for an auction, including the date, the amount of funding that it needs, and the maturity of the bonds to be issued. At the time of the auction, financial institutions submit bids for their own accounts or for their clients.

Bids can be submitted on a competitive or a noncompetitive basis. Competitive bids specify a price that the bidder is willing to pay and a dollar amount of securities to be purchased. Noncompetitive bids specify only a dollar amount of securities to be purchased (subject to a maximum limit). The Treasury ranks the competitive bids in descending order according to the price bid per $100 of par value. All competitive bids are accepted until the point at which the desired amount of funding is achieved. Since November 1998, the Treasury has used the lowest accepted bid price as the price applied to all accepted competitive bids and all noncompetitive bids. Competitive bids are commonly used because many bidders want to purchase more Treasury bonds than the maximum that can be purchased on a noncompetitive basis.

Trading Treasury Bonds

Bond dealers serve as intermediaries in the secondary market by matching up buyers and sellers of Treasury bonds, and they also take positions in these bonds. About 2,000 brokers and dealers are registered to trade Treasury securities, but about 22 so-called primary dealers dominate the trading. These dealers make the secondary market for the Treasury bonds. They quote a bid price for customers who want to sell existing Treasury bonds to the dealers and an ask price for customers who want to buy existing Treasury bonds from them. The dealers profit from the spread between the bid and ask prices. Because of the large volume of secondary market transactions and intense competition among bond dealers, the spread is very narrow. When the Federal Reserve engages in open market operations, it normally conducts trading with the primary dealers of government securities. The primary dealers also trade Treasury bonds among themselves.

Treasury bonds are registered at the New York Stock Exchange, but the secondary market trading occurs over-the-counter (through a telecommunications network). The typical daily transaction volume in government securities (including money market securities) for the primary dealers is about $550 billion. Most of this trading volume occurs in the United States, but Treasury bonds are traded worldwide. They are traded in Tokyo from 7:30 P.M. to 3:00 A.M. New York time. The Tokyo and London markets overlap for part of the time, and the London market remains open until 7:30 A.M., when trading begins in New York.

Investors can contact their broker to buy or sell Treasury bonds. The brokerage firms serve as an intermediary between the investors and the bond dealers. Discount brokers usually charge a fee between $40 and $70 for Treasury bond transactions valued at $10,000. Institutional investors tend to contact the bond dealers directly.

Exhibit 7.3 Example of Bond Price Quotations

RATE	MATURITY DATE	BID	ASK	YIELD
10.75	Aug. 2011	120:17	120:23	8.37%
8.38	Aug. 2013–18	100:09	100:15	8.32%
8.75	Nov. 2013–18	103:05	103:11	8.34%

Online Trading   Investors can also buy bonds through the TreasuryDirect program (www.treasurydirect.gov). They can have the Treasury deduct their purchase from their bank account. They can also reinvest proceeds received when Treasury bonds mature into newly issued Treasury bonds.

Treasury Bond Quotations

Quotations for Treasury bond prices are published in financial newspapers such as *The Wall Street Journal, Barron's,* and *Investor's Business Daily.* They are also provided in *USA Today* and local newspapers. A typical format for Treasury bond quotations is shown in Exhibit 7.3. Each row represents a specific bond. The coupon rate, shown in the first column, will vary substantially among bonds because bonds issued when interest rates were high will have higher coupon rates than those issued when interest rates were low.

The Treasury bonds are organized in the table according to their maturity (shown in the second column), with those closest to maturity listed first. This allows investors to easily find Treasury bonds that have a specific maturity. If the bond contains a call feature allowing the issuer to repurchase the bonds prior to maturity, it is specified beside the maturity date in the second column. For example, the second and third bonds in Exhibit 7.3 mature in the year 2018 but can be called from the year 2013 on.

The bid price (what a bond dealer is willing to pay) and the ask price (what a bond dealer is willing to sell the bond for) are quoted per hundreds of dollars of par value, with fractions (to the right of the colon) expressed as thirty-seconds of a dollar. For example, the first bond listed has a face value of $100,000, so its ask price of 120:23 represents a quote of $120,719. This bond has a much higher price than the other two bonds shown, primarily because it offers a higher coupon rate. However, its yield to maturity is similar to the other yields (see the last column in Exhibit 7.3). From an investor's point of view, the coupon rate advantage over the other two bonds is essentially offset by the high price to be paid for that bond.

Online Quotations   Treasury bond prices are accessible online at www.investingin bonds.com. This website provides the spread between the bid and the ask (offer) prices for various maturities. Treasury bond yields are accessible online at www.federalreserve .gov/releases/H15/. The yields are updated daily and are disclosed for several different maturities.

Stripped Treasury Bonds

The cash flows of bonds are commonly transformed (stripped) by securities firms to create two separate types of securities. In these **stripped securities**, one security represents the principal payment only while the second security represents the interest payments. For example, consider a 10-year Treasury bond with a par value of $100,000 that has a 12 percent coupon rate and semiannual coupon payments. This bond could be stripped into a principal-only (PO) security that will provide $100,000 upon maturity and an interest-only (IO) security that will provide 20 semiannual payments of $6,000 each.

Investors who desire a lump-sum payment in the distant future can choose the PO part, and investors desiring periodic cash inflows can select the IO part. Because the cash flows of the underlying securities are different, so are the degrees of interest rate sensitivity. The 10-year Treasury bond could even be stripped to create a PO security and 20 different IO securities, with each IO security representing one of the semiannual coupon payments.

Stripped Treasury securities are commonly called **STRIPS** (Separate Trading of Registered Interest and Principal of Securities). STRIPS are not issued by the Treasury, but are created and sold by various financial institutions. They can be created for any Treasury security. Since they are components of Treasury securities, they are backed by the U.S. government. They do not have to be held until maturity, as there is an active secondary market. STRIPS have become very popular over time.

Inflation-Indexed Treasury Bonds

The Treasury periodically issues inflation-indexed bonds that provide returns tied to the inflation rate. These bonds, commonly referred to as TIPS (Treasury Inflation-Protected Securities), are intended for investors who wish to ensure that the returns on their investments keep up with the increase in prices over time. The coupon rate offered on TIPS is lower than the rate on typical Treasury bonds, but the principal value is increased by the amount of the U.S. inflation rate (as measured by the percentage increase in the consumer price index) every six months.

EXAMPLE

Consider a 10-year inflation-indexed bond that has a par value of $10,000 and a coupon rate of 4 percent. Assume that during the first six months since the bond was issued, the inflation rate (as measured by the consumer price index) was 1 percent. The principal of the bond is increased by $100 (1% × $10,000). Thus, the coupon payment after six months will be 2 percent (half of the yearly coupon rate) of the new par value, or 2% × $10,100 = $202. Assume that the inflation rate over the next six months is 3 percent. The principal of the bond is increased by $303 (3% × $10,100), which results in a new par value of $10,403. The coupon payment at the end of the year is based on the coupon rate and the new par value, or 2% × $10,403 = $208.06. This process is applied every six months over the life of the bond. If prices double over the 10-year period in which the bond exists, the par value of the bond will also double and thus will be equal to $20,000 at maturity. ●

Inflation-indexed government bonds have become very popular in some other countries including Australia and the United Kingdom; they are especially desirable in countries where inflation tends to be high, such as Brazil and Turkey. They are also becoming popular in the United States. The Treasury historically focused on TIPS with 10-year maturities but is now also offering TIPS with 5-year and 20-year maturities.

Savings Bonds

Savings bonds are issued by the Treasury, but can be purchased from many financial institutions. They are attractive to small investors because they can be purchased with as little as $25. Larger denominations are available as well. The Series EE savings bond provides a market-based rate of interest, while the I savings bond provides a rate of interest that is tied to inflation. The interest accumulates monthly and adds value to the amount received at the time of redemption.

Savings bonds have a 30-year maturity and do not have a secondary market. The Treasury does allow savings bonds issued after February 2003 to be redeemed anytime after a 12-month period, but there is a penalty equal to the last three months of interest.

Like other Treasury securities, the interest income on savings bonds is not subject to state and local taxes, but is subject to federal taxes. For federal tax purposes, investors holding savings bonds can report the accumulated interest on an annual basis or only at the time they redeem the bonds or at maturity.

Federal Agency Bonds

Federal agency bonds are issued by federal agencies. The **Government National Mortgage Association (Ginnie Mae)** issues bonds and uses the proceeds to purchase mortgages that are insured by the Federal Housing Administration (FHA) and by the Veterans Administration (VA). The bonds are backed both by the mortgages that are purchased with the proceeds and by the federal government.

The **Federal National Mortgage Association (Fannie Mae)** and the **Federal Home Loan Mortgage Association (Freddie Mac)** issue bonds and use the proceeds to purchase mortgages in the secondary market. Thus, they channel funds into the mortgage market, thereby ensuring that there is sufficient financing for homeowners who wish to obtain mortgages. Prior to September 2008, these bonds were not backed by the federal government. During the credit crisis in 2008, however, Fannie Mae and Freddie Mac experienced financial problems because they had purchased risky subprime mortgages that had a high frequency of defaults. Consequently, the agencies were unable to issue bonds because investors feared that they might default. In September 2008, the federal government rescued Fannie Mae and Freddie Mac so that they would be able to more easily issue bonds and continue to channel funds into the mortgage market.

MUNICIPAL BONDS

Like the federal government, state and local governments frequently spend more than the revenues they receive. To finance the difference, they issue **municipal bonds**, most of which can be classified as either **general obligation bonds** or **revenue bonds.** Payments on general obligation bonds are supported by the municipal government's ability to tax, whereas payments on revenue bonds must be generated by revenues of the project (tollway, toll bridge, state college dormitory, etc.) for which the bonds were issued. Revenue bonds have generally dominated since 1975.

Credit Risk

Both types of municipal bonds are subject to some degree of credit (default) risk. If a municipality is unable to increase taxes, it could default on general obligation bonds. If it issues revenue bonds and does not generate sufficient revenue, it could default on these bonds.

Nevertheless, in general the risk of default on municipal bonds is low. Less than .5 percent of all municipal bonds issued since 1940 have defaulted. Because there is some concern about the risk of default, investors commonly monitor the ratings of municipal bonds. Moody's, Standard & Poor's, and Fitch Investors Service assign ratings to municipal bonds based on the ability of the issuer to repay the debt. The ratings are important to the issuer because a better rating will cause investors to require a smaller risk premium, and the municipal bonds can be issued at a higher price (lower yield).

Some municipal bonds are insured to protect against default. The issuer pays for this protection so that it can issue the bond at a higher price, which translates into a higher price paid by the investor. Thus, investors indirectly bear the cost of the insurance.

Impact of the Credit Crisis During the credit crisis in 2008 and 2009, state and local governments had more difficulty obtaining funds because of investors' concerns about credit risk. Investors were more cautious because of the weak economy and suspected that some state and local governments might default on their debt. Thus, many municipal bond offerings that were scheduled during the credit crisis had to be postponed.

Characteristics of Municipal Bonds

Revenue bonds and general obligation bonds typically promise semiannual interest payments. Common purchasers of these bonds include financial and nonfinancial institutions as well as individuals. The minimum denomination of municipal bonds is typically $5,000. A secondary market exists for them, although it is less active than the one for Treasury bonds.

Most municipal bonds contain a call provision, which allows the issuer to repurchase the bonds at a specified price before the bonds mature. A municipality may exercise its option to repurchase the bonds if interest rates decline substantially because it can reissue bonds at the lower interest rate and reduce its cost of financing.

Variable-Rate Municipal Bonds   Variable-rate municipal bonds have a floating interest rate based on a benchmark interest rate. The coupon payment adjusts to movements in the benchmark interest rate. Some variable-rate municipal bonds are convertible to a fixed rate until maturity under specified conditions. In general, variable-rate municipal bonds are desirable to investors who expect that interest rates will rise. However, there is the risk that interest rates may decline over time, which would cause the coupon payments to decline as well.

Tax Advantages   One of the most attractive features of municipal bonds is that the interest income is normally exempt from federal taxes. Second, the interest income earned on bonds that are issued by a municipality within a particular state is normally exempt from state income taxes (if any). Thus, investors who reside in states that impose income taxes can reduce their taxes further.

Trading and Quotations

Today, there are more than 1 million different bonds outstanding, and more than 50,000 different issuers of municipal bonds. There are hundreds of bond dealers that can accommodate investor requests to buy or sell municipal bonds in the secondary market, but only five dealers account for more than half of all the trading volume. Bond dealers can also take positions in municipal bonds.

Investors who expect that they will not hold a municipal bond until maturity should consider only bonds that have active secondary market trading. Many municipal bonds have an inactive secondary market. Therefore, it is difficult to know the prevailing market values of these bonds. Although investors do not pay a direct commission on trades, they incur transaction costs in the form of a bid-ask spread on the bonds. This spread can be large, especially for municipal bonds that are rarely traded in the secondary market.

Electronic trading of municipal bonds has become very popular, in part because it enables investors to circumvent the more expensive route of calling brokers. A popular bond website is www.ebondtrade.com. Such websites provide access to information on municipal bonds and allow online buying and selling of municipal bonds.

Yields Offered on Municipal Bonds

The yield offered by a municipal bond differs from the yield on a Treasury bond with the same maturity for three reasons. First, the municipal bond must pay a risk premium to compensate for the possibility of default risk. Second, the municipal bond must pay a slight premium to compensate for being less liquid than Treasury bonds with the same maturity. Third, as explained earlier, the income earned from a municipal bond is exempt from federal taxes. This tax advantage of municipal bonds more than offsets their

Exhibit 7.4 Yield Offered on General Obligation Municipal Bonds over Time

Bond Buyer Go 20-Year Bond Municipal Bond Index

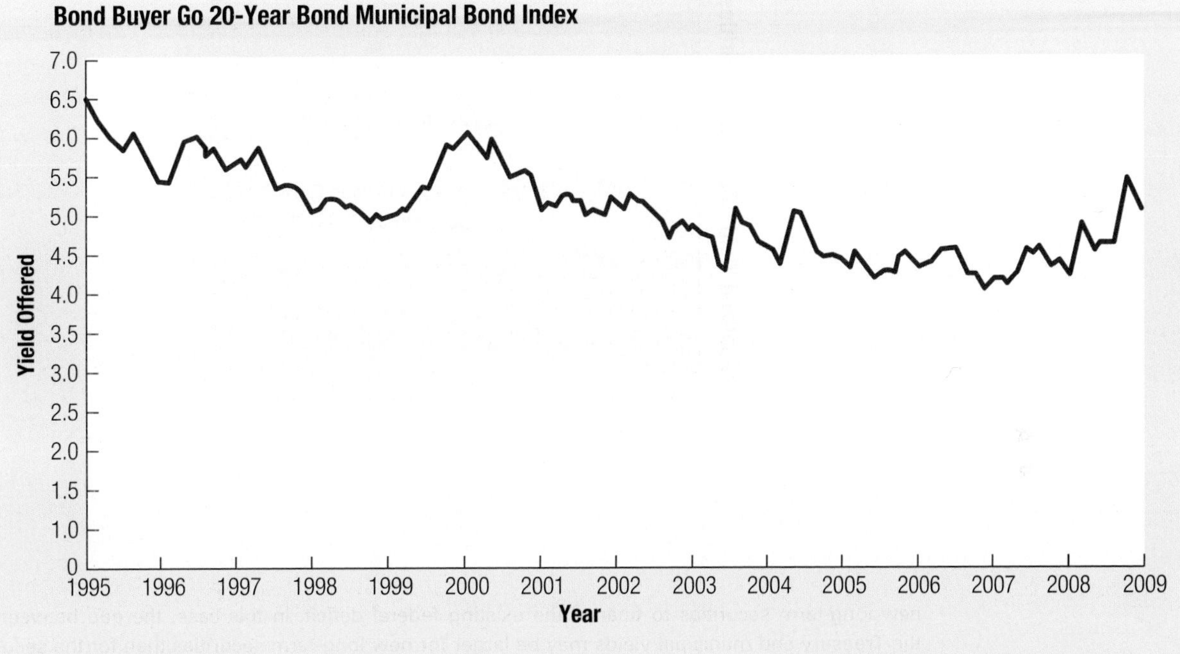

Source: *Federal Reserve.*

two disadvantages and allows municipal bonds to offer a lower yield than Treasury bonds. The yield offered on municipal bonds over time is displayed in Exhibit 7.4.

Yield Curve on Municipal Bonds   At any given time, there are municipal bonds in the secondary market that have only a short time to maturity and others that have longer terms to maturity. A municipal bond yield curve can be constructed from the municipal bonds that are available. An example of a municipal bond yield curve is shown in Exhibit 7.5, which also includes a Treasury yield curve for comparison. Notice that the municipal security yield curve is lower than the Treasury yield curve, which is primarily attributed to the tax differential between the two types of securities. The gap due to the tax differential is offset slightly by the default risk and liquidity differential. The yield on municipal securities is commonly 20 to 30 percent less than the yield offered on Treasury securities with similar maturities.

The shape of a municipal security yield curve tends to be similar to the shape of a Treasury security yield curve for two reasons. First, like the Treasury yield curve, the municipal yield curve is influenced by interest rate expectations. If investors expect interest rates to rise, they tend to favor shorter-term securities, which results in high short-term security prices and low short-term yields in both the municipal and Treasury markets. Second, investors require a premium for longer-term securities with lower liquidity in both the municipal and Treasury markets. If supply conditions differ, the shapes could differ.

EXAMPLE

At a particular point in time, assume that the economy is strong and municipalities experience budget surpluses. Many of them will not have to issue new bonds, so those municipalities that do need long-term funds can more easily find buyers. Meanwhile, the Treasury may still issue

Exhibit 7.5 Annualized Yield Offered on Securities

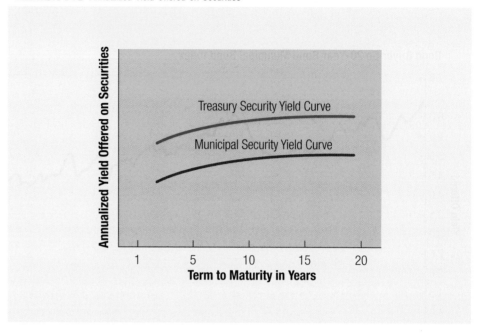

new long-term securities to finance the existing federal deficit. In this case, the gap between the Treasury and municipal yields may be larger for new long-term securities than for the securities that were issued in the past and now have a shorter term to maturity. ●

CORPORATE BONDS

Corporate bonds are long-term debt securities issued by corporations. They promise the owner coupon payments (interest) on a semiannual basis. The minimum denomination is $1,000. Their maturity is typically between 10 and 30 years, although Boeing, Chevron, and other corporations have issued 50-year bonds, and Disney, AT&T, and the Coca-Cola Company issued 100-year bonds. The interest paid by the corporation to investors is tax-deductible to the corporation, which reduces the cost of financing with bonds. Since equity financing does not involve interest payments, it does not offer the same tax advantage. This is a major reason why many corporations rely heavily on bonds to finance their operations. Nevertheless, there is a limit to the amount of funds a corporation can obtain by issuing bonds, because it must be capable of making the coupon payments.

Corporate Bond Offerings

Corporate bonds can be placed with investors through a public offering or a private placement.

Public Offering   Corporations commonly issue bonds through a public offering. A corporation that plans to issue bonds hires an investment bank to underwrite the bonds. The underwriter assesses market conditions and attempts to determine the price at which the corporation's bonds can be sold and the appropriate size (dollar amount) of the offering. The goal is to price the bonds high enough to satisfy the issuer, but also low enough so that the entire bond offering can be placed. If the offering is too large or the price is too high, there may not be enough investors who are willing to purchase the bonds. In this case, the underwriter will have to lower the price in order to sell all the bonds. The issuer registers with the Securities and Exchange Commission (SEC) and submits a prospectus that explains the planned size of the offering, its updated financial condition (supported by financial statements), and its planned use of the funds. Meanwhile, the underwriter distributes the prospectus to other investment banks that it invites to join a syndicate to help place the bonds in the market. Once the SEC approves the issue, the underwriting syndicate attempts to place the bonds. A portion of the bonds that are registered can be shelved for up to two years if the issuer wants to defer placing the entire offering at once.

Underwriters typically try to place newly issued corporate bonds with institutional investors, such as pension funds, bond mutual funds, and insurance companies, because these investors are more likely to purchase large pieces of the offering. Many of these institutional investors may plan to hold the bonds for a long-term period, but if they decide to sell the bonds, they can sell them to other investors.

Private Placement   Some corporate bonds are privately placed rather than sold in a public offering. A private placement does not have to be registered with the SEC. Small firms that borrow relatively small amounts of funds (such as $30 million) may consider private placements rather than public offerings, since they may be able to find an institutional investor that will purchase the entire offering. Although the issuer does not need to register with the SEC, it still needs to disclose financial data to convince any prospective purchasers that the bonds will be repaid in a timely manner. The issuer may hire a securities firm to place the bonds because such firms are normally better able to identify institutional investors that may be interested in purchasing privately placed debt.

The institutional investors that commonly purchase a private placement include insurance companies, pension funds, and bond mutual funds. Since privately placed bonds do not have an active secondary market, they tend to be purchased by institutional investors that are willing to invest for long periods of time. The SEC's Rule 144A creates liquidity for privately placed securities by allowing large institutional investors to trade privately placed bonds (and some other securities) with each other even though the securities are not required to be registered with the SEC.

Characteristics of Corporate Bonds

Corporate bonds can be described according to a variety of characteristics. The bond **indenture** is a legal document specifying the rights and obligations of both the issuing firm and the bondholders. It is very comprehensive (normally several hundred pages) and is designed to address all matters related to the bond issue (collateral, payment dates, default provisions, call provisions, etc.).

Federal law requires that for each bond issue of significant size a **trustee** be appointed to represent the bondholders in all matters concerning the bond issue. The trustee's duties include monitoring the issuing firm's activities to ensure compliance with the terms of the indenture. If the terms are violated, the trustee initiates legal action against the issuing firm and represents the bondholders in that action. Bank trust departments are frequently hired to perform the duties of trustee.

Bonds are not as standardized as stocks. A single corporation may issue more than 50 different bonds with different maturities and payment terms. Some of the characteristics that differentiate one bond from another are identified here.

Sinking-Fund Provision   Bond indentures frequently include a **sinking-fund provision**, or a requirement that the firm retire a certain amount of the bond issue each year. This provision is considered to be an advantage to the remaining bondholders because it reduces the payments necessary at maturity.

Specific sinking-fund provisions can vary significantly among bond issues. For example, a bond with 20 years until maturity could have a provision to retire 5 percent of the bond issue each year. Or it could have a requirement to retire 5 percent each year beginning in the fifth year, with the remaining amount to be retired at maturity. The actual mechanics of bond retirement are carried out by the trustee.

Protective Covenants   Bond indentures normally place restrictions on the issuing firm that are designed to protect the bondholders from being exposed to increasing risk during the investment period. These so-called protective covenants frequently limit the amount of dividends and corporate officers' salaries the firm can pay and also restrict the amount of additional debt the firm can issue. Other financial policies may be restricted as well.

Protective covenants are needed because shareholders and bondholders have different expectations of a firm's management. Shareholders may prefer that managers use a relatively large amount of debt because they can benefit directly from risky managerial decisions that will generate higher returns on investment. In contrast, bondholders simply hope to receive their principal back, with interest. Since they do not share in the excess returns generated by a firm, they would prefer that managerial decisions be conservative. Protective covenants can prevent managers from taking excessive risk and therefore satisfy the preferences of bondholders. If managers are unwilling to accept some protective covenants, they may not be able to obtain debt financing.

WEB

www.investinginbonds
.com

Click on "See
Corporate Market At-
A-Glance" to find data
and other information
about corporate bonds.

Call Provisions   Most bonds include a provision allowing the firm to call the bonds. A **call provision** normally requires the firm to pay a price above par value when it calls its bonds. The difference between the bond's call price and par value is the **call premium.** Call provisions have two principal uses. First, if market interest rates decline after a bond issue has been sold, the firm might end up paying a higher rate of interest than the prevailing rate for a long period of time. Under these circumstances, the firm may consider selling a new issue of bonds with a lower interest rate and using the proceeds to retire the previous issue by calling the old bonds.

EXAMPLE

Four years ago, Mirossa Company issued 10-year bonds that offered a yield of 11 percent. Since then, interest rates have declined, and Mirossa's credit rating has improved. It could issue 10-year bonds today for a yield of 7 percent. The company is sure that it will need funding for the next 10 years. It issues new 10-year bonds at a yield of 7 percent and uses some of the proceeds to call (buy back) the bonds issued four years ago. It reduces its cost of financing as a result of calling these bonds. Ten years from today, Mirossa Company will repay the principal on the newly issued bonds. ●

Second, a call provision may be used to retire bonds as required by a sinking-fund provision. Many bonds have two different call prices: a lower price for calling the bonds to meet sinking-fund requirements and a higher price if the bonds are called for any other reason.

Bondholders normally view a call provision as a disadvantage because it can disrupt their investment plans and reduce their investment returns. As a result, firms must pay slightly higher rates of interest on bonds that are callable, other things being equal.

Bond Collateral   Bonds can be classified according to whether they are secured by collateral and by the nature of that collateral. Usually, the collateral is a mortgage on real property (land and buildings). A **first mortgage bond** has first claim on the specified assets. A **chattel mortgage bond** is secured by personal property.

Bonds unsecured by specific property are called **debentures** (backed only by the general credit of the issuing firm). These bonds are normally issued by large, financially sound firms whose ability to service the debt is not in question. **Subordinated debentures** have claims against the firm's assets that are junior to the claims of both mortgage bonds and regular debentures. Owners of subordinated debentures receive nothing until the claims of mortgage bondholders, regular debenture owners, and secured short-term creditors have been satisfied. The main purchasers of subordinated debt are pension funds and insurance companies.

Low- and Zero-Coupon Bonds In the early 1980s, firms began issuing bonds with coupons roughly half the size of the prevailing rate and later issued bonds with zero coupons. These **low-coupon** or **zero-coupon bonds** are therefore issued at a deep discount from par value. Investors are taxed annually on the amount of interest earned, even though much or all of the interest will not be received until maturity. The amount of interest taxed is the amortized discount. (The gain at maturity is prorated over the life of the bond.) Low- and zero-coupon corporate bonds are purchased mainly for tax-exempt investment accounts (such as pension funds and individual retirement accounts).

To the issuing firm, these bonds have the advantage of requiring low or no cash outflow during their life. Additionally, the firm is permitted to deduct the amortized discount as interest expense for federal income tax purposes, even though it does not pay interest. This adds to the firm's cash flow. Finally, the demand for low- and zero-coupon bonds has been great enough that firms can, in most cases, issue them at a lower cost than regular bonds.

Variable-Rate Bonds The highly volatile interest rates experienced during the 1970s inspired the development of **variable-rate bonds** (also called floating-rate bonds). These bonds affect the investor and borrower as follows: (1) they allow investors to benefit from rising market interest rates over time, and (2) they allow issuers of bonds to benefit from declining rates over time.

Most issues tie their coupon rate to the London Interbank Offer Rate (LIBOR), the rate at which banks lend funds to each other on an international basis. The rate is typically adjusted every three months.

Variable-rate bonds became very popular in 2004, when interest rates were at low levels. Since most investors presumed that interest rates were likely to rise, they were more willing to purchase variable-rate than fixed-rate bonds. In fact, the volume of variable-rate bonds exceeded that of fixed-rate bonds during this time.

Convertibility Another type of bond, known as a **convertible bond**, allows investors to exchange the bond for a stated number of shares of the firm's common stock. This conversion feature offers investors the potential for high returns if the price of the firm's common stock rises. Investors are therefore willing to accept a lower rate of interest on these bonds, which allows the firm to obtain financing at a lower cost.

Corporate Bond Yields and Risk

WEB

http://finance.yahoo
.com/bonds/
composite_bond_rates
Yields on all types of
bonds for various
maturities.

Institutional and individual investors who want an investment that provides stable income may consider purchasing corporate bonds. The interest income earned on corporate bonds represents ordinary income to the bondholders and is therefore subject to federal and state (if any) taxes. Thus, corporate bonds do not provide the same tax benefits to bondholders as municipal bonds.

Yield Curve At a given point in time, the yield curve for corporate bonds will be affected by interest rate expectations, a liquidity premium, and the specific maturity preferences of corporations issuing bonds. Since these are the same factors that affect the yield curve of Treasury bonds, the shape of the yield curve for corporate bonds will also normally be similar to the yield curve for Treasury bonds, except that the curve will be higher to reflect credit risk and less liquidity.

USING THE WALL STREET JOURNAL

Bond Yields

The Wall Street Journal provides information on yields offered by various types of bond issuers, as shown here. It quotes yields on bonds issued by the Treasury, highly rated corporations (DJ Corporate), and low-rated corporations (High-Yield). Borrowers who are considering issuing bonds can review the yields to determine what yield they would have to pay. Investors assess the different yields when deciding which types of bonds to purchase. The risk premium that corporations pay above the Treasury bond yield can be estimated based on the information provided in this table.

Corporate Borrowing Rates and Yields

Bond total return index	Close	YIELD (%) Last	YIELD (%) Week ago	52-WEEK High	52-WEEK Low	TOTAL RETURN (%) 52-wk	TOTAL RETURN (%) 3-yr
Treasury, Ryan ALM	1135.02	1.839	1.563	3.958	1.503	**14.70**	9.06
10-yr Treasury, Ryan ALM	1309.63	2.505	2.086	4.264	2.078	**16.85**	9.75
DJ Corporate	209.53	6.837	6.902	8.872	5.222	**1.26**	3.59
Aggregate, Barclays Capital	1351.34	4.020	3.950	5.670	3.910	**4.09**	5.77
High Yield 100, Merrill Lynch	n.a.	n.a.	13.740	17.034	8.874	**n.a.**	n.a.
Fixed-Rate MBS, Barclays	1464.16	3.420	3.640	5.920	3.330	**8.47**	7.53
Muni Master, Merrill	n.a.	n.a.	3.930	5.021	3.276	**n.a.**	n.a.
EMBI Global, J.P. Morgan	n.a.	n.a.	9.254	12.208	6.567	**n.a.**	n.a.

Sources: J.P. Morgan; Ryan ALM; Ryan Labs; Barclays Capital; Merrill Lynch

Source: Reprinted with permission of Dow Jones & Company, Inc., from *The Wall Street Journal*, January 7, 2009; permission conveyed through the Copyright Clearance Center, Inc.

Default Rate   The general level of defaults on corporate bonds is dependent on economic conditions. When the economy is strong, firms generate higher revenue and are better able to cover their debt payments. When the economy is weak, some firms may not generate sufficient revenue to cover their operating and debt expenses and therefore default on their bonds. In the late 1990s when U.S. economic conditions were strong, the default rate was less than 1 percent, but it exceeded 3 percent in 2002 and during the credit crisis of 2008–2009 when economic conditions were weak. In 2008, the value of bonds that defaulted exceeded $100 billion, versus only $3.5 billion in 2007.

Investor Assessment of Risk   Since credit risk is associated with corporate bonds, investors may consider purchasing corporate bonds only after assessing the issuing firm's financial condition and ability to cover its debt payments. Thus, investors may rely heavily on financial statements created by the issuing firm. This presents an asymmetric information problem in that the firm knows its true condition, but investors do not. Thus, it can be a challenge for investors to properly assess a firm's ability to cover its debt payments.

EXAMPLE

Last year, Spectral Insurance Company considered purchasing bonds that were recently issued by Ladron Company. Spectral assessed Ladron's financial statements to determine whether it would have sufficient cash flows in the future to cover its debt payments. In reviewing the revenue and expenses that Ladron reported for the last year, Spectral noticed that Ladron had a large expense categorized as "nonrecurring," which indicates a onetime expense that should not occur again. Spectral ignored those expenses because it wanted to focus only on the typical operating expenses that will occur every year. After estimating Ladron's future cash flows in this manner, Spectral decided that Ladron would be capable of covering its debt payments and purchased bonds issued by Ladron for $20 million.

Last week, Ladron announced that it must file for bankruptcy because it incurred another huge nonrecurring expense this year. Spectral's mistake was that it trusted Ladron's financial statements. Like many companies, Ladron classified some operating expenses as "nonrecurring expenses" so that it could reduce its reported operating expenses and increase its reported operating earnings. Doing this is misleading, but may be within accounting guidelines. Nevertheless, Spectral incurred major losses on its investments because of the asymmetric information problem. ●

Bond Ratings   Corporate bonds are rated by rating agencies. Corporate bonds that receive higher ratings can be placed at higher prices (lower yields). Therefore, corporations can achieve a lower cost of financing when their bonds are rated highly. Corporations are especially interested in achieving an investment-grade status on their bonds (medium quality or above) because commercial banks will only invest in bonds that have investment-grade status. A corporate bond's rating may change over time if the issuer's ability to repay the debt changes.

Although bond rating agencies are skilled at assessing ability to repay debt, they are also subject to the asymmetric information problem. They commonly consider the financial statements provided by the issuer of bonds when making their assessment and will not necessarily detect any misleading information contained in the financial statements.

Secondary Market for Corporate Bonds

Corporate bonds have a secondary market, so investors who purchase them can sell them to other investors if they prefer not to hold them until maturity. The value of all corporate bonds in the secondary market exceeds $5 trillion. Bonds issued by large well-known corporations in large volume are liquid because they attract a large number of buyers and sellers in the secondary market. Bonds issued by small corporations in small volume are less liquid because there may not be any buyers for those bonds in some periods. Thus, investors who wish to sell these bonds in the secondary market may have to accept a discounted price in order to attract buyers. About 95 percent of the trading volume of corporate bonds is attributed to institutional investors.

Often, a particular company issues many different bonds with variations in maturity, price, and credit rating. Having many different bonds allows investors to find a bond issued by a particular company that fits their desired maturity and other preferences. However, it also creates higher transaction costs because brokers require more time to execute transactions for investors. In addition, some bonds issued by a particular firm may have limited liquidity, because their features are less attractive to investors.

Corporate Bond Listing   Corporate bonds are listed on an over-the-counter market or on an exchange. The over-the-counter bond market is served by bond dealers, who can play a broker role by matching up buyers and sellers. In addition, bond dealers have an inventory of bonds, so they may serve as the counterparty in a bond transaction desired by an investor. For example, if an investor wants to sell bonds that were previously issued by the Coca Cola Company, bond dealers may execute the deal by matching the sellers with investors who want to buy the bonds, or by purchasing the bonds for their own inventories. Dealers commonly handle large transactions, such as those valued at more than $1 million. Information about the trades in the over-the-counter market is provided by the National Association of Securities Dealers' Trade Reporting and Compliance Engine, which is referred to as TRACE. Some bonds also trade on the American Stock Exchange (now part of NYSE Euronext).

More than 1,000 bonds are listed on the New York Stock Exchange (NYSE). Corporations whose stocks are listed on the exchange can list their bonds for free. In 2007, the NYSE developed an electronic bond trading platform as part of its strategy to increase its presence in the corporate bond market. Electronic trading allows more transparency. Investors have access to real-time data and can more easily monitor the bid and ask prices and trading volume of corporate bonds. This market should appeal to investors who want to execute relatively small bond transactions (such as $10,000 or $20,000). The bonds listed on the NYSE are traded through its Automated Bond System (ABS), which is an electronic system used by investment firms that are members of the NYSE. The ABS displays prices and matches buy and sell orders.

Types of Orders   Various bond dealers take positions in corporate bonds and accommodate orders. Individual investors buy or sell corporate bonds through brokers, who communicate the orders to bond dealers. Investors who wish to buy or sell bonds can normally place a **market order;** in this case, the desired transaction will occur at the prevailing market price. Alternatively, they can place a **limit order;** in this case, the transaction will occur only if the price reaches the specified limit. When purchasing bonds, investors use a limit order to specify the maximum limit price they are willing to pay for a bond. When selling bonds, investors use a limit order to specify a minimum limit price at which they are willing to sell their bonds.

Trading Online   Orders to buy and sell corporate bonds are increasingly being placed online. For example, popular online bond brokerage websites are www.schwab.com and http://us.etrade.com. The pricing of bonds is more transparent online because investors can easily compare the bid and ask spreads among brokers. This transparency has encouraged some brokers to narrow their spreads so that they do not lose business to competitors.

Some online bond brokerage services such as Fidelity and Vanguard now charge a commission instead of posting a bid and ask spread. This is a more transparent method of charging investors for their service than using bid and ask prices. In addition, there is a standard fee for every trade, whereas bid and ask spreads may vary among bonds. For example, the fee may be $2 per bond, with a $25 minimum. Thus, an investor who purchases 30 bonds, with a $1,000 par value, would pay a total fee of $60 (computed as $30 \times \$2$). Online bond brokerage services can execute transactions in Treasury and municipal bonds as well. Their fees are generally lower for Treasury bond than corporate bond transactions, but higher for municipal bond transactions.

WEB
─────────
http://averages
.dowjones.com
Links to corporate bond indexes so that you can monitor the general performance of corporate bonds.

Corporate Bond Quotations   The financial press publishes quotations for corporate bonds, just as it does for Treasury bonds, although in a slightly different format (look back at Exhibit 7.3 to review the format for Treasury bonds). Corporate bond quotations also typically include the volume of trading, which is normally measured as the number of bonds traded for that day. As in Treasury bond quotations, the yield to maturity is included. A review of bond quotations on any given day will reveal significant differences among the yields of some bonds. These differences may be due to different risk levels, different provisions (such as call features), or different maturities.

Corporate bond price quotations are accessible online at www.investingin bonds.com. The quotations can be sorted by maturity, credit rating, coupon rate, or other characteristics.

Junk Bonds

Corporate bonds that are perceived to have very high risk are referred to as **junk bonds.** About two-thirds of all junk bond issues are used to finance takeovers (including leveraged buyouts, or LBOs). Some junk bond issues are used by firms to revise their capital structure. The proceeds from issuing bonds are used to repurchase stock, thereby increasing the proportion of debt in the capital structure. Although the newly issued bonds are assigned a low-grade ("junk") quality rating, some institutional investors such as insurance companies and mutual funds are willing to purchase them because of the relatively high yield offered.

Size of the Junk Bond Market   There are currently more than 4,000 junk bond offerings in the United States, with a total market value of more than $600 billion. Junk bonds represent about 25 percent of the value of all corporate bonds and about 5 percent of the value of all bonds (including Treasury and municipal bonds). About one-third of all junk bonds were once rated higher but have been downgraded to below investment grade. The remaining two-thirds were considered to be below investment-grade quality when they were initially issued.

Participation in the Junk Bond Market   There are numerous issuers of junk bonds with more than $1 billion in debt outstanding. The primary investors in junk bonds are mutual funds, life insurance companies, and pension funds. Some bond mutual funds invest only in bonds with high ratings, but there are more than 100 so-called high-yield mutual funds that commonly invest in junk bonds. Individuals account for about one-tenth of all investors in the junk bond market. Recently, some issuers of junk bonds have attempted to attract more individual investors by lowering the minimum denomination to $1,000. High-yield mutual funds allow individual investors to invest in a diversified portfolio of junk bonds with a small investment.

The secondary market for junk bonds in the United States is facilitated by about 20 bond traders (or market makers) that make a market for junk bonds. They execute secondary market transactions for customers and also invest in junk bonds for their own account.

Risk Premium of Junk Bonds   Junk bonds offer high yields that contain a risk premium (spread) to compensate investors for the high risk. Typically, the premium is between 3 and 7 percentage points above Treasury bonds with the same maturity. During periods of weak economies, such as 2002, the difference is larger. Although investors always require a higher yield on junk bonds than other bonds, they require a higher premium when the economy is weak because there is a greater likelihood that the issuer will not generate sufficient cash to cover the debt payments. During the credit crisis in the 2008–2009 period, risk premiums on newly issued junk bonds exceeded 10 percent. Economic conditions were weak, many firms were experiencing financial problems, and investors would consider investing in junk bonds only if the reward was large enough to compensate for the high risk of default.

Performance of Junk Bonds   Junk bonds are generally perceived to offer high returns with high risk. Their performance has varied in different periods depending largely on economic conditions.

During the late 1990s, junk bonds performed very well, and there were few defaults. When the economy weakened during 2001 and 2002, however, the defaults increased. Nevertheless, junk bonds regained their popularity and were commonly used during the period of economic expansion in 2005 and 2006. However, during the credit crisis in 2008, junk bonds valued at more than $25 billion defaulted. These defaults added to investors' fears and explain the high risk premium required for newly issued junk bonds at that time.

How Corporate Bonds Finance Restructuring

Firms can issue corporate bonds to finance the restructuring of their assets and to revise their capital structure. Such restructuring can have a major impact on the firm's degree of financial leverage, the potential return to shareholders, the risk to shareholders, and the risk to bondholders.

Using Bonds to Finance a Leveraged Buyout   A leveraged buyout (LBO) involves the use of debt to purchase shares and take a company private. It is typically financed with senior debt (such as debentures and collateralized loans) and subordinated debt. The senior debt accounts for 50 to 60 percent of LBO financing on average.

To understand how an LBO changes the firm's capital structure, consider the classic example of RJR Nabisco, Inc. In 1988, Kohlberg Kravis Roberts, Inc. (KKR) acquired RJR Nabisco through a $24.7 billion LBO. KKR's equity investment was only about $1.4 billion, less than 6 percent of the purchase price. The debt financing was primarily composed of

WEB

http://bonds.yahoo.
com/glossary1.html
Provides a glossary of
common terms used in
the bond market.

long-term bonds and bank loans. Before the acquisition, RJR's long-term debt was less than its shareholders' equity. After the acquisition, RJR's long-term debt was more than 12 times its shareholders' equity. Annual interest expenses were expected to be more than five times what they were before the acquisition. In 1988, RJR's cash flows totaled $1.8 billion, which was not expected to be sufficient to meet interest payments on the debt. Thus, the company needed additional cash flow to accommodate the substantial increase in financial leverage. As a result of the increase in financial leverage, prices of RJR bonds declined by 20 percent when the LBO was announced. After the LBO, RJR attempted to sell various businesses to improve its cash position.

Many firms (including RJR) go public once their operating performance improves. They typically use some of the proceeds from the stock issuance to retire some outstanding debt, thereby reducing their periodic interest payments on debt. This process is more feasible for firms that can issue shares of stock for high prices because the proceeds will retire a larger amount of outstanding debt. LBOs were popular in the 2004–2007 period, and many of them relied on junk bond financing. Fifteen of the 20 largest LBOs occurred in this period.

Using Bonds to Revise the Capital Structure   Corporations commonly issue bonds in order to revise their capital structure. If they believe that they will have sufficient cash flows to cover their debt payments, they may consider using more debt and less equity, which implies a higher degree of financial leverage. Debt is normally perceived to be a cheaper source of capital than equity, as long as the corporation has the ability to meet its debt payments. Furthermore, a high degree of financial leverage allows the earnings of the firm to be distributed to a smaller group of shareholders. In some cases, corporations issue bonds and use the proceeds to repurchase some of their existing stock. This strategy is referred to as a **debt-for-equity swap.**

When corporations use an excessive amount of debt, they may be unable to make their debt payments. Consequently, they may revise their capital structure by reducing their level of debt. In an equity-for-debt swap, corporations issue stock and use the proceeds to retire existing debt.

GLOBALIZATION OF BOND MARKETS

In recent years, financial institutions such as pension funds, insurance companies, and commercial banks have commonly purchased foreign bonds. For example, pension funds of General Electric, United Technologies Corporation, and IBM frequently invest in foreign bonds with the intention of achieving higher returns for their employees. Many public pension funds also invest in foreign bonds for the same reason. Because of the frequent cross-border investments in bonds, the bond markets have become increasingly integrated among countries. In addition, mutual funds containing U.S. securities are accessible to foreign investors.

Primary dealers of U.S. Treasury notes and bonds have opened offices in London, Tokyo, and other foreign cities to accommodate the foreign demand for these securities. When the U.S. markets close, markets in Hong Kong and Tokyo are opening. As these markets close, European markets are opening. The U.S. market opens as markets in London and other European cities are closing. Thus, the prices of U.S. Treasury bonds at the time the U.S. market opens may differ substantially from the previous day's closing price.

In recent years, low-quality bonds have been issued globally by governments and large corporations. These bonds are referred to as **global junk bonds.** The demand for these bonds has been high as some institutional investors are attracted to their high yields. For example, corporate bonds have been issued by Klabin (Brazil) and Cementos Mexicanos

(Mexico), while government bonds have been issued by Brazil, Mexico, Venezuela, the Czech Republic, and Spain.

The global development of the bond market is primarily attributed to the bond offerings by country governments. In general, bonds issued by foreign governments (referred to as sovereign bonds) are attractive to investors because of the government's ability to meet debt obligations. Nevertheless, some country governments have defaulted on their bonds, including Argentina (1982, 1989, 1990, 2001), Brazil (1986, 1989, 1991), Costa Rica (1989), Russia and other former Soviet republics (1993, 1998), and the former Yugoslavia (1992). Given that sovereign bonds are exposed to credit risk, credit ratings are assigned to them by Moody's and Standard & Poor's. Rating agencies tend to disagree more about the credit risk of sovereign bonds than about bonds issued by U.S. corporations. Perhaps this is due to a lack of consistent information available for country governments, which results in more arbitrary ratings. Also, the process of rating specific countries is still relatively new.

Eurobond Market

Non-U.S. investors who desire dollar-denominated bonds may use the Eurobond market if they prefer bearer bonds to the registered corporate bonds issued in the United States. Alternatively, they may use the Eurobond market because they are more familiar with bond placements within their own country.

An underwriting syndicate of investment banks participates in the Eurobond market by placing the bonds issued. It normally underwrites the bonds, guaranteeing a particular value to be received by the issuer. Thus, the syndicate is exposed to underwriting risk, or the risk that it will be unable to sell the bonds above the price that it guaranteed the issuer.

The issuer of Eurobonds can choose the currency in which the bonds are denominated. The issuer's periodic coupon payments and repayment of principal will normally be in this currency. Moreover, the financing cost from issuing bonds depends on the currency chosen. In some cases, a firm may denominate the bonds in a currency with a low interest rate and use earnings generated by one of its subsidiaries to cover the payments. For example, if the coupon rate on a Eurobond denominated in Swiss francs is 5 percentage points lower than the rate on a dollar-denominated bond, a U.S. firm may consider issuing Swiss franc–denominated bonds and converting the francs to dollars for use in the United States. Then it could instruct a subsidiary in Switzerland to cover the periodic coupon payments with earnings that the subsidiary generates. In this way, a lower financing rate would be achieved without exposure to exchange rate risk.

OTHER TYPES OF LONG-TERM DEBT SECURITIES

In recent years, other types of long-term debt securities have been created. Some of the more popular types are discussed here.

Structured Notes

Firms may also borrow funds by issuing structured notes. For these notes, the amount of interest and principal to be paid is based on specified market conditions. The amount of the repayment may be tied to a Treasury bond price index or even to a stock index or a currency. Sometimes issuers use structured notes to reduce their risk. For example, a structured product may specify that the principal payment will decline if bond prices decline. A bond portfolio manager that needs to borrow funds could partially insulate the portfolio risk by using structured notes, because the required repayments on the notes would decline if the bond market (and therefore the manager's bond portfolio) performed poorly.

Structured notes became very popular in the 1990s when many participants took positions in the notes in their quest for a high return. One of the reasons for the popularity of structured notes is that some investors may be able to use them to bet indirectly on or against a specific market that they cannot bet on directly because of restrictions.

EXAMPLE

The pension fund manager at Cicero Company wants to invest in Brazilian bonds, but the fund has specific restrictions against investing in emerging markets. The restrictions are intended to prevent the manager from taking excessive risk, because he is investing the money that will provide pensions for Cicero's employees when they retire. However, the manager's annual bonus is directly tied to how well the portfolio performs, so he wants to pursue strategies that might generate very large returns. He can invest in a structured note issued by a highly rated investment bank that provides large payments when Brazilian bonds perform well. The pension fund's investment holdings will show that it owns a structured product issued by a highly rated investment bank. In this way, the manager circumvents the restrictions, and his portfolio has a chance to generate a higher return, but it is also exposed to substantial risk. ●

In the early 1990s, the portfolio manager responsible for managing more than $7 billion for Orange County, California, invested in structured notes that would earn high returns if interest rates declined. The rating agencies rated these notes AAA. Apparently, the portfolio manager and the rating agencies did not understand the risk of the structured notes. The portfolio manager guessed wrong, and interest rates increased, which caused the values of the notes to decline substantially. The portfolio manager attempted to make up for the losses by borrowing funds and investing more money in structured notes, but these investments also performed poorly. In 1994, Orange County filed for bankruptcy. Many other state and local governments also suffered losses because their portfolio managers had invested in structured notes. The portfolio managers took excessive risks with the state and local government money. These managers benefited directly by receiving substantial bonuses or raises when their investments generated high returns. Their investments were questioned only after they suffered losses.

Exchange-Traded Notes

Exchange-traded notes (ETNs) are debt instruments in which the issuer promises to pay a return based on the performance of a specific debt index after deducting specified fees. The debt typically has a maturity of 10 to 30 years and is not secured by assets, meaning that investors are subject to default risk. Common issuers of ETNs are securities firms such as Goldman Sachs and Morgan Stanley. ETNs can contain commodities and foreign currencies. They are not legally defined as mutual funds and are not subject to mutual fund regulations. Thus, ETNs have more flexibility to use leverage, which means that the funding for the portfolio of debt instruments is enhanced by borrowed funds. This creates higher potential return for investors in ETNs, but also results in higher risk. The leverage magnifies the gain that investors receive, but also magnifies the loss.

Auction-Rate Securities

Auction-rate securities have been used since the 1980s as a way for borrowers such as municipalities and student loan organizations to borrow for long-term periods while relying on a series of short-term investments by investors. Every 7 to 35 days, the securities can be auctioned off to other investors, and the issuer pays interest based on the new reset rate to the winning bidders. The market for auction-rate securities reached $330 billion in 2008. Corporations and individuals who have cash available commonly invest in auction-rate securities. Investors can invest for a long-term period or can liquidate their securities to fit the investment horizon that they prefer. When investors want to sell, the financial institutions that were serving as intermediaries either find other willing buyers or repurchase the securities.

In 2008, however, the auction-rate market suffered, as some financial institutions were unable to find other buyers and no longer wanted to repurchase the securities. Consequently, when investors wanted to sell their securities at an auction, the financial institutions told them that their investments were frozen and could not be sold because there was not sufficient demand. The values of some of these securities declined substantially, and investors claimed that they had not been informed of the limited liquidity and the risks involved. In response to pressure from the SEC and state regulators, some financial institutions agreed to buy back the securities at face value from individuals who had previously purchased them. These problems occurred after the credit crisis began, when many financial institutions already were holding other types of securities (such as securities backed by subprime mortgages) whose values and liquidity had declined substantially.

SUMMARY

- Bonds are issued to finance government expenditures, housing, and corporate expenditures. Many financial institutions such as commercial banks issue bonds to finance their operations. In addition, most types of financial institutions are major investors in bonds.

- Bonds can be classified in four categories according to the type of issuer: Treasury bonds, federal agency bonds, municipal bonds, and corporate bonds. The issuers are perceived to have different levels of credit risk. In addition, the bonds have different degrees of liquidity, and different provisions. Thus, quoted yields at a given point in time vary across bonds.

- Bond yields vary among countries. Investors are attracted to high bond yields in foreign countries, causing

funds to flow to those countries. Consequently, bond markets have become globally integrated.

- Structured notes are long-term debt instruments that allow investors to bet indirectly on or against a specific market that they cannot bet on directly because of restrictions. Exchange-traded notes (ETNs) are debt instruments in which the issuer promises to pay a return based on the performance of a specific debt index after deducting specified fees. They are not legally defined as mutual funds and therefore are not subject to mutual fund regulations. They also have more flexibility to use leverage, which can achieve higher returns for investors, but also results in higher risk.

POINT COUNTER-POINT

Should Financial Institutions Invest in Junk Bonds?

Point Yes. Financial institutions have managers who are capable of weighing the risk against the potential return. They can earn a significantly higher return when investing in junk bonds than the return on Treasury bonds. Their shareholders benefit when they increase the return on the portfolio.

Counter-Point No. The financial system is based on trust in financial institutions and confidence that the

financial institutions will survive. If financial institutions take excessive risk, the entire financial system is at risk.

Who Is Correct? Use the Internet to learn more about this issue. Offer your own opinion on this issue.

QUESTIONS AND APPLICATIONS

1. Zero-Coupon Bonds What are the advantages and disadvantages to a firm that issues low- or zero-coupon bonds?

2. Bond Downgrade Explain how the downgrading of bonds for a particular corporation affects the prices of those bonds, the return to investors that currently hold these bonds, and the potential return to other investors who may invest in the bonds in the near future.

3.   Debentures What are debentures? How do they differ from subordinated debentures?

4.   Yield Curve for Municipal Securities Explain how the shape of the yield curve for municipal securities compares to the Treasury yield curve. Under what conditions do you think the two yield curves could be different?

5.   Bond Collateral Explain the use of bond collateral, and identify the common types of collateral for bonds.

6.   Calling Bonds As a result of the terrorist attack on September 11, 2001, economic conditions were expected to decline. How do you think this would have affected the tendency of firms to call bonds?

7.   Call Provisions Explain the use of call provisions on bonds. How can a call provision affect the price of a bond?

8.   Global Interaction of Bond Yields If bond yields in Japan rise, how might U.S. bond yields be affected? Why?

9.   Protective Covenants What are protective covenants? Why are they needed?

10.   Impact of Credit Crisis on Junk Bonds Explain how the credit crisis affected the defaults on junk bonds and the risk premiums offered on newly issued junk bonds.

11.   Sinking-Fund Provision Explain the use of a sinking-fund provision. How can it reduce the investor's risk?

12.   Convertible Bonds Why can convertible bonds be issued by firms at a higher price than other bonds?

13.   Bond Indenture What is a bond indenture? What is the function of a trustee, as related to the bond indenture?

14.   Variable-Rate Bonds Are variable-rate bonds attractive to investors who expect interest rates to decrease? Explain. Would a firm that needs to borrow funds consider issuing variable-rate bonds if it expects that interest rates will decrease? Explain.

Advanced Questions

15.   Event Risk An insurance company purchased bonds issued by Hartnett Company two years ago. To-

day, Hartnett Company has begun to issue junk bonds and is using the funds to repurchase most of its existing stock. Why might the market value of those bonds held by the insurance company be affected by this action?

16.   Auction-Rate Securities Explain why the market for auction-rate securities suffered in 2008.

17.   Junk Bonds Merrito, Inc. is a large U.S. firm that issued bonds several years ago. Its bond ratings declined over time, and about a year ago, the bonds were rated in the junk bond classification. Nevertheless, investors were buying the bonds in the secondary market because of the attractive yield they offered. Last week, Merrito defaulted on its bonds, and the prices of most other junk bonds declined abruptly on the same day. Explain why news of Merrito's financial problems could cause the prices of junk bonds issued by other firms to decrease, even when those firms had no business relationships with Merrito. Explain why the prices of those junk bonds with less liquidity declined more than those with a high degree of liquidity.

18.   Exchange-Traded Notes Explain what exchange-traded notes are and how they are used. Why are they risky?

Interpreting Financial News
Interpret the following statements made by Wall Street analysts and portfolio managers:

a. "The values of some stocks are dependent on the bond market. When investors are not interested in junk bonds, the values of stocks ripe for leveraged buyouts decline."

b. "The recent trend in which many firms are using debt to repurchase some of their stock is a good strategy as long as they can withstand the stagnant economy."

c. "Although yields among bonds are related, today's rumors of a tax cut caused an increase in the yield on municipal bonds, while the yield on corporate bonds declined."

Managing in Financial Markets
Forecasting Bond Returns As a portfolio manager for an insurance company, you are about to invest funds in one of three possible investments: (1) 10-year coupon bonds issued by the U.S. Treasury, (2) 20-year zero-coupon bonds issued by the Treasury, or (3) one-year Treasury securities. Each possible investment is perceived to have no risk of default. You plan to maintain this investment for a one-year period. The return of each investment over a one-year horizon will be about the same if interest rates do not change over

the next year. However, you anticipate that the U.S. inflation rate will decline substantially over the next year, while most of the other portfolio managers in the United States expect inflation to increase slightly.

a. If your expectations are correct, how will the return of each investment be affected over the one-year horizon?

b. If your expectations are correct, which of the three investments should have the highest return over the one-year horizon? Why?

c. Offer one reason why you might not select the investment that would have the highest expected return over the one-year investment horizon.

PROBLEMS

1.   Inflation-Indexed Treasury Bond An inflation-indexed Treasury bond has a par value of $1,000 and a coupon rate of 6 percent. An investor purchases this bond and holds it for one year. During the year, the consumer price index increases by 1 percent every six months, for a total increase in inflation of 2 percent. What are the total interest payments the investor will receive during the year?

2.   Inflation-Indexed Treasury Bond Assume that the U.S. economy experienced deflation during the year and that the consumer price index decreased by 1 percent in the first six months of the year and by 2 percent during the second six months of the year. If an investor had purchased inflation-indexed Treasury bonds with a par value of $10,000 and a coupon rate of 5 percent, how much would she have received in interest during the year?

FLOW OF FUNDS EXERCISE

Financing in the Bond Markets

If the economy continues to be strong, Carson Company may need to increase its production capacity by about 50 percent over the next few years to satisfy demand. It would need financing to expand and accommodate the increase in production. Recall that the yield curve is currently upward sloping. Also recall that Carson is concerned about a possible slowing of the economy because of potential Fed actions to reduce inflation. It needs funding to cover payments for supplies. It is also considering issuing stock or bonds to raise funds in the next year.

a. Assume that Carson has two choices to satisfy the increased demand for its products. It could increase production by 10 percent with its existing facilities. In this case, it could obtain short-term financing to cover the extra production expense and then use a portion of the revenue received to finance this level of production in the future. Alternatively, it could issue bonds and use the proceeds to buy a larger facility that would allow for 50 percent more capacity.

b. Carson currently has a large amount of debt, and its assets have already been pledged to back up

its existing debt. It does not have additional collateral. At this point in time, the credit risk premium it would pay is similar in the short-term and long-term debt markets. Does this imply that the cost of financing is the same in both markets?

c. Should Carson consider using a call provision if it issues bonds? Why? Why might Carson decide not to include a call provision on the bonds?

d. If Carson issues bonds, it would be a relatively small bond offering. Should Carson consider a private placement of bonds? What type of investor might be interested in participating in a private placement? Do you think Carson could offer the same yield on a private placement as it could on a public placement? Explain.

e. Financial institutions such as insurance companies and pension funds commonly purchase bonds. Explain the flow of funds that runs through these financial institutions and ultimately reaches corporations that issue bonds such as Carson Company.

INTERNET/EXCEL EXERCISE

1. Go to http://finance.yahoo.com/bonds. Click on "Composite Bond Rates." Compare the rate of a 10-year Treasury bond versus a 10-year municipal bond. Which type of bond would offer you a higher annual yield based on your tax bracket, given that the municipal bond is not subject to federal income taxes? Determine the premium contained in the yield of a 10-year corporate A-rated bond as compared to the 10-year Treasury bonds. Compare that premium to the premium that existed one month ago. Did the premium increase or decrease? Offer an explanation for the change. Is the change attributed to economic conditions?

WSJ EXERCISE

Impact of Treasury Financing on Bond Prices

The Treasury periodically issues new bonds to finance the deficit. Review recent issues of *The Wall Street Journal* or check related online news to find a recent article on such financing. Does the article suggest that financial markets are expecting upward pressure on interest rates as a result of the Treasury financing? What happened to prices of existing bonds when the Treasury announced its intentions to issue new bonds?

8

Bond Valuation and Risk

The specific objectives of this chapter are to:

- explain how bonds are priced,

- identify the factors that affect bond prices,

- explain how the sensitivity of bond prices to interest rates is dependent on particular bond characteristics,

- describe common strategies used to invest in bonds, and

- explain the benefits of diversifying bonds internationally.

EXAMPLE

WEB

www.finpipe.com/valuebnd.htm

More information on the process of valuing bonds.

The values of bonds can change substantially over time. Hence, financial institutions that consider buying or selling bonds closely monitor their values.

BOND VALUATION PROCESS

Bonds are debt obligations with long-term maturities commonly issued by governments or corporations to obtain long-term funds. They are commonly purchased by financial institutions that wish to invest funds for long-term periods.

Bond valuation is conceptually similar to the valuation of capital budgeting projects, businesses, or even real estate. The appropriate price reflects the present value of the cash flows to be generated by the bond in the form of periodic interest (or coupon) payments and the principal payment to be provided at maturity. The coupon payment is based on the coupon rate multiplied by the par value of the bond. Thus, a bond with a 9 percent coupon rate and $1,000 par value pays $90 in coupon payments per year. Because these expected cash flows are known, the valuation of bonds is generally perceived to be easier than the valuation of equity securities.

The current price of a bond should be the present value (*PV*) of its remaining cash flows:

$$PV \text{ of bond} = \frac{C}{(1 + k)^1} + \frac{C}{(1 + k)^2} + \cdots + \frac{C + \text{Par}}{(1 + k)^n}$$

where
C = coupon payment provided in each period
Par = par value
k = required rate of return per period used to discount the bond
n = number of periods to maturity

Consider a bond that has a par value of $1,000, pays $100 at the end of each year in coupon payments, and has three years remaining until maturity. Assume that the prevailing annualized yield on other bonds with similar characteristics is 12 percent. In this case, the appropriate price of the bond can be determined as follows. The future cash flows to investors who would purchase this bond are $100 in Year 1, $100 in Year 2, and $1,100 (computed as $100 in coupon payments plus $1,000 par value) in Year 3. The appropriate market price of the bond is its present value:

$$\begin{aligned} PV \text{ of bond} &= \$100/(1 + .12)^1 + \$100/(1 + .12)^2 + \$1,100/(1 + .12)^3 \\ &= \$89.29 + \$79.72 + \$782.96 \\ &= \$951.97 \end{aligned}$$

This valuation procedure is illustrated in Exhibit 8.1. Because this example assumes that investors require a 12 percent return, *k* equals 12 percent. At the price of $951.97, the bondholders purchasing this bond will receive a 12 percent annualized return. ●

Exhibit 8.1 Valuation of a Three-Year Bond

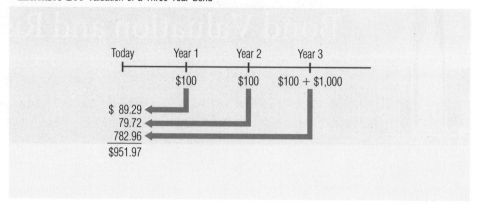

When using a financial calculator, the present value of the bond in the previous example can be determined as follows:

INPUT	3	12	100	1000		
Function Key	N	I	PMT	FV	CPT	PV
Answer						951.97

Impact of the Discount Rate on Bond Valuation

The discount rate selected to compute the present value is critical to accurate valuation. Exhibit 8.2 shows the wide range of present value results at different discount rates, for a $10,000 payment in 10 years. The appropriate discount rate for valuing any asset is the yield that could be earned on alternative investments with similar risk and maturity.

Exhibit 8.2 Relationship between Discount Rate and Present Value of $10,000 Payment to Be Received in 10 Years

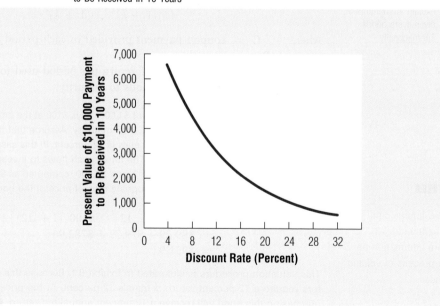

Since investors require higher returns on riskier securities, they use higher discount rates to discount the future cash flows of these securities. Consequently, a high-risk security will have a lower value than a low-risk security even though both securities have the same expected cash flows.

Impact of the Timing of Payments on Bond Valuation

The market price of a bond is also affected by the timing of the payments made to bond-holders. Funds received sooner can be reinvested to earn additional returns. Thus, a dollar to be received soon has a higher present value than one to be received later. The impact of maturity on the present value of a $10,000 payment is shown in Exhibit 8.3, assuming that a return of 10 percent could be earned on available funds. The $10,000 payment has a present value of $8,264 if it is to be paid in two years. This implies that if $8,264 were invested today and earned 10 percent annually, it would be worth $10,000 in two years. Exhibit 8.3 also shows that a $10,000 payment made 20 years from now has a present value of only $1,486, and a $10,000 payment made 50 years from now has a present value of only $85 (based on the 10 percent discount rate).

Valuation of Bonds with Semiannual Payments

In reality, most bonds have semiannual payments. The present value of such bonds can be computed as follows. First, the annualized coupon should be split in half because two payments are made per year. Second, the annual discount rate should be divided by 2 to reflect two six-month periods per year. Third, the number of periods should be doubled to reflect two times the number of annual periods. Incorporating these adjustments, the present value is determined as follows:

$$\begin{matrix} PV \text{ of bond with} \\ \text{semiannual payments} \end{matrix} = \frac{C/2}{[1+(k/2)]^1} + \frac{C/2}{[1+(k/2)]^2} + \cdots + \frac{C/2+\text{Par}}{[1+(k/2)]^{2n}}$$

Exhibit 8.3 Relationship between Time of Payment and Present Value of Payment

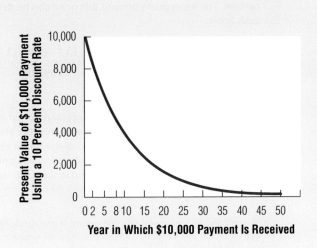

where $C/2$ is the semiannual coupon payment (half of what the annual coupon payment would have been) and $k/2$ is the periodic discount rate used to discount the bond. The last part of the equation shows $2n$ in the denominator exponent to reflect the doubling of periods.

EXAMPLE

As an example of the valuation of a bond with semiannual payments, consider a bond with $1,000 par value, a 10 percent coupon rate paid semiannually, and three years to maturity. Assuming a 12 percent required return, the present value is computed as follows:

$$
\begin{aligned}
PV \text{ of bond} &= \frac{\$50}{(1.06)^1} + \frac{\$50}{(1.06)^2} + \frac{\$50}{(1.06)^3} + \frac{\$50}{(1.06)^4} + \frac{\$50}{(1.06)^5} + \frac{\$50 + \$1,000}{(1.06)^6} \\
&= \$47.17 + \$44.50 + \$41.98 + \$39.60 + \$37.36 + \$740.21 \\
&= \$950.82
\end{aligned}
$$

●

When using a financial calculator, the present value of the bond in the previous example can be determined as follows:[1]

INPUT	6	6	50	1000		
Function Key	N	I	PMT	FV	CPT	PV
Answer						950.82

The remaining examples assume annual coupon payments so that we can focus on the concepts presented without concern about adjusting annual payments.

Relationships between Coupon Rate, Required Return, and Bond Price

Bonds that sell at a price below their par value are called **discount bonds.** The larger the investor's required rate of return relative to the coupon rate, the larger the discount of a bond with a particular par value.

EXAMPLE

Consider a zero-coupon bond (which has no coupon payments) with three years remaining to maturity and $1,000 par value. Assume the investor's required rate of return on the bond is 13 percent. The appropriate price of this bond can be determined by the present value of its future cash flows:

$$
\begin{aligned}
PV \text{of bond} &= \$0/(1+.13)^1 + \$0/(1+.13)^2 + \$1,000/(1+.13)^3 \\
&= \$0 + \$0 + \$693.05 \\
&= \$693.05
\end{aligned}
$$

The very low price of this bond is necessary to generate a 13 percent annualized return to investors. If the bond offered coupon payments, the price would have been higher because those coupon payments would provide part of the return required by investors.

Consider another bond with a similar par value and maturity that offers a 13 percent coupon rate. The appropriate price of the bond would now be

[1]Technically, the semiannual rate of 6 percent is overstated. For a required rate of 12 percent per year, the precise six-month rate would be 5.83 percent. With the compounding effect, which would generate interest on interest, this semiannual rate over two periods would achieve a 12 percent return. Because the approximate semiannual rate of 6 percent is higher than the precise rate, the present value of the bonds is slightly understated.

$$PV \text{ of bond} = \$130/(1+.13)^1 + \$130/(1+.13)^2 + \$1,130/(1+.13)^3$$
$$= \$115.04 + \$101.81 + \$783.15$$
$$= \$1,000$$

Notice that the price of this bond is exactly equal to its par value. This is because the entire compensation required by investors is provided by the coupon payments.

Finally, consider a bond with a similar par value and term to maturity and coupon rate that offers a coupon rate of 15 percent, which is above the investor's required rate of return. The appropriate price of this bond as determined by its present value is

$$PV \text{ of bond} = \$150/(1+.13)^1 + \$150/(1+.13)^2 + \$1,150/(1+.13)^3$$
$$= \$132.74 + \$117.47 + \$797.01$$
$$= \$1,047.22$$

The price of this bond exceeds its par value because the coupon payments are large enough to offset the high price paid for the bond and still provide a 13 percent annualized return. ●

From the examples provided, the following relationships should now be clear. First, if the coupon rate of a bond is below the investor's required rate of return, the present value of the bond (and therefore the price of the bond) should be below the par value. Second, if the coupon rate equals the investor's required rate of return, the price of the bond should be the same as the par value. Finally, if the coupon rate of a bond is above the investor's required rate of return, the price of the bond should be above the par value. These relationships are shown in Exhibit 8.4 for a bond with a 10 percent coupon and a par value of $1,000. If investors require a return of 5 percent and desire a 10-year maturity, they will be willing to pay $1,390 for this bond. If they require a return of 10 percent on this same bond, they will be willing to pay $1,000. If they require a 15 percent return, they will be willing to pay only $745. The relationships described here hold for any bond, regardless of its maturity.

Exhibit 8.4 Relationship between Required Return and Present Value for a 10 Percent Coupon Bond with Various Maturities

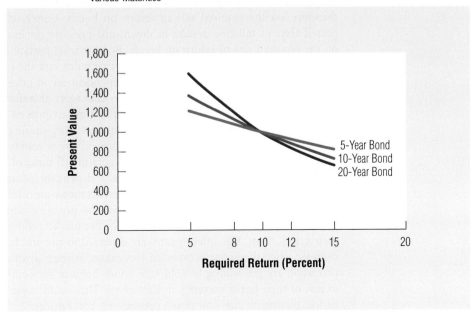

EXPLAINING BOND PRICE MOVEMENTS

As explained earlier, the price of a bond should reflect the present value of future cash flows (coupon payments and the par value), based on a required rate of return (k), so that

$$\Delta P_b = f(\Delta k)$$

Since the required rate of return on a bond is primarily determined by the prevailing risk-free rate (R_f), which is the yield on a Treasury bond with the same maturity, and the credit risk premium (RP) on the bond, the general price movements of bonds can be modeled as

$$\Delta P_b = f(\Delta R_f, \Delta RP)$$

Notice how the bond price is affected by a change in the risk-free rate or the risk premium. An increase in the risk-free rate on bonds results in a higher required rate of return on bonds and therefore causes bond prices to decrease. Thus, bonds are exposed to **interest rate risk**, or the risk that their market value will decline in response to a rise in interest rates. An increase in the credit (default) risk premium also results in a higher required rate of return on bonds and therefore causes bond prices to decrease.

The factors that are commonly monitored by bond market participants because they affect the risk-free rate or default risk premiums, and therefore affect bond prices, are identified next.

Factors That Affect the Risk-Free Rate

The long-term risk-free rate is driven by inflationary expectations (INF), economic growth (ECON), the money supply (MS), and the budget deficit (DEF):

$$\Delta R_f = f(\Delta INF, \Delta ECON, \Delta MS, \Delta DEF)$$
$$+ \quad\quad + \quad\quad ? \quad\quad +$$

The general relationships are summarized next.

Impact of Inflationary Expectations   If the level of inflation is expected to increase, there will be upward pressure on interest rates (as explained in Chapter 2) and, therefore, on the required rate of return on bonds. Conversely, a reduction in the expected level of inflation results in downward pressure on interest rates and, therefore, on the required rate of return on bonds. Bond market participants closely monitor indicators of inflation, such as the consumer price index and the producer price index.

Inflationary expectations are partially dependent on oil prices, which affect the cost of energy and transportation. Bond portfolio managers therefore forecast oil prices and their potential impact on inflation in order to forecast interest rates. A forecast of lower oil prices results in expectations of lower interest rates, causing bond portfolio managers to purchase more bonds. A forecast of higher oil prices results in expectations of higher interest rates, causing bond portfolio managers to sell some of their holdings.

Inflationary expectations are also partially dependent on exchange rate movements. Holding other things equal, inflationary expectations are likely to rise when a weaker dollar is expected, because that will increase the prices of imported supplies. A weaker dollar also prices foreign competitors out of the market, allowing U.S. firms to increase their prices. Thus, U.S. interest rates are expected to rise and bond prices are expected to decrease when the dollar is expected to weaken. Foreign investors anticipating dollar depreciation are less willing to hold U.S. bonds because the coupon payments will convert to less of their home currency in that event. This could cause an immediate net sale of bonds, placing further downward pressure on bond prices.

Expectations of a strong dollar should have the opposite results. A stronger dollar reduces the prices paid for foreign supplies, thus lowering retail prices. In addition, because a stronger dollar makes the prices of foreign products more attractive, domestic firms must maintain low prices in order to compete. Consequently, low inflation and therefore low interest rates are expected, and bond portfolio managers are likely to purchase more bonds.

Impact of Economic Growth

Strong economic growth tends to place upward pressure on interest rates (as explained in Chapter 2), while weak economic conditions place downward pressure on rates. Any signals about future economic conditions will affect expectations about future interest rate movements and cause bond markets to react immediately. For example, any economic announcements (such as measurements of economic growth or unemployment) that signal stronger than expected economic growth tend to reduce bond prices. Investors anticipate that interest rates will rise, causing a decline in bond prices. Therefore, they sell bonds, which places immediate downward pressure on bond prices. Conversely, any economic announcements that signal a weaker than expected economy tend to increase bond prices, because investors anticipate that interest rates will decrease, causing bond prices to rise. Therefore, investors buy bonds, which places immediate upward pressure on bond prices. This explains why sudden news of a possible economic recession can cause the bond market to rally.

Bond market participants closely monitor economic indicators that may signal future changes in the strength of the economy, which signal changes in the risk-free interest rate and in the required return from investing in bonds. Some of the more closely monitored indicators of economic growth include employment, gross domestic product, retail sales, industrial production, and consumer confidence. An unexpected favorable movement in these indicators tends to arouse expectations of an increase in economic growth and an increase in interest rates, which will put downward pressure on bond prices.

Conversely, an unexpected unfavorable movement in these indicators tends to signal a weaker economy, which arouses expectations of lower interest rates and places upward pressure on bond prices. When the credit crisis began in 2008, long-term interest rates declined, which resulted in higher Treasury bond prices.

Impact of Money Supply Growth

When the Federal Reserve increases money supply growth, two reactions are possible (as explained in Chapter 5). First, the increased money supply may result in an increased supply of loanable funds. If demand for loanable funds is not affected, the increased money supply should place downward pressure on interest rates, causing bond portfolio managers to expect an increase in bond prices and thus to purchase bonds based on such expectations.

In a high-inflation environment, however, bond portfolio managers may expect a large increase in the demand for loanable funds (as a result of inflationary expectations), which would cause an increase in interest rates and lower bond prices. Such forecasts would encourage immediate sales of long-term bonds.

Impact of Budget Deficit

As the annual budget deficit changes, so does the federal government's demand for loanable funds (as explained in Chapter 2). An increase in the annual budget deficit over the previous year results in a higher level of borrowing by the federal government, which can place upward pressure on the risk-free interest rate. In other words, increased borrowing by the Treasury can result in a higher required return on Treasury bonds. An increase in borrowing by the federal government can indirectly affect the required rate of return and therefore the yield on all types of bonds.

EXAMPLE

If the Treasury issues an unusually large number of Treasury bonds in the primary market, the result is downward pressure on the market price and upward pressure on the market yield of these bonds. Consequently, holders of corporate bonds with credit risk may then switch to

Treasury bonds because by holding such bonds, they can achieve almost the same yield without exposure to credit risk. This tendency places downward pressure on corporate bond prices and upward pressure on corporate bond yields, restoring the yield differential between corporate bonds and Treasury bonds. Since some investors perceive various bonds as substitutes, their buy and sell decisions will stabilize yield differentials among the bonds. ●

Factors That Affect the Credit (Default) Risk Premium

The credit risk premium tends to be larger for corporate or municipal bonds than for money market securities issued by a given corporation because the probability of a corporation experiencing financial distress is higher for a bond with a longer term to maturity. The general level of credit risk on corporate or municipal bonds can change in response to a change in economic growth (ECON):

$$\Delta RP = f(\Delta \text{ECON})$$

Strong economic growth tends to improve a firm's cash flows and reduce the probability that the firm will default on its debt payments. Conversely, weak economic conditions tend to reduce a firm's cash flows and increase the probability that it will default on its bonds. The credit risk premium is relatively low when economic growth is strong. When the economy is weak, however, the credit risk premium is higher, as investors will provide credit in such periods only if they are compensated for the high degree of credit risk.

Impact of the Credit Crisis on Credit Risk   After the credit crisis began in 2008, numerous U.S. companies defaulted on their bonds. In the most notable case, Lehman Brothers (a large securities firm) filed for bankruptcy and subsequently defaulted on more than $300 billion in bonds and other debt securities. As a result of the defaults of Lehman Brothers and other firms, investors became more concerned about the credit risk of bonds that corporations issued. Many investors shifted their investments from corporate bonds to Treasury bonds because they wanted to avoid credit risk. Consequently, corporations that needed to borrow long-term funds at this time could issue new bonds only if they were willing to offer a relatively high credit risk premium to compensate investors.

Changes in the Credit Risk Premium over Time   Exhibit 8.5 compares yields on Baa-rated corporate bonds and Treasury bonds over time. The yields among securities are highly correlated. Notice that the difference between the corporate and Treasury bond yields widened during periods when the economy was weak, such as during the 2008–2009 credit crisis when investors required a higher credit risk premium. When the credit crisis intensified, the Treasury bond yield declined, but the Baa-rated corporate bond yield increased. Thus, the increase in the risk premium on the Baa-rated corporate bond more than offset the reduction in the risk-free rate.

Changes in Bond Ratings over Time   Recall that bond rating agencies periodically assign a rating to bonds, which is supposed to reflect the likelihood that the issuer will satisfy its bond obligations in a timely manner and in full. A corporate bond's rating can change over time in response to changes in the issuing firm's financial condition. During the credit crisis in the 2008–2009 period, many corporations' bonds experienced downgrades. Corporate high-yield bonds were especially susceptible to downgrades during that period.

Impact of Issuer-Specific Characteristics on Credit Risk   A bond's price can also be affected by factors specific to the issuer of the bond, such as a change in its capital structure. If a firm that issues bonds subsequently obtains additional loans, it may be less

Exhibit 8.5 Comparison of Bond Yields

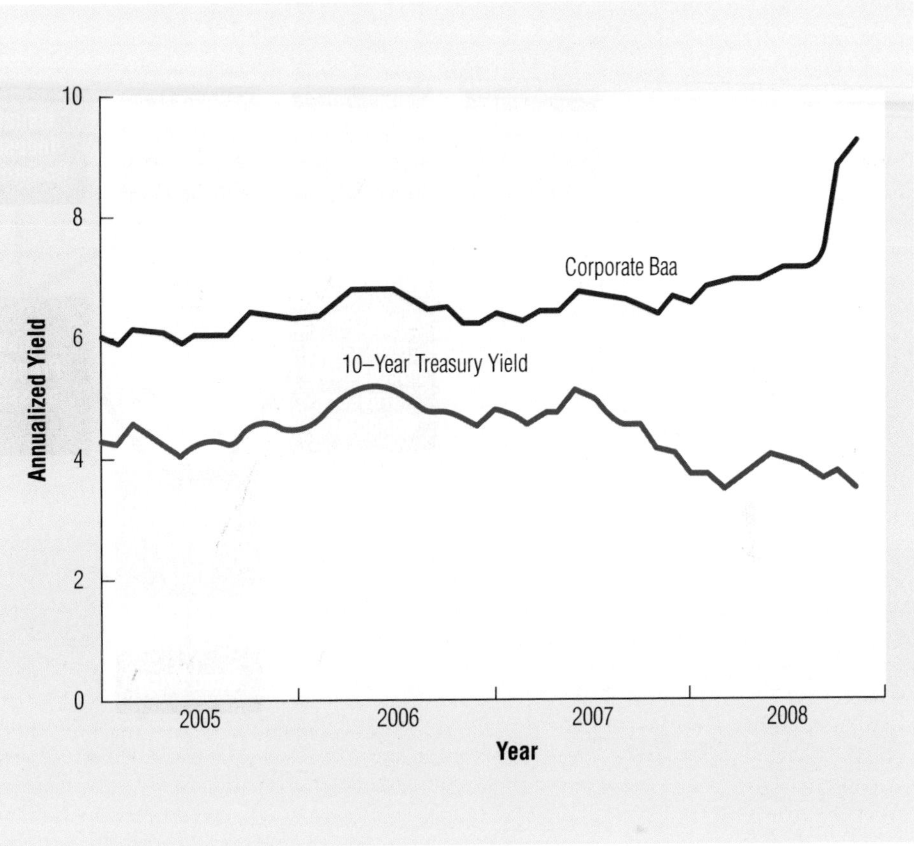

Note: Trends depict quarterly averages of bond yields.
Source: *Federal Reserve 2009.*

capable of making its coupon payments, and its credit risk increases. Consequently, investors would now require a higher rate of return if they were to purchase those bonds in the secondary market, which would cause the market value (price) of the bonds to decrease.

If the bond market is efficient, this would suggest that bond prices fully reflect all available public information. Thus, any new information about a firm that changes its perceived ability to repay its bonds could have an immediate effect on the price of the bonds.

Summary of Factors Affecting Bond Prices

When considering the factors that affect the risk-free rate and the risk premium, the general price movements in bonds can be modeled as

$$\Delta P_b = f(\Delta R_f, \Delta RP)$$
$$= f(\Delta INF, \Delta ECON, \Delta MS, \Delta DEF)$$
$$\quad - \quad\quad ? \quad\quad + \quad\quad -$$

The relationships suggested here assume that other factors are held constant. In reality, other factors are changing as well, which makes it difficult to disentangle the precise impact of each factor on bond prices. The effect of economic growth is uncertain because a high level of economic growth can adversely affect bond prices by causing a higher risk-free rate, but can favorably affect bond prices by lowering the default risk premium.

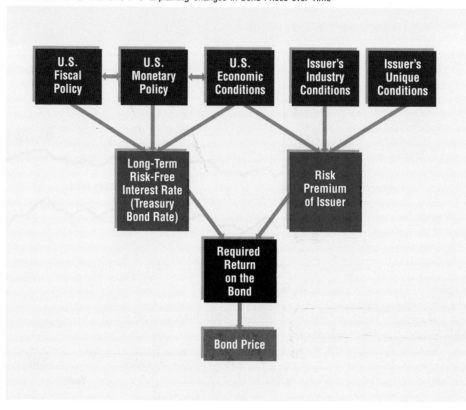

Exhibit 8.6 Framework for Explaining Changes in Bond Prices over Time

To the extent that international conditions affect each of the factors, they also influence bond prices.

Exhibit 8.6 summarizes the underlying forces that can affect the long-term risk-free interest rate and the default risk premium and therefore cause the general level of bond prices to change over time. When pricing Treasury bonds, investors focus on the factors that affect the long-term risk-free interest rate, as the default risk premium is not needed. Thus, the primary difference in the required return of a risky bond (such as a corporate bond) versus a Treasury bond for a given maturity is the default risk premium, which is influenced by economic and industry conditions.

Implications for Financial Institutions

Many financial institutions such as insurance companies, pension funds, and bond mutual funds maintain large holdings of bonds. The values of their bond portfolios are susceptible to changes in the factors described in this section that affect bond prices. Any factors that lead to higher interest rates tend to reduce the market values of financial institution assets and therefore reduce their valuations. Conversely, any factors that lead to lower interest rates tend to increase the market values of financial institution assets and therefore increase their valuations. Many financial institutions attempt to adjust the size of their bond portfolio according to their expectations about future interest rates. When they expect interest rates to rise, they sell bonds and use the proceeds to purchase short-term securities that are less sensitive to interest rate movements. If they anticipate that the risk premiums of risky bonds will increase, they shift toward relatively safe bonds that exhibit less credit risk.

USING THE WALL STREET JOURNAL

Bond Values

The Wall Street Journal provides information on how bond values have changed during the last year, as shown here. Specifically, it provides the total return from investing in bonds from the beginning of the year. It also discloses the range of the yields offered on different types of bonds over the previous year.

Investors can compare the returns earned on their bond investments to the benchmarks provided here.

Source: Republished with permission of Dow Jones & Company, Inc., from *The Wall Street Journal*, April 6, 2007; permission conveyed through the Copyright Clearance Center, Inc.

Tracking Bond Benchmarks

Return on investment and spreads over Treasurys and/or yields paid to investors compared with 52-week highs and lows for different types of bonds

Total return close	YTD total return (%)	Index	Latest	Low	YIELD (%), 52-WEEK RANGE ○ Latest	High
1351.34	−0.2	**Broad market** Barclays Aggregate	4.020	3.910		5.670
1487.92	−0.2	**U.S. Corporate** Barclays Capital	7.600	5.380		9.090
1522.97	0.3	Intermediate	7.610	5.000		9.030
1669.75	−1.9	Long term	7.600	6.420		9.420
340.33	−0.7	Double-A-rated	5.550	4.740		7.610
296.56	unch.	Triple-B-rated	9.560	5.900		10.220
n.a.	n.a.	**High Yield Constrained** Merrill Lynch	n.a.	9.850		22.490
n.a.	n.a.	Triple-C-rated	n.a.	13.528		40.034
n.a.	n.a.	High Yield 100	n.a.	8.874		17.034
n.a.	n.a.	Global High Yield Constrained	n.a.	9.774		22.954
n.a.	n.a.	Europe High Yield Constrained	n.a.	9.362		27.356
1323.62	−0.8	**U.S Agency** Barclays	2.400	2.110		4.310
1218.17	−0.5	10-20 years	2.210	1.950		4.190
2036.27	−3.6	20-plus years	4.410	3.720		5.800
1464.16	0.8	**Mortgage-Backed** Barclays	3.420	3.330		5.920
1432.02	0.8	Ginnie Mae (GNMA)	4.010	3.920		5.940
847.46	0.8	Fannie mae (FNMA)	3.300	3.200		5.910
1319.69	0.8	Freddie Mae (FHLMC)	3.380	3.320		5.940
n.a.	n.a.	**Muni Master** Merrill Lynch	n.a.	3.276		5.021
240.74	1.1	7-12 year	3.800	3.224		5.223
244.43	1.5	12-22 year	5.110	3.931		6.183
204.62	2.1	22-plus year	6.400	4.674		7.171
1556.15	−0.5	**Yankee** Barclays	5.470	4.310		6.420
406.88	−0.9	**Global Government** J.P. Morgan	2.580	2.400		7.870
579.13	−1.3	Canada	3.120	2.140		4.030
250.86	−0.8	EMU	3.870	3.660		6.440
480.88	−1.1	France	3.490	3.270		8.660
363.62	−0.9	Germany	3.220	3.030		9.110
237.25	−0.5	Japan	1.270	1.190		11.100
383.86	−1.0	Netherlands	3.580	1.020		8.690
572.70	−2.0	U.K.	3.730	3.520		5.030
n.a.	n.a.	Emerging Markets **	n.a.	6.567		12.208

* Constrained indexes limit individual issuer concentrations to 2%; the High Yield 100 are the 100 largest bonds   In U.S. - dollar terms Euro-zone bonds
** EMBI Global Index   Sources: Dow Jones Indexes; Merrill Lynch; Barclays Capital; J.P.Morgan

SENSITIVITY OF BOND PRICES TO INTEREST RATE MOVEMENTS

The sensitivity of a bond's price to interest rate movements is dependent on the bond's characteristics. Investors can measure the sensitivity of their bonds' prices to interest rate movements, which will indicate the potential damage to their bond holdings in response to an increase in interest rates (and therefore in the required rate of return on bonds). Two common methods for assessing the sensitivity of bonds to a change in the required rate of return on bonds are (1) bond price elasticity and (2) duration. Each method is described in turn.

Bond Price Elasticity

The sensitivity of bond prices (P) to changes in the required rate of return (k) is commonly measured by the **bond price elasticity** (P^e), which is estimated as

$$P^e = \frac{\text{percent change in } P}{\text{percent change in } k}$$

Exhibit 8.7 compares the price sensitivity of 10-year bonds with $1,000 par value and four different coupon rates: 0 percent, 5 percent, 10 percent, and 15 percent. Initially, the required rate of return (k) on the bonds is assumed to be 10 percent. The price of each bond is therefore the present value of its future cash flows, discounted at 10 percent. The initial price of each bond is shown in Column 2. The top panel shows the effect of a decline in interest rates that reduces the investor's required return to 8 percent. The prices of the bonds based on an 8 percent required return are shown in Column 3. The percentage change in the price of each bond resulting from the interest rate movements is shown in Column 4. The bottom panel shows the effect of an increase in interest rates that increases the investor's required return to 12 percent.

Exhibit 8.7 Sensitivity of 10-Year Bonds with Different Coupon Rates to Interest Rate Changes

EFFECTS OF A DECLINE IN THE REQUIRED RATE OF RETURN					
(1) BONDS WITH A COUPON RATE OF:	(2) INITIAL PRICE OF BONDS WHEN k = 10%	(3) PRICE OF BONDS WHEN k = 8%	(4) = [(3) − (2)]/(2) PERCENTAGE CHANGE IN BOND PRICE	(5) PERCENTAGE CHANGE IN k	(6) = (4)/(5) BOND PRICE ELASTICITY (P^e)
0%	$ 386	$ 463	+19.9%	−20.0%	−.995
5	693	799	+15.3	−20.0	−.765
10	1,000	1,134	+13.4	−20.0	−.670
15	1,307	1,470	+12.5	−20.0	−.625
EFFECTS OF AN INCREASE IN THE REQUIRED RATE OF RETURN					
(1) BONDS WITH A COUPON RATE OF:	(2) INITIAL PRICE OF BONDS WHEN k = 10%	(3) PRICE OF BONDS WHEN k = 12%	(4) = [(3) − (2)]/(2) PERCENTAGE CHANGE IN BOND PRICE	(5) PERCENTAGE CHANGE IN k	(6) = (4)/(5) BOND PRICE ELASTICITY (P^e)
0%	$ 386	$ 322	−16.6%	+20.0%	−.830
5	693	605	−12.7	+20.0	−.635
10	1,000	887	−11.3	+20.0	−.565
15	1,307	1,170	−10.5	+20.0	−.525

The price elasticity for each bond is estimated in Exhibit 8.7 according to the assumed change in the required rate of return. Notice in the exhibit that the price sensitivity of any particular bond is greater for declining interest rates than for rising interest rates. The bond price elasticity is negative in all cases, reflecting the inverse relationship between interest rate movements and bond price movements.

Influence of Coupon Rate on Bond Price Sensitivity   A zero-coupon bond, which pays all of its proceeds to the investor at maturity, is most sensitive to changes in the required rate of return because the adjusted discount rate is applied to one lump sum in the distant future. Conversely, the price of a bond that pays all of its yield in the form of coupon payments is less sensitive to changes in the required rate of return because the adjusted discount rate is applied to some payments that occur in the near future. The adjustment in the present value of such payments in the near future due to a change in the required rate of return is not as pronounced as an adjustment in the present value of payments in the distant future.

Exhibit 8.7 confirms that the prices of zero- or low-coupon bonds are more sensitive to changes in the required rate of return than prices of bonds with relatively high coupon rates. Notice in the exhibit that when the required rate of return declines from 10 percent to 8 percent, the price of the zero-coupon bonds rises from $386 to $463. Thus, the bond price elasticity (P^e) is

$$P^e = \frac{\dfrac{\$463 - \$386}{\$386}}{\dfrac{8\% - 10\%}{10\%}}$$

$$= \frac{+19.9\%}{-20\%}$$

$$= -.995$$

This implies that for each 1 percent change in interest rates, zero-coupon bonds change by 0.995 percent in the opposite direction. Column 6 in Exhibit 8.7 shows that the price elasticities of the higher-coupon bonds are considerably lower than the price elasticity of the zero-coupon bond.

Financial institutions commonly restructure their bond portfolios to contain higher-coupon bonds when they are more concerned about a possible increase in interest rates (and therefore an increase in the required rate of return). Conversely, they restructure their portfolios to contain low- or zero-coupon bonds when they expect a decline in interest rates and wish to capitalize on their expectations by holding bonds that will be very price-sensitive.

Influence of Maturity on Bond Price Sensitivity   As interest rates (and therefore required rates of return) decrease, long-term bond prices (as measured by their present value) increase by a greater degree than short-term bond prices because the long-term bonds will continue to offer the same coupon rate over a longer period of time than the short-term bonds. Of course, if interest rates increase, prices of the long-term bonds will decline by a greater degree.

WEB

http://invest-faq.com
Contains links to many different concepts about bonds, including duration.

Duration

An alternative measure of bond price sensitivity is the bond's **duration**, which is a measurement of the life of the bond on a present value basis. The longer a bond's duration, the greater its sensitivity to interest rate changes. A commonly used measure of a bond's duration (DUR) is

$$DUR = \frac{\sum_{t=1}^{n} \frac{C_t(t)}{(1+k)^t}}{\sum_{t=1}^{n} \frac{C_t}{(1+k)^t}}$$

where

C_t = coupon or principal payment generated by the bond

t = time at which the payments are provided

k = bond's yield to maturity, which reflects the required rate of return by investors

The numerator of the duration formula represents the present value of future payments, weighted by the time interval until the payments occur. The longer the intervals until payments are made, the larger the numerator, and the larger the duration. The denominator of the duration formula represents the discounted future cash flows resulting from the bond, which is the present value of the bond.

EXAMPLE

The duration of a bond with $1,000 par value and a 7 percent coupon rate, three years remaining to maturity, and a 9 percent yield to maturity is

$$DUR = \frac{\frac{\$70}{(1.09)^1} + \frac{\$70(2)}{(1.09)^2} + \frac{\$1,070(3)}{(1.09)^3}}{\frac{\$70}{(1.09)^1} + \frac{\$70}{(1.09)^2} + \frac{\$1,070}{(1.09)^3}}$$

$$= 2.80 \text{ years}$$

By comparison, the duration of a zero-coupon bond with a similar par value and yield to maturity is

$$DUR = \frac{\frac{\$1,000(3)}{(1.09)^3}}{\frac{\$1,000}{(1.09)^3}}$$

$$= 3 \text{ years}$$

The duration of a zero-coupon bond is always equal to the bond's term to maturity. The duration of any coupon bond is always less than the bond's term to maturity because some of the payments occur at intervals prior to maturity. ●

Duration of a Portfolio Bond portfolio managers commonly attempt to immunize their portfolio, that is, insulate it from the effects of interest rate movements. A first step in this process is to determine the sensitivity of their portfolio to interest rate movements. Once the duration of each individual bond is measured, the bond portfolio's duration (DUR_p) can be estimated as

$$DUR_p = \sum_{j=1}^{m} w_j DUR_j$$

where

m = number of bonds in the portfolio

w_j = bond j's market value as a percentage of the portfolio market value

DUR_j = bond j's duration

In other words, the duration of a bond portfolio is the weighted average of bond durations, weighted according to relative market value. Financial institutions concerned with interest rate risk may compare their asset duration to their liability duration. A positive difference means that the market value of the institution's assets is more rate sensitive than the market value of its liabilities. Thus, during a period of rising interest rates, the market value of the assets would be reduced by a greater degree than that of the liabilities. The institution's real net worth (market value of net worth) would therefore decrease.

Modified Duration   The duration measurement of a bond or a bond portfolio can be modified to estimate the impact of a change in the prevailing bond yields on bond prices. The modified duration (denoted as DUR^*) is estimated as

$$DUR^* = \frac{DUR}{(1 + k)}$$

where k represents the prevailing yield on bonds.

The modified duration can be used to estimate the percentage change in the bond's price in response to a 1 percentage point change in bond yields. For example, assume that Bond X has a duration of 8 while Bond Y has a duration of 12. Assuming that the prevailing bond yield is 10 percent, the modified duration is estimated for each bond:

Bond X	Bond Y
$DUR^* = \dfrac{8}{(1 + .10)}$	$DUR^* = \dfrac{12}{(1 + .10)}$
$= 7.27$	$= 10.9$

Given the inverse relationship between the change in bond yields and the response in bond prices, the estimate of modified duration should be applied such that the bond price moves in the opposite direction from the change in bond yields. According to the modified duration estimates, a 1 percentage point increase in bond yields (from 10 percent to 11 percent) would lead to a 7.27 percent decline in the price of Bond X and a 10.9 percent decline in the price of Bond Y. A 0.5 percentage point increase in yields (from 10 percent to 10.5 percent) would lead to a 3.635 percent decline in the price of Bond X (computed as 7.27 × 0.5) and a 5.45 percent decline in the price of Bond Y (computed as 10.9 × 0.5). The percentage increase in bond prices in response to a decrease in bond yields is estimated in the same manner.

The percentage change in a bond's price in response to a change in yield can be expressed more directly with a simple equation:

$$\%\Delta P = -DUR^* \times \Delta y$$

where $\%\Delta P =$ **percentage change in the bond's price**
$\Delta y =$ **change in yield**

The equation above simply expresses the relationship discussed in the preceding paragraphs mathematically. For example, the percentage change in price for Bond X for an increase in yield of 0.2 percentage point would be

$$\%\Delta P = -7.27 \times 0.002$$
$$= -1.45\%$$

Thus, if interest rates rise by 0.2 percentage point, the price of Bond X will drop 1.45 percent. Similarly, if interest rates decrease by 0.2 percentage point, the price of Bond X will increase by 1.45 percent according to the modified duration estimate.

Estimation Errors from Using Modified Duration   If investors rely strictly on modified duration to estimate the percentage change in the price of a bond, they will tend to overestimate the price decline associated with an increase in rates and underestimate the price increase associated with a decrease in rates.

EXAMPLE Consider a bond with a 10 percent coupon that pays interest annually and has 20 years to maturity. Assuming a required rate of return of 10 percent (the same as the coupon rate), the value of the bond is $1,000. Based on the formula provided earlier, this bond's modified duration is 8.514. If investors anticipate that bond yields will increase by 1 percentage point (to 11 percent), then they can estimate the percentage change in the bond's price to be

$$\%\Delta P = -8.514 \times 0.01$$
$$= -0.08514 \text{ or } -8.514\%$$

If bond yields rise by 1 percentage point as expected, the price (present value) of the bond would now be $920.37. (Verify this new price by using the time value function on your financial calculator.) The new price reflects a decline of 7.96 percent [calculated as ($920.37 − $1,000)/$1,000]. The decline in price is less pronounced than was estimated in the previous equation. The difference between the estimated percentage change in price (8.514 percent) and the actual percentage change in price (7.96 percent) is due to convexity. ●

Bond Convexity A more complete formula to estimate the percentage change in price in response to a change in yield will incorporate the property of convexity as well as modified duration.

The estimated modified duration suggests a linear relationship in the response of the bond price to a change in bond yields. This is shown by the straight line in Exhibit 8.8. For a given 1 percentage point change in bond yields from our initially assumed bond yield of 10 percent, the modified duration predicts a specific change in bond price. However, the actual response of the bond's price to a change in bond yields is convex and is represented by the curve in Exhibit 8.8. Notice that if the bond yield (horizontal axis) changes slightly from the initial level of 10 percent, the difference between the expected bond price adjustment according to the modified duration estimate (the straight line in Exhibit 8.8) and the bond's actual price adjustment (the convex curve in Exhibit 8.8) is

Exhibit 8.8 Relationship between Bond Yields and Prices

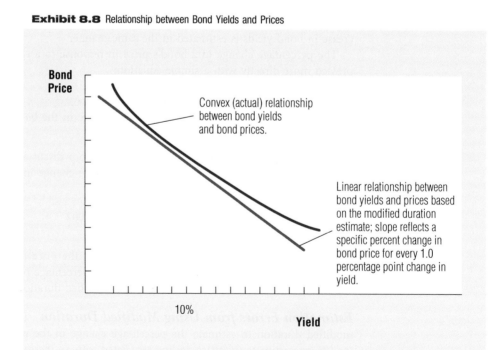

small. For relatively large changes in the bond yield, however, the bond price adjustment as estimated by modified duration is less accurate. The larger the change in the bond yield, the larger the error from estimating the change in bond price in response to the change in yield.

Since a bond's price change in response to a change in yields is positively related to the maturity of the bond, convexity is also more pronounced for bonds with a long maturity. The prices of low- or zero-coupon bonds are more sensitive to changes in yields. Similarly, bond convexity is more pronounced for bonds with low (or no) coupon rates.

Bond Investment Strategies

Many investors value bonds and assess their risk when managing investments. Some investors such as bond portfolio managers of financial institutions commonly follow a specific strategy for investing in bonds. Some of the more common strategies are described here.

Matching Strategy

Some investors create a bond portfolio that will generate periodic income that can match their expected periodic expenses. For example, an individual investor may invest in a bond portfolio that will provide sufficient income to cover periodic expenses after retirement. Alternatively, a pension fund may invest in a bond portfolio that will provide employees with a fixed periodic income after retirement. The matching strategy involves estimating future cash outflows and then developing a bond portfolio that can generate sufficient coupon or principal payments to cover those cash outflows.

Laddered Strategy

With a laddered strategy, funds are evenly allocated to bonds in each of several different maturity classes. For example, an institutional investor might create a bond portfolio with one-fourth of the funds invested in bonds with five years until maturity, one-fourth invested in 10-year bonds, one-fourth in 15-year bonds, and one-fourth in 20-year bonds. In five years, when the bonds that had five years until maturity are redeemed, the proceeds can be used to buy 20-year bonds. Since all the other bonds in the portfolio will have five years less until maturity than they had when the portfolio was created, a new investment in 20-year bonds achieves the same maturity structure that existed when the portfolio was created.

The laddered strategy has many variations, but in general, this strategy achieves diversified maturities and therefore different sensitivities to interest rate risk. Nevertheless, because most bonds are adversely affected by rising interest rates, diversification of maturities in the bond portfolio does not eliminate interest rate risk.

WEB

http://research
.stlouisfed.org
Assess the yield of
30-year Treasury bonds
over the last 24 months.

Barbell Strategy

With the barbell strategy, funds are allocated to bonds with a short term to maturity and bonds with a long term to maturity. The bonds with the short term to maturity provide liquidity if the investor needs to sell bonds in order to obtain cash. The bonds with the long term to maturity tend to have a higher yield to maturity than the bonds with shorter terms to maturity. Thus, this strategy allocates some funds to achieving a relatively high return and other funds to covering liquidity needs.

Interest Rate Strategy

With the interest rate strategy, funds are allocated in a manner that capitalizes on interest rate forecasts. This strategy is very active because it requires frequent adjustments in the bond portfolio to reflect the prevailing interest rate forecast.

Consider a bond portfolio with funds initially allocated equally across various bond maturities. If recent economic events result in an expectation of higher interest rates, the bond portfolio will be revised to concentrate on bonds with short terms to maturity. Because these bonds are the least sensitive to interest rate movements, they will limit the potential adverse effects on the bond portfolio's value. The sales of all the intermediate-term and long-term bonds will result in significant commissions paid to brokers.

Now assume that after a few weeks, new economic conditions result in an expectation that interest rates will decline in the future. Again the bond portfolio will be restructured, but now it will concentrate on long-term bonds. If interest rates decline as expected, this type of bond portfolio will be most sensitive to the interest rate movements and will experience the largest increase in value. ●

Although this type of strategy is rational for investors who believe that they can accurately forecast interest rate movements, it is very difficult for even the most sophisticated investors to consistently forecast future interest rate movements. If investors guess wrong, their portfolio will likely perform worse than if they had used a passive strategy of investing in bonds with a wide variety of maturities.

VALUATION AND RISK OF INTERNATIONAL BONDS

The value of an international bond represents the present value of future cash flows to be received by the bond's local investors. Thus, the bond's value changes over time in response to changes in the risk-free interest rate of the currency denominating the bond and in response to changes in the perceived credit risk of the bond. Since these two factors affect the market price of the bond, they also affect the return on the bond to investors over a particular holding period. An additional factor that affects the return to investors from another country is exchange rate risk. The influence of each of these factors is described next.

Influence of Foreign Interest Rate Movements

As the risk-free interest rate of a currency changes, the required rate of return by investors in that country changes as well. Thus, the present value of a bond denominated in that currency changes. A reduction in the risk-free interest rate of the foreign currency will result in a lower required rate of return by investors who use that currency to invest, which results in a higher value for bonds denominated in that currency. Conversely, an increase in the risk-free rate of that currency results in a lower value for bonds denominated in that currency. In general, the return on a bond denominated in a specific currency over a particular holding period is enhanced if the corresponding interest rate declines over that period; the return is reduced if the corresponding interest rate increases over that period. U.S. bond prices may be rising (due to a reduction in U.S. interest rates), while the prices of bonds denominated in other currencies are decreasing (due to an increase in the interest rates of these currencies).

Influence of Credit Risk

As the perceived credit (default) risk of an international bond changes, the risk premium within the required rate of return by investors is affected. Consequently, the present value of the bond changes. An increase in risk causes a higher required rate of return on the bond and therefore lowers the present value of the bond. A reduction in risk causes a lower required rate of return on the bond and increases the present value of the bond. Thus, investors who are concerned about a possible increase in the credit risk of an international bond monitor economic and political conditions in the relevant country that could affect the credit risk.

Exhibit 8.9 Dollar Cash Flows Generated from a Foreign Bond under Three Scenarios

	YEAR					
SCENARIO I (STABLE POUND)	1	2	3	4	5	6
Forecasted value of pound	$1.50	$1.50	$1.50	$1.50	$1.50	$1.50
Forecasted dollar cash flows	$300,000	$300,000	$300,000	$300,000	$300,000	$3,300,000
SCENARIO II (WEAK POUND)						
Forecasted value of pound	$1.48	$1.46	$1.44	$1.40	$1.36	$1.30
Forecasted dollar cash flows	$296,000	$292,000	$288,000	$280,000	$272,000	$2,860,000
SCENARIO III (STRONG POUND)						
Forecasted value of pound	$1.53	$1.56	$1.60	$1.63	$1.66	$1.70
Forecasted dollar cash flows	$306,000	$312,000	$320,000	$326,000	$332,000	$3,740,000

Influence of Exchange Rate Fluctuations

Changes in the value of the foreign currency denominating a bond affect the U.S. dollar cash flows generated from the bond and thereby affect the return to U.S. investors who invested in the bond. Consider a U.S. financial institution's purchase of bonds with a par value of £2 million, a 10 percent coupon rate (payable at the end of each year), currently priced at par value, and with six years remaining until maturity. Exhibit 8.9 shows how the dollar cash flows to be generated from this investment will differ under three scenarios. The cash flows in the last year also account for the principal payment. The sensitivity of dollar cash flows to the pound's value is obvious.

From the perspective of the investing institution, the most attractive foreign bonds offer a high coupon rate and are denominated in a currency that strengthens over the investment horizon. Although the coupon rates of some bonds are fixed, the future value of any foreign currency is uncertain. Thus, there is a risk that the currency will depreciate and more than offset any coupon rate advantage.

International Bond Diversification

When investors attempt to capitalize on investments in foreign bonds that have higher interest rates than they can obtain locally, they may diversify their foreign bond holdings among countries to reduce their exposure to different types of risk, as explained next.

Reduction of Interest Rate Risk   Institutional investors diversify their bond portfolios internationally to reduce exposure to interest rate risk. If all bonds in a portfolio are from a single country, their values will all be systematically affected by interest rate movements in that country. International diversification of bonds reduces the sensitivity of the overall bond portfolio to any single country's interest rate movements.

Reduction of Credit Risk   Another key reason for international diversification is the reduction of credit (default) risk. Investment in bonds issued by corporations from a single country can expose investors to a relatively high degree of credit risk. The credit risk of corporations is highly dependent on economic conditions. Shifts in credit risk will likely be systematically related to the country's economic conditions. Because economic cycles differ across countries, there is less chance of a systematic increase in the credit risk of internationally diversified bonds. During the credit crisis in the 2008–2009 period, however, there was a perception of higher credit risk (and therefore lower value) for most corporate bonds, regardless of the issuer's country.

Reduction of Exchange Rate Risk

Financial institutions may attempt to reduce their exchange rate risk by diversifying among foreign securities denominated in various foreign currencies. In this way, a smaller proportion of their foreign security holdings will be exposed to the depreciation of any particular foreign currency. Because the movements of many foreign currency values within one continent are highly correlated, U.S. investors may reduce exchange rate risk only slightly when diversifying among securities. For this reason, U.S. financial institutions commonly attempt to purchase securities across continents rather than within a single continent, as a review of the foreign securities purchased by pension funds, life insurance companies, or most international mutual funds will reveal.

The conversion of many European countries to a single currency (the euro) in recent years has resulted in more bond offerings in Europe by European-based firms. Before the introduction of the euro, a European firm needed a different currency in every European country in which it conducted business and therefore borrowed currency from local banks in each country. Now, a firm can use the euro to finance its operations across several European countries and may be able to obtain all the financing it needs with one bond offering in which the bond is denominated in euros. The firm can then use a portion of the revenue (in euros) to pay coupon payments to bondholders who have purchased the bonds. In addition, European investors based in countries where the euro serves as the local currency can now invest in bonds in other European countries that are denominated in euros without being exposed to exchange rate risk.

SUMMARY

- The value of a debt security (such as bonds) is the present value of future cash flows generated by that security, using a discount rate that reflects the investor's required rate of return. As market interest rates rise, the investor's required rate of return increases. The discounted value of bond payments declines when the higher discount rate is applied. Thus, the present value of a bond declines, which forces the bond price to decline.

- Bond prices are affected by the factors that influence interest rate movements, including economic growth, the money supply, oil prices, and the dollar. Bond prices are also affected by a change in credit risk.

- Investors commonly measure the sensitivity of their bond holdings to potential changes in the required rate of return. Two methods used for this purpose are bond price elasticity and duration. Other things being equal, the longer a bond's time to maturity, the more sensitive its price is to interest rate move-

ments. Prices of bonds with relatively low coupon payments are also more sensitive to interest rate movements.

- Common investment strategies used to invest in bonds are the matching strategy, laddered strategy, barbell strategy, and interest rate strategy. The matching strategy focuses on generating income from the bond portfolio that can cover anticipated expenses. The laddered strategy and barbell strategy are designed to cover liquidity needs while also trying to achieve decent returns. The interest rate strategy is useful for investors who believe that they can predict interest rate movements and therefore shift into long-term bonds when they believe interest rates will decline.

- Foreign bonds may possibly offer higher returns, but are exposed to exchange rate risk. Investors can reduce their exposure to exchange rate risk by diversifying among various currency denominations.

POINT COUNTER-POINT

Does Governance of Firms Affect the Prices of Their Bonds?

Point No. Bond prices are primarily determined by interest rate movements and therefore are not affected by the governance of the firms that issued the bonds.

Counter-Point Yes. Bond prices reflect the risk of default. Firms with more effective governance may be

able to reduce their default risk and thereby increase the price of their bonds.

Who Is Correct? Use the Internet to learn more about this issue. Offer your own opinion on this issue.

QUESTIONS AND APPLICATIONS

1.   Impact of Economic Conditions Assume that breaking news causes bond portfolio managers to suddenly expect much higher economic growth. How might bond prices be affected by this expectation? Explain. Now assume that breaking news causes bond portfolio managers to suddenly anticipate a recession. How might bond prices be affected? Explain.

2.   Bond Price Sensitivity Is the price of a long-term bond more or less sensitive to a change in interest rates than the price of a short-term security? Why?

3.   Impact of Oil Prices Assume that oil-producing countries have agreed to reduce their oil production by 30 percent. How would bond prices be affected by this announcement? Explain.

4.   Comparison of Bonds to Mortgages Since fixed-rate mortgages and bonds have similar payment flows, how is a financial institution with a large portfolio of fixed-rate mortgages affected by rising interest rates? Explain.

5.   Bond Price Sensitivity Explain how bond prices may be affected by money supply growth, oil prices, and economic growth.

6.   Coupon Rates If a bond's coupon rate is above its required rate of return, would its price be above or below its par value? Explain.

7.   Impact of War When tensions rise or a war erupts in the Middle East, bond prices in many countries tend to decline. What is the link between problems in the Middle East and bond prices? Would you expect bond prices to decline more in Japan or in the United Kingdom as a result of the crisis? [The answer is tied to how interest rates may change in those countries.] Explain.

8.   Exposure to Bond Price Movements How would a financial institution with a large bond portfolio be affected by falling interest rates? Would it be affected more

than a financial institution with a greater concentration of bonds (and fewer short-term securities)? Explain.

9.   Bond Price Elasticity Explain the concept of bond price elasticity. Would bond price elasticity suggest a higher price sensitivity for zero-coupon bonds or high-coupon bonds that are offering the same yield to maturity? Why? What does this suggest about the market value volatility of mutual funds containing zero-coupon Treasury bonds versus high-coupon Treasury bonds?

10.   Source of Bond Price Movements Determine the direction of bond prices over the last year and explain the reason for it.

11.   Economic Effects on Bond Prices An analyst recently suggested that there will be a major economic expansion, which will favorably affect the prices of high-rated fixed-rate bonds, because the credit risk of bonds will decline as corporations improve their performance. Assuming that the economic expansion occurs, do you agree with the analyst's conclusion? Explain.

12.   Relevance of Bond Price Movements Why is the relationship between interest rates and bond prices important to financial institutions?

13.   Inflation Effects Assume that inflation is expected to decline in the near future. How could this affect future bond prices? Would you recommend that financial institutions increase or decrease their concentration in long-term bonds based on this expectation? Explain.

14.   How Interest Rates Affect Bond Prices Explain the impact of a decline in interest rates on:

a. An investor's required rate of return.

b. The present value of existing bonds.

c. The prices of existing bonds.

15. Required Return on Bonds Why does the required rate of return for a particular bond change over time?

16. Bond Investment Decision Based on your forecast of interest rates, would you recommend that investors purchase bonds today? Explain.

Advanced Questions

17. Impact of the Credit Crisis on Risk Premiums Explain how the prices of bonds were affected by a change in the risk-free rate during the credit crisis. Explain how bond prices were affected by a change in the credit risk premium during this period.

18. International Bonds The pension fund manager of Utterback (a U.S. firm) purchased German 20-year Treasury bonds instead of U.S. 20-year Treasury bonds. The coupon rate was 2 percent lower on the German bonds. Assume that the manager sold the bonds after five years. The yield over the five-year period was substantially more than the yield the manager would have received on the U.S. bonds over the same five-year period. Explain how the German bonds could possibly generate a higher yield than the U.S. bonds for the manager, even if the exchange rate was stable over this five-year period. (Assume that the price of either bond was initially equal to its respective par value.) Be specific.

19. Interaction between Bond and Money Markets Assume that you maintain bonds and money market securities in your portfolio, and you suddenly believe that long-term interest rates will rise substantially tomorrow (even though the market does not share your view), while short-term interest rates will remain the same.

a. How would you rebalance your portfolio between bonds and money market securities?

b. If other market participants suddenly recognize that long-term interest rates will rise tomorrow, and they respond in the same manner as you do, explain how the demand for these securities (bonds and money market securities), supply of these securities for sale, and prices and yields of these securities will be affected.

c. Assume that the yield curve is flat today. Explain how the slope of the yield curve will change tomorrow in response to the market activity.

20. International Bonds A U.S. insurance company purchased British 20-year Treasury bonds instead of U.S. 20-year Treasury bonds because the coupon rate was 2 percent higher on the British bonds. Assume that the insurance company sold the bonds after five years. Its yield over the five-year period was substantially less than the yield it would have received on the U.S. bonds over the same five-year period. Assume that the U.S. insurance company had hedged its exchange rate exposure. Given that the lower yield was not because of default risk or exchange rate risk, explain how the British bonds could possibly generate a lower yield than the U.S. bonds. (Assume that either type of bond could have been purchased at the par value.)

21. How Bond Prices May Respond to Prevailing Conditions Consider the prevailing conditions for inflation (including oil prices), the economy, the budget deficit, and the Fed's monetary policy that could affect interest rates. Based on prevailing conditions, do you think bond prices will increase or decrease during this semester? Offer some logic to support your answer. Which factor do you think will have the biggest impact on bond prices?

22. Impact of the Trade Deficit Bond portfolio managers closely monitor the trade deficit figures, because the trade deficit can affect exchange rates, which can affect inflationary expectations and therefore interest rates.

a. When the trade deficit figure is higher than anticipated, bond prices typically decline. Explain why this reaction may occur.

b. On some occasions, the trade deficit figure has been very large, but the bond markets did not respond to the announcement. Assuming that no other information offset its impact, explain why the bond markets may not have responded to the announcement.

23. Implications of a Shift in the Yield Curve Assume that there is a sudden shift in the yield curve, such that the new yield curve is higher and more steeply sloped today than it was yesterday. If a firm issues new bonds today, would its bonds sell for higher or lower prices than if it had issued the bonds yesterday? Explain.

24. Impact of the Fed Assume that bond market participants suddenly expect the Fed to substantially increase the money supply.

a. Assuming no threat of inflation, how would bond prices be affected by this expectation?

b. Assuming that inflation may result, how would bond prices be affected?

c. Given your answers to (a) and (b), explain why expectations of the Fed's increase in the money supply may sometimes cause bond market participants to disagree about how bond prices will be affected.

Interpreting Financial News

Interpret the following statements made by Wall Street analysts and portfolio managers:

a. "Given the recent uncertainty about future interest rates, investors are fleeing from zero-coupon bonds."

b. "Northern Trust Bank's stock price increased as a result of the abrupt decline in interest rates, which caused investors to revalue Northern Trust's assets."

c. "Bond markets declined when the Treasury flooded the market with its new bond offering."

Managing in Financial Markets

Bond Investment Dilemma As an investor, you plan to invest your funds in long-term bonds. You have $100,000 to invest. You may purchase highly rated municipal bonds at par with a coupon rate of 6 percent; you have a choice of a maturity of 10 years or 20 years. Alternatively, you could purchase highly rated corporate bonds at par with a coupon rate of 8 percent; these bonds also are offered with maturities of 10 years or 20 years. You do not expect to need the funds for five years. At the end of the fifth year, you will definitely sell the bonds because you will need to make a large purchase at that time.

a. What is the annual interest you would earn (before taxes) on the municipal bond? On the corporate bond?

b. Assume that you are in the 20 percent tax bracket. If the level of credit risk and the liquidity for the municipal and corporate bonds are the same, would you invest in the municipal bonds or the corporate bonds? Why?

c. Assume that you expect all yields paid on newly issued notes and bonds (regardless of maturity) to decrease by a total of 4 percentage points over the next two years and to increase by a total of 2 percentage points over the following three years. Would you select the 10-year maturity or the 20-year maturity for the type of bond you plan to purchase? Why?

PROBLEMS

1.   Predicting Bond Values (Use the chapter appendix to answer this problem.) The portfolio manager of Ludwig Company has excess cash that is to be invested for four years. He can purchase four-year Treasury notes that offer a 9 percent yield. Alternatively, he can purchase new 20-year Treasury bonds for $2.9 million that offer a par value of $3 million and an 11 percent coupon rate with annual payments. The manager expects that the required return on these same 20-year bonds will be 12 percent four years from now.

a. What is the forecasted market value of the 20-year bonds in four years?

b. Which investment is expected to provide a higher yield over the four-year period?

2.   Bond Convexity Describe how bond convexity affects the theoretical linear price-yield relationship of bonds. What are the implications of bond convexity for estimating changes in bond prices?

3.   Bond Yields (Use the chapter appendix to answer this problem.) Hankla Company plans to purchase either (1) zero-coupon bonds that have 10 years to maturity, a par value of $100 million, and a purchase price of $40 million, or (2) bonds with similar default risk that have five years to maturity, a 9 percent coupon rate, a par value of $40 million, and a purchase price of $40 million.

Hankla can invest $40 million for five years. Assume that the market's required return in five years is forecasted to be 11 percent. Which alternative would offer Hankla a higher expected return (or yield) over the five-year investment horizon?

4.   Bond Duration A bond has a duration of five years and a yield to maturity of 9 percent. If the yield to maturity changes to 10 percent, what should be the percentage price change of the bond?

5.   Predicting Bond Values (Use the chapter appendix to answer this problem.) Spartan Insurance Company plans to purchase bonds today that have four years remaining to maturity, a par value of $60 million, and a coupon rate of 10 percent. Spartan expects that in three years, the required rate of return on these bonds by investors in the market will be 9 percent. It plans to sell the bonds at that time. What is the expected price it will sell the bonds for in three years?

6.   Bond Duration Determine how the duration of a bond would be affected if the coupons are extended over additional time periods.

7.   Predicting Bond Values (Use the chapter appendix to answer this problem.) Sun Devil Savings has just purchased bonds for $38 million that have a par value of $40 million, five years remaining to maturity, and a coupon rate of 12 percent. It expects the required rate of return on these bonds to be 10 percent two years from now.

a. At what price could Sun Devil Savings sell these bonds two years from now?

b. What is the expected annualized yield on the bonds over the next two years, assuming they are to be sold in two years?

c. If the anticipated required rate of return of 10 percent in two years is overestimated, how would the actual selling price differ from the forecasted price? How would the actual annualized yield over the next two years differ from the forecasted yield?

8.   Bond Elasticity Determine how the bond elasticity would be affected if the bond price changed by a larger amount, holding the change in the required rate of return constant.

9.   Predicting Bond Values (Use the chapter appendix to answer this problem.) Bulldog Bank has just purchased bonds for $106 million that have a par value of $100 million, three years remaining to maturity, and an annual coupon rate of 14 percent. It expects the required rate of return on these bonds to be 12 percent one year from now.

a. At what price could Bulldog Bank sell these bonds one year from now?

b. What is the expected annualized yield on the bonds over the next year, assuming they are to be sold in one year?

10.   Sensitivity of Bond Values

a. How would the present value (and therefore the market value) of a bond be affected if the coupon payments are smaller and other factors remain constant?

b. How would the present value (and therefore the market value) of a bond be affected if the required rate of return is smaller and other factors remain constant?

11.   Bond Value Sensitivity to Exchange Rates and Interest Rates Cardinal Company, a U.S.-based insurance company, considers purchasing bonds denominated in Canadian dollars, with a matu-

rity of six years, a par value of C$50 million, and a coupon rate of 12 percent. Cardinal can purchase the bonds at par. The current exchange rate of the Canadian dollar is $0.80. Cardinal expects that the required return by Canadian investors on these bonds four years from now will be 9 percent. If Cardinal purchases the bonds, it will sell them in the Canadian secondary market four years from now. It forecasts the exchange rates as follows:

YEAR	EXCHANGE RATE OF C$	YEAR	EXCHANGE RATE OF C$
1	$0.80	4	$0.72
2	0.77	5	0.68
3	0.74	6	0.66

a. Refer to earlier examples in this chapter to determine the expected U.S. dollar cash flows to Cardinal over the next four years. Determine the present value of a bond.

b. Does Cardinal expect to be favorably or adversely affected by the interest rate risk? Explain.

c. Does Cardinal expect to be favorably or adversely affected by exchange rate risk? Explain.

12.   Predicting Bond Values A bond you are interested in pays an annual coupon of 4 percent, has a yield to maturity of 6 percent and has 13 years to maturity. If interest rates remain unchanged, at what price would you expect this bond to be selling 8 years from now? Ten years from now?

13.   Valuing a Zero-Coupon Bond Assume that you require a 14 percent return on a zero-coupon bond with a par value of $1,000 and six years to maturity. What is the price you should be willing to pay for this bond?

14.   Bond Valuation You are interested in buying a $1,000 par value bond with 10 years to maturity and an 8 percent coupon rate that is paid semiannually. How much should you be willing to pay for the bond if the investor's required rate of return is 10 percent?

15.   Valuing a Zero-Coupon Bond Assume the following information for existing zero-coupon bonds:

Par value = $100,000

Maturity = 3 years

Required rate of return by investors = 12%

How much should investors be willing to pay for these bonds?

16. Valuing a Zero-Coupon Bond

a. A zero-coupon bond with a par value of $1,000 matures in 10 years. At what price would this bond provide a yield to maturity that matches the current market rate of 8 percent?

b. What happens to the price of this bond if interest rates fall to 6 percent?

c. Given the above changes in the price of the bond and the interest rate, calculate the bond price elasticity.

17. Bond Valuation Assume the following information for an existing bond that provides annual coupon payments:

Par value = $1,000

Coupon rate = 11%

Maturity = 4 years

Required rate of return by investors = 11%

a. What is the present value of the bond?

b. If the required rate of return by investors were 14 percent instead of 11 percent, what would be the present value of the bond?

c. If the required rate of return by investors were 9 percent, what would be the present value of the bond?

18. Predicting Bond Portfolio Value (Use the chapter appendix to answer this problem.) Ash Investment Company manages a broad portfolio with this composition:

	PAR VALUE	PRESENT MARKET VALUE	YEARS REMAINING TO MATURITY
Zero-coupon bonds	$200,000,000	$ 63,720,000	12
8% Treasury bonds	300,000,000	290,000,000	8
11% corporate bonds	400,000,000	380,000,000	10
		$733,720,000	

Ash expects that in four years, investors in the market will require an 8 percent return on the zero-coupon bonds, a 7 percent return on the Treasury bonds, and a 9 percent return on corporate bonds. Estimate the market value of the bond portfolio four years from now.

FLOW OF FUNDS EXERCISE

Interest Rate Expectations, Economic Growth, and Bond Financing

Recall that if the economy continues to be strong, Carson Company may need to increase its production capacity by about 50 percent over the next few years to satisfy demand. It would need financing to expand and accommodate the increase in production. Recall that the yield curve is currently upward sloping. Also recall that Carson is concerned about a possible slowing of the economy because of potential Fed actions to reduce inflation. It needs funding to cover payments for supplies. It is also considering issuing stock or bonds to raise funds in the next year.

a. At a recent meeting, the chief executive officer (CEO) stated his view that the economy will remain strong, as the Fed's monetary policy is not likely to have a major impact on interest rates. So he wants to expand the business to benefit from the expected increase in demand for Carson's products. The next step would be to determine how to finance the expansion. The chief financial officer (CFO) stated that if Carson Company

needs to obtain long-term funds, the issuance of fixed-rate bonds would be ideal at this point in time because she expects that the Fed's monetary policy to reduce inflation will cause long-term interest rates to rise. If the CFO is correct about future interest rates, what does this suggest about future economic growth, the future demand for Carson's products, and the need to issue bonds?

b. If you were involved in the meeting described here, what do you think needs to be resolved before deciding to expand the business?

c. At the meeting described here, the CEO stated: "The decision to expand should not be dictated by whether interest rates are going to increase or not. Bonds should be issued only if the potential increase in interest rates is attributed to a strong demand for loanable funds rather than the Fed's reduction in the supply of loanable funds." What does this statement mean?

INTERNET/EXCEL EXERCISES

Go to www.giddy.org/db/corpspreads.htm. The spreads are listed in the form of basis points (100 basis points = 1 percent) above the Treasury security with the same maturity.

1. First determine the difference between the AAA and CCC spreads. This indicates how much more of a yield is required on CCC-rated bonds versus AAA-rated bonds. Next, determine the difference between AAA and BBB spreads. Then determine the difference between BBB and CCC spreads. Is the difference larger between the AAA and BBB or the BBB and CCC spreads? What does this tell you about the perceived risk of the bonds in these rating categories?

2. Compare the AAA spread for a short-term maturity (such as 2 years) versus a long-term maturity (such as 10 years). Is the spread larger for the short-term or the long-term maturity? Offer an explanation for this.

3. Next, compare the CCC spread for a short-term maturity (such as 2 years) versus a long-term maturity (such as 10 years). Is the spread larger for the short-term or the long-term maturity? Offer an explanation for this. Notice that the difference in spreads for a given rating level among maturities varies with the rating level that you assess. Offer an explanation for this.

Forecasting Bond Prices and Yields

FORECASTING BOND PRICES

To illustrate how a financial institution can assess the potential impact of interest rate movements on its bond holdings, assume that Longhorn Savings and Loan recently purchased Treasury bonds in the secondary market with a total par value of $40 million. The bonds will mature in five years and have an annual coupon rate of 10 percent. Longhorn is attempting to forecast the market value of these bonds two years from now because it may sell the bonds at that time. Therefore, it must forecast the investor's required rate of return and use that as the discount rate to determine the present value of the bonds' cash flows over the final three years of their life. The computed present value will represent the forecasted price two years from now.

To continue with our example, assume the investor's required rate of return two years from now is expected to be 12 percent. This rate will be used to discount the periodic cash flows over the remaining three years. Given coupon payments of $4 million per year (10% × $40 million) and a par value of $40 million, the predicted present value is determined as follows:

$$PV \text{ of bonds two years from now } = \frac{\$4,000,000}{(1.12)^1} + \frac{\$4,000,000}{(1.12)^2} + \frac{\$44,000,000}{(1.12)^3}$$

$$= \$3,571,429 + \$3,188,775 + \$31,318,331$$

$$= \$38,078,535$$

An illustration of this exercise is provided in Exhibit 8A.1, using a time line. The market value of the bonds two years ahead is forecasted to be slightly more than $38 million. This is the amount Longhorn expects to receive if it sells the bonds then.

As a second example, assume that Aggie Insurance Company recently purchased corporate bonds in the secondary market with a par value of $20 million, a coupon rate of 14 percent (with annual coupon payments), and three years until maturity. The firm desires to forecast the market value of these bonds in one year because it may sell the bonds at that time. It expects the investor's required rate of return on similar investments to be 11 percent in one year. Using this information, it discounts the bond's cash flows ($2.8 million in annual coupon payments and a par value of $20 million) over the final two years at 11 percent to determine their present value (and therefore market value) one year from now:

Exhibit 8A.1 Forecasting the Market Value of Bonds

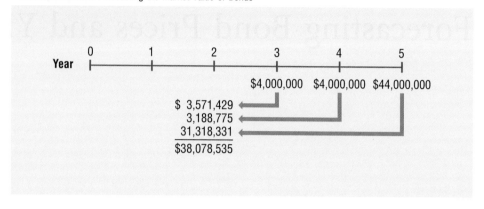

$$PV \text{ of bonds one year from now} = \frac{\$2,800,000}{(1.11)^1} + \frac{\$22,800,000}{(1.11)^2}$$

$$= \$2,522,522 + \$18,504,991$$

$$= \$21,027,513$$

Thus, the market value of the bonds is expected to be slightly more than $21 million one year from now.

FORECASTING BOND YIELDS

The yield to maturity can be determined by solving for the discount rate at which the present value of future payments (coupon payments and par value) to the bondholder would equal the bond's current price. The trial-and-error method can be used by applying a discount rate and computing the present value of the payments stream. If the computed present value is higher than the current bond price, the computation should be repeated using a higher discount rate. Conversely, if the computed present value is lower than the current bond price, try a lower discount rate. Calculators and bond tables are also available to determine the yield to maturity.

If bonds are held to maturity, the yield is known. However, if they are sold prior to maturity, the yield is not known until the time of sale. Investors can, however, attempt to forecast the yield with the methods just demonstrated, in which the forecasted required rate of return is used to forecast the market value (and therefore selling price) of the bonds. This selling price can then be incorporated into the cash flow estimates to determine the discount rate at which the present value of cash flows equals the investor's initial purchase price. Suppose that Wildcat Bank purchases bonds with the following characteristics:

- Par value = $30 million
- Coupon rate = 15 percent (annual payments)
- Remaining time to maturity = 5 years
- Purchase price of bonds = $29 million

The bank plans to sell the bonds in four years. The investor's required rate of return on similar securities is expected to be 13 percent at that time. Given this information, Wildcat forecasts its annualized bond yield over the four-year period in the following manner.

The first step is to forecast the present value (or market price) of the bonds four years from now. To do this, the remaining cash flows (one final coupon payment of $4.5 million plus the par value of $30 million) over the fifth and final year should be discounted (at the forecasted required rate of return of 13 percent) back to the fourth year when the bonds are to be sold:

$$PV \text{ of bond four years from now} = \frac{\$34,500,000}{(1.13)^1}$$

$$= \$30,530,973$$

This predicted present value as of four years from now serves as the predicted selling price in four years.

The next step is to incorporate the forecasted selling price at the end of the bond portfolio's cash flow stream. Then the discount rate that equates the present value of the cash flow stream to the price at which the bonds were purchased will represent the annualized yield. In our example, Wildcat Bank's cash flows are coupon payments of $4.5 million over each of the four years it holds the bonds; the fourth year's cash flows should also include the forecasted selling price of $30,530,973 and therefore sum to $35,030,973. Recall that Wildcat Bank purchased the bonds for $29 million. Given this information, the equation to solve for the discount rate (k) is

$$\$29 \text{ million} = \frac{\$4,500,000}{(1+k)^1} + \frac{\$4,500,000}{(1+k)^2} + \frac{\$4,500,000}{(1+k)^3} + \frac{\$35,030,973}{(1+k)^4}$$

The trial-and-error method can be used to determine the discount rate if a calculator is not available. With a discount rate of 17 percent, the present value would be

$$\begin{aligned} PV \text{ of bonds using} \atop \text{a 17\% discount rate} &= \frac{\$4,500,000}{(1.17)^1} + \frac{\$4,500,000}{(1.17)^2} + \frac{\$4,500,000}{(1.17)^3} + \frac{\$35,030,973}{(1.17)^4} \\ &= \$3,846,154 + \$3,287,311 + \$2,809,667 + \$18,694,280 \\ &= \$28,637,412 \end{aligned}$$

This present value is slightly less than the initial purchase price. Thus, the discount rate at which the present value of expected cash flows equals the purchase price is just slightly less than 17 percent. Consequently, Wildcat Bank's expected return on the bonds is just short of 17 percent.

It should be recognized that the process for determining the yield to maturity assumes that any payments received prior to the end of the holding period can be reinvested at the yield to maturity. If, for example, the payments could be reinvested only at a lower rate, the yield to maturity would overstate the actual return to the investor over the entire holding period.

With a computer program, the financial institution could easily create a distribution of forecasted yields based on various forecasts for the required rate of return four years from now. Without a computer, the process illustrated here must be completed for each forecast of the required rate of return. The computer actually follows the same steps but is much faster.

Financial institutions that forecast bond yields must first forecast interest rates for the point in time when they plan to sell their bonds. These forecasted rates can be used along with information about the securities to predict the required rate of return that will exist for the securities of concern. The predicted required rate of return is applied to cash flows beyond the time of sale to forecast the present value (or selling price) of the bonds at the time of sale. The forecasted selling price is then incorporated when estimating cash flows over the investment horizon. Finally, the yield to maturity on the bonds is determined by solving for the discount rate that equates these cash flows to the initial purchase price. The accuracy of the forecasted yield depends on the accuracy of the forecasted selling price of the bonds, which in turn depends on the accuracy of the forecasted required rate of return for the time of the sale.

FORECASTING BOND PORTFOLIO VALUES

Financial institutions can quantitatively measure the impact of possible interest rate movements on the market value of their bond portfolio by separately assessing the impact on each type of bond and then consolidating the individual impacts. Assume that Seminole Financial, Inc. has a portfolio of bonds with the required return (k) on each type of bond as shown in the upper portion of Exhibit 8A.2. Interest rates are expected to increase, causing an anticipated increase of 1 percent in the required return of each type of bond. Assuming no adjustment in the portfolio, Seminole's anticipated bond portfolio position is displayed in the lower portion of Exhibit 8A.2.

The anticipated market value of each type of bond in the exhibit was determined by discounting the remaining year's cash flows beyond one year by the anticipated required return. The market value of the portfolio is expected to decline by more than $12 million as a result of the anticipated increase in interest rates.

This simplified example assumed a portfolio of only three types of bonds. In reality, a financial institution may have several types of bonds, with several maturities for each type. Computer programs are widely available for assessing the market value of portfolios. The financial institution inputs the cash flow trends of all bond holdings and the anticipated required rates of return for each bond at the future time of concern. The computer uses the anticipated rates to estimate the present value of cash flows at that future time. These present values are then consolidated to determine the forecasted value of the bond portfolio.

Exhibit 8A.2 Forecasts of Bond Portfolio Market Value

PRESENT BOND PORTFOLIO POSITION OF SEMINOLE FINANCIAL, INC.:				
TYPE OF BONDS	PRESENT k	PAR VALUE	YEARS TO MATURITY	PRESENT MARKET VALUE OF BONDS
9% coupon Treasury bonds	9%	$ 40,000,000	4	$ 40,000,000
14% coupon corporate bonds	12%	100,000,000	5	107,207,200
10% coupon gov't agency bonds	10%	150,000,000	8	150,000,000
		$290,000,000		$297,207,200

FORECASTED BOND PORTFOLIO POSITION OF SEMINOLE FINANCIAL, INC.:				
TYPE OF BONDS	FORECASTED k	PAR VALUE	YEARS TO MATURITY AS OF ONE YEAR FROM NOW	FORECASTED MARKET VALUE OF BONDS IN ONE YEAR
9% coupon Treasury bonds	10%	$ 40,000,000	3	$ 39,004,840
14% coupon corporate bonds	13%	100,000,000	4	102,973,000
10% coupon gov't agency bonds	11%	150,000,000	7	142,938,000
		$290,000,000		$284,915,840

The key variable in forecasting the bond portfolio's market value is the anticipated required return for each type of bond. The prevailing interest rates on short-term securities are commonly more volatile than rates on longer-term securities, so the required returns on bonds with three or four years to maturity may change to a greater degree than the longer-term bonds. In addition, as economic conditions change, the required returns of some risky securities could change even if the general level of interest rates remains stable.

FORECASTING BOND PORTFOLIO RETURNS

Financial institutions measure their overall bond portfolio returns in various ways. One way is to account not only for coupon payments but also for the change in market value over the holding period of concern. The market value at the beginning of the holding period is perceived as the initial investment. The market value at the end of that period is perceived as the price at which the bonds would have been sold. Even if the bonds are retained, the measurement of return requires an estimated market value at the end of the period. Finally, the coupon payments must be accounted for as well. A bond portfolio's return is measured the same way as an individual bond's return. Mathematically, the bond portfolio return can be determined by solving for k in the following equation:

$$MVP = \sum_{t=1}^{n} \frac{C_t}{(1+k)^t} + \frac{MVP_n}{(1+k)^n}$$

where MVP = today's market value of the bond portfolio
  C_t = coupon payments received at the end of period t
  MVP_n = market value of the bond portfolio at the end of the investment period of concern
  k = discount rate that equates the present value of coupon payments and the future portfolio market value to today's portfolio market value

To illustrate, recall that Seminole Financial, Inc. forecasted its bond portfolio value for one year ahead. Its annual coupon payments (C) sum to $32,600,000 (computed by multiplying the coupon rate of each type of bond by the respective par value). Using this information, along with today's MVP and the forecasted MVP (called MVP_n), its annual return is determined by solving for k as follows:

$$MVP = \frac{C_1 + MVP_n}{(1+k)^1}$$

$$\$297,207,200 = \frac{\$32,600,0000 + \$284,915,840}{(1+k)^1}$$

$$\$297,207,200 = \frac{\$317,515,840}{(1+k)^1}$$

The discount rate (or k) is estimated to be about 7 percent. (Work this yourself for verification.) Therefore, the bond portfolio is expected to generate an annual return of about 7 percent over the one-year investment horizon. The computations to determine the bond portfolio return can be tedious, but financial institutions use computer programs. If this type of program is linked with another program to forecast future bond prices, a financial institution can input forecasted required returns for each type of bond and let the computer determine projections of the bond portfolio's future market value and its return over a specified investment horizon.

9

Mortgage Markets

CHAPTER OBJECTIVES

The specific objectives of this chapter are to:

■ provide a background on mortgages,

■ describe the common types of residential mortgages,

■ explain the valuation and risk of mortgages,

■ explain mortgage-backed securities, and

■ explain how mortgage problems led to the 2008–2009 credit crisis.

WEB

www.mbaa.org/
News regarding the mortgage markets.

Mortgages are securities used to finance real estate purchases; they are originated by various financial institutions, such as savings institutions and mortgage companies. A secondary mortgage market accommodates originators of mortgages that desire to sell their mortgages prior to maturity. The mortgage markets serve individuals or firms that need long-term funds to purchase real estate. They also serve financial institutions that wish to serve as creditors by lending long-term funds for real estate purchases.

BACKGROUND ON MORTGAGES

A mortgage is a form of debt created to finance investment in real estate. The debt is secured by the property, so if the property owner does not meet the payment obligations, the creditor can seize the property. Financial institutions such as savings institutions and mortgage companies serve as intermediaries by originating mortgages. They consider mortgage applications and assess the creditworthiness of the applicants.

The mortgage represents the difference between the down payment and the value to be paid for the property. The mortgage contract specifies the mortgage rate, the maturity, and the collateral that is backing the loan. The originator charges an origination fee when providing a mortgage. In addition, if it uses its own funds to finance the property, it will earn profit from the difference between the mortgage rate that it charges and the rate that it paid to obtain the funds. Most mortgages have a maturity of 30 years, but 15-year maturities are also available.

How Mortgage Markets Facilitate the Flow of Funds

The means by which mortgage markets facilitate the flow of funds are illustrated in Exhibit 9.1. Financial intermediaries originate mortgages and finance purchases of homes. The financial intermediaries that originate mortgages obtain their funding from household deposits. They also obtain funds by selling some of the mortgages that they originate directly to institutional investors in the secondary market. These funds are then used to finance more purchases of homes, condominiums, and commercial property. Overall, mortgage markets allow households and corporations to increase their purchases of homes, condominiums, and commercial property and thereby finance economic growth.

Institutional Use of Mortgage Markets Mortgage companies, savings institutions, and commercial banks originate mortgages. Mortgage companies tend to sell their mortgages in the secondary market, although they may continue to process payments for the mortgages that they originated. Thus, their income is generated from origination and processing fees, and not from financing the mortgages over a long-term period.

Exhibit 9.1 How Mortgage Markets Facilitate the Flow of Funds

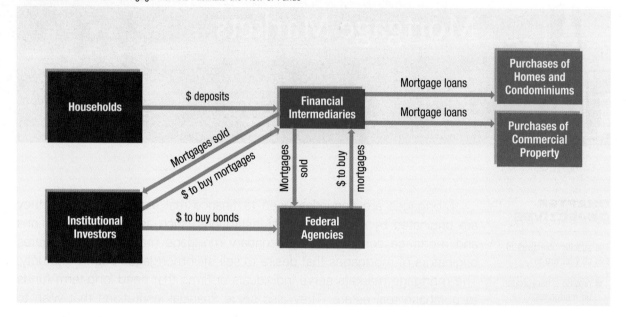

Savings institutions and commercial banks commonly originate residential mortgages. Commercial banks also originate mortgages for corporations that are purchasing commercial property. Savings institutions and commercial banks commonly use funds received from household deposits to provide mortgage financing. However, they also sell some of their mortgages in the secondary market.

The common purchasers of mortgages in the secondary market are savings institutions, commercial banks, insurance companies, pension funds, and some types of mutual funds. The participation by financial institutions in the mortgage market is summarized in Exhibit 9.2.

Exhibit 9.2 Institutional Use of Mortgage Markets

TYPE OF FINANCIAL INSTITUTION	PARTICIPATION IN MORTGAGE MARKETS
Commercial banks and savings institutions	• Originate and service commercial and residential mortgages and maintain mortgages within their investment portfolios. • Bundle packages of mortgages and sell mortgage-backed securities representing the packages of mortgages. • Purchase mortgage-based securities.
Credit unions and finance companies	• Originate mortgages and maintain mortgages within their investment portfolios.
Mortgage companies	• Originate mortgages and sell them in the secondary market.
Mutual funds	• May sell shares and use the proceeds to construct portfolios of mortgage-backed securities.
Securities firms	• Bundle packages of mortgages and sell mortgage-backed securities representing the packages of mortgages. • Offer instruments to help institutional investors in mortgages hedge against interest rate risk.
Insurance companies	• Commonly purchase mortgages or mortgage-backed securities in the secondary market.

Criteria Used to Measure Creditworthiness

When financial institutions consider mortgage applications, they review information that reflects the prospective borrrower's ability to repay the loan. The following are three important criteria that are used to measure a borrower's repayment ability:

- *Level of equity invested by the borrower.* The down payment represents the equity invested by the borrower. The lower the level of equity invested, the higher the probability that the borrower will default. One proxy for this factor is the loan-to-value ratio, which indicates the proportion of the property's value that is financed with debt. When borrowers make relatively small down payments, the loan-to-value ratio is higher, and borrowers have less to lose in the event that they stop making their mortgage payments.
- *Borrower's income level.* Borrowers who have a lower level of income relative to the periodic loan payments are more likely to default on their mortgages. Income determines the amount of funds that borrowers have available per month to make mortgage payments. Income levels change over time, however, so it is difficult for mortgage lenders to anticipate whether prospective borrowers will continue to earn their monthly income over the life of the mortgage, especially given the high frequency of layoffs.
- *Borrower's credit history.* Other conditions being similar, borrowers with a history of credit problems are more likely to default on their loans than those without credit problems.

Classifications of Mortgages

Mortages can be classified in various ways, but two important classifications are prime versus subprime mortgages and insured versus conventional mortages.

Prime versus Subprime Mortgages Mortgages can be classified according to whether the borrower meets the traditional lending standards. Borrowers who obtain "prime" mortgages satisfy the traditional lending standards. "Subprime mortgages" are offered to borrowers who do not qualify for prime loans because they have relatively lower income or high existing debt, or can make only a small down payment. In recent years, especially between 2003 and 2005, many financial institutions such as mortgage companies increased their offerings of subprime loans as a way of expanding their business. In addition, they could charge higher fees (such as appraisal fees) and higher interest rates on the mortgages to compensate for the risk of default. Subprime mortgage rates were commonly 1.5 to 2.5 percentage points above the rates of prime mortgages. Although subprime mortgages enabled some people to purchase homes who otherwise could not have, these mortgages were very susceptible to default. The large number of defaults of subprime mortgages led to the credit crisis that began in 2008, as explained later in this chapter.

Mortgages referred to as Alt-A typically satisfy some but not all of the criteria for prime mortgages. Thus, Alt-A mortgages are generally perceived to have more risk of default than prime loans, but less risk of default than subprime loans.

Insured versus Conventional Mortgages Mortgages are also often classified as federally insured or conventional. Federally insured mortgages guarantee loan repayment to the lending financial institution, thereby protecting it against the possibility of default by the borrower. An insurance fee of 0.5 percent of the loan amount is applied to cover the cost of insuring the mortgage. The guarantor can be either the Federal Housing Administration (FHA) or the Veterans Administration (VA). To qualify for FHA and VA mortgage loans from a financial institution, borrowers must meet various requirements specified by those government agencies. In addition, the maximum mortgage amount is limited by law (although the limit varies among states to account for differences in the cost of housing). The volume of FHA loans has consistently exceeded that of VA loans since 1960. Both types of mortgages have become increasingly popular over the past 30 years.

Financial institutions also provide conventional mortgages. Although not federally insured, they can be privately insured so that the lending financial institutions can still avoid exposure to credit risk. The insurance premium paid for such private insurance will likely be passed on to the borrowers. Lenders can choose to incur the credit risk themselves and avoid the insurance fee. Some participants in the secondary mortgage market purchase only those conventional mortgages that are privately insured (unless the mortgage's loan-to-value ratio is less than 80 percent).

Types of Residential Mortgages

Various types of residential mortgages are available to homeowners, including the following:

- Fixed-rate mortgages
- Adjustable-rate mortgages
- Graduated-payment mortgages
- Growing-equity mortgages
- Second mortgages
- Shared-appreciation mortgages

Fixed-Rate Mortgages

One of the most important provisions in the mortgage contract is the interest rate. It can be specified as a fixed rate or can allow for periodic rate adjustments over time. A **fixed-rate mortgage** locks in the borrower's interest rate over the life of the mortgage. Thus, the periodic interest payment received by the lending financial institution is constant, regardless of how market interest rates change over time. A financial institution that holds fixed-rate mortgages in its asset portfolio is exposed to interest rate risk because it commonly uses funds obtained from short-term customer deposits to make long-term mortgage loans. If interest rates increase over time, the financial institution's cost of obtaining funds (from deposits) will increase. The return on its fixed-rate mortgage loans will be unaffected, however, causing its profit margin to decrease.

Borrowers with fixed-rate mortgages do not suffer from the effects of rising interest rates, but they also fail to benefit from declining rates. Although they can attempt to refinance (obtain a new mortgage to replace the existing mortgage) at the lower prevailing market interest rate, they will incur transaction costs such as closing costs and an origination fee.

Amortizing Fixed-Rate Mortgages   Given the maturity and interest rate on a fixed-rate mortgage, an **amortization schedule** can be developed to show the monthly payments broken down into principal and interest. During the early years of a mortgage, most of the payment reflects interest. Over time, as some of the principal is paid off, the interest proportion decreases.

The lending institution that holds a fixed-rate mortgage will receive equal periodic payments over a specified period of time. The amount depends on the principal amount of the mortgage, the interest rate, and the maturity. If insurance and taxes are included in the mortgage payment, then they, too, influence the amount.

Consider a 30-year (360-month) $100,000 mortgage at an annual interest rate of 8 percent. To focus on the mortgage principal and interest payments, insurance and taxes are

Exhibit 9.3 Example of Amortization Schedule for Selected Years (Based on a 30-Year $100,000 Mortgage at 8 Percent)

PAYMENT NUMBER	PAYMENT OF INTEREST	PAYMENT OF PRINCIPAL	TOTAL PAYMENT	REMAINING LOAN BALANCE
1	$666.66	$ 67.10	$733.76	$99,932.90
2	666.21	67.55	733.76	99,865.35
100	604.22	129.54	733.76	90,504.68
101	603.36	130.40	733.76	90,374.28
200	482.01	251.75	733.76	72,051.18
201	480.34	253.42	733.76	71,797.76
300	244.52	489.24	733.76	36,188.12
301	241.25	492.51	733.76	35,695.61
359	9.68	724.08	733.76	728.91
360	4.85	728.91	733.76	0

not included in this example. A breakdown of the monthly payments into principal versus interest is shown in Exhibit 9.3. In the first month, the interest payment is $666.66, while the principal payment is only $67.10. Note that a larger proportion of interest is paid in the earlier years and a larger portion of principal in the later years. Website calculators are widely available to determine the amortization schedule for any type of mortgage.

An amortization schedule can also be used to compare monthly payments required on a 30-year mortgage versus a 15-year mortgage.

EXAMPLE

A 30-year $100,000 mortgage at 8 percent requires monthly payments (excluding taxes and insurance) of approximately $734. The same mortgage for 15 years would require monthly payments of $956. Total payments for the 30-year loan would be $264,155, versus $172,017 for the 15-year mortgage. Total payments are lower on mortgages with shorter lives, due to the more rapid amortization and lower cumulative interest. ●

For the financial institutions that provide mortgages, 15-year mortgages are subject to less interest rate risk than 30-year mortgages because of the shorter term to maturity.

Adjustable-Rate Mortgages (ARMs)

An **adjustable-rate mortgage (ARM)** allows the mortgage interest rate to adjust to market conditions. Its contract will specify a precise formula for this adjustment. The formula and the frequency of adjustment can vary among mortgage contracts. A common ARM uses a one-year adjustment, with the interest rate tied to the average Treasury bill rate over the previous year (for example, the average T-bill rate plus 2 percent may be specified).

Some ARMs now contain an option clause that allows mortgage holders to switch to a fixed rate within a specified period, such as one to five years after the mortgage is originated (the specific provisions vary).

The fixed rate is typically higher than the adjustable rate at any given point in time when a mortgage is originated. Home buyers attempt to assess future interest rate

USING THE WALL STREET JOURNAL

Mortgage Rates

The Wall Street Journal provides information on mortgage rates, as shown here. Specifically, it provides recently quoted rates for 30-year mortgages and 15-year mortgages. It also provides the range of mortgage rates over the previous year and the change in mortgage rates from three years earlier.

Source: Republished with permission of Dow Jones & Company, Inc., from *The Wall Street Journal*, January 7, 2009, p.C4; permission conveyed through the Copyright Clearance Center, Inc.

Consumer Rates and Returns to Investor

U.S. consumer rates

A consumer rate against its benchmark over the past year

Money market account yields 4.00%
Federal-funds target rate

J F M A M J J A S O N D
2008

Selected rates

Money market accounts

Bankrate.com avg:	**2.10%**
AIG Bank	**3.06%**
Wilmington, DE	866-231-9620
Intervest Natl Bk	**3.10%**
New York, NY	212-218-8383
California First National Bank	**3.05%**
Irvine, CA	800-735-2465
grandyielddirect.com	**2.75%**
New York, NY	800-588-5871
Goldwater Bank	**3.10%**
Scottsdale, AZ	480-281-8200

Interest rate	YIELD/RATE (%) Last (●)	Week ago	52-WEEK RANGE (%) Low 0 3 6 9 12	High	3-yr chg (pct pts)
Federal-funds rate target	**0-0.25**	0.00	0.00	4.25	**-4.25**
Prime rate*	**3.25**	3.25	3.25	7.25	**-4.00**
Libor, 3-month	**1.41**	1.44	1.41	4.82	**-3.14**
Money market, annual yield	**2.10**	2.14	2.09	3.46	**-0.73**
Five-year CD, annual yield	**3.10**	3.19	3.10	4.39	**-1.41**
30-year mortgage, fixed†	**5.44**	5.36	5.36	6.61	**-0.30**
15-year mortgage, fixed†	**5.11**	5.15	4.91	6.22	**-0.21**
Jumbo mortgages, $417,000-plus†	**6.93**	6.87	6.49	7.89	**0.87**
Five-year adj mortgage (ARM)†	**5.87**	5.86	5.01	6.14	**0.53**
New-car loan, 48-month	**6.73**	6.74	6.45	7.14	**0.25**
Home-equity loan, $30,000	**5.20**	5.37	4.64	6.88	**-0.61**

Bankrate.com rates based on survey of over 4,800 online banks. *Base rate posted by 75% of the nation's largest banks.† Excludes closing costs.   Sources: Thomson Reuters; WSJ Market Data Group; Bankrate.com

---

movements at the time a mortgage is originated. If they expect that interest rates will remain somewhat stable or decline during the period they will own the property, they will choose an ARM. Conversely, if they expect that interest rates will increase substantially over time, they will prefer a fixed-rate mortgage.

ARMs from the Financial Institution's Perspective   Because the interest rate of an ARM moves with prevailing interest rates, financial institutions can stabilize their profit margin. If their cost of funds rises, so does their return on mortgage loans. For this reason, ARMs have become very popular over time.

Most ARMs specify a maximum allowable fluctuation in the mortgage rate per year and over the mortgage life, regardless of what happens to market interest rates. These caps are commonly 2 percent per year and 5 percent for the mortgage's lifetime. To the extent that market interest rates move outside these boundaries, the financial institution's profit margin on ARMs could be affected by interest rate fluctuations. Nevertheless, this interest rate risk is significantly less than that of fixed-rate mortgages.

Graduated-Payment Mortgages (GPMs)

A **graduated-payment mortgage (GPM)** allows the borrower to initially make small payments on the mortgage; the payments increase on a graduated basis over the first 5 to 10 years and then level off. GPMs are tailored for families who anticipate higher income and thus the ability to make larger monthly mortgage payments as time passes. In a sense, they are delaying part of their mortgage payment.

Growing-Equity Mortgages

A **growing-equity mortgage** is similar to a GPM in that the monthly payments are initially low and increase over time. Unlike the GPM, however, the payments never level off but continue to increase (typically by about 4 percent per year) throughout the life of the loan. With such an accelerated payment schedule, the entire mortgage may be paid off in 15 years or less.

Second Mortgages

A second mortgage can be used in conjunction with the primary or first mortgage. Some financial institutions may limit the amount of the first mortgage based on the borrower's income. Other financial institutions may then offer a second mortgage, with a maturity shorter than on the first mortgage. In addition, the interest rate on the second mortgage is higher because its priority claim against the property in the event of default is behind that of the first mortgage. The higher interest rate reflects greater compensation as a result of the higher risk incurred by the provider of the second mortgage.

WEB

www.hsh.com/
Detailed information
about mortgage
financing.

Sellers of homes sometimes offer buyers a second mortgage. This practice is especially common when the old mortgage is assumable and the selling price of the home is much higher than the remaining balance on the first mortgage. By offering a second mortgage, the seller can make the house more affordable and therefore more marketable. The seller and the buyer negotiate specific interest rate and maturity terms.

Shared-Appreciation Mortgages

A **shared-appreciation mortgage** allows a home purchaser to obtain a mortgage at a below-market interest rate. In return, the lender providing the attractive loan rate will share in the price appreciation of the home. The precise percentage of appreciation allocated to the lender is negotiated at the origination of the mortgage.

Balloon Payment Mortgages

A **balloon-payment mortgage** requires only interest payments for a three- to five-year period. At the end of this period, the borrower must pay the full amount of the principal (the balloon payment). Because no principal payments are made until maturity, the monthly payments are lower. Realistically, though, most borrowers have not saved enough funds to pay off the mortgage in three to five years, so the balloon payment in effect forces them to request a new mortgage. Therefore, they are subject to the risk that mortgage rates will be higher at the time they refinance the mortgage.

VALUATION AND RISK OF MORTGAGES

Since mortgages are commonly sold in the secondary market, they are continually valued by institutional investors. The market price (P_M) of a mortgage should equal the present value of its future cash flows:

$$P_M = \sum_{t=1}^{n} \frac{C + \text{Prin}}{(1+k)^t}$$

where C represents the interest payment (similar to a coupon payment on bonds), Prin represents the principal payment made each period, and k represents the required rate of return by investors. Similar to bonds, the market value of a mortgage is the present value of the future cash flows to be received by the investor. Unlike bonds, however, the periodic cash flows commonly include a payment of principal along with an interest payment.

The required rate of return on a mortgage is primarily determined by the existing risk-free rate for the same maturity. However, other factors such as credit risk and lack of liquidity will cause the required return on many mortgages to exceed the risk-free rate. The difference between the 30-year mortgage rate and the 30-year Treasury bond rate, for example, is primarily attributed to credit risk and therefore tends to increase during periods when the economy is weak (such as during the credit crisis in 2008).

Since the required rate of return on a fixed-rate mortgage is primarily driven by the prevailing risk-free rate (R_f) and the risk premium (RP), the change in the value (and therefore in the market price) of a mortgage (P_M) can be modeled as

$$\Delta P_M = f(\Delta R_f, \Delta RP)$$
$$\underset{-}{} \quad \underset{-}{}$$

An increase in either the risk-free rate or the risk premium on a fixed-rate mortgage results in a higher required rate of return when investing in the mortgage and therefore causes the mortgage price to decrease.

Risk from Investing in Mortgages

Given the uncertainty of the factors that influence mortgage prices, future mortgage prices (and therefore returns) are uncertain. The uncertainty that financial institutions face from investing in mortgages is due to credit risk, interest rate risk, and prepayment risk, as explained next.

Credit Risk   Credit (default) risk represents the size and likelihood of a loss that investors will experience if borrowers make late payments or even default. Whether investors sell their mortgages prior to maturity or hold them until maturity, they are subject to credit risk. Consequently, investors must weigh the higher potential return from investing in mortgages against the exposure to risk (that the actual return could be lower than the expected return). The probability that a borrower will default is influenced both by economic conditions and by the characteristics specific to the borrower that lenders use to assess a borrower's creditworthiness (level of equity invested by the borrower, the borrower's income level, and the borrower's credit history).

Interest Rate Risk   Financial institutions that hold mortgages are subject to interest rate risk because the values of mortgages tend to decline in response to an increase in interest rates. Mortgages are long term but are commonly financed by some financial institutions with short-term deposits, so the investment in mortgages may create high exposure to interest rate risk. Such mortgages can also generate high returns when interest rates fall, but the potential gains are limited because borrowers tend to refinance (obtain new mortgages at the lower interest rate and prepay their mortgages) when interest rates decline.

When investors hold fixed-rate mortgages until maturity, they do not experience a loss due to a change in interest rates. However, holding fixed-rate mortgages to maturity can create an opportunity cost of what the investors might have earned if they had invested in other securities. For example, if interest rates rise consistently from the time fixed-rate mortgages are purchased until they mature, investors who hold the mortgages to maturity gave up the potential higher return that they would have earned if they had simply invested in money market securities over the same period.

Financial institutions can limit their exposure to interest rate risk by selling mortgages shortly after originating them. However, even institutions that use this strategy are partially exposed to interest rate risk. As a financial institution originates a pool of mortgages, it may commit to a specific fixed rate on some of the mortgages. The mortgages are stored in what is referred to as a mortgage pipeline, until there is a sufficient pool of mortgages to sell. By the time the complete pool of mortgages is originated and sold, interest rates may have risen. In this case, the value of the mortgages in the pool may have declined by the time the pool is sold.

Another way financial institutions can limit interest rate risk is by maintaining adjustable-rate residential mortgages. Alternatively, they could invest in fixed-rate mortgages that have a short time remaining until maturity. However, this conservative strategy may reduce the potential gains that could have been earned.

Prepayment Risk   **Prepayment risk** is the risk that a borrower may prepay the mortgage in response to a decline in interest rates. This type of risk is distinguished from interest rate risk to emphasize that even if investors in mortgages do not need to liquidate the mortgages, they are still susceptible to the risk that the mortgages they hold will be paid off. In this case, the investor receives a payment to retire the mortgage and has to reinvest at the prevailing (lower) interest rates. Thus, the interest rate on the new investment will be lower than the rate that would have been received on the retired mortgages.

Because of prepayments, financial institutions that invest in fixed-rate mortgages may experience only limited benefits in periods when interest rates decline. Although these mortgages offer attractive yields compared to the prevailing low interest rates, they are commonly retired as a result of refinancing.

Financial institutions can insulate against prepayment risk in the same manner that they limit exposure to interest rate risk. They can sell loans shortly after originating them or invest in adjustable-rate mortgages.

MORTGAGE-BACKED SECURITIES

As an alternative to selling their mortgages outright, financial institutions can engage in **securitization**, or the pooling and repackaging of loans into securities called **mortgage-backed securities** (MBS; or **pass-through securities**). These securities are then sold to investors, who become the owners of the loans represented by those securities. Although securitization has enhanced the secondary market for mortgages, it also played a role in the credit crisis that began in 2008.

The Securitization Process

When mortgages are securitized, a financial institution such as a securities firm or commercial bank combine individual mortgages together into packages in (tranches) based on their risk level. Securitization allows the institution to sell smaller mortgage loans that could not be easily sold in the secondary market on an individual basis. When several small mortgage loans are packaged together, they become more attractive to the large institutional investors (such as commercial banks, savings institutions, and insurance companies) that focus on large transactions. The issuer of the MBS assigns a trustee to hold the mortgages as collateral for the investors who purchase the securities. After the securities are sold, the financial institution that issued the MBS receives interest and principal payments on the mortgages and transfers (passes through) the payments to the investors that purchased the securities. The financial institution deducts a fee for servicing the mortgages.

In deciding whether to purchase MBS, investors consider the rating assigned to the securities by a rating agency (such as Moody's, Standard & Poor's, or Fitch). These agencies are hired by the issuers of the securities to assign ratings to the MBS that they plan to sell. Since some investors that purchase MBS may not fully understand the risk of the package of mortgages within a particular tranche, they rely heavily on the credit ratings as an indicator of risk.

The mortgages in a highly rated (low risk) tranche are expected to generate more favorable payments. Thus, MBS within a highly rated tranche can be sold at a higher price. The tranches containing subprime mortgages are assigned a lower credit rating. In 2003, about 13 percent of the value of mortgages packaged to create MBS represented subprime mortgages. By 2007, at least one-third of the value of all mortgages packaged to create MBS were subprime mortgages.

The pricing of MBS is difficult because of the limited transparency. Although there is a secondary market for MBS, it is not very active. There is no centralized reporting system that reports the trading of MBS in the secondary market, as there is for other securities such as stocks and Treasury bonds. The only participants who know the price of the MBS that were traded are the buyer and the seller. In addition, the market price of MBS in one tranche does not necessarily indicate what the market price should be for the MBS in another tranche, because the risk levels may vary between tranches. Given the lack of a centralized reporting system, it is quite possible that a financial institution may overpay when buying MBS.

Mortgage-Backed Securities within CDOs

Some MBS are packaged within a collateralized debt obligation (CDO), which is a package of debt securities backed by collateral that is sold to investors. A CDO may also contain some other nonmortgage types of debt securities such as automobile loans and credit card loans. CDOs became popular in the late 1990s, and by 2007, the value of CDOs issued was about $500 billion.

Like MBS, CDOs can be separated into tranches based on risk. On average, MBS represent about 45 percent of a CDO, but the percentage may be as low as zero or as high as about 90 percent. The MBS that are included in CDOs are commonly subprime mortgages. When economic conditions are favorable, low-rated tranches of CDOs perform well because mortgage defaults are very low and homeowners tend to make their mortgage payments on time. However, when economic conditions weaken, there are more mortgage defaults, and the riskiest tranches of a CDO may suffer major losses. Even highly rated tranches are subject to losses in such periods. Tranches assigned a AAA rating by rating agencies had a risk premium (above the risk-free interest rate) of close to zero in 2005, versus a risk premium of 5 percent in 2008. This significant increase in the premium reflected the additional compensation that investors required when the housing market collapsed in 2008.

When MBS and CDO values deteriorate, financial institutions have more difficulty selling mortgages that they originate. Thus, the activity in the MBS and CDO market influences the volume of funds available to finance new mortgages.

Types of Mortgage-Backed Securities

Five of the more common types of mortgage-backed securities are the following:

- Ginnie Mae mortgage-backed securities
- Fannie Mae mortgage-backed securities
- Publicly issued pass-through securities
- Participation certificates
- Collateralized mortgage obligations (CMOs)

Each type is described in turn.

Ginnie Mae Mortgage-Backed Securities   Ginnie Mae (Government National Mortgage Association) was created in 1968 as a corporation that is wholly owned by the federal government. When financial institutions issue securities that are backed by FHA and VA mortgages, Ginnie Mae guarantees timely payment of principal and interest to investors who purchase these securities. The funds received from their sale are used to finance the mortgages. Thus, Ginnie Mae supplies funds to low- and moderate-income homeowners indirectly by facilitating the flow of funds into the secondary mortgage market.

Fannie Mae Mortgage-Backed Securities   Fannie Mae (Federal National Mortgage Association, or FNMA) was created by the government in 1938 to develop a more liquid secondary market for mortgages. It issues mortgage-backed securities and uses the funds to purchase mortgages in the secondary market. In essence, Fannie Mae channels funds from investors to financial institutions that desire to sell their mortgages. These financial institutions may continue to service the mortgages and earn a fee for this service, while Fannie Mae receives a fee for guaranteeing timely payment of principal and interest to the holders of the MBS. The mortgage payments on mortgages backing these securities are sent to the financial institutions that service the mortgages. The payments are channeled through to the purchasers of MBS, which may be collateralized by conventional or federally insured mortgages.

Publicly Issued Pass-Through Securities (PIPs)   Publicly issued pass-through security (PIPs) are similar to Ginnie Mae mortgage-backed securities, except that they are backed by conventional rather than FHA or VA mortgages. The mortgages backing the securities are insured through private insurance companies.

Participation Certificates (PCs)   Freddie Mac (Federal Home Loan Mortgage Association) was chartered as a corporation by the federal government in 1970 to ensure that sufficient funds flow into the mortgage market. It went public in 1989. It sells **participation certificates (PCs)** and uses the proceeds to finance the origination of conventional mortgages from financial institutions. This provides another outlet (in addition to Fannie Mae) for financial institutions that desire to sell their conventional mortgages in the secondary market.

Fannie Mae, Ginnie Mae, and Freddie Mac enhance liquidity in the mortgage market, as illustrated in Exhibit 9.4. The proceeds received from selling securities are channeled to purchase mortgages in the secondary market from mortgage originators. As a result of Fannie Mae, Ginnie Mae, and Freddie Mac, the secondary mortgage market is more liquid than it otherwise would be. In addition, originators of the mortgages can originate more mortgages because they are not forced to finance the mortgages on their own. Because the mortgage market is more liquid, mortgage rates are more competitive, and housing is more affordable for some homeowners.

Exhibit 9.4 How Fannie Mae, Ginnie Mae, and Freddie Mac Enhance Liquidity in the Mortgage Market

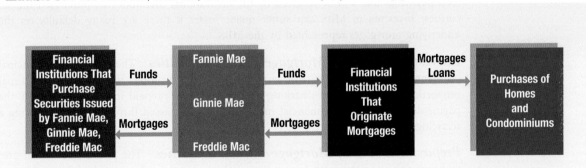

Collateralized Mortgage Obligations (CMOs)   **Collateralized mortgage obligations (CMOs)** have semiannual interest payments, unlike other mortgage-backed securities, which have monthly payments. The CMOs that represent a particular mortgage pool are segmented into tranches (classes). The first tranche has the quickest payback. Any repaid principal is initially sent to owners of the first-tranche CMOs until the total principal amount representing that tranche is fully repaid. Then any further principal payments are sent to owners of the second-tranche CMOs until the total principal amount representing that tranche is fully repaid. This process continues until principal payments are made to owners of the last-tranche CMOs. CMO issues commonly have between 3 and 10 tranches. Individual CMOs have a maximum average life of 10 years.

When interest rates decline, mortgages are prepaid, which accelerates the payments back to the holders of CMOs. This forces investors to reinvest their funds elsewhere under the prevailing (low interest rate) conditions. In some periods, massive mortgage prepayments caused accelerated payments on CMOs. Given the uncertainty about CMOs' maturity (because of the possible prepayment), determining the market valuation of CMOs is very difficult.

The CMOs are sometimes segmented into "interest-only" (IO) and "principal-only" (PO) tranches. Investors in interest-only CMOs receive only interest payments that are paid on the underlying mortgages. When mortgages are prepaid, the interest payments on the underlying mortgages are terminated, and so are payments to investors in interest-only CMOs. For example, mortgage prepayments may cut off the interest rate payments on the CMO after a few years, even though these payments were initially expected to last five years or more. Consequently, investors in these CMOs could lose 50 percent or more of their initial investment. The relatively high yields offered on interest-only CMOs are attributed to their high degree of risk.

Because investors in the principal-only CMO receive principal payments only, they generally receive payments further into the future. Even though the payments to these investors represent principal, the maturity is uncertain because of possible prepayment of the underlying mortgages. For these investors, accelerated prepayment of mortgages is beneficial because they receive their complete payments earlier than expected.

Risk of Mortgage-Backed Securities

Some institutional investors are willing to purchase mortgage-backed securities representing risky mortgages because they expect to earn a higher return. Like mortgages, MBS are subject to credit risk, interest rate risk, and prepayment risk, as explained next.

Credit Risk of Mortgage-Backed Securities   If homeowners are unable to make their payments on some mortgages that were packaged to create MBS, this reduces the total payments that will be received by the institutional investors that purchased the securities. Investors in MBS can suffer major losses if there are many defaults on the underlying mortgages represented by the MBS.

Interest Rate Risk of Mortgage-Backed Securities   The interest and principal payments to owners of MBS can vary over time. For example, if a higher-than-normal proportion of the mortgages backing the securities are prepaid in a specific period, the payments received by the financial institution will be passed through (after deducting a servicing fee) to the security owners.

Prepayment Risk of Mortgage-Backed Securities   The primary source of prepayment risk associated with a mortgage pool results from a borrower's right to prepay a mortgage in part or in full without penalty, which alters the expected life of mortgages depending upon market rates. Some amount of prepayments may occur naturally. When interest rates decline, however, prepayments are accelerated, and the owners of MBS are adversely affected. Owners of MBS are also subject to the possibility that prepayments will decelerate in response to rising interest rates.

MORTGAGE CREDIT CRISIS

In the 2003–2006 period, low interest rates and favorable economic conditions stimulated the demand for new homes. The market values of homes increased substantially, and many institutional investors used funds to invest in mortgages or mortgage-backed securities. Home builders responded to the favorable housing conditions by building more homes. Furthermore, many lenders were so confident that home prices would continue to rise that they reduced the down payment (equity investment) that they required from home buyers. The lenders assumed that even if the home buyers defaulted on the loan, the home's value would serve as sufficient collateral.

In 2006, however, some prospective buyers were less willing to purchase homes because of the abrupt increase in home prices during 2005. Suddenly, the demand for new homes was less than the supply of new and existing homes for sale, and housing prices declined. Along with these conditions, interest rates increased in 2006, which made it more difficult for existing homeowners with adjustable-rate mortgages to make their mortgage payments. In addition, mortgage companies had previously offered mortgages with low initial rates for the first few years. Now these "teaser rates" were expiring on homes that were recently purchased, and these homeowners also faced higher mortgage payments. Consequently, mortgage defaults increased. Because the market values of homes had declined substantially in some areas, in many cases the collateral backing the mortgage was not sufficient to recapture the entire mortgage amount. Even some mortgages that were insured against default by private insurers defaulted because some insurance companies that insured mortgages did not have adequate funds to cover their obligations.

As economic conditions weakened further, mortgage defaults continued to increase. By June 2008, 9 percent of all American homeowners were either behind on their mortgage payments or were in foreclosure. The defaults were much higher on subprime mortgages than on prime mortgages. In 2008, about 25 percent of all outstanding subprime mortgages had late payments of at least 30 days, versus less than 5 percent for prime mortgages. In addition, about 10 percent of outstanding subprime mortgages were subject to foreclosure in 2008, versus less than 3 percent for prime mortgages. The late payments and foreclosures on mortgages resulted in a substantial decline in MBS and CDO values. The values of some MBS and CDOs declined to less than half of the price paid for them when they were first issued.

Who Is to Blame?

The credit crisis illustrated some important problems in the mortgage markets. Various participants in the process of mortgage financing came under criticism, as explained next.

Mortgage Originators The mortgage companies and other financial institutions that originate mortgages are supposed to assess the creditworthiness of prospective homeowners. During the housing boom in the 2003–2005 period, however, some mortgage originators were aggressively seeking new business, without exercising adequate control over quality. In some cases, they approved loans without even verifying the prospective buyer's income. As described earlier, they also reduced the required down payment, based on the incorrect presumption that home prices would not decrease and that the property would be sufficient collateral in the event of default.

Credit Rating Agencies   As described earlier, the mortgage-backed securities that are issued by securities firms and financial institutions are assigned credit ratings by credit rating agencies. In general, the ratings assigned to MBS and CDOs were much higher than what they deserved. According to the Securities and Exchange Commission, many MBS and CDO tranches were overrated for the following reasons. First, credit rating agencies were understaffed and did not do thorough analyses. Second, credit rating agencies did not monitor the performance of the tranches over time and therefore did not detect deterioration in existing tranches. Third, some analysts at rating agencies were motivated to assign a high rating because the issuing firms could more easily sell highly rated tranches and would therefore be more likely to hire the agencies to assign ratings to other tranches in the future.

Some analysts at credit rating agencies apparently understood that there were problems with their ratings. For example, a manager at one agency sent an e-mail to his co-workers saying that assigning high ratings to tranches of MBS was like building a house of cards that would inevitably fall. As another example, an e-mail message by an analyst at a rating agency said that the rating model used by the agency to assess the risk did not capture even half of the risk involved.

In July 2007, Standard & Poor's downgraded the credit ratings of 562 tranches of MBS that represented $6.4 billion in value. However, many critics felt that Standard & Poor's took this action only after it was already obvious that the MBS had been rated too high. The credit rating agencies might try to counter these criticisms by saying that the losses were due to unexpected changes in the housing market. The credit ratings come with a disclaimer in small print that says that investors should not rely on the credit rating to make investment decisions. Nevertheless, investors who suffered major losses on their MBS investments might ask why credit rating agencies are hired to assign ratings if it is not to determine the risk of the MBS.

Financial Institutions That Packaged the MBS   Securities firms, commercial banks, or other financial institutions that packaged the MBS could have verified the credit ratings assigned by the credit rating agencies by making their own assessment of the risk of the MBS. These financial institutions have experience in assessing credit quality.

Institutional Investors That Purchased MBS   Many financial institutions pooled money that they received from individual investors and used the proceeds to invest in MBS. These institutions could have conducted their own assessment of the credit quality of the MBS, as they have experience in assessing credit quality.

Financial Institutions That Insured MBS   A credit default swap (CDS) is a privately negotiated contract that protects investors against the risk of default on particular debt securities such as MBS. The buyer of the CDS provides periodic (usually quarterly) payments to the other party. The seller of the CDS is obligated to provide a payment if the securities specified in the swap agreement default. Some insurance companies (such as American International Group) sold a large amount of CDS contracts, but they might not have been able to cover all of their obligations if many of the MBS defaulted. Consequently, many financial institutions that insured MBS were unable to borrow funds because creditors were afraid that they could go bankrupt if the values of their MBS declined.

Conclusion about Blame   The question of who is to blame will be argued in courtrooms. Participants in the MBS market have filed hundreds of lawsuits claiming that there was a lack of disclosure about the risk of the MBS. Some mortgage companies that originated the mortgages are being sued by securities firms that packaged the mortgages. These securities firms in turn are being sued by the financial institutions that purchased the MBS. Finally, the individuals whose money was used to purchase the MBS are suing these financial institutions for making investments that were not suitable for the investors because of the excessive risk.

Contagion Effects of the Credit Crisis

The impact of the credit crisis extends far beyond the homeowners who lost their homes and the financial institutions that lost money on their mortgage investments. Mortgage insurers that provided insurance to homeowners incurred expenses from foreclosures because the property collateral was worth less than the amount owed on the mortgage. In this way, the problems of the mortgage sector affected the insurance industry. Individual investors whose investments were pooled by mutual funds, hedge funds, and pension funds and used to purchase MBS experienced losses. So did investors who purchased stocks of financial institutions. Several financial institutions went bankrupt, and many employees of financial institutions lost their jobs. Home builders went bankrupt, and many employees in the home building industry lost their jobs. The losses on investments and layoffs contributed to a weaker economy, which made the crisis worse.

International Contagion Effects   Although much of the credit crisis was focused on the United States, the problems were felt internationally as well. Financial institutions in some countries such as the United Kingdom had offered subprime loans, and they also experienced high delinquency and default rates. In addition, some financial institutions based in foreign countries were common purchasers of subprime mortgages that were originated in the United States. Many institutional investors in Asia and Europe had purchased MBS and CDOs that contained subprime mortgages originated in the United States. For example, UBS, a large Swiss bank, incurred a loss of $35 billion from its positions in MBS. Such problems contributed to weaker economies around the world.

Government Programs Implemented in Response to the Crisis

In an effort to stimulate the market for homes and mortgages, the U.S. government implemented various programs. The Housing and Economic Recovery Act of 2008 was passed in July 2008. The act enables some homeowners to keep their existing homes and avoid foreclosure and therefore reduces the excess supply of homes for sale in the market. Specifically, financial institutions can participate in a voluntary program in which they refinance subprime mortgages for homeowners who are at risk of foreclosure. The financial institutions must be willing to create a new mortgage that is no more than 90 percent of the present appraised home value. Since the mortgage value exceeds the home value for many of the qualified homeowners, financial institutions that volunteer for the program essentially forgive a portion of the previous mortgage loan when creating a new mortgage.

Some lenders are willing to participate because forgiving part of the loan may be less costly than the process of foreclosure. For homeowners to qualify, they must live in the home, and their monthly mortgage payment must exceed 31 percent of their monthly income. The Federal Housing Administration provides insurance on these mortgages, which eliminates any credit risk to the financial institutions on these mortgages. Furthermore, any gains that are ultimately received by these homeowners from selling the homes must be shared with the government.

In addition to this program, the Housing and Economic Recovery Act also provided a tax credit for first-time buyers of homes. It also ensured that agencies will provide liquidity to rental housing markets for low-income families.

Impact of the Credit Crisis on Fannie Mae and Freddie Mac

As of 2007, Fannie Mae held about $47 billion in subprime mortgages and/or securities backed by these mortgages, while Freddie Mac held about $124 billion in such securities. Although these companies were chartered by the federal government to provide liquidity to the mortgage market, the compensation of their executives was tied to the companies'

performance, which led to risk taking. This is an example of a moral hazard problem, which occurs when a person or institution does not have to bear the full consequences of its behavior and therefore assumes more risk than it otherwise would. In this case, the executives could take risks knowing that they would benefit if their gambles paid off and that the government would likely bail them out if the gambles failed.

Fannie Mae and Freddie Mac invested heavily in subprime mortgages that required homeowners to pay higher rates of interest. By 2008, many subprime mortgages defaulted, so Fannie Mae and Freddie Mac were left with properties (the collateral) that had a market value substantially below the amount owed on the mortgages that they held. Fannie Mae and Freddie Mac attempted "workouts" in some cases, whereby they renegotiated the terms of mortgage contracts or arranged additional financing for homeowners in order to help them avoid foreclosures.

By the summer of 2008, Fannie Mae and Freddie Mac owned or guaranteed more than $5 trillion of U.S. home mortgages, or about half the value of all outstanding mortgages in the United States. In August 2008, Fannie Mae and Freddie Mac reported losses of more than $14 billion over the previous year. At that time, they held about $84 billion in capital, which represented less than 2 percent of all the mortgages that they held. This was a very small cushion to cover possible losses on their mortgages.

Funding Problems   Because of their poor financial performance, Fannie Mae and Freddie Mac were incapable of raising capital to improve their financial position or to continue their role of supporting the housing market. Their stock values had declined by more than 90 percent from the previous year, so issuing new equity to obtain funds was not a feasible solution. The yield offered on Fannie Mae and Freddie Mac debt securities was 2.5 percent higher than that of Treasury securities with a similar maturity, which reflected the large risk premium that investors were requiring in order to invest in these securities. Thus, the cost of debt to Fannie Mae and Freddie Mac was very high because investors feared that they might not be able to repay their debt. Their cost of debt would have been even higher if all investors had presumed that the government would not bail the two companies out.

The financial problems of Fannie Mae and Freddie Mac created major concerns about mortgage market liquidity. Refer back to Exhibit 9.4 in order to understand the potential impact. Originators of mortgages commonly sell them to Fannie Mae and Freddie Mac. Since Fannie Mae and Freddie Mac could not issue new securities because of their financial problems, their ability to purchase mortgages in the secondary market was limited. Originators of mortgages could not sell them as easily in the secondary market, which reduced the amount of funding available for new mortgages.

Rescue of Fannie Mae and Freddie Mac   In September 2008, the U.S. government took over the management of Fannie Mae and Freddie Mac. Their regulator, the Federal Housing Finance Agency, became responsible for managing them until they are determined to be financially healthy. The CEOs of both companies were removed from their positions, but they left with compensation packages that many critics would say were very forgiving. In the previous year, Fannie Mae's CEO had received income of $11.6 million and Freddie Mac's CEO had received $19.8 million.

The Treasury agreed to provide whatever funding would be necessary to cushion losses from the mortgage defaults. In return, the Treasury received $1 billion of preferred stock in each of the two companies. This arrangement gave Congress time to determine whether and how these companies should be structured in the future. Congress could also establish guidelines that would restrict them from investing in risky mortgages that do not meet specific standards.

The U.S. government rescue of Fannie Mae and Freddie Mac removed the risk of their debt securities defaulting and therefore increased the values of these debt securities. Thus, the government rescue benefited investors who were holding debt securities issued by Fannie Mae or Freddie Mac. Institutional investors holding debt securities issued by these companies might have attempted to dump these securities if they had believed that the government would not back these securities. Without a strong secondary market for mortgages, financial institutions that originate mortgages would not be able to sell mortgages and therefore might have to finance them on their own. This would severely limit the amount of funding for new mortgages. Thus, while the government rescue was primarily focused on ensuring a more liquid secondary market, it indirectly encouraged more originations of new mortgages.

Government Bailout of Financial Institutions

As the credit crisis intensified, many investors were unwilling to invest in mortgage-backed securities because of the risk of continued defaults. Thus, financial institutions that had large holdings of MBS could not easily sell them in the secondary market. On October 3, 2008, the Emergency Economic Stabilization Act of 2008 (also referred to as the bailout act) enabled the Treasury to inject $700 billion into the financial system and improve the liquidity of these financial institutions. A key part of the act was the Troubled Assets Relief Program (TARP), which allows the Treasury to purchase MBS from financial institutions, which would provide them with more cash. A key challenge of this activity has been to determine the proper price at which the securities should be purchased. The secondary market for the securities is not sufficiently active to determine appropriate market prices. The act also allowed the Treasury to invest in the large commercial banks as a means of providing the banks with capital to cushion their losses.

The original proposal for the act was contained in 3 pages, but by the time the act was passed, it was 451 pages long. Although the initial intent was to resolve the credit crisis, the final act contained many other provisions unrelated to the crisis, such as tax breaks for producers of rum in the Virgin Islands, racetrack owners, film producers, and alternative energy producers. These additional provisions were apparently included to satisfy special interests of various House and Senate members and win their approval for the act.

SUMMARY

- Residential mortgages can be characterized by whether they are prime or subprime, whether they are federally insured, the type of interest rate used (fixed or floating), and the maturity. Quoted interest rates on mortgages vary at a given point in time, depending on these characteristics.

- Various types of residential mortgages are available including fixed-rate mortgages, adjustable-rate mortgages, graduated-payment mortgages, growing-equity mortgages, second mortgages, and shared-appreciation mortgages.

- The valuation of a mortgage is the present value of its expected future cash flows, discounted at a discount rate that reflects the uncertainty surrounding

the cash flows. A mortgage is subject to credit risk, interest rate risk, and prepayment risk.

- Mortgage-backed securities (MBS) represent packages of mortgages; the payments on those mortgages are passed through to investors. Five of the more popular types of MBS are Ginnie Mae securities, Fannie Mae securities, publicly issued securities, participation certificates, and collateralized mortgage obligations (CMOs).

- Mortgages were provided liberally without adequate standards (including allowing very low down payments) in the 2003–2006 period. Then a glut in the housing market caused a drastic decline in home prices, with the result that the market values of many homes were lower than the mortgages. Many homeowners defaulted on their mortgages, which led to a credit crisis in the 2008–2009 period. The U.S. government used various strategies to revive the U.S. mortgage market, including an emergency housing recovery act, the rescue of Fannie Mae and Freddie Mac, and a bailout of financial institutions that had heavy investments in mortgages and mortgage-backed securities.

POINT COUNTER-POINT

Is the Trading of Mortgages Similar to the Trading of Corporate Bonds?

Point Yes. In both cases, the issuer's ability to repay the debt is based on income. Both types of debt securities are highly influenced by interest rate movements.

Counter-Point No. The assessment of corporate bonds requires an analysis of the financial statements of the firms that issued the bonds. The assessment of mortgages requires an understanding of the structure of the mortgage market (MBS, CMOs, etc.).

Who Is Correct? Use the Internet to learn more about this issue. Offer your own opinion on this issue.

QUESTIONS AND APPLICATIONS

1. **FHA Mortgages** Distinguish between FHA and conventional mortgages.

2. **Mortgage Rates and Risk** What is the general relationship between mortgage rates and long-term government security rates? Explain how mortgage lenders can be affected by interest rate movements. Also explain how they can insulate against interest rate movements.

3. **ARMs** How does the initial rate on adjustable-rate mortgages (ARMs) differ from the rate on fixed-rate mortgages? Why? Explain how caps on ARMs can affect a financial institution's exposure to interest rate risk.

4. **Mortgage Maturities** Why is the 15-year mortgage attractive to homeowners? Is the interest rate risk to the financial institution higher for a 15-year or a 30-year mortgage? Why?

5. **Balloon-Payment Mortgage** Explain the use of a balloon-payment mortgage. Why might a financial institution prefer to offer this type of mortgage?

6. **Graduated-Payment Mortgage** Describe the graduated-payment mortgage. What type of homeowners would prefer this type of mortgage?

7. **Growing-Equity Mortgage** Describe the growing-equity mortgage. How does it differ from a graduated-payment mortgage?

8. **Second Mortgages** Why are second mortgages offered by some home sellers?

9. **Shared-Appreciation Mortgage** Describe the shared-appreciation mortgage.

10. **Exposure to Interest Rate Movements** Mortgage lenders with fixed-rate mortgages should benefit when interest rates decline, yet research has shown that this favorable impact is dampened. By what?

11. **Mortgage Valuation** Describe the factors that affect mortgage prices.

12. **Selling Mortgages** Explain why some financial institutions prefer to sell the mortgages they originate.

13. **Secondary Market** Compare the secondary market activity for mortgages to the activity for other capital market instruments (such as stocks and bonds). Provide a general explanation for the difference in the activity level.

14. **Financing Mortgages** What types of financial institution finance residential mortgages? What type of financial institution finances the majority of commercial mortgages?

15. **Mortgage Companies** Explain how a mortgage company's degree of exposure to interest rate risk differs from that of other financial institutions.

Advanced Questions

16. **MBS** Describe how mortgage-backed securities (MBS) are used.

17. CMOs Describe how collateralized mortgage obligations (CMOs) are used and why they have been popular.

18. Maturities of MBS Explain how the maturity on mortgage-backed securities can be affected by interest rate movements.

19. How Secondary Mortgage Prices May Respond to Prevailing Conditions Consider current conditions that could affect interest rates, including inflation (including oil prices), the economy, the budget deficit, and the Fed's monetary policy. Based on prevailing conditions, do you think the values of mortgages that are sold in the secondary market will increase or decrease during this semester? Offer some logic to support your answer. Which factor do you think will have the biggest impact on the values of existing mortgages?

20. CDOs Explain collateralized debt obligations (CDOs).

21. Motives for Offering Subprime Mortgages Explain subprime mortgages. Why were mortgage companies aggressively offering subprime mortgages?

22. Subprime versus Prime Mortgage Problems How did the repayment of subprime mortgages compare to that of prime mortgages during the credit crisis?

23. MBS Transparency Explain the problems in valuing mortgage-backed securities.

24. Contagion Effects of Credit Crisis Explain how the credit crisis adversely affected many other people beyond homeowners and mortgage companies.

25. Blame for Credit Crisis Many investors that purchased mortgage-backed securities just before the credit crisis believed that they were misled, because these securities were riskier than they thought. Who is at fault?

26. Avoiding Another Credit Crisis Do you think that the U.S. financial system will be able to avoid another credit crisis like this in the future?

27. Role of Credit Ratings in Mortgage Market Explain the role of credit rating agencies in facilitating the flow of funds from investors to the mortgage market (through mortgage-backed securities).

28. Fannie and Freddie Problems Explain why Fannie Mae and Freddie Mac experienced mortgage problems.

29. Rescue of Fannie and Freddie Explain why the rescue of Fannie Mae and Freddie Mac improves the ability of mortgage companies to originate mortgages.

30. U.S. Treasury Bailout Plan The U.S. Treasury attempted to resolve the credit crisis by establishing a plan to buy mortgage-backed securities held by financial institutions. Explain how the plan could possibly improve the situation for MBS.

31. Assessing the Risk of MBS Why do you think it is difficult for investors to assess the financial condition of a financial institution that has purchased a large amount of mortgage-backed securities?

Interpreting Financial News

Interpret the following comments made by Wall Street analysts and portfolio managers:

a. "If interest rates continue to decline, the interest-only CMOs will take a hit."

b. "Estimating the proper value of CMOs is like estimating the proper value of a baseball player; the proper value is much easier to assess five years later."

c. "When purchasing principal-only CMOs, be ready for a bumpy ride."

Managing in Financial Markets

CMO Investment Dilemma As a manager of a savings institution, you must decide whether to invest in collateralized mortgage obligations (CMOs). You can purchase interest-only (IO) or principal-only (PO) classes. You anticipate that economic conditions will weaken in the future and that government spending (and therefore government demand for funds) will decrease.

a. Given your expectations, would IOs or POs be a better investment?

b. Given the situation, is there any reason why you might not purchase the class of CMOs that you selected in the previous question?

c. Your boss suggests that since CMOs typically have semiannual interest payments, their value at any point in time should be the present value of their future payments. Your boss also says that the valuation of CMOs should be simple. Why is your boss wrong?

PROBLEM

1.   Amortization Use an amortization table (such as www.bloomberg.com/invest/calculators/index.html) that determines the monthly mortgage payment based on a specific interest rate and principal with a 15-year maturity and then for a 30-year maturity. Is the monthly payment for the 15-year maturity twice the amount for the 30-year maturity or less than twice the amount? Explain.

FLOW OF FUNDS EXERCISE

Mortgage Financing

Carson Company currently has a mortgage on its office building through a savings institution. It is attempting to determine whether it should convert its mortgage from a floating rate to a fixed rate. Recall that the yield curve is currently upward sloping. Also recall that Carson is concerned about a possible slowing of the economy because of potential Fed actions to reduce inflation. The fixed rate that it would pay if it refinances is higher than the prevailing short-term rate, but lower than the rate it would pay from issuing bonds.

a. What macroeconomic factors could affect interest rates and therefore affect the mortgage refinancing decision?

b. If Carson refinances its mortgage, it also must decide on the size of a down payment. If it uses more funds for a larger down payment, it will need to borrow more funds to finance its expansion. Should Carson make a minimum down payment or a larger down payment if it refinances the mortgage? Why?

c. Who is indirectly providing the money that is used by companies such as Carson to purchase office buildings? That is, where does the money that the savings institutions channel into mortgages come from?

INTERNET/EXCEL EXERCISE

1.   Assess a mortgage payment schedule such as http://realestate.yahoo.com/calculators/amortization.html. Assume a loan amount of $120,000, an interest rate of 7.4 percent, and a 30-year maturity. Given this information, what is the monthly payment? In the first month, how much of the monthly payment is interest, and how much is principal? What is the outstanding balance after the first year? In the last month of payment, how much of the monthly payment is interest, and how much is principal? Why is there such a difference in the composition of the principal versus interest payment over time?

WSJ EXERCISE

Explaining Mortgage Rate Premiums

Review the "Corporate Borrowing Rates and Yields" table in a recent issue of *The Wall Street Journal* to determine the Treasury bond yield. How do these rates compare to the Fannie Mae yield quoted in the "Borrowing Benchmarks" section? Why do you think there is a difference between the Fannie Mae rate and Treasury bond yields?

Asset Allocation

This problem requires an understanding of how economic conditions influence interest rates and security prices (Chapters 6, 7, 8, and 9).

As a personal financial planner, one of your tasks is to prescribe the allocation of available funds across money market securities, bonds, and mortgages. Your philosophy is to take positions in securities that will benefit most from your forecasted changes in economic conditions. As a result of a recent event in Japan, you expect that in the next month Japanese investors will reduce their investment in U.S. Treasury securities and shift most of their funds into Japanese securities. You expect that this shift in funds will persist for at least a few years. You believe this single event will have a major effect on economic factors in the United States, such as interest rates, exchange rates, and economic growth in the next month. Because the prices of securities in the United States are affected by these economic factors, you must determine how to revise your prescribed allocation of funds across securities.

Questions

1. How will U.S. interest rates be directly affected by the event (holding other factors equal)?

2. How will economic growth in the United States be affected by the event? How might this influence the values of securities?

3. Assume that day-to-day exchange rate movements are dictated primarily by the flow of funds between countries, especially international bond and money market transactions. How will exchange rates be affected by possible changes in the international flow of funds that are caused by the event?

4. Using your answer to (1) only, explain how prices of U.S. money market securities, bonds, and mortgages will be affected.

5. Now use your answer to (2) along with your answer to (1) to assess the impact on security prices. Would prices of risky securities be affected more or less than those of risk-free securities with a similar maturity? Why?

6. Assume that for diversification purposes, you prescribe that at least 20 percent of an investor's funds should be allocated to money market securities, to bonds, and to mortgages. That allows you to allocate the remaining 40 percent however you desire across those securities. Based on all the information you have about the event, prescribe the proper allocation of funds across the three types of U.S. securities. (Assume that the entire investment will be concentrated in U.S. securities.) Defend your prescription.

7. Would you recommend high-risk or low-risk money market securities? Would you recommend high-risk or low-risk bonds? Why?

8. Assume that you would consider recommending that as much as 20 percent of the funds be invested in foreign debt securities. Revise your prescription to include foreign securities if you desire (identify the type of security and the country).

9. If the event of concern increased the demand for, instead of reducing the supply of, loanable funds in the United States, would the assessment of future interest rates be different? What about the general assessment of economic conditions? What about the general assessment of bond prices?

PART 4

Equity Markets

Equity markets facilitate the flow of funds from individual or institutional investors to corporations. Thus, they enable corporations to finance their investments in new or expanded business ventures. They also facilitate the flow of funds between investors. Chapter 10 describes stock offerings and explains how participants in the stock market monitor firms that have publicly traded stock. Chapter 11 explains the valuation of stocks, describes investment strategies involving stocks, and indicates how a stock's performance is measured. Chapter 12 describes the stock market microstructure and explains how orders are placed and executed on stock exchanges.

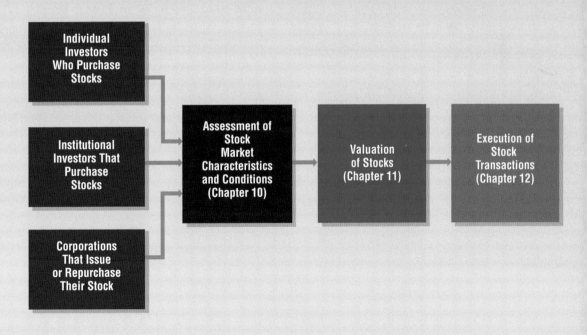

10

Stock Offerings and Investor Monitoring

The specific objectives of this chapter are to:

- explain how stock markets facilitate secondary market trading,

- describe investor participation in the stock markets,

- describe the process of initial public offerings,

- describe the process of secondary offerings,

- explain how the stock market is used to monitor and control firms, and

- describe the globalization of stock markets.

Stock markets facilitate equity investment into firms and the transfer of equity investments between investors.

PRIVATE EQUITY

When a firm is created, its founders typically invest their own money in the business. The founders may also invite some family or friends to invest equity in the business. This is referred to as private equity, as the business is privately held, and the owners cannot sell their shares to the public. Young businesses use debt financing from financial institutions and are better able to obtain loans if they have substantial equity invested. Over time, businesses commonly retain a large portion of their earnings and reinvest it to support expansion. This serves as another means of building equity in the firm.

The founders of many firms dream of going public someday so that they can obtain a large amount of financing to support the firm's growth. They may also hope to "cash out" by selling their original equity investment to others. Normally, however, a firm's owners do not consider going public until they want to sell at least $50 million in stock. A public offering of stock may be feasible only if the firm will have a large enough shareholder base to support an active secondary market. With an inactive secondary market, the shares would be illiquid. Investors who own shares and want to sell them would be forced to sell at a discount from the fundamental value, almost as if the firm was not publicly traded. This defeats the purpose of being public. In addition, there are many fixed costs associated with going public, and these costs will be prohibitive for a firm that is raising only a small amount of funds.

Financing by Venture Capital Funds

Even if a firm wants to sell at least $50 million of stock to the public, it may not have a long enough history of stable business performance to be able to raise money from a large number of investors. Private firms that need a large equity investment but are not yet in a position to go public may attempt to obtain funding from a venture capital (VC) fund. VC funds receive money from wealthy investors and from pension funds that are willing to maintain the investment for a long-term period, such as 5 or 10 years. These investors are not allowed to withdraw their money before a specified deadline. VC funds have participated in a number of businesses that ultimately went public and became very successful, including Apple, Microsoft, and Oracle Corporation.

Venture Capital Market   The venture capital market brings together the private businesses that need equity funding and the VC funds that can provide funding. One way of doing this is through venture capital conferences where each business briefly makes its pitch as to why it will be very successful (and generate high returns to the VC fund) if it receives equity funding. Alternatively, businesses may submit proposals to VC funds. If a VC fund identifies a proposal that it believes has much potential, it may arrange a meeting with the business's owners and request more detailed information. Most proposals are rejected, however, as VC funds recognize that the majority of new businesses ultimately fail.

Terms of a Venture Capital Deal   When a VC fund decides to invest in a business, it will negotiate the terms of its investment, including the amount of funds it is willing to invest. It will also set out clear requirements that the firm must meet, such as providing detailed periodic progress reports. When a VC fund invests in a firm, the fund's managers have an incentive to ensure that the business performs well. Thus, the VC fund managers may serve as advisers to the business. They may also insist on having a seat on the board of directors so that they can influence the firm's future progress. Often, the VC fund provides its funding in stages, based on various conditions that the firm must satisfy. In this way, the VC fund's total investment is aligned with the firm's ability to meet specified financial goals.

Exit Strategy of VC Funds   A VC fund typically plans to exit from its original investment within about four to seven years. One common exit strategy is to sell its equity stake to the public after the business engages in a public stock offering. Many VC funds sell their shares of the businesses in which they invest during the first 6 to 24 months after the business goes public. Alternatively, the VC fund may cash out if the company is acquired by another firm, as the acquirer will purchase the shares owned by the VC fund. Thus, the VC fund commonly serves as a bridge for financing the business until the business either goes public or is acquired.

Financing by Private Equity Funds

Private equity funds pool money provided by institutional investors (such as pension funds and insurance companies) and invest in businesses. They also rely heavily on debt to finance their investments. Unlike VC funds, private equity funds commonly take over businesses and manage them. Their managers typically take a percentage of the profits they earn from their investments in return for managing the fund. They also charge an annual fee for managing the fund. Since they commonly purchase a majority stake or all of a business, they have control to restructure the business as they wish. They sell their stake in the business after several years. If they were able to improve the business substantially while they managed it, they should be able to sell their stake to another firm for a much higher price than they paid for it. Alternatively, they may be able to take the business public through an initial public offering (IPO) and cash out at that time.

PUBLIC EQUITY

When a firm goes public, it issues stock in the **primary market** in exchange for cash. Going public has two effects on the firm. First, it changes the firm's ownership structure by increasing the number of owners. Second, it changes the firm's capital structure by increasing the equity investment in the firm, which allows the firm to either pay off some of its debt, or expand its operations, or both.

The stock that the firm issues is a certificate representing partial ownership in the firm. Like debt securities, common stock is issued by firms in the primary market to obtain long-term funds. The purchaser of stock becomes a part owner of the firm, rather than a creditor, however. This ownership feature attracts many investors who want to have an equity interest in a firm, but do not necessarily want to manage their own firm. Owners of stock can benefit from the growth in the value of the firm and therefore have more to gain than creditors. However, they are also susceptible to large losses, as the values of even the most respected corporations have declined substantially in some periods.

The means by which stock markets facilitate the flow of funds are illustrated in Exhibit 10.1. The stock markets are like other financial markets in that they link the surplus units (that have excess funds) with deficit units (that need funds). Corporations issue new stock so that they will have sufficient funds to expand their operations. Thus, stock markets allow corporations to increase their expenditures and thereby finance economic growth. Stock issued by corporations may be purchased directly by households. Alternatively, households may invest in shares of stock mutual funds, and the managers of these funds use the proceeds to invest in stocks. Other institutional investors such as pension funds and insurance companies also purchase stocks. The massive growth in the stock market has enabled many corporations to expand to a much greater degree and has allowed investors to share in the profitability of corporations.

In addition to the primary market, which facilitates new financing for corporations, there is also a **secondary market** that allows investors to sell the stock they previously purchased to other investors who want to buy the stock. Thus, the secondary market creates liquidity for investors who invest in stocks. In addition to realizing potential gains when they sell their stock, investors may also receive dividends on a quarterly basis from the corporations in which they invest. Some corporations distribute a portion of

Exhibit 10.1 How Stock Markets Facilitate the Flow of Funds

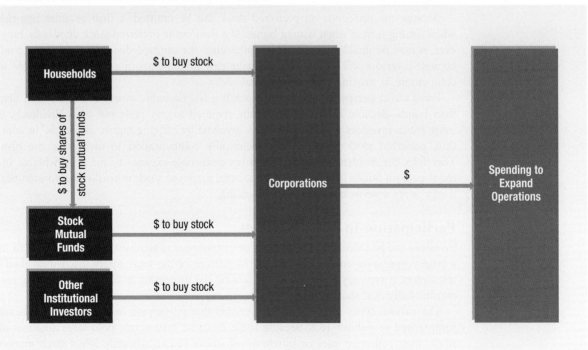

their earnings to shareholders in the form of dividends, but others reinvest all of their earnings so that they can achieve greater growth.

Ownership and Voting Rights

The owners of small companies also tend to be the managers. In publicly traded firms, however, most of the shareholders are not managers. Thus, they must rely on the firm's managers to serve as agents and to make decisions in the shareholders' best interests.

The ownership of **common stock** entitles shareholders to a number of rights not available to other individuals. Normally, only the owners of common stock are permitted to vote on certain key matters concerning the firm, such as the election of the board of directors, authorization to issue new shares of common stock, approval of amendments to the corporate charter, and adoption of bylaws. Many investors assign their vote to management through the use of a proxy. Many other shareholders simply fail to vote at all. As a result, management normally receives the majority of the votes and can elect its own candidates as directors.

Preferred Stock

Preferred stock represents an equity interest in a firm that usually does not allow for significant voting rights. Preferred shareholders technically share the ownership of the firm with common shareholders and are therefore compensated only when earnings have been generated. Thus, if the firm does not have sufficient earnings from which to pay the preferred stock dividends, it may omit the dividend without fear of being forced into bankruptcy. A cumulative provision on most preferred stock prevents dividends from being paid on common stock until all preferred stock dividends (both current and those previously omitted) have been paid. Normally, the owners of preferred stock do not participate in the profits of the firm beyond the stated fixed annual dividend. All profits above those needed to pay dividends on preferred stock belong to the owners of common stock.

Because the dividends on preferred stock can be omitted, a firm assumes less risk when issuing it than when issuing bonds. If a firm omits preferred stock dividends, however, it may be unable to raise new capital until the omitted dividends have been paid, because investors will be reluctant to make new investments in a firm that is unable to compensate its existing sources of capital.

From a cost perspective, preferred stock is a less desirable source of capital for a firm than bonds. Because a firm is not legally required to pay preferred stock dividends, it must entice investors to assume the risk involved by offering higher dividends. In addition, preferred stock dividends are technically compensation to owners of the firm. Therefore, the dividends paid are not a tax-deductible expense to the firm, whereas interest paid on bonds is tax deductible. Because preferred stock normally has no maturity, it represents a permanent source of financing.

Participation in Stock Markets

Investors can be classified as individual or institutional. The investment by individuals in a large corporation commonly exceeds 50 percent of the total equity. Each individual's investment is typically small, however, causing the ownership to be scattered among numerous individual shareholders.

The various types of institutional investors that participate in the stock markets are summarized in Exhibit 10.2. Because some financial institutions hold large amounts of stock, their collective sales or purchases of stocks can significantly affect stock market prices. Institutional investors also have more resources to monitor a corporation, so

Exhibit 10.2 Institutional Use of Stock Markets

TYPE OF FINANCIAL INSTITUTION	PARTICIPATION IN STOCK MARKETS
Commercial banks	• Issue stock to boost their capital base. • Manage trust funds that usually contain stocks.
Stock-owned savings institutions	• Issue stock to boost their capital base.
Savings banks	• Invest in stocks for their investment portfolios.
Finance companies	• Issue stock to boost their capital base.
Stock mutual funds	• Use the proceeds from selling shares to individual investors to invest in stocks.
Securities firms	• Issue stock to boost their capital base. • Place new issues of stock. • Offer advice to corporations that consider acquiring the stock of other companies. • Execute buy and sell stock transactions of investors.
Insurance companies	• Issue stock to boost their capital base. • Invest a large proportion of their premiums in the stock market.
Pension funds	• Invest a large proportion of pension fund contributions in the stock market.

corporations recognize that they must respond to advice or complaints by institutional investors in order to keep them as investors. Many institutional investors own millions of shares of a single firm and therefore are willing to spend time to ensure that managers serve the shareholders' interests.

Financial institutions not only participate in stock markets by investing funds, but sometimes issue their own stock as a means of raising funds. Many stock market transactions involve two financial institutions. For example, an insurance company may purchase the newly issued stock of a commercial bank. If the insurance company someday sells this stock in the secondary market, the purchaser may be a mutual fund or pension fund.

How Investor Decisions Affect Stock Prices   Investors make decisions to buy a stock when its market price is below their valuation, which means they believe the stock is undervalued. They may sell their holdings of a stock when the market price is above their valuation, which means they believe the stock is overvalued. Thus, stock valuation drives their investment decisions. Investors commonly disagree on how to value a stock (as explained in Chapter 11). Thus, some investors may believe a stock is undervalued while others believe it is overvalued. This difference in opinions allows for market trading, because it means that there will be buyers and sellers of the same stock at a given point in time.

When there is a shift in the demand for shares or the supply of shares for sale, the equilibrium price changes. When investors revise their expectations of a firm's performance upward, they revise their valuations upward. If the consensus among investors is a favorable revision of expected performance, there are more buy orders for the stock. Demand for shares exceeds the supply of shares for sale, placing upward pressure on the market price. Conversely, if the consensus among investors is lowered expectations of the firm's future performance, there are more sell orders for the stock. The supply of shares for sale exceeds the demand for shares, placing downward pressure on the market price. Overall, the prevailing market price is determined by the participation of investors in aggregate. Stock transactions between investors in the secondary market do not affect the capital structure of the issuer, but merely transfer shares from one investor to another.

Investor Reliance on Information Investors respond to the release of new information that affects their opinions about a firm's future performance. In general, favorable news about a firm's performance will make investors believe that the firm's stock is undervalued at its prevailing price. The demand for shares of that stock will increase, placing upward pressure on the stock's price. Unfavorable news about a firm's performance will make investors believe that the firm's stock is overvalued at its prevailing price. Some investors will sell their holdings of that stock, placing downward pressure on the stock's price. Thus, information is incorporated into stock prices through its impact on investors' demand for shares and the supply of shares for sale by investors.

Each stock has its own demand and supply conditions and therefore has a unique market price. Nevertheless, new information about macroeconomic conditions commonly causes expectations for many firms to be revised in the same direction and therefore causes stock prices to move in the same direction.

Investors continually respond to new information in their attempt to purchase stocks that are undervalued or sell their stock holdings that are overvalued. When investors properly determine which stocks are undervalued, they can achieve abnormally high returns from investing in those stocks. Thus, the valuation process used by an investor can have a strong influence on the investor's investment performance.

INITIAL PUBLIC OFFERINGS

A corporation first decides to issue stock to the public in order to raise funds. It engages in an **initial public offering** (IPO), which is a first-time offering of shares by a specific firm to the public. An IPO is commonly used not only to obtain new funding but also to offer some founders and VC funds a way to cash out their investment. Even after a firm has gone public, it may need to raise additional equity to support its growth. In that case, it can engage in a secondary offering by issuing additional shares of stock to the public. Some firms have had several secondary offerings to support their expansion. This section describes initial public offerings, and the following section describes secondary offerings.

Process of Going Public

Since firms that engage in an IPO are not well known to investors, they must provide detailed information about their operations and their financial condition. A firm planning on going public normally hires a securities firm that serves as the lead underwriter for the IPO. The lead underwriter is involved in the development of the prospectus and the pricing and placement of the shares.

Developing a Prospectus A few months before the IPO, the issuing firm (with the help of the lead underwriter) develops a prospectus and files it with the **Securities and Exchange Commission (SEC).** The **prospectus** contains detailed information about the firm and includes financial statements and a discussion of the risks involved. It is intended to provide potential investors with the information they need to decide whether to invest in the firm. Within about 30 days, the SEC will assess the prospectus and determine whether it contains all the necessary information. In many cases, before approving the prospectus, the SEC recommends some changes that provide more information about the firm's financial condition.

Once the SEC approves the prospectus, it is sent to institutional investors who may want to invest in the IPO. In addition, the firm's management and the underwriters of the IPO meet with institutional investors. In many cases, the meetings occur in the form of a road show; the firm's managers travel to various cities and put on a presentation for large institutional investors in each city. The institutional investors are informed of the road show in advance so that they can attend if they may be interested in purchasing shares of the IPO. Some institutional investors may even receive separate individual presentations. Institutional investors are targeted because they may be willing to buy large blocks of shares at the time of the IPO. For this reason, they typically have priority over individual investors in purchasing shares during an IPO.

Pricing   The lead underwriter must determine the so-called offer price at which the shares will be offered at the time of the IPO. The price that investors are willing to pay per share is influenced by prevailing market and industry conditions. If other publicly traded firms in the same industry are priced high relative to their earnings or sales, then the price assigned to shares in the IPO will be relatively high.

Before a firm goes public, it attempts to gauge the price that will be paid for its shares. During the road show, the lead underwriter solicits indications of interest in the IPO by institutional investors as to the number of shares that they may demand at various possible offer prices. This process is referred to as bookbuilding.

EXAMPLE

Saint Louis Company has hired Bucknell Investment Company as its lead underwriter for its IPO. Bucknell organizes a road show for a large set of institutional investors that commonly invest in IPO shares. At the road show, managers from St. Louis Company explain the firm's business and how it will use the IPO proceeds. Then Bucknell contacts the investors to request indications of interest. A summary of its findings is provided in Exhibit 10.3. Based on the feedback received, Bucknell decides that an initial offer price of $11 would be appropriate. This price is low enough that it will almost surely result in sufficient demand for 4 million shares, which would provide $44 million to St. Louis Company. Bucknell is concerned that if it sets the price higher, it might not be able to place all of the shares in the IPO. ●

As a result of the bookbuilding process for setting an offer price, many institutional investors pay a lower price than they would have been willing to pay for the shares. In the preceding example, some institutional investors would have paid $13, but the underwriter used an offer price of $11 for all investors to ensure that at least 4 million shares would be sold. Should the issuing firm be satisfied as long as all the shares are placed? What if St. Louis Company firmly believes that all 4 million shares could have been sold at an offer price of $13 per share? In this case, the firm would have received $52 million (4 million shares × $13 per share), but received only $44 million. It gave up $8 million because the underwriter sold the shares for a lower price. In finance terminology, this is referred to as "leaving money on the table." Some issuing firms may be especially concerned that they left money on the table when the market price rises substantially on the day of the IPO, because the price increase may suggest that the demand for shares exceeded the supply of shares for sale on that day. The underwriter might counter that the lower offer price was appropriate because it ensured that all the shares would be sold at

Exhibit 10.3 Summary of Bookbuilding Process Just before the IPO

POSSIBLE OFFER PRICE	TOTAL SHARES DEMANDED	TOTAL PROCEEDS TO ISSUER
$13	3,000,000	$39,000,000
$12	3,500,000	$42,000,000
$11	4,000,000	$44,000,000
$10	4,300,000	$43,000,000

the offering. If the stock price rises over time (which means that the IPO investors benefit from their investment), the issuing firm may more easily engage in another stock offering in the future because it has gained investors' trust.

Some critics suggest that setting a lower offer price provides institutional investors with special favors and may be a way for the securities firm that is underwriting the IPO to attract other business from institutional investors. To the extent that the shares were essentially discounted from their appropriate price, however, the proceeds that the issuing firm receives from the IPO are lower than it deserves.

In some other countries, an auction process is used for IPOs, and investors pay whatever they bid for the shares. The top bidder's order is accommodated first, followed by the next highest bidder, and so on, until all shares are issued. The issuer can set a minimum price at which the bidding must occur for shares to be issued. This process prevents the underwriter from setting the offer price at a level that is intended to please specific institutional investors.

Allocation of IPO Shares   The lead underwriter may rely on a group (called a syndicate) of other securities firms to participate in the underwriting process and share the fees to be received for the underwriting. Each underwriter in the syndicate contacts institutional investors and informs them of the offering. Most of the shares are sold to institutional investors, as it is more convenient for the underwriting syndicate to sell shares in large chunks. Brokerage firms may receive a very small portion (such as 2 percent) of the IPO shares, which they can sell to their individual investors. They normally give priority to their biggest customers.

Transaction Costs   The transaction cost to the issuing firm is usually 7 percent of the funds raised. For example, an IPO of $50 million would result in a transaction cost of $3.5 million (7% × $50 million). In addition, the issuer incurs other costs, such as the cost of assessing whether to go public, compiling data for the prospectus, and ensuring that the prospectus is properly written. It also incurs fees from hiring legal or financial advisers during this process. Thus, the total cost of engaging in an IPO may be close to 10 percent of the total offering.

Underwriter Efforts to Ensure Price Stability

The lead underwriter's performance can be partially measured by the movement in the IPO firm's share price following the IPO. If investors quickly sell an IPO stock in the secondary market, there will be downward pressure on the stock's price. If most stocks placed by a particular underwriter perform poorly after the IPO, institutional investors may no longer want to purchase shares underwritten by that underwriter.

Lockup   The lead underwriter attempts to ensure stability in the stock's price after the offering by requiring a lockup provision, which prevents the original owners of the firm and the VC firms from selling their shares for a specified period (usually six months from the date of the IPO). The purpose of the lockup provision is to prevent downward pressure that could occur if the original owners or VC firms sold their shares in the secondary market. In reality, however, the provision simply defers the possible excess supply of shares sold in the secondary market. When the lockup period expires, the number of shares for sale in the secondary market may increase abruptly, and the share price commonly declines significantly. In fact, some investors who are allowed to sell their shares before the lockup expiration date now recognize this effect and sell their IPO shares just before the expiration date. Consequently, the stock price begins to decline shortly before that date. Some securities firm attempted to avert this effect by having their analysts issue a positive report just before the lockup expiration date, but the SEC mandated a quiet period to prevent such biased reports before the lockup expiration.

Timing of IPOs

IPOs tend to occur more frequently during bullish stock markets, when potential investors are more interested in purchasing new stocks. Prices of stocks tend to be higher in these periods, and issuing firms attempt to capitalize on such prices.

EXAMPLE

In the 2004–2007 period, stocks of most firms were priced high relative to their respective earnings or revenues. Investor demand for new stocks was strong. Firms were more willing to engage in IPOs because they were confident that they could sell all of their shares at relatively high prices.

After the credit crisis began in 2008, the stock market weakened, reducing the valuation of stocks relative to earnings or revenues. For this reason, some firms that planned to go public withdrew their plans. They recognized that their shares would have to be sold for a lower price than they desired. In addition, as economic conditions weakened, some firms cut back on their expansion plans and therefore reduced their need for additional funds. These firms recognized that they should defer their offering until economic conditions were more favorable and stock prices were higher. ●

Initial Returns of IPOs

The initial (first-day) return of IPOs in the United States has averaged about 20 percent over the last 30 years. Such a return is unusual for a single day and exceeds the typical return earned on stocks over an entire year. The initial return on IPOs was especially high for Internet firms during the 1996–1999 period. During 1998, for example, the mean increase in price on the first trading day following the IPO was 84 percent for Internet stocks. Thus, a $1 million investment in each of the Internet IPOs in 1998 would have resulted in a one-day gain of $840,000. Such a high initial return may indicate that the IPO was underpriced, implying that the offer price was lower than it should have been. In that case, the issuer received less than it should have from issuing the shares. The beneficiaries were the institutional investors that were able to purchase the shares at the low offer price.

EXAMPLE

On January 15, 1999, an IPO by an Internet stock called MarketWatch.com jumped from the initial offer price of $17 per share to $130 per share within the first two hours of trading (a return of about 665 percent at that point) and then declined to $97.50 per share by the end of the day. The one-day return for investors who purchased shares at the offer price was about 474 percent. On December 9, 1999, the IPO for VA Linux had an offer price of $30 per share. By the end of the first day, the price was $239, providing for an initial return of 697 percent for investors who purchased shares at the offer price and sold their shares after one day. ●

The media attention given to some successful IPOs of Internet firms that turned some small investors into millionaires attracted many other investors who had never invested in the stock market before. Some investors were investing money that they could not afford to lose, without recognizing the risk involved in investing in Internet stocks. Many of the Internet firms wasted the proceeds of their IPOs and ultimately went bankrupt. The investors who invested in their IPOs lost their entire investments.

Flipping Shares   Some investors who know about the unusually high initial returns on IPOs attempt to purchase the stock at its offer price and sell the stock shortly afterward. This strategy is referred to as flipping. Investors who engage in flipping have no intention of investing in the firm over the long run and are simply interested in capitalizing on the initial return that occurs for many IPOs. If many institutional investors flip their shares, they may cause the market price of the stock to decline shortly after the

USING THE WALL STREET JOURNAL

Recent IPO Performance

The Wall Street Journal provides information on the recent performance of IPOs, as shown here. It identifies firms that went public recently and discloses the return earned by investors who purchased the stock at the time of the IPO.

IPO Scorecard

Performance of selected recent IPOs

Company SYMBOL IPO date/Offer price	Friday's close ($)	Offer price	1st-day close	Company SYMBOL IPO date/Offer price	Friday's close ($)	Offer price	1st-day close
Grand Canyon Edu LOPE Nov. 20/$12.00	18.98	58.2	60.2	Verso Paper VRS May 15/$12.00	1.00	−91.7	−90.0
Rackspace Hosting RAX Aug. 8/$12.50	5.95	−52.4	−40.6	Western Gas Ptnrs L.P. WES May 9/$16.50	14.40	−12.7	−12.7
China Mass Media Adv CMM Aug. 4/$6.80	1.56	−77.1	−76.0	Real Goods Solar, RSOL May 8/$10.00	3.74	−62.6	−57.5
China Distance Edu DL July 30/$7.00	4.19	−40.1	−36.8	Colfax Corporation CFX May 8/$18.00	10.76	−40.2	−48.8
GT Solar Intl SOLR July 24/$16.50	3.63	−78.0	−75.1	Pioneer Sthwst Engy Prtns PSE May 1/$19.00	14.30	−24.7	−27.2
Enrgy Recovery ERII July 2/$8.50	7.95	−6.5	−19.1	Whiting USA Trust I WHX April 25/$20.00	11.20	−44.0	−46.3
HK Highpower Tech HPJ June 19/$3.25	3.19	−1.8	−53.4	Hatteras Fin HTS April 25/$24.00	26.56	10.7	7.6
RHI Entertainment RHIE June 18/$14.00	9.50	−32.1	−29.6	American Wtr Wrks AWK April 23/$21.50	21.12	−1.8	2.5
Safe Bulkers SB May 29/$19.00	7.70	−59.5	−59.3	Intrepid Potash IPI April 22/$32.00	21.41	−33.1	−57.5
American Capital Agcy AGNC May 15/$20.00	20.94	4.7	8.2	Visa V March 19/$44.00	53.44	21.5	−5.4

Sources: WSJ Market Data Group; Reuters

NEW TO THE MARKET

Public Offerings of Stock

IPOs in the U.S. market

None expected this week

Lockup Expirations

None expected this week

Be it an IPO, a bond sale or a merger, the investment banks that work on the deal get their cut. Below, rankings, based on revenues, year to date*

Investment bank	Equity capital markets	Debt capital markets	Mergers and acquisitions	Revenue, in millions($)	Market share(%)
JPMorgan	35	23	42	4551.27	9.34
Goldman Sachs	35	15	50	3690.25	7.57
Merrill Lynch	36	21	44	3432.94	7.04
UBS	30	20	50	3144.68	6.45
Citi	33	29	38	3007.94	6.17
Morgan Stanley	31	19	50	2812.85	5.77
Credit Suisse	30	23	47	2583.56	5.30
Deutsche Bank	23	27	50	2241.92	4.60
Barclays Capital	33	42	26	2043.55	4.19
Bank of America	42	42	16	1543.19	3.17

*When fees are not disclosed Dealogic uses proprietary analytics to calculate them

Source: Dealogic

Other Stock Offerings

Secondaries and follow-ons expected this week in the U.S. market

None expected this week

Off the Shelf

"Shelf registrations" allow a company to prepare a stock or bond for sale, without selling the whole issue at once. Corporations sell as conditions become favorable. Here are the shelf sales, or takedowns, over the last week:

Issuer/Industry	Takedown date/ Registration date	Deal value ($ millions)	Registration (millions)	Bookrunner(s)
SCANA Utility & Energy	Dec. 31 Aug. 7, '07	$88.8	...	M. Stanley

Source: Republished with permission of Dow Jones & Company, Inc., from *The Wall Street Journal*, January 5, 2009, p. C5; permission conveyed through the Copyright Clearance Center, Inc.

IPO. Thus, underwriters are concerned that flipping may place excessive downward pressure on the stock's price. To discourage flipping, some securities firms make more shares of future IPOs available to institutional investors that retain shares for a relatively long period of time. The securities firms may also prevent institutional investors that engage in flipping from participating in any subsequent IPOs that they underwrite.

Google's IPO

On August 18, 2004, Google engaged in an IPO that attracted massive media attention because of Google's name recognition. Google generated $1.6 billion from the offering, more than four times the value of the combined IPOs by Amazon.com, America Online, Microsoft, Netscape, and Priceline.com. The two co-founders, Larry Page and Sergey Brin, sold a portion of their shares within the IPO for about $40 million each, but retained shares valued at $3 billion each. The Google IPO offers interesting insight into the process by which firms obtain equity funding from investors.

Estimating the Stock's Value   Investors attempt to determine the value of the stock that is to be issued so that they can decide whether to invest in the IPO. In the case of Google, some investors used Yahoo! as a benchmark because Yahoo! stock has been publicly traded since 1996. To determine the appropriate price of Google's stock, investors multiplied Google's earnings per share by Yahoo!'s price-earnings ratio. This method had some major limitations, however. First, Google and Yahoo! are not exactly the same type of business. Some investors might argue that Microsoft would have been a better benchmark than Yahoo! for Google. If Google has more growth potential than Yahoo!, it might deserve a higher multiple. In addition, Yahoo! and Google use different accounting methods, so estimating a value by comparing the earnings of the two firms was subject to error. These limitations of valuation are discussed in more detail in Chapter 11, but the main point here is that stock valuations are subject to error, especially for IPOs, because their prices were not market determined in the past.

Even the firm issuing stock in an IPO is unsure of its market value, because it is difficult to judge what investors will be willing to pay for the newly issued stock. Google initially expected that its stock would sell for between $118 and $135 per share, but then revised its estimate to below $100 before the IPO.

Google's Communication to Investors before the IPO   Like any firm that is about to engage in an IPO, Google provided substantial financial information about its operations and recent performance. However, Google was unique in that it communicated in terms that most investors could easily understand. In addition, it emphasized that it would concentrate on long-term growth rather than on short-term goals such as meeting quarterly earnings targets. Many firms focus on meeting short-term earnings targets, because they know that investors obsess over quarterly earnings and that their stock valuations are influenced by earnings. Google maintained that it could make better decisions if it was not subject to the continual strain of having to satisfy a particular short-term earnings target.

The Auction Process   Google's IPO was unique in that it used a Dutch auction process instead of relying almost exclusively on institutional investors. Specifically, it allowed all investors to submit a bid for its stock by a specific deadline. It then ranked the bid prices and determined the minimum price at which it would be able to sell all of the shares that it wished to issue. All bids that were equal to or above that minimum price were accepted, and all bids below the minimum price were rejected.

More than 30 securities firm were involved in the IPO and served as intermediaries between Google and the investors. In a traditional IPO, the securities firms have more responsibility for selling the shares, and they tend to focus on placing the shares with institutional investors. Thus, individual investors rarely have access to an IPO. They commonly obtain shares later on the day of the IPO when some of the institutional investors flip their shares. Typically, the individual investors pay a higher price than the offer price paid by institutional investors.

By using a Dutch auction process, Google allowed individual investors to participate directly in the IPO and therefore to obtain shares at the initial offer price. Nevertheless, some individual investors decided not to participate in the Dutch auction because of the complicated registration process, which required them to complete forms proving that they were financially qualified. Also, some individual investors decided to wait and buy shares after the auction when an initial equilibrium price of the stock would be established.

From Google's perspective, the benefit of the auction process was lower costs (as a percentage of proceeds) than with a traditional IPO. The auction may have saved Google about $20 million in fees. In addition, the auction allowed Google to attract a diversified investor base, including many individual investors. However, such an auction process is unlikely to be as successful for firms that are not as well known to individual investors as Google.

Results of Google's Dutch Auction Google's auction resulted in a price of $85 per share, meaning that all investors whose bids were accepted paid $85 per share. Google was able to sell all of its 19.6 million shares at this price, which generated proceeds of $1.67 billion. Recall that Google initially hoped to sell the shares for between $118 and $135 per share. If it could have sold its shares for $120 per share instead of $85 per share, it would have generated an additional $686 million in proceeds from the IPO.

Trading after the Auction Any transactions that occurred after the auction was completed took place in the secondary market, meaning that investors were buying shares that were previously purchased by other investors. Some investors who obtained shares at the time of the IPO sold (flipped) their shares in the secondary market shortly after the auction was completed. The share price increased by 18 percent to $100.34 by the end of the first day, so investors who obtained shares through the auction and sold them at the end of the first day earned an 18 percent return. This also means that investors who purchased their shares at the end of the first day paid 18 percent more than if they had purchased the shares through the auction.

During the first two days of trading, the trading volume in the secondary market was about 1.7 times the shares issued in the IPO. Clearly, many investors were flipping their shares to benefit from the higher market price after the auction. As of May 2008, Google stock was selling for about $586 per share, or almost seven times its original offer price in 2004. Thus, a $10,000 investment in Google stock at the time of the IPO was worth almost $70,000 in less than four years. However, by April 2009, Google's stock price declined to about $352, which reflects a 40 percent decline from its price 11 months earlier. This example illustrates how the performance from investing in stock is highly influenced by the timing of an investment.

Abuses in the IPO Market

IPOs have received negative publicity because of several abuses. In 2003, regulators issued new guidelines in an effort to prevent such abuses in the future. Some of the more common abuses are described here.

- *Spinning.* Spinning occurs when the underwriter allocates shares from an IPO to corporate executives who may be considering an IPO or other business that will require the help of a securities firm. The underwriter hopes that the executives will remember the favor and hire the securities firm in the future.

- *Laddering.* When there is substantial demand for an IPO, some brokers engage in laddering; that is, they encourage investors to place first-day bids for the shares that are above the offer price. This helps to build upward price momentum. Some investors may be willing to participate to ensure that the broker will reserve some shares of the next hot IPO for them.

- *Excessive commissions.* Some brokers have also charged excessive commissions when demand was high for an IPO. Investors were willing to pay the price because they could normally recover the cost from the return on the first day. Since the underwriter set an offer price significantly below the market price that would occur by the end of the first day of trading, investors were willing to accommodate the brokers. The gain to the brokers was a loss to the issuing firm, however, because its proceeds were less than they would have been if the offer price had been set higher.

Long-Term Performance Following IPOs

There is strong evidence that IPOs of firms perform poorly on average over a period of a year or longer. Thus, from a long-term perspective, many IPOs are overpriced at the time of the issue. Investors may be overly optimistic about firms that go public. To the extent that the investors base their expectations on the firm's performance before the IPO, they should be aware that firms do not perform as well after going public as they did before.

EXAMPLE

Consider the case of MarketWatch.com, whose stock price jumped from the offer price of $17 to $97.50 at the close of the first day. The stock price consistently declined to less than $3 per share or by more than 90 percent within a few years. ●

There is evidence that on average IPOs have poor long-term performance, even when all IPOs over various time periods are considered. This weak performance may be partially attributed to irrational valuations at the time of the IPO, which are corrected over time. Another factor in the poor performance may be the firm's managers, who may spend excessively and use the firm's funds less efficiently than they did before the IPO.

Impact of the Sarbanes-Oxley Act on IPOs

The Sarbanes-Oxley Act of 2002 was intended to improve the accuracy of firms' financial statements. Some of its provisions (discussed in more detail later in the chapter) apply to a firm's reporting process at the time of its IPO. The act requires that a firm have an internal control process in place one year before going public. This requirement has improved the quality of the financial reporting. Since it went into effect, investors have made their decisions based on financial information rather than hype. Another factor that has led to more rational investing in IPOs is the media attention given to all the naïve investors who lost money investing in IPOs without understanding them. Since 2002, initial returns on investments in IPOs have generally been smaller, because the demand for IPO shares is not as excessive. At the same time, however, since the initial pricing is more rational, IPO shares have not experienced the long-term downward corrections that prevailed in the late 1990s.

SECONDARY STOCK OFFERINGS

A **secondary stock offering** is a new stock offering by a specific firm whose stock is already publicly traded. Firms engage in secondary stock offerings to raise more equity so that they can more easily expand their operations. A firm that wants to engage in a secondary stock offering must file the offering with the SEC. It will likely hire a securities firm to advise on the number of shares it can sell, to help develop the prospectus submitted to the SEC, and to place the new shares with investors.

Since there is already a market price for the stock of a firm that engages in a secondary offering, the firm hopes that it can issue shares at the existing market price. Given that a secondary offering may involve millions of shares, however, there may not be sufficient demand by investors at the prevailing market price. In this case, the underwriter will have to reduce the price so that it can sell all the new shares. Many secondary offerings cause the market price to decline by 1 to 4 percent on the day of the offering, which reflects the new price at which the increased supply of shares in the market is equal to the demand for the shares. Because of the potential for a decline in the equilibrium price of all of its shares, a firm considering a secondary stock offering generally monitors stock market movements. It prefers to issue new stock when the market price of its outstanding shares is relatively high and the general outlook for the firm is favorable. Under these conditions, it can issue new shares at a relatively high price, which will generate more funds for a given amount of shares issued.

Corporations sometimes direct their sales of stock toward a particular group, such as their existing shareholders, by giving them **preemptive rights** (first priority) to purchase the new stock. By placing newly issued stock with existing shareholders, the firm avoids diluting ownership. Preemptive rights are exercised by purchasing new shares during the subscription period (which normally lasts a month or less) at the price specified by the rights. Alternatively, the rights can be sold to someone else.

Shelf-Registration

Corporations can publicly place securities without the time lag often caused by registering with the SEC. With this so-called **shelf-registration**, a corporation can fulfill SEC requirements up to two years before issuing new securities. The registration statement contains financing plans over the upcoming two years. The securities are, in a sense, shelved until the firm needs to issue them. Shelf-registrations allow firms quick access to funds without repeatedly being slowed by the registration process. Thus, corporations anticipating unfavorable conditions can quickly lock in their financing costs. Although this is beneficial to the issuing corporation, potential purchasers must realize that the information disclosed in the registration is not continually updated and therefore may not accurately reflect the firm's status over the shelf-registration period.

STOCK REPURCHASES

The notion of asymmetric information means that a firm's managers have information about the firm's future prospects that is not known by the firm's investors. When corporate managers believe that their firm's stock is undervalued, they can use the firm's excess cash to purchase a portion of its shares in the market at a relatively low price based on their valuation of what the shares are really worth. Firms tend to repurchase some of their shares when share prices are at very low levels.

In general, studies have found that stock prices respond favorably to stock repurchase announcements, which implies that investors interpret the announcement as signaling management's perception that the shares are undervalued. Investors respond favorably to this signal.

EXAMPLE

On March 6, 2009, Quest Software announced that it would repurchase up to $100 million of its common stock. Its stock price increased by about 5 percent in response to this announcement, even before Quest repurchased any stock, as investors viewed the announcement as a signal that Quest believed its stock was undervalued. ●

Although many stock repurchase plans are viewed as a favorable signal, some investors may ask why the firm does not use its funds to expand its business instead of buying back its stock. Thus, investors' response to a stock repurchase plan varies with the firm's characteristics.

STOCK EXCHANGES

Any shares of stock that have been issued as a result of an IPO or a secondary offering can be traded by investors in the secondary market. In the United States, stock trading between investors occurs on the organized stock exchanges and the over-the-counter (OTC) market.

Organized Exchanges

Each **organized exchange** has a trading floor where floor traders execute transactions in the secondary market for their clients. Although there are several organized stock exchanges in the United States, the New York Stock Exchange (NYSE) is by far the largest, controlling 80 percent of the value of all organized exchange transactions. The firms listed on the NYSE are typically much larger than those listed on the other exchanges. For some firms, more than 100 million shares are traded on a daily basis.

Individuals or firms that purchase a seat on a stock exchange become members of the exchange and obtain the right to trade securities there. The term *seat* is somewhat misleading because all trading is carried out by individuals standing in groups or by computers. There are 1,366 seats on the NYSE. The price of a seat on the NYSE has exceeded $1 million since 1995. In recent years, the price of a seat has been about $1.5 million.

The NYSE has two broad types of members: floor brokers and specialists. **Floor brokers** are either commission brokers or independent brokers. **Commission brokers** are employed by brokerage houses and execute orders for clients on the floor of the NYSE. Independent brokers trade for their own account and are not employed by any particular brokerage house. However, they sometimes handle the overflow for brokerage houses and handle orders for brokerage houses that do not employ full-time brokers. The fee independent brokers receive depends on the size and liquidity of the order they trade.

Specialists can match orders of buyers and sellers. In addition, they can buy or sell stock for their own account and thereby create more liquidity for the stock.

The Trading Floor   Each organized exchange has a trading floor where the buying and selling of securities take place. The trading floor at the NYSE consists of trading posts and trading booths. The specialists and their clerks maintain 20 trading posts. Above each post, computer monitors display the stocks traded there and the last price for each stock traded at that post. Along the perimeter of the trading floor are about 1,500 trading booths where brokers obtain orders. Once an order is received, the broker will represent that order as an agent at the appropriate trading post. Member firms can also send orders directly to the trading posts through the SuperDot system, which is an electronic system for matching up buy and sell orders for small trades.

The trading that takes place on the floor of an exchange resembles an auction. Any member of the exchange can act as both a seller and a buyer. Those members of the exchange attempting to sell a client's stock strive to obtain the highest price possible, while members purchasing stock for their clients aim for the lowest price possible. When members of the exchange announce the sale of a certain number of shares of a certain stock, they receive bids for that stock by other members. The sellers either accept the highest bid immediately or wait until an acceptable bid is offered.

EXAMPLE

Maria contacts her brokerage firm (which is a member of the NYSE) and says that she wishes to sell 100 shares of IBM. The broker stores the order and transmits it to the NYSE trading floor either directly through a computer or by telephone. On the floor of the NYSE, the order is initially stored in the SuperDot system. Then, depending on the order details, the order is either routed directly to the specialist's trading post or to the broker's trading booth.

If the order is transmitted directly to the trading post from the SuperDot system, the order will appear on the specialist's display book screen. The specialist can use his own funds to purchase the stock at the prevailing market price if he desires. If the order is transmitted to the broker's trading booth, the brokerage firm's clerk receiving the order will inform its floor broker on the NYSE that a new order has arrived. The floor broker takes the order to the appropriate trading post and can execute the sale of 100 shares of IBM. ●

The NYSE now commonly executes trades electronically. In 2006, it acquired Archipelago (an electronic communication network), which improved its technology for electronic trading. Its electronic trading platform is referred to as NYSE Arca. In 2007, the NYSE merged with Euronext (which represents various European exchanges) to form the first global exchange. The merger resulted in a set of six stock exchanges and six derivatives exchanges.

Listing Requirements   The NYSE imposes listing requirements for corporations whose stock is listed there, such as a minimum number of shares outstanding and a minimum level of earnings, cash flow, and revenue over a recent period. Once a stock is listed, the exchange also requires that the share price of the stock be at least $1 per share. As time passes, some new listings occur, along with some delistings when corporations no longer meet the requirements.

The requirement of a minimum number of shares outstanding is intended to ensure adequate liquidity. For a stock to be liquid, there should be many willing buyers and sellers at any time so that an investor can easily buy or sell the stock at the prevailing market price. In a liquid market, the bid price that brokers are willing to pay for a stock should be just slightly less than the ask price at which they would sell the stock.

The NYSE charges an initial fee to firms that wish to have their stock listed and meet the requirements. The fee is dependent on the size of the firm.

Over-the-Counter Market

Stocks not listed on the organized exchanges are traded in the **over-the-counter (OTC) market.** Like the organized exchanges, the OTC market also facilitates secondary market transactions. Unlike the organized exchanges, the OTC market does not have a trading floor. Instead, the buy and sell orders are completed through a telecommunications network. Because there is no trading floor, it is not necessary to buy a seat to trade on this exchange, but it is necessary to register with the SEC.

WEB

www.nasdaq.com
Trends and other statistical information on various Nasdaq indexes.

Nasdaq   Many stocks in the OTC market are served by the **National Association of Securities Dealers Automatic Quotations (Nasdaq)**, which is an electronic quotation system that provides immediate price quotations. Firms that wish to have their prices quoted by the Nasdaq must meet specific requirements on minimum assets, capital, and number of shareholders. More than 3,000 stocks trade on the Nasdaq. Although most stocks listed in the Nasdaq market are relatively small firms, stocks of some very large firms such as Apple and Intel are also traded there. Transaction costs as a percentage of the investment tend to be higher on the Nasdaq than on the NYSE.

The Nasdaq market is composed of two segments, the Nasdaq National Market and the Nasdaq Small Cap Market. The Nasdaq National Market facilitates the trading of large stocks such as Apple and Intel.

Although more stocks are listed on the Nasdaq than on the NYSE, the market value of these stocks is typically much lower than that of stocks listed on the NYSE. The aggregate market value of stocks traded on the Nasdaq is less than one-fourth the aggregate market value of all stocks listed on the NYSE.

In 2007, the NYSE and Nasdaq agencies that regulate trading merged. This reduced the overlap between the rules imposed on firms that execute trades on those exchanges. The firms that execute transactions are now subject to one set of regulations, which makes it easier for them to comply.

OTC Bulletin Board   The OTC Bulletin Board lists stocks that have a price below $1 per share. These stocks are sometimes referred to as penny stocks. More than 3,500 stocks are listed here. Many of these stocks were traded in the Nasdaq market but no longer meet Nasdaq requirements. These stocks are less liquid than those traded on exchanges, as there is a very limited amount of trading. They are typically traded by individual investors only. Institutional investors tend to focus on more liquid stocks that can be easily sold in the secondary market at any time.

Pink Sheets   In addition, the OTC market has another segment known as the "pink sheets" where even smaller stocks are traded. Like the stocks on the OTC Bulletin Board, these stocks typically do not satisfy the Nasdaq's listing requirements. Financial data on them are very limited, if available at all. Even brokers may not be able to obtain information on many of these firms. Families and officers of these firms commonly control much of the stock.

The pink-sheets market provides quotes for about 5,000 stocks. Because the pink-sheets market does not have the regulatory oversight that exists on other exchanges, fraudulent trading is a serious concern. Companies whose stocks are traded on the pink-sheets market do not have to register with the SEC. Some of the stocks have very little trading volume and may not be traded at all for several weeks.

Electronic Stock Exchanges

In the mid-1990s, several electronic stock exchanges were created to execute stock transactions electronically. These electronic exchanges, which are known as electronic communication networks (ECNs), are discussed in more detail in Chapter 12. Two of the best-known ECNs are Instinet and Archipelago, which became very popular because of their ability to execute orders efficiently. In April 2005, Nasdaq acquired Instinet. This enhanced Nasdaq's electronic trading efficiency by making its technological platform more competitive. As a result, Nasdaq may be able to attract more new firms to list there after going public.

Archipelago initially executed orders for Nasdaq and NYSE stocks. Thus, it commonly competed against the NYSE for orders to trade stocks on the NYSE. In January 2006, the NYSE merged with Archipelago. The merger enhanced the NYSE's ability to execute orders efficiently. The merged company is also able to trade Nasdaq-listed stocks through Archipelago's electronic trading system.

Extended Trading Sessions

The NYSE and Nasdaq market offer extended trading sessions beyond normal trading hours. A late trading session enables investors to buy or sell stocks after the market closes, and an early morning session (sometimes referred to as a pre-market session) enables them to buy or sell stocks just before the market opens on the following day. Beyond the sessions offered by the exchanges, some ECNs allow for trading at any time. Since many announcements about firms are made after normal trading hours, investors can attempt to take advantage of this information before the market opens the next day. However, the market liquidity during the extended trading sessions is limited. For example, the total trading volume of a widely traded stock at night may be about 5 percent (or less) of its trading volume during the day. Some stocks are rarely traded at all during the night. Thus, a large trade is more likely to jolt the stock price during an extended trading session because a large price adjustment may be necessary to entice other investors to take the opposite position. Some investors attempt to take advantage of unusual stock price movements during extended trading sessions, but are exposed to the risk that the market price will not adjust in the manner that they anticipated.

Stock Quotations Provided by Exchanges

WEB

www.nasdaq.com
U.S. stock quotes and charts.

The trading of stocks between investors in the secondary market can cause any stock's price to change. Investors can monitor stock price quotations at financial websites and in newspapers. Although the format varies among sources, most quotations provide similar information. Stock prices are always quoted on a per share basis, as in the example in Exhibit 10.4. Use the exhibit to supplement the following discussion of other information in stock quotations.

52-Week Price Range   The stock's highest price and lowest price over the previous 52 weeks are commonly listed just to the left of the stock's name. The high and low

USING THE WALL STREET JOURNAL

Late Trading

The Wall Street Journal provides information on stocks that were heavily traded after normal trading hours, as shown here. Specifically, it indicates the trading volume and the percentage change in the share price after normal trading hours.

Source: Republished with permission of Dow Jones & Company, Inc., from The Wall Street Journal, January 7, 2009; permission conveyed through the Copyright Clearance Center, Inc.

Late Trading

Most-active and biggest movers among NYSE, Amex and Nasdaq issues between 4 p.m. and 6:30 p.m. ET as reported by electronic trading services, securities dealers and regional exchanges. Minimum share price of $3 and minimum after-hours volume of 5,000 shares.

Most-active issues in late trading

Company	Symbol	Volume (000)	Last	Net chg	AFTER HOURS % chg	High	Low
SPDR 500	SPY	14,331	93.00	−0.47	−0.50	93.60	92.71
iShrRus2000	IWM	10,246	50.99	−0.26	−0.51	51.42	50.38
PowerShrs QQQ Tr 1	QQQQ	4,169	31.19	−0.14	−0.45	31.47	31.15
Diamond Tr	DIA	3,364	89.75	−0.40	−0.44	90.21	89.50
iShrMSCIEmrgMkt	EEM	2,169	27.09	−0.01	−0.04	27.25	27.03
Citigroup Inc	C	1,639	7.44	−0.02	−0.27	7.49	7.36
Sprint Nextel	S	1,353	2.33	0.01	0.43	2.35	2.27
Fin'l Sel SPDR	XLF	1,204	12.60	−0.05	−0.40	12.70	12.54

Percentage gainers...

Company	Symbol	Volume (000)	Last	Net chg	AFTER HOURS % chg	High	Low
NetScout Systems	NTCT	19	11.50	1.26	12.30	12.00	10.22
Maguire Props Inc	MPG	77	2.60	0.28	12.07	2.60	1.61
Polycom Inc	PLCM	135	15.30	1.43	10.31	15.30	13.76
Interwoven Inc	IWOV	41	12.75	0.87	7.32	13.03	11.88
F5 Networks Inc	FFIV	650	24.00	1.50	6.67	24.50	20.68
AerCap Hldgs N.V.	AER	22	5.70	0.35	6.62	5.75	5.70
FstFed Fin'l	FED	14	3.05	0.17	5.90	3.05	2.82
James River Coal	JRCC	6	18.52	0.93	5.29	18.52	17.61
Travelzoo Inc	TZOO	29	5.51	0.28	5.26	5.51	5.51
Unifi Inc	UFI	25	2.99	0.14	4.91	2.99	2.99

...And losers

Company	Symbol	Volume (000)	Last	Net chg	AFTER HOURS % chg	High	Low
Dupont Fabros Tech	DFT	8	3.00	−0.68	−18.59	3.00	3.00
Standard Microsys	SMSC	10	14.81	−1.81	−10.89	16.83	14.40
Gaylord Entertain	GET	22	13.06	−1.34	−9.31	13.06	13.06
Domtar Corp	UFS	143	1.91	−0.19	−9.02	2.01	1.91
Cameron Int'l Corp	CAM	58	23.27	−2.16	−8.49	25.43	23.27
Exterran Holdings	EXH	9	24.63	−2.17	−8.10	26.80	24.63
RC2 Corp	RCRC	11	7.62	−0.63	−7.64	7.62	7.62
ArvinMeritor Inc	ARM	8	3.65	−0.30	−7.59	3.96	3.49
Xinyuan Real Estate	XIN	41	3.55	−0.29	−7.55	3.55	3.55
Air Prods & Chem	APD	24	55.10	−4.22	−7.11	59.78	55.10

Exhibit 10.4 Example of Stock Price Quotations

YTD % CHANGE	HI	LO	STOCK	SYM	DIV	YLD%	PE	VOL 100S	LAST	NET CHG
+10.3	121.88	80.06	IBM	IBM	.56	.6	20	71979	93.77	+1.06
Year-to-date percentage change in stock price	Highest price of the stock in this year	Lowest price of the stock in this year	Name of stock	Stock symbol	Annual dividend paid per year	Dividend yield, which represents the annual dividend as a percentage of the prevailing stock price	Price-earnings ratio based on the prevailing stock price	Trading volume during the previous trading day	Closing stock price	Change in the stock price from the close on the day before

prices indicate the range for the stock's price over the last year. Some investors use this range as an indicator of how much the stock price fluctuates. Other investors compare this range to the prevailing stock price because they wish to purchase a stock only when its prevailing price is below its 52-week high.

Notice that IBM's 52-week high price was $121.88 and its low price was $80.06 per share. The low price is about 34 percent below the high price, which suggests a wide difference over the last year. When IBM's stock price hit its 52-week low, the company's market value was more than one-third less than it was when the price reached its 52-week high.

Symbol   Each stock has a specific symbol that is used to identify the firm. This symbol may be used to communicate trade orders to brokers. Ticker tapes at brokerage firms or on financial news television shows use the symbol to identify each firm. If included in the stock quotations, the symbol normally appears just to the right of the firm's name. Each symbol is usually composed of two to four letters. IBM's ticker symbol is the same as its name. Nike's symbol is NKE, the symbol for Home Depot is HD, and the symbol for Motorola is MOT.

Dividend   The annual dividend (DIV) is commonly listed to the right of the firm's name and symbol. It shows the dividends distributed to stockholders over the last year on a per share basis. IBM's dividend is $.56 per share, which indicates an average of $.14 per share for each quarter. The annual dollar amount of dividends paid can be determined by multiplying the dividends per share times the number of shares outstanding.

Dividend Yield   Next to the annual dividend, some stock quotation tables also show the dividend yield (Yld), which is the annual dividend per share as a percentage of the stock's prevailing price. Since IBM's annual dividend is $.56 per share and its prevailing stock price is $93.77, its stock's dividend yield is

$$\text{Dividend yield} = \frac{\text{Dividends paid per share}}{\text{Prevailing stock price}}$$
$$= \frac{\$.56}{\$93.77}$$
$$= .60\%$$

Some firms attempt to provide a somewhat stable dividend yield over time, but other firms do not.

Price-Earnings Ratio   Most stock quotations include the stock's price-earnings (PE) ratio, which represents its prevailing stock price per share divided by the firm's earnings per share (earnings divided by number of existing shares of stock) generated over the last year. IBM's PE ratio of 20 in Exhibit 10.4 is derived by dividing its stock price of $93.77 by the previous year's earnings. PE ratios are closely monitored by some investors who believe that a low PE ratio (relative to other firms in the same industry) signals that the stock is undervalued based on the company's earnings.

Volume   Stock quotations also usually include the volume (referred to as "Vol" or "Sales") of shares traded on the previous day. The volume is normally quoted in hundreds of shares. It is not unusual for several million shares of a large firm's stock to be traded on a single day. Exhibit 10.4 shows that more than 7 million shares of IBM were traded. Some financial media also show the percentage change in the volume of trading from the previous day.

Closing Price Quotations   Stock quotations show the closing price ("Last") on the day (on the previous day if the quotations are in a newpaper). In addition, the change in the price ("Net Chg") is typically provided and indicates the increase or decrease in the stock price from the closing price on the day before.

Stock Index Quotations

Stock indexes serve as performance indicators of specific stock exchanges or of particular subsets of the market. The indexes allow investors to compare the performance of individual stocks with more general market indicators. Some of the more closely monitored indexes are identified next.

Dow Jones Industrial Average   The **Dow Jones Industrial Average (DJIA)** is a price-weighted average of stock prices of 30 large U.S. firms. ExxonMobil, IBM, and the Coca-Cola Company are among the stocks included in the index. Although this index is commonly monitored, it has some limitations as a market indicator. First, because the index is price weighted, it assigns a higher weight over time to those stocks that experience higher prices. Therefore, the index tends to have an upward bias in its estimate of the market's overall performance. Second, because the DJIA is based on only 30 large stocks, it does not necessarily serve as an adequate indicator of the overall market or especially of smaller stocks.

Standard & Poor's (S&P) 500   The **Standard & Poor's (S&P) 500 index** is a value-weighted index of stock prices of 500 large U.S. firms. Because this index contains such a large number of stocks, it is more representative of the U.S. stock market than the DJIA. However, because the S&P 500 index focuses on large stocks, it does not serve as a useful indicator for stock prices of smaller firms.

Wilshire 5000 Total Market Index   The Wilshire 5000 Total Market Index was created in 1974 to reflect the values of 5,000 U.S. stocks. Since more stocks have been added over time, the index now contains more than 5,000 stocks. It represents the broadest index of the U.S. stock market. It is widely quoted in financial media and closely monitored by the Federal Reserve and many financial institutions.

New York Stock Exchange Indexes   The NYSE provides quotations on indexes that it created. The Composite Index represents the average of all stocks traded on the NYSE. This is an excellent indicator of the general performance of stocks traded on the NYSE, but because these stocks represent mostly large firms, the Composite Index is not an appropriate measure of small stock performance. In addition to the Composite Index, the NYSE also provides indexes for four sectors:

1. Industrial
2. Transportation
3. Utility
4. Financial

These indexes are commonly used as benchmarks for comparison to an individual firm or portfolio in that respective sector. Although the indexes are positively correlated, there are substantial differences in their movements during some periods.

Nasdaq Stock Indexes   The **National Association of Securities Dealers** provides quotations on indexes of stocks traded on the Nasdaq. These indexes are useful indicators of small stock performance because many small stocks are traded on the Nasdaq.

USING THE WALL STREET JOURNAL

Stock Market Review

The Wall Street Journal provides detailed information beyond stock index quotations that can be used to review stock market conditions during the previous day.

- The number of stocks that advanced versus the number that declined (useful for determining the general market sentiment).

- Stocks that were the biggest percentage gainers and losers (these stocks may have been the subject of major news on the previous day, causing a large stock price response).

- Stocks with the biggest dollar gains and losses on the previous day.

- Most active stocks (these are usually the stocks of large firms, and they may also have been the subject of major news).

- Volume movers, which are stocks that suddenly experienced a much larger amount of trading volume than their norm.

- Most widely held stocks (these stocks receive more attention because they are so popular among investors).

- A table called "New Highs and Lows":

  - Stocks that reached their highest price on the previous trading day based on prices over the last year.

  - Stocks that reached their lowest price on the previous trading day based on prices over the last year.

MONITORING PUBLICLY TRADED COMPANIES

Since a firm's stock price is normally related to its performance, the return to investors is dependent on how well the firm is managed. A publicly traded firm's managers serve as agents for shareholders by making decisions that are supposed to maximize the stock's price. The separation of ownership (by shareholders) and control (by managers) can result in agency problems because of conflicting interests. Managers may be tempted to serve their own interests rather than those of the investors who own the firm's stock. To attempt to solve these agency problems, various forms of corporate governance are used to monitor managers of corporations.

The easiest way for shareholders to monitor the firm is to monitor changes in its value (as measured by its share price) over time. Since the share price is continuously available, shareholders can quickly detect any abrupt changes in the value of the firm. If the stock price is lower than expected, shareholders may attempt to take action to improve the management of the firm. In addition, publicly traded firms are required to provide financial statements that disclose their financial condition to the public, so investors can also monitor these statements.

Investors also rely on the board of directors of each firm to ensure that its managers make decisions that enhance the firm's performance and maximize the stock price. A firm's board of directors is responsible for supervising its business and affairs. The board attempts to ensure that the business is managed in a way that serves the shareholders. Directors are also responsible for monitoring operations and ensuring that the firm complies with the laws. They cannot oversee every workplace decision, but they can ensure that the firm has a process that can guide some decisions about moral and ethical conduct. They can also ensure that the firm has a system for internal control and reporting.

WEB

http://finance.yahoo
.com/marketupdate/
upgrades?u

List of stocks that were
upgraded or down-
graded by analysts.

Role of Analysts

Analysts can help investors monitor stocks. Analysts are often employed by securities firms and assigned to monitor a small set of publicly traded firms. As part of the monitoring process, they communicate with the high-level managers of the firms that they cover. Because they have expertise in analyzing the financial condition of these firms and in valuing stocks, analysts may detect financial problems within a firm that would not be recognized by most investors. Analysts publicize their opinion of the companies that they monitor for investors by assigning a rating (or recommendation) to the firm's stock such as Strong Buy, Buy, Hold, or Sell.

Though analysts can provide useful information for investors, they tend to be very generous when rating stocks. Thus, their effectiveness in monitoring publicly traded companies is limited. In 2001, the SEC found clear evidence of conflicts of interest for analysts employed by securities firms. Some analysts assigned a rating of "Strong Buy" to stocks that they described as a "piece of junk" or worse in e-mail to co-workers at their securities firms. Some of the e-mail messages confirmed that the main reason the analysts rated a stock highly was so that their securities firm could attract advisory business from corporations and generate fee income. In fact, the bonuses paid to analysts were sometimes based on how much business they generated for their employer.

Stock Exchange Rules   In the 2002–2004 period, the U.S. stock exchanges imposed new rules to prevent some obvious conflicts of interest faced by analysts. First, analysts cannot be supervised by the division that provides advisory services, and their compensation cannot be driven by the amount of advisory business that they generate. This rule was intended to encourage analysts to provide more unbiased ratings of stocks. Second, securities firms must disclose summaries of their analysts' ratings for all the firms that they rate, so that investors can determine whether the ratings are always excessively optimistic.

Accounting Irregularities

To the extent that managers can manipulate the financial statements, they may be able to hide information from investors. In recent years, many firms (including Enron, Tyco, and WorldCom) used unusual accounting methods to create their financial statements. As a result, it was very difficult for investors to ascertain the true financial condition of these firms and therefore to monitor them. The problem was compounded because the auditors hired to audit the financial statements of some firms allowed them to use these irregular accounting methods. A subset of a firm's board members serve on an audit committee, which is supposed to ensure that the audit is done properly, but in some firms, the committee failed to monitor the auditors. Overall, investors' monitoring of some firms was limited because the accountants distorted the financial statements, the auditors did not properly audit, and the audit committees of those firms did not oversee the audit properly.

Sarbanes-Oxley Act

As mentioned earlier, the Sarbanes-Oxley Act was enacted in 2002 to ensure more accurate disclosure of financial information to investors. The act attempts to force accountants to conform to regular accounting standards in preparing a firm's financial statements and to force auditors to take their auditing role seriously. To the extent that the act ensures more accurate financial reporting, it allows investors to more effectively monitor firms and detect when managers are not serving the interests of shareholders. In particular, the act does the following:

- Prevents a public accounting firm from auditing a client firm whose chief executive officer (CEO), chief financial officer (CFO), or other employees with similar job descriptions were employed by the accounting firm within one year prior to the audit. This provision maintains some distance between the audit firm and the client.

- Requires that only outside board members of a firm be on the firm's audit committee, which is responsible for making sure that the audit is conducted in an unbiased manner. Outside board members are more likely to serve the interests of existing and prospective shareholders than inside board members who are part of the firm's management.

- Prevents the members of a firm's audit committee from receiving consulting or advising fees or other compensation from the firm beyond that earned from serving on the board. This provision prevents a firm from providing excessive compensation to the members of an audit committee as a means of paying them off so that they do not closely oversee the audit.

- Requires that the CEO and CFO of firms that are of at least a specified size certify that the audited financial statements are accurate. This provision forces the CFO and CEO to be accountable.

- Specifies major fines or imprisonment for employees who mislead investors or hide evidence. This provision attempts to ensure that a firm's employees will be penalized for their role in distorting the accounting statements.

- Allows public accounting firms to offer nonaudit consulting services to an audit client only if the client's audit committee pre-approves the nonaudit services to be rendered before the audit begins. This provision attempts to ensure that a firm does not pay off an auditor with extra fees for consulting services in return for the auditor's certification that the firm's financial statements are accurate.

The act essentially contains a set of provisions related to a firm's process of recording, auditing, and reporting financial information. It attempts to prevent breakdowns in the process, so that investors can have more confidence in the accuracy of financial statements. Since the act prevents some forms of accounting abuses by publicly traded firms, it should improve the ability of existing and prospective shareholders to monitor these firms.

EXAMPLE

Several managers of Taos Company own shares of the company and would like to cash out soon. Currently, however, the firm's stock price is low because Taos's performance has been weak. As the CFO prepares the income statement for this year, she considers overstating the firm's earnings because she believes this could improve the stock price and allow her to sell her shares for more money. But she is discouraged by several provisions of the Sarbanes-Oxley Act. First, as a result of the process that Taos Company created to comply with the act, the trail of recorded financial information from various employees to the CFO is now very transparent. Thus, she cannot make up numbers because the paper trail will lead back to her. Second, the auditors are more likely to detect any discrepancy because the process for estimating the earnings is more transparent. Third, the auditors are less likely to purposely overlook such a discrepancy because the act attempts to prevent auditors from ignoring discrepancies in exchange for receiving higher fees. Fourth, the act requires the CFO to sign off on the financial statements. She is subject to criminal charges and fines if the financial statements are determined to be misleading. Thus, she cannot pretend that she did not review the financial statements. ●

Although the Sarbanes-Oxley Act has improved transparency, it has not resolved many of the limitations of financial disclosure. Investors still have limited information about the quality of the assets that firms own. Because the information is so limited, investors may be incapable of assigning a reasonable valuation to a stock. This became very obvious during the credit crisis when stock prices of financial institutions gyrated in response to concerns about the mortgages they were holding.

Lehman Brothers was ranked number one in *Barron's* annual survey of corporate performance for large companies. In 2007, *Fortune* magazine put Lehman Brothers at the top of its list of "Most Admired Securities Firms." In March 2007, the value of all of Lehman's stock was about $40 billion. Yet, in September 2008, Lehman filed for bankruptcy, and its stock was worthless. How does a company lose $40 billion in value in 18 months? Some critics would argue that its value should never have been as high as $40 billion because its assets were very susceptible to a major decline in value. Even if Lehman Brothers followed all financial reporting rules under the Sarbanes-Oxley Act, investors might not have had adequate information to assess the quality of its assets. ●

Cost of Being Public   Establishing a process that satisfies the Sarbanes-Oxley provisions can be very costly. For many firms, the cost of adhering to the guidelines of the Sarbanes-Oxley Act exceeds $1 million per year. Consequently, many small publicly traded firms decided to revert back to private ownership as a result of the act. These firms perceived that they would have a higher value if they were private rather than publicly held because they could avoid the substantial reporting costs that are required of publicly traded firms.

Shareholder Activism

If shareholders are displeased with the way managers are managing a firm, they have three general choices. The first is to do nothing and retain the shares in the hope that management's actions will ultimately lead to strong stock price performance. A second choice is to sell the stock. This choice is common among shareholders who do not believe that they can change the firm's management or do not wish to spend the time and money needed to bring about change. A third choice is to engage in **shareholder activisim.** Some of the more common types of shareholder activism are examined here.

Communication with the Firm   Shareholders can communicate their concerns to other investors in an effort to place more pressure on the firm's managers or its board members. For example, shareholders may voice concerns about a firm that expands outside its core businesses, attempts to acquire other companies at excessive prices, or defends against a takeover that the shareholders believe would be beneficial.

Institutional investors commonly communicate with high-level corporate managers and have opportunities to offer their concerns about the firm's operations. The managers may be willing to consider the changes suggested by large institutional investors because they do not want those investors to sell their holdings of the firm's stock.

Some institutional investors have become much more involved in monitoring management, as they have realized that they can enhance the value of their security portfolios by ensuring that the firms in which they invest are properly managed. An institutional investor such as a pension fund, a life insurance company, or a mutual fund that holds a substantial amount of a corporation's stock may request a seat on the corporation's board of directors. Alternatively, the investor may request that the corporation at least replace one of the executives on the board with an outside investor to ensure that the board makes decisions to satisfy shareholders. The hope is that any changes suggested by shareholders result in stronger performance and a higher stock price for the firm.

The California Public Employees' Retirement System (CALPERS) manages the pensions for employees of the state of California. It manages more than $80 billion of securities and commonly maintains large stock positions in some firms. When CALPERS believes that these firms are not being managed properly, it communicates its concerns and sometimes proposes solutions. Some of the firms adjust their management to accommodate CALPERS.

CALPERS periodically announces a list of firms that it believes have serious agency problems. These firms may have been unwilling to respond to CALPERS's concerns about their management style. ●

Firms are especially responsive when institutional investors communicate as a team. Institutional Shareholder Services (ISS), which is part of RiskMetrics Group, organizes institutional shareholders to push for a common cause. After receiving feedback from institutional investors about a particular firm, ISS organizes a conference call with high-ranking executives of the firm so that it can obtain information from the firm. It then announces the time of the conference call to investors and allows them to listen in on the call. The questions focus on institutional shareholders' concerns about the firm's management. Unlike earnings conference calls, which are controlled by firms, ISS runs the conference call. Common questions asked by ISS include:

- Why is your CEO also the chair of the board?
- Why is your executive compensation much higher than the industry norm?
- What is your process for nominating new board members?

Transcripts of the conference calls are available within 48 hours after the call.

Proxy Contest   Shareholders may also engage in proxy contests in an attempt to change the composition of the board. This is a more formal effort than communicating with the firm and is normally considered only if an informal request for a change in the board (through communication with the board) is ignored. A change in the board may be beneficial if it forces the board to make decisions that are more focused on maximizing the stock price. If the dissident shareholders gain enough votes, they can elect one or more directors who share their views. In this case, shareholders are truly exercising their control.

ISS may recommend that shareholders vote a certain way on specific proxy issues. As a result of these more organized efforts, institutional shareholders are having more influence on management decisions. At some firms, they have succeeded in implementing changes that can enhance shareholder value, such as:

- Limiting severance pay for executives who are fired.
- Revising the voting guidelines on the firm's executive compensation policy.
- Requiring more transparent reporting of financial information.
- Imposing ceilings on the CEO's salary and bonus.
- Removing bylaws that prevented takeovers by other firms.
- Allowing for an annual election of all directors so that ineffective directors can be quickly removed from the board.

Shareholder Lawsuits   Investors may sue the board if they believe that the directors are not fulfilling their responsibilities to shareholders. This action is intended to force the board to make decisions that are aligned with the shareholders' interests. Many lawsuits have been filed when corporations prevent takeovers, pursue acquisitions, or make other restructuring decisions that some shareholders believe will reduce the stock's value.

At some firms, the boards have been negligent in representing the shareholders. Nevertheless, since business performance is subject to uncertainty, directors cannot be held responsible every time a key business decision has an unsatisfactory outcome. When directors are sued, the court typically focuses on whether the directors' decisions were reasonable, rather than on whether they increased the firm's profitability. Thus, from the court's perspective, the directors' decision-making process is more relevant than the outcome.

Limited Power of Governance

Although much attention has been given in financial markets to how managers are subject to increased governance, there is some evidence that the governance is not very effective. Consider the following compensation that was paid to executives of companies that either failed or were rescued by the the U.S. government in 2008:

- The CEO of Wachovia received $21 million in 2007.

- The CEO of Washington Mutual received an exit package worth $44 million.

- The CEO of Bear Stearns received an exit package worth $60 million.

- The CEO of Fannie Mae received compensation of about $12 million in 2007.

- The top 11 executives of American International Group received compensation of about $44 million in 2007.

- The CEO of Lehman Brothers reportedly received about $480 million over the eight years leading up to Lehman's bankruptcy in 2008 (the CEO refuted that report and stated to Congress that his compensation was closer to $300 million).

- Four days before Lehman Brothers filed for bankruptcy, its compensation committee awarded $20 million in "special payments" to three executives.

There are numerous examples of executives who continue to receive very high compensation even when the performance of their firm is very weak. In spite of the Sarbanes-Oxley Act, shareholder activism, proxy contests, and shareholder lawsuits, the agency problems of some firms are still severe.

MARKET FOR CORPORATE CONTROL

When corporate managers notice that another firm in the same industry has a low stock price as a result of poor management, they may attempt to acquire that firm. They hope to purchase the business at a low price and improve its management so that they can increase the value of the business. In addition, the combination of the two firms may reduce redundancy in some operations and allow for synergistic benefits. In this way, the managers of the acquiring firm may earn a higher return than if they used their funds for some other type of expansion. In essence, weak businesses are subject to a takeover by more efficient corporations and are therefore subject to the "market for corporate control." Thus, if a firm's stock price is relatively low because of poor performance, it may become an attractive target for other corporations.

A firm may especially benefit from acquisitions when its own stock price has risen. It can use its stock as currency to acquire the shares of a target by exchanging some of its own shares for the target's shares. Some critics claim that acquisitions of inefficient firms typically lead to layoffs and are unfair to employees. The counter to this argument is that without the market for corporate control, firms would be allowed to be inefficient, which is unfair to the shareholders who invested in them. Managers recognize that if their poorly performing business is taken over, they may lose their jobs. Thus, the market for corporate control can encourage managers to make decisions that maximize the stock's value so that they can better avoid takeovers.

In general, studies have found that the share prices of target firms react very positively, but that the share prices of acquiring firms are not favorably affected. Investors may not expect the acquiring firm to achieve its objectives. For example, there is some evidence that firms engaging in acquisitions do not eliminate inefficient operations after the acquisitions, perhaps because of the potential low morale that results from layoffs.

Use of LBOs to Achieve Corporate Control

The market for corporate control is enhanced by the use of **leveraged buyouts (LBOs)**, which are acquisitions that require substantial amounts of borrowed funds. That is, the acquisition requires a substantial amount of financial leverage. Some so-called buyout firms identify poorly managed firms, acquire them (mostly with the use of borrowed funds), improve their management, and then sell them at a higher price than they paid. Alternatively, a group of managers who work for the firm may believe that they can restructure the firm's operations to improve cash flows. The managers may attempt an LBO in the hope that they can improve the firm's performance.

The use of debt to retire a company's stock creates a very highly leveraged capital structure. One favorable aspect of such a revised capital structure is that the ownership of the firm is normally reduced to a small group of people, who may be managers of the firm. Thus, agency costs should be reduced when managers act in their own interests instead of the firm's. A major concern about LBOs, however, is that the firm will experience cash flow problems over time because of the high periodic debt payments that result from the high degree of financial leverage. A firm financed in this way has a high potential return but is risky.

Some firms that engage in LBOs issue new stock after improving the firm's performance. This process is referred to as a **reverse leveraged buyout (reverse LBO).** Whereas an LBO may be used to purchase all the stock of a firm that has not achieved its potential performance (causing its stock to be priced low), a reverse LBO is normally desirable when the stock can be sold at a high price. In essence, the owners hope to issue new stock at a much higher price than they paid when enacting the LBO.

Barriers to the Market for Corporate Control

The power of corporate control to eliminate agency problems is limited due to barriers that can make it more costly for a potential acquiring firm to acquire another firm whose managers are not serving the firm's shareholders. Some of the more common barriers to corporate control are identified next.

Antitakeover Amendments   Some firms have added **antitakeover amendments** to their corporate charter. There are various types of antitakeover amendments. For example, an amendment may require that at least two-thirds of the shareholder votes approve a takeover before the firm can be acquired. Antitakeover amendments are supposed to be enacted to protect shareholders against an acquisition that will ultimately reduce the value of their investment in the firm. However, it may be argued that shareholders are adversely affected by antitakeover amendments.

Poison Pills   **Poison pills** are special rights awarded to shareholders or specific managers on the occurrence of specified events. They can be enacted by a firm's board of directors without the approval of shareholders. Sometimes a target enacts a poison pill to defend against takeover attempts. For example, a poison pill might give all shareholders the right to be allocated an additional 30 percent of shares (based on their existing share holdings) without cost whenever a potential acquirer attempts to acquire the firm. The poison pill makes it more expensive and more difficult for a potential acquiring firm to acquire the target.

Golden Parachutes   A **golden parachute** specifies compensation to managers in the event that they lose their jobs or there is a change in the control of the firm. For example, all managers might have the right to receive 100,000 shares of the firm's stock whenever the firm is acquired. It can be argued that a golden parachute provides managers with security so that they can make decisions that will improve the long-term performance of the firm. That is, managers protected by a golden parachute may be more willing to make decisions that enhance shareholder wealth over the long run even though the decisions adversely affect the stock price in the short run. The counterargument, however, is that a golden parachute allows managers to serve their own interests, rather than shareholder interests, because they receive large compensation even if they are fired.

Golden parachutes can discourage takeover attempts by increasing the cost of the acquisition. A potential acquiring firm recognizes that it will incur the expense associated with the golden parachutes if it acquires a particular target that has enacted golden parachutes prior to the takeover attempt. To the extent that this (or any) defense against takeovers is effective, it disrupts the market for corporate control by allowing managers of some firms to be protected while serving their own interests rather than shareholder interests.

GLOBALIZATION OF STOCK MARKETS

Stock markets are becoming globalized in the sense that barriers between countries have been removed or reduced. Thus, firms in need of funds can tap foreign markets, and investors can purchase foreign stocks. In recent years, many firms have obtained funds from foreign markets through international stock offerings. This strategy may represent an effort by a firm to enhance its global image. Alternatively, because the issuing firm is tapping a larger pool of potential investors, it may more easily place the entire issue of new stock.

Foreign Stock Offerings in the United States

Many of the recent stock offerings in the United States by non-U.S. firms have resulted from privatization programs in Latin America and Europe, whereby businesses that were previously government owned are sold to U.S. shareholders. Some of these businesses are so large that the local stock markets cannot digest the stock offerings. Consequently, U.S. investors are financing many privatized businesses based in foreign countries.

When a non-U.S. firm issues stock in its own country, its shareholder base is quite limited because a few large institutional investors may own most of the shares. By issuing stock in the United States, the firm diversifies its shareholder base; such diversification can reduce share price volatility when large investors sell shares.

Although some large non-U.S. firms have developed a market for their stock in the United States, others are unwilling to do so because of SEC regulations. The SEC requires that any firms desiring to list their stock on a U.S. stock exchange must provide financial statements that satisfy U.S. accounting standards and are compatible with the financial statements of U.S. firms. Non-U.S. firms can avoid the expense of providing these statements if they choose not to list on U.S. exchanges.

Some non-U.S. firms obtain equity financing by using **American depository receipts (ADRs)**, which are certificates representing shares of non-U.S. stock. The use of ADRs circumvents some disclosure requirements imposed on stock offerings in the United States, yet enables non-U.S. firms to tap the U.S. market for funds. The ADR market grew after businesses were privatized in the early 1990s because some of them issued ADRs to obtain financing.

International Placement Process

Securities firms facilitate the international placement of new stock through one or more syndicates across countries. Many securities firms and commercial banks based in the United States provide underwriting and other securities services in foreign countries.

The ability of securities firms to place new shares in foreign markets is somewhat dependent on the stock's perceived liquidity in those markets. A secondary market for the stock must be established in foreign markets to enhance liquidity and make newly issued stocks more attractive. Listing stock on a foreign stock exchange not only enhances the stock's liquidity but may also increase the firm's perceived financial standing when the exchange approves the listing application. Listing on foreign stock exchanges can also protect a firm against hostile takeovers because it disperses ownership and makes it more difficult for other firms to gain a controlling interest. Listing on a foreign stock exchange entails some costs, such as expenses for converting financial data in an annual report into a foreign currency and making financial statements compatible with the accounting standards used in that country. Many countries are complying with a set of international accounting standards, which will allow firms to more easily satisfy the accounting standards when listing their stock on foreign stock exchanges. The U.S. is slowly moving toward some degree of compliance with the international accounting standards.

Global Stock Exchanges

A summary of the world's major stock markets is provided in Exhibit 10.5. Numerous other exchanges also exist. In the past, the growth of many foreign stock markets was limited because their firms relied more on debt financing than equity financing. Recently, however, firms outside the United States have been issuing stock more frequently, which has allowed for substantial growth of non-U.S. stock markets. The percentage of individual versus institutional ownership of shares varies across stock markets. Financial institutions and other firms own a large proportion of the shares outside the United States, and individual investors own a relatively small proportion.

Exhibit 10.5 Comparison of Stock Exchanges (as of 2008)

COUNTRY	MARKET CAPITALIZATION (IN BILLIONS OF $)	NUMBER OF LISTED COMPANIES
Argentina	$ 57	111
Australia	1,298	1,998
Brazil	1,369	404
Chile	212	241
China	4,478	1,530
Greece	264	283
Hong Kong	2,654	1,241
Hungary	46	41
Japan	4,330	2,414
Mexico	3,977	367
Norway	353	248
Russia	211	375
Slovenia	29	87
Spain	1,799	3,537
Switzerland	1,271	341
Taiwan	663	703
United Kingdom	3,851	3,307
United States	19,664	5,965

Source: *World Federation of Exchanges.*

Variation in Characteristics across Stock Markets   The volume of trading activity in each stock market is influenced by legal and other characteristics of the country. Shareholder rights vary among countries, as shareholders in some countries have more voting power and can have a stronger influence on corporate management.

The legal protection of shareholders also varies substantially among countries. Shareholders in some countries can more effectively sue publicly traded firms if their executives or directors commit financial fraud. In general, common law countries such as the United States, Canada, and the United Kingdom allow for more legal protection than civil law countries such as France and Italy.

The government's enforcement of securities laws also varies among countries. If a country has laws to protect shareholders but does not enforce the laws, shareholders are not protected. Some countries tend to have less corporate corruption than others; in these countries, shareholders are less exposed to major losses due to corruption.

In addition, the degree of financial information that must be provided by public companies varies among countries. The variation may be due to the accounting laws set by the government for public companies or to reporting rules enforced by local stock exchanges. Shareholders are less susceptible to losses due to a lack of information if public companies are required to be more transparent in their financial reporting.

In general, more investors are attracted to stock markets in countries that provide voting rights and legal protection for shareholders, strictly enforce the laws, do not tolerate corruption, and impose stringent accounting requirements. These conditions encourage investors to have more confidence in the stock market and allow for greater pricing efficiency. In addition, companies are attracted to the stock market when there are many investors, because they can easily raise funds in the market under these conditions. Conversely, if a stock market does not attract investors, it will not attract companies that need to raise funds. These companies will have to rely on stock markets in other countries or on credit markets to raise funds.

Emerging Stock Markets

Emerging markets enable foreign firms to raise large amounts of capital by issuing stock. These markets also provide a means for investors from the United States and other countries to invest their funds.

Some emerging stock markets are relatively new and small and may not be as efficient as the U.S. stock market. Thus, some stocks may be undervalued, a possibility that has attracted investors to these markets. Because some of these markets are small, however, they may be susceptible to manipulation by large traders. Furthermore, insider trading is more prevalent in many foreign markets because rules against it are not enforced. In general, large institutional investors and insiders based in the foreign markets may have some advantages.

Although international stocks can generate high returns, they may also exhibit high risk. Some of the emerging stock markets are often referred to as casinos because of the wild gyrations in prices that sometimes occur. Large price swings are common because of two characteristics of emerging markets. First, the small number of shares for some firms allows large trades to jolt the equilibrium price. Second, valid financial information about firms is sometimes lacking, causing investors to trade according to rumors. Trading patterns based on continual rumors are more volatile than trading patterns based on factual data.

Methods Used to Invest in Foreign Stocks

Investors can obtain foreign stocks by purchasing shares directly, purchasing American depository receipts (ADRs), investing in international mutual funds, and purchasing exchange-traded funds (ETFs). Each of these methods is explained in turn.

Direct Purchases   Investors can easily invest in stocks of foreign companies that are listed on the local stock exchanges. However, this set of stocks is quite limited. Foreign stocks not listed on local stock exchanges can be purchased through some full-service brokerage firms that have offices in foreign countries, but the transaction costs incurred from purchasing foreign stocks in this manner are high.

American Depository Receipts   An alternative means of investing in foreign stocks is by purchasing ADRs, which, as mentioned earlier, are certificates that represent shares of non-U.S. stocks. Many non-U.S. companies established ADRs in order to develop name recognition in the United States. In addition, some companies wanted to raise funds in the United States.

ADRs are attractive to U.S. investors for several reasons. First, they are closely followed by U.S. investment analysts. Second, companies represented by ADRs are required by the SEC to file financial statements consistent with generally accepted accounting principles in the United States. These statements may not be available for other non-U.S. companies. Third, reliable quotes on ADR prices are consistently available, with existing currency values factored in to translate the price into dollars. A disadvantage, however, is that the selection of ADRs is limited. Also, the ADR market is less active than other stock markets, so ADRs are less liquid than most listed U.S. stocks.

International Mutual Funds   Another way to invest in foreign stocks is to purchase shares of **international mutual funds (IMFs)**, which are portfolios of international stocks created and managed by various financial institutions. Thus, individuals can diversify across international stocks by investing in a single IMF. Some IMFs focus on a specific foreign country, while others contain stocks across several countries or even several continents.

International Exchange-Traded Funds   Exchange-traded funds (ETFs) are passive funds that track a specific index. International ETFs represent international stock indexes. They have become very popular in the last few years. By investing in an international ETF, investors can invest in a specific index representing a foreign country's stock market. An ETF trades like a stock, as it is listed on an exchange, and its value changes in response to trading activity. Although ETFs are denominated in dollars, the net asset value of an international ETF is determined by translating the foreign currency value of the foreign securities into dollars.

WEB

http://finance.yahoo
.com/indices
Click on "World" for
quotations on various
stock market indexes
around the world.

Some international ETFs have been called different names, such as world equity benchmark shares (WEBS) or iShares, by their sponsors. A major difference between ETFs and IMFs is that IMFs are managed, whereas ETFs simply represent an index. If investors prefer that the portfolio be rebalanced by portfolio managers over time, they may prefer an IMF. However, ETFs have lower expenses because they avoid the cost of active portfolio management. The difference in expense ratios between an IMF and an ETF may be 2 percent annually or more.

While the price of a share of each international ETF is denominated in dollars, the underlying securities that make up the index are denominated in non-U.S. currencies. Thus, the return on the ETF will be influenced by the movement of the foreign country's currency against the dollar. This is also true for IMFs. If the foreign currency **appreciates** (increases in value), this will boost the value of the index as measured in dollars. Conversely, if the foreign currency **depreciates** (decreases in value), this will reduce the value of the index as measured in dollars.

SUMMARY

- Stock markets facilitate the transfer of stock ownership between investors. The trading of a stock in the stock market determines its equilibrium price.
- Investors are commonly classified as individual or institutional. The proportion of a firm's shares held by any individual investor tends to be small, which limits the ability of an individual investor to influence the firm's management. Institutional investors have larger equity positions and therefore are more capable of influencing the firm's management. Stock mutual funds, pension funds, and insurance companies are the major institutional investors in the stock market. Securities firms serve as brokers by matching up buyers and sellers in the stock market.
- An initial public offering (IPO) is a first-time offering of shares by a specific firm to the public. Many firms engage in an IPO to obtain funding for additional expansion and to give the founders and venture capital funds a way to cash out their investments. A firm that engages in an IPO must develop a prospectus that is filed with the SEC and uses a road show to promote its offering. It hires an underwriter to help with the prospectus and road show and to place the shares with investors.
- A secondary stock offering is an offering of shares by a firm that already has publicly traded stock. Firms engage in secondary offerings when they need more equity funding to support additional expansion.
- Corporations sometimes serve as investors when they believe that their own business or another business is undervalued. If they believe their own business is undervalued, they can repurchase shares of stock in the secondary market at a relatively low price. If they believe that another poorly performing business is undervalued, they may consider acquiring the shares of that business and then reorganizing the business (replacing managers) to improve its value. This makes poorly performing businesses subject to the market for corporate control.
- Many U.S. firms issue shares in foreign countries, as well as in the United States, so that they can spread their shares among a larger set of investors. In a similar manner, many non-U.S. firms not only issue shares in their own markets but also tap the U.S. market for funds. This strategy not only enlarges the investor base, but also may enhance the global name recognition of a firm. Global stock exchanges exist to facilitate the trading of stocks around the world. U.S. investors invest in foreign stocks by direct purchases on foreign stock exchanges, by purchasing ADRs, by investing in international mutual funds, and by investing in international exchange-traded funds.

POINT COUNTER-POINT

Should a Stock Exchange Enforce Some Governance Standards on the Firms Listed on the Exchange?

Point No. Governance is the responsibility of the firms, and not the stock exchange. The stock exchange should simply ensure that the trading rules of the exchange are enforced and should not intervene in the firms' governance issues.

Counter-Point Yes. By enforcing governance standards such as requiring a listed firm to have a majority of outside members on its board of directors, a stock exchange can enhance its own credibility.

Who Is Correct? Use the Internet to learn more about this issue. Offer your own opinion on this issue.

QUESTIONS AND APPLICATIONS

1. **Shareholder Rights** Explain the rights of common stockholders that are not available to other individuals.

2. **Stock Offerings** What is the danger of issuing too much stock? What is the role of the securities firm that serves as the underwriter, and how can it ensure that the firm does not issue too much stock?

3. IPOs Why do firms engage in IPOs? What is the amount of the fees that the lead underwriter and its syndicate charge a firm that is going public? Why are there many IPOs in some periods and few IPOs in other periods?

4. Venture Capital Explain the difference between obtaining funds from a venture capital firm and engaging in an IPO. Explain how the IPO may serve as a means by which the venture capital firm can cash out.

5. Prospectus and Road Show Explain the use of a prospectus developed before an IPO. Why does a firm do a road show before its IPO? What factors influence the offer price of stock at the time of the IPO?

6. Bookbuilding Describe the process of bookbuilding. Why is bookbuilding sometimes criticized as a means of setting the offer price?

7. Lockups Describe a lockup provision and explain why it is required by the lead underwriter.

8. Initial Return What is the meaning of an initial return for an IPO? Were initial returns of Internet IPOs in the late 1990s higher or lower than normal? Why?

9. Flipping What is the meaning of "flipping" shares? Why would investors want to flip shares?

10. Performance of IPOs How do IPOs perform over the long run?

11. Asymmetric Information Discuss the concept of asymmetric information. Explain why it may motivate firms to repurchase some of their stock.

12. Stock Repurchases Explain why the stock price of a firm may rise when the firm announces that it is repurchasing its shares.

13. Corporate Control Describe how the interaction between buyers and sellers affects the market value of a firm, and explain how that can subject a firm to the market for corporate control.

14. ADRs Explain how ADRs enable U.S. investors to become part owners of foreign companies.

15. NYSE Explain why stocks traded on the NYSE generally exhibit less risk than stocks that are traded on other exchanges.

16. Role of Organized Exchanges Are organized stock exchanges used to place newly issued stock? Explain.

Advanced Questions

17. Role of IMFs How have international mutual funds (IMFs) increased the international integration of capital markets among countries?

18. Spinning and Laddering Describe spinning and laddering in the IPO market. How do you think these actions influence the price of a newly issued stock? Who is adversely affected as a result of these actions?

19. Impact of Accounting Irregularities How do you think accounting irregularities affect the pricing of corporate stock in general? From an investor's viewpoint, how do you think the information used to price stocks changes given that accounting irregularities exist?

20. Impact of Sarbanes-Oxley Act Briefly describe the provisions of the Sarbanes-Oxley Act. Discuss how this act affects the monitoring by shareholders.

21. IPO Dilemma Denton Company plans to engage in an IPO and will issue 4 million shares of stock. It is hoping to sell the shares for an offer price of $14. It hires a securities firm that suggests that the offer price for the stock should be $12 per share to ensure that all the shares will be easily sold. Explain the dilemma for Denton Company. What is the advantage of following the advice of the securities firm? What is the disadvantage? Is the securities firm's incentive to place the shares aligned with that of Denton Company?

22. Variation in Investor Protection among Countries Explain how shareholder protection varies among countries. Explain how enforcement of securities laws varies among countries. Why do these characteristics affect the valuations of stocks?

23. International ETFs Describe international ETFs. Explain how ETFs are exposed to exchange rate risk. How do you think an investor decides whether to purchase an ETF representing Japan, Spain, or some other country?

Interpreting Financial News

Interpret the following statements made by Wall Street analysts and portfolio managers:

a. "The recent wave of IPOs is an attempt by many small firms to capitalize on the recent runup in stock prices."

b. "IPOs transfer wealth from unsophisticated investors to large institutional investors who get in at the offer price and get out quickly."

c. "Firms must be more accountable to the market when making decisions because they are subject to indirect control by institutional investors."

Managing in Financial Markets

Investing in an IPO As a portfolio manager of a financial institution, you are invited to numerous road shows in which firms that are going public promote themselves and the lead underwriter invites you to invest in the IPO. Beyond any specific information about the firm, what other information would you need to decide whether to invest in the upcoming IPO?

PROBLEM

1. Dividend Yield Over the last year, Calzone Corporation paid a quarterly dividend of $0.10 in each of the four quarters. The current stock price of Calzone Corporation is $39.78. What is the dividend yield for Calzone stock?

FLOW OF FUNDS EXERCISE

Contemplating an Initial Public Offering (IPO)

Recall that if the economy continues to be strong, Carson Company may need to increase its production capacity by about 50 percent over the next few years to satisfy demand. It would need financing to expand and accommodate the increase in production. Recall that the yield curve is currently upward sloping. Also recall that Carson is concerned about a possible slowing of the economy because of potential Fed actions to reduce inflation. It is also considering issuing stock or bonds to raise funds in the next year.

a. If Carson issued stock now, it would have the flexibility to obtain more debt and would also be able to reduce its cost of financing with debt. Why?

b. Why would an IPO result in heightened concerns in financial markets about Carson Company's potential agency problems?

c. Explain why institutional investors such as mutual funds and pension funds that invest in stock for long-term periods (at least a year or two) may be more interested in investing in some IPOs than they are in purchasing other stocks that have been publicly traded for several years.

d. Given that institutional investors such as insurance companies, pension funds, and mutual funds are the major investors in IPOs, explain the flow of funds that results from an IPO. That is, what is the original source of the money that is channeled through the institutional investors and provided to the firm going public?

INTERNET/EXCEL EXERCISES

Go to http://ipoportal.edgar-online.com/ipo/home.asp. Review an IPO that is scheduled for the near future. Review the deal information about this IPO.

1. What is the offer amount? How much are total expenses? How much are total expenses as a percentage of the deal amount? How many shares are issued? How long is the lockup period?

2. Review some additional IPOs that are scheduled. What is the range for the offer amount? What is the range for the lockup period length?

WSJ EXERCISE

Assessing Stock Market Movements

Review a recent issue of *The Wall Street Journal.* Indicate whether the market prices increased or decreased, and explain what caused the market's movement.

11

Stock Valuation and Risk

CHAPTER OBJECTIVES

The specific objectives of this chapter are to:

- explain methods of valuing stocks and determining the required rate of return on stocks,

- identify the factors that affect stock prices,

- explain how to measure the risk of stocks, and

- explain the concept of stock market efficiency.

Since the values of stocks change continuously, so do stock prices. Institutional and individual investors constantly value stocks so that they can capitalize on expected changes in stock prices.

STOCK VALUATION METHODS

Investors conduct valuations of stocks when making their investment decisions. They consider investing in undervalued stocks and selling their holdings of stocks that they consider to be overvalued. There are many different methods of valuing stocks. **Fundamental analysis** relies on fundamental financial characteristics (such as earnings) of the firm and its corresponding industry that are expected to influence stock values. **Technical analysis** relies on stock price trends to determine stock values. Our focus is on fundamental analysis. Investors who rely on fundamental analysis commonly use the price-earnings method, the dividend discount model, or the free cash flow model to value stocks. Each of these methods is described in turn.

Price-Earnings (PE) Method

A relatively simple method of valuing a stock is to apply the mean price-earnings (PE) ratio (based on expected rather than recent earnings) of all publicly traded competitors in the respective industry to the firm's expected earnings for the next year.

Consider a firm that is expected to generate earnings of $3 per share next year. If the mean ratio of share price to expected earnings of competitors in the same industry is 15, then the valuation of the firm's shares is

$$\text{Valuation per share} = (\text{Expected earnings of firm per share}) \times (\text{Mean industry PE ratio})$$
$$= \$3 \times 15$$
$$= \$45 \qquad\bullet$$

The logic of this method is that future earnings are an important determinant of a firm's value. Although earnings beyond the next year are also relevant, this method implicitly assumes that the growth in earnings in future years will be similar to that of the industry.

Reasons for Different Valuations This method has several variations, which can result in different valuations. For example, investors may use different forecasts for the firm's earnings or the mean industry earnings over the next year. The previous year's earnings are often used as a base for forecasting future earnings, but the recent year's earnings do not always provide an accurate forecast of the future.

A second reason for different valuations when using the PE method is that investors disagree on the proper measure of earnings. Some investors prefer to use operating earnings or exclude some unusually high expenses that result from onetime events. A third reason is that investors may disagree on which firms represent the industry norm. Some investors use a narrow industry composite composed of firms that are very similar (in terms of size, lines of business, etc.) to the firm being valued; other investors prefer a broad industry composite. Consequently, even if investors agree on a firm's forecasted earnings, they may still derive different values for that firm as a result of applying different PE ratios. Furthermore, even if investors agree on the firms to include in the industry composite, they may disagree on how to weight each firm.

Limitations of the PE Method   The PE method may result in an inaccurate valuation for a firm if errors are made in forecasting the firm's future earnings or in choosing the industry composite used to derive the PE ratio. In addition, some question whether an investor should trust a PE ratio, regardless of how it is derived. In 1994, the mean PE ratio for a composite of 500 large firms was 14. In 1998, the mean PE ratio for this same group of firms was 28, which implies that the valuation for a given level of earnings had doubled. Some investors may interpret such increases in PE ratios as a sign of irrational optimism in the stock market. As of January 2009 (during the credit crisis), the mean PE ratio of these firms was about 12.

Dividend Discount Model

One of the first models used for pricing stocks was developed by John B. Williams in 1931. This model is still applicable today. Williams stated that the price of a stock should reflect the present value of the stock's future dividends, or

$$\text{Price} = \sum_{t=1}^{\infty} \frac{D_t}{(1 + k)^t}$$

where

$$t = \text{period}$$
$$D_t = \text{dividend in period } t$$
$$k = \text{discount rate}$$

The model can account for uncertainty by allowing D_t to be revised in response to revised expectations about a firm's cash flows, or by allowing k to be revised in response to changes in the required rate of return by investors.

EXAMPLE

To illustrate how the dividend discount model can be used to value a stock, consider a stock that is expected to pay a dividend of $7 per share per year forever. This constant dividend represents a perpetuity, or an annuity that lasts forever. The present value of the cash flows (dividend payments) to investors in this example is the present value of a perpetuity. Assuming that the required rate of return (k) on the stock of concern is 14 percent, the present value (PV) of the future dividends is

$$PV \text{ of stock} = D/k$$
$$= \$7/.14$$
$$= \$50 \text{ per share}$$

●

Unfortunately, the valuation of most stocks is not this simple because their dividends are not expected to remain constant forever. If the dividend is expected to grow at a constant rate, however, the stock can be valued by applying the constant-growth dividend discount model:

$$PV \text{ of stock} = D_1/(k - g)$$

where D_1 is the expected dividend per share to be paid over the next year, k is the required rate of return by investors, and g is the rate at which the dividend is expected to grow. For example, if a stock is expected to provide a dividend of $7 per share next year, the dividend is expected to increase by 4 percent per year, and the required rate of return is 14 percent, the stock can be valued as

$$PV \text{ of stock} = \$7/(.14 - .04)$$
$$= \$70 \text{ per share}$$

Relationship with PE Ratio for Valuing Firms   The dividend discount model and the PE ratio may seem to be unrelated, since the dividend discount model is highly dependent on the required rate of return and the growth rate, whereas the PE ratio is driven by the mean multiple of competitors' stock prices relative to their earnings expectations, along with the earnings expectations of the firm being valued. Nevertheless, the PE multiple is influenced by the required rate of return on stocks of competitors and the expected growth rate of competitor firms. When using the PE ratio for valuation, the investor implicitly assumes that the required rate of return and the growth rate for the firm being valued are similar to those of its competitors. When the required rate of return on competitor firms is relatively high, the PE multiple will be relatively low, which results in a relatively low valuation of the firm for its level of expected earnings. When the competitors' growth rate is relatively high, the PE multiple will be relatively high, which results in a relatively high valuation of the firm for its level of expected earnings. Thus, the inverse relationship between required rate of return and value exists when applying either the PE ratio or the dividend discount model. In addition, there is a positive relationship between a firm's growth rate and its value when applying either method.

Limitations of the Dividend Discount Model   The dividend discount model may result in an inaccurate valuation of a firm if errors are made in determining the dividend to be paid over the next year, or the growth rate, or the required rate of return by investors. The limitations of this model are more pronounced when valuing firms that retain most of their earnings, rather than distributing them as dividends, because the model relies on the dividend as the base for applying the growth rate. For example, many Internet-related stocks retain any earnings to support growth and thus are not expected to pay any dividends.

Adjusting the Dividend Discount Model

The dividend discount model can be adapted to assess the value of any firm, even those that retain most or all of their earnings. From the investor's perspective, the value of the stock is (1) the present value of the future dividends to be received over the investment horizon, plus (2) the present value of the forecasted price at which the stock will be sold at the end of the investment horizon. To forecast the price at which the stock can be sold, investors must estimate the firm's earnings per share (after removing any nonrecurring effects) in the year that they plan to sell the stock. This estimate is derived by applying an annual growth rate to the prevailing annual earnings per share. Then, the estimate can be used to derive the expected price per share at which the stock can be sold.

Assume that a firm currently has earnings of $12 per share. Future earnings can be forecasted by applying the expected annual growth rate to the firm's existing earnings (E):

$$\textbf{Forecasted earnings in } n \textbf{ years} = E(1 + G)^n$$

where G is the expected growth rate of earnings and n is the number of years until the stock is to be sold.

If investors expect that the earnings per share will grow by 2 percent per year and expect to sell the firm's stock in three years, the earnings per share in three years are forecasted to be

$$
\begin{aligned}
\textbf{Earnings in three years} &= \$12 \times (1 + .02)^3 \\
&= \$12 \times 1.0612 \\
&= \$12.73
\end{aligned}
$$

The forecasted earnings per share can be multiplied by the PE ratio of the firm's industry to forecast the future stock price. If the mean PE ratio of all other firms in the same industry is 6, the stock price in three years can be forecasted as follows

$$
\begin{aligned}
\textbf{Stock price in three years} &= (\textbf{Earnings in three years}) \times (\textbf{PE ratio of industry}) \\
&= \$12.73 \times 6 \\
&= \$76.38
\end{aligned}
$$

This forecasted stock price can be used along with expected dividends and the investor's required rate of return to value the stock today. If the firm is expected to pay a dividend of $4 per share over the next three years, and if the investor's required rate of return is 14 percent, the present value of expected cash flows to be received by the investor is

$$
\begin{aligned}
PV &= \$4/(1.14)^1 + \$4/(1.14)^2 + \$4/(1.14)^3 + \$76.38/(1.14)^3 \\
&= \$3.51 + \$3.08 + \$2.70 + \$51.55 \\
&= \$60.84
\end{aligned}
$$

In this example, the present value of the cash flows is based on (1) the present value of dividends to be received over the three-year investment horizon, which is $9.29 per share ($3.51 + $3.08 + $2.70), and (2) the present value of the forecasted price at which the stock can be sold at the end of the three-year investment horizon, which is $51.55 per share.

Limitations of the Adjusted Dividend Discount Model   This model may result in an inaccurate valuation if errors are made in deriving the present value of dividends over the investment horizon or the present value of the forecasted price at which the stock can be sold at the end of the investment horizon. Since the required rate of return affects both of these factors, the use of an improper required rate of return will lead to inaccurate valuations. Possible methods for determining the required rate of return are discussed later in the chapter.

Free Cash Flow Model

For firms that do not pay dividends, a more suitable valuation may be the free cash flow model, which is based on the present value of future cash flows. The first step is to estimate the free cash flows that will result from operations. Second, subtract existing liabilities to determine the value of the firm. Third, divide the value of the firm by the number of shares to derive a value per share.

Limitations   The limitation of this model is the difficulty of obtaining an accurate estimate of free cash flow per period. One possibility is to start with forecasted earnings and then add a forecast of the firm's noncash expenses and capital investment and working capital investment required to support the growth in the forecasted earnings. Obtaining accurate earnings forecasts can be difficult, however. Even if earnings can be forecasted accurately, the flexibility of accounting rules can cause major errors in estimating free cash flow based on earnings.

REQUIRED RATE OF RETURN ON STOCKS

When investors attempt to value a firm based on discounted cash flows, they must determine the required rate of return by investors who invest in that stock. Investors require a return that reflects the risk-free interest rate plus a risk premium. Although investors generally require a higher return on firms that exhibit more risk, there is not complete agreement on the ideal measure of risk or the way risk should be used to derive the required rate of return. Two commonly used models for deriving the required rate of return are the capital asset pricing model and the arbitrage pricing model.

Capital Asset Pricing Model

The **capital asset pricing model (CAPM)** is sometimes used to estimate the required rate of return for any firm with publicly traded stock. The CAPM is based on the premise that the only important risk of a firm is **systematic risk,** or the risk that results from exposure to general stock market movements. The CAPM is not concerned with so-called unsystematic risk, which is specific to an individual firm, because investors can avoid that type of risk by holding diversified portfolios. That is, any particular adverse condition (such as a labor strike) affecting one particular firm in an investor's stock portfolio should be offset in a given period by some favorable condition affecting another firm in the portfolio. In contrast, the systematic impact of general stock market movements on stocks in the portfolio cannot be diversified away because most of the stocks would be adversely affected by a general market decline.

The CAPM suggests that the return of an asset (R_j) is influenced by the prevailing risk-free rate (R_f), the market return (R_m), and the covariance between R_j and R_m as follows:

$$R_j = R_f + B_j(R_m - R_f)$$

where B_j represents the beta and is measured as $COV(R_j, R_m)/VAR(R_m)$. This model implies that given a specific R_f and R_m, investors will require a higher return on an asset that has a higher beta. A higher beta reflects a higher covariance between the asset's returns and market returns, which contributes more risk to the portfolio of assets held by the investor.

Estimating the Market Risk Premium   The yield on newly issued Treasury bonds is commonly used as a proxy for the risk-free rate. The terms within the parentheses measure the market risk premium, or the excess return of the market above the risk-free rate. Historical data over 30 or more years can be used to determine the average market risk premium over time. This serves as an estimate of the market risk premium that will exist in the future.

Estimating the Firm's Beta   A firm's **beta** is a measure of its systematic risk, as it reflects the sensitivity of the stock's return to the market's overall return. For example, a stock with a beta of 1.2 means that for every 1 percent change in the market overall, the stock tends to change by 1.2 percent in the same direction. The beta is typically measured with monthly or quarterly data over the last four years or so. It is reported on many financial websites and in investment services such as *Value Line,* or it can be computed by the individual investor who understands how to apply regression analysis. A stock's sensitivity to market conditions may change over time in response to changes in the firm's operating characteristics. Thus, the beta may adjust as time passes, and the stock's value should also adjust in response.

Investors can measure their exposure to systematic risk by determining how the value of their present stock portfolio has been affected by market movements. They can apply regression analysis by specifying the stock portfolio's periodic (monthly or quarterly) return over the last 20 or so periods as the dependent variable and the market's return (as measured by the S&P 500 index or some other suitable proxy) as the independent variable over those same periods. After inputting these data, a computer spreadsheet package such as Excel can be used to run the regression analysis. Specifically, the focus is on the estimation of the slope coefficient by the regression analysis, which represents the estimate of each stock's beta (for more details, see the discussion under "Beta of a Stock" later in the chapter). Additional results of the analysis can also be assessed, such as the strength of the relationship between the firm's returns and market returns. (See Appendix B for more information on using regression analysis.)

Application of the CAPM   Given the risk-free rate, and estimates of the firm's beta and the market risk premium, the required rate of return from investing in the firm's stock can be estimated.

EXAMPLE

Consider a firm that has a beta of 1.2 (based on the application of regression analysis to determine the sensitivity of the firm's return to the market return). Also, assume that the prevailing risk-free rate is 6 percent and that the market risk premium is 7 percent (based on historical data that show that the annual market return has exhibited a premium of 7 percent above the annual risk-free rate). Using this information, the risk premium (above the risk-free rate) is 8.4 percent (computed as the market risk premium of 7 percent times the beta of 1.2). Thus, the required rate of return on the firm is

$$R_j = 6\% + 1.2(7\%)$$
$$= 14.4\%$$

The firm's required rate of return is 14.4 percent, so its estimated future cash flows would be discounted using a discount rate of 14.4 percent to derive the firm's present value. At this same point in time, the required rates of return for other firms could also be determined. Although the risk-free rate and the market risk premium are the same regardless of the firm being assessed, the beta varies across firms. Therefore, at a given point in time, the required rates of return estimated by the CAPM will vary across firms because of differences in their risk premiums, which are attributed to differences in their systematic risk (as measured by beta). ●

Limitations of the CAPM   The CAPM suggests that the return of a particular stock is positively related to its beta. However, a study by Fama and French[1] found that beta was unrelated to the return on stocks over the period 1963–1990.

Subsequently, Chan and Lakonishok[2] reassessed the relationship between stock returns and beta. They found that the relationship varied with the time period used, which implies that it is difficult to make projections about the future based on the findings in

[1]Eugene F. Fama and Kenneth R. French, "The Cross-Section of Expected Stock Returns," *Journal of Finance* (June 1992): 427–465.

[2]Louis K. C. Chan and Josef Lakonishok, "Are the Reports of Beta's Death Premature?" *Journal of Portfolio Management* (Summer 1993): 51–62.

any specific period. Thus, they concluded that although it is appropriate to question whether beta is the driving force behind stock returns, it may be premature to pronounce beta dead.

Furthermore, if beta is a stable measure of the firm's sensitivity to market movements, it would still be useful for determining which stocks are more feasible investments when the stock market is expected to perform well. Thus, investors should still monitor a firm's beta.

Chan and Lakonishok found that firms with the highest betas performed much worse than firms with low betas during market downswings. They also found that high-beta firms outperformed low-beta firms during market upswings. These results support the measurement of beta as an indicator of the firm's response to market upswings or downswings.

Arbitrage Pricing Model

An alternative pricing model is based on the **arbitrage pricing theory (APT).** The APT differs from the CAPM in that it suggests that a stock's price can be influenced by a set of factors in addition to the market. The factors may possibly reflect economic growth, inflation, and other variables that could systematically influence asset prices. The following model is based on the APT:

$$E(R) = B_0 + \sum_{i=1}^{m} B_i F_i$$

where

$$
\begin{aligned}
E(R) &= \text{expected return of asset} \\
B_0 &= \text{a constant} \\
F_i \ldots F_m &= \text{values of factors 1 to } m \\
B_i &= \text{sensitivity of the asset return to particular force}
\end{aligned}
$$

The model suggests that in equilibrium, expected returns on assets are linearly related to the covariance between asset returns and the factors. This is distinctly different from the CAPM, where expected returns are linearly related to the covariance between asset returns and the market. The appeal of the APT is that it allows for factors (such as industry effects) other than the market to influence the expected returns of assets. Thus, the required rate of return may be based not only on the firm's sensitivity to market conditions but also on its sensitivity to industry conditions. A possible disadvantage of the APT is that it is not as well defined as the CAPM. This characteristic could be perceived as an advantage, however, since it allows investors to include whatever factors they believe are relevant in deriving the required rate of return for a particular firm.

FACTORS THAT AFFECT STOCK PRICES

Stock prices are driven by three types of factors: (1) economic factors, (2) market-related factors, and (3) firm-specific factors.

Economic Factors

A firm's value should reflect the present value of its future cash flows. Investors consider various economic factors that affect a firm's cash flows when valuing a firm to determine whether its stock is over- or undervalued.

Impact of Economic Growth   An increase in economic growth is expected to increase the demand for products and services produced by firms and therefore increase a firm's cash flows and valuation. Participants in the stock markets monitor economic indicators such as employment, gross domestic product, retail sales, and personal

WEB

http://biz.yahoo.eom/c/
e.html
Calendar of upcoming
announcements of
economic conditions
that may affect stock
prices.

income because these indicators may signal information about economic growth and therefore affect cash flows. In general, unexpected favorable information about the economy tends to cause a favorable revision of a firm's expected cash flows and therefore places upward pressure on the firm's value. Because the government's fiscal and monetary policies affect economic growth, they are also continually monitored by investors.

Exhibit 11.1 shows the U.S. stock market performance, based on the S&P 500 index, an index of 500 large U.S. stocks. The stock market's strong performance in the late 1990s and in the 2003-2007 period was partially due to the strong economic conditions in the United States at that time. Conversely, the stock market's weak performance in 2002 and in 2008 was partially due to weak economic conditions.

Impact of Interest Rates   One of the most prominent economic forces driving stock market prices is the risk-free interest rate. Investors should consider purchasing a risky asset only if they expect to be compensated with a risk premium for the risk in-

Exhibit 11.1 Stock Market Trend Based on the S&P 500 Index

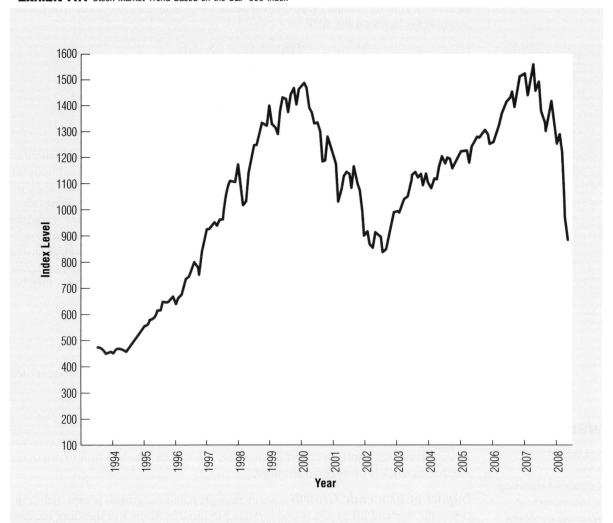

Source: *Federal Reserve.*

WEB

http://research
.stlouisfed.org
Economic information
that can be used to
value securities, in-
cluding money supply
information, gross do-
mestic product, inter-
est rates, and
exchange rates.

curred. Given a choice of risk-free Treasury securities or stocks, investors should purchase stocks only if they are appropriately priced to reflect a sufficiently high expected
return above the risk-free rate.

The relationship between interest rates and stock prices can vary over time. In theory,
a high interest rate should raise the required rate of return by investors and therefore
reduce the present value of future cash flows generated by a stock. However, interest
rates commonly rise in response to an increase in economic growth, so stock prices
may rise in response to an increase in expected cash flows even if investors' required
rate of return rises.

Conversely, a lower interest rate should boost the present value of cash flows and
therefore boost stock prices. However, lower interest rates commonly occur in response
to weak economic conditions, which tend to reduce expected cash flows of firms. Overall,
the effect of interest rates should be considered along with economic growth and other
factors to offer a more complete explanation of stock price movements.

Impact of the Dollar's Exchange Rate Value   The value of the dollar can affect
U.S. stock prices for a variety of reasons. First, foreign investors prefer to purchase U.S.
stocks when the dollar is weak and sell them when it is near its peak. Thus, the foreign
demand for any given U.S. stock may be higher when the dollar is expected to strengthen,
other things being equal. Also, stock prices are affected by the impact of the dollar's changing value on cash flows. Stock prices of U.S. firms primarily involved in exporting could be
favorably affected by a weak dollar and adversely affected by a strong dollar. U.S. importing firms could be affected in the opposite manner.

Stock prices of U.S. companies may also be affected by exchange rates if stock market
participants measure performance by reported earnings. A multinational corporation's
consolidated reported earnings will be affected by exchange rate fluctuations even if the
company's cash flows are not affected. A weaker dollar tends to inflate the reported earnings of a U.S.-based company's foreign subsidiaries. Some analysts argue that any effect
of exchange rate movements on financial statements is irrelevant unless cash flows are
also affected.

The changing value of the dollar can also affect stock prices by affecting expectations
of economic factors that influence the firm's performance. For example, if a weak dollar
stimulates the U.S. economy, it may enhance the value of a U.S. firm whose sales are
dependent on the U.S. economy. A strong dollar could adversely affect such a firm if it
dampens U.S. economic growth. Because inflation affects some firms, a weak dollar
could indirectly affect a firm's stock by putting upward pressure on inflation. A strong
dollar would have the opposite indirect impact. Some companies attempt to insulate
their stock price from the changing value of the dollar, but other companies purposely
remain exposed with the intent to benefit from it.

Market-Related Factors

Market-related factors also drive stock prices. These factors include investor sentiment
and the January effect.

Investor Sentiment   A key market-related factor is investor sentiment, which represents the general mood of investors in the stock market. Since stock valuations reflect
expectations, in some periods the stock market performance is not highly correlated
with existing economic conditions. For example, even though the economy is weak, stock
prices may rise if most investors expect that the economy will improve in the near future. That is, there is a positive sentiment because of optimistic expectations.

Movements in stock prices may be partially attributed to investors' reliance on other investors for stock market valuation. Rather than making their own assessment of a firm's value, many investors appear to focus on the general investor sentiment. This can result in irrational exuberance, whereby stock prices increase without reason.

Given the potential changes in valuation caused by market sentiment, some investors attempt to anticipate future momentum of stock prices by using technical analysis. The rationale behind technical analysis is that if trends in stock prices are repetitive, investors can take positions in stocks when they recognize that a particular trend is occurring. Technical analysis is most commonly used to anticipate short-term movements in stock prices.

Investor sentiment can also be negative. During the credit crisis, investors had a negative outlook, possibly beyond what might be explained by economic factors. In the week of October 6–10, 2008, the U.S. stock market crashed. The average decrease in price for the week was 18 percent, the worst performance ever over a one-week period for U.S. stocks. Throughout the week, the U.S. government stated that market conditions were stable and that investors should not panic, but those statements did not prevent the decline. By the end of the week, stock prices were about 40 percent below those in the previous year.

On the following Monday, the U.S. Treasury announced that it would use about $250 billion to take an equity stake in many financial institutions as part of the Emergency Economic Stabilization Act of 2008, which had been passed a few weeks earlier. Although only limited details were provided, investor sentiment shifted from extremely negative to extremely positive, and stock prices rose by more than 10 percent on average on that day. Just two days later, however, sentiment reversed, and stock prices fell by more than 9 percent on average. This was the largest decline on a single day since the stock market crash in 1987.

The high degree of volatility during this period was driven by the uncertainty about the future. Investor decisions appeared to be influenced more by psychology than by fundamental valuation techniques. Investors were buying stock whenever they noticed market prices moving up and selling stock whenever they saw market prices moving down. These shifts in momentum caused wild swings in the market prices.

January Effect   Because many portfolio managers are evaluated over the calendar year, they tend to invest in riskier small stocks at the beginning of the year and shift to larger (more stable) companies near the end of the year to lock in their gains. This tendency places upward pressure on small stocks in January of every year, causing the so-called January effect. Some studies have found that most of the annual stock market gains occur in January. Once investors discovered the January effect, they attempted to take more positions in stocks in the prior month. This has placed upward pressure on stocks in mid-December, causing the January effect to begin in December.

Firm-Specific Factors

A firm's stock price is affected not only by macroeconomic and market conditions but also by firm-specific conditions. Some firms are more exposed to conditions within their own industry than to general economic conditions, so participants monitor industry sales forecasts, entry into the industry by new competitors, and price movements of the industry's products. Stock market participants may focus on announcements by specific firms that signal information about a firm's sales growth, earnings, or other characteristics that may cause a revision in the expected cash flows to be generated by that firm.

USING THE WALL STREET JOURNAL

Stock Market Indexes

The Wall Street Journal provides information on the recent changes in valuations of stock market indexes, as shown here. Specifically, the returns on various types of stock indexes are disclosed from the previous trading day and from one year ago. Investors can use this information to determine how stocks in different markets or sectors performed.

Source: Republished with permission of Dow Jones & Company, Inc., from *The Wall Street Journal*, January 7, 2009, C4; permission conveyed through the Copyright Clearance Center, Inc.

Major U.S. Stock-Market Indexes

	High	Low	LATEST Close	Net chg	% chg	52-WEEK RANGE High	Low	% chg	%CHG YTD	3-yr. ann.
Dow Jones										
Industrial Average	9088.06	8940.95	9015.10	62.21	0.69	13058.20	7552.29	-28.4	2.7	-6.3
Transportation Avg	3737.01	3626.38	3717.26	90.72	2.50	5492.95	2988.99	-10.4	5.1	-4.1
Utility Average	388.86	376.98	379.53	-2.47	-0.65	550.06	324.57	-30.2	2.4	-3.0
Wilshire 5000	9511.85	9343.13	9437.30	94.17	1.01	14423.75	7471.44	-32.4	3.9	-9.9
Barron's 400	202.52	197.56	200.68	3.12	1.58	318.98	149.12	-31.5	6.0	-10.4
Nasdaq Stock Market										
Nasdaq Composite	1665.63	1636.25	1652.38	24.35	1.50	2549.94	1316.12	-32.3	4.8	-10.5
Nasdaq 100	1286.08	1265.53	1274.49	11.97	0.95	2055.11	1036.51	-33.3	5.2	-9.8
Standard & Poor's										
500 Index	943.85	927.28	934.70	7.25	0.78	1426.63	752.44	-32.8	3.5	-10.1
MidCap 400	563.87	550.49	559.37	8.86	1.61	897.27	417.12	-29.8	3.9	-9.8
SmallCap 600	276.80	271.04	274.79	4.59	1.70	402.07	208.21	-24.8	2.3	-8.8
Other Indexes										
Russell 2000	519.00	507.16	514.71	9.68	1.92	763.27	385.31	-27.0	3.1	-9.7
NYSE Composite	6014.00	5901.51	5968.84	60.41	1.02	9603.01	4651.21	-36.0	3.7	-9.4
Value Line	243.20	235.02	241.45	6.42	2.73	422.64	174.86	-40.5	6.9	-17.2
Alternext Biotech	669.52	656.93	661.68	-1.80	-0.27	886.57	541.81	-15.7	2.2	-2.1
Alternext Pharma	274.30	269.98	271.88	-0.66	-0.24	355.67	234.01	-22.3	-0.4	-6.5
KBW Bank	44.56	43.54	44.11	0.59	1.36	96.11	36.72	-45.3	-0.5	-25.3
PHLX§ Gold/Silver	123.78	117.39	121.45	2.67	2.25	206.37	64.36	-35.6	-1.9	-4.6
PHLX§ Oil Service	144.37	139.15	142.18	6.70	4.95	359.61	104.14	-51.7	17.1	-10.5
PHLX§ Semiconductor	236.12	225.17	234.56	11.27	5.05	421.67	171.32	-35.2	10.6	-23.3
CBOE Volatility	39.33	37.34	38.56	-0.52	-1.33	80.86	16.30	51.6	-3.6	51.9

§Philadelphia Stock Exchange

Sources: **Thomson Reuters**; WSJ Market Data Group

Change in Dividend Policy   An increase in dividends may reflect the firm's expectation that it can more easily afford to pay dividends. A decrease in dividends may reflect the firm's expectation that it will not have sufficient cash flow.

Earnings Surprises   Recent earnings are used to forecast future earnings and therefore to forecast a firm's future cash flows. When a firm's announced earnings are higher than expected, some investors raise their estimates of the firm's future cash flows and therefore revalue its stock upward. Conversely, an announcement of lower than expected earnings can cause investors to reduce their valuation of a firm's future cash flows and its stock.

Acquisitions and Divestitures   The expected acquisition of a firm typically results in an increased demand for the target's stock and therefore raises the stock price. Investors recognize that the target's stock price will be bid up once the acquiring firm attempts to acquire the target's stock. The effect on the acquiring firm's stock is less clear, as it depends on the perceived synergies that could result from the acquisition. Divestitures tend to be regarded as a favorable signal about a firm if the divested assets are unrelated to the firm's core business. The typical interpretation by the market in this case is that the firm intends to focus on its core business.

Expectations   Investors do not necessarily wait for a firm to announce a new policy before they revalue the firm's stock. Instead, they attempt to anticipate new policies so that they can make their move in the market before other investors. In this way, they may be able to pay a lower price for a specific stock or sell the stock at a higher price. For example, they may use the firm's financial reports or recent statements by the firm's executives to speculate on whether the firm will adjust its dividend policy. The disadvantage of trading based on incomplete information is that the investors may not properly anticipate the firm's future policies.

Integration of Factors Affecting Stock Prices

Exhibit 11.2 illustrates the underlying forces that cause a stock's price to change over time. As with the pricing of debt securities, the required rate of return is relevant, as are the economic factors that affect the risk-free interest rate. Stock market participants also monitor indicators that can affect the risk-free interest rate, which affects the required return by investors who invest in stocks. Indicators of inflation (such as the consumer price index and producer price index) and of government borrowing (such as the budget deficit and the volume of funds borrowed at upcoming Treasury bond auctions) also affect the risk-free rate and therefore affect the required return of investors. In general, whenever these indicators signal the expectation of higher interest rates, there is upward pressure on the required rate of return by investors and downward pressure on a firm's value.

In addition, the firm's expected future cash flows are commonly estimated to derive its value, and these cash flows are influenced by economic conditions, industry conditions, and firm-specific conditions. This exhibit provides an overview of what stock market participants monitor when attempting to anticipate future stock price movements.

STOCK RISK

A stock's risk reflects the uncertainty about future returns, such that the actual return may be less than expected. The return from investing in stock over a particular period is measured as

$$R = \frac{(SP - INV) + D}{INV}$$

where

INV = initial investment
D = dividend
SP = selling price of the stock

The main source of uncertainty is the price at which the stock will be sold. Dividends tend to be much more stable than stock prices. Dividends contribute to the immediate return received by investors, but reduce the amount of earnings reinvested by the firm, which limits its potential growth.

Exhibit 11.2 Framework for Explaining Changes in a Firm's Stock Price over Time

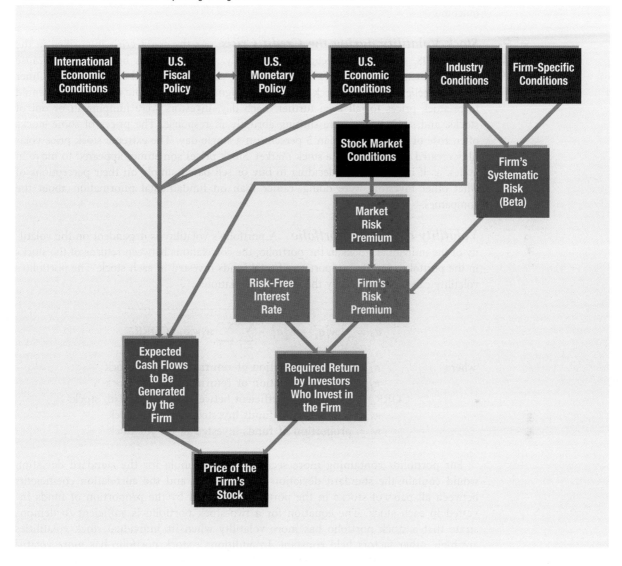

The risk of a stock can be measured by using its price volatility, its beta, and the value-at-risk method. Each of these is discussed in turn.

Volatility of a Stock

A stock's volatility serves as a measure of risk because it may indicate the degree of uncertainty surrounding the stock's future returns. The volatility is often referred to as total risk because it reflects movements in stock prices for any reason, not just movements attributable to stock market movements. A stock's returns over a historical period such as the last 12 quarters may be compiled to estimate future volatility. If the standard deviation of the stock's returns over the last 12 quarters is 3 percent, and if there is no perceived change in volatility, there is a 68 percent probability that the stock's returns will be within 3 percentage points (one standard deviation) of the expected outcome and a 95 percent probability that the stock's returns will be within 6 percentage points (2 standard deviations) of the expected outcome.

Stock Volatility during the Credit Crisis As the credit crisis intensified in the fall of 2008, stock prices declined substantially. Some investors believed that because stocks had experienced such a large decline in price, they must be undervalued. Other investors believed that the stock price decline signaled an economic recession that would force stock prices to fall even further. Each day, investors were jumping in or out of stocks, and stock prices were shifting abruptly in response. The prices of some stocks often rose or fell by more than 5 percent on a single day. The extreme stock price volatility created more fear in the stock market. Stock prices sometimes appeared to move in cycles, as if investors were deciding to buy or sell based simply on their perceptions of what other investors were doing, rather than on fundamental information about the companies.

Volatility of a Stock Portfolio A portfolio's volatility is dependent on the volatility of the individual stocks in the portfolio, the correlations between returns of the stocks in the portfolio, and the proportion of total funds invested in each stock. The portfolio's volatility can be measured by the standard deviation:

$$\sigma_p = \sqrt{w_i^2\sigma_i^2 + w_j^2\sigma_j^2 + \sum_{i=1}^{n}\sum_{j=1}^{n} w_i w_j \sigma_i \sigma_j \text{CORR}_{ij}}$$

where

σ_i = **standard deviation of returns of the *i*th stock**
σ_j = **standard deviation of returns of the *j*th stock**
CORR_{ij} = **correlation coefficient between the *i*th and *j*th stocks**
w_i = **proportion of funds invested in the *i*th stock**
w_j = **proportion of funds invested in the *j*th stock**

For portfolios containing more securities, the formula for the standard deviation would contain the standard deviation of each stock and the correlation coefficients between all pairs of stocks in the portfolio, weighted by the proportion of funds invested in each stock. The equation for a two-stock portfolio is sufficient to demonstrate that a stock portfolio has more volatility when its individual stock volatilities are high, other factors held constant. In addition, a stock portfolio has more volatility when its individual stock returns are highly correlated, other factors held constant. As an extreme example, if the returns of the stocks are all perfectly positively correlated (correlation coefficients = 1.0), the portfolio will have a relatively high degree of volatility because all stocks will experience peaks or troughs simultaneously. Conversely, a stock portfolio containing some stocks with low or negative correlation will exhibit less volatility because the stocks will not experience peaks and troughs simultaneously. Some offsetting effects will occur, smoothing the returns of the portfolio over time.

Beta of a Stock

As explained earlier, a stock's beta measures the sensitivity of its returns to market returns. This measure of risk is used by many investors who have a diversified portfolio of stocks and believe that the unsystematic risk of the portfolio is diversified away (because favorable firm-specific characteristics will offset unfavorable firm-specific characteristics). The beta of a stock can be estimated by obtaining returns of the firm and the stock market over the last 12 quarters and applying regression analysis to derive the slope coefficient as in this model:

$$R_{jt} = B_0 + B_1 R_{mt} + \mu_t$$

where

R_{jt} = return of stock j during period t
R_{mt} = market return during period t
B_0 = intercept
B_1 = regression coefficient that serves as an estimate of beta
μ_t = error term

Some investors or analysts prefer to use monthly returns rather than quarterly returns to estimate the beta. The choice is dependent on the holding period for which one wants to assess sensitivity. If the goal is to assess sensitivity to monthly returns, then monthly data would be more appropriate.

The regression analysis estimates the intercept (B_0) and the slope coefficient (B_1), which serves as the estimate of beta. If the slope coefficient of an individual stock is estimated to be 1.4, this means that for a given return in the market, the stock's expected return is 1.4 times that amount. Such sensitivity is favorable when the stock market is performing well, but unfavorable when the stock market is performing poorly. This implies that the probability distribution of returns is very dispersed, reflecting a wide range of possible outcomes for the individual stock.

Beta serves as a measure of risk because it can be used to derive a probability distribution of returns based on a set of market returns. As explained earlier, beta is useful for investors who are primarily concerned with systematic risk because it captures the movement in a stock's price that is attributable to movements in the stock market. It ignores stock price movements attributable to firm-specific conditions because such unsystematic risk can be avoided by maintaining a diversified portfolio.

EXAMPLE

Exhibit 11.3 shows how the probability distribution of a stock's returns is dependent on its beta. At one extreme, Stock A with a very low beta is less responsive to market movements in either direction, so its possible returns range only from –4.8 percent under poor market conditions to 6 percent under the most favorable market conditions. Stock D with a very high beta has possible returns that range from –11.2 percent under poor market conditions to 14 percent under the most favorable market conditions. ●

Beta of a Stock Portfolio

Participants in the stock market tend to invest in a portfolio of stocks rather than a single stock and therefore are more concerned with the risk of a portfolio than with the risk of an individual stock. The risk of individual stocks is necessary to derive portfolio risk. Portfolio risk is commonly measured by beta or volatility (standard deviation), just as the risk of individual stocks is.

The beta of a stock portfolio can be measured as

$$B_p = \sum w_i B_i$$

That is, the portfolio beta is a weighted average of the betas of stocks that comprise the portfolio, where the weights reflect the proportion of funds invested in each stock. The equation is intuitive as it simply suggests that a portfolio consisting of high-beta stocks will have a relatively high beta. This type of portfolio normally performs poorly relative to other stock portfolios in a period when the market return is negative. The risk of such a portfolio could be reduced by replacing some of the high-beta stocks with low-beta stocks. Of course, the expected return for the portfolio would be lower as a result.

Exhibit 11.3 How Beta Influences Probability Distributions

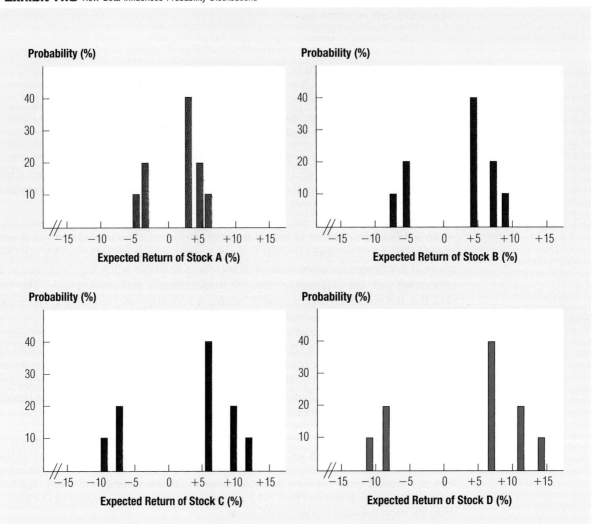

PROBABILITY	R_m	STOCK A's EXPECTED RETURNS, $E(R)$, IF B_i = .6	STOCK B's EXPECTED RETURNS, $E(R)$, IF B_i = .9	STOCK C's EXPECTED RETURNS, $E(R)$, IF B_i = 1.2	STOCK D's EXPECTED RETURNS, $E(R)$, IF B_i = 1.4
10%	−8%	−4.8%	−7.2%	−9.6%	−11.2%
20	−6	−3.6	−5.4	−7.2	−8.4
40	5	3	4.5	6	7
20	8	4.8	7.2	9.6	11.2
10	10	6	9	12	14

The beta of a stock and its volatility are typically related. High-beta stocks are expected to be very volatile because they are more sensitive to market returns over time. Conversely, low-beta stocks are expected to be less volatile because they are less responsive to market returns.

Value at Risk

Value at risk is a risk measurement that estimates the largest expected loss to a particular investment position for a specified confidence level. This method became very popular in the late 1990s after some mutual funds and pension funds experienced abrupt large losses. The value-at-risk method is intended to warn investors about the potential maximum loss that could occur. If the investors are uncomfortable with the potential loss that could occur in a day or a week, they can revise their investment portfolio to make it less risky.

The value-at-risk measurement focuses on the pessimistic portion of the probability distribution of returns from the investment of concern. For example, a portfolio manager might use a confidence level of 90 percent, which estimates the maximum daily expected loss for a stock in 90 percent of the trading days over an upcoming period. The higher the level of confidence desired, the larger the maximum expected loss that could occur for a given type of investment. That is, one may expect that the daily loss from holding a particular stock will be no worse than –5 percent when using a 90 percent confidence level, but no worse than –8 percent when using a 99 percent confidence level. In essence, the more confidence investors have that the actual loss will be no greater than the expected maximum loss, the further they move into the left tail of the probability distribution.

The value at risk is also commonly used to measure the risk of a portfolio. Some stocks may be perceived to have high risk when assessed individually, but low risk when assessed as part of a portfolio. This is because the likelihood of a large loss in the portfolio is influenced by the probabilities of simultaneous losses in all of the component stocks for the period of concern.

Numerous methods can be used when applying value at risk. Three basic methods are discussed next, followed by a discussion of how these methods can be adjusted to improve the assessment of risk in particular situations.

Application Using Historical Returns   An obvious way to use value at risk is to assess historical data. For example, an investor may determine that out of the last 100 trading days, a stock experienced a decline of greater than 7 percent on 5 different days, or 5 percent of the days assessed. This information could be used to infer a maximum daily loss of no more than 7 percent for that stock, based on a 95 percent confidence level for an upcoming period.

Application Using the Standard Deviation   An alternative approach is to measure the standard deviation of daily returns over the previous period and apply it to derive boundaries for a specific confidence level.

Assume that the standard deviation of daily returns for a particular stock in a recent historical period is 2 percent. Also assume that the 95 percent confidence level is desired for the maximum loss. If the daily returns are normally distributed, the lower boundary (the left tail of the probability distribution) is about 1.65 standard deviations away from the expected outcome. Assuming an expected daily return of .1 percent, the lower boundary is

$$.1\% - [1.65 \times (2\%)] = -3.2\%$$

The expected daily return of .1 percent may have been derived from the use of subjective information, or it could be the average daily return from the recent historical period assessed. The lower boundary for a given confidence level can be easily derived for any expected daily return. For example, if the expected daily return is .14 percent, the lower boundary is

$$.14\% - [1.65 \times (2\%)] = -3.16\%$$ ●

Application Using Beta

A third method of estimating the maximum expected loss for a given confidence level is to apply the stock's beta.

EXAMPLE

Assume that the stock's beta over the last 100 days is 1.2. Also assume that the stock market is expected to perform no worse than –2.5 percent on a daily basis based on a 95 percent confidence level. Given the stock's beta of 1.2 and a maximum market loss of –2.5 percent, the maximum loss to the stock over a given day is estimated to be

$$1.2 \times (-2.5\%) = -3.0\%$$

The maximum expected market loss for the 95 percent confidence level can be derived subjectively or by assessing the last 100 days or so (in the same manner described for the two previous methods that can be used to derive a maximum expected loss for an individual stock). ●

Deriving the Maximum Dollar Loss

Once the maximum percentage loss for a given confidence level is determined, it can be applied to derive the maximum dollar loss of a particular investment.

EXAMPLE

Assume that an investor has a $20 million investment in a stock. The maximum dollar loss is determined by applying the maximum percentage loss to the value of the investment. If the investor used beta to measure the maximum expected loss as explained above, the maximum percentage loss over one day would be –3 percent, so the maximum daily loss in dollars is

$$(-3\%) \times \$20,000,000 = \$600,000$$ ●

Since many institutional and individual investors manage stock portfolios, value at risk is commonly applied to assess the maximum possible loss of the entire portfolio. The same three methods used to derive the maximum expected loss of one stock can be applied to derive the maximum expected loss of a stock portfolio for a given confidence level. For instance, the returns of the stock portfolio over the last 100 days or so can be assessed to derive the maximum expected loss. Alternatively, the standard deviation of the portfolio's returns can be estimated over the last 100 days to derive a lower boundary at a specified confidence level. As another alternative, the beta of the portfolio's returns can be estimated over the last 100 days and then applied to a maximum expected daily loss in the stock market to derive a maximum expected loss in the stock portfolio over a given day.

Adjusting the Investment Horizon Desired

An investor who wants to assess the maximum loss over a week or a month can apply the same methods, but should use a historical series that matches the investment horizon. For example, to assess the maximum loss over a given week in the near future, a historical series of weekly returns of that stock (or stock portfolio) can be used.

Adjusting the Length of the Historical Period

The previous examples used a historical series of 100 trading days, but if, for example, conditions have changed such that only the most recent 70 days reflect the general state of market conditions, then those 70 days could be used. However, a subperiod of weak market performance should not be discarded because it could occur again.

Note that because the value-at-risk method measures risk based on historical price movements, it will not reflect new shocks to the stock market. Therefore, the method is not likely to be effective for assessing the maximum expected loss when there are shocks (such as a large unanticipated bankruptcy) to the stock market.

Restructuring the Investment Portfolio When portfolio managers consider the sale of Stock X and the purchase of Stock Y, they should apply value at risk to their potential new portfolio. Then, they can compare the risk of this portfolio to their existing portfolio to decide whether they should make these changes. Even if they plan to increase their investment in some stocks without selling others, they should reapply value at risk to reflect the new proportions of their stock portfolio allocated to each security that result from the restructured portfolio.

FORECASTING STOCK VOLATILITY AND BETA

Since the operations of a particular firm and its competitive environment can change over time, its risk can change as well. Investors are most concerned with the risk of their investments over the future horizon in which they hold those investments so that they can anticipate the range of possible returns that may result.

Methods of Forecasting Stock Price Volatility

Some of the more common methods of forecasting stock price volatility are the historical method, the time-series method, and the implied standard deviation method, which are described next.

Historical Method With the historical method, a historical period is used to derive a stock's standard deviation of returns, and then that estimate is used as the forecast over the future. Although the stock price volatility level may change over time, this method can be useful if there is no obvious trend in volatility, so the best forecast may be the volatility in the most recent period.

Time-Series Method A second method for forecasting stock price volatility is to use a time series of volatility patterns in previous periods.

EXAMPLE

The standard deviation of daily stock returns is determined for each of the last several months. Then, a time-series trend of these standard deviation levels is used to form an estimate for the standard deviation of daily stock returns over the next month. This method differs from the first in that it uses information beyond that contained in the previous month. The forecast may be based on a weighting scheme such as 50 percent times the standard deviation in the last month (month 4), plus 25 percent times the standard deviation in the month before that (month 3), plus 15 percent times the standard deviation in month 2, plus 10 percent times the standard deviation in month 1. ●

This scheme places more weight on the most recent data, but allows data from the last four months to influence the forecast. Normally, the weights and the number of previous periods (lags) that were most accurate (lowest forecast error) in previous periods are used. Various economic and political factors can cause stock price volatility to change abruptly, however, so even sophisticated **time-series models** do not necessarily generate accurate forecasts of stock price volatility.

Implied Standard Deviation A third method for forecasting stock price volatility is to derive the stock's implied standard deviation (ISD) from the stock option pricing model (options are discussed in detail in Chapter 14). The premium on a call option for a stock is dependent on factors such as the relationship between the current stock price and the exercise (strike) price of the option, the number of days until the expiration date of the option, and the anticipated volatility of the stock price movements. There is a formula for estimating the call option premium based on various factors. The actual values of these factors are known, except for the anticipated volatility. However, by plugging in the actual option premium paid by investors for that specific stock, it is possible to derive the anticipated volatility level. Market participants who wish to forecast volatility over a 30-day period will consider a call option on the stock that has 30 days to expiration. This measurement represents the anticipated volatility of the stock over a 30-day period by investors who are trading stocks. Participants may use this measurement as their own forecast of that specific stock's volatility.

Forecasting a Stock Portfolio's Volatility

Portfolio managers who monitor total risk rather than systematic risk are more concerned about stock volatility than about beta. Recall that a stock portfolio's volatility is dependent on the volatility of the individual stocks in the portfolio, as well as their correlations. Since the volatilities and correlations of the individual stocks can change over time, so can the volatility of the portfolio. One method of forecasting portfolio volatility is to first derive forecasts of individual volatility levels as described earlier. Then, the correlation coefficient for each pair of stocks in the portfolio is forecasted by estimating the correlation in recent periods and determining whether there was a trend in the change in correlations. The forecasted volatilities of individual stocks and the correlation coefficients are then used to estimate the future portfolio volatility. This approach explicitly captures the recent trends in individual volatilities and correlations.

Forecasting a Stock Portfolio's Beta

Given that the beta of any stock can change over time and that a stock portfolio's beta is dependent on the betas of its individual stocks, the portfolio's beta is subject to change. One way to forecast a portfolio's beta is to first forecast the betas of the individual stocks in the portfolio and then sum the individual forecasted betas, weighted by the proportion of investment in each stock.

The beta of each individual stock may be forecasted in a subjective manner; for example, a portfolio manager may forecast that a stock's beta will increase from its existing level of .8 to .9 because the firm has initiated a more aggressive growth strategy. Alternatively, the manager can assess a set of historical periods to determine whether there is a trend in the beta over those periods and then apply the trend. For example, a portfolio manager who is attempting to forecast the beta of stocks based on a daily horizon may estimate the betas in each of the previous four 100-day periods. Assume that the beta was estimated to be .6 four periods ago, .62 three periods ago, .7 two periods ago, and .8 last period. This firm's beta appears to have an upward trend, which may support a forecast of a slightly higher beta in the next period. However, the stock's beta will not continually change in one direction.

The same procedure can be used to forecast betas based on a different horizon. For example, a portfolio manager who wants to forecast the beta based on monthly stock returns can attempt to determine the trend by assessing recent 12-month periods.

RISK-ADJUSTED STOCK PERFORMANCE

The performance of a stock or a stock portfolio over a particular period can be measured by its excess return (return above the risk-free rate) over that period divided by its risk. Two common methods of measuring performance are the Sharpe index and the Treynor index.

Sharpe Index

If total variability is thought to be the appropriate measure of risk, a stock's risk-adjusted returns can be determined by the reward-to-variability ratio (also called the **Sharpe index),** computed as

$$\text{Sharpe index} = \frac{\overline{R} - \overline{R}_f}{\sigma}$$

where
$$\overline{R} = \textbf{average return on the stock}$$
$$\overline{R}_f = \textbf{average risk-free rate}$$
$$\sigma = \textbf{standard deviation of the stock's returns}$$

The higher the stock's mean return relative to the mean risk-free rate and the lower the standard deviation, the higher the Sharpe index. This index measures the excess return above the risk-free rate per unit of risk.

EXAMPLE

Assume the following information for two stocks:

- Average return for Sooner stock = 16%
- Average return for Longhorn stock = 14%
- Average risk-free rate = 10%
- Standard deviation of Sooner stock returns = 15%
- Standard deviation of Longhorn stock returns = 8%

$$\text{Sharpe index for Sooner stock} = \frac{16\% - 10\%}{15\%}$$
$$= .40$$
$$\text{Sharpe index for Longhorn stock} = \frac{14\% - 10\%}{8\%}$$
$$= .50$$

Even though Sooner stock had a higher average percentage return, Longhorn stock had a higher performance because of its lower risk. If a stock's average return is less than the average risk-free rate, the Sharpe index for that stock will be negative. ●

Treynor Index

If beta is thought to be the most appropriate type of risk, a stock's risk-adjusted returns can be determined by the **Treynor index,** computed as

$$\text{Treynor index} = \frac{\overline{R} - \overline{R}_f}{B}$$

where B is the stock's beta. The Treynor index is similar to the Sharpe index, except that it uses beta rather than the standard deviation to measure the stock's risk. The higher the Treynor index, the higher the return relative to the risk-free rate, per unit of risk.

Using the information provided earlier on Sooner and Longhorn stock and assuming that Sooner's stock beta is 1.2 and Longhorn's beta is 1.0, the Treynor index is computed for each stock as follows:

$$\text{Treynor index for Sooner stock} = \frac{16\% - 10\%}{1.2}$$
$$= .05$$
$$\text{Treynor index for Longhorn stock} = \frac{14\% - 10\%}{1.0}$$
$$= .04$$

Based on the Treynor index, Sooner stock had the higher performance. ●

A comparison of this example and the previous one shows that the stock determined to have the higher performance is dependent on the measure of risk and therefore on the index used. In some cases, the indexes will lead to the same results. Like the Sharpe index, the Treynor index is negative for a stock whose average return is less than the average risk-free rate.

STOCK MARKET EFFICIENCY

If stock markets are efficient, the prices of stocks at any point in time should fully reflect all available information. As investors attempt to capitalize on new information that is not already accounted for, stock prices should adjust immediately. Investors commonly over- or underreact to information. This does not mean markets are inefficient unless the reaction is biased (consistently over- or underreacting). In this case, investors who recognize the bias will be able to earn abnormally high risk-adjusted returns.

Forms of Efficiency

Efficient markets can be classified into three forms: weak, semistrong, and strong.

Weak-Form Efficiency   **Weak-form efficiency** suggests that security prices reflect all trade-related information, such as historical security price movements and volume of securities trades. Thus, investors will not be able to earn abnormal returns on a trading strategy that is based solely on past price movements.

Semistrong-Form Efficiency   **Semistrong-form efficiency** suggests that security prices fully reflect all public information. The difference between public information and market-related information is that public information also includes announcements by firms, economic news or events, and political news or events. Market-related information is a subset of public information. Thus, if semistrong-form efficiency holds, weak-form efficiency must hold as well. It is possible, however, for weak-form efficiency to hold, while semistrong-form efficiency does not. In this case, investors could earn abnormal returns by using the relevant information that was not immediately accounted for by the market.

Strong-Form Efficiency   **Strong-form efficiency** suggests that security prices fully reflect all information, including private or insider information. If strong-form efficiency holds, semistrong-form efficiency must hold as well. If insider information leads to abnormal returns, however, semistrong-form efficiency could hold, while strong-form efficiency does not.

Inside information gives insiders (such as some employees or board members) an unfair advantage over other investors. For example, if employees of a firm are aware of favorable news about the firm that is not yet disclosed to the public, they may consider purchasing shares or advising their friends to purchase the firm's shares. Though such actions are illegal, they still happen and can create market inefficiencies.

Tests of the Efficient Market Hypothesis

Tests of market efficiency are segmented into three categories, as discussed next.

Test of Weak-Form Efficiency

Weak-form efficiency has been tested by searching for a nonrandom pattern in security prices. If the future change in price is related to recent changes, historical price movements could be used to earn abnormal returns. In general, studies have found that historical price changes are independent over time. Therefore, historical information is already reflected by today's price and cannot be used to earn abnormal profits. Even when some dependence was detected, the transaction costs would offset any excess return earned.

There is some evidence that stocks have performed better in specific time periods. For example, as mentioned earlier, small stocks have performed unusually well in the month of January ("January effect"). Second, stocks have historically performed better on Fridays than on Mondays ("weekend effect"). Third, stocks have historically performed well on the trading days just before holidays ("holiday effect"). To the extent that a given pattern continues and can be used by investors to earn abnormal returns, market inefficiencies exist. In most cases, there is no clear evidence that such patterns persist once they are recognized by the investment community.

One could argue that the stock market is inefficient based on the number of so-called corrections that occur. During the twentieth century, there were more than 100 specific days when the market (as measured by the Dow Jones Industrial Average) declined by 10 percent or more. On more than 300 specific days during the century, the market declined by more than 5 percent. These abrupt declines frequently followed a market runup, which implies that the runup may have been excessive. Thus, a market correction was necessary to remove the excessive runup.

Test of Semistrong-Form Efficiency

Semistrong-form efficiency has been tested by assessing how security returns adjust to particular announcements. Some announcements are specific to a firm, such as an announced dividend increase, an acquisition, or a stock split. Other announcements are economy related, such as an announced decline in the federal funds rate. In general, security prices immediately reflected the information from the announcements. That is, the securities were not consistently over- or undervalued. Consequently, abnormal returns could not consistently be achieved. This is especially true when considering transaction costs.

There is evidence of unusual profits when investing in initial public offerings (IPOs). In particular, the return over the first day following the IPO tends to be abnormally high. One reason for this underpricing is that the securities firms underwriting an IPO intentionally underprice to ensure that the entire issue can be placed. In addition, underwriters are required to exercise due diligence in ensuring the accuracy of the information that they provide to investors about the corporation. Thus, underwriters are encouraged to err on the low side when setting a price for IPOs.

Some analysts might contend that given imperfect information about IPOs, investors will participate only if prices are low. Thus, the potential return must be high enough to compensate for the lack of information about these corporations and the risk incurred. Using this argument, the underpricing does not imply market inefficiencies but rather reflects the high degree of uncertainty.

Test of Strong-Form Efficiency   Tests of strong-form efficiency are difficult, because the inside information used is not publicly available and cannot be properly tested. Nevertheless, many forms of insider trading could easily result in abnormally high returns. For example, there is clear evidence that share prices of target firms rise substantially when the acquisition is announced. If insiders purchased stock of targets prior to other investors, they would normally achieve abnormally high returns. Insiders are discouraged from using this information because it is illegal, not because markets are strong-form efficient.

FOREIGN STOCK VALUATION AND PERFORMANCE

Some of the key concepts in this chapter can be adjusted so that they apply on a global basis, as explained next.

Valuation of Foreign Stocks

Foreign stocks can be valued by using the price-earnings method or the dividend discount model with an adjustment to reflect international conditions.

Price-Earnings (PE) Method   The expected earnings per share of the foreign firm are multiplied by the appropriate PE ratio (based on the firm's risk and local industry) to determine the appropriate price of the firm's stock. Though easy to use, this method is subject to some limitations when valuing foreign stocks. The PE ratio for a given industry may change continuously in some foreign markets, especially when the industry is composed of just a few firms. Thus, it is difficult to determine the proper ratio that should be applied to a specific foreign firm. In addition, the PE ratio for any particular industry may need to be adjusted for the firm's country because reported earnings can be influenced by the country's accounting guidelines and tax laws.

Furthermore, even if U.S. investors are comfortable with their estimate of the proper PE ratio, the value derived by this method is denominated in the local foreign currency (since the estimated earnings are denominated in that currency). Therefore, U.S. investors still need to consider exchange rate effects. Even if the stock is undervalued in the foreign country, it may not necessarily generate a reasonable return for U.S. investors if the foreign currency depreciates against the dollar.

Dividend Discount Model   The dividend discount model can be applied to value foreign stocks by discounting the stream of expected dividends, but with an adjustment to account for expected exchange rate movements. Foreign stocks pay dividends in the currency in which they are denominated. Thus, the cash flow per period to U.S. investors is the dividend (denominated in the foreign currency) multiplied by the value of that foreign currency in dollars. An expected appreciation of the currency denominating the foreign stocks will result in higher expected dollar cash flows and a higher present value. The dividend can normally be forecasted with more accuracy than the value of the foreign currency. Because of exchange rate uncertainty, the value of the foreign stock from a U.S. investor's perspective is subject to more uncertainty than the value of the stock from a local investor's perspective.

International Market Efficiency

Some foreign markets are likely to be inefficient because of the relatively small number of analysts and portfolio managers who monitor stocks in those markets. It is easier to find undervalued stocks when a smaller number of market participants monitor the market. Research has documented that some foreign markets are inefficient, based on slow price responses to new information about specific firms (such as earnings announcements). The inefficiencies are more common in smaller foreign stock markets. Some emerging stock markets are relatively new and small and may not be as efficient as the U.S. stock market. Thus, some stocks may be undervalued, a possibility that has attracted investors to these markets. Because some of these markets are small, however, they may be susceptible to manipulation by large traders. Furthermore, insider trading is more prevalent in many foreign markets because rules against it are not enforced. In general, large institutional investors and insiders based in the foreign markets may have some advantages.

Measuring Performance from Investing in Foreign Stocks

An investor's performance from investing in foreign stocks is most properly measured by considering the objective of the investor. For example, if portfolio managers are assigned to select stocks in Europe, their performance should be compared to the performance of a European index, measured in U.S. dollars. In this way, the performance measurement controls for general market movements and exchange rate movements in the region where the portfolio manager has been assigned to invest funds. Thus, if the entire European market experiences poor performance over a particular quarter, or if the main European currency (the euro) depreciates against the dollar over the period, the portfolio managers assigned to Europe are not automatically penalized. Conversely, if the entire European market experiences strong performance over a particular quarter, or the euro appreciates against the dollar, the managers are not automatically rewarded. Instead, the performance of portfolio managers will be measured relative to the general market conditions of the region to which they are assigned.

Performance from Global Diversification

A substantial amount of research has demonstrated that investors in stocks can benefit by diversifying internationally. Most stocks are highly influenced by the country where their firms are located (although some firms are more vulnerable to economic conditions than others).

Since a given stock market partially reflects the current and/or forecasted state of its country's economy, and economies do not move in tandem, particular stocks of the various markets are not expected to be highly correlated. This contrasts with a purely domestic portfolio (such as all U.S. stocks), in which most stocks are often moving in the same direction and by a somewhat similar magnitude.

Nevertheless, stock price movements among international stock markets are integrated to a degree because some underlying economic factors reflecting the world's general financial condition may systematically affect all markets. Since one country's economy can influence the economies of other countries, expectations about economies across countries may be somewhat similar. Thus, stock markets across countries may respond to some of the same expectations. Integration is an important concept because of its implications about benefits from international diversification. A high degree of integration implies that stock returns of different countries would be affected by common factors. Therefore, the returns of stocks from various countries would move in tandem, allowing only modest benefits from international diversification.

In general, correlations between stock indexes have been higher in recent years than they were several years ago. One reason for the increased correlations is the increased integration of business between countries, which results in more intercountry trade flows and capital flows, causing each country to have more influence on other countries. In particular, many European countries have become more integrated because of the movement to standardize regulations throughout Europe and the use of a single currency (the euro) to facilitate trade between countries.

Integration of Markets during Crises   In many cases, a crisis that adversely affects one large country tends to affect other countries, because economies are globally integrated. As the credit crisis spread in 2008, economic conditions weakened in many countries, and stock markets throughout the world experienced major losses. During the week of October 6–10, 2008, U.S. stock prices declined by 18 percent on average, the largest weekly decline ever in the United States. Stock markets in other countries experienced even more pronounced price declines during that week.

Diversification among Emerging Stock Markets   Emerging markets provide an alternative outlet for investors from the United States and other countries to invest their funds. The potential economic growth rate is relatively high. In addition, investors may achieve extra diversification benefits from investing in emerging markets because their respective economies may not necessarily move in tandem with those of the more developed countries. Thus, the correlation between these stocks and those of other countries is low, and investors can reduce risk by including some stocks from these markets within their portfolio. However, emerging market stocks tend to exhibit a high degree of volatility, which partially offsets the advantage of their low correlations with stocks of other countries.

In addition, these countries are also susceptible to large stock price declines during world crises. For example, during the four-month period ending in September 2008, Russia's stock market experienced a loss of 65 percent, which eliminated $750 billion in equity value. Stocks in emerging markets are more exposed to major government turnovers and other forms of political risk. They also expose U.S. investors to a high degree of exchange rate risk because their local currencies are typically very volatile.

SUMMARY

- Stocks are commonly valued using the price-earnings (PE) method, the dividend discount model, or the free cash flow model. The PE method applies the industry PE ratio to the firm's earnings to derive its value. The dividend discount model estimates the value as the present value of expected future dividends. The free cash flow model is based on the present value of future cash flows.

- Stock prices are affected by those factors that affect future cash flows or the required rate of return by investors. Economic conditions, market conditions, and firm-specific conditions can affect a firm's cash flows or the required rate of return.

- The risk of a stock is measured by its volatility, its beta, or its value-at-risk estimate. Investors are giv-

ing more attention to risk measurement in light of abrupt downturns in the prices of some stocks in recent years.

- Stock market efficiency implies that stock prices reflect all available information. Weak-form efficiency suggests that security prices reflect all trade-related information, such as historical security price movements and the volume of securities trades. Semistrong-form efficiency suggests that security prices fully reflect all public information. Strong-form efficiency suggests that security prices fully reflect all information, including private or insider information. Evidence supports weak-form efficiency to a degree, but there is less support for semistrong or strong-form efficiency.

POINT COUNTER-POINT

Is the Stock Market Efficient?

Point Yes. Investors fully incorporate all available information when trading stocks. Thus, the prices of stocks fully reflect all information.

Counter-Point No. The high degree of stock price volatility offers evidence of how much disagreement there is among stock prices. The fact that many stocks

declined by more than 40 percent during the end of 2008 and beginning of 2009 suggests that stock prices are not always properly valued to reflect available information.

Who Is Correct? Use the Internet to learn more about this issue. Offer your own opinion on this issue.

QUESTIONS AND APPLICATIONS

1. Price-Earnings Model Explain the use of the price-earnings ratio for valuing a stock. Why might investors derive different valuations for a stock when using the PE method? Why might investors derive an inaccurate valuation of a firm when using the PE method?

2. Dividend Discount Model Describe the dividend discount valuation model. What are some limitations of the dividend discount model?

3. Impact of Economic Growth Explain how economic growth affects the valuation of a stock.

4. Impact of Interest Rates How are the interest rate, the required rate of return on a stock, and the valuation of a stock related?

5. Impact of Inflation Assume that the expected inflation rate has just been revised upward by the market. Would the required return by investors who invest in stocks be affected? Explain.

6. Impact of Exchange Rates Explain how the value of the dollar affects stock valuations.

7. Investor Sentiment Explain why investor sentiment can affect stock prices.

8. January Effect Describe the January effect.

9. Earnings Surprises How do earnings surprises affect valuations of stocks?

10. Impact of Takeover Rumors Why can expectations of an acquisition affect the value of the target's stock?

11. Emerging Markets What are the risks of investing in stocks in emerging markets?

12. Stock Volatility during the Credit Crisis Explain how stock volatility changed during the credit crisis.

13. Stock Portfolio Volatility Identify the factors that affect a stock portfolio's volatility and explain their effects.

14. Beta Explain how to estimate the beta of a stock. Explain the logic regarding how beta serves as a measure of the stock's risk.

15. Wall Street In the movie *Wall Street,* Bud Fox is a broker who conducts trades for Gordon Gekko's firm. Gekko purchases shares of firms he believes are undervalued. Various scenes in the movie offer excellent examples of concepts discussed in this chapter.

a. Bud Fox comments to Gordon Gekko that a firm's breakup value is twice its market price. What is Bud suggesting in this statement? How would employees of the firm respond to Bud's statement?

b. When Bud informs Gekko that another investor, Mr. Wildman, is secretly planning to acquire a target firm in Pennsylvania, Gekko tells Bud to buy a large amount of this stock. Why?

c. Gekko says, "Wonder why fund managers can't beat the S&P 500? Because they are sheep." What is Gekko's point? How does it relate to market efficiency?

16. Market Efficiency Explain the difference between weak-form, semistrong-form, and strong-form efficiency. Which of these forms of efficiency is most difficult to test? Which is most likely to be refuted? Explain how to test weak-form efficiency in the stock market.

17. Market Efficiency A consulting firm was hired to determine whether a particular trading strategy could generate abnormal returns. The strategy involved taking positions based on recent historical movements in stock prices. The strategy did not achieve abnormal returns. Consequently, the consulting firm concluded that the stock market is weak-form efficient. Do you agree? Explain.

Advanced Questions

18. Value at Risk Describe the value-at-risk method for measuring risk.

19. Implied Volatility Explain the meaning and use of implied volatility.

20. Leveraged Buyout At the time a management group of RJR Nabisco initially considered engaging in a leveraged buyout, RJR's stock price was less than $70 per share. Ultimately, RJR was acquired by the firm Kohlberg Kravis Roberts (KKR) for about $108 per share. Does the large discrepancy between the stock price before an acquisition was considered versus after the acquisition mean that RJR's price was initially undervalued? If so, does this imply that the market was inefficient?

21. How Stock Prices May Respond to Prevailing Conditions Consider the prevailing conditions that could affect the demand for stocks, including inflation, the economy, the budget deficit, the Fed's monetary policy, political conditions, and the general mood of investors. Based on these conditions, do you think stock prices will increase or decrease during this semester? Offer some logic to support your answer. Which factor do you think will have the biggest impact on stock prices?

22. Application of CAPM to Stock Pricing Explain (using intuition instead of math) why stock prices may decrease in response to a higher risk-free rate according to the CAPM. Explain (using intuition instead of math) why stock prices may increase in this situation even though the risk-free rate increases.

23. Impact of SOX on Stock Valuations Use a stock valuation framework to explain why the Sarbanes-Oxley Act (SOX) could improve the valuation of a stock. Why might SOX cause a reduction in the valuation of a stock?

Interpreting Financial News

Interpret the following statements made by Wall Street analysts and portfolio managers:

a. "The stock market's recent climb has been driven by falling interest rates."

b. "Future stock prices are dependent on the Fed's policy meeting next week."

c. "Given the recent climb in stocks that cannot be explained by fundamentals, a correction is inevitable."

Managing in Financial Markets

Stock Portfolio Dilemma As an investment manager, you frequently make decisions about investing in stocks versus other types of investments and about types of stocks to purchase.

a. You have noticed that investors tend to invest more heavily in stocks after interest rates have declined. You are considering this strategy as well. Is it rational to invest more heavily in stocks once interest rates have declined?

b. Assume that you are about to select a specific stock that will perform well in response to an expected runup in the stock market. You are very confident that the stock market will perform well in the near future. Recently, a friend recommended that you consider purchasing stock of a specific firm because it had decent earnings over the last few years, it has a low beta (reflecting a low degree of systematic risk), and its beta is expected to remain low. You normally rely on beta as a measurement of a firm's systematic risk. Should you seriously consider buying that stock? Explain.

c. You are considering an investment in an initial public offering (IPO) by Marx Company, which has performed very well recently, according to its financial statements. The firm will use some of the proceeds from selling stock to pay off some of its bank loans. How can you apply stock valuation models to estimate this firm's value, when its stock was not publicly traded? Once you estimate the value of the firm, how can you use this information to determine whether to invest in it? What are some limitations in estimating the value of this firm?

d. In the past, your boss assessed your performance based on the actual return on the portfolio of U.S. stocks that you manage. For each quarter in which your portfolio generated an annualized return of at least 20 percent, you received a bonus. Now your boss wants you to develop a method for measuring your performance from managing the portfolio. Offer a method that accurately measures your performance.

e. Assume that you were also asked to manage a portfolio of European stocks. How would your method for measuring your performance in managing this portfolio differ from the method you devised for the U.S. stock portfolio in the previous question?

PROBLEMS

1. Risk-Adjusted Return Measurements Assume the following information over a five-year period:

- Average risk-free rate = 6%
- Average return for Crane stock = 11%
- Average return for Load stock = 14%
- Standard deviation of Crane stock returns = 2%
- Standard deviation of Load stock returns = 4%
- Beta of Crane stock = 0.8
- Beta of Load stock = 1.1

Determine which stock has higher risk-adjusted returns when using the Sharpe index. Which stock has higher risk-adjusted returns when using the Treynor index? Show your work.

2. Measuring Expected Return Assume Mess stock has a beta of 1.2. If the risk-free rate is 7 percent and the market return is 10 percent, what is the expected return of Mess stock?

3. Using the PE Method You found that IBM is expected to generate earnings of $4.38 per share this year and that the mean PE ratio for its industry is 27.195. Using the PE valuation method, what should be the value of IBM shares?

4. Using the Dividend Discount Model Suppose that you are interested in buying the stock of a company that has a policy of paying a $6 per share dividend every year. Assuming no changes in the firm's policies, what is the value of a share of stock if the required rate of return is 11 percent?

5. Using the Dividend Discount Model Micro, Inc. will pay a dividend of $2.30 per share next year. If the company plans to increase its dividend by 9 percent per year indefinitely, and you require a 12 percent return on your investment, what should you pay for the company's stock?

6. Using the Dividend Discount Model Suppose you know that a company *just paid* an annual dividend of $1.75 per share on its stock and that the dividend will continue to grow at a rate of 8 percent per year. If the required return on this stock is 10 percent, what is the current share price?

7. Deriving the Required Rate of Return The next expected annual dividend for Sun, Inc. will be $1.20 per share, and analysts expect the dividend to grow at an annual rate of 7 percent indefinitely. If Sun

stock currently sells for $22 per share, what is the required rate of return?

8. Deriving the Required Rate of Return A share of common stock currently sells for $110. Current dividends are $8 per share annually and are expected to grow at 6 percent per year indefinitely. What is the rate of return required by investors in the stock?

9. Deriving the Required Rate of Return A stock has a beta of 2.2, the risk-free rate is 6 percent, and the expected return on the market is 12 percent. Using the CAPM, what would you expect the required rate of return on this stock to be? What is the market risk premium?

10. Deriving a Stock's Beta You are considering investing in a stock that has an expected return of 13 percent. If the risk-free rate is 5 percent and the market risk premium is 7 percent, what must the beta of this stock be?

11. Measuring Stock Returns Suppose you bought a stock at the beginning of the year for $76.50. During the year, the stock paid a dividend of $0.70 per share and had an ending share price of $99.25. What is the total percentage return from investing in that stock over the year?

12. Measuring the Portfolio Beta Assume the following information:

- Beta of IBM = 1.31
- Beta of LUV = 0.85
- Beta of ODP = 0.94

If you invest 40 percent of your money in IBM, 30 percent in LUV, and 30 percent in ODP, what is your portfolio's beta?

13. Measuring the Portfolio Beta Using the information from Problem 12, suppose that you instead decide to invest $20,000 in IBM, $30,000 in LUV, and $50,000 in ODP. What is the beta of your portfolio now?

14. Value at Risk Assume that IBM has a beta of 1.31.

a. If you assume that the stock market has a maximum expected loss of –3.2 percent on a daily basis (based on a 95 percent confidence level), what is the maximum daily loss for the IBM stock?

b. If you have $19,000 invested in IBM stock, what is your maximum daily dollar loss?

15. Value at Risk If your portfolio beta was calculated to be 0.89 and the stock market has a maximum expected loss of –2.5 percent on a daily basis, what is the maximum daily loss to your portfolio?

16. Dividend Model Relationships

a. When computing the price of a stock with the dividend discount model, how would the price be affected if the required rate of return is increased? Explain the logic of this relationship.

b. When computing the price of a stock using the constant-growth dividend discount model, how would the price be affected if the growth rate is reduced? Explain the logic of this relationship.

17. CAPM Relationships

a. When using the CAPM, how would the required rate of return on a stock be affected if the risk-free rate is lower?

b. When using the CAPM, how would the required rate of return on a stock be affected if the market return is lower?

c. When using the CAPM, how would the required rate of return on a stock be affected if the beta is higher?

18. Value at Risk

a. How is the maximum expected loss on a stock affected by an increase in the volatility (standard deviation), based on a 95 percent confidence interval?

b. Determine how the maximum expected loss on a stock would be affected by an increase in the expected return of the stock, based on a 95 percent confidence interval.

FLOW OF FUNDS EXERCISE

Valuing Stocks

Recall that if the economy continues to be strong, Carson Company may need to increase its production capacity by about 50 percent over the next few years to satisfy demand. It would need financing to expand and accommodate the increase in production. Recall that the yield curve is currently upward sloping. Also recall that Carson is concerned about a possible slowing of the economy because of potential Fed actions to reduce inflation. It is also considering issuing stock or bonds to raise funds in the next year. If Carson goes public, it might even consider using its stock as a means of acquiring some target firms. It would also consider engaging in a secondary offering at a future point in time if the IPO is successful and if its growth continues over time. It would also change its compensation system so that most of its managers would receive about 30 percent of their compensation in shares of Carson stock and the remainder as salary.

a. At the present time, the price-earnings (PE) ratio (stock price per share divided by earnings per share) of other firms in Carson's industry is relatively low but

should rise in the future. Why might this information affect the time at which Carson issues its stock?

b. Assume that Carson Company believes that issuing stock is an efficient means of circumventing the potential for high interest rates. Even if long-term interest rates have increased by the time it issues stock, Carson thinks that it would be insulated by issuing stock instead of bonds. Is this view correct?

c. Carson Company recognizes the importance of a high stock price at the time it engages in an IPO (if it goes public). But why would its stock price be important to Carson Company even after the IPO?

d. If Carson Company goes public, it may be able to motivate its managers by granting them stock as part of their compensation. Explain why the stock may motivate them to perform well. Then explain why the use of stock as compensation may motivate them to use a very short-term focus, even though they are supposed to focus on maximizing shareholder wealth over the long run. How can a firm provide stock as motivation but prevent the managers from using a very short-term focus?

INTERNET/EXCEL EXERCISES

1. Go to http://finance.yahoo.com/7u. Compare the performance of the Dow, Nasdaq, and S&P 500 indexes. Click on each of these indexes and describe the trend for that index since January. Which index has had the best performance?

2. Go to http://finance.yahoo.com/, type in the symbol DELL (for Dell, Inc.) and click on "Get Quotes." Then go to the bottom of the stock price chart and retrieve the end-of-month stock price of Dell over the last 12 months. Record this information on an Excel spreadsheet and estimate the standard deviation of the stock's price movements. [See Appendix B for guidance on how to estimate the standard deviation of a stock's price movements.] Repeat the process for Oracle Corporation (its symbol is ORCL). Which stock is riskier based on your analysis?

3. Assume that the expected return on Dell stock and Oracle stock is 0 percent for the next month. Use the value-at-risk method to determine the maximum expected loss of Dell and Oracle for the next month, based on a 95 percent confidence level.

WSJ EXERCISE

Reviewing Abrupt Shifts in Stock Valuation

Review Section C of a recent issue of *The Wall Street Journal.* Notice that the stocks with the largest one-day gains and losses are shown. Do an Internet search for news about the stock with the biggest gain. What is the reason for the gain? Repeat the exercise for the stock with the biggest loss.

The Link between Accounting and Stock Valuation

In a publicly traded firm, the managers who run the firm are separate from the investors who own it. Managers are hired to serve as agents of the corporation and are expected to serve the interests of the firm's shareholders by making decisions that maximize the value of the firm. The firm's management is required to provide substantial information about the firm's financial condition and performance. Shareholders and other investors use this information to monitor management and to value the firm. For example, if investors use the price-earnings method to derive a valuation, they rely on the reported earnings. If they use the dividend discount model, they may derive an expected growth rate from recently reported earnings or revenue figures. If they use the adjusted dividend discount model, they may rely on financial statements to estimate future cash flows.

If firms provide inaccurate financial information, investors will derive inaccurate valuations, and money will flow to the wrong sources in the stock markets. In addition, inaccurate financial information creates more risk for stocks because investors must worry about the uncertainty surrounding the reported financial statement numbers. If financial statement data are questionable, stock values may decline whenever investors recognize that the earnings or some other proxy used to estimate cash flows is overstated. Investors will require a higher rate of return to hold stocks subject to downside risk because of distorted accounting. Thus, deceptive accounting practices disrupt the stock market and increase the cost of capital raised by issuing stock.

To ensure that managers serve shareholder interests, firms commonly tie managerial compensation to the stock price. For example, managers may be granted stock options that allow them to buy the firm's stock at a specified price over a specified time period (such as the next five years). In this way, the managers benefit directly from a high stock price just like other shareholders and thus should make decisions that result in a high stock price for the shareholders.

Unfortunately, some managers recognize that it may be easier to increase their stock's price by manipulating the financial statements than by improving the firm's operations. When the firm's reported earnings are inflated, investors will likely overestimate the value of its stock, regardless of the method they use to value stocks.

Managers may be tempted to temporarily inflate reported earnings because doing so may temporarily inflate the stock's price. If no limits are imposed on the stock options granted, managers may be able to exercise their options (buying the stock at the price specified in the option contracts) during this period of a temporarily inflated price and immediately sell the stock in the secondary market. They can capitalize on the inflated stock price before other investors realize that the earnings and stock price are inflated.

PROBLEMS WITH CREATIVE ACCOUNTING

Managers would not be able to manipulate a firm's financial information if accounting rules did not allow them to be creative. The accounting for a firm's financial statement items is guided by generally accepted accounting principles (GAAP) set by the Financial Accounting Standards Board (FASB). However, these guidelines allow for substantial flexibility in accounting, which means that there is no standard formula for converting accounting numbers into cash flows. The accounting confusion is compounded by the desire of some managers to inflate their firm's earnings in particular periods when they wish to sell their holdings of the firm's stock. Specifically, the accounting can inflate revenue in a particular period without inflating expenses or defer the reporting of some expenses until a future quarter. Investors who do not recognize that some of the accounting numbers are distorted may overestimate the value of the firm.

Creative accounting can also be used to distort expenses. When a firm discontinues one of its business projects, it commonly records this as a writeoff, or a onetime charge against earnings. Investors tend to ignore writeoffs when estimating future expenses because they do not expect them to occur again. Some firms, however, shift a portion of their normal operating expenses into the writeoff, even though those expenses will occur again in the future. Investors who do not recognize this accounting gimmick will underestimate the future expenses.

As a classic example of shifting expenses, WorldCom attempted to write off more than $7 billion following its acquisition of MCI in 1998. When the Securities and Exchange Commission (SEC) questioned this accounting, WorldCom changed the amount to about $3 billion. If it had succeeded in including the extra $4 billion in the writeoff, it could have reduced its reported operating expenses by $4 billion. Thus, investors who trusted World-Com's income statement would have underestimated its future expenses by about $4 billion per year and therefore would have grossly overestimated the value of the stock.

When firms go beyond the loose accounting guidelines, the SEC may require them to restate their earnings and provide a corrected set of financial statements. In recent years, the SEC has forced hundreds of firms to restate their earnings, but the investors who lost money because they trusted a firm's distorted accounting were not reimbursed.

GOVERNANCE OF ACCOUNTING

Several types of governance can be used to attempt to prevent firms from using distorted accounting, as explained next.

Auditing

Firms are required to hire auditors to audit their financial statements and verify that the statements are within the accounting guidelines. The auditors, however, rely on these firms for their future business. Many large firms pay auditors more than $1 million per year for their auditing services and also for nonauditing services. Thus, the auditors may be tempted to sign off on distorted accounting so that they will be rehired by their clients in the future. If the auditors uphold proper standards that force their clients to revise their reported earnings, they may not be hired again. The temptation to sign off on creative accounting used by client firms is especially strong given the subjectivity allowed by the accounting rules. Auditors may be more willing to sign off on financial statements that are somewhat confusing but do not directly violate accounting rules.

Board of Directors

A firm's board of directors is expected to represent the firm's shareholders. The directors oversee the firm's financial reporting process and should attempt to ensure that the financial information provided by the firm is accurate. However, some boards have not forced managers to accurately disclose the firm's financial condition. A board can be ineffective if it is run by insiders who are the same managers that the board is supposed to monitor. Board members who are managers of the firm (insiders) are less likely to scrutinize the firm's management. In recent years, many firms have increased the proportion of independent board members (outsiders), who are not subject to pressure from the firm's executives. Even some independent board members, however, have strong ties to the firm's executives or receive substantial consulting income beyond their compensation for serving on the board. Thus, they may be willing to overlook distorted accounting or other unethical behavior in order to maintain their existing income stream from the firm.

Several proposals have been made to try to increase the independence of board members. For example, the Commission on Public Trust and Private Enterprise has recommended that corporations consider separating the offices of chair of the board and CEO and that the board chair should be an independent director.

Compensation of Board Members   Some boards are ineffective because of the way the board members are compensated. If board members receive stock options from the firm as compensation, the options' value is tied to the firm's stock price. Consequently, some board members may be tempted to ignore their oversight duties, as they may benefit from selling their shares of the stock (received as compensation) while the price is temporarily inflated. Meanwhile, shareholders who hold their stock for a longer time period will be adversely affected once the market recognizes that the financial statements are distorted.

Board members are more likely to serve the long-term interests of shareholders if they are compensated in a manner that encourages them to maximize the long-term value of the firm. If they are provided stock that they cannot sell for a long-term period, they are more likely to focus on maximizing the long-term value of the firm.

Several regulations have been issued to address the potential abuses resulting from granting stock options to managers and board members. In 2003, the SEC ruled that corporations listed on the New York Stock Exchange (NYSE) or the Nasdaq market must have shareholder approval before giving executives company stock or options. The rules were drafted and approved by the NYSE and Nasdaq. In addition, FASB recently required that corporations expense their executive stock options on their income statements. This increases transparency in financial reporting and might improve corporate governance.

Board's Independent Audit Committee   Some board members may serve on an independent audit committee, which is responsible for monitoring the firm's auditor. The committee is expected to ensure that the audit is completed without conflicts of interest so that the auditors will provide an unbiased audit. Some boards have not prevented distorted audits, however, either because they did not recognize the conflicts of interest or because they were unwilling to acknowledge them.

Role of Credit Rating Agencies

Investors may also rely on credit rating agencies such as Standard & Poor's or Moody's to assess a firm's risk level. However, these agencies do not always detect a firm's financial problems in advance. They normally focus on assessing a firm's risk level based on the financial statements provided, rather than on determining whether the financial statements are accurate. The agencies may assume that the financial statements are accurate because they were verified by an auditor.

Role of the Market for Corporate Control

In the market for corporate control, firms that perform poorly should be acquired and reorganized by other more efficient firms (called raiders). The raiders have an incentive to seek out inefficient firms because they can buy them at a low price (reflecting their poor performance) and remove their inefficient management. Nevertheless, the market for corporate control does not necessarily prevent faulty accounting. First, raiders may not be able to identify firms that inflated their earnings. Second, firms that have inflated their earnings are probably overvalued, and raiders will not want to acquire them at their inflated price. Third, an acquisition involves substantial costs of integrating businesses, and there is the risk that these costs will offset any potential benefits.

THE ENRON SCANDAL

The most famous recent example of the use of creative accounting occurred at Enron Corporation. Enron was formed in 1985 from the merger of two natural gas pipeline companies. It grew relatively slowly until the 1990s when the deregulation of the utilities industry presented new opportunities. Enron began to expand in several directions. It acquired power plants in the United States and also expanded internationally, acquiring a power distributor in Brazil, a power plant in India, and a water company in the United Kingdom, among others. Perhaps most importantly, it took advantage of the new deregulated environment to pioneer the trading of natural gas and electricity. Soon it had branched out beyond simple energy trading to trade such instruments as weather derivatives. In 1999, it introduced Enron Online, an Internet-based trading platform that gave the company the appeal of an "Internet stock" at a time when such stocks were highly desired. The company introduced online trading of metals, wood products, and even broadband capacity, as well as energy. All of this enabled Enron to grow to become the seventh largest firm in the United States in terms of gross revenues by 2000.

Most investors were caught by surprise when Enron began to experience financial problems in October 2001 and then filed for bankruptcy on December 2, 2001. At the time, it was the largest U.S. firm to go bankrupt. In retrospect, Enron's stock may have been overvalued for many years, but some investors and creditors were fooled by its financial statements. The Enron fiasco received much publicity because it demonstrated how a firm could manipulate its financial statements, and therefore manipulate its valuation, in spite of various controls designed to prevent that type of behavior. This section offers some insight into why investor valuations and risk assessments of Enron were so poor.

Enron's Letter to Its Shareholders

If investors trusted the claims made by Enron in its annual report, it is understandable that they would value the stock highly. The letter to shareholders in Enron's 2000 annual report included the following statements:

- "Enron's performance in 2000 was a success by any measure, as we continued to outdistance the competition and solidify our leadership in each of our businesses.
- Enron has built unique and strong businesses that have limitless opportunities for growth.
- At a minimum, we see our market opportunities company-wide tripling over the next five years.

- Enron is laser-focused on earnings per share, and we expect to continue strong performance.
- Enron is increasing earnings per share and continuing our strong return to shareholders.
- The company's total return to shareholders was 89% in 2000, compared with a −9% returned by the S&P 500.
- The 10-year return to Enron shareholders was 1,415%, compared with 383% for the S&P 500.
- We plan to…create significant shareholder value for our shareholders."

Enron's Stock Valuation

Normally, the valuation of a firm is obtained by using the firm's financial statements to derive cash flows and to derive a required rate of return that is used to discount the cash flows. Enron's valuation was excessive because of various irregularities in its financial statements.

Estimating Cash Flows　Since Enron's earnings were distorted, the estimates of its cash flows derived from those earnings were also distorted. Moreover, Enron's earnings were manipulated to create the perception of consistent earnings growth, which tempted investors to apply a high growth rate when estimating future cash flows.

Estimating the Required Rate of Return　Investors can derive a required rate of return as the prevailing long-term risk-free interest rate plus the firm's risk premium. The risk premium can be measured by the firm's existing degree of financial leverage, its ability to cover interest payments with operating earnings, and its sensitivity to market movements.

Until the accounting distortions were publicized, Enron's risk was underestimated. The company concealed much of its debt by keeping it off its consolidated financial statements, as will be explained shortly. Consequently, investors who estimated Enron's sensitivity to market movements using historical data were unable to detect Enron's potential for failure. As a result, they used a lower risk premium than was appropriate. Thus, the financial statements caused investors both to overestimate Enron's future cash flows and to underestimate its risk. Both effects led to a superficially high stock price.

Applying Market Multiples　Given the difficulty of estimating cash flows and the required rate of return, some investors may have tried to value Enron's stock by using market multiples. Determining the appropriate PE multiple for Enron was also difficult, however, because its reported earnings did not represent its real earnings.

Another problem with applying the industry PE method to Enron was the difficulty of identifying the proper industry. One of the company's main businesses was trading various types of energy derivative contracts. Enron did not want to be known as a trading company, however, because the valuations of companies such as securities firms that engage in trading are generally lower for a given level of earnings per share.

Motives of Enron's Management

One of the main reasons for Enron's problems was its management. Managers are expected to maximize the value of the firm's stock. Like many firms, Enron granted stock options to some of its managers as a means of motivating them to make decisions that would maximize the value of its stock. However, Enron's management seemed to focus more on manipulating the financial statements to create a perception of strong business performance than on improving the actual performance. By manipulating the financial statements, Enron consistently met its earnings forecasts and increased its earnings over 20 consecutive quarters leading up to 2001. In this way, it created a false sense of security about its performance, thereby increasing the demand for its stock. This resulted in a superficially high stock price over a period in which some managers sold their stock holdings. Twenty-nine Enron executives or board members sold their holdings of Enron stock for more than $1 billion in total before the stock price plummeted.

Internal Monitoring   Some firms use internal monitoring to ensure some degree of control over managers and encourage them to make decisions that benefit shareholders. Unfortunately, Enron's internal monitoring was also susceptible to manipulation. For example, managers were periodically required to measure the market value of various energy contracts that the company held. Since there was not an active market for some of these contracts, the prevailing valuations of the contracts were arbitrary. Managers used estimates that resulted in very favorable valuations, which in turn led to a higher level of reported performance and higher managerial compensation.

Monitoring by the Board of Directors   The board members serve as representatives of the firm's shareholders and are responsible for ensuring that the managers serve shareholder interests. In fact, board members are commonly compensated with stock so that they have an incentive to ensure that the stock price is maximized. In the case of Enron, some board members followed executives in selling their shares while the stock price was superficially high.

Enron's Financial Statement Manipulation

Some of the methods Enron used to report its financial conditions were inconsistent with accounting guidelines. Other methods were within the rules, but were misleading. Consequently, many investors invested in Enron without recognizing the financial problems that were hidden from the financial statements. Some of these investors lost most or all of their investment.

Accounting for Partnerships   One of the most common methods used by Enron to manipulate its financial statements involved the transfer of assets to partnerships that it owned called special-purpose entities (SPEs). It found outside investors to invest at least 3 percent of each partnership's capital. Under accounting guidelines, a partnership with this minimum level of investment from an outside investor does not have to be classified as a subsidiary. Since Enron did not have to classify its SPEs as subsidiaries, it did not have to include the financial information for them in its consolidated financial statements. Thus, the debt related to the SPEs was removed from Enron's consolidated financial statements. Since most investors focused on the consolidated financial statements, they did not detect Enron's financial problems.

In addition, whenever Enron created a partnership that would buy one of its business segments, it would book a gain on its consolidated financial statements from the sale of the asset to the partnership. Losses from a partnership would be booked on the partnership's financial statements. Thus, Enron was booking gains from its partnerships on its consolidated financial statements while hiding their losses. On November 8, 2001, Enron announced that it was restating its earnings for the previous five years because three of its partnerships should have been included in the consolidated financial statements. This announcement confirmed the suspicion of some investors that previous earnings figures were exaggerated. Enron's previously reported earnings were reduced by about $600 million over the previous five years, but the correction came too late for many investors who had purchased Enron stock when the reported earnings (and share price) were much higher.

Financing of Partnerships   Enron's partnerships were financed by various creditors such as banks. The loans were to be paid off either from the cash flow generated by the assets transferred to the partnership or from the ultimate sale of the assets. When the partnerships performed poorly, they could not cover their debt payments. In some cases, Enron backed the debt with its stock, but as its stock price plummeted, this collateral no longer covered the debt, setting in motion the downward spiral that ultimately led to the company's bankruptcy.

Arthur Andersen's Audit

Investors and creditors commonly presume that financial statements used to value a firm are accurate when they have been audited by an independent accounting firm. In reality, however, the auditor and the firm do not always have an arm's length relationship. The accounting firm that conducts an audit is paid for the audit and recognizes the potential annuity from repeating this audit every year. In addition, accounting firms that provide auditing services also provide consulting services. Enron hired Arthur Andersen both to serve as its auditor and to provide substantial consulting services. In 2000, Arthur Andersen received $25 million in auditing fees from Enron and an additional $27 million in consulting fees.

Although Arthur Andersen was supposed to be completely independent, it recognized that if it did not sign off on the audit, it would lose this lucrative audit and consulting business. Furthermore, the annual bonus an accounting firm pays to its employees assigned to audit a client may be partially based on their billable hours, which would have been reduced if the firm's relationship with such a large client was severed.

Oversight by Investment Analysts

Even if financial statements are contrived, some investors may presume that investment analysts will detect discrepancies. If analysts simply accept the financial statements, however, rather than questioning their accuracy, the analysts will not necessarily serve as a control mechanism. The difficulties analysts faced in interpreting Enron's financial statements are highlighted by a humorous list created by some Enron employees of why the company restructured its operations so frequently. Reason number 7 was "Because the basic business model is to keep the outside investment analysts so confused that they will not be able to figure out that we do not know what we are doing." The humor now escapes some analysts, as well as some creditors and investors.

Another problem, though, is that like the supposedly independent auditors who hope to generate more business for their accounting firm, investment analysts may encounter a conflict of interest when they attempt to rate firms. As explained in Chapter 10, analysts employed by securities firms have been criticized for assigning very high ratings to firms they cover so that their employer may someday receive some consulting business from those firms.

As an example of what can happen to analysts who are "too critical," consider the experience of an analyst at BNP Paribus who downgraded Enron in August 2001, a few months before the company's financial problems became public. At the time, BNP Paribus was providing some consulting services for Enron. The analyst was demoted and then fired shortly after his downgrade of Enron. To the extent that many other analysts were subjected to a similar conflict of interest, it may explain why they did not downgrade Enron until after its financial problems were publicized. Even if analysts had detected financial problems at Enron, they might have been reluctant to lower their rating.

Market for Corporate Control

As explained earlier, if a firm's managers are running a firm into the ground, a raider has an incentive to purchase that firm at a low price and improve it so that it can be sold someday for a much higher price. However, this theory presumes that the stock price of the firm properly reflects its actual business performance. If the firm's financial statements reflect strong performance, a raider will not necessarily realize that the firm is experiencing financial problems. Moreover, even if the raider is able to detect the problems, it will not be willing to pursue a firm whose value is overpriced by the market because of its contrived financial statements.

When Enron's stock price was high, few raiders could have afforded to acquire it. Once the stock price plummeted, Dynegy considered an acquisition of Enron. Dynegy quickly backed off, however, even though the stock price had fallen 90 percent from its high. Dynegy said it was concerned about problems it found when trying to reconcile Enron's cash position with what its financial statements suggested (among other reasons).

Monitoring by Creditors

Enron relied heavily on creditors for its financing. Since Enron's consolidated financial statements showed a superficially high level of earnings and a low level of debt, it had easy access to credit from a wide variety of creditors. Enron maintained a low cost of capital by using contrived statements that concealed its risk. Its balance sheet showed debt of $13 billion, but by some accounts, the actual amount of its debt was $20 billion. The hidden debt concealed Enron's true degree of financial leverage.

Bank of America and J.P. Morgan Chase each had exposure estimated at $500 million. Many other banks had exposure estimated at more than $100 million. They would not have provided so much credit if they had fully understood Enron's financial situation.

Even the debt rating agencies had difficulty understanding Enron's financial situation. On October 16, 2001, Enron announced $2 billion in writeoffs that would reduce its earnings. At this time, Standard & Poor's, the debt rating agency, affirmed Enron's rating at BBB+, along with its opinion that Enron's balance sheet should improve in the future. Over the next 45 days, S&P became more aware of Enron's financial condition and lowered its rating to junk status.

Many of Enron's creditors attempted to sue Enron once it became clear that the financial statements were misrepresented. By that time, however, Enron's value was depleted, as its price had already fallen to less than $1 per share.

PREVENTION OF ACCOUNTING FRAUD

In response to the accounting fraud at Enron and other firms, regulators have attempted to ensure more accurate financial disclosure by firms. Stock exchanges have instituted new regulations for listed firms. The SEC has been given more resources and power to monitor financial reporting. Perhaps the most important regulatory changes have occurred as a result of the Sarbanes-Oxley Act of 2002. Some of the act's more important provisions were summarized in Chapter 10.

DISCUSSION QUESTIONS

The following discussion questions focus on the use of financial statements in the valuation of firms. They should generate much discussion, especially when accounting and finance students are present. These questions can be used in several ways. They may serve as an assignment on a day that the professor is unable to attend class. They are also useful for small group exercises. For each issue, one group could be randomly selected and asked to present their solution. Then, other students not in that group may suggest alternative answers if they feel that the solution can be improved. Each issue does not necessarily have a perfect solution, so students should be able to present different points of view.

1. Should an accounting firm be required to provide only auditing services or consulting services? Explain your answer. If an accounting firm is allowed to offer only one service, might there be any conflicts of interest due to referrals (and finder's fees)?

2. Should members of Congress be allowed to set regulations on accounting and financial matters while receiving donations from related lobbying groups?

3. What alternative sources of information about a firm should investors rely on if they cannot rely on financial statements?

4. Should investors have confidence in ratings by analysts who are affiliated with securities firms that provide consulting services to firms? Explain.

5. Does an analyst who is employed by a securities firm and is assigned to rate firms face a conflict of interest? What is a solution to this potential conflict?

6. How might a firm's board of directors discourage its managers from attempting to manipulate financial statements to create a temporarily high stock price?

7. How can the compensation of a firm's board of directors be structured so that the board members will not be tempted to allow accounting or other managerial decisions that could cause a superficially high price over a short period?

12
Market Microstructure and Strategies

CHAPTER OBJECTIVES

The specific objectives of this chapter are to:

- describe the common types of stock transactions,

- explain how stock transactions are executed,

- explain the role of electronic communication networks (ECNs) in executing transactions,

- describe the regulation of stock transactions, and

- explain how barriers to international stock transactions have been reduced.

WEB

http://finance.yahoo.com/marketupdate/overview?u?u

Overview of stock market performance.

EXAMPLE

Recently, much attention has been given to **market microstructure**, which is the process by which securities such as stocks are traded. For a stock market to function properly, a structure is needed to facilitate the placing of orders, speed the execution of the trades ordered, and provide equal access to information for all investors.

STOCK MARKET TRANSACTIONS

Some of the more common stock market transactions desired by investors are market and limit orders, margin trades, and short sales. Each of these types of transactions is discussed next.

Placing an Order

To place an order to buy or sell a specific stock, an investor contacts a brokerage firm. Brokerage firms serve as financial intermediaries between buyers and sellers of stock in the secondary market. They receive orders from customers and pass the orders on to the exchange through a telecommunications network. The orders are frequently executed a few seconds later. Full-service brokers offer advice to customers on stocks to buy or sell; discount brokers only execute the transactions desired by customers. For a transaction involving 100 shares, a full-service broker may charge a fee of about 4 percent of the transaction amount versus about 1 percent or less for a discount broker. The larger the transaction amount, the lower the percentage charged by many brokers. Some discount brokers charge a fixed price per trade, such as $30 for any trade that is less than 500 shares.

Investors can contact their brokers to determine the prevailing price of a stock. The broker may provide a bid quote if the investor wants to sell a stock or an ask quote if the investor wants to buy a stock. The investor communicates the order to the broker by specifying (1) the name of the stock, (2) whether to buy or sell that stock, (3) the number of shares to be bought or sold, and (4) whether the order is a market or a limit order. A **market order** to buy or sell a stock means to execute the transaction at the best possible price. A **limit order** differs from a market order in that a limit is placed on the price at which a stock can be purchased or sold.

Stock Z is currently selling for $55 per share. If an investor places a market order to purchase (or sell) the stock, the transaction will be executed at the prevailing price at the time the transaction takes place. For example, the price may have risen to $55.25 per share or declined to $54.75 by the time the transaction occurs.

Alternatively, the investor could place a limit order to purchase Stock Z only at a price of $54.50 or less. The limit order can be placed for the day only or for a longer period. Other

303

investors who wish to sell Stock Z may place limit orders to sell the stock only if it can be sold for $55.25 or more. The advantage of a limit order is that it may enable an investor to obtain the stock at a lower price. The disadvantage is that there is no guarantee the market price will ever reach the limit price established by the investor. ●

Stop-Loss Order A **stop-loss order** is a particular type of limit order. The investor specifies a selling price that is below the current market price of the stock. When the stock price drops to the specified level, the stop-loss order becomes a market order. If the stock price does not reach the specified minimum, the stop-loss order will not be executed. Investors generally place stop-loss orders to either protect gains or limit losses.

EXAMPLE

Paul bought 100 shares of Bostner Corporation one year ago at a price of $50 per share. Today, Bostner stock trades for $60 per share. Paul believes that Bostner stock has additional upside potential and does not want to liquidate his position. Nonetheless, he would like to make sure that he realizes at least a 10 percent gain from the stock transaction. Consequently, he places a stop-loss order with a price of $55. If the stock price drops to $55, the stop-loss order will convert to a market order, and Paul will receive the prevailing market price at that time, which will be about $55. If Paul receives exactly $55, his gain from the transaction would be 100 shares × ($55 − $50) = $500. If the price of Bostner stock keeps increasing, the stop-loss order will never be executed. ●

Stop-Buy Order A **stop-buy order** is another type of limit order. In this case, the investor specifies a purchase price that is above the current market price. When the stock price rises to the specified level, the stop-buy order becomes a market order. If the stock price does not reach the specified maximum, the stop-buy order will not be executed.

EXAMPLE

Karen would like to invest in the stock of Quan Company, but only if there is some evidence that stock market participants are demanding that stock. The stock is currently priced at $12. She places a stop-buy order at $14 per share, so if demand for Quan stock is sufficient to push the price to $14, she will purchase the stock. If the price remains below $14, her order will not be executed. ●

Placing an Order Online The mechanics of placing an order have changed substantially in recent years. Now many Internet brokers accept orders online, provide real-time quotes, and provide access to information about firms. The online brokerage business has taken some business away from the full-service and even discount brokerages, but the traditional brokerage firms have responded by offering online services. Many firms that previously required investors to phone in their orders now allow investors to transmit their orders online for a lower commission per trade. Some full-service brokers allow their clients online access to information about any stock of interest.

Some of the more popular online brokerage firms include TD Ameritrade (www .tdameritrade.com), Charles Schwab (www.schwab.com), and E*Trade (www.etrade .com). The typical commission per trade conducted by online brokerage firms is between $5 and $15. Usually, a minimum balance of between $1,000 and $5,000 is required to open an account.

Some online brokerage services offer zero-commission trades. However, investors must maintain a certain amount of funds in their brokerage accounts, and the interest rate paid on these funds is usually low. Thus, the brokerage firms can still profit from these no-commission trades because they can use the funds in the accounts to earn a higher return than they pay the investors as interest. Investors who make frequent trades may benefit from very low or zero commissions, but they should still compare the interest rate earned on account balances and other features before selecting an online brokerage service.

Margin Trading

When investors place an order, they may consider purchasing the stock on margin; in that case, they use cash along with funds borrowed from their broker to make the purchase. The Federal Reserve imposes **margin requirements,** which represent the minimum proportion of funds that must be covered with cash. This limits the proportion of funds that may be borrowed from the brokerage firm to make the investment. Margin requirements were first imposed in 1934, following a period of volatile market swings, to discourage excessive speculation and ensure greater stability. Currently, at least 50 percent of an investor's invested funds must be paid in cash. Margin requirements are intended to ensure that investors can cover their position if the value of their investment declines over time. Thus, with margin requirements, a major decline in stock prices is less likely to cause defaults on loans from brokers and therefore will be less damaging to the financial system.

To purchase stock on margin, investors must establish an account (called a **margin account**) with their broker. Their initial deposit of cash is referred to as the **initial margin.** To meet the requirements imposed by the Federal Reserve, the initial margin must be at least 50 percent of the total investment (although some brokerage firms impose a higher minimum). The brokerage firm can provide financing for the remainder of the stock investment, and the stock serves as collateral. Over time, the market value of the stock will change. Investors are subject to a **maintenance margin,** which is the minimum proportion of equity that an investor must maintain in the account as a proportion of the market value of the stock. The investor's equity position represents what the stock is worth to the investor after paying off the loan from the broker. The New York Stock Exchange (NYSE) and Nasdaq have set the minimum maintenance margin at 25 percent, but some brokerage firms require a higher minimum. If the investor's equity position falls below the maintenance margin, the investor will receive a **margin call** from the brokerage firm and will have to deposit cash to the account in order to boost the equity.

EXAMPLE

Five days ago, Trish purchased 100 shares of Rimax stock at $60 per share through Ohio Brokerage Firm. Thus, the shares were valued at $6,000. Ohio Brokerage required an initial margin of 50 percent. Trish used $3,000 cash as her equity investment and borrowed the remaining $3,000 from Ohio Brokerage to purchase the stock. Ohio Brokerage requires a maintenance margin of 30 percent. Two days later, the price of Rimax stock declined to $50 per share, so the total value of her shares was $5,000. Since Trish still owed the brokerage firm $3,000, her equity position was equal to $2,000 (computed as the market value of the stock minus the $3,000 that is still owed to the broker). The equity position represented 40 percent of the market value of the stock (computed as $2,000/$5,000), which was still above the maintenance margin of 30 percent. Today, the stock price declines to $40 per share, so the market value of the stock is $4,000. Now Trish's equity position is $1,000 (computed as $4,000 – $3,000). This position represents 25 percent of the market value of the stock (computed as $l,000/$4,000). Now this position is below the 30 percent maintenance margin required by Ohio Brokerage. Consequently, Ohio Brokerage calls Trish and informs her that she must deposit sufficient cash to her account to raise her equity position to at least 30 percent of the market value of the stock. ●

WEB

www.bloomberg.com
Discloses today's return for stocks contained in major stock indexes.

Impact on Returns   The return on a stock is affected by the proportion of the investment that is from borrowed funds. Over short-term periods, the return on stocks (*R*) purchased on margin can be estimated as follows:

$$R = \frac{SP - INV - LOAN + D}{INV}$$

where
SP = selling price of stock
INV = initial investment by investor, not including borrowed funds
$LOAN$ = loan payments on borrowed funds, including both principal and interest
D = dividend payments

EXAMPLE

Consider a stock priced at $40 that pays an annual dividend of $1 per share. An investor purchases the stock on margin, paying $20 per share and borrowing the remainder from the brokerage firm at 10 percent annual interest. If, after one year, the stock is sold at a price of $60 per share, the return on the stock is

$$R = \frac{\$60 - \$20 - \$22 + \$1}{\$20}$$

$$= \frac{\$19}{\$20}$$

$$= 95\%$$

In this example, the stock return (including the dividend) would have been 52.5 percent if the investor had used only personal funds rather than borrowing funds. This illustrates how the use of borrowed funds can magnify the returns on an investment.

Any losses are also magnified, however, when borrowed funds are used to invest in stocks. Reconsider the previous example and assume that the stock is sold at a price of $30 per share (instead of $60) at the end of the year. If the investor did not use any borrowed funds when purchasing the stock for $40 per share at the beginning of the year, the return on this investment would be

$$R = \frac{\$30 - \$40 - \$0 + \$1}{\$40}$$

$$= -22.5\%$$

However, if the investor had purchased the stock on margin at the beginning of the year, paying $20 per share and borrowing the remainder from the brokerage firm at 10 percent annual interest, the return over the year would be

$$R = \frac{\$30 - \$20 - \$22 + \$1}{\$20}$$

$$= -55\%$$

●

As these examples illustrate, purchasing stock on margin not only increases the potential return from investing in stock but may magnify the potential losses as well.

Margin Calls As explained earlier, when an investor's equity position falls below the maintenance margin, the investor receives a margin call from the broker, which means that the investor will have to provide more collateral (more cash or stocks) or sell the stock. Because of the potential for margin calls, a large volume of margin lending exposes the stock markets to a potential crisis. A major downturn in the market could result in many margin calls, some of which may force investors to sell their stock holdings if they do not have the cash to build their maintenance margin. Such a response results in more sales of stocks, additional downward pressure on stock prices, and additional margin calls. When the market plummeted during the credit crisis in 2008, investors who did not have cash available to respond to margin calls sold their stock, putting additional downward pressure on stock prices.

Short Selling

In a **short sale,** investors place an order to sell a stock that they do not own. They sell a stock short (or "short the stock") when they anticipate that its price will decline. When they sell short, they are essentially borrowing the stock from another investor and will ultimately have to return that stock to the investor from whom they borrowed it. The short-sellers borrow the stock through a brokerage firm, which facilitates the process. The investors who own the stock are not affected when their shares are borrowed, and are not even aware that their shares were borrowed.

If the price of the stock declines by the time the short-sellers purchase it in the market (to return to the investor from whom they borrowed), the short-sellers earn the difference between the price at which they initially sold the stock versus the price they paid to obtain the stock. Short-sellers must make payments to the investor from whom the stock was borrowed to cover the dividend payments that the investor would have received if the stock had not been borrowed. The short-seller's profit is the difference between the original selling price and the price paid for the stock, after subtracting any dividend payments made. The risk of a short sale is that the stock price may increase over time, forcing the short-seller to pay a higher price for the stock than the price at which it was initially sold.

EXAMPLE

On May 5, the market value of Vizer Company stock was $70 per share. Ed conducted an analysis of Vizer stock and concluded that the price should be much lower. He called his broker and placed an order to sell 100 shares of Vizer stock. Since he did not have shares of Vizer to sell, this transaction was a short sale. Vizer stock does not pay dividends, so Ed did not have to cover dividend payments for the stock that his brokerage firm borrowed and sold for him. The sale of the stock resulted in proceeds of $7,000, which he placed in his account at the brokerage firm. During the next two months, the price of Vizer stock declined. On July 18, Ed placed an order through his brokerage firm to purchase 100 shares of Vizer stock and offset his short position. The market value at the time was $60, so he paid $6,000 for the shares. Thus, Ed earned $1,000 from his short position. This example ignores transaction costs associated with the short sale.

The risk from taking a short position is that the stock's price may rise instead of decline as expected. If the price had increased after Ed created the short position, his purchase price would have been higher than his selling price. In this case, Ed would have incurred a loss on the short position. ●

Measuring the Short Position of a Stock
One measure of the degree of short positions is the ratio of the number of shares that are currently sold short divided by the total number of shares outstanding. For many stocks, this measure is between .5 and 2 percent. A relatively high percentage (such as 3 percent) suggests a large amount of short positions in the market, which implies that a relatively large number of investors expect the stock's price to decline.

Some financial publications disclose the level of short sales for stocks with the short interest ratio, which is the number of shares that are currently sold short divided by the average daily trading volume over a recent period. The higher the ratio, the higher the level of short sales. A short interest ratio of 2.0 for a particular stock indicates that the number of shares currently sold short is two times the number of shares traded per day, on average. A short interest ratio of 20 or more reflects an unusually high level of short sales, indicating that many investors believe that the stock price is currently overvalued. Some stocks have had short interest ratios exceeding 100 at a particular point in time.

The short interest ratio is also measured for the market to determine the level of short sales for the market overall. A high short interest ratio for the market indicates a high level of short selling activity in the market. The largest short positions are periodically disclosed in *The Wall Street Journal*. For each firm with a large short position, the number of shares sold short is disclosed and compared to the corresponding number a month earlier. The change in the overall short position by investors from the previous month is also shown.

Using a Stop-Buy Order to Offset Short Selling
Investors who have established a short position commonly use a stop-buy order to limit their losses.

EXAMPLE

A year ago, Mary sold short 200 shares of Patronum Corporation stock for $70 per share. Patronum's stock currently trades for $80 a share. Consequently, Mary currently has an unrealized loss on the short sale, but she believes that Patronum stock will drop below $70 in the near future. She is unwilling to accept a loss of more than $15 per share on the transaction. Consequently, she places a stop-buy order for 200 shares with a specified purchase price of $85 per share. If Patronum stock increases to $85 per share, the stop-buy order becomes a market order, and Mary will pay approximately $85 per share. If Patronum stock does not increase to $85 per share, the stop-buy order will never be executed. ●

Concerns about Short Selling When the credit crisis intensified in 2008, hedge funds and other investors took large short positions on many stocks, especially those of financial institutions. Some critics argued that the large short sales placed additional downward pressure on prices and created paranoia in the stock market. Such fear could make stock prices decline to a greater degree, which would be beneficial to the short-sellers.

EXAMPLE

Just after the failure of the securities firm Lehman Brothers in September 2008, there were rumors that Morgan Stanley (another securities firm) was unable to obtain financing and was about to fail. During the three-day period from September 15 to 17, 2008, the number of Morgan Stanley shares sold short increased from less than 5 million shares to about 39 million shares. Many of these short sales may have been due to this unfounded rumor. During this three-day period, the stock price of Morgan Stanley declined by one-third. Arguably, much of the decline in the stock price was due to the massive short selling, which was likely triggered by the rumor. ●

Restrictions on Short Selling Following the massive short sales of Morgan Stanley, the Securities and Exchange Commission (SEC) temporarily protected more than 800 firms from short sales. For the most part, the protected firms were financial institutions and other companies that were exposed to the credit crisis, and the SEC was attempting to limit the adverse effect that short sales might have on the stock prices of these firms. The SEC also mandated that traders had to borrow the stock before they could execute a short sale. In some cases, traders were using loopholes in the short sale rules to short stock without borrowing it. The SEC delegated authority to the stock exchanges to identify other firms that should be protected from short sales. Some other countries including Australia, Taiwan, and the Netherlands subsequently instituted their own short selling regulations.

Many critics argued that these restrictions did not affect the general behavior of the speculators who were engaging in short sales. Some short-sellers were focusing on financial institutions that had very little equity and used mostly borrowed funds (financial leverage) to generate large returns on their equity. These short-sellers might argue that the stock prices of these financial institutions were declining not because of the short selling, but because regulators failed to ensure that these financial institutions would have sufficient capital backing their business. Furthermore, even though short sales were banned, speculators have other methods of betting against a stock (such as put options on stock) that could possibly place downward pressure on a stock's price. In October 2008, the ban on short selling was eliminated in the United States, as regulators determined that the ban was not necessarily stabilizing the values of stocks.

However, in 2008 and 2009, the Securities and Exchange Commission imposed new restrictions on short selling. In October 2008, it required that short-sellers borrow and deliver the shares to the buyers within three days. This rule is important because there were many cases in which brokerage firms were allowing speculators to engage in *naked shorting*, whereby they sell a stock short without first borrowing the stock. Therefore, speculators were able to take larger short positions than would have been possible if they were required to first borrow the shares that they were selling, which resulted in more downward pressure on the stock's prices. This new rule by the SEC was a stronger version of an SEC rule implemented to prevent naked short selling in 2005 (called Regulation SHO), but the 2005 rule only applied to specific stocks and was not strictly enforced.

In 2009, the SEC also reinstated the uptick rule (which was previously eliminated in 2007), requiring that speculators can only take a short position after the stock price increases. This rule is intended to prevent short selling in response to a stock's continuous downward price momentum.

HOW STOCK TRANSACTIONS ARE EXECUTED

Transactions on the stock exchanges and the Nasdaq are facilitated by floor brokers, specialists, and market-makers.

Floor Brokers

Floor brokers are situated on the floor of a stock exchange. There are hundreds of computer booths along the perimeter of the trading floor, where floor brokers receive orders from brokerage firms. The floor brokers then fulfill and execute those orders.

EXAMPLE

Bryan Adams calls his broker at Zepellin Securities, where he has a brokerage account, and requests the purchase of 1,000 shares of Clapton, Inc. stock, which is traded on the NYSE. The broker at Zepellin communicates this information to the NYSE trading floor. A floor broker who may be an employee of Zepellin or some other brokerage firm receives the order at a booth and goes to a specific trading post where Clapton stock is traded. There are 20 trading posts on the NYSE, and a different set of stocks is traded at each trading post. The floor broker communicates the desire to purchase 1,000 shares of Clapton stock at a specific price. Other floor brokers who have orders to sell Clapton stock either communicate their willingness to accept the bid or signal the "ask" price at which they would be willing to sell the shares. If the floor brokers can agree on a price, a transaction is executed. The transaction is recorded and transmitted to the tape display. Bryan will likely receive a message from the broker, indicating that the trade was executed, and will receive confirmation in the mail within three days. Bryan provides payment to his brokerage firm within three days. ●

Specialists

Specialists can serve a broker function on stock exchanges by matching up buy and sell orders. They gain from accommodating these orders because their bid and ask prices differ. In addition, they also take positions in specific stocks to which they are assigned.

There are 443 specialists on the NYSE, and each one is typically assigned five to eight stocks. Most of them are employed by one of seven specialist firms. The specialists are required to signal to floor brokers if they have unfilled orders.

Specialists have access to the book (list) of market and limit orders. At the beginning of each day, they set their bid and ask prices to reflect a balance between buy and sell orders. The bid price is the price at which the specialist would purchase the stock; the ask price is the price at which the specialist would sell the stock.

EXAMPLE

The price of Mackin Company stock closed at $32 last night. After the market closed, Mackin announced that it had been awarded a patent on a new invention. Many investors placed orders to buy the stock after hearing this news. Before the market opened on the following morning, the specialist assessed the buy and sell orders for Mackin stock. At a price of $32, there was an imbalance because the demand for the shares was much larger than the supply of shares for sale. The specialist decided that a proper equilibrium price would be about $33 per share. At that price, the quantity of Mackin shares for sale would be equal to the quantity of shares demanded. That is, the higher price would eliminate a portion of the demand (because some investors would be unwilling to pay that price), thereby allowing supply and demand to be equal. He established a bid price of $33.00 and an ask price of $33.02. ●

Making a Market Specialists are required to "make a market" in the stocks that they are assigned. This role is commonly misunderstood. Making a market implies that the specialists stand ready to buy or sell the stocks that they are assigned if no other investors are willing to participate. Making a market does not mean that specialists are offsetting all orders by taking the opposite side of every transaction. In fact, many transactions occur without a specialist's involvement. Specialists participate in about 10 percent of the value of all shares traded; the other transactions are completed on the exchange without their participation.

Making a market does not mean that specialists must prevent a stock price from falling. A large amount of sell orders and a small amount of buy orders for a particular stock will naturally result in a decline in the stock price. Specialists may buy some shares to partially offset this imbalance between supply and demand, but they are buying the shares at the discounted price that resulted from the imbalance. They may sell some shares to partially offset an imbalance when demand exceeds supply, but they are selling the shares at the higher price that resulted from the imbalance. Thus, although specialists incur risk when they take positions on any given day, they commonly earn substantial profits from their positions on average. Since they have access to the book of limit orders on the buy side and sell side, they are sometimes said to be involved in a poker game in which only they can see everyone's cards.

Furthermore, specialists can set the spread to reflect their preferences. If they wish to avoid investing in a stock they are assigned at a particular point in time, they can widen the spread so that their bid price is substantially below the ask price. Under these circumstances, there will be a more favorable bid price for the stock than their bid price, and they can simply serve the broker function by matching buy and sell orders.

EXAMPLE

The specialist for the stock of Closet, Inc. is aware that the equilibrium price is currently $39.99 per share. She notices many limit orders by institutional investors to sell shares of Closet stock at $40 per share. Since she has a large inventory of Closet stock and is concerned because the limit orders suggest possible downward pressure on the price, she decides to sell a large block of her own shares of Closet stock at $39.99. This trade will take priority over the other orders because it is at a slightly lower price. Consequently, the specialist is able to sell her shares ahead of other investors who want to sell their shares. This act, which is referred to as "front-running" (or "penny-jumping"), may even prevent the orders of other investors from being executed if the price reverses as a result. In this example, the specialist who sold a block of shares at $39.99 could cause downward price momentum. Some of the institutional investors who placed limit orders to sell at $40 may have to revise their orders to specify a new lower price in order to sell their shares. They might have been able to sell their shares at $40 if the specialist had not traded in front of them. ●

Specialists may counter that the example shows how they "provide price improvement." In the example, the specialist sold shares at a penny per share less than other investors who were willing to sell their shares. However, the specialist's trade jumped in front of other potential sellers. Although the specialists may argue that they "make a market" for the security, a counterargument is that the investors make the market and specialists only use it to their advantage. The special priority of the specialists is enforced by a "trade-through rule" established by the SEC in 1975, which requires that an order for NYSE-listed stocks must be executed on the exchange that offers the best price for the investor. The intention of the rule was to benefit investors, but it has allowed specialists to have priority in trading, which can place investors at a disadvantage.

Many institutional investors prefer to use automated trading to circumvent the specialists because they believe their orders are handled faster and more fairly. The NYSE's SuperDot system uses automated trading and now accounts for 99 percent of the trading on the NYSE. The "trade-through rule" allows specialists to intervene in place of the SuperDot system or other automated systems (discussed shortly). In the past, the NYSE was slow to respond to the concerns of institutional investors. Given that the specialists own about one-third of the seats on the NYSE and that the NYSE is self-regulated, this is not surprising.

In the 2001–2003 period, the NYSE's regulatory division frequently ignored specialists' violations. Finally, the NYSE's weak self-regulatory efforts and the trading violations prompted the SEC to intervene. In 2004, the SEC investigated several specialist firms for various illegal activities. In addition, the SEC allowed investors to circumvent the trade-through rule. Consequently, trades should occur more quickly, and investors may have a better chance of having their trades executed before the price moves outside the range at which they are willing to buy or sell. They are also more likely to complete their trade without being subjected to front-running by specialists.

Market-Makers on the Nasdaq Transactions in the Nasdaq market are facilitated by so-called **market-makers,** who stand ready to buy specific stocks in response to customer orders made through a telecommunications network. They benefit from the difference (spread) between the bid and ask prices. They also can take positions in stocks. Thus, market-makers serve the Nasdaq market in a manner similar to the specialists on the NYSE. Some market-makers make a market in a few stocks, while others make a market for many stocks. For each stock that is traded in the Nasdaq market, there are 12 market-makers on average. However, stocks that are more actively traded tend to have a larger number of market-makers.

Market-makers take positions to capitalize on the discrepancy between the prevailing stock price and their own valuation of the stock. When many uninformed investors take buy or sell positions that push a stock's price away from its fundamental value, the stock price is distorted as a result of the "noise" caused by the uninformed investors (called **"noise traders"**). Market-makers may take the opposite position of the uninformed investors and therefore stand to benefit if their expectations are correct.

Brokers make the decision on the route by which an order is executed, meaning that they determine whether the order will be filled by a specific market-maker. The spread quoted for a given stock may vary among market-makers. Therefore, the manner by which the trade is routed by the broker can affect the size of the spread. Some market-makers compensate brokers for orders routed to them. So, while a brokerage firm may charge a customer only $10 for a trade, it may also receive a payment from the market-maker. The market-maker may use a wider spread so that it can offer such a payment to the broker. The point is that some customers may pay only $10 for a buy order to be executed, but the order is executed at a price that is relatively high because the market-maker charged a large spread. Customers should attempt to compare not only the fee brokers charge for a trade, but also the spread quoted by the market-maker selected by the brokerage firm. Investors do not have direct control over the routing process, but they can at least select a broker that uses the type of routing process that they prefer. The market is not sufficiently transparent for the routing process to be monitored, but technology may soon allow customers to more easily monitor the routing and the quoted spreads.

Some brokers own market-maker firms; for example, Charles Schwab & Co. owns Mayer & Schweitzer. In this case, investors who are told that they will be charged a very small commission may also incur a transaction fee through the market-maker.

The Spread on Stock Transactions

When investors place an order, they are quoted an ask price, or the price that the broker is asking for that stock. There is also a bid price, or the price at which the broker would purchase the stock. The spread is the difference between the ask price and the bid price and is commonly measured as a percentage of the ask price.

EXAMPLE Boletto Company stock is quoted by a broker as bid $39.80, ask $40.00. The bid-ask spread is

$$\text{Spread} = \frac{\$40.00 - \$39.80}{\$40.00}$$

$$= .5\%$$

This spread of .5 percent implies that if investors purchased the stock and then immediately sold it back before market prices changed, they would incur a cost of .5 percent of their investment for the round-trip transaction. ●

The transaction cost due to the spread is separate from the commission charged by the broker. The spread has declined substantially over time due to more efficient methods of executing orders and increased competition from electronic communications networks.

The spread is influenced by the following factors:

$$\text{Spread} = f(\underset{+}{\text{Order Costs}},\ \underset{+}{\text{Inventory Costs}},\ \underset{-}{\text{Competition}},\ \underset{-}{\text{Volume}},\ \underset{+}{\text{Risk}})$$

Order Costs   Order costs are the costs of processing orders, including clearing costs and the costs of recording transactions.

Inventory Costs   Inventory costs include the cost of maintaining an inventory of a particular stock. There is an opportunity cost because the funds could have been used for some other purpose. If interest rates are relatively high, the opportunity cost of holding an inventory should be relatively high. The higher the inventory costs, the larger the spread that will be established to cover these costs.

Competition   The specialist for a particular stock on the NYSE faces competition from other electronic markets where the stock can be traded. For stocks traded in the Nasdaq market, having multiple market-makers promotes competition. When more market-makers are competing to sell a particular stock, the spread is likely to be smaller.

Volume   Stocks that are more liquid have less chance of experiencing an abrupt change in price. Those stocks that have a large trading volume are more liquid because there is a sufficient number of buyers and sellers at any time. This liquidity makes it easier to sell a stock at any point in time and therefore reduces the risk of a sudden decline in the stock's price.

Risk   If the firm represented by a stock has relatively risky operations, its stock price is normally more volatile over time. Thus, the specialist or market-maker is subject to more risk from holding an inventory in this type of stock and will set a higher spread as a result.

At a given point in time, the spread can vary among stocks. The specialists or market-makers who make a market for a particular stock are exposed to the risk that the stock's price could change abruptly in the secondary market and reduce the value of their position in that stock. Thus, any factors that affect this type of risk to a specialist or a market-maker of a stock can affect the spread of that stock at a given point in time.

Electronic Communication Networks (ECNs)

Electronic communication networks (ECNs) are automated systems for disclosing and sometimes executing stock trades. They were created in the mid-1990s to publicly display buy and sell orders of stock. They were adapted to facilitate the execution of orders and normally service institutional rather than individual investors. In 1997, the SEC allowed ECNs complete access to orders placed in the Nasdaq market. The SEC requires that any quote provided by a market-maker be made available to all market participants. This eliminated the practice of providing more favorable quotes exclusively to proprietary clients. It also resulted in significantly lower spreads between the bid and ask prices quoted on the Nasdaq. ECNs are appealing to investors because they may allow for more efficient execution of trades. ECNs in aggregate now account for more than 30 percent of the total trading volume on the Nasdaq. They also execute a small proportion of all transactions on the NYSE.

Some ECNs focus on market orders. They receive orders and route them through various networks searching for the best price. Other ECNs receive limit orders and electronically match them up with other orders that are still not fulfilled. Exhibit 12.1 shows an example of an ECN book at a given point in time. The book lists the limit buy orders and limit sell orders that are currently not fulfilled. When a new limit order matches an existing order, the transaction is immediately executed, and the matching order is removed from the book. If the new limit order cannot immediately be matched to an existing order on the ECN book, it is added to the book. An ECN can execute a transaction in an average time of about 2 seconds.

EXAMPLE

Assume that the ECN book shown in Exhibit 12.1 is the book for a particular stock and that a new limit order is placed to sell 300 shares of that stock at a price of no less than $32.68. This order can be matched by the order to buy 300 shares at a bid price of $32.68. Upon the execution of this trade, the order on the ECN book to buy 300 shares at a bid price of $32.68 is removed. Assume now that a new limit order is placed to purchase 1,400 shares at a price of no more than $32.80. This order is matched up with the order to sell 400 shares at an ask price of $32.78 and the order to sell 1,000 shares at $32.80. Then those orders are removed from the ECN book because they have been fulfilled. ●

Several ECNs serve the stock market. In 2002, Island, an ECN that facilitates about 20 percent of the total Nasdaq trading volume per day, merged with Instinet, another ECN that commonly facilitates daily stock transactions requested by U.S. financial institutions after the U.S. exchanges are closed. Instinet now executes many transactions for Nasdaq stocks and was acquired by Nasdaq in 2005.

Archipelago, another ECN, was created in 1996 to execute trades of Nasdaq and NYSE stocks electronically. Thus, it commonly competed against the NYSE for orders to trade stocks on the NYSE. Archipelago went public in 2004, and in 2006, it was acquired by the NYSE. The NYSE recognized that its floor trading was not as efficient as an ECN and that it would ultimately need a large ECN to compete in facilitating stock trades. Rather than build a large ECN, it acquired one (now referred to as NYSE Arca) and thus improved its efficiency in executing orders. The NYSE Arca allows all buyers and sellers, including individual investors, brokers, and market-makers, to interact electronically.

Exhibit 12.1 Example of an ECN Book at a Given Point in Time

BID OR ASK?	SHARES	PRICE
Bid	500	$32.50
Bid	300	$32.50
Bid	400	$32.56
Bid	1,000	$32.60
Bid	400	$32.64
Bid	1,200	$32.64
Bid	300	$32.68
Ask	400	$32.78
Ask	1,000	$32.80
Ask	300	$32.84
Ask	500	$32.84
Ask	600	$32.88

ECNs have historically been subjected to regulation by the National Association of Securities Dealers, which includes the market-makers with which the ECNs compete. Consequently, some ECNs have applied to establish their own stock exchanges so that they will not be regulated by their competitors.

Interaction between Direct Access Brokers and ECNs A **direct access broker** is a trading platform on a computer website that allows investors to trade stocks without the use of a broker. The website itself serves as the broker and interacts with ECNs that can execute the trade. Some of the more popular direct access brokers include a division of Charles Schwab (www.schwab.com), Interactive Brokers (www.interactivebrokers.com), and Noble-Trading (www.nobletrading.com). Each of these websites offers a variety of trading platforms, which range from those that are easier to use and offer less information to those that are more complex but provide more information. A monthly fee is usually charged for access to a trading platform; the fee is higher for platforms that offer more information. To use a direct access broker, investors must meet certain requirements, such as maintaining liquid securities valued at more than $50,000. The advantage of a direct access broker is that investors interested in trading a particular stock can monitor the supply of shares for sale at various prices and the demand for shares at various prices on various ECNs. Thus, the market becomes more transparent because investors can visualize the overall supply and demand conditions at various possible prices. Investors can use this information to determine how stock prices may change in the near future.

The use of direct access brokers and ECNs allows computers to match buyers and sellers without relying on the floor brokers or traders on stock exchanges. The trend is toward a floorless exchange where all trades will be executed in cyberspace, and orders will be submitted and confirmed through automated systems. As this technology is implemented across countries, it may ultimately create a single global floorless exchange where investors can easily trade any security in any country by submitting requests from a personal computer.

Program Trading

A common form of computerized trading is **program trading**, which the NYSE defines as the simultaneous buying and selling of a portfolio of at least 15 different stocks that are in the S&P 500 index. This is a narrow definition, as the term is sometimes used in other contexts. The most common program traders are large securities firms. They conduct the trades for their own accounts or for other institutional investors such as pension funds, mutual funds, and insurance companies. The term *program* refers to the use of computers in what is known as the Designated Order Turnaround (DOT) system at the NYSE, which allows traders to send orders to many trading posts at the exchange.

Program trading is commonly used to reduce the susceptibility of a stock portfolio to stock market movements. For example, in one form of program trading, numerous stocks that have become "overpriced" (based on a particular model used to value those stocks) are sold. Program trading can also involve the purchase of numerous stocks that have become "underpriced."

Program trading can be combined with the trading of stock index futures to create **portfolio insurance.** With this strategy, the investor uses futures or options contracts on a stock index. Thus, a decline in the market would result in a gain on the futures or options position, which can offset the reduced market value of the stock portfolio.

Impact of Program Trading on Stock Volatility Program trading is often cited as the reason for a decline or rise in the stock market. The underlying reason for a large amount of program trading, however, is that institutional investors believe that numerous stocks are over- or undervalued. Although program trading can cause share prices to reach a new equilibrium more rapidly, that does not necessarily imply that it causes more volatility in the stock market. A study by Furbush[1] examined the relationship between the intensity of program trading and stock price volatility. Furbush assessed five-minute intervals of stock index prices and stock index futures prices during the week of the October 1987 crash when the Dow Jones Industrial Average declined by more than 20 percent on one day. He found that greater declines in stock prices were not systematically associated with more intense program trading.

A study by Roll[2] compared the magnitude of the October 1987 crash for markets using program trading versus markets in other countries. Roll found that the average share price decline of markets using program trading averaged 21 percent versus a 28 percent decline for other countries. Thus, it does not appear that program trading caused more pronounced losses during the crash.

Some critics have also suggested that program trading instigated the 1987 crash. Roll found, however, that many Asian stock markets where program trading did not exist plunged several hours before the opening of the U.S. market on Black Monday (October 19, 1987).

Collars Applied to Program Trading   Since there is some concern that program trading can cause abrupt stock price movements and therefore cause more market volatility, the NYSE has implemented collars (sometimes referred to as "curbs"), which restrict program trading when the Dow Jones Industrial Average changes by 2 percent from the closing index on the previous trading day. Specifically, when the collars are imposed, program trading that reflects a sell order is allowed only when the last movement in the stock's price was up (an "uptick"). Program trading that reflects a buy order is allowed only when the last movement in the stock's price was down (a "downtick"). These restrictions are intended to prevent program trading from adding momentum to the prevailing direction of stock price movements on a day when stock prices have already moved substantially from the previous closing level. The collars allow program trading on days when it will exert price pressure in the opposite direction of the last price movement so that it may have a stabilizing effect on the market.

REGULATION OF STOCK TRADING

Regulation of stock markets is necessary to ensure that investors are treated fairly. Without regulation, there would be more trading abuses that would discourage many investors from participating in the market. Stock trading is regulated by the individual exchanges and by the SEC. The **Securities Act of 1933** and the **Securities Exchange Act of 1934** were enacted to prevent unfair or unethical trading practices on the security exchanges. As a result of the 1934 act, stock exchanges were empowered and expected to discipline individuals or firms that violate regulations imposed by the exchange. The NYSE states that every transaction made at the exchange is under surveillance. The NYSE uses a computerized system to detect unusual trading of any particular stock that is traded on the exchange. It also employs personnel who investigate any abnormal price or trading volume of a particular stock or unusual trading practices of individuals.

In 2002, the NYSE issued a regulation requiring its listed firms to have a majority of independent directors (not employees of the firm) on their respective boards of directors. This requirement was intended to reduce directors' potential conflicts of interests so that they will concentrate on ensuring that the firm's management is focused on maximizing the stock's value for shareholders.

WEB

www.nyse.com
Regulations imposed on firms that are listed on the NYSE.

---

[1]Dean Furbush, "Program Trading and Price Movement: Evidence from the October 1987 Market Crash," *Financial Management* (Autumn 1989): 68–83.
[2]Richard Roll, "The International Crash of October 1987," *Financial Analysts Journal* (October 1988): 19–35.

Ironically, the NYSE was criticized in 2003 for not abiding by some of the governance guidelines that it was imposing on other firms. In August 2003, the financial media reported that Richard Grasso, chairman of the NYSE, would receive $140 million in deferred compensation. The board members involved in determining Grasso's compensation were criticized for setting a bad example for the firms listed on the exchange. Grasso's annual salary and bonus were much higher than compensation that the chief executive officers of other firms in the financial services industry were receiving.

Circuit Breakers

Stock exchanges can impose **circuit breakers,** which are restrictions on trading when stock prices or a stock index reaches a specified threshold level. In general, circuit breakers are intended to temporarily stop the trading of stocks in response to a very large decline in stock prices within a single day. They may prevent an initial pronounced stock market decline from causing panic selling in the market. More information on circuit breakers is available at www.sec.gov/answers/circuit.htm.

Trading Halts

Stock exchanges may impose trading halts on particular stocks when they believe market participants need more time to receive and absorb material information that could affect the value of a stock. They have imposed trading halts on stocks that are associated with mergers, earnings reports, lawsuits, and other news. A trading halt does not prevent a stock from experiencing a loss in response to news. Instead, the purpose of the halt is to ensure that the market has complete information before trading on the news. A trading halt may last for just a few minutes, or for several hours, or even for several days. Once the stock exchange believes that the market has complete information, it will allow trading to resume. At that time, the dealers at the stock exchange will quote bid and ask prices, based on their view of what the market demand and supply conditions for the stock will be.

Trading halts are intended to reduce stock price volatility, as the market price is adjusted by market forces in response to news. Thus, the halts can prevent excessive optimism or pessimism about a stock by restricting trading until the news about the firm is completely and widely disseminated to the market. However, some critics believe that the trading halts slow the inevitable adjustment in the stock's price to the news. In general, research has found that the stock volatility is relatively high after a halt is lifted, but that the volatility subsides over the next few days.

Securities and Exchange Commission (SEC)

The Securities Act of 1933 and the Securities Exchange Act of 1934 gave the Securities and Exchange Commission authority to monitor the exchanges and required listed companies to file a registration statement and financial reports with the SEC and the exchanges. In general, the SEC attempts to protect investors by ensuring full disclosure of pertinent information that could affect the values of securities. In particular, some of the more relevant SEC regulations require the following:

• Firms must publicly disclose all information about themselves that could affect the value of their securities.
• Employees of firms may take positions in their own firm's securities only during periods when they do not know of inside information that will affect the value of the firm once the information becomes public.
• Participants in security markets who facilitate trades must work in a fair and orderly manner.

The regulations prevent abuses that would give someone an unfair advantage over other investors and therefore could reduce the willingness of investors to invest in security markets. SEC regulations allow all investors to have the same access to public information. The SEC's focus is on sufficient disclosure rather than on accuracy, as it relies on auditors to certify that the financial statements are accurate.

Structure of the SEC   The SEC is composed of five commissioners appointed by the president of the United States and confirmed by the Senate. Each commissioner serves a five-year term. The terms are staggered so that each year one commissioner's term ends and a new appointee is added. The president also selects one of the five commissioners to chair the commission.

The commissioners meet to assess whether existing regulations are successfully preventing abuses and to revise the regulations as needed. Specific staff members of the SEC may be assigned to develop a proposal for a new regulation to prevent a particular abuse that is occurring. When the commission adopts new regulations, they are distributed to the public for feedback before final approval. Some of the more critical proposals are subject to congressional review before final approval.

Key Divisions of the SEC   The SEC has several important divisions that attempt to ensure a fair and orderly stock market. The Division of Corporate Finance reviews the registration statement filed when a firm goes public, corporate filings for annual and quarterly reports, and proxy statements that involve voting for board members or other corporate issues. The Division of Market Regulation requires the orderly disclosure of securities trades by various organizations that facilitate the trading of securities. The Division of Enforcement assesses possible violations of the SEC's regulations and can take action against individuals or firms. An investigation can involve the examination of securities data or transactions; the SEC has the power to obtain information from specific individuals by subpoena. When the SEC finds that action is warranted, it may negotiate a settlement with the individuals or firms that are cited for violations, file a case against them in federal court, or even work with law enforcement agencies if the violations involve criminal activity. Such actions are normally intended to prevent the violations from continuing and to discourage other individuals or firms from engaging in illegal securities activities.

SEC Oversight of Corporate Disclosure   In October 2000, the SEC issued Regulation Fair Disclosure (FD), which requires firms to disclose relevant information broadly to investors at the same time. One of the most important results of Regulation FD is that a firm may no longer provide analysts with information that they could use before the market was aware of the information. Before Regulation FD, some firms would commonly hint to analysts that their earnings would be higher than initially anticipated. Thus, the analysts could advise their preferred clients to purchase the stocks before the price was pushed up by the increased demand for shares by other investors who received the information later.

Since Regulation FD, a firm must announce a change in expected earnings to all investors and other interested parties (such as analysts) at the same time. The firm may disclose the information on its website, through a filing of a document (8-K form) with the SEC, and through a news release. The firm may hold a conference call with analysts after the news is announced, but is expected to include all material information in the announcement. Thus, the conference call will not give analysts an unfair advantage because the key information has already been disclosed. In addition, most firms have now opened up their conference calls to investors, who can listen in by phone or online through a website. Analysts who always relied on their own analytical abilities to develop their recommendations are continuing business as usual, but analysts who relied on what might be considered inside information from firms have had to modify their methods of forming insightful opinions about the firms they cover.

Some analysts suggest that the regulation has caused firms to disclose less information to them and to the public than before. To ensure that they do not violate Regulation FD, some firms may offer less information so that no parties have an unfair advantage. In particular, smaller firms find it expensive to issue a press release every time they have relevant information. The SEC is reviewing Regulation FD and may alter it so that it still allows for a flow of information from firms, while ensuring that investors receive the information at the same time as analysts.

TRADING INTERNATIONAL STOCKS

Although the international trading of stocks has grown over time, until recently it was limited by three barriers: transaction costs, information costs, and exchange rate risk. Now, however, these barriers have been reduced, as explained next.

Reduction in Transaction Costs

Most countries have their own stock exchanges, where the stocks of local, publicly held companies are traded. In recent years, countries have consolidated their exchanges, increasing efficiency and reducing transaction costs. Some European stock exchanges use an extensive cross-listing system (called Eurolist) so that investors in a given European country can easily purchase stocks of companies based in other European countries.

Many international stock exchanges (such as that used in Switzerland and in Belgium) are now fully computerized, so a trading floor is not needed to execute orders. The details of the orders, such as the stock's name, the number of shares to be bought or sold, and the price at which the investor is willing to buy or sell, are fed into a computer system. The system matches buyers and sellers and then sends information confirming the transaction to the financial institution, which then informs the investor that the transaction has been completed.

When there are many more buy orders than sell orders for a given stock, the computer will not be able to accommodate all orders. Some buyers will then increase the price they are willing to pay for the stock. Thus, the price adjusts in response to the demand (buy orders) for the stock and the supply (sell orders) of the stock for sale, as recorded by the computer system. Similar dynamics occur on a trading floor, but the computerized system has documented criteria by which it prioritizes the execution of orders.

Furthermore, the Internet allows investors to use their computers to place orders (through the website of a member of the stock exchange) that will then be executed and confirmed by the computer system back through the Internet to the investor. Thus, all parts of the trading process from the placement of orders to the confirmations that transactions have been executed will be conducted by computers. The ease of placing such orders regardless of the location of the investor and the stock exchange is sure to increase the volume of international stock transactions in the future.

Reduction in Information Costs

Information about foreign stocks is now available on the Internet, enabling investors to make more informed decisions without having to purchase information about these stocks. Consequently, investors should be more comfortable assessing foreign stocks. Differences in accounting rules may still limit the degree to which financial data about foreign companies can be interpreted or compared to data about firms in other countries, but there has been some progress in making accounting standards uniform across countries.

Reduction in Exchange Rate Risk

When investing in a foreign stock denominated in a foreign currency, investors are subject to the possibility that the currency denominating the stock will depreciate against the investor's currency over time. The potential for a major decline in a stock's value simply because of a large degree of depreciation is greater for emerging markets, such as Indonesia or Russia, where the local currency can change by 10 percent or more on a single day.

The ongoing conversion of European countries to a single currency (the euro) should lead to more stock offerings in Europe by U.S. and European-based firms. Previously, a European firm needed a different currency in every European country in which it conducted business; therefore, the firm would borrow currency from local banks in each country. Now, the firm can use the euro to finance its operations across several European countries and may be able to obtain all the financing it needs with one stock offering denominated in euros. The firm can then use a portion of the revenue (in euros) to pay dividends to shareholders who have purchased the stock. In addition, European investors based in countries where the euro serves as the local currency can now invest in stocks in other European countries that are denominated in euros without being exposed to exchange rate risk.

SUMMARY

- Investors engage in various types of stock transactions. They can place an order by phone or online. They can request that a transaction be executed at the prevailing price or only if the stock price reaches a specified level. They can finance a portion of their stock purchase with borrowed funds as a means of increasing the potential return on their investment. They can also sell stocks short.

- Organized stock exchanges are used to facilitate secondary market transactions. Members of the exchanges trade stock for their own accounts or for their clients. The exchanges are served by floor brokers and specialists, who execute transactions. An over-the-counter exchange also exists, where stock transactions are executed through a telecommunications network.

- Electronic communication networks (ECNs) are automated systems for disclosing and sometimes executing stock trades. They facilitate the execution of

orders and normally service institutional rather than individual investors. ECNs can interact with a trading platform on a website (called a direct access broker) that allows investors to trade stocks without the use of a broker.

- Stock markets are regulated to ensure that investors are treated fairly. Stock trading is regulated by the individual exchanges and by the SEC. Many of the regulations are intended to prevent unfair or unethical trading practices on the security exchanges. The stock exchanges and the SEC attempt to prevent the use of inside information by investors.

- As various stock markets have removed their barriers to foreign investors, they have become more globally integrated. Transaction costs, information costs, and exchange rate risk have all been reduced, making it easier for investors to engage in international stock trading.

POINT COUNTER-POINT

Is a Specialist or a Market-Maker Needed?

Point Yes. A specialist or a market-maker can make a market by serving as the counterparty on a transaction. Without specialists or market-makers, stock orders might be heavily weighted toward buys or sells, and price movements would be more volatile.

Counter-Point No. Specialists and market-makers do not prevent stock prices from declining. A stock that

has more selling pressure than buying pressure will experience a decline in price, as it should. The electronic communication networks can serve as the intermediary between buyer and seller.

Who Is Correct? Use the Internet to learn more about this issue. Offer your own opinion on this issue.

QUESTIONS AND APPLICATIONS

1. Orders Explain the difference between a market order and a limit order.

2. Margins Explain how margin requirements can affect the potential return and risk from investing in a stock. What is the maintenance margin?

3. Short Selling Under what conditions might investors consider short selling a specific stock?

4. Short Selling Describe the short selling process. Explain the short interest ratio.

5. Stock Trading Describe the roles played by floor brokers and specialists. Explain how specialists or market-makers may attempt to capitalize on stock price discrepancies.

6. ECNs What are electronic communication networks (ECNs)?

7. SEC Structure and Role Briefly describe the structure and role of the Securities and Exchange Commission (SEC).

8. SEC Enforcement Explain how the Securities and Exchange Commission attempts to prevent violations of SEC regulations.

9. Circuit Breakers Explain how circuit breakers are used to reduce the likelihood of a large stock market crash.

10. Trading Halts Why are trading halts sometimes imposed on particular stocks?

Advanced Questions

11. Reg FD What are the implications of Regulation FD?

12. Stock Exchange Transaction Costs Explain how foreign stock exchanges such as the Swiss stock exchange have reduced transaction costs.

13. Front-Running Describe "front-running." Explain how front-running may prevent limit orders from investors from being executed.

14. Bid-Ask Spread of Penny Stocks Your friend just told you about a penny stock he purchased, which increased in price from $0.10 to $0.50 per share. You start investigating penny stocks, and after conducting a large amount of research, you find a stock with a quoted price of $0.05. Upon further investigation, you notice that the ask price for the stock is $0.08 and that the bid price is $0.01. Discuss the possible reasons for this wide bid-ask spread.

15. Implications of NYSE Compensation The former chairman of the NYSE, Richard Grasso, resigned in 2003 as a result of institutional outrage over his excessive compensation package. Besides setting a bad example for the firms listed on the NYSE, discuss why institutional investors would have been outraged.

16. Ban on Short Selling Why did the SEC impose a temporary ban on short sales of specific stocks in 2008? Do you think a ban on short selling is effective?

Interpreting Financial News

Interpret the following statements made by Wall Street analysts and portfolio managers:

a. "Individual investors who purchase stock on margin might as well go to Vegas."

b. "During a major stock market downturn, specialists suddenly are not available."

c. "The trading floor may become extinct due to ECNs."

Managing in Financial Markets

Focus on Heavily Shorted Stocks As a portfolio manager, you commonly take short positions in stocks that have a high short interest ratio. What is the advantage of focusing on these types of firms? What is a possible disadvantage?

PROBLEMS

1. Buying on Margin Assume that Vogl stock is priced at $50 per share and pays a dividend of $1 per share. An investor purchases the stock on margin, paying $30 per share and borrowing the remainder from the brokerage firm at 10 percent annualized interest. If, after one year, the stock is sold at a price of $60 per share, what is the return to the investor?

2. Buying on Margin Assume that Duever stock is priced at $80 per share and pays a dividend of $2 per share. An investor purchases the stock on margin, paying $50 per share and borrowing the remainder from the brokerage firm at 12 percent annualized interest. If, after one year, the stock is sold at a price of $90 per share, what is the return to the investor?

3. Buying on Margin Suppose that you buy a stock for $48 by paying $25 and borrowing the remaining $23 from a brokerage firm at 8 percent annualized interest. The stock pays an annual dividend of $0.80 per share, and after one year, you are able to sell it for $65. Calculate your return on the stock. Then, calculate the return on the stock if you had used only personal funds to make the purchase. Repeat the problem assuming that only personal funds are used and that at the end of one year you are able to sell the stock at $40.

4. Margin How would the return on a stock be affected by a lower initial investment (and higher loan amount)? Explain the relationship between the proportion of funds borrowed and the return.

FLOW OF FUNDS EXERCISE

Shorting Stocks

Recall that if the economy continues to be strong, Carson Company may need to increase its production capacity by about 50 percent over the next few years to satisfy demand. It would need financing to expand and accommodate the increase in production. Recall that the yield curve is currently upward sloping. Also recall that Carson is concerned about a possible slowing of the economy because of potential Fed actions to reduce inflation. It is also considering issuing stock or bonds to raise funds in the next year.

a. In some cases, a stock's price is too high or too low because of asymmetric information (information known by the firm but not by investors). How can Carson attempt to minimize asymmetric information?

b. Carson Company is concerned that if it issues stock, its stock price over time could be adversely affected by certain institutional investors that take large short positions in a stock. When this happens, the stock's price may be undervalued because of the pressure on the price caused by the large short positions. What can Carson do to counter major short positions taken by institutional investors if it really believes that its stock price should be higher? What is the potential risk involved in this strategy?

INTERNET/EXCEL EXERCISES

1. Go to http://finance.yahoo.com/. Insert the ticker symbol of the firm of your choice in the "Get Quotes" section. Review the statistics provided. What is the average daily trading volume (Avg Vol)? What is the market capitalization of the firm? What is its price-earnings ratio (P/E)? What is the amount of dividends (if any) paid, and what is the dividend yield (Div & Yield)?

2. For the same firm, click on "Key Statistics." What is the firm's beta? What are its return on assets (ROA) and return on equity (ROE)? What is its short ratio?

Stock Market Analysis

This problem requires an understanding of the different methods for valuing stocks.

As a stock portfolio manager, you spend most of your day searching for stocks that appear to be undervalued. In the last few days, you have received information about two stocks that you are assessing—Olympic stock and Kenner stock. Many stock analysts believe that Olympic stock and Kenner stock are undervalued because their price-earnings ratios are lower than the industry average. Olympic, Inc. has a PE ratio of 6, versus an industry PE ratio of 8. Its stock price declined recently in response to an announcement that its quarterly earnings would be lower than expected due to expenses from recent restructuring. The restructuring is expected to improve Olympic's future performance, but its earnings will take a large onetime hit this quarter.

Kenner Company has a PE ratio of 9, versus a PE ratio of 11 in its industry. Its earnings have been decent in recent years, but it has not kept up with new technology and may lose market share to competitors in the future.

Questions

1. Should you still consider purchasing Olympic stock in light of the analysts' arguments about why it may be undervalued?

2. Should you still consider purchasing Kenner stock in light of the analysts' arguments about why it may be undervalued?

3. Some stock analysts have just predicted that the prices of most stocks will fall because interest rates are expected to rise, which would cause investors to use higher required rates of return when valuing stocks. The analysts used this logic to suggest that the present value of future cash flows would decline if interest rates rise. The expected increase in interest rates is due to expectations of a stronger economy, which will result in an increased demand for loanable funds by corporations and individuals. Do you believe that stock prices will decline if the economy strengthens and interest rates rise?

PART 5

Derivative Security Markets

Derivatives are financial contracts whose values are derived from the values of underlying assets. They are widely used to speculate on future expectations or to reduce a security portfolio's risk. The chapters in Part 5 focus on derivative security markets. Each chapter explains how institutional portfolio managers and speculators use these markets. Many financial market participants simultaneously use all these markets, as is emphasized throughout the chapters.

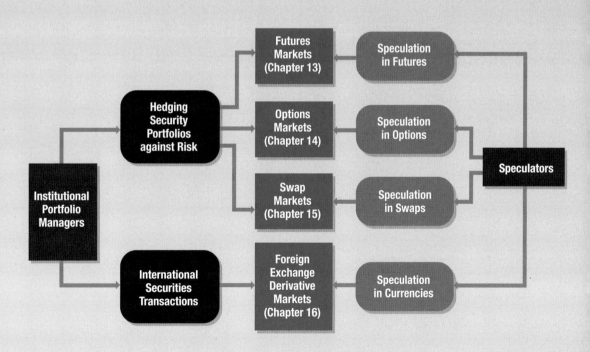

13

Financial Futures Markets

325

CHAPTER OBJECTIVES

The specific objectives of this chapter are to:

- explain how financial futures contracts are valued,

- explain how interest rate futures contracts are used to speculate or hedge, based on anticipated interest rate movements,

- explain how stock index futures contracts are used to speculate or hedge, based on anticipated stock price movements, and

- describe how financial institutions participate in the financial futures markets.

WEB

www.nfa.futures.org/
Information for investors who wish to trade futures contracts.

In recent years, financial futures markets have received much attention because they have the potential to generate large returns to speculators and because they entail a high degree of risk. However, these markets can also be used to reduce the risk of financial institutions and other corporations. Financial futures markets facilitate the trading of financial futures contracts.

BACKGROUND ON FINANCIAL FUTURES

A **financial futures contract** is a standardized agreement to deliver or receive a specified amount of a specified financial instrument at a specified price and date. The buyer of a financial futures contract buys the financial instrument, while the seller of a financial futures contract delivers the instrument for the specified price. Financial futures contracts are traded on organized exchanges, which establish and enforce rules for such trading. Futures exchanges provide an organized marketplace where futures contracts can be traded. They clear, settle, and guarantee all transactions that occur on their exchanges.

The operations of financial futures exchanges are regulated by the Commodity Futures Trading Commission (CFTC). The CFTC approves futures contracts before they can be listed by futures exchanges and imposes regulations to prevent unfair trading practices.

Many of the popular financial futures contracts are on debt securities such as Treasury bills, Treasury notes, Treasury bonds, and Eurodollar CDs. These contracts are referred to as **interest rate futures.** There are also financial futures contracts on stock indexes, which are referred to as **stock index futures.** For each type of contract, the settlement dates at which delivery would occur are in March, June, September, and December.

Purpose of Trading Financial Futures

Financial futures are traded either to speculate on prices of securities or to hedge existing exposure to security price movements. **Speculators** in financial futures markets take positions to profit from expected changes in the price of futures contracts over time. **Hedgers** take positions to reduce their exposure to future movements in interest rates or stock prices.

Many hedgers who maintain large portfolios of stocks or bonds take a futures position to hedge their risk. Speculators commonly take the opposite position and therefore serve as the counterparty on many futures transactions. Thus, speculators provide liquidity to the futures market.

Speculators in futures can be classified according to their methods. **Day traders** attempt to capitalize on price movements during a single day; normally, they close out their futures positions on the same day the positions were initiated. **Position traders** maintain their futures positions for longer periods of time (for weeks or months) and thus attempt to capitalize on expected price movements over a longer time horizon.

Structure of the Futures Market

WEB

www.cmegroup.com/
Offers details about the products offered by the CME Group and also provides price quotations of the various futures contracts.

Most financial futures contracts in the United States are traded through the CME Group, which was formed in July 2007 by the merger of the Chicago Board of Trade (CBOT) and the Chicago Mercantile Exchange (CME). The CBOT had specialized in futures contracts on Treasury bonds and agricultural products, and also traded stock options (described in the next chapter). The CME had specialized in futures contracts on money market securities, stock indexes, and currencies. The CME went public in 2002, while the CBOT went public in 2005. Their merger to form CME Group created the world's largest and most diverse derivatives exchange, which serves international markets for derivative products. As part of the restructuring to increase efficiency, the CME and CBOT trading floors were consolidated into a single trading floor at the CBOT, and their products were consolidated on a single electronic platform, which has reduced operating and maintenance expenses. The CME Group expected that the merger would achieve a cost savings of $150 million in the first two years and result in revenue synergies of at least $75 million. The CME Group has established a plan of continual innovation of new derivative products in the international marketplace. Transactions of new derivative products are typically executed by the CME Group's single electronic platform.

When the futures exchanges were created, they relied on **commission brokers** (also called floor brokers) to execute orders for their customers, which generally were brokerage firms. In addition, **floor traders** (also called **locals**) traded futures contracts for their own account. The commission brokers and floor traders went to a specific location on the trading floor where the futures contract was traded to execute the order. Today, computer technology allows investors to have trades executed electronically. Many electronic communication networks (ECNs) are programmed to consider all possible trades and execute the order at the best possible price.

Market-makers can also execute futures contract transactions for customers. They may facilitate a buy order for one customer and a sell order for a different customer. The market-maker earns the difference between the bid price and the ask price for this trade. The spread has declined significantly in recent years. Market-makers also earn profits when they use their own funds to take positions in futures contracts. Like any investors, they are subject to the risk of losses on their positions.

Over-the-Counter Trading Many types of futures contracts and other derivative contracts are now being sold over the counter, whereby a financial intermediary (such as a commercial bank or an investment bank) finds a counterparty or serves as the counterparty. These over-the-counter arrangements are more personalized and can be tailored to the specific preferences of the parties involved. Such tailoring is not possible for the more standardized futures contracts sold on the exchanges.

Electronic Trading Most futures contracts are now traded electronically. The CME Group has an electronic trading platform called Globex that complements its floor trading. Some futures contracts are traded both on the trading floor and on Globex, while others are traded only on Globex. Transactions can occur on Globex virtually around the clock (closed about one hour per day for maintenance) and on weekends. In 2004, the Chicago Board Options Exchange (CBOE) opened a fully electronic futures exchange.

Trading Futures

Customers who desire to buy or sell futures contracts open accounts at brokerage firms that execute futures transactions. Under exchange requirements, a customer must establish a margin deposit with the broker before a transaction can be executed. This so-called **initial margin** is typically between 5 percent and 18 percent of a futures contract's full value. Brokers commonly require margin deposits above those required by the exchanges. As the futures contract price changes on a daily basis, its value is "marked to market," or revised to reflect the prevailing conditions. When the value of a customer's contract moves in an unfavorable direction, that customer may receive a margin call from the broker, requiring additional funds to be deposited in the margin account. The margin requirements reduce the risk that customers will later default on their obligations.

Type of Orders   Customers can place a market order or a limit order. With a market order, the trade will automatically be executed at the prevailing price of the futures contract. With a limit order, the trade will be executed only if the price is within the limit specified by the customer. For example, a customer may place a limit order to buy a particular futures contract if it is priced no higher than a specified price. Similarly, a customer may place an order to sell a futures contract if it is priced no lower than a specified minimum price.

How Orders Are Executed   Although most trading now takes place electronically, some trades are still conducted on the trading floor. In that case, the brokerage firm communicates its customers' orders to telephone stations located near the trading floor of the futures exchange. The floor brokers accommodate these orders. Each type of financial futures contract is traded in a particular location on the trading floor. The floor brokers make their offers to trade by open outcry, specifying the quantity of contracts they wish to buy or sell. Other floor brokers and traders interested in trading the particular type of futures contract can respond to the open outcry. When two traders on the trading floor reach an agreement, each trader documents the specifics of the agreement (including the price), and the information is transmitted to the customers.

Floor brokers receive transaction fees in the form of a bid-ask spread. That is, they purchase a given futures contract for one party at a slightly lower price than the price at which they sell the contract to another party. For every buyer of a futures contract, there must be a corresponding seller.

The futures exchange facilitates the trading process but does not take buy or sell positions on the futures contract. Instead, the exchange acts as a clearinghouse. A clearinghouse facilitates the trading process by recording all transactions and guaranteeing timely payments on the futures contracts. This precludes the need for a purchaser of a futures contract to check the creditworthiness of the contract seller. In fact, purchasers of contracts do not even know who the sellers are, and vice versa. The clearinghouse also supervises the delivery of contracts as of the settlement date.

INTERPRETING FINANCIAL FUTURES TABLES

Prices of interest rate futures contracts vary from day to day and are reported in the financial media. Assume the information in Exhibit 13.1 appears on a particular day in May 2009 and refers to the previous trading day. From this exhibit, the futures contract specifying delivery of the Treasury bills for June opened at 94.00 (per $100 par value). The highest trading price for the day was 94.26, the low was 94.00, and the closing price (settle price in Column 5) at the end of the day was 94.20. The change in Column 6 is the difference between the settle price and the quoted settle price on the previous trading day.

Exhibit 13.1 Example of Treasury Bill Futures Quotations

TREASURY BILL FUTURES						
(1)	(2)	(3)	(4)	(5)	(6)	(7)
					DISCOUNT	
	OPEN	HIGH	LOW	SETTLE	CHANGE	SETTLE
June 2009	94.00	94.26	94.00	94.20	+.30	5.80
Sept 2009	93.80	94.05	93.80	94.05	+.28	5.95
Dec 2009	93.62	93.79	93.62	93.75	+.24	6.25
Mar 2010	93.45	93.60	93.45	93.60	+.23	6.40

Exhibit 13.1 provides information for T-bill futures contracts with four different settlement months. Once the June settlement date passes, the other months will move up one row in the table, and information on T-bill futures with a settlement date for the following June will appear in the fourth row.

Futures on Treasury bonds and notes are also available and can be used for hedging portfolio positions or for speculation. Specific characteristics of these contracts are shown in Exhibit 13.2 Both Treasury bond and note futures represent a face value of $100,000, which is substantially less than the $1 million face value of securities underlying the T-bill futures contracts.

VALUATION OF FINANCIAL FUTURES

WEB

www.cmegroup.com
Quotations for futures
contracts.

If there are more traders with buy offers than sell offers for a particular contract, the futures price will rise until this imbalance is removed. Price changes on financial futures contracts are indicated on quotation tickers.

The price of any financial futures contract generally reflects the expected price of the underlying security (or index) as of the settlement date. Thus, any factors that influence that expected value should influence the current prices of financial futures. A primary

Exhibit 13.2 Characteristics of Treasury Bond and Note Futures

CHARACTERISTIC OF FUTURES CONTRACT	U.S. TREASURY BOND FUTURES	U.S. TREASURY NOTE FUTURES
Size	$100,000 face value.	$100,000 face value.
Deliverable grade	U.S. Treasury bonds maturing at least 15 years from date of delivery if not callable; coupon is 8%. (The coupon rate on new contracts is periodically adjusted to reflect market interest rate levels.)	U.S. Treasury notes maturing at least $6^1/_2$ years but not more than 10 years from the first day of the delivery month; coupon rate is 6%. (The coupon rate on new contracts is periodically adjusted to reflect market interest rate levels.)
Price quotation	In points ($1,000) and thirty-seconds of a point.	In points ($1,000) and thirty-seconds of a point.
Minimum price fluctuation	One thirty-second ($^1/_{32}$) of a point, or $31.25 per contract.	One thirty-second ($^1/_{32}$) of a point, or $31.25 per contract.
Daily trading limits	Three points ($3,000) per contract above or below the previous day's settlement price.	Three points ($3,000) per contract above or below the previous day's settlement price.
Settlement months	March, June, September, December.	March, June, September, December.

USING THE WALL STREET JOURNAL

Interest Rate Futures

The Wall Street Journal provides information on interest rate futures contracts, as shown here. Specifically, it discloses the recent open price, range (high and low), and final closing (settle) price over the previous trading day. It also provides the amount of existing contracts (open interest). Financial institutions closely monitor interest rate futures prices when considering whether to hedge their interest rate risk.

Source: Republished with permission of Dow Jones & Company, Inc., from *The Wall Street Journal*, January 7, 2009; permission conveyed through the Copyright Clearance Center, Inc.

Interest Rate Futures

Treasury Bonds (CBT)-$100,000; pts 32nds of 100%

March	133-050	133-255	131-235	**132-220**	–10.5	742,060
June	131-230	132-160	130-165	**131-135**	–8.5	1,068

Treasury Notes (CBT)-$100,000; pts 32nds of 100%

March	124-115	124-290	123-090	**124-115**	6.0	1,039,570
June	121-120	122-170	120-175	**122-135**	6.0	14

5 Yr. Treasury Notes (CBT)-$100,000; pts 32nds of 100%

March	118-225	118-310	118-040	**118-217**	2.5	1,017,334

2 Yr. Treasury Notes (CBT)-$200,000; pts 32nds of 100%

March	109-015	109-032	108-275	**108-312**	–1.2	500,509

30 Day Federal Funds (CBT)-$5,000,000; 100 - daily avg.

Jan	99.853	99.858	99.850	**99.853**	.015	68,127
Feb	99.805	99.825	99.805	**99.815**	.020	61,969

1 Month Libor (CME)-$3,000,000; pts of 100%

Jan	99.5800	99.5800	99.5600	**99.5700**	.0125	14,584
Feb	99.5200	99.5300	99.5100	**99.5225**	.0125	7,507

Eurodollar (CME)-$1,000,000; pts of 100%

Jan	98.7000	98.7000	98.6350	**98.6650**	–.0350	157,758
March	98.9200	98.9250	98.8350	**98.9000**	–.0150	1,279,115
June	98.8750	98.9100	98.7850	**98.8850**	.0250	1,007,845
Sept	98.7300	98.8150	98.6350	**98.7750**	.0700	867,930

factor is the current price of the underlying security (or index), which normally serves as a somewhat useful indicator of the future price. As the market price of the financial asset represented by the financial futures contract changes, so will the value of the contract. For example, if the prices of Treasury bonds rise, the value of an existing Treasury bond futures contract should rise because the contract has locked in the price at which Treasury bonds can be purchased.

In addition, some information about economic or market conditions may influence the futures price even though it does not affect the current price. For example, a particular regulatory event anticipated six months from now could possibly affect the futures price even though it does not affect the price of the underlying security. Thus, the futures price is mainly a function of the prevailing price of the underlying security plus an expected adjustment in that price by the settlement date. The futures price should change in response to either changes in the prevailing price or changes in the expected adjustment in that price by the settlement date.

Impact of the Opportunity Cost

Another factor that influences the futures price is the opportunity cost (or benefits) involved in holding a futures contract rather than owning the underlying security. An investor who purchases stock index futures rather than the stocks themselves does not receive the dividends. By itself, this factor would cause the stock index futures to be priced lower than the stocks themselves. However, because the investor's initial investment is much smaller when purchasing the stock index futures, the investor may be able to generate interest income on the remaining funds. By itself, this factor would cause the stock index futures to be priced higher than the stocks themselves. When both factors are considered, the effects are somewhat offsetting.

EXPLAINING PRICE MOVEMENTS OF BOND FUTURES CONTRACTS

Price movements of bond futures contracts are driven by economic conditions. A framework for explaining movements in bond futures prices is provided in Exhibit 13.3

Since Treasury bond futures prices tend to move with the prices of Treasury bonds, participants in the Treasury bond futures market closely monitor the same economic indicators monitored by participants in the Treasury bond market. These indicators may signal future changes in the strength of the economy, which signal changes in the risk-free interest rate and in the required return from investing in bonds. Some of the more closely monitored indicators of economic growth include employment, gross domestic

Exhibit 13.3 Framework for Explaining Changes in Treasury Bond and Treasury Bill Futures Prices over Time

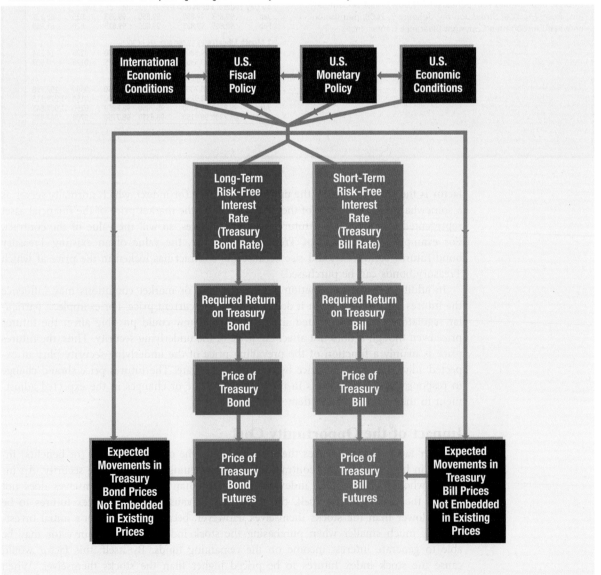

product, retail sales, industrial production, and consumer confidence. When indicators signal an increase in economic growth, participants anticipate an increase in interest rates, which places downward pressure on bond prices and therefore also on Treasury bond futures prices. Conversely, when indicators signal a decrease in economic growth, participants anticipate lower interest rates, which places upward pressure on bond prices and therefore also on Treasury bond futures.

Participants in the Treasury bond futures market also closely monitor indicators of inflation, such as the consumer price index and the producer price index. In general, an unexpected increase in these indexes tends to create expectations of higher interest rates and places downward pressure on bond prices and therefore also on Treasury bond futures prices.

Indicators that reflect the amount of long-term financing are also monitored. For example, announcements about the government deficit or the amount of money that the Treasury hopes to borrow in a Treasury bond auction are closely monitored. Any information that implies more government borrowing than expected tends to signal upward pressure on the long-term risk-free interest rate (the Treasury bond rate), downward pressure on bond prices, and therefore downward pressure on Treasury bond futures prices.

SPECULATING WITH INTEREST RATE FUTURES

The following example explains how speculators use interest rate futures.

EXAMPLE

In February, Jim Sanders forecasts that interest rates will decrease over the next month. If his expectation is correct, the market value of T-bills should increase. Sanders calls a broker and purchases a T-bill futures contract. Assume that the price of the contract was 94.00 (a 6 percent discount) and that the price of T-bills as of the March settlement date is 94.90 (a 5.1 percent discount). Sanders can accept delivery of the T-bills and sell them for more than he paid for them. Because T-bill futures represent $1 million of par value, the nominal profit from this speculative strategy is

Selling price	$949,000	(94.90% of $1,000,000)
− Purchase price	− 940,000	(94.00% of $1,000,000)
= Profit	$9,000	(0.90% of $1,000,000)

In this example, Sanders benefited from his speculative strategy because interest rates declined from the time he took the futures position until the settlement date. If interest rates had risen over this period, the price of T-bills as of the settlement date would have been below 94.00 (reflecting a discount above 6 percent), and Sanders would have incurred a loss.

EXAMPLE

Assume that the price of T-bills as of the March settlement date is 92.50 (representing a discount of 7.5 percent). In this case, the nominal profit from Sanders's speculative strategy is

Selling price	$925,000	(92.50% of $1,000,000)
− Purchase price	− 940,000	(94.00% of $1,000,000)
= Profit	− $15,000	(−1.50% of $1,000,000)

Now suppose instead that, as of February, Sanders had anticipated that interest rates would rise by March. He therefore sold a T-bill futures contract with a March settlement date, obligating him to provide T-bills to the purchaser as of the delivery date. When T-bill prices declined by March, Sanders was able to obtain T-bills at a lower market price in March than the price at which he was obligated to sell those bills. Again, there is always the risk that interest rates (and therefore T-bill prices) will move contrary to expectations. In that case, Sanders would have paid a higher market price for the T-bills than the price at which he could sell them. ●

Exhibit 13.4 Potential Payoffs from Speculating in Financial Futures

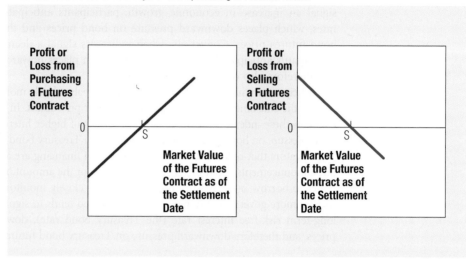

The potential payoffs from trading futures contracts are illustrated in Exhibit 13.4. The left graph represents a purchaser of futures, and the right graph represents a seller of futures. The S on each graph indicates the initial price at which a futures position is created. The horizontal axis represents the market value of the securities represented by a futures contract as of the delivery date. The maximum possible loss when purchasing futures is the amount to be paid for the securities, but this loss will occur only if the market value of the securities falls to zero. The amount of gain (or loss) to a speculator who initially purchased futures will equal the loss (or gain) to a speculator who initally sold futures on the same date (assuming zero transaction costs).

Impact of Leverage

Since investors commonly use a margin account to take futures positions, the return from speculating in interest rate futures should reflect the degree of financial leverage involved. The return is magnified substantially when considering the relatively small margin maintained by many investors.

In the example where Jim Sanders earned a profit of $9,000 on a futures contract, this profit represents 0.90 percent of the value of the underlying contract par value. Consider that Sanders could have taken the interest rate futures position with an initial margin of perhaps $10,000. Under these conditions, the $9,000 profit represents a return of 90 percent over the period of less than two months in which he maintained the futures position.

Just as financial leverage magnifies positive returns, it also magnifies losses. In the example where Sanders lost $15,000 on a futures contract, he would have lost 100 percent of his initial margin and would have been required to add more funds to his margin account when the value of the futures position began to decline. ●

CLOSING OUT THE FUTURES POSITION

Most buyers and sellers of financial futures contracts do not actually make or accept delivery of the financial instrument; instead, they offset their positions by the settlement date. For example, speculators who purchased Treasury bond futures contracts could sell similar futures contracts by the settlement date. Because they now own a contract to receive and a contract to deliver, the obligations net out. The gain or loss from involvement in futures positions depends on the futures price at the time of the purchase versus the futures price at the time of the sale. If the price of the securities represented by the futures contract has risen over the period of concern, speculators who initially purchased interest rate futures will likely have paid a lower futures price than the price at which they can sell the futures contract. Thus, a positive gain will have resulted, and the size of the gain will depend on the degree of movement in the prices of the securities underlying the contract.

Consider the opposite situation (referred to as a "short" position) where the sale of futures is followed by a purchase of futures a few months later to offset the initial short position. If security prices have risen over this period, the earlier contract to sell futures will be priced lower than the later contract to purchase futures. Thus, the speculator will have a loss.

EXAMPLE

Assume that a speculator purchased a futures contract on Treasury bonds at a price of 90–00. One month later, the speculator sells the same futures contract in order to close out the position. At this time, the futures contract specifies 92–10, or 92 and $^{10}/_{32}$ percent of the par value, as the price. Given that the futures contract on Treasury bonds specifies a par value of $100,000, the nominal profit is

Selling price	$92,312	($92^{10}/_{32}$% of $100,000)
− Purchase price	− 90,000	(90.00% of $100,000)
= Profit	$2,312	($2^{10}/_{32}$% of $100,000)

When the initial position is a sale of the futures contract, a purchase of that same type of contract will close out the position. For example, assume a speculator took an initial short position. Using the numbers above, a loss of $2,312 (ignoring transaction costs) will result from closing out the short position one month later. Participants close out a position when they expect that a larger loss will occur if the position is not closed out. If the short position is not closed out before the settlement date, the investor taking that position is obligated to deliver the securities underlying the futures contract at that time. ●

According to estimates, only 2 percent of all futures contracts actually involve delivery, yet this does not reduce their effectiveness for speculation or hedging. Because the contract prices move with the financial instrument representing the contract, an offsetting position at the settlement date generates the same gain or loss as if the instrument were delivered.

HEDGING WITH INTEREST RATE FUTURES

Financial institutions can classify their assets and liabilities by the sensitivity of their market value to interest rate movements. The difference between a financial institution's volume of rate-sensitive assets and rate-sensitive liabilities represents its exposure to interest rate risk. Over the long run, an institution may attempt to restructure its assets or liabilities to balance the degree of rate sensitivity. Restructuring the balance sheet takes time, however. In the short run, the institution may consider using financial futures to hedge its exposure to interest rate movements. A variety of financial institutions use financial futures to hedge their interest rate risk, including mortgage companies, securities dealers, commercial banks, savings institutions, pension funds, and insurance companies.

Using Interest Rate Futures to Create a Short Hedge

Financial institutions most commonly use interest rate futures to create a **short hedge.** Consider a commercial bank that currently holds a large amount of corporate bonds and long-term fixed-rate commercial loans. Its primary source of funds has been short-term deposits. The bank will be adversely affected if interest rates rise in the near future because its liabilities are more rate-sensitive than its assets. Although the bank believes that its bonds are a reasonable long-term investment, it anticipates that interest rates will rise temporarily. Therefore, it hedges against the interest rate risk by selling futures on securities that have characteristics similar to the securities it is holding, so the futures prices will change in tandem with these securities. One possible strategy is to sell Treasury bond futures because the price movements of Treasury bonds are highly correlated with movements in corporate bond prices.

If interest rates rise as expected, the market value of existing corporate bonds held by the bank will decline. Yet, this decline could be offset by the favorable impact of the futures position. The bank locked in the price at which it could sell Treasury bonds. It can purchase Treasury bonds at a lower price just prior to settlement of the futures contract (because the value of bonds will have decreased) and profit from fulfilling its futures contract obligation. Alternatively, it could offset its short position by purchasing futures contracts similar to the type that it sold earlier.

<table>
<tr><td>_EXAMPLE_</td><td>

Assume that Charlotte Insurance Company plans to satisfy cash needs in six months by selling its Treasury bond holdings for $5 million at that time. It is concerned that interest rates might increase over the next three months, which would reduce the market value of the bonds by the time they are sold. To hedge against this possibility, Charlotte plans to sell Treasury bond futures. It sells 50 Treasury bond futures contracts with a par value of $5 million ($100,000 per contract) for 98–16 (or 98 and $^{16}/_{32}$ percent of par value).

Suppose that the actual price of the futures contract declines to 94–16 because of an increase in interest rates. Charlotte can close out its short futures position by purchasing contracts identical to those it has sold. If it purchases 50 Treasury bond futures contracts at the prevailing price of 94–16, its profit per futures contract will be

</td></tr>
</table>

Selling price	$98,500	(98.50% of $100,000)
− Purchase price	− 94,500	(94.50% of $100,000)
= Profit	$4,000	(4.00% of $100,000)

Charlotte had a position in 50 futures contracts, so its total profit from its position will be $200,000 ($4,000 per contract × 50 contracts). This gain on the futures contract position will help offset the reduced market value of Charlotte's bond holdings. Charlotte could also have earned a gain on its position by purchasing an identical futures contract just before the settlement date.

If interest rates rise by a greater degree over the six-month period, the market value of Charlotte's Treasury bond holdings will decrease further. However, the price of Treasury bond futures contracts will also decrease by a greater degree, creating a larger gain from the short position in Treasury bond futures. If interest rates decrease, the futures prices will rise, causing a loss on Charlotte's futures position. But this will be offset by a gain in the market value of Charlotte's bond holdings. In this case, the firm would have experienced better overall performance without the hedge. Firms cannot know whether a hedge of interest rate risk will be beneficial in a future period because they cannot always predict the direction of future interest rates. ●

The preceding example presumes that the **basis,** or the difference between the price of a security and the price of a futures contract, remains the same. In reality, the price of the security may fluctuate more or less than the futures contract used to hedge it. If so, a perfect offset will not result when a given face value amount of securities is hedged with the same face value amount of futures contracts.

Tradeoff from Using a Short Hedge

When one considers both the rising and the declining interest rate scenarios, the advantages and disadvantages of interest rate futures are obvious. Interest rate futures can hedge against both adverse and favorable

Exhibit 13.5 Comparison of Probability Distributions of Returns; Hedged versus Unhedged Positions

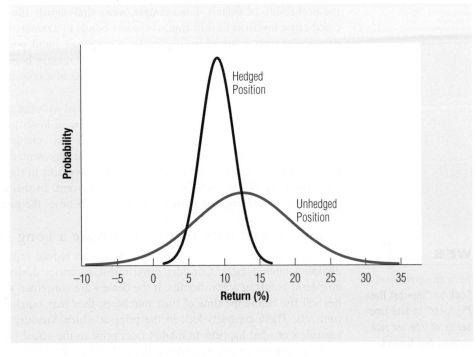

events. Exhibit 13.5 compares two probability distributions of returns generated by a financial institution whose liabilities are more rate-sensitive than its assets. If the institution hedges its exposure to interest rate risk, its probability distribution of returns is narrower than if it does not hedge. The return from hedging would have been higher than without hedging if interest rates increased (see the left side of the graph) but lower if interest rates decreased (see the right side of the graph).

A financial institution that hedges with interest rate futures is less sensitive to economic events. Thus, financial institutions that frequently use interest rate futures may be able to reduce the variability of their earnings over time, which reflects a lower degree of risk. Nevertheless, it should be recognized that hedging is unlikely to remove all uncertainty because it is virtually impossible to perfectly hedge the sensitivity of all cash flows to interest rate movements.

Cross-Hedging   Financial institutions sometimes want to hedge the interest rate risk of assets that cannot be perfectly matched by interest rate futures contracts. In this case, they attempt to identify an asset represented by futures contracts whose market value moves closely in tandem with that of the assets they want to hedge. The use of a futures contract on one financial instrument to hedge a position in a different financial instrument is known as **cross-hedging.** The effectiveness of a cross-hedge depends on the degree of correlation between the market values of the two financial instruments. If the price of the underlying security of the futures contract moves closely in tandem with the security hedged, the futures contract can provide an effective hedge.

For example, a financial institution may take a short position in Treasury bond futures contracts to hedge the interest rate risk of a portfolio of corporate bonds. The Treasury bonds and corporate bonds may be similarly sensitive to interest rate movements (assuming their maturities and coupon payment structures are similar). However, shifts in credit conditions could sever the close relationship between Treasury bond and corporate bond prices because the prices may be affected differently by economic conditions that influence the probability of default. For example, news that signals the possibility of a recession could cause investors to shift from corporate bonds to Treasury bonds. During this transition, the market value of the institution's corporate bond portfolio may decline, while Treasury bond prices are rising. Thus, the sale of Treasury bond futures to hedge against the expected temporary decline in the market value of a corporate bond portfolio would not have been effective.

Even when the futures contract is highly correlated with the portfolio being hedged, the value of the futures contract may change by a higher or lower percentage than the portfolio's market value. If the futures contract value is less volatile than the portfolio value, hedging will require a greater amount of principal represented by the futures contracts. For example, assume that for every percentage movement in the price of the futures contract, the value of the portfolio moves by 1.25 percent. In this case, the value of futures contracts to fully hedge the portfolio would be 1.25 times the principal of the portfolio.

Using Interest Rate Futures to Create a Long Hedge

WEB

www.cmegroup.com
Click on "Interest Rate Products" to find time series of interest rate options and futures.

Some financial institutions use a **long hedge** to reduce exposure to the possibility of declining interest rates. Consider government securities dealers who plan to purchase long-term bonds in a few months. If the dealers are concerned that prices of these securities will rise before the time of their purchases, they may purchase Treasury bond futures contracts. These contracts lock in the price at which Treasury bonds can be purchased, regardless of what happens to market rates prior to the actual purchase of the bonds.

As another example, consider a bank that has obtained a significant portion of its funds from large CDs with a maturity of five years. Also assume that most of its assets represent loans with rates that adjust every six months. This bank would be adversely affected by a decline in interest rates because interest earned on assets would be more sensitive than interest paid on liabilities. To hedge against the possibility of lower interest rates, the bank could purchase T-bill futures to lock in the price on T-bills at a specified future date. If interest rates decline, the gain on the futures position could partially offset any reduction in the bank's earnings due to the reduction in interest rates.

Hedging Net Exposure

Because interest rate futures contracts entail transaction costs, they should be used only to hedge **net exposure,** which reflects the difference between asset and liability positions. Consider a bank that has $300 million in long-term assets and $220 million worth of long-term fixed-rate liabilities. If interest rates rise, the market value of the long-term assets will decline, but the bank will benefit from the fixed rate on the $220 million in long-term liabilities. Thus, the net exposure is only $80 million (assuming that the long-term assets and liabilities are similarly affected by rising interest rates). The financial institution should therefore focus on hedging its net exposure of $80 million by creating a short hedge.

BOND INDEX FUTURES

A bond index futures contract allows for the buying and selling of a bond index for a specified price at a specified date. For financial institutions that trade in municipal bonds, the CME Group offers **Municipal Bond Index (MBI) futures.** The index is based on the **Bond Buyer Index** of 40 actively traded general obligation and revenue bonds. The specific characteristics of MBI futures are shown in Exhibit 13.6 Because MBI futures are based on an index rather than on the bonds themselves, there is no physical exchange of bonds. Instead, these futures contracts are settled in cash.

Exhibit 13.6 Characteristics of Municipal Bond Index Futures

CHARACTERISTICS OF FUTURES CONTRACT	MUNICIPAL BOND INDEX FUTURES
Trading unit	1,000 times the Bond Buyer Municipal Bond Index. A price of 90–00 represents a contract size of $90,000.
Price quotation	In points and thirty-seconds of a point.
Minimum price fluctuation	One thirty-second ($\frac{1}{32}$) of a point, or $31.25 per contract.
Daily trading limits	Three points ($3,000) per contract above or below the previous day's settlement price.
Settlement months	March, June, September, December.
Settlement procedure	Municipal Bond Index futures settle in cash on the last day of trading.

EXAMPLE

Palm Insurance Company will be receiving large cash flows in the near future. Although it plans to use some of the incoming funds to purchase municipal bonds, Palm is concerned that because of the likely downward trend in interest rates, municipal bond prices may increase before it can purchase them. Thus, it purchases MBI futures. If Palm's expectation is correct, the futures position will generate a gain, which can be used to pay for the higher-priced bonds once it has sufficient funds. Conversely, if bond prices fall, Palm will incur a loss from its futures position, but it will be able to purchase bonds at a lower price.

Meanwhile Evergreen Securities has agreed to underwrite bonds for various municipalities. It expects the market prices of bonds to decline in the near future. Such an event could reduce underwriting profits if the market price falls before these bonds are sold. To hedge this risk, Evergreen sells MBI futures. The futures position will generate a gain and offset the reduced underwriting profits if the firm's expectations are correct. ●

STOCK INDEX FUTURES

A stock index futures contract allows for the buying and selling of a stock index for a specified price at a specified date. Futures for various stock indexes are traded at the CME Group. Exhibit 13.7 shows some of the contracts that are available and their valuation.

Exhibit 13.7 Stock Index Futures Contracts

TYPE OF STOCK INDEX FUTURES CONTRACT	CONTRACT IS VALUED AS
S&P 500 index	$250 times index
Mini S&P 500 index	$50 times index
S&P Midcap 400 index	$500 times index
S&P Small Cap index	$200 times index
Nasdaq 100 index	$100 times index
Mini Nasdaq 100 index	$20 times index
Mini Nasdaq Composite index	$20 times index
Russell 2000 index	$500 times index
Nikkei (Japan) 225 index	$5 times index

Source: Republished with permission of Dow Jones & Company, Inc., from *The Wall Street Journal*, January 7, 2009, C9; permission conveyed through the Copyright Clearance Center, Inc.

The S&P 500 index futures contract is valued as the index times $250, so if the index is valued at 1600, the contract is valued at 1600 × $250 = $400,000. Mini S&P 500 index futures contracts are available for small investors. These contracts are valued at $50 times the index, so if the index is valued at 1600, the contract is valued at 1600 × $50 = $80,000 ●

A futures contract on the S&P 500 index represents a composite of 500 large corporations. The purchase of an S&P 500 futures contract obligates the purchaser to purchase the S&P 500 index at a specified settlement date for a specified amount. Thus, participants who expect the stock market to perform well before the settlement date may consider purchasing S&P 500 index futures. Conversely, participants who expect the stock market to perform poorly before the settlement date may consider selling S&P 500 index futures.

Stock index futures contracts have settlement dates on the third Friday in March, June, September, and December. The securities underlying the stock index futures contracts are not deliverable; settlement occurs through a cash payment. On the settlement date, the futures contract is valued according to the quoted stock index. The net gain or loss on the stock index futures contract is the difference between the futures price when the initial position was created and the value of the contract as of the settlement date.

Like other financial futures contracts, stock index futures can be closed out before the settlement date by taking an offsetting position. For example, if an S&P 500 futures contract with a December settlement date is purchased in September, this position can be closed out in November by selling an S&P 500 futures contract with the same December settlement date. When a position is closed out prior to the settlement date, the net gain or loss on the stock index futures contract is the difference between the futures price when the position was created and the futures price when the position is closed out.

Some speculators prefer to trade stock index futures rather than actual stocks because of the smaller transaction costs. The commission for a purchase and subsequent sale of S&P 500 futures contracts is substantially less than the commission for purchasing and selling the equivalent stocks in the S&P 500.

Valuing Stock Index Futures Contracts

The value of a stock index futures contract is highly correlated with the value of the underlying stock index. Nevertheless, the value of the stock index futures contract commonly differs from the price of the underlying asset because of unique features of the stock index futures contract.

Consider that an investor can buy either a stock index or a futures contract on the stock index with a settlement date of six months from now. In either case, the investor will own the stock index in six months, but buying the index rather than the index futures offers distinct advantages and disadvantages. On the favorable side, the buyer of the index receives dividends, whereas the buyer of the index futures does not. On the unfavorable side, the buyer of the index must use funds to buy the index, whereas the buyer of index futures can engage in the futures contract simply by establishing a margin deposit with a relatively small amount of assets (such as Treasury securities) that may generate interest while they are used to satisfy margin requirements.

Assume that the index will pay dividends equal to 3 percent over the next six months. Also assume that the purchaser of the index will borrow funds to purchase the index, at an interest rate of 2 percent over the six-month period. In this example, the advantage of holding the index (a 3 percent dividend yield) relative to holding a futures contract on the index more than offsets the 2 percent cost of financing the purchase of the index. The so-called net financing cost (also called cost of carry) to the purchaser of the underlying assets (the index) is the 2 percent cost of financing minus the 3 percent yield earned on the assets, or −1 percent. A negative cost of carry indicates that the cost of financing is less than the yield earned from dividends.

If the spot price of the index is the same as the futures price, the futures price will be more attractive. In fact, given the information in this example, speculators can engage in arbitrage whereby they earn a risk-free profit without tying up their funds. Specifically, they use borrowed funds to purchase the index at the spot price and simultaneously sell index futures. This strategy generates a 3 percent gain due to the dividend yield and incurs a 2 percent cost of financing, or a net gain of 1 percent without tying up any funds over the six-month period. Such arbitrage puts upward pressure on the spot price of the index (because of the purchases of the index) and downward pressure on the index futures price. Once the futures price is 1 percent less than the spot price, arbitrage will no longer be possible because the 3 percent gain from dividends is offset by the 2 percent cost of financing and the 1 percent discount on the futures price. That is, the -1 percent cost of carry is offset by selling index futures at 1 percent less than the spot rate at which the index was purchased. As this example illustrates, the price of the index futures contract is driven by the underlying index, along with the cost of carry. Arbitrage ensures that as the index value and the cost of carry change over time, so will the price of the index futures contract. In general, the underlying security (or index) tends to change by a much greater degree than the cost of carry, so changes in financial futures prices are primarily attributed to changes in the values of the underlying securities (or indexes). ●

Indicators of Stock Index Futures Prices   Since stock index futures prices are primarily driven by movements in the corresponding stock indexes, participants in stock index futures monitor indicators that may signal changes in the stock indexes. These investors monitor some of the same economic indicators as bond futures participants, but do not necessarily respond to new information in the same way. Furthermore, index futures participants tend to have divergent views on how the new information will affect a stock index. Consequently, although the new information may cause substantial trading of stock index futures, the expected effects on index prices may vary. Thus, the impact of new information on the prices of stock index futures cannot be easily anticipated.

Speculating with Stock Index Futures

Stock index futures can be traded to capitalize on expectations about general stock market movements.

EXAMPLE   Boulder Insurance Company plans to purchase a variety of stocks for its stock portfolio in December, once cash inflows are received. Although the company does not have cash to purchase the stocks immediately, it is anticipating a large jump in stock market prices before December. Given this situation, it decides to purchase S&P 500 index futures. The futures price on the S&P 500 index with a December settlement date is 1500. The value of an S&P 500 futures contract is $250 times the index. Because the S&P 500 futures price should move with the stock market, it will rise over time if the company's expectations are correct. Assume that the S&P 500 index rises to 1600 on the settlement date.

In this example, the nominal profit on the S&P 500 index futures is

Selling price	$400,000	(Index value of 1600 × $250)
− Purchase price	−375,000	(Index value of 1500 × $250)
= Profit	$25,000	

Thus, Boulder was able to capitalize on its expectations even though it did not have sufficient cash to purchase stock. If stock prices had declined over the period of concern, the S&P 500 futures price would have decreased, and Boulder would have incurred a loss on its futures position. ●

Hedging with Stock Index Futures

Stock index futures are also commonly used to hedge the market risk of an existing stock portfolio.

USING THE WALL STREET JOURNAL

Stock Index Futures Contracts

The Wall Street Journal provides information on stock index futures contracts, as shown here. Specifically, it discloses the recent open price, range (high and low), and final closing (settle) price over the previous trading day. It also provides the amount of existing contracts (open interest). Financial institutions closely monitor stock index futures prices when considering whether to hedge their market risk.

Source: Republished with permission of Dow Jones & Company, Inc., from *The Wall Street Journal*, January 7, 2009, C9; permission conveyed through the Copyright Clearance Center, Inc.

Index Futures

DJ Industrial Average (CBT)-$10 x index

March	8914	9040	8890	**8950**	32	9,810

Mini DJ Industrial Average (CBT)-$5 x index

| March | 8945 | 8952 | 8919 | **8950** | 32 | 57,867 |

S&P 500 Index (CME)-$250 x index

| March | 927.30 | 942.00 | 923.70 | **930.50** | 3.10 | 477,461 |
| June | 937.00 | 937.00 | 925.80 | **927.90** | 3.00 | 9,723 |

Mini S&P 500 (CME)-$50 x index

| March | 927.25 | 942.75 | 923.50 | **930.50** | 3.00 | 2,404,780 |
| June | 923.00 | 939.25 | 921.50 | **928.00** | 3.00 | 9,749 |

Nasdaq 100 (CME)-$100 x index

| March | 1263.00 | 1288.00 | 1260.00 | **1271.00** | 6.00 | 20,502 |

Mini Nasdaq 100 (CME)-$20 x index

| March | 1263.8 | 1287.0 | 1259.5 | **1271.0** | 6.0 | 219,837 |
| June | 1278.8 | 1286.5 | 1261.8 | **1271.5** | 5.5 | 1,635 |

Mini Russell 2000 (ICE-US)-$100 x index

| March | 502.50 | 518.60 | 501.30 | **510.50** | 6.90 | 419,447 |
| June | 506.00 | 506.00 ▲ | 506.00 | **508.70** | 6.70 | 450 |

Mini Russell 1000 (ICE-US)-$100 x index

| March | 505.00 | 509.70 ▲ | 501.10 | **503.80** | 2.35 | 15,698 |

U.S. Dollar Index (ICE-US)-$1,000 x index

| March | 83.72 | 84.98 | 83.51 | **83.72** | .14 | 13,017 |
| June | 84.45 | 84.83 | 84.43 | **84.30** | .10 | 2,416 |

Source: Thomson Reuters

EXAMPLE

Glacier Stock Mutual Fund expects the stock market to decline temporarily, causing a temporary decline in its stock portfolio. The fund could sell its stocks with the intent to repurchase them in the near future, but it would incur excessive transaction costs. A more efficient solution is to sell stock index futures. If the fund's stock portfolio is similar to the S&P 500 index, Glacier can sell futures contracts on that index. If the stock market declines as expected, Glacier will generate a gain when closing out the stock index futures position, which will somewhat offset the loss on its stock portfolio. ●

This hedge is more effective when the investor's portfolio is diversified like the S&P 500 index. The value of a less diversified stock portfolio will correlate less with the S&P 500 index, so a gain from selling index futures may not completely offset the loss in the portfolio during a market downturn. Assuming that the stock portfolio moves in tandem with the S&P 500, a full hedge would involve the sale of the amount of futures contracts whose combined underlying value is equal to the market value of the stock portfolio being hedged.

EXAMPLE

Assume that a portfolio manager has a stock portfolio valued at $400,000. Also assume that S&P 500 index futures contracts are available for a settlement date one month from now at a level of 1600, which is about equal to today's index value. The manager could sell S&P 500 futures contracts to hedge the stock portfolio. Since the futures contract is valued at $250 times the index level, the contract will result in a payment of $400,000 at settlement date. One index futures contract will be needed to match the existing value of the stock portfolio. Assuming that the stock index moves in tandem with the manager's stock portfolio, any loss on the portfolio should be offset by the gain on the futures contract. For example, if the stock portfolio declines by about 5 percent over one month, this reflects a loss of $20,000 (5% of $400,000 = $20,000). Yet, the S&P 500 index should also have declined by 5 percent (to a level of 1520). Consequently, the S&P 500 index futures contract that was sold by the manager should result in a gain of $20,000 [(1600 − 1520) × $250], which offsets the loss on the stock portfolio. ●

If the stock market experiences higher prices over the month, the S&P 500 index will rise, creating a loss on the futures contract. The value of the manager's stock portfolio will have increased to offset the loss, however.

Most investors who had hedged their stock portfolios with index futures benefited from the hedge when the credit crisis began in 2008. In particular, hedging during the second half of the year was especially beneficial, since many stocks declined by more than 30 percent during that period.

Test of Suitability of Stock Index Futures The suitability of using stock index futures to hedge can be assessed by measuring the sensitivity of the portfolio's performance to market movements over a period prior to taking a hedge position. The sensitivity of a hypothetical position in futures to those same market movements in that period could also be assessed. A general test of suitability is to determine whether the hypothetical derivative position would have offset adverse market effects on the portfolio's performance. Although it may be extremely difficult to perfectly hedge all of a portfolio's exposure to market risk, for a hedge to be suitable there should be some evidence that such a hypothetical hedge would have been moderately effective for that firm. That is, if the position in financial derivatives would not have provided an effective hedge of market risk over a recent period, a firm should not expect that it will provide an effective hedge in the future. This test of suitability uses only data that were available at the time the hedge was to be enacted.

Determining the Proportion of the Portfolio to Hedge Portfolio managers do not necessarily hedge their entire stock portfolio, because they may wish to be partially exposed in the event that stock prices rise. For instance, if the portfolio in the preceding example was valued at $1.2 million, the portfolio manager could have hedged one-third of the stock portfolio by selling one stock index futures contract. The short position in one index futures contract would reflect one-third of the value of the stock portfolio. Alternatively, the manager could have hedged two-thirds of the stock portfolio by selling two stock index futures contracts. The higher the proportion of the portfolio that is hedged, the more insulated the manager's performance is from market conditions, whether those conditions are favorable or unfavorable. Exhibit 13.8 illustrates the net gain (including the gain on the futures and the gain on the stock portfolio) to the portfolio manager under five possible scenarios for the market return (shown in the first column). If the stock market declines, any degree of hedging is beneficial, but the benefits are greater if a higher proportion of the portfolio was hedged. If the stock market performs well, any degree of hedging reduces the net gain, but the reduction is greater if a higher proportion of the portfolio was hedged. In essence, hedging with stock index futures reduces the sensitivity to both unfavorable and favorable market conditions.

Dynamic Asset Allocation with Stock Index Futures

Institutional investors are increasingly using **dynamic asset allocation,** in which they switch between risky and low-risk investment positions over time in response to changing expectations. This strategy allows managers to increase the exposure of their portfolios when they expect favorable market conditions, and to reduce their exposure when they expect unfavorable market conditions. When they anticipate favorable market movements, stock portfolio managers can purchase stock index futures, which intensify the effects of market conditions. Conversely, when they anticipate unfavorable market

Exhibit 13.8 Net Gain (on Stock Portfolio and Short Position in Stock Index Futures) for Different Degrees of Hedging

SCENARIO FOR MARKET RETURN	PROPORTION OF STOCK PORTFOLIO HEDGED			
	0%	33%	67%	100%
−20%	−20%	−13.4%	−6.7%	0%
−10	−10	−6.7	−3.3	0
0	0	0	0	0
10	+10	+6.7	+3.3	0
20	+20	+13.4	+6.7	0

Note: Numbers are based on the assumption that the stock portfolio moves in perfect tandem with the market.

movements, they can sell stock index futures to reduce the effects that market conditions will have on their stock portfolios. As expectations change frequently, portfolio managers commonly alter their degree of exposure. Stock index futures allow portfolio managers to alter their risk-return position without restructuring their existing stock portfolios. Using dynamic asset allocation in this way avoids the substantial transaction costs that would be associated with restructuring the stock portfolios.

Prices of Stock Index Futures versus Stocks

The prices of index futures and the prices of the stocks representing the index can differ to some degree. To understand why, consider a situation in which many institutional investors anticipate a temporary decline in stock prices. Because they expect the decline to be only temporary, the investors prefer not to liquidate their stock portfolios. As a form of portfolio insurance, they sell stock index futures so that any decline in the market value of their stock portfolio will be offset by a gain on their futures position. When numerous institutional investors sell index futures instead of selling stocks to prepare for a market decline, their actions can cause the index futures price to be below the prevailing stock prices.

In some cases, index futures prices may exceed the prices of the stocks that the index comprises. As favorable information about the stock market becomes available, investors can buy either stock index futures or the actual stocks that make up the index. The futures can be purchased immediately with a small up-front payment. Purchasing actual stocks may take longer because of the time needed to select specific stocks. In addition, a larger up-front investment is necessary. This explains why the price of stock index futures may reflect investor expectations about the market more rapidly than stock prices.

Recent studies have found a high degree of correlation between the stock index futures and the index itself. Price movements in the stock index sometimes lag behind movement in the stock index futures by up to 45 minutes. This confirms that the stock index futures more rapidly reflect new information that can influence expectations about the stock market. Even though the index futures price movements frequently precede stock index movements, the relationship is not consistent enough to develop an exploitable trading strategy in which positions in a stock index are taken based on the most recent movement in the futures index.

Arbitrage with Stock Index Futures

The New York Stock Exchange (NYSE) narrowly defines program trading as the simultaneous buying and selling of at least 15 different stocks that in aggregate are valued at more than $1 million. Program trading is commonly used in conjunction with the trading of stock index futures contracts in a strategy known as **index arbitrage.** Securities firms act as **arbitrageurs** by capitalizing on discrepancies between prices of index futures and stocks. Index arbitrage involves the buying or selling of stock index futures with a simultaneous opposite position in the stocks that the index comprises. The index arbitrage is instigated when prices of stock index futures differ significantly from the stocks represented by the index. For example, if the index futures contract is priced high relative to the stocks representing the index, an arbitrageur may consider purchasing the stocks and simultaneously selling stock index futures. Alternatively, if the index futures are priced low relative to the stocks representing the index, an arbitrageur may purchase index futures and simultaneously sell stocks. An arbitrage profit is attainable if the price differential exceeds the costs incurred from trading in both markets.

Index arbitrage does not cause the price discrepancy between the two markets, but rather responds to it. The arbitrageur's ability to detect price discrepancies between the stock and futures markets is enhanced by computers. Roughly 50 percent of all program trading activity is for the purpose of index arbitrage.

Some critics suggest that the index arbitrage activity of purchasing index futures while selling stocks adversely affects stock prices. However, if index futures did not exist, institutional investors could not use portfolio insurance. In this case, a general expectation of a temporary market decline would be more likely to encourage sales of stocks to prepare for the decline, which would accelerate the drop in prices.

Circuit Breakers on Stock Index Futures

Circuit breakers are trading restrictions imposed on specific stocks or stock indexes. The CME Group imposes circuit breakers on several stock index futures, including the S&P 500 futures contract.

By prohibiting trading for short time periods when prices decline to specific threshold levels, circuit breakers may allow investors to determine whether circulating rumors are true and to work out credit arrangements if they have received a margin call. If prices are still perceived to be too high when the markets reopen, the prices will decline further. Thus, circuit breakers do not guarantee that prices will turn upward. Nevertheless, they may be able to prevent large declines in prices that would be attributed to panic selling rather than to fundamental forces.

SINGLE STOCK FUTURES

A single stock futures contract is an agreement to buy or sell a specified number of shares of a specified stock on a specified future date. Such contracts have been traded on futures exchanges in Australia and Europe since the 1990s. In 2001, the Nasdaq market and the London International Financial Futures and Options Exchange (LIFFE) engaged in a joint venture to create a U.S. market for trading single stock futures. The contracts are available for specific stocks that are traded on the Nasdaq market or NYSE. The nominal size of a contract is 100 shares. Investors can buy or sell singles stock futures contracts through their broker. The orders to buy and sell a specific single stock futures contract are matched electronically. Single stock futures have become increasingly popular. They are regulated by the Commodity Futures Trading Commission (CFTC) and the Securities and Exchange Commission (SEC).

Settlement dates are on the third Friday of the delivery month on a quarterly basis (March, June, September, and December) for the next five quarters, as well as the nearest two months. For example, on January 3, an investor could purchase a stock futures contract for the third Friday in the next two months (January or February), or over the next five quarters (March, June, September, December, and March of the following year). Trading hours are from 9:30 A.M. to 4 P.M. eastern standard time. An investor can buy single stock futures on margin.

Investors who expect a particular stock's price to rise over time may consider buying futures on that stock. To obtain a contract to buy March futures on 100 shares of Zyco stock for $5,000 ($50 per share), an investor must submit the $5,000 payment to the clearinghouse on the third Friday in March and will receive shares of Zyco stock on the settlement date. If Zyco stock is valued at $53 at the time of settlement, the investor can sell the stock in the stock market for a gain of $3 per share or $300 for the contract (ignoring commissions). This gain would likely reflect a substantial return on the investment since the investor had to invest only a small margin (perhaps 20 percent of the contract price) to take a position in futures. If Zyco stock is valued at $46 at the time of settlement, the investor would incur a loss of $4 share, which would reflect a substantial percentage loss on the investment. Thus, single stock futures offer potential high returns but also high risk.

Investors who expect a particular stock's price to decline over time can sell futures contracts on that stock. This activity is somewhat similar to selling a stock short, except that single stock futures can be sold without borrowing the underlying stock from a broker as short-sellers must do. To obtain a contract to sell March futures of Zyco stock, an investor must deliver Zyco stock to the clearinghouse on the third Friday in March and will receive the payment specified in the futures contract.

Investors can close out their position at any time by taking the opposite position. For example, assume that shortly after the investor purchased futures on Zyco stock with a March delivery at $50 per share, the stock price declines. Rather than incur the risk that the price could continue to decline, the investor could sell a Zyco futures contract with a March delivery. If this contract specifies a price of $48 per share, the investor's gain will be the difference between the selling price and the buying price, which is −$2 per share or −$200 for the contract.

The Chicago Board Options Exchange and the CME Group recently engaged in a joint venture called OneChicago, which provides another market for trading single stock futures. The contract specifications are similar to those established by Nasdaq and LIFFE. The contracts are traded electronically.

RISK OF TRADING FUTURES CONTRACTS

Users of futures contracts must recognize the various types of risk exhibited by such contracts and other derivative instruments.

Market Risk

Market risk refers to fluctuations in the value of the instrument as a result of market conditions. Firms that use futures contracts to speculate should be concerned about market risk. If their expectations about future market conditions are wrong, they may suffer losses on their futures contracts. Firms that use futures contracts to hedge are less concerned about market risk because if market conditions cause a loss on their derivative instruments, they should have a partial offsetting gain on the positions that they were hedging.

Basis Risk

A second type of risk is **basis risk,** or the risk that the position being hedged by the futures contracts is not affected in the same manner as the instrument underlying the futures contract. This type of risk applies only to those firms or individuals who are using futures contracts to hedge. For example, consider a bond portfolio manager who uses Treasury bond futures contracts to hedge a portfolio of Treasury bonds that have, on average, five years remaining until maturity. The value of the Treasury bond futures may not necessarily move in tandem with the value of the Treasury bond portfolio, because the maturities (and the duration) of the bond portfolio and the underlying securities in the futures contract are not exactly the same. Therefore, a short position in Treasury bond futures contracts will not perfectly offset the impact of interest rate movements on the Treasury bond portfolio.

Liquidity Risk

A third type of risk is **liquidity risk,** which refers to potential price distortions due to a lack of liquidity. For example, a firm may purchase a particular bond futures contract to speculate on expectations of rising bond prices. However, when it attempts to close out its position by selling an identical futures contract, it may find that there are no willing buyers for this type of futures contract at that time. In this case, the firm will have to sell the futures contract at a lower price. Users of futures contracts may reduce liquidity risk by using only those futures contracts that are widely traded.

Credit Risk

A fourth type of risk is **credit risk,** which is the risk that a loss will occur because a counterparty defaults on the contract. This type of risk exists for over-the-counter transactions, in which a firm or individual relies on the creditworthiness of a counterparty.

The possibility that counterparties will not fulfill their obligations is not a concern when trading futures and other derivatives on exchanges, because the exchanges normally guarantee that the provisions of the contract will be honored. The financial intermediaries that make the arrangements in the over-the-counter market can also take some steps to reduce this type of risk. First, the financial intermediary can require that each party provide some form of collateral to back up its position. Second, the financial intermediary can serve as a guarantor (for a fee) in the event that the counterparty does not fulfill its obligation.

Prepayment Risk

Prepayment risk refers to the possibility that the assets to be hedged may be prepaid earlier than their designated maturity. Suppose a commercial bank sells Treasury bond futures in order to hedge its holdings of corporate bonds, and just after the futures position is created, the bonds are called by the corporation that initially issued them. If interest rates subsequently decline, the bank will incur a loss from its futures position without a corresponding gain from its bond position (because the bonds were called earlier).

As a second example, consider a savings and loan association with large holdings of long-term fixed-rate mortgages that are mostly financed by short-term funds. It sells Treasury bond futures to hedge against the possibility of rising interest rates; then, after the futures position is established, interest rates decline, and many of the existing mortgages are prepaid by homeowners. The savings and loan association will incur a loss from its futures position without a corresponding gain from its fixed-rate mortgage position (because the mortgages were prepaid).

Operational Risk

A sixth type of risk is **operational risk,** which is the risk of losses as a result of inadequate management or controls. For example, firms that use futures contracts to hedge are exposed to the possibility that the employees responsible for their futures positions do not fully understand how values of specific futures contracts will respond to market conditions. Furthermore, those employees may take more speculative positions than the firms desire if the firms do not have adequate controls to monitor their positions.

REGULATION IN THE FUTURES MARKETS

Given recent cases in which firms incurred major losses on futures contracts or other derivative securities, there is more awareness about **systemic risk,** or the risk that a particular event (such as financial problems at one particular firm) could spread adverse effects among several firms or among financial markets. The concern about systemic risk stems from the intertwined relationships among firms that engage in derivative securities trading that obligates them to make future payments to each other.

EXAMPLE

Nexus, Inc. requests several transactions in derivative securities, in which it buys futures on Treasury bonds in an over-the-counter market. Bangor Bank accommodates Nexus by taking the opposite side of the transactions. The bank's positions in these contracts also serve as a hedge against its existing exposure to interest rate risk. As time passes, Nexus experiences financial problems. As interest rates rise and the value of a Treasury bond futures contract declines, Nexus will take a major loss on the futures transactions. It files for bankruptcy, as it is unable to fulfill its obligation to buy the Treasury bonds from Bangor Bank at the settlement date. Bangor Bank was relying on this payment to hedge its exposure to interest rate risk. Consequently, Bangor Bank experiences financial problems and cannot make the payments on other over-the-counter derivatives contracts that it has with three other financial institutions. These financial institutions were relying on those funds to cover their own obligations on derivative contracts with several other firms. These firms may then be unable to honor their payment obligations resulting from the derivative contract agreements, causing the adverse effects to spread further. ●

Lengthy delays in payment could also disrupt the financial markets. Systemic risk is more pronounced as a result of the increasing use of over-the-counter markets for the trading of derivative securities.

Various regulators have attempted to reduce systemic risk by ensuring that participants in derivative securities markets have adequate collateral to back their derivative positions and that the participants fully disclose their exposure to risk resulting from derivative positions. For example, the Federal Reserve System monitors the commercial banks that participate in the derivative securities markets to ensure that they have adequate capital. During the credit crisis in 2008 and 2009, much more attention has been focused on limiting systemic risk.

Accounting regulators revised accounting standards in 1994 to require more disclosure about derivative positions. Specifically, firms are now required to report both their objectives in using derivative securities and the means by which they plan to achieve those objectives. The accounting guidelines also encourage firms to measure the impact of various possible economic scenarios on their derivative positions. There is an ongoing effort to make the accounting rules more consistent among derivative securities in the United States and throughout other countries as well. The accounting regulations are being reassessed due to the impact of the credit crisis.

INSTITUTIONAL USE OF FUTURES MARKETS

Exhibit 13.9 summarizes the manner in which various types of financial institutions participate in futures markets. Financial institutions generally use futures contracts to reduce risk, as has already been illustrated by several examples. Some commercial banks and savings institutions use a short hedge to protect against a possible increase in interest

Exhibit 13.9 Institutional Use of Futures Markets

TYPE OF FINANCIAL INSTITUTION	PARTICIPATION IN FUTURES MARKETS
Commercial banks	• Take positions in futures contracts to hedge against interest rate risk.
Savings institutions	• Take positions in futures contracts to hedge against interest rate risk.
Securities firms	• Execute futures transactions for individuals and firms. • Take positions in futures contracts to hedge their own portfolios against stock market or interest rate movements.
Mutual funds	• Take positions in futures contracts to speculate on future stock market or interest rate movements. • Take positions in futures contracts to hedge their portfolios against stock market or interest rate movements.
Pension funds	• Take positions in futures contracts to hedge their portfolios against stock market or interest rate movements.
Insurance companies	• Take positions in futures contracts to hedge their portfolios against stock market or interest rate movements.

rates. Some bond mutual funds, pension funds, and life insurance companies take short positions in interest rate futures to insulate their bond portfolios from a possible increase in interest rates. Stock mutual funds, pension funds, and insurance companies take short positions in stock index futures to partially insulate their respective stock portfolios from adverse stock market movements.

GLOBALIZATION OF FUTURES MARKETS

The trading of financial futures also requires the assessment of international financial market conditions. The flow of foreign funds into and out of the United States can affect interest rates and therefore the market value of Treasury bonds, corporate bonds, mortgages, and other long-term debt securities. Portfolio managers assess international flows of funds to forecast changes in interest rate movements, which in turn affect the value of their respective portfolios. Even speculators assess international flows of funds to forecast interest rates so that they can determine whether to take short or long futures positions.

Non-U.S. Participation in U.S. Futures Contracts

Financial futures contracts on U.S. securities are commonly traded by non-U.S. financial institutions that maintain holdings of U.S. securities. These institutions use financial futures to reduce their exposure to U.S. stock market or interest rate movements.

Foreign Stock Index Futures

Foreign stock index futures have been created to either speculate on or hedge against potential movements in foreign stock markets. Expectations of a strong foreign stock market encourage the purchase of futures contracts on the representative index. Conversely, if firms expect a decline in the foreign market, they will consider selling futures on the representative index. In addition, financial institutions with substantial investments in a particular foreign stock market can hedge against a temporary decline in that market by selling foreign stock index futures.

Exhibit 13.10 Popular Foreign Stock Index Futures Contracts

NAME OF STOCK FUTURES INDEX	DESCRIPTION
Nikkei 225	225 Japanese stocks
Toronto 35	35 stocks on Toronto stock exchange
Financial Times Stock Exchange 100	100 stocks on London stock exchange
Barclays share price	40 stocks on New Zealand stock exchange
Hang Seng	33 stocks on Hong Kong stock exchange
Osaka	50 Japanese stocks
All Ordinaries share price	307 Australian stocks

Some of the more popular foreign stock index futures contracts are identified in Exhibit 13.10. Numerous other foreign stock index futures contracts have been created. In fact, futures exchanges have been established in Ireland, France, Spain, and Italy. Financial institutions around the world can use futures contracts to hedge against temporary declines in their asset portfolios. Speculators can take long or short positions to speculate on a particular market with a relatively small initial investment. Financial futures on debt instruments (such as futures on German government bonds) are also offered by numerous exchanges in non-U.S. markets, including the London International Financial Futures Exchange, Singapore International Monetary Exchange (SIMEX), and Sydney Futures Exchange (SFE). In 2001, the LIFFE was acquired by Euronext, an alliance of European stock exchanges.

Electronic trading of futures contracts is creating an internationally integrated futures market. As mentioned earlier, the CME Group has instituted Globex, a round-the-world electronic trading network. It allows financial futures contracts to be traded even when the trading floor is closed.

Currency Futures Contracts

A **currency futures contract** is a standardized agreement to deliver or receive a specified amount of a specified foreign currency at a specified price (exchange rate) and date. The settlement months are March, June, September, and December. Some companies act as hedgers in the currency futures market by purchasing futures on currencies that they will need in the future to cover payables or by selling futures on currencies that they will receive in the future. Speculators in the currency futures market may purchase futures on a foreign currency that they expect to strengthen against the U.S. dollar or sell futures on currencies that they expect to weaken against the U.S. dollar.

Purchasers of currency futures contracts can hold the contract until the settlement date and accept delivery of the foreign currency at that time, or they can close out their long position prior to the settlement date by selling the identical type and number of contracts before then. If they close out their long position, their gain or loss is determined by the futures price when they created the position versus the futures price at the time the position was closed out. Sellers of currency futures contracts either deliver the foreign currency at the settlement date or close out their position by purchasing an identical type and number of contracts prior to the settlement date.

SUMMARY

- A financial futures contract is a standardized agreement to deliver or receive a specified amount of a specified financial instrument at a specified price and date. As the market value of the underlying instrument changes, so will the value of the financial futures contract. As the market value of the underlying instrument rises, there is a greater demand for the futures contract that has locked in the price of the instrument.

- An interest rate futures contract locks in the price to be paid for a specified debt instrument. Speculators who expect interest rates to decline can purchase interest rate futures contracts, because the market value of the underlying debt instrument should rise. Speculators who expect interest rates to rise can sell interest rate futures contracts, because the market value of the underlying debt instrument should decrease.

  Financial institutions (or other firms) that desire to hedge against rising interest rates can sell interest rate futures contracts. Financial institutions that desire to hedge against declining interest rates can purchase these contracts. If interest rates move in the anticipated direction, the financial institutions will gain from their futures position, which can partially offset any adverse effects of the interest rate movements on their normal operations.

- Speculators who expect stock prices to increase can purchase stock index futures contracts; speculators who expect stock prices to decrease can sell these contracts. Stock index futures can be sold by financial institutions that expect a temporary decline in stock prices and wish to hedge their stock portfolios.

- Depository institutions such as commercial banks and savings institutions commonly sell interest rate futures contracts to hedge against a possible increase in interest rates. Bond mutual funds, pension funds, and insurance companies also sell interest rate futures contracts to hedge their bond portfolios against a possible increase in interest rates.

  Stock mutual funds, pension funds, and insurance companies frequently sell stock index futures contracts to hedge their stock portfolios against a possible temporary decrease in stock prices.

POINT COUNTER-POINT

Has the Futures Market Created More Uncertainty for Stocks?

Point Yes. Futures contracts encourage speculation on indexes. Thus, an entire market can be influenced by the trading of speculators.

Counter-Point No. Futures contracts are commonly used to hedge portfolios and therefore can reduce the effects of weak market conditions. Moreover, investing in stocks is just as speculative as taking a position in futures markets.

Who Is Correct? Use the Internet to learn more about this issue. Offer your own opinion on this issue.

QUESTIONS AND APPLICATIONS

1. Futures Contracts Describe the general characteristics of a futures contract. How does a clearinghouse facilitate the trading of financial futures contracts?

2. Futures Pricing How does the price of a financial futures contract change as the market price of the security it represents changes? Why?

3. Hedging with Futures Explain why some futures contracts may be more suitable than others for hedging exposure to interest rate risk.

4. Treasury Bond Futures Will speculators buy or sell Treasury bond futures contracts if they expect interest rates to increase? Explain.

5. Gains from Purchasing Futures Explain how purchasers of financial futures contracts can offset their position. How is their gain or loss determined? What is the maximum loss to a purchaser of a futures contract?

6. Gains from Selling Futures Explain how sellers of financial futures contracts can offset their position. How is their gain or loss determined?

7. Hedging with Futures Assume a financial institution has more rate-sensitive assets than rate-sensitive liabilities. Would it be more likely to be adversely affected by an increase or a decrease in interest rates? Should it purchase or sell interest rate futures contracts in order to hedge its exposure?

8. Hedging with Futures Assume a financial institution has more rate-sensitive liabilities than rate-sensitive assets. Would it be more likely to be adversely affected by an increase or a decrease in interest rates? Should it purchase or sell interest rate futures contracts in order to hedge its exposure?

9. Hedging Decision Why do some financial institutions remain exposed to interest rate risk, even when they believe that the use of interest rate futures could reduce their exposure?

10. Long versus Short Hedge Explain the difference between a long hedge and a short hedge used by financial institutions. When is a long hedge more appropriate than a short hedge?

11. Impact of Futures Hedge Explain how the probability distribution of a financial institution's returns is affected when it uses interest rate futures to hedge. What does this imply about its risk?

12. Cross-Hedging Describe the act of cross-hedging. What determines the effectiveness of a cross-hedge?

13. Hedging with Bond Futures How might a savings and loan association use Treasury bond futures to hedge its fixed-rate mortgage portfolio (assuming that its main source of funds is short-term deposits)? Explain how prepayments on mortgages can limit the effectiveness of the hedge.

14. Stock Index Futures Describe stock index futures. How could they be used by a financial institution that is anticipating a jump in stock prices but does not yet have sufficient funds to purchase large amounts of stock? Explain why stock index futures may reflect investor expectations about the market more quickly than stock prices.

15. Selling Stock Index Futures Why would a pension fund or insurance company even consider selling stock index futures?

16. Index Arbitrage Explain how index arbitrage may be used.

17. Circuit Breakers Explain the use of circuit breakers.

Advanced Questions

18. Hedging with Futures Elon Savings and Loan Association has a large number of 30-year mortgages with floating interest rates that adjust on an annual basis and obtains most of its funds by issuing five-year certificates of deposit. It uses the yield curve to assess the market's anticipation of future interest rates. It believes that expectations of future interest rates are the major force affecting the yield curve. Assume that a downward-sloping yield curve with a steep slope exists. Based on this information, should Elon consider using financial futures as a hedging technique? Explain.

19. Hedging Decision Blue Devil Savings and Loan Association has a large number of 10-year fixed-rate mortgages and obtains most of its funds from short-term deposits. It uses the yield curve to assess the market's anticipation of future interest rates. It believes that expectations of future interest rates are the major force affecting the yield curve. Assume that an upward-sloping yield curve with a steep slope exists. Based on this information, should Blue Devil consider using financial futures as a hedging technique? Explain.

20. How Futures Prices May Respond to Prevailing Conditions Consider the prevailing conditions for inflation (including oil prices), the economy, the budget deficit, and other conditions that could affect the values of futures contracts. Based on prevailing conditions, would you prefer to buy or sell Treasury bond futures at this time? Would you prefer to buy or sell stock index futures at this time? Assume that you would close out your position at the end of your semester. Offer some logic to support your answers. Which factor is most influential on your decision regarding Treasury bond futures and on your decision regarding stock index futures?

Interpreting Financial News

Interpret the following statements made by Wall Street analysts and portfolio managers:

a. "The existence of financial futures contracts allows our firm to hedge against temporary market declines without liquidating our portfolios."

b. "Given my confidence in the market, I plan to use stock index futures to increase my exposure to market movements."

c. "We used currency futures to hedge the exchange rate exposure of our international mutual fund focused on German stocks."

Managing in Financial Markets
Managing Portfolios with Futures Contracts

As a portfolio manager, you are monitoring previous investments that you made in stocks and bonds of U.S. firms, as well as stocks and bonds of Japanese firms. Though you plan to keep all of these investments over the long run, you are willing to hedge against adverse effects on your investments that result from economic conditions. You expect that over the next year, U.S. and Japanese interest rates will decline, the U.S. stock market will perform poorly, the Japanese stock market will perform well, and the Japanese yen (the currency) will depreciate against the dollar.

a. Should you consider taking a position in U.S. bond index futures to hedge your investment in U.S. bonds? Explain.

b. Should you consider taking a position in Japanese bond index futures to hedge your investment in Japanese bonds? Explain.

c. Should you consider taking a position in U.S. stock index futures to hedge your investment in U.S. stocks? Explain.

d. Should you consider taking a position in Japanese stock index futures to hedge your investment in Japanese stocks? (Note: The Japanese stock index is denominated in yen and therefore is used to hedge stock movements, not currency movements.)

e. Should you consider taking a position in Japanese yen futures to hedge the exchange rate risk of your investment in Japanese stocks and bonds?

PROBLEMS

1. Profit from T-bill Futures Spratt Company purchased T-bill futures contracts when the quoted price was 93.50. When this position was closed out, the quoted price was 94.75. Determine the profit or loss per contract, ignoring transaction costs.

2. Profit from T-bill Futures Suerth Investments, Inc. purchased T-bill futures contracts when the quoted price was 95.00. When this position was closed out, the quoted price was 93.60. Determine the profit or loss per contract, ignoring transaction costs.

3. Profit from T-bill Futures Toland Company sold T-bill futures contracts when the quoted price was 94.00. When this position was closed out, the quoted price was 93.20. Determine the profit or loss per contract, ignoring transaction costs.

4. Profit from T-bill Futures Rude Dynamics, Inc. sold T-bill futures contracts when the quoted price was 93.26. When this position was closed out, the

quoted price was 93.90. Determine the profit or loss per contract, ignoring transaction costs.

5. Profit from T-bond Futures Egan Company purchased a futures contract on Treasury bonds that specified a price of 91–00. When the position was closed out, the price of the Treasury bond futures contract was 90–10. Determine the profit or loss, ignoring transaction costs.

6. Profit from T-bond Futures R. C. Clark sold a futures contract on Treasury bonds that specified a price of 92–10. When the position was closed out, the price of the Treasury bond futures contract was 93–00. Determine the profit or loss, ignoring transaction costs.

7. Profit from Stock Index Futures Marks Insurance Company sold S&P 500 stock index futures that specified an index of 1690. When the position was closed out, the index specified by the futures contract was 1720. Determine the profit or loss, ignoring transaction costs.

FLOW OF FUNDS EXERCISE

Hedging with Futures Contracts

Recall that if the economy continues to be strong, Carson Company may need to increase its production capacity by about 50 percent over the next few years to satisfy demand. It would need financing to expand and accommodate the increase in production. Recall that the yield curve is currently upward sloping. Also recall that Carson is concerned about a possible slowing of the economy because of potential Fed actions to reduce inflation. Carson currently relies mostly on commercial loans with floating interest rates for its debt financing.

a. How could Carson use futures contracts to reduce the exposure of its cost of debt to interest rate move-ments? Be specific about whether it would use a short hedge or a long hedge.

b. Will the hedge that you described in the previous question perfectly offset the increase in debt costs if interest rates increase? Explain what drives the profit from the short hedge, versus what drives the higher cost of debt to Carson if interest rates increase.

INTERNET/EXCEL EXERCISES

1. Go to http://futuresource.quote.com/. Review the charts for an equity index product such as the S&P 500. Explain how the price pattern moved recently.

2. Now compare that pattern to the actual trend of the S&P 500, which is provided at http://finance.yahoo .com/7u (just click on "S&P 500" there to access the charts). Describe the relationship between the movements in S&P 500 futures and movements in the S&P 500 index.

14

Options Markets

CHAPTER OBJECTIVES

The specific objectives of this chapter are to:

- explain how stock options are used to speculate,

- explain why stock option premiums vary,

- explain the use of stock index options, and

- explain the use of options on futures.

WEB

www.cboe.com

The volume of calls versus the volume of puts—used to assess their respective popularity.

Stock options can be used by speculators to benefit from their expectations and by financial institutions to reduce their risk. Options markets facilitate the trading of stock options.

BACKGROUND ON OPTIONS

Options are classified as calls or puts. A **call option** grants the owner the right to purchase a specified financial instrument for a specified price (called the **exercise price** or **strike price**) within a specified period of time. There are two major differences between purchasing an option and purchasing a futures contract. First, to obtain an option, a premium must be paid in addition to the price of the financial instrument. Second, the owner of an option can choose to let the option expire on the so-called expiration date without exercising it. That is, call options grant a right, but not an obligation, to purchase a specified financial instrument. The seller (sometimes called the **writer**) of a call option is obligated to provide the specified financial instrument at the price specified by the option contract if the owner exercises the option. Sellers of call options receive an up-front fee (the premium) from the purchaser as compensation.

A call option is said to be **in the money** when the market price of the underlying security exceeds the exercise price, **at the money** when the market price is equal to the exercise price, and **out of the money** when it is below the exercise price.

The second type of option is known as a **put option.** It grants the owner the right to sell a specified financial instrument for a specified price within a specified period of time. As with call options, owners pay a premium to obtain put options. They can exercise the options at any time up to the expiration date but are not obligated to do so.

A put option is said to be "in the money" when the market price of the underlying security is below the exercise price, "at the money" when the market price is equal to the exercise price, and "out of the money" when it exceeds the exercise price.

Call and put options specify 100 shares for the stocks to which they are assigned. Most small standardized transactions are executed electronically, while complex transactions are executed by competitive open outcry between exchange members. Premiums paid for call and put options are determined by the participants engaged in trading. The premium for a particular option changes over time as it becomes more or less desirable to traders.

Participants can close out their option positions by making an offsetting transaction. For example, purchasers of an option can offset their positions at any time by selling an identical option. The gain or loss is determined by the premium paid when purchasing the option versus the premium received when selling an identical option. Sellers of options can close out their positions at any time by purchasing an identical option.

The stock options just described are known as "American-style" stock options. They can be exercised at any time until the expiration date. In contrast, "European-style" stock options can be exercised only just before expiration.

Markets Used to Trade Options

The Chicago Board Options Exchange (CBOE), which was created in 1973, is the most important exchange for trading options. It serves as a market for options on more than 2,000 different stocks. Before the creation of the CBOE, some stock options were exchanged between financial institutions, but the contracts were customized and exchanged largely through personal agreements. In contrast, the options listed on the CBOE have a standardized format, as will be explained shortly. The standardization of the contracts on the CBOE proved to be a major advantage because it allowed for easy trading of existing contracts (a secondary market). With standardization, the popularity of options increased, and the options became more liquid. Since there were numerous buyers and sellers of the standardized contracts, buyers and sellers of a particular option contract could be matched.

Options are also traded at the CME Group, which was formed in July 2007 by the merger of the Chicago Board of Trade (CBOT) and the Chicago Mercantile Exchange (CME). As discussed in Chapter 13, the CME Group serves international markets for derivative products. To increase efficiency and reduce operating and maintenance expenses after the merger, the CME Group consolidated the CME and CBOT trading floors into a single trading floor at the CBOT and consolidated the products of the CME and CBOT on a single electronic platform. Transactions of new derivative products typically are executed by the CME Group's electronic platform.

As the popularity of stock options increased, various stock exchanges began to list options. In particular, the American Stock Exchange (acquired by NYSE Euronext in 2008), the Nasdaq, and the Philadelphia Stock Exchange (acquired by the Nasdaq market in 2008) list options on many different stocks, as does the International Securities Exchange, which was the first fully electronic U.S. options exchange. Today, any particular options contract may be traded on various exchanges, and the competition among the exchanges may result in more favorable prices for customers.

Listing Requirements Each exchange has its own requirements for the stocks for which it creates options. One key requirement is a minimum trading volume of the underlying stock, as the volume of options traded on a particular stock will normally be higher if the stock trading volume is high. The decision to list an option is made by each exchange, not by the firms represented by the options contracts.

Role of the Options Clearing Corporation (OCC) Like a stock transaction, the trading of an option involves a buyer and a seller. The sale of an option imposes specific obligations on the seller under specific conditions. The exchange itself does not take positions in option contracts, but provides a market where the options can be bought or sold. The Options Clearing Corporation (OCC) serves as a guarantor on option contracts traded in the United States, which means that the buyer of an option contract does not have to be concerned that the seller will back out of the obligation.

Regulation of Options Trading Options trading is regulated by the Securities and Exchange Commission (SEC) and by the various option exchanges. The regulation is intended to ensure fair and orderly trading. For example, it attempts to prevent insider trading (trading based on information that insiders have about their firms and that is not yet disclosed to the public). It also attempts to prevent price fixing among floor brokers that could cause wider bid-ask spreads that would impose higher costs on customers.

How Option Trades Are Executed

When options exchanges were created, floor brokers were available to execute orders for brokerage firms. They went to a specific location on the trading floor where the option was traded to execute the order. Today, computer technology allows investors to have trades executed electronically. Many electronic communication networks (ECNs) are programmed to consider all possible trades and execute the order at the best possible price.

Market-makers can also execute stock option transactions for customers. They earn the difference between the bid price and the ask price for this trade. The spread has declined significantly in recent years. Market-makers also generate profits or losses when they invest their own funds in options.

Types of Orders

As with stocks, an investor can use either a market order or a limit order for an option transaction. A market order will result in the immediate purchase or sale of an option at the prevailing market price of the option. With a limit order, the transaction will occur only if the market price is no higher or lower than a specified price limit. For example, an investor may request the purchase of a specific option only if it can be purchased at or below some specified price. Conversely, an investor may request to sell an option only if it can be sold for some specified limit or more.

Online Trading   Option contracts can also be purchased or sold online. Many online brokerage firms, including E*Trade and TD Ameritrade, facilitate options orders. Online option contract orders are commonly routed to computerized networks on options exchanges, where they are executed. For these orders, computers handle the order from the time it is placed until it is executed.

Stock Option Quotations

Financial newspapers and other financial media publish quotations for stock options. Exhibit 14.1 provides an example of McDonald's stock options as of May 1, when the stock was priced at about $45.62 per share. There are more options on McDonald's stock than are shown here, with additional exercise prices and expiration dates. Each row represents a specific option on McDonald's stock. The first column lists the exercise (strike) price, and the second column lists the expiration date. (The expiration date for stock options traded on the CBOE is the Saturday following the third Friday of the specified month.) The third and fourth columns show the volume and the most recently quoted premium of the call option with that exercise price and expiration date. The fifth and sixth columns show the volume and the most recently quoted premium of the put option with that exercise price and expiration date.

A comparison of the premiums among the four options illustrates how specific factors affect option premiums. First, a comparison of the first and third rows (to control for the same expiration date) reveals that an option with a higher exercise price has a lower call

Exhibit 14.1 McDonald's Stock Option Quotations

	STRIKE	EXP.	VOLUME	CALL	VOLUME	PUT
McDonald's	45	Jun	180	4½	60	2¾
	45	Oct	70	5¾	120	3¾
	50	Jun	360	1⅛	40	5⅛
	50	Oct	90	3½	40	6½

option premium and a higher put option premium. A comparison of the second and fourth rows further confirms this relationship. Second, comparing the first and second rows (to control for the same exercise price) reveals that an option with a longer term to maturity has a higher call option premium and a higher put option premium. A comparison of the third and fourth rows further confirms this relationship.

SPECULATING WITH STOCK OPTIONS

Stock options are frequently traded by investors who are attempting to capitalize on their expectations. When investors purchase an option that does not cover (hedge) their existing investments, the option can be referred to as "naked" (uncovered). Since speculators trade options to gamble on price movements rather than to hedge existing investments, their positions in options are naked. Whether speculators purchase call options or put options depends on their expectations.

In some cases, speculators borrow a portion of the funds that they use to invest in stock options. The use of borrowed funds can magnify their gains, but it can also magnify their losses. The gains and losses described in this chapter would be more pronounced if the speculators cited in the examples used borrowed funds for a portion of their investment.

Speculating with Call Options

Call options can be used to speculate on the expectation of an increase in the price of the underlying stock.

EXAMPLE   Pat Jackson expects Steelco stock to increase from its current price of $113 per share but does not want to tie up her available funds by investing in stocks. She purchases a call option on Steelco with an exercise price of $115 for a premium of $4 per share. Before the option's expiration date, Steelco's price rises to $121. At that time, Jackson exercises her option, purchasing shares at $115 per share. She then immediately sells those shares at the market price of $121 per share. Her net gain on this transaction is measured below:

Amount received when selling shares	$121 per share
− Amount paid for shares	− $115 per share
− Amount paid for the call option	− $ 4 per share
= Net gain	$ 2 per share
	or $200 for one contract

Pat's net gain of $2 per share reflects a return of 50 percent (not annualized). ●

If the price of Steelco stock had not risen above $115 before the option's expiration date, Jackson would have let the option expire. Her net loss would have been the $4 per share she initially paid for the option, or $400 for one option contract. This example reflects a 100 percent loss, as the entire amount of the investment is lost.

The potential gains or losses from this call option are shown in the left portion of Exhibit 14.2, based on the assumptions that (1) the call option is exercised on the expiration date, if at all, and (2) if the call option is exercised, the shares received are immediately sold. Exhibit 14.2 shows that the maximum loss when purchasing this option is the premium of $4 per share. For stock prices between $115 and $119, the option is exercised, and the purchaser of a call option incurs a net loss of less than $4 per share. The stock price of $119 is a break-even point, because the gain from exercising the option exactly offsets the premium paid for it. At stock prices above $119, a net gain is realized.

The right portion of Exhibit 14.2 shows the net gain or loss to a writer of the same call option, assuming that the writer obtains the stock only when the option is exercised.

Exhibit 14.2 Potential Gains or Losses on a Call Option: Exercise Price = \$115, Premium = \$4

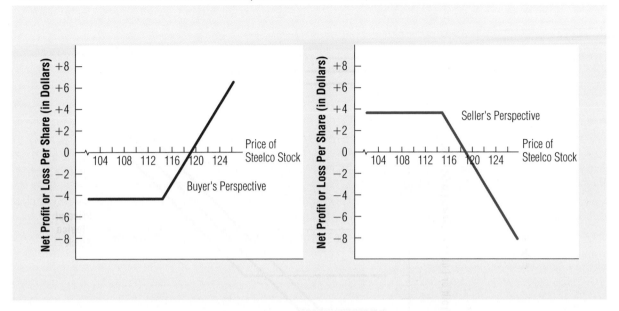

Under this condition, the call option writer's net gain (loss) is the call option purchaser's net loss (gain), assuming zero transaction costs. The maximum gain to the writer of a call option is the premium received.

Several call options are available for a given stock, and the risk-return potential will vary among them. Assume that three types of call options were available on Steelco stock with a similar expiration date, as described in Exhibit 14.3. The potential gains or losses per unit for each option are also shown in Exhibit 14.3, assuming that the option is exercised on the expiration date, if at all. It is also assumed that if the speculators exercise the call option, they immediately sell the stock. This comparison of different options for a given stock illustrates the various risk-return tradeoffs from which speculators can choose.

Purchasers of call options are normally most interested in returns (profit as a percentage of the initial investment) under various scenarios. For this purpose, the contingency graph can be revised to reflect returns for each possible price per share of the underlying stock. The first step is to convert the profit per unit into a return for each possible price, as shown in Exhibit 14.4. For example, for the stock price of \$116, Call Option 1 generates a return of 10 percent (\$1 per share profit as a percentage of the \$10 premium paid), Call Option 2 generates a loss of about 14 percent (\$1 per share loss as a percentage of the \$7 premium paid), and Call Option 3 generates a loss of 75 percent (\$3 per share loss as a percentage of the \$4 premium paid).

The data can be transformed into a contingency graph as shown in Exhibit 14.5. This graph illustrates that for Call Option 1 both the potential losses and the potential returns in the event of a high stock price are relatively low. Conversely, the potential losses for Call Option 3 are relatively high, but so are the potential returns in the event of a high stock price.

Speculating with Put Options

Put options can be used to speculate on the expectation of a decrease in the price of the underlying stock.

Exhibit 14.3 Potential Gains or Losses for Three Call Options (Buyer's Perspective)

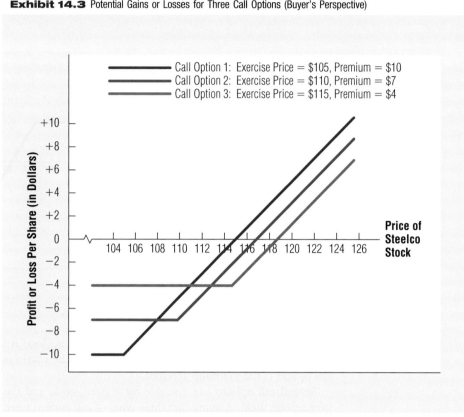

Exhibit 14.4 Potential Returns on Three Different Call Options

PRICE OF STEELCO	OPTION 1: EXERCISE PRICE = $105 PREMIUM = $10		OPTION 2: EXERCISE PRICE = $110 PREMIUM = $7		OPTION 3: EXERCISE PRICE = $115 PREMIUM = $4	
	PROFIT PER UNIT	PERCENTAGE RETURN	PROFIT PER UNIT	PERCENTAGE RETURN	PROFIT PER UNIT	PERCENTAGE RETURN
$104	−$10	−100%	−$7	−100%	−$4	−100%
106	−9	−90	−7	−100	−4	−100
108	−7	−70	−7	−100	−4	−100
110	−5	−50	−7	−100	−4	−100
112	−3	−30	−5	−71	−4	−100
114	−1	−10	−3	−43	−4	−100
116	1	10	−1	−14	−3	−75
118	3	30	1	14	−1	−25
120	5	50	3	43	1	25
122	7	70	5	71	3	75
124	9	90	7	100	5	125
126	11	110	9	129	7	175

Exhibit 14.5 Potential Returns for Three Call Options (Buyer's Perspective)

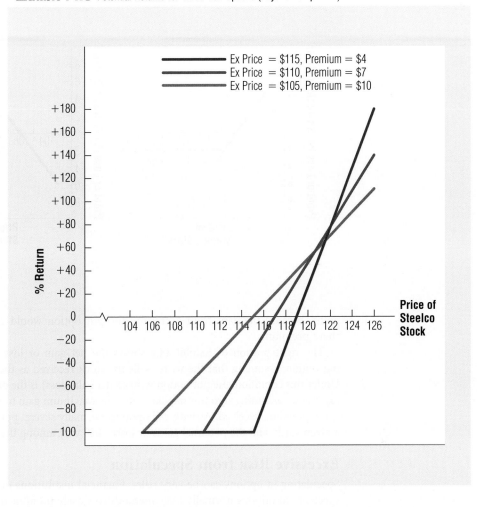

A put option on Steelco is available with an exercise price of $110 and a premium of $2. If the price of Steelco stock falls below $110, speculators could purchase the stock and then exercise their put options to benefit from the transaction. However, they would need to make at least $2 per share on this transaction to fully recover the premium paid for the option. If the speculators exercise the option when the market price is $104, their net gain is measured as follows:

Amount received when selling shares	$110 per share
− Amount paid for shares	− $104 per share
− Amount paid for the put option	− $ 2 per share
= Net gain	$ 4 per share

The net gain here is 200 percent, or twice as much as the amount paid for the put options. ●

The potential gains or losses from the put option described here are shown in the left portion of Exhibit 14.6, based on the assumptions that (1) the put option is exercised on the expiration date, if at all, and (2) the shares would be purchased just before the put option is exercised. Exhibit 14.6 shows that the maximum loss when purchasing this option is $2 per share. For stock prices between $108 and $110, the purchaser of a put option incurs a net loss of less than $2 per share. The stock price of $108 is a break-even

Exhibit 14.6 Potential Gains or Losses on a Put Option: Exercise Price = $110, Premium = $2

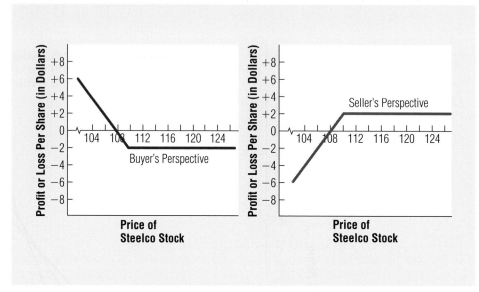

point, because the gain from exercising the put option would exactly offset the $2 per share premium.

The right portion of Exhibit 14.6 shows the net gain or loss to a writer of the same put option, assuming that the writer sells the stock received as the put option is exercised. Under this condition, the put option writer's net gain (loss) is the put option purchaser's net loss (gain), assuming zero transaction costs. The maximum gain to the writer of a put option is the premium received. As with call options, normally several put options are available for a given stock, and the potential gains or losses will vary among them.

Excessive Risk from Speculation

Speculating in options can be very risky. Financial institutions or other corporations that speculate in options normally have methods to closely monitor their risk and to measure their exposure to possible option market conditions. In several cases, however, a financial institution or a corporation incurred a major loss on options positions because of a lack of oversight over its options trading.

EXAMPLE

In 1995, Barings PLC, an investment bank in the United Kingdom, incurred losses of more than $1 billion as a result of positions in stock options and other derivative instruments. A brief summary of the Barings case identifies the reasons for the substantial losses and indicates measures that other firms can take to ensure that they will not experience such losses.

In 1992, Nicholas Leeson, a clerk in Barings's London office, was sent to manage the accounting at a Singapore subsidiary called Barings Futures. Shortly after he began his new position in Singapore, Leeson took and passed the examinations required to trade on the floor of the Singapore International Monetary Exchange (SIMEX). Barings Futures served as a broker on this exchange for some of its customers. In less than one year after he arrived in Singapore, Leeson was trading derivative contracts on the SIMEX as an employee of Barings Futures. He then began to trade for the firm's own account rather than just as a broker, trading options on the Nikkei (Japanese) stock index. At the same time, he also continued to serve as the accounting manager for Barings Futures. In this role Leeson was able to conceal losses on any derivative positions, so the financial reports to Barings PLC showed massive profits.

In January 1995, an earthquake in Japan led to a major decline in Japanese stock prices, and the Nikkei index declined. This caused a loss exceeding the equivalent of $100 million on

Leeson's options positions. Leeson attempted to recover these losses by purchasing Nikkei index futures contracts, but the market declined further over the next two months. Leeson's losses accumulated, exceeding the equivalent of $300 million. Leeson had periodically needed funds to cover margin calls as his positions declined in value. Barings PLC met the funding requests to cover the equivalent of millions of dollars to satisfy the margin calls and did not recognize that the margin calls were signaling a major problem.

In late February 1995, an accounting clerk at Barings who noticed some discrepancies met with Leeson to reconcile the records. During the meeting, when Leeson was asked to explain specific accounting entries, he excused himself and never returned. He left Singapore that night and faxed his resignation to Barings PLC from Kuala Lumpur, Malaysia. The next day, employees of the Singapore office reviewed Leeson's private records and realized that he had accumulated major losses. At this point, Barings PLC asked the Bank of England (the central bank) for assistance in resolving the situation. When Barings PLC and the Bank of England investigated, they found that Leeson had accumulated losses of more than the equivalent of $1 billion—more than double the entire amount of equity of Barings PLC. Barings was insolvent and was acquired by a Dutch firm called Internationale Nederlanden Groep (ING). Later that year, Leeson was extradited to Singapore and pleaded guilty to charges of fraud. He was sentenced to prison for six and one-half years. Until Barings discovered the losses, Leeson was scheduled to earn an annual bonus exceeding the equivalent of $600,000. ●

Any firms that use futures or other derivative instruments can draw a few obvious lessons from the Barings collapse. First, firms should closely monitor the trading of derivative contracts by their employees to ensure that derivatives are being used within the firm's guidelines. Second, firms should separate the reporting function from the trading function so that traders cannot conceal trading losses. Third, when firms receive margin calls on derivative positions, they should recognize that there may be potential losses on their derivative instruments, and they should closely evaluate those positions. The Barings case provided a wake-up call to many firms, which recognized the need to establish guidelines for their employees who take derivative positions and to more closely monitor the actions of these employees.

DETERMINANTS OF STOCK OPTION PREMIUMS

Stock option premiums are determined by market forces. Any characteristic of an option that results in many willing buyers but few willing sellers will place upward pressure on the option premium. Thus, the option premium must be sufficiently high to equalize the demand by buyers and the supply that sellers are willing to sell. This generalization applies to both call options and put options. The specific characteristics that affect the demand and supply conditions, and therefore affect the option premiums, are described below.

Determinants of Call Option Premiums

Call option premiums are affected primarily by the following factors:

- Market price of the underlying instrument (relative to the option's exercise price)
- Volatility of the underlying instrument
- Time to maturity of the call option

Influence of the Market Price   The higher the existing market price of the underlying financial instrument relative to the exercise price, the higher the call option premium, other things being equal. A financial instrument's value has a higher probability of increasing well above the exercise price if it is already close to or above the exercise price. Thus, a purchaser would be willing to pay a higher premium for a call option on that instrument.

Exhibit 14.7 Relationship between Exercise Price and Call Option Premium on KSR Stock

EXERCISE PRICE	PREMIUM FOR APRIL EXPIRATION DATE
$130	11⅝
135	7½
140	5¼
145	3¼
150	1⅞

The influence of the market price of an instrument (relative to the exercise price) on the call option premium can also be understood by comparing options with different exercise prices on the same instrument at a given point in time.

EXAMPLE

Consider the data shown in Exhibit 14.7 for KSR call options quoted on February 25, 2010, with a similar expiration date. The stock price of KSR was about $140 at that time. The premium for the call option with the $130 exercise price was almost $10 higher than the premium for the option with the $150 exercise price. This example confirms that a higher premium is required to lock in a lower exercise price on call options. ●

Influence of the Stock's Volatility The greater the volatility of the underlying stock, the higher the call option premium, other things being equal. If a stock is volatile, there is a higher probability that its price will increase well above the exercise price. Thus, a purchaser would be willing to pay a higher premium for a call option on that stock. To illustrate, call options on small stocks normally have higher premiums than call options on large stocks because small stocks are typically more volatile.

Influence of the Call Option's Time to Maturity The longer the call option's time to maturity, the higher the call option premium, other things being equal. A longer time period until expiration allows the owner of the option more time to exercise the option. Thus, there is a higher probability that the instrument's price will move well above the exercise price before the option expires.

The relationship between the time to maturity and the call option premium is illustrated in Exhibit 14.8 for KSR call options quoted on February 25, 2010, with a similar exercise price of $135. The premium was $4.50 per share for the call option with a March expiration month versus $7.50 per share for the call option with an April expiration month. The difference reflects the additional time in which the April call option can be exercised.

Determinants of Put Option Premiums

The premium paid on a put option is dependent on the same factors that affect the premium paid on a call option. However, the direction of influence varies for one of the factors, as explained next.

Exhibit 14.8 Relationship between Time to Maturity and Call Option Premium on KSR Stock

EXPIRATION DATE	PREMIUM FOR OPTION WITH A $135 EXERCISE PRICE
March	4½
April	7½
July	13¼

Exhibit 14.9 Relationship between Exercise Price and Put Option Premium on KSR Stock

EXERCISE PRICE	PREMIUM FOR JUNE EXPIRATION DATE
$130	1⅞
135	3⅛
140	5⅜
145	8½
150	12¼

Influence of the Market Price   The higher the existing market price of the underlying financial instrument relative to the exercise price, the lower the put option premium, other things being equal. A financial instrument's value has a higher probability of decreasing well below the exercise price if it is already close to or below the exercise price. Thus, a purchaser would be willing to pay a higher premium for a put option on that instrument. This influence on the put option premium differs from the influence on the call option premium, because a lower market price is preferable from the perspective of put option purchasers.

The influence of the market price of an instrument (relative to the exercise price) on the put option premium can also be understood by comparing options with different exercise prices on the same instrument at a given point in time. For example, consider the data shown in Exhibit 14.9 for KSR put options with a similar expiration date quoted on February 25, 2010. The premium for the put option with the $150 exercise price was more than $9 per share higher than the premium for the option with the $135 exercise price. The difference reflects the more favorable price at which the stock can be sold when holding the put option with the higher exercise price.

Influence of the Stock's Volatility   The greater the volatility of the underlying stock, the higher the put option premium, other things being equal. This relationship also held for call option premiums. If a stock is volatile, there is a higher probability of its price deviating far from the exercise price. Thus, a purchaser would be willing to pay a higher premium for a put option on that stock, because its market price is more likely to decline well below the option's exercise price.

Influence of the Put Option's Time to Maturity   The longer the time to maturity, the higher the put option premium, other things being equal. This relationship also held for call option premiums. A longer time period until expiration allows the owner of the option more time to exercise the option. Thus, there is a higher probability that the instrument's price will move well below the exercise price before the option expires.

The relationship between the time to maturity and the put option premium is shown in Exhibit 14.10 for KSR put options with a similar exercise price of $135 quoted on

Exhibit 14.10 Relationship between Time to Maturity and Put Option Premium on KSR Stock

EXPIRATION DATE	PREMIUM FOR OPTION WITH A $135 EXERCISE PRICE
March	½
April	3⅛
July	7¼

February 25, 2010. The premium was $7.25 per share for the put option with a July expiration month versus $.50 per share for the put option with a March expiration month. The difference reflects the additional time in which the put option with the July expiration date can be exercised.

EXPLAINING CHANGES IN OPTION PREMIUMS

Exhibit 14.11 identifies the underlying forces that cause option prices to change over time. Economic conditions and market conditions can cause abrupt changes in the stock price or in the anticipated volatility of the stock price over the time remaining until option expiration. These changes would have a major impact on the stock option's premium.

Exhibit 14.11 Framework for Explaining Why a Stock Option's Premium Changes over Time

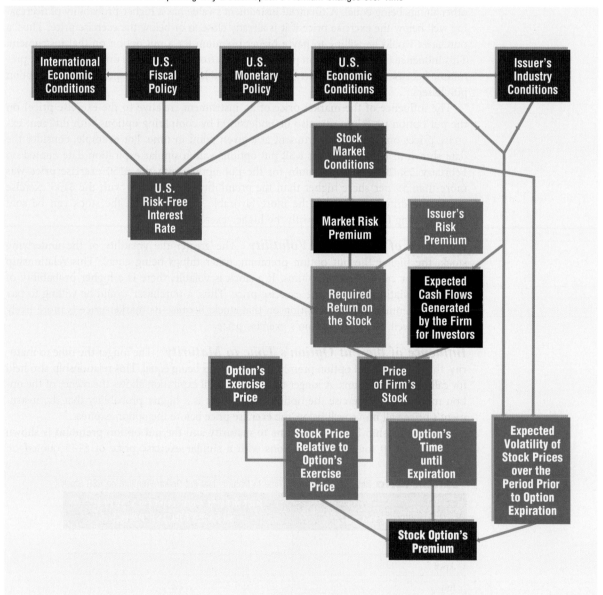

Indicators Monitored by Participants in the Options Market

Since the premiums paid on stock options are highly influenced by the price movements of the underlying stocks, participants in the stock option market closely monitor the same indicators that are monitored when trading the underlying stocks. Participants who have an options position or are considering taking a position monitor several indicators for the set of underlying stocks, including economic indicators, corresponding industry-specific conditions, and firm-specific conditions. Participants trading stock options may assess a given set of information differently than those who trade stocks, however. For example, an owner of a call option representing a particular stock may not be as concerned about the possibility of a labor strike as an owner of the firm's stock would be, because the call option limits the downside risk.

EXAMPLE

During the fall of 2008, the credit crisis intensified, and stock volatility increased substantially. Consequently, premiums for options increased substantially as well. Under these conditions, more portfolio managers wanted to hedge their stock positions, but they had to pay a higher price for put options. The sellers of put options recognized that their risk had increased due to the higher volatility and priced the put options accordingly. ●

Traders of options tend to monitor economic indicators because economic conditions affect cash flows of firms and, therefore, can affect expected stock valuations and stock option premiums. Economic conditions can also affect the premiums by affecting the expected stock volatility. Therefore, these traders closely monitor economic indicators such as a change in the Federal Reserve's federal funds rate target, the employment level, and the gross domestic product.

HEDGING WITH STOCK OPTIONS

Call and put options on selected stocks and stock indexes are commonly used for hedging against possible stock price movements. Financial institutions such as mutual funds, insurance companies, and pension funds manage large stock portfolios and are the most common users of options for hedging.

Hedging with Call Options

Call options on a stock can be used to hedge a position in that stock.

EXAMPLE

Portland Pension Fund owns a substantial amount of Steelco stock. It expects that the stock will perform well in the long run, but is somewhat concerned that the stock may perform poorly over the next few months because of temporary problems Steelco is experiencing. The sale of a call option on Steelco stock can hedge against such a potential loss. This is known as a **covered call,** because the option is covered, or backed, by stocks already owned.

If the market price of Steelco stock rises, the call option will likely be exercised, and Portland will fulfill its obligation by selling its Steelco stock to the purchaser of the call option at the exercise price. Conversely, if the market price of Steelco stock declines, the option will not be exercised. Consequently, Portland would not have to sell its Steelco stock, and the premium received from selling the call option would represent a gain that could partially offset the decline in the price of the stock. In this case, although the market value of the institution's stock portfolio is adversely affected, the decline is at least partially offset by the premium received from selling the call option.

Assume that Portland Pension Fund purchased Steelco stock at the market price of $112 per share. To hedge against a temporary decline in Steelco's stock price, Portland sells call options on Steelco stock with an exercise price of $110 per share for a premium of $5 per share. The net profit to Portland when using covered call writing is shown in Exhibit 14.12 for various possible scenarios. For comparison purposes, the profit that Portland would earn if it did not use

Exhibit 14.12 Risk-Return Tradeoff from Covered Call Writing

							EXPLANATION OF PROFIT PER SHARE FROM COVERED CALL WRITING					
MARKET PRICE OF STEELCO AS OF THE EXPIRATION DATE	PRICE AT WHICH PORTLAND PENSION FUND SELLS STEELCO STOCK		PREMIUM RECEIVED FROM WRITING THE CALL OPTION		PRICE PAID FOR STEELCO STOCK		PROFIT OR LOSS PER SHARE
$104	$104	+	$5	–	$112	=	–$3
105	105	+	5	–	112	=	–2
106	106	+	5	–	112	=	–1
107	107	+	5	–	112	=	0
108	108	+	5	–	112	=	1
109	109	+	5	–	112	=	2
110	110	+	5	–	112	=	3
111	110	+	5	–	112	=	3
112	110	+	5	–	112	=	3
113	110	+	5	–	112	=	3
114	110	+	5	–	112	=	3
115	110	+	5	–	112	=	3
116	110	+	5	–	112	=	3
117	110	+	5	–	112	=	3
118	110	+	5	–	112	=	3
119	110	+	5	–	112	=	3
120	110	+	5	–	112	=	3

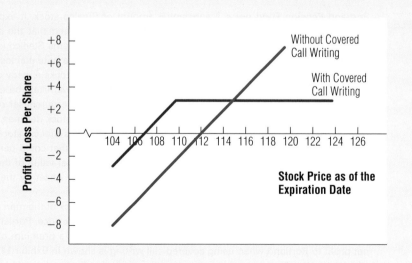

covered call writing but sold the stock on the option's expiration date is also shown (see the diagonal line) for various possible scenarios. Notice that the results with covered call writing are not as bad as without covered call writing when the stock performs poorly, but not as good when the stock performs well. ●

The table in Exhibit 14.12 explains the profit or loss per share from covered call writing. At any price above $110 per share as of the expiration date, the call option would be exercised, and Portland would have to sell its holdings of Steelco stock at the exercise price of $110 per share to the purchaser of the call option. The net gain to Portland would be $3 per share, determined as the premium of $5 per share, received when writing the option, minus the $2 per share difference between the price paid for the Steelco stock and the price at which the stock is sold. Comparing the profit or loss per scenario with versus without covered call writing, it is clear that covered call writing limits the upside potential return on stocks but also reduces the risk.

Hedging with Put Options

Put options on stock are also used to hedge stock positions.

Reconsider the example in which Portland Pension Fund was concerned about a possible temporary decline in the price of Steelco stock. Portland could hedge against a temporary decline in Steelco's stock price by purchasing put options on that stock. In the event that Steelco's stock price declines, Portland would likely generate a gain on its option position, which would help offset the reduction in the stock's price. If Steelco's stock price does not decline, Portland would not exercise its put option. ●

Put options are typically used to hedge when portfolio managers are mainly concerned about a temporary decline in a stock's value. When portfolio managers are mainly concerned about the long-term performance of a stock, they are likely to sell the stock itself rather than hedge the position.

Using Options to Measure a Stock's Risk

Recall that one of the measures of a stock's risk is the standard deviation of its returns. Stock options are commonly used to derive the market's anticipation of a stock's standard deviation over the life of the option. Recall that a stock option's premium is influenced by factors such as the prevailing stock price, the time to expiration, and the volatility of the stock. The price of an option is often determined by using a formula (see the chapter appendix) based on the values of these factors, including a guess at the market's anticipation of the stock's volatility over the remaining life of the option.

Although market participants' anticipated volatility of a stock is not observable, the stock option formula can be used to derive an estimate for a specific stock's volatility. By plugging in values for the factors that affect a particular stock option's premium and for the prevailing premium, it is possible to derive the implied standard deviation of a stock. Thus, the implied standard deviation is derived by determining what its value must be, given the values of other factors that affect the stock option's premium and given the prevailing option premium.

When a firm experiences an event that creates more uncertainty, its implied standard deviation increases. For example, if a firm's CEO suddenly resigns, the implied standard deviation will likely increase. The premium to be paid for a stock option will increase in response, even if the stock price itself does not change. An increase in uncertainty results in a higher implied standard deviation for the stock, which means that the writer of an option requires a higher premium to compensate for the anticipated increase in the stock's volatility.

Options on ETFs and Stock Indexes

Options are also traded on exchange-traded funds (ETFs) and stock indexes. ETFs are funds that are designed to mimic particular indexes and are traded on an exchange. Thus, an ETF option provides the right to trade a specified ETF at a specified price by a specified expiration date. Since ETFs are traded like stocks, options on ETFs are traded like options on stocks. Investors who exercise a call option on an ETF will receive delivery of the ETF in their account. Investors who exercise a put option on an ETF will have the ETF transferred from their account to the counterparty on the put option.

A **stock index option** provides the right to trade a specified stock index at a specified price by a specified expiration date. Call options on stock indexes allow the right to purchase the index, and put options on stock indexes allow the right to sell the index. If and when the index option is exercised, the cash payment is equal to a specified dollar amount multiplied by the difference between the index level and the exercise price.

Options on stock indexes are somewhat similar to options on ETFs. However, the values of stock indexes change only at the end of each trading day, whereas ETF values can change throughout the day. Therefore, an investor who wants to capitalize on the expected movement of an index within a particular day will trade options on ETFs. An investor who wants to capitalize on the expected movement of an index over a longer period of time (such as a week or several months) can trade options on either ETFs or indexes.

Options on indexes have become popular for speculating on general movements in the stock market overall. Speculators who anticipate a sharp increase in stock market prices overall may consider purchasing call options on one of the market indexes. Conversely, speculators who anticipate a stock market decline may consider purchasing put options on these indexes.

A sampling of options that are traded on ETFs and on stock indexes is provided in Exhibit 14.13. In general, investors can trade options on ETFs or indexes to speculate on expected changes in broad markets or specific sectors.

Hedging with Stock Index Options

Financial institutions and other firms commonly take positions in options on ETFs or indexes to hedge against market or sector conditions that would adversely affect their asset portfolio or cash flows. The following discussion is based on the use of options on stock indexes, but options on ETFs could be used in the same manner.

Financial institutions such as insurance companies and pension funds maintain large stock portfolios whose values are driven by general market movements. If the stock portfolio is broad enough, any changes in its value will likely be highly correlated with the market movements. For this reason, portfolio managers consider purchasing put options on a stock index to protect against stock market declines. The put options should be purchased on the stock index that most closely mirrors the portfolio to be hedged. If the stock market experiences a severe downturn, the market value of the portfolio declines, but the put options on the stock index will generate a gain because the value of the index will be less than the exercise price. The greater the market downturn, the greater the decline in the market value of the portfolio, but the greater the gain from holding put options on a stock index. Thus, this offsetting effect minimizes the overall impact on the firm.

If the stock market rises, the put options on the stock index will not be exercised. Thus, the firm will not recover the cost of purchasing the options. This situation is similar to purchasing other forms of insurance, but not using them. Some portfolio managers may still believe the options were worthwhile for temporary protection against downside risk.

Exhibit 14.13 Sampling of ETFs and Indexes on Which Options Are Traded

SAMPLING OF ETFs ON WHICH OPTIONS ARE TRADED	
iShares Nasdaq Biotechnology	iShares Russell 1000 Growth Index Fund
iShares Goldman Sachs Technology Index	Energy Select Sector SPDR
iShares Goldman Sachs Software Index	Financial Select Sector SPDR
iShares Russell 1000 Index Fund	Utilities Select Sector SPDR
iShares Russell 1000 Value Index Fund	Health Care Select Sector SPDR
SAMPLING OF INDEXES ON WHICH OPTIONS ARE TRADED	
Asia 25 Index	S&P SmallCap 600 Index
Euro 25 Index	Nasdaq 100 Index
Mexico Index	Russell 1000 Index
Dow Jones Industrial Average	Russell 1000 Value Index
Dow Jones Transportation Average	Russell 1000 Growth Index
Dow Jones Utilities Average	Russell Midcap Index
S&P 100 Index	Goldman Sachs Internet Index
S&P 500 Index	Goldman Sachs Software Index
Morgan Stanley Biotechnology Index	

Hedging with Long-Term Stock Index Options **Long-term equity anticipations (LEAPs)** are used by option market participants who want options with longer terms until expiration. For example, LEAPs on the S&P 100 and S&P 500 indexes are available, with expiration dates extending at least two years ahead. Each of these indexes is revised to one-tenth its normal size when applying LEAPs. This results in smaller premiums, which makes the LEAPs more affordable to smaller investors.

The transaction costs for hedging over a long period are lower than the costs of continually repurchasing short-term put options each time the options expire or are exercised. Furthermore, the costs of continually repurchasing put options are uncertain, whereas the costs of purchasing a put option on a long-term index option are known immediately.

Dynamic Asset Allocation with Stock Index Options

Dynamic asset allocation involves switching between risky and low-risk investment positions over time in response to changing expectations. Some portfolio managers use stock index options as a tool for dynamic asset allocation. For example, when portfolio managers anticipate favorable market conditions, they purchase call options on a stock index, which intensify the effects of the market conditions. Essentially, the managers are using stock index options to increase their exposure to stock market conditions. Conversely, when they anticipate unfavorable market movements, they can purchase put options on a stock index to reduce the effects that market conditions will have on their stock portfolios.

Because stock options are available with various exercise prices, portfolio managers can select an exercise price that provides the degree of protection desired. For example, assume an existing stock index is quite similar to the managers' stock portfolio and that they want to protect against a loss beyond 5 percent. If the prevailing level of the index is 400, the managers can purchase put options that have an exercise price of 380, because that level is 5 percent lower than 400. If the index declines to a level below 380, the managers will exercise the options, and the gain from doing so will partially offset the reduction in the stock portfolio's market value.

This strategy is essentially a form of insurance, where the premium paid for the put option is similar to an insurance premium. Because the index must decline by 5 percent before the option will possibly be exercised, this is similar to the "deductible" that is common in insurance policies. If portfolio managers desire to protect against even smaller losses, they can purchase a put option that specifies a higher exercise price on the index, such as 390. To obtain the extra protection, however, they would have to pay a higher premium for the option. In other words, the cost of the portfolio insurance would be higher because of the smaller "deductible" desired.

In another form of dynamic asset allocation, portfolio managers sell (write) call options on stock indexes in periods when they expect the stock market to be very stable. This strategy does not create a perfect hedge, but it can enhance the portfolio's performance in periods when stock prices are stagnant or declining.

Portfolio managers can adjust the risk-return profile of their investment position by using stock index options rather than restructuring their existing stock portfolios. This form of dynamic asset allocation avoids the substantial transaction costs associated with restructuring the stock portfolios.

Using Index Options to Measure the Market's Risk

Just as a stock's implied volatility can be derived from information about options on that stock, a stock index's implied volatility can be derived from information about options on that stock index. The same factors that affect the option premium on a stock affect the option premium on an index. Thus, the premium on an index option is positively related to the expected volatility of the underlying stock index. If investors want to estimate the expected volatility of the stock index, they can use software packages to insert values for the prevailing option premium and the other factors (except volatility) that affect an option premium.

OPTIONS ON FUTURES CONTRACTS

In recent years, the concept of options has been applied to futures contracts to create options on futures contracts (sometimes referred to as "futures options"). An option on a particular futures contract allows the right (but not an obligation) to purchase or sell that futures contract for a specified price within a specified period of time. Thus, options on futures grant the power to take the futures position if favorable conditions occur but the flexibility to avoid the futures position (by letting the option expire) if unfavorable conditions occur. As with other options, the purchaser of options on futures pays a premium.

Options are available on stock index futures. They are used for speculating on expected stock market movements or hedging against adverse market conditions. Individuals and financial institutions use them in a manner similar to the way stock index options are used.

Options are also available on interest rate futures, such as Treasury note futures or Treasury bond futures. The settlement dates of the underlying futures contracts are usually a few weeks after the expiration date of the corresponding options contracts.

A call option on interest rate futures grants the right to purchase a futures contract at a specified price within a specified period of time. A put option on financial futures grants the right (again, not an obligation) to sell a particular financial futures contract at a specified price within a specified period of time. Because interest rate futures contracts can hedge interest rate risk, options on interest rate futures might be considered by any financial institution that is exposed to this risk, including savings institutions, commercial banks, life insurance companies, and pension funds.

Speculating with Options on Futures

Speculators who anticipate a change in interest rates should also expect a change in bond prices. They could take a position in options on Treasury bond futures to capitalize on their expectations.

Speculation Based on an Expected Decline in Interest Rates   If speculators expect a decline in interest rates, they may consider purchasing a call option on Treasury bond futures. If their expectations are correct, the market value of Treasury bonds will rise, and the price of a Treasury bond futures contract will rise as well. The speculators can exercise their option to purchase futures at the exercise price, which will be lower than the value of the futures contract.

EXAMPLE

Kelly Warden expects interest rates to decline and purchases a call option on Treasury bond futures. The exercise price on Treasury bond futures is 94–32 (94 and $^{32}/_{64}$ percent of $100,000, or $94,500). The call option is purchased at a premium of 2–00 (or 2 percent of $100,000), which equals $2,000. Assume that interest rates do decline and as a result, the price of the Treasury bond futures contract rises over time and is valued at 99–00 ($99,000) shortly before the option's expiration date. At this time, Kelly decides to exercise the option and closes out the position by selling an identical futures contract (to create an offsetting position) at a higher price than the price at which she purchased the futures. Kelly's net gain from this speculative strategy is

Selling price of T-bond futures	$99,000	(99.00% of $100,000)
− Purchase price of T-bond futures	− $94,500	(94.50% of $100,000)
− Call option premium paid	− $ 2,000	(2.00% of $100,000)
=Net gain to purchaser of call option of futures	$2,500	(2.50% of $100,000)

This net gain of $2,500 represents a return on investment of 125 percent. ●

The seller of the call option will have the opposite position to the buyer. Thus, the gain (or loss) to the buyer will equal the loss (or gain) to the seller of the call option.

EXAMPLE

Ellen Rose sold the call option purchased by Kelly Warden in the previous example. Ellen is obligated to purchase and provide the futures contract at the time the option is exercised. Her net gain from this speculative strategy is

Selling price of T-bond futures	$94,500	(94.50% of $100,000)
− Purchase price of T-bond futures	− $99,000	(99.00% of $100,000)
− Call option premium received	+ $ 2,000	(2.00% of $100,000)
=Net gain to seller of call option of futures	− $ 2,500	(−2.50% of $100,000)

In the absence of transaction costs, Ellen's loss is equal to Kelly's gain. If the Treasury bond futures price had remained below the exercise price of 94–32 ($94,500) until the expiration date, the option would not have been exercised; in that case, the net gain from purchasing the call option on Treasury bond futures would have been −$2,000 (the premium paid for the option), and the net gain from selling the call option would have been $2,000. ●

When interest rates decline, the buyers of call options on Treasury bonds may simply sell their previously purchased options just before expiration. If interest rates rise, the options will not be desirable. In that case, buyers of call options on Treasury bond futures will let their options expire, and their loss will be the premium paid for the call options on futures. Thus, the loss from purchasing options on futures is more limited than the loss from simply purchasing futures contracts.

Some speculators who expect interest rates to remain stable or decline may be willing to sell a put option on Treasury bond futures. If their expectations are correct, the price of a futures contract will likely rise, and the put option will not be exercised. Therefore, sellers of the put option would earn the premium that was paid to them when they sold the option.

Speculation Based on an Expected Increase in Interest Rates   If speculators expect interest rates to increase, they can benefit from purchasing a put option on Treasury bond futures. If their expectations are correct, the market value of Treasury bonds will decline, and the price of a Treasury bond futures contract will decline as well. The speculators can exercise their option to sell futures at the exercise price, which will be higher than the value of the futures contract. They can then purchase futures (to create an offsetting position) at a lower price than the price at which they sold futures. If interest rates decline, the speculators will likely let the options expire, and their loss will be the premium paid for the put options on futures.

EXAMPLE

John Drummer expects interest rates to increase and purchases a put option on Treasury bond futures. Assume the exercise price on Treasury bond futures is 97–00 ($97,000) and the premium paid for the put option is 3–00 ($3,000). Assume that interest rates do increase and as a result, the price of the Treasury bond futures contract declines over time and is valued at 89–00 ($89,000) shortly before the option's expiration date. At this time, John decides to exercise the option and closes out the position by purchasing an identical futures contract. John's net gain from this speculative strategy is

Selling price of T-bond futures	$97,000	(97.00% of $100,000)
− Purchase price of T-bond futures	− $89,000	(89.00% of $100,000)
− Put option premium received	− $ 3,000	(3.00% of $100,000)
=Net gain to purchaser of put option on future	$ 5,000	(5.00% of $100,000)

John's net gain of $5,000 represents a return on investment of about 167 percent. ●

The person who sold the put option on Treasury bond futures to John in this example incurred a loss of $5,000, assuming that the position was closed out (by selling an identical futures contract) on the same date that John's position was closed out. If the Treasury bond futures price had remained above the exercise price of 97–00 until the expiration date, the option would not have been exercised, and John would have lost $3,000 (the premium paid for the put option).

Some speculators who anticipate an increase in interest rates may be willing to sell a call option on Treasury bond futures. If their expectations are correct, the price of the futures contract will likely decline, and the call option will not be exercised.

HEDGING WITH OPTIONS ON FUTURES

Options on futures contracts are also used to hedge against risk. Put options on interest rate futures can be purchased to hedge bond portfolios, and put options on stock index futures can be purchased to hedge stock portfolios.

Hedging with Options on Interest Rate Futures

Financial institutions commonly hedge their bond or mortgage portfolios with options on interest rate futures contracts. The position they take on the options contract is designed to create a gain that can offset a loss on their bond or mortgage portfolio, while allowing some upside potential.

EXAMPLE

Emory Savings and Loan Association has a large number of long-term fixed-rate mortgages that are mainly supported by short-term funds and would therefore be adversely affected by rising interest rates. As the previous chapter showed, sales of Treasury bond futures can

Exhibit 14.14 Results from Hedging with Put Options on Treasury Bond Futures

	SCENARIO 1: • INTEREST RATES RISE • T-BOND FUTURES PRICE DECLINES TO 91-00	SCENARIO 2: • INTEREST RATES DECLINE • T-BOND FUTURES PRICE INCREASES TO 104-00
Effect on Emory's spread	Spread is reduced.	Spread is increased, but mortgage prepayments may occur.
Effect on T-bond futures price	Futures price decreases.	Futures price increases.
Decision on exercising the put option	Exercise put option.	Do not exercise put option.
Selling price of T-bond futures	$98,000	Not sold
− Purchase price of T-bond futures	− $91,000	Not purchased
− Price paid for put option	− $ 2,000	− $2,000
= Net gain per option	$ 5,000	− $2,000

partially offset the adverse effect of rising interest rates in such a situation. Recall that if interest rates decline instead, the potential increase in Emory's interest rate spread (difference between interest revenues and expenses) would be partially offset by the loss on the futures contract.

One potential limitation of selling interest rate futures to hedge mortgages is that households may prepay their mortgages. If interest rates decline and most fixed-rate mortgages are prepaid, Emory will incur a loss on the futures position without an offsetting gain on its spread. To protect against this risk, Emory can purchase put options on Treasury bond futures. Assume that Emory purchases put options on Treasury bond futures with an exercise price of 98–00 ($98,000) for a premium of 2–00 ($2,000) per contract. The initial Treasury bond futures price is 99–00 at the time. First, assume that interest rates rise, causing the Treasury bond futures price to decline to 91–00. In this scenario, Emory will exercise its right to sell Treasury bond futures and offset its position by purchasing identical futures contracts, generating a net gain of $5,000 per contract, as shown in Exhibit 14.14. The gain on the futures position helps to offset the reduction in Emory's spread that occurs because of the higher interest rates.

Now consider a second scenario in which interest rates decline, causing the Treasury bond futures price to rise to 104–00. In this scenario, Emory does not exercise the put options on Treasury bond futures because the futures position would result in a loss. ●

The preceding example shows how a put option on futures offers more flexibility than simply selling futures. However, a premium must be paid for the put option. Financial institutions that wish to hedge against rising interest rate risk should compare the possible outcomes from selling interest rate futures contracts versus purchasing put options on interest rate futures in order to hedge interest rate risk.

Hedging with Options on Stock Index Futures

Financial institutions and other investors commonly hedge their stock portfolios with options on stock index futures contracts. The position they take on the options contract is designed to create a gain that can offset a loss on their stock portfolio, while allowing some upside potential.

EXAMPLE

You currently manage a stock portfolio that is valued at $400,000 and plan to hold these stocks over a long-term period. However, you are concerned that the stock market may experience a temporary decline over the next three months and that your stock portfolio will probably decline by about the same degree as the market. You want to create a hedge so that your portfolio will decline no more than 3 percent from its present value, but you would like to maintain any upside potential. You can purchase a put option on index futures to hedge your stock portfolio. Put options on S&P 500 index futures are available with an expiration date about three months from now.

Assume that the S&P 500 index level is currently 1600, and that one particular put option on index futures has a strike price of 1552 (which represents a 3 percent decline from the prevailing index level) and a premium of 10. Since the options on S&P 500 index futures are priced at $250 times the quoted premium, the dollar amount to be paid for this option is 10 × $250 = $2,500. If the index level declines below 1552 (reflecting a decline of more than 3 percent), you may exercise the put option on index futures, which gives you the right to sell the index for a price of 1552. At the settlement date of the futures contract, you will receive $250 times the differential between the futures price of 1552 and the prevailing index level. For example, if the market declines by 5 percent, the index will decline from 1600 to 1520. There will be a gain on the index futures contract of (1552 − 1520) × $250 = $8,000. Meanwhile, a 5 percent decline in the value of the portfolio reflects a loss of $20,000 (5 percent of $400,000 = $20,000). The $8,000 gain (excluding the premium paid) from the options contract reduces the overall loss to $12,000, or 3 percent of the portfolio. ●

Determining the Degree of the Hedge with Options on Stock Index Futures

In the previous example, any loss less than 3 percent is not hedged. When using put options to hedge, various strike prices exist for an option on a specific stock index and for a specific expiration date. For example, put options on the S&P 500 index may be available with strike prices of 1760, 1800, 1840, and so on. The higher the strike price relative to the prevailing index value, the higher the price at which the investor can lock in the sale of the index. However, a higher premium must be paid to purchase put options with a higher strike price. From a hedging perspective, this simply illustrates that a higher price must be paid to be "insured" (or protected) against losses resulting from stock market downturns. This concept is analogous to automobile insurance, where a person must pay a higher premium for a policy with a lower deductible.

Selling Call Options to Cover the Cost of Put Options

In the previous example, the cost of hedging with a put option on index futures is $2,500. Given your expectations of a weak stock market over the next three months, you could generate some fees by selling call options on S&P 500 index futures to help cover the cost of purchasing put options.

Assume that there is a call option on S&P 500 index futures with a strike price of 1648 (3 percent above the existing index level) and a premium of 10. You can sell a call option on index futures for $2,500 (10 × $250) and use the proceeds to pay the premium on the put option. The obvious disadvantage of selling a call option to finance the purchase of the put option is that it limits your upside potential. For example, if the market rises by 5 percent over the three-month period, the S&P 500 index level will rise to 1680. The difference between this level and the strike price of 1648 on the call option forces you to make a payment of (1680 − 1648) × $250 = $8,000 to the owner of the call option. This partially offsets the gain to your portfolio that resulted from the favorable market conditions. ●

When attempting to hedge larger portfolios than the one in the previous example, additional put options would be purchased to hedge the entire portfolio against a possible decline in the market. For example, if your stock portfolio was $1.2 million instead of $400,000 as in the previous example, you would need to purchase three put options on S&P 500 index futures contracts. Since each index futures contract would have a value of $400,000, you would need a short position in three index futures contracts to hedge the entire stock portfolio (assuming that the index and the stock portfolio move in tandem).

INSTITUTIONAL USE OF OPTIONS MARKETS

Exhibit 14.15 summarizes the uses of options by various types of financial institutions; some of these were illustrated in the previous examples. Although options positions are sometimes taken by financial institutions for speculative purposes, they are more commonly used for hedging. Savings institutions and bond mutual funds use options on interest rate futures to hedge interest rate risk. Stock mutual funds, insurance companies, and pension funds use stock index options and options on stock index futures to hedge their stock portfolios.

J.P. Morgan Chase, Citigroup, and some other commercial banks have aggressively penetrated the options market by offering options and other derivative securities to various firms. These banks commonly serve as an intermediary between two parties that take derivative positions in an over-the-counter market.

Options as Compensation

Firms sometimes distribute stock options to executives and other managers as a reward for good performance. For example, a manager may receive a salary along with call options on 10,000 shares of stock that have an exercise price above the prevailing price and an expiration date of five years from today. The purpose of awarding options as compensation is to increase the managers' incentive to make decisions that increase the value of the firm's stock. With options, their compensation is more directly aligned with the value of the firm's stock.

Distortion between Performance and Option Compensation   Many option compensation programs do not account for general market conditions, however. For example, managers who earned stock options when market conditions were weak may have earned low compensation even though their firm performed relatively well, because the stock prices of most firms were weak in this period. Conversely, the managers who received stock options when market conditions were more favorable may have earned very high compensation even

Exhibit 14.15 Institutional Use of Options Markets

TYPE OF FINANCIAL INSTITUTION	PARTICIPATION IN OPTIONS MARKETS
Commercial banks	• Sometimes offer options to businesses.
Savings institutions	• Sometimes take positions in options on futures contracts to hedge interest rate risk.
Mutual funds	• Stock mutual funds take positions in stock index options to hedge against a possible decline in prices of stocks in their portfolios. • Stock mutual funds sometimes take speculative positions in stock index options in an attempt to increase their returns. • Bond mutual funds sometimes take positions in options on futures to hedge interest rate risk.
Securities firms	• Serve as brokers by executing stock option transactions for individuals and businesses.
Pension funds	• Take positions in stock index options to hedge against a possible decline in prices of stocks in their portfolio. • Take positions in options on futures contracts to hedge their bond portfolios against interest rate movements.
Insurance companies	• Take positions in stock index options to hedge against a possible decline in prices of stocks in their portfolio. • Take positions in options on futures contracts to hedge their bond portfolios against interest rate movements.

though their firm performed relatively poorly, because the stock prices of most firms increased substantially at this time. Since compensation from holding options is driven more by general market conditions than by the relative performance of a firm's managers, options are not always effective at rewarding good performance.

How Stock Option Compensation Can Destroy Shareholder Value Another concern with using options as compensation is that managers with substantial options may be tempted to manipulate the stock's price upward in the short term, even though doing so adversely affects the stock price in the long term. For example, they might use accounting methods that defer the reporting of some expenses until next year, while accelerating the reporting of some revenue. In this way, short-term earnings will appear favorable, but earnings in the following period will be reduced. When the managers believe that the stock price has peaked, they can exercise their options and then sell their shares in the secondary market. Firms can prevent the wrongful use of options by requiring that managers hold them for several years before exercising them.

Many firms were very willing to provide option compensation to their CEOs and other executives because they did not have to treat the options as an expense. Until 2006, firms did not have to report their options as an expense, but could claim them as a tax deduction. If Enron Corporation had reported its option compensation as expenses on its income statements over the five-year period before its bankruptcy in 2001, its net income would have been reduced by $600 million. Since options did not have to be reported as an expense on the income statements, some firms were overly generous in awarding options. Global Crossing's CEO earned $730 million from options before the firm filed for bankruptcy. Cisco Systems awarded its CEO an additional 6 million new options in a year in which its stock price declined by 72 percent. Largely as a result of options, CEO compensation jumped to 500 times the average compensation of employees in a firm.

Backdating Options Some firms also allowed their CEOs to backdate options that they were granted to an earlier period when the stock price was lower. This enabled the CEOs to exercise the options at a lower exercise price. This backdating took place in the late 1990s and early 2000s but was not recognized until 2006. Backdating is completely inconsistent with the idea of granting options to encourage managers to focus on maximizing the stock price. Instead, CEOs benefit when the options are backdated to a period when the stock price was weak. Although stock options potentially could be used in ways that would encourage executives to serve the interests of shareholders, in many cases executives have abused their rights because of weak governance by the board of directors.

GLOBALIZATION OF OPTIONS MARKETS

The globalization of stock markets has resulted in the need for a globalized market in stock options. Options on stock indexes representing various countries are now available. Options exchanges have been established in numerous countries, including Australia, Austria, Belgium, France, Germany, and Singapore. U.S. portfolio managers who maintain large holdings of stocks from specific countries are heavily exposed to the conditions of those markets. Rather than liquidate the portfolio of foreign stocks to protect against a possible temporary decline, the managers can purchase put options on the foreign stock index of concern. Portfolio managers residing in these countries can also use this strategy to hedge their stock portfolios.

Portfolio managers desiring to capitalize on the expectation of temporary favorable movements in foreign markets can purchase call options on the corresponding stock indexes. Thus, the existence of options on foreign stock indexes allows portfolio managers to hedge or speculate based on forecasts of foreign market conditions. The trading of options on foreign stock indexes avoids the transaction costs associated with buying and selling large portfolios of foreign stocks.

Currency Options Contracts

A **currency call option** provides the right to purchase a specified currency for a specified price within a specified period of time. Corporations involved in international business transactions use currency call options to hedge future payables. If the exchange rate at the time payables are due exceeds the exercise price, corporations can exercise their options and purchase the currency at the exercise price. Conversely, if the prevailing exchange rate is lower than the exercise price, corporations can purchase the currency at the prevailing exchange rate and let the options expire.

Speculators purchase call options on currencies that they expect to strengthen against the dollar. If the foreign currency strengthens as expected, they can exercise their call options to purchase the currency at the exercise price and then sell the currency at the prevailing exchange rate.

A **currency put option** provides the right to sell a specified currency for a specified price within a specified period of time. Corporations involved in international business transactions may purchase put options to hedge future receivables. If the exchange rate at the time they receive payment in a foreign currency is less than the exercise price, they can exercise their option by selling the currency at the exercise price. Conversely, if the prevailing exchange rate is higher than the exercise price, they can sell the currency at the prevailing exchange rate and let the options expire.

Speculators purchase put options on currencies they expect to weaken against the dollar. If the foreign currency weakens as expected, the speculators can purchase the currency at the prevailing spot rate and exercise their put options to sell the currency at the exercise price.

For every buyer of a currency call or put option, there must be a seller (or writer). A writer of a call option is obligated to sell the specified currency at the specified strike price if the option is exercised. A writer of a put option is obligated to purchase the specified currency at the specified strike price if the option is exercised. Speculators may be willing to write call options on foreign currencies that they expect to weaken against the dollar or write put options on those they expect to strengthen against the dollar. If a currency option expires without being exercised, the writer earns the up-front premium received.

SUMMARY

- Stock options are traded on exchanges, just as many stocks are. Orders submitted by a brokerage firm are transmitted to a trading floor, where floor brokers execute the trades. Many trades are executed electronically.

- Speculators purchase call options on stocks whose prices are expected to rise and purchase put options on those expected to decrease. They purchase call options on interest rate futures contracts when they expect interest rates to decrease. They buy currency call options when they expect foreign currencies to strengthen and currency put options when they expect foreign currencies to weaken.

- The premium of a call option is influenced by the characteristics of the option and of the underlying stock that can affect the potential gains. First, the higher the market price of the stock relative to the exercise price, the higher the premium. Second, the higher the stock's volatility, the higher the premium. Third, the longer the term until expiration, the higher the premium.

For put options, the higher the market price of the stock relative to the exercise price, the lower the premium. The volatility of the underlying stock and the term to expiration are related to the put option premium in the same manner as they are to the call option premium.

■ Index options can be used to speculate on movements in stock indexes, with a small investment.

■ Put options on stock indexes can be purchased to hedge a stock portfolio whose movements are somewhat similar to that of the stock index.

■ Options on stock index futures can be used to speculate on movements in the value of the stock index futures contract. Put options on stock index futures can be purchased to hedge portfolios of stocks that move in tandem with the stock index.

POINT COUNTER-POINT

If You Were a Major Shareholder of a Publicly Traded Firm, Would You Prefer That Stock Options Be Traded on That Stock?

Point No. Options can be used by investors to speculate, and excessive trading of the options may push the stock price away from its fundamental price.

Counter-Point Yes. Options can be used by investors to temporarily hedge against adverse movements in the stock, so they may reduce the selling pressure on the stock in some periods.

Who Is Correct? Use the Internet to learn more about this issue. Offer your own opinion on this issue.

QUESTIONS AND APPLICATIONS

1. Options versus Futures Describe the general differences between a call option and a futures contract.

2. Speculating with Call Options How are call options used by speculators? Describe the conditions in which their strategy would backfire. What is the maximum loss that could occur for a purchaser of a call option?

3. Speculating with Put Options How are put options used by speculators? Describe the conditions in which their strategy would backfire. What is the maximum loss that could occur for a purchaser of a put option?

4. Selling Options Under what conditions would speculators sell a call option? What is the risk to speculators who sell put options?

5. Factors Affecting Call Option Premiums Identify the factors affecting the premium paid on a call option. Describe how each factor affects the size of the premium.

6. Factors Affecting Put Option Premiums Identify the factors affecting the premium paid on a put option. Describe how each factor affects the size of the premium.

7. Leverage of Options How can financial institutions with stock portfolios use stock options when they expect stock prices to rise substantially but do not yet have sufficient funds to purchase more stock?

8. Hedging with Put Options Why would a financial institution holding ABC stock consider buying a put option on this stock rather than simply selling the stock?

9. Call Options on Futures Describe a call option on interest rate futures. How does it differ from purchasing a futures contract?

10. Put Options on Futures Describe a put option on interest rate futures. How does it differ from selling a futures contract?

Advanced Questions

11. Hedging Interest Rate Risk Assume a savings institution has a large amount of fixed-rate mortgages and obtains most of its funds from short-term deposits. How could it use options on financial futures to hedge its exposure to interest rate movements? Would futures or options on futures be more appropriate if the institution is concerned that interest rates will decline, causing a large number of mortgage prepayments?

12. Hedging Effectiveness Three savings and loan institutions (S&Ls) have identical balance sheet compositions: a high concentration of short-term deposits that are used to provide long-term, fixed-rate mortgages. The S&Ls took the following positions one year ago.

NAME OF S&L	POSITION
LaCrosse	Sold financial futures
Stevens Point	Purchased put options on interest rate futures
Whitewater	Did not take any position in futures

Assume that interest rates declined consistently over the last year. Which of the three S&Ls would have achieved the best performance based on this information? Explain.

13. Change in Stock Option Premiums Explain how and why the option premiums may change in response to a surprise announcement that the Fed will increase interest rates even if stock prices are not affected.

14. Speculating with Stock Options The price of Garner stock is $40. There is a call option on Garner stock that is at the money, with a premium of $2.00. There is a put option on Garner stock that is at the money, with a premium of $1.80. Why would investors consider writing this call option and this put option? Why would some investors consider buying this call option and this put option?

15. How Stock Index Option Prices May Respond to Prevailing Conditions Consider the prevailing conditions that could affect the demand for stocks, including inflation, the economy, the budget deficit, the Fed's monetary policy, political conditions, and the general mood of investors. Based on prevailing conditions, would you consider purchasing stock index options at this time? Offer some logic to support your answer. Which factor do you think will have the biggest impact on stock index option prices?

16. Backdating Stock Options Explain what backdating stock options entails. Is backdating consistent with rewarding executives who help to maximize shareholder wealth?

17. Merger between the CME and the CBOT What are potential benefits of the merger between the CME and the CBOT? Are there any potential disadvantages due to the merger?

Interpreting Financial News

Interpret the following comments made by Wall Street analysts and portfolio managers:

a. "Our firm took a hit because we wrote put options on stocks just before the stock market crash."

b. "Before hedging our stock portfolio with options on index futures, we search for the index that is most conducive."

c. "We prefer to use covered call writing to hedge our stock portfolios."

Managing in Financial Markets

Hedging with Stock Options As a stock portfolio manager, you have investments in many U.S. stocks and plan to hold these stocks over a long-term period. However, you are concerned that the stock market may experience a temporary decline over the next three months and that your stock portfolio will probably decline by about the same degree as the market. You are aware that options on S&P 500 index futures are available. The following options on S&P 500 index futures are available and have an expiration date about three months from now:

STRIKE PRICE	CALL PREMIUM	PUT PREMIUM
1372	40	24
1428	24	40

The options on S&P 500 index futures are priced at $250 times the quoted premium. Currently, the S&P 500 index level is 1400. The strike price of 1372 represents a 2 percent decline from the prevailing index level, and the strike price of 1428 represents an increase of 2 percent above the prevailing index level.

a. Assume that you want to take an options position to hedge your entire portfolio, which is currently valued at about $700,000. How many index option contracts should you take a position in to hedge your entire portfolio?

b. Assume that you want to create a hedge so that your portfolio will lose no more than 2 percent from its present value. How can you take a position in options on index futures to achieve this goal? What is the cost to you as a result of creating this hedge?

c. Given your expectations of a weak stock market over the next three months, how can you generate some fees from the sale of options on S&P 500 index futures to help cover the cost of purchasing options?

PROBLEMS

1. Writing Call Options A call option on Illinois stock specifies an exercise price of $38. Today, the stock's price is $40. The premium on the call option is $5. Assume the option will not be exercised until maturity, if at all. Complete the following table:

ASSUMED STOCK PRICE AT THE TIME THE CALL OPTION IS ABOUT TO EXPIRE	NET PROFIT OR LOSS PER SHARE TO BE EARNED BY THE WRITER (SELLER) OF THE CALL OPTION
$37	
39	
41	
43	
45	
48	

2. Purchasing Call Options A call option on Michigan stock specifies an exercise price of $55. Today, the stock's price is $54 per share. The premium on the call option is $3. Assume the option will not be exercised until maturity, if at all. Complete the following table for a speculator who purchases the call option:

ASSUMED STOCK PRICE AT THE TIME THE CALL OPTION IS ABOUT TO EXPIRE	NET PROFIT OR LOSS PER SHARE TO BE EARNED BY THE SPECULATOR
$50	
52	
54	
56	
58	
60	
62	

3. Purchasing Put Options A put option on Iowa stock specifies an exercise price of $71. Today, the stock's price is $68. The premium on the put option is $8. Assume the option will not be exercised until maturity, if at all. Complete the following table for a speculator who purchases the put option (and currently does not own the stock):

ASSUMED STOCK PRICE AT THE TIME THE PUT OPTION IS ABOUT TO EXPIRE	NET PROFIT OR LOSS PER SHARE TO BE EARNED BY THE SPECULATOR
$60	
64	
68	
70	
72	
74	
76	

4. Writing Put Options A put option on Indiana stock specifies an exercise price of $23. Today, the stock's price is $24. The premium on the put option is $3. Assume the option will not be exercised until maturity, if at all. Complete the following table:

ASSUMED STOCK PRICE AT THE TIME THE PUT OPTION IS ABOUT TO EXPIRE	NET PROFIT OR LOSS PER SHARE TO BE EARNED BY THE WRITER (OR SELLER) OF THE PUT OPTION
$20	
21	
22	
23	
24	
25	
26	

5. Covered Call Strategy

a. Evanston Insurance, Inc. has purchased shares of stock E at $50 per share. It will sell the stock in six months. It considers using a strategy of covered call writing to partially hedge its position in this stock. The exercise price is $53, the expiration date is six months, and the premium on the call option is $2. Complete the following table:

POSSIBLE PRICE OF STOCK E IN 6 MONTHS	PROFIT OR LOSS PER SHARE IF A COVERED CALL STRATEGY IS USED	PROFIT OR LOSS PER SHARE IF A COVERED CALL STRATEGY IS NOT USED
$47		
50		
52		
55		
57		
60		

b. Assume that each of the six stock prices in the first column in the table has an equal probability of occurring. Compare the probability distribution of the profits (or losses) per share when using covered call writing versus not using it. Would you recommend covered call writing in this situation? Explain.

6. Put Options on Futures Purdue Savings and Loan Association purchased a put option on Treasury bond futures with a September delivery date and an exercise price of 91–16. The put option has a premium of 1–32. Assume that the price of the Treasury bond futures decreases to 88–16. Should Purdue exercise the option or let it expire? What is Purdue's net gain or loss after accounting for the premium paid on the option?

7. Call Options on Futures Wisconsin, Inc. purchased a call option on Treasury bond futures at a premium of 2–00. The exercise price is 92–08. If the price of the Treasury bond futures rises to 93–08, should Wisconsin exercise the call option or let it expire? What is Wisconsin's net gain or loss after accounting for the premium paid on the option?

8. Call Options on Futures DePaul Insurance Company purchased a call option on an S&P 500 futures contract. The option premium is quoted as $6. The exercise price is 1430. Assume the index on the futures contract becomes 1440. Should DePaul exercise the call option or let it expire? What is the net gain or loss to DePaul after accounting for the premium paid for the option?

9. Covered Call Strategy Coral, Inc. has purchased shares of stock M at $28 per share. Coral will sell the stock in six months. It considers using a strategy of covered call writing to partially hedge its position in this stock. The exercise price is $32, the expiration date is six months, and the premium on the call option is $2.50. Complete the following table:

POSSIBLE PRICE OF STOCK M IN 6 MONTHS	PROFIT OR LOSS PER SHARE IF COVERED CALL STRATEGY IS USED
$25	
28	
33	
36	

10. Hedging with Bond Futures Smart Savings Bank desired to hedge its interest rate risk. It considered two possibilities: (1) sell Treasury bond futures at a price of 94–00, or (2) purchase a put option on Treasury bond futures. At the time, the price of Treasury bond futures was 95–00. The face value of Treasury bond futures was $100,000. The put option premium was 2–00, and the exercise price was 94–00. Just before the option expired, the Treasury bond futures price was 91–00, and Smart Savings Bank would have exercised the put option at that time, if at all. This is also the time when it would have offset its futures position, if it had sold futures. Determine the net gain to Smart Savings Bank if it had sold Treasury bond futures versus if it had purchased a put option on Treasury bond futures. Which alternative would have been more favorable, based on the situation that occurred?

FLOW OF FUNDS EXERCISE

Hedging with Options Contracts

Carson Company would like to acquire Vinnet, Inc., a publicly traded firm in the same industry. Vinnet's stock price is currently much lower than the prices of other firms in the industry because it is inefficiently managed. Carson believes that it could restructure Vinnet's operations and improve its performance. It is about to contact Vinnet to determine whether Vinnet will agree to an acquisition. Carson is somewhat concerned that investors may learn of its plans and buy Vinnet stock in anticipation that Carson will need to pay a high premium (perhaps a 30 percent premium above the prevailing stock price) in order to complete the acquisition. Carson decides to call a bank about its risk, as the bank has a brokerage subsidiary that can help it hedge with stock options.

a. How can Carson use stock options to reduce its exposure to this risk? Are there any limitations to this

strategy, given that Carson will ultimately have to buy most or all of the Vinnet stock?

b. Describe the maximum possible loss that may be directly incurred by Carson as a result of engaging in this strategy.

c. Explain the results of the strategy you offered in the previous question if Vinnet plans to avoid the acquisition attempt by Carson.

INTERNET/EXCEL EXERCISES

1. Go to www.cboe.com. Under "Quotes," select "Delayed Quotes Classic." Insert the ticker symbol for a stock option in which you are interested. Assess the results. Did the premium ("Net") on the call options increase or decrease today? Did the

premium on the put options increase or decrease today?

2. Based on the changes in the premium, do you think the underlying stock price increased or decreased? Explain.

WSJ EXERCISE

Assessing Stock Option Information

Obtain recent stock options data for a particular stock or stock index in which you are interested. Go to http://online.wsj.com/mdc/public/page/marketsdata.html and click on "Stocks" and then click on "Listed Option Quotes" Complete the following table (use the same expiration month for all quoted premiums):

NAME OF STOCK _____		
EXERCISE PRICE	PREMIUM ON CALL OPTION	PREMIUM ON PUT OPTION

Explain the relationship between the option's time to maturity and (1) the call option premium and (2) the put option premium.

Obtain recent stock options data for a particular stock or stock index in which you are interested. Using *The Wall Street Journal*, complete the following table (use the same exercise price for all quoted premiums):

NAME OF STOCK _____		
EXERCISE PRICE	PREMIUM ON CALL OPTION	PREMIUM ON PUT OPTION

Explain the relationship between the option's exercise price and (1) the call option premium and (2) the put option premium.

Obtain recent stock options data for a particular stock or stock index in which you are interested. Use a recent issue of *The Wall Street Journal* to complete the following table:

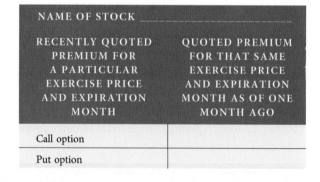

NAME OF STOCK _____	
RECENTLY QUOTED PREMIUM FOR A PARTICULAR EXERCISE PRICE AND EXPIRATION MONTH	QUOTED PREMIUM FOR THAT SAME EXERCISE PRICE AND EXPIRATION MONTH AS OF ONE MONTH AGO
Call option	
Put option	

Explain why the call option premium increased or decreased. Determine the percentage change in the premium. Do the same for the put option premium.

Option Valuation

The Binomial Pricing Model

The binomial option-pricing model was originally developed by William F. Sharpe. An advantage of the model is that it can be used to price both European-style and American-style options with or without dividends. European options are put or call options that can be exercised only at maturity; American options can be exercised at any time prior to maturity.

Assumptions of the Binomial Pricing Model

The following are the main assumptions of the binomial pricing model:

1. The continuous random walk underlying the Black-Scholes model can be modeled by a discrete random walk with the following properties:

- The asset price changes only at discrete (noninfinitesimal) time steps.
- At each time step, the asset price may move either up or down; thus, there are only two returns, and these two returns are the same for all time steps.
- The probabilities of moving up and down are known.

2. The world is risk-neutral. This allows the assumption that investors' risk preferences are irrelevant and that investors are risk-neutral. Furthermore, the return from the underlying asset is the risk-free interest rate.

Using the Binomial Pricing Model to Price Call Options

The following is an example of how the binomial pricing model can be employed to price a call option (that is, to determine a call option premium). To use the model, we need information for three securities: the underlying stock, a risk-free security, and the stock option.

Assume that the price of Gem Corporation stock today is $100. Furthermore, it is estimated that Gem stock will be selling for either $150 or $70 in one year. That is, the stock is expected to either rise by 50 percent or fall by 30 percent. Also assume that the annual risk-free interest rate on a one-year Treasury bill is 10 percent, continuously compounded. Assume that a T-bill currently sells for $100. Since interest is continuously compounded, the T-bill will pay interest of $100 \times (e^{10} - 1)$, or $10.52.

Currently, a call option on Gem stock is available with an exercise price of $100 and an expiration date one year from now. Since the call option is an option to buy Gem stock, the option will have a value of $50 if the stock price is $150 in one year.

Conversely, the call option will have a value of $0 if the stock price is $70. Our objective is to value this call option using the binomial pricing model.

The first step in applying the model to this call option is to recognize that three investments are involved: the stock, a risk-free security, and the call option. Using the information given above, we have the following payoff matrix in one year:

SECURITY	PRICE IF STOCK IS WORTH $150 IN ONE YEAR	PRICE IF STOCK IS WORTH $70 IN ONE YEAR	CURRENT PRICE
Gem stock	$150.00	$70.00	$100.00
Treasury bill	110.52	110.52	100.00
Call option	50.00	0.00	?

The objective of the binomial pricing model is thus to determine the current price of the call option. The key to understanding the valuation of the call option using the binomial pricing model is that the option's value must be based on a combination of the value of the stock and the T-bill. If this were not the case, arbitrage opportunities would result. Consequently, in either the up or the down state, the payoff of a portfolio of N_s shares of Gem stock and N_b T-bills must be equal to the value of the call option in that state. Using the payoff matrix above, we thus get a system of two equations:

$$150N_s + 110.52N_b = 50$$
$$70N_s + 110.52N_b = 0$$

Since we are dealing with two linear equations with two unknowns, we can easily solve for the two variables by substitution. Doing so gives the following values for the number of shares and the number of T-bills in the investor's *replicating* portfolio:

$$N_s = 0.625$$
$$N_b = -0.3959$$

In other words, the payoffs of the call option on Gem stock can be replicated by borrowing $39.59 at the risk-free rate and buying 0.625 shares of Gem stock for $62.50 (since one share currently sells for $100). Since the payoff of this replicating portfolio is the same as that for the call, the cost to the investor must be the value of the call. In this case, since $39.59 of the outlay of $62.50 is financed by borrowing, the outlay to the investor is $62.50 − $39.59 = $22.91. Thus, the call option premium must be $22.91.

In equation form, the value of the call option (V) can thus be written as

$$V_0 = N_sP_s + N_bP_b$$

The computation of the N's can be simplified somewhat. More specifically,

$$N_s = h = \frac{P_{ou} - P_{od}}{P_{su} - P_{sd}}$$

where
P_{ou} = value of the option in the up state
P_{od} = value of the option in the down state
P_{su} = price of Gem stock in the up state
P_{sd} = price of Gem stock in the down state

This is also referred to as the *hedge ratio*.

The amount borrowed (BOR) in the example above is equal to the product of the number of risk-free securities in the replicating portfolio and the price of the risk-free security:

$$N_b P_b = \text{BOR} = PV(hP_{sd} - P_{od})$$

where
$$PV = \textbf{present value of a continuously compounded sum}$$
$$h = \textbf{hedge ratio}$$

Thus, the value of the call option can be expressed more simply as

$$V_0 = hP_s + \text{BOR}$$

To illustrate why the relationships discussed so far should hold, assume for the moment that a call option on Gem stock is selling for a premium of $25 (that is, the call option is overpriced). In this case, investors are presented with an arbitrage opportunity to make an instantaneous, riskless profit. More specifically, investors could write a call, buy the stock, and borrow at the risk-free rate. Now assume the call option on Gem stock is selling for a premium of only $20 (that is, the call option is underpriced). Using arbitrage, investors would buy a call, sell the stock short, and invest at the risk-free rate.

Using the Binomial Pricing Model to Price Put Options

Continuing with the example of Gem Corporation, the only item that changes in the payoff matrix when the option is a put option (that is, an option to sell Gem stock) is the value of the option at expiration in the up and down states. Specifically, if Gem stock is worth $150 in one year, the put option will be worthless; if Gem stock is worth only $70 in one year, the put option will be worth $30. Since the value of the risk-free security is contingent only on the T-bill interest rate, it will be unaffected by the fact that we are now dealing with a put option.

The hedge ratio and the amount borrowed can now be easily determined using the formulas introduced previously. Specifically, the hedge ratio is

$$h = \frac{0 - 30}{150 - 70} = -0.375$$

The amount borrowed is

$$\text{BOR} = PV[-0.375(70) - 30] = \frac{-56.25}{e^{RT}} = -50.90$$

Thus, to replicate the put option, the investor would sell short 0.375 Gem shares and lend $50.90 at the risk-free rate. Thus, the net amount the investor must put up is $50.90 − $37.50 = $13.40. Accordingly, this is the fair value of the put.

Put-Call Parity

With some mathematical manipulation, the following relationship can be derived between the prices of puts and calls (with the same exercise price and time to expiration):

$$P_p = P_c + \frac{E}{e^{RT}} - P_s$$

where
$$P_p = \textbf{price of a put option}$$
$$P_c = \textbf{price of a call option}$$
$$E = \textbf{exercise price of the option}$$
$$e^{RT} = \textbf{present value operator for a continuously compounded sum,}$$
$$\textbf{discounted at interest rate } R \textbf{ for } T \textbf{ years}$$
$$P_s = \textbf{price of the stock}$$

Using the example of Gem Corporation,

$$P_p = \$22.91 + \frac{\$100}{e^{.1}} - \$100 = \$13.39$$

THE BLACK-SCHOLES OPTION-PRICING MODEL FOR CALL OPTIONS

In 1973, Black and Scholes devised an option-pricing model that motivated further research on option valuation that continues to this day.

Assumptions of the Black-Scholes Option-Pricing Model

The following are some of the key assumptions underlying the Black-Scholes option-pricing model:

1. The risk-free rate is known and constant over the life of the option.
2. The probability distribution of stock prices is lognormal.
3. The variability of a stock's return is constant.
4. The option is to be exercised only at maturity, if at all.
5. There are no transaction costs involved in trading options.
6. Tax rates are similar for all participants who trade options.
7. The stock of concern does not pay cash dividends.

The Black-Scholes Partial Differential Equation

The Black-Scholes option-pricing model was one of the first to introduce the concept of a *riskless hedge*. Assume that an amount π is invested in a risk-free asset. Thus, the investor would see a return of $r\pi dt$ over a time interval dt. If an appropriately selected portfolio, with a current value of π consisting of a company's stock and an offsetting position in an option on that stock, returns more than $r\pi dt$ over a time interval dt, an investor could conduct arbitrage by borrowing at the risk-free rate and investing in the portfolio. Conversely, if the portfolio returns less than $r\pi dt$, the investor would short the portfolio and invest in the risk-free asset. In either case, the arbitrageur would make a riskless, no-cost, instantaneous profit. Thus, the return on the portfolio and on the riskless asset must be more or less equal.

Using this argument, Black and Scholes developed what has become known as the *Black-Scholes partial differential equation*:

$$\frac{\partial V}{\partial t} + \frac{1}{2}\sigma^2 S^2 \frac{\partial^2 V}{\partial S^2} + rS\frac{\partial V}{\partial S} - rV = 0$$

where

V = **value of an option**
S = **price of the underlying stock**
r = **risk-free rate of return**
t = **a measure of time**
σ^2 = **variance of the underlying stock's price**
∂ and ∂^2 = **first- and second-order partial derivatives**

The Black-Scholes Option-Pricing Model for European Call Options

In order to price an option, the partial differential equation must be solved for V, the value of the option. Assuming that the risk-free interest rate and stock price volatility are constant, solving the Black-Scholes partial differential equation results in the familiar Black-Scholes formula for European call options:

$$V = SN(d_1) - Ee^{-rT}N(d_2)$$

where

$V = $ **value of the call option**

$S = $ **stock price**

$N(\cdot) = $ **cumulative distribution function for a standardized normal random variable**

$E = $ **exercise price of the call option**

$e = $ **base e antilog or 2.7183**

$r = $ **risk-free of return for one year assuming continuous compounding**

$T = $ **time remaining to maturity of the call option, expressed as a fraction of a year**

The terms $N(d_1)$ and $N(d_2)$ deserve further elaboration. N represents a cumulative probability for a unit normal variable, where

$$d_1 = \frac{\ln(S/E) + \left(r + \frac{1}{2}\sigma^2\right)(T)}{\sigma\sqrt{T}}$$

and

$$d_2 = \frac{\ln(S/E) + \left(r - \frac{1}{2}\sigma^2\right)(T)}{\sigma\sqrt{T}}$$

$$= d_1 - \sigma\sqrt{T}$$

where $\ln(S/E)$ represents the natural logarithm and σ represents the standard deviation of the continuously compounded rate of return on the underlying stock.

Using the Black-Scholes Option-Pricing Model to Price a European Call Option

To illustrate how the Black-Scholes equation can be used to price a call option, assume you observe a call option on MPB Corporation stock expiring in six months with an exercise price of $70. Thus, $T = .50$ and $E = \$70$. Furthermore, the current price of MPB stock is $72, and the stock has a standard deviation of 0.10. Moreover, the annual risk-free rate is 7 percent. Solving for d_1 and, d_2 we get

$$d_1 = \frac{\ln(72/70) + [0.07 + 0.5(0.10)^2](0.5)}{0.10\sqrt{0.5}} = 0.9287$$

$$d_2 = 0.9287 - 0.10\sqrt{0.50} = 0.8580$$

Using a table that identifies the area under the standard normal distribution function (see Exhibit 14.A1), the cumulative probability can be determined. Because d_1 is 0.9287, the cumulative probability from zero to 0.9287 is about 0.3235 (from Exhibit 14.A1, using linear interpolation). Because the cumulative probability for a unit normal variable from minus infinity to zero is 0.50, the cumulative probability from minus infinity to 0.9287 is 0.50 + 0.3235 = 0.8235.

For d_2, the cumulative probability from zero to 0.8580 is 0.3045. Therefore, the cumulative probability from minus infinity to 0.8580 is 0.50 + 0.3042 = 0.8042.

Exhibit 14A.1 Institutional Use of Options Markets

d	0.00	0.01	0.02	0.03	0.04	0.05	0.06	0.07	0.08	0.09
0.0	0.0000	0.0040	0.0080	0.0120	0.0160	0.0199	0.0239	0.0279	0.0319	0.0359
0.1	0.0398	0.0438	0.0478	0.0517	0.0557	0.0596	0.0636	0.0675	0.0714	0.0753
0.2	0.0793	0.0832	0.0871	0.0910	0.0948	0.0987	0.1026	0.1064	0.1103	0.1141
0.3	0.1179	0.1217	0.1255	0.1293	0.1331	0.1368	0.1406	0.1443	0.1480	0.1517
0.4	0.1554	0.1591	0.1628	0.1664	0.1700	0.1736	0.1772	0.1808	0.1844	0.1879
0.5	0.1915	0.1950	0.1985	0.2019	0.2054	0.2088	0.2123	0.2157	0.2190	0.2224
0.6	0.2257	0.2291	0.2324	0.2357	0.2389	0.2422	0.2454	0.2486	0.2517	0.2549
0.7	0.2580	0.2611	0.2642	0.2673	0.2704	0.2734	0.2764	0.2794	0.2823	0.2852
0.8	0.2881	0.2910	0.2939	0.2967	0.2995	0.3023	0.3051	0.3078	0.3106	0.3133
0.9	0.3159	0.3186	0.3213	0.3238	0.3264	0.3289	0.3315	0.3340	0.3365	0.3389
1.0	0.3413	0.3438	0.3461	0.3485	0.3508	0.3531	0.3554	0.3577	0.3599	0.3621
1.1	0.3643	0.3665	0.3686	0.3708	0.3729	0.3749	0.3770	0.3790	0.3810	0.3830
1.2	0.3849	0.3869	0.3888	0.3907	0.3925	0.3944	0.3962	0.3980	0.3997	0.4015
1.3	0.4032	0.4049	0.4066	0.4082	0.4099	0.4115	0.4131	0.4147	0.4162	0.4177
1.4	0.4192	0.4207	0.4222	0.4236	0.4251	0.4265	0.4279	0.4292	0.4306	0.4319
1.5	0.4332	0.4345	0.4357	0.4370	0.4382	0.4394	0.4406	0.4418	0.4429	0.4441
1.6	0.4452	0.4463	0.4474	0.4484	0.4495	0.4505	0.4515	0.4525	0.4535	0.4545
1.7	0.4554	0.4564	0.4573	0.4582	0.4591	0.4599	0.4608	0.4616	0.4625	0.4633
1.8	0.4641	0.4649	0.4656	0.4664	0.4671	0.4678	0.4686	0.4693	0.4699	0.4706
1.9	0.4713	0.4719	0.4726	0.4732	0.4738	0.4744	0.4750	0.4756	0.4761	0.4767
2.0	0.4773	0.4778	0.4783	0.4788	0.4793	0.4798	0.4803	0.4808	0.4812	0.4817
2.1	0.4821	0.4826	0.4830	0.4834	0.4838	0.4842	0.4846	0.4850	0.4854	0.4857
2.2	0.4861	0.4866	0.4868	0.4871	0.4875	0.4878	0.4881	0.4884	0.4887	0.4890
2.3	0.4893	0.4896	0.4898	0.4901	0.4904	0.4906	0.4909	0.4911	0.4913	0.4916
2.4	0.4918	0.4920	0.4922	0.4925	0.4927	0.4929	0.4931	0.4932	0.4934	0.4936
2.5	0.4938	0.4940	0.4941	0.4943	0.4945	0.4946	0.4948	0.4949	0.4951	0.4952
2.6	0.4953	0.4955	0.4956	0.4957	0.4959	0.4960	0.4961	0.4962	0.4963	0.4964
2.7	0.4965	0.4966	0.4967	0.4968	0.4969	0.4970	0.4971	0.4972	0.4973	0.4974
2.8	0.4974	0.4975	0.4976	0.4977	0.4977	0.4978	0.4979	0.4979	0.4980	0.4981
2.9	0.4981	0.4982	0.4982	0.4982	0.4984	0.4984	0.4985	0.4985	0.4986	0.4986
3.0	0.4987	0.4987	0.4987	0.4988	0.4988	0.4989	0.4989	0.4989	0.4990	0.4990

Now that $N(d_1)$ and $N(d_2)$ have been estimated, the call option value can be estimated:

$$V_c = (\$72 \times 0.8235) - \left(\frac{\$70}{e^{0.07 \times 0.50}} \times 0.8045 \right) = \$4.91$$

Thus, a call option on MPB stock should sell for a premium of $4.91.

Put-Call Parity

Using the Black-Scholes option-pricing model, the same relationship exists between the price of a call and that of a put as in the binomial option-pricing model. Thus, we have

$$P_p = P_c + \frac{E}{e^{RT}} - P_s$$

Deriving the Implied Volatility

In the example of deriving the value of a call option, an estimate of the stock's standard deviation was used. In some cases, investors want to derive the market's implied volatility rather than a valuation of the call option. The volatility is referred to as "implied" under these circumstances because it is not directly observable in the market. The implied volatility can be derived with some software packages by inputting values for the other variables (prevailing stock price, exercise price, option's time to expiration, and interest rate) in the call option–pricing model and also inputting the market premium of the call option. Instead of deriving a value for the call option premium, the prevailing market premium of the call option is used along with these other variables to derive the implied volatility. The software package will also show how the stock's implied volatility is affected for different values of the call option premium. If the market premium of the call option increases and other variables have not changed, this reflects an increase in the implied volatility. This relationship can be verified by plugging in a slightly higher market premium in the software program and checking how the implied volatility changes in response to a higher premium. The point is that investors can detect changes in the implied volatility of a stock by monitoring how the stock's call option premium changes over short intervals of time.

AMERICAN VERSUS EUROPEAN OPTIONS

American Call Options

An American call option is an option to purchase stock that can be exercised at any time prior to maturity. However, the original Black-Scholes model was developed to price European call options, which are options to purchase stock that can be exercised only at maturity. Naturally, European puts could be directly derived using the put-call parity relationship. Consequently, the question is whether the Black-Scholes equation can be used to price American call options.

In general, early exercise of a call may be justified only if the asset makes a cash payment such as a dividend on a stock. If there are no dividends during the life of the option, early exercise would be equivalent to buying something earlier than you need it and then giving up the right to decide later whether you really wanted it. If, however, it is possible to save a little money doing so, early purchase/exercise can sometimes be justified. Early exercise is not appropriate every time there is a dividend, but if early exercise is justified, it should occur just before the stock goes ex-dividend. This minimizes the amount of time value given up and still results in receiving the dividend. Thus, if there are no dividends on the underlying stock, the Black-Scholes model can be used to price American call options. If the underlying stock pays dividends, however, the Black-Scholes model may not be directly applicable. Conversely, the binomial option-pricing model can be used to price American call options that pay dividends.

American Put Options

Suppose you purchase a European put option. If the value of the underlying asset goes to zero, then the option has reached its maximum value. It allows you to sell a worthless asset for the exercise price. Since the option is European, however, it cannot be exercised prior to maturity. Its value will simply be the present value of the exercise price, and, of course, this value will gradually rise by the time value of money until expiration, at which time the option will be exercised. Clearly, this is a situation where you would wish the option were American, and if it were, you would exercise it as soon as the asset value goes to zero.

The example above indicates that there would be a demand for an option that allowed early exercise. It is not necessary, however, for the asset price to go to zero. The European put price must be at least the present value of the exercise price minus the asset price. Clearly, the present value of the exercise price minus the asset price is less than the exercise price minus the asset price, which is the amount that could be claimed if the put could be exercised early. Thus, an American put will sell for more than the European put, and the Black-Scholes option-pricing model cannot be used to price an American put option. There is a point where the right to exercise early is at its maximum value, and at that point the American put would be exercised. Finding that point is difficult, but to do so is to unlock the mystery of pricing the American put.

The only surefire way to price the American put correctly is to use a numerical procedure such as the binomial model. The procedure is akin to partitioning a two-dimensional space of time and the asset price into finer points and solving either a difference or a differential equation at each time point. The process starts at expiration and successively works its way back to the present by using the solution at the preceding step. Thus, a closed-form solution does not exist. American puts can be viewed as an infinite series of compound options (that is, an option on an option). At each point in time, the holder of the put has the right to decide whether to exercise it or not. The decision not to exercise the put is tantamount to a decision to exercise the compound option and obtain a position in a new compound option, which can be exercised an instant later. This proceeds on to the expiration day. This logic can lead to an intuitive but complex mathematical formula that contains an infinite number of terms. Thus, the holders of American puts face an infinite series of early exercise decisions. Only at an instant before the asset goes ex-dividend do the holders know that they should wait to exercise. This is because they know the asset will fall in value an instant later, so they might as well wait an instant and benefit from the decline in value.

15
Swap Markets

CHAPTER OBJECTIVES

The specific objectives of this chapter are to:

■ describe the types of interest rate swaps that are available,

■ explain the risks of interest rate swaps,

■ identify other interest rate derivative instruments that are commonly used,

■ explain how credit default swaps are used to reduce credit risk, and

■ describe how the swap markets have become globalized.

Many firms have inflow and outflow payments that are not equally sensitive to interest rate patterns. Consequently, they are exposed to interest rate risk. Interest rate swap contracts have been established to reduce these risks. In addition, credit default swap contracts have been established to reduce credit risk.

BACKGROUND

An **interest rate swap** is an arrangement whereby one party exchanges one set of interest payments for another. In the most common arrangement, fixed-rate interest payments are exchanged for floating-rate interest payments over time. The provisions of an interest rate swap include the following:

- The **notional principal** value to which the interest rates are applied to determine the interest payments involved.

- The fixed interest rate.

- The formula and type of index used to determine the floating rate.

- The frequency of payments, such as every six months or every year.

- The lifetime of the swap.

For example, a swap arrangement may involve an exchange of 11 percent fixed-rate payments for floating payments at the prevailing one-year Treasury bill rate plus 1 percent, based on $30 million of notional principal, at the end of each of the next seven years. Other money market rates are sometimes used instead of the T-bill rate to index the interest rate.

Although each participant in the swap agreement owes the other participant at each payment date, the amounts owed are typically netted out so that only the net payment is made. If a firm owes 11 percent of $30 million (the notional principal) but is supposed to receive 10 percent of $30 million on a given payment date, it will send a net payment of 1 percent of the $30 million, or $300,000.

The market for swaps is facilitated by over-the-counter trading rather than trading on an organized exchange. Given the uniqueness of the provisions in each swap arrangement, swaps are less standardized than other derivative instruments such as futures or options. Thus, a telecommunications network is more appropriate than an exchange to work out specific provisions of swaps.

Interest rate swaps became more popular in the early 1980s when corporations were experiencing the effects of large fluctuations in interest rates. Although some manufacturing companies were exposed to interest rate movements, financial institutions were exposed to a greater degree and became the primary users of interest rate swaps. Initially, only those institutions wishing to swap payments on amounts of $10 million or more engaged in interest rate swaps. In recent years, however, swaps have been conducted on smaller amounts as well.

Use of Swaps for Hedging

Financial institutions such as savings institutions and commercial banks in the United States traditionally had more interest rate-sensitive liabilities than assets and therefore were adversely affected by increasing interest rates. Conversely, some financial institutions in other countries (such as some commercial banks in Europe) had access to long-term fixed-rate funding but used funds primarily for floating-rate loans. These institutions were adversely affected by declining interest rates.

By engaging in an interest rate swap, both types of financial institutions could reduce their exposure to interest rate risk. Specifically, a U.S. financial institution could send fixed-rate interest payments to a European financial institution in exchange for floating-rate payments. This type of arrangement is illustrated in Exhibit 15.1. In the event of rising interest rates, the U.S. financial institution receives higher interest payments from the floating-rate portion of the swap agreement, which helps to offset the rising cost of obtaining deposits. In the event of declining interest rates, the European financial institution provides lower interest payments in the swap arrangement, which helps to offset the lower interest payments received on its floating-rate loans.

In our example, the U.S. financial institution forgoes the potential benefits from a decline in interest rates, while the European financial institution forgoes the potential benefits from an increase in interest rates. The interest rate swap enables each institution to offset any gains or losses that result specifically from interest rate movements. Consequently,

Exhibit 15.1 Illustration of an Interest Rate Swap

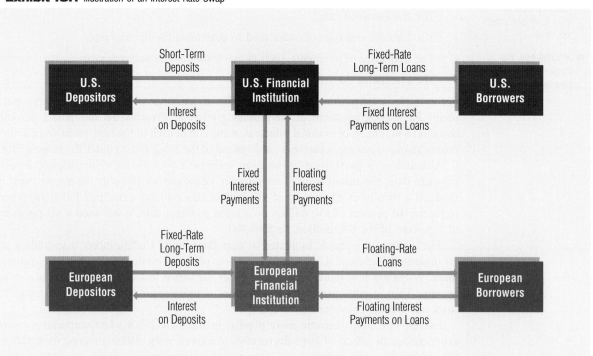

as interest rate swaps reduce interest rate risk, they can also reduce potential returns. Most financial institutions that anticipate that interest rates will move in a favorable direction do not hedge their positions. Interest rate swaps are primarily used by financial institutions that would be adversely affected by the expected movement in interest rates.

A primary reason for the popularity of interest rate swaps is the existence of market imperfections. If the parties involved in a swap could easily access funds from various markets without having to pay a premium, they would not need to engage in swaps. Using our previous example, a U.S. financial institution could access long-term funds directly from the European market, while the European institution could access short-term funds directly from the U.S. depositors. However, a lack of information about foreign institutions and convenience encourages individual depositors to place deposits locally. Consequently, swaps are necessary for some financial institutions to obtain the maturities or rate sensitivities on funds that they desire.

Use of Swaps for Speculating

Interest rate swaps are sometimes used by financial institutions and other firms for speculative purposes. For example, a firm may engage in a swap to benefit from its expectations that interest rates will rise, even if its other operations are not exposed to interest rate movements. When the swap is used for speculating rather than for hedging, any loss on the swap positions will not be offset by gains from other operations.

EXAMPLE

Gibson Greetings, Inc. incurred a loss of almost $17 million in 1994 as a result of its positions in interest rate swaps. In the same year, Procter & Gamble incurred a loss of about $157 million as a result of its positions in interest rate swaps. Procter & Gamble then claimed that Bankers Trust (a commercial bank that served as an intermediary and an adviser on interest rate swaps) did not properly advise it about the risk of its swap positions.

Also in 1994, Orange County, California, lost more than $2 billion as a result of its positions in interest rate swaps and other derivative securities. It was positioned to generate large gains if interest rates declined. Interest rates increased instead, however, and the treasurer of the county took more positions to make up for those losses. He continued to take positions in anticipation that interest rates would decline, but the rates kept on rising throughout 1994. By December 1994, the treasurer resigned, and Orange County announced that it would be filing for bankruptcy.

The substantial losses incurred in these cases encouraged firms to more closely monitor the actions of their managers who take derivative positions to ensure that those positions are aligned with the firm's goals. ●

PARTICIPATION BY FINANCIAL INSTITUTIONS

Financial institutions participate in the swap markets in various ways, as summarized in Exhibit 15.2. Financial institutions such as commercial banks, savings institutions, insurance companies, and pension funds that are exposed to interest rate movements commonly engage in swaps to reduce interest rate risk.

A second way to participate in the swap market is by acting as an intermediary. Some commercial banks and securities firms serve in this capacity by matching up firms and facilitating the swap arrangement. Financial institutions that serve as intermediaries for swaps charge fees for their services. They may even provide credit guarantees (for a fee) to each party in the event that the counterparty does not fulfill its obligation. Under these circumstances, the parties engaged in swap agreements assess the creditworthiness of the intermediary that is backing the swap obligations. For this reason, participants in the swap market prefer intermediaries that have a high credit rating.

Exhibit 15.2 Participation of Financial Institutions in Swap Markets

FINANCIAL INSTITUTION	PARTICIPATION IN SWAP MARKETS
Commercial banks	• Engage in swaps to reduce interest rate risk. • Serve as an intermediary by matching up two parties in a swap. • Serve as a dealer by taking the counterparty position to accommodate a party that desires to engage in a swap.
Savings and loan associations and savings banks	• Engage in swaps to reduce interest rate risk.
Finance companies	• Engage in swaps to reduce interest rate risk.
Securities firms	• Serve as an intermediary by matching up two parties in a swap. • Serve as a dealer by taking the counterparty position to accommodate a party that desires to engage in a swap.
Insurance companies	• Engage in swaps to reduce interest rate risk.
Pension funds	• Engage in swaps to reduce interest rate risk.

A third way to participate is by acting as a dealer in swaps. The financial institution takes the counterparty position in order to serve a client. In such a case, the financial institution may be exposing itself to interest rate risk unless it has recently taken the opposite position as a counterparty for another swap agreement.

TYPES OF INTEREST RATE SWAPS

In response to firms' diverse needs, a variety of interest rate swaps have been created. The following are some of the more commonly used swaps:

- Plain vanilla swaps
- Forward swaps
- Callable swaps
- Putable swaps
- Extendable swaps
- Zero-coupon-for-floating swaps
- Rate-capped swaps
- Equity swaps

Some types of interest rate swaps are more effective than others at offsetting any unfavorable effects of interest rate movements on the U.S. institution. However, those swaps also offset any favorable effects to a greater degree. Other types of interest rate swaps do not provide as effective a hedge but allow the institution more flexibility to benefit from favorable interest rate movements.

Plain Vanilla Swaps

In a **plain vanilla swap,** sometimes referred to as a fixed-for-floating swap, fixed-rate payments are periodically exchanged for floating-rate payments. The earlier example of the U.S. and European institutions involved this type of swap.

Consider the exchange of payments under different interest rate scenarios in Exhibit 15.3 when using a plain vanilla swap. Although infinite possible interest rate scenarios exist, only two scenarios are considered: (1) a consistent rise in market interest rates and (2) a consistent decline in market interest rates.

Exhibit 15.3 Illustration of a Plain Vanilla (Fixed-for-Floating) Swap

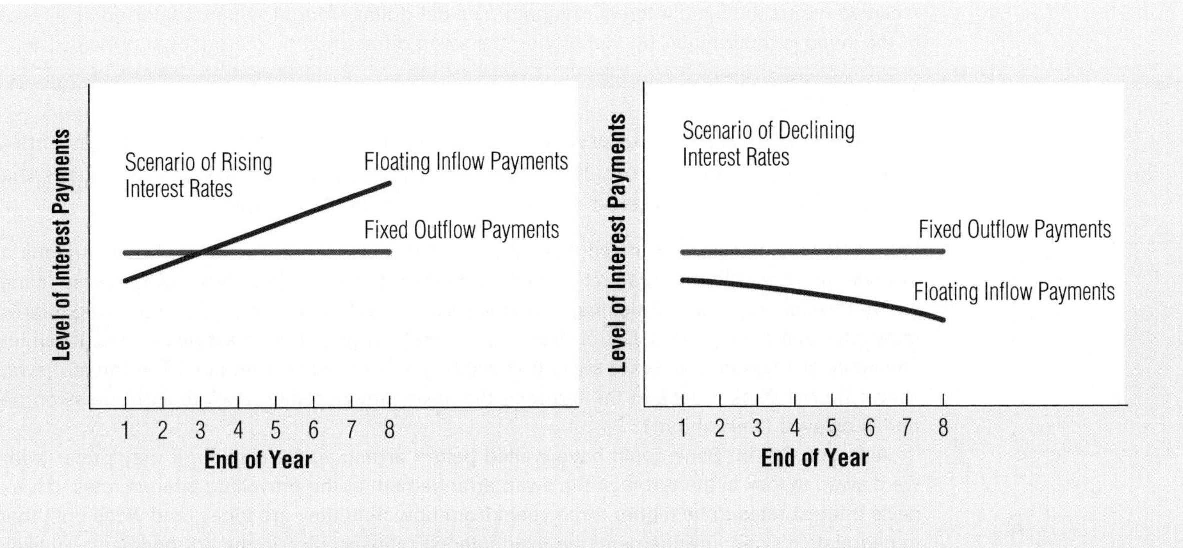

EXAMPLE

The Bank of Orlando has negotiated a plain vanilla swap in which it will exchange fixed payments of 9 percent for floating payments equal to LIBOR plus 1 percent at the end of each of the next five years. LIBOR is the **London Interbank Offer Rate,** or the interest rate charged on loans between European banks. The LIBOR varies among currencies; for swap examples involving U.S. firms, the LIBOR on U.S. dollars would normally be used. Assume the notional principal is $100 million.

Two scenarios for LIBOR are shown in Exhibit 15.4. The first scenario (in the top panel of Exhibit 15.4) reflects rising U.S. interest rates, which cause LIBOR to increase. The second scenario (in the lower panel) reflects declining U.S. interest rates, which cause LIBOR to

Exhibit 15.4 Possible Effects of a Plain Vanilla Swap Agreement (Fixed Rate of 9 Percent in Exchange for Floating Rate of LIBOR + 1 Percent)

	YEAR				
SCENARIO I	1	2	3	4	5
LIBOR	7.0%	7.5%	8.5%	9.5%	10.0%
Floating rate received	8.0%	8.5%	9.5%	10.5%	11.0%
Fixed rate paid	9.0%	9.0%	9.0%	9.0%	9.0%
Swap differential	−1.0%	−0.5%	+0.5%	+1.5%	+2.0%
Net dollar amount received based on notional value of $100 million	−$1,000,000	−$500,000	+$500,000	+$1,500,000	+$2,000,000

	YEAR				
SCENARIO II	1	2	3	4	5
LIBOR	6.5%	6.0%	5.0%	4.5%	4.0%
Floating rate received	7.5%	7.0%	6.0%	5.5%	5.0%
Fixed rate paid	9.0%	9.0%	9.0%	9.0%	9.0%
Swap differential	−1.5%	−2.0%	−3.0%	−3.5%	−4.0%
Net dollar amount received based on notional value of $100 million	−$1,500,000	−$2,000,000	−$3,000,000	−$3,500,000	−$4,000,000

decrease. The swap differential derived for each scenario represents the floating interest rate received minus the fixed interest rate paid. The net dollar amount to be transferred as a result of the swap is determined by multiplying the swap differential by the notional principal. ●

Forward Swaps

A **forward swap** involves an exchange of interest payments that does not begin until a specified future point in time. It is useful for financial institutions or other firms that expect to be exposed to interest rate risk at a future point in time.

Detroit Bank is currently insulated against interest rate risk. Three years from now, it plans to increase its proportion of fixed-rate loans (in response to consumer demand for these loans) and reduce its proportion of floating-rate loans. To prevent the adverse effects of rising interest rates after that point in time, Detroit Bank may want to engage in interest rate swaps. It can immediately arrange for a forward swap that will begin three years from now. The forward swap allows Detroit Bank to lock in the terms of the arrangement today, even though the swap period is delayed (see Exhibit 15.5).

Although Detroit Bank could have waited before arranging for a swap, it may prefer a forward swap to lock in the terms of the swap arrangement at the prevailing interest rates. If it expects interest rates to be higher three years from now than they are today, and waits until then to negotiate a swap arrangement, the fixed interest rate specified in the arrangement will likely be higher. A forward interest rate swap may allow Detroit Bank to negotiate a fixed rate today that is less than the expected fixed rate on a swap negotiated in the future. Because Detroit Bank will be exchanging fixed payments for floating-rate payments, it wants to minimize the fixed rate used for the swap agreement. ●

The fixed rate negotiated on a forward swap will not necessarily be the same as the fixed rate negotiated on a swap that begins immediately. The pricing conditions on any swap are based on expected interest rates over the swap lifetime.

Like any interest rate swap, forward swaps involve two parties. Our example of a forward swap involves a U.S. institution that expects interest rates to rise and wants to immediately lock in the fixed rate that it will pay when the swap period begins. The party that takes the opposite position in the forward swap will likely be a firm that will be adversely affected by declining interest rates and expects interest rates to decline. This firm

Exhibit 15.5 Illustration of a Forward Swap

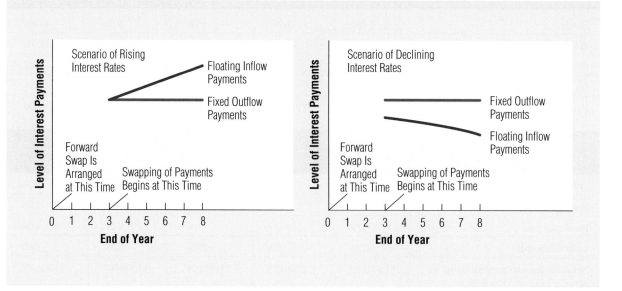

would prefer to lock in the prevailing fixed rate, because that rate is expected to be higher than the applicable fixed rate when the swap period begins. Because this institution will be receiving the fixed interest payments, it wishes to maximize the fixed rate specified in the swap arrangement.

Callable Swaps

Another use of interest rate swaps is through **swap options** (or **swaptions**). A **callable swap** provides the party making the fixed payments with the right to terminate the swap prior to its maturity. It allows the fixed-rate payer to avoid exchanging future interest payments if it desires.

EXAMPLE

Reconsider the U.S. institution that wanted to swap fixed interest payments for floating interest payments to reduce any adverse effects of rising interest rates. If interest rates decline, the interest rate swap arrangement offsets the potential favorable effects on this institution. A callable swap allows the institution to terminate the swap in the event that interest rates decline (see Exhibit 15.6). ●

The disadvantage of a callable swap is that the party given the right to terminate the swap pays a premium that is reflected in a higher fixed interest rate than the party would pay without the call feature. The party may also incur a termination fee in the event that it exercises its right to terminate the swap arrangement.

Putable Swaps

A **putable swap** provides the party making the floating-rate payments with a right to terminate the swap. To illustrate, reconsider the European institution that wanted to exchange floating-rate payments for fixed-rate payments to reduce the adverse effects of declining interest rates. If interest rates rise, the interest rate swap arrangement offsets the potential favorable effects on the financial institution. A putable swap allows the institution to terminate the swap in the event that interest rates rise (see Exhibit 15.7). As

Exhibit 15.6 Illustration of a Callable Swap

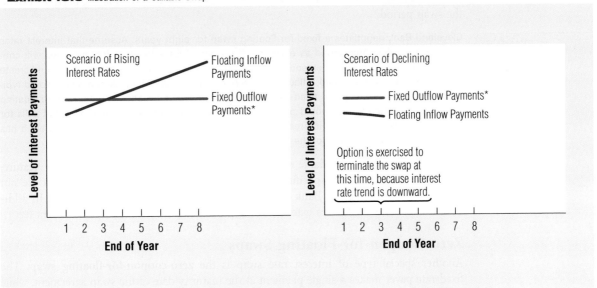

*Note that the fixed outflow payments in a callable swap are slightly higher than those of a plain vanilla swap because the payer of the fixed outflow payments incurs the cost for the option to terminate the swap before it matures.

Exhibit 15.7 Illustration of a Putable Swap

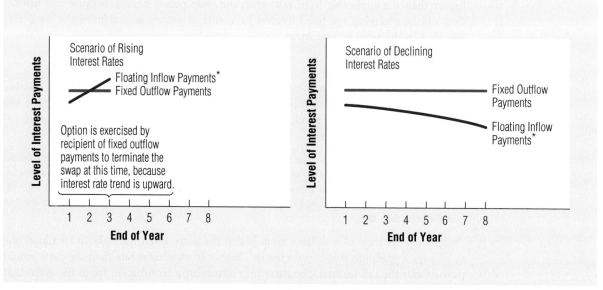

*Note that the floating inflow payments in a putable swap are slightly higher than those of a plain vanilla swap because the payer of the floating inflow payments incurs the cost for the option to terminate the swap before it matures.

with callable swaps, the party given the right to terminate the swap pays a premium. For putable swaps, the premium is reflected in a higher floating rate than would be paid without the put feature. The party may also incur a termination fee in the event that it exercises its right to terminate the swap arrangement.

Extendable Swaps

An **extendable swap** contains a feature that allows the fixed-for-floating party to extend the swap period.

Cleveland Bank negotiates a fixed-for-floating swap for eight years. Assume that interest rates increase over this time period as expected. If Cleveland Bank believes interest rates will continue to rise, it may prefer to extend the swap period (see Exhibit 15.8). Although it could create a new swap, the terms would reflect the current economic conditions. A new swap would typically involve an exchange of fixed payments at the prevailing higher interest rate for floating payments. Cleveland Bank would prefer to extend the previous swap agreement that calls for fixed payments at the lower interest rate that existed at the time the swap was created. It has additional flexibility because of the extendable feature. ●

The terms of an extendable swap reflect a price paid for the extendability feature. That is, the interest rates specified in a swap agreement allowing an extension are not as favorable for Cleveland Bank as they would have been without the feature. In addition, if Cleveland Bank does extend the swap period, it may have to pay an extra fee.

Zero-Coupon-for-Floating Swaps

Another special type of interest rate swap is the **zero-coupon-for-floating swap**. The fixed-rate payer makes a single payment at the maturity date of the swap agreement, while the floating-rate payer makes periodic payments throughout the swap period. For example, consider a financial institution that primarily attracts short-term deposits and currently has large holdings of zero-coupon bonds that it purchased several years ago. At the time it

Exhibit 15.8 Illustration of an Extendable Swap

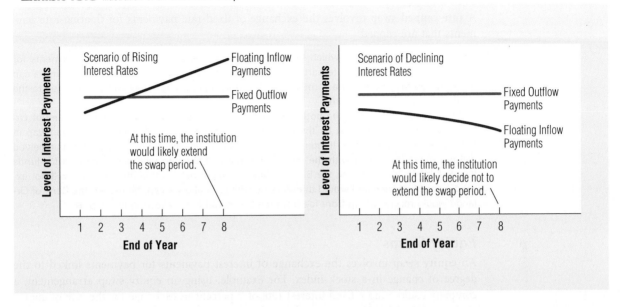

purchased the bonds, it expected interest rates to decline. Now it has become concerned that interest rates will rise over time, which will not only increase its cost of funds but also reduce the market value of the bonds. This financial institution can request a swap period that matches the maturity of its bond holdings. If interest rates rise over the period of concern, the institution will benefit from the swap arrangement, thereby offsetting any adverse effects on the institution's cost of funds. The other party in this type of transaction might be a firm that expects interest rates to decline (see Exhibit 15.9). Such a firm would be willing to provide floating-rate payments based on this expectation, because the payments will decline over time, while the single payment to be received at the end of the swap period is fixed.

Exhibit 15.9 Illustration of a Zero-Coupon-for-Floating Swap

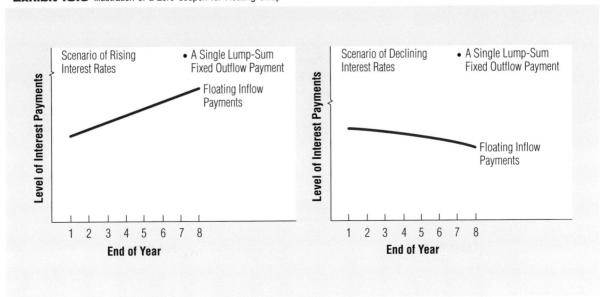

Rate-Capped Swaps

A **rate-capped swap** involves the exchange of fixed-rate payments for floating-rate payments that are capped.

EXAMPLE

Reconsider the example in which the Bank of Orlando arranges to swap fixed payments for floating payments. The counterparty may want to limit its possible payments by setting a cap or ceiling on the interest rate it must pay. The floating-rate payer pays an up-front fee to the fixed-rate payer for this feature.

In this case, the size of the potential floating payments to be received by the Bank of Orlando would now be limited by the cap, which may reduce the effectiveness of the swap in hedging its interest rate risk. If interest rates rise above the cap, the floating payments received will not move in tandem with the interest the Bank of Orlando will pay depositors for funds (see Exhibit 15.10). However, the Bank of Orlando might believe that interest rates will not exceed a specified level and would therefore be willing to allow a cap. Moreover, the Bank of Orlando would receive an up-front fee from the counterparty for allowing this cap. ●

Equity Swaps

An **equity swap** involves the exchange of interest payments for payments linked to the degree of change in a stock index. For example, using an equity swap arrangement, a company could swap a fixed interest rate of 7 percent in exchange for the rate of appreciation on the S&P 500 index each year over a four-year period. If the stock index appreciates by 9 percent over the year, the differential is 2 percent (9 percent received minus 7 percent paid), which will be multiplied by the notional principal to determine the dollar amount received. If the stock index appreciates by less than 7 percent, the company will have to make a net payment. This type of swap arrangement may be appropriate for portfolio managers of insurance companies or pension funds that are managing stocks and bonds. The swap would enhance their investment performance in bullish stock market periods without requiring the managers to change their existing allocation of stocks and bonds.

Exhibit 15.10 Illustration of a Rate-Capped Swap

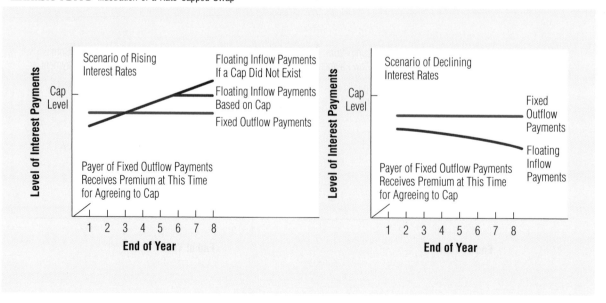

Other Types of Swaps

A variety of other swaps are also available, and additional types will be created to accommodate firms' future needs.

Use of Swaps to Accommodate Financing Preferences   Some interest rate swaps are combined with other financial transactions such as the issuance of bonds. Corporate borrowers may be able to borrow at a more attractive interest rate when using floating-rate debt than when using fixed-rate debt. Yet, if they want to make fixed payments on their debt, they can swap fixed-rate payments for floating-rate payments and use the floating-rate payments received to cover their coupon payments. Alternatively, some corporations may prefer to borrow at a floating rate but find it advantageous to borrow at a fixed rate. These corporations can issue fixed-rate bonds and then swap floating-rate payments in exchange for fixed-rate payments.

EXAMPLE

Quality Company is a highly rated firm that prefers to borrow at a variable rate. Risky Company is a low-rated firm that prefers to borrow at a fixed rate. These companies would pay the following rates when issuing either variable-rate or fixed-rate Eurobonds:

	FIXED-RATE BOND	VARIABLE-RATE BOND
Quality Company	9%	LIBOR + $^1/_2$%
Risky Company	$10^1/_2$%	LIBOR + 1%

Based on the information given, Quality Company has an advantage when issuing either fixed-rate or variable-rate bonds, but its advantage is greater when issuing fixed-rate bonds. Quality Company could issue fixed-rate bonds while Risky Company issues variable-rate bonds. Quality could then provide variable-rate payments to Risky in exchange for fixed-rate payments.

Assume that Quality negotiated with Risky to provide variable-rate payments at LIBOR plus $^1/_2$ percent in exchange for fixed-rate payments of $9^1/_2$ percent. This interest rate swap is shown in Exhibit 15.11. Quality Company benefits, because its fixed-rate payments received on the swap exceed the payments owed to bondholders by $^1/_2$ percent. Its variable-rate payments to

Exhibit 15.11 Illustration of an Interest Rate Swap to Reconfigure Bond Payments

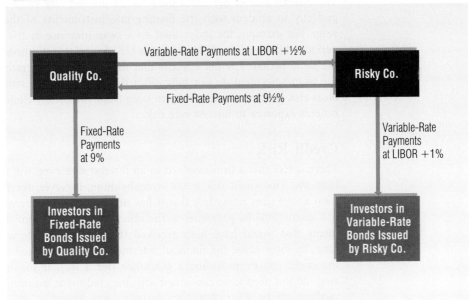

Risky Company are the same as what it would have paid if it had issued variable-rate bonds. Risky is receiving LIBOR plus $\frac{1}{2}$ percent on the swap, which is $\frac{1}{2}$ percent less than what it must pay on its variable-rate bonds. Yet, it is making fixed payments of $9\frac{1}{2}$ percent, which is 1 percent less than it would have paid if it had issued fixed-rate bonds. Overall, it saves $\frac{1}{2}$ percent per year on financing costs. ●

Two limitations of the swap just described are worth mentioning. First, the process of searching for a suitable swap candidate and negotiating the swap terms entails a cost in time and resources. Second, each swap participant faces the risk that the counterparty could default on payments. For this reason, financial intermediaries may match up participants and sometimes assume the credit (default) risk involved (for a fee).

Tax Advantage Swaps   Some swaps have recently been used by firms for tax purposes.

Columbus, Inc. has expiring tax loss carryforwards from previous years. To utilize the carryforwards before they expire, it may engage in a swap that calls for receipt of a large up-front payment with somewhat less favorable terms over time. Columbus may realize an immediate gain on the swap, with possible losses in future years. The tax loss carryforwards from previous years can be applied to offset any taxes on the immediate gain from the swap. Any future losses realized from future payments due to the swap agreement may be used to offset future gains from other operations.

Meanwhile, Ann Arbor, Inc. expects future losses but will realize large gains from operations in this year. It can take a position opposite to that of Columbus. That is, Ann Arbor will arrange for a swap in which it makes an immediate large payment and receives somewhat favorable terms on future payments. This year the firm will incur a tax loss on the swap, which can be used to offset some of its gains from other operations and thereby reduce its tax liability. ●

RISKS OF INTEREST RATE SWAPS

Several types of risk must be considered when engaging in interest rate swaps. Three of the more common types of risks are basis risk, credit risk, and sovereign risk.

Basis Risk

The interest rate of the index used for an interest rate swap will not necessarily move perfectly in tandem with the floating-rate instruments of the parties involved in the swap. For example, the index used on a swap may rise by 0.7 percent over a particular period, while the cost of deposits to a U.S. financial institution rises by 1.0 percent over the same period. The net effect is that the higher interest rate payments received from the swap agreement do not fully offset the increase in the cost of funds. This so-called **basis risk** prevents the interest rate swap from completely eliminating the financial institution's exposure to interest rate risk.

Credit Risk

There is risk that a firm involved in an interest rate swap will not meet its payment obligations. This credit risk is not overwhelming, however, for the following reasons. As soon as the firm recognizes that it has not received the interest payments it is owed, it will discontinue its payments to the other party. The potential loss is a set of net payments that would have been received (based on the differential in swap rates) over time. In some cases, the financial intermediary that matched up the two parties incurs the credit risk by providing a guarantee (for a fee). If so, the parties engaged in the swap do not need to be concerned with the credit risk, assuming that the financial intermediary will be able to cover any guarantees promised.

Concerns about a Swap Credit Crisis   The willingness of large banks and securities firms to provide guarantees has increased the popularity of interest rate swaps, but it has also raised concerns that widespread adverse effects might occur if any of these intermediaries cannot meet their obligations. If a large bank that has taken numerous swap positions and guaranteed many other swap positions fails, there could be a number of defaults on swap payments. These defaults could cause cash flow problems for other swap participants and force them to default on some of their payment obligations on swaps or other financial agreements. In this way, given the global integration of the swap network, defaults by a single large financial intermediary could be transmitted throughout the world. In fact, when American International Group (AIG) was rescued by the federal government during the credit crisis (as discussed later in this chapter), the potential damage throughout the swap network was cited as a reason for the rescue.

Because of the potential damage that a single shock could cause throughout the swap network, various regulators have considered methods of reducing credit risk in the market. For example, bank regulators have considered forcing banks to maintain more capital if they provide numerous guarantees on swap payments. Other proposals include creating a regulatory agency that would oversee the swap market and minimize credit risk and requiring more complete disclosure of swap positions and guarantees created by financial intermediaries. Given the large growth in swaps, the concerns about credit risk in the market will continue to receive much attention.

Sovereign Risk

Sovereign risk reflects potential adverse effects resulting from a country's political conditions. Various political conditions could prevent the counterparty from meeting its obligation in the swap agreement. For example, the local government might take over the counterparty and then decide not to meet its payment obligations. Alternatively, the government might impose foreign exchange controls that prohibit the counterparty from making its payments.

Sovereign risk differs from credit risk because it is dependent on the financial status of the government rather than the counterparty itself. A counterparty could have very low credit risk but conceivably be perceived as having high sovereign risk because of its government. It does not have control over some restrictions that are imposed by its government.

Pricing Interest Rate Swaps

The setting of specific interest rates for an interest rate swap is referred to as pricing the swap. The pricing is influenced by several factors, including prevailing market interest rates, availability of counterparties, and credit and sovereign risk.

Prevailing Market Interest Rates

The fixed interest rate specified in a swap is influenced by supply and demand conditions for funds with the appropriate maturity. For example, a plain vanilla (fixed-for-floating) interest rate swap structured when interest rates are very high would have specified a much higher fixed interest rate than one structured when interest rates were low. In general, the interest rates specified in a swap agreement reflect the prevailing interest rates at the time of the agreement.

Availability of Counterparties

Swap pricing is also determined by the availability of counterparties. When numerous counterparties are available for a particular desired swap, a party may be able to negotiate a more attractive deal. For example, consider a U.S. financial institution that wants a fixed-for-floating swap. If several European institutions are willing to serve as the counterparty, the U.S. institution may be able to negotiate a slightly lower fixed rate.

The availability of counterparties can change in response to economic conditions. For example, in a period when interest rates are expected to rise, many institutions will want a fixed-for-floating swap, but few institutions will be willing to serve as the counterparty. The fixed rate specified on interest rate swaps will be higher under these conditions than in a period when many financial institutions expect interest rates to decline.

Credit and Sovereign Risk

A party involved in an interest rate swap must assess the probability of default by the counterparty. For example, a firm that desires a fixed-for-floating swap will likely require a lower fixed rate applied to its outflow payments if the credit risk or sovereign risk of the counterparty is high. If a well-respected financial intermediary guarantees payments by the counterparty, however, the fixed rate will be higher.

FACTORS AFFECTING THE PERFORMANCE OF INTEREST RATE SWAPS

As Exhibit 15.12 shows, the performance of an interest rate swap is affected by several underlying forces; the most important are the forces that influence interest rate movements. The impact of the underlying forces on the performance of an interest rate swap depends on the party's swap position. For example, to the extent that strong economic growth can increase interest rates, it will be beneficial for a party that is swapping fixed-rate payments for floating-rate payments, but it will adversely affect a party that is swapping floating-rate payments for fixed-rate payments.

The diagram in Exhibit 15.12 can be adjusted to fit any currency. For an interest rate swap involving an interest rate benchmark denominated in a foreign currency, the economic conditions of that country are the primary forces that determine interest rate movements in that currency and therefore the performance of the interest rate swap.

Since the performance of a particular interest rate swap position is normally influenced by future interest rate movements, participants in the interest rate swap market closely monitor indicators that may affect these movements. Among the more closely watched indicators are indicators of economic growth (employment, gross domestic product), indicators of inflation (consumer price index, producer price index), and indicators of government borrowing (budget deficit, expected volume of funds borrowed at upcoming Treasury bond auctions).

INTEREST RATE CAPS, FLOORS, AND COLLARS

In addition to the more traditional forms of interest rate swaps, three other interest rate derivative instruments are commonly used:

- Interest rate caps
- Interest rate floors
- Interest rate collars

These instruments are normally classified separately from interest rate swaps, but they do result in interest payments between participants. Each of these instruments can be used by financial institutions to capitalize on expected interest rate movements or to hedge their interest rate risk.

Exhibit 15.12 Framework for Explaining Net Payments Resulting from an Interest Rate Swap

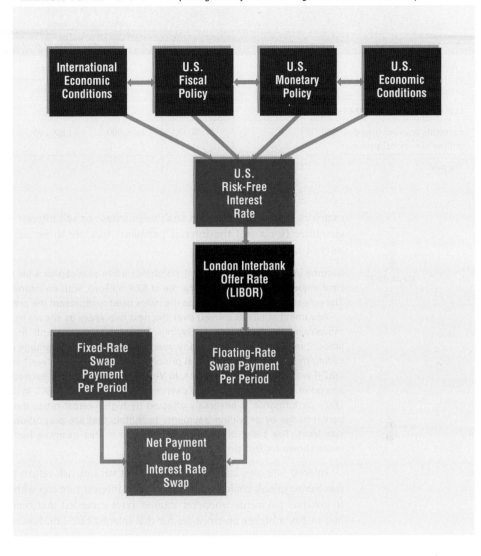

Interest Rate Caps

An **interest rate cap** offers payments in periods when a specified interest rate index exceeds a specified ceiling (cap) interest rate. The payments are based on the amount by which the interest rate exceeds the ceiling, multiplied by the notional principal specified in the agreement. A fee is paid up-front to purchase an interest rate cap, and the lifetime of a cap commonly ranges between three and eight years.

The typical purchaser of an interest rate cap is a financial institution that is adversely affected by rising interest rates. If interest rates rise, the payments received from the interest rate cap agreement will help offset any adverse effects.

The seller of an interest rate cap receives the fee paid up-front and is obligated to provide periodic payments when the prevailing interest rates exceed the ceiling rate specified in the agreement. The typical seller of an interest rate cap is a financial institution that expects interest rates to remain stable or decline.

Large commercial banks and securities firms serve as dealers for interest rate caps, in which they act as the counterparty on the transaction. They also serve as brokers,

Exhibit 15.13 Illustration of an Interest Rate Cap

		END OF YEAR:				
	0	1	2	3	4	5
LIBOR		6%	11%	13%	12%	7%
Interest rate ceiling		10%	10%	10%	10%	10%
LIBOR's percent above the ceiling		0%	1%	3%	2%	0%
Payments received (based on $60 million of notional principal)		$0	$600,000	$1,800,000	$1,200,000	$0
Fee paid	$2,400,000					

matching up participants that wish to purchase or sell interest rate caps. They may even guarantee (for a fee) the interest payments that are to be paid to the purchaser of the interest rate cap over time.

EXAMPLE

Assume that Buffalo Savings Bank purchases a five-year cap for a fee of 4 percent of notional principal valued at $60 million (so the fee is $2.4 million), with an interest rate ceiling of 10 percent. The agreement specifies LIBOR as the index used to represent the prevailing market interest rate.

Assume that LIBOR moved over the next five years as shown in Exhibit 15.13. Based on the movements in LIBOR, Buffalo Savings Bank received payments in three of the five years. The amount received by Buffalo in any year is based on the percentage points above the 10 percent ceiling multiplied by the notional principal. For example, in Year 1 the payment is zero because LIBOR was below the ceiling rate. In Year 2, however, LIBOR exceeded the ceiling by 1 percentage point, so Buffalo received a payment of $600,000 (1% × $60 million). To the extent that Buffalo's performance is adversely affected by high interest rates, the interest rate cap creates a partial hedge by providing payments to Buffalo that are proportionately related to the interest rate level. The seller of the interest rate cap in this example had the opposite payments of those shown for Buffalo in Exhibit 15.13. ●

Interest rate caps can be devised to meet various risk-return profiles. For example, Buffalo Savings Bank could have purchased an interest rate cap with a ceiling rate of 9 percent to generate payments whenever interest rates exceeded that ceiling. The bank would have had to pay a higher up-front fee for this interest rate cap, however.

Interest Rate Floors

An **interest rate floor** offers payments in periods when a specified interest rate index falls below a specified floor rate. The payments are based on the amount by which the interest rate falls below the floor rate, multiplied by the notional principal specified in the agreement. A fee is paid up-front to purchase an interest rate floor, and the lifetime of the floor commonly ranges between three and eight years. The interest rate floor can be used to hedge against lower interest rates in the same manner that the interest rate cap hedges against higher interest rates. Any financial institution that purchases an interest rate floor will receive payments if interest rates decline below the floor, which will help offset any adverse interest rate effects.

The seller of an interest rate floor receives the fee paid up-front and is obligated to provide periodic payments when the interest rate on a specified money market instrument falls below the floor rate specified in the agreement. The typical seller of an interest rate floor is a financial institution that expects interest rates to remain stable or rise. Large commercial banks or securities firms serve as dealers and/or brokers of interest rate floors, just as they do for interest rate swaps or caps.

Exhibit 15.14 Illustration of an Interest Rate Floor

		END OF YEAR:				
	0	1	2	3	4	5
LIBOR		6%	11%	13%	12%	7%
Interest rate floor		8%	8%	8%	8%	8%
LIBOR's percent below the floor		2%	0%	0%	0%	1%
Payments received (based on $60 million of notional principal)		$1,200,000	$0	$0	$0	$600,000
Fee paid	$2,400,000					

EXAMPLE

Assume that Toland Finance Company purchases a five-year interest rate floor for a fee of 4 percent of notional principal valued at $60 million (so the fee is $2.4 million), with an interest rate floor of 8 percent. The agreement specifies LIBOR as the index used to represent the prevailing interest rate.

Assume that LIBOR moved over the next five years as shown in Exhibit 15.14. Based on the movements in LIBOR, Toland received payments in two of the five years. The dollar amount received by Toland in any year is based on the percentage points below the 8 percent floor multiplied by the notional principal. For example, in Year 1, LIBOR was 2 percentage points below the interest rate floor, so Toland received a payment of $1.2 million (2% × $60 million). The seller of the interest rate floor in this example had the opposite payments of those shown for Toland in Exhibit 15.14. ●

Interest Rate Collars

An **interest rate collar** involves the purchase of an interest rate cap and the simultaneous sale of an interest rate floor. In its simplest form, the fee received up-front from selling the interest rate floor to one party can be used to pay the fee for purchasing the interest rate cap from another party. Any financial institution that desires to hedge against the possibility of rising interest rates can purchase an interest rate collar. The hedge results from the interest rate cap, which will generate payments to the institution if interest rates rise above the interest rate ceiling.

Because the collar also involves the sale of an interest rate floor, the financial institution is obligated to make payments if interest rates decline below the floor. Yet, if interest rates rise as expected, the rates will remain above the floor, so the financial institution will not have to make payments.

EXAMPLE

Assume that Pittsburgh Bank's performance is inversely related to interest rates. It anticipates that interest rates will rise over the next several years and decides to hedge its interest rate risk by purchasing a five-year interest rate collar, with LIBOR as the index used to represent the prevailing interest rate. The interest rate cap specifies a fee of 4 percent of notional principal valued at $60 million (so the fee is $2.4 million), with an interest rate ceiling of 10 percent. The interest rate floor specifies a fee of 4 percent of notional principal valued at $60 million and an interest rate floor of 8 percent.

Assume that LIBOR moved over the next five years as shown in Exhibit 15.15. Based on the movements in LIBOR, the payments received from purchasing the interest rate cap and the payments made from selling the interest rate floor are derived separately over each of the five years. Because the fee received from selling the interest rate floor was equal to the fee paid for the interest rate cap, the initial fees offset. The net payments received by Pittsburgh Bank as a result of purchasing the collar are equal to the payments received from the interest rate cap minus the payments made as a result of the interest rate floor. In the years when interest rates were relatively high, the net payments received by Pittsburgh Bank were positive.

Exhibit 15.15 Illustration of an Interest Rate Collar (Combined Purchase of Interest Rate Cap and Sale of Interest Rate Floor)

		END OF YEAR:				
	0	1	2	3	4	5
Purchase of interest rate cap:						
LIBOR		6%	11%	13%	12%	7%
Interest rate ceiling		10%	10%	10%	10%	10%
LIBOR's percent above the ceiling		0%	1%	3%	2%	0%
Payments received		$0	$600,000	$1,800,000	$1,200,000	$0
Fee paid	$2,400,000					
Sale of interest rate floor:						
Interest rate floor		8%	8%	8%	8%	8%
LIBOR's percent below the floor		2%	0%	0%	0%	1%
Payments made		$1,200,000	$0	$0	$0	$600,000
Fee received	$2,400,000					
Fee received minus fee paid	$0					
Payments received minus payments made		−$1,200,000	+$600,000	+$1,800,000	+$1,200,000	−$600,000

As this example illustrates, when interest rates are high, the collar can generate payments, which may offset the adverse effects of the high interest rates on the bank's normal operations. Although the net payments were negative in those years when interest rates were low, the performance of the bank's normal operations should have been strong. Like many other hedging strategies, the interest rate collar reduces the sensitivity of the financial institution's performance to interest rate movements. ●

CREDIT DEFAULT SWAPS

A **credit default swap (CDS)** is a privately negotiated contract that protects investors against the risk of default on particular debt securities. The swap involves two parties that have different needs or expectations about the future performance of particular debt securities. One party is the buyer, who is willing to provide periodic (usually quarterly) payments to the other party. The seller receives the payments from the buyer. It is obligated to provide a payment to the buyer if the securities specified in the swap agreement default. In this case, the seller pays the par value of the securities in exchange for the securities. Alternatively, the securities may be auctioned off by the buyer, and the seller must pay the buyer of the CDS the difference between the par value of the securities and the price at which those securities were sold.

The buyer of a CDS receives protection if the securities specified in the CDS contract default. Financial institutions purchase CDS contracts to protect their own investments in debt securities against default risk. The seller of a CDS expects that the CDS is unlikely to default. If its expectations come true, it will not have to make a payment and therefore benefits from the quarterly payments it receives over the life of the CDS contract.

The maturity of a CDS is typically between 1 and 10 years, but the most common maturity is 5 years. The notional value of the securities represented by a CDS contract is typically between $10 million and $20 million. The CDS contracts are traded over-the-counter and are not backed by an organized exchange. Therefore, each party must consider the ability of the counterparty to make payments when it participates in a CDS contract. Furthermore, there is a secondary market for CDS contracts, meaning that the counterparty can sell the CDS to another financial institution, subject to the approval of the other party on the contract.

When the securities protected by a CDS contract decline in price because of conditions that increase the likelihood of their default, the seller of the CDS must post a higher level of collateral to back its position. This is intended to ensure that the seller of the CDS does not default on its position.

Development of the CDS Market

Credit default swaps were created in the 1990s as a way to protect investors that purchased bonds against default risk. Over time CDS contracts were adapted to protect investors that purchased mortgage-backed securities. The CDS market grew rapidly, representing $4 trillion of debt securities in 2003, $25 trillion in 2006, and $62 trillion in 2008. One reason for this rapid growth was that many financial institutions that invested in mortgage-backed securities wanted to purchase CDS contracts in order to protect against default. Other financial institutions that believed the mortgage-backed securities were safe served as the counterparties in order to generate periodic income. In addition, some financial institutions that had no exposure to mortgage-backed securities were buying CDS contracts so that they could benefit if these securities defaulted. Thus, some institutions were using the CDS market as a means of betting on an outcome that had nothing to do with their business, almost like betting on a sports event at a casino. The main participants in the CDS market are insurance companies, hedge funds, and securities firms.

Payments on a Credit Default Swap

Holding maturity and notional value constant, the payments required on a new CDS are positively related to the default risk. For example, a CDS on $10 million of debt securities that have a relatively low likelihood of default may require an annual payment of 1 percent or $100,000 per year (spread into quarterly payments). Conversely, a CDS on $10 million of riskier debt securities might require an annual payment of 3 percent, or $300,000 per year. A seller of a CDS requires more compensation to provide protection against default if the likelihood of default is higher.

In periods when economic growth is strong, the payments required on a CDS contract on most securities should be relatively low, because the default risk is usually low under these conditions. Conversely, when economic conditions are weak, the payments required on a CDS contract on most securities should be relatively high, because the default risk is high.

How CDSs Affect Debtor-Creditor Negotiations

Normally, when a firm encounters financial problems, its creditors attempt to work with the firm to prevent it from going bankrupt. They may be willing to help the debtor firm avoid bankruptcy by accepting a fraction of what they are owed, since they may receive even less if the firm files for bankruptcy. If the creditors have purchased a CDS contract, however, they may benefit more if the debtor firm goes bankrupt because they will receive payment from the seller of the CDS. Thus, creditors who hold CDS contracts have less incentive to help a debtor firm avoid bankruptcy.

Impact of the Credit Crisis on the CDS Market

Many financial institutions accumulated large holdings of mortgage-backed securities during the housing boom in the 2003–2005 period. They may have believed that the return was favorable and that the risk was negligible because home prices were rising consistently. As the housing market began to weaken in 2006, they purchased CDS contracts as protection against the default of these mortgage-backed securities.

Impact of Lehman Brothers' Failure   The securities firm Lehman Brothers was a major participant in the CDS market. When it went bankrupt in September 2008, it did not cover all of its CDS obligations. Thus, many financial institutions that had purchased CDS contracts from Lehman to protect against the default of mortgage-backed securities were not protected once the firm went bankrupt. Since the CDS market is over-the-counter, there was little information about the exposure of financial institutions to CDS contracts. The credit crisis illustrated how protection provided to buyers of a CDS is only as good as the creditworthiness of the CDS seller.

Impact of AIG's Financial Problems   American International Group (AIG), the world's largest insurance company, frequently sold CDS contracts as a means of generating periodic revenue. By 2008, it was on the sale side of CDS contracts representing about $440 billion in debt securities. Many of its CDS contracts obligated AIG to cover risky mortgage-backed securities that represented subprime mortgages. As housing conditions weakened further, rumors circulated that AIG might not be able to cover all the future claims on its CDS contracts due to defaults. The federal government was concerned that if AIG could not satisfy its obligations, all the financial institutions that had purchased CDS contracts from AIG would lose their protection and could possibly fail. In September 2008, the Federal Reserve injected billions of dollars into AIG because it feared that AIG's failure could cause major damage to the financial sector. In the following months, the bailout continued. By early 2009, AIG had received $150 billion in government funds.

GLOBALIZATION OF SWAP MARKETS

The market for interest rate swaps is not restricted to the United States. As mentioned earlier, European financial institutions commonly have the opposite exposure to interest rate risk and therefore take swap positions counter to the positions desired by U.S. financial institutions. Manufacturing corporations from various countries that are exposed to interest rate risk also engage in interest rate swaps.

Interest rate swaps are executed in various countries and are denominated in many different currencies. Dollar-denominated interest rate swaps account for about half the value of all interest rate swaps outstanding.

Given that swap participants are from various countries, the banks and securities firms that serve as intermediaries have a globalized network of subsidiaries. In this way, they can link participants from various countries. One obvious barrier to the global swap market is the lack of information about participants based in other countries. Thus, concerns about credit risk may discourage some participants from engaging in swaps. This barrier is reduced when international banks and securities firms that serve as intermediaries are willing to back the payments that are supposed to occur under the provisions of the swap agreement.

Financial institutions from numerous countries participated in the credit default swap market. Some of them were attempting to protect against default risk of their investments in bonds issued by governments around the world. In fact, some of the most popular CDS contracts were written on bonds issued by governments of emerging markets such as Brazil, Russia, and Turkey. Because CDS contracts were traded internationally, the credit crisis spread globally as participants began to realize that their counterparties might not be able to fulfill their obligations.

Currency Swaps

A **currency swap** is an arrangement whereby currencies are exchanged at specified exchange rates and at specified intervals. It is essentially a combination of currency futures contracts, although most futures contracts are not available for periods in the distant future. Currency swaps are commonly used by firms to hedge their exposure to exchange rate fluctuations.

EXAMPLE

Springfield Company is a U.S. firm that expects to receive 2 million British pounds (£) in each of the next four years. It may want to lock in the exchange rate at which it can sell British pounds over the next four years. A currency swap will specify the exchange rate at which the £2 million can be exchanged in each year. Assume the exchange rate specified by a swap is $1.70 (the spot exchange rate at the time of the swap arrangement), so Springfield will receive $3.4 million (£2 million × $1.70 per £) in each of the four years. Conversely, if the firm does not engage in a currency swap, the dollar amount received will depend on the spot exchange rate at the time the pounds are converted to dollars.

The impact of the currency swap is illustrated in Exhibit 15.16. This exhibit also shows the payments that would have been received under two alternative scenarios if the currency swap had not been arranged. Note that the payments received from the swap would have been less favorable than the unhedged strategy if the pound appreciated against the dollar over that period. However, the payments received from the swap would have been more favorable than the unhedged strategy if the pound depreciated against the dollar over that period. The currency swap arrangement reduces the firm's exposure to changes in the pound's value. ●

The large commercial banks that serve as financial intermediaries sometimes take positions. That is, they may agree to swap currencies with a firm rather than simply search for a suitable swap candidate.

Exhibit 15.16 Impact of Currency Swaps

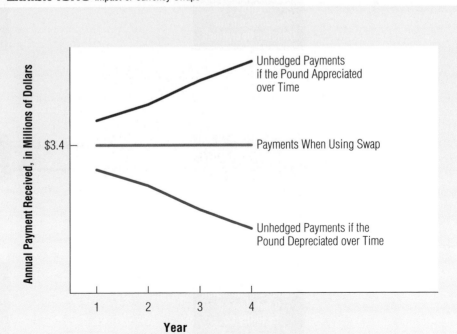

Like interest rate swaps, currency swaps are available in several variations. Some currency swap arrangements allow one of the parties an option to terminate the contract. That party incurs a premium for the option, which is either charged up-front or reflected in the exchange rates specified in the swap arrangement.

Using Currency Swaps to Hedge Bond Payments

Although currency swaps are commonly used to hedge payments on international trade, they may also be used in conjunction with bond issues to hedge foreign cash flows.

EXAMPLE

Philly Company, a U.S. firm, wants to issue a bond denominated in euros (the currency now used in several European countries) because it could make payments with euro inflows to be generated from ongoing operations. Philly, however, is not well known to investors who would consider purchasing euro-denominated bonds. Another firm, Windy Company, wants to issue dollar-denominated bonds because its inflow payments are mostly in dollars, but Windy is not well known to the investors who would purchase these bonds. If Philly is known in the dollar-denominated market and Windy is known in the euro-denominated market, the following transactions are appropriate. Philly can issue dollar-denominated bonds, while Windy issues euro-denominated bonds. Philly can exchange euros for dollars to make its bond payments. Windy will receive euros in exchange for dollars to make its bond payments. This currency swap is illustrated in Exhibit 15.17. ●

Risk of Currency Swaps

The same types of risk applicable to interest rate swaps may also apply to currency swaps. First, basis risk can exist if the firm cannot obtain a currency swap on the currency it is exposed to and uses a related currency instead.

Exhibit 15.17 Illustration of a Currency Swap

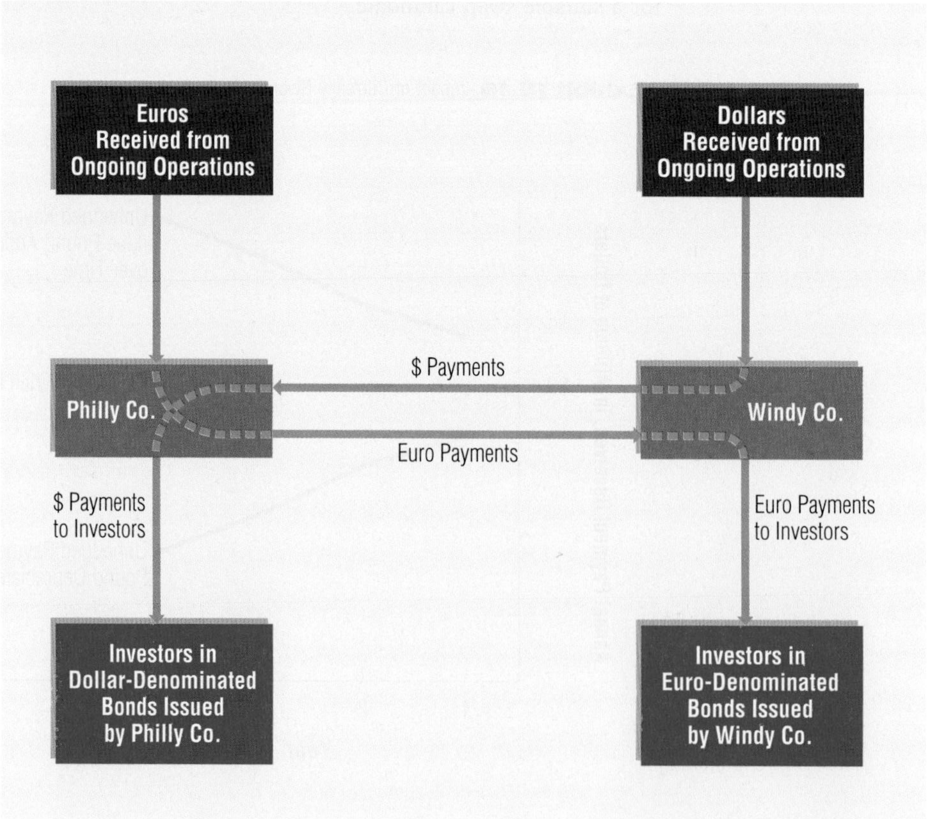

For example, consider a U.S. firm with cash inflows in British pounds that cannot find a counterparty to enact a swap in pounds. The firm may enact a swap in euros because movements in the euro and the pound against the dollar are highly correlated. To be specific, the firm will enact a currency swap to exchange euros for dollars. As it receives pounds, it will convert them to euros and then exchange the euros for dollars as specified by the swap arrangement. The exchange rate between pounds and euros is not constant, however, so basis risk exists.

Currency swaps can also be subject to credit risk, which reflects the possibility that the counterparty may default on its obligation. The potential loss is somewhat limited, however, because one party can stop exchanging its currency if it no longer receives currency from the counterparty.

A third type of risk is sovereign risk, which reflects the possibility that a country may restrict the convertibility of a particular currency. In this case, a party involved in a swap arrangement may not be able to fulfill its obligation because its government prohibits the local currency from being converted to another currency. This scenario is less likely in countries that encourage free trade of goods and securities across borders.

SUMMARY

- Various types of interest rate swaps are used to reduce interest rate risk. Some of the more popular types of interest rate swaps are plain vanilla swaps, forward swaps, callable swaps, putable swaps, extendable swaps, rate-capped swaps, and equity swaps. Each type of swap accommodates a particular need of financial institutions or other firms that are exposed to interest rate risk.

- When engaging in interest rate swaps, the participants can be exposed to basis risk, credit risk, and sovereign risk. Basis risk prevents the interest rate swap from completely eliminating the swap user's exposure to interest rate risk. Credit risk reflects the possibility that the counterparty on a swap agreement may not meet its payment obligations. Sovereign risk reflects the possibility that political conditions could prevent the counterparty in a swap agreement from meeting its payment obligations.

- In addition to the traditional forms of interest rate swaps, three other interest rate derivative instruments are commonly used to hedge interest rate risk: interest rate caps, interest rate floors, and interest rate collars. Interest rate caps offer payments when a specified interest rate index exceeds the interest rate

ceiling (cap) and therefore can hedge against rising interest rates. Interest rate floors offer payments when a specified interest rate index falls below a specified interest rate floor; they can be used to hedge against declining interest rates. An interest rate collar involves the purchase of an interest rate cap and the simultaneous sale of an interest rate floor and is used to hedge against rising interest rates.

- Credit default swaps are commonly purchased by financial institutions to protect against default on specific debt securities that they previously purchased. These swaps are sold by financial institutions that are willing to insure against the securities' default. As some financial institutions with major positions in credit default swaps experienced financial problems during the credit crisis in 2008, they were unable to cover their obligations. The credit crisis intensified due to the uncertainty surrounding potential losses of financial institutions that had positions in credit default swaps.

- The interest rate swap market has become globalized in the sense that financial institutions from various countries participate. Interest rate swaps are available in a variety of currencies.

POINT COUNTER-POINT

Should Financial Institutions Engage in Interest Rate Swaps for Speculative Purposes?

Point Yes. They have expertise in forecasting future interest rate movements and can generate gains for their shareholders by taking speculative positions.

Counter-Point No. They should use their main business to generate gains for their shareholders. They

should serve as intermediaries for swap transactions only in order to generate transaction fees or should take a position only if it is to hedge their exposure to interest rate risk.

Who Is Correct? Use the Internet to learn more about this issue. Offer your own opinion on this issue.

QUESTIONS AND APPLICATIONS

1. Hedging with Interest Rate Swaps Bowling Green Savings & Loan uses short-term deposits to fund fixed-rate mortgages. Explain how Bowling Green can use interest rate swaps to hedge its interest rate risk.

2. Decision to Hedge with Interest Rate Swaps Explain the types of cash flow characteristics that would cause a firm to hedge interest rate risk by swapping floating-rate payments for fixed payments. Why would some firms avoid the use of interest rate swaps, even when they are highly exposed to interest rate risk?

3. Role of Securities Firms in Swap Market Describe the possible roles of securities firms in the swap market.

4. Hedging with Swaps Chelsea Finance Company receives floating inflow payments from its provision of floating-rate loans. Its outflow payments are fixed because of its recent issuance of long-term bonds. Chelsea is somewhat concerned that interest rates will decline in the future. Yet, it does not want to hedge its interest rate risk because it believes interest rates may increase. Recommend a solution to Chelsea's dilemma.

5. Basis Risk Comiskey Savings provides fixed-rate mortgages of various maturities, depending on what customers want. It obtains most of its funds from issuing certificates of deposit with maturities ranging from one month to five years. Comiskey has decided to engage in a fixed-for-floating swap to hedge its interest rate risk. Is Comiskey exposed to basis risk?

6. Fixed-for-Floating Swaps Shea Savings negotiates a fixed-for-floating swap with a reputable firm in South America that has an exceptional credit rating. Shea is very confident that there will not be a default

on inflow payments because of the very low credit risk of the South American firm. Do you agree? Explain.

7. Fixed-for-Floating Swaps North Pier Company entered into a two-year swap agreement, which would provide fixed-rate payments for floating-rate payments. Over the next two years, interest rates declined. Based on these conditions, did North Pier Company benefit from the swap?

8. Equity Swap Explain how an equity swap could allow Marathon Insurance Company to capitalize on expectations of a strong stock market performance over the next year without altering its existing portfolio mix of stocks and bonds.

9. Swap Network Explain how the failure of a large commercial bank could cause a worldwide swap credit crisis.

10. Currency Swaps Markus Company purchases supplies from France once a year. Would Markus be favorably affected if it establishes a currency swap arrangement and the dollar strengthens? What if it establishes a currency swap arrangement and the dollar generally weakens?

11. Basis Risk Explain basis risk as it relates to a currency swap.

12. Sovereign Risk Give an example of how sovereign risk is related to currency swaps.

13. Use of Interest Rate Swaps Explain why some companies that issue bonds engage in interest rate swaps in financial markets. Why do they not simply issue bonds that require the type of payments (fixed or variable) that they prefer to make?

14. Use of Currency Swaps Explain why some companies that issue bonds engage in currency swaps. Why do they not simply issue bonds in the currency that they would prefer to use for making payments?

Advanced Questions

15. Rate-Capped Swaps Bull and Finch Company wants a fixed-for-floating swap. It expects interest rates to rise far above the fixed rate that it would have to pay and to remain very high until the swap maturity date. Should it consider negotiating for a rate-capped swap with the cap set at two percentage points above the fixed rate? Explain.

16. Forward Swaps Rider Company negotiates a forward swap to begin two years from now, in which it will swap fixed payments for floating-rate payments. What will be the effect on Rider if interest rates rise substantially over the next two years? That is, would Rider have been better off by using a forward swap than by simply waiting two years before negotiating the swap? Explain.

17. Swap Options Explain the advantage of a swap option to a financial institution that wants to swap fixed payments for floating payments.

18. Callable Swaps Back Bay Insurance Company negotiated a callable swap involving fixed payments in exchange for floating payments. Assume that interest rates decline consistently up until the swap maturity date. Do you think Back Bay might terminate the swap prior to maturity? Explain.

19. Credit Default Swaps Credit default swaps were once viewed as a great innovation for making mortgage markets more stable. Recently, however, the swaps have been criticized for making the credit crisis worse. Why?

Interpreting Financial News

Interpret the following comments made by Wall Street analysts and portfolio managers:

a. "The swaps market is another Wall Street–developed house of cards."

b. "As a dealer in interest rate swaps, our bank takes various steps to limit our exposure."

c. "The regulation of commercial banks, securities firms, and other financial institutions that participate in the swaps market could create a regulatory war."

Managing in Financial Markets

Assessing the Effects of an Interest Rate Collar As a manager of a commercial bank, you just purchased a three-year interest rate collar, with LIBOR as the interest rate index. The interest rate cap specifies a fee of 2 percent of notional principal valued at $100 million and an interest rate ceiling of 9 percent. The interest rate floor specifies a fee of 3 percent of notional principal valued at $100 million and an interest rate floor of 7 percent. Assume that LIBOR is expected to be 6 percent, 10 percent, and 11 percent, respectively, at the end of each of the next three years.

a. Determine the net fees paid, and also determine the expected *net* payments to be received as a result of purchasing the interest rate collar.

b. Assuming you are very confident that interest rates will rise, should you consider purchasing a callable swap instead of the collar? Explain.

c. Explain the conditions in which your purchase of an interest rate collar could backfire.

PROBLEMS

1. Vanilla Swaps Cleveland Insurance Company has just negotiated a three-year plain vanilla swap in which it will exchange fixed payments of 8 percent for floating payments of LIBOR plus 1 percent. The notional principal is $50 million. LIBOR is expected to be 7 percent, 9 percent, and 10 percent, respectively, at the end of each of the next three years.

a. Determine the net dollar amount to be received (or paid) by Cleveland each year.

b. Determine the dollar amount to be received (or paid) by the counterparty on this interest rate swap each year based on the forecasts of LIBOR assumed above.

2. Interest Rate Caps Northbrook Bank purchases a four-year cap for a fee of 3 percent of notional principal valued at $100 million, with an interest rate ceiling of 9 percent and LIBOR as the index representing the market interest rate. Assume that LIBOR is expected to be 8 percent, 10 percent, 12 percent, and 13 percent, respectively, at the end of each of the next four years.

a. Determine the initial fee paid, and also determine the expected payments to be received by Northbrook if LIBOR moves as forecasted.

b. Determine the dollar amount to be received (or paid) by the seller of the interest rate cap based on the forecasts of LIBOR assumed above.

3.   Interest Rate Floors Iowa City Bank purchases a three-year interest rate floor for a fee of 2 percent of notional principal valued at $80 million, with an interest rate floor of 6 percent and LIBOR representing the interest rate index. The bank expects LIBOR to be 6 percent, 5 percent, and 4 percent, respectively, at the end of each of the next three years.

a. Determine the initial fee paid, and also determine the expected payments to be received by Iowa City if LIBOR moves as forecasted.

b. Determine the dollar amounts to be received (or paid) by the seller of the interest rate floor based on the forecasts of LIBOR assumed above.

FLOW OF FUNDS EXERCISE

Hedging with Interest Rate Derivatives

Recall that if the economy continues to be strong, Carson Company may need to increase its production capacity by about 50 percent over the next few years to satisfy demand. It would need financing to expand and accommodate the increase in production. Recall that the yield curve is currently upward sloping. Also recall that Carson is concerned about a possible slowing of the economy because of potential Fed actions to reduce inflation. Carson currently relies mostly on commercial loans with floating interest rates for its debt financing. It has contacted Blazo Bank about the use of interest rate derivatives to hedge the risk.

a. How could Carson use interest rate swaps to reduce the exposure of its cost of debt to interest rate movements?

b. What is a possible disadvantage of Carson using the interest rate swap hedge as opposed to no hedge?

c. How could Carson use an interest rate cap to reduce the exposure of its cost of debt to interest rate movements?

d. What is a possible disadvantage of Carson using the interest cap hedge as opposed to no hedge? Explain the tradeoff from using an interest rate swap versus an interest rate cap.

INTERNET/EXCEL EXERCISES

Go to www.economagic.com/fedbog.htm.

1. Review the recent annualized rate for a short-term security such as the 1-year Treasury rate versus a long-term security such as the 10-year Treasury rate. Based on this information, do you think that the market expects interest rates to rise over time? Explain.

2. Assume that you need long-term funds and can borrow at the short-term Treasury rate. Based on the existing interest rates, would you consider engaging in a swap of a floating rate in exchange for a fixed rate? Explain.

WSJ EXERCISE

Impact of Interest Rates on a Swap Arrangement

Use a recent issue of *The Wall Street Journal* to determine how short-term interest rates have changed over the last year (assess the Treasury yield for a three-month maturity based on the yield curve shown for today versus the yield curve shown for a year ago). The three-month Treasury bill rate at the present time and one year ago are quoted in the Money & Investing section of *The Wall Street Journal*. Explain whether the interest rate movement would have had a favorable impact on a firm that initiated a fixed-for-floating swap agreement one year ago.

16

Foreign Exchange Derivative Markets

In recent years, various derivative instruments have been created to manage or capitalize on exchange rate movements. These so-called **foreign exchange derivatives** (or "forex" derivatives) include forward contracts, currency futures contracts, currency swaps, and currency options. Foreign exchange derivatives account for about half of the daily foreign exchange transaction volume.

The potential benefits from using foreign exchange derivatives are dependent on the expected exchange rate movements. Thus, it is necessary to understand why exchange rates change over time before exploring the use of foreign exchange derivatives.

FOREIGN EXCHANGE MARKETS

As international trade and investing have increased over time, so has the need to exchange currencies. Foreign exchange markets consist of a global telecommunications network among the large commercial banks that serve as financial intermediaries for such exchange. These banks are located in New York, Tokyo, Hong Kong, Singapore, Frankfurt, Zurich, and London. Foreign exchange transactions at these banks have been increasing over time.

At any point in time, the price at which banks will buy a currency (bid price) is slightly lower than the price at which they will sell it (ask price). Like markets for other commodities and securities, the market for foreign currencies is more efficient because of financial intermediaries (commercial banks). Otherwise, individual buyers and sellers of currency would be unable to identify counterparties to accommodate their needs.

Institutional Use of Foreign Exchange Markets

Exhibit 16.1 summarizes the ways financial institutions utilize the foreign exchange markets and foreign exchange derivatives. The degree of international investment by financial institutions is influenced by potential return, risk, and government regulations. Commercial banks use international lending as their primary form of international investing. Mutual funds, pension funds, and insurance companies purchase foreign securities. In recent years, technology has reduced information costs and other transaction costs associated with purchasing foreign securities, prompting an increase in institutional purchases of foreign securities. Consequently, financial institutions are increasing their use of the foreign exchange markets to exchange currencies. They are also increasing their use of foreign exchange derivatives to hedge their investments in foreign securities.

417

Exhibit 16.1 Institutional Use of Foreign Exchange Markets

TYPE OF FINANCIAL INSTITUTION	USES OF FOREIGN EXCHANGE MARKETS
Commercial banks	• Serve as financial intermediaries in the foreign exchange market by buying or selling currencies to accommodate customers. • Speculate on foreign currency movements by taking long positions in some currencies and short positions in others. • Provide forward contracts to customers. • Some commercial banks offer currency options to customers; unlike the standardized currency options traded on an exchange, these options can be tailored to a customer's specific needs.
International mutual funds	• Use foreign exchange markets to exchange currencies when reconstructing their portfolios. • Use foreign exchange derivatives to hedge a portion of their exposure.
Brokerage firms and securities firms	• Some brokerage firms and securities firms engage in foreign security transactions for their customers or for their own accounts.
Insurance companies	• Use foreign exchange markets when exchanging currencies for their international operations. • Use foreign exchange markets when purchasing foreign securities for their investment portfolios or when selling foreign securities. • Use foreign exchange derivatives to hedge a portion of their exposure.
Pension funds	• Require foreign exchange of currencies when investing in foreign securities for their stock or bond portfolios. • Use foreign exchange derivatives to hedge a portion of their exposure.

WEB

www.bloomberg.com
Spot rates of currencies and cross-exchange rates among currencies.

Exchange Rate Quotations

The **direct exchange rate** specifies the value of a currency in U.S. dollars. For example, the Mexican peso may have a value such as $.10, while the British pound may have a value such as $2.00. The **indirect exchange rate** specifies the number of units of a currency equal to a U.S. dollar. For example, the indirect exchange rate of the peso may be 10 pesos per dollar, while the indirect exchange rate of the British pound may be .50 pounds equal one dollar. Notice that the indirect exchange rate is the reciprocal of the direct exchange rate.

Forward Rate   For widely used currencies, **forward rates** are available and are commonly quoted next to the respective spot rates. The forward rates indicate the rate at which a currency can be exchanged in the future. If the forward rate is above the spot rate, it contains a premium. If the forward rate is below the spot rate, it contains a negative premium (also called a discount).

Cross-Exchange Rates   Most exchange rate quotation tables express currencies relative to the dollar. In some instances, however, the exchange rate between two nondollar currencies is needed.

EXAMPLE   If a Canadian firm needs Mexican pesos to buy Mexican goods, it is concerned about the value of the Mexican peso relative to the Canadian dollar. This type of rate is known as a cross-exchange rate because it reflects the amount of one foreign currency per unit of another foreign currency. Cross-exchange rates can be easily determined with the use of foreign exchange quotations. The general formula follows:

$$\text{Value of 1 unit of Currency A in units of Currency B}$$
$$= \text{Value of Currency A in \$/Value of Currency B in \$}$$

If the peso is worth $.07, and the Canadian dollar (C$) is worth $.70, the value of the peso in Canadian dollars is calculated as follows:

$$\text{Value of peso in C\$} = \text{Value of peso in \$}/\text{Value of C\$ in \$} = \$.07/\$.70 = .10$$

Thus, a Mexican peso is worth C$.10. The exchange rate can also be expressed as the number of pesos equal to one Canadian dollar. This figure can be computed by taking the reciprocal: .70/.07 = 10.0, which indicates that a Canadian dollar is worth 10.0 pesos according to the information provided. ●

Types of Exchange Rate Systems

From 1944 to 1971, the exchange rate at which one currency could be exchanged for another was maintained by governments within 1 percent of a specified rate. This period was known as the **Bretton Woods era,** because the agreement establishing the system was negotiated at the Bretton Woods Conference in Bretton Woods, New Hampshire. The manner by which governments were able to control exchange rates is discussed later in the chapter.

By 1971, the U.S. dollar was clearly overvalued. That is, its value was maintained only by central bank intervention. In 1971, an agreement among all major countries (known as the **Smithsonian Agreement**) allowed for devaluation of the dollar. In addition, the Smithsonian Agreement called for a widening of the boundaries from 1 percent to $2^{1}/_{4}$ percent around each currency's set value. Governments intervened in the foreign exchange markets whenever exchange rates threatened to wander outside the boundaries.

In 1973, the boundaries were eliminated. Since then, the exchange rates of major currencies have been floating without any government-imposed boundaries. A government may still intervene in the foreign exchange markets to influence the market value of its currency, however. A system with no boundaries in which exchange rates are market determined but are still subject to government intervention is called a **dirty float.** This can be distinguished from a **freely floating system,** in which the foreign exchange market would be totally free from government intervention.

Some countries today use a pegged exchange rate system. Hong Kong has tied the value of its currency (the Hong Kong dollar) to the U.S. dollar (HK$78 = $1) since 1983. In 2000, El Salvador set its currency (the colon) to be valued at 8.75 per dollar.

China's currency (the yuan) was pegged to the U.S. dollar until 2005. Many U.S. politicians argued that China was maintaining its currency at a level that was too low. The low value of the yuan meant that China's products were priced cheap in dollars. In 2005, U.S. exports to China were about $50 billion, but U.S. imports from China were about $250 billion, resulting in a balance of trade deficit of $200 billion with China. Thus, U.S. politicians claimed that China was creating jobs at U.S. expense by preventing the yuan's value from floating. In July 2005, China revalued the yuan by 2.1 percent against the dollar and implemented a new system that allowed the yuan to float within narrow boundaries based on a set of major currencies. This change has had only a very limited effect on the relative pricing of Chinese versus U.S. products, however, and therefore on the balance of trade between the two countries.

A country that pegs its currency does not have complete control over its local interest rates because they must be aligned with the interest rates of the currency to which its currency is tied.

EXAMPLE

If Hong Kong lowers its interest rates to stimulate its economy, its interest rates will be lower than U.S. interest rates. Investors based in Hong Kong will then be enticed to exchange Hong Kong dollars for U.S. dollars and invest in the United States where interest rates are higher. Since the Hong Kong dollar is tied to the U.S. dollar, the investors will be able to exchange their investment proceeds back to Hong Kong dollars at the end of the investment period without concern about exchange rate risk because the exchange rate is fixed. ●

As the example illustrates, Hong Kong no longer has control of its interest rates, as it is subject to movements in U.S. interest rates. Nevertheless, a country may view such an arrangement as advantageous because its interest rates (and therefore its economic conditions) might be much more volatile if they were not tied to the U.S. interest rates. Hong Kong's interest rate is typically equal to the U.S. interest rate plus a premium for risk. For example, when the Hong Kong government borrows funds, its interest rate is equal to the U.S. Treasury rate plus a small risk premium. As the U.S. Treasury rate changes, so does Hong Kong's interest rate.

In addition, because the Hong Kong dollar's value is fixed relative to the U.S. dollar, its value moves in tandem with the U.S. dollar against other currencies, including other Asian currencies. Thus, if the Japanese yen depreciates against the U.S. dollar, it will also depreciate against the Hong Kong dollar.

One concern about pegging a currency is that its value may change dramatically when the controls are removed. Many governments such as Argentina, Indonesia, and Russia have imposed restrictions to prevent their exchange rate from fluctuating, but when the controls were removed, the exchange rate abruptly adjusted to a new market-determined level.

FACTORS AFFECTING EXCHANGE RATES

The value of a currency adjusts to changes in demand and supply conditions, moving toward equilibrium. In equilibrium, there is no excess or deficiency of that currency.

EXAMPLE

A large increase in the U.S. demand for European goods and securities will result in an increased demand for euros. Because the demand for euros will then exceed the supply of euros for sale, the market-makers (commercial banks) will experience a shortage of euros and will respond by increasing the quoted price of euros. Therefore, the euro will **appreciate,** or increase in value.

Conversely, if European corporations begin to purchase more U.S. goods and European investors purchase more U.S. securities, the opposite forces will occur. There will be an increased sale of euros in exchange for dollars, causing a surplus of euros in the market. The value of the euro will therefore **depreciate,** or decline, until it once again achieves equilibrium. ●

In reality, both the demand for euros and the supply of euros for sale can change simultaneously. The adjustment in the exchange rate will depend on the direction and magnitude of these changes.

Supply of and demand for a currency are influenced by a variety of factors, including (1) differential inflation rates, (2) differential interest rates, and (3) government intervention. These factors are discussed in the following subsections.

Differential Inflation Rates

Begin with an equilibrium situation and consider what will happen to the U.S. demand for euros and the supply of euros for sale if U.S. inflation suddenly becomes much higher than European inflation. The U.S. demand for European goods will increase, reflecting an increased U.S. demand for euros. In addition, the supply of euros to be sold for dollars will decline as the European desire for U.S. goods decreases. Both forces will place upward pressure on the value of the euro.

Under the reverse situation, where European inflation suddenly becomes much higher than U.S. inflation, the U.S. demand for euros will decrease, while the supply of euros for sale increases, placing downward pressure on the value of the euro.

A well-known theory about the relationship between inflation and exchange rates, **purchasing power parity (PPP),** suggests that the exchange rate will, on average, change by a percentage that reflects the inflation differential between the two countries of concern.

EXAMPLE

Assume an initial equilibrium situation where the British pound's spot rate is $1.60, U.S. inflation is 3 percent, and British inflation is also 3 percent. If U.S. inflation suddenly increases to 5 percent, the British pound will appreciate against the dollar by approximately 2 percent according to PPP. The rationale is that as a result of the higher U.S. prices, U.S. demand for British goods will increase, placing upward pressure on the pound's value. Once the pound appreciates by 2 percent, the purchasing power of U.S. consumers will be the same whether they purchase U.S. goods or British goods. Although the prices of the U.S. goods will have risen by a higher percentage, the British goods will then be just as expensive to U.S. consumers because of the pound's appreciation. Thus, a new equilibrium exchange rate results from the change in U.S. inflation. ●

In reality, exchange rates do not always change as suggested by the PPP theory. Other factors that influence exchange rates (discussed next) can distort the PPP relationship. Thus, all these factors must be considered when assessing why an exchange rate has changed. Furthermore, forecasts of future exchange rates must account for the potential direction and magnitude of changes in all factors that affect exchange rates.

Differential Interest Rates

Interest rate movements affect exchange rates by influencing the capital flows between countries. An increase in interest rates may attract foreign investors, especially if the higher interest rates do not reflect an increase in inflationary expectations.

EXAMPLE

Assume U.S. interest rates suddenly become much higher than European interest rates. The demand by U.S. investors for European interest-bearing securities decreases, as these securities become less attractive. In addition, the supply of euros to be sold in exchange for dollars increases as European investors increase their purchases of U.S. interest-bearing securities. Both forces put downward pressure on the euro's value.

In the reverse situation, opposite forces occur, resulting in upward pressure on the euro's value. In general, the currency of the country with a higher increase (or smaller decrease) in interest rates is expected to appreciate, other factors held constant. ●

Central Bank Intervention

Central banks commonly consider adjusting a currency's value to influence economic conditions. For example, the U.S. central bank may wish to weaken the dollar to increase demand for U.S. exports, which can stimulate the economy. However, a weaker dollar can also cause U.S. inflation by reducing foreign competition (by raising the prices of foreign goods to U.S. consumers). Alternatively, the U.S. central bank may prefer to strengthen the dollar to intensify foreign competition, which can reduce U.S. inflation.

Direct Intervention   A country's government can intervene in the foreign exchange market to affect a currency's value. Direct intervention occurs when a country's central bank (such as the Federal Reserve Bank for the United States or the European Central Bank for European countries that use the euro) sells some of its currency reserves for a different currency.

EXAMPLE

Assume that the Federal Reserve and the European Central Bank desire to strengthen the value of the euro against the dollar. They use dollar reserves to purchase euros in the foreign exchange market. In essence, they dump dollars in the foreign exchange market and increase the demand for euros. ●

Central bank intervention can be overwhelmed by market forces, however, and therefore may not always succeed in reversing exchange rate movements. In fact, the efforts of the Fed and the European Central Bank to boost the value of the euro in 2000 were not successful. Nevertheless, central bank intervention may significantly affect the foreign exchange markets in two ways. First, it may slow the momentum of adverse exchange rate movements. Second, commercial banks and other corporations may reassess their foreign exchange strategies if they believe the central banks will continue to intervene.

Indirect Intervention   The Fed can affect the dollar's value indirectly by influencing the factors that determine its value. For example, the Fed can attempt to lower interest rates by increasing the U.S. money supply (assuming that inflationary expectations are not affected). Lower U.S. interest rates tend to discourage foreign investors from investing in U.S. securities, thereby putting downward pressure on the value of the dollar. Or, to boost the dollar's value, the Fed can attempt to increase interest rates by reducing the U.S. money supply. It has commonly used this strategy along with direct intervention in the foreign exchange market. Indirect intervention can be an effective means of influencing a currency's value.

When countries experience substantial net outflows of funds (which put severe downward pressure on their currency), they commonly use indirect intervention by raising interest rates to discourage excessive outflows of funds and therefore limit any downward pressure on the value of their currency. This adversely affects local borrowers (government agencies, corporations, and consumers), however, and may weaken the economy.

Indirect Intervention during the Peso Crisis   In 1994, Mexico experienced a large balance of trade deficit, perhaps because the peso was stronger than it should have been and encouraged Mexican firms and consumers to buy an excessive amount of imports. By December 1994, there was substantial downward pressure on the peso. On December 20, 1994, Mexico's central bank devalued the peso by about 13 percent. Mexico's stock prices plummeted, as many foreign investors sold their shares and withdrew their funds from Mexico in anticipation of further devaluation in the peso. On December 22, the central bank allowed the peso to float freely, and it declined by 15 percent. This was the beginning of the so-called Mexican peso crisis. The central bank increased interest rates as a form of indirect intervention to discourage foreign investors from withdrawing their investments in Mexico's debt securities. The higher interest rates increased the cost of borrowing for Mexican firms and consumers, thereby slowing economic growth.

Indirect Intervention during the Asian Crisis   In the fall of 1997, many Asian countries experienced weak economies, and their banks suffered from substantial defaults on loans. Concerned about their investments, investors began to withdraw their funds from these countries. Some countries (such as Thailand and Malaysia) increased their interest rates as a form of indirect intervention to encourage investors to leave their funds in Asia. However, the higher interest rates increased the cost of borrowing for firms that had borrowed funds there, making it more difficult for them to repay their loans. In addition, the high interest rates discouraged new borrowing by firms and weakened the economies (see Appendix 16A for a more comprehensive discussion of the Asian crisis).

During the Asian crisis, investors also withdrew funds from Brazil and reinvested them in other countries, causing major capital outflows and putting extreme downward pressure on the currency (the real). At the end of October, the central bank of Brazil responded by doubling its interest rates from about 20 percent to about 40 percent. This action discouraged investors from pulling funds out of Brazil because they could now earn twice the interest from investing in some securities there. Although the bank's action was successful in defending the real, it reduced economic growth because the cost of borrowing funds was too high for many firms.

Indirect Intervention during the Russian Crisis   A similar situation occurred in Russia in May 1998. Over the previous four months, the Russian currency (the ruble) had consistently declined, and stock market prices had declined by more than 50 percent. Since the lack of confidence in Russia's currency and stocks could cause massive outflows of funds, the Russian central bank attempted to prevent further outflows by tripling interest rates (from about 50 percent to 150 percent). The ruble was temporarily stabilized, but stock prices continued to decline as investors were concerned that the high interest rates would reduce economic growth.

Foreign Exchange Controls

Some governments attempt to use foreign exchange controls (such as restrictions on the exchange of the currency) as a form of indirect intervention to maintain the exchange rate of their currency. When there is severe pressure, however, they tend to let the currency float temporarily toward its market-determined level and set new bands around that level. For example, during the mid-1990s, Venezuela imposed foreign exchange controls on its currency (the bolivar). In April 1996, Venezuela removed its controls on foreign exchange, and the bolivar declined by 42 percent the next day. This result suggests that the market-determined exchange rate of the bolivar was substantially lower than the exchange rate artificially set by the government.

FORECASTING EXCHANGE RATES

Market participants who use foreign exchange derivatives tend to take positions based on their expectations of future exchange rates. For example, U.S. portfolio managers may take positions in foreign exchange derivatives to hedge the exposure of their British stocks, if they anticipate a decline in the value of the British pound. Speculators may take positions in foreign exchange derivatives to benefit from the expectation that the Japanese yen will strengthen. Thus, the initial task is to develop a forecast of specific exchange rates. Although there are various techniques for forecasting, no specific technique stands out. Most techniques have had limited success in forecasting future exchange rates. Most forecasting techniques can be classified as one of the following:

- Technical forecasting
- Fundamental forecasting
- Market-based forecasting
- Mixed forecasting

Technical Forecasting

WEB

www.oanda.com
Historical exchange rates.

Technical forecasting involves the use of historical exchange rate data to predict future values. For example, the fact that a given currency has increased in value over four consecutive days may provide an indication of how the currency will move tomorrow. In some cases, a more complex statistical analysis is applied. For example, a computer program can be developed to detect particular historical trends.

There are also several **time-series models** that examine moving averages and thus allow a forecaster to develop some rule, such as "The currency tends to decline in value after a rise in moving average over three consecutive periods." Normally, consultants who use such a method will not disclose their particular rule for forecasting. If they did, their potential clients might apply the rules themselves rather than pay for the consultant's advice.

Technical forecasting of exchange rates is similar to technical forecasting of stock prices. If the pattern of currency values over time appears random, then technical forecasting is not appropriate. Unless historical trends in exchange rate movements can be identified, examination of past movements will not be useful for indicating future movements.

Fundamental Forecasting

Fundamental forecasting is based on fundamental relationships between economic variables and exchange rates. Given current values of these variables along with their historical impact on a currency's value, corporations can develop exchange rate projections. For example, high inflation in a given country can lead to depreciation in its currency. Of course, all other factors that may influence exchange rates should also be considered.

A forecast may arise simply from a subjective assessment of the degree to which general movements in economic variables in one country are expected to affect exchange rates. From a statistical perspective, a forecast would be based on quantitatively measured impacts of factors on exchange rates.

Market-Based Forecasting

Market-based forecasting, the process of developing forecasts from market indicators, is usually based on either (1) the spot rate or (2) the forward rate.

Use of the Spot Rate   To clarify why the spot rate can serve as a market-based forecast, assume the British pound is expected to appreciate against the dollar in the very near future. This will encourage speculators to buy the pound with U.S. dollars today in anticipation of its appreciation, and these purchases could force the pound's value up immediately. Conversely, if the pound is expected to depreciate against the dollar, speculators will sell off pounds now, hoping to purchase them back at a lower price after they decline in value. Such action could force the pound to depreciate immediately. Thus, the current value of the pound should reflect the expectation of the pound's value in the very near future. Corporations can use the spot rate to forecast, since it represents the market's expectation of the spot rate in the near future.

Use of the Forward Rate   The forward rate can serve as a forecast of the future spot rate, because speculators would take positions if there was a large discrepancy between the forward rate and expectations of the future spot rate.

EXAMPLE

The 30-day forward rate of the British pound is $1.40, and the general expectation of speculators is that the future spot rate of the pound will be $1.45 in 30 days. Since speculators expect the future spot rate to be $1.45, and the prevailing forward rate is $1.40, they might buy pounds 30 days forward at $1.40 and then sell them when received (in 30 days) at the spot rate existing then. If their forecast is correct, they will earn $.05 ($1.45 − $1.40) per pound. If a large number of speculators implement this strategy, the substantial forward purchases of pounds will cause the forward rate to increase until this speculative demand stops. Perhaps this speculative demand will terminate when the forward rate reaches $1.45, since at this rate, no profits will be expected by implementing the strategy. The forward rate should move toward the market's general expectation of the future spot rate. In this sense, the forward rate serves as a market-based forecast because it reflects the market's expectation of the spot rate at the end of the forward horizon (30 days from now in this example). ●

Mixed Forecasting

Because no single forecasting technique has been found to be consistently superior to the others, some multinational corporations (MNCs) use a combination of forecasting techniques. This method is referred to as **mixed forecasting.** Various forecasts for a particular currency value are developed using several forecasting techniques. Each of the techniques used is assigned a weight so that the weights total 100 percent; the techniques thought to be more reliable are assigned higher weights. The actual forecast of the currency by the MNC will be a weighted average of the various forecasts developed.

Foreign Exchange Derivatives

Foreign exchange derivatives can be used to speculate on future exchange rate movements or to hedge anticipated cash inflows or outflows in a given foreign currency. As foreign security markets have become more accessible, institutional investors have increased their international investments, which has increased their exposure to exchange rate risk. Some institutional investors use foreign exchange derivatives to hedge their exposure. The most popular foreign exchange derivatives are forward contracts, currency futures contracts, currency swaps, and currency options contracts.

Forward Contracts

Forward contracts are contracts typically negotiated with a commercial bank that allow the purchase or sale of a specified amount of a particular foreign currency at a specified exchange rate (the forward rate) on a specified future date. A **forward market** facilitates the trading of forward contracts. This market is not in one physical place, but is essentially a telecommunications network through which large commercial banks match participants who wish to buy a currency forward with other participants who wish to sell a currency forward.

Many of the commercial banks that offer foreign exchange on a spot basis also offer forward transactions for the widely traded currencies. By enabling a corporation to lock in the price to be paid for a foreign currency, forward purchases or sales can hedge the corporation's risk that the currency's value may change over time.

EXAMPLE

St. Louis Insurance Company plans to invest about $20 million in Mexican stocks two months from now. Because the Mexican stocks are denominated in pesos, the amount of stock that can be purchased is dependent on the peso's value at the time of the purchase. If St. Louis Insurance Company is concerned that the peso will appreciate by the time of the purchase, it can buy pesos forward to lock in the exchange rate. ●

A corporation receiving payments denominated in a particular foreign currency in the future can lock in the price at which the currency can be sold by selling that currency forward.

EXAMPLE

The pension fund manager of Gonzaga, Inc. plans to liquidate the fund's holdings of British stocks in six months, but anticipates that the British pound will depreciate by that time. The pension fund manager can insulate the future transaction from exchange rate risk by negotiating a forward contract to sell British pounds six months forward. In this way, the British pounds received when the stocks are liquidated can be converted to dollars at the exchange rate specified in the forward contract. ●

The large banks that accommodate requests for forward contracts are buying forward from some firms and selling forward to others for a given date.

EXAMPLE

Corvalis Company will need 1 million euros in one year. It can purchase euros one year forward from Utah Bank. If the forward rate of the euro is $1.25, the firm will need $1,250,000 ($1.25 × 1,000,000 euros) in one year, regardless of how the euro's value changes over the year. Meanwhile Salem Company will be receiving 1 million euros in one year and is concerned that the euro may depreciate by the time it receives them. It calls Utah Bank, which quotes a rate of $1.24 to buy the euros from Salem Company in one year. Thus, Salem will exchange the euros for dollars at Utah Bank and will receive $1,240,000 ($1.24 × 1,000,000 euros). Utah Bank earned $.01 per unit or $10,000 on the spread between its ask price of $1.25 for euros one year forward and its bid price of $1.24 for euros one year forward. ●

Many types of financial institutions rely on the forward market to hedge the exchange rate risk resulting from their holdings of foreign securities.

If a bank's forward purchase and sale contracts do not even out for a given date, the bank is exposed to exchange rate risk.

Nebraska Bank has contracts committed to selling C$100 million and purchasing C$150 million 90 days from now. It will receive C$50 million more than it sells. An increase in the Canadian dollar's value 90 days from now will be advantageous, but if the Canadian dollar depreciates, the bank will be adversely affected by its exposure to the exchange rate risk. ●

Estimating the Forward Premium   The forward rate of a currency will sometimes exceed the existing spot rate, thereby exhibiting a premium. At other times, it will be below the spot rate, exhibiting a discount. Forward contracts are sometimes referred to in terms of their percentage premium or discount rather than their actual rate. For example, assume that the spot rate (S) of the Canadian dollar is $.70 while the 180-day ($n = 180$) forward rate ($FR$) is $.71. The forward rate premium (p) would be

$$p = \frac{FR - S}{S} \times \frac{360}{n}$$
$$= \frac{\$.71 - \$.70}{\$.70} \times \frac{360}{180}$$
$$= 2.86\%$$

This premium simply reflects the percentage by which the forward rate exceeds the spot rate on an annualized basis.

Currency Futures Contracts

WEB

www.cmegroup.com
Click on "FX Products"
to find quotes on currency futures
contracts.

An alternative to the forward contract is a currency futures contract, which is a standardized contract that specifies an amount of a particular currency to be exchanged on a specified date and at a specified exchange rate. A firm can purchase a futures contract to hedge payables in a foreign currency by locking in the price at which it could purchase that specific currency at a particular point in time. To hedge receivables denominated in a foreign currency, it could sell futures, thereby locking in the price at which it could sell that currency. A futures contract represents a standard number of units. Currency futures contracts also have specific maturity (or "settlement") dates from which the firm must choose.

Futures contracts differ from forward contracts in that they are standardized, whereas forward contracts can specify whatever amount and maturity date the firm desires. Forward contracts have this flexibility because they are negotiated with commercial banks rather than on a trading floor.

Currency Swaps

A currency swap is an agreement that allows one currency to be periodically swapped for another at specified exchange rates. It essentially represents a series of forward contracts. Commercial banks facilitate currency swaps by serving as the intermediary that links two parties with opposite needs. Alternatively, commercial banks may be willing to take the position counter to that desired by a particular party. In such a case, they expose themselves to exchange rate risk unless the position they have assumed will offset existing exposure.

Currency Options Contracts

Another instrument used for hedging is the currency option. Its primary advantage over forward and futures contracts is that it provides a right rather than an obligation to purchase or sell a particular currency at a specified price within a given period.

USING THE WALL STREET JOURNAL

Currency Futures Contracts

The Wall Street Journal provides information on currency futures contracts, as shown here. Specifically, it discloses the recent open price, range (high and low), and final closing (settle) price over the previous trading day. It also provides the amount of existing contracts (open interest).

Source: Republished with permission of Dow Jones & Company, Inc., from *The Wall Street Journal*, January 7, 2009, p. C9; permission conveyed through the Copyright Clearance Center, Inc.

Currency Futures

Japanese Yen (CME)-¥12,500,000; $ per 100¥

	Open	High	Low	Settle	Change	Open Int
March	1.0744	1.0782	1.0567	**1.0645**	−.0099	103,588
June	1.0697	1.0794	1.0608	**1.0664**	−.0100	3,799

Canadian Dollar (CME)-CAD 100,000; $ per CAD

March	.8398	.8500	.8331	**.8474**	.0067	47,891
June	.8478	.8506	.8347	**.8484**	.0066	2,144

British Pound (CME)-£62,500; $ per £

March	1.4675	1.4982	1.4486	**1.4920**	.0213	79,592
June	1.4571	1.4959	1.4495	**1.4916**	.0210	1,223

Swiss Franc (CME)-CHF 125,000; $ per CHF

March	.9011	.9038	.8870	**.8964**	−.0066	24,449
June	.8898	.8999	.8898	**.8983**	−.0068	350

Australian Dollar (CME)-AUD 100,000; $ per AUD

March	.7100	.7230	.6991	**.7209**	.0102	36,028
Sept	.7045	.7045	.7045	**.7142**	.0097	151

Mexican Peso (CME)-MXN 500,000; $ per 10MXN

Jan	...	...	...	**.74825**	.00925	0
March	.72775	.73925	.72725	**.73700**	.00925	16,813

Euro (CME)-€125,000; $ per €

March	1.3603	1.3628	1.3283	**1.3492**	−.0081	117,378
June	1.3480	1.3582	1.3265	**1.3467**	−.0081	908

WEB

www.cmegroup.com
Click on "FX Products" to find quotes on currency options contracts.

A currency call option provides the right to purchase a particular currency at a specified price (called the exercise price) within a specified period. This type of option can be used to hedge future cash payments denominated in a foreign currency. If the spot rate remains below the exercise price, the option will not be exercised, because the firm could purchase the foreign currency at a lower cost in the spot market. A fee (or a premium) must be paid for options, however, so there is a cost to hedging with options, even if the options are not exercised.

A put option provides the right to sell a particular currency at a specified price (exercise price) within a specified period. If the spot rate remains above the exercise price, the option will not be exercised, because the firm could sell the foreign currency at a higher price in the spot market. Conversely, if the spot rate is below the exercise price at the time the foreign currency is received, the firm can exercise its put option.

When deciding whether to use forward, futures, or options contracts for hedging, a firm should consider the following characteristics of each contract. First, if the firm requires a tailor-made hedge that cannot be matched by existing futures contracts, a forward contract may be preferred. Otherwise, forward and futures contracts should generate somewhat similar results.

The choice of either an obligation type of contract (forward or futures) or an options contract depends on the expected trend of the spot rate. If the currency denominating payables appreciates, the firm will benefit more from a futures or forward contract than from a call option contract. The call option contract requires an up-front fee, but it is a wiser choice when the firm is less certain of the future direction of a currency. The call option can hedge the firm against possible appreciation but still allow the firm to ignore the contract and use the spot market if the currency depreciates. Put options may be preferred over futures or forward contracts for hedging receivables when future currency movements are very uncertain, because the firm has the flexibility to let the options expire if the currencies strengthen.

Conditional Currency Options
Some currency options are structured with a conditional premium, meaning that the premium is conditioned on the actual movement in the currency's value over the period of concern.

Canyon Company, a U.S.-based MNC, needs to sell British pounds that it will receive in 60 days. Assume it can negotiate a traditional currency put option on pounds in which the exercise price is $1.70 and the premium is $.02 per unit.

Alternatively, Canyon can negotiate with a commercial bank to obtain a conditional currency option that has an exercise price of $1.70 and a so-called trigger of $1.74. If the pound's value falls below the exercise price by the expiration date, Canyon will exercise the option, receiving $1.70 per pound, and does not need to pay a premium for the option. If the pound's value is between the exercise price ($1.70) and the trigger ($1.74), the option will not be exercised, and Canyon will not need to pay a premium. If the pound's value exceeds the trigger of $1.74, Canyon will pay a premium of $.04 per unit. Notice that this premium may be higher than the premium Canyon would pay if it purchases a basic put option. Canyon may not mind this outcome, however, because it will be receiving a high dollar amount from converting its pound receivables in the spot market.

Canyon must determine whether the potential advantage of the conditional option (avoiding the payment of a premium under some conditions) outweighs the potential disadvantage (paying a higher premium than the premium for a traditional put option on British pounds). The potential advantage and disadvantage are illustrated in Exhibit 16.2. At exchange rates below or

Exhibit 16.2 Comparison of Conditional and Basic Currency Options

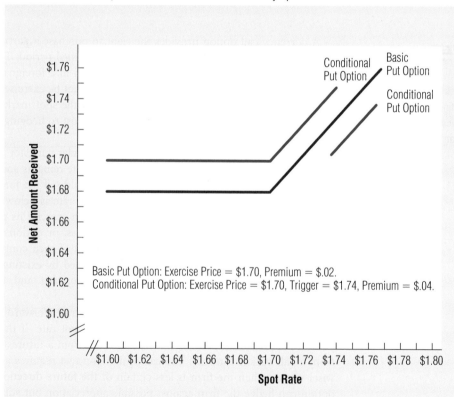

equal to the trigger level ($1.74), the conditional option will result in a larger payment to Canyon by the amount of the premium that would have been paid for the basic option. Conversely, at exchange rates above the trigger level, the conditional option results in a lower payment to Canyon, as its premium of $.04 exceeds the premium of $.02 per unit paid on a basic option. The choice of a basic option versus a conditional option is dependent on the firm's expectations of the currency's exchange rate over the period of concern. If Canyon is very confident that the pound's value will not exceed $1.74, it will prefer the conditional currency option. ●

Conditional currency options are also available for U.S. firms that need to purchase a foreign currency in the near future. For example, a conditional call option on the pound may specify an exercise price of $1.70 and a trigger of $1.67. If the pound's value remains above the trigger of the call option, a premium will not have to be paid for the call option. If the pound's value falls below the trigger, however, a large premium (such as $.04 per unit) will be required. Some conditional options require a premium if the trigger is reached anytime up until the expiration date; others require a premium only if the exchange rate is beyond the trigger as of the expiration date.

Use of Foreign Exchange Derivatives for Speculating

The forward, currency futures, and currency options markets may be used for speculating as well as for hedging. A speculator who expects the Singapore dollar to appreciate could consider any of these strategies:

1. Purchase Singapore dollars forward; when they are received, sell them in the spot market.
2. Purchase futures contracts on Singapore dollars; when the Singapore dollars are received, sell them in the spot market.
3. Purchase call options on Singapore dollars; at some point before the expiration date, when the spot rate exceeds the exercise price, exercise the call option and then sell the Singapore dollars received in the spot market.

Conversely, a speculator who expects the Singapore dollar to depreciate could consider any of these strategies:

1. Sell Singapore dollars forward and then purchase them in the spot market just before fulfilling the forward obligation.
2. Sell futures contracts on Singapore dollars; purchase Singapore dollars in the spot market just before fulfilling the futures obligation.
3. Purchase put options on Singapore dollars; at some point before the expiration date, when the spot rate is less than the exercise price, purchase Singapore dollars in the spot market and then exercise the put option.

Speculating with Currency Futures   As an example of speculating with currency futures, consider the following information:

- Spot rate of the British pound is $1.56 per pound.
- Price of a futures contract is $1.57 per pound.
- Expectation of the pound's spot rate as of the settlement date of the futures contract is $1.63 per pound.

Given that the future spot rate is expected to be higher than the futures price, you could buy currency futures. You would receive pounds on the settlement date for $1.57. If your expectations are correct, you would then sell the pounds for $.06 more per unit than you paid for them. The risk of your speculative strategy is that the pound may decline rather than increase in value. If it declines to $1.55 by the settlement date, you would have sold the pounds for $.02 less per unit than you paid.

To account for uncertainty, speculators may develop a probability distribution for the future spot rate:

FUTURE SPOT RATE OF BRITISH POUND	PROBABILITY
$1.50	10%
1.59	20
1.63	50
1.66	20

This probability distribution suggests that four outcomes are possible. For each possible outcome, the anticipated gain or loss can be determined:

POSSIBLE OUTCOME FOR FUTURE SPOT RATE	PROBABILITY	GAIN OR LOSS PER UNIT
$1.50	10%	−$.07
1.59	20	.02
1.63	50	.06
1.66	20	.09

This analysis measures the probability and potential magnitude of a loss from the speculative strategy.

Speculating with Currency Options

Consider the information from the previous example and assume that a British call option is available with an exercise price of $1.57 and a premium of $.03 per unit. Recall that your best guess of the future spot rate was $1.63. If your guess is correct, you will earn $.06 per unit on the difference between what you paid (the exercise price of $1.57) and the price for which you could sell a pound ($1.63). After the premium paid for the option ($.03 per unit) is deducted, the net gain is $.03 per unit.

The risk of purchasing this option is that the pound's value might decline over time. If so, you will be unable to exercise the option, and your loss will be the premium paid for it. To assess the risk involved, a probability distribution can be developed. In Exhibit 16.3, the probability distribution from the previous example is applied here. The distribution of net gains from the strategy is shown in the sixth column.

Exhibit 16.3 Estimating Speculative Gains from Options Using a Probability Distribution

(1) POSSIBLE OUTCOME FOR FUTURE SPOT RATE	(2) PROBABILITY	(3) WILL THE OPTION BE EXERCISED BASED ON THIS OUTCOME?	(4) GAIN PER UNIT FROM EXERCISING OPTION	(5) PREMIUM PAID PER UNIT FOR THE OPTION	(6) NET GAIN OR LOSS PER UNIT
$1.50	10%	No	—	$.03	−$.03
1.59	20	Yes	$.02	.03	−.01
1.63	50	Yes	.06	.03	.03
1.66	20	Yes	.09	.03	.06

Speculators should always compare the potential gains from currency options and currency futures contracts to determine which type of contract (if any) to trade. It is possible for two speculators to have similar expectations about potential gains from both types of contracts, yet prefer different types of contracts because they have different degrees of risk aversion.

INTERNATIONAL ARBITRAGE

Exchange rates in the foreign exchange market are market determined. If they become misaligned, various forms of arbitrage will occur, forcing realignment. Common types of international arbitrage are explained next.

Locational Arbitrage

Locational arbitrage is the act of capitalizing on a discrepancy between the spot exchange rate at two different locations by purchasing the currency where it is priced low and selling it where it is priced high.

EXAMPLE

The exchange rates of the European euro quoted by two banks differ, as shown in Exhibit 16.4. The ask quote is higher than the bid quote to reflect the transaction costs charged by each bank. Because Baltimore Bank is asking $1.046 for euros and Sacramento Bank is willing to pay (bid) $1.050 for euros, an institution could execute locational arbitrage. That is, it could achieve a risk-free return without tying funds up for any length of time by buying euros at one location (Baltimore Bank) and simultaneously selling them at the other location (Sacramento Bank). ●

As locational arbitrage is executed, Baltimore Bank will begin to raise its ask price on euros in response to the strong demand. In addition, Sacramento Bank will begin to lower its bid price in response to the excess supply of euros it has recently received. Once Baltimore's ask price is at least as high as Sacramento's bid price, locational arbitrage will no longer be possible. Because some financial institutions (particularly the foreign exchange departments of commercial banks) watch for locational arbitrage opportunities, any discrepancy in exchange rates among locations should quickly be alleviated.

Triangular Arbitrage

If the quoted cross rate between two foreign currencies is not aligned with the two corresponding exchange rates, there is a discrepancy in the exchange rate quotations. Under this condition, investors can engage in **triangular arbitrage,** which involves buying or selling the currency that is subject to a mispriced cross-exchange rate.

EXAMPLE

If the spot rate is $.07 for the Mexican peso and $.70 for the Canadian dollar, the cross-exchange rate should be C$1 = 10 pesos (computed as $.70/$.07). Assume that the Canadian dollar/peso exchange rate is quoted as C$1 = 10.3 pesos. In this case, the quote for the Canadian dollar is higher than it should be. An investor could benefit by using U.S. dollars to buy Canadian dollars, using those Canadian dollars to buy pesos, and then using the pesos to buy U.S. dollars. These transactions would be executed at about the same time before the exchange rates change. With $1,000, you could buy C$1,428.57 (computed as 1,000 divided by .70), convert those Canadian dollars into 14,714 pesos (computed as 1,428.57 × 10.3), and then convert the pesos into $1,030 (computed as 14,714 × .07). Thus, you would have a gain of $30. The gain would be much larger if you engaged in triangular arbitrage with a larger amount of money. ●

Exhibit 16.4 Bank Quotes Used for Locational Arbitrage Example

	BID RATE ON EUROS	ASK RATE ON EUROS
Sacramento Bank	$1.050	$1.056
Baltimore Bank	$1.042	$1.046

Whenever there is a discrepancy in exchange rates, financial institutions with large amounts of money will engage in triangular arbitrage, causing the quoted exchange rates to quickly adjust. The arbitrage transaction of using U.S. dollars to buy Canadian dollars will cause the exchange rate of the Canadian dollar to rise with respect to the U.S. dollar. The arbitrage transaction of using Canadian dollars to buy pesos will cause the value of the Canadian dollar to depreciate against the peso. The arbitrage transaction of using pesos to buy U.S. dollars will cause the value of the peso to depreciate against the U.S. dollar. Once the cross-exchange rate adjusts to its appropriate level, triangular arbitrage will no longer be feasible. The rates may adjust within a matter of seconds in response to the market forces. Quoted cross-exchange rates normally do not reflect a discrepancy because if they did, financial institutions would capitalize on the discrepancy until the exchange rates were realigned.

Covered Interest Arbitrage

The coexistence of international money markets and forward markets forces a special relationship between a forward rate premium and the interest rate differential of two countries, known as **interest rate parity.** The equation for interest rate parity can be written as

$$p = \frac{(1 + i_h)}{(1 + i_f)} - 1$$

where

$p =$ **forward premium of foreign currency**
$i_h =$ **home country interest rate**
$i_f =$ **foreign interest rate**

EXAMPLE

The spot rate of the New Zealand dollar is $.50, the one-year U.S. interest rate is 9 percent, and the one-year New Zealand interest rate is 6 percent. Under conditions of interest rate parity, the forward premium of the New Zealand dollar will be

$$p = \frac{(1 + 9\%)}{(1 + 6\%)} - 1$$
$$\simeq 2.8\%$$

This means that the forward rate of the New Zealand dollar will be about $.514, to reflect a 2.8 percent premium above the spot rate. ●

A review of the equation for interest rate parity suggests that if the interest rate is lower in the foreign country than in the home country, the forward rate of the foreign currency will exhibit a premium. In the opposite situation, the forward rate will exhibit a discount.

Interest rate parity suggests that the forward rate premium (or discount) should be about equal to the differential in interest rates between the countries of concern. If the relationship does not hold, market forces should occur that will restore the relationship. The act of capitalizing on the discrepancy between the forward rate premium and the interest rate differential is called **covered interest arbitrage.**

EXAMPLE

The spot rate and the one-year forward rate of the Canadian dollar are $.80. The Canadian interest rate is 10 percent, while the U.S. interest rate is 8 percent. U.S. investors can take advantage of the higher Canadian interest rate without being exposed to exchange rate risk by executing covered interest arbitrage. Specifically, they will exchange U.S. dollars for Canadian dollars and invest at the rate of 10 percent. They will simultaneously sell Canadian dollars one year forward. Because they are able to purchase and sell Canadian dollars for the same price, their return is the 10 percent interest earned on their investment. ●

As the U.S. investors demand Canadian dollars in the spot market while selling Canadian dollars forward, they place upward pressure on the spot rate and downward pressure on the one-year forward rate of the Canadian dollar. Thus, the Canadian dollar's forward rate will exhibit a discount. Once the discount becomes large enough, the interest rate advantage in Canada will be offset. What U.S. investors gain on the higher Canadian interest rate is offset by having to buy Canadian dollars at a higher (spot) rate than the selling (forward) rate. Consequently, covered interest arbitrage will no longer generate a return that is any higher for U.S. investors than an alternative investment in the United States. Once the forward discount (or premium) offsets the interest rate differential in this manner, interest rate parity exists.

The interest rate parity equation determines the forward discount that the Canadian dollar must exhibit to offset the interest rate differential:

$$p = \frac{(1 + i_h)}{(1 + i_f)} - 1$$
$$= \frac{(1 + 8\%)}{(1 + 10\%)} - 1$$
$$\simeq -1.82\%$$

If the forward rate is lower than the spot rate by 1.82 percent, the interest rate is offset, and covered interest arbitrage would yield a return to U.S. investors similar to the U.S. interest rate.

The existence of interest rate parity prevents investors from earning higher returns from covered interest arbitrage than can be earned in the United States. Nevertheless, international investing may still be feasible if the investing firm does not simultaneously cover in the forward market. Of course, failure to do so usually exposes the firm to exchange rate risk; if the currency denominating the investment depreciates over the investment horizon, the return on the investment is reduced.

SUMMARY

- Exchange rates are influenced by differential inflation rates, differential interest rates, and central bank intervention. There is upward pressure on a foreign currency's value when its home country has relatively low inflation or relatively high interest rates. Central banks can place upward pressure on a currency by purchasing that currency in the foreign exchange markets (by exchanging other currencies held in reserve for that currency). Alternatively, they can place downward pressure on a currency by selling that currency in the foreign exchange markets in exchange for other currencies.

- Exchange rates can be forecasted using technical, fundamental, and market-based methods. Each method has its own advantages and limitations.

- Foreign exchange derivatives include forward contracts, currency futures contracts, currency swaps, and currency options contracts. Forward contracts can be purchased to hedge future payables or sold

to hedge future receivables in a foreign currency. Currency futures contracts can be used in a manner similar to forward contracts to hedge payables or receivables in a foreign currency. Currency swaps can be used to lock in the exchange rate of a foreign currency to be received or purchased at a future point in time. Currency call options can be purchased to hedge future payables in a foreign currency, while currency put options can be purchased to hedge future receivables in a foreign currency. Currency options offer more flexibility than the other foreign exchange derivatives, but a premium must be paid for them.

Foreign exchange derivatives can also be used to speculate on expected exchange rate movements. When speculators expect a foreign currency to appreciate, they can lock in the exchange rate at which they may purchase that currency by purchasing forward contracts, futures contracts, or call options on that currency. When speculators expect a currency to depreciate, they can lock in the exchange rate at which they may sell that currency by selling forward contracts or futures contracts on that currency. They could also purchase put options on that currency.

■ International arbitrage ensures that foreign exchange market prices are set properly. If exchange rates vary among the banks that serve the foreign exchange market, locational arbitrage will be possible. Foreign exchange market participants will purchase a currency at the bank with a low quote and sell it to another bank where the quote is higher. If a quoted cross-exchange rate is misaligned with the corresponding exchange rates, triangular arbitrage will be possible. This involves buying or selling the currency that is subject to the mispriced exchange rate. If the interest rate differential is not offset by the forward rate premium (as suggested by interest rate parity), covered interest arbitrage will be possible. This involves investing in a foreign currency and simultaneously selling the currency forward. Arbitrage will occur until interest rate parity is restored.

POINT COUNTER-POINT

Do Financial Institutions Need to Consider Foreign Exchange Market Conditions When Making Domestic Security Market Decisions?

Point No. If there is no exchange of currencies, there is no need to monitor the foreign exchange market.

Counter-Point Yes. Foreign exchange market conditions can affect an economy or an industry and therefore affect the valuation of securities. In addition, the valuation of a firm can be affected by currency movements because of its international business.

Who Is Correct? Use the Internet to learn more about this issue. Offer your own opinion on this issue.

QUESTIONS AND APPLICATIONS

1.   Exchange Rate Systems Explain the exchange rate system that existed during the 1950s and 1960s. How did the Smithsonian Agreement in 1971 revise it? How does today's exchange rate system differ?

2.   Dirty Float Explain the difference between a freely floating system and a dirty float. Which type is more representative of the U.S. system?

3.   Impact of Quotas Assume that European countries impose a quota on goods imported from the United States, and the United States does not plan to retaliate. How could this affect the value of the euro? Explain.

4.   Impact of Capital Flows Assume that stocks in the United Kingdom become very attractive to U.S. investors. How could this affect the value of the British pound? Explain.

5.   Impact of Inflation Assume that Mexico suddenly experiences high and unexpected inflation. How could this affect the value of the Mexican peso according to purchasing power parity (PPP) theory?

6.   Impact of Economic Conditions Assume that Switzerland has a very strong economy, putting upward pressure on both inflation and interest rates. Explain how these conditions could put pressure on the value of the Swiss franc, and determine whether the franc's value will rise or fall.

7.   Central Bank Intervention The Bank of Japan desires to decrease the value of the Japanese yen against the dollar. How could it use direct intervention to do this?

8.   Bank Speculation When would a commercial bank take a short position in a foreign currency? A long position?

9.   Risk from Speculating Seattle Bank was long in Australian dollars and short in Canadian dollars. Explain a possible future scenario that could adversely affect the bank's performance.

10. Impact of a Weak Dollar How does a weak dollar affect U.S. inflation? Explain.

11. Speculating with Foreign Exchange Derivatives Explain how U.S. speculators could use foreign exchange derivatives to speculate on the expected appreciation of the Japanese yen.

Advanced Questions

12.   Interaction of Capital Flows and Yield Curve Assume a horizontal yield curve exists. How do you think the yield curve would be affected if foreign investors in short-term securities and long-term securities suddenly anticipate that the value of the dollar will strengthen? (You may find it helpful to refer back to the discussion of the yield curve in Chapter 3.)

13.   How the Euro's Value May Respond to Prevailing Conditions Consider the prevailing conditions for inflation (including oil prices), the economy, interest rates, and any other factors that could affect exchange rates. Based on these conditions, do you think the euro's value will likely appreciate or depreciate against the dollar for the remainder of this semester? Offer some logic to support your answer. Which factor do you think will have the biggest impact on the euro's exchange rate?

Interpreting Financial News

Interpret the following statements made by Wall Street analysts and portfolio managers:

a. "Our use of currency futures has completely changed our risk-return profile."

b. "Our use of currency options resulted in an upgrade in our credit rating."

c. "Our strategy of using forward contracts to hedge backfired on us."

Managing in Financial Markets

Using Forex Derivatives for Hedging You are the manager of a stock portfolio for a financial institution, and about 20 percent of the stock portfolio that you manage is in British stocks. You expect the British stock market to perform well over the next year, and plan to sell the stocks one year from now (and will convert the British pounds received to dollars at that time). However, you are concerned that the British pound may depreciate against the dollar over the next year.

a. Explain how you could use a forward contract to hedge the exchange rate risk associated with your position in British stocks.

b. If interest rate parity exists, does this limit the effectiveness of a forward rate as a hedge?

c. Explain how you could use an options contract to hedge the exchange rate risk associated with your position in stocks.

d. Assume that although you are concerned about the potential decline in the pound's value, you also believe that the pound could appreciate against the dollar over the next year. You would like to benefit from the potential appreciation but also wish to hedge against the possible depreciation. Should you use a forward contract or options contracts to hedge your position? Explain.

PROBLEMS

1.   Currency Futures Using the following information, determine the probability distribution of per unit gains from selling Mexican peso futures:

- Spot rate of peso is $.10.
- Price of peso futures per unit is $.102.
- Your expectation of the peso spot rate at maturity of the futures contract is:

POSSIBLE OUTCOME FOR FUTURE SPOT RATE	PROBABILITY
$.09	10%
.095	70
.11	20

2.   Currency Call Options Using the following information, determine the probability distribution of net gains per unit from purchasing a call option on British pounds:

- Spot rate of British pound is $1.45.
- Premium on British pound option is $.04 per unit.
- Exercise price of a British pound option is $1.46.
- Your expectation of the British pound spot rate prior to the expiration of the option is:

POSSIBLE OUTCOME FOR FUTURE SPOT RATE	PROBABILITY
$1.48	30%
1.49	40
1.52	30

3.   Locational Arbitrage Assume the following exchange rate quotes on British pounds:

	BID	ASK
Orleans Bank	$1.46	$1.47
Kansas Bank	1.48	1.49

Explain how locational arbitrage would occur. Also explain why this arbitrage will realign the exchange rates.

4.   Covered Interest Arbitrage Assume the following information:

- British pound spot rate = $1.58
- British pound one-year forward rate = $1.58
- British one-year interest rate = 11%
- U.S. one-year interest rate = 9%

Explain how U.S. investors could use covered interest arbitrage to lock in a higher yield than 9 percent. What would be their yield? Explain how the spot and forward rates of the pound would change as covered interest arbitrage occurs.

5.   Covered Interest Arbitrage Assume the following information:

- Mexican one-year interest rate = 15%
- U.S. one-year interest rate = 11%

If interest rate parity exists, what would be the forward premium or discount on the Mexican peso's forward rate? Would covered interest arbitrage be more profitable to U.S. investors than investing at home? Explain.

FLOW OF FUNDS EXERCISE

Hedging with Foreign Exchange Derivatives

Carson Company expects that it will receive a large order from the government of Spain. If the order occurs, Carson will be paid about 3 million euros. All of Carson's expenses are in dollars. Carson would like to hedge this position. Carson has contacted a bank with brokerage subsidiaries that can help it hedge with foreign exchange derivatives.

a. How could Carson use currency futures to hedge its position?

b. What is the risk of hedging with currency futures?

c. How could Carson use currency options to hedge its position?

d. Explain the advantage and disadvantage to Carson of using currency options instead of currency futures.

INTERNET/EXCEL EXERCISES

Use the website www.oanda.com to assess exchange rates.

1. What is the most recent value of the Australian dollar in U.S. dollars? For large transactions, how many British pounds does a U.S. dollar buy?

2. Review the pound's value over the past year. Offer a possible explanation for the recent movements in the pound's value.

3. What is the most recent value of the Hong Kong dollar in U.S. dollars? Do you notice anything unusual about this value over time? What could explain an exchange rate trend such as this?

WSJ EXERCISE

Assessing Exchange Rate Movements

Use a recent issue of *The Wall Street Journal* to determine how a particular currency's value has changed against the dollar since the beginning of the year. The table called "Currencies" lists the percentage change in many currencies since the beginning of the year.

Impact of the Asian Crisis on Foreign Exchange Markets and Other Financial Markets

The Asian crisis provides an excellent example of the linkages between the foreign exchange markets and all of the major financial markets. During the crisis, problems in the foreign exchange markets caused abrupt price movements in securities in all markets. In fact, the high degree of integration among financial markets today makes each financial market susceptible to events in any other financial market.

CRISIS IN THAILAND

Until July 1997, Thailand was one of the world's fastest-growing economies. In fact, Thailand was the fastest-growing country over the 1985–1994 period. Thai consumers spent freely, which resulted in lower savings than in other Southeast Asian countries. The high level of spending and low level of saving put upward pressure on prices of real estate and products and on the local interest rate. Normally, countries with high inflation tend to have a weak currency because of forces from purchasing power parity. Prior to July 1997, however, Thailand's currency (the baht) was linked to the dollar; this link made Thailand an attractive site for foreign investors, because they could earn a high interest rate on invested funds while being protected (until the crisis) from a large depreciation in the baht.

Flow of Funds Situation

The large inflow of funds made Thailand highly susceptible to a massive outflow of funds if the foreign investors ever lost confidence in the Thai economy. Given the large amount of risky loans and the potential for a massive outflow of funds, Thailand was sometimes described as a house of cards, waiting to collapse.

Export Competition

During the first half of 1997, the dollar strengthened against the Japanese yen and European currencies. Since the baht was linked to the dollar over this period, the baht strengthened against the yen and European currencies as well, and Thailand's products became more expensive to various importers.

Pressure on the Thai Baht

The baht experienced downward pressure in July 1997 when some foreign investors recognized its potential weakness. The outflow of funds expedited the currency's weakening as foreign investors exchanged their baht for their home currencies. The baht's value relative to the dollar was pressured by the large sales of baht in exchange for dollars. On July 2, 1997, the baht was detached from its link to the dollar. Thailand's central bank attempted to maintain the baht's value by intervention. Specifically, it swapped its baht reserves for dollar reserves at other central banks and then used its dollar reserves to purchase the baht in the foreign exchange market (the swap agreement required Thailand to reverse this transaction by exchanging dollars for baht at a future date). The bank hoped that its intervention would offset the sales of baht by foreign investors in the foreign exchange market, but its efforts were overwhelmed by market forces. The supply of baht for sale exceeded the demand for baht in the foreign exchange market, which caused the government to surrender in its effort to defend the baht's value. In July 1997, the value of the baht plummeted, declining by more than 20 percent against the dollar over a five-week period.

Rescue Package for Thailand

On August 5, 1997, the International Monetary Fund (IMF) and several countries agreed to provide Thailand with a $16 billion rescue package. Japan and the IMF each contributed $4 billion, and other countries provided the rest. This was the second largest bailout plan for a single country (Mexico received $50 billion in 1995). In return for the monetary support, Thailand agreed to reduce its budget deficit, prevent inflation from rising above 9 percent, raise its value-added tax from 7 to 10 percent, and clean up the financial statements of its banks, which had many undisclosed bad loans.

SPREAD OF THE CRISIS THROUGHOUT SOUTHEAST ASIA

The crisis in Thailand proved contagious to other countries in Southeast Asia. The Southeast Asian economies are somewhat integrated because of their trade contacts. The crisis weakened Thailand's economy and therefore reduced Thai demand for products from the other countries of Southeast Asia. As the demand for the other countries' products declined, so did their national incomes and their own demand for products from other Southeast Asian countries.

The other Southeast Asian countries were similar to Thailand in that they had relatively high interest rates, and their governments tended to stabilize their currency. Consequently, these countries had also attracted a large amount of foreign investment, but the foreign investors now realized that the other countries were vulnerable as well. These investors began to withdraw funds from these countries.

Impact of the Asian Crisis on South Korea

South Korea also experienced financial problems, as many of its corporations were unable to repay their loans. On December 3, 1997, the IMF agreed to a $55 million rescue package for South Korea. The World Bank and the Asian Development Bank joined with the IMF to provide a standby credit line of $35 billion. In exchange for the funding, South Korea agreed to reduce its economic growth and to impose restrictions on its conglomerates to prevent excessive borrowing. These measures led to some bankruptcies and unemployment, because the banks could no longer automatically provide loans to all conglomerates that needed funds unless the funding was economically justified.

Impact of the Asian Crisis on Japan

Japan was also affected by the Asian crisis for several reasons. It exports products throughout Southeast Asia, and many of its corporations have subsidiaries in other Asian countries and were therefore affected by the local economic conditions. Many of Japan's corporations experienced financial distress and could not repay their loans.

During the spring of 1998, the Japanese yen continued to weaken against the dollar. The yen's decline placed more pressure on other Asian currencies, because the Asian countries wanted to gain a competitive advantage in exporting to the United States as a result of their weak currencies. In April 1998, the Bank of Japan used more than $20 billion to purchase yen in the foreign exchange market. This effort to boost the yen's value was unsuccessful.

EFFECTS ON ASIAN CURRENCIES

In July and August of 1997, the values of the Malaysian ringgit, Singapore dollar, Philippine peso, Taiwan dollar, and Indonesian rupiah also declined. The Philippine peso was devalued in July. Malaysia initially attempted to maintain the ringgit's value within a narrow band, but then surrendered and let the ringgit float to its market-determined level.

In August 1997, Bank Indonesia (the central bank) used more than $500 million in direct intervention to purchase rupiah in the foreign exchange market in an attempt to boost the currency's value. By mid-August, however, the bank gave up on its effort to maintain the rupiah's value within a band and let the rupiah float to its natural level. This decision to let the rupiah float may have been influenced by the failure of Thailand's costly efforts to maintain the baht. The market forces were too strong and could not be offset by direct intervention. In the spring of 1998, the IMF provided Indonesia with a rescue package worth about $43 billion.

Impact of the Asian Crisis on Hong Kong

On October 23, 1997, prices on the Hong Kong stock market declined by 10.2 percent on average; considering the three previous trading days as well, the cumulative four-day effect was a decline of 23.3 percent. The decline was primarily attributed to speculation that Hong Kong's currency might be devalued and that it could experience financial problems similar to those of the Southeast Asian countries. The decline of almost one-fourth in the market value of Hong Kong companies over a four-day period demonstrated the perceived exposure of Hong Kong to the crisis.

Hong Kong maintained its pegged exchange rate system during this period, as its dollar was tied to the U.S. dollar. Nevertheless, it had to increase interest rates to discourage investors from transferring their funds out of the country.

Impact of the Asian Crisis on China

Ironically, China did not experience the adverse economic effects of the crisis because its growth in the years prior to the crisis was not as strong as that of the countries in Southeast Asia. The Chinese government had more control over economic conditions than other Asian governments because it still owned most real estate and controlled most of the banks that provided credit to support growth. Thus, China experienced fewer bankruptcies as a result of the crisis. In addition, the government was able to maintain the value of the Chinese currency (the yuan) against the dollar, which limited speculative flows of funds out of China. Although interest rates increased during the crisis, they remained relatively low. This allowed Chinese firms to obtain funding at a reasonable cost and enabled them to continue to meet their interest payments.

Nevertheless, concerns about China mounted because it relies heavily on exports to stimulate its economy and was now at a competitive disadvantage relative to the Southeast Asian countries whose currencies had depreciated. Thus, importers from the United States and Europe shifted some of their purchases to countries where the currencies had weakened substantially. In addition, the decline in the other Asian currencies against the Chinese yuan encouraged Chinese consumers to purchase imports rather than locally manufactured products.

Impact of the Asian Crisis on Russia

During the crisis, investors also lost confidence in the value of the Russian ruble and began to transfer funds out of Russia. In response to the downward pressure these outflows placed on the ruble, the central bank of Russia engaged in direct intervention, using dollars to purchase rubles in the foreign exchange market. It also used indirect intervention, raising interest rates to make them more attractive to investors and discourage additional outflows.

In July 1998, the IMF organized a loan package (with some help from Japan and the World Bank) worth $22.6 billion to Russia. The package required that Russia boost its tax revenue, reduce its budget deficit, and create a more capitalist environment for its businesses.

During August 1998, Russia's central bank frequently intervened to prevent the ruble from declining substantially. On August 26, however, it gave up its fight to defend the ruble's value, and market forces caused the ruble to decline by more than 50 percent against most currencies on that day. This led to fears of a new crisis, and the next day (called "Bloody Thursday") paranoia swept stock markets around the world. Some stock markets (including the U.S. markets) experienced declines of more than 4 percent.

Impact of the Asian Crisis on Latin American Countries

The Asian crisis also affected Latin American countries. Countries such as Chile, Mexico, and Venezuela were adversely affected because they export to Asia and demand for their products declined due to the weak Asian economies. In addition, the Latin American countries lost business as other importers switched to Asian products because the substantial depreciation of the Asian currencies had made those goods cheaper than those of Latin America.

The adverse effects on Latin American countries placed pressure on Latin American currency values, as there was concern that speculative outflows of funds would weaken these currencies in the same way that Asian currencies had weakened. In particular, Brazil's currency (the real) came under pressure in late October 1997. Some speculators believed that because most Asian countries had failed to maintain their currencies within bands, Brazil, too, would be unable to stabilize its currency.

In a form of direct intervention, the central bank of Brazil used about $7 billion of reserves to purchase real in the foreign exchange market and protect the currency from depreciation. The bank also used indirect intervention by raising short-term interest rates. This encouraged foreign investment in Brazil's short-term securities to capitalize on the high interest rates and also encouraged local investors to invest locally rather than in foreign markets. The increase in interest rates signaled that the bank was serious about maintaining the stability of the real. This type of intervention is costly, however, because it increases the cost of borrowing for households, corporations, and government agencies and thus can reduce economic growth. If Brazil's currency had weakened, the speculative forces might have spread to the other Latin American currencies as well.

The Asian crisis also caused bond ratings of many large corporations and government agencies in Latin America to be downgraded. For example, in November 1997, when top-grade government-backed bonds in South Korea were reduced to junk-level status in the international credit markets, rumors that banks were dumping Asian bonds created fears that all emerging market debt would be dumped in the bond markets. Furthermore, there was concern that many banks experiencing financial problems (because their loans were not being repaid) would sell bond holdings in the secondary market to raise funds. Consequently, prices of bonds issued in emerging markets, including those of Latin American countries, declined.

Impact of the Asian Crisis on Europe

During the Asian crisis, European countries were experiencing strong economic growth. Nevertheless, many European firms were adversely affected by the crisis. Like firms in Latin America, some firms in Europe experienced reduced demand for their exports to Asia. In addition, they lost some exporting business to Asian exporters as a result of the weakened Asian currencies that reduced Asian prices from an importer's perspective.

Impact of the Asian Crisis on the United States

The effects of the Asian crisis were even felt in the United States. Stock values of U.S. firms such as IBM, Motorola, Hewlett-Packard, and Nike that conducted much business in Asia were adversely affected. Many U.S. engineering and construction firms were adversely affected as Asian countries curtailed their plans to improve infrastructure. Stock values of U.S. exporters to those countries were adversely affected because of the decline in spending by Asian consumers and corporations and because the weakening of the Asian currencies made U.S. products more expensive.

LESSONS FROM THE ASIAN CRISIS

The Asian crisis demonstrated that financial markets can be exposed to the financial problems of other countries, as explained next.

Exposure to Effects on Exchange Rates

The Asian crisis demonstrated that currencies are susceptible to depreciation in response to a lack of confidence in central banks' ability to stabilize their local currencies. If investors and firms had believed that the central banks could prevent the free fall in currency values, they would not have transferred their funds to other countries. This would have removed the downward pressure on the currency values.

Exhibit 16A.1 shows how exchange rates of some Asian currencies changed against the U.S. dollar within one year of the crisis (from June 1997 to June 1998). In particular, the currencies of Indonesia, Malaysia, South Korea, and Thailand declined substantially.

Exposure to Effects on Interest Rates

The Asian crisis also demonstrated how much interest rates could be affected by the flow of funds out of countries. Exhibit 16A.2 illustrates how interest rates changed from June 1997 (just before the crisis) to June 1998 for various Asian countries. The increases in interest rates can be attributed to the indirect interventions intended to prevent the local currencies from depreciating further, or to the massive outflows of funds, or to both of these conditions. In particular, interest rates in Indonesia, Malaysia, and Thailand increased substantially from their precrisis levels. Countries whose local currencies experienced more depreciation had higher upward adjustments. Since the substantial increases in interest rates (which tend to reduce economic growth) may have been caused by the outflows of funds, they may be indirectly due to the lack of confidence of investors and firms in the ability of the Asian central banks to stabilize their local currencies.

Exhibit 16A.1 How Exchange Rates Changed during the Asian Crisis (June 1997–June 1998)

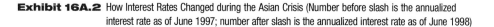

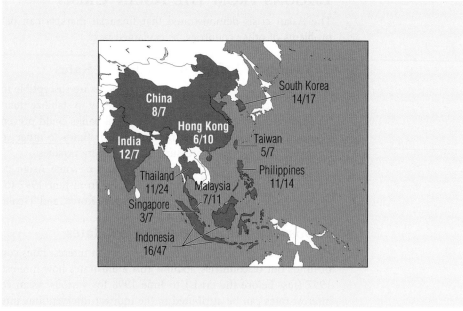

Exhibit 16A.2 How Interest Rates Changed during the Asian Crisis (Number before slash is the annualized interest rate as of June 1997; number after slash is the annualized interest rate as of June 1998)

Exposure to Effects on Security Prices

Exhibit 16A.3 provides a summary of how the Asian crisis affected financial market prices in Thailand. The exhibit is equally applicable to the other Asian countries that experienced financial distress during the crisis. For clarity, bonds, bank loans, and money market instruments are combined and simply referred to as debt securities in the exhibit.

Exhibit 16A.3 How the Asian Crisis Affected Thailand's Security Prices

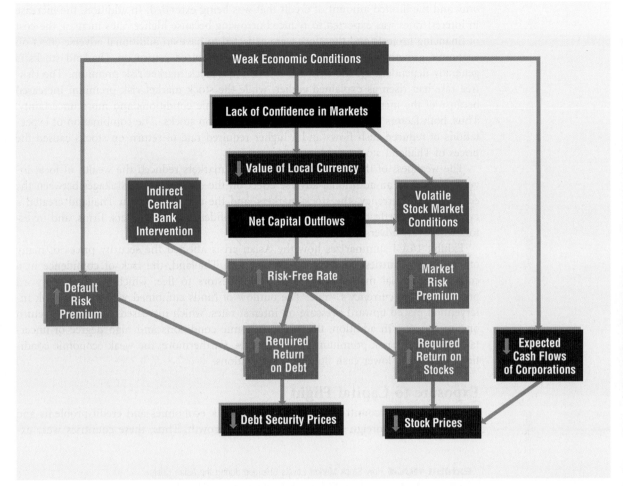

The initial conditions that instigated the crisis in Thailand were a weak economy, heavy reliance on foreign funding to finance growth, and excessive credit problems. These conditions scared investors and encouraged them to sell their investments and withdraw their funds from Thailand. The prices of debt securities issued in Thailand are primarily driven by the required rate of return by investors who may purchase debt securities, which is influenced by the local risk-free rate and the default risk premium. During the crisis, Thailand experienced higher interest rates because of the speculative outflows by investors, which reduced the supply of funds available, and because of the central bank's efforts to boost interest rates. The default risk premium increased because of the weak economic conditions and the increased market awareness of the credit problems experienced by many local firms. In fact, the rescue package provided by the IMF may even have increased the default risk premium because the IMF required that the local banks increase credit standards, which may have made it more difficult for firms in Thailand to obtain funding and pushed them one step closer to bankruptcy. Since the risk-free rate increased and the default risk premium increased, the required rate of return on Thailand's debt securities increased, and prices of debt securities decreased.

Stock prices in Thailand are dependent on the expected cash flows of the firms that issued the stocks and the required rate of return by investors who may invest in them.

The expected cash flows for firms in Thailand were reduced because of the weak economy and the limited amount of credit that was being extended. In addition, the increase in interest rates was expected to reduce borrowing because higher rates increase the cost of financing projects and therefore were expected to have an additional adverse effect on economic growth and expected cash flows. The required return on Thailand stocks is generally dependent on the risk-free rate and the stock market risk premium. The risk-free rate had risen as explained earlier, while the stock market risk premium increased because of the increased awareness of poor economic conditions and more uncertainty. Thus, both factors caused a higher required return on stocks. The combination of expectations of reduced cash flows and a higher required rate of return on stocks caused the prices of Thailand stocks to plummet.

The weakness of the stock and debt security markets reduced the wealth of local investors and had an additional adverse effect on the economy. The linkages between the economy, the currency, the stock markets, and the debt markets in Thailand created a cycle of adverse effects, further reducing the confidence of consumers, firms, and investors with every adverse effect.

Exhibit 16A.4 summarizes how the Asian crisis affected the security prices of many other Asian countries. In these countries, as in Thailand, the lack of confidence in a country's financial markets caused foreign investors to flee, which placed downward pressure on the currency's value. The outflow of funds combined with central bank intervention placed upward pressure on interest rates, which increased the required return on investments. In addition, the weak economic conditions and high degree of uncertainty raised the risk premium on investments. Furthermore, the weak economic conditions resulted in lower cash flows for corporations.

Exposure to Capital Flight

Many other Asian countries also experienced weak economies and credit problems and relied heavily on foreign investment to finance growth. Thus, these countries were ex-

Exhibit 16A.4 How Stock Market Levels Changed during the Asian Crisis

posed to the same type of speculative outflows as Thailand. The crisis in Thailand soon infected them.

Some Latin American countries also had weak economies and credit problems, and their currencies were subject to potential depreciation. This scared foreign investors and caused some speculative outflows of funds from these countries as well. Consequently, these countries also experienced an increase in interest rates, which adversely affected the stock and debt security markets.

The impact of the Asian crisis on prices in stock and debt security markets does not imply that every adverse situation will adversely affect all markets simultaneously. It is unusual for an event to cause higher interest rates, default risk premiums, and market risk premiums in one country and simultaneously affect other countries. Nevertheless, an obvious lesson from the Asian crisis is that when countries rely on funding (investments) from foreign investors to support their growth, they are susceptible to the massive withdrawal of that funding if adverse conditions within the country scare investors. Any countries that are exposed to an abrupt outflow of funds are exposed to a potential abrupt increase in interest rates, which can harm stock markets and debt security markets and reduce economic growth.

Degree of Global Integration

The Asian crisis also demonstrated how integrated country economies are, especially during a crisis. Just as the U.S. and European economies can affect emerging markets, they are susceptible to conditions in emerging markets. Even if a central bank can withstand the pressure on its currency that is caused by conditions in other countries, it is not necessarily able to insulate its economy from other countries that are experiencing financial problems.

DISCUSSION QUESTIONS

The following discussion questions related to the Asian crisis illustrate how foreign exchange market conditions are integrated with other financial markets around the world. Thus, participants in any of these markets must understand the dynamics of the foreign exchange market. These questions can be used in several ways. They may serve as an assignment on a day that the professor is unable to attend class. They are especially useful for group exercises. The class could be divided into small groups; each group will assess all of the issues and determine a solution. Each group should have a spokesperson. For each issue, one group will be randomly selected and asked to present their solution; then other students not in that group may suggest alternative answers if they feel that the solution can be improved. Some of the issues have no perfect solution, which allows students to present different points of view.

1. Was the depreciation of the Asian currencies during the Asian crisis due to trade flows or capital flows? Why might the degree of movement over a short period depend on whether the reason is trade flows or capital flows?

2. Why do you think the Indonesian rupiah was more exposed to an abrupt decline in value than the Japanese yen during the Asian crisis (even though the economies of Indonesia and Japan experienced the same degree of weakness)?

3. During the Asian crisis, direct intervention did not prevent depreciation of currencies. Offer your explanation for why the interventions did not work.

4. During the Asian crisis, some local firms in Asia borrowed dollars rather than local currency to support local operations. Why did they borrow dollars when they really needed their local currency to support operations? Why did this strategy backfire?

5. The Asian crisis showed that a currency crisis could affect interest rates. Why did the crisis place upward pressure on interest rates in Asian countries? Why did it place downward pressure on U.S. interest rates?

6. If high interest rates reflect high expected inflation, how would expectations of Asian exchange rates change after interest rates in Asia increased? Why? Is the underlying reason logical?

7. During the Asian crisis, why did the discount on the forward rate of Asian currencies change? Do you think it increased or decreased? Why?

8. During the Asian crisis, the Hong Kong stock market declined substantially over a four-day period due to concerns in the foreign exchange market. Why would stock prices decline due to concerns in the foreign exchange market? Why would some countries be more susceptible to this type of situation than others?

9. On August 26, 1998, when Russia decided to let the ruble float freely, the ruble declined by 50 percent. On the following day, "Bloody Thursday," stock markets around the world (including the U.S. markets) declined by more than 4 percent. Why do you think the decline in the ruble had such a global impact on stock prices? Was the markets' reaction rational? Would the effect have been different if the ruble's plunge had occurred at an earlier time, such as four years earlier? Why?

10. Normally, a weak local currency is expected to stimulate the local economy. Yet it appears that the weak currencies of Asia adversely affected their economies. Why do you think the weakening of the currencies did not initially improve the countries' economies during the crisis?

11. During the Asian crisis, Hong Kong and China successfully intervened (by raising their interest rates) to protect their local currencies from depreciating. Nevertheless, these countries were also adversely affected by the Asian crisis. Why do you think the actions to protect the values of their currencies affected their economies? Why do you think the weakness of other Asian currencies against the dollar and the stability of the Hong Kong and Chinese currencies against the dollar adversely affected their economies?

12. Why do you think the values of bonds issued by Asian governments declined during the crisis? Why do you think the values of Latin American bonds declined in response to the crisis?

13. Why do you think the depreciation of the Asian currencies adversely affected U.S. firms? (There are at least three reasons, each related to a different type of exposure of some U.S. firms to exchange rate risk.)

14. During the Asian crisis, the currencies of many Asian countries declined even though their respective governments attempted to intervene with direct intervention or by raising interest rates. Given that the abrupt depreciation of currencies was attributed to an abrupt outflow of funds in the financial markets, what alternative action by the Asian governments might have been more successful in preventing a substantial decline in their currency's value? Are there any possible adverse effects of your proposed solution?

Currency Option Pricing

Understanding what drives the premiums paid for currency options makes it easier to recognize the various factors that must be monitored when anticipating future movements in currency option premiums. Since participants in the currency options market typically take positions based on their expectations of how the premiums will change over time, they can benefit from understanding how options are priced.

BOUNDARY CONDITIONS

The first step in pricing currency options is to recognize boundary conditions that force the option premium to be within lower and upper bounds.

Lower Bounds

The call option premium (C) has a lower bound of at least zero or the spread between the underlying spot exchange rate (S) and the exercise price (X), whichever is greater, as shown here:

$$C \geq \text{MAX}(0, S - X)$$

This floor is enforced by arbitrage restrictions. For example, assume that the premium on a British pound call option is $.01, while the spot rate of the pound is $1.62 and the exercise price is $1.60. In this example, the spread $(S - X)$ exceeds the call premium, which would allow for arbitrage. One could purchase the call option for $.01 per unit, immediately exercise the option at $1.60 per pound, and then sell the pounds in the spot market for $1.62 per unit. This would generate an immediate profit of $.01 per unit. Arbitrage would continue until the market forces realigned the spread $(S - X)$ to be less than or equal to the call premium.

The put option premium (P) has a lower bound of zero or the spread between the exercise price (X) and the underlying spot exchange rate (S), whichever is greater, as shown next:

$$P \geq \text{MAX}(0, X - S)$$

This floor is also enforced by arbitrage restrictions. For example, assume that the premium on a British pound put option is $.02, while the spot rate of the pound is $1.60 and the exercise price is $1.63. One could purchase the pound put option for $.02 per unit, purchase pounds in the spot market at $1.60, and immediately exercise the option

447

by selling the pounds at \$1.63 per unit. This would generate an immediate profit of \$.01 per unit. Arbitrage would continue until the market forces realigned the spread $(X - S)$ to be less than or equal to the put premium.

Upper Bounds

The upper bound for a call option premium is equal to the spot exchange rate (S), as shown:

$$C \leq S$$

If the call option premium ever exceeds the spot exchange rate, one could engage in arbitrage by selling call options for a higher price per unit than the cost of purchasing the underlying currency. Even if those call options were exercised, one could provide the currency that was purchased earlier (the call option was covered). The arbitrage profit in this example would be the difference between the amount received when selling (which is the premium) and the cost of purchasing the currency in the spot market. Arbitrage would occur until the call option's premium was less than or equal to the spot rate.

The upper bound for a put option is equal to the option's exercise price (X), as shown here:

$$P \leq X$$

If the put option premium ever exceeds the exercise price, one could engage in arbitrage by selling put options. Even if the put options were exercised, the proceeds received from selling the put options would exceed the price paid (which is the exercise price) at the time of exercise.

Given these boundaries that are enforced by arbitrage, option premiums lie within these boundaries.

APPLICATION OF PRICING MODELS

Although boundary conditions can be used to determine the possible range for a currency option's premium, they do not precisely indicate the appropriate premium for the option. However, pricing models have been developed to price currency options. Based on information about an option (such as the exercise price and time to maturity) and about the currency (such as its spot rate, standard deviation, and interest rate), pricing models can derive the premium on a currency option. The currency option pricing model of Biger and Hull (1983) is

$$C = e^{-R_f^* T} S \cdot N(d_1) - e^{-R_f T} X \cdot N(d_1 - \sigma\sqrt{T})$$

where

$d_1 = \{[\text{In}(S/X) + (R_f - R_f^* + (\sigma^2/2))T]/\sigma\sqrt{T}\}$
C = price of the currency call option
S = underlying spot exchange rate
X = exercise price
R_f = U.S. riskless rate of interest
R_f^* = foreign riskless rate of interest
σ = instantaneous standard deviation of the return on a holding of foreign currency
T = time to option maturity expressed as a fraction of a year
$N(\cdot)$ = standard normal cumulative distribution function

This equation is based on the stock option pricing model (OPM) when allowing for continuous dividends. Since the interest gained on holding a foreign security (R_f^*) is equivalent to a continuously paid dividend on a stock share, this version of the OPM holds completely. The key transformation in adapting the stock OPM to value currency options is the substitution of exchange rates for stock prices. Thus, the percentage change of exchange rates is assumed to follow a diffusion process with constant mean and variance.

Bodurtha and Courtadon (1987)[1] have tested the predictive ability of the currency option pricing model. They computed pricing errors from the model using 3,326 call options. The model's average percentage pricing error for call options was −6.90 percent, which is smaller than the corresponding error reported for the dividend-adjusted Black-Scholes stock OPM. Hence, the currency option pricing model has been more accurate than the counterpart stock OPM.

The model developed by Biger and Hull is sometimes referred to as the European model because it does not account for early exercise.[2] Unlike American currency options, European currency options do not allow for early exercise (before the expiration date). The extra flexibility of American currency options may justify a higher premium than on European currency options with similar characteristics. However, there is not a closed-form model for pricing American currency options. Although various techniques are used to price American currency options, the European model is commonly applied to price American currency options because it can be just as accurate. Bodurtha and Courtadon (1987) found that the application of an American currency option pricing model does not improve predictive accuracy. Their average percentage pricing error was −7.07 percent for all sample call options when using the American model.

Given all other parameters, the currency option pricing model can be used to impute the standard deviation σ. This implied parameter represents the option's market assessment of currency volatility over the life of the option.

Pricing Currency Put Options According to Put-Call Parity

Given the premium of a European call option (C), the premium for a European put option (P) on the same currency and with the same exercise price (X) can be derived from put-call parity as follows:

$$P = C + Xe^{-R_f T} - Se^{-R_f^* T}$$

where R_f is the riskless rate of interest, R_f^* is the foreign rate of interest, and T is the option's time to maturity expressed as a fraction of the year. If the actual put option premium is less than is suggested by the put-call parity equation just shown, arbitrage can be conducted. Specifically, one could (1) buy the put option, (2) sell the call option, and (3) buy the underlying currency. The purchases would be financed with the proceeds from selling the call option and from borrowing at the rate R_f. Meanwhile, the foreign currency that was purchased can be deposited to earn the foreign rate R_f^*. Regardless of the scenario for the path of the currency's exchange rate movement over the life of the option, the arbitrage will result in a profit. First, if the exchange rate is equal to the exercise price such that each option expires worthless, the foreign currency can be converted in the spot market to dollars, and this amount will exceed the amount required to repay the loan. Second, if the foreign currency appreciates and therefore exceeds the exercise price, there will be a loss from the call option being exercised. Although the put option would expire, the foreign currency would be converted in the spot market to

[1]James N. Bodurtha, Jr., and George R. Courtadon, "Efficiency Tests of the Foreign Currency Options Market," *Journal of Finance* (March 1987): 151–161.

[2]Nahum Biger and John Hull, "The Valuation of Currency Options," *Financial Management* (Spring 1983): 24–28.

dollars, and this amount will exceed the amount required to repay the loan and the amount of the loss on the call option. Third, if the foreign currency depreciates and therefore is below the exercise price, the amount received from selling the put option plus the amount received from converting the foreign currency to dollars will exceed the amount required to repay the loan. Since the arbitrage generates a profit under any exchange rate scenario, it will force an adjustment in the option premiums so that put-call parity is no longer violated.

If the actual put option premium is more than is suggested by put-call parity, arbitrage would again be possible. The arbitrage strategy would be the reverse of that used when the actual put option premium is less than suggested by put-call parity (as just described). The arbitrage would force an adjustment in option premiums so that put-call parity is no longer violated. The arbitrage that can be applied when there is a violation of put-call parity on American currency options differs slightly from the arbitrage applicable to European currency options. Nevertheless, the concept still holds that the premium of a currency put option can be determined according to the premium of a call option on the same currency and with the same exercise price.

Choosing among Derivative Securities

This problem requires an understanding of futures contracts (Chapter 13), options markets (Chapter 14), interest rate swap markets (Chapter 15), and foreign exchange derivative markets (Chapter 16). It also requires an understanding of how economic conditions affect interest rates and security prices.

Assume that the United States just experienced a mild recession. As a result, interest rates have declined to their lowest levels in a decade. The U.S. interest rates appear to be influenced more by changes in the demand for funds than by changes in the supply of U.S. savings, because the savings rate does not change much regardless of economic conditions. The yield curve is currently flat. The federal budget deficit has improved lately and is not expected to rise substantially.

The federal government recently decided to reduce personal tax rates significantly for all tax brackets as well as corporate tax rates. The U.S. dollar has just recently weakened. Economies of other countries were somewhat stagnant but have improved in the past quarter. Your assignment is to recommend how various financial institutions should respond to the preceding information.

Questions

1. A savings institution holds 50 percent of its assets as long-term fixed-rate mortgages. Virtually all of its funds are in the form of short-term deposits. Which of the following strategies would be most appropriate for this institution?

- Use a fixed-for-floating swap.
- Use a swap of floating payments for fixed payments.
- Use a put option on interest rate futures contracts.
- Remain unhedged.

Defend your recommendation.

2. An insurance company maintains a large portfolio of U.S. stocks. Which of the following would be more appropriate?

- Sell stock index futures contracts.
- Remain unhedged.

Defend your recommendation.

3.   A pension fund maintains a large bond portfolio of U.S. bonds. Which of the following would be most appropriate?

- Sell bond index futures.
- Buy bond index futures.
- Remain unhedged.

Defend your recommendation.

4.   An international mutual fund sponsored by a U.S. securities firm consists of bonds evenly allocated across the United States and the United Kingdom. One of the portfolio managers has decided to hedge all the assets by selling futures on a popular U.S. bond index. The manager has stated that because the fund concentrates only on risk-free Treasury bonds, the only concern is interest rate risk. Assuming that interest rate risk is the only risk of concern, will the hedge described above be effective? Why or why not? Is there any other risk that deserves to be considered? If so, how would you hedge that risk?

Midterm Self-Exam

MIDTERM REVIEW

You have just completed all of the chapters focused on the financial markets. Here is a brief summary of some of the key points in those chapters.

Chapter 1 provides an overview of the types of financial markets, the securities that are traded within those markets, and the financial institutions that serve those markets. Chapter 2 explains how general interest rate levels are driven by factors that affect the demand for loanable funds (such as inflation and economic growth) and the supply of loanable funds (such as the Fed's monetary policy). Chapter 3 explains how interest rates vary among securities due to differences in credit risk, liquidity, tax status, and term to maturity. Chapter 4 describes the Fed's monetary policy, while Chapter 5 explains how the Fed's policy adjusts the supply of loanable funds to affect interest rates and economic conditions.

Chapter 6 explains how money market securities serve investors whose primary need is liquidity rather than high returns. Chapters 7 through 12 describe the characteristics, pricing, and risk of capital market securities. In particular, Chapters 7 through 9 focus on long-term debt securities and explain how sensitive the market values of long-term debt are to interest rate movements. Chapter 10 describes how stocks are placed and how institutional investors attempt to ensure that managers of publicly traded companies make decisions that maximize the stock's value. Chapter 11 shows how the value of a stock is influenced by the factors that influence the firm's future cash flows or risk. Chapter 12 describes how stocks are traded and how the trading is regulated. Because money market securities, long-term debt securities, and stocks have different characteristics, they serve different investors. In addition, the sensitivity of their prices to various factors differs among securities. Therefore, investors are able to allocate their investments in securities to reflect their specific return and risk preferences.

Chapter 13 explains how interest rate futures contracts can be sold to speculate on expectations of rising rates, as well as how these contracts can be sold to speculate on expectations of declining interest rates. It also explains how interest rate futures can be sold to hedge the interest rate risk of portfolios containing long-term debt securities and how stock index futures contracts can be used to hedge the market risk of stock portfolios. Chapter 14 explains how call options can be used to speculate on expectations of rising stock prices, while put options can be used to speculate on expectations of declining stock prices. It also explains how put options on stock indexes can be used to hedge stock portfolios, while put options on bond index futures can be used to hedge long-term debt security portfolios. Chapter 15 explains how interest rate swaps can be used to speculate on expectations of rising or declining interest rates, while Chapter 16 explains how foreign exchange markets are used to facilitate the trading of international securities.

This exam does not cover all of the concepts that have been presented up to this point. It is simply intended to allow you to test yourself on a general overview of key concepts. Try to simulate taking an exam by answering all of the questions without using your book and your notes. The answer key for this exam is provided just after this exam. If you have any wrong answers, you should re-read the related material and then redo any exam questions that you had wrong.

This exam may not necessarily match the level of rigor in your course. Your instructor may provide specific information about how this Midterm Self-Exam relates to the coverage and rigor of the midterm exam in your course.

MIDTERM SELF-EXAM

1. Explain the meaning of asymmetric information and how it can have an impact on trading in the stock market.

2. In the last year, the one-year risk-free interest rate increased from 3 to 7 percent.

a. What is a likely reason for the large increase in the risk-free rate?

b. In the last year, the 10-year risk-free rate declined from 7 to 6 percent. How can you reconcile the change in the short-term interest rate with the change in the long-term interest rate? What does the shift in the yield curve imply about future interest rates according to expectations theory?

3. The prevailing yield on a B-rated corporate bond is 7 percent. Explain how the yield offered on new B-rated bonds could be affected if economic conditions deteriorate. There are two forces that deserve consideration.

4. Consider the components that determine the prevailing yield of a highly rated corporate bond, such as the risk-free rate, default risk premium, and liquidity premium. The yield offered on a corporate bond in the secondary market changes over time. Which component do you think is typically the main source of changes in the yield offered on a highly rated corporate bond over time? Explain.

5. Recently, economic conditions have weakened. Although consumer prices have not increased in the last year, oil prices have risen by 20 percent in the last month. The Fed wants to show its dedication to controlling inflation and therefore decides to restrict the money supply and increase the target federal funds rate by .5 percent.

a. If you were on the FOMC, would you support the Fed's decision? Explain.

b. Explain how prices of money market securities would change in response to this policy. Why might bond prices be more sensitive to the change in the Fed's policy than money market securities? Why might bond prices be less sensitive to change in the Fed's policy than money market securities?

6. Assume that the Fed decided to reduce the federal funds rate by .5 percent today and that this decision was not anticipated by the financial markets.

a. Why might the change in monetary policy affect the yields paid by corporations when they issue corporate bonds?

b. Why might the change in monetary policy have no effect on the yields paid by corporations when they issue corporate bonds?

7. Why do bond market participants pay close attention to the fiscal policy decisions of the U.S. government?

8. A Treasury bond's coupon and principal payments are guaranteed. Does this mean that the value of the Treasury bond is almost constant over time? Explain.

9. Offer a logical explanation for why higher expected inflation could affect the yield on new 30-year fixed-rate mortgages. Why are secondary price movements of fixed-rate mortgages correlated with price movements of corporate bonds?

10. Assume that the Fed uses monetary policy to reduce the target federal funds rate. Also assume that the market does not anticipate this reduction. Use the CAPM framework to explain why this policy could enhance the prices of stocks.

11. Assume that the standard deviation of a stock's monthly returns is 4 percent. The expected return of the stock over the next month is zero. Using the VAR method, estimate the maximum expected loss for a month based on a 95 percent confidence level.

12. Based on what you learned in the chapters on the bond markets and stock markets, are these markets complements or substitutes from an issuer's perspective? From an investor's perspective?

13. Explain why a publicly traded firm's ability to place stock in a secondary offering is dependent on the stock's liquidity in the secondary market.

14. Why would a publicly traded firm go private? Why might the Sarbanes-Oxley Act encourage some publicly traded firms to go private?

15. Why does the market for corporate control affect stock valuations? Offer a reason why the market for corporate control will not always force corporate managers to serve shareholders.

16. Charleston Investment Company just purchased Renfro stock for $50. It engages in a covered call strategy in which it sells call options on Renfro stock. A call option on Renfro stock is available with an exercise price of $52, a one-year expiration date, and a premium of $2. Assume the buyers of the call option will exercise the option on the expiration date, if it is feasible to do so. Charleston will sell the stock at the end of one year even if the option is not exercised. Determine the net profit per share for Charleston based on the following possible prices for Renfro stock at the end of one year:

  a. $45

  b. $49

  c. $50

  d. $53

  e. $55

17. a. Compare the purchase of stock index futures versus index options. Why might institutional investors use futures to hedge their stock portfolios in some periods and options to hedge their stock portfolios in other periods?

  b. Explain the tradeoff involved when purchasing a put option with an exercise price that is at the money versus deep out of the money to hedge a stock portfolio.

18. Assume that interest rate parity exists. Assume U.S. investors plan to invest in a government security denominated in a foreign currency.

a. If the security has a higher interest rate than the U.S. interest rate, will the forward rate of the currency exhibit a discount? Explain.

b. If the investors engage in covered interest arbitrage, will they achieve a return that is higher than, lower than, or the same as the foreign interest rate? Explain.

c. If the investors engage in covered interest arbitrage, will they achieve a return that is higher than, lower than, or the same as the U.S. interest rate? Explain.

ANSWERS TO MIDTERM SELF-EXAM

1. Asymmetric information occurs because managers of publicly traded firms have more information about their firms than investors who do not work at the firm. Consequently, the valuation of firms by investors is limited because there may be private information about the firms that they do not have. This can result in improper pricing of stocks and a wide dispersion among investors regarding the proper valuation of stocks.

2. a. Common reasons for higher interest rates include a stronger economy, higher inflation, and a more restrictive monetary policy.

b. The yield curve had a steep upward slope one year ago. Now the yield curve has a slight downward slope. According to expectations theory, based on the prevailing yield curve, interest rates are expected to decline in the future.

3. If deteriorating economic conditions cause a decline in the demand for loanable funds, the risk-free interest rate will decline. However, the risk premium should increase because the chance of default by the issuer of the bonds will be higher as a result of the weaker economy.

4. Changes in the risk-free rate can have a major impact on the yield offered on a corporate bond. The default risk premium and liquidity premium may change, but normally they have less impact on the yield offered over time.

5. a. No, because the policy will not necessarily have any impact on oil prices, but it will slow economic growth and the economy is already weak,

b. Prices of money market securities will decline in response to the Fed's policy change because the interest rate and therefore the required rate of return on short-term securities will increase, and the present value of their cash flows will be reduced. When the Fed reduces the money supply in order to increase the federal funds rate, this shift could also possibly affect long-term interest rates. If so, the required rate of return on bonds will change, and long-term bond prices will decline in response. However, if the Fed's policy has no effect on long-term interest rates, the prices of long-term bonds should not change. In this case, bond prices are less sensitive than money market security prices to the Fed's policy.

6. a. The short-term and long-term markets for debt securities are partially integrated. Therefore, when the Fed increases the money supply in order to reduce the federal funds rate, some of the increased funds in the financial system may be used to invest in bonds. The additional funds supplied to the bond market can reduce the rate that corporations must pay when they borrow by issuing bonds,

b. Sometimes, when the Fed increases the money supply, most of the additional funds are channeled into short-term debt securities rather than long-term debt securities. In this case, there may be no effect on the yields offered on new corporate bonds.

7. The U.S. government's fiscal policy can affect the budget deficit, which can influence interest rates and thereby affect bond prices.

8. No. Movements in the long-term interest rate cause movements in the required rate of return, which can have a major impact on the valuation of Treasury bonds.

9. The higher inflationary expectations may result in a higher demand for and a smaller supply of loanable funds, which would drive interest rates higher. This results in a higher long-term risk-free interest rate, which is a key component of the required rate of return when investing in long-term fixed-rate mortgages.

10. The lower target federal funds rate may result in a lower long-term risk-free rate, which increases the present value of future cash flows generated by the stock. In addition, the lower interest rate may stimulate borrowing and spending by consumers, which could increase demand for the firm's products and therefore increase cash flows.

11. $0 - (1.64 \times 4\%) = -6.56\%$

12. Issuers may view the markets as complements because they may use both types of markets to raise funds. In some cases, however, the markets serve as substitutes because a firm may tap only one market or the other.

Investors may view the markets as complements because they may use both types of markets to invest funds. In some cases, however, the markets serve as substitutes because an investor may tap only one market or the other at a given point in time when investing funds.

13. Most investors that purchase publicly traded stock want to be able to sell the stock easily in the secondary market in the future. If a stock is illiquid, investors may not be able to sell the stock easily because there may be no interested investors who are willing to purchase the stock. Thus, investors may have to sell the stock at a discount because of the illiquidity.

14. A publicly traded firm may go private if its managers believe that it is undervalued in the public market. Thus, the managers may suggest that the firm use cash and debt to repurchase all of its outstanding stock. The Sarbanes-Oxley Act increased the reporting requirements for publicly traded firms, which increased the cost of financial reporting by more than $1 million per year for some publicly traded firms. Some firms decided that the benefits of being public were less than the costs of being public, and they went private to avoid the reporting requirements.

15. The market for corporate control may encourage some efficient firms to acquire other inefficient firms whose stock prices are relatively low because these firms have performed poorly. The efficient firms may be able to restructure the firms that they purchase and improve their performance. Thus, the market for corporate control allows for a change in control so that more efficient managers replace weak managers.

The market for corporate control does not cure every weak firm. There is limited information about firms, which may discourage other firms from trying to acquire them. For example, these weak firms could have many legal problems that might have to be assumed by any firm that acquires them.

16. a. −$3

    b. $1

    c. $2

    d. $4

    e. $4

17. a. Institutional investors may prefer to hedge with stock index futures when they are less confident about stock market conditions, because they forgo the potential gain if market conditions are favorable. Index options may be more desirable when the investors want to hedge but also believe there is a reasonable chance that market conditions will be favorable. They must pay a premium for such flexibility.

b. When purchasing a stock index option that is deep out of the money in order to hedge against market declines, a lower premium is paid. However, the hedge is less effective because the exercise price is low. The stock portfolio is only hedged against very large losses. Purchasing a stock index put option at the money to hedge against market declines will insulate a stock portfolio even if losses are small. However, the premium paid for this type of option is very high.

18. a. Yes, based on the interest rate parity formula.

b. Lower, because there is a discount on the forward rate.

c. The same, based on interest rate parity.

PART 6

Commercial Banking

The chapters in Part 6 focus on commercial banking. Chapter 17 identifies the common sources and uses of funds for commercial banks, and Chapter 18 describes the regulations that are imposed on sources and uses of funds and other banking operations. Chapter 19 explains how banks manage their sources and uses of funds to deal with risk. Chapter 20 explains how commercial bank performance can be measured and monitored to assess previous managerial policies.

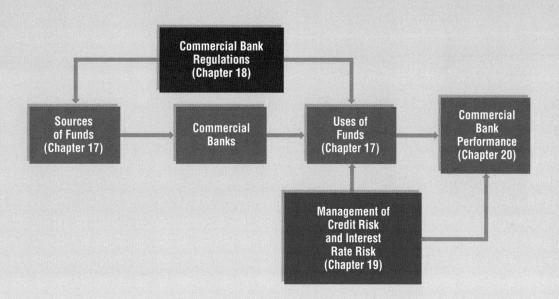

17

Commercial Bank Operations

CHAPTER OBJECTIVES

The specific objectives of this chapter are to:

■ describe the most common sources of funds for commercial banks,

■ explain the most common uses of funds for commercial banks, and

■ describe typical off-balance sheet activities for commercial banks.

Measured by total assets, commercial banks are the most important type of financial intermediary. Like other financial intermediaries, they perform a critical function of facilitating the flow of funds from surplus units to deficit units.

BACKGROUND ON COMMERCIAL BANKS

Up to this point, the text has focused on the role and functions of financial markets. From this point forward, the emphasis is on the role and functions of financial institutions. Recall from Chapter 1 that financial institutions commonly facilitate the flow of funds between surplus units and deficit units. Commercial banks represent a key financial intermediary because they serve all types of surplus and deficit units. They offer deposit accounts with the size and maturity characteristics desired by surplus units. They repackage the funds received from deposits to provide loans of the size and maturity desired by deficit units. They have the ability to assess the creditworthiness of deficit units that apply for loans, so that they can limit their exposure to credit (default) risk on the loans they provide.

Bank Market Structure

In 1985, more than 14,000 banks were located in the United States. Since then, the market structure has changed dramatically. Banks have been consolidating for several reasons. One reason is that interstate banking regulations were changed in 1994 to allow banks more freedom to acquire other banks across state lines. Consequently, banks in a particular region are now subject to competition not only from other local banks but also from any bank that may penetrate that market. This has prompted banks to become more efficient in order to survive. They have pursued growth as a means of capitalizing on economies of scale (lower average costs for larger scales of operations) and enhanced efficiency. Acquisitions have been a convenient way to grow quickly.

As a result of this trend, there are only about half as many banks today as there were in 1985, and consolidation is still occurring. Exhibit 17.1 shows how the number of banks has declined over time, thereby increasing concentration in the banking industry. The largest 100 banks now account for about 75 percent of all bank assets versus about 50 percent in 1985. The largest banks have increased their market share of total commercial and industrial loans. Banks have also acquired many other types of financial service firms in recent years.

Many banks are owned by bank holding companies, which are companies that own at least 10 percent of a bank. The holding company structure allows more flexibility to

461

Exhibit 17.1 Consolidation among Commercial Banks over Time

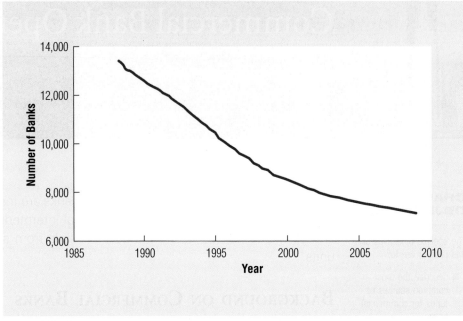

Source: *Federal Reserve.*

borrow funds, issue stock, repurchase the company's own stock, and acquire other firms. Bank holding companies may also avoid some state banking regulations.

The operations, management, and regulation of a commercial bank vary with the types of services offered. Therefore, the different types of financial services (such as banking, securities, and insurance) are discussed in separate chapters. This chapter on commercial bank operations applies to both independent commercial banks and commercial bank units that are part of a financial conglomerate formed by combining a bank and other financial services firms.

The primary operations of commercial banks can be most easily identified by reviewing their main sources of funds, their main uses of funds, and the off-balance sheet activities that they provide, as explained in this chapter.

BANK SOURCES OF FUNDS

WEB

www.fdic.gov

Statistics on bank sources and uses of funds.

To understand how any financial institution (or subsidiary of the institution) obtains funds and uses funds, its balance sheet can be reviewed. Its reported liabilities and equity indicate its sources of funds, while its reported assets indicate its uses of funds. The major sources of commercial bank funds are summarized as follows:

Deposit Accounts

1. Transaction deposits
2. Savings deposits
3. Time deposits
4. Money market deposit accounts

Borrowed Funds

1. Federal funds purchased (borrowed)
2. Borrowing from the Federal Reserve banks

3. Repurchase agreements
4. Eurodollar borrowings

Long-Term Sources of Funds

1. Bonds issued by the bank
2. Bank capital

Each source of funds is briefly described in the following subsections.

Transaction Deposits

A **demand deposit account,** or checking account, is offered to customers who desire to write checks against their account. A conventional demand deposit account requires a small minimum balance and pays no interest. From the bank's perspective, demand deposit accounts are classified as transaction accounts that provide a source of funds that can be used until withdrawn by customers (as checks are written).

Another type of transaction deposit is the **negotiable order of withdrawal (NOW) account,** which pays interest as well as providing checking services. Because NOW accounts at most financial institutions require a larger minimum balance than some consumers are willing to maintain in a transaction account, traditional demand deposit accounts are still popular.

Electronic Transactions   Some transactions originating from transaction accounts have become much more efficient as a result of electronic banking. Most employees in the United States have direct deposit accounts, which allow their paychecks to be directly deposited to their transaction account (or other accounts). Social Security recipients have their checks directly deposited to their bank accounts. Computer banking enables bank customers to view their bank accounts online, pay bills, make credit card payments, order more checks, and transfer funds between accounts.

Bank customers use automated teller machines (ATMs) to make withdrawals from their transaction accounts, add deposits, check account balances, and transfer funds. Debit cards allow bank customers to use a card to make purchases and have their bank account debited to reflect the amount spent. Banks also allow preauthorized debits, in which specific periodic payments are automatically transferred from a customer's bank account to a particular recipient. Preauthorized debits are commonly used to cover recurring monthly expenses such as utility bills, car loan payments, and mortgage payments.

Savings Deposits

The traditional savings account is the passbook savings account, which does not permit check writing. Passbook savings accounts continue to attract savers with a small amount of funds, as such accounts often have no required minimum balance.

Time Deposits

Time deposits are deposits that cannot be withdrawn until a specified maturity date. The two most common types of time deposits are certificates of deposit (CDs) and negotiable certificates of deposit.

Certificates of Deposit   A common type of time deposit is a retail **certificate of deposit** (or retail **CD**), which requires a specified minimum amount of funds to be deposited for a specified period of time. Banks offer a wide variety of CDs to satisfy depositors' needs. Annualized interest rates offered on CDs vary among banks, and even among maturity types at a single bank. There is no secondary market for retail CDs. Depositors must leave their funds in the bank until the specified maturity, or they will normally forgo a portion of their interest as a penalty.

CD rates are easily accessible on numerous websites. For example, Bank-Rate (www.bankrate.com) and Bank CD-Rate Scanner (www.bankcd.com) identify banks that are paying the highest rates on CDs at any point in time. Because of easy access to CD rate information online, many depositors invest in CDs at banks far away to earn a higher rate than that offered by local banks. Some banks allow depositors to invest in CDs online by providing a credit card number.

In recent years, some financial institutions have begun to offer CDs with a callable feature (referred to as **callable CDs**). That is, they can be called by the financial institution, forcing an earlier maturity. For example, a bank could issue a callable CD with a five-year maturity, callable after two years. In two years, the financial institution will likely call the CD if it can obtain funds at a lower rate over the following three years than the rate paid on that CD. Depositors who invest in callable CDs earn a slightly higher interest rate, which compensates them for the risk that the CD may be called.

Negotiable Certificates of Deposit   Another type of time deposit is the **negotiable CD (NCD)**, offered by some large banks to corporations. NCDs are similar to retail CDs in that they have a specified maturity date and require a minimum deposit. Their maturities are typically short term, and their minimum deposit requirement is $100,000. A secondary market for NCDs does exist.

The level of large time deposits is much more volatile than that of small time deposits, because investors with large sums of money frequently shift their funds to wherever they can earn higher rates. Small investors do not have as many options as large investors and are less likely to shift in and out of small time deposits.

Money Market Deposit Accounts

Money market deposit accounts (MMDAs) differ from conventional time deposits in that they do not specify a maturity. MMDAs are more liquid than retail CDs from the depositor's point of view. However, they offer a lower interest rate than CDs. MMDAs differ from NOW accounts in that they provide limited check-writing ability (they allow only a limited number of transactions per month), require a larger minimum balance, and offer a higher yield.

The remaining sources of funds to be described are of a nondepository nature. Such sources are necessary when a bank temporarily needs more funds than are being deposited. Some banks use nondepository funds as a permanent source of funds.

Federal Funds Purchased

The federal funds market allows depository institutions to accommodate the short-term liquidity needs of other financial institutions. Federal funds purchased (or borrowed) represent a liability to the borrowing bank and an asset to the lending bank that sells them. Loans in the federal funds market are typically for one to seven days. Such loans can be rolled over so that a series of one-day loans can take place. The intent of federal funds transactions is to correct short-term fund imbalances experienced by banks. A bank may act as a lender of federal funds on one day and as a borrower shortly thereafter, as its fund balance changes on a daily basis.

The interest rate charged in the federal funds market is called the **federal funds rate.** Like other market interest rates, it moves in reaction to changes in demand or supply or both. If many banks have excess funds and few banks are short of funds, the federal funds rate will be low. Conversely, a high demand by many banks to borrow in the federal funds market relative to a small supply of excess funds available at other banks will result in a higher federal funds rate. The federal funds rate is typically the same for all banks borrowing in the federal funds market, although a financially troubled bank may have to pay a higher rate. The federal funds rate is quoted on an annualized basis (using a 360-day year) even though the loans are usually for terms less than one week. It typically is between .25 percent and 1.00 percent above the Treasury bill rate. The difference increases when the perceived risk of banks increases.

The federal funds market is typically most active on Wednesday, because that is the final day of each particular settlement period for which each bank must maintain a specified volume of reserves required by the Fed. Banks that were short of required reserves on average over the period must compensate with additional required reserves before the settlement period ends. Large banks frequently need temporary funds and therefore are common borrowers in the federal funds market.

Borrowing from the Federal Reserve Banks

Another temporary source of funds for banks is the Federal Reserve System, which serves as the U.S. central bank. Along with other bank regulators, the Federal Reserve district banks regulate certain activities of banks. They also provide short-term loans to banks (as well as to some other depository institutions). This form of borrowing by banks is often referred to as borrowing at the discount window. The interest rate charged on these loans is known as the **primary credit lending rate.**

As of January 2003, the primary credit lending rate was to be set at a level above the federal funds rate at any point in time. This was intended to ensure that banks rely on the federal funds market for normal short-term financing and borrow from the Fed only as a last resort.

Loans from the Federal Reserve are short term, commonly from one day to a few weeks. To ensure that the need for funds is justified, banks that wish to borrow at the Federal Reserve must first obtain the Fed's approval. Like the federal funds market, loans from the Fed are mainly used to resolve a temporary shortage of funds. If a bank needs more permanent sources of funds, it will develop a strategy to increase its level of deposits.

The Federal Reserve is intended to be a source of funds for banks that experience unanticipated shortages of reserves. Frequent borrowing to offset reserve shortages implies that the bank has a permanent rather than a temporary need for funds and should therefore satisfy this need with a more permanent source of funds. The Fed may disapprove of continuous borrowing by a bank unless there are extenuating circumstances, such as that the bank was experiencing financial problems and could not obtain temporary financing from other financial institutions.

Repurchase Agreements

A **repurchase agreement (repo)** represents the sale of securities by one party to another with an agreement to repurchase the securities at a specified date and price. Banks often use a repo as a source of funds when they expect to need funds for just a few days. The bank simply sells some of its government securities (such as Treasury bills) to a corporation with a temporary excess of funds and buys those securities back shortly thereafter. The government securities involved in the repo transaction serve as collateral for the corporation providing funds to the bank.

Repurchase agreement transactions occur through a telecommunications network connecting large banks, other corporations, government securities dealers, and federal funds brokers. The federal funds brokers match up firms or dealers that need funds (wish to sell and later repurchase their securities) with those that have excess funds (are willing to purchase securities now and sell them back on a specified date). Transactions are typically in blocks of $1 million. Like the federal funds rate, the yield on repurchase agreements is quoted on an annualized basis (using a 360-day year) even though the loans are for short-term periods. The yield on repurchase agreements is slightly less than the federal funds rate at any given point in time, because the funds loaned out are backed by collateral and are therefore less risky.

Eurodollar Borrowings

If a U.S. bank is in need of short-term funds, it may borrow dollars from those banks outside the United States (typically in Europe) that accept dollar-denominated deposits, or **Eurodollars.** Some foreign banks or foreign branches of U.S. banks accept large short-term deposits and make short-term loans in dollars. Because U.S. dollars are widely used as an international medium of exchange, the Eurodollar market is very active.

Bonds Issued by the Bank

Like other corporations, banks own some fixed assets such as land, buildings, and equipment. These assets often have an expected life of 20 years or more and are usually financed with long-term sources of funds, such as through the issuance of bonds. Common purchasers of such bonds are households and various financial institutions, including life insurance companies and pension funds. Banks do not finance with bonds as much as most other corporations, because they have fewer fixed assets than corporations that use industrial equipment and machinery for production. Therefore, banks have less need for long-term funds.

Bank Capital

Bank capital generally represents funds attained through the issuance of stock or through retaining earnings. With either form, the bank has no obligation to pay out funds in the future. This distinguishes bank capital from all the other sources of funds, which represent a future obligation by the bank to pay out funds. Bank capital as defined here represents the equity or net worth of the bank. Capital can be classified as primary or secondary. Primary capital results from issuing common or preferred stock or retaining earnings, while secondary capital results from issuing subordinated notes and bonds.

A bank's capital must be sufficient to absorb operating losses in the event that expenses or losses exceed revenues, regardless of the reason for the losses. Although long-term bonds are sometimes considered to be secondary capital, they are a liability to the bank and therefore do not appropriately cushion against operating losses.

While the issuance of new stock increases a bank's capital, it dilutes the ownership of the bank because the proportion of the bank owned by existing shareholders decreases. In addition, the bank's reported earnings per share are reduced when additional shares of stock are issued, unless earnings increase by a greater proportion than the increase in outstanding shares. For these reasons, banks generally attempt to avoid issuing new stock unless absolutely necessary.

Bank regulators are concerned that banks may maintain a lower level of capital than they should and have therefore imposed capital requirements on them. Because capital can absorb losses, a higher level of capital is thought to enhance a bank's safety and may increase the public's confidence in the banking system.

In 1988, regulators imposed new risk-based capital requirements that were completely phased in by 1992. Under this system, the required level of capital for each bank is dependent on its risk. Assets with low risk are assigned relatively low weights, and assets with high risk are assigned high weights. The capital level is set as a percentage of the risk-weighted assets. Therefore, riskier banks are subject to higher capital requirements. The same risk-based capital guidelines have been imposed in several other industrialized countries. Additional details are provided in the next chapter.

Exhibit 17.2 Bank Sources of Funds (as a Proportion of Total Liabilities)

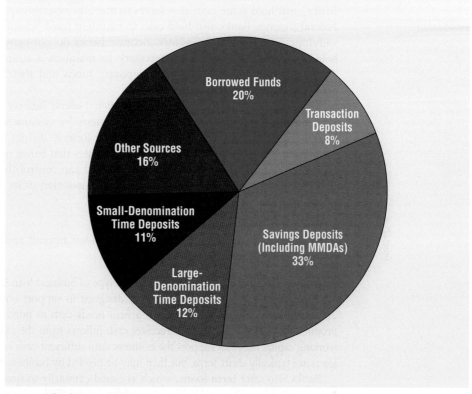

Source: *Federal Reserve, 2009.*

Distribution of Bank Sources of Funds

Exhibit 17.2 shows the distribution of bank sources of funds. Transaction and savings deposits make up 41 percent of all bank liabilities. The distribution of bank sources of funds is influenced by bank size. Smaller banks rely more heavily on savings deposits than larger banks do because small banks concentrate on household savings and therefore on small deposits. Much of this differential is made up in large time deposits (such as NCDs) for very large banks. In addition, the larger banks rely more on short-term borrowings than do small banks. The impact of the differences in the composition of fund sources on bank performance is discussed in Chapter 20.

USES OF FUNDS BY BANKS

Having identified the main sources of funds, bank uses of funds can be discussed. The more common uses of funds by banks include the following:

- Cash
- Bank loans
- Investment in securities
- Federal funds sold (loaned out)
- Repurchase agreements
- Eurodollar loans
- Fixed assets

Cash

Banks must hold some cash as reserves to meet the reserve requirements enforced by the Federal Reserve. Banks also hold cash to maintain some liquidity and accommodate any withdrawal requests by depositors. Because banks do not earn income from cash, they hold only as much cash as is necessary to maintain a sufficient degree of liquidity. They can tap various sources for temporary funds and therefore are not overly concerned with maintaining excess reserves.

Banks hold cash in their vaults and at their Federal Reserve district bank. Vault cash is useful for accommodating withdrawal requests by customers or for qualifying as required reserves, while cash held at the Federal Reserve district banks represents the major portion of required reserves. The Fed mandates that banks maintain required reserves because they provide a means by which the Fed can control the money supply. The required reserves of each bank depend on the composition of its deposits.

Bank Loans

The main use of bank funds is for loans. The loan amount and maturity can be tailored to the borrower's needs.

Types of Business Loans   A common type of business loan is the **working capital loan** (sometimes called a self-liquidating loan), designed to support ongoing business operations. There is a lag between the time when a firm needs cash to purchase raw materials used in production and the time when it receives cash inflows from the sales of finished products. A working capital loan can support the business until sufficient cash inflows are generated. These loans are typically short term, but they may be needed by businesses on a frequent basis.

Banks also offer **term loans,** which are used primarily to finance the purchase of fixed assets such as machinery. With a term loan, a specified amount of funds is loaned out, for a specified period of time and a specified purpose. The assets purchased with the borrowed funds may serve as partial or full collateral on the loan. Maturities on term loans commonly range from 2 to 5 years and are sometimes as long as 10 years. When banks offer term loans, they typically impose **protective covenants,** which specify specific conditions for the borrower that may protect the bank from loan default. For example, a bank may specify a maximum level of dividends that the borrower can pay to its shareholders each year. This protective covenant is intended to ensure that the borrower has sufficient cash to repay its loan on time.

Term loans can be amortized so that the borrower makes fixed periodic payments over the life of the loan. Alternatively, the bank can periodically request interest payments, with the loan principal to be paid off in one lump sum (called a **balloon payment**) at a specified date in the future. This is known as a **bullet loan.** Several combinations of these payment methods are also possible. For example, a portion of the loan may be amortized over the life of the loan, while the remaining portion is covered with a balloon payment.

As an alternative to providing a term loan, the bank may purchase the assets and lease them to the firm in need. This method, known as a **direct lease loan,** may be especially appropriate when the firm wishes to avoid adding more debt to its balance sheet. Because the bank is the owner of the assets, it can depreciate them over time for tax purposes.

A more flexible financing arrangement is the **informal line of credit,** which allows the business to borrow up to a specified amount within a specified period of time. This is useful for firms that may experience a sudden need for funds but do not know precisely when. The interest rate charged on any borrowed funds is typically adjustable in accordance with prevailing market rates. Banks are not legally obligated to provide funds to the business, but they usually honor the arrangement to avoid harming their reputation.

Exhibit 17.3 Prime Rate over Time

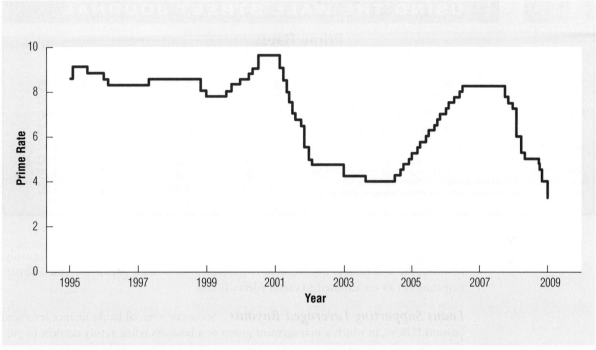

Source: *Federal Reserve 2009.*

An alternative to the informal line of credit is the **revolving credit loan,** which obligates the bank to offer up to some specified maximum amount of funds over a specified period of time (typically less than five years). Because the bank is committed to provide funds when requested, it normally charges businesses a commitment fee (of about one-half of 1 percent) on any unused funds.

The interest rate charged by banks on loans to their most creditworthy customers is known as the **prime rate.** Banks periodically revise the prime rate in response to changes in market interest rates, which reflect changes in the bank's cost of funds. Thus, the prime rate moves in tandem with the Treasury bill rate and other market interest rates. The prime rate in recent years is shown in Exhibit 17.3. It decreased during the weak economy in 2001, increased during the strong economy in 2003–2006, and then decreased during the credit crisis in 2008. The prime rate tends to adjust in response to changes in other interest rates that influence the bank's cost of funds. When economic conditions are weak, however, the spread between the prime rate and the bank's cost of funds tends to widen because banks require a higher premium to compensate for credit risk.

Loan Participations   Some large corporations wish to borrow a larger amount of funds than any individual bank is willing to provide. To accommodate a corporation, several banks may be willing to pool their available funds in what is referred to as a **loan participation.** One of the banks serves as the lead bank by arranging for the documentation, disbursement, and payment structure of the loan. The main role of the other banks is to supply funds that are channeled to the borrower by the lead bank. The borrower may not even realize that other banks have provided much of the funds. As interest payments are received, the lead bank passes the payments on to the other participants in proportion to the original loan amounts they provided. The lead bank receives fees for servicing the loan in addition to its share of interest payments.

Prime Rates

The Wall Street Journal provides quotes on the prime rate charged by U.S. banks, as shown here. It also quotes the prime rate charged by banks in other countries. Corporations closely monitor the prime rate because changes in the prime rate may influence their cost of financing.

Source: Republished with permission of Dow Jones & Company, Inc., from *The Wall Street Journal*, January 7, 2009, p. C9; permission conveyed through the Copyright Clearance Center, Inc.

Prime rates

U.S.	3.25	3.25	7.25	3.25
Canada	3.50	3.50	6.00	3.50
Euro zone	2.50	2.50	4.25	2.50
Japan	1.675	1.675	1.875	1.675
Switzerland	0.52	2.02	4.56	0.52
Britain	2.00	2.00	5.50	2.00
Australia	4.25	4.25	7.25	4.25
Hong Kong	5.00	5.00	7.00	5.00

The lead bank is expected to ensure that the borrower repays the loan. Normally, however, the lead bank is not required to guarantee the interest payments. Thus, all participating banks are exposed to credit (default) risk.

Loans Supporting Leveraged Buyouts   Some commercial banks finance leveraged buyouts (LBOs), in which a management group or a business relies mostly on debt to purchase the equity of another business. Firms request LBO financing because they perceive that the market value of certain publicly held shares is too low. The borrowers are highly leveraged, however, and may experience cash flow pressure during periods when sales are lower than normal. It is desirable that these firms have access to equity funds because it can serve as a cushion during periods of poor economic conditions. Although these firms prefer not to go public again during such periods, they are at least capable of doing so. Banks financing these firms can, as a condition of the loan, require that the firms reissue stock if they experience cash flow problems.

Some banks originate the loans designed for LBOs and then sell them to other financial institutions, such as insurance companies, pension funds, and foreign banks. In this way, they can generate fee income by servicing the loans while avoiding the credit risk associated with the loans.

Bank regulators monitor the amount of bank financing provided to corporate borrowers that have a relatively high degree of financial leverage. These loans, known as **highly leveraged transactions (HLTs),** are defined by the Federal Reserve as credit that results in a debt-to-asset ratio of at least 75 percent. In other words, the level of debt is at least three times the level of equity. About 60 percent of HLT funds are used to finance LBOs, while some of the funds are used to repurchase only a portion of the outstanding stock. HLTs are usually originated by a large commercial bank, which provides 10 to 20 percent of the financing itself. Other financial institutions participate by providing the remaining 80 to 90 percent of the funds needed.

Collateral Requirements on Business Loans   Commercial banks are increasingly accepting intangible assets (such as patents, brand names, and licenses to franchises and distributorships) as collateral for commercial loans. This change is especially important to service-oriented companies that do not have tangible assets.

Lender Liability on Business Loans   In recent years, businesses that previously obtained loans from banks are filing lawsuits, claiming that the banks terminated further financing without sufficient notice. These so-called lender liability suits have been prevalent in the farming, grocery, clothing, and oil industries.

Volume of Business Loans   The volume of business loans provided by commercial banks changes over time in response to economic conditions. When the economy is strong, businesses are more willing to finance expansion. When economic conditions are weak, businesses defer expansion plans and therefore do not need as much financing. During the 2004–2006 period, economic growth increased, resulting in a major increase in business loans provided by banks. During the credit crisis of 2008–2009, however, the volume of loans decreased.

Types of Consumer Loans   Commercial banks provide **installment loans** to individuals to finance purchases of cars and household products. These loans require the borrowers to make periodic payments over time.

Banks also provide credit cards to consumers who qualify, enabling them to purchase various goods without having to reapply for credit on each purchase. Credit card holders are assigned a maximum limit, based on their income and employment record, and a fixed annual fee may be charged. This service often involves an agreement with VISA or Master-Card. If consumers pay off the balance each month, they normally are not charged interest. Bank rates on credit card balances are sometimes about double the rate charged on business loans. State regulators can impose **usury laws** that restrict the maximum rate of interest charged by banks, and these laws may be applied to credit card loans as well. A federal law requires that banks abide by the usury laws of the state where they are located rather than the state where the consumer lives.

Assessing the applicant's creditworthiness is much easier for consumer loans than for corporate loans. An individual's cash flow is typically simpler and more predictable than a firm's cash flow. In addition, the average loan amount to an individual is relatively small, warranting a less detailed credit analysis.

Since the interest rate on credit card loans and personal loans is typically much higher than the cost of funds, many commercial banks have pursued these types of loans as a means of increasing their earnings. The most common method of increasing such loans is to use more lenient guidelines when assessing the creditworthiness of potential customers. However, there is an obvious tradeoff between the potential return and exposure to credit risk. When commercial banks experience an increase in defaults on credit card loans and other personal loans, they respond by increasing their standards for extending credit card loans and personal loans. This results in a reduced allocation of funds to credit card loans, which also reduces the potential returns of the bank. When the economy weakened during the credit crisis in 2008 and 2009, for example, many banks raised their standards for credit card loans and reduced the amount of credit that they would allow consumers to have. As economic conditions improve, commercial banks tend to increase their allocation of funds toward credit card loans.

Real Estate Loans   Banks also provide real estate loans. For residential real estate loans, the maturity on a mortgage is typically 15 to 30 years, although shorter-term mortgages with a balloon payment are also common. The loan is backed by the residence purchased. During the economic expansion in the 2004–2006 period, many banks offered subprime loans to home buyers with questionable credit quality. These mortgages were given to home buyers who had relatively lower income, high existing debt, or only a small down payment to use to purchase a home. Many commercial banks expected to benefit from subprime mortgage loans because they could charge up-front fees (such as appraisal fees) and higher interest rates on the mortgages to compensate for the risk of default. Furthermore, they presumed that real estate values would continue to rise, so the residence backing the loan would serve as adequate collateral. In 2008, however, there were many defaults on subprime mortgages. As of January 2009, about 10 percent of all homeowners with mortgages were either late on their payments or subject to foreclosure. Banks and other financial institutions were forced to take over the ownership of many homes, which led to an excess supply of homes in the housing market. Consequently, the prices of homes declined substantially, which further reduced the collateral value of the homes taken back by the banks. Thus, banks that originated mortgages and held them as assets were adversely affected by the credit crisis.

Commercial banks also provide commercial real estate loans, such as loans to build shopping malls. In general, during the early 2000s banks required more stringent standards for borrowers to qualify for commercial real estate loans. Therefore the default rate on commercial real estate loans provided by commercial banks was low compared to the default rate on residential loans during the credit crisis. In addition, commercial banks commonly retain the commercial real estate loans that they originate as assets. Banks and other financial institutions are likely to use greater diligence in assessing real estate loan applicants when they retain the mortgages that they originate.

Investment in Securities

Banks purchase various types of securities. One advantage of investing funds in securities rather than loans is that the securities tend to be more liquid. In addition, banks can easily invest in securities, whereas they need more resources to assess loan applicants and service loans. However, they normally expect to generate higher rates of return on funds used to provide loans.

Treasury and Agency Securities   Banks purchase Treasury securities as well as securities issued by agencies of the federal government. Government agency securities can be sold in the secondary market, but the market is not as active as it is for Treasury securities. Furthermore, government agency securities are not a direct obligation of the federal government. Therefore, credit risk exists, although it is normally thought to be very low. Banks that are willing to accept the slight possibility of credit risk and less liquidity from investing in government agency securities can earn a higher return than on Treasury securities with a similar maturity.

Federal agency securities are commonly issued by federal agencies, such as the Federal National Mortgage Association (called Fannie Mae) and the Federal Home Loan Mortgage Corporation (called Freddie Mac). Funds received by the agencies issuing these securities are used to purchase mortgages from various financial institutions. Such securities have maturities that can range from one month to 25 years. Unlike interest income from Treasury securities, interest income from federal agency securities is subject to state and local income taxes. The values of the mortgages held by Fannie Mae and Freddie Mac declined in 2008 due to the large amount of late payments and mortgage defaults during the credit crisis. Consequently, there were concerns that Fannie Mae and Freddie Mac might not be able to cover their debt security payments. In September 2008, the U.S. government took control of Fannie Mae and Freddie Mac, thereby ensuring the safety of the debt securities issued by these agencies.

Corporate and Municipal Bonds   Banks also purchase corporate and municipal bonds. Although corporate bonds are subject to credit risk, they offer a higher return than Treasury or government agency securities. Municipal bonds exhibit some degree of risk but can also provide an attractive return to banks, especially when their after-tax return is considered. The interest income earned from municipal securities is exempt from federal taxation. Banks purchase only **investment-grade securities,** which are rated as "medium quality" or higher by rating agencies.

Mortgage-Backed Securities   Banks also commonly purchase mortgage-backed securities (MBS), which represent packages of mortgages. Banks tend to purchase mortgages within a particular tranche that is categorized as having relatively low risk. During the credit crisis in 2008 and 2009, however, there were many defaults on mortgages within tranches that had been assigned high ratings by rating agencies. Consequently, banks that had invested in MBS experienced losses during the credit crisis. The market value of MBS at any bank is difficult to measure because the MBS are not standardized and the secondary market transactions between parties are not conducted through an organized exchange. Thus, two banks could have an equal proportion of their assets classified as MBS, but one bank's MBS may be much riskier than the other bank's MBS.

Federal Funds Sold

Some banks often lend funds to other banks in the federal funds market. The funds sold, or lent out, will be returned at the time specified in the loan agreement, with interest. The loan period is typically very short, such as a day or a few days. Small banks are common providers of funds in the federal funds market. If the transaction is executed by a broker, the borrower's cost on a federal funds loan is slightly higher than the lender's return, because the broker matching up the two parties charges a transaction fee.

Repurchase Agreements

Recall that from the borrower's perspective, a repurchase agreement (repo) transaction involves repurchasing the securities it had previously sold. From a lender's perspective, the repo represents a sale of securities that it had previously purchased. Banks can act as the lender (on a repo) by purchasing a corporation's holdings of Treasury securities and selling them back at a later date. This provides short-term funds to the corporation, and the bank's loan is backed by these securities.

Eurodollar Loans

Branches of U.S. banks located outside the United States and some foreign-owned banks provide dollar-denominated loans to corporations and governments. These so-called Eurodollar loans are common because the dollar is frequently used for international transactions. Eurodollar loans are short term and denominated in large amounts, such as $1 million or more.

Fixed Assets

Banks must maintain some amount of fixed assets, such as office buildings and land, so that they can conduct their business operations. However, this is not a concern to the bank managers who decide how day-to-day incoming funds will be used. They direct these funds into the other types of assets already identified.

Summary of Bank Uses of Funds

The distribution of bank uses of funds is illustrated in Exhibit 17.4. Loans of all types make up about 64 percent of bank assets, while securities account for about 21 percent of bank assets. The distribution of assets for an individual bank varies with the type of bank. For example, smaller banks tend to have a relatively large amount of household loans and government securities; larger banks have a higher level of business loans (including loans to foreign firms).

The distribution of bank uses of funds indicates how commercial banks operate. In recent years, however, banks have begun to provide numerous services that are not

Exhibit 17.4 Bank Uses of Funds (as a Proportion of Total Assets)

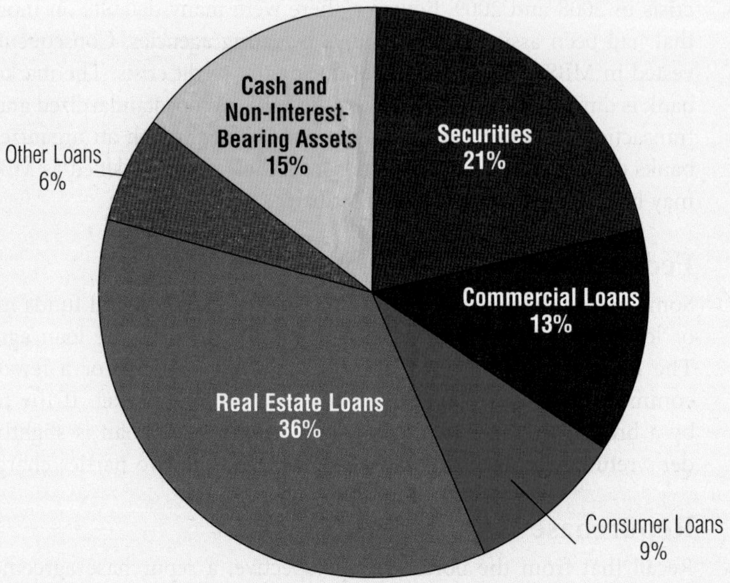

Source: *The Federal Reserve, 2009.*

indicated on their balance sheet. These services differ distinctly from banks' traditional operations that focused mostly on channeling deposited funds into various types of loans and investments.

Commercial Bank Balance Sheet A commercial bank's sources of funds represent its liabilities or equity, while its uses of funds represent its assets. Each commercial bank determines its own composition of liabilities and assets, which determines its specific operations.

EXAMPLE

Exhibit 17.5 shows the balance sheet of Hornet Bank. The bank's assets are shown on the left side of the balance sheet. The second column indicates the dollar amount of each asset, and the third column shows the size of each asset in proportion to total assets to illustrate how Hornet Bank distributes its funds. Hornet's main assets are commercial and consumer loans, as well as securities. The balance sheet shows the bank's holdings at a particular point in time. It frequently revises the composition of its assets in response to economic conditions. When the economy improves and creditworthy businesses want to expand, Hornet Bank will sell some of its holdings of Treasury securities and use the funds to provide more corporate loans.

Hornet Bank's liabilities and stockholders' equity are shown on the right side of the balance sheet. Hornet obtains funds from various types of deposits. It incurs some expenses from all types of deposits. In particular, it must hire employees to serve depositors. The composition of Hornet's liabilities determines its interest expenses, because it does not pay interest on demand deposits but pays a relatively high interest rate on large CDs.

Hornet also incurs expenses from managing its assets. Its main expense is the cost of hiring employees to assess the creditworthiness of businesses and households that request loans. In general, Hornet wants to generate enough income from its assets so that it can cover its expenses and provide a reasonable return to its shareholders. Its primary source of income is

Exhibit 17.5 Balance Sheet of Hornet Bank as of June 30, 2009

ASSETS	DOLLAR AMOUNT (IN MILLIONS)	PROPORTION OF TOTAL ASSETS	LIABILITIES AND STOCK-HOLDERS' EQUITY	DOLLAR AMOUNT (IN MILLIONS)	PROPORTION OF TOTAL LIABILITIES AND STOCK-HOLDERS' EQUITY
Cash (includes required reserves)	$ 50	5%	Demand deposits	$ 250	25%
Commercial loans	400	40%	NOW accounts	60	6%
Consumer loans	250	25%	Money market deposit accounts	200	20%
Treasury securities	80	8%	Short-term CDs	250	25%
Corporate securities	120	12%	CDs with maturities beyond one year	120	12%
Federal funds sold (lent out)	10	1%	Federal funds purchased (borrowed)	0	0%
Repurchase agreements	20	2%	Long-term debt	30	3%
Eurodollar loans	0	0%			
Fixed assets	70	7%	Common stock issued	50	5%
			Retained earnings	40	4%
TOTAL ASSETS	$1,000	100%	TOTAL LIABILITIES AND STOCKHOLDERS' EQUITY	$1,000	100%

the interest received on the business loans that it provides. Its capital is shown on the balance sheet as common stock issued and retained earnings. ●

Exhibit 17.6 shows how commercial banks use the key balance sheet items to finance economic growth. They channel funds from their depositors to households and thereby finance household spending. They channel funds from depositors to corporations and thereby finance corporate expansion. They also use some deposits to purchase Treasury and municipal securities and thereby finance spending by the Treasury and municipalities.

Off-Balance Sheet Activities

Banks commonly engage in off-balance sheet activities, which generate fee income without requiring an investment of funds. These activities do create a contingent obligation for banks, however. The following are some of the more popular off-balance sheet activities:

- Loan commitments
- Standby letters of credit
- Forward contracts on currencies
- Interest rate swap contracts
- Credit default swap contracts

Exhibit 17.6 How Commercial Banks Finance Economic Growth

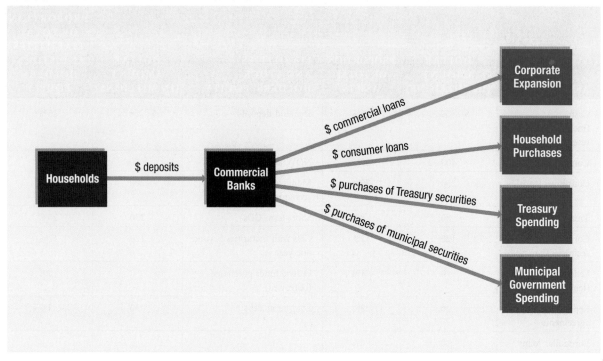

Loan Commitments

A **loan commitment** is an obligation by a bank to provide a specified loan amount to a particular firm upon the firm's request. The interest rate and purpose of the loan may also be specified. The bank charges a fee for offering the commitment.

One type of loan commitment is a **note issuance facility (NIF),** in which the bank agrees to purchase the commercial paper of a firm if the firm cannot place its paper in the market at an acceptable interest rate. Although banks earn fees for their commitments, they could experience illiquidity if numerous firms request their loans at the same time.

Standby Letters of Credit

A **standby letter of credit (SLC)** backs a customer's obligation to a third party. If the customer does not meet its obligation, the bank will. The third party may require that the customer obtain an SLC to complete a business transaction. For example, consider a municipality that wants to issue bonds. To ensure that the bonds are easily placed, a bank could provide an SLC that guarantees payment of interest and principal. In essence, the bank uses its credit rating to enhance the perceived safety of the bonds. In return for the guarantee, the bank charges a fee to the municipality. The bank should be willing to provide SLCs only if the fee received compensates for the possibility that the municipality will default on its obligation.

Forward Contracts on Currencies

A forward contract on currency is an agreement between a customer and a bank to exchange one currency for another on a particular future date at a specified exchange rate. Banks engage in forward contracts with customers that desire to hedge their exchange rate risk. For example, a U.S. bank may agree to purchase 5 million euros in one year from a firm for $1.10 per euro. The bank may simultaneously find another firm that wishes to exchange 5 million euros for dollars in one year. The bank can serve as an intermediary and accommodate both requests, earning a transaction fee for its services. However, it is exposed to the possibility that one of the parties will default on its obligation.

Interest Rate Swap Contracts

Banks also serve as intermediaries for interest rate swaps, whereby two parties agree to periodically exchange interest payments on a specified notional amount of principal. Once again, the bank receives a transaction fee for its services. If it guarantees payments to both parties, it is exposed to the possibility that one of the parties will default on its obligation. In that event, the bank must assume the role of that party and fulfill the obligation to the other party.

Some banks facilitate currency swaps (for a fee) by finding parties with opposite future currency needs and executing a swap agreement. Currency swaps are somewhat similar to forward contracts, except that they are usually for more distant future dates.

Credit Default Swap Contracts

Credit default swaps are privately negotiated contracts that protect investors against the risk of default on particular debt securities. Some commercial banks and other financial institutions buy them in order to protect their own investments in debt securities against default risk. Other banks and financial institutions sell them. The banks that sell credit default swaps receive periodic coupon payments for the term of the swap agreement. A typical term of a credit default swap is five years. If there are no defaults on the debt securities, the banks that sold the credit default swaps benefit because they are not required to make any payments. However, when there are defaults on the debt securities, the sellers of credit default swaps must make payments to the buyers to cover the damages. In essence, the sellers of credit default swaps are providing insurance against default.

These contracts were heavily used to protect against the default risk from investing in mortgage-backed securities. During the credit crisis in 2008, commercial banks that sold credit default swap contracts incurred major expenses because of the high frequency of defaults on mortgage-backed securities. Conversely, commercial banks that purchased credit default swap contracts reduced the adverse impact of defaults on mortgage-backed securities (assuming that the counterparty that sold them the swaps did not default on its obligation).

INTERNATIONAL BANKING

Until historical barriers against interstate banking were largely removed in 1994, some U.S. commercial banks were better able to achieve growth by penetrating foreign markets than by expanding at home. Many U.S. banks have expanded internationally to improve their prospects for growth and to diversify so that their business will not be dependent on a single economy.

Global Competition in Foreign Countries

The most common way for U.S. commercial banks to expand internationally is by establishing branches, full-service banking offices that can compete directly with other banks located in a particular area. Before establishing foreign branches, a U.S. bank must obtain the approval of the Federal Reserve Board. Among the factors considered by the Fed are the bank's financial condition and experience in international business. Commercial banks may also consider establishing agencies, which can provide loans but cannot accept deposits or provide trust services.

U.S. banks have recently established foreign subsidiaries wherever they expect more foreign expansion by U.S. firms, such as in Southeast Asia and Eastern Europe. Recently, expansion has also been focused on Latin America. The banks offer banker's acceptances, foreign exchange services, credit card services, and other household services.

As an example of the diversity in international banking services, consider the case of Citigroup. Citigroup offers a number of key services to firms around the world including foreign exchange transactions, forecasting, risk management, cross-border trade finance, acquisition finance, cash management services, and local currency funding. Citigroup serves not only large multinational corporations, such as Coca-Cola, Dow Chemical, IBM, and Sony, but also small firms that need international banking services. By spreading itself across the world, Citigroup can typically handle the banking needs of all of a multinational corporation's subsidiaries.

Impact of the Euro on Global Competition

The inception of the euro has stimulated increased bank expansion throughout Europe. The use of a single currency in a number of European countries simplifies transactions because the majority of a bank's transactions between those countries are now denominated in euros. Use of the euro also reduces exposure to exchange rate risk, as banks can accept deposits in euros and use euros to lend funds or invest in securities. The use of a single currency throughout many European countries may also encourage firms to engage in a bond or stock offering to support their European business, as the euro can be used to support most of that business. Commercial banks can serve as intermediaries by underwriting and placing the debt or the equity issued by firms.

Given the potential advantages of a single currency, U.S. banks and European banks are expanding throughout Europe by acquiring existing banks. The single currency makes it easier to achieve economies of scale and enables banks' internal reporting systems to be more efficient. As banks expand and capitalize on economies of scale, the global competition has become more intense. Furthermore, the euro enables businesses in Europe to more easily compare the prices of services offered by banks based in different European countries. This also forces banks to be more competitive.

SUMMARY

- The most common sources of commercial bank funds are deposit accounts, borrowed funds, and long-term sources of funds. The common types of deposit accounts are transaction deposits, savings deposits, time deposits, and money market deposit accounts. These accounts vary in terms of liquidity (for the depositor) and the interest rates offered.

  Commercial banks can solve temporary deficiencies in funds by borrowing from other banks (federal funds market), from the Federal Reserve, or from other sources by issuing short-term securities such as repurchase agreements. When banks need long-

term funds to support expansion, they may use retained earnings, issue new stock, or issue new bonds.

- The most common uses of funds by commercial banks are bank loans and investment in securities. Banks can use excess funds by providing loans to other banks or by purchasing short-term securities.

- Banks engage in off-balance sheet activities such as loan commitments, standby letters of credit, forward contracts, and swap contracts. These types of activities generate fees for commercial banks. However, they also reflect commitments by the banks, which can expose them to more risk.

POINT COUNTER-POINT

Should Banks Engage in Other Financial Services Besides Banking?

Point No. Banks should focus on what they do best.

Counter-Point Yes. Banks should increase their value by engaging in other services. They can appeal to cus-tomers who want to have all their financial services provided by one financial institution.

Who Is Correct? Use the Internet to learn more about this issue. Offer your own opinion on this issue.

QUESTIONS AND APPLICATIONS

1.   Bank Balance Sheet Create a balance sheet for a typical bank, showing its main liabilities (sources of funds) and assets (uses of funds).

2.   Bank Sources of Funds What are four major sources of funds for banks? What alternatives does a bank have if it needs temporary funds? What is the most common reason that banks issue bonds?

3.   CDs Compare and contrast a retail CD and a negotiable CD.

4.   Money Market Deposit Accounts How does a money market deposit account differ from other bank sources of funds?

5.   Federal Funds Define federal funds, federal funds market, and federal funds rate. Who sets the federal funds rate? Why is the federal funds market more active on Wednesday?

6.   Federal Funds Market Explain the use of the federal funds market in facilitating bank operations.

7.   Borrowing from the Federal Reserve De-scribe the process of "borrowing at the Federal Reserve." What rate is charged, and who sets it? Why do banks commonly borrow in the federal funds mar-ket rather than through the Federal Reserve?

8.   Repurchase Agreements How does the yield on a repurchase agreement differ from a loan in the federal funds market? Why?

9.   Bullet Loan Explain the advantage of a bullet loan.

10. Bank Use of Funds Why do banks invest in securities, even though loans typically generate a higher return? Explain how a bank decides the appropriate percentage of funds that should be allocated to each type of asset.

11. Bank Capital Explain the dilemma faced by banks when determining the optimal amount of capital to hold. A bank's capital is less than 10 percent of its assets. How do you think this percentage would com-pare to that of manufacturing corporations? How would you explain this difference?

12. HLTs Would you expect a bank to charge a higher rate on a term loan or a highly leveraged transaction (HLT) loan? Why?

13. Credit Crisis Explain how some mortgage op-erations by some commercial banks (along with other financial institutions) played a major role in instigating the credit crisis.

14. Bank Use of Credit Default Swaps Explain how banks have used credit default swaps.

Interpreting Financial News

Interpret the following comments made by Wall Street analysts and portfolio managers:

a. "Lower interest rates may reduce the size of banks."

b. "Banks are no longer as limited when competing with other financial institutions for funds targeted for the stock market."

c. "If the demand for loans rises substantially, interest rates will adjust to ensure that commercial banks can accommodate the demand."

Managing in Financial Markets

Managing Sources and Uses of Funds As a consultant, you have been asked to assess a bank's sources and uses of funds and to offer recommenda-tions on how it can restructure its sources and uses of funds to improve its performance. This bank has tra-ditionally focused on attracting funds by offering cer-tificates of deposit (CDs). It offers checking accounts and money market deposit accounts (MMDAs), but it has not advertised these accounts because it has obtained an adequate amount of funds from the CDs. It pays about 3 percentage points more on its CDs than on its MMDAs, but the bank prefers to know the precise length of time it can use the deposited funds. (The CDs have a specified maturity while the MMDAs do not.) Its cost of funds has historically been higher than that of most banks, but it has not been concerned because its earnings have been relatively high. The bank's use of funds has historically focused on local real estate loans to build shopping malls and apartment complexes. The real estate loans have provided a very high

return over the last several years. However, the demand for real estate in the local area has slowed.

a. Should the bank continue to focus on attracting funds by offering CDs, or should it push its other types of deposits?

b. Should the bank continue to focus on real estate loans? If the bank reduces its real estate loans, where should the funds be allocated?

c. How will the potential return on the bank's uses of funds be affected by your restructuring of the asset portfolio? How will the cost of funds be affected by your restructuring of the bank's liabilities?

FLOW OF FUNDS EXERCISE

Services Provided by Financial Conglomerates

Carson Company is attempting to compare the services offered by different banks, as it would like to have all services provided by one bank.

a. Explain the different types of services provided by a financial institution that may allow Carson Company to obtain funds or to hedge its risk.

b. Review the services that you listed in the previous question. What services could provide financing to Carson Company? What services could hedge Carson's exposure to risk?

INTERNET/EXCEL EXERCISE

1. Go to the website www.chase.com. List the various services offered by Chase that were listed in this chapter. For each, state whether the service provided by the

bank reflects an asset (use of funds) or a liability (source of funds) for the bank. What interest rates does Chase offer on its CDs?

18

Bank Regulation

Bank regulations are designed to maintain public confidence in the financial system by preventing commercial banks from becoming too risky.

CHAPTER OBJECTIVES

The specific objectives of this chapter are to:

■ describe the key regulations imposed on commercial banks,

■ explain capital requirements of banks, and

■ explain how regulators monitor banks.

WEB

www.federal reserve .gov/bankinforeg/ reglisting.htm
Detailed descriptions of bank regulations from the Federal Reserve Board.

WEB

www.federalreserve .gov
Click on "Banking Information & Regulation" to find key bank regulations at the website of the Board of Governors of the Federal Reserve System.

BACKGROUND

The banking industry has experienced substantial changes in recent years. The industry has become more competitive due to deregulation. Today, banks have considerable flexibility in the services they offer, the locations where they operate, and the rates they pay depositors for deposits. Although generally viewed as favorable, this flexibility is creating intense competition among banks and even between banks and other financial institutions that now offer bank services.

Many banks have expanded across the country by opening new branches or making acquisitions in an attempt to use their resources efficiently. Others have diversified across services to capitalize on economies of scope. Many banks have expanded beyond their traditional banking business and now offer other financial services. Bank regulators have attempted to manage the speed of integration between banks and other financial services firms.

Bank regulation is needed to protect customers who supply funds to the banking system. By preventing bank runs that might occur if customers became concerned about the safety of their deposits, regulation ensures a safer banking environment. Regulators also attempt to enhance the safety of the banking system by overseeing individual banks. The regulators do not attempt to manage individual banks, but do impose some discipline so that banks assuming more risk are forced to create their own form of protection against the possibility that they will default. In this way, regulators are shifting more of the burden of risk assessment to the individual banks themselves.

REGULATORY STRUCTURE

The regulatory structure of the banking system in the United States is dramatically different from that of other countries. It is often referred to as a **dual banking system** because it includes both a federal and a state regulatory system. There are more than 6,000 separately owned commercial banks in the United States, supervised by three federal agencies and 50 state agencies. The regulatory structure in other countries is much simpler.

A charter from either a state or the federal government is required to open a commercial bank in the United States. A bank that obtains a state charter is referred to as a state bank; a bank that obtains a federal charter is known as a national bank. All national banks are required to be members of the Federal Reserve System (the Fed). The federal

481

charter is issued by the Comptroller of the Currency. An application for a bank charter must be submitted to the proper supervisory agency, should provide evidence of the need for a new bank, and should disclose how the bank will be operated. Regulators determine if the bank satisfies general guidelines to qualify for the charter.

State banks may decide whether they wish to be members of the Federal Reserve System. The Fed provides a variety of services for commercial banks and controls the amount of funds within the banking system. About 35 percent of all banks are members of the Federal Reserve. These banks are generally larger than the norm; their combined deposits make up about 70 percent of all bank deposits. Both member and nonmember banks can borrow from the Fed, and both are subject to the Fed's reserve requirements.

Regulators

National banks are regulated by the Comptroller of the Currency, while state banks are regulated by their respective state agency. Banks that are insured by the **Federal Deposit Insurance Corporation (FDIC)** are also regulated by the FDIC. Because all national banks must be members of the Federal Reserve and all Fed member banks must hold FDIC insurance, national banks are regulated by the Comptroller of the Currency, the Fed, and the FDIC. State banks are regulated by their respective state agency, the Fed (if they are Fed members), and the FDIC. The Comptroller of the Currency is responsible for conducting periodic evaluations of national banks, the Fed holds the same responsibility for state-chartered banks that are members of the Fed, and the FDIC is responsible for state-chartered banks that are not members of the Fed.

Because of the regulatory overlap, it has often been argued that a single regulatory agency should be assigned the role of regulating all commercial banks and savings institutions. The momentum for consolidation increased in 1989, when the Financial Institutions Reform, Recovery, and Enforcement Act (FIRREA) was passed. One of the provisions of FIRREA allows commercial banks to acquire either healthy or failing savings and loan associations (S&Ls). Prior to FIRREA, banks could not acquire S&Ls.

Regulation of Bank Ownership

Commercial banks can be either independently owned or owned by a **bank holding company (BHC).** Although some multibank holding companies (owning more than one bank) exist, one-bank holding companies are more common. More banks are owned by holding companies than are owned independently. The holding company structure became popular after 1970, when the Bank Holding Company Act of 1956 was amended to allow BHCs to engage in various nonbanking activities, such as leasing, mortgage banking, and data processing. As a result, BHCs have greater potential for product diversification.

REGULATION OF BANK OPERATIONS

Banks are regulated according to how they obtain funds, how they use their funds, and the types of financial services that they can offer. Some of the most important regulations are discussed here.

Regulation of Deposit Insurance

Federal deposit insurance has existed since the creation of the FDIC in 1933 as a response to the bank runs that occurred in the late 1920s and early 1930s. During the 1930–1932 period during the Great Depression, about 5,100 banks failed, representing more than 20 percent of the existing banks at that time. The initial wave of failures caused depositors to withdraw their deposits from other banks, fearing that the failures would spread. Their actions actually caused more banks to fail. If deposit insurance had been available, depositors might not have removed their deposits, and some bank failures might have been avoided.

The FDIC preserves public confidence in the U.S. financial system by providing deposit insurance to commercial banks and savings institutions. The FDIC is managed by a board of five directors, who are appointed by the president. Its headquarters is in Washington, D.C., but it has six regional offices and other field offices throughout the country. Today, the FDIC's insurance funds are responsible for insuring deposits of more than $3 trillion.

Insurance Limits

The specified amount of deposits per person insured by the FDIC is $100,000. The insured deposits make up 80 percent of all commercial bank balances, as very large deposit accounts are insured only up to the $100,000 limit. Deposits in foreign branches of U.S. banks are not insured by the FDIC, however. As a result of the credit crisis in 2008, the amount of deposits insured was temporarily increased to $250,000 through 2013 as part of the Emergency Economic Stabilization Act of 2008 (also referred to as the bailout act). This act was intended to resolve the liquidity problems of financial institutions and restore confidence in the banking system.

In general, deposit insurance has allowed depositors to deposit funds under the insured limits in any insured depository institution without the need to assess the institution's financial condition. In addition, the insurance system prevents bank runs on deposits because insured depositors believe that their deposits are backed by the U.S. government even if the insured depository institution fails. When a bank fails, insured depositors normally have access to their money in a few days.

Risk-Based Deposit Premiums

Banks insured by the FDIC must pay annual insurance premiums. Until 1991, all banks obtained insurance for their depositors at the same rate. Because the riskiest banks were more likely to fail, they were being indirectly subsidized by safer banks. This system encouraged some banks to assume more risk because they could still attract deposits from depositors who knew they would be covered regardless of the bank's risk. The act of insured banks taking on more risk because their depositors are protected is referred to as a **moral hazard problem.** As a result of many banks taking excessive risks, bank failures increased during the 1980s and early 1990s. The balance in the FDIC's insurance fund declined because the FDIC had to reimburse depositors who had deposits at the banks that failed.

The moral hazard problem prompted bank regulators and Congress to search for a way to discourage banks from taking excessive risk and to replenish the FDIC's insurance fund. As a result of the Federal Deposit Insurance Corporation Improvement Act (FDICIA) of 1991, risk-based deposit insurance premiums were phased in. Consequently, bank insurance premiums are now aligned with the risk of banks, thereby reducing the moral hazard problem.

Before 2006, the Bank Insurance Fund was used to collect premiums and provide insurance for banks, while the Savings Association Insurance Fund (SAIF) was used to collect premiums and provide insurance for savings institutions. In 2006, the two insurance funds were merged into one insurance fund called the **Deposit Insurance Fund**, which is regulated by the FDIC.

The deposit insurance premiums were increased in 2009, because the FDIC used substantial reserves during the credit crisis to reimburse depositors of failed banks. The range of premiums was set between 12 cents and 50 cents per $100, with most banks paying between 12 and 14 cents. The FDIC's reserves are currently about $45 billion, or about 1 percent of all insured deposits.

Regulation of Deposits

Three regulatory acts created more competition for bank deposits over time, as discussed next.

DIDMCA   In 1980, the **Depository Institutions Deregulation and Monetary Control Act (DIDMCA)** was enacted to (1) to deregulate the banking (and other depository institutions) industry and (2) improve monetary policy. Because this chapter focuses on regulation and deregulation, only the first goal is discussed here.

The DIDMCA was a major force in deregulating the banking industry and increasing competition among banks. It removed interest rate ceilings on deposits, allowing banks and other depository institutions to make their own decisions on what interest rates to offer for time and savings deposits. In addition, it allowed banks to offer NOW accounts.

The DIDMCA has had a significant impact on the banking industry, most importantly by increasing competition among depository institutions.

Garn-St Germain Act   Banks and other depository institutions were further deregulated in 1982 as a result of the **Garn-St Germain Act.** The act came at a time when some depository institutions (especially savings institutions) were experiencing severe financial problems. One of its more important provisions permitted depository institutions to offer money market deposit accounts (MMDAs), which have no minimum maturity and no interest ceiling. These accounts allow a maximum of six transactions per month (three by check). They are very similar to the traditional accounts offered by **money market mutual funds** (whose main function is to sell shares and pool the funds to purchase short-term securities that offer market-determined rates). Because MMDAs offer savers similar benefits, they allow depository institutions to compete against money market funds in attracting savers' funds.

A second key deregulatory provision of the Garn-St Germain Act permitted depository institutions (including banks) to acquire failing institutions across geographic boundaries. This allowed some banks to circumvent restrictions (imposed by the **McFadden Act of 1927** and the Douglas Amendment to the Bank Holding Company Act of 1956) that prevented them from crossing state lines. The intent was to reduce the number of failures that require liquidation, as the chances of finding a potential acquirer for a failing institution improve when geographic barriers are removed. Also, competition was expected to increase, as depository institutions previously barred from entering specific geographic areas could do so by acquiring failing institutions.

Interstate Banking Act   In September 1994, Congress passed the Reigle-Neal Interstate Banking and Branching Efficiency Act, which removed interstate branching restrictions and thereby further increased the competition among banks for deposits. Nationwide interstate banking enabled banks to grow and achieve **economies of scale**. It also allowed banks in stagnant markets to penetrate markets where economic conditions were more favorable. Banks in all markets were pressured to become more efficient as a result of the increased competition.

Regulation of Bank Loans

Since loans represent the key asset of commercial banks, they are regulated to limit a bank's exposure to default risk.

Regulation of Highly Leveraged Transactions   As a result of concern about the popularity of highly leveraged loans (for supporting leveraged buyouts and other activities), bank regulators monitor the amount of highly leveraged transactions (HLTs).

HLTs are commonly defined as loan transactions in which the borrower's liabilities are valued at more than 75 percent of total assets.

Regulation of Foreign Loans Regulators also monitor a bank's exposure to loans to foreign countries. Because regulators require banks to report significant exposure to foreign debt, investors and creditors have access to more detailed information about the composition of bank loan portfolios.

Regulation of Loans to a Single Borrower Banks are restricted to a maximum loan amount of 15 percent of their capital to any single borrower (up to 25 percent if the loan is adequately collateralized). This forces them to diversify their loans to a degree.

Regulation of Loans to Community Banks are also regulated to ensure that they attempt to accommodate the credit needs of the communities in which they operate. The Community Reinvestment Act (CRA) of 1977 (revised in 1995) requires banks to meet the credit needs of qualified borrowers in their community, even those with low or moderate incomes. The CRA is not intended to force banks to make high-risk loans but rather to ensure that lower-income (and qualified) borrowers receive the loans that they request. Each bank's performance in this regard is evaluated periodically by its respective regulator.

Regulation of Bank Investment in Securities

Banks are not allowed to use borrowed or deposited funds to purchase common stock, although they can manage stock portfolios through trust accounts that are owned by individuals. Banks can invest only in bonds that are investment-grade quality (as measured by a Baa rating or higher by Moody's or a BBB rating or higher by Standard & Poor's). The regulations on bonds are intended to prevent banks from taking excessive risks.

Regulation of Securities Services

The Banking Act of 1933 (better known as the **Glass-Steagall Act**) separated banking and securities activities. The act was prompted by problems during 1929 when some banks sold some of their poor-quality securities to their trust accounts established for individuals. Some banks also engaged in insider trading, buying or selling corporate securities based on confidential information provided by firms that had requested loans. The Glass-Steagall Act prevented any firm that accepted deposits from underwriting stocks and bonds of corporations.

The separation of securities activities from banking activities was intended to prevent potential conflicts of interest. For example, the concern was that if a bank was allowed to underwrite securities, it might advise its corporate customers to purchase these securities and could threaten to cut off future loans if the customers did not oblige.

WEB

www.federalreserve
.gov/bankinforeg/
default.htm
Links to regulations of
securities services of-
fered by banks.

Financial Services Modernization Act In 1999, Congress passed the **Financial Services Modernization Act** (also called the Gramm-Leach-Bliley Act), which essentially repealed the Glass-Steagall Act. The 1999 act allows affiliations between banks, securities firms, and insurance companies. It also allows bank holding companies to engage in any financial activity through their ownership of subsidiaries. Consequently, a single holding company can engage in traditional banking activities, securities trading, underwriting, and insurance. The act also requires that the holding company be well managed and have sufficient capital in order to expand its financial services. The Securities and Exchange Commission (SEC) regulates any securities products that are created, but the bank subsidiaries that offer the securities products are regulated by bank regulators.

Although many commercial banks had previously pursued securities services, the 1999 act increased the degree to which banks can offer these services. Furthermore, it allowed securities firms and insurance companies to acquire banks. Under the act, commercial banks must have a strong rating in community lending (meaning that they have been willing to actively provide loans in lower-income communities) in order to pursue additional expansion in securities and other nonbank activities.

Since the Financial Services Modernization Act was passed, there has been much more consolidation of financial institutions. Many of the larger financial institutions are able to offer all types of financial services through their various subsidiaries. Since individuals commonly use financial institutions to deposit funds, obtain mortgage loans and consumer loans (such as an automobile loan), purchase shares of mutual funds, order stock transactions (brokerage), and purchase insurance, they can obtain all their financial services from a single financial conglomerate. Since firms commonly use financial institutions to maintain a business checking account, obtain loans, issue stocks or bonds, have their pension fund managed, and purchase insurance services, they can receive all of their financial services from a single financial conglomerate.

The Financial Services Modernization Act also offers benefits to financial institutions. By offering more diversified services, financial institutions can reduce their reliance on the demand for any single service that they offer. This diversification may result in less risk for the institution's consolidated business, assuming that the new services are not subject to a much higher degree of risk than its traditional services.

The individual units of a financial conglomerate may generate some new business simply because they are part of the conglomerate and offer convenience to clients who already rely on its other services. Each financial unit's list of existing clients represents a potential source of new clients for the other financial units to pursue.

Regulation of Insurance Services

As with securities services, banks have been eager to offer insurance services. The arguments for and against bank involvement in insurance are quite similar to those regarding bank involvement in securities. Banks could increase competition in the insurance industry, as they would be able to offer services at a lower cost. In addition, they could offer their customers the convenience of one-stop shopping (especially if the bank could also offer securities services).

In 1998, regulators allowed the merger between Citicorp and Traveler's Insurance Group, which essentially paved the way for the consolidation of bank and insurance services. Passage of the Financial Services Modernization Act in the following year confirmed that banks and insurance companies could merge and consolidate their operations. These events encouraged banks and insurance companies to pursue mergers as a means of offering a full set of financial services.

Regulation of Off-Balance Sheet Transactions

Banks offer a variety of off-balance sheet commitments. For example, banks provide letters of credit to back commercial paper issued by corporations. They also act as the intermediary on interest rate swaps and usually guarantee payments over the specified period in the event that one of the parties defaults on its payments.

Various off-balance sheet transactions have become popular because they provide fee income. That is, banks charge a fee for guaranteeing against the default of another party and for facilitating transactions between parties. Nevertheless, off-balance sheet transactions also expose the banks to risk. If, during a severe economic downturn, many corporations should default on their commercial paper or on payments specified by interest rate swap agreements, the banks that provided guarantees would incur large losses.

Bank exposure to off-balance sheet activities has become a major concern of regulators. Banks could be riskier than their balance sheets indicate because of these transactions. The risk-based capital requirements are higher for banks that conduct more off-balance sheet activities. In this way, regulators discourage banks from excessive off-balance sheet activities.

Regulation of Credit Default Swaps   Credit default swaps are a type of off-balance sheet transaction that became very popular in the 2004–2008 period as a means of protecting against the risk of default on bonds and mortgage-backed securities. A swap allows a commercial bank to make periodic payments to a counterparty in return for protection in the event that its holdings of mortgage-backed securities default. While some commercial banks purchased these swaps as a means of protecting their assets against default, other commercial banks sold them (to provide protection) as a means of generating fee income. By 2008, credit default swaps represented $62 trillion of mortgage-backed securities or other types of securities.

When commercial banks purchase credit default swaps to protect their assets against possible default, these assets are not subject to capital requirements. Yet, if the sellers of the credit default swaps are overexposed, they may not be able to provide the protection they promised. Thus, the banks that purchased credit default swaps might not be protected if the sellers default. As the credit crisis intensified in 2008 and 2009, regulators became concerned about credit default swaps because of the lack of transparency regarding the exposure of each commercial bank and the credibility of the counterparties on the swaps. They increased their oversight of this market and asked commercial banks to provide more information about their credit default swap positions. Congress is also considering possible laws that could ensure that credit default swaps do not lead to another financial crisis.

Regulation of the Accounting Process

Publicly traded banks, like other publicly traded companies, are required to provide financial statements that indicate their recent financial position and performance. In the 2001–2002 period, the accounting scandals at Enron, WorldCom, and some other firms led to a lack of confidence in the financial information disclosed by firms. In some cases, executives sold their holdings of their firm's stock during a period when the firm's reported earnings were exaggerated, causing the stock's market price to be higher than the firm's actual earnings warranted. Investors are less willing to invest in firms whose earnings may be exaggerated. The Sarbanes-Oxley (SOX) Act was enacted in 2002 to ensure a more transparent process for reporting on a firm's productivity and financial condition. The act requires firms to implement an internal reporting process that can be easily monitored by executives and makes it impossible for executives to pretend that they did not know about fraudulent reporting. Although publicly traded banks were not the cause of the accounting scandals, they also must follow the guidelines specified in the SOX Act.

Some of the key provisions of the act require banks to improve their internal control processes and establish a centralized database of information. In addition, executives are now more accountable for a bank's financial statements because they must personally verify the accuracy of the statements. One negative effect of the SOX Act is that publicly traded banks have incurred expenses of more than $1 million per year to comply with its provisions. Nevertheless, investors may have more confidence in the financial statements now that there is greater accountability that could discourage fraudulent accounting.

REGULATION OF CAPITAL

Banks are subject to capital requirements, which force them to maintain a minimum amount of **capital** (or equity) as a percentage of total assets. They rely on their capital as a cushion against possible losses. If a bank has insufficient capital to cover losses, it will not be able to cover its expenses and will fail. Thus, much attention is focused on bank capital levels. Banks commonly boost their capital levels by retaining earnings or by issuing stock to the public. However, a bank that is performing poorly cannot easily build its capital for the following reasons. If it is performing poorly, it has no earnings that it can retain to build its capital. In addition, the bank's stock price is probably depressed because it has been performing poorly, and it might not receive a sufficient amount of funds if it tried to issue stock at the prevailing stock price. Furthermore, investors may not have much interest in purchasing new shares of stock of a bank that is very weak and is desperate to build capital, because they may expect that the bank will fail.

Banks can increase their capital by reducing their dividends, which enables them to retain a larger amount of their earnings (if they have earnings). However, a cut in dividends might signal to existing shareholders that the bank is desperate for capital, and this could cause its stock price to decline further. This type of effect could make it more difficult for the bank to issue stock in the future.

Many of these requirements are set out in international agreements, known as the Basel Accords. In addition, value-at-risk models may be used to assess banks' risk and determine capital requirements.

Basel I Accord

In the first Basel Accord (often called Basel I) in 1988, the central banks of 12 major countries agreed to establish uniform capital requirements. A key provision in the Basel Accord bases the capital requirements on a bank's risk level. Banks with greater risk are required to maintain a higher level of capital, which discourages banks from excessive exposure to credit risk. By the end of 1992, banks were required to have a capital ratio of at least 8 percent of risk-weighted assets, with a minimum Tier 1 capital ratio of 4 percent. Tier 1 capital consists mostly of shareholders' equity, retained earnings, and preferred stock, while Tier 2 capital includes loan loss reserves (up to a specified maximum) and subordinated debt.

Assets are weighted according to risk. Very safe assets such as cash are assigned a zero weight, while very risky assets are assigned a 100 percent weight. Because the required capital is set as a percentage of risk-weighted assets, riskier banks are subject to more stringent capital requirements.

In 1996, the Basel Accord was amended so that other factors that affect bank risk are also considered. The amendment mandates that a bank's capital level also account for its sensitivity to market conditions, such as stock prices, interest rates, and exchange rates.

Basel II Accord

In recent years, banking regulators who form the so-called Basel Committee have been working on a new accord (called Basel II) that will refine the risk measures and increase the transparency of a bank's risk to its customers. The goal is to properly account for a bank's risk so that the bank's capital requirements are in line with its corresponding risk. This is a major challenge because different banks may have different risk levels even though they all have the same composition of corporate loans, household mortgage loans, and other types of loans. Risk levels could differ if, for example, some banks required better collateral to back their loans. In addition, some banks may take positions in derivative securities that can reduce their credit risk, while other banks may have positions in derivative securities that increase their credit risk. The Basel II Accord attempts to account for such differences among banks.

Specifically, the Basel II Accord has three major parts:

1. Revise the measurement of credit risk.
2. Explicitly account for operational risk.
3. Require more disclosure about exposure to risk.

Revised Measures of Credit Risk

Banks can continue to use the traditional standardized approach to calculating credit risk, in which they categorize their assets and assign risk weights to the categories. To improve the calculation, however, the categories are being refined to account for possible differences in risk levels of loans within a category.

EXAMPLE

As a result of Basel II, a bank's loans that are past due will be assigned a higher weight. This adjustment inflates the size of these assets for the purpose of determining minimum capital requirements. Thus, banks with more loans that are past due will be forced to maintain a higher level of capital (other things being equal). ●

An alternative method of calculating credit risk, called the internal ratings-based (IRB) approach, would also be available. A bank would provide summary statistics about its loans to the Basel Committee, which would apply preexisting formulas to the statistics to determine the required capital level for that bank.

Accounting for Operational Risk

The Basel Committee defines operational risk as the risk of losses resulting from inadequate or failed internal processes or systems. The Basel Accord did not explicitly account for this type of risk. The Basel Committee wants to encourage banks to improve their techniques for controlling operational risk because doing so could reduce failures in the banking system. By imposing higher capital requirements on banks with higher levels of operational risk, Basel II would provide an incentive for banks to reduce their operational risk. Initially, banks will be allowed to use their own methods for assessing their exposure to operational risk. The Basel Committee suggests that a bank's average annual income over the last three years may serve as an indicator. The annual income represents the size of a bank's operations and thus may reflect the degree of the bank's operational risk. The committee plans to develop a more sophisticated process to assess operational risk over time.

Public Disclosure of Exposure to Risk

The Basel Committee plans to require banks to provide more information to existing and prospective shareholders about their exposure to different types of risk. Whereas the other provisions of Basel II focus on ensuring that a bank's capital requirements are based on its risk, this provision would increase the information available about a bank's risk. By making banks' risk more transparent to investors, this provision may cause banks to use more conservative management.

Implementation of the Basel II Accord

The provisions of the Basel II Accord are not directly enforceable. However, some countries have established new guidelines for their banks that are adapted from parts of the accord. In particular, the United States, Canada, and countries in the European Union have created regulations for their banks that conform to some parts of the Basel II Accord. Many Asian countries plan to implement the Basel II guidelines over time.

Use of the VAR Method to Determine Capital Requirements

Under the 1996 amendment to the Basel Accord, the capital requirements on large banks that have substantial trading businesses (such as interest rate derivatives, foreign exchange derivatives, and underwriting services) were adjusted to incorporate their own internal measurements of general market risk, which reflects exposure to movements in market forces such as interest rates, stock prices, and exchange rates. The capital requirements imposed to cover general market risk are based on the bank's own assessment of risk when applying a value-at-risk (VAR) model. Recall that participants in the stock market commonly use this model to assess the risk of a stock portfolio. It is used in a somewhat similar manner to assess the risk of a bank.

The VAR model can be applied in various ways to determine capital requirements. In general, a bank defines the VAR as the estimated potential loss from its trading businesses that could result from adverse movements in market prices. Banks typically use a 99 percent confidence level, meaning that there is a 99 percent chance that the loss on a given day will be more favorable than the VAR estimate. When applied to a daily time horizon, the actual loss from a bank's trading businesses should not exceed the VAR estimated loss on more than 1 out of every 100 days. Banks estimate the VAR by assessing the probability of specific adverse market events (such as an abrupt change in interest rates) and the possible sensitivity in response to those events. Banks with a higher maximum loss based on a 99 percent confidence interval are subject to higher capital requirements.

This focus on daily price movements forces banks to continuously monitor their trading positions so that they are immediately aware of any losses. Many banks now have access to the market values of their trading businesses at the end of every day. If banks used a longer-term horizon (such as a month), larger losses might build up before being recognized.

Testing the Validity of a Bank's VAR   The validity of a bank's estimated VAR is assessed by comparing the actual daily trading gains or losses to the estimated VAR over a particular period. If the VAR is estimated properly, only 1 percent of the actual daily trading days should show results that are worse than the estimated VAR. In reality, banks may not be very concerned if all their trading results exceed their estimated VAR, because this suggests that their risk may have been overestimated for that period. However, they would be concerned (as would regulators) if the actual results from the trading businesses were frequently worse than the estimated VAR.

Limitations of the VAR Model   The VAR model was generally not effective at detecting the risk of banks during the credit crisis. The VAR model failed to recognize the degree to which the value of bank assets (such as mortgages or mortgage-backed securities) could decline under adverse conditions. The use of historical data from before 2007 did not capture the risk of mortgages because investments in mortgages during that period normally resulted in low defaults. Thus, the VAR model was not adequate for predicting the possible estimated losses. Many banks experienced larger losses than they thought was possible in 2008, and they had to use up some of their capital to absorb these losses. Thus, their capital proved to be deficient.

Bank-Imposed Stress Tests   Some banks supplement the VAR estimate with their own stress tests.

EXAMPLE

Georgia Bank wants to estimate the loss that would occur in response to an extreme adverse market event. First, it identifies an extreme event that could occur, such as an increase in interest rates on one day that is 10 standard deviations from the mean daily change in interest rates. The mean and standard deviation of daily interest rate movements may be based on a recent historical period, such as the last 300 days. Georgia Bank then uses this scenario along with the typical sensitivity of its trading businesses to such a scenario to estimate the loss on its trading businesses as a result. It may then repeat this exercise based on a scenario of a decline in the market value of stocks that is 10 standard deviations from the mean daily change in stock prices. It may even estimate the possible losses in its trading businesses from an adverse scenario in which interest rates increase and stock prices decline substantially on a given day. ●

Regulatory Stress Tests during the Credit Crisis   Regulators closely monitor bank capital levels during periods of weak economic conditions, because banks may need to rely on their capital to cushion losses and avoid bankruptcy. During the credit crisis in the 2008–2009 period, bank regulators periodically infused their own funds into some banks, thereby taking partial ownership of the banks. In April 2009, they applied stress tests to the 19 largest bank holding companies to determine if the banks had enough capital. These banks account for about half of all loans provided by U.S. banks. This type of regulatory assessment of bank capital may be frequently applied in the future to ensure that banks have sufficient capital.

One of the stress tests applied to banks in April 2009 involved forecasting the likely effect on the banks' capital levels if the recession existing at that time lasted longer than expected. Since many of the banks were already incurring losses at the time, this adverse scenario would cause them to incur larger losses and to incur losses farther into the future. As a result, the banks would have to periodically use a portion of their capital to cover their losses, resulting in a reduction in their capital over time.

The potential impact of an adverse scenario such as a deeper recession varies among banks. During the credit crisis, banks that had a larger proportion of real estate assets were expected to suffer larger losses if economic conditions worsened, because real estate values were very sensitive to economic conditions. Thus, the banks with considerable exposure to real estate values were more likely to experience capital deficiencies if the recession lasted longer than expected. Regulators focused on banks that did not do well on the stress tests in April 2009 in order to ensure that these banks would have sufficient capital even if the recession lasted for a longer period of time. These banks could attempt to raise capital by issuing stock to the public. However, if they believed that they would not be able to raise sufficient funds from issuing stock to the public, they could issue preferred stock to the Federal Reserve.

HOW REGULATORS MONITOR BANKS

WEB

www.fdic.gov
Information about specific bank regulations.

Bank regulators typically conduct an on-site examination of each commercial bank at least once a year. During the examination, regulators assess the bank's compliance with existing regulations and its financial condition. In addition to on-site examinations, regulators periodically monitor commercial banks with computerized monitoring systems, based on data provided by the banks on a quarterly basis.

CAMELS Ratings

Regulators monitor banks to detect any serious deficiencies that might develop so that they can correct the deficiencies before the bank fails. The more failures they can prevent, the more confidence the public will have in the banking industry. The evaluation approach described here is used by the FDIC, the Federal Reserve, and the Comptroller of the Currency.

The single most common cause of bank failure is poor management. Unfortunately, no reliable measure of poor management exists. Therefore, the regulators rate banks on the basis of six characteristics, which together comprise the **CAMELS ratings,** so named for the acronym that identifies the six characteristics:

- Capital adequacy

- Asset quality

- Management

- Earnings

- Liquidity

- Sensitivity

Each of the CAMELS characteristics is rated on a 1-to-5 scale, with 1 indicating outstanding and 5 very poor. A composite rating is determined as the mean rating of the six characteristics. Banks with a composite rating of 4.0 or higher are considered to be problem banks. They are closely monitored, because their risk level is perceived to be very high.

Capital Adequacy   Because adequate bank capital is thought to reduce a bank's risk, regulators determine the **capital ratio** (typically defined as capital divided by assets). Regulators have become increasingly concerned that some banks do not hold enough capital, so they have increased capital requirements. If banks hold more capital, they can more easily absorb potential losses and are more likely to survive. Banks with higher capital ratios are therefore assigned a higher capital adequacy rating. Even a bank with a relatively high level of capital could fail, however, if the other components of its balance sheet have not been properly managed. Thus, regulators must evaluate other characteristics of banks in addition to capital adequacy.

Because a bank's capital requirements are dependent on the value of its assets, they are subject to the accounting method that is used in the valuation process. Fair value accounting is used to measure the value of bank assets. That is, a bank is required to periodically mark its assets to market so that it can revise the amount of needed capital based on the reduced market value of the assets. During the credit crisis, the secondary market for mortgage-backed securities and mortgage loans was very illiquid, such that banks would have had to sell these assets at very low prices (large discounts). Consequently, the fair value accounting method forced the banks to "write down" the value of their assets.

Given a decline in a bank's book value of assets, and no associated change in its book value of liabilities, a bank's balance sheet is balanced by reducing its capital. Thus, many banks were required to replenish their capital in order to meet the capital requirements, and some banks came under extra scrutiny by regulators. Some banks satisfied the capital requirements by selling some of their assets, but they would have preferred not to sell assets during this period because there were not many buyers and the market price of these assets was low. An alternative method of meeting capital requirements is to issue new stock, but since bank stock values were so low during the credit crisis, this was not a viable option at that time.

Banks complained that their capital was reduced because of the fair value accounting rules. They argued that their assets should have been valued higher if the banks intended to hold them until the credit crisis ended and the secondary market for these assets became more liquid. If the banks' assets had been valued in this manner, their writedowns of assets would have been much smaller, and the banks could have more easily met the capital requirements. As a result of the banks' complaints, the fair value accounting rules were modified somewhat in 2009.

Asset Quality   Each bank makes its own decisions as to how deposited funds should be allocated, and these decisions determine its level of credit (default) risk. Regulators therefore evaluate the quality of the bank's assets, including its loans and its securities.

The Fed considers the 5 Cs to assess the quality of the loans extended by Skyler Bank, which it is examining:

- Capacity—the borrower's ability to pay.

- Collateral—the quality of the assets that back the loan.

- Condition—the circumstances that led to the need for funds.

- Capital—the difference between the value of the borrower's assets and its liabilities.

- Character—the borrower's willingness to repay loans, as measured by its payment history on the loan and credit report.

From an assessment of a sample of Skyler Bank's loans, the Fed determines that the borrowers have excessive debt, minimal collateral, and low capital levels. Thus, the Fed concludes that Skyler Bank's asset quality is weak. ●

Rating an asset portfolio can be difficult, however, as the following example illustrates.

A bank currently has 1,000 loans outstanding to firms in a variety of industries. Each loan has specific provisions as to how it is secured (if at all) by the borrower's assets; some of the loans have short-term maturities, while others are for longer terms. Imagine the task of assigning a rating to this bank's asset quality. Even if all the bank's loan recipients are current on their loan repayment schedules, this does not guarantee that the bank's asset quality deserves a high rating. The economic conditions existing during the period of prompt loan repayment may not persist in the future. Thus, an appropriate examination of the bank's asset portfolio should incorporate the portfolio's exposure to potential events (such as a recession). The reason for the regulatory examination is not to grade past performance, but to detect any problem that could cause the bank to fail in the future. ●

Because of the difficulty in assigning a rating to a bank's asset portfolio, it is possible that some banks will be rated lower or higher than they deserve.

Management   Each of the characteristics examined relates to the bank's management. In addition, regulators specifically rate the bank's management according to administrative skills, ability to comply with existing regulations, and ability to cope with a changing environment. They also assess the bank's internal control systems, which may indicate how well the bank's management would detect its own financial problems. This evaluation is clearly subjective.

Earnings   Although the CAMELS ratings are mostly concerned with risk, earnings are very important. Banks fail when their earnings become consistently negative. A profitability ratio commonly used to evaluate banks is **return on assets (ROA),** defined as earnings after taxes divided by assets. In addition to assessing a bank's earnings over time, it is also useful to compare the bank's earnings with industry earnings. This allows for an evaluation of the bank relative to its competitors. In addition, regulators are concerned about how a bank's earnings would change if economic conditions change.

Liquidity   Some banks commonly obtain funds from some outside sources (such as the Federal Reserve or the federal funds market), but regulators would prefer that banks not consistently rely on these sources. Such banks are more likely to experience a liquidity crisis whereby they are forced to borrow excessive amounts of funds from outside sources. If existing depositors sense that the bank is experiencing a liquidity problem, they may withdraw their funds, compounding the problem.

Sensitivity   Regulators also assess the degree to which a bank might be exposed to adverse financial market conditions. Two banks could be rated similarly in terms of recent earnings, liquidity, and other characteristics, and yet one bank may be much more sensitive than the other to financial market conditions. Regulators began to explicitly consider banks' sensitivity to financial market conditions in 1996 and added this characteristic to what were previously referred to as the CAMEL ratings. In particular, regulators place much emphasis on a bank's sensitivity to interest rate movements. Many banks have liabilities that are repriced more frequently than their assets and are therefore adversely affected by rising interest rates. Banks that are more sensitive to rising interest rates are more likely to experience financial problems.

Limitations of the CAMELS Rating System   The CAMELS rating system is essentially a screening device. Because there are so many banks, regulators do not have the resources to closely monitor each bank on a frequent basis. The rating system identifies what are believed to be problem banks. Over time, some problem banks improve and are removed from the "problem list," while others may deteriorate further and ultimately fail. Still other banks are added to the problem list.

Although examinations by regulators may help detect problems experienced by some banks in time to save them, many problems still go unnoticed, and by the time they are detected, it may be too late to find a remedy. Because financial ratios measure current or past performance rather than future performance, they do not always detect problems in time to correct them. Thus, although an analysis of financial ratios can be useful, the task of assessing a bank is as much an art as it is a science. Subjective opinion must complement objective measurements to provide the best possible evaluation of a bank.

Any system used to detect financial problems may err in one of two ways. It may classify a bank as safe when in fact it is failing or as very risky when in fact it is safe. The first type of mistake is more costly, because some failing banks are not identified in time to help them. To avoid this mistake, bank regulators could lower their benchmark composite rating. However, if they did, many more banks would be on the problem list requiring close supervision, and regulators' limited resources would be spread too thin.

Corrective Action by Regulators

When a bank is classified as a problem bank, regulators thoroughly investigate the cause of its deterioration. Corrective action is often necessary. Regulators may examine such banks frequently and thoroughly and discuss with bank management possible remedies to cure the key problems. For example, regulators may request that a bank boost its capital level or delay its plans to expand. They can require that additional financial information be periodically updated to allow continued monitoring. They have the authority to remove particular officers and directors of a problem bank if doing so would enhance the bank's performance. They even have the authority to take legal action against a problem bank if the bank does not comply with their suggested remedies. Such a drastic measure is rare, however, and would not solve the existing problems of the bank.

Funding the Closure of Failing Banks

If a failing bank cannot be saved, it will be closed. The FDIC is responsible for the closure of failing banks. It must decide whether to liquidate the failed bank's assets or to facilitate the acquisition of that bank by another bank. When liquidating a failed bank, the FDIC draws from its Deposit Insurance Fund to reimburse insured depositors. After reimbursing depositors, the FDIC attempts to sell any marketable assets (such as securities and some loans) of the failed bank. The cost to the FDIC of closing a failed bank is the difference between the reimbursement to depositors and the proceeds received from selling the failed bank's assets.

An alternative solution is for the FDIC to provide some financial support to facilitate another bank's acquisition of the failed bank. The financial support is necessary because the acquiring bank recognizes that the market value of the failed bank's assets is less than its liabilities. The FDIC may be willing to provide funding if doing so would be less costly than liquidating the failed bank. Whether a failing bank is liquidated or acquired by another bank, it loses its identity.

On some occasions, the government has given preferential treatment to certain large troubled banks. In some cases, for example, the government has provided short-term loans to a distressed bank or insured all its deposits, even those above the insurance limit, in an effort to encourage depositors to leave their funds in the troubled bank. Or the government might orchestrate a takeover of the troubled bank in a manner that enables the shareholders to receive at least some payment for their shares (ordinarily, when a failed bank is acquired, shareholders lose their investment). Such intervention by the government is very controversial, however.

Argument for Government Rescue

Those who think that the government should sometimes intervene to help troubled banks argue that news of a large bank failure could trigger bank runs at other large banks and might prevent these banks from securing the funds that they need for their operations. This might cause failures at other banks that could have been avoided if the government had rescued the large failing bank.

If all financial institutions that were weak during the credit crisis had been allowed to fail without any intervention, the FDIC might have had to use all of its reserves to reimburse depositors. To the extent that FDIC intervention can reduce the degree of losses at depository institutions, it may reduce the cost to the government (and therefore the taxpayers).

Argument against Government Rescue

Those who oppose government rescues say that when the federal government rescues a large bank, it sends a message to the banking industry that large banks will not be allowed to fail. Consequently, large banks may take excessive risks without concern about failure. If a large bank's risky ventures (such as loans to very risky borrowers) pay off, the return will be high. If they do not pay off, the federal government will bail the bank out. If large banks can be sure that they will be rescued, their shareholders will benefit because they face limited downside risk.

Some critics recommend a policy of letting the market work, meaning that no financial institution would ever be bailed out. In this case, managers of a troubled bank would be held accountable for their bad management because their jobs would be terminated due to the failure of the bank. In addition, shareholders would more closely monitor the bank managers to make sure that they do not take excessive risk.

Government Assistance to Bear Stearns

The credit crisis led to new arguments about government rescues of failing financial institutions. In March 2008, Bear Stearns, a large securities firm, was about to go bankrupt. Bear Stearns had facilitated many transactions in financial markets, and its failure would have delayed these transactions, causing liquidity problems for many individuals and firms that were to receive cash as a result of the transactions. The Federal Reserve provided short-term loans to Bear Stearns to ensure that it had adequate liquidity. The Fed then backed the acquisition of Bear Stearns by J.P. Morgan Chase by providing a loan so that J.P. Morgan Chase could afford the acquisition.

At this point, the question was whether the Federal Reserve (a regulator of commercial banks) should be assisting a securities firm such as Bear Stearns that it did not regulate. Some critics (including Paul Volcker, a previous chair of the Fed) suggested that the rescue of a firm other than a commercial bank should be the responsibility of Congress and not the Fed. The Fed's counter was that it recognized that a number of financial transactions would potentially be frozen if it did not intervene. Thus, it was acting in an attempt to stabilize the financial system rather than in its role as a regulator of commercial banks.

Then, in September 2008, Lehman Brothers, another large securities firm, was allowed to go bankrupt without any assistance from the Fed, whereas American International Group (AIG, a large insurance company) was rescued by the Fed. Some critics asked why some large financial institutions were bailed out but others were not. At what point does a financial institution become sufficiently large or important that it deserves to be rescued? This question will continue to trigger heated arguments.

Global Bank Regulations

Although the division of regulatory power between the central bank and other regulators varies among countries, each country has a system for monitoring and regulating commercial banks. Most countries also maintain different guidelines for deposit insurance. Differences in regulatory restrictions can allow some banks a competitive advantage in a global banking environment.

Historically, Canadian banks were not as restricted in offering securities services as U.S. banks and therefore control much of the Canadian securities industry. Recently, Canadian banks have begun to enter the insurance industry. European banks have had much more freedom than U.S. banks in offering securities services such as underwriting corporate securities. Many European banks are allowed to invest in stocks.

Japanese commercial banks have some flexibility to provide investment banking services, but not as much as European banks. Perhaps the most obvious difference between Japanese and U.S. bank regulations is that Japanese banks are allowed to use depositor funds to invest in stocks of corporations. Thus, Japanese banks are not only creditors of firms, but are also their shareholders.

As regulatory intervention continues in the banking industry, updated information will be posted on the companion website at www.cengage.com/international within the material for Chapter 18.

Summary

- Banks are regulated on the deposit insurance that they must maintain, their loan composition, the bonds that they are allowed to purchase, and the financial services that they can offer. In general, regulations on deposits and financial services have been loosened in recent decades in order to allow more competition among banks.

- Capital requirements are intended to ensure that banks have a cushion against any losses. The requirements have become more stringent and are risk adjusted so that banks with more risk are required to maintain a higher level of capital.

- Bank regulators monitor banks by focusing on six criteria: capital, asset quality, management, earnings, liquidity, and sensitivity to financial market conditions. The regulators assign ratings to these criteria to determine whether corrective action is necessary. When a bank is failing, the FDIC or other government agencies consider whether it can be saved. In some cases, large banks have been rescued, which has led to opposing arguments about whether a bank should be rescued just because of its size. During the credit crisis, the failures and rescues of some large financial institutions reignited the controversy.

POINT COUNTER-POINT

Should Regulators Intervene to Take Over Weak Banks?

Point Yes. Intervention could turn a bank around before weak management results in failure. Bank failures require funding from the FDIC to reimburse depositors up to the deposit insurance limit. This cost could be avoided if the bank's problems are corrected before it fails.

Counter-Point No. Regulators will not necessarily manage banks any better. Also, this would lead to ex-

cessive government intervention each time a bank experienced problems. Banks would use a very conservative management approach to avoid intervention, but this approach would not necessarily appeal to their shareholders who want high returns on their investment.

Who Is Correct? Use the Internet to learn more about this issue. Offer your own opinion on this issue.

QUESTIONS AND APPLICATIONS

1.   Regulation of Bank Sources and Uses of Funds How are a bank's balance sheet decisions regulated?

2.   Off-Balance Sheet Activities Provide examples of off-balance sheet activities. Why are regulators concerned about them?

3.   Moral Hazard and the Credit Crisis Explain why the moral hazard problem may have received so much attention during the credit crisis.

4.   FDIC Insurance What led to the establishment of FDIC insurance?

5.   Glass-Steagall Act Briefly describe the Glass-Steagall Act. Then explain how the related regulations have changed.

6.   DIDMCA Describe the main provisions of the DIDMCA that relate to deregulation.

7.   CAMELS Ratings Explain how the CAMELS ratings are used.

8.   Uniform Capital Requirements Explain how the uniform capital requirements established by the Basel Accord can discourage banks from taking excessive risk.

9.   FIRREA Explain how the Financial Institutions Reform, Recovery, and Enforcement Act (FIRREA) has resulted in increasing integration between the commercial banking industry and the savings institution industry.

10. HLTs Describe highly leveraged transactions (HLTs), and explain why a bank's exposure to HLTs is closely monitored by regulators.

11. Bank Underwriting Why might banks be even more interested in underwriting corporate debt issues

since the higher capital requirements were imposed on them?

12. Moral Hazard Explain the moral hazard problem as it relates to deposit insurance.

13. Economies of Scale How do economies of scale in banking relate to the issue of interstate banking?

14. Contagion Effects How can the financial problems of one large bank affect the market's risk evaluation of other large banks?

15. Regulating Bank Failures Why are bank regulators more concerned about a large bank failure than a small bank failure, aside from the difference in direct cost to the FDIC?

16. Financial Services Modernization Act Describe the Financial Services Modernization Act of 1999. Explain how it affected commercial bank operations and changed the competitive landscape among financial institutions.

17. Impact of SOX Act on Banks Explain how the Sarbanes-Oxley Act improved the transparency of banks. Why could the act have a negative impact on some banks?

18. Conversion of Securities Firms to BHCs Explain how the conversion of a securities firm to a bank holding company (BHC) structure might reduce its risk.

19. Capital Requirements during the Credit Crisis Explain how the accounting method applied to mortgage-backed securities made it more difficult for banks to satisfy capital requirements during the credit crisis.

20. Fed Assistance to Bear Stearns Explain why regulators might argue that the assistance that they provided to Bear Stearns was necessary.

21. Fed Aid to Nonbanks Should the Fed have the power to provide assistance to firms such as Bear Stearns that are not commercial banks?

22. Regulation of Credit Default Swaps Why were bank regulators concerned about credit default swaps during the credit crisis?

Interpreting Financial News

Interpret the following comments made by Wall Street analysts and portfolio managers:

a. "The FDIC recently subsidized a buyer for a failing bank, which had different effects on FDIC costs than if the FDIC had closed the bank."

b. "Bank of America has pursued the acquisition of many failed banks because it sees potential benefits."

c. "By allowing a failing bank time to resolve its financial problems, the FDIC imposes an additional tax on taxpayers."

Managing in Financial Markets
Effect of Bank Strategies on Bank Ratings

A bank has asked you to assess various strategies it is considering and explain how they could affect its regulatory review. Regulatory reviews include an assessment of capital, asset quality, management, earnings, liquidity, and sensitivity to financial market conditions. Many types of strategies can result in more favorable regulatory reviews based on some criteria but less favorable reviews based on other criteria. The bank is planning to issue more stock, retain more of its earnings, increase its holdings of Treasury securities, and reduce its business loans. The bank has historically been rated favorably by regulators, but believes that these strategies will result in an even more favorable regulatory assessment.

a. Which regulatory criteria will be affected by the bank's strategies? How?

b. Do you believe that the strategies planned by the bank will satisfy its shareholders? Is it possible for the bank to use strategies that would satisfy both regulators and shareholders? Explain.

c. Do you believe that the strategies planned by the bank will satisfy the bank's managers? Explain.

FLOW OF FUNDS EXERCISE

Impact of Regulation and Deregulation on Financial Services

Carson Company relies heavily on commercial banks for funding and for some other services.

a. Explain how the services provided by a commercial bank (just the banking, not the nonbank, services) to Carson may be limited due to bank regulation.

b. Explain the types of nonbank services that Carson Company can receive from the subsidiaries of a commercial bank as a result of deregulation. How might Carson Company be affected by the deregulation that allows subsidiaries of a commercial bank to offer nonbank services?

INTERNET/EXCEL EXERCISE

1. Browse the most recent Quarterly Banking Profile at www.fdic.gov/bank/analytical/index.html. Click on "Industry Analysis" and then on "Failed Banks."

Describe how regulators responded to one recent bank failure listed here.

WSJ EXERCISE

Impact of Bank Regulations

Using a recent issue of *The Wall Street Journal*, summarize an article that discussed a particular commercial bank regulation that has recently been passed or is currently being considered by regulators. (You may wish to use *The Wall Street Journal Index* in the library to identify a specific article on a commercial banking regulation or bill.) Would this regulation have a favorable or unfavorable impact on commercial banks? Explain.

19
Bank Management

CHAPTER
OBJECTIVES

The specific objectives of
this chapter are to:

■ describe the
underlying goal of
bank management,

■ explain how banks
manage liquidity,

■ explain how banks
manage interest rate
risk,

■ explain how banks
manage credit risk,
and

■ explain integrated
bank management.

The performance of any commercial bank depends on the management of the bank's assets, liabilities, and capital. Increased competition has made efficient management essential for survival.

BANK MANAGEMENT GOALS AND STRUCTURE

The underlying goal behind the managerial policies of a bank is to maximize the wealth of the bank's shareholders. Thus, bank managers should make decisions that maximize the price of the bank's stock.

In some cases, managers are tempted to make decisions that are in their own best interests rather than shareholder interests. For example, decisions that result in growth may be intended to increase employee salaries, as larger banks tend to provide more employee compensation. In addition, the compensation to a bank's loan officers may be tied to loan volume, which encourages a loan department to extend loans without concern about risk. As these examples suggest, banks can incur agency costs, or costs resulting from managers maximizing their own wealth instead of shareholder wealth. To prevent agency problems, some banks provide stock as compensation to managers. These managers may be more likely to maximize shareholder wealth because they are shareholders as well. Also, if managerial decisions conflict with the goal of maximizing shareholder wealth, the share price will not achieve its maximum. Therefore, the bank may become a takeover target, as other banks may perceive it as undervalued, with the potential to improve under their own management. In this way, managers can be disciplined to maximize shareholder wealth.

Board of Directors

A bank's board of directors oversees the operations of the bank and attempts to ensure that managerial decisions are in the best interests of the shareholders. Bank boards tend to have more directors and a higher percentage of outside directors than boards of other types of firms. Some of the more important functions of bank directors are to

- Determine a compensation system for the bank's executives.
- Ensure proper disclosure of the bank's financial condition and performance to investors.
- Oversee growth strategies such as acquisitions.
- Oversee policies for changing the capital structure, including decisions to raise capital or to engage in stock repurchases.
- Assess the bank's performance and ensure that corrective action is taken if the performance is weak due to poor management.

Bank directors are liable if they do not fulfill their duties. The Sarbanes-Oxley (SOX) Act, described in the previous chapter, has had a major effect on the monitoring conducted by the board members of commercial banks. Recall that this act requires publicly traded firms to implement a more thorough internal control process to ensure more accurate financial reporting to shareholders. As a result of the SOX Act, directors are now held more accountable for their oversight because the internal process requires them to document their assessment and opinion of key decisions made by the bank's executives. Furthermore, directors more frequently hire outside legal and financial advisers to aid in assessing key decisions (such as acquisitions) by bank executives to determine whether the decisions are justified.

Overview of Bank Management

A bank's management involves the management of its sources of funds (liabilities) and its uses of funds (assets). Its management will affect its performance (as measured from its income statement) in the following ways. First, its decisions on sources of funds will heavily influence its interest expenses on the income statement. Its asset structure will heavily influence its interest revenue on the income statement. Its asset structure also affects its expenses because an emphasis on commercial loans will result in a high labor cost for assessing loan applicants.

Management of Operations

Like any business, a bank is exposed to operating risk resulting from the bank's general business operations. Specifically, banks are subject to risk related to information (sorting, processing, transmitting through technology), execution of transactions, damaged relationships with clients, legal issues (lawsuits by employees and customers), and regulatory issues (increased costs due to new compliance requirements or penalties due to lack of compliance). While these forms of risk should be recognized, the focus of this chapter is on managing financial risk, such as liquidity risk, interest rate risk, and credit risk. The management of each type of financial risk is discussed in turn.

MANAGING LIQUIDITY

Banks can experience illiquidity when cash outflows (due to deposit withdrawals, loans, etc.) exceed cash inflows (new deposits, loan repayments, etc.). They can resolve any cash deficiency either by creating additional liabilities or by selling assets. Banks have access to various forms of borrowing, such as the federal funds market. They also maintain some assets that can readily be sold in the secondary market. The decision on how to obtain funds depends on the situation. If the need for funds is temporary, an increase in short-term liabilities (from the federal funds market) may be appropriate. If the need is permanent, however, a policy for increasing deposits or selling liquid assets may be appropriate.

Because some assets are more marketable than others, the bank's asset composition can affect its degree of liquidity. At an extreme, banks could ensure sufficient liquidity by using most of their funds to purchase Treasury securities. However, they must also be concerned with achieving a reasonable return on their assets, which often conflicts with the liquidity objective. Although Treasury securities are liquid, their yield is low relative to bank loans or investments in other securities. Recent research has shown that high-performance banks are able to maintain relatively low (but sufficient) liquidity. Banks should maintain the level of liquid assets that will satisfy their liquidity needs but use their remaining funds to satisfy their other objectives. As the secondary market for loans has become active, banks are better able to satisfy their liquidity needs with a higher proportion of loans while striving for higher profitability.

Use of Securitization to Boost Liquidity

The ability to securitize assets such as automobile and mortgage loans can enhance a bank's liquidity position. The process of securitization commonly involves the sale of assets by the bank to a trustee, who issues securities that are collateralized by the assets. The bank may still service the loans, but it passes through the interest and principal payments received to the investors who purchased the securities. Banks are more liquid as a result of securitization because they effectively convert future cash flows into immediate cash. In most cases, the process includes a guarantor who, for a fee, guarantees future payments to investors who purchased the securities. The loans that collateralize the securities normally exceed the amount of the securities issued or are backed by an additional guarantee from the bank that sells the loans.

Collateralized Loan Obligations (CLOs)   As one form of securitization, commercial banks can obtain funds by packaging their commercial loans with those of other financial institutions as collateralized loan obligations (CLOs) and then selling securities that represent ownership of these loans. The banks earn a fee for selling these loans.. The pool of loans might be perceived to be less risky than a typical individual loan within the pool because the loans were provided to a diversified set of borrowers. The securities that are issued to investors who invest in the loan pool represent various classes. For example, one class of notes issued to investors may be BB-rated notes, which offer an interest rate of LIBOR (London Interbank Offer Rate) plus 3.5 percent. If there are loan defaults by the corporate borrowers whose loans are in the pool, this group of investors will be the first to suffer losses. Another class may consist of BBB-rated notes that offer a slightly lower interest rate. Investors in these notes are slightly less exposed to defaults on the loans. The AAA-rated notes offer investors the most protection against loan defaults but provide the lowest interest rate, such as LIBOR plus .25 percent. Insurance companies and pension funds are common investors in CLOs.

Banks learned during the credit crisis that all AAA-rated CLOs are not risk-free. Their CLOs experienced substantial defaults in 2008. The AAA rating was apparently based on an assumption of much better economic conditions than the crisis conditions that occurred in the second half of 2008.

Liquidity Problems

There have been many cases of banks experiencing liquidity problems. However, the liquidity problems are typically preceded by other financial problems such as major defaults on their loans. Healthy banks tend to have easy access to liquidity. A bank that is performing poorly has less ability to obtain short-term funds because it may not be able to repay the credit that it desires.

MANAGING INTEREST RATE RISK

The performance of a bank is highly influenced by the interest payments earned on its assets relative to the interest paid on its liabilities (deposits). The difference between interest payments received versus interest paid is measured by the **net interest margin** (also referred to sometimes as "spread"):

$$\text{Net interest margin} = \frac{\text{Interest revenues} - \text{Interest expenses}}{\text{Assets}}$$

In some cases, net interest margin is defined to include only the earning assets, excluding any assets that do not generate a return to the bank (such as required reserves). Because the rate sensitivity of a bank's liabilities normally does not perfectly match that of the assets, the net interest margin changes over time. The change depends on whether bank assets are more or less rate sensitive than bank liabilities, the degree of difference in rate sensitivity, and the direction of interest rate movements.

The composition of a bank's balance sheet will determine how its profitability is influenced by interest rate fluctuations. If a bank expects interest rates to consistently decrease over time, it will consider allocating most of its funds to rate-insensitive assets, such as long-term and medium-term loans (all with fixed rates) as well as long-term securities. These assets will continue to provide the same periodic yield. As interest rates decline, the bank's cost of funds will decrease, and its overall return will increase.

If a bank expects interest rates to consistently increase over time, it will consider allocating most of its funds to rate-sensitive assets such as short-term commercial and consumer loans, long-term loans with floating interest rates, and short-term securities. The short-term instruments will mature soon, so reinvestment will be at a higher rate if interest rates increase. The longer-term instruments will continue to exist, so the bank will benefit from rising interest rates only if it uses floating rates.

During a period of rising interest rates, a bank's net interest margin will likely decrease if its liabilities are more rate sensitive than its assets, as illustrated in Exhibit 19.1. Under the opposite scenario, where market interest rates are declining over time, rates offered on new bank deposits, as well as those earned on new bank loans, will be affected by the decline in interest rates. The deposit rates will typically be more sensitive if their turnover is quicker, as illustrated in Exhibit 19.2.

To manage interest rate risk, a bank measures the risk and then uses its assessment of future interest rates to decide whether and how to hedge the risk. Methods of assessing the risk are described next, followed by a discussion of the hedging decision and methods of reducing interest rate risk.

Methods Used to Assess Interest Rate Risk

No method of measuring interest rate risk is perfect, so commercial banks use a variety of methods to assess their exposure to interest rate movements. The following are the most common methods of measuring interest rate risk:

- Gap analysis
- Duration analysis
- Regression analysis

Exhibit 19.1 Impact of Increasing Interest Rates on a Bank's Net Interest Margin (If the Bank's Liabilities Are More Rate Sensitive Than Its Assets)

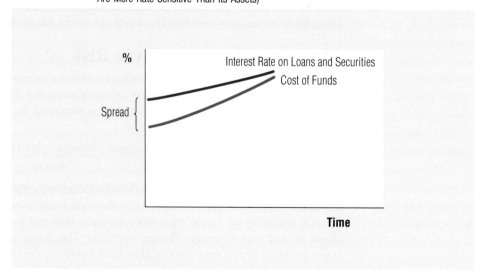

Exhibit 19.2 Impact of Decreasing Interest Rates on a Bank's Net Interest Margin (If the Bank's Liabilities Are More Rate Sensitive Than Its Assets)

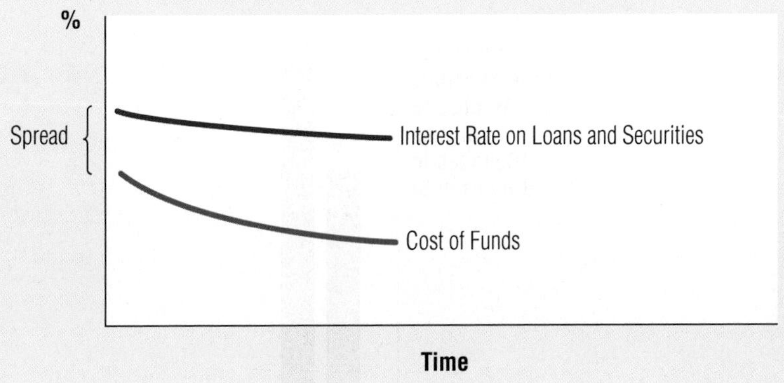

Gap Analysis   Banks can attempt to determine their interest rate risk by monitoring their **gap** over time, defined here as

$$\text{Gap} = \text{Rate-sensitive assets} - \text{Rate-sensitive liabilities}$$

An alternative formula is the **gap ratio,** which is measured as the volume of rate-sensitive assets divided by rate-sensitive liabilities. A gap of zero (or gap ratio of 1.00) indicates that rate-sensitive assets equal rate-sensitive liabilities, so the net interest margin should not be significantly influenced by interest rate fluctuations. A negative gap (or gap ratio of less than 1.00) indicates that rate-sensitive liabilities exceed rate-sensitive assets. Banks with a negative gap are typically concerned about a potential increase in interest rates, which could reduce their net interest margin.

EXAMPLE

Kansas City (K.C.) Bank had interest revenues of $80 million last year and $35 million in interest expenses. About $400 million of its $1 billion in assets are rate sensitive, while $700 million of its liabilities are rate sensitive. K.C. Bank's net interest margin is

$$\text{Net interest margin} = (\$80,000,000 - \$35,000,000)/\$1,000,000,000$$
$$= .045, \text{ or } 4.5\%$$

K.C. Bank's gap is

$$\text{Gap} = \$400,000,000 - \$700,000,000$$
$$= -\$300,000,000$$

K.C. Bank's gap ratio is

$$\text{Gap ratio} = \$400,000,000/\$700,000,000$$
$$= .5714, \text{ or } 57.14\%$$

Based on the gap analysis of K.C. Bank, an increase in market interest rates would cause its net interest margin to decline from its recent level of 4.5 percent. Conversely, a decrease in interest rates would cause its net interest margin to increase above 4.5 percent. ●

Exhibit 19.3 Interest-Sensitive Assets and Liabilities: Illustration of the Gap Measured for Various Maturity Ranges for Deacon Bank

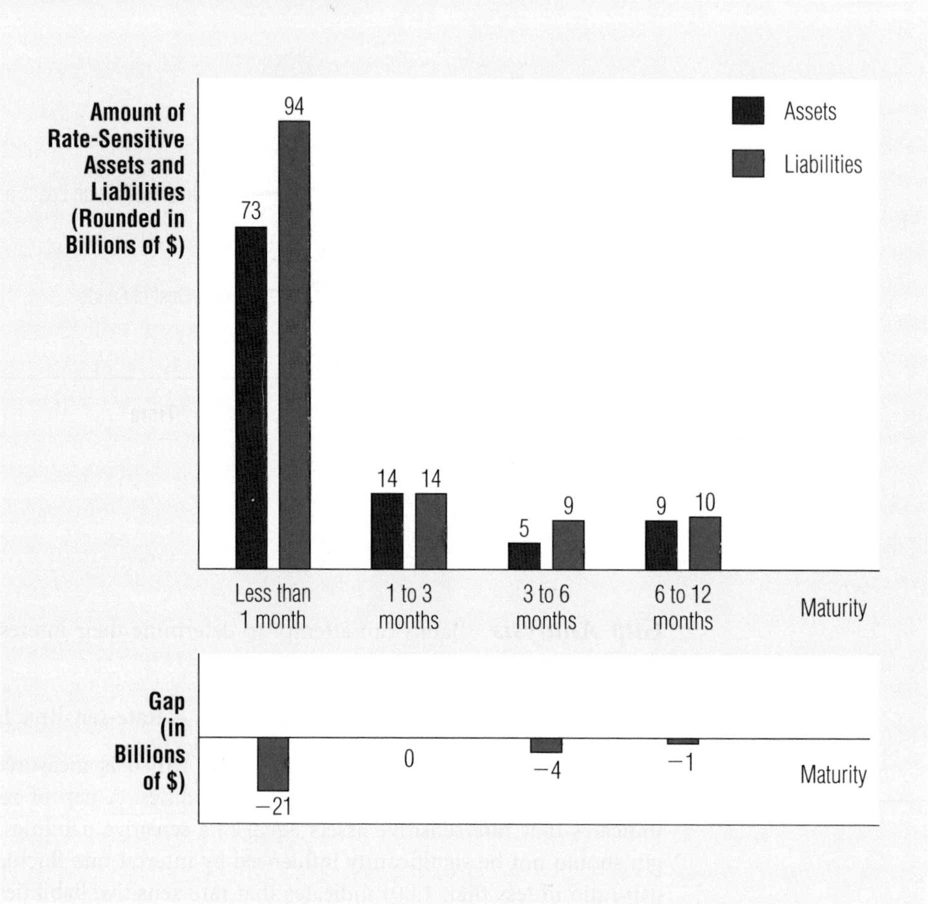

Many banks classify interest-sensitive assets and liabilities into various categories based on the time of repricing. Then the bank can determine the gap in each category so that its exposure to interest rate risk can be assessed.

EXAMPLE

Deacon Bank compares the interest rate sensitivity of its assets versus its liabilities as shown in Exhibit 19.3. It has a negative gap in the less-than-1-month maturity range, the 3- to 6-month range, and the 6- to 12-month range. Thus, the bank may hedge this gap if it believes that interest rates are rising. ●

Although the gap as described here is an easy method for measuring a bank's interest rate risk, it has limitations. Banks must decide how to classify their liabilities and assets as rate sensitive versus rate insensitive. For example, should a Treasury security with a year to maturity be classified as rate sensitive or rate insensitive? How short must a maturity be to qualify for the rate-sensitive classification?

Each bank may have its own classification system, because there is no perfect measurement of the gap. Whatever system is used, there is a possibility that the measurement will be misinterpreted.

EXAMPLE

Spencer Bank obtains much of its funds by issuing CDs with seven-day and one-month maturities as well as money market deposit accounts (MMDAs). Assume that it typically uses these funds to provide loans with a floating rate, adjusted once per year. These sources of funds and uses of funds will likely be classified as rate sensitive. Thus, the gap will be close to zero, implying that the bank is not exposed to interest rate risk. Yet, there is a difference in the degree of rate sensitivity between the bank's sources and uses of funds. The rates paid by the bank on its sources of funds will change more frequently than the rates earned on its uses of funds. Thus, Spencer Bank's net interest margin would likely be reduced during periods of rising interest rates. This exposure would not be detected by the gap measurement. ●

Duration Measurement   An alternative approach to assessing interest rate risk is to measure duration. Some assets or liabilities are more rate sensitive than others, even if the frequency of adjustment and the maturity are the same. A 10-year zero-coupon bond is more sensitive to interest rate fluctuations than a 10-year bond that pays coupon payments. Thus, the market value of assets in a bank that has invested in zero-coupon bonds will be very susceptible to interest rate movements. The duration measurement can capture these different degrees of sensitivity. In recent years, banks and other financial institutions have used the concept of **duration** to measure the sensitivity of their assets to interest rate movements. There are various measurements for an asset's duration; one of the more common is

$$DUR = \frac{\sum_{t=1}^{n} \frac{C_t(t)}{(1+k)^t}}{\sum_{t=1}^{n} \frac{C_t}{(1+k)^t}}$$

where C_t represents the interest or principal payments of the asset, t is the time at which the payments are provided, and k is the required rate of return on the asset, which reflects the asset's yield to maturity. The duration of each type of bank asset can be determined, and the duration of the asset portfolio is the weighted average (based on the relative proportion invested in each asset) of the durations of the individual assets.

The duration of each type of bank liability can also be estimated; the duration of the portfolio is estimated as the weighted average of the durations of the liabilities. The bank can then estimate its **duration gap,** which is commonly measured as the difference between the weighted duration of the bank's assets and the weighted duration of its liabilities, adjusted for the firm's asset size:

$$DURGAP = \frac{(DURAS \times AS)}{AS} - \frac{(DURLIAB \times LIAB)}{AS}$$
$$= DURAS - [DURLIAB \times (LIAB/AS)]$$

where DURAS is the average duration of the bank's assets, DURLIAB is the weighted average of the bank's liabilities, AS represents the market value of the assets, and LIAB represents the market value of the liabilities. A duration gap of zero suggests that the bank's value should be insensitive to interest rate movements, meaning that the bank is not exposed to interest rate risk. For most banks, the average duration of assets exceeds the average duration of liabilities, so the duration gap is positive. This implies that the market value of the bank's assets is more sensitive to interest rate movements than the value of its liabilities because the asset durations are higher on average. Thus, if interest rates rise, banks with positive duration gaps will be adversely affected. Conversely, if interest rates decline, banks with positive duration gaps will benefit. The larger the duration gap, the more sensitive the bank should be to interest rate movements.

Other things being equal, assets with shorter maturities have shorter durations; also, assets that generate more frequent coupon payments have shorter durations than those that generate less frequent payments. Banks and other financial institutions concerned with interest rate risk use duration to compare the rate sensitivity of their entire asset and liability portfolios. Because duration is especially critical for a savings institution's operations, a numerical example showing the measurement of the duration of a savings institution's entire asset and liability portfolio is provided in Chapter 21.

Although duration is a valuable technique for comparing the rate sensitivity of various securities, its capabilities are limited when applied to assets that can be terminated on a moment's notice. For example, consider a bank that offers a fixed-rate five-year loan that can be paid off early without penalty. If the loan is not paid off early, it is perceived as rate insensitive. Yet, there is the possibility that the loan will be terminated anytime over the five-year period. In this case, the bank would reinvest the funds at a rate dependent on market rates at that time. Thus, the funds used to provide the loan *can* be sensitive to interest rate movements, but the degree of sensitivity depends on when the loan is paid off. In general, loan prepayments are more common when market rates decline, because borrowers refinance by obtaining lower-rate loans to pay off existing loans. The point here is that the possibility of prepayment makes it impossible to perfectly match the rate sensitivity of assets and liabilities.

Regression Analysis   Gap analysis and duration analysis are based on the bank's balance sheet composition. Alternatively, a bank can assess interest rate risk by simply determining how performance has historically been influenced by interest rate movements. To do this, a proxy must be identified for bank performance and for prevailing interest rates, and a model that can estimate the relationship between the proxies must be chosen. A common proxy for performance is return on assets, return on equity, or the percentage change in stock price. To determine how performance is affected by interest rates, regression analysis can be applied to historical data. For example, using an interest rate proxy called i, the S&P 500 stock index as the market, and the bank's stock return (R) as the performance proxy, the following regression model could be used:

$$R = B_0 + B_1 R_m + B_2 i + \mu$$

where R_m is the return on the market; B_0, B_1, and B_2 are regression coefficients; and μ is an error term. The regression coefficient B_2 in this model can also be called the interest rate coefficient, because it measures the sensitivity of the bank's performance to interest rate movements. A positive (negative) coefficient suggests that performance is favorably (adversely) affected by rising interest rates. If the interest rate coefficient is not significantly different from zero, this suggests that the bank's stock returns are insulated from interest rate movements.

Models similar to that just described have been tested for the portfolio of all publicly traded banks to determine whether bank stock levels are affected by interest rate movements. The vast majority of this research has found that bank stock levels are inversely related to interest rate movements (the B_2 coefficient is negative and significant). These results can be attributed to the common imbalance between a bank's rate-sensitive liabilities and its assets. Because banks tend to have a negative gap (their liabilities are more rate sensitive than their assets), rising interest rates reduce bank performance. These results are generalized for the banking industry and do not apply to every bank.

Because a bank's assets and liabilities are replaced over time, exposure to interest rate risk must be continually reassessed. As exposure changes, the reaction of bank performance to a particular interest rate pattern will change.

When a bank uses regression analysis to determine its sensitivity to interest rate movements, it may combine this analysis with the so-called value-at-risk (VAR) method to determine how its market value would change in response to specific interest rate movements. The VAR method can be applied by combining a probability distribution of interest rate movements with the interest rate coefficient (measured from the regression analysis) to determine a maximum expected loss due to adverse interest rate movements. For example, if the bank determines from applying the regression model to monthly data that its interest rate regression coefficient is −2.4, this implies that for a 1 percentage point increase in interest rates, the value of the bank would decline by 2.4 percent. Assume that the bank determines at the 99 percent confidence level that the change in the interest rate should be no worse than an increase of 2.0 percent. For a 2 percentage point increase, the value of the bank is expected to decline by 4.8 percent (computed as 2.0 percent multiplied by the regression coefficient of −2.4). Thus, the maximum expected loss due to interest rate movements (based on a 99 percent confidence level) is a 4.8 percent loss in market value.

Whether to Hedge Interest Rate Risk

A bank can consider its measurement of its interest rate risk along with its forecast of interest rate movements to determine whether it should consider hedging its risk. The general conclusions resulting from a bank's analysis of its interest rate risk are presented in Exhibit 19.4. This exhibit shows the three methods that are commonly used by banks to measure their interest rate risk. Since none of these measures is perfect for all situations, some banks measure interest rate risk using all three methods. Other banks prefer just one of the methods. The use of any method along with an interest rate forecast can help a bank determine whether it should consider hedging its interest rate risk. However, since interest rate movements cannot always be accurately forecasted, banks should not be overly aggressive in attempting to capitalize on interest rate forecasts. They should assess the sensitivity of their future performance to each possible interest rate scenario that could occur to ensure that they can survive any possible scenario.

In general, the three methods of measuring interest rate risk should lead to a similar conclusion. If a bank has a negative gap, its average asset duration is probably larger than its liability duration (positive duration gap), and its past performance level is probably inversely related to interest rate movements. If a bank recently revised the composition of its assets or liabilities, it may wish to focus on the gap or the duration gap, as regression analysis is based on a historical relationship that may no longer exist. Banks can use their analysis of gap along with their forecast of interest rates to make their hedging decision. If banks decide to hedge their interest rate risk, they must consider the methods of hedging, which are described next.

Methods Used to Reduce Interest Rate Risk

Interest rate risk can be reduced by

- Maturity matching
- Using floating-rate loans
- Using interest rate futures contracts
- Using interest rate swaps
- Using interest rate caps

Maturity Matching One obvious method of reducing interest rate risk is to match each deposit's maturity with an asset of the same maturity. For example, if the bank receives funds for a one-year CD, it could provide a one-year loan or invest in a security with a one-year maturity. Although this strategy would avoid interest rate risk, it cannot be implemented effectively. Banks receive a large volume of short-term deposits and would not be able to match up maturities on deposits with the longer loan maturities. Borrowers rarely request funds for a period as short as one month or even six months. In addition, the deposit amounts are typically small relative to the loan amounts. A bank would have difficulty combining deposits with a particular maturity to accommodate a loan request with the same maturity.

Exhibit 19.4 Framework for Managing Interest Rate Risk

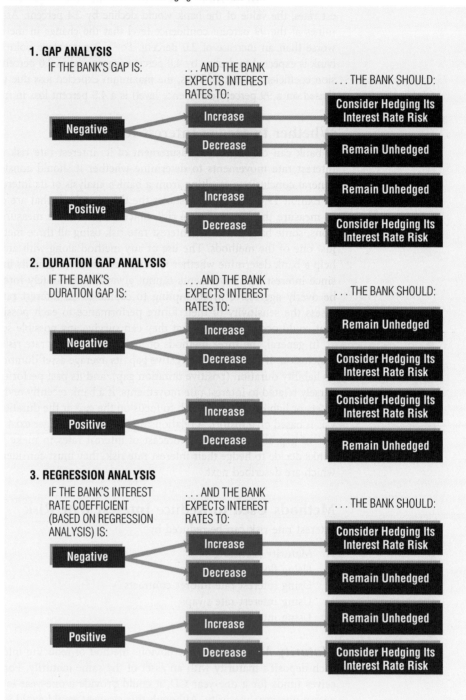

Using Floating-Rate Loans An alternative solution is to use floating-rate loans, which allow banks to support long-term assets with short-term deposits without overly exposing themselves to interest rate risk. Floating-rate loans cannot, however, completely eliminate the risk. If the cost of funds is changing more frequently than the rate on assets, the bank's net interest margin is still affected by interest rate fluctuations.

When banks reduce their exposure to interest rate risk by replacing long-term securities with more floating-rate commercial loans, they increase their exposure to credit risk, because the commercial loans provided by banks typically have a higher frequency of default than the securities they hold. In addition, bank liquidity risk would increase, because loans are not as marketable as securities.

Using Interest Rate Futures Contracts Large banks frequently use interest rate futures and other types of derivative instruments to hedge interest rate risk. A common method of reducing interest rate risk is to use interest rate futures contracts, which lock in the price at which specified financial instruments can be purchased or sold on a specified future settlement date. Recall that the sale of a futures contract on Treasury bonds prior to an increase in interest rates will result in a gain, because an identical futures contract can be purchased later at a lower price once interest rates rise. Thus, a gain on the Treasury bond futures contracts can offset the adverse effects of higher interest rates on a bank's performance. The size of the bank's position in Treasury bond futures is dependent on the size of its asset portfolio, the degree of its exposure to interest rate movements, and its forecasts of future interest rate movements.

Exhibit 19.5 illustrates how the use of financial futures contracts can reduce the uncertainty about a bank's net interest margin. The sale of CD futures, for example, reduces the potential adverse effect of rising interest rates on the bank's interest expenses. Yet, it also reduces the potential favorable effect of declining interest rates on the bank's interest

Exhibit 19.5 Effect of Financial Futures on the Net Interest Margin of Banks That Have More Rate-Sensitive Liabilities Than Assets

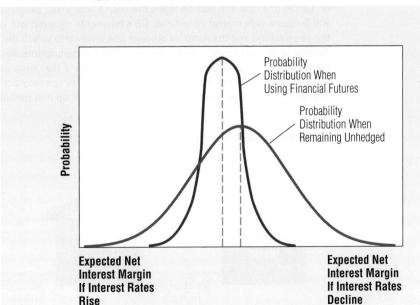

expenses. Assuming that the bank initially had more rate-sensitive liabilities, its use of futures would reduce the impact of interest rates on its net interest margin.

Using Interest Rate Swaps   Commercial banks can hedge interest rate risk by engaging in an interest rate swap, which is an arrangement to exchange periodic cash flows based on specified interest rates. A fixed-for-floating swap allows one party to periodically exchange fixed cash flows for cash flows that are based on prevailing market interest rates.

A bank whose liabilities are more rate sensitive than its assets can swap payments with a fixed interest rate in exchange for payments with a variable interest rate over a specified period of time. If interest rates rise, the bank benefits because the payments to be received from the swap will increase while its outflow payments are fixed. This can offset the adverse impact of rising interest rates on the bank's net interest margin. In 2004, interest rates were unusually low, causing banks to take swap positions that protected against a possible increase in interest rates. These banks benefited from their swap positions as interest rates rose in the 2005–2007 period.

An interest rate swap requires another party that is willing to provide variable-rate payments in exchange for fixed-rate payments. Financial institutions that have more rate-sensitive assets than liabilities may be willing to assume such a position, because they could reduce their exposure to interest rate movements in this manner. A financial intermediary is typically needed to match up the two parties that desire an interest rate swap. Some securities firms and large commercial banks serve in this role.

EXAMPLE   Assume that Denver Bank (DB) has large holdings of 11 percent fixed-rate loans. Because its sources of funds are mostly interest rate sensitive, DB desires to swap fixed-rate payments in exchange for variable-rate payments. It informs Colorado Bank of its situation, because it knows that this bank commonly engages in swap transactions. Colorado Bank searches for a client and finds that Brit Eurobank desires to swap variable-rate dollar payments in exchange for fixed dollar payments. Colorado Bank then develops the swap arrangement illustrated in Exhibit 19.6. DB will swap fixed-rate payments in exchange for variable-rate payments based on LIBOR (the rate charged on loans between Eurobanks). Because the variable-rate payments will fluctuate with market conditions, DB's payments received will vary over time. The length of the swap period and the notional amount (the amount to which the interest rates are applied to determine the payments) can be structured to the participants desires'. Colorado Bank, the financial intermediary conducting the swap, charges a fee, such as .1 percent of the notional amount per year. Some financial intermediaries for swaps may act as the counterparty and exchange the payments desired, rather than just match up two parties.

Exhibit 19.6 Illustration of an Interest Rate Swap

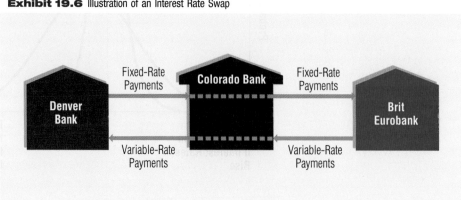

Exhibit 19.7 Comparison of Denver Bank's Spread: Unhedged versus Hedged

	POSSIBLE LIBOR RATES IN THE FUTURE					
UNHEDGED STRATEGY	7%	8%	9%	10%	11%	12%
Average rate on existing mortgages	11%	11%	11%	11%	11%	11%
Average cost of deposits	6	7	8	9	10	11
Spread	5	4	3	2	1	0
HEDGING WITH AN INTEREST RATE SWAP						
Fixed interest rate earned on fixed-rate mortgages	11	11	11	11	11	11
Fixed interest rate owed on swap arrangement	9	9	9	9	9	9
Spread on fixed-rate payments	2	2	2	2	2	2
Variable interest rate earned on swap arrangement	7	8	9	10	11	12
Variable interest rate owed on deposits	6	7	8	9	10	11
Spread on variable-rate payments	1	1	1	1	1	1
Combined total spread when using the swap	3	3	3	3	3	3

Now assume that the fixed payments to be paid are based on a fixed rate of 9 percent. Also assume that LIBOR is initially 7 percent and that DB's cost of funds is 6 percent. Exhibit 19.7 shows how DB's spread is affected by various possible interest rates when unhedged versus when hedged with an interest rate swap. If LIBOR remains at 7 percent, DB's spread would be 5 percent if unhedged and only 3 percent when using a swap. However, if LIBOR increases beyond 9 percent, the spread when using the swap exceeds the unhedged spread because the higher cost of funds causes a lower unhedged spread. The swap arrangement would provide DB with increased payments that offset the higher cost of funds. The advantage of a swap is that it can lock in the spread to be earned on existing assets, or at least reduce the possible variability of the spread. ●

When interest rates decrease, a bank's outflow payments would exceed inflow payments on a swap. However, the spread between the interest rates received on existing fixed-rate loans and those paid on deposits should increase, offsetting the net outflow from the swap. During periods of declining interest rates, fixed-rate loans are often prepaid, which could result in a net outflow from the swap without any offsetting effect.

Using Interest Rate Caps   An alternative method of hedging interest rate risk is an interest rate cap, an agreement (for a fee) to receive payments when the interest rate of a particular security or index rises above a specified level during a specified time period. Various financial intermediaries (such as commercial banks and brokerage firms) offer interest rate caps. During periods of rising interest rates, the cap provides compensation, which can offset the reduction in the spread during such periods.

International Interest Rate Risk

When a bank has foreign currency balances, the strategy of matching the overall interest rate sensitivity of assets to that of liabilities will not automatically achieve a low degree of interest rate risk.

EXAMPLE

California Bank has deposits denominated mostly in euros, while its floating-rate loans are denominated mostly in dollars. It matches its average deposit maturity with its average loan maturity. However, the difference in currency denominations creates interest rate risk. The deposit and loan rates are dependent on the interest rate movements of the respective currencies. The performance of California Bank will be adversely affected if the interest rate on the euro increases and the U.S. interest rate decreases. ●

Even though a bank matches the mix of currencies in its assets and its liabilities, it can still be exposed to interest rate risk if the rate sensitivities differ between assets and liabilities for each currency.

Oklahoma Bank uses its dollar deposits to make dollar loans and its euro deposits to make euro loans. It has short-term dollar deposits and uses the funds to make long-term dollar loans. It also has medium- and long-term fixed-rate deposits in euros and uses those funds to make euro loans with adjustable rates. An increase in U.S. rates will reduce the spread on Oklahoma Bank's dollar loans versus deposits, because the dollar liabilities are more rate sensitive than the dollar assets. In addition, a decline in interest rates on the euro will decrease the spread on the euro loans versus deposits, because the euro assets are more rate sensitive than the euro liabilities. Thus, exposure to interest rate risk can be minimized only if the rate sensitivities of assets and liabilities are matched for each currency. ●

Managing Credit Risk

Most of a bank's funds are used either to make loans or to purchase debt securities. For either use of funds, the bank is acting as a creditor and is subject to credit (default) risk, or the possibility that credit provided by the bank will not be repaid. The types of loans provided and the securities purchased will determine the overall credit risk of the asset portfolio. A bank can also be exposed to credit risk if it serves as a guarantor on interest rate swaps and other derivative contracts in which it is the intermediary.

Measuring Credit Risk

An important part of managing credit risk is to measure it. This requires a credit assessment of loan applicants. Banks employ credit analysts who review the financial information of corporations applying for loans and evaluate their creditworthiness. The evaluation should indicate the probability that a firm can meet its loan payments so that the bank can decide whether to grant the loan.

Determining the Collateral   When a bank assesses a request for credit, it must decide whether to require collateral that can back the loan in the event that the borrower is unable to make the payments. For example, if a firm applies for a loan to purchase machinery, the loan agreement may specify that the machinery will serve as collateral. When a bank serves as an intermediary and a guarantor on derivative contracts, it commonly attempts to require collateral such as securities owned by the client.

Determining the Loan Rate   If the bank decides to grant the loan, it can use its evaluation of the firm to determine the appropriate interest rate. Loan applicants deserving of a loan may be rated on a basis of 1 to 5 (1 being the highest quality), reflecting their degree of credit risk. The rating dictates the premium to be added to the base rate. For example, a rating of 5 may dictate a 2 percentage point premium above the prime rate (the rate a bank offers to its most creditworthy customers), while a rating of 3 may dictate a 1 percentage point premium. Given the current prime rate along with the rating of the potential borrower, the loan rate can be determined.

Some loans to high-quality (low-risk) customers are commonly offered at rates below the prime rate. This does not necessarily mean that the bank has reduced its spread. It may instead imply that the bank has redefined the prime rate to represent the appropriate loan rate for borrowers with a moderate risk rating. Thus, a discount would be attached to the prime rate when determining the loan rate for borrowers with a superior rating.

Tradeoff between Credit Risk and Return

If a bank wants to minimize credit risk, it can use most of its funds to purchase Treasury securities, which are virtually free of credit risk. However, these securities may not generate a much higher yield than the average overall cost of obtaining funds. In fact, some bank sources of funds can be more costly to banks than the yield earned on Treasury securities.

At the other extreme, a bank concerned with maximizing its return could use most of its funds to provide credit card and consumer loans. While this strategy may allow a bank to achieve a high return, these types of loans experience more defaults than other types of loans. Thus, the bank may experience high loan losses, which could offset the high interest payments it received from those loans that were repaid. A bank that pursues the high potential returns associated with credit card loans or other loans that generate relatively high interest payments must accept a high degree of credit risk. Because riskier assets offer higher returns, a bank's strategy to increase its return on assets will typically entail an increase in the overall credit risk of its asset portfolio. Thus, a bank's decision to create a very safe versus a moderate or high-risk asset portfolio is dependent on its risk-return preferences.

Expected Return and Risk of Subprime Mortgage Loans   Many commercial banks aggressively funded subprime mortgage loans in the 2004–2006 period by originating the mortgages or purchasing mortgage-backed securities that represented subprime mortgages. The banks pursuing this strategy expected that they would earn a relatively high interest rate compared to prime mortgages and that the subprime mortgages would have low default risk because the home serves as collateral. What the banks did not anticipate was that a credit crisis would occur in the 2008–2009 period and that the value of many homes would decline far below the amount owed on the mortgage. The banks were forced to initiate mortgage foreclosures and sell the homes at a large discount in the weak housing market. Alternatively, some banks worked out arrangements with homeowners who were behind in their mortgage payments, but the banks had to provide more favorable terms so that the homeowners could afford the mortgage. Banks incurred major expenses from these arrangements. The lesson from the subprime mortgage situation is that when banks use loan strategies to achieve relatively high returns, they must recognize the risk from those strategies.

Reducing Credit Risk

Although all consumer and commercial loans exhibit some credit risk, banks can use several methods to reduce this risk.

Industry Diversification of Loans   Banks should diversity their loans to ensure that their customers are not dependent on a common source of income. For example, a bank in a small farming town that provides consumer loans to farmers and commercial loans to farm equipment manufacturers is highly susceptible to credit risk. If the farmers experience a bad growing season because of poor weather conditions, they may be unable to repay their consumer loans. Furthermore, the farm equipment manufacturers would simultaneously experience a drop in sales and may be unable to repay their commercial loans.

When a bank's loans are too heavily concentrated in a specific industry, it should attempt to expand its loans into other industries. In this way, if one particular industry experiences weakness (which will lead to loan defaults by firms in that industry), loans provided to other industries will be insulated from that industry's conditions. However, a bank's loan portfolio may still be subject to high credit risk even though its loans are diversified across industries.

International Diversification of Loans   Many banks reduce their exposure to U.S. economic conditions by diversifying their loan portfolio internationally. They use a country risk assessment system to assess country characteristics that may influence the ability of a government or corporation to repay its debt. In particular, the country risk assessment focuses on a country's financial and political conditions. Banks tend to focus on countries to which they have assigned a high rating. Once a bank establishes a branch in a foreign country, however, it is committed to international loans in that country. After extending loans, a bank cannot recall them just because country conditions have deteriorated.

Diversifying loans across countries can often reduce the loan portfolio's exposure to any single economy or event. If diversification across geographic regions means that the bank must accept loan applicants with very high risk, however, the bank is defeating its purpose. Furthermore, international diversification does not necessarily avoid adverse economic conditions. The credit crisis adversely affected most countries and therefore affected the ability of borrowers around the world to repay their loans.

Selling Loans   Banks can eliminate loans that are causing excessive risk to their loan portfolios by selling them in the secondary market. Most loan sales enable the bank originating the loan to continue servicing the loan by collecting payments and monitoring the borrower's collateral. However, the bank that originated the loan is no longer funding the loan, and the loan is therefore removed from the bank's assets. Bank loans are commonly purchased by other banks and some other financial institutions, such as pension funds and insurance companies, and some mutual funds.

Revising the Loan Portfolio in Response to Economic Conditions   Banks continuously assess both the overall composition of their loan portfolios and the economic environment. As economic conditions change, so does the risk of a bank's loan portfolio. A bank is typically more willing to extend loans during strong economic conditions, since businesses are more likely to meet their loan payments under those conditions. During weak economic conditions, the bank is more cautious and reduces the amount of new loans that are extended to businesses. Under these conditions, the bank typically increases the credit it extends to the Treasury by purchasing more Treasury securities. Nevertheless, its loan portfolio may still be heavily exposed to economic conditions because some of the businesses that have already borrowed may be unable to repay their loans.

Ideally, banks would use an aggressive approach when they can capitalize on favorable economic conditions but insulate themselves during adverse economic conditions. Economic conditions cannot always be accurately forecasted for several years in advance, however, so even well-managed banks will experience defaults on loans. This is a cost of doing business.

MANAGING MARKET RISK

From a bank management perspective, market risk results from changes in the value of securities due to changes in financial market conditions such as interest rate movements, exchange rate movements, and equity prices. As banks pursue new services related to the trading of securities, they have become much more susceptible to market risk. For example, some banks now provide loans to special partnerships called hedge funds, which use the borrowed funds to invest in stocks or derivative securities. Thus, these loans may not be repaid if the prices of the stocks or derivative securities held by the hedge funds decline substantially.

The increase in banks' exposure to market risk is also attributed to their increased participation in the trading of derivative contracts. Many banks now serve as intermediaries between firms that take positions in derivative securities and will be exchanging payments in the future. For some of these transactions, a bank serves as a guarantor to one of the parties if the counterparty in the transaction does not fulfill its payment obligation. If derivative security prices change abruptly and cause several parties involved in these transactions to default, a bank that served as a guarantor will suffer major losses. Furthermore, banks that purchase debt securities issued in developing countries are subject to abrupt losses as a result of abrupt swings in the economic or currency conditions in those countries.

The need to monitor the positions of banks with substantial trading businesses was reinforced by the shocking $488 million loss reported by Bankers Trust (now part of Deutsche Bank) in October 1998. The loss was attributed to markdowns on Russian and Latin American debt securities held by Bankers Trust, adverse currency movements, and a reduction in its securities underwriting business. If Bankers Trust had been using a system that monitored the market values of its positions on a daily basis, it might have been able to reduce its losses.

Measuring Market Risk

Banks commonly measure their exposure to market risk by applying the value-at-risk (VAR) method, which involves determining the largest possible loss that would occur as a result of changes in market prices based on a specified percent confidence level. To estimate this loss, the bank first determines an adverse scenario (such as a 20 percent decline in derivative security prices) that has a 1 percent chance of occurring. Then it estimates the impact of that scenario on its investment or loan positions, based on the sensitivity of the values of its investments to the scenario. All of the losses that would occur from its existing positions are summed to determine the estimated total loss to the bank under this scenario. This estimate reflects the largest possible loss at the 99 percent confidence level, as there is only a 1-in-100 chance that such an unfavorable scenario would occur. By determining its exposure to market risk, the bank can ensure that it has sufficient capital to cushion against the adverse effects of such an event.

Bank Revisions of Market Risk Measurements   Banks continually revise their estimate of market risk in response to changes in their investment and credit positions and to changes in market conditions. When market prices become more volatile, banks recognize that market prices could change to a greater degree and typically increase their estimate of their potential losses due to market conditions.

Relationship between a Bank's Market Risk and Interest Rate Risk   A bank's market risk is partially dependent on its exposure to interest rate risk. Banks give special attention to interest rate risk, however, because it is commonly the most important component of market risk. Moreover, many banks assess interest rate risk by itself when evaluating their positions over a longer time horizon. For example, a bank might assess interest rate risk by itself over the next year using the methods described earlier in the chapter. In this case, the bank might use the assessment to alter the maturities on the deposits it attempts to obtain or on its uses of funds. Conversely, banks' assessment of market risk tends to be focused on a shorter-term horizon, such as the next month. Nevertheless, they may still use their assessment of market risk to alter their operations, as explained next.

Methods Used to Reduce Market Risk

If a bank determines that its exposure to market risk is excessive, it can reduce its involvement in the activities that cause the high exposure. For example, it could reduce the amount of transactions in which it serves as guarantor for its clients or reduce its investment in foreign debt securities that are subject to adverse events in a specific region. Alternatively, it could attempt to take some trading positions to offset some of its exposure to market risk. It could also sell some of its securities that are heavily exposed to market risk.

INTEGRATED BANK MANAGEMENT

WEB

www.fdic.gov
Statistical overview of
how banks have performed in recent years.

Bank management of assets, liabilities, and capital is integrated. A bank's asset growth can be achieved only if it obtains the necessary funds. Furthermore, growth may require an investment in fixed assets (such as additional offices) that will require an accumulation of bank capital. Integration of asset, liability, and capital management ensures that all policies will be consistent with a cohesive set of economic forecasts. An integrated management approach is necessary to manage liquidity risk, interest rate risk, and credit risk.

Application

Assume that you are hired as a consultant by Atlanta Bank to evaluate its favorable and unfavorable aspects. Atlanta Bank's balance sheet is shown in Exhibit 19.8. A bank's balance sheet can best be evaluated by converting the actual dollar amounts of balance sheet components to a percentage of assets. This conversion enables the bank to be compared with its competitors. Exhibit 19.9 shows each balance sheet component as a percentage of total assets for Atlanta Bank (derived from Exhibit 19.8). To the right of each bank percentage is the assumed industry average percentage for a sample of banks with a similar amount of assets. For example, the bank's required reserves are 4 percent of assets (the same as the industry average), its floating-rate commercial loans are 30 percent of assets (versus an industry average of 20 percent), and so on. The same type of comparison is provided for liabilities and capital on the right side of the exhibit. A comparative analysis relative to the industry can indicate the management style of Atlanta Bank.

It is possible to evaluate the potential level of interest revenues, interest expenses, noninterest revenues, and noninterest expenses for Atlanta Bank relative to the industry. Furthermore, it is possible to assess the bank's exposure to credit risk and interest rate risk as compared to the industry.

A summary of Atlanta Bank based on the information in Exhibit 19.9 is provided in Exhibit 19.10. Although its interest expenses are expected to be above the industry average, so are its interest revenues. Thus, it is difficult to determine whether Atlanta Bank's net interest margin will be above or below the industry average. Because it is more heavily concentrated in risky loans and securities, its credit risk is higher than that of the average bank; nevertheless, its interest rate risk is less because of its relatively high concentration of medium-term CDs and floating-rate loans. A gap measurement of Atlanta Bank can be conducted by first identifying the rate-sensitive liabilities and assets, as follows:

RATE-SENSITIVE ASSETS	AMOUNT (IN MILLIONS)	RATE-SENSITIVE LIABILITIES	AMOUNT (IN MILLIONS)
Floating-rate loans	$3,000	NOW accounts	$1,200
Floating-rate mortgages	500	MMDAs	2,000
Short-term Treasury securities	1,000	Short-term CDs	1,500
	$4,500		$4,700

Exhibit 19.8 Balance Sheet of Atlanta Bank (in Millions of Dollars)

ASSETS			LIABILITIES AND CAPITAL		
Required reserves		$ 400	Demand deposits		$ 500
Commercial loans			NOW accounts		1,200
Floating-rate	3,000		MMDAs		2,000
Fixed-rate	1,100		CDs		
Total		4,100	Short-term	1,500	
Consumer loans		2,500	From 1 to 5 yrs.	3,800	
Mortgages			Total		5,300
Floating-rate	500		Long-term bonds		200
Fixed-rate	None		CAPITAL		800
Total		500			
Treasury securities					
Short-term	1,000				
Long-term	None				
Total		1,000			
Corporate securities					
High-rated	None				
Moderate-rated	1,000				
Total		1,000			
Municipal securities					
High-rated	None				
Moderate-rated	None				
Total		None			
Fixed assets		500			
TOTAL ASSETS		$10,000	TOTAL LIABILITIES AND CAPITAL		$10,000

$$\text{Gap} = \$4{,}500 \text{ million} - \$4{,}700 \text{ million}$$
$$= -\$200 \text{ million}$$
$$\text{Gap ratio} = \frac{\$4{,}500 \text{ million}}{\$4{,}700 \text{ million}}$$
$$= .957$$

The gap measurements suggest somewhat similar rate sensitivity on both sides of the balance sheet.

The future performance of Atlanta Bank relative to the industry depends on future economic conditions. If interest rates rise, it will be more insulated than other banks. If interest rates fall, other banks will likely benefit to a greater degree. Under conditions of a strong economy, Atlanta Bank would likely benefit more than other banks because of its aggressive lending approach. Conversely, an economic slowdown could cause more loan defaults, and Atlanta Bank would be more susceptible to possible defaults than

Exhibit 19.9 Comparative Balance Sheet of Atlanta Bank

ASSETS			LIABILITIES AND CAPITAL		
	PERCENTAGE OF ASSETS FOR ATLANTA BANK	AVERAGE PERCENTAGE FOR INDUSTRY		PERCENTAGE OF TOTAL FOR ATLANTA BANK	AVERAGE PERCENTAGE FOR INDUSTRY
Required reserves	4%	4%	Demand deposits	5%	17%
Commercial loans			NOW accounts	12	8
Floating-rate	30	20	MMDAs	20	20
Fixed-rate	11	11	CDs		
Total	41	31	Short-term	15	35
Consumer loans	25	20	From 1 to 5 yrs.	38	10
Mortgages			Long-term bonds	2	2
Floating-rate	5	7	CAPITAL	8	8
Fixed-rate	0	3			
Total	5	10			
Treasury securities					
Short-term	10	7			
Long-term	0	8			
Total	10	15			
Corporate securities					
High-rated	0	5			
Moderate-rated	10	5			
Total	10	10			
Municipal securities					
High-rated	0	3			
Moderate-rated	0	2			
Total	0	5			
Fixed assets	5	5		—	—
TOTAL ASSETS	100%	100%	TOTAL LIABILITIES AND CAPITAL	100%	100%

other banks. This could be confirmed only if more details were provided (such as a more comprehensive breakdown of the balance sheet).

Management of Bank Capital   An evaluation of Atlanta Bank should also include an assessment of its capital. Atlanta Bank's future performance is influenced by the amount of capital that it holds. It needs to maintain at least the minimum capital ratio required by regulators. However, if Atlanta Bank maintains too much capital, each shareholder will receive a smaller proportion of any distributed earnings. A common measure of the return to the shareholders is the **return on equity (ROE),** measured as

Exhibit 19.10 Evaluation of Atlanta Bank Based on Its Balance Sheet

	MAIN INFLUENTIAL COMPONENTS	EVALUATION OF ATLANTA BANK RELATIVE TO INDUSTRY
Interest expenses	All liabilities except demand deposits.	Higher than industry average because it concentrates more on high-rate deposits than the norm.
Noninterest expenses	Loan volume and checkable deposit volume.	Possibly higher than the norm; its checkable deposit volume is less than the norm, but its loan volume is greater than the norm.
Interest revenues	Volume and composition of loans and securities.	Potentially higher than industry average because its assets are generally riskier than the norm.
Exposure to credit risk	Volume and composition of loans and securities.	Higher concentration of loans than industry average; it has a greater percentage of risky assets than the norm.
Exposure to interest rate risk	Maturities on liabilities and assets; use of floating-rate loans.	Lower than the industry average; it has more medium-term liabilities, fewer assets with very long maturities, and more floating-rate loans.

$$\text{ROE} = \frac{\text{Net profit after taxes}}{\text{Equity}}$$

The term *equity* represents the bank's capital. The return on equity can be broken down as follows:

$$\text{ROE} = \text{Return on assets (ROA)} \times \text{Leverage measure}$$

$$\frac{\text{Net profit after taxes}}{\text{Equity}} = \frac{\text{Net profit after taxes}}{\text{Assets}} \times \frac{\text{Assets}}{\text{Equity}}$$

The ratio (assets/equity) is sometimes called the **leverage measure,** because leverage reflects the volume of assets a firm supports with equity. The greater the leverage measure, the greater the amount of assets per dollar's worth of equity. The above breakdown of ROE is useful because it can demonstrate how Atlanta Bank's capital can affect its ROE. For a given level of return on assets (ROA), a higher capital level reduces the bank's leverage measure and therefore reduces its ROE.

If Atlanta Bank is holding an excessive amount of capital, it may not need to rely on retained earnings to build its capital and can distribute a high percentage of its earnings to shareholders (as dividends). Thus, its capital management is related to its dividend policy. If Atlanta Bank is expanding, it may need more capital to support construction of new buildings, office equipment, and other expenses. In this case, it would need to retain a larger proportion of its earnings to support its expansion plans.

MANAGING RISK OF INTERNATIONAL OPERATIONS

Banks that are engaged in international banking face additional types of risk.

WEB

www.risknews.net
Links to risk-related information in international banking.

Exchange Rate Risk

When a bank providing a loan requires that the borrower repay in the currency denominating the loan, it may be able to avoid exchange rate risk. However, some international loans contain a clause that allows repayment in a foreign currency, thus allowing the borrower to avoid exchange rate risk.

In many cases, banks convert available funds (from recent deposits) to whatever currency corporations want to borrow. Thus, they create an asset denominated in that currency, while the liability (deposits) is denominated in a different currency. If the liability currency appreciates against the asset currency, the bank's profit margin is reduced.

All large banks are exposed to exchange rate risk to some degree. They can attempt to hedge this risk in various ways.

EXAMPLE

Cameron Bank, a U.S. bank, converts dollar deposits into a British pound (£) loan for a British corporation, which will pay £50,000 in interest per year. Cameron Bank may attempt to engage in forward contracts to sell £50,000 forward for each date when it will receive those interest payments. That is, it will search for corporations that wish to purchase £50,000 on the dates of concern. ●

In reality, a large bank will not hedge every individual transaction, but will instead net out the exposure and be concerned only with net exposure. Large banks enter into several international transactions on any given day. Some reflect future cash inflows in a particular currency, while others reflect cash outflows in that currency. The bank's exposure to exchange rate risk is determined by the net cash flow in each currency.

Settlement Risk

International banks that engage in large currency transactions are exposed not only to exchange rate risk as a result of their different currency positions, but also to settlement risk, or the risk of a loss due to settling their transactions. For example, a bank may send its currency to another bank as part of a transaction agreement, but it may not receive any currency from the other bank if that bank defaults before sending its payment.

The failure of a single large bank could create more losses if other banks were relying on receivables from the failed bank to make future payables of their own. Consequently, there is concern about systemic risk, or the risk that many participants will be unable to meet their obligations because they did not receive payments on obligations due to them.

PARTICIPATION IN FINANCIAL MARKETS

In order to manage their operations, commercial banks rely heavily on financial markets, as explained in Exhibit 19.11. They rely on the money markets to obtain funds, the mortgage and bond markets to use some of their funds, and the futures, options, and swaps markets to hedge their risk.

Exhibit 19.11 Participation of Commercial Banks in Financial Markets

FINANCIAL MARKET	PARTICIPATION BY COMMERCIAL BANKS
Money markets	As banks offer deposits, they must compete with other financial institutions in the money market along with the Treasury to obtain short-term funds. They serve households that wish to invest funds for short-term periods.
Mortgage markets	Some banks offer mortgage loans on homes and commercial property and therefore provide financing in the mortgage market.
Bond markets	Commercial banks purchase bonds issued by corporations, the Treasury, and municipalities.
Futures markets	Commercial banks take positions in futures to hedge interest rate risk.
Options markets	Commercial banks take positions in options on futures to hedge interest rate risk.
Swaps markets	Commercial banks engage in interest rate swaps to hedge interest rate risk.

SUMMARY

- The underlying goal of bank management is to maximize the wealth of the bank's shareholders, which implies maximizing the price of the bank's stock (if the bank is publicly traded). A bank's board of directors needs to monitor bank managers to ensure that managerial decisions are intended to serve shareholders.

- Banks manage liquidity by maintaining some liquid assets such as short-term securities and ensuring easy access to funds (through the federal funds market).

- Banks measure their sensitivity to interest rate movements so that they can assess their exposure to interest rate risk. Common methods of measuring interest rate risk include gap analysis and duration analysis. Some banks use regression analysis to determine the sensitivity of their earnings or stock returns to interest rate movements.

- Banks can reduce their interest rate risk by matching maturities of their assets and liabilities or by using

floating-rate loans to create more rate sensitivity in their assets. Alternatively, they may use interest rate futures contracts or interest rate swaps. If they are adversely affected by rising interest rates, they could sell financial futures contracts or engage in a swap of fixed-rate payments for floating-rate payments.

- Banks manage credit risk by carefully assessing the borrowers who apply for loans and by limiting the amount of funds they allocate toward risky loans (such as credit card loans). They also diversify their loans across borrowers of different regions and industries so that the loan portfolio is not heavily susceptible to financial problems in any single region or industry.

- An evaluation of a bank includes an assessment of its exposure to interest rate movements and credit risk. This assessment can be used along with a forecast of interest rates and economic conditions to forecast the bank's future performance.

POINT COUNTER-POINT

Can Bank Failures Be Avoided?

Point No. Banks are in the business of providing credit. When economic conditions deteriorate, there will be loan defaults and some banks will not be able to survive.

Counter-Point Yes. If banks focus on providing loans to creditworthy borrowers, most loans will not default even during recessionary periods.

Who Is Correct? Use the Internet to learn more about this issue. Offer your own opinion on this issue.

QUESTIONS AND APPLICATIONS

1. Integrating Asset and Liability Management What is accomplished when a bank integrates its liability management with its asset management?

2. Liquidity Given the liquidity advantage of holding Treasury bills, why do banks hold only a relatively small portion of their assets as T-bills?

3. Illiquidity How do banks resolve illiquidity problems?

4. Managing Interest Rate Risk If a bank expects interest rates to decrease over time, how might it alter the rate sensitivity of its assets and liabilities?

5. Rate Sensitivity List some rate-sensitive assets and some rate-insensitive assets of banks.

6. Managing Interest Rate Risk If a bank is very uncertain about future interest rates, how might it insulate its future performance from future interest rate movements?

7. Net Interest Margin What is the formula for the net interest margin? Explain why it is closely monitored by banks.

8. Managing Interest Rate Risk Assume that a bank expects to attract most of its funds through short-term CDs and would prefer to use most of its funds to provide long-term loans. How could it follow this strategy and still reduce interest rate risk?

9. Bank Exposure to Interest Rate Movements According to this chapter, have banks been able to insulate themselves against interest rate movements? Explain.

10. Gap Management What is a bank's gap, and what does it attempt to determine? Interpret a negative gap. What are some limitations of measuring a bank's gap?

11. Duration How do banks use duration analysis?

12. Measuring Interest Rate Risk Why do loans that can be prepaid on a moment's notice complicate the bank's assessment of interest rate risk?

13. Bank Management Dilemma Can a bank simultaneously maximize return and minimize default risk? If not, what can it do instead?

14. Bank Exposure to Economic Conditions As economic conditions change, how do banks adjust their asset portfolios?

15. Bank Loan Diversification In what two ways should a bank diversify its loans? Why? Is international diversification of loans a viable solution to credit risk? Defend your answer.

16. Commercial Borrowing Do all commercial borrowers receive the same interest rate on loans?

17. Bank Dividend Policy Why might a bank retain some excess earnings rather than distribute them as dividends?

18. Managing Interest Rate Risk If a bank has more rate-sensitive liabilities than rate-sensitive assets, what will happen to its net interest margin during a period of rising interest rates? During a period of declining interest rates?

19. Floating-Rate Loans Does the use of floating-rate loans eliminate interest rate risk? Explain.

20. Managing Exchange Rate Risk Explain how banks become exposed to exchange rate risk.

Advanced Questions

21. Bank Exposure to Interest Rate Risk Oregon Bank has branches overseas that concentrate on short-term deposits in dollars and floating-rate loans in British pounds. Because it maintains rate-sensitive assets and liabilities of equal amounts, it believes it has essentially eliminated its interest rate risk. Do you agree? Explain.

22. Managing Interest Rate Risk Dakota Bank has a branch overseas with the following balance sheet characteristics: 50 percent of the liabilities are rate sensitive and denominated in Swiss francs; the remaining 50 percent of liabilities are rate insensitive and are denominated in dollars. With regard to assets,

50 percent are rate sensitive and are denominated in dollars; the remaining 50 percent of assets are rate insensitive and are denominated in Swiss francs.

a. Is the performance of this branch susceptible to interest rate movements? Explain.

b. Assume that Dakota Bank plans to replace its short-term deposits denominated in U.S. dollars with short-term deposits denominated in Swiss francs, because Swiss interest rates are currently lower than U.S. interest rates. The asset composition would not change. This strategy is intended to widen the spread between the rate earned on assets and the rate paid on liabilities. Offer your insight on how this strategy could backfire.

c. One consultant has suggested to Dakota Bank that it could avoid exchange rate risk by making loans in whatever currencies it receives as deposits. In this way, it will not have to exchange one currency for another. Offer your insight on whether there are any disadvantages to this strategy.

Interpreting Financial News

Interpret the following comments made by Wall Street analysts and portfolio managers:

a. "The bank's biggest mistake was that it did not recognize that its forecasts of a strong local real estate market and declining interest rates could be wrong."

b. "Banks still need some degree of interest rate risk to be profitable."

c. "The bank used interest rate swaps so that its spread is no longer exposed to interest rate movements. However, its loan volume and therefore its profits are still exposed to interest rate movements."

Managing in Financial Markets

Hedging with Interest Rate Swaps As a manager of Stetson Bank, you are responsible for hedging Stetson's interest rate risk. Stetson has forecasted its cost of funds as follows:

YEAR	COST OF FUNDS
1	6%
2	5%
3	7%
4	9%
5	7%

It expects to earn an average rate of 11 percent on some assets that charge a fixed interest rate over the next five years. It considers engaging in an interest rate swap in which it would swap fixed payments of 10 percent in exchange for variable-rate payments of LIBOR plus 1 percent. Assume LIBOR is expected to be consistently 1 percent above Stetson's cost of funds.

a. Determine the spread that would be earned each year if Stetson uses an interest rate swap to hedge all of its interest rate risk. Would you recommend that Stetson use an interest rate swap?

b. Although Stetson has forecasted its cost of funds, it recognizes that its forecasts may be inaccurate.

Offer a method that Stetson can use to assess the potential results from using an interest rate swap while accounting for the uncertainty surrounding future interest rates.

c. The reason for Stetson's interest rate risk is that it uses some of its funds to make fixed-rate loans, as some borrowers prefer fixed rates. An alternative method of hedging interest rate risk is to use adjustable-rate loans. Would you recommend that Stetson use only adjustable-rate loans to hedge its interest rate risk? Explain.

PROBLEMS

1. Net Interest Margin Suppose a bank earns $201 million in interest revenue but pays $156 million in interest expense. It also has $800 million in earning assets. What is its net interest margin?

2. Calculating Return on Assets If a bank earns $169 million net profit after tax and has $17 billion invested in assets, what is its return on assets?

3. Calculating Return on Equity If a bank earns $75 million net profits after tax and has $7.5 billion invested in assets and $600 million equity investment, what is its return on equity?

4. Managing Risk Use the balance sheet for San Diego Bank in Exhibit A and the industry norms in Exhibit B to answer the following questions:

Exhibit A Balance Sheet for San Diego Bank (in Millions of Dollars)

ASSETS			LIABILITIES AND CAPITAL		
Required reserves		$ 800	Demand deposits		$ 800
Commercial loans			NOW accounts		2,500
Floating-rate	None		MMDAs		6,000
Fixed-rate	7,000		CDs		
Total		7,000	Short-term	9,000	
Consumer loans		5,000	From 1 to 5 yrs.	None	
Mortgages			Total		9,000
Floating-rate	None		Federal funds		500
Fixed-rate	2,000		Long-term bonds		400
Total		2,000	CAPITAL		800
Treasury securities					
Short-term	None				
Long-term	1,000				
Total		1,000			
Long-term corporate securities					
High-rated	None				
Moderate-rated	2,000				
Total		2,000			

ASSETS			LIABILITIES AND CAPITAL		
Long-term municipal securities					
High-rated	None				
Moderate-rated	1,700				
Total		1,700			
Fixed assets		500			
TOTAL ASSETS		$20,000	TOTAL LIABILITIES and CAPITAL		$20,000

Exhibit B Industry Norms in Percentage Terms

ASSETS		LIABILITIES AND CAPITAL	
Required reserves	4%	Demand deposits	17%
Commercial loans		NOW accounts	10
Floating-rate	20	MMDAs	20
Fixed-rate	11	CDs	
Total	31	Short-term	35
Consumer loans	20	From 1 to 5 yrs.	10
Mortgages		Total	45
Floating-rate	7	Long-term bonds	2
Fixed-rate	3	CAPITAL	6
Total	10		
Treasury securities			
Short-term	7		
Long-term	8		
Total	15		
Long-term corporate securities			
High-rated	5		
Moderate-rated	5		
Total	10		
Long-term municipal securities			
High-rated	3		
Moderate-rated	2		
Total	5		
Fixed assets	5		
TOTAL ASSETS	100%	TOTAL LIABILITIES and CAPITAL	100%

a. Estimate the gap and the gap ratio and determine how San Diego Bank would be affected by an increase in interest rates over time.

b. Assess San Diego's credit risk. Does it appear high or low relative to the industry? Would San Diego Bank perform better or worse than other banks during a recession?

c. For any type of bank risk that appears to be higher than the industry, explain how the balance sheet could be restructured to reduce the risk.

5. Measuring Risk Montana Bank wants to determine the sensitivity of its stock returns to interest rate movements, based on the following information:

Use a regression model in which Montana's stock return is dependent on the stock market return and the interest rate. Determine the relationship between the interest rate and Montana's stock return by assessing the regression coefficient applied to the interest rate. Is the sign of the coefficient positive or negative? What does it suggest about the bank's exposure to interest rate risk? Should Montana Bank be concerned about rising or declining interest rate movements in the future?

QUARTER	RETURN ON MONTANA STOCK	RETURN ON MARKET	INTEREST RATE
1	2%	3%	6.0%
2	2	2	7.5
3	−1	−2	9.0
4	0	−1	8.2
5	2	1	7.3
6	−3	−4	8.1
7	1	5	7.4
8	0	1	9.1
9	−2	0	8.2
10	1	−1	7.1
11	3	3	6.4
12	6	4	5.5

FLOW OF FUNDS EXERCISE

Managing Credit Risk

Recall that Carson Company relies heavily on commercial banks for loans. When the company was first established with equity funding from its owners, Carson Company could easily obtain debt financing, as the financing was backed by some of the firm's assets. However, as Carson expanded, it continually relied on extra debt financing, which increased its ratio of debt to equity. Some banks were unwilling to provide more debt financing because of the risk that Carson would not be able to repay additional loans. A few banks were still willing to provide funding, but they required an extra premium to compensate for the risk.

a. Explain the difference in the willingness of banks to provide loans to Carson Company. Why is there a difference between banks when they are assessing the same information about a firm that wants to borrow funds?

b. Consider the flow of funds for a publicly traded bank that is a key lender to Carson Company. This bank received equity funding from shareholders, which it uses to establish its business. It channels bank deposit funds, which are insured by the Federal Deposit Insurance Corporation (FDIC), to provide loans to Carson Company and other firms. The depositors have no idea how the bank uses their funds, as their deposits are insured, yet the FDIC is not preventing the bank from making risky loans. So who is monitoring the bank? Do you think the bank is taking more risk than its shareholders desire? How does the FDIC discourage the bank from taking too much risk? Why might the bank ignore the FDIC's efforts to discourage excessive risk taking?

INTERNET/EXCEL EXERCISES

1. Assess the services offered by an Internet bank. Describe the types of online services offered by the bank. Do you think an Internet bank such as this offers higher or lower interest rates than a "regular" commercial bank? Why or why not?

2. Go to http://finance.yahoo.com/, enter the symbol BK (Bank of New York Mellon Corporation), and click on "Get Quotes." Click on "5y" just below the stock price trend to review the stock price movements over the last five years. Check the S&P box just above the graph and click on "Compare" in order to compare the trend of Bank of New York Mellon with the movements in the S&P stock index. Has Bank of New York Mellon Corporation performed better or worse than the index? Offer an explanation for its performance.

3. Go to http://finance.yahoo.com/, enter the symbol WFC (Wells Fargo Bank), and click on "Get Quotes."

Retrieve stock price data at the beginning of the last 20 quarters. Then go to http://research.stlouisfed.org/fred2/ and retrieve interest rate data at the beginning of the last 20 quarters for the three-month Treasury bill. Record the data on an Excel spreadsheet. Derive the quarterly return of Wells Fargo Bank. Derive the quarterly change in the interest rate. Apply regression analysis in which the quarterly return of Wells Fargo Bank is the dependent variable and the quarterly change in the interest rate is the independent variable (see Appendix B for more information about using regression analysis). Is there a positive or negative relationship between the interest rate movement and the return of Wells Fargo Bank stock? Is the relationship significant? Offer an explanation for this relationship.

WSJ EXERCISE

Bank Management Strategies

Summarize an article in *The Wall Street Journal* that discussed a recent change in managerial strategy by a particular commercial bank. (You may wish to do an Internet search in the online version of *The Wall Street Journal* to identify an article on a commercial bank's change in strategy.) Describe the change in managerial strategy. How will the bank's balance sheet be affected by this change? How will the bank's potential return and risk be affected? What reason does the article give for the bank's decision to change its strategy?

20
Bank Performance

The specific objectives of this chapter are to:

- identify the factors that affect the valuation of a commercial bank,

- compare the performance of banks in different size classifications over recent years, and

- explain how to evaluate the performance of banks based on financial statement data.

A commercial bank's performance is examined for various reasons. Bank regulators identify banks that are experiencing severe problems so that they can be remedied. Shareholders need to determine whether they should buy or sell the stock of various banks. Investment analysts must be able to advise prospective investors on which banks to select for investment. Commercial banks also evaluate their own performance over time to determine the outcomes of previous management decisions so that changes can be made where appropriate. Without persistent monitoring of performance, existing problems can remain unnoticed and lead to financial failure in the future.

VALUATION OF A COMMERCIAL BANK

Commercial banks (or commercial bank units that are part of a financial conglomerate) are commonly valued by their managers as part of their efforts to monitor performance over time and to determine the proper mix of services that will maximize the value of the bank. Banks may also be valued by other financial institutions that are considering an acquisition. An understanding of commercial bank valuation is useful because it identifies the factors that determine a commercial bank's value. The value of a commercial bank can be modeled as the present value of its future cash flows:

$$V = \sum_{t=1}^{n} \frac{E(CF_t)}{(1+k)^t}$$

where $E(CF_t)$ represents the expected cash flow to be generated in period t, and k represents the required rate of return by investors who invest in the commercial bank. Thus, the value of a commercial bank should change in response to changes in its expected cash flows in the future and to changes in the required rate of return by investors:

$$\Delta V = f[\Delta E(CF), \Delta k]$$
$$\quad\quad\quad + \quad\quad -$$

Factors That Affect Cash Flows

The change in a commercial bank's expected cash flows may be modeled as

$$\Delta E(CF) = f(\Delta ECON, \Delta R_f, \Delta INDUS, \Delta MANAB)$$
$$\quad\quad\quad\quad + \quad\quad - \quad\quad ? \quad\quad +$$

527

where ECON represents economic growth, R_f represents the risk-free interest rate, INDUS represents prevailing bank industry conditions (including regulations and competition), and MANAB represents the abilities of the commercial bank's management.

Change in Economic Growth

Economic growth can enhance a commercial bank's cash flows by increasing the household or business demand for loans. During periods of strong economic growth, loan demand tends to be higher, allowing commercial banks to provide more loans. Since loans tend to generate better returns to commercial banks than investment in Treasury securities or other securities, expected cash flows should be higher. Another reason cash flows may be higher is that fewer loan defaults normally occur during periods of strong economic growth.

Furthermore, the demand for other financial services provided by commercial banks tends to be higher during periods of strong economic growth. For example, brokerage, insurance, and financial planning services typically receive more business when economic growth is strong, because households have relatively high levels of disposable income.

Change in the Risk-Free Interest Rate

Interest rate movements may be inversely related to a commercial bank's cash flows. If the risk-free interest rate decreases, other market rates may also decline, which may result in a stronger demand for the commercial bank's loans. Second, commercial banks rely heavily on short-term deposits as a source of funds, and the rates paid on these deposits are typically revised in accordance with other interest rate movements. Banks' uses of funds (such as loans) are normally also sensitive to interest rate movements, but to a smaller degree. Therefore, when interest rates fall, the depository institution's cost of obtaining funds declines more than the decline in the interest earned on its loans and investments. Conversely, an increase in interest rates could reduce a commercial bank's expected cash flows because the interest paid on deposits may increase to a greater degree than the interest earned on loans and investments.

Change in Industry Conditions

One of the most important industry characteristics that can affect a commercial bank's cash flows is regulation. If regulators reduce the constraints imposed on commercial banks, banks' expected cash flows should increase. For example, when regulators eliminated certain geographic constraints, commercial banks were able to expand across new regions in the United States. As regulators reduced constraints on the types of businesses that commercial banks could pursue, the banks were able to expand by offering other financial services (such as brokerage and insurance services).

Another important industry characteristic that can affect a bank's cash flows is technological innovation, which can improve efficiencies and therefore enhance cash flows. The level of competition is an additional industry characteristic that can affect cash flows, because a high level of competition may reduce the bank's volume of business or reduce the prices it can charge for its services. As regulation has been reduced, competition has intensified. While some commercial banks benefit, other banks may lose some of their market share.

Change in Management Abilities

Of the four characteristics that commonly affect the cash flows, the only one over which the bank has control is management skills. It cannot dictate economic growth, interest rate movements, or regulations, but it can select its managers and its organizational structure. The managers can attempt to make internal decisions that will capitalize on the external forces (economic growth, interest rates, regulatory constraints) that the bank cannot control.

As the management skills of a commercial bank improve, so should its expected cash flows. For example, skillful managers will recognize how to revise the composition of the bank's assets and liabilities to capitalize on existing economic or regulatory conditions. They can capitalize on economies of scale by expanding specific types of businesses and by offering a diversified set of services that accommodate specific customers. They may restructure operations and use technology in a manner that can reduce expenses. They may also use derivative securities to alter the bank's potential return and risk. Thus, even if the other external forces are unchanged, a commercial bank's expected cash flows (and therefore value) can change in response to a change in its management skills.

Factors That Affect the Required Rate of Return by Investors

The required rate of return by investors who invest in a commercial bank can be modeled as

$$\Delta k = f(\Delta R_f, \Delta RP)$$
$$\quad\quad + \quad +$$

where R_f represents a change in the risk-free interest rate, and RP represents the risk premium of the bank.

Change in the Risk-Free Rate   When the risk-free rate increases, so does the return required by investors. Recall that the risk-free rate of interest is driven by inflationary expectations (INF), economic growth (ECON), the money supply (MS), and the budget deficit (DEF):

$$\Delta R_f = f(\Delta INF, \Delta ECON, \Delta MS, \Delta DEF)$$
$$\quad\quad\quad + \quad\quad + \quad\quad - \quad\quad +$$

High inflation, economic growth, and a high budget deficit place upward pressure on interest rates, while money supply growth places downward pressure on interest rates (assuming it does not cause inflation).

Change in the Risk Premium   If the risk premium on a commercial bank rises, so will the required rate of return by investors who invest in the bank. The risk premium can change in response to changes in economic growth, industry conditions, or management abilities:

$$\Delta RP = f(\Delta ECON, \Delta INDUS, \Delta MANAB)$$
$$\quad\quad\quad - \quad\quad\quad ? \quad\quad\quad -$$

High economic growth results in less risk for a commercial bank because its loans and investments in debt securities are less likely to default.

Bank industry characteristics such as regulatory constraints, technological innovations, and the level of competition can affect the risk premium on banks. Regulatory constraints may include a minimum level of capital required of banks. The most prominent regulatory change in recent years has been the reduction in constraints on services, which has allowed commercial banks to diversify their offerings to reduce risk. Conversely, this change may allow commercial banks to engage in some services that are riskier than their traditional services and to pursue some services that they cannot provide efficiently. Thus, the reduction in regulatory constraints could increase the risk premium required by investors.

An improvement in management skills may reduce the perceived risk of a commercial bank. To the extent that more skillful managers allocate funds to assets that exhibit less risk, they may reduce the risk premium required by investors who invest in the bank.

Exhibit 20.1 provides a framework for valuing a commercial bank, based on the preceding discussion. In general, the valuation is favorably affected by economic growth, lower interest rates, a reduction in regulatory constraints (assuming the bank focuses on services that it can provide efficiently), and an improvement in the bank's management abilities.

Exhibit 20.1 Framework for Valuing a Commercial Bank

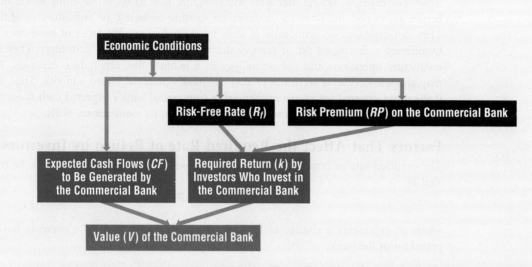

- A stronger economy leads to an increased demand for loans (interest income) and other services provided by the commercial bank (noninterest income), fewer loan defaults, and better cash flows
- A lower risk-free rate can enhance the valuation of bank assets that do not have an adjustable interest rate, such as some consumer and mortgage loans. It can also increase the valuations of bonds. Commercial banks that have a higher proportion of these types of assets will benefit more from a decline in the risk-free rate and will be adversely affected to a greater degree by an increase in the risk-free rate
- The valuation is also influenced by industry conditions and the commercial bank's management (not shown in the diagram). These factors affect the risk premium (and therefore the required return by investors) and the expected cash flows to be generated by the commercial bank.

PERFORMANCE OF BANKS

WEB

www.fdic.gov
Information about the performance of commercial banks.

Exhibit 20.2 summarizes the performance of all U.S.-chartered insured commercial banks during particular years. Each item is measured as a percentage of assets to control for growth when assessing the changes in each characteristic over time. Exhibit 20.2 serves as a useful reference point for assessing each of the performance proxies discussed throughout this chapter. Bank performance is shown over time to illustrate how performance can change. The following discussion examines the items in the first column of Exhibit 20.2 in the order listed; these income statement items are also the key income and expense items that affect a bank's performance.

Interest Income and Expenses

Gross interest income (in Row 1 of Exhibit 20.2) is interest income generated from all assets. It is affected by market rates and the composition of assets held by banks. Gross interest income tends to increase when interest rates rise and decrease when interest rates decline. It increased from 2003 to 2006 for all types of banks because of the general increase in market interest rates. It decreased in 2008 when interest rates declined.

The gross interest income varies among banks of different sizes because of the rates they may charge on particular types of loans (size classifications are discussed later in the chapter). Small banks tend to make more loans to small local businesses, which may allow them to charge higher interest rates than the money center banks and large banks charge on loans they provide to larger businesses. The rates charged to larger businesses tend to be lower because they generally have more options for obtaining funds than small local businesses do.

Exhibit 20.2 Performance Summary of All Insured Commercial Banks (2001–2008). All items in the exhibit are estimated as a proportion of total assets

ITEM	2001	2003	2006	2007	2008
1. Gross interest income	6.40%	4.66%	5.85%	5.94%	5.78
2. Gross interest expenses	2.98	1.32	2.80	2.99	2.70
3. Net interest income	3.42	3.32	3.05	2.95	3.08
4. Noninterest income	2.51	2.57	2.36	2.10	2.06
5. Loan loss provision	.68	.47	.27	.54	.72
6. Noninterest expenses	3.56	3.42	3.13	3.09	3.10
7. Securities gains (losses)	.07	.08	−.01	−.01	.00
8. Income before tax	1.77	2.08	2.00	1.41	1.32
9. Taxes	.59	.67	.61	.43	.37
10. Net income	1.17	1.41	1.39	.98	.95
11. Cash dividends provided	.87	1.08	.87	.82	.80
12. Retained earnings	.30	.33	.52	.16	.15

Source: *Federal Reserve.*

Gross interest expenses (in Row 2) represent interest paid on deposits and on other borrowed funds (from the federal funds market). These expenses are affected by market rates and the composition of the bank's liabilities. Gross interest expenses will normally be higher when market interest rates are higher. The gross interest expenses will vary among banks depending on how they obtain their deposits. Banks that rely more heavily on NOW accounts, money market deposit accounts, and CDs instead of checking accounts for deposits will incur higher gross interest expenses.

Net interest income (in Row 3 of Exhibit 20.2) is the difference between gross interest income and interest expenses and is measured as a percentage of assets. This measure is commonly referred to as net interest margin. It has a major effect on the bank's performance. Banks need to earn more interest income than their interest expenses in order to cover their other expenses. Yet competition prevents them from charging excessive rates (and earning excessive income). In general, the net interest margin of all banks in aggregate has remained somewhat stable over time. Exhibit 20.3 shows the trends of gross interest income and gross interest expenses for banks as a percentage of assets. The trends increase when market interest rates rise and decrease when market interest rates decline. The difference between the two trends represents the net interest margin trend, which is somewhat stable over time.

Noninterest Income and Expenses

Noninterest income (in Row 4 of Exhibit 20.2) results from fees charged on services provided, such as lockbox services, banker's acceptances, cashier's checks, and foreign exchange transactions. During the 1990s, banks increased their noninterest income, as they offered more fee-based services. Since 2000, however, noninterest income has declined because of more intense competition among financial institutions offering fee-based services. Noninterest income is usually higher for money center, large, and medium banks than for small banks. This difference occurs because the larger banks tend to provide more services for which they can charge fees.

The **loan loss provision** (in Row 5) is a reserve account established by the bank in anticipation of loan losses in the future. It should increase during periods when loan

Exhibit 20.3 Comparison of Gross Interest Income and Gross Interest Expenses (as a Percentage of Assets) over Time

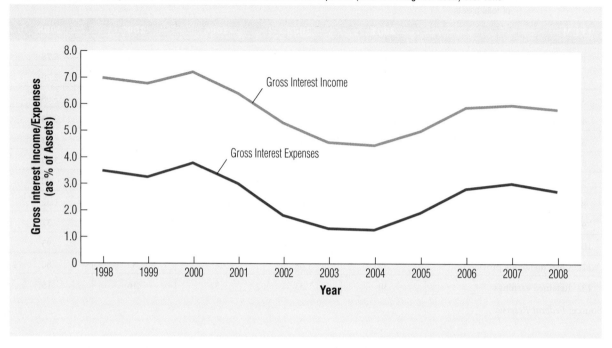

losses are more likely, such as during a recessionary period. In many cases, there is a lagged impact because some borrowers survive the recessionary period but never fully recover from it and subsequently fail. The amount of loan losses is influenced by the volume of loans provided and economic conditions.

The reporting of a bank's earnings requires managerial judgment on the amount of existing loans that will default. This can cause two banks with similar loan portfolios to have different earnings. A bank with conservative management may account for larger loan losses, which reduces the reported earnings now. Conversely, a bank with more aggressive management may understate the likely level of loan losses, which essentially defers the bad news until a future point in time. This lack of transparency can be beneficial in the short run to the bank with more aggressive management. Since the stock price is partially driven by earnings, the bank may be able to keep its stock price artificially high by understating its loan losses (and therefore overstating its earnings). If managerial compensation is tied to the bank's short-term stock price movements or earnings, managers may be tempted to understate loan losses.

Noninterest expenses (in Row 6 of Exhibit 20.2) include salaries, office equipment, and other expenses not related to the payment of interest on deposits. Noninterest expenses are partially dependent on personnel costs associated with the credit assessment of loan applications, which in turn are affected by the bank's asset composition (proportion of funds allocated to loans). Noninterest expenses also depend on the liability composition because small deposits are more time-consuming to handle than large deposits. Banks offering more nontraditional services will incur higher noninterest expenses, although they expect to offset the higher costs with higher noninterest income.

Securities gains and losses (in Row 7 of Exhibit 20.2) result from the bank's sale of securities. They have been negligible, when all banks in aggregate are considered. An individual bank's gains or losses might be more significant.

Income before tax (in Row 8 of Exhibit 20.2) is obtained by summing net interest income, noninterest income, and securities gains and subtracting from this sum the provision for loan losses and noninterest expenses. Bank income has generally declined in recent years (see the later discussion of the impact of the credit crisis).

Net Income

The key income statement item, according to many analysts, is **net income** (in Row 10 of Exhibit 20.2), which accounts for any taxes paid.

Return on Assets   The net income figure shown in Exhibit 20.2 is measured as a percentage of assets and therefore represents the **return on assets (ROA)**. The ROA is influenced by all previously mentioned income statement items and therefore by all policies and other factors that affect those items.

Return on Equity   An alternative measure of overall bank performance is **return on equity (ROE)**. A bank's ROE is affected by the same income statement items that affect ROA as well as by the bank's degree of financial leverage.

$$ROE = ROA \times Leverage\ measure$$

$$\frac{Net\ income}{Equity\ capital} = \frac{Net\ income}{Total\ assets} \times \frac{Total\ assets}{Equity\ capital}$$

The leverage measure is simply the inverse of the capital ratio (when only equity counts as capital). The higher the capital ratio, the lower the leverage measure and the lower the degree of financial leverage. For a given positive level of ROA, a bank's ROE will be higher if it uses more financial leverage.

Impact of the Credit Crisis on Net Income   Commercial banks were adversely affected in several ways by the subprime mortgage problems that intensified during the credit crisis that began in 2008. First, many commercial banks held mortgages as assets and experienced late payments or defaults on some of these mortgages. Second, they had invested in mortgage-backed securities, which generated poor returns because of late payments or defaults on the mortgages represented by these securities. Third, some commercial banks had sold credit default swap contracts, which obligated them to cover damages resulting from defaults on mortgage-backed securities. Fourth, some commercial banks experienced a reduction in loan demand during the credit crisis, because businesses reduced or delayed their expansion plans. The first three reasons are directly due to the credit risk of mortgages, while the fourth reason is an indirect effect of the credit crisis. The obvious lesson to banks was that they should have been more careful in assessing the risk of the assets that they were purchasing. Their expertise is supposed to be in assessing creditworthiness, but they presumed that many of the assets they purchased were creditworthy without conducting a thorough assessment.

HOW TO EVALUATE A BANK'S PERFORMANCE

Up to this point, the discussion has focused mostly on the performance of the overall industry. Although this information can be beneficial, analysts often need to evaluate an individual bank's performance, in which case financial statements are used. Analysts may also wish to compare a bank's performance with that of banks of the same size. Similarly, a bank will normally use banks within its same size classification as a benchmark to evaluate its performance. The Federal Reserve provides bank performance summaries for banks in four size classifications: money center banks (the 10 largest banks that serve money centers such as New York), large banks (ranked 11 to 100 in size), medium banks (ranked 101 to 1,000 in size), and small banks (ranked lower than 1,000 in size).

Exhibit 20.4 Influence of Bank Policies and Other Factors on a Bank's Income Statement

INCOME STATEMENT ITEM AS A PERCENTAGE OF ASSETS	BANK POLICY DECISIONS AFFECTING THE INCOME STATEMENT ITEM	UNCONTROLLABLE FACTORS AFFECTING THE INCOME STATEMENT ITEM
(1) Gross interest income	• Composition of assets • Quality of assets • Maturity and rate sensitivity of assets • Loan pricing policy	• Economic conditions • Market interest rate movements
(2) Gross interest expenses	• Composition of liabilities • Maturities and rate sensitivity of liabilities	• Market interest rate movements
(3) Net interest income = (1) − (2)		
(4) Noninterest income	• Service charges • Nontraditional activities	• Regulatory provisions
(5) Noninterest expenses	• Composition of assets • Composition of liabilities • Nontraditional activities • Efficiency of personnel • Costs of office space and equipment • Marketing costs • Other costs	• Inflation
(6) Loan losses	• Composition of assets • Quality of assets • Collection department capabilities	• Economic conditions • Market interest rate movements
(7) Pretax return on assets = (3) + (4) − (5) − (6)		
(8) Taxes	• Tax planning	• Tax laws
(9) After-tax return on assets = (7) − (8)		
(10) Financial leverage, measured here as (assets/equity)	• Capital structure policies	• Capital structure regulations
(11) Return on equity = (9) × (10)		

Exhibit 20.4 identifies some of the key policy decisions that influence a bank's income statement. This exhibit also identifies factors not controlled by the bank that affect the bank's income statement.

WEB

www.fdic.gov/quicklinks/analysts.html

Financial data for individual commercial banks so that their performance can be evaluated. The site also provides a quarterly outlook for the banking industry.

Examination of Return on Assets (ROA)

The ROA will usually reveal when a bank's performance is not up to par, but it does not indicate the reason for the poor performance. Its components must be evaluated separately. Exhibit 20.5 identifies the factors that affect bank performance as measured by the ROA and ROE. If a bank's ROA is less than desired, the bank is possibly incurring excessive interest expenses. Banks typically know what deposit rate is necessary to attract deposits and therefore are not likely to pay excessive interest. Yet, if all a bank's sources of funds require a market-determined rate, the bank will face relatively high interest expenses. A relatively low ROA could also be due to low interest received on loans and securities because the bank has been overly conservative with its funds or was locked

Exhibit 20.5 Breakdown of Performance Measures

MEASURES OF BANK PERFORMANCE	FINANCIAL CHARACTERISTICS INFLUENCING PERFORMANCE	BANK DECISIONS AFFECTING FINANCIAL CHARACTERISTICS
(1) Return on assets (ROA)	Net interest margin	Deposit rate decisions
		Loan rate decisions
		Loan losses
	Noninterest revenues	Bank services offered
	Noninterest expenses	Overhead requirements
		Efficiency
		Advertising
	Loan losses	Risk level of loans provided
(2) Return on equity (ROE)	ROA	See above
	Leverage measure	Capital structure decision

into fixed rates prior to an increase in market interest rates. High interest expenses and/ or low interest revenues (on a relative basis) will reduce the net interest margin and therefore reduce the ROA.

A relatively low ROA may also result from insufficient noninterest income. Some banks have made a much greater effort than others to offer services that generate fee (noninterest) income. Because a bank's net interest margin is somewhat dictated by interest rate trends and balance sheet composition, many banks attempt to focus on noninterest income to boost their ROA.

A bank's ROA can also be damaged by heavy loan losses. Yet, if the bank is too conservative in attempting to avoid loan losses, its net interest margin will be low (because of the low interest rates received from very safe loans and investments). Because of the obvious tradeoff here, banks generally attempt to shift their risk-return preferences according to economic conditions. They may increase their concentration of relatively risky loans during periods of prosperity when they may improve their net interest margin without incurring excessive loan losses. Conversely, they may increase their concentration of relatively low-risk (and low-return) investments when economic conditions are less favorable.

A low ROA may also be attributed to excessive noninterest expenses, such as overhead and advertising expenses. Any waste of resources due to inefficiencies can lead to relatively high noninterest expenses.

Application

Consider the performance characteristics for Bank of America and the industry in Exhibit 20.6. Because of differences in accounting procedures, the information may not be perfectly comparable. The industry data are based on the class of money center banks. Bank of America's income before tax has typically exceeded the industry norm. A comparison with the industry figures indicates that although Bank of America's net interest margin was recently lower than the norm, so were its noninterest expenses. In addition, its noninterest income was recently higher than the norm. Bank of America has generally performed relatively well over time, primarily because of its relatively low noninterest expenses. However, its loan loss provisions almost tripled in 2008 (during the credit crisis), primarily because of existing and anticipated mortgage loan problems. Investors and regulators were concerned that even this large increase in loan loss provisions might not fully absorb Bank of America's future loan losses. Consequently, the U.S. Treasury purchased preferred stock from

Exhibit 20.6 Comparison of Bank of America's Expenses and Income to the Industry

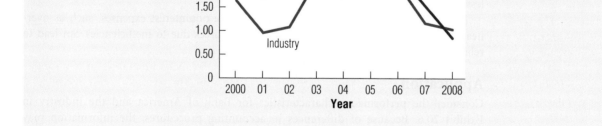

Source: *Bank of America's Annual Report; and the Federal Reserve Bulletin, various issues.*

Bank of America as a means of injecting additional capital into the bank. In addition, Bank of America issued stock to the public in May 2009.

Any particular bank will perform a more thorough evaluation of itself than that shown here. For example, Bank of America's annual reports typically provide a comprehensive explanation for its performance in recent years, along with a discussion of how it plans to improve its performance over time.

SUMMARY

- A bank's value is dependent on its expected future cash flows and the required rate of return by investors who invest in the bank. The bank's expected cash flows are influenced by economic growth, interest rate movements, regulatory constraints, and the abilities of the bank's managers. The required rate of return by investors who invest in the bank is influenced by the prevailing interest rate (which is affected by other economic conditions) and the risk premium (which is affected by economic growth, regulatory constraints, and the management abilities of the bank). In general, the value of commercial banks is favorably affected by strong economic growth, declining interest rates, and strong management abilities.

- A bank's performance can be evaluated by comparing its income statement items (as a percentage of total assets) to a control group of other banks with a similar size classification. The performance of the bank may be compared to the performance of a control group of banks. Any difference in performance between the bank and the control group is typically because of differences in net interest margin, loan loss reserves, noninterest income, or noninterest expenses.

If the bank's net interest margin is relatively low, it either is relying too heavily on deposits with higher interest rates or is not earning adequate interest on its loans. If the bank is forced to boost loan loss reserves, this suggests that its loan portfolio may be too risky. If its noninterest income is relatively low, the bank is not providing enough services that generate fee income. If the bank's noninterest expenses are relatively high, its cost of operations is excessive. There may be other specific details that make the assessment more complex, but the key problems of a bank can usually be detected with the approach described here.

- A common measure of a bank's overall performance is its return on assets (ROA). The ROA of a bank is partially determined by movements in market interest rates, as many banks benefit from lower interest rates. In addition, the ROA is highly dependent on economic conditions, because banks can extend more loans to creditworthy customers and may also experience a higher demand for their services.

  Another useful measure of a bank's overall performance is return on equity (ROE). A bank can increase its ROE by increasing its financial leverage, but its leverage is constrained by capital requirements.

POINT COUNTER-POINT

Does a Bank's Income Statement Clearly Indicate the Bank's Performance?

Point Yes. The bank's income statement can be partitioned to determine its performance and the underlying reasons for its performance.

Counter-Point No. The bank's income statement can be manipulated because the bank may not fully recognize loan losses (will not write off loans that are likely to default) until a future period.

Who Is Correct? Use the Internet to learn more about this issue. Offer your own opinion on this issue.

QUESTIONS AND APPLICATIONS

1.   Interest Income How can gross interest income rise, while the net interest margin remains somewhat stable for a particular bank?

2.   Impact on Income If a bank shifts its loan policy to pursue more credit card loans, how will its net interest margin be affected?

3.   Noninterest Income What has been the trend in noninterest income in recent years? Explain.

4.   Net Interest Margin How could a bank generate higher income before tax (as a percentage of assets) when its net interest margin has decreased?

5.   Net Interest Income Suppose a bank generates net interest income as a percentage of assets of 1.50 percent. Based on past experience, would the bank experience a loss or a gain? Explain.

6. Noninterest Income Why have large money center banks' noninterest income levels typically been higher than those of smaller banks?

7. Bank Leverage What does the assets/equity ratio of a bank indicate?

8. Analysis of a Bank's ROA What are some of the more common reasons why a bank may experience a low ROA?

9. Loan Loss Provisions Explain why loan loss provisions of most banks could increase in a particular period.

10. Evaluating a Bank's Performance When evaluating a bank, what are some of the key aspects to review?

11. Weak Performance What are likely reasons for weak bank performance?

12. Bank Income Statement Assume that SUNY Bank plans to liquidate Treasury security holdings and use the proceeds for small business loans. Explain how this strategy will affect the different income statement items. Also identify any income statement items where the effects of this strategy are more difficult to estimate.

Interpreting Financial News

Interpret the following comments made by Wall Street analysts and portfolio managers:

a. "The three most important factors that determine a local bank's bad debt level are the bank's location, location, and location."

b. "The bank's profitability was enhanced by its limited use of capital."

c. "Low risk is not always desirable. Our bank's risk has been too low, given the market conditions. We will restructure operations in a manner to increase risk."

Managing in Financial Markets

Forecasting Bank Performance As a manager of Hawaii Bank, you anticipate the following:

- Loan loss provision at end of year = 1 percent of assets
- Gross interest income over the next year = 9 percent of assets
- Noninterest expenses over the next year = 3 percent of assets
- Noninterest income over the next year = 1 percent of assets
- Gross interest expenses over the next year = 5 percent of assets
- Tax rate on income = 30 percent
- Capital ratio (capital/assets) at end of year = 5 percent

a. Forecast Hawaii Bank's net interest margin.

b. Forecast Hawaii Bank's earnings before taxes as a percentage of assets.

c. Forecast Hawaii Bank's earnings after taxes as a percentage of assets.

d. Forecast Hawaii Bank's return on equity.

e. Hawaii Bank is considering a shift in its asset structure to reduce its concentration of Treasury bonds and increase its volume of loans to small businesses. Identify each income statement item that would be affected by this strategy, and explain whether the forecast for that item would increase or decrease.

Problem

1. Assessing Bank Performance Select a bank whose income statement data are available. Using recent income statement information about the commercial bank, assess its performance. How does the performance of this bank compare to the performance of other banks? Is its return on equity higher or lower than the ROE of other banks as reported in this chapter? What is the main reason why its ROE is different from the norm? (Is it due to its interest expenses? Its noninterest income?)

Flow of Funds Exercise

How the Flow of Funds Affects Bank Performance

In recent years, Carson Company has requested the services listed below from Blazo Financial, a financial conglomerate. These transactions have created a flow of funds between Carson Company and Blazo.

a. Classify each service according to how Blazo benefits from the service.

- Advising on possible targets that Carson may acquire
- Futures contract transactions
- Options contract transactions
- Interest rate derivative transactions
- Loans
- Line of credit
- Purchase of short-term CDs
- Checking account

b. Explain why Blazo's performance from providing these services to Carson Company and other firms will decline if economic growth is reduced.

c. Given the potential impact of slow economic growth on a bank's performance, do you think that commercial banks would prefer that the Fed use a tight-money policy or a loose-money policy?

INTERNET/EXCEL EXERCISES

1. Go to www.suntrust.com. Click on "Investor Relations" and then on "Annual Reports." Use the income statement to determine SunTrust's performance. Describe SunTrust's performance in recent years.

2. Has SunTrust's ROA increased since the year before? Explain what caused its ROA to change over the last year. Has its net interest margin changed since last year? How has its noninterest income (as a percentage of assets) changed over the last year? How have its noninterest expenses changed over the last year? How have its loan loss reserves changed in the last year? Discuss how SunTrust's recent strategy and economic conditions might explain the changes in these components of its income statement.

WSJ EXERCISE

Assessing Bank Performance

Using a recent issue of *The Wall Street Journal*, summarize an article that discussed the recent performance of a particular commercial bank. Does the article suggest that the bank's performance was better or worse than the norm? What is the reason given for the performance?

Forecasting Bank Performance

This problem requires an understanding of banks' sources and uses of funds (Chapter 17), bank management (Chapter 19), and bank performance (Chapter 20). It also requires the use of spreadsheet software such as Microsoft Excel. The data provided can be input onto a spreadsheet to more easily complete the necessary computations. A conceptual understanding of commercial banking is needed to interpret the computations.

As an analyst of a medium-sized commercial bank, you have been asked to forecast next year's performance. In June you were provided with information about the sources and uses of funds for the upcoming year. The bank's sources of funds for the upcoming year are as follows:

SOURCES OF FUNDS	DOLLAR AMOUNT (IN MILLIONS)	INTEREST RATE TO BE OFFERED
Demand deposits	$5,000	0%
Time deposits	2,000	6%
1-year NCDs	3,000	T-bill rate + 1%
5-year NCDs	2,500	1-year NCD rate + 1%

The bank also has $1 billion in capital.

The bank's uses of funds for the upcoming year are as follows:

USES OF FUNDS	DOLLAR AMOUNT (IN MILLIONS)	INTEREST RATE	LOAN LOSS PERCENTAGE
Loans to small businesses	$4,000	T-bill rate + 6%	2%
Loans to large businesses	2,000	T-bill rate + 4%	1
Consumer loans	3,000	T-bill rate + 7%	4
Treasury bills	1,000	T-bill rate	0
Treasury bonds	1,500	T-bill rate + 2%	0
Corporate bonds	1,100	Treasury bond rate + 2%	0

The bank also has $900 million in fixed assets. The interest rates on loans to small and large businesses are tied to the T-bill rate and will change at the beginning of each new year. The forecasted Treasury bond rate is tied to the future T-bill rate, based on the expectation that an upward-sloping yield curve will exist at the beginning of next year. The corporate bond rate is tied to the Treasury bond rate, allowing for a risk premium of 2 percent. Consumer loans will be provided at the beginning of next year, and interest rates will be fixed over the lifetime of the loan. The remaining time to maturity on all assets except T-bills exceeds three years. As the one-year T-bills mature, the funds are to be reinvested in new one-year T-bills (all T-bills are to be purchased at the beginning of the year). The bank's loan loss percentage reflects the percentage of bad loans. Assume that no interest will be received on these loans. In addition, assume that this percentage of loans will be accounted for as loan loss reserves (assume that they should be subtracted when determining before-tax income).

The bank has forecasted its noninterest revenues to be $200 million and its noninterest expenses to be $740 million. A tax rate of 34 percent can be applied to the before-tax income in order to estimate after-tax income. The bank has developed the following probability distribution for the one-year T-bill rate that will exist as of the beginning of next year:

POSSIBLE T-BILL RATE	PROBABILITY
8%	30%
9	50
10	20

Questions

1. Using the information provided, determine the probability distribution of return on assets (ROA) for next year by completing the following table:

INTEREST RATE SCENARIO (POSSIBLE T-BILL RATE)	FORECASTED ROA	PROBABILITY
8%		
9		
10		

2. Will the bank's ROA next year be higher or lower if market interest rates are higher? (Use the T-bill rate as a proxy for market interest rates.) Why? The information provided did not assume any required reserves. Explain how including required reserves would affect the forecasted interest revenue, ROA, and ROE.

3. The bank is considering a strategy of attempting to attract an extra $1 billion as one-year negotiable certificates of deposit (NCDs) to replace $1 billion of five-year NCDs. Develop the probability distribution of ROA based on this strategy:

INTEREST RATE SCENARIO	FORECASTED ROA BASED ON THE STRATEGY OF INCREASING ONE-YEAR NCDs	PROBABILITY
8%		
9		
10		

4. Is the bank's ROA likely to be higher next year if it uses the strategy of attracting more one-year NCDs?

5. What would be an obvious concern about a strategy of using more one-year NCDs and fewer five-year NCDs beyond the next year?

6. The bank is considering a strategy of using $1 billion to offer additional loans to small businesses instead of purchasing T-bills. Using all the original assumptions provided, determine the probability distribution of ROA (assume that noninterest expenses would not be affected by this change in strategy).

INTEREST RATE SCENARIO (POSSIBLE T-BILL RATE)	FORECASTED ROA IF AN EXTRA $1 BILLION IS USED FOR LOANS TO SMALL BUSINESSES	PROBABILITY
8%		
9		
10		

7. Would the bank's ROA likely be higher or lower over the next year if it allocates the extra funds to small business loans?

8. What is the obvious risk of such a strategy beyond the next year?

9. The strategy of attracting more one-year NCDs could affect noninterest expenses and revenues. How would noninterest expenses be affected by the strategy? How would noninterest revenues be affected by the strategy?

10. Now assume that the bank is considering a strategy of increasing its consumer loans by $1 billion instead of using the funds for loans to small businesses. Using this information along with all the original assumptions provided, determine the probability distribution of ROA.

INTEREST RATE SCENARIO (POSSIBLE T-BILL RATE)	POSSIBLE ROA IF AN EXTRA $1 BILLION IS USED FOR CONSUMER LOANS	PROBABILITY
8%		
9		
10		

11. Other than possible changes in the economy that may affect credit risk, what key factor will determine whether this strategy is beneficial beyond one year?

12. Now assume that the bank wants to determine how its forecasted return on equity (ROE) next year would be affected if it boosts its capital from $1 billion to $1.2 billion. (The extra capital would not be used to increase interest or noninterest revenues.) Using all the original assumptions provided, complete the following table:

INTEREST RATE SCENARIO (POSSIBLE T-BILL RATE)	FORECASTED ROE IF CAPITAL = $1 BILLION	FORECASTED ROE IF CAPITAL = $1.2 BILLION	PROBABILITY
8%			
9			
10			

Briefly state how the ROE will be affected if the capital level is increased.

PART 7

Nonbank Operations

The chapters in Part 7 cover the key nonbank operations. Each chapter is devoted to a particular type of operation, with a focus on sources of funds, uses of funds, regulations, management, and recent performance. Some of the institutions discussed are independent; others are units (subsidiaries) of financial conglomerates. Each financial institution's interactions with other institutions and its participation in financial markets are also emphasized in these chapters.

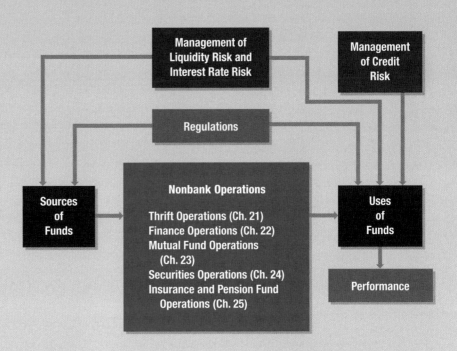

21

Thrift Operations

The specific objectives of this chapter are to:

- identify the key sources and uses of funds for savings institutions,

- describe the exposure of savings institutions to various types of risk,

- explain the valuation of a savings institution,

- describe how savings institutions have been exposed to recent crises,

- describe the main sources and uses of funds for credit unions, and

- describe the exposure of credit unions to various forms of risk.

The term *thrift institution* (or *savings institution*) is normally used to refer to a depository institution that specializes in mortgage lending. These institutions were created to accept deposits and channel the funds for mortgage loans. Some thrift operations are independent financial institutions, while others are units (subsidiaries) of financial conglomerates. Sometimes credit unions are also considered to be thrift institutions. For this reason, credit unions are also covered in this chapter.

BACKGROUND ON SAVINGS INSTITUTIONS

Savings institutions include savings banks and savings and loan associations (S&Ls). S&Ls are the most dominant type. While S&Ls are spread across the entire country, savings banks are mainly concentrated in the northeastern United States. Although savings banks have had more flexibility in their investing practices than S&Ls, the difference has narrowed over time. The two types of thrifts now have very similar sources and uses of funds. Therefore, the remainder of the chapter focuses on savings institutions, abbreviated as SIs. Most SIs are small, with assets of less than $1 billion.

Ownership of Savings Institutions

Savings institutions are classified as either stock owned or **mutual** (owned by depositors). Although most SIs are mutual, many SIs have shifted their ownership structure from depositors to shareholders through what is known as a **mutual-to-stock conversion.** This conversion allows SIs to obtain additional capital by issuing stock.

Beyond having the capability to boost capital, stock-owned institutions also provide their owners with greater potential to benefit from their performance. The dividends and/or stock price of a high-performance institution can grow, thereby providing direct benefits to the shareholders. Conversely, the owners (depositors) of a mutual institution do not benefit directly from high performance. Although they have a pro rata claim to the mutual SI's net worth while they maintain deposits there, their claim is eliminated once they close their account.

Because of the difference in owner control, stock-owned institutions are more susceptible to unfriendly takeovers. It is virtually impossible for another firm to take control of a mutual institution, because management generally holds all voting rights. From the owners' perspective, the stock-owned institution may seem more desirable because the owners may have more influence on managerial decisions.

When a mutual SI is involved in an acquisition, it first converts to a stock-owned SI. If it is the acquiring firm, it then arranges to purchase the existing stock of the institution to be acquired. Conversely, if it is to be acquired, its stock is purchased by the acquiring institution. This process is often referred to as a **merger-conversion.**

Some SIs have been acquired by commercial banks that wanted to diversify their operations. Even after such an acquisition, the SI may still maintain its operations, but under the ownership of the commercial bank. Consolidation and acquisitions have caused the number of mutual and stock SIs to decline consistently over the years. There are less than half as many SIs today as in 1994.

While consolidation among SIs has resulted in a smaller number of institutions, the total assets of SIs in aggregate have increased. The total assets of stock SIs have more than doubled since 1994, while the total assets of mutual SIs have remained steady.

REGULATION OF SAVINGS INSTITUTIONS

WEB

www.ots.treas.gov
Background on laws
and regulations
imposed on savings
institutions.

Savings institutions are regulated at both the state and federal levels. All federally chartered SIs are regulated by the Office of Thrift Supervision (OTS). State-chartered SIs are subject to some oversight by the state that has chartered them, but the states have no authority over federally chartered institutions.

The insuring agency for both S&Ls and savings banks is the Deposit Insurance Fund (DIF), which is administered by the Federal Deposit Insurance Corporation (FDIC) and insures deposits up to $100,000 per depositor (this level was raised to $250,000 until 2013). The DIF was formed on March 31, 2006, as a result of the merger of the **Savings Association Insurance Fund (SAIF),** which had formerly insured S&Ls, and the Bank Insurance Fund (BIF), which had insured savings banks. The FDIC charges the SIs annual insurance premiums, which are placed in the DIF. If an SI fails, the FDIC uses funds from the DIF to reimburse depositors.

Regulatory Assessment of Savings Institutions

Regulators conduct periodic on-site examinations to ensure that SIs have the minimum level of capital required and maintain their exposure to risk within a tolerable range. SIs are monitored using the CAMELS rating in a manner similar to commercial banks. They are assessed according to their capital adequacy, asset quality, management, earnings, liquidity, and sensitivity to market conditions. If an SI receives a composite CAMELS rating of 4 or higher, it is classified as a "problem" and receives close attention. It may be subject to corrective action by the Office of Thrift Supervision. Exhibit 21.1 shows the number of problem thrifts and their aggregate asset level in recent years. In general, the number and aggregate asset level of problem SIs have been low in recent years. During the credit crisis that began in 2008, however, the number and asset level of problem SIs increased, primarily as a result of the large number of subprime (low quality) mortgage loans that defaulted.

Deregulation of Services

In recent years, SIs have been granted more flexibility to diversify the products and services they provide. In recent years, SIs have been granted more flexibility to diversify the products and services they provide. They have diversified their business by merging with other businesses specializing in real estate, insurance, and brokerage. By offering discount brokerage service and other nontraditional services, an SI can attract customers searching for a one-stop shop.

SOURCES AND USES OF FUNDS

Like commercial banks, SIs serve as valuable financial intermediaries. However, their sources and uses of funds are different from those of commercial banks, so their management also differs from that of commercial banks.

Exhibit 21.1 Problem Thrifts over Time (Based on CAMELS Ratings)

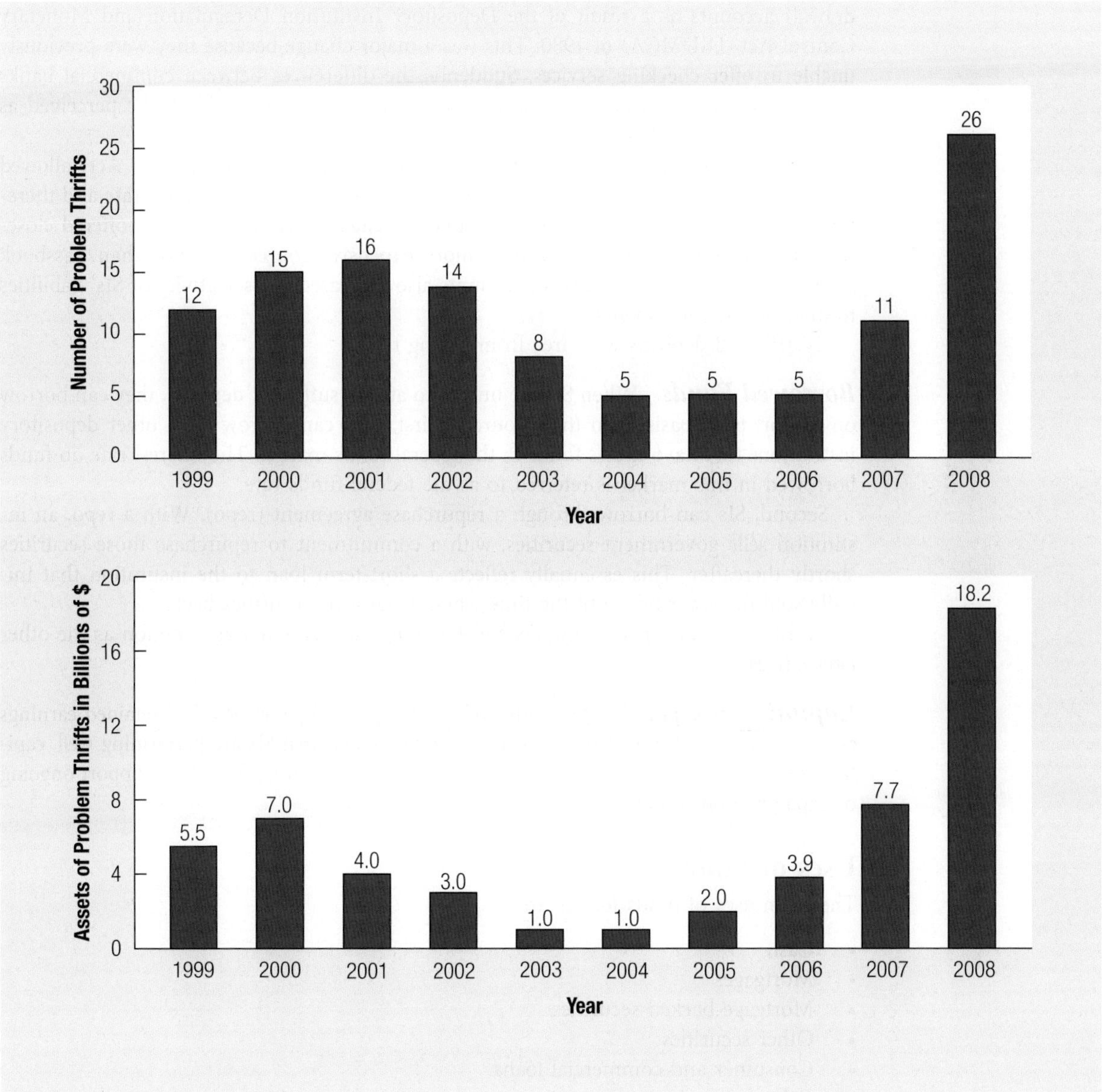

Sources of Funds

WEB

http://research
.stlouisfed.org/fred2
Time-series data on
various savings rates
and total savings
breakdown.

The main sources of funds for SIs are described next.

Deposits   Savings institutions obtain most of their funds from a variety of savings and time deposits, including passbook savings, retail certificates of deposit (CDs), and money market deposit accounts (MMDAs). Before 1978 SIs focused primarily on passbook savings accounts. During the early and mid-1970s, market interest rates exceeded the passbook savings rate, so many savers transferred their funds from SIs to alternative investments, a process known as **disintermediation.** Because disintermediation reduced the volume of savings at SIs, it reduced the amount of mortgage financing available.

In 1981 SIs across the country were allowed to offer NOW (negotiable order of withdrawal) accounts as a result of the Depository Institution Deregulation and Monetary Control Act (DIDMCA) of 1980. This was a major change because they were previously unable to offer checking services. Suddenly, the differences between commercial banks and SIs were not so obvious to savers. NOW accounts enabled SIs to be perceived as full-service financial institutions.

The creation of MMDAs in 1982 (as a result of the Garn-St Germain Act) allowed SIs to offer limited checking combined with a market-determined interest rate and therefore to compete against money market funds. Because these new accounts offered close-to-market interest rates, they were a more expensive source of funds than passbook savings. The new types of deposit accounts also increased the sensitivity of SIs' liabilities to interest rate movements.

By 1986, all deposits were free from ceiling rates.

Borrowed Funds   When SIs are unable to attract sufficient deposits, they can borrow on a short-term basis from three sources. First, they can borrow from other depository institutions that have excess funds in the federal funds market. The interest rate on funds borrowed in this market is referred to as the federal funds rate.

Second, SIs can borrow through a repurchase agreement (repo). With a repo, an institution sells government securities, with a commitment to repurchase those securities shortly thereafter. This essentially reflects a short-term loan to the institution that initially sold the securities until the time when it buys the securities back.

Third, SIs can borrow at the Federal Reserve, but this is not as common as the other alternatives.

Capital   The **capital** (or net worth) of an SI is primarily composed of retained earnings and funds obtained from issuing stock. During periods when SIs are performing well, capital is boosted by additional retained earnings. Capital is commonly used to support ongoing or expanding operations.

Uses of Funds

The main uses of funds for SIs are

- Cash
- Mortgages
- Mortgage-backed securities
- Other securities
- Consumer and commercial loans
- Other uses

Cash   Savings institutions maintain cash to satisfy reserve requirements enforced by the Federal Reserve System and to accommodate withdrawal requests of depositors. In addition, some SIs hold correspondent cash balances at other financial institutions in return for various services.

Mortgages   Mortgages are the primary asset of SIs. They typically have long-term maturities and can usually be prepaid by borrowers. About 90 percent of the mortgages originated are for homes or multifamily dwellings, while 10 percent are for commercial properties. The volume of mortgage originations increased substantially in the 2003–2006 period, which enhanced the overall performance of SIs. This increase was attributed to the stronger economy in that period. In addition, some SIs increased their volume of mortgage originations by providing many subprime mortgages, which allow more liberal credit standards when assessing mortgage applicants. However, defaults on mortgages increased in the 2007–2008 period, in part because some SIs had been too liberal with their credit standards.

Mortgages can be sold in the secondary market, although their market value changes in response to interest rate movements, so they are subject to interest rate risk as well as credit (default) risk. To protect against interest rate risk, SIs use a variety of techniques, discussed later in the chapter.

Mortgage-Backed Securities   Some savings institutions purchase mortgage-backed securities. The return on these securities is highly influenced by the default rate on the underlying mortgages. During the credit crisis, there were many defaults, and savings institutions that had purchased mortgage-backed securities commonly experienced losses.

Other Securities   All SIs invest in securities such as Treasury bonds and corporate bonds. These securities provide liquidity, as they can quickly be sold in the secondary market if funds are needed.

Consumer and Commercial Loans   Many SIs are attempting to increase their consumer loans and commercial loans. As a result of the DIDMCA and the Garn-St Germain Act, the lending guidelines for federally chartered SIs were loosened, and many state-chartered SIs were also granted more lending flexibility by their respective states. Specifically, federally chartered SIs are allowed to invest up to 30 percent of their assets in nonmortgage loans and securities. A maximum of 10 percent of assets can be used to provide non–real estate commercial loans.

Savings institutions have taken advantage of the deregulatory acts by providing corporate and consumer loans with maturities typically ranging between one and four years. Because consumer and corporate loan maturities closely match their liability maturities, SIs that reduce their fixed-rate mortgage loans in favor of consumer loans reduce their exposure to interest rate risk. However, offering these loans results in some noninterest costs. The increased emphasis on corporate and consumer loans can affect an SI's overall degree of credit risk. The loss rate on mortgage loans is normally perceived to be lower than the loss rate on consumer loans. During the credit crisis in the 2008–2009 period, however, the loss rate on subprime mortgages increased substantially.

Other Uses of Funds   Savings institutions can provide temporary financing to other institutions through the use of repurchase agreements. In addition, they can lend funds on a short-term basis through the federal funds market. Both methods allow them to efficiently use funds that they will have available for only a short period of time.

Balance Sheet of Savings Institutions

The sources of funds represent liabilities or equity of an SI, while the uses of funds represent assets. Each SI determines its own composition of liabilities and assets, which determines its specific operations.

EXAMPLE

Exhibit 21.2 summarizes the main sources and uses of funds of SIs by showing the balance sheet of Ashland Savings. The assets are shown on the left side of the balance sheet. The second column shows the dollar amount, and the third column shows the size of each asset in proportion to the total assets, to illustrate how Ashland Savings distributes its funds. Ashland's main asset is mortgage loans. The allocation of assets by Ashland Savings reflects the average allocation for all SIs. Allocations vary considerably among SIs, however, as some institutions maintain a much larger amount of mortgages than others.

Ashland Savings incurs some expenses from all types of deposits. Specifically, it hires employees to serve depositors. Its composition of liabilities determines its interest expenses, since it must pay a higher interest rate on large CDs than on small savings deposits. Ashland also incurs

Exhibit 21.2 Balance Sheet of Ashland Savings as of June 30, 2009

ASSETS	DOLLAR AMOUNT (IN MILLIONS)	PROPORTION OF TOTAL ASSETS	LIABILITIES AND STOCK HOLDERS' EQUITY	DOLLAR AMOUNT (IN MILLIONS)	PROPORTION OF TOTAL LIABILITIES AND STOCKHOLDERS' EQUITY
Cash (includes required reserves)	$ 60	6%	Savings deposits	$ 100	10%
Single-family mortgages	500	50%	NOW accounts	50	5%
Multifamily mortgages	50	5%	Money market deposit accounts	300	30%
Other mortgages	40	4%	Short-term CDs	360	36%
Mortgage-backed securities	70	7%	CDs with maturities beyond one year	100	10%
Other securities	100	10%			
Consumer loans	70	7%			
Commercial loans	40	4%			
Fixed assets	70	7%	Common stock issued	50	5%
			Retained earnings	40	4%
TOTAL ASSETS	$1,000	100%	TOTAL LIABILITIES AND STOCKHOLDERS' EQUITY	$1,000	100%

expenses from managing its assets. In particular, it hires employees to assess the creditworthiness of individuals and businesses that request loans. In general, Ashland wants to generate enough income from its assets to cover its expenses and provide a reasonable return to its shareholders. Its primary source of income is interest received from the mortgage loans that it provides. Its capital is shown on the balance sheet as common stock issued and retained earnings. ●

Exhibit 21.3 shows how savings institutions use the key balance sheet items to finance economic growth. They channel funds from their depositors with surplus funds to other households that purchase homes. They also channel funds to support investment in commercial property. They serve a major role in the development of the housing and commercial property market. They also use some deposits to purchase Treasury and municipal securities and thereby finance spending by the Treasury and municipalities.

Exposure to Risk

Like commercial banks, SIs are exposed to liquidity risk, credit risk, and interest rate risk. However, because their sources and uses of funds differ from those of banks, their exposure to risk varies as well.

Liquidity Risk

Since SIs commonly use short-term liabilities to finance long-term assets, they depend on additional deposits to accommodate withdrawal requests. If new deposits are not

Exhibit 21.3 How Savings Institutions Finance Economic Growth

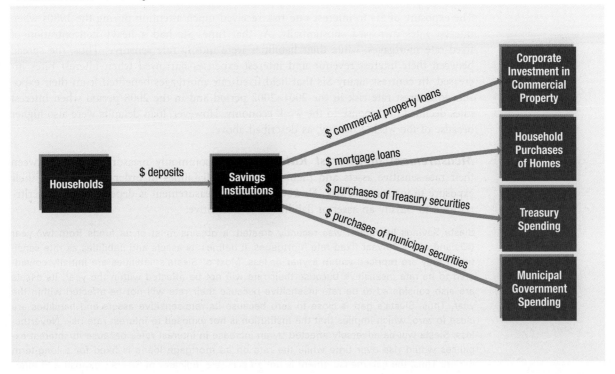

sufficient to cover withdrawal requests, these institutions can experience liquidity problems. To remedy this situation, they can obtain funds through repurchase agreements or borrow funds in the federal funds market. These sources of funds will resolve only a short-term shortage, however. They will not be appropriate if a longer-term liquidity problem exists.

An alternative way to remedy a problem of insufficient liquidity is to sell assets in exchange for cash. Savings institutions can sell their Treasury securities or even some of their mortgages in the secondary market. Although the sale of assets can boost liquidity, it also reduces the institution's size and possibly its earnings. Therefore, minor liquidity deficiencies are typically resolved by increasing liabilities rather than selling assets.

Credit Risk

Because mortgages represent the primary asset, they are the main reason for credit risk at SIs. Although Federal Housing Authority (FHA) and Veterans Administration (VA) mortgages originated by SIs are insured against credit risk, conventional mortgages are not. Private insurance can normally be obtained for conventional mortgages, but SIs often incur the risk themselves rather than pay for the insurance. If they perform adequate credit analysis on their potential borrowers and geographically diversify their mortgage loans, they should be able to maintain a low degree of credit risk.

Some SIs increased their concentration of subprime (low quality) mortgage loans in order to strive for a higher return on their assets. This strategy failed as many of the loans defaulted during the credit crisis in the 2008–2009 period.

Interest Rate Risk

The exposure of SIs to interest rate risk received much attention during the 1980s when interest rates increased substantially. At that time, SIs had a heavy concentration of fixed-rate mortgages, while their liabilities were mostly rate sensitive. Thus, the spread between their interest revenue and interest expenses narrowed when interest rates increased. In contrast, many SIs that held fixed-rate mortgages benefited from their exposure to interest rate risk in the 2001–2002 period and in the 2008 period when interest rates declined in response to the weak economy. However, loan defaults were also higher because of the weak economy, as described above.

Measurement of Interest Rate Risk

SIs commonly measure the gap between their rate-sensitive assets and their rate-sensitive liabilities in order to determine their exposure to interest rate risk. However, the gap measurement is dependent on the criteria used to classify an asset or liability as rate sensitive.

EXAMPLE

Siesta Savings Institution was recently created. It obtains most of its funds from two-year CDs and offers 30-year fixed-rate mortgages. It defines its assets and liabilities as rate sensitive if they are repriced within a year or less. Most of Siesta's liabilities are initially considered to be rate insensitive because their rate will not be affected within the year. Its assets are also considered to be rate insensitive because their rate will not be affected within the year. Thus, Siesta's gap is close to zero because its rate-sensitive assets and liabilities are close to zero, which implies that the institution is not exposed to interest rate risk. Nevertheless, Siesta will be adversely affected by an increase in interest rates because its interest expenses would rise over time while the rate on its mortgage loans is fixed for a long-term period. Thus, the gap measurement is not an accurate indicator of Siesta's exposure to interest rate risk. ●

Given the limitations of the gap measurement, some SIs measure the duration of their respective assets and liabilities to determine the imbalance in sensitivity of interest revenue versus expenses to interest rate movements. An example follows.

EXAMPLE

Tucson Savings Institution (TSI) desires to measure the duration of its assets and liabilities. It first needs to classify each balance sheet component into various maturity categories, as shown in Exhibit 21.4. The rates on most adjustable-rate mortgages are adjusted every year, which is why the amounts under the longer-term categories show zero. The average duration for each category is provided below the dollar amount. Some fixed-rate mortgages are classified in the earlier term categories, because they are maturing or will be sold soon. The duration of .91 for adjustable-rate mortgages is a weighted average of their durations, computed as (7,000/27,000).30 + (15,000/27,000).80 + (4,000/27,000)1.9 + (1,000/27,000)2.9.

The durations for fixed-rate mortgages and investment securities were computed in a similar manner. The duration for total assets of 2.76 years was computed as a weighted average of the individual assets: (27,000/61,000).91 + (20,000/61,000) 5.32 + (14,000/61,000)2.65 = 2.76.

A similar procedure was used to estimate the duration of liabilities. NOW accounts and passbook savings have no specified maturity, but their rate is adjusted less frequently than the rate on MMDAs, which is why MMDAs have a shorter duration. The total liability duration is about .45. TSI's total asset duration is more than six times its liability duration. Thus, its future performance is highly exposed to interest rate movements. Its market value would decrease substantially in response to an increase in interest rates. TSI can reduce its exposure to interest rate risk by reducing the proportion of its assets in the long-duration categories. ●

Financial institutions use computer programs to estimate their asset and liability duration and apply sensitivity analysis to proposed balance sheet adjustments. For example, TSI could determine how its asset and liability duration would change if it engaged in a promotional effort to issue five-year deposits and used the funds to offer adjustable-rate mortgages.

Exhibit 21.4 Duration Schedule for Tucson Savings Institution (Dollar Amounts are in Thousands)

| | RATE READJUSTMENT PERIOD | | | | | | | |
ASSETS	LESS THAN 6 MONTHS	6 MONTHS TO 1 YEAR	1–3 YEARS	3–5 YEARS	5–10 YEARS	10–20 YEARS	OVER 20 YEARS	TOTAL
Adjustable-rate mortgages								
Amount ($)	$7,000	$15,000	$4,000	$1,000	$0	$0	$0	$27,000
Average duration (yr)	.30	.80	1.90	2.90	0	0	0	.91
Fixed-rate mortgages								
Amount ($)	500	500	1,000	1,000	2,000	10,000	5,000	20,000
Average duration (yr)	.25	.60	1.80	2.60	4.30	5.50	7.60	5.32
Investment securities								
Amount ($)	2,000	3,000	4,000	2,000	1,000	0	2,000	14,000
Average duration (yr)	.20	.70	1.70	3.20	5.30	0	8.05	2.65
Total amount ($)	$9,500	$18,500	$9,000	$4,000	$3,000	$10,000	$7,000	$61,000

Asset duration = 2.76

LIABILITIES								
Fixed-maturity deposits								
Amount ($)	$14,000	$9,000	$2,000	$1,000	$0	$0	$0	$26,000
Duration (yr)	.30	.60	1.80	2.80	0	0	0	.62
NOW accounts								
Amount ($)	4,000	0	0	0	0	0	0	4,000
Duration (yr)	.40	0	0	0	0	0	0	.40
MMDAs								
Amount ($)	15,000	0	0	0	0	0	0	15,000
Duration (yr)	.20	0	0	0	0	0	0	.20
Passbook accounts								
Amount ($)	13,000	0	0	0	0		0	13,000
Duration (yr)	.40	0	0	0	0	0	0	.40
Total amount ($)	$46,000	$9,000	$2,000	$1,000	$0	$0	$0	$58,000

Liability duration = .45

MANAGEMENT OF INTEREST RATE RISK

Savings institutions can use a variety of methods to manage their interest rate risk, including the following:

- Adjustable-rate mortgages
- Interest rate futures contracts
- Interest rate swaps

Adjustable-Rate Mortgages (ARMs)

The interest rates on adjustable-rate mortgages (ARMs) are tied to market-determined rates such as the one-year Treasury bill rate and are periodically adjusted in accordance with the formula stated in the ARM contract. A variety of formulas are used. ARMs enable SIs to maintain a more stable spread between interest revenue and interest expenses.

Although ARMs reduce the adverse impact of rising interest rates, they also reduce the favorable impact of declining interest rates. Suppose an SI that obtains most of its funds from short-term deposits uses the funds to provide fixed-rate mortgages. If interest rates decline and the SI does not hedge its exposure to interest rate risk, the spread will increase. If the SI uses ARMs as a hedging strategy, however, the interest on loans will decrease during a period of declining rates, so the spread will not widen.

While ARMs reduce the risks of SIs, they expose consumers to interest rate risk. Although ARMs typically have a maximum cap limiting the increase in interest rates (such as 2 percent per year and 5 percent over the loan life), the impact on household mortgage payments is still significant. Because some homeowners prefer fixed-rate mortgages, most SIs continue to offer them and therefore incur interest rate risk. Thus, additional strategies besides the use of ARMs are necessary to reduce this risk.

Interest Rate Futures Contracts

An interest rate futures contract allows for the purchase of a specific amount of a particular debt security for a specified price at a future point in time. Sellers of futures contracts are obligated to sell the securities for the contract price at the stated future point in time.

Some SIs use Treasury bond futures contracts because the cash flow characteristics of Treasury bonds resemble those of fixed-rate mortgages. Like mortgages, Treasury bonds offer fixed periodic payments, so their market value moves inversely to interest rate fluctuations. Savings institutions that sell futures contracts on these securities can effectively hedge their fixed-rate mortgages. If interest rates rise, the market value of the securities represented by the futures contract will decrease. The SIs will benefit from the difference between the market value at which they can purchase these securities in the future and the futures price at which they will sell the securities. This can offset the reduced spread between their interest revenue and interest expenses during the period of rising interest rates.

Although the concept of using interest rate futures to guard against interest rate risk is simple, the actual application is more complex. It is difficult to perfectly offset the potential reduction in the spread with a futures position.

Interest Rate Swaps

Another strategy for reducing interest rate risk is the interest rate swap, which allows an SI to swap fixed-rate payments (an outflow) for variable-rate payments (an inflow). The fixed-rate outflow payments can be matched against the fixed-rate mortgages held so that a certain spread can be achieved. In addition, the variable-rate inflows due to the swap can be matched against the variable cost of funds. In a rising rate environment, the institution's fixed-rate outflow payments from the swap agreement remain fixed, while the variable-rate inflow payments due to the swap increase. This favorable result can partially offset the normally unfavorable impact of rising interest rates on an SI's spread. However, an interest rate swap also reduces the favorable impact of declining interest rates. Inflow interest payments decrease, while the outflow interest payments remain the same during a period of declining rates.

Conclusions about Interest Rate Risk

Many SIs have used the strategies just described to reduce their interest rate risk. Although these strategies are useful, it is virtually impossible to completely eliminate the risk. One reason for this is the potential prepayment of mortgages. Homeowners often pay off their mortgages before maturity without much advance notice to the SI. Consequently, SIs do not really know the actual maturity of the mortgages they hold and cannot perfectly match the interest rate sensitivity of their assets and liabilities.

INTERACTION WITH OTHER FINANCIAL INSTITUTIONS

The roles of SIs overlap with those of other financial institutions. Thus, SIs interact with various types of financial institutions, as summarized in Exhibit 21.5. Savings institutions compete with commercial banks and money market mutual funds to obtain funds as well as with commercial banks and finance companies in lending funds. Their hedging of interest rate risk is facilitated by investment companies that act as financial intermediaries for interest rate swaps. Their ability to sell mortgages in the secondary market is enhanced by insurance companies that purchase them.

Many SIs have other financial institutions as subsidiaries that provide a variety of services, including consumer finance, trust company, mortgage banking, discount brokerage, and insurance.

Participation in Financial Markets

As SIs interact with other financial institutions, they rely on various financial markets, as summarized in Exhibit 21.6. Mortgage markets provide a source of funds to SIs that desire to issue mortgage-backed securities or sell their mortgages in the secondary market.

Exhibit 21.5 Interactions between Savings Institutions and Other Financial Institutions

TYPE OF FINANCIAL INSTITUTION	INTERACTION WITH SAVINGS INSTITUTIONS
Commercial banks	• Compete with SIs in attracting deposits, providing consumer loans, and providing commercial loans. • Have merged with SIs in recent years.
Finance companies	• Compete with SIs in providing consumer and commercial loans.
Money market mutual funds	• Compete with SIs in attracting short-term investments from investors.
Investment companies and brokerage firms	• Serve SIs that wish to engage in interest rate swaps and interest rate caps. • Have agreements with SIs to offer brokerage services to their customers.
Insurance companies	• Purchase mortgages from SIs in the secondary market.

Exhibit 21.6 Participation of Savings Institutions in Financial Markets

FINANCIAL MARKET	HOW SAVINGS INSTITUTIONS PARTICIPATE IN THIS MARKET
Money markets	• Compete with other depository institutions for short-term deposits by issuing commercial paper.
Mortgage markets	• Sell mortgages in the secondary market and issue mortgage-backed securities.
Bond markets	• Purchase bonds for their investment portfolios. • Issue bonds to obtain long-term funds.
Futures markets	• Hedge against interest rate movements by taking positions in interest rate futures.
Options markets	• Hedge against interest rate movements by purchasing put options on interest rate futures.
Swap markets	• Hedge against interest rate movements by engaging in interest rate swaps.

Bond markets serve as a use of funds for SIs with excess funds and as a source of funds for SIs that issue new bonds in the primary market or sell bond holdings in the secondary market. Futures markets and options markets have enabled SIs to reduce interest rate risk that results from their investment in mortgages and bonds.

VALUATION OF A SAVINGS INSTITUTION

Savings institutions (or SI operating units that are part of a financial conglomerate) are commonly valued by their managers to monitor progress over time or by other financial institutions that are considering an acquisition. The value of an SI can be modeled as the present value of its future cash flows. Thus, the value of an SI should change in response to changes in its expected cash flows in the future and to changes in the required rate by investors:

$$\Delta V = f[\Delta E(CF), \Delta k]$$
$$\qquad\qquad\quad + \qquad -$$

Factors That Affect Cash Flows

The change in an SI's expected cash flows may be modeled as

$$\Delta E(CF) = f(\Delta ECON, \Delta R_f, \Delta INDUS, \Delta MANAB)$$
$$\qquad\qquad\quad + \qquad - \qquad ? \qquad\qquad +$$

where ECON represents economic growth, R_f represents the risk-free interest rate, INDUS represents the industry conditions to which SIs are exposed, and MANAB represents abilities of the SI's management.

Economic Growth   Economic growth can enhance an SI's cash flows by increasing household demand for consumer loans or mortgage loans, thereby allowing the SI to provide more loans. In addition, loan defaults are normally reduced in periods of strong economic growth. Furthermore, the demand for other financial services (such as real estate and insurance services) provided by SIs tends to be higher during periods of strong economic growth when households have relatively high levels of disposable income.

Change in the Risk-Free Interest Rate   An SI's cash flows may be inversely related to interest rate movements. First, if the risk-free interest rate decreases, other market rates may also decline, and the result may be a stronger demand for the SI's loans. Second, SIs rely heavily on short-term deposits as a source of funds, and the rates paid on these deposits are typically revised in accordance with other interest rate movements. Savings institutions' assets (such as consumer loans and mortgage loans) commonly have fixed rates, so interest income does not adjust to interest rate movements until those assets reach maturity or are sold. Therefore, when interest rates fall, an SI's cost of obtaining funds declines more than the decline in the interest earned on its loans and investments. An increase in interest rates can reduce the SI's expected cash flows because the interest paid on deposits may increase more than the interest earned on loans and investments.

Change in Industry Conditions   Savings institutions are exposed to industry conditions such as regulatory constraints, technology, and competition. If regulatory constraints are reduced, the expected cash flows of some SIs should increase. For example, when regulators reduced constraints on the services that could be offered, SIs were able to provide more services for their customers. At the same time, however, a reduction in regulations can cause some of the less efficient SIs to lose market share and therefore experience a reduction in cash flows.

Change in Management Abilities   An SI has control over the composition of its managers and its organizational structure. Its managers attempt to make internal decisions that will capitalize on the external forces (economic growth, interest rates, regulatory constraints) that the institution cannot control. Thus, the management skills of an SI influence its expected cash flows. For example, skillful managers will recognize whether to increase the funds allocated to fixed-rate mortgages based on expectations of future interest rates. They can capitalize on regulatory changes by offering a diversified set of services that accommodate specific customers. They can use technology in a manner that reduces expenses. They may also use derivative securities to alter the potential return and the exposure of the SI to interest rate movements.

Factors That Affect the Required Rate of Return

The required rate of return by investors who invest in an SI can be modeled as

$$\Delta k = f(\Delta R_f, \Delta RP)$$
$$+ \quad +$$

where ΔR_f represents a change in the risk-free interest rate, and ΔRP represents a change in the risk premium.

An increase in the risk-free rate results in a higher return required by investors. High inflation, economic growth, and a high budget deficit place upward pressure on interest rates, while money supply growth places downward pressure on interest rates (assuming it does not cause inflation). Thus, a substantial increase in inflation or in the budget deficit typically results in lower valuations of SIs.

Change in the Risk Premium   If the risk premium on an SI rises, so will the required rate of return by investors who invest in the SI. High economic growth results in less risk for an SI because its consumer loans, mortgage loans, and investments in debt securities are less likely to default. The effect of industry conditions on SIs can be mixed. A reduction in regulatory constraints on services can reduce the risk of SIs as they diversify their offerings, or it can increase their risk if they engage in some services that are riskier than their traditional services. An improvement in management skills may reduce the perceived risk of the SIs and therefore reduce the risk premium.

Exhibit 21.7 provides a framework for valuing an SI, based on the preceding discussion. In general, the value of an SI is favorably affected by strong economic growth, a reduction in interest rates, and high-quality management. The sensitivity of an SI's value to these conditions depends on its own characteristics. For example, the value of an SI that emphasizes real estate and insurance services will be more sensitive to regulations that restrict or limit the offering of these services than will the value of an SI that focuses on traditional mortgage lending. The latter institution may be more sensitive to interest rate movements.

WEB

www.fdic.gov
Information about the performance of savings institutions.

WEB

www.ots.treas.gov
Review of performance of savings institutions overall.

EXPOSURE OF SAVINGS INSTITUTIONS TO CRISES

SIs were devastated by the savings institution crisis during the late 1980s and by the credit crisis in the 2008–2009 period.

Savings Institution Crisis in the Late 1980s

One reason for the crisis of the late 1980s was an increase in interest rates. Those SIs that had provided long-term mortgages were adversely affected, because the interest they earned on assets remained constant while the interest they paid on liabilities increased. Consequently, their net interest income declined.

Exhibit 21.7 Framework for Valuing a Savings Institution

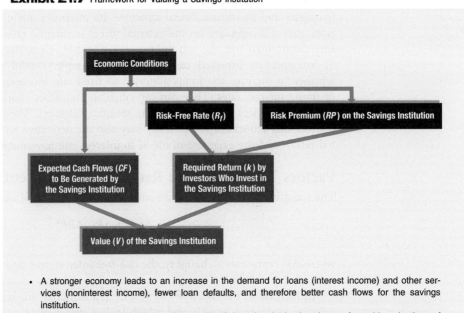

- A stronger economy leads to an increase in the demand for loans (interest income) and other services (noninterest income), fewer loan defaults, and therefore better cash flows for the savings institution.
- A lower risk-free rate leads to a lower cost of deposits obtained and more favorable valuations of the mortgages held by the savings institution.
- The valuation is also influenced by industry conditions and the saving institution's management (not shown in the diagram). These factors affect the risk premium (and therefore the required return by investors) and the expected cash flows to be generated by the savings institution. In particular, regulatory changes can affect the level of competition and therefore affect the savings institution's cash flows and risk premium.

In addition, many SIs had been making commercial loans without much expertise in assessing the ability of firms to repay their loans. Many loan defaults occurred in the Southwest, where economies were devastated by a decline in oil prices. Layoffs in the oil industry resulted, causing a decline in income. Real estate prices dropped so dramatically that when SIs foreclosed on the bad real estate loans, the property that had served as collateral was worth less than the loans. Although some housing loans defaulted, the major loan losses were in commercial real estate, such as office complexes. Some SIs also experienced losses on their investments in junk bonds.

Many SIs experienced a cash flow deficiency as a result of their loan losses, as the inflows from loan repayments were not sufficient to cover depositor withdrawals. Consequently, they were forced to offer higher interest rates on deposits to attract more funds. As depositors became aware of the crisis, they began to withdraw their savings from SIs, which exacerbated the illiquidity problem.

Fraud   In addition, many SIs experienced financial problems because of various fraudulent activities. In one of the most common types of fraud, managers used depositors' funds to purchase personal assets, including yachts, artwork, and automobile dealerships. At many SIs, there had clearly been a lack of oversight by executives and by the board of directors, which allowed some managers to serve their own interests rather than shareholder interests. Many of the problems of the SIs could have been reduced if proper governance had been applied.

Provisions of the FIRREA   To prevent further failures and restore confidence, the Financial Institutions Reform, Recovery, and Enforcement Act (FIRREA) was enacted in 1989.

Among other things, the FIRREA increased penalties for officers of SIs and other financial institutions convicted of fraud, revised the regulation of SIs, and raised the capital requirements for SIs. It also allowed commercial banks to acquire SIs. In addition, SIs were required to sell off any holdings of junk bonds and prohibited from investing in them in the future.

The Resolution Trust Corporation (RTC) was formed to deal with insolvent SIs. The RTC liquidated the assets of the insolvent SIs and reimbursed depositors or sold the SIs to other financial institutions. By the time the RTC was closed at the end of 1995, it had either liquidated or found a buyer for 747 insolvent SIs. It had also recovered $394 billion from liquidating assets and another $2.4 billion from legal settlements.

Beyond restoring confidence in the SI industry, the FIRREA significantly improved conditions for SIs over the next 15 years. SIs slowly built their capital and sold off risky assets. Nevertheless, many SIs pursued risky strategies again in the 2004–2006 period, which led to major problems for them during the credit crisis, as described next.

The Credit Crisis

Following the enactment of the FIRREA, the performance of SIs improved for several years. In particular, SIs experienced strong performance in the 2003–2006 period when the U.S. economy was strong and mortgage originations increased substantially. During this period, some SIs or their subsidiaries offered subprime mortgage loans, which were granted to borrowers who did not qualify for conventional mortgages. Lenders charge a premium of 3 percentage points or more on subprime mortgage loans over the rate charged on conventional mortgages. In addition, they charge additional fees at the time the loan is originated. Because of the large spread between the rate earned on subprime mortgages and the cost of obtaining funds, many SIs entered this market. Some of them were very aggressive and originated loans without properly screening the loan applicants. The subprime mortgage loans were commonly fixed at a low rate for the first two years and then were to adjust in line with market interest rates after that. As market interest rates increased in the 2005–2006 period, many subprime mortgage borrowers could not meet their monthly payments. Furthermore, the economy weakened in the 2007–2008 period, and home prices plummeted. The values of many homes were substantially less than the respective mortgage balances on the homes. Consequently, there were many mortgage foreclosures. By January 2009, about 10 percent of all mortgages were experiencing late payments or were in foreclosure.

Some SIs originated subprime loans and then immediately sold them to institutional investors in the secondary market. These institutions were less exposed to credit risk because they limited their holdings of subprime mortgages. However, the financial firms that focused entirely on subprime mortgages and maintained the mortgages after originating them experienced poor performance in the 2007–2008 period when many borrowers could not cover their mortgage payments. Several subprime lenders went bankrupt. The lesson was that the higher premium charged on these risky loans exists because the borrowers are more likely to default, especially when interest rates rise. Some subprime lenders did not anticipate that market interest rates would rise in the 2005–2006 period or that the higher mortgage payments resulting from the higher market interest rates would cause so many loan defaults. Even the subprime lenders that sold all the mortgages they created were adversely affected by the credit crisis, because once the economy weakened, the level of mortgage originations declined substantially.

Many SIs invested heavily in mortgage-backed securities without recognizing the potential credit risk of these securities. They incurred losses on these investments because of late payments or defaults on the mortgages represented by these securities. Some SIs sold credit default swap contracts on mortgage-backed securities, which required them to cover damages when some mortgage-backed securities held by other financial institutions defaulted.

In general, the adverse effects of the credit crisis in the 2008–2009 period were very similar to the adverse effects during the savings institution crisis in the late 1980s. Both crises were caused by lenders that attempted to generate very high returns without recognizing the risk involved.

Notable Failures during the Credit Crisis   The financial problems of SIs were highlighted by several large failures, including Countrywide Financial (the second largest SI), IndyMac (the eighth largest SI), and Washington Mutual (the largest SI). Countrywide Financial used a very aggressive strategy in which it approved subprime mortgage loans of questionable quality. It financed some of its loans and sold many other loans in the secondary market, while continuing to service those loans. Many of these loans defaulted in 2007. In January 2008, Countrywide Financial was failing and was acquired by Bank of America.

In July 2008, as rumors circulated about the possible failure of IndyMac (with $32 billion of mortgage assets), depositors began to withdraw an average of $100 million per day. This created even more severe problems for IndyMac, which caused the FDIC to intervene and take it over.

In September 2008, Washington Mutual became the largest depository institution ever to fail in the United States. Like IndyMac, Washington Mutual suffered liquidity problems as its depositors were withdrawing funds because of rumors about its financial problems. It held assets of $307 billion. The main reason for Washington Mutual's failure was its heavy investment in mortgages and mortgage-backed securities. The FDIC seized the assets of Washington Mutual and then sold most of them to J.P. Morgan Chase. As a result of this acquisition, J.P. Morgan Chase became the second largest commercial bank in the United States.

CREDIT UNIONS

Credit unions (CUs) are nonprofit organizations composed of members with a common bond, such as an affiliation with a particular labor union, church, university, or even residential area. A qualified person can typically become a member of a CU by depositing $5 or more into an account. Credit unions serve as intermediaries for their members. They accept deposits from members who have excess funds and channel most of the funds to those members who want to finance the purchase of a car or other assets.

There are about 10,200 CUs in the United States. Although the number of CUs now exceeds the number of commercial banks, the total assets of CUs are less than one-tenth the amount of total assets in commercial banks.

Ownership of Credit Unions

WEB

www.findcu.com

Identifies credit unions in all states.

Because CUs do not issue stock, they are technically owned by the depositors. The deposits are called shares, and interest paid on the deposits is called a dividend. Because CUs are nonprofit organizations, their income is not taxed. Like savings institutions and commercial banks, CUs can be federally or state chartered. If the state does not offer a charter, a federal charter is necessary.

Although a few CUs (such as the Navy Federal CU) have assets of more than $1 billion, most are very small. Federally chartered CUs are growing at a faster rate than state-chartered CUs, and their total assets are now significantly larger than the aggregate assets of state-chartered CUs.

Because CUs are owned by members, their objective is to satisfy those members. CUs offer interest on share deposits to members who invest funds. In addition, they provide loans to members who are in need of funds. Thus, as mentioned earlier, they act as intermediaries by repackaging deposits from member savers and providing them as loans to member borrowers. If CUs accumulate earnings, they can use the earnings to either offer higher rates on deposits or reduce rates on loans. Growth can allow CUs to be more diversified and more efficient if economies of scale exist.

Advantages and Disadvantages of Credit Unions

As mentioned earlier, CUs are nonprofit and therefore are not taxed. This creates a major advantage for CUs over other types of financial institutions. Credit unions can offer higher deposit rates and lower loan rates than their competitors and still achieve a satisfactory level of performance, because their profits are not taxed and they do not have to achieve a desired return for shareholders. In addition, their noninterest expenses are relatively low, because their office and furniture are often donated or provided at a very low cost through the affiliation of their members.

Some characteristics of CUs can be unfavorable. Their employees may not have the incentive to manage operations efficiently. In addition, the common bond requirement for membership restricts a given CU from growing beyond the potential size of that particular affiliation. The common bond also limits the ability of CUs to diversify. This is especially true when all members are employees of a particular institution. If that institution lays off a number of workers, many members may simultaneously experience financial problems and withdraw their share deposits or default on their loans. This could cause the CU to become illiquid at a time when more members need loans to survive the layoff.

Even when the common bond does not represent a particular employer, many CUs are unable to diversify geographically because all members live in the same area. Thus, an economic slowdown in this area would have an adverse impact on most members. Furthermore, CUs cannot diversify among various products the way that commercial banks and savings institutions do. They are created to serve the members and therefore concentrate heavily on providing loans to members. Finally, in the event that CUs do need funds, they are unable to issue stock because they are owned by depositors rather than shareholders.

To try to overcome some of these disadvantages as well as to better diversify their services and take greater advantage of economies of scale, CUs increasingly have been merging. Consequently, some CUs now draw their members from a number of employers, organizations, and other affiliations. CUs are also trying to diversify their products by offering traveler's checks, money orders, and life insurance to their members.

Credit Union Sources of Funds

Credit unions obtain most of their funds from share deposits by members. The typical deposit is similar to a passbook savings account deposit at commercial banks or savings institutions, as it has no specified maturity and is insured up to $100,000 ($250,000 in 2009). CUs also offer share certificates, which provide higher rates than share deposits but require a minimum amount (such as $500) and a specified maturity. The share certificates offered by CUs compete against the retail CDs offered by commercial banks and SIs. The proportion of funds obtained through regular share deposits is relatively large compared to the counterpart passbook accounts offered by other depository institutions. This characteristic allows CUs to obtain much of their funds at a relatively low cost.

In addition to share deposits and certificates, most CUs also offer checkable accounts called share drafts, which became more popular in the early 1990s. These accounts can pay interest and allow an unlimited amount of checks to be written. They normally require a minimum balance to be maintained. Share drafts offered by CUs compete against the NOW accounts and MMDAs offered by commercial banks and SIs.

If a CU needs funds temporarily, it can borrow from other CUs or from the **Central Liquidity Facility (CLF).** The CLF acts as a lender for CUs to accommodate seasonal funding and specialized needs or to boost the liquidity of troubled CUs.

Like other depository institutions, CUs maintain capital. Their primary source of capital is retained earnings. In recent years, CUs have boosted their capital, which helps cushion against any future loan losses. Given that CUs tend to use conservative management, their capital ratio is relatively high compared with other depository institutions.

Credit Union Uses of Funds

Credit unions use the majority of their funds for loans to members. These loans finance automobiles, home improvements, and other personal expenses. They are typically secured and carry maturities of five years or less. Some CUs offer long-term mortgage loans, but many prefer to avoid loans with long maturities. In addition to providing loans, CUs purchase government and agency securities to maintain adequate liquidity.

Regulation of Credit Unions

WEB

www.ncua.gov
Background on the
NCUA.

Federal CUs are supervised and regulated by the **National Credit Union Administration (NCUA),** which is composed of three board members, one of whom chairs the board.

The NCUA employs a staff of examiners to monitor CUs. The examiners conduct assessments of all federally chartered CUs as well as any state-chartered CUs applying for federal insurance. Each CU completes a semiannual call report that provides financial information. From this information, the NCUA examiners derive financial ratios that measure the financial condition of the CU. The ratios are then compared to an industry norm to detect any significant deviations. Then a summary of the CU, called a Financial Performance Report, is completed to identify any potential problems that deserve special attention in the future.

As part of the assessment, the examiners classify each CU into a specific risk category, ranging from Code 1 (low risk) to Code 5 (high risk). This is intended to serve as an early warning system so that CUs that are experiencing problems or are in potential danger can be closely monitored in the future. The criteria used to assess risk are capital adequacy, asset quality, management, earnings, liquidity, and sensitivity to market conditions. This CAMELS system is very similar to the FDIC's system for tracking the commercial banks it insures. In 1999, the NCUA implemented a Corporate Risk Information System (CRIS), which provides a more detailed analysis of each CU's risk. In addition, CUs are required to maintain a capital ratio of 8 percent of risk-weighted assets.

Regulation of State-Chartered Credit Unions   State-chartered CUs are regulated by their respective states. The degree to which CUs can offer various products and services is influenced by the type of charter and by their location. In addition to services and rates, loans offered by CUs to officers and directors of CUs also carry certain limitations.

Insurance for Credit Unions   About 90 percent of CUs are insured by the **National Credit Union Share Insurance Fund (NCUSIF),** which is administered by the NCUA. The CUs typically pay an annual insurance premium of one-twelfth of 1 percent of share deposits. A supplemental premium is added if necessary. Some states require their CUs to be federally insured; others allow insurance to be offered by alternative insurance agencies.

The NCUSIF was created in 1970, without any contributing start-up capital from the U.S. Treasury and Federal Reserve. All federally chartered CUs are required to obtain insurance from the NCUSIF. State-chartered CUs are eligible for NCUSIF insurance only if they meet various guidelines. The maximum insurance per depositor is $100,000 ($250,000 in 2009).

The NCUSIF sets aside a portion of its funds as reserves to cover expenses resulting from CU failures each year. Given the low number of failures, the reserves have been more than adequate to cover these expenses.

Exposure of Credit Unions to Risk

Like other depository institutions, CUs are exposed to liquidity risk, credit risk, and interest rate risk. Their balance sheet structure differs from that of other institutions, however, so their exposure to each type of risk also differs.

Liquidity Risk of Credit Unions If a CU experiences an unanticipated wave of withdrawals without an offsetting amount of new deposits, it could become illiquid. It can borrow from the Central Liquidity Facility to resolve temporary liquidity problems, but if the shortage of funds is expected to continue, the CU must search for a more permanent cure. Other depository institutions have greater ability to boost deposit levels because they can tap various markets. Because the market for a CU is restricted to those consumers who qualify as members, CUs have less ability to quickly generate additional deposits.

Credit Risk of Credit Unions Because CUs concentrate on personal loans to their members, their exposure to credit (default) risk is primarily derived from those loans. Most of their loans are secured, which reduces the loss to CUs in the event of default. Poor economic conditions can have a significant impact on loan defaults. Some CUs will perform much better than others because of more favorable economic conditions in their area. However, even during favorable economic periods, CUs with very lenient loan policies could experience losses. A common concern is that CUs may not conduct a thorough credit analysis of loan applicants; the loans provided by CUs are consumer oriented, however, so an elaborate credit analysis generally is not required.

While CUs are normally viewed as the most conservative of all depository institutions, even they felt the adverse effects of the credit crisis that began in 2008. Some CUs suffered large losses due to late payments or defaults on mortgages that they provided. They also experienced some losses on mortgage-backed securities in which they had invested. Credit unions are restricted from investing in risky securities, but some of the mortgage-backed securities that they purchased were highly rated at the time of purchase. As housing conditions worsened, the demand for securities backed by mortgages declined, and the values of mortgage-backed securities declined as well.

Interest Rate Risk of Credit Unions The majority of maturities on consumer loans offered by CUs are short term, causing their asset portfolios to be rate sensitive. Because their sources of funds are also generally rate sensitive, movements in interest revenues and interest expenses of CUs are highly correlated. Therefore, the spread between interest revenues and interest expenses remains somewhat stable over time, regardless of how interest rates change.

SUMMARY

- The main sources of funds for SIs are deposits and borrowed funds. The main uses of funds for SIs are mortgages, mortgage-backed securities, and other securities.

- Savings institutions are exposed to credit risk as a result of their heavy concentration in mortgages, mortgage-backed securities, and other securities. They attempt to diversify their investments to reduce credit risk.

   Savings institutions are highly susceptible to interest rate risk, because their asset portfolios are typ-

ically less rate sensitive than their liability portfolios to interest rate movements. They can reduce their interest rate risk by using interest rate futures contracts or interest rate swaps.

- The valuation of an SI is a function of its expected cash flows and the required return by its investors. The expected cash flows are influenced by economic growth, interest rate movements, regulatory constraints, and the abilities of the institution's managers. The required rate of return is influenced by the prevailing risk-free rate and the risk premium. The risk premium is lower when economic conditions are strong. A reduction in regulatory constraints can reduce the risk premium by allowing the SI to diversify its services, but may increase the risk premium if the institution pursues services that it cannot provide efficiently.

- In the late 1980s, many SIs experienced heavy losses from loan defaults, adverse interest rate movements, and fraud. These adverse effects led to the SI crisis. In 1989, the FIRREA was passed to resolve the crisis. Specifically, the FIRREA boosted capital requirements, increased penalties for fraud, and prohibited SIs from purchasing junk bonds. Nevertheless, many SIs pursued aggressive mortgage lending strategies in the 2004–2006 period, which led to ma-

jor problems during the credit crisis of 2008–2009. SIs that had used liberal standards to expand their mortgage business experienced heavy losses.

- Credit unions obtain most of their funds from share deposits by members. If they experience a cash deficiency, they can borrow from other CUs or from the Central Liquidity Facility (CLF). They use the majority of their funds for personal loans to members.

- Credit unions are exposed to liquidity risk because they could experience an unanticipated wave of deposit withdrawals. They are also exposed to credit risk as a result of personal loans to members.

Because the personal loans offered by CUs are short term, they are rate sensitive like the liabilities. Thus, the interest rate risk of CUs is typically less than that of other depository institutions.

POINT COUNTER-POINT

Can All Savings Institutions Avoid Failure?

Point Yes. If SIs use conservative management by focusing on adjustable-rate mortgages with limited default risk, they can limit their risk and avoid failure.

Counter-Point No. Some SIs will be crowded out of the market for high-quality adjustable-rate mortgages

and will have to take some risk. There are too many SIs, and some that have weaker management will inevitably fail.

Who Is Correct? Use the Internet to learn more about this issue. Offer your own opinion on this issue.

QUESTIONS AND APPLICATIONS

1. SI Sources and Uses of Funds Explain in general terms how savings institutions differ from commercial banks with respect to their sources of funds and uses of funds. Discuss each source of funds for SIs. Identify and discuss the main uses of funds for SIs.

2. Ownership of SIs What are the alternative forms of ownership of a savings institution?

3. Regulation of SIs What criteria are used by regulators to examine a thrift institution?

4. MMDAs How did the creation of money market deposit accounts influence the overall cost of funds for a savings institution?

5. Offering More Diversified Services Discuss the entrance of savings institutions into consumer and commercial lending. What are the potential risks and rewards of this strategy? Discuss the conflict between diversification and specialization of SIs.

6. Liquidity and Credit Risk Describe the liquidity and credit risk of savings institutions, and discuss how each is managed.

7. ARMs What is an adjustable-rate mortgage (ARM)? Discuss potential advantages such mortgages offer a savings institution.

8. Use of Financial Futures Explain how savings institutions could use interest rate futures to reduce interest rate risk.

9. Use of Interest Rate Swaps Explain how savings institutions could use interest rate swaps to reduce interest rate risk. Will SIs that use swaps perform better or worse than those that were unhedged during a period of declining interest rates? Explain.

10. DIDMCA What effect did the Depository Institution Deregulation and Monetary Control Act

(DIDMCA) of 1980 and the Garn-St Germain Act of 1982 have on savings institutions?

11. Hedging Interest Rate Movements If market interest rates are expected to decline over time, will a savings institution with rate-sensitive liabilities and a large amount of fixed-rate mortgages perform best by (a) using an interest rate swap, (b) selling financial futures, or (c) remaining unhedged? Explain.

12. Exposure to Interest Rate Risk The following table discloses the interest rate sensitivity of two savings institutions (dollar amounts are in millions).

	INTEREST SENSITIVITY PERIOD			
	WITHIN 1 YEAR	FROM 1 TO 5 YEARS	FROM 5 TO 10 YEARS	OVER 10 YEARS
Lawrence S&L				
Interest-earning assets	$ 8,000	$3,000	$7,000	$3,000
Interest-bearing liabilities	11,000	6,000	2,000	1,000
Manhattan S&L				
Interest-earning assets	1,000	1,000	4,000	3,000
Interest-bearing liabilities	2,000	2,000	1,000	1,000

Based on this information only, which institution's stock price would likely be affected more by a given change in interest rates? Justify your opinion.

13. SI Crisis What were some of the more obvious reasons for the savings institution crisis of the late 1980s?

14. FIRREA Explain how the Financial Institutions Reform, Recovery, and Enforcement Act (FIRREA) reduced the perceived risk of savings institutions.

15. Background on CUs Who are the owners of credit unions? Explain the tax status of CUs and the reason for that status. What is the typical size range of CUs? Give reasons for that range.

16. Sources of CU Funds Describe the main source of funds for credit unions. Why might the average cost of funds to CUs be relatively stable even when market interest rates are volatile?

17. Regulation of CUs Who regulates credit unions? What are the regulators' powers? Where do CUs obtain deposit insurance?

18. Risk of CUs Explain how credit union exposure to liquidity risk differs from that of other financial institutions. Explain why CUs are more insulated from interest rate risk than some other financial institutions.

19. Advantages and Disadvantages of CUs Identify some advantages of credit unions. Identify disadvantages of CUs that relate to their common bond requirement.

20. Impact of the Credit Crisis Explain how the credit crisis in the 2008–2009 period affected some savings institutions. Compare the causes of the credit crisis to the causes of the SI crisis in the late 1980s.

Interpreting Financial News

Interpret the following comments made by Wall Street analysts and portfolio managers:

a. "Deposit insurance can fuel a crisis because it allows weak SIs to grow."

b. "Thrifts are no longer so sensitive to interest rate movements, even if their asset and liability compositions have not changed."

c. "Many SIs did not understand that higher returns from subprime mortgages must be weighed against risk."

Managing in Financial Markets

Hedging Interest Rate Risk As a consultant to Boca Savings & Loan Association, you notice that a large portion of its 15-year fixed-rate mortgages are financed with funds from short-term deposits. You believe the yield curve is useful in indicating the market's anticipation of future interest rates and that the yield curve is primarily determined by interest rate expectations. At the present time, Boca has not hedged its interest rate risk. Assume that a steep upward-sloping yield curve currently exists.

a. Boca asks you to assess its exposure to interest rate risk. Describe how Boca will be affected by rising interest rates and by a decline in interest rates.

b. Given the information about the yield curve, would you advise Boca to hedge its exposure to interest rate risk? Explain.

c. Explain why your advice to Boca may possibly backfire.

Flow of Funds Exercise

Market Participation by Savings Institutions

Rimsa Savings is a savings institution that provided Carson Company with a mortgage for its office building. Rimsa recently offered to refinance the mortgage if Carson Company will change to a fixed-rate loan from an adjustable-rate loan.

a. Explain the interaction between Carson Company and Rimsa Savings.

b. Why is Rimsa willing to allow Carson Company to transfer its interest rate risk to Rimsa? (Assume that there is an upward-sloping yield curve.)

c. If Rimsa maintains the mortgage on the office building purchased by Carson Company, who is the ultimate source of the money that was provided for the office building? If Rimsa sells the mortgage in the secondary market to a pension fund, who is the source that is essentially financing the office building? Why would a pension fund be willing to purchase this mortgage in the secondary market?

Internet/Excel Exercises

1. Assess the recent performance of savings institutions using the website www2.fdic.gov/qbp/index.asp. Click on "Quarterly Banking Profile," then on "Savings Institution" section, and summarize the general performance of SIs in the last two years.

2. Retrieve the annual report of Heritage Financial Corporation (ticker symbol is HFWA) or another savings institution of your choice. To access income statement information, go to http://finance.yahoo.com, enter the ticker symbol, and click on "Get Quotes." Then click on "SEC Filings" to retrieve recent income statements. Review the SI's recent performance. Has its income as a percentage of assets increased since the year before? Explain what caused this change over the last year. Has the SI's net interest margin changed since last year? How has its noninterest income (as a percentage of assets) changed over the last year? How have its noninterest expenses changed over the last year? How have its loan loss reserves changed in the last year? Discuss how the SI's recent strategy and eco-

nomic conditions may explain the changes in these components of its income statement.

3. Go to http://finance.yahoo.com/, enter the symbol HFWA (Heritage Financial Corporation), and click on "Get Quotes." Then, retrieve stock price data at the beginning of the last 20 quarters. Then go to http://research.stlouisfed.org/fred2/ and retrieve interest rate data at the beginning of the last 20 quarters for the three-month Treasury bill. Record the data on an Excel spreadsheet. Derive the quarterly return of Heritage Financial. Derive the quarterly change in the interest rate. Apply regression analysis in which the quarterly return of Heritage Financial is the dependent variable and the quarterly change in the interest rate is the independent variable (see Appendix B for more information about using regression analysis). Is there a positive or negative relationship between the interest rate movement and the stock return of Heritage Financial? Is the relationship significant? Offer an explanation for this relationship.

WSJ Exercise

Assessing the Performance of Savings Institutions

Using a recent issue of *The Wall Street Journal*, summarize an article that discussed the recent performance of a particular savings institution. Does the article suggest that the SI's performance was better or worse than the norm? What reason is given for the unusual level of performance?

22
Finance Operations

CHAPTER OBJECTIVES

The specific objectives of this chapter are to:

■ identify the main sources and uses of finance company funds,

■ describe how finance companies are exposed to various forms of risk,

■ identify the factors that determine the values of finance companies, and

■ explain how finance companies interact with other financial institutions.

Finance companies provide short- and intermediate-term credit to consumers and small businesses. Although other financial institutions provide this service, only finance companies specialize in it. Many finance companies operate with a single office, while others have hundreds of offices across the country and even in foreign countries. Consumer finance operations can be conducted by an independent finance company or a unit (subsidiary) of a financial conglomerate.

TYPES OF FINANCE COMPANIES

Finance companies have more than $1 trillion in assets. In aggregate, the amount of their business is similar to that of savings institutions. Some finance companies are independently owned, while others are subsidiaries of financial institutions or other corporations. For example, some very large finance companies are subsidiaries of General Motors, Ford Motor Company, Citigroup, American Express, Capital One, and General Electric.

Finance companies are commonly classified into the different types described below according to the specific services that they offer. Some finance companies could fit in every category because they offer all types of services.

Consumer Finance Companies

Consumer finance companies provide financing for customers of retail stores or wholesalers. For example, a consumer finance company can sponsor a credit card for a retailer so that the retailer can offer its own credit card for its customers. The customers can purchase products there on credit, which is provided by the finance company.

Many consumer finance companies also provide personal loans directly to individuals to finance purchases of large household items. Some consumer finance companies also provide mortgage loans.

Business Finance Companies

Business finance companies offer loans to small businesses. For example, they may provide loans to finance inventory. The business uses the loan to purchase materials that are used in the production process. Once the products are manufactured and sold, the business uses the revenue to pay off the loan. Business finance companies also provide financing in the form of credit cards that are used by a business's employees for travel or for making purchases on behalf of the business.

Captive Finance Subsidiaries

A **captive finance subsidiary (CFS)** is a wholly owned subsidiary whose primary purpose is to finance sales of the parent company's products and services, provide wholesale financing to distributors of the parent company's products, and purchase receivables of the parent company. The actual business practices of a CFS typically include various types of financing apart from just the parent company business. When a captive is formed, the captive and the parent company draw up an operating agreement containing specific stipulations, such as the type of receivables that qualify for sale to the captive and specific services to be provided by the parent.

The motive for creating a CFS can be easily understood by considering the automobile industry. Historically, automobile manufacturers were unable to finance dealers' inventories and had to demand cash from each dealer. Many dealers were unable to sell cars on an installment basis because they needed cash immediately. Banks were the primary source of capital to dealers. However, banks viewed automobiles as luxury items not suitable for bank financing and were unwilling to buy the installment plans created from automobile sales. For this reason, the automobile manufacturers became involved in financing.

The number of CFSs grew most rapidly between 1946 and 1960 as a result of liberalized credit policies and a need to finance growing inventories. By 1960 more than 100 CFSs existed.

Advantages of Captive Finance Subsidiaries

There are several advantages to maintaining a CFS. A CFS can be used to finance distributor or dealer inventories until a sale occurs, making production less cyclical for the manufacturer. It can serve as an effective marketing tool by providing retail financing. It can also be used to finance products leased to others.

A CFS allows a corporation to clearly separate its manufacturing and retailing activities from its financing activities. Therefore, analysis of each segment of the parent company is less expensive and easier. Also, when lending to a CFS rather than a division of the parent company, the lender does not have to be so concerned about the claims of others. Unlike commercial banks, a CFS has no reserve requirements and no legal prohibitions on how it obtains or uses funds. Furthermore, a firm with a CFS can gain a competitive advantage because sale items such as automobiles and housing may depend on the financing arrangements available.

CFSs have diversified their financing activities to include more than just the parent company's product installment plans. General Electric Capital Corporation (GECC) has been the most innovative of all the CFSs. Its financing includes industrial and equipment sales, consumer installment credit, and second mortgage loans on private residences.

SOURCES AND USES OF FUNDS

Finance companies are distinctly different from commercial banks and savings institutions in that they do not rely heavily on deposits. Their sources and uses of funds are described next.

Sources of Funds

The main sources of funds for finance companies are

- Loans from banks
- Commercial paper
- Deposits
- Bonds
- Capital

Loans from Banks   Finance companies commonly borrow from commercial banks and can consistently renew the loans over time. For this reason, bank loans can provide a continual source of funds, although some finance companies use bank loans mainly to accommodate seasonal swings in their business.

Commercial Paper   Although commercial paper is available only for short-term financing, finance companies can continually roll over their issues to create a permanent source of funds. Only the most well-known finance companies have traditionally been able to issue commercial paper to attract funds, because unsecured commercial paper exposes investors to the risk of default. In the past, small or medium-sized finance companies had difficulty placing unsecured commercial paper. In recent years, as secured commercial paper has become popular, more finance companies have access to funds through this market.

The best-known finance companies can issue commercial paper through direct placement, thereby avoiding a transaction fee and lowering their cost of funds. Most companies, however, utilize the services of a commercial paper dealer.

Deposits   Under certain conditions, some states allow finance companies to attract funds by offering customer deposits similar to those of the depository institutions discussed in previous chapters. Although deposits have not been a major source of funds for finance companies, they may become more widely used where legal.

Bonds   Finance companies in need of long-term funds can issue bonds. The decision to issue bonds versus some alternative short-term financing depends on the company's balance sheet structure and its expectations about future interest rates. When the company's assets are less interest rate sensitive than its liabilities and when interest rates are expected to increase, bonds can provide long-term financing at a rate that is completely insulated from rising market rates. If the finance company is confident that interest rates will rise, it might consider using the funds obtained from bonds to offer loans with variable interest rates. Conversely, when interest rates decline, finance companies may use more long-term debt to lock in the cost of funds over an extended period of time.

Capital   Finance companies can build their capital base by retaining earnings or by issuing stock. Like other financial institutions, finance companies maintain a low level of capital as a percentage of total assets. Several finance companies have engaged in initial public offerings of stock so that they could expand their businesses.

Uses of Finance Company Funds

Finance companies use funds for

- Consumer loans
- Business loans and leasing
- Real estate loans

Each use of funds is described in turn.

WEB

www.nfcc.org
More detailed information about consumer loans.

Consumer Loans   Finance companies extend consumer loans in the form of personal loans. One of the most popular types is the automobile loan offered by a finance company that is owned by a car manufacturer. For example, General Motors Acceptance Corporation (GMAC) finances purchases of automobiles built by General Motors. Ford Motor Company and Chrysler also have their own finance companies. Subsidiaries of automobile manufacturers may offer unusually low rates to increase automobile sales.

In addition to offering automobile loans, finance companies offer personal loans for home improvement, mobile homes, and a variety of other personal expenses. Personal loans are often secured by a co-signer or by real property. The maturities on personal loans are typically less than five years.

Finance company loans are subject to ceiling interest rates on the loans provided and to a maximum length on the loan maturity. These regulations are imposed by states, and they vary among the states. Because ceiling rates are now sufficiently above market rates, they normally do not interfere with the rate-setting decisions of finance companies. Finance companies are also subject to state regulations on intrastate business. If a finance company wishes to set up a new branch, it must convince regulators that the branch would serve the needs of the people in that location.

Some finance companies also offer credit card loans through a particular retailer. For example, a retail store may sell products to customers on credit and then sell the credit contract to a finance company. Customers make payments to the finance company under the terms negotiated with the retail store. The finance company is responsible for the initial credit approval and for processing the credit card payments. The retailer can benefit from the finance company's credit allowance through increased sales; the finance company benefits by obtaining increased business. Finance companies increase their customer base in this way and are accessible for additional financing for those customers who prove to be creditworthy. The specific arrangement between a finance company and retailer can vary.

The main competition to finance companies in the consumer loan market comes from commercial banks and credit unions. Finance companies have consistently provided more credit to consumers than credit unions have, but they are a distant second to commercial banks. Savings institutions have recently entered this market and are now also considered a major competitor.

Business Loans and Leasing   In addition to consumer loans, finance companies also provide business (commercial) loans. Companies commonly obtain these loans from the time they purchase raw materials until cash is generated from sales of the finished goods. Such loans are short term but may be renewed, as many companies permanently need financing to support their cash cycle. Business loans are often backed by inventory or accounts receivable.

Some finance companies provide loans to support leveraged buyouts (LBOs). These loans are generally riskier than other business loans but offer a higher expected return. In 2001, some highly leveraged firms experienced financial problems, and exposure to LBO loans received more attention.

Finance companies commonly act as **factors** for accounts receivable; that is, they purchase a firm's receivables at a discount and are responsible for processing and collecting the balances of these accounts. The finance company incurs any losses due to bad debt. Factoring reduces a business's processing costs and also provides short-term financing, as the business receives cash from the finance company earlier than it would have obtained funds from collecting the receivables.

Another way finance companies provide financing is by leasing. They purchase machinery or equipment and then lease it to businesses that prefer to avoid the additional debt on their balance sheet that purchases would require. Avoiding debt can be important to a business that is already close to its debt capacity and is concerned that additional debt will adversely affect its credit rating.

Real Estate Loans   Finance companies offer real estate loans in the form of mortgages on commercial real estate and second mortgages on residential real estate. The offering of second mortgages has become increasingly popular over time. These mortgages are typically secured and historically have had a relatively low default rate.

Exhibit 22.1 How Finance Companies Finance Economic Growth

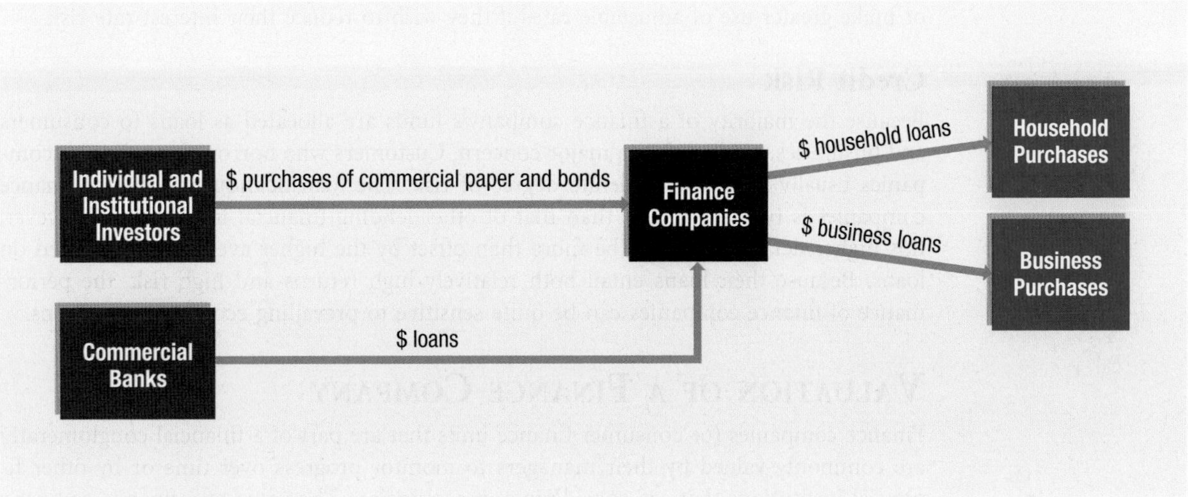

In the 2003–2006 period, however, some finance companies offered subprime (low quality) mortgage loans, which experienced a higher default rate that resulted in losses for the companies during the credit crisis.

Summary of Uses of Funds   The particular allocation of a finance company's uses of funds depends on whether the company is focused on business or consumer lending. Some finance companies, such as GE Capital, provide all types of services. Exhibit 22.1 summarizes the sources and uses of funds by illustrating how finance companies finance economic growth. They channel funds from institutional investors who purchase the securities they issue to households and small businesses that need funds.

Risks Faced by Finance Companies

Finance companies, like other financial institutions, are exposed to three types of risks:

- Liquidity risk
- Interest rate risk
- Credit risk

Because finance companies' characteristics differ from those of other financial institutions, their degree of exposure to each type of risk differs as well.

Liquidity Risk

Finance companies generally do not hold assets that could be easily sold in the secondary market. Thus, if they are in need of funds, they have to borrow. However, their balance sheet structure does not call for much liquidity. Virtually all of their funds are from borrowings rather than deposits anyway. Consequently, they are not susceptible to unexpected deposit withdrawals. Overall, the liquidity risk of finance companies is less than that of other financial institutions.

Interest Rate Risk

Both liability and asset maturities of finance companies are short or intermediate term. Therefore, they are not as susceptible to increasing interest rates as savings institutions are. Finance companies can still be adversely affected, however, because their assets are typically not as rate sensitive as their liabilities. They can shorten their average asset life or make greater use of adjustable rates if they wish to reduce their interest rate risk.

Credit Risk

Because the majority of a finance company's funds are allocated as loans to consumers and businesses, credit risk is a major concern. Customers who borrow from finance companies usually exhibit a moderate degree of risk. The loan delinquency rate of finance companies is typically higher than that of other lending financial institutions. However, this higher default level may be more than offset by the higher average rate charged on loans. Because their loans entail both relatively high returns and high risk, the performance of finance companies can be quite sensitive to prevailing economic conditions.

VALUATION OF A FINANCE COMPANY

Finance companies (or consumer finance units that are part of a financial conglomerate) are commonly valued by their managers to monitor progress over time or by other financial institutions that are considering an acquisition. The value of a finance company can be modeled as the present value of its future cash flows. Thus, the value of a finance company should change in response to changes in its expected cash flows in the future and to changes in the required rate of return by investors:

$$\Delta V = f[\Delta E(CF), \Delta k]$$
$$\qquad\qquad + \qquad -$$

Factors That Affect Cash Flows

The change in a finance company's expected cash flows may be modeled as

$$\Delta E(CF) = f(\Delta ECON, \Delta R_f, \Delta INDUS, \Delta MANAB)$$
$$\qquad\qquad\quad + \qquad - \qquad ? \qquad\quad +$$

where ECON represents economic growth, R_f represents the risk-free interest rate, INDUS represents industry conditions (such as regulatory constraints), and MANAB represents the abilities of the finance company's management.

Economic Growth   Economic growth can enhance a finance company's cash flows by increasing household demand for consumer loans, thereby allowing the finance company to provide more loans. In addition, loan defaults are normally reduced in periods of strong growth. The valuation of finance companies can be very sensitive to economic conditions because they commonly offer relatively risky loans; thus, loan repayments are sensitive to economic conditions.

Change in the Risk-Free Interest Rates   A finance company's cash flows may be inversely related to interest rate movements. If the risk-free interest rate decreases, other market rates may also decline, and as a result, there may be stronger demand for the finance company's loans. Second, finance companies rely heavily on short-term funds, and the rates paid on these funds are typically revised in accordance with other interest rate movements. Finance companies' assets (such as consumer loans) commonly have fixed rates, so interest income does not adjust to interest rate movements until those assets reach maturity. Therefore, when interest rates fall, the finance company's cost of obtaining funds declines more than the decline in the interest earned on its loans and investments. An increase in interest rates could reduce the finance company's expected cash flows because the interest paid on its sources of funds increases, while the interest earned on its existing loans and investments does not.

Change in Industry Conditions Industry conditions include regulatory constraints, technology, and competition within the industry. Some finance companies may be valued higher if state regulators give them the opportunity to generate economies of scale by expanding throughout the state. However, this would result in more competition, causing some finance companies to gain at the expense of others.

Change in Management Abilities A finance company has control over the composition of its managers and its organizational structure. Its managers attempt to make internal decisions that will capitalize on the external forces (economic growth, interest rates, regulatory constraints) that the institution cannot control. Thus, the management skills of a finance company can influence its expected cash flows. In particular, finance companies need skilled managers to analyze the creditworthiness of potential borrowers and assess how future economic conditions may affect their ability to repay their loans. Finance company managers may also capitalize on technology by advertising to consumers and accepting loan applications over the Internet.

Factors That Affect the Required Rate of Return

The required rate of return by investors who invest in a finance company can be modeled as

$$\Delta k = f(\Delta R_f, \Delta RP)$$
$$+ \qquad +$$

where ΔR_f represents a change in the risk-free interest rate, and ΔRP represents a change in the risk premium.

The risk-free interest rate is normally expected to be positively related to inflation, economic growth, and the budget deficit level, but inversely related to money supply growth (assuming it does not cause inflation). The risk premium on a finance company is inversely related to economic growth because there is less uncertainty about loan repayments when economic conditions are strong. The risk premium is also inversely related to the company's management skills, as more skillful managers may be able to focus on financial services that reduce the finance company's exposure to risk.

Exhibit 22.2 provides a framework for valuing a finance company, based on the preceding discussion. In general, the value of a finance company is favorably affected by strong economic growth, a reduction in interest rates, and skilled management. The sensitivity of a finance company's value to these conditions depends on its own characteristics. The higher the risk tolerance reflected in the loans provided by a finance company, the more sensitive its valuation to changes in economic growth (and therefore in the ability of borrowers to repay their loans).

INTERACTION WITH OTHER FINANCIAL INSTITUTIONS

Finance companies and their subsidiaries often interact with other financial institutions, as summarized in Exhibit 22.3. Because of their concentration in consumer lending, finance companies are more closely related to commercial banks, savings institutions, and credit unions. However, those finance companies with subsidiaries that specialize in other financial services compete with insurance companies and pension plans.

Because finance companies compete with savings institutions in providing consumer loans, they are able to increase their market share when savings institutions experience financial problems. Furthermore, some finance companies (such as Household International, Inc.) have acquired savings institutions. Before being acquired by the British-based conglomerate HSBC Holdings in 2003, Household International, Inc. acquired

Exhibit 22.2 Framework for Valuing a Finance Company

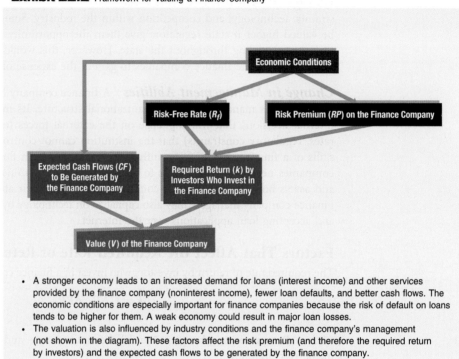

- A stronger economy leads to an increased demand for loans (interest income) and other services provided by the finance company (noninterest income), fewer loan defaults, and better cash flows. The economic conditions are especially important for finance companies because the risk of default on loans tends to be higher for them. A weak economy could result in major loan losses.
- The valuation is also influenced by industry conditions and the finance company's management (not shown in the diagram). These factors affect the risk premium (and therefore the required return by investors) and the expected cash flows to be generated by the finance company.

numerous branches of depository institutions across the country in an effort to diversify its services. Like many other finance companies, Household became a diversified financial services company.

Participation in Financial Markets

Finance companies utilize various financial markets to manage their operations, as summarized in Exhibit 22.4. For their core business, finance companies use financial markets mainly to obtain funds. However, the subsidiaries of finance companies often utilize financial markets to invest funds or to hedge investment portfolios against interest rate risk or market risk. They may even diversify their financial services in foreign countries. As large finance companies expand internationally, they are better able to use the international bond and commercial paper markets as a source of funds.

Exhibit 22.3 Interaction between Finance Companies and Other Financial Institutions

TYPE OF FINANCIAL INSTITUTION	INTERACTION WITH FINANCE COMPANIES
Commercial banks and savings institutions	• Compete with finance companies for consumer loan business (including credit cards), commercial loans, and leasing.
Credit unions	• Compete with finance companies for consumer loan business.
Securities firms	• Underwrite bonds that are issued by finance companies.
Pension funds	• Compete with insurance subsidiaries of finance companies that manage pension plans.
Insurance companies	• Compete directly with insurance subsidiaries of finance companies.

Exhibit 22.4 Participation of Finance Companies in Financial Markets

TYPE OF FINANCIAL MARKET	PARTICIPATION BY FINANCE COMPANIES
Money markets	• Finance companies obtain funds by issuing commercial paper.
Bond markets	• Finance companies issue bonds as a method of obtaining long-term funds. • Subsidiaries of finance companies commonly purchase corporate and Treasury bonds.
Mortgage markets	• Finance companies purchase real estate and also provide loans to real estate investors. • Subsidiaries of finance companies commonly purchase mortgages.
Stock markets	• Finance companies issue stock to establish a capital base. • Subsidiaries of finance companies commonly purchase stocks.
Futures markets	• Subsidiaries of finance companies that offer insurance-related services sometimes use futures contracts to reduce the sensitivity of their bond portfolio to interest rate movements and may also trade stock index futures to reduce the sensitivity of their stock portfolio to stock market movements.
Options markets	• Subsidiaries of finance companies that offer insurance-related services sometimes use options contracts to protect against temporary declines in particular stock holdings.
Swap markets	• Finance companies may engage in interest rate swaps to hedge their exposure to interest rate risk.

Some finance companies have recently acquired insurance companies to enter the insurance business. They have also acquired commercial banks located in various states. In addition, the larger finance companies have diversified into a variety of nonfinancial businesses as well.

MULTINATIONAL FINANCE COMPANIES

Some finance companies are large multinational corporations with subsidiaries in several countries. For example, GE Money provides consumer finance services in 55 countries and serves more than 130 million customers around the world. It provides products and services in local currencies where it does business.

SUMMARY

- The main sources of finance company funds are loans from banks, sales of commercial paper, bonds, and capital. The main uses of finance company funds are consumer loans, business loans, leasing, and real estate loans.
- Finance companies are exposed to credit risk as a result of their consumer loans, business loans, and real estate loans. They are also exposed to liquidity risk because their assets are not very marketable in the secondary market. They may also be exposed to interest rate risk.
- Finance companies are valued as the present value of their expected cash flows. Their valuation is

highly dependent on economic conditions, because there are more requests for loans by qualified borrowers when economic conditions are favorable. In addition, the amount of loan defaults is normally lower when the economy is strong.

- Finance companies compete with depository institutions (such as commercial banks, savings institutions, and credit unions) that provide loans to consumers and businesses. Many finance companies have insurance subsidiaries that compete directly with other insurance subsidiaries.

POINT COUNTER-POINT

Will Finance Companies Be Replaced by Banks?

Point Yes. Commercial banks specialize in loans and can provide the services that are provided by finance companies. The two types of financial institutions will eventually merge into one.

Counter-Point No. Finance companies and commercial banks tend to target different markets for loans.

Thus, commercial banks will not replace finance companies because they do not serve the same market.

Who Is Correct? Use the Internet to learn more about this issue. Offer your own opinion on this issue.

QUESTIONS AND APPLICATIONS

1. Exposure to Interest Rate Risk Is the cost of funds obtained by finance companies very sensitive to market interest rate movements? Explain.

2. Issuance of Commercial Paper How are small and medium-sized finance companies able to issue commercial paper? Why do some well-known finance companies directly place their commercial paper?

3. Finance Company Affiliations Explain why some finance companies are associated with automobile manufacturers. Why do some of these finance companies offer below-market rates on loans?

4. Uses of Funds Describe the major uses of funds by finance companies.

5. Credit Card Services Explain how finance companies benefit from offering consumers a credit card.

6. Leasing Services Explain how finance companies provide financing through leasing.

7. Regulation of Finance Companies Describe the kinds of regulations that are imposed on finance companies.

8. Liquidity Position Explain how the liquidity position of finance companies differs from that of depository institutions such as commercial banks.

9. Exposure to Interest Rate Risk Explain how the interest rate risk of finance companies differs from that of savings institutions.

10. Exposure to Credit Risk Explain how the default risk of finance companies differs from that of other lending financial institutions.

Interpreting Financial News

Interpret the following comments made by Wall Street analysts and portfolio managers:

a. "During a credit crunch, finance companies tend to generate a large amount of business."

b. "Some finance companies took a huge hit as a result of the last recession because they opened their wallets too wide before the recession occurred."

c. "During periods of strong economic growth, finance companies generate unusually high returns without any hint of excessive risk; but their returns are at the mercy of the economy."

Managing in Financial Markets

Managing a Finance Company As a manager of a finance company, you are attempting to increase the spread between the rate earned on your assets and the rate paid on your liabilities.

a. Assume that you expect interest rates to decline over time. Should you issue bonds or commercial paper in order to obtain funds?

b. If you expect interest rates to decline, will you benefit more from providing medium-term fixed-rate loans to consumers or floating-rate loans to businesses?

c. Why would you still maintain some balance between medium-term fixed-rate loans and floating-rate loans to businesses, even if you anticipate that one type of loan will be more profitable under a cycle of declining interest rates?

FLOW OF FUNDS EXERCISE

How Finance Companies Facilitate the Flow of Funds

Carson Company has sometimes relied on debt financing from Fente Finance Company. Fente has been willing to lend money even when most commercial banks were not. Fente obtains funding from issuing commercial paper and focuses mostly on channeling the funds to borrowers.

a. Explain how finance companies are unique by comparing Fente's net interest income, noninterest income, noninterest expenses, and loan losses to those of commercial banks.

b. Explain why Fente performs better than commercial banks in some periods.

c. Describe the flow of funds channeled through finance companies to firms such as Carson Company. What is the original source of the money that is channeled to firms or households that borrow from finance companies?

INTERNET/EXCEL EXERCISES

1. Go to www.gmaccf.com. Describe the services offered by GMAC Commercial Finance.

2. Retrieve the annual report of American International Group (its ticker symbol is AIG), which owns a large consumer finance company, or select your own consumer finance company. To access income statement information, go to http://finance .yahoo.com, enter the ticker symbol, and click on "Get Quotes." Then click on "SEC Filings."

Review the consumer finance company's recent performance. Has its income as a percentage of assets increased since the year before? Explain what caused this change over the last year. How have its operating expenses changed over the last year? Discuss how the finance company's recent strategy and economic conditions may explain the changes in these components of its income statement.

WSJ EXERCISE

Finance Company Performance

Using a recent issue of *The Wall Street Journal,* summarize an article that discussed the recent performance of a particular finance company. Does the article suggest that the finance company's performance was better or worse than the norm? What was the reason for the unusual level of performance?

23

Mutual Fund Operations

CHAPTER OBJECTIVES

The specific objectives of this chapter are to:

- explain how characteristics vary among mutual funds,

- describe the various types of stock and bond mutual funds,

- describe the characteristics of money market funds, and

- describe other types of funds.

A **mutual fund** is an investment company that sells shares and uses the proceeds to manage a portfolio of securities. Mutual funds have grown substantially in recent years, and they serve as major suppliers of funds in financial markets.

BACKGROUND ON MUTUAL FUNDS

Mutual funds serve as a key financial intermediary. They pool investments by individual investors and use the funds to accommodate financing needs of governments and corporations in the primary markets. They also frequently invest in securities in the secondary market.

Mutual funds provide an important service not only for corporations and governments that need funds, but also for individual investors who wish to invest funds. Small investors are unable to diversify their investments because of their limited funds. Mutual funds offer a way for these investors to diversify. Some mutual funds have holdings of 50 or more securities, and the minimum investment may be only $250 to $2,500. Small investors could not afford to create such a diversified portfolio on their own. Moreover, the mutual fund uses experienced portfolio managers, so investors do not have to manage the portfolio themselves. Some mutual funds also offer liquidity because they are willing to repurchase an investor's shares upon request. They also offer various services, such as 24-hour telephone or Internet access to account information, money transfers between different funds operated by the same firm, consolidated account statements, check-writing privileges on some types of funds, and tax information.

A mutual fund hires portfolio managers to invest in a portfolio of securities that satisfies the desires of investors. Like other portfolio managers, the managers of mutual funds analyze economic and industry trends and forecasts and assess the potential impact of various conditions on companies. They adjust the composition of their portfolio in response to changing economic conditions.

Because of their diversification, management expertise, and liquidity, mutual funds have grown at a rapid pace. The growth of mutual funds is illustrated in Exhibit 23.1. Today, there are more than 8,000 different mutual funds, with total assets exceeding $10 trillion. The value of mutual fund assets more than doubled between 1993 and 2008. Over the last 25 years, total mutual fund assets have increased by more than 23 times. More than 88 million households now own shares of one or more mutual funds.

Exhibit 23.1 Growth in Mutual Funds

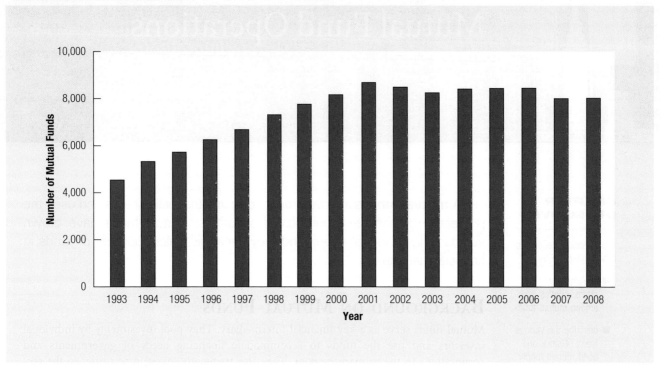

Note: The numbers shown here include money market funds.

Source: *Investment Company Institute.*

Types of Funds

Funds are classified as open-end or closed-end funds. Each type of mutual fund is described in turn.

Open-End Funds   **Open-end funds** are open to investment from investors at any time. Investors can purchase shares directly from the open-end fund at any time. In addition, investors can sell (redeem) their shares back to the open-end fund at any time. Thus, the number of shares of an open-end fund is always changing. When the fund receives additional investments, it invests in additional securities. It maintains some cash on hand in case redemptions exceed investments on a given day. If there are substantial redemptions, the fund will have to sell some of its securities to obtain sufficient funds to accommodate the redemptions. There are many different categories of open-end mutual funds, allowing investors to invest in a fund that fits their particular investment objective. Investors can select from thousands of open-end mutual funds to meet their particular return and risk profile. When the term *mutual fund* is used, it normally refers to the open-end type just described.

Closed-End Funds   **Closed-end funds** do not repurchase (redeem) the shares they sell. Instead, investors must sell the shares on a stock exchange just like corporate stock. The market price of a closed-end fund can deviate from the aggregate value of the underlying stocks. For some closed-end funds, the shares are priced higher than the aggregate value of the respective portfolio. This often occurs when the shares represent stocks of countries that have investment restrictions. Investors from the United States who want to invest in those stocks are willing to pay a premium beyond the market value of the stocks because they cannot easily obtain the stocks otherwise. For other closed-end funds, the shares are priced at a discount relative to the underlying stocks. This may occur because some of the stocks held by the closed-end funds are illiquid, and if a fund sold a large amount of those shares in the secondary market, it would have to sell them at a discount. The premium or discount on a closed-end fund can change over time.

The number of outstanding shares sold by a closed-end investment company usually remains constant and is equal to the number of shares originally issued. However, some closed-end funds engage in secondary offerings of new shares and use the proceeds to expand their investment portfolios.

There are about 670 closed-end funds. Approximately 70 percent of these funds invest mainly in bonds or other debt securities, while the other 30 percent focus on stocks. The closed-end stock funds represent particular sectors or countries, which enables investors to invest in a portfolio of stocks that reflects a particular sector or country. Unlike open-end funds, closed-end funds can be sold short. This allows investors to capitalize on their expectations that stock prices of a particular sector or country will decline. The total market value of closed-end funds is less than $300 billion and thus is much smaller than the total market value of open-end funds. In addition, the growth of closed-end funds has been less than that of open-end funds.

Comparison to Depository Institutions

Mutual funds are like depository institutions in that they repackage the proceeds received from individuals to make various types of investments. Nevertheless, investing in mutual funds is distinctly different from depositing money in a depository institution in that it represents partial ownership, whereas deposits represent a form of credit. Thus, the investors share the gains or losses generated by the mutual fund, while depositors simply receive interest on their deposits. Individual investors view mutual funds as an alternative to depository institutions. In fact, much of the money invested in mutual funds in the 1990s came from depository institutions. When interest rates decline, many individuals withdraw their deposits and invest in mutual funds.

Regulation

Mutual funds must adhere to a variety of federal regulations. They must register with the Securities and Exchange Commission (SEC) and provide interested investors with a prospectus that discloses details about the components of the fund and the risks involved. Mutual funds are also regulated by state laws, many of which attempt to ensure that investors fully understand the fund.

If a mutual fund distributes at least 90 percent of its taxable income to shareholders, it is exempt from taxes on dividends, interest, and capital gains distributed to shareholders. The shareholders are, of course, subject to taxation on these forms of income.

Information Contained in a Prospectus Since July 1993, mutual funds have been required to disclose in the prospectus the names of their portfolio managers and the length of time that they have been employed by the fund in that position. Many investors regard this information as relevant because the performance of a mutual fund is highly dependent on its portfolio managers. Mutual funds must also disclose their performance record over the past 10 years in comparison to a broad market index. They must also state in the prospectus how their performance was affected by market conditions.

Specifically, a mutual fund prospectus contains the following information:

1. The minimum amount of investment required.
2. The investment objective of the mutual fund.
3. The return on the fund over the past year, the past three years, and the past five years.
4. The exposure of the mutual fund to various types of risk.

5. The services (such as check writing, ability to transfer money by telephone, etc.) offered by the mutual fund.
6. The fees incurred by the mutual fund (such as management fees) that are passed on to the investors.

Estimating the Net Asset Value

The **net asset value (NAV)** of a mutual fund indicates the value per share. It is estimated each day by first determining the market value of all securities comprising the mutual fund (any cash is also accounted for). Any interest or dividends accrued from the mutual fund are added to the market value. Then any expenses are subtracted, and the amount is divided by the number of shares of the fund outstanding.

EXAMPLE

Newark Mutual Fund has 20 million shares issued to its investors. It used the proceeds to buy stock of 55 different firms. A partial list of its stock holdings is shown below:

NAME OF STOCK	NUMBER OF SHARES	PREVAILING SHARE PRICE	MARKET VALUE
Aztec Co.	10,000	$40	$ 400,000
Caldero, Inc.	20,000	30	600,000
⋮	⋮	⋮	⋮
Zurkin, Inc.	8,000	70	560,000
Total market value of shares today			$500,020,000
+ Interest and dividends received today			+10,000
− Expenses incurred today			−30,000
= Market value of fund			$500,000,000

$$\text{Net asset value} = \text{Market value of fund/number of shares}$$
$$= \$500{,}000{,}000/20{,}000{,}000$$
$$= \$25 \text{ per share} \qquad\bullet$$

The SEC monitors the reporting of the NAV by mutual funds. When a mutual fund pays its shareholders dividends, its NAV declines by the per-share amount of the dividend payout.

Distributions to Shareholders

Mutual funds can generate returns to their shareholders in three ways. First, they can pass on any earned income (from dividends or coupon payments) as dividend payments to the shareholders. Second, they distribute the capital gains resulting from the sale of securities within the fund. A third type of return to shareholders is through mutual fund share price appreciation. As the market value of a fund's security holdings increases, the fund's NAV increases, and the shareholders benefit when they sell their mutual fund shares.

Although investors in a mutual fund directly benefit from any returns generated by the fund, they are also directly affected if the portfolio generates losses. Because they own the shares of the fund, there is no other group of shareholders to whom the fund must be accountable. This differs from commercial banks and stock-owned savings institutions, which obtain their deposits from one group of investors and sell shares of stock to another.

Exhibit 23.2 Distribution of Investment in Mutual Funds

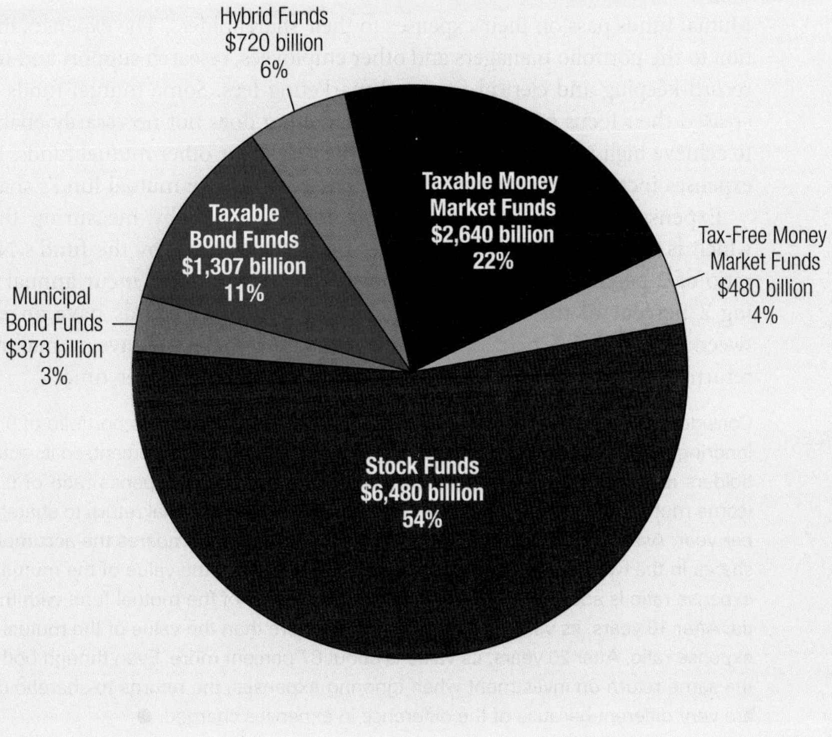

Source: *Investment Company Institute.*

Mutual Fund Classifications

Mutual funds are commonly classified as stock (or equity) mutual funds, bond mutual funds, or money market mutual funds, depending on the types of securities in which they invest. The distribution of investments in these three classes of mutual funds is shown in Exhibit 23.2. Stock funds are dominant when measured by the market value of total assets among mutual funds. Many investment companies offer a family of many different mutual funds so that they can accommodate the diverse preferences of investors. With one phone call, an investor can normally transfer money from one mutual fund to another within the same family; transfers can also be requested online.

Management of Mutual Funds

Each mutual fund is managed by one or more portfolio managers, who must focus on the stated investment objective of that fund. These managers tend to purchase stocks in large blocks. They prefer liquid securities that can easily be sold in the secondary market at any time. Since open-end mutual funds allow shareholders to buy shares at any time, their managers continuously seek new investments. They may maintain a small amount of cash for liquidity purposes. If there are more redemptions than sales of shares at a given point in time, the managers can use the cash to cover the redemptions. If the cash is not sufficient to cover the redemptions, they sell some of their holdings of securities to obtain the cash they need.

Since closed-end funds are closed to new investment or redemptions by shareholders, their portfolio managers do not need to plan for new investment. In addition, they do not need to hold cash because the fund does not allow redemptions. Shareholders of closed-end funds sell their shares in the secondary market rather than redeem their shares with the fund.

Expenses Incurred by Shareholders

Mutual funds pass on their expenses to their shareholders. The expenses include compensation to the portfolio managers and other employees, research support and investment advice, record-keeping and clerical fees, and marketing fees. Some mutual funds have recently increased their focus on marketing, but marketing does not necessarily enable a mutual fund to achieve high performance relative to the market or other mutual funds. In fact, marketing expenses increase the expenses that are passed on to the mutual fund's shareholders.

Expenses can be compared among mutual funds by measuring the expense ratio, which is equal to the annual expenses per share divided by the fund's NAV. An expense ratio of 2 percent in a given year means that shareholders incur annual expenses reflecting 2 percent of the value of the fund. Many mutual funds have an expense ratio between 0.6 and 1.5 percent. A high expense ratio can have a major impact on the returns generated by a mutual fund for its shareholders over time.

EXAMPLE

Consider two mutual funds, each of which generates a return on its portfolio of 9.2 percent per year, ignoring expenses. One mutual fund has an expense ratio of 3.2 percent, so its actual return to shareholders is 6 percent per year. The other mutual fund has an expense ratio of 0.2 percent per year (some mutual funds have expense ratios at this level), so its actual return to shareholders is 9 percent per year. Assume you have $10,000 to invest. Exhibit 23.3 compares the accumulated value of your shares in the two mutual funds over time. After five years, the value of the mutual fund with the low expense ratio is about 20 percent higher than the value of the mutual fund with the high expense ratio. After 10 years, its value is about 40 percent more than the value of the mutual fund with the high expense ratio. After 20 years, its value is about 87 percent more. Even though both mutual funds had the same return on investment when ignoring expenses, the returns to shareholders after expenses are very different because of the difference in expenses charged. ●

Exhibit 23.3 How the Accumulated Value Can Be Affected by Expenses (Assume Initial Investment of $10,000 and a Return before Expenses of 9.2 Percent)

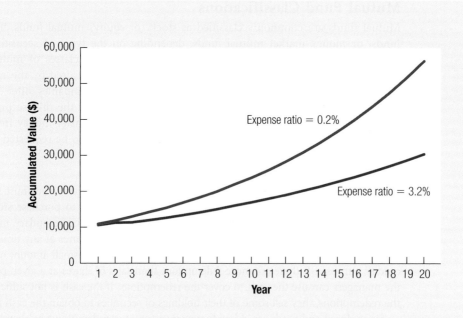

Thus, the higher the expense ratio, the lower the return for a given level of portfolio performance. Mutual funds with lower expense ratios tend to outperform others that have a similar investment objective. That is, funds with higher expenses are generally unable to generate higher returns that could offset those expenses. Since expenses can vary substantially among mutual funds, investors should review the annual expenses of any fund before making an investment.

Sales Load

Mutual funds can also be classified as either **load,** meaning that there is a sales charge, or **no-load,** meaning that the funds are promoted strictly by the mutual fund of concern. Load funds are promoted by registered representatives of brokerage firms, who earn a sales charge typically ranging between 3 percent and 8.5 percent. Investors in a load fund pay this charge through the difference between the bid and ask prices of the load fund. Loads, commissions, and bid-ask spreads are not included in the expense ratio of a mutual fund.

Some investors may feel that the sales charge is worthwhile, because the brokerage firm helps determine the type of fund that is appropriate for them. Other investors who feel capable of making their own investment decisions often prefer to invest in no-load funds. Some no-load mutual funds can be purchased through a discount broker for a relatively low fee (such as 1 to 2 percent), although investors receive no advice from the discount broker.

EXAMPLE

As an example of the potential advantage of no-load funds, consider separate $10,000 investments in no-load and load funds. Assuming an 8.5 percent load fee, the actual investment in the load fund is $9,150. If the value of both funds grows by 10 percent per year, the investment in the no-load fund will be worth $2,204 more than the investment in the load fund after 10 years. ●

In recent years, some small no-load funds have become load funds because they could not attract investors without a large budget for national advertising. As a load fund, they will be recommended by various brokers and financial planners, who will earn a commission on any shares sold.

Types of Loads   Mutual funds charge different types of loads: front-end loads and back-end loads.

A **front-end load** is paid only once, at the time you invest money in a mutual fund. The legal limit on front-end loads is 8.5 percent, but most funds charge 5.75 percent or less. Mutual funds with a front-end load often offer discounts like breakpoints, right of accumulation, letters of intent, or free transfers. Breakpoints are basically volume discounts, which means that the percentage load becomes smaller as you invest more. Such discounts often start at $25,000. Many funds waive their loads entirely for investments of more than $1 million. A right of accumulation is a discount based on the total amount of money you invest in the fund family (as opposed to just the individual fund). Letters of intent are often used for investors who invest only a small amount today but commit themselves to additional purchases over the next year. With this setup, the investor is entitled to the breakpoint discount today even though he or she has not yet invested enough money to actually qualify for it. Of course, if the investor fails to invest the additional funds, the fund will retroactively collect the higher fee from the account. Free transfers allow investors to move money between funds with no additional load, provided the money stays in the same family.

A **back-end load** (also known as a rear load or reverse load) is a withdrawal fee assessed when you withdraw money from the mutual fund. Back-end loads are often between 5 and 6 percent for the first year but decline by a certain percentage each subsequent year. Some mutual funds have features that can minimize the back-end load. For example, some funds permit investors to withdraw dividends and capital gains at any time without a charge. Other funds allow a certain percentage withdrawal of the investment each year without incurring a load. Also, many funds allow for free transfers within the fund family without incurring additional charges.

12b-1 Fees

In 1980, the SEC allowed mutual funds to charge shareholders a distribution fee, also called a 12b-l fee in reference to SEC rule 12b-l. In some cases, funds have used the proceeds from 12b-l fees to pay commissions to brokers whose clients invested in the fund. In essence, the fee substituted for the load (sales charge) that was directly charged to investors in load funds. A fund that states that it does not charge a sales load may charge shareholders 12b-1 fees and use the proceeds to pay commissions to brokers. Some shareholders who believe that they are not incurring a cost on a no-load fund do pay a commission indirectly through the 12b-l fees. The fees are generally included in a fund's expense ratio as part of its marketing expenses. These fees are controversial because many mutual funds do not clarify how they use the money received from the fees.

Governance of Mutual Funds

A mutual fund is usually run by an investment company, whose owners are different from the shareholders in the mutual funds. In fact, some managers employed by mutual funds invest their money in the investment company rather than in the mutual funds that they manage. Thus, the investment company may have an incentive to charge high fees to the shareholders of the mutual fund. The expenses charged to the fund represent income generated by the investment company. Although valid expenses are incurred in running a mutual fund, the expenses charged by some investment companies may be excessive. Many mutual funds have grown substantially over time and should be able to capitalize on economies of scale. Nevertheless, their expense ratios have generally increased over time. Competition is expected to ensure that mutual funds will charge shareholders only reasonable expenses, but many investors are not aware of the expenses that they are charged.

Connection between Fees and Agency Problems   The large fees at some mutual funds are due to agency problems. Managers of mutual funds are expected to serve their shareholders. However, they may focus on serving their own interests rather than those of shareholders. The managers provide very limited information about how they spend the money that they receive from fees. Since many mutual funds that charge high fees do not outperform funds with lower fees, the way they use the proceeds from the fees deserves to be questioned. Unfortunately, many shareholders do not recognize all the fees that they are charged by some mutual funds or how the fees affect the return on their investment. This may explain why some mutual funds that charge high fees continue to attract investments from shareholders.

Mutual funds, like corporations, are subject to some forms of governance that are intended to ensure that the managers are serving the shareholders. Each mutual fund has a board of directors who are supposed to represent the fund's shareholders. The effectiveness of the boards is questionable, however. The SEC requires that a majority of the directors of a mutual fund board be independent (not employed by the fund). However, an employee of the company can retire and qualify as an independent board member just two years later. In addition, the average annual compensation paid to the board members of large mutual funds exceeds $100,000. Thus, some board members may be willing to avoid confrontation with management if doing so enables them to keep their positions. This same criticism is also leveled at boards of publicly traded companies. Another problem is that board members of a mutual fund family commonly oversee all funds in the entire family. Consequently, they may concentrate on general issues that are not particular to any one fund and spend a relatively small amount of time on any individual fund within the family.

Mutual funds also have a compliance officer who is supposed to ensure that the fund's operations are in line with its objective and guidelines for trading rules. Until recently, however, some compliance officers reported to the investment company instead of the mutual fund's board of directors. As a result of scandals, compliance officers are now reporting to the board.

Late Trading Scandal

In 2003, mutual funds received unfavorable publicity because some of the funds were allowing their large clients to buy or sell the fund's shares after the stock exchange's 4 P.M. closing but at the 4 P.M. prices. Thus, if favorable news about the market occurred after 4 P.M., the clients could buy fund shares at a price that was less than what was appropriate. This late trading, as it is called, is distinctly different from night trading (or after-hours trading) in the stock market where trades occur at prevailing market prices. Late trading of mutual funds involves engaging in a trade on prices that are "stale" or no longer appropriate. It is a clear violation of laws established by the SEC in 1968. Other shareholders of the mutual fund who were not able to trade on the inside information are adversely affected by these actions. The scandal was a major blow to mutual funds because they were commonly viewed as a safe way to diversify among firms and avoid exposure to possible scandals such as accounting irregularities that could affect a firm's stock price. Although many mutual funds were completely innocent, it was difficult for investors to identify the funds that had violated the rules.

As soon as this problem was publicized, the SEC began to investigate mutual funds and fined some of them heavily. The SEC was concerned that investors might come to mistrust all mutual funds (even those that were innocent) and withdraw their investments; massive redemptions could adversely affect the values of the securities that the funds invest in. Consequently, the SEC and other agencies of the federal government took steps to restore investor confidence in mutual funds including prosecuting managers of mutual funds who violated the rules.

Corporate Control by Mutual Funds

Regardless of whether mutual funds monitor their own management effectively, they have the power to monitor the management of the firms in which they invest. Since mutual funds invest large amounts of money in some stocks, they become major shareholders of firms. For example, Fidelity is the largest shareholder of more than 700 firms in which it owns stock. Portfolio managers of many mutual funds serve on the board of directors of various firms. Even when a fund's managers do not serve on a firm's board, the firm may still attempt to satisfy them so that they do not sell their holdings of the firm's stock. To illustrate the importance of mutual funds, Fidelity typically accounts for at least 5 percent of all the trading on the New York Stock Exchange on a given day. Fidelity is commonly one of the first institutional investors to be asked whether it wants to invest in a firm's new offerings of stock. Fidelity has more than 200 analysts who assess the financial condition of firms. Many firms discuss any major policy changes with analysts and portfolio managers of mutual funds to convince them that the changes should have a favorable effect on performance over time. In this way, a firm may discourage the funds from selling their holdings of the firm's stock and may even persuade them to purchase more.

MUTUAL FUND CATEGORIES

Because investors have various objectives, no single portfolio can satisfy everyone. Consequently, a variety of mutual funds have been created. Investors select stock or bond mutual funds with characteristics that fit their preferences. Some investors need mutual funds that can generate income, while others do not. Some investors want to earn a high return and are willing to tolerate a high level of risk, while others need a fund that is very conservative and offers more stable returns.

Stock Mutual Fund Categories

The more popular stock mutual fund categories include

- Growth funds
- Capital appreciation funds
- Growth and income funds
- International and global funds
- Specialty funds
- Index funds
- Multifund funds

Growth Funds   For investors who desire a high return and are willing to accept a moderate degree of risk, **growth funds** are appropriate. These funds are typically composed of stocks of companies that have not fully matured and are expected to grow at a higher than average rate in the future. The primary objective of a growth fund is to generate an increase in investment value, with less concern about the generation of steady income. Growth funds may entail different degrees of risk. Some concentrate on companies that have existed for several years but are still experiencing growth, while others concentrate on relatively young companies.

Capital Appreciation Funds   Also known as aggressive growth funds, **capital appreciation funds** are composed of stocks that have potential for very high growth but may also be unproven. These funds are suited to investors who are willing to risk a possible loss in value. As the economy changes, portfolio managers of capital appreciation funds constantly revise the portfolio composition to take full advantage of their expectations. They sometimes even use borrowed money to support their portfolios, thereby using leverage to increase their potential return and risk.

Growth and Income Funds   Some investors are looking for potential for capital appreciation along with some stability in income. For these investors, a **growth and income fund,** which contains a unique combination of growth stocks, high-dividend stocks, and fixed-income bonds, may be most appropriate.

International and Global Funds   In recent years, awareness of foreign securities has been increasing. Investors historically avoided foreign securities because of the high information and transaction costs associated with purchasing them and monitoring their performance. International mutual funds were created to enable investors to invest in foreign securities without incurring these excessive costs.

The returns on international stock mutual funds are affected not only by foreign companies' stock prices but also by the movements of the currencies that denominate these stocks. As a foreign currency's value strengthens against the U.S. dollar, the value of the foreign stock as measured in U.S. dollars increases. Thus, U.S. investors can benefit not only from higher stock prices but also from a strengthened foreign currency (against the dollar). Of course, they can also be adversely affected if the foreign currencies denominating the stocks depreciate.

An alternative to an international mutual fund is a global mutual fund, which includes some U.S. stocks in its portfolio. International and global mutual funds have historically included stocks from several different countries to limit the portfolio's exposure to economic conditions in any single foreign economy.

In recent years, some new international mutual funds have been designed to fully benefit from a particular emerging country or continent. Although the potential return from such a strategy is greater, so is the risk, because the entire portfolio value is sensitive to a single economy. For investors who prefer minimum transaction costs, mutual funds have begun to offer index funds. Each of these funds is intended to mirror a stock index of a particular country or group of countries. For example, Vanguard offers a fund representing a European stock index and a Pacific Basin stock index. Because these mutual funds simply attempt to mirror an existing stock index, they avoid the advisory and transaction costs that are common to other mutual funds. International funds are discussed further at the end of this chapter.

Specialty Funds   Some mutual funds, called **specialty funds,** focus on a group of companies sharing a particular characteristic. For example, there are industry-specific funds such as energy, banking, and high-tech funds. Some funds include only stocks of firms that are likely takeover targets. Other mutual funds specialize in options or other commodities, such as precious metals. There are also mutual funds that invest only in socially conscious firms. The risk of specialty funds varies with the particular characteristics of each fund.

Some specialty funds focus their investment on Internet companies. Internet funds performed extremely well in the late 1990s when stock prices of Internet companies surged, but poorly in the 2000–2002 period. Investors who want to invest in technology but do not have any insight about specific companies commonly invest in these mutual funds.

Index Funds   Some mutual funds are designed to simply match the performance of an existing stock index. For example, Vanguard offers an **index fund** that is designed to match the S&P 500 index. Index funds are composed of stocks that, in aggregate, are expected to move in line with a specific index. They contain many of the same stocks contained in the corresponding index and tend to have very low expenses because they require little portfolio management and execute a relatively small number of transactions.

Index funds have become very popular over time as investors recognize that most mutual funds do not outperform indexes. Furthermore, investors benefit because the expenses of index funds are much lower than the expenses of actively managed mutual funds. Index funds are very similar to exchange-traded funds (ETFs—to be discussed later in the chapter). The primary difference is that index funds are not traded throughout the day, whereas ETFs are.

Multifund Funds   In recent years, **multifund mutual funds** have been created. A multifund mutual fund's portfolio managers invest in a portfolio of different mutual funds. A multifund mutual fund achieves even more diversification than a typical mutual fund because it contains several mutual funds. However, investors incur two types of management expenses: (1) the expenses of managing each individual mutual fund and (2) the expenses of managing the multifund mutual fund.

Bond Mutual Fund Categories

Investors in bonds are primarily concerned about interest rate risk, credit (default) risk, and tax implications. Thus, most bond funds can be classified according to either their maturities (which affect interest rate risk) or the type of bond issuers (which affects credit risk and taxes incurred).

Income Funds   For investors who are mainly concerned with stability of income rather than capital appreciation, **income funds** are appropriate. These funds are usually composed of bonds that offer periodic coupon payments and vary in exposure to risk. Income funds composed of only corporate bonds are susceptible to credit risk, while those composed of only Treasury bonds are not. A third type of income fund contains bonds backed by government agencies, such as the Government National Mortgage Association (GNMA, or Ginnie Mae). These funds are normally perceived to be less risky than a fund containing corporate bonds. Those income funds exhibiting more credit risk will offer a higher potential return, other things being equal.

The market values of even medium-term income funds are quite volatile over time because of their sensitivity to interest rate movements. Thus, income funds are best suited for investors who rely on the fund for periodic income and plan to maintain the fund over a long period of time.

Tax-Free Funds   Investors in high tax brackets have historically purchased municipal bonds as a way to avoid taxes. Because these bonds are susceptible to default, a diversified portfolio is desirable. Mutual funds containing municipal bonds allow investors in high tax brackets with even small amounts of money to avoid taxes while maintaining a low degree of credit risk.

High-Yield (Junk) Bond Funds   Investors desiring high returns and willing to incur high risk may wish to consider bond portfolios with at least two-thirds of the bonds rated below Baa by Moody's or BBB by Standard & Poor's. These portfolios are sometimes referred to as **high-yield** (or **junk bond) funds.** Typically, the bonds were issued by highly leveraged firms. The issuing firm's ability to repay the bonds is very sensitive to economic conditions.

International and Global Bond Funds   International bond funds contain bonds issued by corporations or governments based in other countries. Global bond funds differ from international bond funds in that they contain U.S. as well as foreign bonds. Global funds may be more appropriate for investors who want a fund that includes U.S. bonds within a diversified portfolio, whereas investors in international bond funds may already have a sufficient investment in U.S. bonds and prefer a fund that focuses entirely on foreign bonds. International and global bond funds provide U.S. investors with an easy way to invest in foreign bonds. However, these funds are subject to risk. Like bond funds containing U.S. bonds, these funds are subject to credit risk, based on the financial position of the corporations or governments that issued the bonds. They are also subject to interest rate risk, as the bond prices are inversely related to the interest rate movements in the currency denominating each bond. These funds are also subject to exchange rate risk, as the NAV of the funds is determined by translating the foreign bond holdings to dollars. Thus, when the foreign currency denominating the bonds weakens, the translated dollar value of those bonds will decrease.

Maturity Classifications   Since the interest rate sensitivity of bonds is dependent on the maturity, bond funds are commonly segmented according to the maturities of the bonds they contain. Intermediate-term bond funds invest in bonds with 5 to 10 years remaining until maturity. Long-term bond funds typically contain bonds with 15 to 30 years until maturity. The bonds in these funds normally have a higher yield to maturity and are more sensitive to interest rate movements than the bonds in intermediate-term funds. For a given type of bond fund classification (such as municipal or tax-free), various alternatives with different maturity characteristics are available, so investors can select a fund with the desired exposure to interest rate risk.

The variety of bond funds available can satisfy investors who desire combinations of the features described here. For example, investors who are concerned about interest rate risk and credit risk could invest in bond funds that focus on Treasury bonds with intermediate terms to maturity. Investors who expect interest rates to decline but are concerned about credit risk could invest in a long-term Treasury bond fund. Investors who expect interest rates to decline and are not concerned about credit risk may invest in high-yield bond funds. Investors who wish to avoid federal taxes on interest income and are concerned about interest rate risk may consider short-term municipal bond funds.

Asset Allocation Funds

Asset allocation funds contain a variety of investments (such as stocks, bonds, and money market securities). The portfolio managers adjust the compositions of these funds in response to expectations. For example, a given asset allocation fund will tend to concentrate more heavily on bonds if interest rates are expected to decline; it will focus on stocks if a strong stock market is expected. These funds may even concentrate on international securities if the portfolio managers forecast favorable economic conditions in foreign countries.

Growth and Size of Mutual Funds

Exhibit 23.4 shows how the number of mutual funds has grown over time. The relative growth of investment in stock mutual funds versus bond mutual funds is illustrated in Exhibit 23.5, based on asset size. In the 1980s, investment in bond funds exceeded that of stock funds, but since the mid-1990s, investment in stock funds has been higher, as investors have substantially increased their investment in stock funds in response to the generally higher returns in the stock market.

Growth funds, income funds, international and global funds, and long-term municipal bond funds are the most popular types of funds. Growth and income funds are the most

Exhibit 23.4 Growth in the Number of Stock Funds and Bond Funds

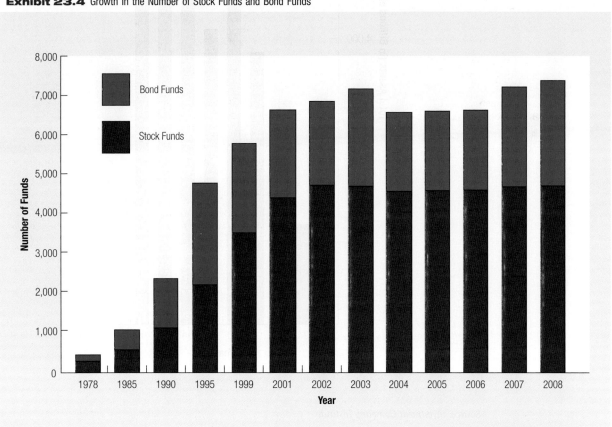

Source: *Investment Company Institute.*

Exhibit 23.5 Investment in Bond and Stock Mutual Funds

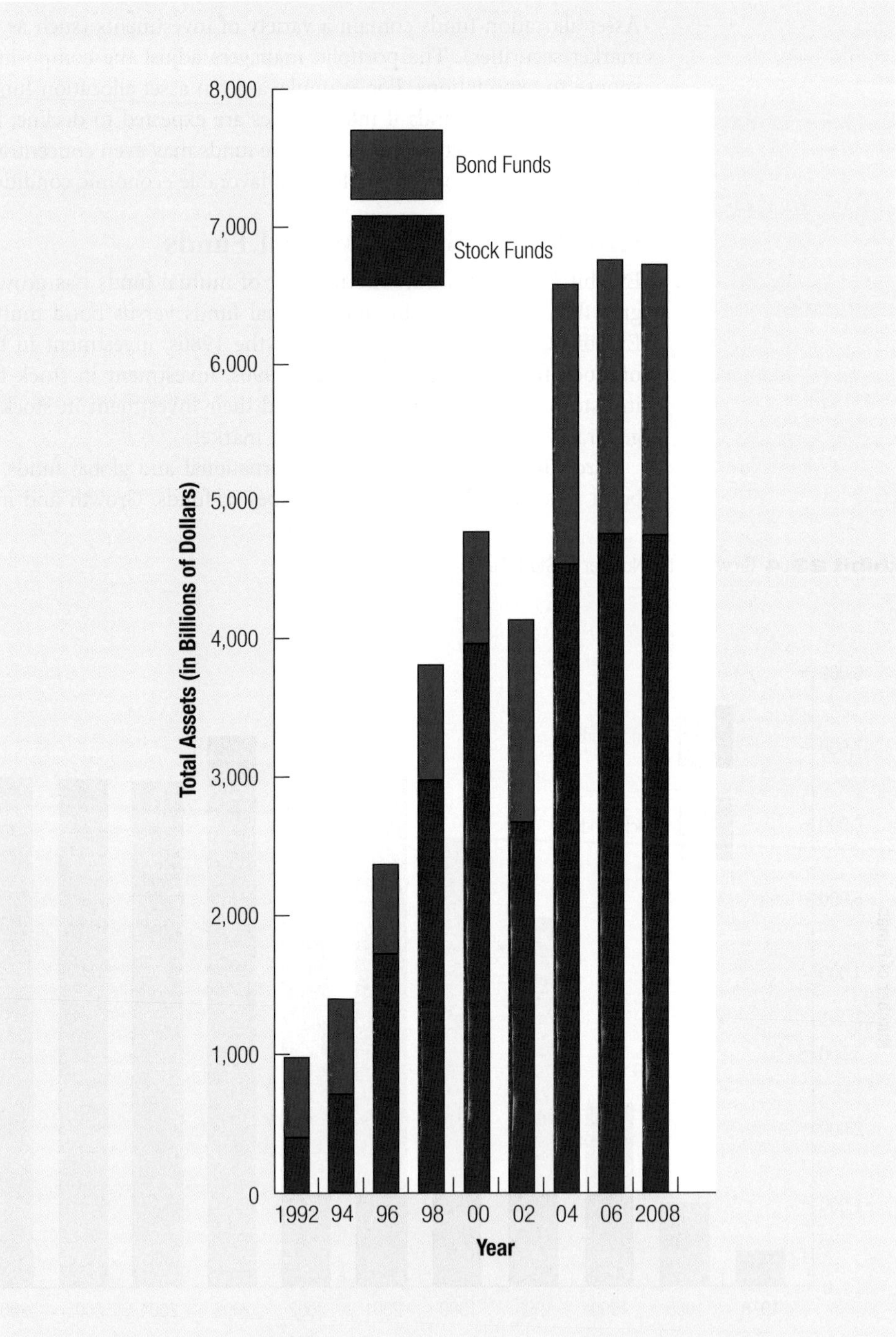

Source: *Investment Company Institute.*

popular when measured according to total assets. Although mutual funds originally targeted more conservative investors, new kinds of funds have recently been created to accommodate all types of investors. Exhibit 23.6 shows the composition of all mutual fund assets in aggregate. Common stocks are clearly the dominant asset maintained by mutual funds.

Exhibit 23.6 Distribution of Aggregate Mutual Fund Assets

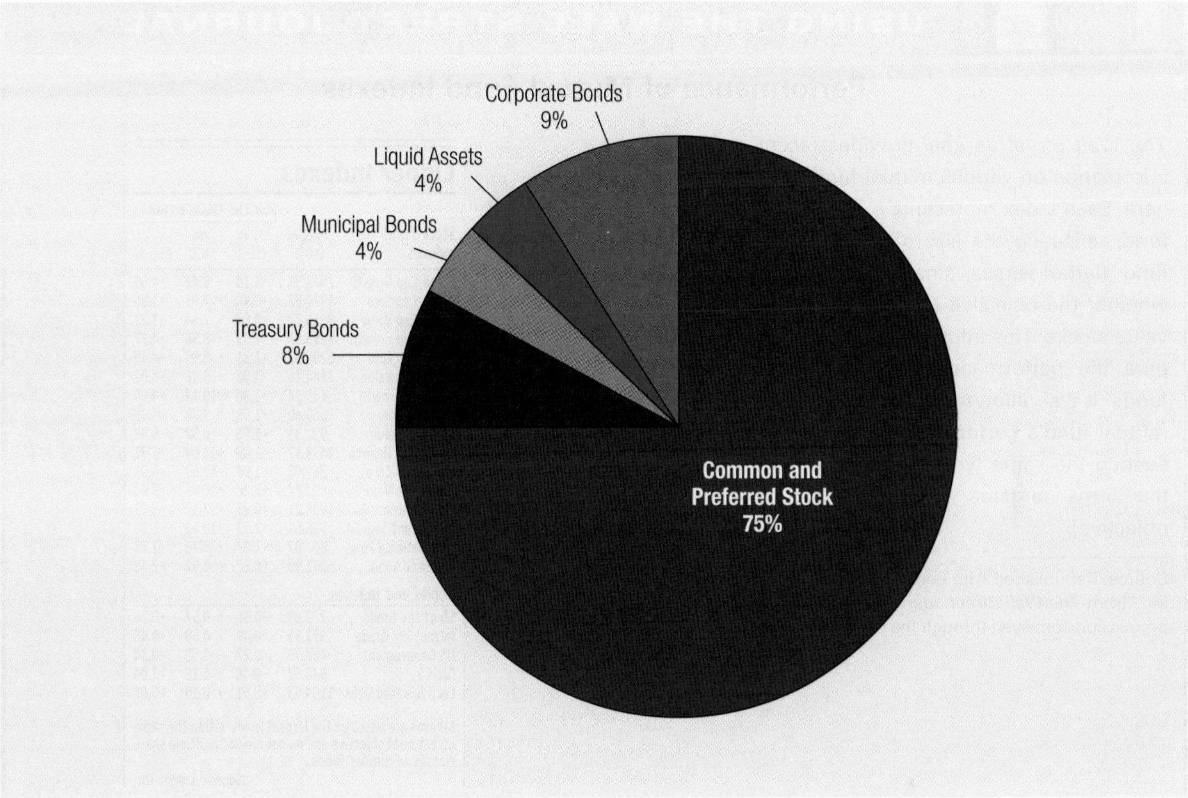

Source: *Investment Company Institute.*

WEB

http://biz.yahoo.com/p/
top.html
Links to information
about mutual funds,
including a list of the
top-performing funds.

PERFORMANCE OF MUTUAL FUNDS

Investors in mutual funds closely monitor the performance of these funds. They also monitor the performance of other mutual funds in which they may invest in the future. In addition, portfolio managers of a mutual fund closely monitor its performance, as their compensation is typically influenced by the performance level.

Performance of Stock Mutual Funds

The change in the performance (measured by risk-adjusted returns) of an open-end mutual fund focusing on stocks can be modeled as

$$\Delta\text{PERF} = f(\Delta\text{MKT}, \Delta\text{SECTOR}, \Delta\text{MANAB})$$

where MKT represents general stock market conditions, SECTOR represents conditions in the specific sector (if there is one) on which the mutual fund is focused, and MANAB represents the abilities of the mutual fund's management.

Change in Market Conditions A mutual fund's performance is usually closely related to market conditions. In fact, some mutual funds (index funds) attempt to resemble a particular stock market index.

To measure the sensitivity of a mutual fund's exposure to market conditions, investors estimate its beta. A mutual fund's beta is estimated in the same manner as a stock's beta. Mutual funds with high betas are more sensitive to market conditions and therefore have more potential to benefit from favorable market conditions. If unfavorable market

USING THE WALL STREET JOURNAL

Performance of Mutual Fund Indexes

The Wall Street Journal provides recent performance information on various mutual fund indexes, as shown here. Each index represents a particular type of mutual fund, reflecting the size of the firms targeted by the fund (large versus small capitalization stocks) and whether the objective is to invest in growth stocks or value stocks. This information allows investors to compare the performance of different types of mutual funds. It also allows investors to compare a particular mutual fund's performance to that of an index representing the same type of funds (based on the size of the firms targeted and the value versus growth objective).

Source: Republished with permission of Dow Jones & Company, Inc., from *The Wall Street Journal*, January 7, 2009, p. C13; permission conveyed through the Copyright Clearance Center, Inc.

Lipper Indexes

Stock-Fund Indexes	PRELIM CLOSE	PERCENT CHANGE FROM		
		PREV CLOSE	WK AGO	DEC. 31
Large-Cap Growth	2541.53	+1.10	+ 8.42	+4.65
Large-Cap Core	1974.02	+0.94	+ 7.93	+3.86
Large-Cap Value	8816.32	+0.87	+ 7.34	+3.27
Multi-Cap Growth	2293.57	+0.89	+ 8.56	+4.37
Multi-Cap Core	6291.32	+1.31	+ 8.99	+4.45
Multi-Cap Value	3684.16	+1.08	+ 8.48	+4.02
Mid-Cap Growth	613.74	+1.30	+10.17	+4.90
Mid-Cap Core	609.40	+1.53	+ 9.78	+4.35
Mid-Cap Value	922.39	+1.86	+10.92	+5.48
Small-Cap Growth	438.97	+1.39	+10.04	+3.91
Small-Cap Core	369.08	+1.99	+10.63	+4.03
Small-Cap Value	603.84	+2.28	+10.98	+3.98
Equity Income Fd	3934.21	+0.75	+ 7.17	+3.03
Science and Tech Fd	516.61	+2.53	+10.42	+6.36
International Fund	867.07	+1.07	+ 5.76	+2.73
Balanced Fund	5061.90	+0.82	+ 4.97	+2.48

Bond-Fund Indexes

Short Inv Grade	273.89	−0.36	+ 0.57	+0.26
Intmdt Inv Grade	337.55	−0.49	+ 0.59	+0.46
US Government	487.79	+0.27	− 0.58	−0.34
GNMA	538.52	+0.48	+ 1.18	+1.04
Corp A-Rated Debt	1184.53	+0.51	+ 0.15	−0.02

Indexes are based on the largest funds within the same investment objective and do not include multiple share classes of similar funds.

Source: Lipper Inc.

conditions occur, however, they are subject to a more pronounced decline in their NAV and therefore in their price.

When the credit crisis intensified in the third quarter of 2008, many stock indexes had losses of more than 25 percent. Stock mutual funds also experienced very poor returns. Stock mutual funds with higher risk experienced more pronounced losses. Even relatively safe stock mutual funds experienced losses in that quarter.

Change in Sector Conditions   The performance of a stock mutual fund focused on a specific sector is influenced by market conditions in that sector. Mutual funds that focus on U.S. technology stocks experience very high performance whenever the technology sector performs well. Energy mutual funds have achieved very high performance in some periods when the energy sector performed well and very poor performance in other periods when the energy sector performed poorly. During the credit crisis, stock mutual funds focused on financial institutions suffered severe losses because that sector was devastated by the credit crisis.

Change in Management Abilities   In addition to market and sector conditions, a mutual fund's performance may also be affected by the abilities of its managers. Mutual funds in the same sector can have different performance levels because of differences in management abilities. If the portfolio managers of one mutual fund in the sector can select stocks that generate higher returns, that fund should generate higher returns. Also important is a mutual fund's operating efficiency, which affects the expenses incurred by the fund and therefore affects its value. A fund that is managed efficiently such that its expenses are low may be able to achieve higher returns for its shareholders even if its portfolio performance is about the same as that of other mutual funds in the same sector.

Performance from Diversifying among Funds

The performance of any given mutual fund may be primarily driven by a single economic factor. For example, the performance of growth stock funds may be highly dependent on the stock market's performance (market risk). The performance of any bond mutual fund is highly dependent on interest rate movements (interest rate risk). The performance of any international mutual fund is influenced by the dollar's value (exchange rate risk). When all securities in a given mutual fund are similarly influenced by an underlying economic factor, the fund does not achieve full diversification benefits. For this reason, some investors diversify among different types of mutual funds so that only a portion of their entire investment is susceptible to a particular type of risk. Diversification among types of mutual funds can substantially reduce the volatility of returns on the overall investment.

Performance of Closed-End Stock Funds

The performance of closed-end stock funds is essentially driven by the same factors that influence open-end (mutual) stock funds. In addition, however, the performance of closed-end stock funds is affected by a change in their premium or discount.

Some closed-end funds, especially those focusing on securities of a foreign country, can have large premiums or discounts relative to their NAVs. If a fund's premium increases relative to its NAV (or if its discount is reduced), the return to the fund's shareholders is increased. Some investment strategies focus on investing in closed-end funds that are priced at a large discount from their NAV. This is based on the premise that closed-end funds with large discounts in price are undervalued. Applying this strategy will not always generate high risk-adjusted returns, however, because the market price of some closed-end funds with large discounts continues to decline over time (their discount becomes larger).

Performance of Bond Mutual Funds

The change in the performance of an open-end mutual fund focusing on bonds can be modeled as

$$\Delta \text{PERF} = f(\Delta R_f, \Delta RP, \text{CLASS}, \Delta \text{MANAB})$$

where R_f represents the risk-free rate, RP represents the risk premium, CLASS represents the classification of the bond fund, and MANAB represents the abilities of the fund's managers.

Change in the Risk-Free Rate   The prices of bonds tend to be inversely related to changes in the risk-free interest rate. In periods when the risk-free interest rate declines substantially, the required rate of return by bondholders declines, and most bond funds perform well. Those bond funds that are focused on bonds with longer maturities are more exposed to changes in the risk-free rate.

Change in the Risk Premium   The prices of bonds tend to decline in response to an increase in the risk premiums required by investors who purchase bonds. When economic conditions deteriorate, the risk premium required by bondholders usually increases, which results in a higher required rate of return (assuming no change in the risk-free rate) and lower prices on risky bonds. In periods (such as during the credit crisis) when risk premiums increase, prices of risky bonds tend to decrease, and bond mutual funds focusing on risky bonds perform poorly.

Change in Management Abilities   The performance levels of bond mutual funds in a specific bond classification can vary due to differences in the abilities of the funds' managers. If the portfolio managers of one bond fund in that classification can select bonds that generate higher returns, that bond fund should generate higher returns. Also important is a bond fund's operating efficiency, which affects the expenses incurred by the fund and therefore affects the fund's value. A bond fund that is managed efficiently such that its expenses are low may be able to achieve higher returns for its shareholders even if its portfolio performance is about the same as that of other bond mutual funds in the same classification.

Research on Mutual Fund Performance

A variety of studies have attempted to assess mutual fund performance over time. Measuring mutual fund performance solely by return is not a valid test, because the return will likely be highly dependent on the performance of the stock and bond markets during the period of concern. An alternative measure of performance is to compare the mutual fund return to the return of a benchmark market index (such as the Dow Jones Industrial Average or the S&P 500 index).

Most studies that assess mutual fund performance find that mutual funds do not outperform the market, especially when accounting for the type of securities that each fund invests in. Furthermore, mutual funds that have high expense ratios tend to perform worse. Even when returns are adjusted to account for risk, mutual funds have, on average, failed to outperform the market. Advocates of market efficiency suggest that beyond insider information, market prices should already reflect any good or bad characteristics of each stock, making it difficult to construct a portfolio whose risk-adjusted returns will consistently outperform the market. Even if mutual funds do not outperform the market, they can still be attractive to investors who wish to diversify and who prefer that a portfolio manager make their investment decisions.

MONEY MARKET FUNDS

Money market mutual funds, sometimes called money market funds (MMFs), are portfolios of money market (short-term) instruments constructed and managed by investment companies. The portfolio is divided into shares that are sold to individual investors. Because investors can participate in some MMFs with as little as $1,000, they are able to invest in money market instruments that they could not afford on their own. Most MMFs allow check-writing privileges, although there may be restrictions on the number of checks written per month or on the minimum amount of the check.

MMFs send periodic account statements to their shareholders to update them on any changes in their balance. They also send shareholders periodic updates on any changes in the asset portfolio composition, providing a breakdown of the names of securities and amounts held in the MMF portfolio.

Because the sponsoring investment company is willing to purchase MMFs back at any time, investors can liquidate their investment whenever they desire. In most years, additional sales exceed redemptions, allowing the companies to build their MMF portfolios by purchasing more securities. When redemptions exceed sales, the company accommodates the amount of excessive redemptions by selling some of the assets contained in the MMF portfolios.

Exhibit 23.7 illustrates the growth in assets of MMFs over time. As investors increase their investment in MMFs, the asset level increases. When economic conditions are weak, investment in MMFs tends to increase, as investors become more concerned about the risks of stocks and bonds.

MMFs can be distinguished from one another and from other mutual funds by the composition, maturity, and risk of their assets. Each of these characteristics is described next.

Exhibit 23.7 Growth in Money Market Fund Assets

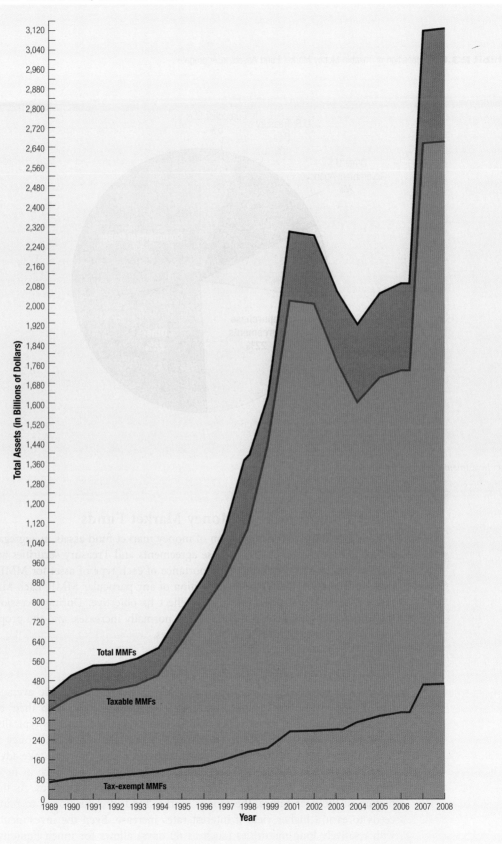

Source: *Investment Company Institute.*

Exhibit 23.8 Composition of Taxable Money Market Fund Assets in Aggregate

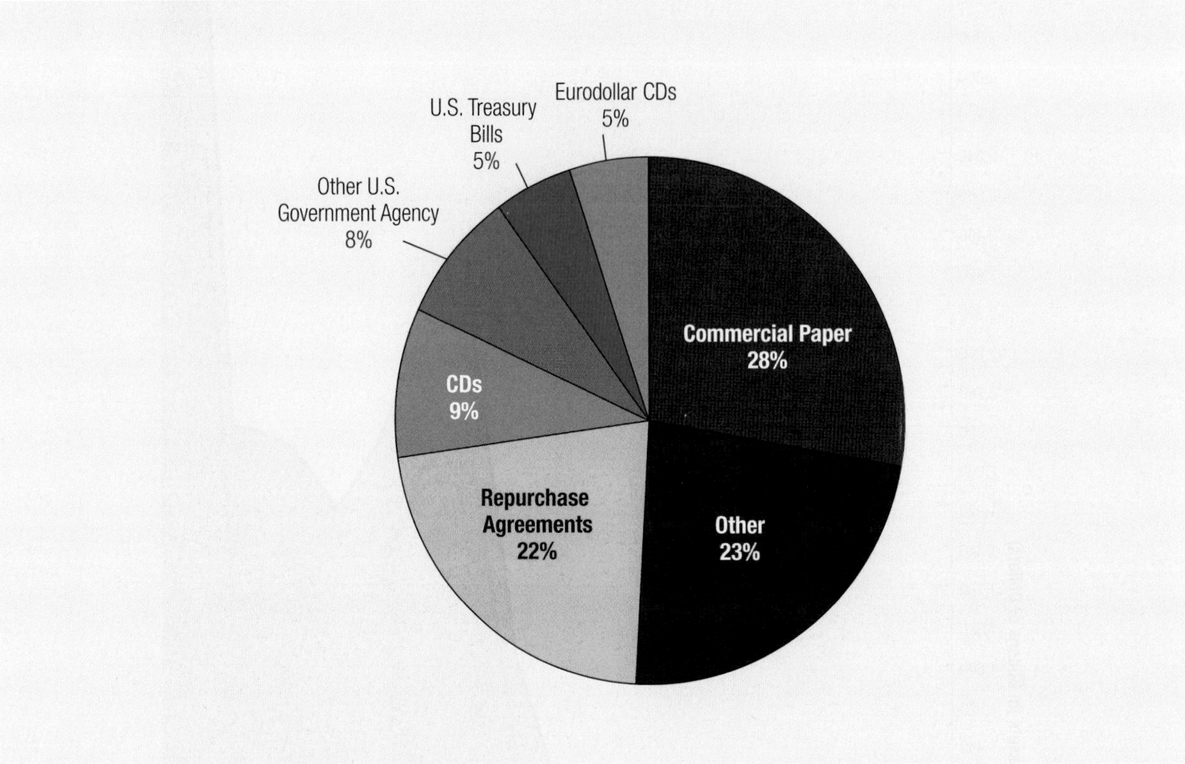

Source: *Investment Company Institute.*

Asset Composition of Money Market Funds

Exhibit 23.8 shows the composition of money market fund assets in aggregate. Commercial paper dominates, but repurchase agreements and Treasury securities are also popular. This composition reflects the importance of each type of asset for MMFs overall and does not represent the typical composition of any particular MMF. Each MMF is usually more concentrated in whatever assets reflect its objective. During recessionary periods, the proportion of Treasury bills in MMFs normally increases, and the proportion of the more risky money market securities decreases.

Maturity of Money Market Funds

Exhibit 23.9 shows the average maturity of MMFs over time. The average maturity is determined by individual asset maturities, weighted according to their relative value. The average maturity of securities held by money market funds is typically between 30 days and 60 days. When money market yields are relatively high, money market funds tend to invest in securities with longer maturities so that they can take advantage of the prevailing yields. Conversely, when interest rates are very low (such as in 2009), money market funds tend to invest in securities with very short maturities. As these securities mature in the near future, the money market funds are positioned to reinvest the proceeds to earn a higher yield if interest rates increase. Even the investment in securities with relatively long maturities (such as 60 days) allows for much liquidity since many of the money market securities can easily be sold in the secondary market.

Exhibit 23.9 Weighted Average Maturity of Money Market Fund Assets

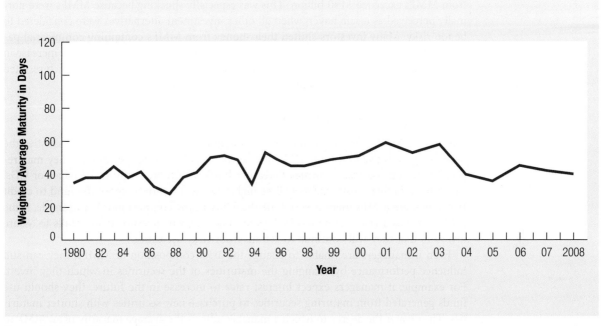

Source: *Investment Company Institute.*

Risk of Money Market Funds

From an investor's perspective, MMFs usually have a low level of credit risk. There may be some concern that an economic downturn could cause frequent defaults on commercial paper or that several banking failures could cause defaults on Eurodollar certificates of deposit and banker's acceptances. These instruments subject to credit risk have short-term maturities, however. Thus, MMFs can quickly shift away from securities issued by any particular corporations that may fail in the near future.

Because MMFs contain instruments with short-term maturities, their market values are not too sensitive to movements in market interest rates (as are mutual funds containing long-term bonds). Although the short-maturity characteristic is sometimes perceived as an advantage, it also causes the returns on MMFs to decline in response to decreasing market interest rates. For this reason, some investors choose to invest in an MMF offered by an investment company that also offers a bond mutual fund. During periods when interest rates are expected to decline, a portion of the investor's funds can be transferred from the MMF to the bond mutual fund upon the investor's request.

The expected returns on MMFs are low relative to bonds or stocks because of the following factors. First, the credit risk of MMFs is normally perceived to be lower than that of corporate bonds. Second, MMFs have less interest rate risk than bond funds. Third, they consistently generate positive returns over time, whereas bond and stock funds can experience negative returns. Because MMFs are normally characterized as having relatively low risk and low expected returns, they are popular among investors who need a conservative investment medium. Furthermore, they provide liquidity with their check-writing privileges.

Risk of Money Market Funds during the Credit Crisis   During the credit crisis, investors became concerned about the risk of MMFs that were focused on commercial paper. Much commercial paper is issued by financial institutions, and investors feared that

their commercial paper could default. In one week during September 2008, withdrawals from MMFs exceeded $140 billion. This was especially shocking because MMFs were normally perceived as a safe haven when all other investment alternatives were considered to be too risky. Many investors shifted their money from MMFs containing commercial paper to MMFs containing Treasury bills. The shift in the flow of funds caused an increase in the yield on commercial paper and a decrease in the yield on Treasury bills, which resulted in a larger risk premium being offered on commercial paper.

Management of Money Market Funds

The role of MMF portfolio managers is to maintain an asset portfolio that satisfies the underlying objective of a fund. If the managers expect a stronger economy, they may replace maturing risk-free securities (Treasury bills) with more commercial paper or CDs. The return on these instruments will be higher but will not overexpose the fund to credit risk. For some MMFs there is very little flexibility in the composition. For example, some MMFs may as a rule maintain a high percentage of their investment in T-bills to assure investors that they will continue to refrain from risky securities.

Even if managers are unable to change the asset composition of MMFs, they can still influence performance by changing the maturities of the securities in which they invest. For example, if managers expect interest rates to increase in the future, they should use funds generated from maturing securities to purchase new securities with shorter maturities. The greater the degree to which a manager adjusts the average maturity of an MMF to capitalize on interest rate expectations, the greater the reward or penalty. If the expectation turns out to be correct, the MMF will yield relatively high returns, and vice versa.

Although individual investors and institutions do not manage the portfolio composition or maturity of an MMF, they have a variety of MMFs from which to choose. If they expect a strong economy, they may prefer an MMF that contains securities with some risk that offer higher returns than T-bills. If they expect interest rates to increase, they could invest in MMFs with a short average maturity. They are in a sense managing their investment by choosing an MMF with the characteristics they prefer. Some investment companies offer several MMFs, allowing investors to switch from one fund to another based on their expectations of economic conditions.

Regulation and Taxation of Money Market Funds

As a result of the Securities Act of 1933, sponsoring companies must provide full information on any MMFs they offer. In addition, they must provide potential investors with a current prospectus that describes the fund's investment policies and objectives. The Investment Company Act of 1940 contains numerous restrictions that prevent a conflict of interest by the fund's managers.

Earnings generated by an MMF are generally passed on to the fund's shareholders in the form of interest payments or converted into additional shares. If the fund distributes at least 90 percent of its income to its shareholders, the fund itself is exempt from federal taxation. This tax rule is designed to avoid double taxation. Although the fund can avoid federal taxes on its income, shareholders are subject to taxes on the income they receive, regardless of whether it is in the form of interest payments or additional shares.

OTHER TYPES OF FUNDS

In recent years, several other types of funds have become very popular. These include exchange-traded funds, venture capital funds, private equity funds, hedge funds, and real estate investment trusts. Each type is described in turn.

Exchange-Traded Funds

Exchange-traded funds (ETFs) are designed to mimic particular stock indexes and are traded on a stock exchange just like stocks. They can be purchased on margin, just like stocks. They differ from open-end mutual funds in that their shares are traded on an exchange, and their share price changes throughout the day. Also unlike an open-end fund, an ETF has a fixed number of shares. ETFs differ from most open-end and closed-end funds in that they are not actively managed. The management goal of an ETF is to mimic an index so that the share price of the ETF moves in line with that index. Because ETFs are not actively managed, they normally do not have capital gains and losses that must be distributed to shareholders. ETFs have become very popular in recent years because they are an efficient way for investors to invest in a particular stock index.

ETFs are commonly classified as broad-based, sector, or global, depending on the specific index that they mimic. The broad-based funds are the most popular, but both sector and global ETFs have experienced substantial growth in recent years.

A popular ETF is the so-called PowerShares QQQ, or Cube (its trading symbol is QQQQ), which was created by the Bank of New York. Cubes are traded on the Nasdaq and represent the Nasdaq 100 index, which consists of many technology firms. Thus, Cubes are ideal for investors who believe that technology stocks will perform well but do not want to select individual technology stocks. Cubes are also commonly sold short by investors who expect that technology stocks will decline in value.

Another example of an ETF is the Standard & Poor's Depository Receipt (SPDR or Spider), which is a basket of stocks matched to the S&P 500 index. Spiders enable investors to take positions in the index by purchasing shares. Thus, investors who anticipate that the stock market as represented by the S&P 500 will perform well may purchase shares of Spiders, especially when their expectations reflect the composite as a whole rather than any individual stock within the composite. Spiders trade at one-tenth the S&P 500 value, so if the S&P 500 is valued at 1400, a Spider is valued at $140. Thus, the percentage change in the price of the shares over time is equivalent to the percentage change in the value of the S&P 500 index.

Diamond ETFs are shares of the Dow Jones Industrial Average (DJIA) and are measured as one one-hundredth of the DJIA value. Midcap Spiders are shares that represent the S&P 400 Midcap Index. There are also Sector Spiders, which are intended to match a specific sector index. For example, a Technology Spider is a fund representing 79 technology stocks from the S&P 500 composite. World equity benchmark shares (WEBs), which are designed to track stock indexes of specific countries, are another type of ETF. Barclays Bank has created several different ETFs (which it calls iShares) that represent specific countries.

One disadvantage of ETFs is that each purchase of additional shares must be done through the exchange where they are traded. Investors incur a brokerage fee from purchasing the shares just as if they had purchased shares of a stock. This cost is especially important to investors who plan to frequently add to their investment in a particular ETF.

Like closed-end funds, ETFs can be sold short. In fact, investors more commonly short ETFs than closed-end funds, because ETFs are more liquid, which makes it easier to execute the short sales. The shares of ETFs sold short represent about 19 percent of all ETF shares on average. This ratio is about 10 times larger than it is for individual stocks. It is attributed to investors who may more commonly bet on price declines of sectors or countries in aggregate rather than individual stocks. In addition, some of the short selling of ETFs is conducted by investors in order to hedge a portion of their existing assets. For example, a financial institution that currently holds a very large portfolio of technology stocks may be concerned about the price movements during the next week even though it has confidence in those stocks over the long run. It could take a short position in a technology stock ETF over the next week to hedge its holdings of individual technology stocks.

Venture Capital Funds

Venture capital (VC) funds use money that they receive from wealthy individuals and some institutional investors to invest in companies. They pool the money that is invested in the fund and use the proceeds to create a diversified equity portfolio. These funds typically require a large minimum investment (such as $100,000 or more) and therefore exclude small investors. A fund charges investors fees for managing the fund, such as 1 to 2 percent of the dollar value of its portfolio per year. Unlike mutual funds, VC funds typically invest in privately held firms rather than publicly traded firms, so their investments are not liquid. They invest in young, growing firms that need equity funding but are not ready or willing to go public. They may invest in businesses that are just being created, that have existed for only a few years, or that are in a later stage of growth. More than half of all VC investing is in businesses that are being created.

Venture capital funds tend to focus on technology firms, which have the potential for high returns but also exhibit a high level of risk. They receive numerous business proposals from businesses that need funding, but invest in less than 1 percent of all the businesses that submit proposals. Sequoia Capital and Menlo Ventures are examples of popular VC funds.

The VC fund managers typically have some experience in running a business. When a VC fund provides equity funding, it becomes a partial owner and may expect to have some control (such as a seat on the board of directors) over the business. Thus, the VC fund managers may also be advisers to the business. Because VC funds invest in risky business ventures, a high percentage of their ventures fail. Even with a high failure rate, however, a fund can still perform well because some of its ventures may be major success stories. Many businesses that ultimately became famous, including Apple, Microsoft, and Oracle Corporation, were partially supported with venture capital in their earlier years.

A VC fund typically plans to exit from its original investment within about four to seven years. If the business goes public, the fund commonly can sell its stake (shares) in the secondary market between 6 and 24 months after the initial public offering (IPO). More than half of businesses that go public are partially backed by VC funds before the IPO. Many businesses backed by venture capital never become large enough to go public. They are typically acquired by other firms, and the VC funds receive payment for their stake in the business.

Private Equity Funds

Private equity funds pool money provided by individual and institutional investors and buy majority (or entire) stakes in businesses. Such a fund is usually created as a limited liability partnership, and the general partners develop a business plan for investing in businesses and managing the businesses that they acquire. They promote their business plan to attract funds from outside investors who become limited partners of the fund. Private equity funds appeal to institutional investors such as pension funds and insurance companies because they have the potential to earn very high returns. They also appeal to university endowments and individuals who can afford to invest $1 million or more.

A private equity fund is typically closed to outside investors once it has reached its funding goal. The fund may be opened again to obtain more funding if it develops new plans for investing additional money. The fund managers commonly distribute 80 percent of the profits from their investments to their investors and retain 20 percent for themselves.

When a private equity fund purchases a business, it assumes control and is able to restructure the business in a manner that will improve its performance. These funds usually purchase private businesses, but sometimes they acquire public companies. They commonly purchase businesses that are struggling and have potential to improve. Thus, a private equity fund may purchase a business at a low price, restructure its operations to improve it, and sell the business for a much higher price than it paid. Examples of businesses purchased by private equity funds include Dunkin' Donuts, Hertz, La Quinta, and Neiman Marcus.

Among the most popular private equity funds are Blackstone, Permira, Apollo Investment, Providence Equity, Carlyle Group, Kohlberg Kravis Roberts (KKR), and Texas Pacific Group. Each of these private equity funds has more than $10 billion in assets. At the other extreme, some private equity funds have less than $10 million in assets. Some major private equity funds are owned by commercial banks. Examples include Credit Suisse Private Equity and Barclays Private Equity. The United States has the largest market for private equity, followed by the United Kingdom, but private equity investments are increasing rapidly throughout Europe and Asia.

The Market for Private Equity Businesses

The market for private businesses is not as efficient as the market for publicly traded stocks. Information about private businesses is very limited, so private equity fund managers may see opportunities to buy a business at a low price and improve it. The potential to capitalize on inefficiencies in this market has attracted much more investment in private equity and has led to the creation of many new private equity funds. In recent years, considerable money has flowed into private equity funds, as investors want to benefit from the high potential returns. Although private equity funds in aggregate raise more than $500 billion per year, these funds also commonly restructure the businesses they buy to rely on more debt financing. This enables them to use less equity per deal and to spread their investments across more deals. It also results in a higher degree of financial leverage for the businesses in which they invest. Thus, the funds can generate a higher rate of return on their equity investment from a given level of business profit, but the increased leverage increases the risk that the business will be unable to repay the debt.

A potential problem is that the large inflow of money into private equity funds could result in too much money chasing too few deals. The intense competition could cause some private equity funds to pay too much for some acquisitions in order to outbid competitors. This may result in a winner's curse, meaning that the winning bidders get the target firms but have paid too much money for them. It is more difficult for private equity firms to perform well in an environment in which there is intense competition with other bidders.

Vulture Funds

A vulture fund is a type of private equity fund that purchases distressed assets of a firm that is in or near bankruptcy, or securities issued by such a firm. For example, a vulture fund may purchase the debt securities of a bankrupt firm at a steep discount. When a firm files for bankruptcy, its equity is commonly eliminated, and its creditors have claims on its assets. If the firm emerges from bankruptcy, the vulture fund will exchange some of its debt for equity in the firm and become the majority owner. The goal of the vulture fund will be to improve the firm's performance and thereby boost the value of its shares, so that the fund can ultimately sell its shares to other investors.

Views of Private Equity Funds

Private equity funds are viewed favorably because of their ability to improve weak businesses. Their investment in businesses is commonly intended to improve sales, increase profits, enhance efficiency, and increase value. Thus, private equity funds have the potential to generate high returns for their investors. Furthermore, some of the businesses they buy experience substantial growth and add new employees following private equity investment. Thus, private equity funds can stimulate economic growth and employment.

Some critics, however, suggest that private equity funds distribute too much of the return on their investment to their managers, and not enough to the investors. In addition, some private equity funds have performed poorly for their investors. Union lobbyists argue that private equity funds are too eager to fire employees after buying a company in order to achieve short-term efficiency, but at the expense of reducing the company's long-term performance. Social and environmental advocates are concerned that private equity funds may not consider the social and environmental consequences of the actions they take to enhance the value of businesses such as hospitals or casinos.

Hedge Funds

WEB

www.sec.gov/
answers/hedge.htm
Provides information
on hedge funds.

Hedge funds sell shares to wealthy individuals and financial institutions and use the proceeds to invest in securities. They differ from an open-end mutual fund in several ways. First, they require a much larger initial investment (such as $1 million), whereas mutual funds typically allow a minimum investment in the range of $250 to $2,500. Second, many hedge funds are not "open" in the sense that they may not always accept additional investments or accommodate redemption requests unless advance notice is provided. Some hedge funds permit investors to withdraw their investments, but require advance notice of 30 days or more. Third, hedge funds have been subject to minimal regulation. They provide very limited information to prospective investors. Fourth, hedge funds invest in a wide variety of investments to achieve high returns. Consequently, they tend to take more risk than mutual funds. Although some hedge funds have performed well, many have failed.

Most hedge funds are organized as limited partnerships. There are at least 9,000 hedge funds, with a combined market value of about $2 trillion. The investment strategies used by hedge funds include investing in derivative securities and selling stocks short. In recent years, some hedge funds have purchased businesses that they manage, similar to private equity funds. When a hedge fund purchases securities, it is simply attempting to capitalize on a market inefficiency (improper market valuation of a security). When it buys a business, it attempts to capitalize on inefficiencies in the management of the firm. The hedge fund either oversees or replaces managers to improve the performance of the business, with a goal of ultimately selling the business for a much higher price than it paid. In some cases, a hedge fund purchases distressed assets of a bankrupt firm, similar to a vulture fund.

Use of Financial Leverage Hedge funds commonly use borrowed funds to complement the equity that they receive and invest. This use of financial leverage allows them to make more investments with a given amount of equity, and can magnify the returns.

EXAMPLE

Durham Hedge Fund uses $3 of borrowed funds for every $1 of equity that it invests. It can obtain $4 of assets for each $1 of equity that it invests. If its investment results in a +20 percent return on assets (ROA), this represents a return on its equity (ROE) investment of

$$\text{ROE} = \text{ROA} \times (\text{Assets}/\text{Equity})$$
$$= 20\% \times 4$$
$$= 80\%$$

If Durham Hedge Fund used only equity (no borrowed funds) to invest in assets, its return on equity would have been only 20 percent, the same as its return on assets. The financial leverage in this example allowed the hedge fund to magnify its returns to investors by four times the return on assets. ●

Financial leverage can also magnify negative returns (losses) and therefore increases the risk to investors.

EXAMPLE

Consider the previous example in which Durham Hedge Fund used $3 of borrowed funds for every $1 of equity that it invests. But now assume that its investment results in a −20 percent return on the assets (ROA). This represents a return on its equity (ROE) investment of

$$\text{ROE} = \text{ROA} \times (\text{Assets}/\text{Equity})$$
$$= -20\% \times 4$$
$$= -80\%$$

If this hedge fund used only equity (no borrowed funds) to invest in assets, its return on equity would have been −20 percent. ●

Hedge Fund Fees

Hedge funds charge a management fee of between 1 and 2 percent of the investment per year. In addition, they charge an incentive fee that is based on the return of the fund. The typical incentive fee is 20 percent of the return.

EXAMPLE

Consider a hedge fund that charges a management fee of 2 percent and an incentive fee of 20 percent of the annual return. In the most recent year, the fund earned a return of 15 percent. The investors in this fund would have paid an incentive fee of 3 percent (computed as 20 percent of the 15 percent return) along with a 2 percent management fee, or a total fee of 5 percent of their total investment. Considering that some index mutual funds have a very small management fee and no incentive fee, this hedge fund would have been a better investment only if its performance exceeded that of index funds by about 5 percent in that year. ●

Financial Problems Experienced by LTCM

One of the best-known hedge funds was Long-Term Capital Management (LTCM), which was managed by a group of partners who had a very strong track record in the field of finance. In fact, two of its partners, Robert Merton and Myron Scholes (co-creator of the Black-Scholes pricing model for options), received the Nobel Prize in economics. LTCM was created in 1994 and earned relatively high returns in the mid-1990s, which caused more wealthy investors and financial institutions to invest in the fund.

LTCM relied heavily on financial leverage to boost its returns. By 1998, LTCM had about $5 billion in equity and $125 billion in debt to support its $130 billion portfolio, a ratio of $25 of debt for every dollar of equity. Furthermore, some of its investments were in financial derivative positions that magnify returns beyond the level of the underlying securities. From May to July of 1998, LTCM experienced losses of about 16 percent due to volatile market movements. In August 1998, Russia defaulted on some of its bonds, which aroused general concern about bond credit risk throughout the world. At the time, LTCM had investments in relatively risky bonds and lost more than $2 billion or about 40 percent of its total capital. After accounting for the loss, its existing debt of $125 billion was about 50 times its remaining equity. On September 23, 1998, the Federal Reserve Bank of New York organized a rescue of LTCM by 14 large commercial banks and securities firms. These firms provided a capital infusion of $3.6 billion, which gave them a 90 percent stake in LTCM. The rescue plan was intended to prevent LTCM from defaulting on all of its derivative contract positions, which could have caused the counterparties of those positions to lose billions of dollars. In addition, LTCM would have defaulted on some of its loans at a time when the debt markets had just recently been shaken by the Russian bond default; thus, a default on loans by LTCM would have added to a potential international debt crisis. Asian countries were still suffering from the Asian crisis, and additional market paranoia would have resulted in more capital flows out of countries where funds were needed. Nevertheless, some critics suggest that LTCM was given preferential treatment because it was too big to fail.

Performance of Hedge Funds during the Credit Crisis

Some hedge funds failed during the credit crisis in 2008 because they had invested heavily in mortgage-related securities just before subprime mortgage values collapsed. Their losses, which were magnified because of their use of financial leverage, wiped out all of their equity. Some hedge funds that used excessive borrowing received margin calls from their lenders when the values of their investments declined during the credit crisis. They had to sell some investments such as mortgage-backed securities and stocks in order to obtain cash to post more collateral.

Short Selling by Hedge Funds   One reason for the success of some hedge funds is that they can take a very large short position (selling stocks that they do not own) on overvalued stocks. In some cases, firms have issued misleading financial statements, causing their stock prices to be higher than their actual earnings justified. Hedge funds thoroughly investigate such firms, because a fund can earn very large returns by shorting the stocks of these firms before other investors (and various regulators or credit agencies that attempt to detect financial fraud) recognize that the financial statements are misleading. For example, some hedge funds took large short positions in the stocks of Enron, Tyco, and Krispy Kreme. Once the media reported that the financial statements of these firms were questionable, the prices of these stocks declined, and the hedge funds closed out their positions.

During the credit crisis in 2008, hedge funds were accused of making market conditions worse by taking short positions in some of the financial institutions that held subprime mortgages or other mortgage-related securities. The SEC imposed temporary restrictions on short sales of stocks of financial institutions that were highly exposed to subprime mortgages. The hedge funds would likely justify their short sale strategies by arguing that the financial institutions with subprime mortgages were overvalued because they had not been fully transparent about their exposure. To the extent that the hedge funds push the stock closer to its proper value, they make the market more efficient. The arguments about whether hedge funds should be allowed to take large short positions in any stock will continue.

Madoff Fund Scandal   Bernard Madoff managed a large well-respected hedge fund that included various institutions, charities, and wealthy individuals among its investors. The fund reportedly earned favorable returns every year. When some investors wanted to cash out of their investments in December 2008, however, there was no money available for them. Madoff admitted that he had been periodically using money from new investors to pay off investors who wanted to cash out of the fund. The potential losses to investors were estimated to be as high as $50 billion, making this possibly the biggest financial scandal in U.S. history.

One major lesson from this scandal is that hedge funds deserve closer scrutiny from regulators than they have received in the past. A second lesson is that the SEC's oversight of hedge funds should be reviewed. The SEC was alerted several times over the previous nine years to possible irregularities in the Madoff fund, but it failed to detect the fraud.

Hedge Funds of Funds   Since the minimum investment in some hedge funds may be $1 million or more, most small investors are unable to invest in them. However, some "hedge funds of funds" have been created to pool smaller investments by individuals and invest in hedge funds. Thus, the investors who invest in a hedge fund of funds are essentially owners of a diversified set of hedge funds. The typical minimum investment to invest in a hedge fund of funds is between $25,000 and $100,000.

The performance of hedge funds of funds is difficult to monitor because these funds do not have to report to the SEC. However, those that have reported to the SEC have generally experienced weaker performance than that of a basic stock index fund. One reason for the weak performance is the high fees imposed on the investors. The sponsor of a fund of funds has a portfolio manager who decides how to allocate the money, and the costs incurred from that management are charged to investors. In addition, the money is invested in other hedge funds that also charge fees. Thus, investors in a hedge fund of funds essentially pay for two layers of fees resulting from the management of their money.

Real Estate Investment Trusts

A **real estate investment trust (REIT)** (pronounced "reet") is a closed-end fund that invests in real estate or mortgages. Like other mutual funds, REITs allow small investors to participate with a low minimum investment. The funds are pooled to invest in mortgages and in commercial real estate. REITs generate income for shareholders by passing through rents on real estate or interest payments on mortgages. Most existing REITs can be sold on stock exchanges, so investors can sell them at any time. The composition of a REIT is determined by its portfolio manager, who is presumed to have expertise in real estate investments. In the early and mid-1970s, many of the mortgages held by REITs defaulted. Consequently, investors' interest in REITs declined. Since that time, however, REITs have grown substantially. Although the price of a REIT is somewhat influenced by its portfolio composition, it is basically determined by supply and demand. Even if the portfolio has performed well in the past, the REIT's share value may be low if investors are unwilling to invest in it.

REITs can be classified as **equity REITs,** which invest directly in properties, or **mortgage REITs,** which invest in mortgage and construction loans. A third type of REIT, called a hybrid, invests in both properties and mortgages.

Equity REITs are sometimes purchased to hedge against inflation, as rents and property values tend to rise with inflation. Their performance varies according to the perceived future value of the real estate held in each portfolio. REITs that have concentrated in potential high-growth properties are expected to generate a higher return than those with a more nationally diversified portfolio. However, they are also susceptible to more risk if the specific locations experience slow growth.

Because mortgage REITs essentially represent a fixed-income portfolio, their market value will be influenced by interest rate movements. As interest rates rise, the market value of mortgages declines, and therefore the demand for mortgage REITs declines. If interest rates are expected to decrease, mortgage REITs become more attractive. Mortgage REITs are also influenced by credit risk since the mortgages are subject to possible default.

Impact of Credit Crisis on REITs   During the credit crisis in the 2008–2009 period, many mortgages experienced late payments or default. Consequently, mortgage REITs experienced losses during that period. In particular, those REITs that invested heavily in subprime mortgages suffered severe losses.

INTERACTION WITH OTHER FINANCIAL INSTITUTIONS

Mutual funds and other types of funds interact with various financial institutions, as described in Exhibit 23.10. They serve as an investment alternative for portfolio managers of financial institutions such as insurance companies and pension funds.

Some funds are subsidiaries of commercial banks. At least 100 commercial banks such as Citigroup and Bank of America now offer mutual funds. This provides them with a means of retaining customer funds when customers wish to switch from bank deposits to stock or bond mutual funds. Since many customers periodically switch their savings between bank deposits and stocks (or bonds), commercial banks may be able to attract more funds in their mutual funds as they lose deposits, and vice versa. Their mutual funds also attract funds from investors who are not bank customers.

Exhibit 23.10 Interaction between Mutual Funds and Other Financial Institutions

TYPE OF FINANCIAL INSTITUTION	INTERACTION WITH MUTUAL FUNDS
Commercial banks and savings institutions (SIs)	• Money market mutual funds invest in certificates of deposit at banks and SIs and in commercial paper issued by bank holding companies. • Some commercial banks (such as Citigroup and J.P. Morgan Chase) have investment company subsidiaries that offer mutual funds. • Some stock and bond mutual funds invest in securities issued by banks and SIs.
Finance companies	• Some money market mutual funds invest in commercial paper issued by finance companies. • Some stock and bond mutual funds invest in stocks and bonds issued by finance companies.
Securities firms	• Mutual funds hire securities firms to execute security transactions for them. • Some mutual funds own a discount brokerage subsidiary that competes with other securities firms for brokerage services.
Insurance companies	• Some stock mutual funds invest in stocks issued by insurance companies. • Some insurance companies (such as Kemper) have investment company subsidiaries that offer mutual funds. • Some insurance companies invest in mutual funds.
Pension funds	• Pension fund portfolio managers invest in mutual funds.

Use of Financial Markets

Each type of fund uses a particular financial market, as described in Exhibit 23.11. Because the main function of mutual funds is to invest, all securities markets are commonly used. The futures and options markets are also utilized to hedge against interest rate risk or market risk. Some specialized mutual funds take speculative positions in futures contracts.

Many of the transactions by mutual funds in the financial markets finance economic growth, as illustrated in Exhibit 23.12. Mutual funds are major participants in stock and

Exhibit 23.11 How Mutual Funds Utilize Financial Markets

TYPE OF MARKET	HOW MUTUAL FUNDS USE THAT MARKET
Money markets	• Money market mutual funds invest in various money market instruments, such as Treasury bills, commercial paper, banker's acceptances, and certificates of deposit.
Bond markets	• Some bond mutual funds invest mostly in bonds issued by the U.S. Treasury or a government agency. Others invest in bonds issued by municipalities or firms. • Foreign bonds are sometimes included in a bond mutual fund portfolio.
Mortgage markets	• Some bond mutual funds invest in bonds issued by the Government National Mortgage Association (GNMA, or "Ginnie Mae"), which uses the proceeds to purchase mortgages that were originated by some financial institutions.
Stock markets	• Numerous stock mutual funds purchase stocks with various degrees of risk and potential return.
Futures markets	• Some bond mutual funds periodically attempt to hedge against interest rate risk by taking positions in interest rate futures contracts.
Options markets	• Some stock mutual funds periodically hedge specific stocks by taking positions in stock options. • Some mutual funds take positions in stock options for speculative purposes.
Swap markets	• Some bond mutual funds engage in interest rate swaps to hedge interest rate risk.

Exhibit 23.12 How Mutual Funds Finance Economic Growth

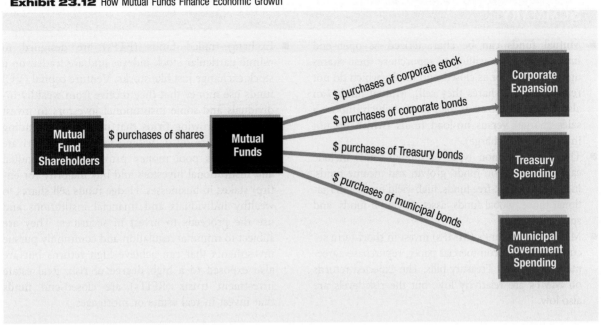

bond offerings and thereby finance corporate expansion. They are also major participants in bond offerings by the Treasury and municipalities and thereby finance government spending.

GLOBALIZATION THROUGH MUTUAL FUNDS

International and global mutual funds have facilitated international capital flows and thereby have helped create a global securities market. They can reduce the excessive transaction costs that might be incurred by small investors who attempt to invest in foreign securities on their own. They also increase the degree of integration among stock markets. As international markets become more accessible, the volume of U.S. investment in foreign securities will become more sensitive to events and financial market conditions in those countries.

Mutual funds are popular not only in the United States but in other countries as well. The types of investment companies that sponsor mutual funds vary across countries. Insurance companies are the most common sponsor of mutual funds in the United Kingdom, while banks dominate in France, Germany, and Italy.

European countries have recently agreed to allow their respective mutual fund shares to be sold across their borders. The shares are under the supervision of their home country but are subject to marketing rules of the countries where they are being marketed. This deregulatory step in Europe may provide the momentum for other countries to do the same.

Qualified companies are allowed to sell mutual fund shares in Mexico. Consequently, many U.S. companies that commonly sponsor mutual funds, such as securities firms, commercial banks, and insurance companies, are generating new business in Mexico.

SUMMARY

- Mutual funds can be characterized as open-end funds (which are willing to repurchase their shares upon demand) or as closed-end funds (which do not repurchase the shares they sell). Mutual funds can also be characterized as load funds (which impose a sales charge) versus no-load funds (which do not impose a sales charge).
- The more common types of mutual funds include capital appreciation funds, growth and income funds, income funds, tax-free funds, high-yield funds, international funds, global funds, asset allocation funds, and specialty funds.
- Money market funds (MMFs) invest in short-term securities, such as commercial paper, repurchase agreements, CDs, and Treasury bills. The expected returns on MMFs are relatively low, but the risk levels are also low.

- Exchange-traded funds (ETFs) are designed to mimic particular stock indexes and are traded on a stock exchange just like stocks. Venture capital (VC) funds use money that they receive from wealthy individuals and some institutional investors to invest in young, growing firms that need equity funding but are not ready or willing to go public. Private equity funds pool money provided by individual and institutional investors and buy majority (or entire) stakes in businesses. Hedge funds sell shares to wealthy individuals and financial institutions and use the proceeds to invest in securities. They are subject to minimal regulation and commonly pursue investments that can achieve high returns but are also exposed to a high degree of risk. Real estate investment trusts (REITs) are closed-end funds that invest in real estate or mortgages.

POINT COUNTER-POINT

Should Mutual Funds Be Subject to More Regulation?

Point No. Mutual funds can be monitored by their shareholders (just like many firms), and the shareholders can enforce governance.

Counter-Point Yes. Mutual funds need to be governed by regulators because they are accountable for such a large amount of money. Without regulation,

there could be massive withdrawals from mutual funds when unethical behavior by managers of mutual funds is publicized.

Who Is Correct? Use the Internet to learn more about this issue. Offer your own opinion on this issue.

QUESTIONS AND APPLICATIONS

1. Mutual Fund Services Explain why mutual funds are attractive to small investors. How can mutual funds generate returns to their shareholders?

2. Open- versus Closed-End Funds How do open-end mutual funds differ from closed-end mutual funds?

3. Load versus No-Load Mutual Funds Explain the difference between load and no-load mutual funds.

4. Use of Funds Like mutual funds, commercial banks and stock-owned savings institutions sell shares,

but the proceeds received by mutual funds are used in a different way. Explain.

5. Risk of Treasury Bond Funds Support or refute the following statement: Investors can avoid all types of risk by purchasing a mutual fund that contains only Treasury bonds.

6. Fund Selection Describe the ideal mutual fund for investors who wish to generate tax-free income and also maintain a low degree of interest rate risk.

7.   Exposure to Exchange Rate Movements
Explain how changing foreign currency values can affect the performance of international mutual funds.

8.   Components of Mutual Funds Considering all stock and bond mutual funds in aggregate, what type of security is dominant?

9.   Tax Effects on Mutual Funds Explain how the income generated by a mutual fund is taxed when the fund distributes at least 90 percent of its taxable income to shareholders.

10.   Performance According to research, have mutual funds outperformed the market? Explain. Would mutual funds be attractive to some investors even if they are not expected to outperform the market? Explain.

11.   Money Market Funds How do money market funds differ from other types of mutual funds in terms of how they use the money invested by shareholders? Which security do MMFs invest in most often? How can an MMF accommodate shareholders who wish to sell their shares when the amount of proceeds received from selling new shares is less than the amount needed?

12.   Risk of Money Market Funds Explain the relative risk of the various types of securities in which a money market fund may invest.

13.   Risk of Mutual Funds Is the value of a money market fund or a bond fund more susceptible to rising interest rates? Explain.

14.   Diversification among Mutual Funds
Explain why diversification across different types of mutual funds is highly recommended.

15.   Tax Effects on Money Market Funds
Explain how the income generated by a money market fund is taxed if it distributes at least 90 percent of its income to shareholders.

16.   REITs Explain the difference between equity REITs and mortgage REITs. Which type would likely be a better hedge against high inflation? Why?

Advanced Questions

17.   Comparing Management of Open-versus Closed-end Funds Compare the management of a closed-end fund with that of an open-end fund. Given the differences in the funds' characteristics, explain why the management of liquidity is different in the open-end fund as compared to the closed-end fund. Assume that the funds are the same size and have the same goal to invest in stocks and to earn a very high return. Which portfolio manager do you think will achieve a larger increase in the fund's net asset value? Explain.

18.   Selecting a Type of Mutual Fund Consider the prevailing conditions that could affect the demand for stocks, including inflation, the economy, the budget deficit, the Fed's monetary policy, political conditions, and the general mood of investors. Based on current conditions, recommend a specific type of stock mutual fund that you think would perform well. Offer some logic to support your recommendation.

19.   Comparing Hedge Funds and Mutual Funds Explain why hedge funds may be able to achieve higher returns for their investors than mutual funds. Explain why hedge funds and mutual funds may have different risks. When the market is overvalued, why might hedge funds be better able to capitalize on the excessive market optimism than mutual funds?

20.   How Private Equity Funds Can Improve Business Conditions Describe private equity funds. How can they improve business conditions? Money that individual and institutional investors previously invested in stocks is now being invested in private equity funds. Explain why this should result in improved business conditions.

21.   Source of Mutual Fund versus Private Equity Fund Returns Equity mutual funds and private equity funds generate returns for their investors in different ways. Explain this difference. Which type of fund do you think would be better able to capitalize on a weak publicly traded firm that has ignored all forms of shareholder activism?

Interpreting Financial News

Interpret the following comments made by Wall Street analysts and portfolio managers:

a. "Just because a mutual fund earned a 20 percent return in one year, that does not mean that investors should rush into it. The fund's performance must be market adjusted."

b. "An international mutual fund's performance is subject to conditions beyond the fund manager's control."

c. "Small mutual funds will need to merge to compete with the major players in terms of efficiency."

Managing in Financial Markets

Investing in Mutual Funds As an individual investor, you are attempting to invest in a well-diversified portfolio of mutual funds so that you will be somewhat insulated from any type of economic shock that may occur.

a. An investment adviser recommends that you buy four different U.S. growth stock funds. Since these funds contain over 400 different U.S. stocks, the adviser says that you will be well insulated from any economic shocks. Do you agree? Explain.

b. A second investment adviser recommends that you invest in four different mutual funds that are focused on different countries in Europe. The adviser says that you will be completely insulated from U.S. economic conditions and that your portfolio will therefore have low risk. Do you agree? Explain.

c. A third investment adviser recommends that you avoid exposure to the stock markets by investing your money in four different U.S. bond funds. The adviser says that because bonds make fixed payments, these bond funds have very low risk. Do you agree? Explain.

FLOW OF FUNDS EXERCISE

How Mutual Funds Facilitate the Flow of Funds

Carson Company is considering a private placement of bonds with Venus Mutual Fund.

a. Explain the interaction between Carson and Venus. How would Venus serve Carson's needs, and how would Carson serve the needs of Venus?

b. Why does Carson interact with Venus Mutual Fund instead of trying to obtain the funds directly from individuals who invested in Venus Mutual Fund?

c. Would Venus Mutual Fund serve as a better monitor of Carson Company than the individuals who provided money to the mutual fund? Explain.

INTERNET/EXCEL EXERCISES

1. Assess today's mutual fund performance, using the website www.bloomberg.com/markets/. Under "Market Data," click on "Mutual Funds." What is the best-performing mutual fund today in terms of the yield-to-date (YTD)? What is the net asset value (NAV) of this fund, and what is its YTD? What is the five-year return on this fund, and what is its YTD this year? Do you think mutual fund rankings change frequently? Why or why not?

2. Go to http://screen.yahoo.com/funds.html. Describe the constraints that you would impose when selecting funds. Impose those constraints on the category, past performance, ratings, and other characteristics, and then allow the screener to screen the mutual funds for you. List one or more mutual funds that satisfied your criteria.

3. Go to http://finance.yahoo.com/, enter the symbol MVC (for the closed-end fund MVC Capital that invests in U.S. stocks), and click on "Get Quotes." Click on "5y" just below the stock price trend to review the stock price movements over the last five years. Check the S&P box just above the graph and click on "Compare" in order to compare the trend of MVC's price with the movements in the S&P stock index. Does it appear that MVC's performance is influenced by general stock market movements?

4. Go to http://finance.yahoo.com/, enter the symbol DNP (for the closed-end fund DNP Select Income Fund that invests in bonds), and click on "Get Quotes." Retrieve stock price data at the beginning of the last 20 quarters. Then go to http://research.stlouisfed.org/fred2/ and retrieve interest rate data at the beginning of the last 20 quarters for the three-month T-bill. Record the data on an Excel spreadsheet. Derive the quarterly return of DNP. Derive the quarterly change in the interest rate. Apply regression analysis in which the quarterly return of DNP is the dependent variable and the quarterly change in the interest rate is the independent variable (see Appendix B for more information about using regression analysis). Is there a positive or negative relationship between the interest rate movement and the stock return of DNP? Is the relationship significant? Offer an explanation for this relationship.

WSJ Exercise

Performance of Mutual Funds

Using an issue of *The Wall Street Journal,* summarize an article that discussed the recent performance of a specific mutual fund. Has this mutual fund's performance been better or worse than the norm? What reason is given for the particular level of performance?

24
Securities Operations

CHAPTER OBJECTIVES

The specific objectives of this chapter are to:

■ describe the key functions of securities firms,

■ explain the exposure of securities firms to risk,

■ identify the factors that affect the valuation of securities firms, and

■ explain how the credit crisis affected securities firms.

WEB

http://finance.yahoo.com

Search engine for information about any publicly traded stocks in the United States.

Securities firms serve as important intermediaries by helping governments and firms raise funds. They also facilitate the transactions between investors in the secondary market.

SERVICES PROVIDED BY SECURITIES FIRMS

Securities firms provide several different services. They facilitate stock and bond offerings, and facilitate corporate restructuring activities. Since these services are commonly categorized as investment banking, the securities firms that provide these services are commonly referred to as *investment banks*.

Some securities firms provide brokerage services for investors who want to either buy or sell various types of securities in the secondary market. The securities firms that provide these services are commonly referred to as *brokerage firms*.

Many securities firms provide both investment banking services and brokerage services. Some of these firms are independent, but many of them are part of a financial conglomerate. Recently, some securities firms have become part of a bank holding company structure. Nevertheless, their securities operations are distinctly different from commercial banking operations and therefore deserve coverage as a separate chapter. The services provided by securities firms are described in detail next.

Facilitating New Stock Offerings

A securities firm acts as an intermediary between a corporation issuing securities and investors by providing the following services:

- Origination
- Underwriting
- Distribution
- Advising

Origination When a corporation decides to publicly issue stock, it may contact a securities firm. The securities firm can recommend the appropriate amount of stock to issue because it can anticipate the amount of stock that the market can likely absorb without causing a reduction in the stock price. It evaluates the corporation's financial condition to determine the appropriate price for the newly issued stock. If the corporation has issued stock to the public before, the price should be the same as the market price on its outstanding stock. If not, the securities firm will compare the corporation's financial characteristics with those of other similar firms in the same industry that have stock outstanding to help determine the proper valuation of the corporation and therefore the price at which the stock should be sold.

The issuing corporation then registers with the Securities and Exchange Commission (SEC). All information relevant to the security, as well as the agreement between the issuer and the securities firm, must be provided in the **registration statement,** which is intended to ensure that accurate information is disclosed by the issuing corporation. Some publicly placed securities do not require registration if the issue is very small or is sold entirely within a particular state. Included in the required registration information is the **prospectus,** which discloses relevant financial data on the firm and provisions applicable to the security. The prospectus can be issued only after the registration is approved, which typically takes 20 to 40 days. SEC approval does not guarantee the quality or safety of the securities to be issued; it simply acknowledges that a firm is disclosing accurate information about itself.

The securities firm along with the issuing firm may meet with institutional investors who may be interested in the offering. They engage in a road show in which they travel to various cities where they meet with institutional investors to discuss the issuing firm's plans for using the funds that will be obtained from the offering.

WEB

www.sec.gov/edgar
.shtml
Identifies upcoming
IPOs and the securities
firms that are involved
in the underwriting
process.

Underwriting   The original securities firm may form an **underwriting syndicate** by asking other securities firms to underwrite a portion of the stock. Each participating securities firm shares in the underwriting fees charged to the issuer. Some of the more well-known securities firms for underwriting include Bank of America's Merrill Lynch division, Goldman Sachs, and Morgan Stanley.

The term *underwrite* is sometimes wrongly interpreted to mean that the underwriting syndicate guarantees the price at which shares will be sold. However, stock offerings are normally based on a **best-efforts agreement,** whereby the securities firm does not guarantee a price to the issuing corporation. In such a case, the issuing corporation bears the risk because it does not receive a guaranteed price from the securities firm on the stock to be issued.

When securities firms facilitate initial public offerings (IPOs), they attempt to price the stock high enough to satisfy the issuing firm. The higher the average price at which the shares are issued, the greater the proceeds received by the issuing firm. If the securities firms price the stock too high, however, they will not be able to place the entire issue. The reputation of the underwriting syndicate is at stake when it attempts to place the stock of the issuing firm. It knows that other corporations that may issue stock in the future will monitor its ability to place the stock.

Securities firms must also attempt to satisfy the institutional investors that may invest in the IPO. The higher the price institutional investors pay for the stock being issued, the lower the return they earn on their investment when they sell the stock. Underwriting syndicates recognize that other institutional investors monitor stock prices after offerings to determine whether the initial offer price charged by the syndicate was appropriate. If the institutional investors do not earn reasonable returns on their investment, they may not invest in future IPOs. Since securities firms rely on institutional investors when placing shares of newly issued stock, they want to maintain a good relationship with them.

Research documents that securities firms tend to underprice IPOs. That is, institutional investors that invest at the offer price earn high returns on average if they retain the investment for a short-term period, such as three months or less. Much of the return occurs within the first few days after the IPO. Consequently, the returns to investors who purchase the shares shortly after the IPO are generally poor.

Distribution of Stock   Once all agreements between the issuing firm, the originating securities firm, and other participating securities firms are complete and the registration is approved by the SEC, the stock may be sold. The prospectus is distributed to all potential purchasers of the stock, and the issue is advertised to the public. In some cases, the issue sells within hours. If the issue does not sell as expected, the underwriting syndicate will likely have to reduce the price to complete the sale. The demand for the stock is somewhat influenced by the sales force involved in selling the stock. Some securities firms participating in a syndicate have brokerage subsidiaries that can sell stock on a retail level. Others may specialize in underwriting but still utilize a group of brokerage firms to sell the newly issued stock. The brokers earn a commission on the amount they sell but do not guarantee a specific amount of sales.

When a corporation publicly places stock, it incurs two types of **flotation costs,** or costs of placing the securities. First, it must pay fees to the underwriters who place the stock with investors. Second, it incurs **issue costs** including printing, legal, registration, and accounting expenses. Because these issue costs are not significantly affected by the size of the issue, flotation costs as a percentage of the value of securities issued are lower for larger issues.

Advising　The securities firm acts as an adviser throughout the **origination** stage. Even after the stock is issued, the securities firm may continue to provide advice on the timing, amount, and terms of future financing. Included with this advice are recommendations on the appropriate type of financing (bonds, stocks, or long-term commercial loans).

Private Placements of Stocks　Securities firms are also hired to facilitate private placements of stock. With a **private placement** (or direct placement), an entire stock offering may be placed with a small set of institutional investors and not offered to the general public. Under the SEC's Rule 144A, firms may engage in private placements of stock without filing the extensive registration statement that is required for public placements. Consequently, the issuing firm's costs of reporting are lower than with a public placement. In addition, the underwriting services are more manageable because an underwriting syndicate may not be necessary.

Institutional investors that are willing to hold the stock for a long period of time are prime candidates for participating in a private placement. Since all the stock is held by a small set of institutional investors, there will not be an established secondary market for the stock. Thus, the institutional investors may expect a higher return on the stock to compensate for the lack of liquidity.

Facilitating New Bond Offerings

A securities firm's role in placing bonds is somewhat similar to its role in placing stock. The four main services of a securities firm in placing bonds are explained in turn.

Origination　The securities firm may suggest a maximum amount of bonds that should be issued, based on the issuer's characteristics. If the issuer already has a high level of outstanding debt, the bonds may not be well received by the market, because the issuer's ability to meet the debt payments will be questionable. Consequently, the bonds will need to offer a relatively high yield, which will increase the cost of borrowing to the issuer.

Next, the coupon rate, the maturity, and other provisions are decided, based on the characteristics of the issuing firm. The asking price on the bonds is determined by evaluating market prices of existing bonds that are similar in their degree of risk, term to maturity, and other provisions.

Issuers of bonds must register with the SEC. The registration statement contains information about the bonds to be issued, states the agreement between the securities firm and the issuer, and also includes a prospectus with financial information about the issuer.

Underwriting Bonds   Some issuers of bonds, particularly public utilities, may solicit competitive bids on the price of bonds from various securities firms so that they can select the firm with the highest bid. Securities firms provide several services to the issuer, however, so price is not the only consideration. Corporations typically select a securities firm based on reputation rather than competitive bids.

Bonds can often be sold in large blocks to financial institutions. In contrast, a stock issue must be segmented into smaller pieces and is more difficult to sell. The main concern of institutional investors that purchase bonds is the credit risk of the issuer, which may be easier to assess than the risk of newly issued stock.

As with stocks, the securities firm may organize an underwriting syndicate of securities firms to participate in placing the bonds. Each securities firm assumes a portion of the risk. Of course, the potential income earned by the original securities firm is reduced, too. If the securities firm is uncomfortable guaranteeing a price to the issuer, it may offer only a best-efforts agreement.

Distribution of Bonds   Upon SEC approval of the registration, a prospectus is distributed to all potential purchasers of the bonds, and the issue is advertised to the public. The asking price on the bonds is normally set at a level that will ensure a sale of the entire issue. The flotation costs generally range from 0.5 percent to 3 percent of the value of the bonds issued, which can be significantly lower than the flotation costs of issuing common or preferred stock.

Advising   As with a stock placement, a securities firm that places bonds for issuers may serve as an adviser to the issuer even after the placement is completed. Most issuers of bonds will need to raise long-term funds in the future and will consider the securities firm's advice on the type of securities to issue at that time.

Private Placements of Bonds   If an issuing corporation knows of a potential purchaser for its entire issue, it may be able to sell its securities directly without offering the bonds to the general public (or using the underwriting services of a securities firm). This private placement avoids the underwriting fee. Corporations have been increasingly using private placements. Potential purchasers of securities that are large enough to buy an entire issue include insurance companies, commercial banks, pension funds, and bond mutual funds. Securities can even be privately placed with two or more of these institutions. Private placements of bonds are more common than private placements of stocks.

The price paid for privately placed securities is determined by negotiations between the issuing corporation and the purchaser. Although the securities firm is not needed here for underwriting, it may advise the issuing corporation on the appropriate terms of the securities and identify potential purchasers.

Unlike the standardized provisions of a publicly placed issue, the provisions of a privately placed issue can be tailored to the desires of the purchaser. A possible disadvantage of a private placement is that the demand may not be as strong as for a publicly placed issue, because only a fraction of the market is targeted. This could force a lower price for the bonds, resulting in a higher cost of financing for the issuing firm.

By facilitating bond offerings, securities firms serve as important financial intermediaries between corporations (and governments) and institutional investors. Exhibit 24.1 illustrates how they influence the flow of funds and help corporations and governments raise funds, thereby facilitating economic growth.

Facilitating Leveraged Buyouts

Securities firms facilitate leveraged buyouts (LBOs) in the following ways. First, they assess the market value of the firm (or division) of concern so that the acquirer does not

Exhibit 24.1 How Securities Firms Facilitate Economic Growth

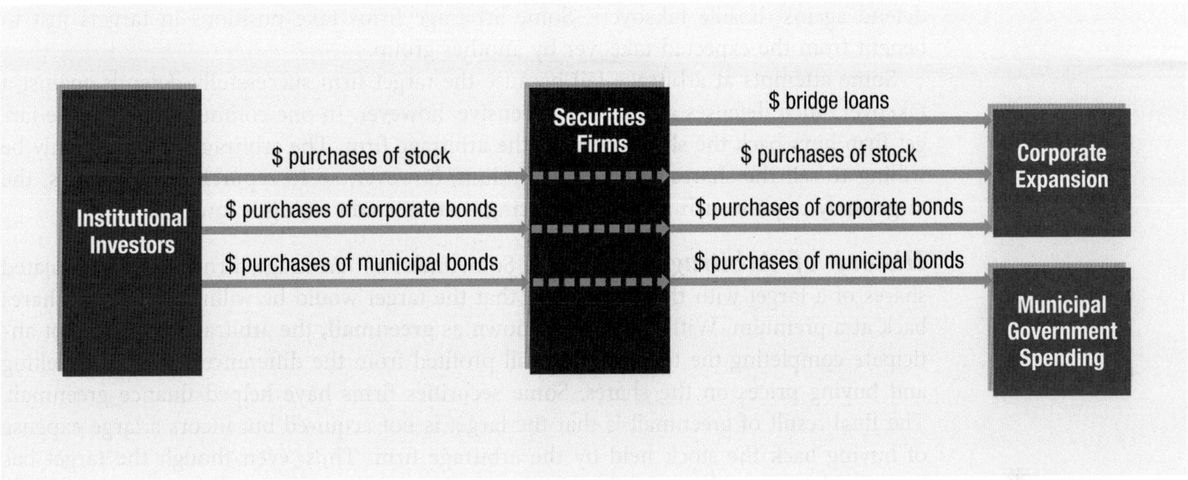

pay more than the target firm's value. Second, they arrange financing, in which they may provide a **bridge loan** that provides temporary financing until the acquirer has access to other funds. They may also help the acquirer issue securities to raise funds. Third, they help the acquirer purchase any common stock of the target that is outstanding. Finally, they may be retained in an advisory capacity.

The acquirer may not be able to afford an LBO because of constraints on the amount of funds it can borrow. The securities firm may therefore consider purchasing a portion of the firm's assets, thereby providing the client with some financial support. It will either try to sell these assets immediately or hold them for some time. Some securities firms have generated substantial returns on such deals by selling the assets later at a much higher price than the purchase price. Nevertheless, such transactions may pose a significant risk to a securities firm because there is no guarantee that the assets will sell at a premium.

Facilitating Arbitrage

Some securities firms also facilitate **arbitrage activity,** which in the securities industry involves purchasing undervalued shares and reselling them at a higher price. The securities firms work closely with **arbitrage firms** (which specialize in arbitrage) by searching for undervalued firms and raising funds for the arbitrage firms. It is sometimes difficult to distinguish between arbitrage and an LBO because both activities involve an attempt to purchase an undervalued firm, mostly with borrowed funds. LBOs, however, are commonly executed by management or other employees, who may plan to maintain ownership of the firm. Sometimes arbitrage activity is referred to as a hostile LBO.

In a common form of arbitrage, a firm is acquired, and then its individual divisions are sold off. This **asset stripping,** as it is called, is motivated by the perception that the sum of the parts is sometimes greater than the whole.

Securities firms generate fee income from advising arbitrage firms and also receive a commission on the bonds issued to support the arbitrage activity. They also receive fees from divestitures of divisions. When the fund raising is not expected to be complete before the acquisition is initiated, securities firms provide bridge loans. Because the acquisitions are largely financed with borrowed funds, arbitrage firms essentially pay off their debts with the target's cash flow.

When hostile (uninvited) takeovers became popular, some securities firms offered advice on takeover defense maneuvers. Sometimes these securities firms found themselves simultaneously financing some hostile takeovers while advising other firms on how to defend against hostile takeovers. Some arbitrage firms take positions in targets just to benefit from the expected takeover by another group.

Some attempts at arbitrage fail because the target firm successfully defends against a takeover. Such defenses are usually expensive, however. In one common defense, the target firm buys back the shares held by the arbitrage firm. The arbitrage firm may only be willing to sell the shares back at a premium, however, so to repurchase the shares, the target may require such massive financing that its credit rating is lowered.

History of Arbitrage Activity   Sometimes an arbitrage firm has accumulated shares of a target with the expectation that the target would be willing to buy its shares back at a premium. With this tactic, known as **greenmail,** the arbitrage firm did not anticipate completing the takeover but still profited from the difference between its selling and buying prices on the shares. Some securities firms have helped finance greenmail. The final result of greenmail is that the target is not acquired but incurs a large expense of buying back the stock held by the arbitrage firm. Thus, even though the target has been singled out as being undervalued (possibly as a result of inefficient management), it is still run by the same management.

Arbitrage activity has been criticized because it often results in excessive financial leverage and risk for corporations. In addition, the restructuring of divisions after acquisitions results in corporate layoffs. Because some securities firms facilitate arbitrage activity, they are criticized as well. Nevertheless, arbitrage helps eliminate managerial inefficiencies. If a firm is not efficiently managed, it should become a target so that an acquirer can restructure the firm and enable it to reach its full potential. In addition, shareholders of a target firm can benefit from arbitrage activity because the share price generally rises as the arbitrage firm purchases shares.

Arbitrage Divisions of Securities Firms   Many securities firms have an arbitrage division that engages in arbitrage activity far beyond seeking undervalued companies to acquire. An arbitrage division is normally composed of traders with an exceptional ability to value assets. The securities firm allocates funds to the division, and the traders attempt to generate a high return for the firm. They often attempt to take advantage of a discrepancy between prices of two securities whose returns are normally highly correlated. For example, a trader may identify two securities that have almost identical future expected payoffs but are selling at different prices. Therefore, the trader will buy (take a long position in) the security that appears to be undervalued and take a short position in the security that is priced relatively high. The trader's firm benefits if the prices of the two securities ultimately converge. If the market conditions are generally favorable, the prices of both stocks will likely rise, but the undervalued stock should rise by a greater degree than the other stock. If the market conditions are unfavorable, the prices of both stocks will likely decline, but the undervalued stock should decline by a lower degree than the other stock. Therefore, the gain on the short position should be larger than the loss on the long position.

Facilitating Corporate Restructuring

Another critical function of securities firms is providing advice on corporate restructuring. A key component of the advisory function is the valuation of a business. Securities firms assess the potential value of target firms so that they can advise corporations on whether to merge and on the appropriate price to offer. The valuation process is also used for advising on potential divestitures and on LBOs. Securities firms not only assist with valuations but also help firms with the process of implementing a merger, acquisition, or divestiture.

Advising on Corporate Restructuring Many securities firms have expertise at assessing how corporate restructuring could change the valuation of a business. They assess potential synergies that might result from combining two businesses. In some cases, they conclude that the sum of the two separate parts is worth less than the whole. In other words, the combination of the two businesses may be worth more than the sum of their values if they remained separate. Consequently, one of the businesses may be able to realize benefits from acquiring the other, even after considering the premium above the target's market value that it will likely have to pay.

In other situations, securities firms may suggest that the sum of the parts of a particular business will be worth more than the whole if their ownership is separated. In this case, the securities firm may suggest that the firm engage in a carve-out and sell one of its units to new shareholders through an IPO. The proceeds of the IPO go to the parent firm. The parent benefits if the funds raised exceed the present value of the future cash flows that the unit would generate if it was retained. Although estimating the future cash flows of a unit can be difficult, securities firms normally have experience in such valuations.

Alternatively, a securities firm may advise the firm to spin off a unit by creating new shares representing the unit and distributing them to existing shareholders. Consequently, the firm's old shares no longer represent ownership of the unit, so their price will decline. Together, however, the sum of the values of both the old and the new shares may exceed the value of the firm's shares before the spin-off. The separation of a subsidiary from its parent may also reduce asymmetric information problems between managers and investors. Because the unit is now valued separately, monitoring its performance is easier than it was when the unit was just one component of a firm with many different businesses. In addition, now that the unit has a market value, its managers can be compensated with stocks or stock options to align their compensation directly with the unit's value.

Financing Mergers and Acquisitions Many mergers and acquisitions require outside financing, and securities firms that are able to raise large amounts of funds in the capital markets are more likely to be chosen as advisers for mergers and acquisitions. In recent years, securities firms have loaned their own funds to companies involved in a merger or acquisition. In some cases, they have even provided equity financing, whereby they become part owner of the acquired firms.

Exhibit 24.2 illustrates how securities firms participate in an acquisition. Note how many different functions the securities firms may perform for the acquiring firms, all of which generate fees or interest. The securities firms can help finance an acquisition by (1) providing loans to the acquirer, (2) underwriting bonds or stock for the acquirer, and (3) investing their own equity in the acquirer's purchase of the target.

Providing Brokerage Services

Securities firms commonly serve as brokers by executing buy or sell orders desired by their customers. They execute large orders placed by institutional investors, such as an order to purchase 100,000 shares of a specific stock. They also execute orders placed by individuals. They also execute short sale transactions for their customers.

Full-Service versus Discount Brokerage Services Brokerage firms can be classified by the services they provide. **Full-service brokerage firms** provide information and personalized advice and execute orders. **Discount brokerage firms** only execute orders upon request and do not provide advice. They are often unable to maintain a long-term relationship with clients, because they provide a service difficult to differentiate from competitors. Their required minimum opening balance is typically in the range of $1,000 to $3,000. Most discount brokers do offer some degree of research on stocks on a website exclusively for their clients.

Exhibit 24.2 Participation of Securities Firms in an Acquisition

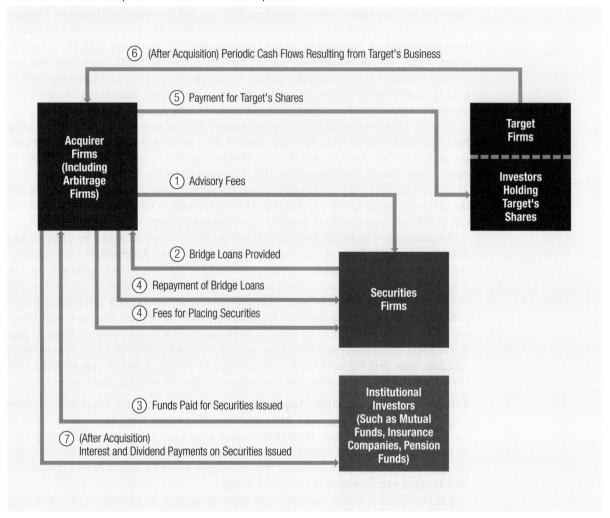

Although discount brokers still concentrate on executing stock transactions, they have expanded their services to include precious metals, options, and municipal bonds. Some also offer credit cards, cash management accounts, 24-hour phone service, and research reports. Many discount brokerage firms are owned by large commercial banks, which were historically prohibited from offering full-service brokerage services.

Online Orders   Many investors now place orders online rather than calling brokers. Brokerage firms have reduced their costs by implementing online order systems because the online format is less expensive than having brokers receive the orders by phone. On-line trading has become very competitive, however, with numerous brokerage firms fighting for market share. Consequently, the prices charged for online orders are very low. The fee for an online order to trade 100 shares of stock is typically $20 or less for investors who have an established account with the brokerage firm.

Management of Customer Accounts   Some securities firms not only execute transactions for customers, but also manage the portfolios of securities owned by the customers. That is, the firm decides when to buy or sell securities owned by the customers. Securities firms commonly provide this type of service to manage the pension funds of companies, but the service may also be offered to individuals. The securities firm charges a management fee for its services, which may be expressed as an annual percentage (such as 1 percent) of the assets that are managed. The firm may also charge fees for any securities transactions that it executes on behalf of the customer.

Investing Their Own Funds

Securities firms commonly use some of their funds to invest in a wide range of securities, including stocks, bonds, mortgage-backed securities, and various types of derivatives. These investment operations have supplemented the profits of many securities firms. In several cases, however, securities firms have experienced financial problems as a result of taking on excessive risk in their investment operations.

Barings Bank Barings Bank was established in 1763 and became one of the most prominent financial institutions in England, offering commercial and securities services. In 1995, Nick Leeson, a trader of currencies at Barings' Singapore branch, circumvented trading restrictions and invested much more money than Barings realized. By the time his excessive trading was discovered, his account had suffered losses of more than $600 million, which wiped out Barings' capital. The insolvent bank was eventually acquired by the Dutch firm ING. The lesson of this story was that better controls were necessary to prevent individual traders from taking excessive risk.

Société Générale In 2008, Société Générale, a large French bank, incurred $7.2 billion in trading losses due to huge unauthorized trades by Jérôme Kerviel, one of its employees. Kerviel's assignment was to take positions in European stock indexes for the company. During 2007, he circumvented the company's computerized controls on the size of the positions that he could take. His supervisors were unaware of the size of his positions.

Bear Stearns In 2008, the Wall Street securities firm Bear Stearns suffered major losses from investing in mortgage-backed securities. It had relied heavily on borrowed funds (financial leverage) in order to magnify its return on investment. However, its return was negative, so its losses were magnified. Furthermore, once creditors recognized its difficulties, they cut off their credit, and Bear Stearns suffered liquidity problems. It was ultimately saved from bankruptcy by the U.S. government, as explained later in this chapter.

Lehman Brothers Lehman Brothers, another Wall Street securities firm, also suffered financial problems due to bad investments in mortgage-backed securities and heavy reliance on borrowed funds. It filed for bankruptcy in September 2008, as explained later in this chapter.

Underlying Cause of Investment Problems The underlying cause of the problems experienced by the four securities firms described above is the huge incentive to take risk. Individuals are assigned to make investment decisions for the firm. They have a great incentive to take risks with the money they invest because they can earn huge rewards based on their return on investment. Many employees have earned millions of dollars in one year as investors for securities firms. Given the potential reward, it is not surprising that some employees have been willing to take excessive risk in this capacity. Furthermore, many financial institutions do not have adequate controls to prevent employees from taking too much risk. After Nick Leeson's trading destroyed Barings Bank, many financial institutions were expected to impose tighter controls to prevent employees from making such risky investments. Yet the Leeson case occurred more than ten years before the other three cases described here, so it apparently did not prompt some securities firms to revise their incentive policies or improve their controls over investment operations. As long as employees can earn huge bonuses when the securities firm's investments perform well, they will have an enormous incentive to take on risk.

WEB

www2.goldmansachs
.com

Information on a securities firm's performance and services provided.

Summary of Services Provided

Exhibit 24.3 summarizes the services that are commonly provided by securities firms. The proportion of income derived from each type of service in any particular year varies among securities firms. When IPOs are hot, some securities firms that offer investment banking generate significant income from underwriting fees. When there is more acquisition activity, securities firms that offer advisory services for corporate restructuring generate much of their income from advisory fees. When market conditions are favorable, the trading volume tends to increase, and securities firms will generate more income from trading commissions.

Some securities firms such as Goldman Sachs and Morgan Stanley emphasize investment banking and therefore generate a higher proportion of income from underwriting and advising fees. Conversely, many small securities firms emphasize brokerage services and therefore generate a higher proportion of their income from trading commissions.

Some securities firms attempt to diversify their services so that they can capitalize on economies of scope and also possibly reduce their exposure if the demand for any particular service is weak. However, the demand is highly correlated across services. When market conditions are weak, the volume of IPOs, secondary market trades, and acquisitions is usually low. Thus, securities firms will likely perform poorly under these conditions.

Exhibit 24.3 Sources of Income for a Securities Firm

INVESTMENT BANKING SERVICES	
Underwriting	Fees from underwriting stock offerings by firms or underwriting bond offerings by firms and government agencies
Advising	Fees for providing advice to firms about: • Identifying potential targets • Valuing targets • Identifying potential acquirers • Protecting against takeovers
Restructuring	Fees for facilitating: • Mergers • Divestitures • Carve-outs • Spin-offs
BROKERAGE SERVICES	
Management fees	Fees for managing an individual's or a firm's securities portfolio
Trading commissions	Fees for executing securities trades requested by individuals or firms in the secondary market
Margin interest	Interest charged to investors who buy securities on margin
INVESTING ITS OWN FUNDS	
Investing	Profits from investing in securities

Exhibit 24.4 Interaction between Securities Firms and Other Financial Institutions

TYPE OF FINANCIAL INSTITUTION	INTERACTION WITH SECURITIES FIRMS
Commercial banks and savings institutions	• Compete with securities firms that provide brokerage services. • Compete directly with securities firms to provide merger advisory services.
Mutual funds	• Rely on securities firms to execute trades. • Are sometimes owned by securities firms. • Purchase newly issued securities that are underwritten by securities firms.
Insurance companies	• Receive advice from securities firms on what securities to buy or sell. • Rely on securities firms to execute securities transactions. • Receive advice from securities firms on how to hedge against interest rate risk and market risk. • Purchase stocks and bonds that are underwritten by securities firms. • May compete directly with securities firms to sell mutual funds to investors. • May provide financing for LBOs to securities firms. • May acquire or merge with a securities firm in order to offer more diversified services.
Pension funds	• Receive advice from securities firms on what securities to buy or sell. • Rely on securities firms to execute securities transactions. • Receive advice from securities firms on how to hedge against interest rate risk and market risk. • Purchase newly issued securities that are underwritten by securities firms.

Interaction with Other Financial Institutions

When securities firms provide their financial services, they commonly interact with various types of financial institutions as summarized in Exhibit 24.4. They offer investment advice and execute security transactions for financial institutions that maintain security portfolios. They also compete against those financial institutions that have brokerage subsidiaries. Furthermore, they compete with some commercial banks that are now allowed to underwrite securities and sponsor mutual funds. Because securities firms commonly offer banking and insurance services, and many insurance companies and commercial banks offer securities services, it is sometimes difficult to distinguish among financial institutions. Some savings institutions that experienced financial problems have been acquired by securities firms and operate as wholly owned subsidiaries.

Participation in Financial Markets

When securities firms provide financial services, they participate in all types of financial markets as summarized in Exhibit 24.5. Their investment banking divisions participate in the primary markets by placing newly issued securities, while the brokerage divisions concentrate mostly on executing secondary market transactions for investors. Both the investment banking and brokerage divisions serve as advisers to financial market participants.

WEB

www.seclaw.com/
secrules.htm
Federal rules and
regulations related to
securities firms.

REGULATION OF SECURITIES FIRMS

Securities firms are subject to a wide variety of regulations. The SEC plays a key role in regulation by enforcing financial disclosure laws that attempt to ensure that investors who buy or sell securities have access to financial information. These laws give

Exhibit 24.5 Participation of Securities Firms in Financial Markets

TYPE OF FINANCIAL MARKET	PARTICIPATION BY SECURITIES FIRMS
Money markets	• Some securities firms have created money market mutual funds, which invest in money market securities. • Securities firms underwrite commercial paper and purchase short-term securities for their own investment portfolios.
Bond markets	• Securities firms underwrite bonds in the primary market, advise clients on bonds to purchase or sell, and serve as brokers for bond transactions in the secondary market. • Some bond mutual funds have been created by securities firms. • Securities firms facilitate mergers, acquisitions, and LBOs by placing bonds for their clients. • Securities firms purchase bonds for their own investment portfolios.
Mortgage markets	• Securities firms underwrite securities that are backed by mortgages for various financial institutions.
Stock markets	• Securities firms underwrite stocks in the primary market, advise clients on what stocks to purchase or sell, and serve as brokers for stock transactions in the secondary market. • Securities firms purchase stocks for their own investment portfolios.
Futures markets	• Securities firms advise large financial institutions on how to hedge their portfolios with financial futures contracts. • Securities firms serve as brokers for financial futures transactions.
Options markets	• Securities firms advise large financial institutions on how to hedge portfolios with options contracts. • Securities firms serve as brokers for options transactions.
Swap markets	• Some securities firms engage in interest rate swaps to reduce their exposure to interest rate risk. • Many securities firms serve as financial intermediaries in swap markets.

the SEC the power to require publicly traded companies to provide sufficient financial information to existing or prospective investors.

Stock exchanges and the Nasdaq market are expected to prevent unfair or illegal practices, ensure orderly trading, and address customer complaints. Stock exchanges have regulatory divisions, while the Nasdaq market is regulated by the National Association of Securities Dealers (NASD). Both the exchanges and the NASD have surveillance departments that monitor trading patterns and behavior by specialists, market-makers, and floor traders. They also have enforcement divisions that investigate possible violations and can take disciplinary actions. They can take legal actions as well and sometimes work with the SEC to correct cases of market trading abuse. While the SEC tends to establish general guidelines that can affect trading on security exchanges, the day-to-day regulation of exchange trading is the responsibility of the exchange.

Regulation of trading behavior is necessary to ensure that investors who place orders are properly accommodated. This can establish credibility within the systems used to execute securities transactions. However, the exchanges have been criticized because they tend to react to abuses only after they have been publicized by the media. Consequently, some investors question whether their trades are properly executed.

In addition to the SEC, NASD, and exchanges, the Federal Reserve Board has some regulatory influence because it determines the credit limits (margin requirements) on securities purchased. The **Securities Investor Protection Corporation (SIPC)** offers insurance on cash and securities deposited at brokerage firms and can liquidate failing brokerage firms. The insurance limit is $500,000, including $100,000 against claims on cash. The SIPC uses premiums assessed on brokers that are registered with the SEC to maintain its insurance fund. In addition to its insurance fund, the SIPC has a $500 million revolving line of credit with a group of banks and can borrow up to $1 billion from the SEC. Because the SIPC boosts investor confidence in the securities industry, economic efficiency is increased, and market concerns are less likely to cause a run on deposits of cash and securities at securities firms.

Several regulatory events that were mentioned in previous chapters had a direct or indirect effect on securities firms. Here is a summary of recent regulatory events that are related to securities firms.

Financial Services Modernization Act

In the 1990s, financial institutions focusing on different types of financial services found numerous loopholes in regulations. To clarify the situation, Congress enacted the Financial Services Modernization Act of 1999, which allowed banking, securities activities, and insurance to be consolidated. As a result, financial institutions no longer need to search for loopholes. Specifically, the act provides for a special holding company structure that enables a financial holding company to own subsidiaries that focus on various financial services. Firms that adopt this structure are regulated by the Federal Reserve. Capital requirements for the bank subsidiaries are imposed by bank regulators. Capital requirements for the insurance subsidiaries are subject to state insurance regulators.

The Financial Services Modernization Act resulted in the creation of more financial conglomerates that include securities firms. One of the key benefits to securities firms in a financial conglomerate is cross-listing. When individuals use brokerage services of a securities firm, that firm may steer them to do their banking with the affiliated commercial bank or to obtain a mortgage with the affiliated savings institution. When firms use investment banking services of a securities firm, that firm may steer them to do their banking with the affiliated commercial bank. The other types of financial institutions that form the conglomerate can reciprocate by steering their customers toward the securities firm. Thus, the bundling of financial services can generate more business for each type of financial institution that is part of the financial conglomerate. However, just as a financial conglomerate can increase market share by pulling business away from other financial institutions, it may lose market share when other financial conglomerates use their bundling of financial services to attract customers.

The Financial Services Modernization Act of 1999 created a more competitive environment for securities firms by allowing commercial banks, securities firms, and insurance companies to merge. It removed limitations on the degree to which banks could offer securities services, which resulted in more intense competition from the banks. Some banks acquired securities services and attempted to market these new services to their existing customer base. In the most prominent example of a bank expanding into securities services, Citicorp merged with Traveler's Insurance Company, creating the financial conglomerate named Citigroup. Since Traveler's Insurance Group already owned Smith Barney, the merger was a massive consolidation of banking, securities, and insurance services. This merger occurred in 1998, the year before the passage of the Financial Services Modernization Act. Nevertheless, the act was still critical, because it allowed Citigroup to retain its banking, securities, and insurance services. The act not only created more competition among securities firms, but also made the offerings of securities services more efficient. Many individual and corporate customers need banking, securities, and insurance services and may prefer the convenience of obtaining all services from one financial institution. The conglomerate form can be difficult to manage, however, and in later years Citigroup itself sold some of the businesses it previously acquired, including much of Traveler's Insurance.

Regulation FD

In October 2000, the SEC enacted Regulation Fair Disclosure (FD), which requires firms to disclose any significant information simultaneously to all market participants. This rule was partially intended to prevent firms from leaking information to analysts. Before Regulation FD, sometimes a firm's chief financial officer would leak information to an analyst about the firm's earnings or other relevant financial details. Some analysts capitalized on the information by disclosing it to their key clients. These analysts also implicitly rewarded the firm that provided the inside information by assigning a high rating to its stock. Small investors were left out of the loop and were at a competitive disadvantage.

As a result of Regulation FD, firms more frequently provide their information in the form of news releases or conference calls rather than leaking it to a few analysts. Thus, analysts no longer have inside information, as all market participants receive the information at the same time. To the extent that Regulation FD has limited leaks to analysts, it may have limited their performance and credibility. Since analysts are commonly employees of securities firms, the securities firms have been affected as well. Those analysts who relied on inside information when providing their insight to clients have lost their competitive advantage, while analysts who relied on their own analysis rather than information leaks have gained a competitive edge.

Analyst Compensation and Ratings

In the 2001–2002 period, the process by which analysts rated stocks was widely criticized. Firms recognize that the demand for their stock may be partially dictated by the rating assigned by an analyst. When they need underwriting or advisory services from a securities firm, they are more likely to hire a firm whose analysts rate their stock highly. Securities firms also recognize that they are more likely to attract business from a firm if they give its stock a high rating, regardless of their real opinion of the stock. In fact, some analysts were spending much of their time generating new business, and their compensation was sometimes aligned with the business they brought to the securities firm. Consequently, analysts were tempted to inflate the ratings they assigned to stocks, and the investors who relied on the ratings to make investment decisions were misled.

In 2002, in an attempt to prevent the obvious conflict of interest, the SEC implemented new rules, as summarized here.

WEB

www.sec.gov
How the SEC monitors
securities trading
activity and enforces
securities laws.

- If a securities firm underwrites an IPO, its analysts cannot promote the stock for the first 40 days after the IPO. Thus, the price of the stock should be driven by factors other than hype provided by the underwriter's analysts in the first 40 days.

- An analyst's compensation cannot be directly aligned with the amount of business that the analyst brings to the securities firm. Analysts cannot be supervised by the investment banking department within the securities firm. This rule is intended to prevent the investment bankers from pressuring the analysts to provide high rankings of firms in order to attract more underwriting business from those firms.

- An analyst's rating must also divulge any recent investment banking business provided by the securities firm that assigned the rating.

Rules Preventing Abuses in the IPO Market

In the 2001–2003 period, various abuses in the IPO market were highly publicized.

- Some securities firms that served as underwriters on IPOs allocated shares to corporate executives who were considering an IPO for their own firm. Some critics viewed this process, referred to as *spinning,* as an implicit bribe to obtain the future business of the firm.

- Some securities firms that served as underwriters of IPOs encouraged institutional investors to place bids above the offer price on the first day that the shares traded as a condition for being allowed to participate in the next IPO. They also charged excessive commissions to investors in some cases when the demand for the IPO shares was well in excess of the supply.

The SEC investigated cases of abuse and imposed fines on some securities firms. In addition, it enacted rules to prevent such abuses from occurring in the future.

Repeal of the Trade-Through Rule

As explained in Chapter 12, specialists serve the New York Stock Exchange by matching up buyers and sellers of a stock and can also take a position in the stock. As a result of the trade-through rule, specialists were sometimes able to jump ahead of other orders (called *penny-jumping*), thereby preventing other investors from having their orders executed. In 2004, the SEC ruled that investors could circumvent the trade-through rule to avoid penny-jumping by specialists. Consequently, investors may have a better chance to have their trades executed.

RISKS OF SECURITIES FIRMS

The operations conducted by securities firms create exposure to market risk, interest rate risk, credit risk, and exchange rate risk, as explained next.

Market Risk

Securities firms offer many services that are linked to stock market conditions. When stock prices are rising, there is normally a greater volume of stock offerings and secondary market transactions. Because securities firms typically are needed to facilitate these transactions, they benefit from a bullish stock market. Those securities firms that sponsor mutual funds typically benefit from the large investment in mutual funds during a bullish market.

Some securities firms take equity positions in the stocks they underwrite (especially the IPOs). They also commonly take a partial equity interest in target firms acquired by their client firms. These firms tend to benefit from a bullish stock market. Acquisitions tend to be more numerous during favorable stock market conditions. Given their participation in advising and financing acquisitions, securities firms can generate more business under these conditions.

When the stock market is depressed, stock transactions tend to decline, causing a reduction in business for securities firms. Although securities firms have diversified into different services, the demand for many of these services is tied to stock market conditions. Thus, the performance of most securities firms is highly sensitive to the stock market cycles.

Interest Rate Risk

The performance of securities firms can be sensitive to interest rate movements for the following reasons. First, the market values of bonds held as investments by securities firms increase as interest rates decline. Second, lower interest rates can encourage investors to withdraw deposits from depository institutions and invest in the stock market, thereby increasing stock transactions. Thus, the performance of some securities firms is inversely related to interest rate movements.

Credit Risk

Many securities firms offer bridge loans and other types of credit to corporations. The securities firms are subject to the possibility that these corporations will default on their loans. The probability of default tends to increase during periods when economic conditions deteriorate.

Exchange Rate Risk

Many securities firms have operations in foreign countries. The earnings remitted by foreign subsidiaries are reduced when the foreign currencies weaken against the parent firm's home currency. In addition, the market values of securities maintained as investments and denominated in foreign currencies decline as the currencies weaken against the parent firm's home currency.

WEB

www.bloomberg.com
Insert the ticker symbol for any securities firm and click on "News" to review news about specific securities firms and the industry overall.

VALUATION OF A SECURITIES FIRM

Securities firms (or securities operating units that are part of a financial conglomerate) are commonly valued by their managers to monitor progress over time or by other financial institutions that are considering an acquisition. The value of a securities firm can be modeled as the present value of its future cash flows. Thus, the value of a securities firm should change in response to changes in its expected cash flows in the future and to changes in the required rate of return by investors:

$$\Delta V = f[\underset{+}{\Delta E(CF)}, \underset{-}{\Delta k}]$$

Factors That Affect Cash Flows

The change in a securities firm's expected cash flows may be modeled as

$$\Delta E(CF) = f(\underset{+}{\Delta ECON}, \underset{-}{\Delta R_f}, \underset{?}{\Delta INDUS}, \underset{+}{\Delta MANAB})$$

where ECON represents economic growth, R_f represents the risk-free interest rate, INDUS represents industry conditions, and MANAB represents the abilities of the securities firm's management.

Economic Growth   Economic growth can enhance a securities firm's cash flows because it increases the level of income of firms and households and can increase the demand for the firm's services. Specifically, the volume of brokerage activity tends to increase when households have more income, and corporations are more likely to hire securities firms to help them raise funds for expansion when economic conditions are favorable. During periods of strong economic growth, debt securities maintained by securities firms are less likely to default. In addition, equity security investments by securities firms should perform well because the firms represented by these securities should generate relatively high cash flows.

Change in the Risk-Free Interest Rate   Some of a securities firm's assets (such as bonds) are adversely affected by rising interest rates, so the valuation of a security firm may be inversely related to interest rate movements.

Change in Industry Conditions   Securities firms can be affected by industry conditions, including regulations, technology, and competition. For example, regulatory constraints can restrict firms from offering specific banking services or set the margin limits for investors. If regulators reduce the regulatory constraints, the expected cash flows of a securities firm should increase. Loosening of regulations to allow other financial institutions to offer securities services reduces the expected cash flows of securities firms.

Change in Management Abilities   A securities firm has control over the composition of its managers and its organizational structure. Its managers can attempt to make internal decisions that will capitalize on the external forces (economic growth, interest rates, regulatory constraints) that the firm cannot control. Thus, the management skills of a securities firm can influence its expected cash flows. In particular, securities firms need skillful management to create new financial services that may complement the brokerage services they already offer to individuals. Skillful management is also needed to create new products (such as specialized derivative instruments) that will be used by firms.

Factors That Affect the Required Rate of Return

The required rate of return by investors who invest in a securities firm can be modeled as

$$\Delta k = f(\Delta R_f, \Delta RP)$$
$$+ \quad +$$

where ΔR_f represents a change in the risk-free interest rate, and ΔRP represents a change in the risk premium. The risk-free interest rate is normally expected to be positively related to inflation, economic growth, and the budget deficit level, but inversely related to money supply growth (assuming it does not cause inflation). The risk premium on a securities firm is inversely related to economic growth and the company's management skills. Industry conditions such as regulatory constraints may discourage securities firms from taking excessive risk. However, the removal of regulatory barriers to entry in the securities industry may increase the risk of securities firms.

Exhibit 24.6 provides a framework for valuing a securities firm, based on the preceding discussion. In general, the value of a securities firm is favorably affected by strong economic growth, a reduction in interest rates, and strong management capabilities.

IMPACT OF THE CREDIT CRISIS ON SECURITIES FIRMS

During the credit crisis in 2008, securities firms experienced a number of problems. Various types of debt securities such as mortgages that they had purchased defaulted. As the credit crisis intensified, institutional investors that commonly purchased debt securities were less willing to participate after noticing the higher default rates on credit. Thus, some credit markets became inactive, and firms that wanted to borrow funds could not obtain credit. Consequently, the fees earned by securities firms for facilitating debt offerings declined. Stock prices plummeted, so firms did not want to issue stock, and the fees earned by securities firms for facilitating stock offerings also declined. Merger volume declined as well, and therefore so did the fees earned by securities firms for facilitating merger transactions.

Government Assistance to Bear Stearns

Bear Stearns was a leading financial intermediary of securities linked to low quality (subprime) mortgages that were sold in the secondary market. It also owned many mortgage-backed securities. As the credit crisis intensified, the value of its mortgage-backed securities

Exhibit 24.6 Framework for Valuing a Securities Firm

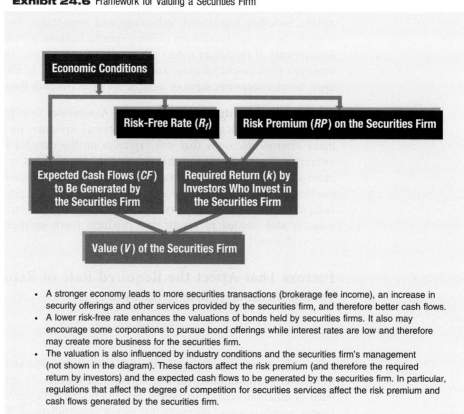

- A stronger economy leads to more securities transactions (brokerage fee income), an increase in security offerings and other services provided by the securities firm, and therefore better cash flows.
- A lower risk-free rate enhances the valuations of bonds held by securities firms. It also may encourage some corporations to pursue bond offerings while interest rates are low and therefore may create more business for the securities firm.
- The valuation is also influenced by industry conditions and the securities firm's management (not shown in the diagram). These factors affect the risk premium (and therefore the required return by investors) and the expected cash flows to be generated by the securities firm. In particular, regulations that affect the degree of competition for securities services affect the risk premium and cash flows generated by the securities firm.

declined. In fact, Bear owned two hedge funds that collapsed because of their heavy investment in subprime mortgage securities. From March 2007 until March 2008, it wrote down $3 billion of its assets so that their valuation was more closely in line with the true market value.

Bear's Liquidity Problems   By March 2008, Bear Stearns was suffering from liquidity problems. Some of the financial institutions that were providing loans to the firm were no longer willing to provide funding because they were doubtful that Bear would be able to repay the loans. Bear was not in a position to raise funds with an equity offering because its stock price was slipping and would have fallen further if the company had signaled its need for funding with a secondary stock offering.

On Thursday, March 13, Bear Stearns secretly notified the Federal Reserve that it was experiencing liquidity problems and would have to file for bankruptcy the next day if it could not obtain funds.

Fed Intervention   The next morning the Fed's Board of Governors met to discuss the situation. The Board of Governors recognized that the bankruptcy of Bear Stearns could be contagious and create chaos in the financial markets. Since Bear facilitated various financial transactions, its bankruptcy could cause liquidity problems for all the people and firms that were relying on it to complete financial transactions in its intermediary role.

On Friday, March 14, 2008, it was announced that J.P. Morgan Chase (a commercial bank) was going to offer a loan to Bear Stearns. Rather than calming the markets, however, the announcement validated the suspicion that Bear Stearns lacked adequate liquidity, and its stock price immediately declined from about $57 to $30. This illustrates the limitations in the information that investors have about a firm's financial condition. Bear's valuation declined 47 percent in one day because the degree of the company's liquidity problems was not known until the announcement of the financing from J.P. Morgan Chase.

During the weekend, Fed officials met with executives from Bear Stearns and J.P. Morgan Chase. Before the financial markets opened on Monday, March 17, 2008, the Fed had extended a $30 billion credit line to J.P. Morgan Chase to help it acquire Bear Stearns. The Fed's role was critical because it would allow J.P. Morgan Chase to obtain more permanent financing for the acquisition over time. J.P. Morgan Chase initially offered to pay $2 per share for Bear Stearns, but about a week later, it agreed to pay $10 per share. This was still substantially less than the market value of Bear Stearns on Friday, March 14. At that time, its share price was about $30, but investors were not yet fully aware of the extent of its liquidity problems. A year earlier its share price was about $100. The collateral for the loan extended by the Fed was a pool of mortgage-backed securities owned by Bear Stearns. The Fed held the collateral. If Bear had liquidated this collateral in order to obtain cash, it would have placed more downward pressure on the market value of mortgage-backed securities.

The Fed also allowed J.P. Morgan Chase an 18-month exemption on capital requirements that are imposed on commercial banks. This was to allow J.P. Morgan Chase time to absorb Bear's assets and to sell off high-risk assets that could require a higher capital level.

On Monday, March 17, the Fed also announced that it was willing to provide emergency loans to about 20 primary dealers that serve as key financial intermediaries for the large Treasury securities transactions in the secondary market. It also committed to loans of up to $200 billion of Treasury securities to primary dealers for a term of 28 days (rather than overnight) in exchange for other types of securities. These provisions were also intended to calm the financial markets.

The Fed's assistance to Bear Stearns offered only limited help to its stockholders. Most of the stockholders that had invested in Bear before its liquidity problems surfaced lost most of their investment. Instead, the major beneficiaries of the Fed's intervention were the creditors that had provided credit to Bear Stearns; if Bear had failed and been liquidated, they would probably have received only a small fraction of the credit that they had provided.

Potential Contagion Effects of Bear Stearns' Problems

The Fed's assistance to Bear Stearns led to questions about whether there should be a consistent policy for dealing with financial institutions that are deemed too big to fail. In general, the typical strategy would be to allow the equity value of the failing firm to be dictated by market forces, meaning that equity investors would lose their entire investment. Creditors would have rights to the remaining value of the firm, but in liquidation they would receive only a portion of the funds they had loaned to the firm. But the Fed's intervention protected the creditors holding debt securities that were issued by Bear Stearns.

The Fed's justification for its intervention was that Bear Stearns was a major provider of clearing operations for many types of financial transactions. If it had gone bankrupt, these financial transactions might have been frozen or delayed, which could have resulted in a liquidity crisis for many individuals and firms that were to receive cash as a result of the transactions. Bear Stearns also served as a counterparty to various types of financial agreements. If Bear had defaulted on all of its counterparty positions, this could have caused problems for the financial institutions on the other side of those agreements, which could have created chaos in financial markets.

The concern about the contagion effects of the failure of large securities firms is quite similar to the concern about big commercial banks failing. Consider their roles in financial markets. Securities firms provide business loans. They serve as intermediaries to facilitate the flow of equity funding in the primary market and commonly attempt to stabilize the prices of the stocks that they are responsible for issuing. They also serve as intermediaries in the primary and secondary markets for debt securities. In other words, Bear Stearns was viewed as a critical intermediary not because of its size but because of its role in facilitating financial transactions. That is, Bear Stearns may have been viewed as "too entangled" (in financial transactions) to fail.

Criticism of the Fed's Assistance to Bear Stearns   Some critics (including Paul Volcker, a previous chair of the Fed) have questioned the Fed's role in aiding Bear Stearns, since Bear was a securities firm, not a commercial bank. They suggest that providing assistance to a firm other than a commercial bank should be the responsibility of Congress and not the Fed. Some critics argue that securities firms have an unfair advantage over commercial banks, because they have access to funds from the Fed but are not subject to bank regulations such as capital requirements.

In addition, a rescue can cause a moral hazard problem, meaning that financial institutions may pursue high-risk opportunities in order to achieve high returns with the assumption that they will be bailed out if their strategies fail. Managers who pursue such strategies may be able to keep their jobs if the firm is rescued before it fails. The Fed's actions also raise the question of what other types of firms might be aided by the Fed rather than Congress. Some people, though, might counter that the Fed is in a better position to intervene when a potential bankruptcy could undermine the financial system.

Failure of Lehman Brothers

Lehman Brothers specialized in the underwriting of fixed-income securities such as bonds and in asset management for companies and wealthy individuals. In 2006, it was ranked number one in *Barron's* annual survey of corporate performance for large companies. In 2007, it was ranked at the top of *Fortune* magazine's list of "Most Admired Securities Firms." By 2008, it had grown to become the fourth largest securities firm in the United States. However, Lehman had considerable exposure to mortgage-backed securities, which led to financial problems in 2008. Following the Federal Reserve's aid to Bear Stearns in March 2008, media attention focused on Lehman's financial problems. The firm had a relatively low level of cash, and its high degree of financial leverage created more pressure. For every dollar of equity, it had about $30 of debt. Furthermore, some of its debt was short term and therefore could be cut off (not renewed) if creditors sensed that Lehman was experiencing financial problems.

Lehman's Liquidity Problems   Since the stock price of Lehman Brothers had declined substantially, it was unable to raise sufficient funds through a stock offering. In addition, concerns about its creditworthiness prevented it from obtaining credit at a reasonable cost. The growing concerns about Lehman led some clients to cut their business ties, which further reduced its cash inflows. From March 2008 to September 2008, its stock price declined by about 85 percent. Lehman looked for a financial institution that had sufficient cash to acquire it, so it could continue operating, but its efforts were unsuccessful. On September 15, 2008, it filed for bankruptcy.

Rescue Decisions   The story of Lehman leads to the question of why Bear Stearns received help from the Fed but Lehman did not. Lehman fit the mold of Bear Stearns in that it played a similar role in facilitating financial transactions and therefore was "too entangled" to fail. Furthermore, Lehman's business size was larger than that of Bear Stearns, as it had $630 billion in assets. Nevertheless, the Federal Reserve and the U.S. Treasury did not offer support to the financial institutions that considered acquiring Lehman. One possible reason was that the aid to Bear Stearns may have been intended to prevent chaos in financial markets. By the time Lehman failed, its demise was anticipated to a degree.

Yet, *one day* after Lehman Brothers filed for bankruptcy, the Federal Reserve announced that it would (with support from the Treasury) lend up to $85 billion to American International Group (AIG), an insurance company. AIG's annual revenue is more than $100 billion. It experienced financial problems because it sold insurance to offer protection on mortgage-backed securities, and the values of these securities declined. The Fed stated that the failure of AIG could have added to the existing financial market fragility. If AIG filed for bankruptcy and had to liquidate all of its assets, its massive investments in stocks and bonds would be sold in the secondary market. Furthermore, most large firms have insurance policies with AIG and would have suffered losses from their policies if AIG failed. The day before AIG was bailed out, rating agencies lowered its credit rating, a move that caused some investors to anticipate a possible bankruptcy and sell their holdings of bonds issued by AIG and other insurance companies.

Some people in the securities industry questioned why a large insurance company such as AIG was bailed out by the government, but a large securities firm such as Lehman Brothers was not. While both firms were large and had transactions that entangled them with other firms, the Fed and Treasury must have believed that the potential impact of AIG's failure would have been more devastating to the financial sector.

Impact of the Crisis on Regulatory Reform

The Federal Reserve's assistance to Bear Stearns and offer of temporary financing to other securities firms provided a rationale for the Fed to require that securities firms meet specified regulations such as capital requirements just like commercial banks. Historically, securities firms were subject to looser regulations than those imposed on commercial banks. In particular, securities firms were not subject to the capital requirements imposed on banks and therefore could use more debt to support their operations. They used a higher degree of financial leverage, which magnified their positive returns, but also magnified their losses. The problems of Bear Stearns and Lehman Brothers illustrated how the high degree of financial leverage used by securities firms could create excessive risk to the firms and to the financial system.

The momentum for regulatory reform of financial services continued when Merrill Lynch was acquired by Bank of America. Like Bear Stearns and Lehman, Merrill Lynch experienced major losses from its mortgage-backed securities. Its stock price had been declining, and its access to new capital was limited because of investor concerns about its financial condition. While the Federal Reserve was the primary regulator of Bank of America's operations, the SEC was the primary regulator of Merrill Lynch's operations. But when Merrill Lynch was acquired by Bank of America, it was subject to oversight by the Federal Reserve.

Conversion of Securities Firms to BHCs   During the credit crisis, some securities firms were unable to access funds by issuing securities. They did not want to issue stock while stock prices were weak. In addition, they were unable to issue debt securities because investors were concerned about their financial condition. The lack of funding deepened the financial problems of Bear Stearns and Merrill Lynch before they were acquired and of Lehman Brothers before it went bankrupt. As a result of the consolidation during the credit crisis, Goldman Sachs and Morgan Stanley were the only two large securities firms remaining. They applied to become bank holding companies (BHCs), and the Fed approved the requests in September 2008. This new structure gave the firms more flexibility to obtain financing. While securities firms were allowed to borrow short-term funds from the Federal Reserve during the credit crisis, their conversion to a BHC structure would give them permanent access to Federal Reserve funding.

A BHC can have commercial banking and securities subsidiaries. The commercial banking subsidiary can accept deposits and perform the functions of commercial banks, such as lending to businesses. It can create some stability for the company overall because it has steady access to deposits that are insured up to a limit. The securities subsidiary performs the traditional securities functions such as advising and underwriting securities for client firms.

Overall, the BHC structure results in a greater degree of regulatory oversight by the Federal Reserve. The companies will need to satisfy capital requirements established by the Fed. These requirements are higher than the capital normally maintained by securities firms. Consequently, the securities firms may be viewed as safer as a result of their conversion to BHCs.

GLOBALIZATION OF SECURITIES FIRMS

Since 1986 many securities firms have increased their presence in foreign countries. In October 1986, the so-called **Big Bang** allowed for deregulation in the United Kingdom. With the commission structure competitive instead of fixed, British securities firms recognized that they would have to rely more on other services, as commission income would be reduced by competitive forces. Commercial banks from the United States have established investment banking subsidiaries overseas, where regulations do not attempt to separate banking and securities activities.

Most large securities firms have established a presence in foreign markets. For example, Morgan Stanley has offices in Frankfurt, London, Melbourne, Sydney, Tokyo, and Zurich. Becoming internationalized can give securities firms several possible advantages. First, their international presence allows them to place securities in various markets for corporations or governments. Second, some corporations that are heavily involved with international mergers and acquisitions prefer advice from securities firms that have subsidiaries in all potential markets. Third, institutional investors that invest in foreign securities prefer securities firms that can easily handle such transactions.

Growth in International Joint Ventures

In recent years, securities firms have expanded their international business by engaging in joint ventures with foreign securities firms. In this way, they penetrate foreign markets but have a limited stake in each project. Many securities firms have also increased their global presence by facilitating privatizations of firms in foreign markets such as Latin America and Eastern Europe.

Growth in International Securities Transactions

The growth in international securities transactions has created more business for the larger securities firms. For example, many stock offerings are now conducted across numerous countries, as some corporations attempt to achieve global name recognition. In addition, an international stock offering can avoid the downward pressure on the stock's price that might occur if the entire issue is sold in the domestic country. Large securities firms facilitate international stock offerings by creating an international syndicate to place the securities in various countries. Those securities firms that have established a global presence receive most of the requests for international stock offerings.

Growth in Latin America   As a result of the North American Free Trade Agreement (NAFTA), U.S. securities firms have increased their business in Mexico and other Latin American countries. Securities firms have facilitated the increased trading of stocks, bonds, and other securities between the United States and Mexico. They are also facilitating mergers between firms from both countries.

Growth in Japan   The Japanese government now allows foreign securities firms to enter its markets. Goldman Sachs has acquired a seat on the Tokyo Stock Exchange, as have other U.S. and non-US. securities firms. Nevertheless, there are still explicit and implicit barriers to entry or at least limits on the degree of penetration by non-Japanese firms. Some securities firms complain that restrictions are excessive or vague. Although Japanese securities firms enter other financial markets, non-Japanese securities firms account for a tiny fraction of transactions on the Tokyo Stock Exchange.

SUMMARY

- Securities firms help corporations raise capital, provide advice on mergers and acquisitions, and may even help finance acquisitions. Some securities firms commonly acquire firms and restructure them.

- Securities firms facilitate new issues of stock by advising on how much stock the firm can issue, determining the appropriate price for the stock, underwriting the stock, and distributing the stock. Securities firms facilitate new issues of bonds in a somewhat similar manner.

- Brokerage firms execute securities transactions for their clients and also may manage their clients' portfolios of securities. Full-service brokerage firms provide information and advice and execute the securities transactions desired by their clients. Discount brokers tend to focus exclusively on executing security transactions for their clients.

- Securities firms are exposed to market risk because their volume of business is larger when stock market conditions are stronger. They are subject to interest rate risk because their underwriting business is sensitive to interest rate movements. They also hold some long-term financial assets whose values decline in response to higher interest rates. Securities firms are also subject to credit risk, since they commonly provide loans to some of their business clients.

- The value of a securities firm is affected by any factors that can affect its future cash flows or the required rate of return by investors. The value is enhanced when economic conditions are strong, because the demand for the firm's services increases when economic conditions are strong.

- As a result of the credit crisis, several major securities firms experienced financial problems, which were partially due to their high degree of financial leverage. Bear Stearns was failing and was aided by the Federal Reserve. Bear's operations were acquired by J.P. Morgan Chase. Lehman Brothers filed for bankruptcy. Merrill Lynch was acquired by Bank of America. Goldman Sachs and Morgan Stanley applied and were approved to become bank holding companies. These changes led to a major reduction in the financial leverage and risk-taking behavior of securities firms.

POINT COUNTER-POINT

Should Analysts Be Separated from Securities Firms to Prevent Conflicts of Interest?

Point No. Securities firms are known for their ability to analyze companies and value them. Investors may be more comfortable when analysts work within a securities firm, because they have access to substantial information.

Counter-Point Yes. Analysts have a conflict of interest, because they may be unwilling to offer negative

views about a company that is a client of their securities firm.

Who Is Correct? Use the Internet to learn more about this issue. Offer your own opinion on this issue.

QUESTIONS AND APPLICATIONS

1. Regulation of Securities Activities Explain the role of the SEC, the NASD, and the stock exchanges in regulating the securities industry.

2. SIPC What is the purpose of the SIPC?

3. Investment Banking Services How do securities firms facilitate leveraged buyouts? Why are securities firms that are better able to raise funds in the capital markets preferred by corporations that need advice on proposed acquisitions?

4. Origination Process Describe the origination process for corporations that are about to issue new stock.

5. Underwriting Function Describe the underwriting function of a securities firm.

6. Best-Efforts Agreement What is a best-efforts agreement?

7. Failure of Lehman Brothers Why did Lehman Brothers experience financial problems during the credit crisis?

8. Direct Placement Describe a direct placement of bonds. What is an advantage of a private placement? What is a disadvantage?

9. International Expansion Explain why securities firms from the United States have expanded into foreign markets.

10. Arbitrage Activities Explain how some securities firms facilitate arbitrage activity in the securities industry.

11. Asset Stripping What is asset stripping?

12. Greenmail How have some arbitrage firms attempted to benefit from greenmail tactics?

13. Valuation Discrepancy A division of Spence, Inc. has experienced a major decline in sales. Assume that the corporation prefers not to lay off any employees as a general policy. It is often suggested that this division may become a primary target for arbitrage firms. Given that the value of a division is the sum of its discounted cash flows, explain why the value of this division to an arbitrage firm may exceed its value to Spence, Inc.

14. Access to Inside Information Why do securities firms typically have some inside information that could affect future stock prices of other firms?

15. Sensitivity to Stock Market Conditions Most securities firms experience poor profit performance during periods in which the stock market performs poorly. Given what you know about securities firms, offer some possible reasons for these reduced profits.

16. Conversion to BHC Structure Explain how the credit crisis encouraged some securities firms to convert to a bank holding company (BHC) structure. Why might the expected return on equity be lower for securities firms that convert to a BHC structure?

Interpreting Financial News

Interpret the following comments made by Wall Street analysts and portfolio managers:

a. "The stock prices of most securities firms took a hit because of the recent increase in interest rates."

b. "Now that commercial banks are allowed more freedom to offer securities services, there may be a shakeout in the underwriting arena."

c. "Chaos in the securities markets can be good for some securities firms."

Managing in Financial Markets
Assessing the Operations of Securities Firms

As a consultant, you are assessing the operations of a securities firm.

a. The securities firm relies heavily on full-service brokerage commissions. Do you think the firm's heavy reliance on these commissions is risky? Explain.

b. If this firm attempts to enter the underwriting business, would it be an easy transition?

c. In recent years, the stock market volume has increased substantially, and this securities firm has performed very well. In the future, however, many institutional and individual investors may invest in indexes rather than in individual stocks. How would this affect the securities firm?

FLOW OF FUNDS EXERCISE

How Securities Firms Facilitate the Flow of Funds

Recall that Carson Company has periodically borrowed funds, but contemplates a stock or bond offering so that it can expand by acquiring some other businesses. It has contacted Kelly Investment Company, a securities firm.

a. Explain how Kelly Investment Company can serve Carson and how it will serve other clients as well when it serves Carson. Also explain how Carson Company can serve Kelly Investment Company.

b. In a securities offering, Kelly Investment Company would like to do a good job for its clients, which include both the issuer and institutional investors. Explain Kelly's dilemma.

c. The issuing firm in an IPO hopes that there will be strong demand for its shares at the offer price, which will ensure that it receives a reasonable amount of proceeds from its offering. In some previous IPOs, the share price by the end of the first day was more than 80 percent above the offer price at the beginning of the day. This reflects a very strong demand relative to the

price at the end of the day. In fact, it probably suggests that the IPO was fully subscribed at the offer price and that some institutional investors who purchased the stock at the offer price flipped their shares near the end of the first day to individual investors who were willing to pay the market price. Do you think that the issuing firm would be pleased that its stock price increased by more than 80 percent on the first day? Explain. Who really benefits from the increase in price on the first day?

d. Continuing the previous question, assume that the stock price drifts back down to near the original offer price over the next three weeks (even though the general stock market conditions were stable over this period) and then moves in tandem with the market over the next several years. Based on this information, do you think the offer price was appropriate? If so, how can you explain the unusually high one-day return on the stock? Who benefited from this stock price behavior, and who was adversely affected?

INTERNET/EXCEL EXERCISES

1. Go to www2.goldmansachs.com. Using this website, describe the different types of financial services offered by Goldman Sachs. Summarize its main business. Is Goldman Sachs focused on brokerage, investment banking, or a combination of these? Describe its performance over the last year. Explain why its performance was higher or lower than normal. Was the change in its performance due to the economy, recent interest rate movements, the stock market's performance, or changes in the amount of stock-trading or merger activity?

2. Retrieve information about Morgan Stanley (ticker symbol is MS) or another publicly traded securities firm of your choice. Go to the firm's website and retrieve its most recent annual report or access information from http://finance.yahoo.com by entering the ticker symbol and clicking on "Get Quotes." Then click on "SEC Filings" to retrieve income statement information. Review the security firm's recent performance. Has its income as a percentage of assets increased since the year before? Explain what caused this change over the last year. How have the firm's operating expenses changed over the last year? Discuss how the firm's recent strategy and economic conditions may explain the changes in these components of its income statement.

3. Go to http://finance.yahoo.com/, enter the symbol MS (Morgan Stanley), and click on "Get Quotes." Click on "5y" just below the stock price trend to review the stock price movements over the last five years. Check the S&P box just above the graph and click on "Compare" in order to compare the trend of Morgan Stanley's stock price with the movements in the S&P stock index. Has Morgan Stanley performed better or worse than the index? Offer an explanation for its performance.

4. Go to http://finance.yahoo.com/, enter the symbol MS (Morgan Stanley), and retrieve stock price data at the beginning of the last 20 quarters. Then go to http://research.stlouisfed.org/fred2/ and retrieve interest rate data at the beginning of the last 20 quarters for the three-month Treasury bill. Record the data on an Excel spreadsheet. Derive the quarterly return of Morgan Stanley. Derive the quarterly change in the interest rate. Apply regression analysis in which the quarterly return of Morgan Stanley is the dependent variable and the quarterly change in the interest rate is the independent variable (see Appendix B for more information about using regression analysis). Is there a positive or negative relationship between the interest rate movement and the stock return of Morgan Stanley? Is the relationship significant? Offer an explanation for this relationship.

WSJ EXERCISE

Performance of Securities Firms

Using a recent issue of *The Wall Street Journal,* summarize an article that discussed the recent performance of a particular securities firm. Does the article suggest that the securities firm's performance was better or worse than the norm? What reason is given for the particular level of performance?

25

Insurance and Pension Fund Operations

CHAPTER OBJECTIVES

The specific objectives of this chapter are to:

- describe the main operations of insurance companies,

- explain the exposure of insurance companies to various forms of risk,

- identify the factors that affect the value of insurance companies,

- describe the common types of private pension plans, and

- explain how pension funds are managed.

WEB

www.insure.com
Information about more than 200 insurance companies.

Insurance companies and pension funds were created to provide insurance and retirement funding for individuals, firms, and government agencies. They serve financial markets by supplying funds to a variety of financial and nonfinancial corporations as well as government agencies. Some insurance and pension operations are independent companies, while others are units (or subsidiaries) of financial conglomerates.

BACKGROUND

Insurance companies provide various forms of insurance and investment services to individuals and charge a fee (called a premium) for this financial service. In general, the insurance provides a payment to the insured (or a named beneficiary) under conditions specified by the insurance policy contract. These conditions typically result in expenses or lost income, so the insurance is a means of financial protection. It reduces the potential financial damage incurred by individuals or firms due to specified conditions.

Common types of insurance offered by insurance companies include life insurance, property and casualty insurance, health insurance, and business insurance. Many insurance companies offer multiple types of insurance.

An individual's decision to purchase insurance may be influenced by the likelihood of the conditions that would result in receiving an insurance payment. Individuals who are more exposed to specific conditions that cause financial damage will purchase insurance against those conditions. Consequently, the insurance industry faces an **adverse selection problem,** meaning that those who are most likely to need insurance are most likely to purchase it. Furthermore, insurance can cause the insured to take more risks because they are protected. This is known as the **moral hazard problem** in the insurance industry.

Insurance companies employ underwriters to calculate the risk of specific insurance policies. The companies decide what types of policies to offer based on the potential level of claims to be paid on those policies and the premiums that they can charge.

Determinants of Insurance Premiums

The premium charged by an insurance company for each insurance policy is based on the probability of the condition under which the company will have to provide a payment to the insured (or the insured's beneficiary) and the potential size of the payment. The premium may also be influenced by the degree of competition within the industry for the specific type of insurance offered. Insurance companies can estimate the present value of a payment that they will have to make for a specific insurance policy. The premium charged for that insurance is influenced by the present value of the expected payment. The premium will also contain a markup to cover overhead expenses and to provide a profit beyond expenses.

The insurance premium is higher when there is more uncertainty about the size of the payment that may ultimately have to be made. Insurance companies recognize that the timing of the payout of any particular policy may be difficult to predict, but are more concerned with the total flow of payments in any particular period. That is, if they have 20,000 policies, they may not know which policies will require payment this month, but may be able to predict the typical amount of payments per month.

Insurance companies tend to charge lower premiums when they provide services to all employees of a corporation through group plans. The lower premium represents a form of quantity discount in return for being selected to provide a particular type of insurance to all employees.

Dilemma When Setting Insurance Premiums
When insurance companies assess the probability of a condition that will result in a payment to the insured (or the insured's beneficiary), they rely on statistics about the general population. Individuals, however, have private information about themselves that is not available to the insurance company. This results in the adverse selection problem mentioned earlier. Those who have private information that makes them more likely to need insurance will buy it, while those who have private information that makes them less likely to need insurance will not buy it. For the insurance industry, the adverse selection problem means that people who have insurance are more likely to suffer losses (and therefore to file claims) than people who do not have insurance.

EXAMPLE

An insurance company representative arrives on a college campus and asks all students whether they want to purchase insurance in case any of the property (such as stereo equipment) in their dorm rooms is stolen. Beth declines the offer because she always locks the door when she leaves her dorm room. Conversely, Randy decides to buy the insurance because he never locks his dorm room and realizes that he may need the insurance. Even though Randy is a higher risk to the insurance company, he pays the same premium for the insurance as other students because the insurance company does not have the private information about his behavior.

Assume the insurance company sets the premium based on historical police reports showing that 3 percent of all students on the campus have property stolen from their dorm rooms. Now consider that many careless students like Randy buy the insurance while many careful students like Beth do not. Since the students who purchase the insurance often forget to lock their dorm rooms, they are more likely to have property stolen than the norm. Conversely, the students who do not purchase the insurance generally lock their dorm rooms and thus are less likely to have property stolen than the norm. In general, this adverse selection problem means that the insurance company will likely experience more stolen property claims than it anticipated. If the company does not consider the adverse selection problem when setting its premiums, the premiums may be too low. ●

A related problem is the moral hazard problem, which, as mentioned earlier, means that some people take more risks once they are insured. This problem can also cause insurance companies to set their premiums too low if they do not take this tendency into account.

EXAMPLE

Refer back to the previous example in which the insurance company offers insurance to students in case property is stolen from their dorm rooms. Assume that Mina purchases this insurance even though she is normally very careful about locking her dorm room. Once she has insurance, she decides that she does not need to worry about locking her room because she is protected if her property is stolen. At the time Mina purchased the insurance, she was less likely to have property stolen than other students who were more careless than she was. But once she had insurance, she became a high risk because she changed her behavior as a result of having insurance. ●

As a result of the adverse selection and moral hazard problems, insurance companies need to assess the probability of a loss incurred by the people who obtain insurance rather than by the population in general. By doing this, the companies can charge premiums that more closely fit the likelihood that those who have insurance will file claims to cover their losses.

Investments by Insurance Companies

Insurance companies invest the insurance premiums and fees received from other services until the funds are needed to pay insurance claims. In some cases, the claims occur several years after the premiums are received. Thus, the performance of insurance companies is partially dependent on the return on the invested funds. Their investment decisions balance the goals of return, liquidity, and risk. They want to generate a high rate of return while maintaining risk at a tolerable level. They need to maintain sufficient liquidity so that they can easily access funds to accommodate claims by policyholders. Those insurance companies whose claims are less predictable need to maintain more liquidity.

Regulation of Insurance Companies

The insurance industry is highly regulated by state agencies (called commissions in some states), although the degree of regulation varies among states. Each state attempts to make sure that insurance companies are providing adequate services, and the state also approves the rates insurers may charge. Insurance company agents must be licensed. In addition, the forms used for policies must be approved by the state to ensure that they do not contain misleading wording.

State regulators also evaluate the asset portfolios of insurance companies to ensure that investments are reasonably safe and that adequate reserves are maintained to protect policyholders. For example, some states have limited an insurance company's investment in junk bonds to no more than 20 percent of total assets.

WEB

www.naic.org
Links to information about insurance regulations.

The **National Association of Insurance Commissioners (NAIC)** facilitates cooperation among the various state agencies whenever an insurance issue is a national concern. It attempts to maintain a degree of uniformity in common reporting issues. It also conducts research on insurance issues and participates in legislative discussions.

The Insurance Regulatory Information System (IRIS) has been developed by a committee of state insurance agencies to assist in each state's regulatory duties. The IRIS compiles financial statements, lists of insurers, and other relevant information pertaining to the insurance industry. In addition, it assesses the companies' respective financial statements by calculating 11 ratios that are then evaluated by NAIC regulators to monitor the financial health of a company. The NAIC provides all state insurance departments with IRIS assessment results that can be used as a basis for comparison when evaluating the financial health of any company. The regulatory duties of state agencies often require a comparison of the financial ratios of a particular insurance company to the industry norm. Use of the industry norm facilitates the evaluation.

Assessment System   The regulatory system is designed to detect any problems in time to search for a remedy before the company deteriorates further. The more commonly used financial ratios assess a variety of relevant characteristics, including the following:

- The ability of the company to absorb either losses or a decline in the market value of its investments
- Return on investment
- Relative size of operating expenses
- Liquidity of the asset portfolio

Regulators monitor these characteristics to ensure that insurance companies do not become overly exposed to credit risk, interest rate risk, and liquidity risk.

Regulation of Capital   Insurance companies have been required to report a risk-based capital ratio to insurance regulators. The ratio was created by the NAIC and is intended to force those insurance companies with a higher exposure to insurance claims, potential losses on assets, and interest rate risk to hold a higher level of capital. The application of risk-based capital ratios not only discourages insurance companies from excessive exposure to risk, but also forces companies that take high risks to back their business with a large amount of capital. Consequently, there is less likelihood of failures in the insurance industry.

Regulation of Failed Insurance Companies   If an insurance company files for bankruptcy, the insurance commissioner proposes a plan within the court system on how the assets should be distributed to the creditors. If the company is to be liquidated, property insurance policies are canceled, and state guaranty funds, which are funded by solvent insurers, are used to cover claims based on limits set by state laws. The limits can vary among states. The state insurance department will typically assume management of the failed insurance company to preserve the remaining assets and ensure that policyholders' rights are maintained. Owners of life insurance, health insurance, or annuities can have their policies assumed by other insurance companies.

Regulation of Financial Services Offered   Before 1999, insurance operations were mostly separated from other types of financial services. In 1998, Citicorp merged with Traveler's Insurance Company, resulting in the financial conglomerate named Citigroup. This merger forced Congress to deal with the issue of whether insurance operations can be offered along with all other types of financial services. In 1999, Congress passed the Financial Services Modernization Act, which allowed insurance companies to merge with commercial banks and securities firms. Some banks acquired insurance companies, which then marketed their insurance services under the bank's brand name to the bank's existing customer base.

LIFE INSURANCE OPERATIONS

Since life insurance companies are a dominant force in the insurance industry, they receive more attention in this chapter. In aggregate, they generate more than $100 billion in premiums each year and serve as key financial intermediaries by investing their funds in financial markets.

Life insurance companies compensate (provide benefits to) the beneficiary of a policy upon the policyholder's death. They charge policyholders a premium that should reflect the probability of making a payment to the beneficiary as well as the size and timing of the payment. Despite the difficulty of forecasting the life expectancy of a given individual, life insurance companies have historically forecasted with reasonable accuracy the benefits they will have to provide beneficiaries. Because they hold a large portfolio of policies, these companies use actuarial tables and mortality figures to forecast the percentage of policies that will require compensation over a given period, based on characteristics such as the age distribution of policyholders.

Life insurance companies also commonly offer employees of a corporation a **group life policy.** This service has become quite popular and has generated a large volume of business in recent years. Group policies can be provided at a low cost because of the high volume. Group life coverage now makes up about 40 percent of total life insurance coverage, up from only 26 percent in 1974.

Ownership

There are about 1,000 life insurance companies, classified as having either stock or mutual ownership. A stock-owned company is owned by its shareholders, while a mutual life insurance company is owned by its policyholders. Most of the U.S. life insurance companies are stock owned, and in recent years some mutual life insurance companies have converted to become stock owned. As in the savings institutions industry, a primary reason for the conversions is to gain access to capital by issuing stock. The mutual companies are relatively large and account for more than 46 percent of the total assets of all life insurance companies.

Types of Life Insurance

Some of the more common types of life insurance policies are described here.

WEB

www.insurance.com/
default.aspx
Provides quotes on any
type of insurance.

Whole Life Insurance   From the perspective of the insured policyholders, **whole life insurance** protects them until death or as long as the premiums are promptly paid. In addition, a whole life policy provides a form of savings to the policyholder. It builds a cash value that the policyholder is entitled to even if the policy is canceled.

From the perspective of the life insurance company, whole life policies generate periodic (typically, quarterly or semiannual) premiums that can be invested until the policyholder's death, when benefits are paid to the beneficiary. The amount of benefits is typically fixed.

Term Insurance   **Term insurance** is temporary, providing insurance only over a specified term, and does not build a cash value for policyholders. The premiums paid represent only insurance, not savings. Term insurance, however, is significantly less expensive than whole life insurance. Policyholders must compare the cash value of whole life insurance to the additional costs to determine whether it is preferable to term insurance. Those who prefer to invest their savings themselves will likely opt for term insurance.

People who need more insurance now than later may choose decreasing term insurance, in which the benefits paid to the beneficiary decrease over time. Families with mortgages commonly select this form of insurance. As time passes, the mortgage balance decreases, and the family is more capable of surviving without the breadwinner's earnings. Thus, less compensation is needed in later years.

Variable Life Insurance   Under **variable life insurance,** the benefits awarded by the life insurance company to a beneficiary vary with the assets backing the policy. Flexible-premium variable life insurance policies are available, allowing flexibility on the size and timing of payments.

Universal Life Insurance   **Universal life insurance** combines the features of term and whole life insurance. It specifies a period of time over which the policy will exist but also builds a cash value for the policyholder over time. Interest is accumulated from the cash value until the policyholder uses those funds. Universal life insurance allows flexibility on the size and timing of the premiums, too. The growth in a policy's cash value is dependent on the pace of the premiums. The premium payment is divided into two portions. The first is used to pay the death benefit identified in the policy and to cover any administrative expenses. The second is used for investments and reflects savings for the policyholder. The Internal Revenue Service prohibits the value of these savings from exceeding the policy's death benefits.

Sources of Funds

Life insurance companies obtain much of their funds from premiums, as shown in Exhibit 25.1. Total premiums (life plus health insurance) represent about 31 percent

Exhibit 25.1   Distribution of U.S. Life Insurance Company Income

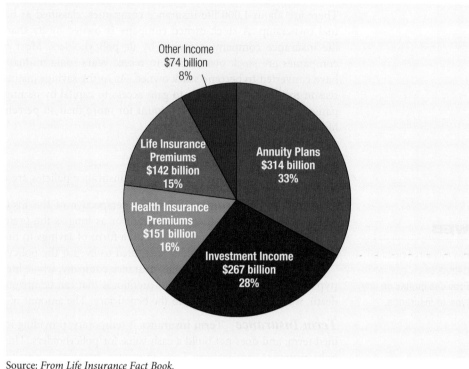

Source: *From Life Insurance Fact Book.*

of total income. The most important source of funds, however, is the provision of **annuity plans,** which offer a predetermined amount of retirement income to individuals. Annuity plans have become very popular and now generate proportionately more income to insurance companies than in previous years. More information about the annuities provided by numerous life insurance companies can be found at www.annuity.com. The third largest source of funds is investment income, which results from the investment of funds received from premium payments.

Capital   Insurance companies build capital by retaining earnings or issuing new stock. They use capital as a means of financing investment in fixed assets, such as buildings, and as a cushion against operating losses. Since a relatively large amount of capital can enhance safety, insurance companies are required to maintain adequate capital. Insurance companies are required to maintain a larger amount of capital when they are exposed to a higher degree of risk. Their risk can be measured by assessing the risk of their assets (as some assets are more exposed to losses than others) and their exposure to the types of insurance they provide.

Insurance companies maintain an adequate capital level not only to cushion potential losses, but also to reassure their customers. When customers purchase insurance, the benefits are received at a future point in time. The customers are more comfortable purchasing insurance from an insurance company that has an adequate capital level and is therefore likely to be in existence at the time the benefits are to be provided.

Uses of Funds

The uses of funds by life insurance companies strongly influence their performance. Life insurance companies are major institutional investors. Exhibit 25.2, which shows the

Exhibit 25.2 Assets of U.S. Life Insurance Companies

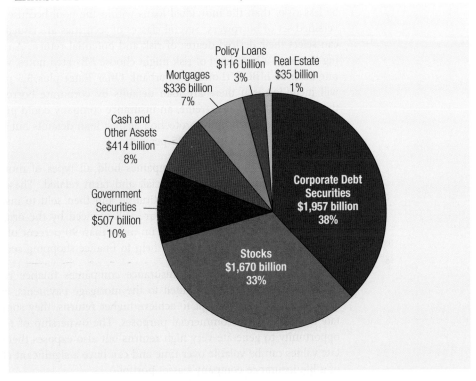

assets of life insurance companies, indicates how funds have been used. The main assets are described in the following subsections.

Government Securities   Life insurance companies invest in U.S. Treasury securities, state and local government bonds, and foreign bonds. They maintain investments in U.S. Treasury securities because of their safety and liquidity, but also invest in bonds issued by foreign governments in an attempt to enhance profits.

Corporate Securities   Corporate bonds are the most popular asset of life insurance companies. Companies usually hold a mix of medium- and long-term bonds for cash management and liquidity needs. Although corporate bonds provide a higher yield than government securities, they have a higher degree of credit (default) risk. Some insurance companies focus on high-grade corporate bonds, while others invest a portion of their funds in junk bonds.

Because life insurance companies expect to maintain a portion of their long-term securities until maturity, this portion can be somewhat illiquid. Thus, they have the flexibility to obtain some high-yielding, directly placed securities when they can directly negotiate the provisions. Because such nonstandard securities are less liquid, life insurance companies balance their asset portfolios with other more liquid securities. A minor portion of corporate securities are foreign. The foreign holdings typically represent industrialized countries and are therefore considered to have low credit risk. Of course, the market values of these foreign bonds are still susceptible to interest rate and currency fluctuations.

In addition to buying individual corporate bonds, insurance companies invest in packages of corporate bonds, called collateralized loan obligations (CLOs). Commercial banks combine numerous existing commercial loans into a pool and sell securities that represent ownership of these loans. The pool of loans making up a CLO is perceived to be less risky than the individual loans within the pool because the loans represent a diversified set of borrowers. Several classes of securities are issued, so insurance companies can select their desired degree of risk and potential return. An insurance company willing to accept a high level of risk might choose BB-rated notes, which offer a high interest rate such as LIBOR (London Interbank Offer Rate) plus 3.5 percent. But the company will incur losses if there are loan defaults by corporate borrowers whose loans are in the pool. At the other extreme, an insurance company could purchase AAA-rated notes, which provide much more protection against loan defaults but offer a much lower interest rate, such as LIBOR plus .25 percent.

Mortgages   Life insurance companies hold all types of mortgages, including one to four family, multifamily, commercial, and farm related. These mortgages are typically originated by another financial institution and then sold to insurance companies in the secondary market. The mortgages are still serviced by the originating financial institution. Commercial mortgages make up more than 90 percent of the total mortgages held by life insurance companies. They help to finance shopping centers and office buildings.

Real Estate   Although life insurance companies finance real estate by purchasing mortgages, their return is limited to the mortgage payments, as they are simply acting as a creditor. In an attempt to achieve higher returns, they sometimes purchase real estate and lease it for commercial purposes. The ownership of real estate offers them the opportunity to generate very high returns but also exposes them to greater risk. Real estate values can be volatile over time and can have a significant effect on the market value of a life insurance company's asset portfolio.

Policy Loans   Life insurance companies lend a small portion of their funds to whole life policyholders (called *policy loans*). Whole life policyholders can borrow up to their policy's cash value (or a specified proportion of the cash value). The rate of interest is sometimes guaranteed over a specified period of time, as stated in the policy. Other sources of funds for individuals typically do not guarantee an interest rate at which they can borrow. For this reason, policyholders tend to borrow more from life insurance companies during periods of rising interest rates, when alternative forms of borrowing would be more expensive.

Summary of Uses of Funds   Exhibit 25.3 summarizes the uses of funds by illustrating how insurance companies finance economic growth. They channel funds received from insurance premiums to purchase stocks and bonds issued by corporations. They purchase bonds issued by the Treasury and municipalities and thereby finance government spending. They also use some of their funds to purchase household and commercial real estate.

Asset Management of Life Insurance Companies

Because life insurance companies tend to receive premiums from policyholders for several years before paying out benefits to a beneficiary, their performance can be significantly affected by their asset portfolio management. Like other financial institutions, they adjust their asset portfolios to counter changes in the factors that affect their risk. If they expect a downturn in the economy, they may reduce their holdings of corporate stocks and real estate. If they expect higher interest rates, they may reduce their holdings of fixed-rate bonds and mortgages.

To cope with the existing forms of risk, life insurance companies attempt to balance their portfolios so that any adverse movements in the market value of some assets will be offset by favorable movements in others. For example, assuming that interest rates will

Exhibit 25.3 How Insurance Companies Finance Economic Growth

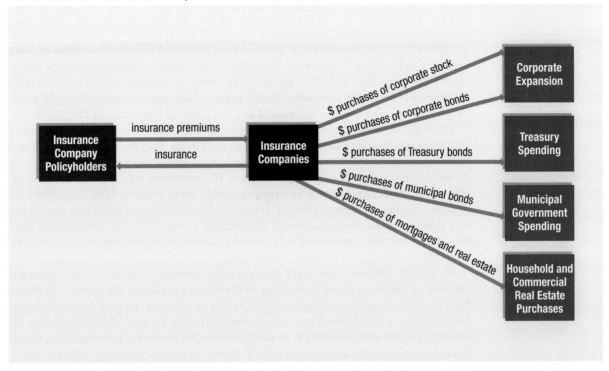

move in tandem with inflation, life insurance companies can use real estate holdings to partially offset the potential adverse effect of inflation on bonds. When higher inflation causes higher interest rates, the market value of existing bonds decreases, whereas the market values of real estate holdings tend to increase with inflation. Conversely, an environment of low or decreasing inflation may cause real estate values to stagnate but have a favorable impact on the market value of bonds and mortgages (because interest rates would likely decline). Although such a strategy may be useful, it is much easier to implement on paper than in practice. Because real estate values can fluctuate to a great degree, life insurance companies allocate only a limited amount of funds to real estate. In addition, real estate is less liquid than most other assets.

Many insurance companies are diversifying into other businesses by offering a wide variety of financial products. Such a strategy not only provides diversification but also enables these companies to offer packages of products to policyholders who desire to cover all these needs at once.

Overall, life insurance companies want to earn a reasonable return while maintaining their risk at a tolerable level. The degree to which they avoid or accept the various forms of risk depends on their degree of risk aversion. Companies that accept a greater amount of risk in their asset portfolios are likely to generate a higher return. If market conditions move in an unexpected manner, however, they will be more severely damaged than companies that employed a more conservative approach.

OTHER TYPES OF INSURANCE OPERATIONS

In addition to life insurance, other common types of insurance operations include property and casualty insurance, health insurance, business insurance, bond insurance, and mortgage insurance. Each of these types of insurance is described in turn.

Property and Casualty Insurance

Property and casualty (PC) insurance protects against fire, theft, liability, and other events that result in economic or noneconomic damage. Property insurance protects businesses and individuals from the impact of financial risks associated with the ownership of property, such as buildings, automobiles, and other assets. Casualty insurance protects policyholders from potential liabilities for harm to others as a result of product failure or accidents. PC insurance companies charge policyholders a premium that should reflect the probability of a payout to the insured and the potential magnitude of the payout.

There are about 3,800 individual PC companies. The largest providers of PC insurance are State Farm Insurance Group, Allstate Insurance Group, Farmers Insurance Group, and Nationwide Insurance Enterprise. No single company controls more than 10 percent of the PC insurance market. Although there are more PC companies than life insurance companies, the PC insurance business in aggregate is only about one-fourth as large as the life insurance business in aggregate (based on assets held). Nevertheless, the PC insurance business generates about the same amount of insurance premiums as the life insurance business. Many insurance companies now diversify their business, offering both life and PC insurance.

PC and life insurance have very different characteristics. First, PC policies often last one year or less, as opposed to the long-term or even permanent life insurance policies. Second, PC insurance encompasses a wide variety of activities, ranging from auto insurance to business liability insurance. Life insurance is more focused. Third, forecasting the amount of future compensation to be paid is more difficult for PC insurance than for life insurance. PC compensation depends on a variety of factors, including inflation, hurricanes, trends in terrorism, and the generosity of courts in lawsuits. Because of the greater uncertainty, PC insurance companies need to maintain more liquid asset portfolios. Earnings can be quite volatile over time, as the premiums charged may be based on highly overestimated or underestimated compensation.

Cash Flow Underwriting   A unique aspect of the PC insurance industry is its cyclical nature. As interest rates rise, companies tend to lower their rates so as to write more policies and acquire more premium dollars to invest. They are hoping losses will hold off long enough to make the cheaper premiums profitable through increased investment income. As interest rates decline, the price of insurance rises to offset decreased investment income. This method of adapting prices to interest rates is called **cash flow underwriting.** It can backfire for companies that focus on what they can earn in the short run and ignore what they will pay out later. A company that does not accurately predict the timing of the cycle can experience inadequate reserves and a drain on cash.

Uses of Funds   The primary uses of funds for PC insurance companies are illustrated in Exhibit 25.4. Municipal bonds dominate, followed by corporate bonds, and then by common stock. The amount of common stock holdings has been more volatile than that of the other components. The most obvious difference in the asset structure of PC companies relative to life insurance companies is the much higher concentration of government (municipal, Treasury, and government agency) securities.

Property and Casualty Reinsurance   PC companies commonly obtain **reinsurance,** which effectively allocates a portion of their return and risk to other insurance companies. It is similar to a commercial bank's acting as the lending agent by allowing other banks to participate in the loan. A particular PC insurance company may agree to insure a corporation but spread the risk by inviting other insurance companies to participate. Reinsurance allows a company to write larger policies because a portion of the risk involved will be assumed by other companies.

Exhibit 25.4   Assets of Property and Casualty Insurance Companies

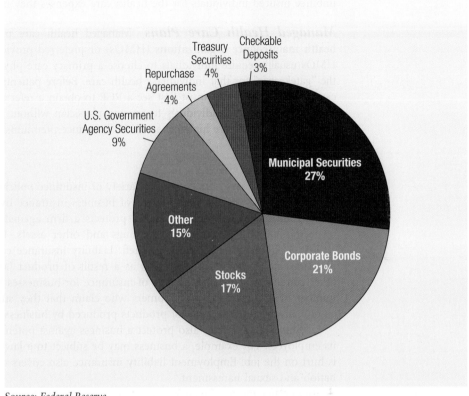

Source: *Federal Reserve.*

The number of companies willing to offer reinsurance has declined significantly because of generous court awards and the difficulty of assessing the amount of potential claims. Reinsurance policies are often described in the insurance industry as "having long tails," which means that the probability distribution of possible returns on reinsurance is widely dispersed. Although many companies still offer reinsurance, their premiums have increased substantially in recent years. If the desire to offer reinsurance continues to decline, the primary insurers will be less able to "sell off" a portion of the risk they assume when writing policies. Consequently, they will be under pressure to more closely evaluate the risk of the policies they write.

Health Care Insurance

Insurance companies provide various types of health care insurance, including coverage for hospital stays, visits to physicians, and surgical procedures. They serve as intermediaries between the health care providers and the recipients of health care. Since the cost of health care is so high, individuals seek health care insurance as a form of protection against conditions that cause them to incur large health care expenses.

Types of Health Care Plans   Insurance companies offer two types of health care plans: managed health care plans and indemnity plans. The primary difference between the two types of plans is that individuals who are insured by a managed care plan may choose only specified health care providers (hospitals and physicians) who participate in the plan. Individuals who are insured under an indemnity plan can usually choose any provider of health care services. The payment systems of the two types of plans are also distinctly different. The premiums for managed health care plans are generally lower, and payment is typically made directly to the provider. In contrast, indemnity plans reimburse insured individuals for the health care expenses they incur.

Managed Health Care Plans   Managed health care plans can be classified as **health maintenance organizations (HMOs)** or preferred provider organizations (PPOs). HMOs usually require individuals to choose a primary care physician (PCP). The PCP is the "gatekeeper" for that individual's health care. Before patients insured under an HMO can see a specialist, they must first see a PCP to obtain a referral for the specialist. PPOs usually allow insured individuals to see any physician without a referral. However, PPO insurance premiums are higher than HMO insurance premiums.

Business Insurance

Insurance companies provide a wide variety of insurance policies that protect businesses from many types of risk. Some forms of business insurance overlap with property and casualty insurance. Property insurance protects a firm against the risk associated with ownership of property, such as buildings and other assets. It can provide insurance against property damage by fire or theft. Liability insurance can protect a firm against potential liability for harm to others as a result of product failure or a wide range of other conditions. This is a key type of insurance for businesses because of the increasing number of lawsuits filed by customers who claim that they suffered physical injury or emotional distress as a result of products produced by businesses.

Liability insurance can also protect a business against potential liability for claims by its employees. For example, a business may be subject to a lawsuit by an employee who is hurt on the job. Employment liability insurance also covers claims of wrongful termination and sexual harassment.

Some other forms of business insurance are separate from property and casualty insurance. Key employee insurance provides a financial payout if specified employees of a business become disabled or die. The insurance is intended to enable the business to replace the skills of the key employees so that the business can continue. Business interruption insurance protects against losses due to a temporary closing of the business. Credit line insurance covers debt payments owed to a creditor if a borrower dies. Fidelity bond insurance covers losses due to dishonest employees. Marine insurance covers losses due to damage during transport. Malpractice insurance protects business professionals from losses due to lawsuits by dissatisfied customers. Surety bond insurance covers losses due to a contract not being fulfilled. Umbrella liability insurance provides additional coverage beyond that provided by the other existing insurance policies.

Bond Insurance

Bond insurance protects the investors that purchase bonds in the event that the bond issuers default on their bonds. About 40 percent of all municipal bonds are backed by insurance. Municipalities are willing to pay for the insurance because it allows them to more easily sell their bonds at lower prices; thus, the insurance reduces their cost of borrowing. The risk of default may be minimized when an insurance company insures the bonds. Many insurance companies, including Ambac Financial Group and MBIA, Inc., provide bond insurance.

The insurance on bonds is only as good as the insurance company's ability to cover claims, however. It is possible that both a bond issuer and the insurer backing the bond issuer might not satisfy their obligations, which could cause major losses to institutional investors holding these bonds. A downgrade in the credit rating of a bond insurer is a signal that there is a greater likelihood that the insurance company could not cover a claim in the event that the bond defaults. Thus, bonds insured by this company will need to offer higher yields in order to compensate for the higher risk. Existing bonds insured by this insurer will experience a decline in price to reflect the higher risk of loss from holding these bonds.

During the credit crisis in 2008, the credit ratings of several large insurance companies were assessed for possible downgrade, and this aroused concerns that many insured bonds might suffer major losses. Consequently, the prices of these insured bonds declined. Some mutual funds that invest heavily in municipal bonds may only be willing to hold bonds that are insured by a company that is assigned the highest credit rating. This situation illustrates the importance of creditworthy insurance companies in facilitating the flow of funds from bond issuers to institutional investors such as mutual funds.

Mortgage Insurance

Mortgage insurance protects the lender that provides mortgage loans in the event that homeowners cannot cover their payments and default on their mortgages. The insurance is normally intended to cover the lender's losses when the lender is forced to foreclose on the home and sells it for less than the prevailing mortgage amount.

Mortgage lenders commonly require homeowners to obtain mortgage insurance. Sometimes, obtaining the insurance may allow a homeowner to qualify for a lower interest rate on the mortgage. The insurance companies that sell mortgage insurance typically receive periodic insurance premiums for providing this insurance. In the event of a mortgage default, they cover the damages to the creditor.

Credit Default Swaps as a Form of Mortgage Insurance

Some insurance companies provide insurance on mortgages by taking a position in credit default swaps, which are privately negotiated contracts that protect investors against the risk of default on particular debt securities. An institutional investor that previously purchased mortgage securities may become concerned that these securities could perform poorly. Therefore, it may be willing to engage in a credit default swap in which it will make monthly or quarterly payments to the counterparty.

Insurance companies commonly serve as the counterparty and have to make payments only if there is a default on the securities covered by the swap. In this event, the insurance companies have to pay the face value of the securities covered by the swap in exchange for those securities. When there are no defaults on the debt securities, the insurance companies benefit from their swap positions because they not required to make any payments. When there are defaults, however, the insurance companies can incur large expenses to cover the payments.

Insurance companies reduce their exposure to various types of insurance through diversification. They have numerous policyholders, and an adverse event that causes an insurance claim from one policyholder is unlikely to happen to many other policyholders at the same time. However, credit defaults on mortgage-backed securities can occur across financial institutions at the same time if mortgage qualification standards are low and the economy is weak. Consequently, diversification among credit default swaps on mortgage-backed securities does not effectively reduce risk. Insurance companies that sold credit default swaps were highly exposed to mortgage conditions during the credit crisis.

INTERACTION WITH OTHER FINANCIAL INSTITUTIONS

Insurance companies interact with financial institutions in several ways, as summarized in Exhibit 25.5. They compete in one form or another with all types of financial institutions. Those insurance companies that have merged with brokerage firms offer a wide variety of securities-related services. Several insurance companies offer mutual funds to investors.

Exhibit 25.5   Interaction between Insurance Companies and Other Financial Institutions

TYPE OF FINANCIAL INSTITUTION	INTERACTION WITH INSURANCE COMPANIES
Commercial banks and savings institutions (SIs)	• Compete with insurance companies to finance leveraged buyouts. • Merge with insurance companies in order to offer various insurance-related services. • Compete with insurance companies to provide insurance-related services. • Provide loans to insurance companies.
Finance companies	• Are sometimes acquired by insurance companies.
Securities firms	• Compete directly with insurance companies in offering mutual funds. • Compete with insurance companies to finance leveraged buyouts. • Underwrite new issues of stocks and bonds that are purchased by insurance companies.
Brokerage firms	• Compete directly with insurance companies in offering securities-related services. • Compete directly with insurance companies in offering insurance-related services. • Serve as brokers for insurance companies that buy stocks or bonds in the secondary market.
Pension funds	• Are sometimes managed by insurance companies.

Some state insurance regulators have allowed commercial banks to underwrite and sell insurance, which will result in more intense competition in the insurance industry.

Participation in Financial Markets

The manner in which insurance companies use their funds indicates their form of participation in the various financial markets. Insurance companies are common participants in the stock, bond, and mortgage markets because their asset portfolios are concentrated in these securities. They also use the money markets to purchase short-term securities for liquidity purposes. Although their participation in money markets is less than in capital markets, they have recently increased their holdings of money market instruments such as Treasury bills and commercial paper. Some insurance companies use futures and options markets to hedge the impact of interest rates on bonds and mortgages and to hedge against anticipated movements in stock prices. Insurance companies generally participate in the futures, options, and swap markets for risk reduction rather than speculation. Exhibit 25.6 summarizes the manner in which insurance companies participate in financial markets.

Exhibit 25.6   Participation of Insurance Companies in Financial Markets

FINANCIAL MARKET	HOW INSURANCE COMPANIES PARTICIPATE IN THIS MARKET
Money markets	• Maintain a portion of their funds in money market securities, such as Treasury bills and commercial paper, to maintain adequate liquidity.
Bond markets	• Purchase bonds for their portfolios.
Mortgage markets	• Purchase mortgages and mortgage-backed securities for their portfolios.
Stock markets	• Purchase stocks for their portfolios.
Futures markets	• May sell futures contracts on bonds or a bond market index to hedge their bond and mortgage portfolios against interest rate risk. • May take positions in stock market index futures to hedge their stock portfolios against market risk.
Options markets	• Purchase call options on particular stocks that they plan to purchase in the near future. • Purchase put options or write call options on stocks they own that may experience a temporary decline in price.
Swap markets	• Engage in interest rate swaps to hedge the exposure of their bond and mortgage portfolios to interest rate risk.

EXPOSURE TO RISK

The major types of risk faced by insurance companies are interest rate risk, credit risk, market risk, and liquidity risk.

Interest Rate Risk

Because insurance companies carry a large amount of fixed-rate long-term securities, the market value of their asset portfolios can be very sensitive to interest rate fluctuations. When interest rates increase, insurance companies are unable to fully capitalize on these rates, because they have much of their funds tied up in long-term bonds.

Insurance companies have been reducing their average maturity on securities. In addition, they have been investing in long-term assets that offer floating rates, such as commercial mortgages. Both strategies reduce the impact of interest rate movements on the market value of their assets.

As insurance companies have become more aware of their exposure to interest rate risk and more knowledgeable about techniques to hedge the risk, they are increasingly utilizing futures contracts and interest rate swaps to manage their exposure.

Credit Risk

The corporate bonds, mortgages, state and local government securities, and real estate holdings in insurance companies' asset portfolios are subject to credit risk. To deal with this risk, some insurance companies typically invest only in securities assigned a high credit rating. They also diversify among securities issuers so that the repayment problems experienced by any single issuer will have only a minor impact on the overall portfolio. Other insurance companies, however, have invested heavily in risky assets, such as junk bonds.

Market Risk

A related risk to insurance companies is market risk. A good example of market risk was the credit crisis, which significantly reduced the market value of the stock holdings of insurance companies. The value of the companies' real estate holdings was also adversely affected by the economic downturn.

Liquidity Risk

An additional risk to insurance companies is liquidity risk. A high frequency of claims at a single point in time could force a company to liquidate assets at a time when the market value is low, thereby depressing its performance. Claims due to death are not likely to occur simultaneously, however. Life insurance companies can therefore reduce their exposure to this risk by diversifying the age distribution of their customer base. If the customer base becomes unbalanced and is heavily concentrated in the older age group, life insurance companies should increase their proportion of liquid assets to prepare for a higher frequency of claims.

WEB

http://finance.yahoo
.com/insurance
Information about
individual insurance
companies and
updates on the
industry.

VALUATION OF AN INSURANCE COMPANY

Insurance companies (or insurance company units that are part of a financial conglomerate) are commonly valued by their managers to monitor progress over time or by other financial institutions that are considering an acquisition. The value of an insurance company can be modeled as the present value of its future cash flows. Thus, the value of an insurance company should change in response to changes in its expected cash flows in the future and to changes in the required rate of return by investors:

$$\Delta V = f[\Delta E(CF), \Delta k]$$
$$\quad\quad\quad + \quad\quad -$$

Factors That Affect Cash Flows

The change in an insurance company's expected cash flows may be modeled as

$$\Delta E(CF) = f(\Delta \text{PAYOUT}, \Delta \text{ECON}, \Delta R_f, \Delta \text{INDUS}, \Delta \text{MANAB})$$
$$\quad\quad\quad\quad\quad - \quad\quad\quad + \quad\quad - \quad\quad ? \quad\quad\quad +$$

where PAYOUT represents insurance payouts to beneficiaries, ECON represents economic growth, R_f represents the risk-free interest rate, INDUS represents industry conditions, and MANAB represents the abilities of the insurance company's management.

Change in Payouts The payouts on insurance claims are somewhat stable for most life insurance companies with a diversified set of customers. In contrast, the payouts on property and casualty claims can be volatile for PC companies. The September 11, 2001 attack on the United States serves as an example of how a single event can cause billions of dollars worth of liabilities.

Change in Economic Conditions Economic growth can enhance an insurance company's cash flows because it increases the level of income of firms and households and can increase the demand for the company's services. During periods of strong economic growth, debt securities maintained by insurance companies are less likely to default. In addition, equity securities maintained by insurance companies should perform well because the firms represented by these securities should generate relatively high cash flows.

Change in the Risk-Free Interest Rate Some of an insurance company's assets (such as bonds) are adversely affected by rising interest rates. Thus, the valuation of an insurance company may be inversely related to interest rate movements.

Change in Industry Conditions Insurance companies are subject to industry conditions, including regulatory constraints, technology, and competition within the industry. For example, they now compete against various financial institutions when offering some services. As regulators have reduced barriers, competition within the insurance industry has become more intense.

Change in Management Abilities An insurance company has control over the composition of its managers and its organizational structure. Its managers can attempt to make internal decisions that will capitalize on the external forces (economic growth, interest rates, regulatory constraints) that the company cannot control. Thus, the management skills of an insurance company can influence its expected cash flows. In particular, skillful management is needed to determine the likelihood of events that will necessitate quick and massive payouts to policyholders. Managers must be able to estimate the present value of cash inflows from insurance premiums and the present value of future cash outflows resulting from payouts to policyholders. This analysis determines the types of insurance offered by the company and the size of the premiums charged on insurance. Insurance company managers must also be capable of analyzing the creditworthiness of firms issuing the bonds that they may purchase.

Factors That Affect the Required Rate of Return by Investors

The required rate of return by investors who invest in an insurance company can be modeled as

$$\Delta k = f(\Delta R_f, \Delta RP)$$
$$\quad\quad\quad + \quad\quad +$$

where ΔR_f represents a change in the risk-free interest rate, and ΔRP represents a change in the risk premium.

Exhibit 25.7   A Framework for Valuing an Insurance Company

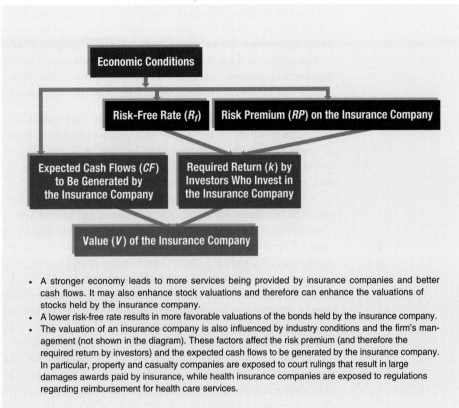

- A stronger economy leads to more services being provided by insurance companies and better cash flows. It may also enhance stock valuations and therefore can enhance the valuations of stocks held by the insurance company.
- A lower risk-free rate results in more favorable valuations of the bonds held by the insurance company.
- The valuation of an insurance company is also influenced by industry conditions and the firm's management (not shown in the diagram). These factors affect the risk premium (and therefore the required return by investors) and the expected cash flows to be generated by the insurance company. In particular, property and casualty companies are exposed to court rulings that result in large damages awards paid by insurance, while health insurance companies are exposed to regulations regarding reimbursement for health care services.

The risk-free interest rate is normally expected to be positively related to inflation, economic growth, and the budget deficit level, but inversely related to money supply growth (assuming it does not cause inflation). The risk premium on an insurance company is inversely related to economic growth and the company's management skills. It can also be affected by industry conditions, such as regulatory constraints. Some constraints (such as capital constraints) discourage insurance companies from taking excessive risk; other constraints, such as those on the services that can be offered, may increase risk because they limit the degree of diversification. The risk premium on PC companies can also change in response to the degree of expected terrorism.

Exhibit 25.7 provides a framework for valuing an insurance company, based on the preceding discussion. In general, the value of an insurance company is favorably affected by strong economic growth, a reduction in interest rates, and strong management capabilities. The sensitivity of an insurance company's value to these conditions is dependent on its own characteristics. The higher the risk tolerance reflected in the types of insurance offered, the more sensitive the company's valuation to events (such as catastrophes) that could trigger massive payouts to policyholders.

Impact of the Credit Crisis

As the credit crisis intensified in 2008, many insurance companies experienced losses. Those insurance companies that had invested some of their funds in mortgage-backed securities experienced losses on their investments. Some insurance companies had sold private mortgage insurance to offer protection on mortgages and had to cover insurance claims filed by creditors when homeowners defaulted on their mortgage payments. Other insurance companies incurred losses from their credit default swaps. As defaults occurred during the credit crisis, some insurance companies that had engaged in credit default swaps had to scramble for funds to cover their obligations or boost their collateral on the swap agreements. These moves were necessary because regulators had not required the companies to set aside reserves when they took their positions. Beyond these direct effects, economic conditions weakened in response to the credit crisis. Consequently, the demand for various insurance products offered by insurance companies declined.

Government Rescue of AIG   American International Group (AIG) is the largest insurance company in the world, with annual revenue of more than $100 billion and operations in more than 130 countries. In 2008, AIG experienced severe financial problems because it had sold credit default swaps to offer protection on mortgage-backed securities, and the values of these securities declined.

Since credit default swaps are traded in an over-the-counter market rather than on an organized exchange, no organized exchange stands behind a swap agreement. Thus, a financial institution that purchases a credit default swap to protect against defaults on its holdings of securities could still suffer damages if the counterparty defaults on the swap agreement. AIG had sold credit default swaps covering about $440 billion in debt securities, many of which represented subprime mortgages. If AIG failed, all of the financial institutions that had purchased credit default swaps from AIG to protect the value of their holdings in mortgage-backed securities could lose their protection and might fail as a result.

Faced with the prospect that the failure of AIG could be contagious to the insurance industry and the rest of the financial sector, in September 2008 the Federal Reserve bailed out AIG with support from the U.S. Treasury. The Fed may have viewed AIG as too big and too entangled with other financial institutions to fail. The bailout allowed AIG to borrow up to $85 billion from the Federal Reserve over a two-year period, and the government received an equity stake of about 80 percent of AIG. As part of the agreement, AIG was required to sell off some of its businesses in order to increase its liquidity. Its CEO, who had been in office for only three months before the bailout, was offered a $22 million severance package by the company, but refused it in light of AIG's financial distress. The head of AIG's finance division was allowed to keep $34 million in bonuses and was receiving $1 million per month for consulting since leaving the company about seven months before the bailout.

Regulation of Credit Default Swaps   In 2000, the New York State Insurance Department declared that credit default swaps were not a form of insurance and therefore were not subject to regulation. Thus, insurance companies could take a position in them to provide insurance, without maintaining reserves in the event of default. Left unregulated, credit default swaps grew rapidly. In 2008, credit default swap contracts represented $62 trillion of assets. This was at least twice the value of all stocks on the New York Stock Exchange and about 10 times the value of all U.S. corporate debt at that time. As the financial problems of some insurance companies were publicized due to their exposure to credit default swaps, in September 2008 the New York State Insurance Department reversed its position and decided that credit default swaps do reflect insurance. Other state insurance departments will likely follow its lead. Regulations can vary from state to state, however, so the safety of an insurance company may depend on the state in which its parent is located.

Indicators of Value and Performance

Some of the more common indicators of an insurance company's value and performance are available in investment service publications such as *Value Line*. A time-series assessment of the dollar amount of life insurance and/or PC insurance premiums indicates the growth in the company's insurance business. A time-series analysis of investment income can be used to assess the performance of the company's portfolio managers. However, the dollar amount of investment income is affected by several factors that are not under the control of portfolio managers, such as the amount of funds received as premiums that can be invested in securities and market interest rates. In addition, a relatively low level of investment income may result from a high concentration in stocks that pay low or no dividends rather than from poor performance.

Because insurance companies have unique characteristics, the financial ratios of other financial institutions are generally not applicable. An insurance company's liquidity can be measured using the following ratio:

$$\text{Liquidity ratio} = \frac{\text{Invested assets}}{\text{Loss reserves and unearned premium reserves}}$$

The higher the ratio, the more liquid the company. This ratio can be evaluated by comparing it to the industry average.

The profitability of insurance companies is often assessed using the return on net worth (or policyholders' surplus) as a ratio, as follows:

$$\text{Return on net worth} = \frac{\text{Net profit}}{\text{Policyholders' surplus}}$$

Net profit consists of underwriting profits, investment income, and realized capital gains. Changes in this ratio over time should be compared to changes in the industry norms, as the norm is quite volatile over time. The return on net worth tends to be quite volatile for PC insurance companies because of the volatility in their claims.

Although the net profit reflects all income sources and therefore provides only a general measure of profitability, various financial ratios can be used to focus on a specific source of income. For example, underwriting gains or losses are measured by the net underwriting margin:

$$\text{Net underwriting margin} = \frac{\text{Premium income} - \text{Policy expenses}}{\text{Total assets}}$$

When policy expenses exceed premium income, the net underwriting margin is negative. As long as other sources of income can offset such a loss, however, net profit will still be positive.

MULTINATIONAL INSURANCE COMPANIES

Some life insurance companies are multinational corporations with subsidiaries and joint ventures in several countries. By expanding their international business, insurance companies may reduce their exposure to the U.S. economy. However, they must comply with foreign regulations regarding services offered in foreign countries. The differences in regulations among countries increase the information costs of entering foreign markets.

Many U.S. insurance companies have recently established insurance subsidiaries in less developed countries that are underinsured. For example, less than 3 percent of the people in Mexico have life or home insurance, and less than 25 percent have automobile insurance. The lack of a developed insurance market offers much potential to U.S. insurance companies. In addition, the economic growth in Mexico resulting from the North American Free Trade Agreement (NAFTA) has created more demand for commercial insurance.

BACKGROUND ON PENSION FUNDS

Pension plans provide a savings plan for employees that can be used for retirement. They receive premiums from the employer and/or the employee. In aggregate, most of the contributions come from the employer. Pension funds are major investors in stocks, bonds, and various types of loan packages such as mortgage-backed securities.

Public Pension Funds

Public pension funds can be either state, local, or federal. The best-known government pension fund is Social Security. In addition to that system, all government employees and almost half of all nongovernment employees participate in other pension funds.

Many public pension plans are funded on a pay-as-you-go basis. Thus, existing employee and employer contributors are essentially supporting previous employees. At some point, this strategy could cause the future benefits owed to outweigh contributions to such an extent that the pension fund would be unable to fulfill its promises or would have to obtain more contributions to do so.

Private Pension Plans

Private pension plans are created by private agencies, including industrial, labor, service, nonprofit, charitable, and educational organizations. Some pension funds are so large that they are major investors in corporate securities.

Defined-Benefit Plans   Private pension funds can be classified by the way contributions are received and benefits are paid. With a **defined-benefit plan**, contributions are dictated by the benefits that will eventually be provided. The future pension obligations of a defined-benefit plan are uncertain because the obligations are stated in terms of fixed payments to retirees. These payments are dependent on salary levels, retirement ages, and life expectancies. Even if future payment obligations can be accurately predicted, the amount the plan needs today will be uncertain because of the uncertain rate of return on today's investments. The higher the future return on the plan's investments, the fewer the funds that must be invested today to satisfy future payments.

Many defined-benefit plans used optimistic projections of the rate of return to be earned on their investments, which created the appearance that their existing investments were adequate to cover future payment obligations. This allowed the corporations to reduce their contributions (an expense) to the plan and thereby increase their earnings. When projected rates of return on the pension funds were overestimated, however, the pension funds became underfunded, or inadequate to cover future payment obligations.

Some pension funds have recently made investments that offer high potential returns in order to justify their high projected rates of return. These investments, which include real estate, junk bonds, and international securities, also carry a high degree of risk. Thus, it is possible that some pension plans could be substantially underfunded if these investments perform poorly.

Defined-Contribution Plans   In contrast, a **defined-contribution plan** provides benefits that are determined by the accumulated contributions and the fund's investment performance. Some firms match a portion of the contribution made by their employees. With this type of plan, a firm knows with certainty the amount of funds to contribute, whereas that amount is undetermined in a defined-benefit plan. With a defined-contribution plan, however, the benefits to the participants are uncertain. Firms commonly hire an investment company to manage the pension portfolios of employees.

Defined-contribution plans outnumber defined-benefit plans, but defined-benefit plans have more participants and a greater aggregate value of assets. New plans allow employees more flexibility to choose what they want. In recent years, defined-benefit plans have commonly been replaced by defined-contribution plans. Employees can often decide the pace of their contributions and how their contributions will be invested. Common investment alternatives include stocks, investment-grade bonds, real estate, and money market securities. Communications from the benefits coordinator to the employees have become much more important, because employees now have more influence on their pension plan contributions and the investment approach used to invest the premiums.

Pension Fund Participation in Financial Markets

To set up a pension fund, a sponsor corporation establishes a trust pension fund through a commercial bank's trust department or an insured pension fund through an insurance company. The financial institution that is delegated the task of managing the pension fund then receives periodic contributions and invests them. Many of the transactions by pension funds in the financial markets finance economic growth, as illustrated in Exhibit 25.8. Pension funds are major participants in stock and bond offerings and thereby finance corporate expansion. They are also major participants in bond offerings by the Treasury and municipalities and thereby finance government spending.

Many of pension funds' investments in the stock, bond, and mortgage markets require the brokerage services of securities firms. Managers of pension funds instruct securities firms on the type and amount of investment instruments to purchase. Exhibit 25.9 summarizes the interaction between pension funds and other financial institutions.

Exhibit 25.8 How Pension Funds Finance Economic Growth

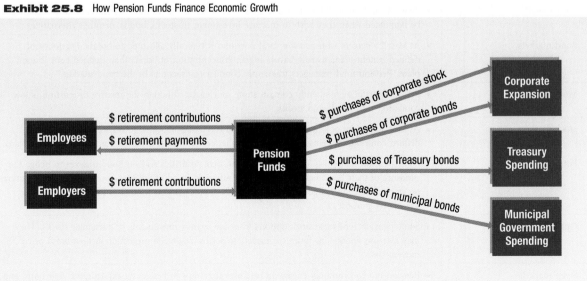

Exhibit 25.9   Interaction between Pension Funds and Other Financial Institutions

TYPE OF FINANCIAL INSTITUTION	INTERACTION WITH PENSION FUNDS
Commercial banks	• Sometimes manage pension funds. • Sell commercial loans to pension funds in the secondary market.
Insurance companies	• Create annuities for pension funds.
Mutual funds	• Serve as investments for some pension funds.
Securities firms	• Execute securities transactions for pension funds. • Offer investment advice to pension portfolio managers. • Underwrite newly issued stocks and bonds that are purchased by pension funds.

Exhibit 25.10 summarizes how pension fund managers participate in various financial markets. Because pension fund portfolios are normally dominated by stocks and bonds, the participation of pension fund managers in the stock and bond markets is obvious. Pension fund managers also participate in money and mortgage markets to fill out the remainder of their portfolios. They sometimes utilize the futures and options markets as well in order to partially insulate their portfolio performance from interest rate and/or stock market movements.

Pension Regulations

WEB

www.eric.org
Information about
pension guidelines.

The regulation of pension funds varies with the type of plan. All plans must comply with the set of Internal Revenue Service tax rules that apply to pension fund income. For defined-contribution plans, the sponsoring firm's main responsibility is its contributions to the fund.

Exhibit 25.10   Participation of Pension Funds in Financial Markets

FINANCIAL MARKET	HOW PENSION FUNDS PARTICIPATE IN THIS MARKET
Money markets	• Pension fund managers maintain a small proportion of liquid money market securities that can be liquidated when they wish to increase investment in stocks, bonds, or other alternatives.
Bond markets	• At least 25 percent of a pension fund portfolio is typically allocated to bonds. Portfolios of defined-benefit plans usually have a higher concentration of bonds than defined-contribution plans. Pension fund managers frequently conduct transactions in the bond market.
Mortgage markets	• Pension portfolios frequently contain some mortgages, although the relative proportion is low compared with bonds and stocks.
Stock markets	• At least 30 percent of a pension fund portfolio is typically allocated to stocks. In general, defined-contribution plans usually have a higher concentration of stocks than defined-benefit plans.
Futures markets	• Some pension funds use futures contracts on debt securities and on bond indexes to hedge the exposure of their bond holdings to interest rate risk. In addition, some pension funds use futures on stock indexes to hedge against market risk. Other pension funds use futures contracts for speculative purposes.
Options markets	• Some pension funds use stock options to hedge against movements of particular stocks. They may also use options on futures contracts to secure downside protection against bond price movements.
Swap markets	• Pension funds commonly engage in interest rate swaps to hedge the exposure of their bond and mortgage portfolios to interest rate risk.

Erisa   Defined-contribution plans are also subject to guidelines specified by the **Employee Retirement Income Security Act (ERISA)** of 1974 (also called the Pension Reform Act) and its 1989 revisions. This act requires a pension fund to choose one of two vesting schedule options, which determine when an employee has a legal right to the contributed funds:

1. One hundred percent vesting after five years of service.
2. Graded vesting, with 20 percent vesting in the third year, 40 percent in the fourth, 60 percent in the fifth, 80 percent in the sixth, and 100 percent in the seventh year.

ERISA also requires that any contributions be invested in a prudent manner, meaning that pension funds should concentrate their investments in high-grade securities. Although this was implicitly expected before, ERISA made this so-called fiduciary responsibility (monitored by the U.S. Department of Labor) explicit to encourage portfolio managers to serve the interests of the employees rather than themselves. Pension plans can face legal ramifications if they do not comply.

In addition, ERISA allows employees changing employers to transfer any vested amount into the pension plan of their new employer or to invest it in an Individual Retirement Account (IRA). With either alternative, taxes on the vested amount are still deferred until retirement when the funds become available.

The Pension Benefit Guaranty Corporation

ERISA established the **Pension Benefit Guaranty Corporation (PBGC)** to provide insurance on pension plans. This federally chartered agency guarantees that participants of defined-benefit pension plans will receive their benefits upon retirement. If the pension fund is incapable of fully providing the benefits promised, the PBGC will make up the difference. The PBGC does not receive government support. It is financed by annual premiums, income from assets acquired from terminated pension plans, and income generated by investments. It also receives employer-liability payments when an employer terminates its pension plan.

About 44 million Americans, or one-third of the workforce, have pension plans insured by the PBGC. As a wholly owned independent government agency, it differs from other federal regulatory agencies in that it has no regulatory powers.

The PBGC monitors pension plans periodically to determine whether they can adequately provide the benefits they have guaranteed. If a plan is judged inadequate, it is terminated, and the PBGC (or a PBGC appointee) takes control as the fund manager. The PBGC has a claim on part of a firm's net worth if it is needed to support the underfunded pension assets.

The PBGC's funding requirements depend on all the pension funds it monitors. Because the market values of these funds are similarly susceptible to economic conditions, funding requirements are volatile over time. A poor economic environment will depress stock prices and simultaneously reduce the asset values of most pension funds.

Pension Protection Act of 2006

If a company's defined-benefit pension plan is underfunded, the Pension Protection Act of 2006 requires the company to increase its contributions to the pension plan so that it will be fully funded within seven years. Prior to the act, some corporations' pension plans were underfunded by more than $1 billion. During the credit crisis in 2008, many large companies experienced losses on their pension portfolios because of their investments in mortgage-backed securities and stocks. Thus, the gap between what they needed to pay their retired employees versus the amount of funds available in their pension plans increased. Consequently, some companies had to revise their operating plans for 2009 in order to contribute more cash to their pension plans. When companies use more of their cash to boost underfunded pension plans, they have less cash to use for other purposes. Thus, their operating performance may suffer when they have to increase contributions to their pension plans.

PENSION FUND MANAGEMENT

Regardless of the manner in which funds are contributed to a pension plan, the funds received must be managed (invested) until needed to pay benefits. Private pension portfolios are dominated by common stock. Public pension portfolios are somewhat evenly invested in corporate bonds, stock, and other credit instruments.

Pension fund management can be classified according to the strategy used to manage the portfolio. With a **matched funding** strategy, investment decisions are made with the objective of generating cash flows that match planned outflow payments. An alternative strategy is **projective funding,** which offers managers more flexibility in constructing a pension portfolio that can benefit from expected market and interest rate movements. Some pension funds segment their portfolios, with part used for matched funding and the rest for projective funding.

An informal method of matched funding is to invest in long-term bonds to fund long-term liabilities and intermediate bonds to fund intermediate liabilities. The appeal of matching is the assurance that future liabilities are covered regardless of market movements. Matching limits the manager's discretion, however, because it allows only investments that match future payouts. For example, portfolio managers required to use matched funding would need to avoid callable bonds, because these bonds could potentially be retired before maturity. This requirement precludes consideration of many high-yield bonds. In addition, each liability payout may require a separate investment to which it can be perfectly matched; this would require several small investments and increase the pension fund's transaction costs.

Pension funds that are willing to accept market returns on bonds can purchase bond index portfolios that have been created by investment companies. The bond index portfolio may include investment-grade corporate bonds, Treasury bonds, and U.S. government agency bonds. It does not include the entire set of these bonds but includes enough of them to mirror market performance. Investing in a market portfolio is a passive approach that does not require any analysis of individual bonds. Some pension funds are not willing to accept a totally passive approach, so they compromise by using only a portion of their funds to purchase a bond market portfolio.

Equity portfolio indexes that mirror the stock market are also available for passive portfolio managers. These index funds have become popular over time, as they avoid transaction costs associated with frequent purchases and sales of individual stocks.

Management of Insured versus Trust Portfolios

Some pension plans are managed by life insurance companies. Contributions to such plans, called **insured plans,** are often used to purchase annuity policies so that the life insurance companies can provide benefits to employees upon retirement.

As an alternative, some pension funds are managed by the trust departments of financial institutions, such as commercial banks. The trust department invests the contributions and pays benefits to employees upon retirement. Although the day-to-day investment decisions of the trust department are controlled by the managing institution, the corporation owning the pension normally specifies general guidelines that the institution should follow. These guidelines might include

- The percentage of the portfolio that should be used for stocks or bonds
- A desired minimum rate of return on the overall portfolio
- The maximum amount to be invested in real estate
- The minimum acceptable quality ratings for bonds

- The maximum amount to be invested in any one industry
- The average maturity of bonds held in the portfolio
- The maximum amount to be invested in options
- The minimum size of companies in which to invest

There is a significant difference in the asset composition of pension portfolios managed by life insurance companies and those managed by trust departments. Assets managed by insurance companies are designed to create annuities, whereas the assets managed by a trust department still belong to the corporation. The insurance company becomes the legal owner of the assets and is allowed to maintain only a small portion of its assets as equities. Therefore insurance companies concentrate on bonds and mortgages. Conversely, the pension portfolios managed by trusts concentrate on stocks.

Pension portfolios managed by trusts offer potentially higher returns than insured plans and also have a higher degree of risk. The average return of trust plans is much more volatile over time.

Management of Portfolio Risk

Pension fund portfolio managers are very concerned about interest rate risk. If they hold long-term, fixed-rate bonds, the market value of their portfolio will decrease during periods when interest rates increase. They may periodically hedge against interest rate movements by selling bond futures contracts.

Many portfolio managers periodically sell futures contracts on stock indexes to hedge against market downturns. Portfolio managers of pension funds can obtain various types of insurance to limit the risk of the portfolio. For example, a policy could insure beyond a specified decline (such as 10 percent) in the asset value of a pension fund. This insurance allows managers to use more aggressive investment strategies. The cost of the insurance depends on the provisions of the contract and the length of time the portfolio is to be insured.

The pension funds of some companies, such as Lockheed Martin, simply concentrate investment in stocks and bonds and do not employ immunization techniques (to hedge the portfolio against risk). Lockheed Martin has generally focused on highly liquid investments so that the proportion of stocks and bonds within the portfolio can be revised in response to market conditions.

Corporate Control by Pension Funds

Pension funds in aggregate hold a substantial portion of the common stock outstanding in the United States. These funds are increasingly using their ownership as a means of influencing policies of the corporations whose stock they own. In particular, the California Pension Employees Retirement System (CALPERS) and the New York State Government Retirement Fund have taken active roles in questioning specific policies and suggesting changes to the board of directors at some corporations. Corporate managers consider the requests of pension funds because of the large stake the pension funds have in the corporations. As pension funds exert some corporate control to ensure that the managers and board members serve the best interests of shareholders, they can benefit because of their position as large shareholders.

WEB

www.bloomberg.com
Links to corporate directory search (database with over 10,000 U.S. companies, links to financial data, quotes, company news, etc.).

PERFORMANCE OF PENSION FUNDS

Pension funds commonly maintain a portfolio of stocks and a portfolio of bonds. Since pension funds focus on investing pension contributions until payments are provided, the performance of the investments is critical to the pension fund's success.

Pension Fund's Stock Portfolio Performance

The change in the performance (measured by risk-adjusted returns) of a pension fund's portfolio focusing on stocks can be modeled as

$$\Delta PERF = f(\Delta MKT, \Delta MANAB)$$

where MKT represents general stock market conditions, and MANAB represents the abilities of the pension fund's management.

Change in Market Conditions   The stock portfolio's performance is usually closely related to market conditions. Most pension funds' stock portfolios performed well in the late 1990s when stock market conditions were very favorable. They performed poorly when the economy weakened in the 2000–2002 period but performed better when the economy improved during the 2003–2007 period.

Change in Management Abilities   Stock portfolio performance can vary among pension funds in a particular time period because of differences in management abilities. The composition of the stocks in a pension fund's portfolio is determined by the fund's portfolio managers. In addition, a pension fund's operating efficiency affects the expenses the fund incurs and therefore affects its performance. A fund that is managed efficiently such that its expenses are low may be able to achieve higher returns even if its portfolio performance is about the same as the performance of other pension funds' portfolios.

Pension Fund's Bond Portfolio Performance

The change in the performance of a pension fund's bond portfolio can be modeled as

$$\Delta PERF = f(\Delta R_f, \Delta RP, \Delta MANAB)$$

where R_f represents the risk-free rate, RP represents the risk premium, and MANAB represents the abilities of the portfolio managers.

Impact of Change in the Risk-Free Rate   The prices of bonds tend to be inversely related to changes in the risk-free interest rate. In periods when the risk-free interest rate declines substantially, the required rate of return by bondholders declines, and most bond portfolios managed by pension funds perform well.

Impact of Change in the Risk Premium   The prices of bonds tend to be inversely related to changes in the risk premiums required by investors who purchase bonds. When economic conditions deteriorate, the risk premium required by bondholders usually increases, which results in a higher required rate of return (assuming no change in the risk-free rate) and lower prices on risky bonds. In periods when risk premiums increase, bond portfolios of pension funds that contain a high proportion of risky bonds perform poorly.

Impact of Management Abilities   The performance levels of bond portfolios can vary due to differences in management abilities. If a pension fund's portfolio managers can effectively adjust the bond portfolio in response to accurate forecasts of changes in interest rates or shifts in bond risk premiums, that fund's bond portfolio should experience relatively high performance. In addition, a pension fund's operating efficiency affects the expenses it incurs. If a bond portfolio is managed efficiently such that its expenses are low, it may be able to achieve relatively high returns even if its investments perform the same as those of other pension funds.

Performance Evaluation

If a manager has the flexibility to adjust the relative proportion of stocks versus bonds, the portfolio performance should be compared to a benchmark representing a passive strategy. For example, assume that the general long-run plan is a balance of 60 percent bonds and 40 percent stocks. Also assume that management has decided to create a more bond-intensive portfolio in anticipation of lower interest rates. The risk-adjusted returns on this actively managed portfolio could be compared to a benchmark portfolio composed of 60 percent bond index plus 40 percent stock index.

Any difference between the performance of the pension portfolio and the benchmark portfolio would result from (1) the manager's shift in the relative proportion of bonds versus stocks and (2) the composition of bonds and stocks within the respective portfolios. A pension portfolio could conceivably have stocks that outperform the stock index and bonds that outperform the bond index yet be outperformed by the benchmark portfolio when the shift in the relative bond/stock proportion backfires. In this example, a period of rising interest rates could cause the pension portfolio to be outperformed by the benchmark portfolio.

In many cases, the performances of stocks and bonds in a pension fund are evaluated separately. Stock portfolio risk is usually measured by the portfolio's beta, or the sensitivity to movements in a stock index (such as the S&P 500). Bond portfolio risk can be measured by the bond portfolio's sensitivity to a bond index or to a particular proxy for interest rates.

Performance of Pension Portfolio Managers

Many pension funds hire several portfolio managers to manage the assets. The general objective of portfolio managers is to make investments that will earn a large enough return to adequately meet future payment obligations. Some research has found that managed pension portfolios perform no better than market indexes. Based on these results, pension funds might consider investing in indexed mutual funds, which would perform as well as the market without requiring the pension plan to incur expenses for portfolio management.

Performance during the Credit Crisis

Pension funds commonly invest in mortgages and mortgage-backed securities. Those pension funds that had a high concentration of those securities during the credit crisis of 2008 experienced poor performance. For example, the state of Washington lost $90 million on its investment in securities issued by Lehman Brothers (which filed for bankruptcy after experiencing severe losses in mortgage-related securities), while the state of New York lost hundreds of millions of dollars on its investment in similar securities. During the 15-month period ending in October 2008, the value of assets held in retirement accounts declined by $2 trillion. Much of this loss was attributed to the large decline in stock valuations over this period.

The impact was also felt in foreign countries, as many foreign pension funds had invested in securities representing mortgages or the financial institutions that failed because of mortgage-related problems. For example, Norway's pension fund lost hundreds of millions of dollars because of its investment in Lehman Brothers securities.

SUMMARY

- Insurance companies offer insurance on life, property, health, business, bonds, and mortgages. Insurance companies commonly use their funds to invest in government securities, corporate securities, mortgages, and real estate.

- Insurance companies are exposed to interest rate risk, as they tend to maintain large bond portfolios whose values decline when interest rates rise. They are also exposed to credit risk and market risk, as a result of their investments in corporate debt securities, mortgages, stocks, and real estate.

- The value of an insurance company is based on its expected cash flows and the required rate of return by investors. The payouts of claims are somewhat predictable for life insurance firms, so they tend to have stable cash flows. In contrast, the payouts of claims for property and casualty insurance and other types of insurance services are subject to much uncertainty.

- Pension funds provide a savings plan for retirement. For defined-benefit pension plans, the contributions are dictated by the benefits that are specified. For defined-contribution pension plans, the benefits are determined by the accumulated contributions and the returns on the pension fund investments.

- Pension funds can use a matched funding strategy, in which investment decisions are made with the objective of generating cash flows that match planned outflow payments. Alternatively, pension funds can use a projective funding strategy, which attempts to capitalize on expected market or interest rate movements.

POINT COUNTER-POINT

Should Pension Fund Managers Be More Involved with Corporate Governance?

Point No. Pension fund managers should focus on assessing stock valuations and determining which stocks are undervalued or overvalued. If pension funds own stocks of firms that perform poorly, the pension fund managers can penalize those firms by dumping those stocks and investing their money in other stocks. If pension funds focus too much on corporate governance, they will lose sight of their goal of serving the pension recipients.

Counter-Point Yes. To the extent that pension funds can use governance to improve the performance of the firms in which they invest, they can improve the funds' performance. In this way, they also improve the returns to the pension recipients.

Who Is Correct? Use the Internet to learn more about this issue. Offer your own opinion on this issue.

QUESTIONS AND APPLICATIONS

1. **Life Insurance** How is whole life insurance a form of savings to policyholders?

2. **Whole Life versus Term Insurance** How do whole life and term insurance differ from the perspective of insurance companies? From the perspective of the policyholders?

3. **Universal Life Insurance** Identify the characteristics of universal life insurance.

4. **Group Plan** Explain group plan life insurance.

5. **Assets of Life Insurance Companies** What are the main assets of life insurance companies? Iden-

tify the main categories. What is the main use of funds by life insurance companies?

6. **Financing the Real Estate Market** How do insurance companies finance the real estate market?

7. **Policy Loans** What is a policy loan? When are policy loans popular? Why?

8. **Managing Interest Rates** Why are life insurance equity values sensitive to interest rate movements? What are two strategies that reduce the impact of changing interest rates on the market value of life insurance companies' assets?

9. Managing Credit Risk and Liquidity Risk
How do insurance companies manage credit risk and liquidity risk?

10. Liquidity Risk Discuss the liquidity risk experienced by life insurance and property and casualty (PC) insurance companies.

11. PC Insurance What purpose do property and casualty (PC) insurance companies serve? Explain how the characteristics of PC insurance and life insurance differ.

12. Cash Flow Underwriting Explain the concept of cash flow underwriting.

13. Impact of Inflation on Assets Explain how a life insurance company's asset portfolio may be affected by inflation.

14. Reinsurance What is reinsurance?

15. NAIC What is the NAIC, and what is its purpose?

16. PBGC What is the main purpose of the Pension Benefit Guaranty Corporation (PBGC)?

17. Defined-Benefit versus Defined-Contribution Plan Describe a defined-benefit pension plan. Describe a defined-contribution plan, and explain how it differs from a defined-benefit plan.

18. Guidelines for a Trust What type of general guidelines may be specified for a trust that is managing a pension fund?

19. Management of Pension Portfolios Explain the general difference in the composition of pension portfolios managed by trusts versus those managed by insurance companies. Explain why this difference occurs.

20. Private versus Public Pension Funds Explain the general difference between private pension funds versus public pension funds.

21. Exposure to Interest Rate Risk How can pension funds reduce their exposure to interest rate risk?

22. Pension Agency Problems The objective of the pension fund manager for McCanna, Inc. is not the same as the objective of McCanna's employees participating in the pension plan. Why?

23. ERISA Explain how ERISA affects employees who frequently change employers.

24. Adverse Selection and Moral Hazard Problems in Insurance Explain the adverse selection and moral hazard problems in insurance. Gorton Insurance Company wants to properly price its auto insurance, which protects against losses due to auto accidents. If Gorton wants to avoid the adverse selection and moral hazard problems, should it assess the behavior of insured people, uninsured people, or both groups? Explain.

Interpreting Financial News
Interpret the following comments made by Wall Street analysts and portfolio managers:

a. "Insurance company stocks may benefit from the recent decline in interest rates."

b. "Insurance company portfolio managers may serve as shareholder activists to implicitly control a corporation's actions."

c. "If a life insurance company wants a portfolio manager to generate sufficient cash to meet expected payments to beneficiaries, it cannot expect the manager to achieve relatively high returns for the portfolio."

Managing in Financial Markets
Assessing Insurance Company Operations As a consultant to an insurance company, you have been asked to assess the asset composition of the company.

a. The insurance company has recently sold a large amount of bonds and invested the proceeds in real estate. Its logic was that this would reduce the exposure of its assets to interest rate risk. Do you agree? Explain.

b. This insurance company currently has a small amount of stock. The company expects that it will need to liquidate some of its assets soon to make payments to beneficiaries. Should it shift its bond holdings (with short terms remaining until maturity) into stock in order to strive for a higher rate of return before it needs to liquidate this investment?

c. The insurance company maintains a higher proportion of junk bonds than most other insurance companies. In recent years, junk bonds have performed very well during a period of strong economic growth, as the yields paid by junk bonds have been well above those of high-quality corporate bonds. There have been very few defaults over this period. Consequently, the insurance company has proposed that it invest more heavily in junk bonds, as it believes that the concerns about junk bonds are unjustified. Do you agree? Explain.

FLOW OF FUNDS EXERCISE

How Insurance Companies Facilitate the Flow of Funds

Carson Company is considering a private placement of equity with Secura Insurance Company.

a. Explain the interaction between Carson Company and Secura. How will Secura serve Carson's needs, and how will Carson serve Secura's needs?

b. Why does Carson interact with Secura Insurance Company instead of trying to obtain the funds directly from individuals who pay premiums to Secura?

c. If Secura's investment performs well, who benefits? Is it worthwhile for Secura to closely monitor Carson Company's management? Explain.

INTERNET/EXCEL EXERCISES

1. Obtain a life insurance quotation online, using the website www.eterm.com. Fill in information about you (or a family member or friend) and obtain a quotation for a $1 million life insurance policy. What are the monthly and annual premiums for the various term lengths? Next, leaving all other information unchanged, change your gender. Are the premiums the same or different? Do you think insurance premiums are higher or lower for insurance companies operating entirely through the Internet?

2. Select a publicly traded insurance company of your choice. Go to its website and retrieve its most recent annual report. Summarize the company's main business. Is it focused on life insurance, auto insurance, health insurance, or a combination of these? Describe its performance over the last year. Explain why its performance was higher or lower than normal. Was the change in its performance due to the economy, the impact of recent interest rate movements on its asset portfolio, the stock market's performance, or a change in the frequency and size of insurance claims?

3. Go to http://finance.yahoo.com/, enter the symbol MET (MetLife, Inc.), and click on "Get Quotes." Click on "5y" just below the stock price trend to review the stock price movements over the last five years. Check the S&P box just above the graph and click on "Compare" in order to compare the trend of MetLife's stock price with the movements in the S&P stock index. Has MetLife performed better or worse than the index? Offer an explanation for its performance.

4. Go to http://finance.yahoo.com/, enter the symbol MET (MetLife, Inc.), and click on "Get Quotes." Retrieve stock price data at the beginning of the last 20 quarters. Then go to http://research.stlouisfed.org/fred2/ and retrieve interest rate data at the beginning of the last 20 quarters for the three-month Treasury bill. Record the data on an Excel spreadsheet. Derive the quarterly return of MetLife. Derive the quarterly change in the interest rate. Apply regression analysis in which the quarterly return of MetLife, Inc. is the dependent variable and the quarterly change in the interest rate is the independent variable (see Appendix B for more information about using regression analysis). Is there a positive or negative relationship between the interest rate movement and the stock return of MetLife? Is the relationship significant? Offer an explanation for this relationship.

WSJ EXERCISE

Insurance Company Performance

Using an issue of *The Wall Street Journal,* summarize an article that discussed the recent performance of a particular insurance company. Does the article suggest that the insurance company's performance was better or worse than the norm? What reason is given for the particular level of performance?

Assessing the Influence of Economic Conditions across a Financial Conglomerate's Units

This problem requires an understanding of the operations and asset compositions of savings institutions (Chapter 21), finance companies (Chapter 22), mutual funds (Chapter 23), securities firms (Chapter 24), and insurance companies (Chapter 25).

A diversified financial conglomerate has five units (subsidiaries). One unit conducts thrift operations; the second unit conducts consumer finance operations; the third, mutual fund operations; the fourth, securities operations; and the fifth, insurance operations. As a financial analyst for the conglomerate's holding company, you have been asked to assess all of the units and indicate how each unit will be affected as economic conditions change and which units will be affected the most.

In the past few months, all economic indicators have been signaling the possibility of a recession. Stock prices have already declined as the demand for stocks has decreased significantly. It appears that the pessimistic outlook will last for at least a few months. Economic conditions are already somewhat stagnant and are expected to deteriorate further in future months. During that time, firms will not consider mergers, new stock issues, or new bond issues.

An economist at your financial conglomerate believes that individual investors will overreact to the pessimistic outlook. Once stock prices are low enough, some firms will acquire target firms whose stock appears to be undervalued. In addition, some firms will buy back some of their own stock once they believe it is undervalued. Although these activities have not yet occurred, the economist believes it is only a matter of time.

Questions

1. Your strategy is to identify the units that will be less adversely affected by the recession. You believe that the units' different characteristics will cause some of them to be affected more than others.

2. Currently, each unit employs economists who develop forecasts for interest rates and other economic conditions. When assessing potential economic effects on each unit, what are the disadvantages of this approach versus having just one economist at the holding company provide forecasts?

Final Self-Exam

FINAL REVIEW

Chapters 17 to 25 are focused on financial institutions. Here is a brief review of the chapters.

Chapter 17 explains how banks obtain most of their funds from deposits and allocate most of their funds toward loans or securities. Chapter 18 explains how banks are regulated according to the services they offer and the capital that they must maintain, and how regulators monitor their risk over time. Chapter 19 explains how banks manage their sources and uses of funds (within regulatory constraints) in a manner to achieve their return and risk preferences. Chapter 20 shows how a bank's performance is highly influenced by what it charges on loans versus what it pays on deposits (which affects its net interest margin), its income earned from services (noninterest income), and its level of noninterest expenses.

Chapter 21 explains that savings institutions are similar to banks in the manner by which they obtain funds, but use most of their funds to invest in mortgages or mortgage-related securities. This results in a higher exposure to interest rate risk, but savings institutions can hedge that risk. Chapter 22 explains that finance companies differ from banks and savings institutions in that they typically obtain their funds by issuing commercial paper and target their use of funds toward consumers or small businesses. In general, the credit risk of their assets is higher than that of commercial banks or savings institutions. Chapter 23 identifies the types of mutual funds and explains how the performance and risk vary across funds. In general, a mutual fund's asset portfolio is much more risky than those of other financial institutions. Chapter 24 describes how securities firms channel funds through financial markets. The investment banking portion of a securities firm places new securities with investors and thereby helps corporations obtain financing. The brokerage portion of a securities firm channels funds between investors in the secondary market. Chapter 25 explains how insurance companies obtain funds from the premiums they charge while pension funds rely on retirement contributions from employees or their respective employers. Insurance companies and pension funds are major investors in the bond and stock markets.

This self-exam allows you to test your understanding of some of the key concepts covered in the chapters on financial institutions. It does not replace the end-of-chapter questions, nor does it cover all the concepts. It is simply intended to allow you to test yourself on a general overview of key concepts. Try to simulate taking an exam by answering the questions without using your book and your notes. The answers to this exam are provided at the end of the questions so that you can grade your exam. If you have any wrong answers, you should reread the related material and then redo the questions that you had wrong.

This exam may not necessarily match the level of rigor in your course. Your instructor may offer you specific information about how this Final Self-Exam relates to the coverage and rigor of the final exam in your course.

FINAL SELF-EXAM

1. Flagstaff Bank currently has assets heavily concentrated in secured loans and Treasury securities, while Mesa Bank has assets concentrated in consumer loans and credit card loans. The managerial capabilities of the two banks are similar. Mesa Bank's performance was much better than that of Flagstaff Bank last year, but Flagstaff Bank's performance is much better than that of Mesa Bank this year. Explain why the relative performance of the two banks is likely to change over time.

2. The Sarbanes-Oxley Act of 2002 requires publicly traded firms to be more transparent in their reporting. This may reduce the asymmetric information problem between firms (including banks) and their investors. Do you think the Sarbanes-Oxley Act will eliminate the need for CAMELS ratings?

3. Kentucky Bank has a new board of directors who believe that the bank has opportunities for major growth and want to ensure that the CEO makes good investment decisions to expand the bank's business. To give the CEO a strong incentive to perform well, the board set the CEO's quarterly compensation in line with the return on equity. The CEO immediately decided to repurchase as many shares as possible while barely meeting the bank's capital requirements. Why would the CEO take this action? Will the compensation structure remove agency problems?

4. Last year, Alabama Bank had a net interest margin of 3 percent, noninterest income was 1.5 percent of assets, noninterest expenses were 3 percent of assets, and loan loss reserves were .5 percent of assets. Alabama Bank wants to employ a strategy of using more of its resources to offer financial services. It expects that it can increase its noninterest income by .5 percent as a percentage of assets. What other components (or ratios) of the income statement may be affected by this strategy?

5. Maryland Savings Institution maintains most of its assets in fixed-rate mortgages of between 10 and 30 years. Most of its deposits have maturities of less than one year. Assume that the Fed implements a restrictive monetary policy.

a. Explain how that monetary policy will affect interest rates.

b. Assuming that interest rates change as expected, how will that affect the spread between interest revenue and interest expenses?

c. Should Maryland hedge its asset portfolio, based on its expectations? If so, how should it hedge? If it should hedge, explain any limitations of the hedge.

6. How do financial institutions vary in terms of their main uses of funds?

7. Explain the role that insurance companies and pension funds play in financial markets.

8. Explain why a stock market benefits more when financial institutions are investors than when individual investors invest all their money directly into the stock market themselves.

9. Discuss the following: Money market funds attract money from investors who do not know what else to do with their money. Thus, money market funds are merely a last resort when there are no better alternatives for investment. Since they invest only in short-term securities, they do not play a role in financing economic growth.

10. Closed-end funds tend to hold stocks that are less liquid than stocks held by open-end funds.

a. Do you think this characteristic is an advantage for closed-end funds that want to achieve high returns?

b. Why is it easier for closed-end funds to manage a portfolio of less liquid stocks than it would be for open-end funds?

11. Discuss the strategy of an investor who invests all of his money in four mutual funds that focus on growth companies. The investor believes he is fully insulated from market conditions because each fund contains 40 different stocks.

12. For a given type of mutual fund classification, what is a key characteristic that causes some mutual funds to outperform others?

13. When a securities firm serves as an underwriter for an initial public offering (IPO), is the firm working for the issuer or the institutional investors that may purchase shares? Explain the dilemma.

14. Do stock analysts reduce market inefficiencies?

15. Why might the value of an insurance company be affected by interest rate movements?

16. Should financial institutions be regulated in order to reduce their risk? Offer at least one argument for regulation and one argument against regulation.

17. Consider the typical sources and uses of funds at commercial banks, savings institutions, and securities firms. Explain the risk of each type of institution based on its typical sources and uses of funds.

Answers to Final Self-Exam

1. Under favorable economic conditions, Mesa Bank should perform better because it earns higher returns on its loans as long as the borrowers repay their loans (higher risk). Under unfavorable economic conditions, Flagstaff Bank should perform better because Mesa will likely experience many loan defaults, while Flagstaff will not.

2. Even if investors have more information, they may not be able to detect banks that have financial problems. In addition, CAMELS ratings are intended to detect financial problems of banks early so that there is time to correct the problems. This can prevent bank failures and therefore allow for a more stable banking system.

3. The stock repurchase will reduce equity so that the profits in the near future will result in a higher return on equity. This will enhance the CEO's compensation, but will not necessarily enhance the bank's value in the long run. In fact, the decreased equity will restrict the growth of the bank. Thus, this compensation structure will not remove agency problems.

4. Alabama Bank will incur more expenses when attempting to expand its financial services. This will increase the ratio of noninterest expenses to assets, and this increase could offset any increase in revenue.

5. **a.** Interest rates will rise.

b. The spread will decrease because short-term deposit rates will increase, while long-term rates may not be affected as much or at all.

c. Maryland should hedge. It could sell interest rate futures. However, if it does sell interest rate futures and interest rates decline, it will incur a loss on its interest rate futures position, which may offset most of its gain from operations.

6. Commercial banks serve corporate borrowers, savings institutions serve home-owners, finance companies serve consumers and small businesses, while mutual funds, insurance companies, and pension funds serve corporate borrowers (investing in stocks and bonds and money market securities issued by corporations).

7. Insurance companies and pension funds are suppliers of funds and add much liquidity to the financial markets. They may also make the stock market more efficient because if a stock's price deviates from its fundamental value, they may take a position to capitalize on the discrepancy, and this should push the stock toward its fundamental value.

8. Institutional investors pool funds that come from many individuals and take much bigger stakes in a specific stock. Thus, the institutional investors have an incentive to make the correct investment choices (because of the large investment) and then to monitor the companies in which they invest. As a result, there is more governance over companies than if stocks were owned only by small investors.

9. Money market funds provide liquidity to investors, which is necessary even when investors have alternative investments that pay higher returns. In addition, money market funds play a major role in financing the budget deficit as they invest heavily in Treasury securities. They also channel funds to corporations in the form of commercial paper. Since the Treasury and corporations frequently reissue short-term securities, they are sometimes using the short-term securities to finance long-term investment.

10. a. The investment in illiquid stocks may be an advantage because it allows the closed-end funds to pursue stocks that are not followed by most investors. These stocks are more likely to be mispriced than other stocks,

b. Closed-end funds do not have to accommodate redemptions whereas open-end funds do. Thus, closed-end funds do not need to worry about selling some of their stock holdings just for the purpose of satisfying redemptions.

11. These mutual funds will all be adversely affected during a weak economy because firms that have high growth potential will probably experience weak performance when economic conditions are weak. There is not sufficient demand under these conditions.

12. Mutual funds with a low expense ratio tend to perform better than those with higher expense ratios.

13. A securities firm attempts to satisfy the issuer of stock by ensuring that the price is sufficiently high, but it must also ensure that it can place all the shares. It also wants to satisfy investors who invest in the IPO. If the investors incur losses because they paid too much for the shares, they may not want to purchase any more stock from that underwriter in the future.

14. Some stock analysts may be able to detect when a specific stock is underpriced or overpriced in the market, and they can communicate their opinion through their stock ratings, which may cause investors to capitalize on the information. This could push stock prices closer to their fundamental values and reduce market inefficiencies. During the stock market bubble in the year 2000, however, analysts were overly optimistic about stocks and were not paying attention to fundamentals of the companies. Thus, they may have been a partial cause of the stock market bubble.

15. The value of an insurance company is partially influenced by the value of its asset portfolio. Its asset portfolio contains bonds. The market value of the bonds is inversely related to interest rate movements.

16. Regulation may be able to reduce failures of financial institutions, which may stabilize the financial system. The flow of funds into financial institutions will be larger if the people who provide the funds can trust that the financial institutions will not fail. However, regulation can also restrict competition. In some cases, it results in subsidies to financial institutions that are performing poorly. Thus, regulation can prevent firms from operating efficiently.

17. Commercial banks are exposed to default risk due to their commercial and consumer loans. They are exposed to interest rate risk because the maturities on some of their assets (especially bonds and some term loans) may be longer than the maturities on their liabilities. Savings institutions are exposed to default risk due to their mortgage loans (although these loans are normally backed by the home) and consumer loans. They are exposed to interest rate risk because the maturities on their fixed-rate mortgages are longer than the maturities on their liabilities. Securities firms are exposed to market risk from taking equity positions and to default risk when providing bridge loans. Their operations are especially sensitive to financial market activity. When financial transactions such as mergers and stock trades decline, their business declines because they serve as intermediaries for many types of financial transactions.

APPENDIX A
Comprehensive Project

One of the best ways to gain a clear understanding of the key concepts explained in this text is to apply them directly to actual situations. This comprehensive project enables you to apply numerous concepts regarding financial markets and institutions discussed throughout the text to actual situations. The tasks in this project can be categorized as follows:

Part I. Applying Financial Markets Concepts

Part II. Applying Financial Institutions Concepts

Part III. Measuring Stock Performance

At the beginning of the school term, you should complete two tasks. First, compile the information on financial markets needed to fill in the blank spaces in steps (a) through (j) in Part I. This information will be needed when applying financial markets concepts in the questions that follow (Part I of the project). Second, obtain the information on financial institutions identified at the beginning of Part II below. This information will be needed when applying financial institutions concepts in the questions that follow (Part II of the project).

PART I. APPLYING FINANCIAL MARKETS CONCEPTS

The exercises on financial markets concepts require you to measure the change in the yields and values of securities over the school term and explain why the values changed. In doing so, you will apply the concepts in the chapters on financial markets to actual situations.

At the beginning of the school term and near the end of the term, use an issue of *The Wall Street Journal (WSJ)* or various financial websites to obtain the information requested here. Your professor will identify the dates to use as the beginning and end of the term. The dates will allow you sufficient time to assess the changes in the yields and values of securities so that you can answer the questions. Your professor will explain the specific format of the assignment, such as whether any parts are excluded or whether students should work in teams. Your professor will also indicate whether the answers will be handed in, presented to the class, or both. A commonly used format is to divide the project into parts and assign a team of students to present their answers to one specific part. Each student will be a member of one of the teams. All students may still be required to hand in answers to all parts of the project, even though their team's presentation focuses on only one part.

	BEGINNING OF TERM	END OF TERM

a. Stock Market Index Information:

S&P 500 (stock) index level: _____ _____

Nasdaq Composite (stock) index level: _____ _____

DJ World: _____ _____

b. Interest Rate Information:

Prime rate: _____ _____

Federal funds rate: _____ _____

Commercial paper rate (90 days): _____ _____

Certificate of deposit rate (3-month): _____ _____

Treasury bill rate (13 weeks): _____ _____

Treasury bill rate (26 weeks): _____ _____

c. Bond Yield Information:

Treasury long-term bond yield: _____ _____

DJ Corporate bond yield: _____ _____

Corporate (Master) bond yield: _____ _____

High-yield corporate bond yield: _____ _____

Tax-exempt (7–12 yr) bond yield: _____ _____

d. Use Stock Exchange Quotations to record the stock price and dividend of one stock from each stock exchange in which you would like to invest.

New York Stock Exchange: Stock price: _____ _____

Name of firm _____ Dividend: _____ _____

Nasdaq Market: Stock price: _____ _____

Name of firm _____ Dividend: _____ _____

e. Use Futures Prices Quotations to record the recent ("settle") price of:

Treasury bond futures with the first
settlement date beyond your school term: _____ _____

S&P 500 index futures with the first
settlement date beyond your school term: _____ _____

British pound futures with the first
settlement date beyond your school term: _____ _____

f. Use an Options Quotations table to select a call option on a firm where you expect the stock price to increase (select the option with the first expiration month beyond the end of the school term):

Name of firm: _____

Expiration month: _____

Strike price: _____

Stock price: _____ _____

Option premium: _____ _____

g. Use an Options Quotations table to select a put option on a firm where you expect the stock price to decrease (select the option with the first expiration month beyond the end of the school term):

Name of firm: _____

Expiration month: _____

Strike price: _____

Stock price: _____   _____   _____

Option premium: _____   _____   _____

h. Use a Currency Exchange Rate table in the *WSJ* to record exchange rates:

Exchange rate of the British pound (in $): _____   _____

Exchange rate of the Japanese yen (in $): _____   _____

Exchange rate of the Mexican peso (in $): _____   _____

i. Use Currency Options data (if available) to select a call option on a foreign currency that you expect will strengthen against the dollar (select the option with the first expiration month beyond the end of the school term):

Currency: _____

Expiration month: _____

Strike price: _____

Currency's existing value: _____   _____

Option premium: _____   _____

j. Use Currency Options data (if available) to select a put option on a foreign currency that you expect will weaken against the dollar (select the option with the first expiration month beyond the end of the school term):

Currency: _____

Expiration month: _____

Strike price: _____

Currency's existing value: _____   _____

Option premium: _____   _____

1. Explaining changes in interest rates (from Chapter 2)

a. Compare the 13-week Treasury bill rate (which is a proxy for short-term interest rates) at the end of the school term to the rate that existed at the beginning of the school term.

b. Recall that Chapter 2 offered reasons why interest rates change over time. Apply the concepts in that chapter to explain why you think interest rates have changed over the school term.

2. Comparing yields among securities (from Chapter 3)

a. What is the difference between the yield on corporate high-quality bonds and the yield on Treasury bonds as of the end of the school term?

b. Apply the concepts discussed in Chapter 3 to explain why this premium exists.

c. What is the difference between the yield on long-term Treasury bonds and the yield on long-term municipal bonds as of the end of the school term?

d. Apply the concepts discussed in Chapter 3 to explain why this difference exists.

3.   Assessing the forecasting ability of the yield curve (from Chapter 3)

a.   What was the difference between the 26-week T-bill yield and the 13-week T-bill yield at the beginning of the school term?

b.   Does this imply that the yield curve had an upward or downward slope at that time?

c.   Assuming that this slope can be primarily attributed to expectations theory, did the direction of the slope indicate that the market expected higher or lower interest rates in the future?

d.   Did interest rates move in that direction over the school term?

4.   Explaining shifts in the yield curve over time (from Chapter 3)

a.   What was the difference between the long-term Treasury bond yield and the 13-week T-bill yield at the beginning of the school term?

b.   What is the difference between the long-term Treasury bond yield and the 13-week T-bill yield at the end of the school term?

c.   Given your answers to the two previous questions, describe how the yield curve changed over the school term. Explain the changes in expectations about future interest rates that are implied by the shift in the yield curve over the school term.

5.   The Fed's influence on interest rates (from Chapter 5)

a.   Did the Fed change the federal funds rate over the school term?

b.   Do you think the movements in interest rates over the school term were caused by the Fed's monetary policy? Explain.

6.   Measuring and explaining premiums on money market securities (from Chapter 6)

a.   What is the difference between the yield on 90-day commercial paper and the yield on 13-week T-bills as of the end of the school term? Apply the concepts discussed in Chapter 6 to explain why this premium exists.

b.   Compare the premium on the 90-day commercial paper yield (relative to the 13-week T-bill yield) that exists at the end of the school term to the premium that existed at the beginning of the term. Apply the concepts discussed in Chapter 6 to explain why the premium may have changed over the school term.

7.   Explaining bond premiums and price movements (from Chapter 8)

a.   What is the difference between the yield on high-yield corporate bonds at the end of the school term versus the yield on high-quality corporate bonds as of the beginning of the school term? Apply the concepts discussed in Chapter 8 to explain why this premium exists.

b.   Compare the long-term Treasury bond yield at the end of the school term to the long-term Treasury bond yield that existed at the beginning of the school term. Given the direction of this change, did prices of long-term bonds rise or fall over the school term?

c.   Compare the change in the yields of Treasury, municipal, and corporate bonds over the school term. Did the yields of all three types of securities move in the same direction and by about the same degree? Apply the concepts discussed in Chapter 8 to explain why yields of different types of bonds move together.

d.   Compare the premium on high-yield corporate bonds (relative to Treasury bonds) at the beginning of the school term to the premium that existed at the end of the school term. Did the premium increase or decrease? Apply the concepts discussed in Chapter 8 to explain why this premium changed over the school term.

8. Explaining mortgage rates (from Chapter 9)

a.   Compare the rate paid by a homeowner on a 30-year mortgage to the rate (yield) paid by the Treasury on long-term Treasury bonds as of the end of the school term. Explain the difference.

b.   Compare the 30-year mortgage rate at the end of the school term to the 30-year mortgage rate that existed at the beginning of the school term. What do you think is the primary reason for the change in 30-year mortgage rates over the school term?

9. Explaining stock price movements (from Chapter 11)

a.   Determine the return on the stock market over your school term, based on the percentage change in the S&P 500 index level over the term. Annualize this return by multiplying the return times $(12/m)$, where m is the number of months in your school term. Apply concepts discussed in Chapter 11 to explain why the market return was high or low over your school term.

b.   Repeat the previous question for smaller stocks by using the Nasdaq Composite instead of the S&P 500 index. What was the annualized return on the Nasdaq Composite over your school term?

c.   Explain why the return on the Nasdaq Composite was high or low over your school term.

d.   Determine the return over the school term on the stock in which you chose to invest. The return is $(P_t - P_{t-1} + D)/P_{t-1}$, where P_t is the stock price as of the end of the school term, P_{t-1} is the stock price at the beginning of the school term, and D is the dividend paid over the school term. In most cases, one quarterly dividend is paid over a school term, which is one-fourth of the annual dividend amount per share shown in stock quotation tables.

e.   What was your return over the school term on the stock you selected from the New York Stock Exchange? What was your return over the school term on the stock you selected from the Nasdaq market? Apply the concepts discussed in Chapter 11 to explain why you think these three stocks experienced different returns over the school term.

10. Measuring and explaining futures price movements (from Chapter 13)

a.   Assume that you purchased an S&P 500 futures contract at the beginning of the school term, with the first settlement date beyond the end of the school term. Also assume that you sold an S&P 500 futures contract with this same settlement date at the end of the school term. Given that this contract has a value of the futures price times $250, determine the difference between the dollar value of the contract you sold and the dollar amount of the contract that you purchased.

b.   Assume that you invested an initial margin of 20 percent of the amount that you would owe to purchase the S&P 500 index at the settlement date. Measure your return from taking a position in the S&P 500 index futures as follows. Take the difference determined in the previous question (which represents the dollar amount of the gain on the futures position), and divide it by the amount you originally invested (the amount you originally invested is 20 percent of the dollar value of the futures contract that you purchased).

c.   The return that you just derived in the previous question is not annualized. To annualize your return, multiply it by $(12/m)$, where m is the number of months in your school term.

d.   Apply the concepts discussed in Chapter 13 to explain why your return on your S&P 500 index futures position was low or high over the school term.

e.   Assume that you purchased a Treasury bond futures contract at the beginning of the school term with the first settlement date beyond the end of the school term. Also assume that you sold this same type of futures contract at the end of the school term. Recall that Treasury bond futures contracts are priced relative to a $100,000 face value, and the fractions are in thirty-seconds. What was the dollar value of the futures contract at the beginning of the school term when you purchased it?

f.   What was the dollar value of the Treasury bond futures contract at the end of the school term when you sold it?

g.   What was the difference between the dollar value of the Treasury bond futures contract when you sold it and the value when you purchased it?

h.   Assume that you invested an initial margin of 20 percent of the amount that you would owe to purchase the Treasury bonds at the settlement date. Your investment is equal to 20 percent of the dollar value of the Treasury bond futures contract as of the time you purchased the futures. Determine the return on your futures position, which is the difference you derived in the previous question as a percentage of your investment.

i.   The return that you just derived in the previous question is not annualized. To annualize your return, multiply your return times $(12/m)$, where m is the number of months in your school term.

j.   Apply the concepts discussed in Chapter 13 to explain why the return on your Treasury bond futures position was low or high.

11. Measuring and explaining option price movements (from Chapter 14)

a.   Assume that you purchased a call option (representing 100 shares) on the specific stock that you identified in Part I (f) of this project. What was your return from purchasing this option? [Your return can be measured as $(\text{Prem}_t - \text{Prem}_{t-1})/\text{Prem}_{t-1}$, where Prem_{t-1} represents the premium paid at the beginning of the school term and Prem_t represents the premium at which the same option can be sold at the end of the school term.] If the premium for this option is not quoted at the end of the school term, measure the return as if you had exercised the call option at the end of the school term (assuming that it is feasible to exercise the option at that time). That is, the return is based on purchasing the stock at the option's strike price and then selling the stock at its market price at the end of the school term.

b.   Annualize the return on your option by multiplying the return you derived in the previous question by $(12/m)$, where m represents the number of months in your school term.

c.   Compare the return on your call option to the return that you would have earned if you had simply invested in the stock itself. Notice how the magnitude of the return on the call option is much larger than the magnitude of the return on the stock itself. That is, the gains are larger and the losses are larger when investing in call options on a stock instead of the stock itself.

d.   Assume that you purchased a put option (representing 100 shares) on the specific stock that you identified in Part I (g) of this project. What was your return from purchasing this option? [Your return can be measured as $(\text{Prem}_t - \text{Prem}_{t-1})/\text{Prem}_{t-1}$, where Prem_{t-1} represents the premium paid at the beginning of the school term and Prem_t represents the premium at which the same option can be sold at the end of the school term.] If the premium for this option is not quoted at the end of the school term, measure the return as if you had exercised the put option at the end of the school term (assuming that it is feasible to exercise the option at that time). That is, the return is based on purchasing the stock at its market price and then selling the stock at the option's strike price at the end of the school term.

12. Determining swap payments (from Chapter 15)

a.   Assume that at the beginning of the school term, you engaged in a fixed-for-floating rate swap in which you agreed to pay 6 percent in exchange for the prevailing 26-week T-bill rate that exists at the end of the school term. Assume that your swap agreement specifies the end of the school term as the only time at which a swap will occur and that the notional amount is $10 million. Determine the amount that you owe on the swap, the amount you are owed on the swap, and the difference. Did you gain or lose as a result of the swap?

13. Measuring and explaining exchange rate movements (from Chapter 16)

a.   Determine the percentage change in the value of the British pound over the school term. Did the pound appreciate or depreciate against the dollar?

b.   Determine the percentage change in the value of the Japanese yen over the school term. Did the yen appreciate or depreciate against the dollar?

c.   Determine the percentage change in the value of the Mexican peso over the school term. Did the peso appreciate or depreciate against the dollar?

d.   Determine the per unit gain or loss if you had purchased British pound futures at the beginning of the term and sold British pound futures at the end of the term.

e.   Given that a single futures contract on British pounds represents 62,500 pounds, determine the dollar amount of your gain or loss.

PART II. APPLYING FINANCIAL INSTITUTIONS CONCEPTS

Obtain an annual report of (1) a commercial bank, (2) a savings and loan association, (3) a securities firm, and (4) an insurance company. The annual reports will allow you to relate the theory in specific related chapters to the particular financial institution of concern. The exercises in Part II of the Comprehensive Project require the use of these annual reports. The annual reports can be obtained by calling the Shareholder Services department for each financial institution, or they may be available online. Also, order a prospectus of a specific mutual fund in which you are interested. The prospectus can be obtained from the specific investment company that sponsors the mutual fund, or it may be available online.

1. Commercial bank operations (from Chapter 17)

For the commercial bank that you selected at the beginning of the term, use its annual report or any other related information to answer the following questions:

a.   Identify the types of deposits that the commercial bank uses to obtain most of its funds.

b.   Identify the main uses of funds by the bank.

c.   Summarize any statements made by the commercial bank in its annual report about how recent or potential regulations will affect its performance.

d.   Does it appear that the bank is attempting to enter the securities industry by offering securities services? If so, explain how.

e.   Does it appear that the bank is attempting to enter the insurance industry by offering insurance services? If so, explain how.

2. Commercial bank management (from Chapter 19)

For the commercial bank that you selected at the beginning of the term, use its annual report or any other related information to answer the following questions:

a. Assess the bank's balance sheet as well as any comments in its annual report about the gap between its rate-sensitive assets and its rate-sensitive liabilities. Does it appear that the bank has a positive gap or a negative gap?

b. Does the bank use any methods to reduce its gap and therefore reduce its exposure to interest rate risk?

c. Summarize any statements made by the bank in its annual report about how it attempts to limit its exposure to credit risk on the loans it provides.

3. Commercial bank performance (from Chapter 20)

For the commercial bank that you selected at the beginning of the term, use its annual report or any other related information to answer the following questions:

a. Determine the bank's interest income as a percentage of its total assets.

b. Determine the bank's interest expenses as a percentage of its total assets.

c. Determine the bank's net interest margin.

d. Determine the bank's noninterest income as a percentage of its total assets.

e. Determine the bank's noninterest expenses (do not include the addition to loan loss reserves here) as a percentage of its total assets.

f. Determine the bank's addition to loan loss reserves as a percentage of its total assets.

g. Determine the bank's return on assets.

h. Determine the bank's return on equity.

i. Identify the bank's income statement items described previously that would be affected if interest rates rise in the next year, and explain how they would be affected.

j. Identify the bank's income statement items described previously that would be affected if U.S. economic conditions deteriorate, and explain how they would be affected.

4. Savings institutions (from Chapter 21)

For the savings institution (SI) that you selected at the beginning of the term, use its annual report or any other related information to answer the following questions:

a. Identify the types of deposits that the SI uses to obtain most of its funds.

b. Identify the main uses of funds by the SI.

c. Summarize any statements made by the SI in its annual report about how recent or potential regulations will affect its performance.

d. Assess the SI's balance sheet as well as any comments in its annual report about the gap between its rate-sensitive assets and its rate-sensitive liabilities. Does it appear that the SI has a positive gap or a negative gap?

e. Does the SI use any methods to reduce its gap and therefore reduce its exposure to interest rate risk?

f. Summarize any statements made by the SI in its annual report about how it attempts to limit its exposure to credit risk on the loans it provides.

g. Determine the SI's interest income as a percentage of its total assets.

h. Determine the SI's interest expenses as a percentage of its total assets.

i. Determine the SI's noninterest income as a percentage of its total assets.

j. Determine the SI's noninterest expenses (do not include the addition to loan loss reserves here) as a percentage of its total assets.

   k. Determine the SI's addition to loan loss reserves as a percentage of its total assets.

   l. Determine the SI's return on assets.

  m. Determine the SI's return on equity.

   n. Identify the SI's income statement items described previously that would be affected if interest rates rise in the next year, and explain how they would be affected.

   o. Identify the SI's income statement items described previously that would be affected if U.S. economic conditions deteriorate, and explain how they would be affected.

5. Mutual funds (from Chapter 23)

For the mutual fund that you selected at the beginning of the term, use its prospectus or any other related information to answer the following questions:

a. What is the investment objective of this mutual fund? Do you consider this mutual fund to have low risk, moderate risk, or high risk?

b. What was the return on the mutual fund last year? What was the average annual return over the last three years?

c. What is a key economic factor that influences the return on this mutual fund? (That is, are the fund's returns highly influenced by U.S. stock market conditions? By U.S. interest rates? By foreign stock market conditions? By foreign interest rates?)

d. Must any fees be paid when buying or selling this mutual fund?

e. What was the expense ratio for this mutual fund over the last year? Does this ratio seem high to you?

6. Securities firms (from Chapter 24)

For the securities firm that you selected at the beginning of the term, use its annual report or any other related information to answer the following questions:

a. What are the main types of business conducted by the securities firm?

b. Summarize any statements made by the securities firm in its annual report about how it may be affected by existing or potential regulations.

c. Describe the recent performance of the securities firm, and explain why the performance has been favorable or unfavorable.

7. Insurance companies (from Chapter 25)

For the insurance company that you selected at the beginning of the term, use its annual report or any other related information to answer the following questions:

a. How does the insurance company allocate its funds? (That is, what is its asset composition?)

b. Is the insurance company exposed to interest rate risk? Explain.

c. Does the insurance company use any techniques to hedge its exposure to interest rate risk?

d. Summarize any statements made by the insurance company in its annual report about how it may be affected by existing or potential regulations.

e. Describe the recent performance of the insurance company (using any key financial ratios that measure its income). Explain why its recent performance was strong or weak.

PART III. MEASURING STOCK PERFORMANCE

This part of the project enables you to analyze the risk and return characteristics of one particular stock that you own or would like to purchase. You should input your data on Excel or an alternative electronic spreadsheet. Perform the following tasks:

a.   Obtain stock price data at the end of each of the last 16 quarters, and fill in that information in Column A of your electronic spreadsheet. Historical stock price data are available on the Yahoo! finance website and on other websites. Your professor may offer some suggestions on where to obtain this information.

b.   Obtain the data on dividend per share for this firm for each of the last 16 quarters, and input that information in Column B of your electronic spreadsheet. When you obtain dividend data, recognize that the dividend is often listed on an annual basis. In this case, divide the annual dividend by 4 to obtain the quarterly dividend.

c.   Use "compute" statements to derive the quarterly return on your stock in Column C of your electronic spreadsheet. The return on the stock during any quarter is computed as follows. First, compute the stock price at the end of that quarter minus the stock price at the end of the previous quarter, then add the quarterly dividend, and then divide by the stock price at the end of the previous quarter.

d.   Input the S&P 500 stock index level as of the end of each of the 16 quarters in Column D of your electronic spreadsheet.

e.   Use "compute" statements to derive the quarterly stock market return in Column E, which is equal to the percentage change in the S&P 500 index level from the previous quarter.

f.   Using the tools in an electronic package, run a regression analysis in which your quarterly stock return (Column C) represents the dependent variable, and the stock market return (Column E) represents the independent variable. This analysis can be easily run by Excel or Lotus.

g.   Based on your regression results, what is the relationship between the market return and your stock's return? (The slope coefficient represents the estimate of your firm's beta, which is a measure of its systematic risk.)

h.   Based on your regression results, does it appear that there is a significant relationship between the market return and your stock's return? (The t-statistic for the slope coefficient can be assessed to determine whether there is a significant relationship.)

i.   Based on your regression results, what proportion of the variation in the stock's returns can be explained by movements (returns) in the stock market overall? (The R-SQUARED statistic measures the proportion of variation in the dependent variable that is explained by the independent variable in a regression model like the one described previously.) Does it appear that the stock's return is driven mainly by stock market movements or by other factors that are not captured in the regression model?

j.   What is the standard deviation of your stock's quarterly returns over the 16-quarter period? (You can easily compute the standard deviation of your column of stock return data by using a compute statement.) What is the standard deviation of the quarterly stock market returns (as measured by quarterly returns on the S&P 500 index) over the 16-quarter period? Is your stock more volatile than the stock market in general? If so, why do you think it is more volatile than the market?

k.   Assume that the average risk-free rate per quarter over the 16-quarter period is 1.5 percent. Determine the Sharpe index for your stock. (The Sharpe index is equal to your stock's average quarterly return minus the average risk-free rate, divided by the standard deviation of your stock's returns.) Determine the Treynor index for your stock. (The Treynor index is equal to your stock's average quarterly return minus the average risk-free rate, divided by the estimated beta of your stock.)

Using Excel to Conduct Analyses

Excel spreadsheets are useful for organizing numerical data. In addition, they can execute computations for you. Excel not only allows you to compute general statistics such as average and standard deviations of cells, but also can be used to conduct regression analysis. This appendix begins by describing the use of Excel to compute general statistics. Then, a background of regression analysis is provided, followed by a discussion of how Excel can be used to run regression analysis.

GENERAL STATISTICS

Some of the more popular computations are discussed here.

Creating a Compute Statement

If you want to determine the percentage change in a value from one period to the next, type the compute statement in a cell where you want to see the result. For example, assume that you identify the month and year in Column A and record the stock price of Dell, Inc. at the beginning of that month in Column B. To assess the performance or risk characteristics of stocks, you should first convert the stock price data into "returns." This allows you to compare performance and risk among different stocks. Since Dell does not pay a dividend, the return from investing in Dell stock over a period is simply the percentage change in the price. Assume you want to compute the monthly percentage change in the stock price. In cell C2, you can create a compute statement to derive the percentage change in price from the beginning of the first month until the beginning of the second month. A compute statement begins with an = sign. The proper compute statement to compute a percentage change for cell B2 is =(B2-B1)/B1. Assume that in cell C3, you want to derive the percentage change in Dell's stock price as of the month in cell B3 from the previous month B2. Type the compute statement =(B3-B2)/B2 in cell C3.

Using the COPY Command

If you need to repeat a particular compute statement for several different cells, you can use the COPY command as follows:

1. Place the cursor in the cell with the compute statement that you want to copy to other cells.
2. Click "Edit" and then click "Copy" on your menu bar.
3. Highlight the cells where you want that compute statement copied.
4. Hit the Enter key.

For example, assume that you have 30 monthly prices of Dell stock in Column B and have already calculated the percentage change in the stock price in cell C2 as explained above. (You did not have a percentage change in cell C1 because you needed two dates [cells B1 and B2] to derive your first percentage change.) You can place the cursor on cell C2, click "Edit" and then click "Copy" on your menu bar, highlight cells C3 to C30, and then hit the Enter key.

Computing an Average

You can compute the average of a set of cells as follows. Assume that you want to determine the mean monthly return on Dell stock shown in cells C2 to C30. Go to any blank cell (such as cell C31), and type the compute statement =AVERAGE(C2:C30).

Computing a Standard Deviation

You can compute the standard deviation of a set of cells as follows. Assume that you want to determine the standard deviation of the returns on Dell stock. In cell C32 (or in any blank cell where you want to see the result), type the compute statement =STDEV(C2:C30).

REGRESSION ANALYSIS

Various software packages are available to run regression analysis. The Excel package is recommended because of its simplicity. The following example illustrates the ease with which regression analysis can be run.

Assume that a financial institution wishes to measure the relationship between the change in the interest rate in a given period (Δi_t) and the change in the inflation rate in the previous period (ΔINF_{t-1}); that is, the financial institution wishes to assess the lagged impact of inflation on interest rates. Assume that the data over the last 20 periods are as follows:

COLUMN A PERIOD	COLUMN B Δi_t	COLUMN C ΔINF_{t-1}
1	.50%	.90%
2	.65	.75
3	−.70	−1.20
4	.50	.30
5	.40	.60
6	−.30	−.20
7	.60	.85
8	.75	.45
9	.10	−.05
10	1.10	1.35
11	.90	1.10
12	−.65	−.80
13	−.20	−.35
14	.40	.55
15	.30	.40
16	.60	.75

COLUMN A PERIOD	COLUMN B Δi_t	COLUMN C ΔINF_{t-1}
17	−.05	−.10
18	1.30	1.50
19	−.55	−.70
20	.15	.25

Assume the firm applies the following regression model to the data:

$$\Delta i_t = b_0 + b_1 \Delta INF_{t-1} + \mu$$

where Δi_t = **change in the interest rate in period t**
ΔINF_{t-1} = **change in the inflation rate in period $t-1$ (the previous period)**
b_0 and b_1 = **regression coefficients to be estimated by regression analysis**
μ = **error term**

Regression Analysis Using Excel

In our example, Δi_t is the dependent variable, and ΔINF_{t-1} is the independent variable. The first step is to input the two columns of data that were provided earlier (Columns B and C) into a file using Excel. Then you can perform regression analysis as follows. Click the Tools menu and then click "Data Analysis." If "Data Analysis" does not appear on your Tools menu, select "Add Ins." Select "Analysis Toolpak" and click "OK." You should now be able to choose "Data Analysis" from your Tools menu. Once you click "Data Analysis," you are presented with a new menu in which you should select "Regression." For "Input Y Range," identify the range of the dependent variable ($B$1:$B$20 in our example). Then for "Input X Range," identify the range of the independent variable ($C$1:CC20 in our example). Click "OK," and within a few seconds, the regression analysis will be complete. For our example, the output is as follows:

SUMMARY OUTPUT	
Multiple R	0.96884081
R-SQUARE	0.93865251
Adjusted R-SQUARE	0.93524431
Standard Error	0.1432744
Observations	20

ANOVA					
	df	SS	MS	F	SIGNIFICANCE F
Regression	1	5.653504056	5.653504	275.4105	2.34847E-12
Residual	18	0.369495944	0.020528		
Total	19	6.023			

	COEFFICIENTS	STANDARD ERROR	t STAT	P-VALUE	LOWER 95%	UPPER 95%
Intercept	0.0494173	0.035164424	1.405321	0.176951	−0.024460473	0.123295
X Variable 1	0.75774079	0.045659421	16.5955	2.35E-12	0.661813835	0.853668

The estimate of the so-called slope coefficient is about .76, which suggests that every 1 percent change in the inflation rate is associated with a .76 percent change (in the same direction) in the interest rate. The t-statistic is 16.6, which suggests that there is a significant relationship between Δi_t and ΔINF_{t-1}. The R-SQUARED statistic suggests that about 94 percent of the variation in Δi_t is explained by ΔINF_{t-1}. The correlation between Δi_t and ΔINF_{t-1} can also be measured by the correlation coefficient, which is the square root of the R-SQUARED statistic.

If you have more than one independent variable (multiple regression), you should place the independent variables next to each other in the file. Then, for the X-RANGE, identify this block of data. The output for the regression model will display the coefficient and standard error for each of the independent variables. The t-statistic can be estimated for each independent variable to test for significance. For multiple regression, the R-SQUARED statistic represents the percentage of variation in the dependent variable explained by the model as a whole.

Using Regression Analysis to Forecast

The regression results can be used to forecast future values of the dependent variable. In our example, the historical relationship between Δi_t and ΔINF_{t-1} can be expressed as

$$\Delta i_t = b_0 + b_1(\Delta INF_{t-1})$$

Assume that last period's change in inflation (ΔINF_{t-1}) was 1 percent. Given the estimated coefficients derived from regression analysis, the forecast for this period's Δi_t is

$$\Delta i_t = .0494\% + .7577(1\%)$$
$$= .8071\%$$

There are some obvious limitations that should be recognized when using regression analysis to forecast. First, if other variables that influence the dependent variable are not included in the model, the coefficients derived from the model may be improperly estimated. This can cause inaccurate forecasts. Second, some relationships are contemporaneous rather than lagged, which means that last period's value for ΔINF could not be used. Instead, a forecast would have to be derived for ΔINF, to use as input for forecasting Δi_t. If the forecast for ΔINF is poor, the forecast for Δi_t will likely be poor even if the regression model is properly specified.

Glossary

A

adjustable-rate mortgage (ARM) Mortgage that requires payments that adjust periodically according to market interest rates.

adverse selection problem In an insurance context, the problem for the insurance industry stemming from the fact that those who are most likely to purchase insurance are also those who are most likely to need it.

American depository receipts (ADRs) Certificates representing ownership of foreign stocks.

amortization schedule Schedule developed from the maturity and interest rate on a mortgage to determine monthly payments broken down into principal and interest.

annuity Even stream of payments over a given period of time.

annuity plans Plans provided by insurance companies that offer a predetermined amount of retirement income to individuals.

antitakeover amendments Changes in the corporate charter that make it more difficult and costly for the firm to be taken over by a potential acquiring firm.

appreciate Increase in the value of a foreign currency.

arbitrage activity In the securities industry, the purchasing of undervalued shares and the resale of these shares for a higher profit.

arbitrage firms (arbitrageurs) Securities firms that capitalize on discrepancies between prices of index futures and stocks.

arbitrage pricing theory (APT) Theory on the pricing of assets, which suggests that stock prices may be driven by a set of factors in addition to the market.

ask quote (ask price) Price at which a seller is willing to sell.

asset stripping A strategy of acquiring a firm, breaking it into divisions, segmenting the divisions, and then selling them separately.

at the money Refers to an option in which the prevailing price of the underlying security is equal to the exercise price.

B

back-end load A withdrawal fee assessed when money is withdrawn from a mutual fund.

balloon payment A required lump-sum payment of the principal of a loan.

balloon-payment mortgage Mortgage that requires payments for a three- to five-year period; at the end of the period, full payment of the principal is required.

banker's acceptance Agreement in which a commercial bank accepts responsibility for a future payment; it is commonly used for international trade transactions.

bank holding company (BHC) Company that owns a commercial bank.

Bank Insurance Fund Reserve fund used by the FDIC to close failing banks until 2006 when it was replaced by the Deposit Insurance Fund; the fund was supported with deposit insurance premiums paid by commercial banks.

basis Difference between the price movement of a futures contract and the price movement of the underlying security.

basis risk As applied to interest rate swaps, risk that the index used for an interest rate swap does not move perfectly in tandem with the floating-rate instrument specified in a swap arrangement. As applied to financial futures, risk that the futures prices do not move perfectly in tandem with the assets that are hedged.

bearer bonds Bonds that require the owner to clip coupons attached to the bonds and send them to the issuer to receive coupon payments.

behavioral finance The application of psychology to make financial decisions.

Beige Book A consolidated report of economic conditions in each of the Federal Reserve districts; used by the FOMC in formulating monetary policy.

best-efforts agreement Arrangement in which the securities firm does not guarantee a price on securities to be issued by a corporation, but states only that it will give its best effort to sell the securities at a reasonable price.

beta Sensitivity of an asset's returns to market returns; measured as the covariance between asset returns and market returns divided by the variance of market returns.

bid quote (bid price) Price a purchaser is willing to pay for a specific security.

Big Bang Deregulatory event in London in 1986 that allowed investment firms trading in the United States and Japan to trade in London and eliminated the fixed commission structure on securities transactions.

Board of Governors Composed of seven individual members appointed by the president of the United States; also called the Federal Reserve Board. The board helps regulate commercial banks and control monetary policy.

Bond Buyer Index Index based on 40 actively traded general obligation and revenue bonds.

bond price elasticity Sensitivity of bond prices to changes in the required rate of return.

bonds Debt obligations with long-term maturities issued by governments or corporations.

Bretton Woods era Period from 1944 to 1971, when exchange rates were fixed (maintained within 1 percent of a specified rate).

bridge loans Funds provided as temporary financing until other sources of long-term funds can be obtained; commonly provided by securities firms to firms experiencing leveraged buyouts.

broker One who executes securities transactions between two parties.

bullet loan Loan structured so that interest payments and the loan principal are to be paid off in one lump sum at a specified future date.

business finance companies Finance companies that concentrate on purchasing credit contracts from retailers and dealers.

C

call option Contract that grants the owner the right to purchase a specified financial instrument for a specified price within a specified period of time.

call premium Difference between a bond's call price and its par value.

call provision (call feature) Provision that allows the initial issuer of bonds to buy back the bonds at a specified price.

callable certificates of deposit (CDs) CDs that can be called by the financial institution, forcing an earlier maturity.

callable swap (swaption) Swap of fixed-rate payments for floating-rate payments, whereby the party making the fixed payments has the right to terminate the swap prior to maturity.

CAMELS ratings Characteristics used to rate bank risk.

capital As related to banks, capital is mainly composed of retained earnings and proceeds received from issuing stock.

capital appreciation funds Mutual funds composed of stocks of firms that have potential for very high growth, but may be unproven.

capital asset pricing model (CAPM) Theory that suggests the return of an asset is influenced by the risk-free rate, the market return, and the covariance between asset returns and market returns.

capital markets Financial markets that facilitate the flow of long-term funds.

capital market securities Long-term securities, such as bonds, whose maturities are more than one year.

capital ratio Ratio of capital to assets.

captive finance subsidiary (CFS) Wholly owned subsidiary of a finance company whose primary purpose is to finance sales of the parent company's products and purchase receivables of the parent company.

cash flow underwriting   Method by which insurance companies adapt insurance premiums to interest rates.

Central Liquidity Facility (CLF)   Facility that acts as a lender for credit unions to accommodate seasonal funding and specialized needs or to boost liquidity.

certificate of deposit (CD)   Deposit offered by depository institutions that specifies a maturity, a deposit amount, and an interest rate.

chattel mortgage bond   Bond that is secured by personal property.

circuit breakers   Used to temporarily halt the trading of some securities or contracts on an exchange.

closed-end funds   Mutual funds that do not repurchase the shares they sell.

coincident economic indicators   Economic indicators that tend to reach their peaks and troughs at the same time as business cycles.

collateralized mortgage obligations (CMOs)   Represent securities that are backed by mortgages; segmented into classes (or tranches) that dictate the timing of the payments.

commercial paper   Short-term securities (usually unsecured) issued by well-known creditworthy firms.

commission brokers (floor brokers)   Brokers who execute orders for their customers.

common stock   Securities representing partial ownership of a corporation.

consumer finance companies   Finance companies that concentrate on direct loans to consumers.

contagion effects   Adverse effects of a single firm that become contagious throughout the industry.

convertible bonds   Bonds that can be converted into a specified number of the firm's common stock.

corporate bonds   Bonds issued by corporations in need of long-term funds.

covered call   Sale of a call option to partially cover against the possible decline in the price of a stock that is being held.

covered interest arbitrage   Act of capitalizing on higher foreign interest rates while covering the position with a simultaneous forward sale.

credit crunch   A period during which banks are less willing to extend credit; normally results from an increased probability that some borrowers will default on loans.

credit default swap   A privately negotiated contract that protects investors against the risk of default on particular debt securities.

credit risk   The risk of loss that will occur when a counterparty defaults on a contract.

cross-hedging   The use of a futures contract on one financial instrument to hedge a financial institution's position in a different financial instrument.

crowding-out effect   Phenomenon that occurs when insufficient loanable funds are available for potential borrowers, such as corporations and individuals, as a result of excessive borrowing by the Treasury. Because limited loanable funds are available to satisfy all borrowers, interest rates rise in response to the increased demand for funds, thereby crowding some potential borrowers out of the market.

currency call option   Contract that grants the owner the right to purchase a specified currency for a specified price, within a specified period of time.

currency futures contract   Standardized contract that specifies an amount of a particular currency to be exchanged on a specified date and at a specified exchange rate.

currency put option   Contract that grants the owner the right to sell a specified currency for a specified price, within a specified period of time.

currency swap   An agreement that allows the periodic swap of one currency for another at specified exchange rates; it essentially represents a series of forward contracts.

D

day traders   Traders of financial futures contracts who close out their contracts on the same day that they initiate them.

dealers   Securities firms that make a market in specific securities by adjusting their inventories.

debentures   Bonds that are backed only by the general credit of the issuing firm.

debt-for-equity swap   An exchange of debt for an equity interest in the debtor's assets.

debt securities   Securities that represent credit provided to the initial issuer by the purchaser.

default risk Credit risk; risk that loans provided or securities purchased will default, cutting off principal and/or interest payments.

defensive open market operations Implemented to offset the impact of other market conditions that affect the level of funds.

deficit units Individual, corporate, or government units that need to borrow funds.

defined-benefit plan Pension plan in which contributions are dictated by the benefits that will eventually be provided.

defined-contribution plan Pension plan in which benefits are determined by the accumulated contributions and on the fund's investment performance.

demand deposit account Deposit account that offers checking services.

demand-pull inflation Inflation caused by excess demand for goods.

Deposit Insurance Fund Reserve fund used by the FDIC to close failing banks. The fund is supported by deposit insurance premiums paid by commercial banks.

Depository Institutions Deregulation and Monetary Control Act (DIDMCA) Act that deregulated some aspects of the depository institutions industry, such as removing the ceiling interest rates on deposits and allowing NOW accounts nationwide.

depreciate Decrease in the value of a foreign currency.

derivative instruments Instruments created from a previously existing security.

derivative markets Markets that allow for the buying or selling of derivative securities.

derivative securities Financial contracts whose values are derived from the values of underlying assets.

direct access broker A trading platform for a computer website that allows investors to trade stocks without using a broker.

direct exchange rate The value of a currency in U.S. dollars.

direct lease loan Occurs when a bank purchases assets and then leases the assets to a firm.

dirty float System whereby exchange rates are market determined without boundaries, but subject to government intervention.

discount bonds Bonds that sell below their par value.

discount brokerage firms Brokerage firms that focus on executing transactions.

discount rate Interest rate charged on loans provided by the Federal Reserve to depository institutions.

disintermediation Process in which savers transfer funds from intermediaries to alternative investments with market-determined rates.

Dow Jones Industrial Average Index of stocks representing 30 large firms.

dual banking system Regulatory framework of the banking system, composed of federal and state regulators.

duration Measurement of the life of a bond on a present value basis.

duration gap Difference between the average duration of a bank's assets versus its liabilities.

dynamic asset allocation Switching between risky and low-risk investment positions over time in response to changing expectations.

dynamic open market operations Implemented to increase or decrease the level of funds.

E

economies of scale Reduction in average cost per unit as the level of output increases.

effective yield Yield on foreign money market securities adjusted for the exchange rate.

Employee Retirement Income Security Act (ERISA) Act that provided three vesting schedule options from which a pension fund could choose. It also stipulated that pension contributions be invested in a prudent manner and that employees can transfer any vested pension amounts to new employers as they switch employers.

employee stock ownership plans (ESOPs) Plans to offer periodic contributions of a corporation's stock to participating employees; ESOPs have been used as a means of preventing a takeover.

equity REIT REIT (real estate investment trust) that invests directly in properties.

equity securities Securities such as common stock and preferred stock that represent ownership in a business.

equity swap   Swap arrangement involving the exchange of interest payments for payments linked to the degree of change in a stock index.

Euro-commercial paper (Euro-CP)   Securities issued in Europe without the backing of a bank syndicate.

Eurodollar certificate of deposit   Large U.S. dollar–denominated deposits in non-U.S. banks.

Eurodollar floating-rate CDs (FRCDs)   Eurodollar CDs with floating interest rates that adjust periodically to the LIBOR.

Eurodollar loans   Short-term loans denominated in dollars provided to corporations and governments by branches of U.S. banks located outside the United States and some foreign-owned banks.

Eurodollar market   Market in Europe in which dollars are deposited and loaned for short time periods.

Eurodollars   Large dollar-denominated deposits accepted by banks outside the United States.

Euronotes   Notes issued in European markets in bearer form, with short-term maturities.

event risk   An increase in the perceived risk of default on bonds resulting from the restructuring of debt or an acquisition.

exchange rate risk   Risk that currency values will change in a manner that adversely affects future cash flows.

exchange-traded funds (ETFs)   Mutual funds that are designed to mimic particular stock indexes and are traded on a stock exchange like stocks.

exercise price (strike price)   Price at which the instrument underlying an option contract can be purchased (in the case of a call option) or sold (in the case of a put option).

extendable swap   Swap of fixed payments for floating payments that contains an extendable feature allowing the party making fixed payments to extend the swap period if desired.

F

factor   Firm that purchases accounts receivable at a discount and is responsible for processing and collecting on the balances of these accounts; finance companies commonly have subsidiaries that serve as factors.

Federal Deposit Insurance Corporation (FDIC)   Federal agency that insures the deposits of commercial banks.

Federal Deposit Insurance Corporation Improvement Act (FDICIA)   Legislation enacted in 1991 to penalize banks that engage in high-risk activities and reduce the regulatory costs of closing troubled banks.

federal funds market   Market that facilitates the flow of funds from banks that have excess funds to banks that are in need of funds.

federal funds rate   Interest rate charged on loans between depository institutions.

Federal Home Loan Mortgage Association (Freddie Mac)   Issues mortgage-backed securities and uses the proceeds to purchase mortgages.

Federal National Mortgage Association (Fannie Mae)   Issues mortgage-backed securities and uses the funds to purchase mortgages.

Federal Open Market Committee (FOMC)   Composed of the seven members of the Board of Governors plus the presidents of five Federal Reserve district banks. The main role of the FOMC is to control monetary policy.

Federal Reserve   Central bank of the United States.

Federal Reserve district bank   A regional government bank that facilitates operations within the banking system by clearing checks, replacing old currency, providing loans to banks, and conducting research; there are 12 Federal Reserve district banks.

financial futures contract   Standardized agreement to deliver or receive a specified amount of a specified financial instrument at a specified price and date.

Financial Institutions Reform, Recovery, and Enforcement Act (FIRREA)   Act intended to enhance the safety of savings institutions; prevented savings institutions from investing in junk bonds, increased capital requirements, and increased the penalties for fraud.

financial market   Market in which financial assets (or securities) such as stocks and bonds are traded.

Financial Services Modernization Act (Gramm-Leach-Bliley Act)   Legislation enacted in 1999 that allows affiliations between banks, securities firms, and insurance companies; repealed the Glass-Steagall Act.

first mortgage bond   Bond that has first claim on specified assets as collateral.

Fisher effect   Positive relationship between interest rates and expected inflation.

fixed-rate mortgage   Mortgage that requires payments based on a fixed interest rate.

floor brokers Individuals who facilitate the trading of stocks on the New York Stock Exchange by executing transactions for their clients.

floor traders (locals) Members of a futures exchange who trade futures contracts for their own account.

flotation costs Costs of placing securities.

flow-of-funds accounts Reports on the amount of funds channeled to and from various sectors.

foreign exchange derivatives Instruments created to lock in a foreign exchange transaction, such as forward contracts, futures contracts, currency swaps, and currency options contracts.

foreign exchange market The financial market that facilitates the exchange of currencies.

forward contract Contract typically negotiated with a commercial bank that allows a customer to purchase or sell a specified amount of a particular foreign currency at a specified exchange rate on a specified future date.

forward market Market that facilitates the trading of forward contracts; commercial banks serve as intermediaries in the market by matching up participants who wish to buy a currency forward with other participants who wish to sell the currency forward.

forward rate In the context of the term structure of interest rates, the market's forecast of the future interest rate. In the context of foreign exchange, the exchange rate at which a specified currency can be purchased or sold at a specified future point in time.

forward swap Involves an exchange of interest payments that does not begin until a specified future point in time.

freely floating system System whereby exchange rates are market determined, without any government intervention.

front-end load A fee paid when money is invested in a mutual fund.

full-service brokerage firms Brokerage firms that provide complete information and advice about securities, in addition to executing transactions.

fundamental analysis Method of valuing stocks that relies on fundamental financial characteristics (such as earnings) about the firm and its corresponding industry.

fundamental forecasting Is based on fundamental relationships between economic variables and exchange rates.

futures contract Standardized contract allowing one to purchase or sell a specified amount of a specified instrument (such as a security or currency) for a specified price and at a specified future point in time.

G

gap Defined as rate-sensitive assets minus rate-sensitive liabilities.

gap ratio Measured as the value of rate-sensitive assets divided by the value of rate-sensitive liabilities.

Garn-St Germain Act Act passed in 1982 that allowed for the creation of money market deposit accounts (MMDAs), loosened lending guidelines for federally chartered savings institutions, and allowed failing depository institutions to be acquired by other depository institutions outside the state.

general obligation bonds Bonds that provide payments that are supported by the municipal government's ability to tax.

Glass-Steagall Act Act in 1933 that separated commercial banking and investment banking activities; largely repealed in 1999.

global crowding out Situation in which excessive government borrowing in one country can cause higher interest rates in other countries.

global junk bonds Low quality bonds issued globally by governments and corporations.

golden parachute Provisions that allow specific employees to receive specified compensation if they are terminated from their positions.

Government National Mortgage Association (Ginnie Mae) Agency that guarantees the timely payment of principal and interest to investors who purchase securities backed by mortgages.

graduated-payment mortgage (GPM) Mortgage that allows borrowers to initially make small payments on the mortgage; the payments are increased on a graduated basis.

greenmail The accumulation of shares of a target, followed by sale of the shares back to the target; the target purchases the shares back (at a premium) to remove the threat of a takeover.

gross interest expense Interest paid on deposits and on other borrowed funds.

gross interest income Interest income generated from all assets.

group life policy   Policy provided to a group of policyholders with some common bond.

growing-equity mortgage   Mortgage where the initial monthly payments are low and increase over time.

growth and income funds   Mutual funds that contain a combination of growth stocks, high-dividend stocks, and fixed-income bonds.

growth funds   Mutual funds containing stocks of firms that are expected to grow at a higher than average rate; for investors who are willing to accept a moderate degree of risk.

H

health maintenance organizations (HMOs)   Intermediaries between purchasers and providers of health care.

hedge funds   Mutual funds that sell shares to wealthy individuals and financial institutions and use the proceeds to invest in securities; require a larger investment than open-end mutual funds, are subject to less regulation, and tend to be more risky.

hedgers   Participants in financial futures markets who take positions in contracts to reduce their exposure to risk.

high-yield funds   Mutual funds composed of bonds that offer high yields (junk bonds) and have a relatively high degree of credit risk.

highly leveraged transactions (HLTs)   Credit provided that results in a debt-to-asset ratio of at least 75 percent.

I

immunize   The act of insulating a security portfolio from interest rate movements.

impact lag   Lag time between when a policy is implemented by the government and the time when the policy has an effect on the economy.

imperfect markets   Markets in which buyers and sellers of securities do not have full access to information and cannot always break down securities to the precise size they desire.

implementation lag   Lag time between when the government recognizes a problem and the time when it implements a policy to resolve the problem.

income funds   Mutual funds composed of bonds that offer periodic coupon payments.

indenture   Legal document specifying the rights and obligations of both the issuing firm and the bondholders.

index arbitrage   Act of capitalizing on discrepancies between prices of index futures and stocks.

index funds   Mutual funds that are designed to match the performance of an existing stock index.

indirect exchange rate   The value of a currency specified as the number of units of that currency equal to a U.S. dollar.

informal line of credit   Financing arrangement that allows a business to borrow up to a specified amount within a specified period of time.

initial margin   A margin deposit established by a customer with a brokerge firm before a margin transaction can be executed.

initial public offering (IPO)   A first-time offering of shares by a specific firm to the public.

installment loans   Loans to individuals to finance purchases of cars and household products.

insured plans   Pension plans that are used to purchase annuity policies so that the life insurance companies can provide benefits to employees upon retirement.

interest-inelastic   Insensitive to interest rates.

interest rate cap   Arrangement that offers a party interest payments in periods when the interest rate on a specific money market instrument exceeds a specified ceiling rate; the payments are based on the amount by which the interest rate exceeds the ceiling as applied to the notional principal specified in the agreement.

interest rate collar   The purchase of an interest rate cap and the simultaneous sale of an interest rate floor.

interest rate floor   Agreement in which one party offers an interest rate payment in periods when the interest rate on a specified money market instrument is below a specified floor rate.

interest rate futures   Financial futures contracts on debt securities such as Treasury bills, notes, or bonds.

interest rate parity   Theory that suggests the forward discount (or premium) is dependent on the interest rate differential between the two countries of concern.

interest rate risk   Risk that an asset will decline in value in response to interest rate movements.

interest rate swap   Arrangement whereby one party exchanges one set of interest payments for another.

international mutual fund Portfolio of international stocks created and managed by a financial institution; individuals can invest in international stocks by purchasing shares of an international mutual fund.

in the money Describes a call option whose premium is above the exercise price or a put option whose premium is below the exercise price.

investment-grade bonds Bonds that are rated Baa or better by Moody's and BBB or better by Standard & Poor's.

investment-grade securities Securities that are rated as "medium" quality or higher by rating agencies.

issue costs Cost of issuing stock, including printing, legal registration, and accounting expenses.

J

junk bonds Corporate bonds that are perceived to have a high degree of risk.

junk commercial paper Low-rated commercial paper.

L

lagging economic indicators Economic indicators that tend to rise or fall a few months after business-cycle expansions and contractions.

leading economic indicators Economic indicators that tend to rise or fall a few months before business-cycle expansions and contractions.

letter of credit (L/C) Guarantee by a bank on the financial obligations of a firm that owes payment (usually an importer).

leveraged buyout (LBO) A buyout of a firm that is financed mostly with debt.

leverage measure Measure of financial leverage; defined as assets divided by equity.

limit orders Requests by customers to purchase or sell securities at a specified price or better.

liquidity Ability to sell assets easily without loss of value.

liquidity premium theory (liquidity preference theory) Theory that suggests the yield to maturity is higher for illiquid securities, other things being equal.

liquidity risk Potential price distortions due to a lack of liquidity.

load funds Mutual funds that have a sales charge imposed by brokerage firms that sell the funds.

loan commitment Obligation by a bank to provide a specified loan amount to a particular firm upon the firm's request.

loan loss provision A reserve account established by a bank in anticipation of loan losses in the future.

loan participation Arrangement in which several banks pool funds to provide a loan to a corporation.

loanable funds theory Theory that suggests the market interest rate is determined by the factors that control the supply and demand for loanable funds.

locational arbitrage Arbitrage intended to capitalize on a price (such as a foreign exchange rate quote) discrepancy between two locations.

London Interbank Offer Rate (LIBOR) Interest rate charged on interbank loans.

long hedge The purchase of financial futures contracts to hedge against a possible decrease in interest rates.

long-term equity anticipations (LEAPs) Stock options with relatively long-term expiration dates.

low-coupon bonds Bonds that pay low coupon payments; most of the expected return to investors is attributed to the large discount in the bond's price.

M

M1 Definition of the money supply; composed of currency held by the public plus checking accounts.

M2 Definition of the money supply; composed of Ml plus savings accounts, small time deposits, MMDAs, and some other items.

M3 Definition of the money supply; composed of M2 plus large time deposits and other items.

maintenance margin A margin requirement that reduces the risk that participants will later default on their obligations.

margin account An account established with a broker that allows the investor to purchase stock on margin by putting up cash for part of the cost and borrowing the remainder from the broker.

margin call Call from a broker to participants in futures contracts (or other investments) informing them that they must increase their equity.

margin requirements The proportion of invested funds that must be paid in cash versus borrowed; set by the Federal Reserve.

market-based forecasting   Process of developing forecasts from market indicators.

market-makers   Individuals who facilitate the trading of stocks on the Nasdaq by standing ready to buy or sell specific stocks in response to customer orders made through a tele-communications network.

market microstructure   Process by which securities are traded.

market orders   Requests by customers to purchase or sell securities at the market price existing when the order reaches the exchange floor.

market risk   Risk that the stock market experiences lower prices in response to adverse economic conditions or pessimistic expectations.

matched funding   Strategy in which investment decisions are made with the objective of matching planned outflow payments.

McFadden Act of 1927   Act preventing all banks from establishing branches across state lines.

merger-conversion   Procedure used in acquisitions whereby a mutual S&L converts to a stock-owned S&L before either acquiring or being acquired by another firm.

mixed forecasting   The use of a combination of forecasting techniques, resulting in a weighted average of the various forecasts developed.

money market deposit account (MMDA)   Deposit account that pays interest and allows limited checking and does not specify a maturity.

money market mutual funds   Mutual funds that concentrate their investment in money market securities.

money markets   Financial markets that facilitate the flow of short-term funds.

money market securities   Short-term securities, such as Treasury bills or certificates of deposit, whose maturities are one year or less.

moral hazard problem   In a banking context, refers to the deposit insurance pricing system that existed until the early 1990s; insurance premiums per $100 of deposits were similar across all commercial banks. This system caused an indirect subsidy from safer banks to risky banks and encouraged banks to take excessive risk. In an insurance context, the problem for the insurance industry stemming from the fact that those who have insurance may take more risks because they are protected against losses.

mortgage-backed securities (MBS)   Securities isssued by a financial institution that are backed by a pool of mortgages; also called *pass-through securities.*

mortgage REIT   A REIT (real estate investment trust) that invests in mortgage and construction loans.

multifund mutual fund   A mutual fund composed of different mutual funds.

Municipal Bond Index (MBI) futures   Futures contract allowing for the future purchase or sale of municipal bonds at a specified price.

municipal bonds   Debt securities issued by state and local governments, which can usually be classified as either general obligation bonds or revenue bonds.

mutual fund   An investment company that sells shares representing an interest in a portfolio of securities.

mutual S&Ls   S&Ls that are owned by depositors.

mutual-to-stock conversion   Procedure by savings institutions to shift the ownership structure from depositors to shareholders.

N

National Association of Insurance Commissioners (NAIC)   Agency that facilitates cooperation among the various state agencies when an insurance issue is a concern.

National Association of Securities Dealers (NASD)   Regulator of the securities industry.

National Association of Securities Dealers Automatic Quotations (Nasdaq)   A service for the over-the-counter market that reports immediate price quotations for many of the stocks.

National Credit Union Administration (NCUA)   Regulator of credit unions; the NCUA participates in the creation of new CUs, examines the financial condition of CUs, and supervises any liquidations or mergers.

National Credit Union Share Insurance Fund (NCUSIF)   Agency that insures deposits at credit unions.

negotiable certificate of deposit (NCD)   Deposit account with a minimum deposit of $100,000 that requires a specified maturity; there is a secondary market for these deposits.

net asset value (NAV)   Financial characteristic used to describe a mutual fund's value per share; estimated as the market value of the securities comprising the mutual fund, plus any accrued interest or dividends, minus any expenses. This value is divided by the number of shares outstanding.

net exposure   In the context of futures markets, the difference between asset and liability positions.

net interest margin   Estimated as interest revenues minus interest expenses, divided by assets.

noise traders   Uninformed investors whose buy and sell positions push the stock price away from its fundamental value.

noise trading   Theory used to explain that stock prices may deviate from their fundamental values as a result of the buy and sell positions of uninformed investors (called "noise traders"); a market correction may not eliminate the discrepancy if the informed traders are unwilling to capitalize on the discrepancy (because of uncertainty surrounding the stock's fundamental value).

no-load funds   Mutual funds that do not have a sales charge, meaning that they are not promoted by brokerage firms.

noninterest expenses   Expenses, such as salaries and office equipment, that are unrelated to interest payments on deposits or borrowed funds.

noninterest income   Income resulting from fees charged or services provided.

note issuance facility (NIF)   Commitment in which a bank agrees to purchase the commercial paper of a firm if the firm cannot place its paper in the market at an acceptable interest rate.

notional principal   Value to which interest rates from interest rate swaps are applied to determine the interest payments involved.

NOW (negotiable order of withdrawal) accounts   Deposit accounts that allow unlimited checking and pay interest.

O

open-end funds   Mutual funds that are willing to repurchase the shares they sell from investors at any time.

Open Market Desk   Division of the New York Federal Reserve district bank that is responsible for conducting open market operations.

open market operations   The Fed's buying and selling of government securities (through the Trading Desk).

operational risk   The risk of losses as a result of inadequate management or controls.

option premium   Price paid for an option contract.

organized exchange   Visible marketplace for secondary market transactions.

origination   Decisions by a firm (with the help of a securities firm) on how much stock or bonds to issue, the type of stock (or bonds) to be issued, and the price at which the stock (or bonds) should be sold.

out of the money   Describes a call option whose premium is below the exercise price or a put option whose premium is above the exercise price.

over-the-counter (OTC) market   Market used to facilitate transactions of securities not listed on organized exchanges.

P

participation certificates (PCs)   Certificates sold by the Federal Home Loan Mortgage Association; the proceeds are used to purchase conventional mortgages from financial institutions.

pass-through securities   Securities issued by a financial institution and backed by a group of mortgages. The mortgage interest and principal are sent to the financial institution, which then transfers the payments to the owners of the pass-through securities after deducting a service fee. Also called *mortgage-backed securities.*

Pension Benefit Guaranty Corporation (PBGC)   Established as a result of ERISA to provide insurance on pension plans.

perfect markets   Markets in which all information about any securities for sale would be freely and continuously available to investors. Furthermore, all securities for sale could be broken down into any size desired by investors, and transaction costs would be nonexistent.

plain vanilla swap   Involves the periodic exchange of fixed-rate payments for floating-rate payments.

poison pills   Special rights awarded to shareholders or specific managers on the occurrence of specified events; used to defend against takeover attempts.

policy directive   Statement provided by the FOMC to the Trading Desk regarding the target money supply range.

portfolio insurance   Program trading combined with the trading of stock index futures to hedge against market movements.

position traders   Traders of financial futures contracts who maintain their futures positions for relatively long periods (such as weeks or months) before closing them out.

preemptive rights   Priority given to a particular group of people to purchase newly issued stock, before other investors are given the opportunity to purchase the stock.

preferred habitat theory   Theory that suggests that although investors and borrowers may normally concentrate on a particular natural maturity market, certain events may cause them to wander from it.

preferred stock   Securities representing partial ownership of a corporation, without significant voting rights; it provides owners dividends, but normally does not provide a share of the firm's profits.

prepayment risk   The possibility that the assets to be hedged may be prepaid earlier than their designated maturity; also applies to mortgages.

primary market   Market where securities are initially issued.

prime rate   Interest rate charged on loans by banks to their most creditworthy customers.

private placement   Process in which a corporation sells new securities directly without using underwriting services.

privatization   Process of converting government ownership of businesses to private ownership.

program trading   The simultaneous buying and selling of a portfolio of at least 15 different stocks valued at more than $1 million.

projective funding   Strategy that offers pension fund managers some flexibility in constructing a pension portfolio that can benefit from expected market and interest rate movements.

prospectus   A pamphlet that discloses relevant financial data on the firm and provisions applicable to the security.

protective covenants   Restrictions enforced by a bond indenture (or a bank loan) that protect the bondholders (or the bank) from an increase in risk; such restrictions may include limits on the dividends paid, the salaries paid, and the additional debt the firm can issue.

purchasing power parity (PPP)   Theory that suggests exchange rates adjust, on average, by a percentage that reflects the inflation differential between the two countries of concern.

pure expectations theory   Theory suggesting that the shape of the yield curve is determined solely by interest rates.

put option   Contract that grants the owner the right to sell a specified financial instrument for a specified price within a specified period of time.

putable swap   Swap of fixed-rate payments for floating-rate payments whereby the party making floating-rate payments has the right to terminate the swap.

R

rate-capped swap   Swap arrangement involving fixed-rate payments for floating-rate payments, whereby the floating payments are capped.

real estate investment trust (REIT)   Closed-end mutual fund that invests in real estate or mortgages.

real estate mortgage conduit (REMIC)   Allows financial institutions to sell mortgage assets and issue mortgage-backed securities.

real interest rate   Nominal interest rate adjusted for inflation.

recognition lag   Lag time between when a problem arises and when it is recognized by the government.

registered bonds   Require the issuer to maintain records of who owns the bonds and automatically send coupon payments to the owners.

registration statement   Statement of relevant financial information disclosed by a corporation issuing securities, which is intended to ensure that accurate information is disclosed by the issuing corporation.

Regulation Q   Bank regulation that limited the interest rate banks could pay on deposits.

reinsurance   Manner by which insurance companies can allocate a portion of their return and risk to other insurance companies, which share in insuring large policies.

repurchase agreement (repo)   Agreement in which a bank (or some other firm) sells some of its government security holdings, with a commitment to purchase those securities back at a later date. This agreement essentially reflects a loan from the time the firm sold the securities until the securities are repurchased.

reserve requirement ratio   Percentage of deposits that commercial banks must maintain as required reserves. This ratio is sometimes used by the Fed as a monetary policy tool.

Resolution Trust Corporation (RTC)   Agency created in 1989 to help bail out failing savings institutions. The RTC liquidated an institution's assets and reimbursed depositors or sold the savings institution to another depository institution.

retail certificate of deposit (retail CD)   Deposit requiring a specific minimum amount of funds to be deposited for a specified period of time.

return on assets (ROA)   Defined as net income divided by assets.

return on equity (ROE) Defined as net income divided by equity.

revenue bonds Bonds that provide payments that are supported by the revenue generated by the project.

reverse leveraged buyout (reverse LBO) Process of issuing new stock after engaging in a leveraged buyout and improving the firm's performance.

reverse repo The purchase of securities by one party from another with an agreement to sell them in the future.

revolving credit loan Financing arrangement that obligates the bank to loan some specified maximum amount of funds over a specified period of time.

S

S&P 500 Index Futures Futures contract allowing for the future purchase or sale of the S&P 500 index at a specified price.

Savings Association Insurance Fund (SAIF) Insuring agency for S&Ls from 1989 until 2006.

secondary market Market where securities are resold.

secondary stock offering A new stock offering by a firm that already has stock outstanding.

securities Certificates that represent a claim on the issuer.

Securities Act of 1933 Intended to ensure complete disclosure of relevant information on publicly offered securities and prevent fraudulent practices in selling these securities.

Securities and Exchange Commission (SEC) Agency that regulates the issuance of securities, disclosure rules for issuers, the exchanges, and participating brokerage firms.

Securities Exchange Act of 1934 Intended to ensure complete disclosure of relevant information on securities traded in secondary markets.

securities gains and losses Bank accounting term that reflects the gains or losses generated from the sale of securities.

Securities Investor Protection Corporation (SIPC) Offers insurance on cash and securities deposited at brokerage firms.

securitization Pooling and repackaging of loans into securities, which are sold to investors.

segmented markets theory Theory that suggests investors and borrowers choose securities with maturities that satisfy their forecasted cash needs.

semistrong-form efficiency Security prices reflect all public information, including announcements by firms, economic news or events, and political news or events.

shared-appreciation mortgage Mortgage that allows a home purchaser to pay a below-market interest rate; in return, the lender shares in the appreciation of the home price.

shareholder activism Actions taken by shareholders to correct a firm's deficiencies so that the stock price may improve.

Sharpe index Measure of risk-adjusted return; defined as the asset's excess mean return beyond the mean risk-free rate, divided by the standard deviation of returns of the asset of concern.

shelf-registration Registration with the SEC in advance of public placement of securities.

short hedge The sale of financial futures contracts to hedge against a possible increase in interest rates.

short selling The sale of securities that are borrowed, with the intent of buying those securities to repay what was borrowed.

Single European Act of 1987 Act that called for a reduction in barriers between European countries. This allowed for easier trade and capital flows throughout Europe.

sinking-fund provision Requirement that the firm retire a specific amount of the bond issue each year.

Smithsonian Agreement Agreement among major countries to devalue the dollar against some currencies and widen the boundaries around each exchange rate from 1 percent to 2.25 percent.

sovereign risk As applied to swaps, risk that a country's political conditions could prevent one party in the swap from receiving payments due.

specialists Individuals who facilitate the trading of stocks on the New York Stock Exchange by taking positions in specific stocks; they stand ready to buy or sell these stocks on the trading floor.

specialty funds Mutual funds that focus on a group of companies sharing a particular characteristic.

speculators Those who take positions to benefit from future price movements.

spot exchange rate Present exchange rate.

spread Used to represent the difference between bid and ask quotes. This term is also sometimes used to reflect the difference between the average interest rate earned on assets and the average interest rate paid on liabilities.

Standard & Poor's 500 index   Index of stocks of 500 large firms.

standby letter of credit   Agreement that backs a customer's financial obligation.

stock index futures   Financial futures contracts on stock indexes.

stock index option   Provides the right to trade a specified stock index at a specified price by a specified expiration date.

stop-buy order   Order to purchase a particular security when the price reaches a specified level above the current market price; often used in short sales.

stop-loss order   Order of a sale of a specific security when the price reaches a specified minimum.

strike price (exercise price)   Price at which an option can be exercised.

stripped securities   Securities that are stripped of their coupon payments to create two separate types of securities: (1) a principal-only part that pays a future lump sum, and (2) an interest-only part that pays coupon payments, but no principal.

STRIPS   Stripped Treasury securities; acronym for Separate Trading of Registered Interest and Principal of Securities.

strong-form efficiency   Security prices fully reflect all information, including private (insider) information.

subordinated debentures   Debentures that have claims against the firm's assets that are junior to the claims of both mortgage bonds and regular debentures.

surplus units   Individual, business, or government units that have excess funds that can be invested.

swap options (swaptions)   Options on interest rate swaps.

systematic risk   Risk that is attributable to market movements and cannot be diversified away.

T

T-bill discount   Percentage by which the price paid for a Treasury bill is less than the par value.

technical analysis   Method of forecasting future stock prices with the use of historical stock price patterns.

technical forecasting   Involves the use of historical exchange rate data to predict future values.

term insurance   Temporary insurance over a specified term; the policy does not build a cash value.

term loan   Business loan used to finance the purchase of fixed assets.

term structure of interest rates   Relationship between the term remaining until maturity and the annualized yield of debt securities.

theory of rational expectations   Suggests that the public will consider the historical effects of money supply growth when forecasting the effects of prevailing money supply growth.

time deposits   Deposits that cannot be withdrawn until a specified maturity date.

time-series model   Examines moving averages and allows forecasters to develop rules.

Trading Desk   Located at the New York Federal Reserve district bank, it is used to carry out orders from the FOMC about open market operations.

Treasury bills   Securities issued by the Treasury that have maturities of one year or less.

Treynor index   Measure of risk-adjusted return; defined as the asset's excess mean return beyond the mean risk-free rate, divided by the beta of the asset of concern.

triangular arbitrage   Buying or selling a currency that is subject to a mispriced cross exchange rate.

trustee   Appointed to represent the bondholders in all matters concerning the bond issue.

U

underwrite   Act of guaranteeing a specific price to the initial issuer of securities.

underwriting spread   Difference between the price at which a securities firm expects to sell securities and the price it is willing to pay the issuing firm.

underwriting syndicate   Group of securities firms that are required to underwrite a portion of a corporation's newly issued securities.

universal life insurance   Combines the features of term and whole life insurance. It specifies a period of time over which the policy will exist but also builds a cash value for policyholders over time.

usury laws   Laws that enforce a maximum interest rate that can be imposed on loans to households.

V

variable life insurance Insurance in which benefits awarded by the life insurance company to a beneficiary vary with the assets backing the policy.

variable-rate bonds Bonds whose coupon rates adjust to market interest rates over time.

W

weak-form efficiency Theory that suggests that security prices reflect all market-related data, such as historical security price movements and volume of securities traded.

whole life insurance Insurance that protects the insured policyholder until death or as long as premiums are promptly paid; the policy builds a cash value that the policyholder is entitled to even if the policy is canceled.

working capital loan Business loan designed to support ongoing operations, typically for a short-term period.

writer The seller of an option contract.

Y

yield curve Curve depicting the relationship between the term remaining until maturity and the annualized yield of Treasury securities.

yield to maturity Discount rate at which the present value of future payments would equal the security's current price.

Z

zero-coupon bonds Bonds that have no coupon payments.

zero-coupon-for-floating swap Swap arrangement calling for one party to swap a lump-sum payment at maturity in exchange for periodic floating-rate payments.

Index

52-week price range, 245

A

Abnormal returns, 61, 284–285, 289
ABS. *See* Automated Bond System
Accounts receivable, 31, 129, 570, 695
Adjustable-rate mortgage, 208–210, 213, 217,
    221–222, 552–554, 564, 691
Adjusted dividend discount model, 266, 294
ADR. *See* American depository receipt
Advisory committee, 81, 83–84
After-tax yield, 51–53, 72–74
Agency cost, 255, 499
Agency problem, 249, 253–255, 262, 499, 586,
    669, 673–674
Aggregate demand for loanable funds, 32, 34–35
Aggregate supply of loanable funds, 35
AICPA. *See* American Institute of Certified
    Public Accountants
AIG. *See* American International Group
Allstate Insurance Group, 650
Amazon.com, 238
America Online, 238
American currency option, 449–450
American depository receipt, 256, 258–261, 691
American Express, 15, 567
American International Group, 12, 28, 218,
    254, 403, 410, 496, 577, 635, 658
American Stock Exchange, 163, 354
American-style option, 383
Ameritrade, 304, 355
Amex. *See* American Stock Exchange
Analyst, 24, 43, 46, 66, 72, 97, 119, 146, 170,
    193, 195, 218, 223, 236, 250, 259, 261,
    271, 277, 285–286, 290–291, 300, 302,
    315, 317–318, 320, 322, 350, 379, 415,
    435, 479, 498, 512, 522, 527, 533–534,
    538, 540, 565, 576, 587, 611, 628, 638,
    669, 671, 674–676
Annuity, 264, 300, 644, 646, 662, 664–665, 691,
    697
Annuity plan, 646, 691

Antitakeover amendment, 255, 691
APT. *See* Arbitrage pricing model
Arbitrage, 267, 269, 338–339, 342–343, 350,
    384–386, 417, 431–434, 436, 447–450, 456,
    619–620, 622, 638, 691, 693, 697–698, 703
Arbitrage firm, 619–620, 622, 638, 691
Arbitrage pricing model, 267, 269, 691
Arbitrage restriction, 447
Arbitrageur, 343, 386, 691
ARM. *See* Adjustable-rate mortgage
Arthur Andersen, 300
Asian crisis, 422, 437–446, 605
Asian Development Bank, 438
Ask quote, 16, 86, 303, 431, 691, 702
Asset allocation fund, 591, 610
Asset quality, 492–493, 496, 498, 546, 562
Asset stripping, 619, 638, 691
Asymmetric information, 11–12, 162–163, 242,
    261, 321, 454, 456, 621, 673
At the money, 353, 379, 455, 458, 691
ATM. *See* Automated teller machine
Audit committee, 250–251, 296
Automated Bond System, 163
Automated teller machine, 463

B

B/A. *See* Banker's acceptance
Backdating options, 376
Back-end load, 585, 691
Bailout act, 22, 139, 221, 483
Balloon-payment mortgage, 211, 222, 691
Bank failure, 483, 491, 495, 497–498, 521, 674
Bank holding company, 83–84, 129, 136–137,
    461–462, 482, 484–485, 491, 497, 608, 615,
    636–638, 691
Bank Holding Company Act, 482, 484
Bank Insurance Fund, 483, 546, 691
Bank of America, 14, 24, 301, 498, 535–536,
    560, 607, 635, 637
Bank of Canada, 95
Bank of England, 361
Bank of Japan, 95, 434, 439

Bank of New York, 86, 526, 601, 605
Banker's acceptance, 125, 133–137, 145–146,
    148, 478, 531, 599, 608, 691
Bankers Trust, 393, 515
Banking Act of 1933, 485, 497, 695–696
Banking syndicate, 143
Barbell strategy, 189, 192
Barclays Bank, 601
Barings PLC, 360–361
Basel Accord, 488–490, 497
Basel Committee, 488–489
Basel II Accord, 488–489
Basis, 3, 5, 15, 48, 53, 83, 120, 126–127, 132,
    143, 148, 151–152, 155, 158, 161, 185, 198,
    210, 213, 231, 242, 245, 247, 280, 286, 291,
    327, 334, 343–344, 350, 402, 412–414,
    425–426, 464–466, 468, 491–492, 494,
    512, 515, 535, 548–549, 568, 643, 660, 686,
    692, 694, 696
Basis risk, 344, 402, 412–414, 692
Bear Stearns, 12, 28, 92, 96, 132, 146, 254, 495,
    498, 623, 631–637
Bearer bond, 149, 167, 692
Before-tax yield, 51–53, 70–71, 73–74
Beige Book, 85, 96, 692
Beneficiary, 237, 633, 641–642, 644–645, 648,
    656, 669, 704
Best-efforts agreement, 616, 618, 638, 692
Beta, 267–269, 275–284, 288–292, 321, 593,
    667, 686, 692, 703
Bid quote, 303, 431, 692
Bid-ask spread, 156, 311, 320, 327, 354, 585
Big Bang, 636, 692
Binomial pricing model, 383–385
Black Monday, 315
Black-Scholes option-pricing model, 386–387,
    389–390
Black-Scholes partial differential equation, 386
Bloody Thursday, 440, 446
BNP Paribas, 300
Board of directors, 12, 83, 230, 232, 249, 252,
    255, 260, 296, 299, 302, 315, 376, 499, 521,
    558, 586–587, 602, 665, 673

Board of Governors, 18, 81–85, 90, 95, 477, 481, 627, 632, 692, 695
Boeing, 158
Bond Buyer Index, 336, 692
Bond convexity, 188–189, 197
Bond dealer, 152–153, 156, 163–164
Bond index futures, 336–337, 351, 452–453
Bond market, 114, 149–151, 153, 155, 157, 159, 161, 163–167, 169–171, 178–179, 181, 194–195, 330, 441, 455–456, 520, 555–556, 575, 596, 608, 626, 654, 662, 664
Bond mutual fund, 24, 114–115, 150–151, 159, 165, 182, 347, 349, 375, 579, 583, 587, 589, 591, 595–596, 599, 607–608, 611, 618, 626
Bond price elasticity, 184–185, 192–193, 497, 692
Bond rating, 49, 72, 163, 170, 180, 440
Bookbuilding, 235, 261
Boundary conditions, 447–448
Bretton Woods era, 419, 692
Bridge loan, 619, 622, 630, 676, 692
Broker, 15–17, 23, 132–133, 137, 152, 156, 163–164, 190, 240, 243–244, 247, 260, 289, 303–307, 309–314, 319–320, 326–327, 331, 343–344, 354–355, 360, 375, 377, 405–406, 465, 473, 585–586, 617, 621–622, 626–627, 637, 654, 692–694, 696, 698
Brokerage firm, 21, 151–152, 236, 243, 247, 259, 303–309, 311, 320–321, 326–327, 355, 377, 418, 511, 555, 585, 615, 617, 621–622, 627, 637, 653–654, 694, 696, 698, 700, 702
Budget deficit, 39–40, 42–43, 45–47, 53, 76, 94, 111–112, 116, 125, 152, 178–179, 194, 223, 274, 290, 350, 379, 404, 438, 440, 451, 457, 529, 557, 573, 611, 631, 657, 675
Budget surplus, 157
Bullet loan, 468, 479, 692
Bullish stock market, 237, 400, 629
Business demand for loanable funds, 30, 35, 43
Business insurance, 19, 641, 649, 652, 659
Business interruption insurance, 652
Bylaws, 232, 253

C

California Public Employees' Retirement System, 252–253, 665
Call feature, 153, 164, 397, 692
Call option, 282, 353, 355–363, 365–372, 374–389, 427, 429–430, 433, 435, 447–450, 453, 455, 654, 678–679, 682, 692–693, 695, 698, 700
Call premium, 56, 160, 379, 447, 692
Callable CD, 464
Callable swap, 394, 397–398, 413, 415, 692
CALPERS. See California Public Employees' Retirement System
CAMELS rating, 491–494, 497, 546–547, 673–674, 692
Cap, 210, 222, 244, 337, 400, 404–408, 413, 415–416, 507, 511, 554–555, 697
Capital adequacy, 492, 546, 562

Capital appreciation fund, 588, 610, 692
Capital asset pricing model, 267–269, 290–292, 455, 692
Capital budgeting, 173
Capital flight, 444
Capital gain, 7, 581–582, 585, 601, 659
Capital market, 4–8, 15, 22–23, 53–54, 116, 149, 222, 230, 261, 453, 621, 638, 654, 692
Capital market securities, 4, 6–8, 15, 22, 53–54, 149, 453, 692
Capital ratio, 488, 492, 518, 533, 538, 562, 644, 692
Capital requirements, 466, 481, 487–490, 492, 496–498, 537, 559, 564, 627, 633–636, 673, 695
Capital structure, 16, 164–166, 180, 230, 234, 255, 499, 534–535
CAPM. See Capital asset pricing model
Captive finance subsidiary, 568, 692
Carve-out, 621, 624
Cash flow underwriting, 650, 669, 693
Cashier's check, 531
CBOE. See Chicago Board of Options Exchange
CBOT. See Chicago Board of Trade
CD. See Certificate of deposit
CD futures, 509
CDO. See Collateralized default obligation
CDS. See Collateralized default swap
Central bank, 76, 81, 93–96, 99, 103, 361, 419, 421–423, 433–434, 438–441, 443–445, 448, 465, 496, 695
Central Liquidity Facility, 561, 563–564, 693
Certificate of deposit, 6, 53, 64, 108, 125, 131, 136, 140, 142, 146–148, 325, 336, 350, 414, 463–464, 474–475, 479–480, 504, 507, 509, 516–518, 521, 523–524, 531, 539, 541, 547, 549–550, 552, 561, 598–600, 608, 610, 678, 692–693, 695, 699, 701
CFS. See Captive finance subsidiary
CFTC. See Commodity Futures Trading Commission
Charles Schwab, 304, 311, 314
Chattel mortgage bond, 160, 693
Chicago Board of Options Exchange, 8, 326, 353–355, 382
Chicago Board of Trade, 326, 354, 379
Chicago Mercantile Exchange, 326, 336–337, 343–344, 348, 354, 379
Circuit breaker, 316, 320, 343, 350, 693
Cisco, 376
Citicorp, 486, 627, 644
Citigroup, 14, 375, 478, 567, 607–608, 627–628, 644
CLF. See Central Liquidity Facility
Closed-end fund, 580–581, 583–584, 595, 601, 607, 610–612, 674–675, 693
Closing cost, 208
CME. See Chicago Mercantile Exchange
CME Group, 326, 336–337, 343–344, 348, 354
CMO. See Collateralized mortgage obligation
CNA Insurance, 16
Coca-Cola Company, 158, 248
Coincident economic indicator, 100, 693

Collar, 315, 404, 407–408, 413, 415, 697
Collateral, 22, 50, 92–93, 132, 159–160, 170–171, 205, 213–214, 217, 219–220, 300, 305–306, 345–346, 409, 465–466, 468, 470, 472, 489, 493, 512–514, 558, 606, 633, 658, 695
Collateralized default obligation, 214, 217–219, 223
Collateralized default swap, 218, 408–410
Collateralized mortgage obligation, 214, 216, 221–223, 693
Commercial loan, 15, 20, 333, 352, 146, 470, 474–476, 500–501, 509, 513, 516–518, 523–524, 548–550, 555, 558, 570, 574, 617, 647, 662
Commercial mortgage, 222, 648, 655
Commercial paper, 6, 16, 28, 53, 55, 73, 93, 96, 125, 129–133, 136–140, 143, 145–148, 476, 486–487, 555, 568–569, 571, 574–577, 598–600, 608, 610, 626, 654, 672, 675, 678, 680, 693, 695, 698, 700
Commercial paper dealer, 130, 137, 569
Commercial paper yield curve, 131, 146
Commission broker, 243, 326, 693
Commodity Futures Trading Commission, 325, 343
Community Reinvestment Act, 485
Compensating balance, 130
Competitive bid, 127, 145, 152, 618
Comptroller of the Currency, 83, 482, 491
Conditional currency option, 428–429
Conference Board, 100
Confidence level, 279–280, 291, 293, 455, 490, 507, 515
Constant-growth dividend discount model, 265, 292
Consumer Advisory Council, 83
Consumer confidence survey, 100
Consumer finance, 20, 83, 555, 567, 572, 575, 577, 671, 693
Consumer finance operation, 20, 567, 671
Consumer loan, 19–20, 471, 474–476, 486, 502, 513, 517–518, 523–524, 540–542, 549–550, 555–557, 563, 569–570, 572–575, 673, 676
Consumer price index, 100–101, 138, 154, 171, 178, 274, 331, 404
Contagion effect, 219, 223, 497, 633–634, 693
Contingency graph, 357
Conventional mortgage, 207–208, 215, 222, 551, 559, 700
Convertible bond, 161, 170, 693
Corporate bond, 53–55, 71–74, 77, 149–150, 158–167, 169–170, 179–180, 182, 192, 195–196, 199, 202, 222, 333–336, 345, 347, 454–456, 472, 540–541, 549, 589–590, 593, 599, 609, 619, 647, 649–651, 655, 661, 664, 669, 680, 693, 698
Corporate charter, 232, 255, 691
Correlation coefficient, 276, 282, 690
Cost of capital, 112, 118, 294, 301
Cost of carry. See Net financing cost
Country risk, 514
Covariance, 267, 269, 692
Covered call, 365–367, 379–381, 455, 693

Covered interest arbitrage, 432–434, 436, 456, 693

CRA. *See* Community Reinvestment Act

Credit crisis, 4, 7, 21–24, 27–28, 35, 37, 39, 43, 50, 54, 66, 68, 81, 90, 92, 95–97, 105, 110–111, 116, 118, 129, 132, 139, 141, 146, 155–156, 162, 165, 169–170, 179–180, 191, 194, 205, 207, 212–213, 217, 219, 221–223, 237, 251, 264, 272, 276, 288–289, 306, 308, 341, 346, 365, 403, 409–410, 413–415, 469, 471–473, 477, 479, 483, 487, 490–492, 495–498, 501, 513–514, 533, 535, 546, 549, 551, 557, 559–560, 563–565, 571, 594–595, 599, 605–607, 615, 631, 635–638, 653, 655, 657–658, 663, 667

Credit crunch, 105, 576, 693

Credit line insurance, 652

Credit rating, 50, 133, 160, 163–164, 167, 214, 218, 223, 296, 393, 414, 435, 476, 570, 620, 635, 652–653, 655

Credit risk. *See* Default risk

Credit risk premium, 49, 54–55, 69, 72, 146, 171, 178, 180, 195

Credit union, 15, 17–19, 22, 24, 84, 114, 206, 545, 560–565, 570, 573–575, 693, 699

Cross-exchange rate, 418, 431, 434

Cross-hedging, 335, 350, 693

Crowding-out effect, 40, 116, 693

Cube, 601

Curb. *See* Collar

Currency call option, 377, 427, 433, 435, 448, 693

Currency futures contract, 327, 348, 411, 417, 425–427, 431, 433, 693

Currency futures market, 348

Currency option, 114, 377, 417–418, 425–431, 433, 435–436, 447–450, 679, 696

Currency option pricing, 447–449

Currency options market, 429, 447, 449

Currency put option, 377, 428, 433, 449–450, 693

Currency swap, 411–415, 417, 425–426, 433, 477, 693, 696

D

Day trader, 325, 693

Dealer, 13, 16, 23, 86–87, 90, 92, 96, 126, 129–132, 134, 137, 143, 152–153, 156, 163–164, 166, 244, 248, 314, 316, 333, 336, 394, 405–406, 415, 465, 568–569, 626, 633, 692–693, 699

Debenture, 160–161, 165, 170, 693, 703

Debt-to-asset ratio, 470, 697

Default premium. *See* Credit risk premium

Default risk, 46, 49–50, 52–56, 70–74, 105, 119, 126, 129–130, 133–135, 138–139, 145–146, 155–157, 161–162, 167–169, 171, 178–182, 190–196, 208, 212, 216, 219, 221, 345, 391, 402–404, 408–410, 413–414, 443, 445, 453–454, 456, 459, 461, 469–472, 477, 484, 488–489, 492, 499–500, 509, 512–513, 516, 519,

521–522, 525, 533, 542–543, 549–551, 559, 563–564, 571–572, 575–576, 589–590, 599–600, 605, 607, 618, 629–630, 637, 644, 647, 655, 668–669, 672, 684, 676, 693–694, 697

Defensive open market operations, 88, 694

Deficit unit, 3–4, 12–17, 22–23, 25, 45, 119, 123, 149, 231, 461, 694

Defined-benefit plan, 660–662, 669, 694

Defined-contribution plan, 660–663, 669, 694

Dell, 292–293, 687–688

Demand deposit account, 90, 463, 694

Demand for loanable funds, 29–32, 34–37, 39, 41–46, 66, 102, 106, 110, 112, 116–118, 121, 179, 197, 322, 453, 456, 698

Demand-pull inflation, 101, 103, 117, 694

Depository Institutions, 6, 14–19, 22, 24, 29, 39, 82–84, 87, 90–92, 95–96, 105, 115, 126, 131, 133, 135–137, 349, 464–465, 483–484, 495, 545, 548, 555, 560–564, 569, 574–576, 581, 630, 693–696, 701

Depository Institutions Deregulation and Monetary Control Act of 1980, 90, 484, 497, 548–549, 564–565, 694

Deregulation Act. *See* Depository Institutions Deregulation and Monetary Control Act of 1980

Derivative security, 6, 8–9, 323, 326, 328, 330, 332, 334, 336, 338, 340, 342, 344, 346, 348, 350, 352, 354, 356, 358, 360, 362, 364, 366, 368, 370, 372, 374–376, 378, 380, 382, 384, 386, 388, 390, 392–394, 396, 398, 400, 402, 404, 406, 408, 410, 412, 414, 416, 418, 420, 422, 424, 426, 428, 430, 432, 434, 436, 438, 440, 442, 444, 446, 448, 450–452, 489, 514–515, 529, 557, 604, 694

Designated Order Turnaround system, 314

Deutsche Bank, 515

Diamond, 601

DIDMCA. *See* Depository Institutions Deregulation and Monetary Control Act of 1980

Direct access broker, 314, 319, 694

Direct exchange rate, 418, 694

Direct intervention, 421–422, 434, 439–440, 445–446

Direct lease loan, 468, 694

Dirty float, 419, 434, 694

Discount bonds, 176, 694

Discount broker, 152, 303, 585, 621–622, 637

Discount rate, 10, 91, 150–151, 174–176, 185, 192, 199–203, 221, 264, 268, 694, 704

Discount window, 82, 91–92, 96, 465

Disintermediation, 547, 694

Disposable income, 29, 40–41, 528, 556

District bank. *See* Federal Reserve district bank

Diversification, 189, 191, 225, 256, 287–288, 482, 486, 513–514, 522, 564, 579, 589, 595, 611, 649, 653, 657

Divestiture, 274, 619–620, 624

Dividend discount model, , 263–266, 286, 288–289, 291–292, 294

Dividend policy, 273–274, 519, 522

Dividend yield, 246–247, 262, 321, 338–339

Division of Corporate Finance, 317

Division of Enforcement, 317

Division of Market Regulation, 317

DJIA. *See* Dow Jones Industrial Average

DOT system. *See* Designated Order Turnaround system

Douglas Amendment, 484

Dow Chemical, 478

Dow Jones Industrial Average, 8, 248, 285, 315, 369, 596, 601, 694

Dow Jones Utilities Average, 369

Downtick, 315

Downward-sloping yield curve, 66, 72, 350

Dual banking system, 481, 694

Duration, 100, 184–189, 192, 197, 345, 502, 505–508, 521–522, 552–553, 694

Duration analysis, 502, 506, 521–522

Duration gap, 505, 507–508, 694

Dutch auction, 239–240

Dynamic asset allocation, 341–342, 369–370, 694

Dynamic open market operations, 694

Dynegy, 301

E

E*Trade, 304, 355

Earnings per share, 239, 247, 265–266, 286, 292, 298, 466

Earnings surprise, 273, 289

ECB. *See* European Central Bank

ECNs. *See* Electronic communications networks

Economies of scale, 19, 22, 461, 478, 484, 497, 529, 561, 573, 586, 694

Economies of scope, 19, 481, 624

ECU. *See* European Currency Unit

Effective yield, 143–144, 147, 694

Efficiency. *See* Market efficiency

Electronic communications networks, 245, 303, 312–314, 319–320, 326, 355

Emergency Economic Stabilization Act of 2008, 22, 139, 221, 272, 483

Emerging market, 21, 168, 258, 288–289, 319, 410, 441, 445

Employee Retirement Income Security Act, 663, 669, 694, 700

Enron, 11, 50, 250, 297–301, 376, 487, 606

Enron Online, 297

Equilibrium interest rate, 35–38, 41, 43, 45, 102, 112

Equilibrium price, 10, 233, 239, 241, 258, 260, 309–310

Equity REIT, 607, 611, 694

Equity swap, 166, 394, 400, 413–414, 693, 695

Equity-for-debt swap, 166

Equivalent before-tax yield, 51

ERISA. *See* Employee Retirement Income Security Act

ERM. *See* Exchange rate mechanism

ETF. *See* Exchange-traded fund

ETNs. *See* Exchange-traded notes

Eurobank, 143, 510

Eurobond, 167, 401

Euro-commercial paper, 143, 695
Eurodollar, 88, 141–142, 325, 463, 466–467, 473, 475, 598–599, 695
Eurodollar certificate of deposit, 142, 599, 695
Eurodollar deposit, 142
Eurodollar floating-rate CDs, 142–143, 695
Eurodollar market, 142, 466, 695
Eurolist, 318
Euronext, 163, 243, 348, 354
Euronotes, 143, 695
European Central Bank, 94–96, 421
European currency option, 449–450
European Union, 93, 489
Exchange controls, 403, 423
Exchange rate risk, 114, 145, 167, 190, 192, 194, 196, 261, 288, 318–319, 351, 419, 425–426, 432–433, 435, 446, 476, 478, 519–520, 522, 590, 595, 629–630, 695
Exchange-traded fund, 258–261, 368–369, 589, 600–602, 610, 695
Exchange-traded notes, 168–170
Exercise price, 282, 353, 355–365, 367–382, 384–385, 387, 389–390, 427–430, 435, 447–450, 455, 458, 678–679, 682–683, 691, 695, 698, 700, 703
Expectations theory. *See* Pure expectations theory
Expense ratio, 259, 584–586, 596, 675, 685
Expiration date, 236–237, 282, 353–357, 359, 362–364, 366–372, 374–375, 379–381, 384, 428–429, 449, 455, 698, 703
Extendable swap, 394, 398–399, 413, 695
Extended trading session, 245
ExxonMobil, 248

F

Fannie Mae. *See* Federal National Mortgage Association
Fannie Mae mortgage-backed securities, 214–215
Farmers Insurance Group, 650
FASB. *See* Financial Accounting Standards Board
FDICIA. *See* Federal Deposit Insurance Corporation Improvement Act
Federal Advisory Council, 83
Federal agency bond, 149–151, 155, 169
Federal Deposit Insurance Corporation, 482–483, 525, 546, 695
Federal Deposit Insurance Corporation Improvement Act, 483, 695
Federal funds, 14–15, 86–89, 92, 100, 109, 113, 118–120, 125, 133–134, 136–137, 143, 145, 285, 365, 454–457, 462, 464–467, 473, 475, 478–479, 493, 500, 521, 523, 531, 548–549, 551, 678, 680, 695
Federal funds broker, 133, 137, 465
Federal funds market, 14–15, 86, 88, 92, 133, 136–137, 143, 464–465, 473, 478–479, 493, 500, 521, 531, 548–549, 551, 695
Federal funds rate, 86–89, 92, 98, 109, 113, 118–120, 133–134, 143, 285, 365, 454–457, 464–466, 479, 548, 678, 680, 695

Federal funds target rate, 109
Federal Home Loan Mortgage Association, 155, 215, 695, 700
Federal Housing Administration, 155, 207–208, 215, 219, 222, 551
Federal National Mortgage Association, 28, 155, 214–215, 219–224, 254, 472, 695
Federal Open Market Committee, 39, 81, 83–86, 95–96, 98, 109, 112–113, 118–120, 133, 454, 692, 695, 700, 703
Federal Reserve Act, 81
Federal Reserve Board. *See* Board of Governors
Federal Reserve district bank, 81–86, 96, 133, 465, 468, 695, 700, 703
Federal Reserve float, 88
Federally insured mortgage, 207, 215
FHA. *See* Federal Housing Administration
Fidelity, 164, 587, 652
Finance company, 15–19, 22, 24–25, 47, 73, 97, 114, 119, 129–130, 136–137, 148–149, 151, 206, 233, 394, 407, 414, 555, 567–577, 608, 654, 671–672, 675, 692–693, 695
Financial Accounting Standards Board, 295–296
Financial conglomerate, 19–20, 22, 462, 480, 486, 527, 538, 543, 545, 556–567, 572, 615, 627, 630, 641, 644, 655, 671
Financial futures contract, 325–329, 332, 338, 347–350, 370, 509, 521, 626, 693, 695, 697–698, 700, 702–703
Financial Institutions Reform, Recovery, and Enforcement Act, 482, 497, 558–559, 564–565, 695
Financial leverage, 165–166, 168–169, 255, 298, 301, 308, 332, 378, 470, 519, 533–535, 537–538, 588, 603–606, 620, 623, 634–635, 637, 698
Financial Performance Report, 562
Financial planner, 225, 585
Financial Services Modernization Act, 485–486, 497, 627, 644, 695
FIRREA. *See* Financial Institutions Reform, Recovery, and Enforcement Act
First mortgage, 160, 211, 695
First mortgage bond, 160, 695
Fiscal policy, 39, 41–42, 94, 97, 110–111, 117–118, 121, 138, 182, 275, 330, 364, 405, 455, 457
Fisher effect, 39, 695
Fitch Investor Service, 129
Fixed asset, 466–468, 473, 475, 516–518, 524, 541, 550, 646, 703
Fixed-for-floating swap. *See* Plain vanilla swap
Fixed-rate mortgage, 115, 193, 208, 210, 212–213, 221–222, 345, 350, 372–373, 378–379, 414, 451, 455, 457, 511, 549, 552–554, 557, 565, 673, 676, 695
Fixed-rate bond, 161, 193, 401–402, 648, 665
Flight to quality, 72, 139
Flipping, 237–238, 240, 261
Floating-rate bond. *See* Variable-rate bond
Floating-rate loan, 47, 74, 392, 396, 414, 507, 509, 511, 516, 519, 521–522, 576
Floating-rate mortgage, 516

Floor broker, 243, 309, 314, 319–320, 326–327, 354–355, 377, 693, 696
Floor trader, 242, 326, 626, 696
Flotation cost, 617–618, 696
FOMC. *See* Federal Open Market Committee
Ford, 567, 569
Forecasting error, 64
Foreign bond, 166– 191–192, 590, 608, 647
Foreign demand for loanable funds, 32, 35
Foreign exchange derivative, 323, 417–419, 421, 423, 425, 427, 429, 431, 433–436, 439, 441, 443, 445, 449, 451, 490, 696
Foreign exchange derivative market, 323, 417, 419, 421, 423, 425, 427, 429, 431, 433, 435, 439, 441, 443, 445, 449, 451
Foreign exchange market, 13, 93, 95, 417–422, 431, 433–434, 437–440, 445–446, 454, 696
Foreign stock index futures, 347–348
Forward contract, 417–418, 425–427, 433–435, 475–478, 520, 693, 696
Forward market, 425, 432–433, 696
Forward rate, 59–64, 69–73, 75, 418, 424–426, 432–436, 446, 456, 458, 696
Forward swap, 394, 396, 413, 415, 696
Franchise, 470
Fraud, 11, 258, 301, 361, 558–559, 564, 606, 695
FRCDs. *See* Eurodollar floating-rate CDs
Freddie Mac. *See* Federal Home Loan Mortgage Association
Free cash flow model, 263, 266, 288
Freely floating system, 419, 434, 696
Front-end load, 585, 696
Front-running, 310–311, 320, 629
FSLIC. *See* Federal Savings and Loan Insurance Corporation
Full-service broker, 303–304
Fundamental analysis, 263, 696
Fundamental forecasting, 423–424, 696
Futures contract, 325–341, 343–353, 361, 370–375, 377–378, 381, 411, 417, 425–427, 429, 431, 433–435, 451, 453, 507, 509, 521, 539, 553–554, 563, 575, 608, 626, 654–655, 662, 665, 681–683, 692–693, 695–700, 702–703
Futures market, 323, 325–327, 329–331, 333, 335, 337, 339, 341, 343, 345–349, 351, 520, 555–556, 575, 608, 626, 654, 662, 697, 700
Futures options, 370, 372, 520, 555, 654

G

GAAP. *See* Generally accepted accounting principles
Gap, 157–158, 502–508, 516–517, 521–522, 525, 552, 663, 684, 694, 696
Gap analysis, 502–503, 506, 508, 521
Gap ratio, 503, 517, 525, 696
Garn-St Germain Act, 484, 548–549, 565, 696
GDP. *See* Gross domestic product
GECC. *See* General Electric Credit Corporation
General Electric, 15, 166, 567–568
General Electric Credit Corporation, 568

General Motors, 567, 569

General Motors Acceptance Corporation, 569, 577

General obligation bond, 155–156, 696, 699

Generally accepted accounting principles, 259, 295

Gibson Greetings, Inc., 393

Ginnie Mae. *See* Government National Mortgage Association

Ginnie Mae mortgage-backed securities, 214–215

Glass-Steagall Act. *See* Banking Act of 1933

Global crowding out, 116, 696

Global integration, 13, 403, 445

Global junk bond, 166, 696

Global mutual fund, 588, 609

GLOBEX, 326, 348

GMAC. *See* General Motors Acceptance Corporation

Golden parachute, 255–266, 696

Goldman Sachs, 16, 24, 168, 369, 616, 624, 636–637, 639

Google, 4, 10, 238–240

Governance, 12, 193, 249, 254, 260, 295–296, 316, 376, 558, 586, 610, 668, 675

Government agency, 3–6, 13–14, 16–17, 19, 21, 49, 102, 125–126, 149, 208, 422, 440, 472, 496, 590, 598, 608, 624, 641, 650–651, 663–664

Government agency securities, 472, 650–651

Government demand for loanable funds, 31–32, 35, 43

Government National Mortgage Association, 155, 214–215, 221, 590, 608, 696

Government securities dealer, 86–87, 126, 132, 336, 465

GPM. *See* Graduated-payment mortgage

Graduated-payment mortgage, 208, 210–211, 221–222, 696

Gramm-Leach-Bliley Act. *See* Financial Services Modernization Act

Great Depression, 11, 482

Greenmail, 620, 638, 696

Greenspan, Alan, 83

Gross domestic product, 85, 99, 122, 138, 179, 269, 271, 365, 404

Gross interest expenses, 531–532, 534, 538, 696

Gross interest income, 530–532, 534, 537–538, 696

Group life policy, 644, 697

Growing-equity mortgage, 208, 211, 222, 697

Growth and income fund, 588, 591, 610, 697

Growth fund, 588, 591, 697

H

Health insurance, 20, 641, 644–646, 649, 657, 670

Health maintenance organization, 652, 697

Hedge fund, 219, 308, 409, 514, 600, 604–607, 610–611, 632, 697

Hedge ratio, 384–385

Hedgers, 325, 348, 697

Hewlett-Packard, 441

Highly leveraged transaction, 470, 479, 484–485, 497, 697

HLT. *See* Highly leveraged transaction

HMO. *See* Health maintenance organization

Holding period return, 151

Holiday effect, 285

Home Depot, 247

Hostile takeover, 257, 620

Household demand for loanable funds, 29–30, 35, 42–43, 45

Household International Inc., 573

Hybrid fund, 583

I

IBA. *See* Interstate Banking Act

IBF. *See* Investment bank

IBM, 24–25, 166, 243, 246–248, 291, 441, 478

IMF. *See* International Monetary Fund

Impact lag, 105, 697

Imperfect market, 23, 697

Implementation lag, 105, 118, 697

Implied standard deviation, 281–282, 367

Implied volatility, 290, 370, 389

In the money, 45, 87, 89–91, 94, 99, 118, 121–122, 136, 139–140, 146, 148, 194, 353, 416, 520, 698

Income fund, 588–591, 610, 612, 697

Indenture, 159–160, 169, 697, 701

Independent broker, 243

Index arbitrage, 342–343, 350, 697

Index mutual fund, 605

Index of Leading Economic Indicators, 100

Indirect exchange rate, 418, 697

Indirect intervention, 422–423, 440–441

Individual retirement account, 16, 161, 663

Industrial loan, 100, 461

Industrial production index, 99

Inflation rate, 38–39, 47, 70, 76, 101, 107–108, 110, 117, 119, 154, 171, 289, 420, 433, 688–690

Inflation-indexed bond, 154

Informal line of credit, 468–469, 697

Information cost, 318–319, 417, 659

ING. *See* Internationale Nederlanden Groep

Initial margin, 305, 327, 332, 681–682, 697

Initial public offering, 27, 229–230, 234–242, 260–262, 285, 290, 292, 569, 602, 616, 621, 624, 628–629, 639, 674–675, 697

Inside board member, 251

Insider trading, 258, 286–287, 354, 485

Installment credit, 100, 568

Installment debt, 29

Installment loan, 471, 697

Instinet, 245, 313

Institutional Shareholder Services Inc., 253

Insurance commissioner, 643–644, 699

Insurance premium, 19, 208, 370, 483, 546, 562, 641–643, 646, 648–650, 652–653, 656, 658, 670, 691, 693–694, 699

Insurance Regulatory Information System, 643

Insured plan, 664–665, 697

Intel, 244

Interest rate cap, 404–408, 413, 415–416, 507, 511, 555, 697

Interest rate collar, 404, 407–408, 413, 415, 697

Interest rate derivative, 391, 404, 413, 416, 490, 539

Interest rate floor, 404, 406–408, 413, 415–416, 697

Interest rate futures contract, 325, 327, 329, 335–336, 349–350, 370, 372–373, 377, 451, 453, 507, 509, 521, 553–554, 563, 608

Interest rate parity, 432–436, 455, 458, 697

Interest rate risk, 139–140, 142, 178, 186, 189, 191, 196, 206, 208–210, 212–213, 216, 221–222, 329, 333–335, 346–347, 349–350, 370, 373, 375, 378, 381, 391–394, 396, 400, 402, 404, 407, 410, 413–414, 452–453, 459, 499–512, 515–516, 519–523, 525, 543, 549–550, 552–556, 563–566, 571–572, 574–576, 589–590, 595, 599, 608, 610, 625–626, 629, 637, 644, 654–655, 662, 665, 668–669, 672, 676, 684–685, 697

Interest rate strategy, 189, 192

Interest rate swap, 391–394, 396–398, 401–406, 410, 412–416, 451, 454, 475, 477, 486–487, 507, 510–512, 520–523, 553–555, 563–565, 575, 608, 626, 654–655, 662, 692, 697, 700, 703

Interest-inelastic, 32, 34, 697

Interest-only CMO, 216

Internal ratings-based approach, 489

International arbitrage, 417, 431, 434

International debt crisis, 605

International Monetary Fund, 259, 438–440, 443

International money market, 141–142, 432

International mutual fund, 192, 258–261, 351, 418, 452, 588–589, 595, 611, 698

International Securities Exchange, 354

International stock offering, 256, 637

International syndicate, 637

International trade, 85, 133, 141–142, 412, 417, 691

Internationale Nederlanden Groep, 361, 623

Internet broker, 304

Internet fund, 589

Interstate Banking Act, 484

Inventory cost, 312

Inverted yield curve. *See* Downward-sloping yield curve

Investment bank, 25, 158–159, 167–168, 326, 360, 615

Investment Company Act, 600

Investment-grade bonds, 50, 661, 698

Investor sentiment, 95, 271–272, 289

Investor's Business Daily, 153

IPO. *See* Initial public offering

IRB approach. *See* Internal ratings-based approach

IRIS. *See* Insurance Regulatory Information System

Irregular accounting method, 250

ISD. *See* Implied standard deviation

ishares, 259, 369, 601

Island, 140, 313
ISS Inc. *See* Institutional Shareholder Services Inc.
Issue cost, 617, 698

J

J.P. Morgan Chase, 14, 92, 301, 375, 495, 560, 608, 632–633, 637
January effect, 271–272, 285, 289
Joint venture, 343–344, 636, 659
Junk bond, 164–166, 169–170, 558–559, 564, 590, 643, 647, 655, 660, 669, 695–698
Junk bond fund, 590
Junk commercial paper, 129, 698

K

Key employee insurance, 652
Kohlberg Kravis Roberts, Inc., 165, 290, 603

L

L/C. *See* Letter of credit
Labor union, 560
Laddered strategy, 189, 192
Laddering, 240, 261
Lagging economic indicator, 100, 698
Late trading, 245–246, 587
LBO. *See* Leveraged buyout
Lead underwriter, 234–236, 261–262
Leading economic indicator, 100, 118, 698
LEAPs. *See* Long-term equity anticipations
Leasing, 482, 569–570, 574–576
Lehman Brothers, 12, 27–28, 93, 129, 139, 146, 180, 252, 252, 308, 410, 496, 623, 634–638, 667
Lender liability suit, 471
Letter of credit, 134–135, 475–476, 478, 486, 698, 703
Leverage. *See* Financial leverage
Leverage measure, 519, 533, 535, 698
Leveraged buyout, 164–166, 170, 255, 290, 470, 484, 570, 618–620, 625–626, 638, 654, 692, 698, 702
Liability insurance, 650, 652
Liberty Mutual, 16
LIBOR, 142–143, 161, 395, 401–402, 405–408, 415–416, 501, 510–511, 523, 648, 695, 698
License, 470
Life insurance, 63, 165, 192, 252, 347, 370, 466, 561, 641, 644–650, 655–656, 658–659, 664–665, 668–670, 697, 703–704
LIFFE. *See* London International Financial Futures and Options Exchange
Limit order, 164, 303–304, 309–310, 313, 320, 327, 355, 698
Line of credit, 130, 136, 148, 468–469, 539, 627, 697
Liquidity premium, 55–56, 61–66, 69–73, 75–76, 161, 454, 456, 698
Liquidity premium theory, 56, 61, 64, 70–71, 698
Liquidity ratio, 659

Liquidity risk, 55–56, 345, 500, 509, 516, 543, 550, 563–565, 571, 575, 644, 655, 669, 698
Listing requirements, 243–244, 354
Load fund, 585–586, 610, 698, 700
Loan commitment, 475–475, 478, 698
Loan loss provision, 531, 535–536, 538, 698
Loan participation, 469, 698
Loanable funds theory, 29, 39, 698
Loan-to-value ratio, 207–208
Locational arbitrage, 431, 434, 436, 698
Lockbox, 531
Lockheed Martin, 665
Lockup provision, 236, 261
London Interbank Offer Rate. *See* LIBOR
London International Financial Futures and Options Exchange, 343–344, 348
Long hedge, 336, 350, 352, 698
Long-Term Capital Management, 605
Long-term equity anticipations, 369, 698
Loose money policy. *See* Stimulative monetary policy
Low-coupon bond, 185, 698
LTCM. *See* Long-Term Capital Management

M

M1, 87–88, 698
M2, 87–88, 100, 698
M3, 87–88, 698
Madoff, Bernard, 606
Maintenance margin, 350–306, 320, 698
Making a market, 16, 309–310
Malpractice insurance, 652
Managed health care plan, 651–652
Management fee, 582, 605, 623–624
Managerial compensation, 294, 299, 532
Margin account, 305, 327, 332, 698
Margin call, 305–306, 327, 343, 361, 606, 698
Margin requirement, 83, 305, 320, 327, 338, 627, 698
Margin trade, 303
Marginal tax rate, 51
Marine insurance, 652
Market efficiency, 10, 21, 61, 245, 248, 263, 284–286, 288–289, 313, 318, 326, 354, 449, 461, 484, 534–535, 594, 596, 603–604, 611, 627, 666, 702–704
Market for corporate control, 254–256, 260–261, 297, 301, 455, 457
Market imperfections, 14, 393
Market microstructure, 227, 303, 305, 307, 309, 311, 313, 315, 317, 319, 321, 699
Market order, 164, 303–304, 307, 313, 320, 327, 355, 699
Market risk, 139, 267–268, 275, 291, 339–341, 344, 364, 444–445, 453, 490, 514–516, 574, 595, 608, 625, 629, 637, 654–655, 662, 668, 676, 699
Market risk premium, 139, 267–268, 275, 291, 364, 444–445
Market-based forecasting, 423–424, 699
Market-maker, 309, 311–314, 319–320, 326, 355, 420, 626, 699
MarketWatch.com, 237, 241

Matched funding, 664, 668, 699
Matching strategy, 189, 192
Maturity matching, 507
Mayer & Schweitzer, 311
MBI futures. *See* Municipal Bond Index futures
McDonald's, 355
McFadden Act, 484, 699
MCI, 295
Member bank, 81–84, 482
Menlo Ventures, 602
Merger, 16, 21–22, 243, 245, 297, 316, 326, 354, 379, 486, 546, 620–621, 624–627, 631, 636–637, 639, 644, 671, 676, 699
Merger-conversion, 546, 699
Merrill Lynch, 28, 616, 635–637
Microsoft, 229, 238–239, 540, 602
Mini Nasdaq 100, 100, 337
Mini S&P 500, 337–338
Mixed forecasting, 423–424, 699
MMDA. *See* Money market deposit account
MMF. *See* Money market mutual fund
MNC. *See* Multinational corporation
Modified duration, 187–189
Monetary Control Act of 1980. *See* Depository Institutions Deregulation and Monetary Control Act of 1980
Monetary policy, 34, 39, 42, 46, 79, 81–86, 88–122, 138, 182, 194, 197, 223, 270, 275, 290, 330, 364, 379, 405, 453–456, 484, 611, 673, 680, 692, 695, 701
Money center bank, 530, 533, 535, 538
Money market deposit account, 87–88, 462, 464, 467, 475, 478–480, 484, 504, 516–518, 523–524, 531, 547–548, 550, 552–553, 561, 564, 696, 698–699
Money market mutual fund, 15, 24, 87–88, 136, 484, 555, 583, 596–600, 608, 610–611, 626, 699
Money market security, 4, 6, 15, 29, 53, 71, 114, 123, 125–126, 128, 134, 137–149, 152, 180, 194, 212, 225–226, 326, 453–454, 456, 591, 598, 626, 654, 661–662, 675, 680, 694, 699
Money order, 561
Money supply growth, 44–45, 84, 86–87, 91, 96, 103, 105–107, 118, 179, 193, 529, 557, 573, 631, 657, 703
Moody's Investor Service, 50, 129, 167, 296, 485, 590, 698
Moral hazard problem, 220, 483, 497, 634, 641–643, 699
Morgan Stanley, 16, 168, 308, 369, 616, 624, 636–637, 639–640
Morgan Stanley Biotechnology Index, 369
Mortgage loan, 15, 115, 206–208, 210, 213, 219, 471, 486, 492, 501, 513, 520, 530, 535, 545–546, 549–552, 556–557, 559–560, 562, 567–568, 571, 653, 676
Mortgage market, 28, 114, 123, 155, 205–209, 211, 213, 215, 217, 219–223, 415, 520, 555, 575, 608, 626, 654, 661–662
Mortgage origination. *See* Origination
Mortgage pass-through security, 213–215, 699–700

Mortgage rate, 112, 205, 207–208, 210–212, 215, 222, 224, 681
Mortgage REIT, 607, 611, 699
Mortgage-backed securities, 7, 21–22, 27–28, 92–93, 206, 213–218, 221–223, 409–410, 473, 477, 487, 490, 492, 497, 513, 533, 548–549, 555, 559–560, 563, 606, 623, 631, 633–635, 653–654, 657–658, 660, 663, 667, 695, 699–700
Motorola, 247, 441
Multibank holding companies, 482
Multifund fund, 588–589
Multinational corporation, 15, 424, 428, 478, 575, 659
Multinational finance companies, 575
Multinational insurance companies, 659
Multiplier effect, 91
Municipal bond, 31, 53, 71–72, 113, 149–151, 155–157, 161, 164, 169–170, 172, 180, 195, 336–337, 472, 583, 590–591, 593, 609, 619, 622, 649–650, 652–653, 661, 679, 699
Municipal Bond Index futures, 336–337, 699
Municipal bond yield curve, 157
Municipal government, 21, 32–33, 35, 476, 551, 609, 619, 646, 661
Municipal security, 52, 92, 157–158, 170, 472, 475–476, 517–518, 524, 550–551, 651
Mutual fund, 15, 17–20, 22, 24, 27, 87–88, 114–115, 136, 150–151, 159, 164–166, 168–169, 182, 192–193, 206, 219, 231, 233, 252, 258–262, 279, 314, 340, 347, 349, 351, 365, 375, 417–418, 452, 484, 486, 514, 543, 555, 579–596, 599, 601–605, 607–613, 618, 622, 625–626, 629, 653–654, 662, 667, 671–672, 674–675, 683, 685, 691–693, 695–702
Mutual life insurance company, 645
Mutual-to-stock conversion, 545, 699

N

NADAL, 11
NAFTA. *See* North American Free Trade Agreement
NAIC. *See* National Association of Insurance Commissioners
Naked options, 356
Naked shorting, 308
NASD. *See* National Association of Securities Dealers
Nasdaq. *See* National Association of Securities Dealers Automatic Quotations
Nasdaq 100 index, 337, 369, 601
Nasdaq National Market, 244
Nasdaq Small Cap Market, 244
National Association of Insurance Commissioners, 643–644, 669, 699
National Association of Securities Dealers, 163, 244, 248, 314, 626–627, 638, 699
National Association of Securities Dealers Automatic Quotations, 4, 244–245, 248, 292, 296, 305, 309, 311–313, 337, 343–344, 354, 369, 601, 626, 678, 681, 699

National Association of Securities Dealers' Trade Reporting and Compliance Engine, 163
National bank, 83, 481–482
National Credit Union Administration, 561–562, 699
National Credit Union Share Insurance Fund, 562, 699
National income, 99, 438
Nationwide Insurance Enterprise, 650
NAV. *See* Net asset value
Navy Federal Credit Union, 15, 560
NCD. *See* Negotiable certificate of deposit
NCUA. *See* National Credit Union Administration
NCUSIF. *See* National Credit Union Share Insurance Fund
Negotiable certificate of deposit, 6, 53, 125, 131–132, 135–137, 139–140, 142, 145–147, 463–464, 467, 540–542, 699
Negotiable order of withdrawal account, 87, 463–464, 475, 484, 516–518, 523–524, 531, 548, 550, 552–553, 561, 694, 700
Net asset value, 259, 582, 584, 590, 594–595, 611–612, 699
Net demand for funds, 43
Net exposure, 336, 520, 700
Net financing cost, 338–339
Net interest income, 531–532, 534, 537, 557, 577
Net interest margin, 501–503, 505, 509–510, 516, 521–523, 531, 535–539, 566, 672–673, 684, 700
Net present value, 30
Net underwriting margin, 659
Net worth, 187, 466, 548, 659, 663
Netscape, 238
New York Stock Exchange, 4, 8, 152, 163, 242–245, 248, 261, 296, 305, 309–316, 320, 342–343, 354, 587, 629, 658, 678, 681, 696, 702
New York Stock Exchange Composite Index, 248
NIF. *See* Note issuance facility
Nike, 9, 441
Nikkei 225 Stock Average, 337, 348, 360–361
NobleTrading, 314
Noise trader, 311, 700
No-load fund, 585–586, 610, 700
Nominal interest rate, 39, 45, 70, 101, 701
Noncompetitive bid, 127, 145, 152
Noninterest expenses, 516, 519, 531–539, 541–542, 561, 566, 577, 672–674, 684, 700
Noninterest income, 530–532, 534–539, 558, 566, 574, 577, 672–673, 684, 700
Nonprofit organization, 560
North American Free Trade Agreement, 637, 659
Note issuance facility, 476, 700
Notional principal, 391, 395–396, 400, 405–407, 415–416, 697, 700
NOW account. *See* Negotiable order of withdrawal account
NPV. *See* Net present value
NYSE. *See* New York Stock Exchange

O

OCC. *See* Options Clearing Corporation
Off-balance sheet activity, 462, 475, 478, 487, 497
Off-balance sheet transaction, 486–487
Offer price, 153, 235–237, 239–241, 261, 616, 629, 639
Office of Thrift Supervision, 546, 557
Oil prices, 46, 85, 101, 107–110, 114–115, 118, 121, 178, 192–194, 223, 350, 435, 454, 456, 558
One-bank holding company, 482
OneChicago, 344
Open interest, 329, 340, 427
Open Market Desk. *See* Trading Desk
Open market operation, 84, 86–91, 93, 96, 103, 106, 118, 152, 694, 700, 703
Open-end fund, 580–581, 601, 610–611, 674–675, 700
Operating risk, 500
Operational risk, 345, 489, 700
Opportunity cost, 31, 212, 312, 329
Option contract, 295, 353–356, 379, 427, 692–693, 695, 700–701, 704
Option market, 360, 365, 369
Option premium, 282, 353, 355–356, 361–365, 367, 370–372, 378–379, 381–384, 389, 447–450, 678–679, 700
Options Clearing Corporation, 354, 494
Oracle Corporation, 229, 293, 602
Orange County, California, 168, 393
Order cost, 312
Organizational structure, 20, 81, 528, 557, 573, 631, 656
Organized exchange, 242–244, 261, 325, 391, 408, 473, 658, 700
Origination, 205, 208, 211, 215, 221, 548, 559, 615, 617, 638, 700
Origination fee, 205, 208
OTC bulletin board, 244
OTC market. *See* Over-the-counter market
OTS. *See* Office of Thrift Supervision
Out of the money, 353, 455, 458, 700
Outside board member, 251
Overhead, 535, 642
Over-the-counter market, 163, 242, 244, 345–346, 375, 658, 699–700

P

Pacific Basin stock index, 589
Participation certificate, 214–2
Passbook savings account. S
Patent, 309, 470
PBGC. *See* Pension Bene Corporation
PC. *See* Participation
PC insurance. *See* insurance
PE method. *See*
PE ratio. *See*
Pegged exch
Penny sto
Penny-ju

Pension Benefit Guaranty Corporation, 663, 669, 700
Pension fund, 16–19, 21–22, 24, 27–28, 63, 114–115, 136–137, 150–151, 159, 161, 165–166, 168, 171, 182, 189, 192, 194, 206, 219, 229–231, 233, 252, 260, 262, 279, 314, 333, 347, 349–350, 365–368, 370, 375, 393–394, 400, 417–418, 425, 452, 466, 470, 486, 501, 514, 543, 566, 574, 602, 607–608, 618, 622–623, 625, 641, 643, 645, 647, 649, 651, 653–655, 657, 659–669, 672–673, 675, 694, 701
Perpetuity, 264
Peso crisis, 422
Philadelphia Stock Exchange, 354
Pink sheet, 244–245
PIPs. *See* Publicly issued pass-through securities
Plain vanilla swap, 394–395, 398, 404, 414–416, 451, 510
Poison pill, 255, 700
Policy directive, 86–88, 96, 700
Policy loan, 647–648, 668
Political risk, 288
Portfolio beta, 277, 291
Portfolio insurance, 314, 342–343, 370, 700
Position trader, 325, 700
PowerShares, 601
PPO. *See* Preferred provider organization
PPP. *See* Purchasing power parity
Precious metal, 589, 622
Preemptive right, 241–242, 700
Preferred habitat theory, 64, 71, 701
Preferred provider organization, 652
Preferred stock, 22, 220, 232, 466, 488, 491, 535, 593, 618, 694, 701
Premium. *See* Option premium
Prepayment risk, 212–213, 216, 221, 345, 701
~ index, 48, 100–101, 138, 154, 167, 171, ~74, 331, 404
~ethod, 263–264, 286, 288–289,
~47, 263–266, 286,

Property and casualty insurance, 20, 641, 649–652, 658–659, 668–669
Prospectus, 159, 234, 236, 241, 260–261, 581, 600, 616–618, 683, 685, 701
Protective covenant, 160, 170, 468, 701
Proxy contest, 253–254
Proxy statement, 317
Publicly issued pass-through securities, 214–215
Purchasing power parity, 420–421, 434, 437, 701
Pure expectations theory, 56, 60–62, 64–67, 70–71, 73, 106, 454, 456, 680, 701
Put option, 208, 353, 355–357, 359–365, 367–374, 376–382, 385, 389–390, 427–429, 433–434, 447–451, 453, 455, 458, 555, 654, 679, 982, 693, 695, 698, 700–701
Putable swap, 394, 397–398, 413, 701
Put-call parity, 385, 389, 449–450

R

Raider, 297, 301
Rate-capped swap, 394, 400, 413, 415, 701
Rating agency, 72, 213, 218, 301
Real estate investment trust, 600, 607, 610–611, 694, 699, 701
Real estate loan, 471–472, 474, 480, 558, 569–570, 575
Real interest rate, 39, 45–47, 70, 701
Recession. *See* Recessionary period
Recessionary period, 29, 45, 66, 72, 74, 95, 97, 117–118, 121–122, 131, 146, 179, 194, 276, 336, 451, 491, 493, 521, 525, 532, 576, 598, 671
Recognition lag, 105, 118, 701
Registered bond, 149, 701
Registration statement, 242, 316–317, 616–617, 701
Regression analysis, 48, 120, 148, 268, 277, 502, 506–508, 521, 525–526, 566, 612, 640, 670, 686–690
Regression model. *See* Regression analysis
Regulation Fair Disclosure, 317, 628
Regulation Q, 701
Reigle-Neal Interstate Banking and Branching Efficiency Act. *See* Interstate Banking Act
Reinsurance, 650–651, 669, 701
See Real estate investment trust
~ortfolio, 384–385
~hase agreement

~47
~ent, 87–88, 125, 132–133,
~–147, 463, 465–467, 473,
~9, 548–549, 551, 598, 610,

~irement ratio, 90–91, 96, 701
~quirements, 81, 83–84, 90–91, 93,
~96, 142, 468, 482, 548, 568, 701
~tial construction, 85, 112
~ential mortgage, 7, 15, 205–206, 208, 213, ~221–222
~esolution Trust Corporation, 559, 701

Restrictive monetary policy, 101, 103–104, 107–110, 114, 117–118, 456, 539, 673
Retail CD. *See* Certificate of deposit
Retail sales index, 99
Return on assets, 321, 493, 506, 513, 519, 523, 533–535, 537–539, 541–542, 604–605, 684–685, 701
Return on equity, 321, 506, 518–519, 523, 533–535, 537–538, 541–542, 604–605, 638, 673–674, 684–685, 702
Return on net worth, 659
Revenue bond, 155–156, 336, 692, 699, 702
Reverse LBO, 255, 702
Reverse repo, 132, 702
Revolving credit loan, 469, 702
Reward-to-variability ratio. *See* Sharpe index
Riding the yield curve, 66
Risk aversion, 431, 649
Risk management, 8, 478
Risk-adjusted return, 283–284, 291, 593, 595–596, 666–667, 702–703
Riskless hedge, 386
RJRNabisco, Inc., 165, 290
ROA. *See* Return on assets
Road show, 235, 260–262, 616
ROE. *See* Return on equity
RTC. *See* Resolution Trust Corporation
Rule 144A, 159, 617
Russell 1000, 369
Russell 2000, 337
Russian crisis, 422

S

S&L. *See* Savings and loan association
S&P 100 index, 369
S&P 400 Midcap Index, 601
S&P 500 index, 248, 268, 270, 314, 337–341, 352, 369, 374, 379, 400, 589, 596, 601, 678, 681, 686, 702–703
S&P 500 index futures, 338–341, 374, 379, 678, 681, 702
S&P SmallCap 600, 600, 369
SAIF. *See* Savings Association Insurance Fund
Sarbanes-Oxley Act, 12, 241, 250–252, 254, 261, 290, 301, 455, 457, 487, 497, 500, 673
Savings account, 87, 90, 463, 547, 561, 698
Savings and loan association, 15, 24, 84, 132, 151, 345, 350, 372, 379, 381, 394, 482, 545–546, 565, 683, 699, 702
Savings Association Insurance Fund, 483, 546, 702
Savings bank, 7, 15, 84, 233, 381, 394, 406, 545–546
Savings bond, 154–155
Savings deposit, 88, 462–463, 467, 478, 484, 549–550
Savings institution, 15, 17–19, 21–22, 64, 84, 114, 136–137, 149–150, 205–206, 213, 223–224, 233, 333, 346–347, 349, 370, 375, 378, 392–393, 451, 482–484, 497, 545–558, 560–561, 563–568, 570–571, 573–576, 582, 608, 610, 625, 627, 645, 654, 671–676, 684, 695–696, 699, 701

~15, 221, 700
~e Savings account
~fit Guaranty
~certificate
~roperty and casualty
~Price-earnings method
~Price-earnings ratio
~ange rate system, 419, 439
~k, 244, 320
~mping. *See* Front-running